THE
GALAXY ON EARTH

Also by Richard Leviton

Seven Steps to Better Vision

The Imagination of Pentecost: Rudolf Steiner and Contemporary Spirituality

Brain Builders! A Lifelong Guide to Sharper Thinking, Better Memory, and an Age-Proof Mind

Weddings by Design: A Guide to Non-Traditional Ceremonies

Looking for Arthur: A Once and Future Travelogue

Physician: Medicine and the Unsuspected Battle for Human Freedom

The Healthy Living Space: 70 Practical Ways to Detoxify the Body and Home

What's Beyond That Star: A Chronical of Geomythic Adventure

THE
GALAXY ON EARTH

A TRAVELER'S GUIDE TO THE PLANET'S VISIONARY GEOGRAPHY

RICHARD LEVITON

HAMPTON ROADS
PUBLISHING COMPANY, INC.

for the evolving human spirit

Cover design by Marjoram Productions
Galaxy image: Digital imagery © copyright 2002 PhotoDisc, Inc.
Earth image: © 2002 Image Ideas, Inc. and Index Stock Imagery
Table 5: Photo © 2002 Corbis Images/John Aikins; Illustrations by Anne L. Louque
Dodecahedron by Anne L. Louque

Hampton Roads Publishing Company, Inc.
1125 Stoney Ridge Road
Charlottesville, VA 22902

434-296-2772
fax: 434-296-5096
e-mail: hrpc@hrpub.com
www.hrpub.com

If you are unable to order this book from your local
bookseller, you may order directly from the publisher.
Call 1-800-766-8009, toll-free.
Library of Congress Catalog Card Number: 2001098001
ISBN 1-57174-222-0
10 9 8 7 6 5 4 3 2 1
Printed on acid-free paper in the United States

Dedication

For Mike Booth, for reminding me and for great company on the journey; for Blaise, for thinking it all up and sharing it with us; for Leon LeGant, for showing me how to see it better; for Frank DeMarco, for opening the door; and for Judith Lewis, just because.

Acknowledgments

Hearty thanks to Charles Sides, author of *Motorcycle Enlightenment* and enthusiastic researcher into the Mysteries, for his excellent research assistance.

Table of Contents

Foreword

My idea of a holy site used to be a tropical beach with crystal-clear water and a five-star resort. Three events changed my perspective. One, I was asked if I wanted to accompany some acquaintances on a trip to Asian holy sites. "Sure," I said, "where are they?" A month later I was traveling in Thailand, Nepal, India, and Bhutan. One morning in Katmandu, Nepal, I rose early, crawled up a ladder to the rooftop of the hotel, looked through the mist, and saw the Sambogaya Temple on a distant hill. Suddenly I began crying uncontrollably. Something about the site triggered my emotion.

Two, I was sitting at my computer working on a novel when I received an e-mail from Frank DeMarco, a friend and co-owner of Hampton Roads Publishing Company. "Interested in traveling to Cuzco and Machu Picchu?" he wrote. "Sure," I replied. "Where are they?" Several months later I was in Peru climbing Huena Picchu, the mountain overlooking Machu Picchu. I had no trouble ascending the steps, but when I reached a ledge high above Machu Picchu I froze, unable to even stand. Cowering against the rocks, I managed to continue on the trail, crawl through the small cave, and stop at what felt like a safer location. There we decided to sit, rest, and meditate. When I closed my eyes, I had the experience

of a young girl who was about to be sacrificed by being pushed off the mountain. I felt as if I mentally communicated with her and helped relieve her fears. When Frank and I returned to the same ledge on the way down, I was able to stand and even take a photograph.

Three, having completed my novel shortly after our return from Peru, I was sitting at my desk asking the universe, somewhat jokingly, what I should do for my next project. At that precise moment, the telephone rang and startled me. The call was from Richard Leviton asking if I wanted to research holy sites for his next book. "Sure," I said, "where are they?" My assignment would consist of researching each site for its physical location, mythological and legendary origins, religious associations, celebrated holidays, and visitors' impressions.

I began the project by reading earlier works by Richard Leviton in which he wrote about the "ley" of the land. He stated, "Native cultures teach us of a sacralized, mythopoeic landscape in which human consciousness has a special, if not essential, role." He asked, "How can we regain this seamless perception of landscape and human consciousness in a way that is appropriate to our times and temperament . . . ?" He continued, "Along the way, we come up against some of the oldest mysteries of the world: how was the Earth (and our respective section of it) created, by whom or what, for what reason, and what is our human role within it? What is the *spiritual* purpose of the landscape? How does consciousness interface with the landscape?"

The questions intrigued me and I knew the holy sites that I was about to research contained some of those answers. I started with Cuzco and Machu Picchu and realized that my visit could have been helpful had I searched for more information than the best "Gringo" hotels in the Inca Valley.

As I worked with each site, I discovered that I became interested in some, uninterested in others, and angered by the atrocities committed at others. I was enthralled by Rennes-le-Chateau and felt as if I were stepping into an abyss where time and space no longer existed. I wanted to stand at the top of Montsegur. I wanted to visit Iona Island where it's said the veil is thin between the worlds. I wanted to live at St. Catherine's Monastery and scale the three thousand steps to the summit of Mount Sinai. I wanted to climb Wu-T'ai Shan Mountain and experience Borobudur where I could ascend to the stupa of ultimate truth. I wanted to participate in the Hajj, the pilgrimage to Mecca, and see the Great Mosque and the Black Stone. I wanted to say, "I am here, O Lord. I am here." But I discovered that "Saudi Arabia is closed to tourists and Mecca itself is off limits to all non-Muslims." I wanted to take the pilgrimage to Santiago de Compostela. But I stayed home and continued working.

I spent more than a year collecting information and assembling it, but still not comprehending its essence. I submitted the material and declared myself finished. But now, writing this foreword two years later, I realize that many of the sites continue to affect me and only a few have faded from memory. It is, therefore, with great anticipation that I look forward to the publication of *The Galaxy on Earth,* a book that takes readers another step into a mysterious and fascinating world in which Richard Leviton navigates so well.

Charles Sides

Preface

The key is, *as above, so below, and in the middle, too.*

That phrase may mean nothing to you now. By the time you have gotten halfway through this book, you will be hard put to believe it was not always obvious to you. You will see the world differently, and will experience yourself differently. Indeed, it would not be too much to say that this book provides you a way—regardless of whether you travel widely, occasionally, or not at all—to become more fully yourself, and to see the world truly for the first time.

The ideas in this book can change your life, as they have changed mine. My friend Charles Sides mentioned in his preface that he and I went to Machu Picchu together. What he did not mention is that when we climbed Huena Picchu, the mountain that towers over the city, we went through an old tunnel and found ourselves looking across the Urubamba River at the wonderful mountain of Putucusi. I had carried with me a printed version of a meditation that Richard had led me though at Monticello (another sacred site) some months before. I pulled out that piece of paper and led Charles through it, with remarkable results that made believers of us both.

That meditation is included in this book, and it is part of the passport Richard provides you. It's a passport that is sorely needed. For five centuries, since the Renaissance, we in the West have been held captive by the mistaken idea that the material world is all that is real. That idea has traveled worldwide, and holds almost every culture in thrall, even as the West begins, slowly, sluggishly, to shake it off.

There is death in that idea. Nations can die of it. Civilizations can die of it. Just possibly, the world could die of it. Clearly, individuals can. And, oddly, many people who think of themselves as religious are as firmly entrapped in this perceptual materialism as are the militant atheists. For it is not so different to say, on the one hand, "this world is all there is," and to say, on the other hand, "there is another world, a spiritual world, but it is separate from this one."

It is true, this world is paralleled by the Other Side. But it is also true that *this world, this material reality*, is as holy as anywhere else. The question is, can you perceive it? Can you *learn to* perceive it? And what would happen to you when you did?

In *The Galaxy on Earth*, Richard Leviton sketches the world's hidden reality. He provides instructions on how to experience this reality firsthand. And he grounds esoteric knowledge in mythology, history, and travelers' impressions, which opens new links to portions of our cultural heritage that have been forgotten or misread.

That's a lot to accomplish in one book. And of the things he accomplished, I am quite sure that providing a key to personal experience is the greatest. Indeed, one day while I was editing this book, I called him up and said, "I feel like I have been living in the presence of angels all day." It was a wonderful experience, one I hope you experience as well.

—Frank DeMarco, chairman
Hampton Roads Publishing Co., Inc.

Table 1. Geomantic Features

Abydos, Egypt

Crown of the Ancient of Days; Underworld Entrance; Landscape Zodiac; Dome

Acropolis, Athens, Greece

Dome; Major Egregor Point; Palladium; Grail Castle; Tree of Life; Arc of Developing Consciousness; Ray Master Sanctuary; Underworld Entrance

Afrasiab, Samarkand, Uzbekistan

Dome; Underworld Entrance; Soma Temple

Avebury, England

Planetary Umbilicus; Oroboros Line Grounding Point; Master Dome; Tree of Life

Banaras, India

Dome; Cosmic Egg; Landscape Zodiac; Ixion's Wheel; Soma Temple; Crown of the Ancient of Days; Epiphany Focus

Bayreuth, Germany

Dome; Grail Castle; National Egregor Point

Brocken, Harz Mountains, Germany

Landscape Zodiac; Lucifer Binding Site

Carnac, France

Dome; Landscape Zodiac; Virgo Albion Brow Chakra

Chaco Canyon, New Mexico, United States

Dome; Time Portal; Dragon; Landscape Zodiac; Leo Albion Solar Plexus Chakra

Chichen Itza, Mexico

Landscape Zodiac; Dome; Lucifer Binding Site; Tree of Life; Labyrinth; Control Bubble

Citamparam, India

Dome; Emerald for Sagittarius Albion; Lucifer Binding Site

Clingman's Dome, Tennessee, United States

Dome; Labyrinth; Scorpio Albion Crown Chakra

Croagh Patrick, Ireland

Dome; Naga City; Control Bubble

Cumae, Naples, Italy

Dome Cap; Avalon; Dragon; Underworld Entrance; Landscape Zodiac

# of Fifty-Six Sites at a Glance

Cusco, Peru

Dome; Ixion's Wheel; Solar Logos Residence; Egregor Grounding Point; Camalate Center; Cyclopean City; Crown of the Ancient of Days; Mount Olympus

Delphi, Mount Parnassus, Greece

Dome; Dragon; Vibrating Stone; Oroboros Line Anchor Point; Shambhala Doorway; Avalon; Grail Castle

Dome of the Rock, Jerusalem, Israel

Dome; Grail Castle; Lucifer Binding Site

Dornach, Switzerland

Aquarius Albion Emerald; Landscape Zodiac; Golden Egg; Dome

Easter Island, Chile

Planetary Energy Receptor; Golden Pillars; Labyrinth; Dome

Edfu, Egypt

Mithraeum; Golden Egg; Silver Egg

Ephesus, Turkey

Ray Master Sanctuary; Landscape Zodiac

Externsteine, Detmold, Germany

Dome Cap; Universe Dome Merudanda

Gediminas Hill, Vilnius, Lithuania

Dome Cap; Landscape Zodiac; Mithraeum; Lucifer Binding Site

Glastonbury, England

Domes; Dragon; Avalon; Cretan Labyrinth; Underworld Entrance; Arc of Developing Consciousness; Pointer's Ball; Grail Castle; Interdimensional Portal; Tree of Life; Soma Temple; Shambhala Doorway; Golden Egg; Silver Egg; Perpetual Choir; Vibrating Stone; Ixion's Wheel; Landscape Zodiac; Virgo Albion Heart Chakra; Mobile Shambhallic Focus; Planetary *Anahata* Heart Chakra; New Jerusalem

Hardwar, India

Dome; Epiphany Focus; Soma Temple

Hill Cumorah, Palmyra, New York, United States

Dome; Dragon; Palladium; Pointer's Ball; Tree of Life; Three Star Temple; Scorpio Albion Emerald

Hill of Tara, Ireland

Dome; Mount Olympus; Palladium; Avalon; Landscape Zodiac; Emerald; Gnome Egg; National Egregor Point

Iona Island, Scotland

Dome; Chakra Template

Table 1. Geomantic Features

Jasna Gora, Czestochowa, Poland

Dome; Ray Master Sanctuary; Tree of Life; Golden Pillars; Palladium

Lourdes, France

Dome Cap; Ray Master Sanctuary

Machu Picchu, Peru

Dome; Mithraeum; Labyrinth; Activated Dome Paradise Crystal

Monticello, Charlottesville, Virginia, United States

Dome Cap; Mount Olympus; Avalon; Scorpio Albion *Ananda-kanda* Chakra; Landscape Zodiac; Palladium; Tree of Life

Mont-Royal, Montreal, Quebec, Canada

Dome; Lily; Ray Master Sanctuary; Scorpio Albion Foot Chakra

Mont-Saint-Michel, France

Dome Cap; Dragon; Michaelion

Montsegur, France

Dome; Grail Castle

Montserrat, Spain

Dome; Grail Castle; Tree of Life; Avalon

Mount Damavand, Iran

Dome; Cosmic Egg; Underworld Entrance; Naga City; Grail Castle; Soma Temple

Mount Etna, Taormina, Sicily, Italy

Dome; Mithraeum; Ixion's Wheel; Underworld Entrance

Mount Fuji, Japan

Dome; Soma Temple

Mount Haleakala, Maui, Hawaii, United States

Dome; Mithreaum

Mount Holyoke, Hadley, Massachusetts, United States

Dome; Pointer's Ball; Underworld Entrance; Landscape Zodiac; Golden Egg; Scorpio Albion Root Chakra

Mount Ida, Crete, Greece

Dome; Major Egregor Grounding Point; Cretan Labyrinth; Cosmic Egg; Planetary Energy Receptor

Mount Kailash, Tibet

Dome; Etheric Umbilicus for Albion; Dragon; Naga City; Avalon; Shambhala Entrance; Og-Min Cave Heavens

Mount Temahani, Raiatea, Society Islands

Dome; Avalon; Dragon; Epiphany Focus

# of Fifty-Six Sites at a Glance (continued)

Mycenae, Greece

Dome; Cyclopean City; Landscape Zodiac; Avalon; Mithraeum; Grail Castle; Camalate Center; Soma Temple; Albion Chakra

Newgrange, Ireland

Dome Cap; Pointer's Ball; Ray Master Sanctuary

Rennes-le-Chateau, France

Dome Cap; Landscape Zodiac; National Egregor Point; Ray Master Sanctuary; Arc of Developing Consciousness; Pointer's Ball

Santiago de Compostela, Spain

Dome; Three Star Temple; Tree of Life

Sedona, Arizona, United States

Landscape Zodiac; Domes; Dragon; Silver Egg; Epiphany Focus; Mount Olympus; Labyrinth; Tree of Life; Pointer's Ball; Gnome Egg; Shambhala Doorway; Leo Albion Solar Plexus Chakra; Ixion's Wheel

Teotihuacan, Mexico

Domes; Mesoamerican Control Temple; Planetary Solar Plexus Chakra; Epiphany Focus; Tree of Life; Landscape Zodiac; Ixion's Wheel; Pointer's Ball; Golden Egg; Palladium; Labyrinth; Lucifer Binding Site

Tetford, England

Dome; Golden Egg; Silver Egg; Mount Olympus; Tree of Life; Lily; Palladium; Gnome Egg; Dragon; Grail Castle; Stargate; Soma Temple

Thebes, Greece

Dome Cap; Cyclopean City; Dragon; Ray Master Sanctuary; Shambhala Doorway; Golden Pillars; Silver Egg

Troy, Turkey

Dome; Cyclopean City; Palladium; Mount Olympus; Avalon; Solar Logos Residence; Camalate Center; Landscape Zodiac; Tree of Life

Uluru, Alice Springs, Australia

Dome; Dragon; Planetary Solar Plexus Chakra; Mount Olympus

Wawel Hill, Cracow, Poland

Dome; Dragon; Golden Egg; Interdimensional Portal; Aquarian Albion Hand Chakra

Wu-T'ai Shan, China

Dome; Shambhala Entrance; Michaelion

Part One

Geomancy, Cosmology, and a Planet of Sacred Sites

Getting a Taste of the Earth's Energy Body: The Earth in the Star

When it comes to understanding and interacting with the mysteries of the Earth and its holy sites, everyone has an equal opportunity and open invitation. You might even say it's everyone's birthright. So here is a simple but immediate way to be introduced to the subject, a way to make it feel more real.

First Meditation

Sit in a comfortable chair in a room that is free of distractions. Relax and place both feet, uncrossed, on the floor. Close your eyes and take a few deep breaths. Do this without effort or strain. Spend a few moments observing your breathing, noting that the inhales and exhales come and go without effort on your part.

As you relax into the natural rhythm of your breathing, allow your lips to form a little smile with each out-breath, as if you are amused, or feeling affectionate.

Focus your attention on a point two inches above your belly button and the same distance inside. Imagine a pinprick of light at that spot, a tiny blazing star of brilliant light. It is very tiny but brighter than seems possible. As you exhale, *breathe* to this little bright star with a smile. Let every exhale work as a bellows, making the star just a little brighter.

As you exhale, send your smile to that little pinprick of brilliant light, to that little blazing star at the center of your body. Breathe to it with some

fondness, as if somehow it is an old, almost forgotten friend, suddenly returned to you after a long absence. Breathe to this star with a sense of fondness, affection, and with a smile of recognition. It may surprise you to notice from time to time that it seems the star is twinkling at you, even winking, if this were possible. No effort is required—just a smile and your natural breathing.

You may notice that this point of light begins to grow a bit larger. It may be the size of a marble now. Soon it becomes the size of a golf ball. Now a peach. Now a softball. Now a basketball. Continue to breathe with the sense of quiet fondness to this growing point of light.

Now picture the planet Earth as seen from space. You have probably seen the now world-famous NASA space photographs of our blue-white planet seen from many miles out in space. Place this image of the blue-white planet Earth inside your blazing star at the center of your body. Simply put the Earth inside the star, and continue to breathe to it with fondness and regard.

You may wish to amplify that fondness to something called Love from Above. This is the way the spiritual world regards physical humans and our planet. Try it. Allow yourself for a moment to be in the spiritual world breathing as Love from Above—fondly, with affection and regard—to the blue-white planet Earth inside the blazing star at the center of your being. For this star is not only inside your body, it is also (and more really) at the center of your being.

Allow yourself to feel like a parent to the Earth. Allow yourself to feel that in some way you are a kind of cosmic parent to the Earth, that you are nurturing it inside this blazing star at the center of your being. Continue to breathe as Love from Above to the Earth inside your star for a few moments. . . .

You have just reversed your normal relationship to the Earth, and you have just made an essential discovery about the subject of holy sites.

Usually we think of ourselves as completely dependent on the physical Earth to nurture and sustain us. But who sustains the planet? As spiritual beings, *we* do.

How on Earth do we do this?

We have something the planet needs: the blazing star at the center of our being. You might think that's merely an artifact of a contrived meditation, but it isn't. Rather, it is an introduction to an actual *fact* about the spiritual nature of being human. It is also, as we'll see, the key to the mysteries of sacred sites and what this book calls visionary geography.

The spiritual world gave us this star. It's a point of light—a little reminder, if you wish—from the highest source. As spiritual beings, we are supposed to maintain the Earth through this star. From a spiritual perspective—that is, when we think of ourselves as spiritual beings occupying physical bodies—we are actually in a parental role with respect to the planet. That is why we put the Earth inside the star and breath to it as Love from Above. This little star is central to everything.

We have a star; the Earth has a star; each of the planet's numerous holy sites has a star. The galaxy has billions of stars, among them a special one akin to the one we, the planet, and holy sites have. Recognition is everything here—that is, recognizing the star. It is hoped, by those Above, that we will each recognize our own star and recognize the planet's star, and that through this recognition in two realms we will make the Earth our home away from home. This will make more sense as the book unfolds.

A Perpetual Harmonic Convergence Highlights a Planet of Sacred Sites

During the highly publicized and widely ridiculed Harmonic Convergence of August 1987, thousands of people all around the planet gravitated towards holy sites famous and obscure for up to a week. Expectations were high for cosmic epiphanies: UFOs, celestial beings, mythic saviors, religious progenitors returning to their temples after a long hiatus.

Putting aside the millennial expectations, whether grounded in fantasy or reality, the entire event had a larger, more obvious message. People in diverse cultures believed that by spending time at recognized sacred sites their experience would be amplified. People flocked to the pyramids at Giza, to Mount Shasta, Machu Picchu, Uluru, Stonehenge. . . . It was a bit like musical chairs: everyone hoped to be seated at some high profile sacred site at the right time. For a week, the world's preeminent holy sites were more prestigious, more desirable, than the most luxuriously chic travel destinations.

For one week in August 1987, holy sites around the Earth became *the* place to be for the millennially attuned. Why? The general notion was that places like these somehow facilitated mystical experiences. They somehow produced exaltations in consciousness. They healed; they revealed; they transformed you. This is the subject of *The Galaxy on Earth*.

Many sites were rich in attribution and allegation: UFOs had been sighted; people had been abducted by aliens; angels had been glimpsed; bushes had burned with celestial light; fairy lights had been observed; revelations from God had been received; saints had thrived there; apparitions had been beheld; miraculous cures had been achieved; the gods had once dwelt there; holy objects had been hidden there.

Suddenly the world of myth, for so long relegated derisively to the far edges of academic study and cultural awareness, was a key. In fact, at the core of the Harmonic Convergence was a myth. According to the Zapotec Indians of southern Mexico, the great plumed serpent god, Quetzalcoatl, was slated to return to the Tule tree, set in the courtyard of El Templo del Santa Maria, a small church about six miles from Oaxaca. From there he would distribute seeds of "his" heart planetwide. Quetzalcoatl, to the Zapotecs, the Lord of the Tree of Life, had been away from his temple for a thousand years. He had buried his heart under the massive Tule tree long ago; now with his imminent return, this buried heart would burst into billions of tiny sparks and scintillate around the planet. Everyone would get a spark. The Harmonic Convergence was merely the rallying call sent out around the world to get people ready.

But why at El Templo del Santa Maria? Why was this majestic myth focused on this seemingly insignificant Mexican churchyard and a gigantic old tree? And what made it holy in the first place? Again, the answers are at the heart of *The Galaxy on Earth* and are central to the concept of sacred sites.

Picture it: thousands, probably millions, of people around the planet perched meditatively at holy sites, on mountaintops, in cathedrals, by ruined ancient cities, at stone circles, atop Mayan pyramids, in city parks, waiting, expectant, faithful, as dawn broke on August 17, 1987. Never mind what they thought might—or should—happen. Focus instead on the convergence of expectancy. Millions of humans were concerned about the same global thing that morning: Was something astonishingly mythic about to happen?

Regardless of what happened—or what people think happened or didn't happen—Harmonic Convergence awakened a generation of humans to the fact that the planet has *many* holy sites, perhaps thousands, which have to do with experiences in consciousness and possible encounters with a higher reality and which are worth visiting.

Many gained a new respect for myths and the improbable claims of folklore. Many gained the impression that indigenous peoples might know some valuable things about these subjects. Some, if they acknowledged the fact in front of them, realized that the planet was dotted with sacred sites, as copious as dandelions on a spring lawn.

It gave us, as Westerners not living particularly close to the land, a new way of thinking about the planet as a whole, and it gave us lots of new places to visit and a new reason for doing so. It gave us a fleeting glimpse of the possibility that, even today, myths are living in the landscape.

The Increasing Popularity of Sacred Sites Tourism

In the years since the Harmonic Convergence, travel to designated holy sites around the Earth has gained considerable popularity among Westerners. Many people set off on their own pilgrimages of meaning and meditation; others join guided tours by experts or celebrities promising revelations of ancient intent and experiences of potent energy. Some go with agendas, themes, specific quests; others travel with an open slate, free to peregrinate wherever the spirit leads them.

The important point is that many now feel inspired, urged, even compelled, to go. As one scholar puts it, at a time when social and geographic mobility are at a peak, "new topophilia," or love of the land, is emerging, based on ancient sacred sites "felt to be inherently special places . . . through which one can reconnect both with the past and the energies therein."[1]

In many respects these observations encapsulate the direction of this book: what is *inherent* to these places that makes them *special*? What are the *energies* there and how do you *reconnect* with them? In fact, to say reconnect, rather than connect, implies a preexisting relationship, which happens to be a major theme in this book.

New names have sprung into circulation to describe the holy sites. You now hear terms like power places, power points, mysterious places, sacred centers, mystical places, vortexes, places of peace and power, spiritual sites, sacred places, spiritual oases. Old names such as archeological ruins, ancient temples, shrines, megalithic sites, lost cities, and pilgrimage routes suddenly have a new vibrancy, a renewed relevance.

The important point is that an increasing number of people are visiting them with some measure of the same expectancy that characterized the Harmonic Convergence. In a sense, whereas a previous generation dutifully attended synagogue or church every weekend, a new generation is attending sacred sites, natural "churches" in the landscape.

People flock to holy sites because in some way, hard for them to explain, merely being present at such places is good for their development as humans. It deepens their meditations, provides insights, confirms intuitions, aligns their intentions. It gives them a taste of the antiquity of some of the planet's sites, a brush with the enigma of its myths; it makes them wonder what it's all about. The idea of sacred sites is even moving into the mainstream.

There is no shortage of sacred sites tour guides or claims for what's possible on such a pilgrimage. Their claims may seem a bit inflated at times, but they are intriguingly suggestive. What are these "mysterious and magical energies"? How do you "tune" into them? How can they affect consciousness? How can they produce "transformations" in our life and identity? Perhaps a deeper question is this: why are there holy sites in the first place? How did they get there? What makes them holy? Why are they distributed around the planet? And what is the basis

for their distribution? Do they form a global pattern? And if they do, what is the origin of this pattern? How did it get here on Earth? What is the intent of the entire pattern?

These are the questions about sacred sites for which *The Galaxy on Earth* provides novel yet eminently practical answers.

The Gaia Hypothesis: Seeing the Planet As a Whole Living System

Important conceptual models emerged in the 1970s that prepared the way for the Harmonic Convergence, for sacred sites tourism in the 1990s, and beyond. One was by British atmospheric scientist James Lovelock, who made the persuasive case that the planet was a single "geophysiological" unit capable of responding as a whole to differing environmental conditions much the way a biological organism does.

Lovelock called his model the Gaia Hypothesis, borrowing the ancient Greek term *Ge,* or more popularly, Gaia, to refer to the planet as a living, intelligent organism, as an integrated planetary ecosystem. Of course, Lovelock was not prepared to take his model into animistic thinking; his was a model of the planet as a self-regulating (homeostatic) system capable of managing its own temperature and chemistry despite perturbations, from changes produced either by its inhabitants or the cosmos.

Lovelock noted that the remarkable consistency of an essentially unstable atmosphere over billions of years suggested some automatic regulating agency and control mechanism. He wasn't ready to accord this system any kind of self-awareness, but modeled his geophysiological planet as an active feedback process that operates unconsciously and automatically. He said that the global "feedback" derives from all the living organisms present on the planet, including us.[2] Even though Lovelock's Gaian model was mechanistic, it enlarged our thinking to consider systems on a planetary scale.

Another major intellectual stimulus came with the introduction of acupuncture and traditional Chinese medicine to the United States, at the same time that awareness of ancient Vedic and Hindu models of consciousness and human subtle anatomy began to achieve some circulation among the intellectually adventurous in the West.

These new inputs to Western thinking encouraged the generalized notion that the human being is more than the apparent physical organism and its physiological processes. Traditional Chinese medicine schooled us in the idea that subtle energy coursed through our system along channels called meridians, which contained points where the subtle energy, called *qi* (pronounced "chee"), could be interacted with. Similarly, the subtler anatomy models of ancient India taught that the body has a series of primary energy centers, arrayed along the spinal column from the base of the spine to the top of the head. These centers are called *chakras,* meaning "spinning wheels," which is a description of their appearance on an energy level as reported by clairvoyants. Generally associated with specific planets, colors, sounds, and other symbolic images, chakras feed an intricate system of an estimated 72,000 tiny energy streams called *nadis* and numerous minor energy centers in the palms, soles of the feet, and behind the knees, among other places.

The meridians of *qi,* the *chakras,* and *nadis* are all part of a generalized energy field surrounding the body called the aura. Psychics who can see the aura report that it is like an everchanging dance of color that reflects both the stable and momentary aspects of the life of our mind, body, emotions, and soul.

The aura can be affected by other people, places, landscapes, buildings, even solar and lunar events. In fact, traditional Chinese medicine models the ways in which extraplanetary energies cyclically influence the meridians, speaking of celestial stems and branches. Some acupuncture scholars contend the stems actually relate to the twelve-year cycle of Jupiter. Many Chinese names for the treatment points have names evocative of the heavens. For example, an acupoint on the neck called *Tian You* means "Celestial Window"; a point called *Tian Chong* near the hairline means "Celestial Hub." Translations of other acupoint names on the body mean Upper Star, Sun and Moon, Celestial Well, Celestial Pillar, Celestial Connection, Celestial Countenance, Celestial Gathering, Celestial Storehouse.[3]

Acupuncturists also note that some key acupoints in the solar plexus region have Chinese names that pertain to stars in the constellations Ursa Major (Great Bear) and Ursa Minor (Little Bear). Three points on the Stomach meridian, for example, are named after the pole star (Polaris), the pivot around which the galaxy is believed to revolve.

According to two noted acupuncture scholars, acupoints were deliberately given astronomical names. "The Chinese envisioned a microcosmic universe in the body that mirrored the universe itself," they say. "We can see that not only the specific areas of the abdomen, below and around the umbilicus, were named after highly significant stars and constellations, but also the general nature of the body was reflected in the analogy thus created."[4]

In other words, the subtle energy topography of the body, according to acupuncture, is based on a cosmological model.

By the turn of the twenty-first century, the idea that the human is more than meets the non-psychic eye was fairly well established among a growing percentage of the West. While most people did not see *qi,* meridians, *chakras, nadis,* or the aura, they felt confident in postulating that they probably existed and did something like what the psychics claimed they did. All of these features seem to have something to do with the structures and functions of consciousness, and if you follow them back far enough to where they come from (relying on clues from the esoteric literature), they have something to do with the stars, planets, and cosmos in general.

If humans have this complex subtle energy as the underpinning of their anatomy and physiology, might not the planet? If human physiology appears to have another layer of subtle, non-chemical energy exchanges and influences, and if the Earth itself is modeled as a self-regulating geophysiological organism, then surely it's possible it too has a comparable subtle energy body with numerous parts and functions. And if the Earth has such an energy body, is it based on the same principles and does it have the same components as the human energy body?

If you follow the implications of sacred sites tourism and the Gaia Hypothesis far enough, you end up wondering if the Earth itself has a multilayered spiritual body, just as we do, and if there are ways we can interact with it, even heal it. You begin to suspect that perhaps the hundreds of identified holy sites might be part of a global pattern, part of Earth's mystical terrain. You get a feeling that they might, like the human body's subtle counterparts, pertain in some way to the life of the cosmos.

"It is helpful to know that in Daoist mythology the Earth was seen as suspended and cocooned within a vast network or web of threads hanging down from heaven that controlled terrestrial events."[5] If we could *see* the planet psychically, what would our vision reveal? Exploring these questions occupies a large measure of *The Galaxy on Earth*.

A Deeper Sense of Place: The Numinous and the Cosmological in the Landscape

Artists, novelists, philosophers, even historians of religion were intuiting aspects of an answer to this question—what comprises the sense of place?—during most of the twentieth century. Sensitive writers such as D. H. Lawrence and Henry Miller visited Mexico and Greece, respectively, and came away with an unshakable sense of something holy, mysterious, numinous in those landscapes. D. H. Lawrence found the landscape of Mexico heavy, even oppressive at times. He had no doubt that it exerted an effect on human consciousness, although to him it was a baleful one. The Mexican landscape put Lawrence's heroine, Kate, in *The Plumed Serpent*, in a state of "violent anger," of "burning, furious rage." To Lawrence it seemed that something must be coming out of the Earth, "some effluence, some vibration which militated against the very composition of the blood and nerves of human beings."[6]

Similarly, the British writer Lawrence Durrell said that an intimate knowledge of the landscape could, if scientifically developed, yield a viable political science. You could understand what gives a Greek his Greekness. "Human beings are expressions of their landscape," said Durrell, and in the particularities of a landscape you can find "the secret springs of a national essence."

Durrell said that as a novelist he sees characters "almost as functions of a landscape." He also suggested that the "secret springs" could be identified if you get still enough, if you close your eyes and breathe through your nose. You will hear a whispered message, "for all landscapes ask the same question in the same whisper. 'I am watching you—are you watching yourself in me?'"[7]

Henry Miller, touring Greece in the late

1930s, stopped at Mycenae to collect impressions. Perhaps he closed his eyes and breathed through his nose as Durrell advised, for they were correspondents. To Miller, it seemed the gods had once walked the Earth at this "hoary scene." Neither archeologists nor historians have yet penetrated the secret of this astonishing antique site, understanding of which "defies the feeble processes of the intellectual mind."

At Phaestos, Miller marveled at the "ultimate violet light" that makes everything Greek seem "holy, natural, and familiar" and which inspires one to want to bathe in the sky. At Eleusis, everything speaks of "blinding, joyous illumination," and even the rocks are "quite mad," having been exposed for centuries to this "divine illumination." The road to Epidaurus, Miller said, is like "the road to creation." Its landscape "installs itself in the open places of the heart." Epidaurus "is a bowl from which to drink the pure spirit." Athens is permeated with "a violet-blue reality which envelops you with a caress"; its air is like champagne, "a tonic, a revivifier."[8]

The American novelist William Maxwell evoked a similar quality of awesome upliftment in his description of Chartres Cathedral. "They felt in the presence of some vast act of understanding," he wrote of a young couple visiting the cathedral in the 1940s. The place reduced their speaking to whispers. "Their breathing, their heartbeat, seemed to be affected."[9]

The film *Field of Dreams* is a vivid example of the wakening of a preexistent sacred site in contemporary awareness. The movie's hero learns through his intuition that part of his Iowa cornfield wants to be a baseball diamond, as improbable and illogical as this seems. He builds the baseball park and discovers it is an intermediate place for spirits from the astral world and living humans—in other words, a crack between the worlds. People will come to this improbable baseball park because the site on which it stands has

reverted to its original essence: it was always a sacred site, a doorway between the worlds, and now it is one again.

It is a reclaimed, reawakened site with a specific purpose: to facilitate the working out of unexpressed, unfulfilled wishes and dreams, of both the living and the dead. Without using any of the identifying terms—geomancy, sacred sites, crack between the worlds—the movie perfectly illustrates the birth of geomantic awareness in the modern psyche and provides a new, even startling way of viewing the landscape.

Contemporary pilgrims to mystical sites have attempted to characterize that quality that affects the breathing and heartbeat and that renders speech to whispers. One says a sacred site is a place "graced with the presence of unconditioned being," where "the unfettered energy and life of the domain of the gods makes itself known" in our physical world.[10] Another says sacred places are sites where once "the gods showed forth"; they are "holy ground that blazed with meaning."

Holy sites provide "confirmation that the mystery exists" in a world that wants to deny the sacred and downgrade it as superstition, confirmation that the "presence" still abides behind the façade of cultural memory. They satisfy our desire for "the deeply real," to be in a place where time stops "and we are seized by the mysteries."[11] Yet another comments that holy places awaken the human spirit and "the land acts as a catalyst" to spark us on all levels, moving us "through a doorway that transforms our consciousness."[12]

A British writer and commentator on holy sites and the role of pilgrimage characterized such numinous places as landscape temples. They are "part of the very body of the living Earth, points where Earth-energy is focused, vortices of power and light which mark where Heaven and Earth meet, where ethereal space unites with the field of gravity." In his view, landscape temples are part of Earth's innate structure, and they often take the form of "chakra temples" in accordance with the energy hierarchy of subtle centers in the human. We are "integrally" part of the Earth, so "if you wish to understand in what sense the Earth is a living creature, look into yourself."[13]

Still another writer with clairvoyant insight speaks of the ancient landscape temple as "an invisible energetic fabric penetrating a landscape, thus expressing its divine being." Landscapes have a "spiritual-soul dimension" and exhibit "invisible geometric structures," he adds. They "represent the spiritual level of the Earth composed of divine qualities embodied by different places and landscapes."[14]

French Orientalist Alain Danielou, an insightful scholar of religion, writes that a sacred place is where the visible and invisible lie "very close" to each other, where there exist subtle doorways enabling the sensitive to "tumble suddenly into another world." Such places are in fact the "gates" of Heaven; they are "privileged" places where you can sense "invisible presences," or "feel a special atmosphere which is outside of time or in another dimension of space." Together they comprise a landscape best described as "sacred geography."[15]

Mircea Eliade, the preeminent University of Chicago historian of religions, shamanism, yoga, and other archaic techniques of ecstasy and illumination, put the matter in even broader, more fundamental terms. After all, what is the sacred? How would we define it? Eliade conceived of sacred sites in the context of the sacred and the profane. Sacred space reveals the presence of the divine and reiterates the cosmological origin of the world and reality, said Eliade; the profane space is a place that hides this or does not reveal it.

The sacred space is where the origin of things, the ultimate center of creation, breaks through from the No-Time that preceded Time. Every sacred space provides a fundamental orientation for human consciousness, giving it its primordial bearings as to how the spiritual world once manifested in the physical, where the gods once revealed themselves in a glorious "hierophany." Sanctuaries are "'doors of the gods' and hence places of passage between Heaven and Earth."

The sacred reveals "absolute reality"; it founds the world; and it imparts a "cosmicized territory" upon the Earth. Here the sacred burst forth into the mundane world, ordering everything around it in accordance with its divinely mandated pattern. This is true of any sacred ground, be it a Vedic fire altar or a Gothic cathedral. Not only did the gods communicate sacrality and consecrate the ground in places, says Eliade, "They manifested the different modalities of the sacred in the very structure of the world and of cosmic phenomena." He further stated that it seems the gods created the world in such a way that it reflected their existence, somehow mirroring divine life and its aspects.[16]

Eliade's phrases "cosmicized" and "different modalities of the sacred in the very structure of the world" are central to *The Galaxy on Earth.* They imply an overall patterning, both purposeful and mystical, to the array of sacred sites around the world.

He uses many terms—cosmic topography, mystical geography, cosmographic schemas, mythical geography—to suggest a kind of mythically templated primordial landscape in which the gods revealed themselves at particular sites in such a way as to forever leave an imprint on the planet. Such places have remained sacred and they put people back in touch with that origin. The origin is cosmic; it is the cosmos itself; and the templating of the Earth in an antique time is the imparting of a cosmic imprint. "It must be understood that the cosmicization of unknown territories is always a consecration; to organize a space is to repeat the paradigmatic work of the gods."[17]

In Eliade's view, sites are holy because they were once touched—"consecrated"—by the revelation and presence of the "gods," by some awesome organizing spiritual presence. We might say that awesome presence acted like a computer disk inserted into a hard drive: a great deal of information about the structure and hierarchy of the cosmos was deposited and "downloaded" into a relatively small space, there to await human investigation.

Hence, a sacred space is one marked by a "superabundance of reality." It is a place impregnated with what we refer to as the mythical, the No-Time before Time when the gods performed primordial genitive acts that still echo with meaning today. Sacred time and space reveal that mythical moment and make it present, vital, urgent, fructifying, shockingly real, full of life and revelation once more.

The sacred is a place where "the real unveils itself" and the holy irrupts into human life, such that this act "opens communication" between the cosmic planes and Earth. It establishes a cosmological center in the midst of profane chaos. Such a place "cosmicizes chaos, but also sanctifies" our world by making it like that of the gods, which presumably was "a pure and holy cosmos, as it was in the beginning, when it came fresh from the Creator's hands."[18] In other words, the sacred bears an imprint of the gods, of the celestial world, of the origins of ours, and this imprint immediately organizes our world in accordance with a supramundane model—Eliade's "pure and holy cosmos."

A valuable umbrella term for Eliade's sense of cosmic freshness is *numinous*. Back in 1923, the German philosopher Rudolf Otto sought an expanded definition of the term "holy." He wanted to broaden its definition beyond the scope of "mere goodness" so that it encompassed the "non-rational factor" in the idea of the divine. He coined the term *numinous* to denote the awe and attraction characteristic of our communion with the divine; the root of his word is the Latin *numen*, which suggests the spirit or deity present in a locality or in an object. "The numinous is thus felt as objective and outside the self," and is something "to which the mind turns spontaneously," Otto wrote. It is characterized by a quality of the soul he called *mysterium tremendum*, being in the presence of an inexpressible, tremendous mystery.

Such a feeling may sweep over the mind "like a gentle tide," evoking a mood of deepest worship; it may come on "thrillingly vibrant and resonant"; or it may "burst in sudden eruption up from the depths of the soul" or "lead to the strangest excitements, to intoxicated frenzy, to transport, and to ecstasy."

This *mysterium tremendum*, which is the face of the numinous, has several marked features such as awefulness, overpoweringness, or majesty, a sense of energy and urgency, the quality of being "wholly other," the manifesting of "something uniquely attractive and fascinating," said Otto.[19]

Conveniently for us in our quest to understand sacred sites, Otto's definitions of the holy and the numinous neatly encapsulate many of the key experiences consistently reported by visitors and pilgrims to the world's numerous holy places. These places are numinous.

Ironically, Otto's explanation of the "wholly other" aspect of the *mysterium tremendum* is both on and off the point. He said its kind and character are "incommensurable with our own, and before which we therefore recoil in a wonder that strikes us chill and numb."[20] When we first encounter a sacred site and make a direct contact with its structures and energy, it *can* seem as though we have met something wholly other; it can be a little intimidating, even dreadful in a salutary way. Yet when we probe deeper into the mysteries of Eliade's "cosmicized" world, we begin to sense a familiarity, an ancestral remembering. These sites have something to do with us. We suspect somewhere deep within us that we are looking into a mirror, although the "face" reflected back is not our everyday human face, but a far older one, a face made of stars.

Envisioning the Earth As a Planet Scintillating with Stars

Here is a second easy way to get introduced to the numinous planet we live on.

Second Meditation

Let's return to the little blazing star just above the navel. Take a moment to refocus your attention on your breathing. On the exhale, allow a little smile to appear on your face, and send this smile to the tiny brilliant pinprick of light just above your navel. Just breathe for a few moments to this star, sending to it a feeling of kind regard, fondness, even a dash of Love from Above.

As before, allow the star to come closer to you. Allow it to enlarge, to become brighter, clearer, more present in your awareness. Without any effort, continue to breathe to it as Love from Above, allowing it to grow larger at its own rate. It may be the size of a marble now. Soon it becomes the size of a golf ball. Now a peach. Now a softball. Now a basketball. Continue to breathe with this sense of quiet fondness to this growing point of light.

Now, as before, bring to mind the NASA photograph of the Earth as a blue-white planet floating in space. Put this image inside the star, and continue to breathe to the star and the Earth with a feeling of quiet fondness and familiarity.

As you continue to breathe as Love from Above and without any effort to the blue-white Earth inside the star, notice that many pinpricks of light are appearing across the planet's surface. Thousands of stars now dot the planet's surface, creating a scintillating effect, as if you were observing many thousands of lightning bugs on a summer's night, each emitting a phosphorescent flicker.

It is as if you are looking at a night sky from deep in the desert, far from city lights. More stars than you can count twinkle across the Earth's surface. It is as if you are looking at a galaxy overlaid on rivers, lakes, oceans, mountains, deserts, steppes, glaciers, suburban neighborhoods, forests, grain fields, prairies, cities, and canyons. Somehow everything on Earth is dressed up in stars.

As you continue to breathe as Love from Above to the thousands of stars on the Earth's surface, you see that some are in groups and you recognize some of the patterns they form. For a moment, as you breathe to this image as Love from Above, celestial figures take shape amidst the stars on the Earth's surface, as if the stars were illuminated pins marking the place where their heavenly bodies could appear.

There is the Big Dipper; there is the Little Dipper; there is Orion the Hunter with his glorious belt of three stars; there is Orion's dog, Canis Major, with the bright star in its neck, Sirius; there is the big "W" formed by Cassiopeia, the Ethiopian queen in her starry chair; there is serpentine Draco, dragon of the galaxy; there are the Pleiades sisters, huddling in the neck of Taurus the Bull.

For a moment, as you maintain your calm focus on your exhales, allow yourself to see the forms made by the stars in this mythological tableau: the Bears, Orion, the Dog, Cassiopeia, Draco, the Pleiades. As the planet slowly rotates, you see there are thousands more stars and many more constellations. There isn't a place on Earth that doesn't have stars twinkling upon it like sequins on a dress. . . .

Taking Myths Seriously As a Guide to the Visionary Geography of Earth

This is more than an imaginative image, or an analogy for the worldwide prevalence of holy sites. It is in fact a true and accurate image of the planet's spiritual body, as hinted at by clairvoyants and mystics as well as certain religious traditions.

A few examples will help paint the picture. British novelist Doris Lessing portrayed one of her characters mystically surveying the Earth from a distance. He observed a "colored spinning membrane" and an "enclosing web of subtle light" touching the Earth; he saw patterns of light, colors, textures, and "pulses of faint or strong light," all part of a "great web of patterning oscillations and quiverings."[21]

A psychic described her clairvoyant impressions off the Earth as "a fishnet web of light lines," with "lines of light radiating from the intersections of the planet's surface to link with the web network surrounding other planets."[22] A dowser saw the planet as "a geometrically precise web" or "a vast multilayered cobweb" punctuated with "grids of light, focal points," and as a "receptor web complex with nexi of entrance." He compared it to a micrograph of nerve cells and their ganglia, suggesting it was the circulation and nervous system of the planet.[23]

Don Juan Matus, the Yaqui mentor of Carlos Castaneda, described the Earth as "a gigantic sentient being" inside a "luminous cocoon" that entraps cosmic energies, or in Castaneda's terms, "the Eagle's emanations."[24] Don Juan further told Castaneda that certain power spots are doors or holes in this world, and "if you are formless you can go through one of those holes into the unknown, into another world."[25]

What happens when somebody goes through one of those holes? It's all in the tale of Rip van Winkle, published by Washington Irving in 1820, which describes the otherworldly adventures of Rip when he journeys alone into the Catskills, the "fairy mountains" up the Hudson River in New York State. It may be fiction but it describes something true.

One day Rip climbed high into the mountains until he was looking down "into a deep mountain glen, wild, lonely, and shagged." A peculiar short square-built "old fellow" came out of nowhere and invited Rip to follow him. Rip found himself in a hollow, like an amphitheater, in which dozens of these squat, bearded old fellows were bowling and drinking. They offered Rip a flagon, and he accepted it. The liquor made him drowsy and he fell asleep, to be awakened by the sunshine—twenty years later.

The twenty years had seemed like a single night to Rip. Somehow he had stepped outside of time, through one of those holes into the unknown. He had partied with spirit beings—most likely gnomes—and had tasted the otherworld. The oldest inhabitant of Rip's village confirmed that the Catskills had long been known to be "haunted by strange beings" and "odd-looking personages" dressed "in a quaint outlandish fashion" who liked to bowl ninepins "in the hollow of the mountain." Even the great discoverer of the site, Hendrick Hudson, had experienced the otherworldly activities up in the mountains.[26]

Rip van Winkle's adventure outside of time parallels the Hindu model of holy sites, called *tirthas*. A *tirtha* is a crossing place, ford, doorway, or pilgrimage place, a place where you can easily and safely cross over from this world into the next, travel from the mundane to the sacred, behold an apparition of the gods.

It's a threshold that readily reveals the divine, where the presence of the spiritual is the "most luminous, most powerful, and most transparent." A *tirtha* is a location charged with purity, goodness, and auspiciousness. A *tirtha* is like a bridge over a river, "a spiritual ford where earth and heaven meet, or where one 'crosses over' the river of *samsara*—this round of repeated birth and death—to reach the 'far shore' of liberation."[27]

At a *tirtha*, human prayers easily rise up to the spiritual realms, and the good thoughts and influences of the gods make their divine descents, or *avataras*, to our realm. In fact, even the words convey this two-way movement of spirit, as *tirtha* and *avatara* come from similar roots: *tr* means "to cross over," and *avatr* means "to cross down."

It is as if the gods descend and throw open the doors of the *tirthas*, highlighting Don Juan's psychic "holes" in the landscape. This "showing forth" by the denizens of the celestial worlds is a hierophany across the landscape, creating "a living sacred geography" of holy sites.[28] In India, "the gods have shown forth in thousands of places" such that "the whole of India's geography is engraved with traces of mythic events."[29]

In fact, India's cultural memory of its sanctified landscape is one of the richest on the planet. There are holy sites throughout the Indian subcontinent and a copious store of mythic and legendary stories to account for them. Some of India's most ancient sacred texts, such as the *Mahabharata, Ramayana,* and the Puranas, catalog *tirthas,* and their epic adventures turn on the peregrinations of heroes across this sanctified landscape.

One Purana enumerates eighty-one *tirthas;* another counts sixty-two; the *Mahabharata* recounts 270; and according to a modern scholarly consensus based on seven sources and three authorities, there are at least eighty-four sacred places worthy of pilgrimage in modern India.[30]

In India, pilgrimage to sacred sites has always been regarded as a ritual, and *tirthayatra* originally meant "journeys to the sacred fords," while now it more generally denotes a pilgrimage. People journeyed to the *ksetras*, or holy places, to detect the activities of the gods, believing if they approached the *ksetra* in the right way, they could hope "for direct involvement in the divine world."[31]

Indian religious myths state that the subcontinent has seven sacred cities, four divine abodes, 108 "seats" of the Goddess Shakti, sixty-eight places where Shiva's *linga* appeared spontaneously from the Earth, seven sacred rivers, and twelve places where Shiva's *linga* manifested as a column of light. It's a map of pilgrimage sites, myths, a secret landscape of the gods. Every site has a presiding deity; every *tirtha* has a story of when the gods showed forth; each site has a connection to the cosmos; and each brings merit and illumination to those who undertake the *tirthayatra*.

In India, any traveler is immediately aware of the omnipresence of pilgrims at the holy sites. It's estimated that twenty million people visit the eighteen hundred Hindu shrines of India every year. But when you factor in the Buddhist sites, that number grows fantastically because legend holds that the relics of the Buddha were scattered to 84,000 *stupas* throughout India, each of them numinous.[32]

India is a whole and full sacred geography, "a body-cosmos," formed of a network of thousands of *tirthas* and places where the spiritual worlds broke through into the physical. All of these *tirthas* constitute "the very bones of India as a cultural unit."[33] In India, the myth in the landscape—the sacred, visionary geography—is its soul as a nation. You could say its soul is distributed throughout its 62, 81, 84, 108, or 270 *tirthas*.

In fact, India's soul has a name: Sati, Shiva's consort. The story goes that Sati, a representation of the generalized Goddess MahaDevi, killed herself. Shiva (one of Hinduism's three major gods) was beside himself with grief, and carried Sati's corpse around with him, neglecting his celestial duties. Vishnu (another of Hinduism's three big gods) sliced Sati's body up into dozens of pieces and distributed them throughout the Indian subcontinent. Every place a body part fell was known thereafter as a *Sati pitha,* or seat of Sati.

The number of *Sati pithas* (also called *Sakta pithas*) varied from four to 110, but whatever the correct count, the essential point was that the goddess's body was distributed throughout the landscape. In effect, India was sown with the pieces of her body; the landscape was sacralized by her distributed body. Sati as a celestial being or principle became grounded at these landscape sites. You could say "the Indian subcontinent *is* the goddess Sati," that "India is the Devi's living body."

Naturally, temples were established at the *Sati pithas,* but their function was mostly to "mark, specify, or objectify the sacrality of the local geography."[34] If anything, the preexisting sacrality of the site amplified the sacredness of the temple.

Another example of the same geomythic idea is in Tibet. That land was once mythically seen as the supine body of a demoness named Srin-mo. The only way to force this fierce demoness into submission was to erect temples at various key points on her body (including some at the country's capital, Lhasa) so as to pin her down. All of Tibet was considered "the flesh-eating red-faced" Srin-mo demoness.

Under the guidance of Padmasambhava, a hero of Tibetan culture, at least thirteen Buddhist temples set within a series of three concentric squares were specifically designed and placed to pin down and immobilize her head, shoulders, arms, legs, and feet. Like the dismembered body of Sati in India, Srin-mo "provides no less than the organic unity of the land, the totality of the context in which civilization could thrive."[35]

According to the distinguished French scholar Jean Richer, classical Greece may also have had a "sacred geography" based on a twelvefold division of the country into zodiacal wheels. Richer says the activities of the gods and heroes were coordinated with numerous astrologically founded sites. The ancient Greek theory of landscape alignments was based on the cult of a great solar god. "The sites of the most ancient temples of Greece had probably been selected by priests, the great initiates of a heliacal [solar] religion."

The same geomantic understanding that led to the siting of megalithic monuments throughout Europe, says Richer, "may have dictated the choice of the great temple sites." Physical and textual evidence supports the theory that the ancient Greeks wove a "fabric of correspondences" between the sky (and the course of the Sun through the signs or constellations of the zodiac), the inhabited parts of the Earth, and its cities.

In fact, Richer says, "astral beliefs and zodiacal geography" played a major role in the scheme of colonization and city-building throughout the Greco-Roman civilization, and one could by using deductive reasoning and the study of artifacts such as coin images reconstruct the diagrams influential in the colonization of Greece.[36]

Eliade coined the word *hierophany* to refer to an act of manifestation of the sacred. A hierophany happens when "something sacred shows itself to us." The term is an excellent one to use in reference to the sacred geography of not only India, Tibet, or Greece, but the entire planet. The history of religions, Eliade suggests, could be seen as a succession of many hierophanies, each one a "mysterious act," when something manifests from "a wholly different order, a reality that does not belong to our world."[37]

Let's say hierophanies happen at *tirthas.* The sacred manifests at holy sites. The gods show forth at fords and crossing-over points on the planet's surface. We go to such places to get a glimpse of these spiritual presences, to experience a hierophany. To get a sense of where to go—where the *tirthas* lie in the landscape—consult the myths. One working assumption of *The Galaxy on Earth* is that myths encode information about the planet's visionary geography, once you figure out how to read them.[38]

Most people regard myths as curiosities from an antique time, as raw material for symbolic psychological systems, or as ridiculously unreal artifacts from a primitive, fanciful deep past. For many people, the term "myth" is an all-purpose pejorative.

But metaphysics shows myths to be door-openers, living keys to an esoteric understanding of the landscape. In fact, quite often myths are keenly tied to specific localities. For convenience, I use the term *geomythic* to indicate the myth in the landscape.[39]

Some examples of geomyths are: Mount Etna in Sicily is said to be the site of the forge of Hephaistos, the smith-god of Mount Olympus. The Cyclopes are said also to have a smithy deep underneath the volcanic mountain and, once, Zeus imprisoned the monster Typhon under this mountain. Legend has it that the Polish city of Cracow was founded by the mythical ruler Krak on Wawel Hill above a cave occupied by a "ravenous" dragon. Mycenae in Greece was said to have been founded by Perseus, son of Zeus, while the ancient city's ring wall and its massive Gate with Lions was supposed to have been constructed by the Cyclopes. Samarkand in Uzbekistan was supposedly founded by two-thousand-year-old Afrasiab, the "Alive King of the Dead" and son of the Goddess Anakhita who came from Sirius in the Golden Age. Under Mount Damavand in Iran, King Solomon incarcerated a host of fallen angels or, alternatively, the demon Biourasf whose groans sound like volcanic rumblings. Ngai, the god who created humans, lives on *Kere Nyaga,* the "Mountain of Brightness," also known as Mount Kenya in Africa. Haleakala, a volcanic crater on Maui in Hawaii is known as the House

of the Sun because this is the place from which the demigod Maui lassoed the Sun.

Many more examples could be given. Stories about gods having forges under mountains, Cyclopes building huge walls, monsters imprisoned under volcanoes, ravening dragons inside hills, creator gods atop mountains—these are examples of geomyths, myths living in the landscape. They live in the landscape in the sense that, in a given locality, people remember (though disbelieve) the old stories told about their hills, mountains, caves, and grottoes. But more important, geomyths are guides to the esoteric landscape.

Bear in mind that geomyths are written in a kind of metaphysical shorthand. These geomyths are astonishingly old, and their frame of reference is inherently psychic. They presume a common and widespread ability to perceive the subtle landscape—far more common and widespread than it is today. They presume a deeper sense of embeddedness between humans and planet. Their reality starts on the other side of the *tirtha,* once you've passed through that peculiar "hole" in the landscape.

The geomythic language was also symbolic. Cyclopes, birthplaces of the Sun, Kings of the Dead, and hill-sequestered dragons meant something specific in initiates' language, something not quite literal, not quite what the words themselves suggest, yet not that far off either.

The paradoxical truth of myths is that you should take them almost literally but not as necessarily happening in our three-dimensional matter-bound reality. If you dismiss the myths out of hand, you run the risk of missing the *tirthas,* or failing to understand how to *use* them—for these sacred crossing-over points are *meant* to be used by us.

The language of geomyths is also sometimes analogy. When a site such as Montsegur, a craggy rock outcropping in the French Pyrenees, is said to be the location of the Grail Castle called *Munsalvaesche* of the Arthurian legends, it is true, but not quite literally. There is indeed a Grail Castle at Montsegur, but not a physical one, and it's more accurate to say the castle is *over* Montsegur. It's not a castle, architecturally speaking, but a defined, enclosed space; nor is the Holy Grail actually present if you're thinking of it in conventional terms as a dish, platter, vessel, cauldron, or cup blessed by Christ at the Last Supper. Yet the essential experience implied by the term "Grail Castle" is accessible at Montsegur.

You can definitely have a Grail experience inside a specially prepared spiritual space accessed at the top of the mountain. What is exciting is that Montsegur is not the Earth's only access to a Grail Castle. More than 140 such sites around the planet offer an equivalent experience, though couched in different mythic, cultural, and metaphysical language. The trick—and, intellectually, the fun—is to find geomythic equivalencies across myth systems and cultures, to find the common threads among perhaps ten different and seemingly contradictory descriptions of the Grail Castle.

This detective work is an engaging fusion of scholarship and clairvoyance. It is very helpful if you have had the opportunity to visit a Grail Castle in person (in a visionary sense). It also helps if you know the basic Western myth of the Fisher King.

The Fisher King occupies the Grail Castle in a desolate area known as the Wasteland. He lies on a couch every day, unable to get about due to a wound in his thigh or groin. He used to be known as the Rich Fisher King but now he's the Wounded Fisher King. The Holy Grail is borne before him every day in a solemn, mystical procession, but he can't partake of it or use it to heal himself. Only a Grail Knight specially initiated can heal him. One day, such a knight arrives, heals the King, the Wasteland is rejuvenated, and things are good again.

As I explain in more detail in part 2, the essential aspects of the Grail Castle are deep

memory, cosmic knowledge, healing, abundance of the food and drink of the gods, wondrous hospitality, among others. These are valuable clues for locating other Grail Castles amidst the veils and cultural nuances of different myth systems.

If you come across a myth about a sacred place in an unfamiliar culture that bears semblance to any of these qualities, you know you're on the trail of a probable Grail Castle, and your clairvoyance can fine-tune the identification.

This is, to me, a persuasive reason for taking myths seriously: they are accurate maps to the visionary geography of Earth. Discovering and interpreting these geomythic maps is like being part of a grand detective story; only we know *who* did it—the Supreme Butler, if you will—but we don't know *what* "he" and "his" assistants (the angelic hierarchy) actually did.

They left us a huge mirror—the planet—and all we have to do is look into the mirror and recognize the reflected face. The only thing is, it's not our face, but a face we as everyday men and women have never seen before. Despite this, it's our face from a time long ago, before we were ever born.

It starts to make more sense when you realize you are looking through symbols and analogies into a spiritual experience referenced to a specific landscape site. There is, in fact, a master list of forty-one design features of sacred sites. The forty-one have different functions, they produce different experiences, and—once you become familiar with them—they feel different, too. Generically, they are all sacred places, in that they evoke an experience of the holy and numinous; but specifically, they achieve this quality of sacredness through strikingly different ways and means.

This will become clearer in part 2. There I show that the geomyths can be extracted from the larger body of mythology to describe different energy structures and processes on the planet. These different features comprise the global network of *tirthas* and the patterns they make. When I say "patterns," you might wish to recall the meditative image from above of stars and constellations overlaid on the physical Earth.

The Galaxy on Earth proposes ways of conceptualizing and interpreting those patterns. In fact, an old word from English perfectly describes this process: geomancy. It comes from the Greek, *Ge,* for "Earth," and *mantos,* for "divination," and it has an elegant double-nuanced meaning. Geomancy means *divining* the secrets of the patterning and organization of the Earth, and it means the process of *divinizing* the Earth by figuring out its secrets, by *seeing*—which is to say, acknowledging—its essence.

A geomantic site is one in which the sacred has shone forth into the world; it is a *tirtha,* a place in which a previous hierophany is still trembling the landscape; it is a place worthy of our pilgrimage and attention.

In this type of approach, mythology is one of the most valuable resources we have for reconstituting a memory of the original templating of the Earth in that long ago hierophanic moment when the gods showed forth and left their numinous traces around the Earth. I use the term visionary geography to denote the hierophanic, geomythic, geomantic landscape—a planet of holy sites. It is a landscape of visions, one in which you need to be visionary to see things. It is a landscape purposeful and relevant to humans. It pertains to consciousness, the structure and processes of the galaxy, and the reason we and the planet are here.

A Marvelous Cosmic Mystery upon the Earth

Not only are there a great many sacred sites on Earth, and not only are they distributed uniformly around the planet, but when seen as a whole, they express a pattern. That pattern is a template of an edited, condensed version of the galaxy. The galaxy, astrophysicists estimate, contains perhaps one hundred billion stars. That's too many—too rich an infusion—for a planet, or at least, for our planet. So we have a smaller amount.

Although the number may seem fantastic or improbable, about 85,000 different stars are represented across the surface of the planet, corresponding to the Earth's many thousands of holy sites and made present by large energy canopies called domes. The stars are selected on the basis of their magnitude (or brightness), from Earth's vantage point, and in terms of their function and status in the galaxy.

The fact of the galaxy on Earth implies that the entire Earth is by definition extraterrestrial in nature. There are many doorways built into the fabric itself through which Pleiadians, Sirians, Arcturians, Vegans, and other fabulous or inimical beings from the ET pantheon can rightfully have egress to our planet. I say "rightfully" because it was designed that way. This is just one feature of the complete model, what some call the planetary grid, the sacred sites matrix, or Earth's energy topology—or in this book, visionary geography.

Let's consider the big picture. The astonishing fact is that to account for Earth's visionary geography you need to explain the origin and design principles of the planet, and to do that you need a spiritualized conception of the galaxy. You need a conception that relates the structures of the galaxy to the structures of human consciousness, using the Earth as an interface. I refer to this triple-layered model as the galaxy on Earth.

The representation of thousands of stars on the planet's surface is only one feature among the forty-one basic design features I mentioned previously. Also present are many structures, "places," and processes found in the spiritual worlds and often described in the world's religious, spiritual, and mythic traditions. Not only are individual stars represented, but miniaturized versions of the galaxy are templated in the landscape. The Celtic myths referred to this star-mapped landscape as Avalon and the Summer Country.

Hindu mythology talks of the cosmic mountain called Mount Meru and its eight Celestial Cities arrayed around it. These eight Celestial Cities are present on the Earth, and so is the one archetypal Mount Meru. Persian mystics spoke of the cosmic mountain, Mount Qaf. It is the same as—and different from—Mount Meru, the cosmic mountain that is replicated many times across the Earth. Homer and Virgil recounted their heroes entering the Underworld and Land of the Dead through certain portals in the landscape. These Underworld entrances are present on the planet, almost two thousand of them. If you have the pluck, you can pass through them and find out what's inside.

Greek and Norse myths say the major gods dwell in a special place, called Mount Olympus or Asgard, respectively. The Hindus called it Indra's City of Amaravati and the Sumerians knew it as the *Ekur*. These homes of the gods are present in multiple expressions in the planet's grid system. The Greek, Chinese, and Vedic myths say the world originally emerged from a Cosmic Egg; there are Cosmic Eggs on Earth. The Chinese, Norse, and Hindu stories say that the world was generated from the body of a primordial giant, P'an ku, Ymir, or Purusha. Representations of this primogenitive cosmic giant or Universal Man are found in the planet's energy topology.

Norse myth describes the massive Midgard serpent wrapped around the base of the Tree of Life; other myths claim dragons lurk in caves, grottoes, hills, glens, lakes, inside mountains. These stories are factual: dragons are present in the sacred sites matrix, though they aren't quite what you would think. The variously described ten "families" or choirs of angels are associated with the various geomantic features mentioned throughout this book. There are even wormholes or "quick ways" by which you can travel almost instantaneously from one site to another across the planet. Many more correlations between the galaxy and Earth could be listed.

So how did all this galactic stuff get here on Earth? Was it brought? Did somebody come with a giant cookie cutter or stamp? Did people construct their temples in imitation of these mythic archetypes?

My next book, *The Emerald Modem,* gives the full answer to these and many related questions, but the short answers are no, no, and no. The energy topology was here *before* the Earth was. It is in fact a truer Earth than the Earth we know. It's the mold, the organizing field.

Imagine a transparent skin around the planet, like an aura. In this auric skin are all the features I've mentioned, and many I haven't. It is a multidimensional matrix teeming with galactic life. The physical planet emerges from this auric matrix as if the galactic matrix births it, and the planet retains copious birthmarks, imprints of all this teeming life of the galaxy.

In fact, the galactic matrix and the physical planet are one and the same, occupying the same space in different dimensions. Earth's visionary geography lies close to the physical skin of the planet the way heat waves ripple just a bit above a hot summer landscape.

It isn't even correct to say the galaxy is *imprinted* on the Earth. It is present, to borrow a phrase from the Australian Aborigines, as a Dreaming in the Earth—*as* the Earth. Where there is a physical mountain, there is also a star; where there is a human settlement, there is an Avalon, or miniaturized galaxy; where there is a rounded hill, there is also a dragon sitting on a horde of gems; where there is a physical temple, there may also be the home of the gods.

It is misleading to see this galactic skin as situated only on the Earth's surface. If you could see this with double vision, you would behold a galaxy and a planet occupying the same point in space. The globe of Earth is a miniature galaxy, brimming with stars and pulsating with lines of connection. Everything in the celestial world is here on Earth as part of its visionary geography. The planets and stars are here; the constellations are here. The residences—the "Celestial Cities," as the *Mahabharata* calls them—of the gods, the temples of spiritual beings and the angelic hierarchy, are here. The processes that they supervise—that is, their essences—are here. And everything that's in the human body is here too: the organs, the chakras, the *nadis,* the myriad strands of connection between sites popularly called ley lines.

In fact, this is a key point. All the galaxy on Earth is but a magnificent planetary mirror of the spiritual organization of the human. It's us, projected outside to make a world around us. Ironically, it's highly solipsistic: everywhere you go, it's you; you're walking in yourself; seeing yourself; catching yourself at yet another unexpected angle. As I said earlier, however, the you you're watching is the Big You, the cosmic you, the Self you always are, before you ever came here.

Henry Corbin, the marvelous scholar of Persian mysticism, put this revelation elegantly when he said a moment comes when "the soul discovers itself to be the earthly counterpart of another being with which it forms a totality that is dual in structure." These two parts are "the transcendent celestial Self and the earthly Self." The soul came from this transcendent Self in the original days of creation and long before coming to the Earth, but as souls we forgot all about it. "This Self had become strange to it while the soul slumbered in the world of ordinary consciousness."[40]

Remembering the Self is what the Earth's visionary geography facilitates for us. That's why it's here: to help us wake from this long slumber of forgetting *and,* once awake, not to feel like a stranger. This is a crucial consideration. When you start to wake up, and sense a preexistence in a spiritual realm, when the soul at last starts to find itself, it "experiences itself as exiled, terrified, and disoriented by and among the common norms," says Corbin. The soul discovers itself to be "alone in a world formerly familiar."[41]

The soul feels itself to be a stranger in the world and starts looking around for a way out of here. That's where visionary geography comes in; that's where it is an act of grace. The way out of here is *here,* in the world within the world, the holy terrain behind the mundane one.

As Above, So Below, and in the Middle Too: A Rational Cosmological Template

As I said, *how* the galaxy got here on Earth requires a book in itself, so let's try an easier question. *Why* is the galaxy on Earth?

It's here so we will feel at home on the planet, our home away from home, so we won't feel constantly exiled and alone. To explain this statement would require a history of the human race. For the sake of brevity, let's accept the assertion of mystics and spiritual teachers that we ultimately derive from the spiritual worlds and the Supreme Being. Let's assume, in a neutral way, that in some form we once existed in something like a Garden of Eden in the spiritual worlds, then decided to incarnate in human bodies on a physical planet. Let's put aside the moral spin on the concept of a "fall" and think of it only as a falling away from full awareness.

For most of us, it's hard—on most days, nearly impossible—to remember much of our widely rumored spiritual origins. On our better days, we take it on faith. Not remembering puts us on edge, a little anxious, alienated, a bit estranged from things.

Let's say it was the intention—and a brilliant idea—to fashion the Earth to serve to wake us up gradually and restore our full memory of our cosmic and spiritual origins. Let's say some clever and compassionate beings designed the planet's energy matrix to work as a mirror, to show us our cosmic better halves.

It's a little strange for us at first, as if we woke up in somebody else's body, and a mighty big body at that. We travel to sacred sites, looking into the mirror at each. Eventually we recognize the face. Keep at it long enough and you get total recall.

A little phrase attributed to Hermes Trismegistus, the magus of the old Mysteries, says, "as above, so below." The "above" is the galaxy and the celestial realms; the "below" is us, humans in bodies. The concept is that the structures, contents, and processes of the galaxy are found in the human. This has a practical advantage. If you want to understand how the cosmos works, figure out how the human does; or if you want to plumb the depths of the human organization, master the design principles of the cosmos.

Left out of this handy axiom—just five words, but they make all the difference—is *and in the middle too.* The middle is planet Earth, templated with the same galactic imprint as the human. This gives us three things in a set: galaxy, planet, human. To understand the human and the galaxy, study the Earth. To remember how you came from the galaxy, study the Earth. To overcome your homesickness and sense of alienation, study the Earth.

Even better, to *return* to the galaxy while *remaining* on Earth in your body, study the Earth. Everything we need to remember our spiritual origins is here as part of the planet, as Earth's soul. Think of it as Gaia's secret galactic life.

It's helpful to be able to remember in full where we came from, but we didn't come here only to remember. We came here to participate in an experiment, to see to what degree total recall

is possible in material human bodies, and then to see how far we can take it. This long experiment is called evolution—in this case, the evolution of consciousness. What are the limits? How long will it take? Do we, like golfers, need a bit of a handicap? The answers are: I don't know, I don't know, and yes. Our handicap is the Earth's galactic template. It gives us a leg up on the mystery. The various structures in the Earth's energy matrix (described briefly in part 2) make it possible for human consciousness to wake up, remember, and evolve, to test the limits, to stretch the galactic membrane around the planet.

A remarkable essay by the Persian mystical philosopher Muhyiddin Ibn 'Arabi (died 1240 A.D.), called "The Earth which Was Created from What Remained of the Clay of Adam," gives another way of describing this correspondence between the planet and us. Ibn 'Arabi writes that after God created Adam as the origin and archetype of all human bodies, "there remained a surplus of the leaven of the clay."

First, God created a palm tree, which to Ibn 'Arabi symbolized the celestial Earth, then God laid out an immense Earth inside another tiny bit of original clay about the size of a sesame seed. According to Ibn 'Arabi, "the whole of our universe is to be found there in that Earth in its entirety . . . and that same Earth has hidden in it so many marvels and strange things" that we can't count them.

The Earth created from the leaven of Adam's clay is the "Earth of True Reality." Ibn 'Arabi also speaks of "that Earth, with its immensity and the multitude of universes which have been constituted *from it* and *in it*." For mystics, this is where theophanic visions take place, where revelations of the gods happen.[42]

Ibn 'Arabi, from our point of view, was talking in initiates' code. When he says Adam, he doesn't mean the Biblical flesh and blood Adam, husband to Eve, but rather the cosmic archetype of this human. This creation is formally called

Adam Kadmon by the Qabalists but, as mentioned earlier, certain myths describe "him" as Ymir, P'an Ku, Protogonas, or Purusha. William Blake called "him" the "Ancient Man" and the "Giant Albion." By celestial Earth and Earth of True Reality, Ibn 'Arabi is referring to what I have called the Earth's energy topology, its matrix of sacred sites, or the auric skin of the galaxy templated upon the planet—its *visionary* geography.

Ibn 'Arabi's celestial Earth is a visionary place. It's a mystical terrain, a realm of hierophanies, the place where you get visions of the galaxy, where you walk among the stars, where you recall yourself. The celestial Earth is the "inmost secret of man."[43] The planet's array of holy sites is where you divine this inmost secret and claim it for yourself. It's where you see Adam in the mirror.

Draping the Giant Albion, the Ancient Man, over the Planet

Let's immerse ourselves again in the Earth's visionary geography to keep these concepts alive, vital, and grounded in experience.

Third Meditation

First, let's retrace our steps from the previous two exercises. Make yourself comfortable again, feet on the floor, eyes closed, attention on your breathing. Bring the blazing star at your belly into focus again, and smile to it as you exhale. Without effort, allow the star to enlarge, to move closer to you until it becomes the size of a beach ball.

Place the image of the blue-white planet Earth inside this star and continue to breathe to it as Love from Above. Notice the drifting, swirling clouds, the huge landmasses, the even huger sheets of water. Visualize yourself standing on this blue-white planet. Don't worry about how it's possible; give yourself the benefit of the doubt for the moment. There you are, standing like a giant on this blue-white planet inside a membrane of starlight. It feels like the seashore here.

While continuing to hold this image steady by breathing with Love from Above as you exhale, allow yourself a luxurious sigh as you lie down on this planet as if it were no bigger than a large beach ball. Let your backbone stretch, so much, in fact, that your legs wrap themselves all the way around the beach-ball planet and touch the back of your head.

Don't bother trying to figure out how this is possible. There you are, lying on your back on a wonderful beach ball. Your back muscles and spine are so relaxed that somehow you are completely wrapped around this beach ball and your feet are touching the back of your head.

Continue to breathe to this image with Love from Above. As you look at your body making this O-shape around the blue-white beach ball of a planet, you become aware that there are many points of twinkling light within you. There are, in fact, thousands of tiny stars in your body, with lines of light connecting them. You also notice eggs of light all around the inside of your body, like a lawn on Easter Sunday just before the egg hunt begins. Some eggs are golden, some silver, some translucent white, some like pock-marked golf balls.

You see temples, palaces, and rotundas filled with majestic beings of light. You see glorious spinning wheels of constellations, and you see some of the living shapes they represent: dog, bear, hunter, ship, shepherd, bull, centaur, goat.

All of this is inside your body draped luxuriously over the blue-white planet. The more you look, the harder it is to tell where your body ends and the planet's begins. The stars and eggs and palaces and wheels seem as much inside your body as within the planet. Continue to breathe to this image as Love from Above and without any effort. Allow yourself to feel that you are this huge cosmic body draped over the Earth and that you are this blue-white Earth too. . . .

This little exercise gives us an introductory sense of the meaning of Albion, Blake's ancient and giant human. This is the Qabalists' Adam Kadmon, the primordial vast human-shaped being whose "body" encompassed the universe. The Qabalists say that God's idea of perfect existence was Adam Kadmon and that as Gershom Scholem, the eminent scholar of Judaic mysteries, explains, Adam Kadmon was the "first configuration of the divine light."

Humanity before its "Fall" into material incarnation was conceived as a "cosmic being which contains the whole world in itself," says Scholem.[44] Adam's great soul contained and concentrated "the entire soul structure of mankind"; he was stretched out from one end of the world to another; his enormous size filled the universe and he concentrated the power of the whole universe in himself. Adam Kadmon, says Scholem, is "the mystical structure of God as He reveals Himself."[45]

Bear in mind of course that Adam Kadmon is a name originally written in Hebrew as an initiate's code involving both mathematical and occult references; in other words, it's not a gender-specific name. But the more obvious question is this: what does Albion or Adam Kadmon have to do with visionary geography?

Albion is the pattern behind the pattern. The first pattern is the visionary geography formed when all the sacred sites are seen as a whole. They represent the galaxy on Earth. But what is the galaxy? That's where the second pattern comes in.

The pattern revealed by the galaxy—the Qabalist's Adam Kadmon or Blake's Albion—is the "transcendent celestial Self" Henry Corbin reminded us of earlier. This is the half we forgot, but which comes to us as a guide when we start to remember.

If the universe was originally expressed as a gigantic human figure and this figure contained everything in existence including the soul of humanity, then if we're headed in the opposite direction—upstream, so to speak, back to the source, swimming against the flow of emanations—then the everything that is in existence will reproduce for us the image of Adam Kadmon. In other words, if the Qabalists are right, everything in the universe—all the stars, dragons, planets, eggs, spiritual beings, residences of the gods—comes out of the vast celestial body of Adam Kadmon. The end result, among others, is planet Earth.

That's the downstream flow of emanation, the course of differentiation. Going back, we *reassemble* all the parts—the stars, eggs, rotundas, angelic choirs, and the rest—to get the greater whole: Adam Kadmon. The universe, the galaxy on Earth, and the embodied human are in effect intermediate zones between Adam Kadmon above and its reflection below. Actually, it's another case of *as above, so below, and in the middle too.* Adam Kadmon above (God's first configuration), Adam Kadmon below (us), and in the middle too (the galaxy on Earth—Albion draped across the planet).

Humanity, the generic human, is the grand symbol of the Mysteries, explained esotericist Manly Hall. The perennial pursuit of the world's Mystery schools and esoteric teachings has been to model and experience the equivalencies between human being and cosmic being according to the principle that the macrocosm (the galaxy) is expressed and copied in the microcosm (the human). Esotericists, Hall said, "believed firmly that if once they could discover and classify the parts of man, they would possess the master key to the whole mystery of life." We live, Hall added, "isolated in the midst of an incomprehensible whole."[46] The genius of the Earth's sacred geography is that it enables us to penetrate this incomprehensible whole and to find the master key.

Some key energy structures of the Earth—for convenience, let's call them inner plane temples—can be correlated with esoterically known parts of the human anatomy. I have alluded to the correspondence between body chakras and energy lines and similar features in the Earth's visionary geography. There are many other correspondences.

An Earth temple structure called a Cosmic Egg has an equivalence in the human energy anatomy in the form of the *Brahmarandhra* chakra, a minor chakra located at the top of the brain and considered to be an aspect of the seventh, or crown, chakra. This energy center in the head is believed to provide one with information and perceptions of a cosmic, exalted nature.

Cosmic Eggs (discussed in detail in part 2) have a rich mythic resume, but in truth they are geomyths because they are found in the Earth's visionary geography, notably at a very holy place in India called Banaras. If you are at Banaras, or any of the other Cosmic Egg locations around the planet, you stand in an environment that energetically matches an energy center in your brain.

Hindu mythology describes eight Celestial Cities constellated around the divine city called Mount Meru. All of these "cities" are found in the planet's visionary geography (again, see part 2 for details). One is traditionally called Yasovati, the City of Isana, according to the Indian Puranas. Yasovati is actually a temple structure for the Moon and Soma (or Amrita), the fabled nectar of immortality favored by the gods. I call them Soma Temples, to keep it simple. In the human subtle anatomy, this Celestial City corresponds to the Soma or Amrita chakra in the brain associated with the crown chakra.

This center is known as the "City of Freedom," and like the Cosmic Egg chakra, it affords deep and liberating insights into reality. If you were to stand in the ruins of the ancient city of Ur (in modern Iraq) or at Barbury Castle, a large Earth circle bounded by a ditch on a long walkway called the Ridgeway in Wiltshire, England, you would be in an environment that energetically matches this energy center in your head.

Perpetual Star-Infused Pilgrimage: Asking Gaia Where It Hurts

So what do we *do* with this cosmological and geomythic information? To some degree, we are already doing it: we visit holy places hoping for a touch of the numinous. We know they're sacred, but we don't quite understand why. We want to contribute something, but we're not sure what is actually effective. It doesn't hurt to ask the planet itself.

Fourth Meditation

Let's try another exercise. As before, we first retrace our steps. Make yourself comfortable again, feet on the floor, eyes closed, attention on your breathing. Bring the blazing star at your belly into focus again, and smile to it as you exhale. Without effort, allow the star to enlarge, to move closer to you, to become the size of a golf ball, then a softball, then a beach ball. Place the image of the blue-white planet Earth inside this star and continue to breathe to it as Love from Above.

Now ask Gaia to reveal herself to you, to give you an image of her appearance. Gaia is different from Albion. Albion is something on the order of Gaia's celestial soul, whereas Gaia is more like the physical body of the planet expressed as a single sentient cosmic being. This needn't be a female, goddess image, though we are comfortable speaking of Mother Nature and Mother Earth.

Don't forget, the Earth is a planet—a *being*—in the solar system and galaxy. Gaia then is a way of referring to this totality of the planet and all its processes, life forms, features, and history.

Without straining or making any effort and while continuing to focus on your breathing and exhaling with a gentle smile and a quality of Love from Above, allow an image of Gaia to appear before you as the sentient expression of planet Earth. If no image comes into view, you have still made contact, and it's the contact that is relevant to this exercise. Ask Gaia where it hurts. Ask where you could send some Love from Above as you hold "her" body within your star at the center of your being.

You may see a picture; you may hear a few words; you may perceive a location; you may get a blank screen. It doesn't matter. Your intent is the key. Breathe to the planet as Love from Above; Gaia will take your good intent, your star-infused breathing, and put it to good use. Continue to breathe to the planet as Love from Above, remembering that your breath is its life. . . .

The results from this simple exercise can be arresting. Some people feel sad or cry; some are shown toxic sites, such as dumps, spill-sites, nuclear radiation storage facilities, or undiscovered land mines; others are shown geological fracture zones, seeds of potential earthquakes; or human burial places that were disturbed by inappropriate building; or ancient places of conflict, war, destruction, violence, rape, and mass death.

You might be shown places to visit; you might have the sense you've been specifically invited. You may have the sense of the planet as a being whose body is full of festering sores, untreated wounds, broken bones, ripped skin, black and blue marks, cuts, scrapes, abrasions, burns—if this were a person, you'd rush him to the ER at once. But how do you rush a planet to the emergency room?

You don't. You bring the ER room to the injury. You're already doing it by breathing as Love from Above to the Earth inside your star.

The Earth has many wounds, many of them psychic in nature. Terrible things have happened at sites where today there is no evidence of the previous depraved indifference to human life. Thousands were killed on a battlefield or in extermination camps, or in black magic rituals practiced at stepped pyramids in the jungle, but today there may be no physical trace. Yet the psychic residue of terrible, intense human trauma remains like a toxin at such places, perpetually influencing physical events within its range. You can do something about this, if you wish.

Retrace your steps, as above, from blazing star at your belly, to beach-ball size, to blue-white planet inserted inside it, breathing to it as Love from Above. Ask Gaia to show you a place of toxicity or pain somewhere on or in the Earth, or bring to mind a picture of such a place, such as the concentration camps at Auschwitz, or the battleground near Verdun, or ground zero at Hiroshima. See this place as being inside your star.

Spend a few moments breathing as Love from Above to it. Such places are highly toxic and deeply infected on an energy and consciousness level, so do not expect to work miracles in a few minutes, but every breath of star-infused attention helps clear the air at such places and makes it easier for beneficial physical changes to take place.

This is something you can give to Gaia any time you visit a holy site within "her" visionary geography. It's an act of spiritual geomancy in accordance with that old contract between us and the planet: Gaia maintains us as physical beings, and we are to maintain "her" spiritually by looking after her holy sites and infusing them with our stars.

This idea of reciprocal maintenance is part of William Blake's grand story, a story so big it's better to call it a myth. I mentioned that you could see Albion as Gaia's soul. That's essentially the way Blake saw it, except he called Gaia "Vala." But Blake's Albion was in a state of desolation, exile, pain, and near amnesia. He had turned away from the divine vision, shunned his spiritual emanations, was "sick, diseased, despairing in darkness and solitude."

"Albion groans in the deep slumbers of Death upon his Rock," wrote Blake in his magisterial poem *Jerusalem: The Emanation of the Giant Albion* in 1804. In the dark, unknown night, in his "long & cold repose," Albion stretched out "his Giant beauty" on the ground, in pain and tears, "self-exiled from the face of light & shine of morning."[47]

This esoteric knowledge of the geomythic landscape has political application. Conflict within Earth's visionary geography explains why China took over Tibet's holy city, Lhasa, and why it destroyed most of Tibet's temples. It is why war waged in Sarajevo for years; why Jerusalem has been fiercely contested for millennia; why Washington keeps bombing Baghdad; why a prison was erected on Alcatraz Island in San Francisco Bay; why one of the bloodiest battles of World War I was fought at Verdun; why the Mormons founded Salt Lake City; why Rome is the "Eternal City"; why the Zapotec Indians occupied Monte Alban to maintain their empire in Southern Mexico; why the British fought to maintain control of the Falklands.

The list is long. In fact, knowledge of star wars in the geomythic landscape could open up productive new branches of study in political science, history, and economics. Knowledge of the esoteric landscape is believed to have been used by the Knights Templar of Europe in the eleventh and twelfth centuries in siting future cathedrals; and by Nazi Germany in the 1930s and 1940s in its campaign to take over Europe. If you control even a small number of holy sites in the planet's visionary geography, you can potentially control everything that happens in that area. Empires can be maintained this way.

Thus we get a sense of why Albion feels so alienated from the world, so turned away from the divine vision. Albion's alienation is a metaphor for *our* estrangement from the Earth's visionary geography. His desolation and darkened vision is a metaphor for the global psychic toxicity we live within.

The cumulative effect of projecting human emotions into the ethers around the planet for millennia has been to create a toxic cloud of pain in the planet's aura. This toxic envelope continuously feeds back to us our own negativity, creating a fierce circulating loop of unexpiated pain that is hard—but not impossible—to break. The human body can be detoxified and emotionally purged; so can the planet. Planetary detoxification is one of the benefits to Gaia from responsible sacred sites tourism.

By responsible, I mean, literally, providing a response in accordance with the need of the place. In most cases, the most effective response we can make is to give back our star to the site. Gaia needs stars. Your star, my star, everyone's star. To Gaia, the star is what the "transcendent celestial Self" is to us: a potent reminder, a friendly gesture, the start of the healing process. Of course, we are not really giving our star away; when we leave a site, it goes with us. But it's the gesture of *recognition* that makes the contribution.

There is an elegant, majestic word for this planetary healing process: *Tikkun*. It is used in Qabalistic thinking and Judaic mysticism to denote a restoration of the original cosmic order and unity, the time before the "Fall," before the exile into incarnation. In Tikkun, all things are redeemed from their exile and everything is restored to its rightful place; all the broken pieces are mended, all the scattered sparks of light are collected, all things are restored to their original contact with God.

As Gershom Scholem explains, "The task of man is seen to consist in the direction of his whole inner purpose towards the restoration of the original harmony which was disturbed by the original defect . . ."[48] You could say all the parts of Adam Kadmon's vast cosmic body, spread out across the universe and forgetful of their home, come back to him. Blake foresaw the healing of Albion. The time will come, he wrote, "When all Albion's injuries shall cease, and when we shall/Embrace him, tenfold bright, rising from his tomb in immortality."[49]

This idea was put in more neutral terms in India's sacred scripture, the Rig Veda. The Vedic name for the universe expressed as a human figure was Prajapati, whose name meant Lord of Creatures. (Later the name Purusha became interchangeable with Prajapati.) Prajapati was the Vedic way of conceiving of the entire cosmos as a great living being, a single vast organism. The aim of the Vedic sacrificial fire ritual was to "reconstitute, replenish, rebuild, or reinvigorate Prajapati by gathering his dispersed energy."[50]

In other words, the fire ritual was a way of renewing Prajapati, who had sacrificed his cosmic body so that all of creation could exist. The Vedas saw the matter as a perpetual cycle: Prajapati "creatively releases his ascetic power into the world and is then continuously renourished in the sacrificial cult."[51] It was a simple feedback loop in which the cosmos maintained its creations and these in turn maintained the cosmos—and of course the most efficacious place to do this reciprocal maintenance was the Earth's sacred geography.

Keeping in mind these variations on the theme, what does Tikkun mean on a practical level for those visiting holy sites? It means you visit nodes within the planet's visionary geography with the understanding that they are parts in a vast context, a "fallen" celestial being who is the soul of Gaia and that this being, ultimately, is but a reflection of each of us. Your own quest to wake up, to gain spiritual insight, however you describe your spiritual, interior processes, gets *traction* at the holy sites.

You can move. You can expand. You can remember. You can make the landscape the temple for your meditations. This is what the Grail Quest involved: men and women traversing the geomythic landscape, finding parts of themselves in the mirrors of the visionary geography, eventually putting together an image of their "transcendent celestial Self." As you search for yourself in the geomythic landscape, you simultaneously contribute to Gaia's Tikkun.

Understanding the galaxy on Earth means you can refine your quest. Each of the forty-one basic design features described in part 2 refers to a stage, function, and process in consciousness. Each is relevant to us because each reflects to us a part of our spiritual constitution. They are workshops for our remembering.

For deep cosmic memory confirming your immortality as a spiritual being, visit a Grail Castle. To climb the cosmic mountain and ascend to the source of everything, visit a Cosmic Egg. To experience the Solar Logos, visit a Mithraeum. To revisit the Garden of Eden and have a near-death experience without physical injury, visit an Underworld entrance. To experience the angelic family called the Hashmallim, visit a dome and its dome caps. To walk among the stars in Avalon, visit a Landscape Zodiac. To converse with the evolved humans, celestial beings, and other spirits comprising the Hierarchy, pass through a Shambhallic doorway.

In addition to the classic consciousness-related features of Earth's visionary geography, other noteworthy, even surprising, things happen at sacred sites these days. Think of the Earth's web of sites as a prepared matrix capable of accommodating other otherworldly or supernatural events and visitations. UFO sightings are common to nodes in this geography; some speculate that sacred sites act as dimensional doorways making it easier for UFOs (presumed to exist in a different level of reality where matter is less solid) to come through into our reality.

Marian apparitions—that is, spectral daytime visions of the Virgin Mary—are common at pre-existing holy sites; in some instances, they rededicate a site with a new quality of holiness; in others they introduce a seemingly new site to the geomantic roster.

Crop circles, those enigmatic and usually geometric designs appearing in fields of standing grain, tend to appear near preexisting sacred sites. Often they get as close as possible to the extant sites—notably, megalithic sites such as Avebury and Silbury Hill in Wiltshire, England.

It's as if the world's visionary geography is being added to, amended, reinvigorated, as we watch, and we can feel these sites bristling with energy. We can describe it, but can we explain it? What is this energy we're feeling at the world's holy sites?

What Is the Energy Everybody's Talking About? The Star Is the Key

One January I went to Mount Shasta, a 14,000-foot peak in Northern California, for a week of meditation in the landscape. I wasn't planning on scaling the mountain, but I wanted to get a little off the mountain road and onto the great mountain's "skin," covered though it was by about eight feet of snow. I drove up the access road one morning around five, parked, and got out of my car. There was nobody around. It was still dark, though I could make out a bit of Shasta's slopes. I clutched my snowshoes and held my breath.

God, that mountain was scary. No, it was intimidating. Formidable. Majestic. I felt it throughout my body; I was shivering inside. I was in no physical danger, yet I felt at risk. What was in danger, of course, was my sense of self, my identity. Hinduism has an evocative term to denote the experience of an ordinary person

spending a few moments in the presence of a spiritual teacher. The word is *darshan* and it denotes the sense of imbibing the reality and implications of a more awake person. Standing before a mountain like Mount Shasta before dawn is a *darshan.*

I hiked across the snowfields for about twenty minutes, then found a place to sit, near a few conifers. I sat on my snowshoes so I wouldn't sink into the snow. I did the Blazing Star meditation and put Mount Shasta in the star, then I relaxed, and laughed. I had been in awe of myself. I was quaking in my snowshoes over a *darshan* with myself. Of course, I mean my Self, not the personality.

It is more accurate to say I was in awe of the Self of which Mount Shasta, numinous and exalted in its own right, is but a mirror, an aspect.

It makes sense when you think about it. If the galaxy is found on Earth, and this templated galaxy represents the very large terrestrially displayed body of a celestial being, which is God's idea of perfect existence, then the "energy" we sense at a sacred site in this galactic matrix upon Earth is what we might call the outer edge of the aura of this vast being. This is the big picture, the grand view. But the energy is arrayed in layers, in a hierarchy of exaltation.

From the top down, then, it goes: God, Prajapati (or Purusha, Adam Kadmon, or Albion, etc.), the angelic families, the myriads of stars (celestial beings), planet Earth, a particular holy site, you sitting at one of these sites. In sensing the "energy" at a node in Earth's sacred geography, you have perhaps one or two cells of your index finger touching the penumbra of the presence of all of creation.

Here's another description of apprehending the energy of a holy site. The German-Bolivian Buddhist monk, Lama Anagarika Govinda, made a pilgrimage to Tibet's Mount Kailash in 1948 and wrote about it in a memorable work called *The Way of the White Clouds.*

On first seeing "the dazzling dome of Kailas, the 'Jewel of the Snows,'" from a distance, Govinda was filled with "an immense peace" that filled the landscape and the heart of the pilgrim, he said, leaving him immune to personal concerns and possessed of the magnificent equanimity "of one who knows that nothing can happen to him other than what belongs to him already from eternity."

Govinda said that beholding Mount Kailash was like being face-to-face with the eternal, on the threshold of the "Throne of the Gods." He said that one cannot attempt to penetrate the energy field of Mount Kailash and the "mystery of ultimate reality" it embodies without risking one's life and sanity. This is the "price one has to pay for being admitted to the divine presence on the most sacred spot on Earth."[52]

One surprising irony of Earth's visionary geography is that the underlying energy at holy sites is not Earth energy at all, but cosmic energy, the energy of individual stars. Most of the planet's key geomantic sites (numbering almost 85,000) are energized by domes or their satellites, and each dome is the holographic presence of a specific star. The "Earth" energy you sense at holy sites is actually the spiritual reality of stars *on* the Earth.

As I said earlier, at a sacred site, you look into the face of the Supreme Being before you to whatever extent you can see it. Maybe it's easier to work at this from the ground up.

Take Sedona, Arizona, or Glastonbury, England. Both sacred sites attract thousands of visitors each year. Sedona, set in the striking red rocks of the high desert, has ET, UFO, and vortex attributions; Glastonbury, set in the rolling green hills of Somerset, has Celtic overtones of King Arthur, Avalon, and the Grail. In both cases, the energy exists in at least two layers: first, whatever preexisting pure sacrality the sites originally possessed; and second, the overlay of centuries of human visitation, projection, manipulation, and pollution of that original energy quality.

In practical terms, this means the energy you "tune into" at Sedona or Glastonbury may be only the secondary layer, representing the aspirations, and sometimes the delusions, overlaid by human visitors. While meditating at such sites, you may sense that you are in the midst of a dense dark fog full of swirling images, none of them yours.

A holy site can get congested, even toxic, if not regularly cleansed and purified of unprocessed human energies. In fact, the purification of sacred sites was once a regular part of ritual practice, so it is no judgment or condemnation to mention that some sites are in need of energy cleansing.[53]

Let's say you are able to discern the original surface at a place like Sedona or Glastonbury. Then it's a matter of determining which of the forty-one basic design features this particular site embodies. Is it a dome, a Grail Castle, a Mithraeum, a dragon, a Mount Olympus? Each has a different energy signature; each feels different; each, to inner sight, will look different; each, when you interact with it, will produce a different experience.

But this can be complicated. Isn't there some guide to conduct us through this labyrinth of sites in Earth's visionary geography?

There is, and in fact we have been using it throughout this chapter for the express purpose of guiding souls through the labyrinth of the Earth energy grid. It's the Blazing Star at the core of the four meditative exercises. The star is not only the guide but the answer to the inevitable—and justified—question about epistemology: "How do you *know* all this? Who says you're right?" If I hadn't written this book, I'd be asking the same questions.

The elegance of the star is that *you* can verify everything. Some things may look a little different, or get described from a different perspective, but the essentials are consistent. That's because visionary geography is a mystical science that produces results that can be corroborated. It's intellectually convenient to compare the science of visionary geography to acupuncture, which has a vocabulary, an accepted terrain of operations, a scheme of effects, and a *modus operandi* of treatment that requires training to master.

In 1984, I was invited to begin training in the mystical science of sacred geography under the tutelage of some excellent teachers in England named Blaise. Blaise is neither English nor even human. Blaise is a term I use to refer to a congeries of angels who had a lot to do with the original design and implementation of the planet's visionary geography and who today remain vitally involved in its maintenance and evolution. The Hebrews in their scheme of angelology call them the *Ofanim*, which means "the Wheels."

Paradoxically, Blaise is the Blazing Star that we have used in the four meditations. Even better, Blaise is something you already have access to; you had it before you ever picked up this book.[54]

One ramification of the axiom *As above, so below, and in the middle too* is that everything in the celestial world is represented in the human organization. The Austrian clairvoyant scientist Rudolf Steiner explained in great detail some years ago that all the families of angels (he described ten) participate in the processes of physiology and consciousness in the human being.[55] If we, as the ancient wisdom teachings all attest, are a breathing, walking microcosm of the grand and manifold mysteries of creation, then everything in Heaven is in us. The rightful place of the Ofanim then is at the center of our being, accessed two inches above the belly button and two inches inside.

This is only half the equation. The Ofanim—Blaise—sit in every human as the tiny blazing pinprick of light at the center of our being, as a spiritual umbilicus to Heaven, but they also sit in the Earth in an equivalent way. When you understand this, there is nothing, ultimately, about the Earth's visionary geography that will not make sense.

There is one place on Earth that is the planet's own "spiritual" umbilicus to the cosmos. It's called Avebury, and it's a stone circle twenty-eight acres in size in central Wiltshire in England. Two roads crisscross at Avebury and a small village nestles among the huge stones. That's where the Ofanim planted themselves, so to speak, where they buried the star, for Earth.

The geomantic significance of Avebury is discussed in part 3 under "Avebury," but I'll make a few comments here to secure this point. Every time we focus our breathing on the Blazing Star inside us, it puts us instantaneously in resonance with the Ofanim and the star at Avebury. The star at Avebury is the planet's umbilicus; it connects the Earth to the cosmos—Mother Cosmos, if you like—just as a physical umbilicus connects the fetus to the mother.

If all the planet's sacred sites are cups of water, the water from all the cups comes from Avebury and flows back to Avebury. Avebury is the seed for the Earth's sacralized landscape. Everything starts and ends at the Avebury umbilicus.

If you accept this premise—and you can verify it for yourself by visiting Avebury with attention on your star—then you see how every person can, if they wish, interact with this visionary geography for their benefit and the planet's. The star is the door-opener, the elucidator, and the season's pass. The star is also, as I said, the proof.

During my training, I was introduced to sites, often thrown in at the deep end, and told to "experience." I took notes, asked questions, checked texts for clues, and then I asked to be thrown in at the deep end again, and again. I realized I liked swimming. Through a combination of direct (guided) experience, clairvoyant insight, and textual research, I was able to put together some aspects of a very large picture.

The scope and details of this picture are continuously being amended and upgraded through more experience, insight, and research. One needs to be shamelessly eclectic, studying all extant myth systems for clues, for *tools*. The world's mythic repertory is a toolbox; you need to find the tools that open the door you're trying to go through.

One especially helpful technique is finding mythic equivalencies. One tradition knows a figure as Anfortas, the Wounded Fisher King; another as Ea, Lord of the Abyss; another as Noah and his Ark; and still another as Vishnu's first incarnation as Matsya, the Fish. These three are the same figure, as seen through German, Sumerian, Biblical, and Vedic filters. If you can find the same figure or geomythic feature in a different cultural context, penetrate to its essentials and understand it, then it illuminates all the other expressions of that same figure.

If you have had the good fortune to visit the Fisher King's "castle," then your insight benefits even more from discovering the mythic equivalencies because you can match myth with experience. This is appropriate since it seems myth is an initiate's code for referencing the geomythic landscape and for maintaining the knowledge of this referencing over long periods of time.

In fact, for me, myths and legends are an invaluable research tool, providing an "early warning" of a site's possible geomantic significance. Myths attributing giants, dragons, Sun or Moon gods to a site are always a good indication that the site in question has significant geomantic importance, that its temple structures have been teased out of the mythic description. So, in many respects, the most important question one could ask of a myth is: *where* did it take place? The more specific the myth is about location, the more likely it is a fairly accurate, if veiled, memory of geomantic significance.

Another technique of great value is holding data and theories up to the yardstick of organic and geometric laws. As I explain in *The Emerald Modem*, many of the basic functions described by mathematics, such as pi, phi (the golden ratio), and e (the principle of logarithmic expansion, or Napier's constant) are operative in the Earth's energy grid.

Certain fundamental shapes described by geometry as the five Platonic Solids are central to the design feature of the planet's energy body. The specific quantities of design features—144 Grail Castles, 1,080 Silver Eggs, 1,746 domes—are meaningful and purposefully chosen numbers that have mathematical and spiritual significance.[56]

All features are replicated and more or less uniformly distributed across the globe. Grail Castles, landscape chakras, and ley lines are global, not merely local, because Earth's visionary geography is based on the same design principles found in nature from DNA to sunflowers to galaxies.

In fact, you can learn a lot about the distribution of dome caps from a dome by studying the array of petals on a mature sunflower. Both are based on the botanical principle of phyllotaxis, which in turn is based on the golden ratio, and describes the basis by which leaves are distributed with respect to the stem.

So model-building and picture-describing, in terms of the Earth's sacred geography, must be in accordance with the principles of geometry, math, and organic form. This requirement can then be used as a touchstone for assessing results. You can check your speculations and interpretations against the laws of geometry and organic design, and you can cross-check by finding examples from other myth systems.

For example, consider the mythic equivalencies for merely one geomythic idea, discussed above: the world being created from the body of a vast celestial being, variously called Adam Kadmon, Ymir, Purusha, Albion, Prajapati, Protogonas, P'an Ku, Sati, Srin-mo. When you collate the data from these nine equivalent myths (and there are more) you start to feel like you're walking on epistemologically solid ground, that this mythic idea has some basis in reality and that it has global applications.

Along the way remarkable discoveries await you. In *The Galaxy on Earth*, you will learn why the gods almost always live on mountaintops, and why the *Mahabharata* frequently describes the shimmering majesty of celestial beings (seen from afar by mortals) as they walk around on the tops of the highest mountains. It has to do with domes.

You will find out why Rama, Hanuman, and the monkey hordes had to fight the ten-headed demon Ravanna to reclaim the Celestial City of Lanka; why Saint Patrick had to "imprison" a "demon" inside Croagh Patrick in Ireland; why Zeus did the same to the giant dragon-demon Typhon under Mount Etna in Sicily; and why Thraetona imprisoned the demon Dahak under Mount Damavand in Iran. And you will understand why Grail Knights have always described the Grail Castle as *Caer Sidi*, the Revolving, Spinning Castle, the entry into which is exceedingly difficult because the doors keep shifting location. You'll see why dragons always guard vast jewel hordes inside caves.

The method of *The Galaxy on Earth* is to operate in this spirit of eclecticism, empiricism, clairvoyance, and scholarship. The goal is to give you a frame of reference, an orientation, a starting point, for your exploration of any of the sites discussed in the book.

A few comments about my methodology. First, the sites covered are not meant to comprise a definitive list, nor is their listing hierarchical or in any way a ranking of importance. I selected these sites partly for their geographic and cultural-mythic variations, and for the particular geomantic feature each exemplifies. I left out some geomantically big ticket items, such as the

Giza pyramids, Rome, and Stonehenge, because they require too detailed a coverage to compress into a few pages. Others, such as Mecca in Saudi Arabia or the ancient Sumerian and Babylonian sites in Iraq, I did not include because most readers will be unable to visit them.

Second, the presentation of the historical, archeological, and legendary aspects of sites is deliberately selective, limited to the data most relevant to the geomantic reality of the site. Other information may be pertinent to an overall appreciation of a site, but it is not strictly needed to get a geomantic interpretation of the site.

Third, in part 2, various geomantic structures and mythic personages are given names, usually drawn from one mythic-metaphorical system. This is mostly for convenience and is not meant as an endorsement or preference for one mythic vocabulary over another. To most in the West, the Greek and Norse legends and names are more familiar than the Egyptian and Chinese. While I give multicultural tables of equivalencies (how a deity or celestial site is known in different myth systems), I tend to use one name or description to serve as a generic term for the deity or structure found in many cultures.

Fourth, you will often encounter abbreviated discussions and words seemingly in code in the geomantic commentary section under each site. The book would be inconveniently long if I described each geomantic feature or geomythic archetype afresh and comprehensively each time it came up at a site. Spend some time on part 2 familiarizing yourself with the terms and concepts, or frequently resort to this pivotal section for fuller explanations of concepts, characters, and features that are only briefly described under the geomantic commentary sections.

If you read, for example, about Croagh Patrick in Ireland and are mystified by terms such as Celestial City of Raksovati, Control Bubble, Churning the Ocean of Milk, and flooding the

Summer Country, resort to part 2 for help. To adequately explain even one feature, such as a Celestial City, requires a comprehensive new model of the universe, and that would take a lot of pages. Part 2 itself is only a brief explanation of the geomantic features and geomythic archetypes; a fuller discussion is found in *The Emerald Modem.*

Fifth, you may find the geomantic interpretations surprising, unusual, perhaps even shocking. It is reasonable, I propose, to expect the spiritual world to be arrestingly *different* from our physical world. If the two weren't different, they'd be the same, which is to say, there would be no revelation, no Mystery, no awakening possible.

Ultimately, the geomantic discussions are analogical and metaphorical. Most levels of human cognition seem only to involve the mental production of ever more elaborate *comparisons:* The temple of the gods on Mount Olympus is *like* an elegant, symmetrically arrayed, twelve-chambered white marble structure with a large central open feature. A dome is *like* a globular canopy of light overlaid upon a mountain. But a comparison is helpful when you're negotiating virgin territory. In most cases, the further you venture into this land of visionary geography, the more it will seem familiar, and something that you want to learn more about.

The Galaxy on Earth offers a practical way to fine-tune and deepen your geomythic immersion. It gives you the opportunity to engage a specific heightened experience; it provides a rational, mythically enriched framework with which to begin your interpretations of your encounters with the numinous. And it equips you (perhaps even inspires you) to conduct your spiritual quest for understanding, insight, and awakening in the context of the entire planet seen as a single initiation temple with thousands of doors and signs in all known languages.

Bear in mind that your quest also benefits the Earth. Most sensitive people today agree the planet is in need of nurturing. When you bring your Blazing Star to a holy site and breath to it there, it feeds the Earth with a nourishing blend of human and angelic energy.

In the next decade or so it is likely that the Earth will continue to generate turbulence in the four elements. If you can send the planet a little Love from Above, this may reduce the severity of the cleansing activities the planet deems necessary to get humanity's attention. (It will also identify you to the Earth as somebody of value to Her well-being. It is not a guarantee, but this might be useful if you find yourself in the midst of a natural disaster. The planet tends to look after Her own.)

The book shows how the myths, legends, mystical reports, and history and archeological aspects of a site are clues to the site's geomantic structure, and how this structure, once revealed, *validates* the attributions. This then indicates the way into an interactive experience with the holy site. Each site description reviews the basic physical and historical facts of the site, its legendary and mythic attributions, and the experiential reports on the site by travelers, mystics, and psychics. Then the site's geomythic function is identified and discussed, and the clues present in the first three categories of information—site description, mythic attributions, travelers' experiences—are highlighted to show how structure, memory, and experience encode to varying extents a site's essential nature.

Surprisingly, the keys to the sites were left at the sites themselves. It's the proverbial open secret, somewhat amusing when you catch on, and certainly enlightening once you start working with it.

Part Two

An A-Z Inventory of the Light Pattern Library of the Earth Grid

Creating a Geomythic Reality

This section of *The Galaxy on Earth* provides a brief glossary for forty-one key geomantic features referenced in part 3 in the context of actual sites. The Earth's visionary geography has more than forty-one geomantic features, but these are the ones that have been most prevalent among the fifty-six holy sites considered.

The purpose of this glossary is to provide generic descriptions of the different features so that when you encounter them in part 3, or even better, at the actual site, you will have some conceptual understanding of their nature. I recommend that you read this glossary before part 3, then refer to it as the various features are mentioned in relation to a site.

All the temple structures we encounter in the Earth's visionary geography are building blocks for creating a reality that makes sense. You could think of the variety of features as elements in a light pattern library. Numerous patterns in light work together to create our reality; they are its blueprint. They are also the mark of the creator, a bit like a manufacturer's seal, enabling us to divine a few of the thoughts behind the spiritual beings that created our world.

Even better, and what makes the system relevant to humans, is that the light pattern library that comprises Earth's subtle body is the same one that structures our consciousness. This puts us and the Earth in resonance, and it puts us both in resonance with the galaxy, the even grander expression of the light patterns. This demonstrates the marvelous principle of *As above, so below, and in the middle too.*

Even though these forty-one features are described here as discrete temple structures offering different types of experiences, they are all part of a larger unitary reality. The trouble is that unitary reality is too big for us to experience in a way that would make sense to us. It would be like trying to read all the books in a library at once. Instead, we read one book at a time, which means, we walk the Earth's geomythic landscape and encounter and assimilate one type of temple after the next, depending on the type of mystical experience we are seeking. A knowledge of the types of experiences each geomantic feature can produce helps us fine-tune our use of the geomythic landscape (see table 2).

Three examples vividly make this point. First, say you have sustained a near-death experience (NDE) and are struggling to integrate its baffling details of encounters and events in the spiritual worlds. You can use one of the Earth's 1,746 Underworld Entrances as a way of deepening your NDE, of bringing more of its contents to consciousness, and of using these remembered details as a foundation for going further into that realm without having to have another NDE.

Another possibility has to do with making contact with deceased family and friends or ancestors. The Hindus have a ritual called *shraddha,* in which they make sacrifices to honor their ancestors. It is a tradition at least two thousand years old, which finds particular application at the Hindu side of Gaya (as in Bodh Gaya) in India. Pilgrims to Gaya perform various rituals, do

Table 2

Practical Uses for the Light Pattern Library—A Selection

Feature	Application
Albion	Meet the terrestrial version of the Primal Human
Arc of Developing Consciousness	Walk through a unitive consciousness corridor
Avalon	Collect and "digest" a golden apple of wisdom
Chakra	Have your energies be resonant with the planet's
Cosmic Egg	Experience Heaven and Earth before their separation
Domes	Experience individual stars as celestial beings
Dragons	Master and assimilate the dragon energies within you
Emerald	Enter the Heart within the Heart
Epiphany Focus	Experience the Christ as a living energy
Gnome Egg	Get initiated into elemental energy
Golden Egg	Birth the Christ Child in consciousness
Grail Castle	Regain deep cosmic memory, heal multilifetime wounds
Interdimensional Portal	Encounter the Pleiadian Council of Light
Ixion's Wheel	Receive a Solar Logos initiation
Labyrinth	Download celestial light codings from the Hall of Records
Landscape Zodiacs	Integrate your horoscope dynamics
Lily	Experience purified human consciousness
Lucifer Binding Site	Deal with your Shadow
Mithraeum	Visit Calypso's Pleiadian Time Cave
Mount Olympus	Integrate the 14 rays of creation
Naga City	Experience the undifferentiated cosmos and creative chaos
Palladium	Meet the Supreme Being
Pointer's Ball	Walk between the dimensions of reality
Ray Master Sanctuary	Enjoy individual Ray Master encounters and initiations
Shambhala	Visit the seat of Earth's spiritual government
Silver Egg	Be guided into the Mysteries by Hermes-Thoth
Soma Temple	Have a go at the Fountain of Youth
Three Star Temple	Integrate angelic, human, elemental energies
Tree of Life	Experience the hierarchy of energies and dimensions
Underworld Entrances	Deepen awareness of near-death experience events
Vibrating Stone	Touch an object from the Andromeda galaxy

fasts, make prayers, and beseech Yama the death god to treat their ancestors well and to bring them peace. (The *shraddha,* one of the most extensive of Hindu pilgrimage rituals, is also used "as a means of warding off their fear of ghosts and of spirits.")[57]

Second, say you have had a brush with the angelic world, and would like more of that wonderful, exalted state of being. A Three Star Temple can provide this. All you need to interact with this temple is a Blazing Star, which every human already has as a birthright (see part 1). There your own Blazing Star interacts with one in the landscape, and interacts with two other versions of itself, in the purely angelic and elemental realms. You get to experience what it's like to fuse the three stars and three realms within consciousness. You get to experience how the human is the balance point between the angelic and elemental realms.

Third, say you remember a secret childhood interest you once had in the Little Folk, the fairies, gnomes, or other seemingly magical denizens of some invisible realm. Maybe you remember the *fun* of the interaction. That's how it was for me when I reencountered the gnomes as an adult and remembered the grand times we had had when I was young and suitably impressionable. To renew your relationship with the elemental world, a Gnome Egg is the way. There are plenty to go around—some 60,600 on Earth.

The gnomes, the elementals or Nature spirits for the earth element, are the beings who most closely work with people engaged in geomantic activities. If you immerse yourself in the geomythic landscape, you will inevitably encounter them, to your advantage, because they know their way around and can be excellent guides to the minutiae of local geomythic domains (see table 1 at the front of the book for locations of these and other features).

Let's take this a step further into the mystical possibilities. Say you are an astronomy buff or are familiar with the star myths from one or more cultures. For a direct experience of a star, unmediated by textbooks or anybody else's opinion, visit a dome (see table 3 for listings).

I once had an experience at a dome that pertained to the Pleiades (in the neck of Taurus) and Orion, the Great Hunter. In the Greek myths, Orion was said to be perpetually chasing the Seven Sisters of the Pleiades so as, presumably, to ravish them, as the male Greek mythic characters were wont to do. I discovered that the myth had it backwards. Orion protects the Pleiades from ravishment by other star beings or inimical energies. Orion as a celestial being can also heal karmic wounds sustained by Pleiadians within the human incarnational stream. I learned this firsthand by spending some time in meditation at the grounds of Mount Palomar, near San Diego in Southern California. That mountain is the dome for one of the stars in Orion, and by being there, I got to experience a little of Orion's nature.

How do you access these light-pattern library features? The easiest way is to follow the meditation in part 1 involving the Earth in the Blazing Star. Instead of the Earth, put the specific site in the Blazing Star. If you are at Lourdes in France, put the cathedral, grotto, and whatever else you can picture from the site inside your star. This reverses your relationship with the site, and by extension, with the Earth. You are now assuming the rightful human role as geomantic interface between galaxy and planet, spiritual hierarchy and matter.

Focus your attention on the Lourdes within your star and breathe as Love from Above to this image. Let things develop from there. If you consciously work with spiritual beings, guides, angels, or subtle plane teachers, ask them for assistance in clarifying your vision and facilitating appropriate visionary information or experiences to enter your awareness.

Table 3
Stars Corresponding to Domes on Earth

Achernar, alpha Eridani	Machu Picchu, Peru
Albireo, beta Cygnus	Montserrat, Spain
Alchiba, alpha Corvus	Mt. Bugarach, Rennes-le-Chateau, France
Aldebaran, alpha Taurii (Taurus)	Dome of the Rock, Jerusalem, Israel
Al Giedi, alpha Capricorn	Mount Ida, Crete, Greece
Alioth, epsilon Ursae Majoris	Easter Island, Chile
Alnitak, zeta Orion	Cathedral Rock, Sedona, Arizona, U.S.
Alpha Centauri, Rigel Centaurus	Banaras, India
Alpha Fornacis	Bayreuth, Germany
Alpha Volantis, Piscis Volans (Flying Fish)	Mount Vesuvius (Cumae), Naples, Italy
Alphecca, alpha Coruna Borealis	Tiryns, near Mycenae, Greece
Alpheratz, alpha Andromeda	Troy, Turkey
Alshain, beta Aquila, the Eagle	Lake Titicaca, Peru, near Cusco
Altair, alpha Aquilae	Tenochtitlan (Teotihuacan), Mexico City, Mexico
Anser, beta Vulpecula, the Fox	Mount Vesuvius (Cumae), Naples, Italy
Antares, alpha Scorpii (Scorpio)	Chalice Hill, Glastonbury, England
Arcturus, alpha Boötes	Chaco Canyon, New Mexico, U.S.
Arneb, alpha Lepus (the Hare)	Dornach, Switzerland
Beta Crateris (Crater, the Cup)	Afrasiab, Samarkand, Uzbekistan
Canopus, alpha Carinae	Iona Island, Scotland
Capella, alpha Auriga	Acropolis, Athens, Greece
Cursa, beta Eridani	Santiago de Compostela, Spain
Delta Boötes	Grand Jer Mountain, Lourdes, France
Delta Cephei (Cepheus)	Externsteine/Grotenburg, Detmold, Germany
Delta Hydra	Wawel Hill, Cracow, Poland
Delta Perseus	Mount Haleakala, Maui, Hawaii, U.S.
Deneb, alpha Cygnus	Jasna Gora, Czestochowa, Poland
Denebola, beta Leonis	Wilson Mountain, Sedona, Arizona, U.S.
Dubhe, alpha Ursae Majoris	Wu-T'ai Shan, China
Dumbbell Nebula, M27, Vulpecula	Mount Fuji, Japan

Epsilon Cephei	Abydos, Egypt
Gamma Corona Borealis	Mycenae, Greece
Gamma Delphinus	Mont-Royal, Montreal, Quebec, Canada
Lambda Boötes	Schnebly Hill, Sedona, Arizona, U.S.
Maiaplacidus, beta Argo Navis	Mt. Nonotuck (Mount Holyoke), Hadley, Massachusetts, U.S.
Merak, beta Ursae Majoris	Cerro Gordo, Teotihuacan, Mexico
Merope, epsilon Pleiades	Beckery, Glastonbury, England
Mintaka, delta Orion	Montsegur, France
Murzim, beta Canis Majoris	Mount Kailash, Tibet
Nusakan, beta Corona Borealis	Mount Etna, Taormina, Sicily, Italy
Nu Taurii (Taurus)	Chichen Itza, Mexico
Polaris, alpha Ursae Minoris	Hardwar, India
Praesepe, epsilon Cancer	Mt. Temahani, Raiatea, Society Islands
Procyon, alpha Canis Minoris	Boynton Canyon, Sedona, Arizona, U.S.
Ras al Hawwa, alpha Ophiuchus Serpentarius	Mt. Damavand, Iran
Rastaban, beta Draconis	Uluru, Alice Springs, Australia
Rigel, beta Orion	Mount Holyoke, Hadley, Massachusetts, U.S.
Rotanev, beta Delphinus	Clingman's Dome, Tennessee, U.S.
Sa'd al Bahaim, theta Pegasus	Juozapines Hill, (Gediminas Hill), Vilnius, Lithuania
Sadalmelik, alpha Aquarius	Tetford, England
Sadalsuud, beta Aquarius	Steep Hill, Lincoln, England
S Camelopardalis	Croagh Patrick, Ireland
Seginus, gamma Boötes	Hill of Tara, Ireland
Sirius, alpha Canis Major	Carnac, France
Spica, alpha Virginis (Virgo)	Glastonbury Tor, Glastonbury, England
Star 15, Lynx	Cusco, Peru
Theta Ophiuchi (Ophiuchus)	Citamparam, India
Thuban, alpha Draconis	Delphi, Mt. Parnassus, Greece
Vega, alpha Lyra	Brown's Hill, Monticello, Charlottesville, Virginia, U.S.
Wezen, delta Canis Majoris	Mt. Kithairon, Thebes, Greece
Zosma, delta Leonis (Leo)	Hill Cumorah, Palmyra, New York, U.S.

Table 4

A Geomancer's Do-It-Yourself Toolkit

Here are tips for evaluating a sacred site, or discovering a new one.

Function	Indication
1. Tune into your Star	Proof of spiritual presence and galaxy on Earth feature
2. Assess the terrain	Domes, Cosmic Eggs on mountains, zodiacs on settled flatland and valleys
3. Study the site myths	Clues about the type of geomythic temple present
4. Note references to gods and their functions	Could be Ray Masters
5. Consider reports of mystics	Clues about the type of experience you may have there

---

If you are conversant with the gnomes, ask them for help; their observations can be surprisingly useful. When I was focusing my attention on Sedona, Arizona, for part 3, for several days running the gnomes told me about different aspects and problems with this site, all of which I used. Probably your best and most reliable guide to the geomythic terrain of any site is the star itself. It knows the pattern well; if you are open to it, let the star show you. See table 4 for more ideas on this.

Remember two things: First, you may have a deep visionary experience yet not see anything or even remember any details *that* day. It doesn't mean the contents of the experience were not registered in your subtle being bodies. They will eventually percolate into your awareness, perhaps through dream images or sudden daytime inspirations or pictures. Carlos Castaneda always said it took him years to remember all the wild and crazy things he did while in the "second attention."

Second, whatever happens, whatever you are aware of, or not, the moment you put the site in your star you are benefiting the Earth, giving some angelic light back to it. As Woody Allen once said, showing up is worth ninety percent. When you breathe as Love from Above to Lourdes within your star—and of course, to any site of whatever size or scale—you are helping to heal the planet.

If you know something in advance about the site's geomantic features—say you are at Montsegur in the French Pyrenees and know it is a Grail Castle—then after you have put the site in the star, you could allow your mind to form the generic image of the Grail Castle, using some of the conceptual and perceptual references in this book.

Be prepared for your Grail Castle to look altogether different from what is described in *The Galaxy on Earth*; on the other hand, it may be similar. It is not too important; focus on the energy essence. Things are in form, after all, only for the purposes of illustration. When you get the point, the form doesn't matter.

Albion

QUANTITY: 445

EQUIVALENT NAMES: Purusha; Ymir; Adam Kadmon; P'an-ku; Primordial Man; the Goddess Sati; the Srin-mo Demoness.

LOCATIONS: There is one for the entire planet, one each for the twelve pentagonal divisions of the Earth's surface, and one each for the 432 zodiacs.

DESCRIPTION: In ancient times it was the name for the Isle of Britain, but here the name derives from William Blake, who used it to describe the original human. Albion represents the entirety of the galaxy expressed as a generic human figure that contains all the stars and planets. In myth, it is the cosmic being who sacrifices his body to create the world.

The cosmic blueprint for this, Adam Kadmon, is described by Qabala; the imprint of that archetype on the Earth is called Albion, and it exists geomythically on three levels.

First, Albion is the summation of a Landscape Zodiac; its numerous stars are his wings or auric field, while the central energy line, or Oroboros Line, dividing the zodiac in half is the chakra column in his body. When a zodiac has been "worked" on and "activated" through the cooperation of the elemental, human, and angelic communities, its Albion awakens. Its inner life is the galaxy filtered through the life of humanity over time.

Second, each of the twelve pentagonal divisions of the Earth's prime energy body is at its highest and most complete level an Albion. For simplicity's sake, we could refer to these divisions as *Albion plates.* Each is a template for the full expression of Albion, although, technically, each Albion plate is a hologram of the single planetary Albion.

Also, each Albion plate is under a particular zodiacal influence for a 2,400-year period, such as Scorpio, Taurus, Leo, and the rest. You could think of it as a lamp turned on directly over each Albion plate; the light radiates onto the plate for the duration of this time period, influencing everything in that Albion plate—people, biological life, temple structures—with its specific flavor

of zodiacal energy. Each Albion plate is always under one of these twelve zodiacal energies, an influence that supports large trends in human consciousness, identity, and behavior. Each of these Albions contains eighty-one chakras, nine major and seventy-two minor.

Third, the Earth as a totality has one Albion whose consciousness when fully integrated and awakened will include the awarenesses of the Albions from the Landscape Zodiacs as well as the twelve pentagonal Earth face Albions. This single prime Albion represents and contains the totality of the human conscious experience on the Earth, light and dark, remembered and suppressed, from humanity's beginning. It is like humanity's collective higher Self. It will eventually awaken to its galactic origin and identity as part of the Earth's destiny, and as the Earth's long slumbering soul will awaken to "marry" the planet.

Arc of Developing Consciousness

QUANTITY: 174,060

EQUIVALENT NAMES: Parting of the Red Sea.

LOCATIONS: Acropolis; Glastonbury; Rennes-le-Chateau.

DESCRIPTION: The Arc is a particular kind of parabolic curve of consciousness, extending from one site to another in a curve, usually over a space of under ten miles, with a starting point and a grounding point, created by the intersection of ley line energy from the dome cap spiral lines in a vicinity.

The Arc is an etheric bridge that links one reality with another. Visually, it resembles a walled corridor, whose walls are at least one hundred feet tall. It is as if you are walking through the gap made by the parting of the Red Sea, between the motionless towering walls of water. The Red Sea in this metaphor would be the normal flow and inundation of our familiar spacetime reality. The Arc is a corridor outside of our accustomed spacetime framework. It is a unitive consciousness corridor in which you experience no distance or time duration. You enter at what seems to be the root chakra or grounding point and end up at the starting point or crown chakra, but there is no movement. Once inside the corridor, between the Land of Goshen and the Land of Promise there is no separation, no time, no distance. It's a zone of missing time.

The moment you enter the corridor you experience its entirety. You are walking through the parted sea, in a different or insulated dimension, moving quickly from Egypt to the Promised Land. The Promised Land, geomantically, is the consciousness of the star god whose body is extrapolated across the landscape in the form of forty-eight dome caps. Your awareness, in the corridor, now encompasses all that.

The Arc has to do with Love from Above and the process of individuation. It is the combination of grace and precipitation in the process of moving from the personal to the collective. It gives us the opportunity to experience unitive consciousness, as an experimental time-out from our normal individuation-focused reality. It facilitates the evolution of human awareness into the unitive state.

The feature was originally extrapolated into the landscape by one of the Ray Masters (for the first ray, known as Apollo, El Morya, and possibly Moses—see Ray Master Sanctuaries, below). There are approximately 14,505 Arcs per Albion plate.

The Arcs are usually present with a Pointer's Ball and share the same point of access; their function is complementary. As an example, the Arc in Glastonbury is about eight miles long, extending from the Tor, across Pointer's Ball to a small copse called Park Wood in Butleigh, to the site of a former stone circle called Lugshorn in the village of Compton Dundon.

Avalon: Temple of the Golden Apple

QUANTITY: 144

EQUIVALENT NAMES: Celestial City of Gandhavati; City of Vayu; the Summer Country; *Emain Ablach;* Floating Island of Aeolia; Gardens of the Hesperides; Venusberg.

LOCATIONS: Cumae; Delphi, Mount Parnassus; Glastonbury; Monticello; Montserrat; Mount Kailash; Mount Temahani; Mycenae; Teach Cormaic (Hill of Tara); Troy.

DESCRIPTION: This is a paradisiacal realm in the astral plane whose chief function is the cultivation, protection, and dispensing of golden apples, which are the fruits or encapsulations of higher spiritual wisdom. The Celtic name Avalon means "Isle of Apples," and it was a place of leisure and recuperation to which the Celtic magus Merlin retired and to which the mortally wounded King Arthur was taken to recover until the next round of incarnation. In that myth, Morgan le Fay and her eight priestesses preside over Avalon.

In the Vedic account of the eight Celestial Cities that surround Mount Meru, Gandhavati lies in the northwest, presided over by Vayu, Lord of the Wind. Other denizens of this city include the Gandharvas (celestial musicians), Apsaras (celestial dancing maidens), and the Nine Muses of Greek myth.

Avalon in a large sense is a single golden apple, the realm where the energies of the Sun and Moon mingle, where Time (the Greek Helios) and Space (the Vedic Soma) dance, creating the Day of Brahma, or a unit of spacetime known as the *kalpa,* about 4.3 billion years. In Avalon there is the continuous sacred marriage *(hieros gamos)* of the Year (Helios, Time) and the daughters of Space (the twenty-seven *Nakshatras* of King Soma). They dance the duration of the Day, which is the time content of the golden apple expressed as the life of stars.

Camalate Center

QUANTITY: 26
EQUIVALENT NAMES: Unavailable.
LOCATIONS: Cusco; Mycenae; Troy.
DESCRIPTION: This is a physical Mystery training and geomantic maintenance center that is found periodically in a different location around the Earth. The Arthurian myths contain the most vivid recollection of some aspects of its nature, a cadre of collegial Knights of the Round Table, presided over by King Arthur (an expression of the Solar Logos) and his magus, Merlin.

There have been 26 Camalate Centers in various cultures and locations, and their work has included servicing the Earth's geomythic body, working with the spiritual worlds on implementing galactic and planetary agendas, acting as a bridge between the angelic and elemental kingdoms, and birthing the Christ consciousness in matter.

The Camalate Center is based on a cosmic archetype and an astral model prototype. Its purpose is to ground the energies and consciousness of eight key stars or constellations central to the evolution of humanity and planet. These include: Sirius (Canis Major, Greater Dog); Canopus (Argo Navis); Orion; Pleiades (in Taurus); Arcturus (in Boötes); Cepheus; Cygnus; and Great Bear (Ursa Major). Each of these oversees one of the eight Celestial Cities.

The Camalate Center, as well as its affiliate stars, pertains to the inner heart chakra of the human and planet, called the *Ananda-kanda,* said by Hindu tantric models of the chakras to have eight petals and to hang like a pendant below the main, outer heart chakra, the *Anahata.*

Celestial Cities

QUANTITY: 8 types; 3,654 replicas of all 8 types
EQUIVALENT NAMES: See individual listings.
LOCATIONS: Too many to list.
DESCRIPTION: The Sanskrit Puranas recount how eight Celestial Cities surround the great golden city of Mount Meru on the peak of the world's cosmic mountain. The three chief Hindu gods, Brahma, Shiva, and Vishnu, dwell in Mount Meru. Each of the eight cities is a realm of a particular god and quality, and each has a specific cardinal or inter-cardinal direction, such as north or northwest. The gods of these cities are collectively known as the *Lokapalas,* the Guardians of the Directions.

In terms of Earth geomancy, these cities also have affiliations with the Earth's inner heart chakra, the *Ananda-kanda,* and the Camalate Centers. In this book, I have in most cases found more familiar, equivalent names from Western myth traditions to refer to these dimensions. Here is a summary map of their locations and functions:

East: City of Sakra or Amaravati, home of Indra, King of the gods; realm of the primary superintendent gods, the fourteen Ray Masters of the Great Bear: Mount Olympus.

Southeast: City of Tejovati, realm of the fire god, Agni; realm of the wild untamed Sun god, prototype of Time: Mithraeum.

South: City of Samyamani, realm of Yama, Lord of Death; the equivalent of the Greek Hades, King of the Dead, transition point out of planetary spheres: Underworld.

Southwest: City of Nirrti or Raksovati, realm of the Raksasas, Nagas, and cosmic serpent, Ananta-Sesa; primordial creative energy: Naga City.

West: City of Suddhavati, domain of King Varuna; also known as the Western Paradise, Blessed Isles, realm of the spiritual hierarchy: Shambhala.

Northwest: City of Gandhavati, domain of King Vayu, Lord of the Winds, realm of the Gandharvas and Apsaras; prototype of spacetime: Avalon.

North: City of Sankara, Yasovati, or Lanka, realm of Kubera, lord of wealth and endless riches; deep cosmic memory: Grail Castle.

Northeast: City of Soma or Kantimati, the Moon god, source of the Elixir of Immortality culled from the Ocean of Milk; prototype of Space: Soma Temple.

Chakras

QUANTITY: 36,014

EQUIVALENT NAMES: Planetary spheres; Planetary Logoi; Titans.

LOCATIONS: Too many to list.

DESCRIPTION: Chakras are the energy centers by which the level of consciousness associated with the seven planetary spheres enters the physical. The chakras transmit and holographically present the energies of Mars, Mercury, Venus, Jupiter, Saturn, and the Sun and Moon. These are not the physical planets, however, but spheres of cosmic influence bounded and defined by certain energy attributes conventionally assigned to the planets by astrology.

These qualities are sometimes individually called a Planetary Logos, which is like a god or deity of that domain of consciousness. Each chakra is a hologram of the presence and consciousness level of what the Greeks called the Titans.

In the Earth's visionary geography, chakras exist at different levels, and accuracy in attribution of chakras to landscape sites is one of the hardest things to achieve because of this multidimensionality. While all seven chakras work inter-

dependently and none is inherently better or worse, higher or lower, they comprise a hierarchy or cascade of energies and consciousness.

Here are some of the levels at which chakras exist in the Earth grid: Each Landscape Zodiac has a chakra hierarchy, running up the "spine" of the Albion and along the Oroboros Line that cleaves the zodiac in two. Each Albion plate has a chakra hierarchy in the form of energy centers.

The unitary planetary Albion also has a chakra hierarchy, but here it is a matter of forty-nine centers: seven major centers with seven aspects each plus one extra, making fifty. For each chakra, there is one site where all seven aspects line up, and that place can rightly be called the root chakra or heart chakra, or whatever. For example, Uluru in Australia and Teotihuacan in Mexico are both aspects of the Earth's solar plexus center, and Glastonbury in England is (the outer aspect of) the unitary Earth heart chakra.

Within an Albion, at any of its three levels of expression, are also seventy-two minor chakras or energy centers as defined by traditional Hindu yogic models. The original Albion's body encompasses the entire planet. This figure has nine major and seventy-two minor chakras, or eighty-one. Next, the planet has twelve equal surface divisions defined in geometry as pentagons (five-sided polyhedra), what I am calling Albion plates. There is an Albion for each of the twelve plates, and each has nine major and seventy-two minor chakras, or eighty-one. That gives 972 for the planet.

But that's only the top level. The system is a fractal, and a hologram with repeating patterns on each level. There are also Albions for each of the 432 Landscape Zodiacs, each of which has eighty-one chakras. Globally that gives another 34,992 chakras.

Thus on the three levels of Albions, there are 36,045 chakras on the Earth. You can see how it is difficult to be accurate with this complexity. You could legitimately identify a landscape chakra, but the tricky part is to know to which level of the system it pertains.

In most cases, a chakra hierarchy must be part of an Albion, his inner energy centers, as generated by a Landscape Zodiac. But in some instances, such as at Iona in Scotland, and Cusco in Peru, a dome may generate a chakra template independent of the presence of a Landscape Zodiac or Albion.

Control Bubbles

QUANTITY: 238
EQUIVALENT NAMES: Not available.
LOCATIONS: Chichen Itza; Croagh Patrick; Charlottesville, Virginia.
DESCRIPTION: The name is based on the visual appearance and perceived function of these structures which are equally distributed around the Earth, seventeen per Albion plate. These are arcane aspects of the Earth's visionary geography, kept out of public knowledge for obvious reasons; namely, to protect them from misuse.

The "bubble" appears like a beehive globular cell or spherical greenhouse; the glass panes comprise numerous smaller squares of glass; all of it is a hologram for the various geomantic aspects within the scope of control of this bubble. Spiritual or angelic beings work in these bubbles to regulate the "mixture" of angelic and cosmic energies flowing into and through the system and to keep the energies of the human, elemental, and angelic realms in balance.

Cosmic Egg

QUANTITY: 48
EQUIVALENT NAMES: Cosmic Mountain; Kashi; Egg of Brahma; Mundane Egg; *Shi'ur Komah;* Mount Kaf.
LOCATIONS: Banaras; Mount Damavand; Mount Ida.

DESCRIPTION: This is a concentrated energy field, globular in shape, that contains all the energies, structures, and potentialities of creation before Heaven was separated from Earth. Earth here does not mean the physical planet, but Gaia, which is not our planet, but substance, from the subtlest to the grossest, at all levels of existence. Heaven is the unmanifest realm of potential.

The Cosmic Egg is that condition of unity *before* the separation, when all the stars and planets, the Sun and Moon, were inside the Earth, and the Earth was still in Heaven. The Greeks said the Cosmic Egg resided in the stream of Oceanos, the primal river god, that flowed in a circle from the outermost edge of the Earth, back upon himself in a circular flux.

Most myths that describe Cosmic Eggs say that a primordial creator being, such as Brahma, the Hindu creator god, was birthed from the egg. As such, the Cosmic Egg is also what the Jewish mystics call the *Shi'ur Komah,* the mystical shape of the Godhead, as experienced by Moses on Mount Sinai, site of a Cosmic Egg.

The egg as the shape of the Godhead explains why a Cosmic Egg is the archetypal cosmic mountain, the consummate source of connection with the Godhead who presides over the Seven Heavens from a higher point. This higher point is referred to in Islamic mysticism as the Orient, while the Seven Heavens and everything below are called the Occident. Islamic mysticism calls the cosmic mountain, especially the Orient part, Mount Kaf.

Geomantically, Cosmic Eggs tend to be positioned at the root chakra point of a Landscape Zodiac or at a place that serves to stabilize the zodiac in the landscape. The eggs assist in landscape or grid activations and in Earth feature, or geomythic, amplifications. They also afford one profound mystical experiences.

Crown of the Ancient of Days

QUANTITY: 12

EQUIVALENT NAMES: Gorgon Medusa's Head; Brahma's Fifth Head.

LOCATIONS: Abydos; Banaras; Golgotha (see Dome of the Rock); Hansen's Mountain (see Monticello); Sacsaywaman (Cusco).

DESCRIPTION: Various myths speak of the severed head of a prime god, such as Brahma (Hindu), Bran the Blessed (Welsh), or Osiris (Egyptian), that is then installed at a specific landscape site for the benefit of others. Qabala speaks of the "Vast Countenance" and the "White Head" as epithets to evoke the otherwise ineffable and transcendent reality of the Supreme Being, or what are variously called the Ancient of Days, the Concealed of the Concealed, the Primordial Point.

This feature is also referred to as a Crown because it occupies the topmost position on the energy hierarchy called the Tree of Life, a position called *Kether*, which means "Crown." We could think of this feature as a hologram of an aspect of the Supreme Being present in twelve places around the Earth, one per Albion plate, peering omnisciently into our realm through vantage points in the visionary geography. Some are well-remembered by myth, such as the fifth head of Brahma at Banaras, the buried head of Osiris at Abydos, and the Noble Head of Bran the Blessed at the White Mount (St. Paul's Cathedral) in London.

The public or even mythic memory of other Crowns, such as the one near Monticello in Charlottesville, Virginia, has been entirely lost. Others, such as the Crown at the Hill of Skulls, or Golgotha, in Jerusalem, are in an in-between state, as it were, staring our understanding directly in the face without our comprehending their import.

Cyclopean Cities

QUANTITY: 6,300

EQUIVALENT NAMES: Stone Cities.

LOCATIONS: Cusco; Mycenae; Thebes; Troy.

DESCRIPTION: Here we have a case where we must take certain myths as literally true. If, for example, we read that the huge, cyclopean stones of Mycenae in Greece were originally placed there by the gods or giants, or that the walls of Troy were built in a year by the gods Apollo and Poseidon, then we must take the claim at face value. In the earliest days of the Earth, there were in fact many such massive stone edifices or citadels, what for convenience's sake I call Cyclopean Cities.

The term "cyclopean" is commonly used to describe the size of the stones at places such as Myceanae, Troy, and Sacsaywaman at Cusco in Peru, and it is also a reference to the mythical Cyclopes, the one-eyed giants presumed to have placed these stones. Again, the mythic clues must be believed because in fact the Elohim, a family of angels charged with physically installing most of the Earth's geomantic structures, especially the various types of stone works, are the same beings that myth remembers as Cyclopes.

In the planet's primordial days, the Elohim as Cyclopes erected 6,300 such cities of stone. It is shocking to contemplate what the planet must have felt like, energetically, in those days when the 6,300 Cyclopean Cities were intact and that nearly all of them today are vanished from the planet, and only a handful remain even as ruins.

What were they for? In *Shikasta*, Doris Lessing's marvelous recounting of esoteric lore about the planet masquerading as a science fiction novel, she calls these structures stone cities. They were built by the giants (who were eighteen feet tall, she says) and each exemplified a mathematical principle, symbol, and shape. One was a Square City, another a Triangle City, a third the

Rhomboid City. These cities were placed upon preexisting energy lines and had to do with "the basis and foundation of the transmitting systems of the Lock between Canopus and Rohanda . . . now poor Shikasta." The Lock was Lessing's term for the Earth energy grid and its cosmic connections to specific stars.[58]

In addition to the aspects suggested by Lessing, the Cyclopean Cities were dimensional matrices, both formed and formless, interfacing in the third dimension. The Cyclopean Cities fed into human and planetary reality possibilities to go beyond the present state of affairs as they were then. Even though very few of these cities are left in the physical plane, they are still on the planet like memories in the light field.

The Elohim helped to build them, but they were assisted by the Hyperboreans (primarily Pleiadians), the angelic family known as the Ofanim, the Archangel Metatron, and many of the Time Lords. The Time Lords rule time and count among their ranks the biblical prophet Enoch and the Archangel Metatron. These beings are particularly concerned with the fourth dimension.

Domes

QUANTITY: 1,746

EQUIVALENT NAMES: Residences of the gods.

LOCATIONS: See table 3.

DESCRIPTION: These are one of the central geomantic features in the Earth's visionary geography, responsible in many cases for making a site sacred. The dome is like a globular lampshade or etheric energy canopy, usually at least a few miles in diameter, and often more, set over mountains like an aureole. Various well-executed religious domes, such as the Dome of the Rock in Jerusalem, St. Paul's Cathedral dome in London, or Brunelleschi's dome in Florence, are excellent physical images of the subtler energy field of a dome.

In most cases, domes actually produced the mountains, summoning them up out of the soft clay of the Earth in its earliest days to be the physical aspects of the homes of the gods. Most of the Earth's 1,746 domes are situated over mountains, most of which were at one time volcanoes.

Their heat was so intense that the domes invariably also summoned up the water from deep inside the Earth to cool the landscape under the dome; that is why dowsers so often detect water tables, spirals, pools, and "domes" at sacred sites. It's an appropriate balance of fire above, water below.

The domes were distributed around the Earth in accordance with a plan to produce a specific energy matrix capable of supporting the evolution of higher consciousness among humans. Each dome represented the holographic presence of one of the 1,746 stars most relevant to human evolution on Earth. (I often provide physical data about the corresponding star—its size, distance, and brightness—to make its presence more real and grounded for the reader.)

The star affiliations are not a matter of archeo-astronomical alignment; they are the virtual or holographic presence of the actual star itself on the Earth. The different major stars in a given constellation are not necessarily next to one another on the landscape, but may be distributed all over the Earth.

The domes, from our vantage point, exist in between what we know as matter and what we experience as spirit, traveling faster than the speed of light and thus flickering between the dimensions of matter and spirit. They were like "spaceships" or UFOs, but that would be too parochial a description. You could not necessarily walk up to a dome and tap it with your knuckles and hear a sound, yet they had a palpable presence, as they occupied a more or less visually definable space.

They were sent to Earth from elsewhere in the galaxy as a way of preparing this planet for

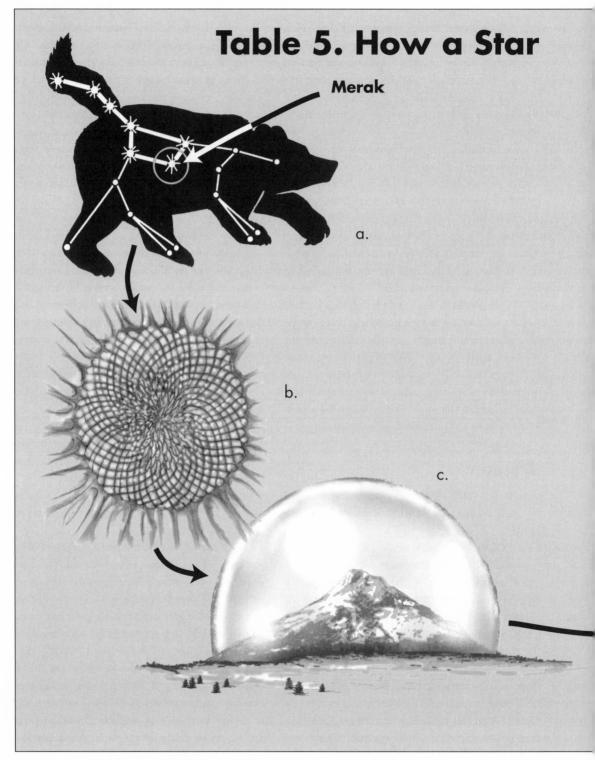

Table 5. How a Star

Merak

a.

b.

c.

Becomes a Dome

(a) Of the galaxy's billions of stars, 1,746 are selected for imprinting on the Earth, such as the beta star called Merak, in the Big Dipper, itself part of the constellation called the Great Bear (Ursae Majoris). (b) Each of the 1,746 domes represents a different star on the Earth, and its energy is imprinted in the Earth's subtle atmosphere. The dome itself generates an array of 48 smaller energy centers called dome caps; these are distributed in a geometric manner which resembles the way a sunflower head distributes its seeds. The total array of dome and dome caps may extend many miles across a landscape. (c) Seen with clairvoyant vision, the dome over a mountain is like a shimmering energy canopy, typically in variations of lilacs or golds. The dome itself is much bigger, taller, and wider than the physical mountain. (d) Experientially, standing inside a dome is like standing under a domed ceiling in a cathedral. It is likely that the original architectural impulse for domed cathedrals came from a perception of an energy dome in the landscape. This image gives you a fair idea of what the inside of a dome looks like, only it would be much larger.

d.

higher conscious evolution. The domes "came" here three times, and each dome returned to its predesignated spot. The first dome presence seeded the planet with the star pattern; the second brought up the water; the third activated the light patterns. The domes are expected to make a fourth arrival at some point in Earth's history.

During the first two "dome arrivals," there were no humans on Earth; during the third, in the early Lemurian time period (an estimated eighteen million years ago), some humans were aware of them. Certain myth systems, such as the Sumerian, remember the domes as the homes of the gods, and rightly so, because various high celestial beings were present in the domes.

An Islamic mystical tradition speaks of the *Xvarnah*, or "Light of Glory," which is the aura of a star as a celestial being. The *Xvarnah* is "the Energy operative from the initial instant of the formation of the world," which is involved in the world's final transfiguration. The Light of Glory is "the all-luminous substance, the pure luminesence of which Ohrmazd's [Ahura-Mazda, the creator god] creatures were constituted at their origin . . . the Energy of sacral light which gives coherence to their being."[59] The dome is the robe of glory, the *Aura Gloriae* or luminous halo, of a celestial being we think of as a star.

Now for the paradox. Technically, the domes have left the Earth, yet they were so bright and so intensely present that even their residual imprint is powerful enough to render and sustain a site in a state of high sacrality and numinosity.

The domes were interconnected by way of what we sense today as straight-running lines. Some of what dowsers describe as straight ley lines are residual impressions of these lines.

All 1,746 domes have two light filaments—one gold, one silver—that connect the dome from its topmost cap to a central master dome at Avebury in England. They carry the energies received at Avebury from the Earth's two princi-pal umbilical "parents," namely, Sirius in Canis Major, the Greater Dog (the gold line), and Canopus in Argo Navis, the Ship (the silver line). These are the two brightest stars in our galaxy. In other words, each dome is vicariously or indirectly connected to Sirius and Canopus.

Dome Caps

QUANTITY: 83,808

EQUIVALENT NAMES: Residences of the gods.

LOCATIONS: Too numerous to list.

DESCRIPTION: Each dome could generate up to forty-eight subsidiary energy centers, miniature domes, called dome caps, in a manner similar to the way a plant arrays its leaves around the central stalk. This array is based on the mathematical function called phi, or the Golden Mean, and it is found throughout nature, from the shape of seashells to galaxies. The dome caps are connected to the "mother" dome by way of spiral lines determined by phi.

Seen from above in vision, the dome and its dome caps resemble a mature, fully flowering sunflower head whose petals are arrayed in accordance with the Golden Mean principle. The dome and its dome caps could well occupy a circular extent of the landscape fifty miles or more in diameter. A dome cap diameter can vary in size from one-half mile to nine miles.

Working together, the 1,746 domes and 83,808 dome caps play the predominant role in making Earth's visionary geography sites holy. In fact, in contemplating this vast combined number—85,554—you realize you do not have to travel far to encounter either a dome or dome cap. Nearly all the Earth's physical surface is energized and uplifted by a dome or dome cap or the radiating proximity of their presence.

Dragons

QUANTITY: 1,067: 1 primary, 13 major, 1,053 minor

EQUIVALENT NAMES: Uluru, the Rainbow Serpent; *Jormundgandr, Midgardsormr,* or *Nidhoggr* (Norse); Oroboros, Ladon, Draco (Greek); Tiamat (Babylonian); Fafnir (Teutonic); Svarbhanu, Ananta-Sesa, Shakti Kundalini (Hindu).

LOCATIONS: Chaco Canyon (major); Cumae (minor); Delphi, Mount Parnassus (major); Glastonbury (major); Hill Cumorah (minor); Mount Kailash (minor); Mont Saint-Michel (minor); Bell Rock, Sedona (minor); Mount Temahani (minor); Tetford (minor); Thebes (minor); Uluru (major); Wawel Hill (minor).

DESCRIPTION: Most of what myth says about dragons is true, except that you do not *slay* the dragon but *activate* it, releasing its energies to enrich the landscape. In their early work in establishing the Earth's energy matrix, the fourteen Ray Masters of the Great Bear relied on the thirteen major dragons to ground their energies so as to use them effectively on the Earth. Within the human biological sphere, the dragon is Shakti Kundalini, the dragon goddess coiled three and a half times at the base of the spine.

Each of the thirteen major dragons is a hologram of the one oroboric dragon, whose energy body encircles the planet; and each of the thirteen dragons generates eighty-one minor dragons. The minor dragons tend to be situated at the largest dome caps within domes where they guard the entrance into a large geomythic temple domain and help to energize the interior of the temple. They are often shown coiled around or beneath a tree laden with golden apples, which symbolize the higher spiritual wisdom available in that particular temple, or set deep in a cave guarding a jewel horde, which carries the same symbolism.

Myth tends to blur the distinction between serpent and dragon, and we often end up with an image of a large snake with wings and call it a dragon. One way to visualize a landscape dragon is to picture a Celtic torc, a kind of necklace where the two halves do not quite touch. Where they would touch is the dragon's head, while the rest of the circle would be the coils of the dragon's body.

A more abstract concept comes from Qabala, which speaks of the 231 Gates. Take the twenty-two letters of the Hebrew alphabet and place them at equal distances on the periphery of a circle; then connect them in pairs across the diameter of the circle so as not to repeat any pairs. Only 231 combinations are possible, and these are called the Gates. The resulting image is a complex matrix of crisscrossing lines within a sphere.

The image makes more sense when you factor in what the letter pairs do. Dragon myths often speak of a dragon slayer who after tasting dragon's blood becomes clairvoyant to the communications of nature or a master of higher knowledge and power. The Hebrews say the twenty-two letters of their alphabet are living primary creative energies that God used to create all existence.

Put more simply, the letters are magical invocations that can create or destroy reality, generate myriads of stars or eliminate them. Think of the letters then as the dragon's fiery breath. The dragons were placed in the landscape so as to serially release some of this foundational creative fire as needed into the Earth's visionary topography.

On an initiatory level, the dragons pertain to the polarity in the dome lines, both straight and spiral, and to the point at which a person is able to activate a realization within of the human dragon and its energies. This is encountering the dragon, both inner and outer, with the outer mirroring and precipitating the awareness of the inner dragon. The desired result is to "slay" the dragon so as to release its light to flow through the dome lines and the body.

Egregors

QUANTITY: 81: 9 major, 72 minor

EQUIVALENT NAMES: Watchers; Guardians; National Protector Beings.

LOCATIONS: Bayreuth; Cusco; Mount Ida; Rennes-le-Chateau.

DESCRIPTION: An egregor (from the Greek *egregoros,* meaning "Watcher" or "Guardian") is an astral being that embodies the essence of a people or landscape and which watches and guards people who have a common purpose, be it a city, province, or country. The egregor also embodies the occult power that directs the destiny of a polis. For France, it is the cock or rooster; for England, the matron (or lion); for the U.S., the eagle; for Russia, the bear. In fact, the egregor as the nation can become a "person," a discrete entity, though it does not have to be human form.

Qabalistic tradition holds that there are seventy-two national angelic regents, assigned one per country or ethnic group. Each nation has an angel set over it as a spiritual leader, and these terrestrial angels oversee public affairs and the doings of princes and magistrates, as the old texts put it, to protect from outside pressures a region or ethnic group assigned to its care.

In the original organization of the Earth, its surface area was divided into twelve equal pentagons or Albion plates. To nine of these were assigned a major egregor, in accordance with the (then) nine distinct major landmasses, while three were left vacant as their area mostly encompassed water. Each of the (then) seventy-two major subdivisions of these major landmasses was assigned an egregor, to help evolve the people who would emerge from and assimilate the energies of that specific landscape. At either level, we could conceive of these egregors as landscape angels specific to preassigned regions and peoples.

Egregors can be evoked through magic ritual to accomplish a purpose, including the overcoming of the people it protects. Apparently the ancient Romans were aware of the occult advantages of this, and used it in their attacks on enemy or foreign cities. It is said that the Romans, when besieging a city, would find out the name of the city's guardian spirit. They would then call forth the protective divinities of that polis by means of a magical spell, and overcome those divinities with magical rites, making it easier to conquer the people and their city.

Emerald

QUANTITY: 445

EQUIVALENT NAMES: The Heart within the Heart; Cintamani; Lia Fail.

LOCATIONS: Citamparam; Dornach; Hill Cumorah; Hill of Tara

DESCRIPTION: This is an energy structure with expressions on many levels. In the human realm, it is an electromagnetic doorway about two inches long on the right side of the sternum, and it resembles a double-terminated, six-sided emerald placed vertically starting at the third rib down. It is the Heart within the Heart, which means a secret portal outside spacetime positioned between the outer *(Anahata)* and inner *(Ananda-kanda)* aspects of the heart chakra. Thus the emerald exists in every human being as a birthright.

On the level of the planet, each Landscape Zodiac has one site that corresponds to the emerald, or esoteric heart center, for its Albion figure. Then each Albion for a pentagonal face, or Albion plate, has a site that is the emerald for that anthropomorphic figure. Next, the planet itself has one prime site where the original copy of the emerald was placed for the benefit of the entire planet.

Finally, on a geometric level, all aspects of the Earth's complex visionary geography and the planet itself are contained within a single planet-sized emerald, which we might think of as the Earth's higher being body. All of these emeralds interconnect and work like a computer modem, affording us linkups across time and space throughout not only the Earth but also the galaxy. I refer to this function as the *Emerald Modem*.

Originally, the emerald came from the crown of the Lord of Light, also known as Lucifer, the Light-Bearer, and described in early Hebrew texts as God's chief archangel, emblazoned with jewels and lights. The emerald makes individuated consciousness possible—the unique sense of I-ness and its cognitive reach, the "fire" that Prometheus (Lucifer) "stole" from the gods for humanity—and is what enables us to transcend or escape the conventional spacetime dimension. It is the basis and means of profound mystical experiences.

The Hindu yogic tradition knows the emerald as the *Hridayam,* as the foundation of the Mind, the very core of one's being, the place that attracts everything else to it in the end, the dwelling place of the Ultimate Divine within each human, pure consciousness beyond space and time. The twelfth-century German esoteric writer, Wolfram von Eschenbach, in his *Parzival* spoke of a "forever incorruptible" green stone brought to Earth by the angels and called the Grail. It was the "very fruit of bliss," he wrote. Experientially, the Holy Grail is found *inside* the emerald.

At the inception of the Earth's visionary topography, the prime holograph of the emerald was installed at what is now known as the Templo del Santa Maria, a modest Catholic church and grounds with a massive two-thousand-year-old tree a half-dozen miles from Oaxaca in Southern Mexico. This site, by virtue of holding the Earth's prime emerald, is one of three aspects of the Earth's heart chakra. Not surprisingly, it is the Heart within the Heart, the emerald.

Epiphany Focus

QUANTITY: One new one each year.
EQUIVALENT NAMES: Not available.

LOCATIONS: Banaras; Sedona; Mount Temahani; Teotihuacan.
DESCRIPTION: Ever since 4,000 B.C., the Christ as a cosmic being has focused "his" consciousness like a laser beam on a single geomantic site on Earth for a week in January, culminating on January 6, the day Orthodox Christianity and Rudolf Steiner's Anthroposophy still observe as Epiphany.

Like a dimmer switch slowly turned on to full, there is a buildup of this Christ beam in the week leading up to January 6, then it reaches its fullness on that day. The specific site receives the Christ consciousness on behalf of the planet, then allows it to be distributed through the local, regional, and global systems through the geomantic network of the Earth.

Since this practice began, more than six thousand sites have been irradiated by this Epiphany Focus. Human participation in this weeklong event, provided one knows the site ahead of time so as to physically go there, affords a remarkable spiritual experience referred to as the Christed Initiation in the Buddha Body.

Gnome Egg

QUANTITY: 10,660
EQUIVALENT NAMES: Not available.
LOCATIONS: Hill of Tara; Sedona; Tetford.
DESCRIPTION: A Gnome Egg looks like a huge transparent pockmarked golf ball set part way into the ground, usually in remote or protected places away from human habitation. The egg is the local or regional headquarters for the elementals of the earth called gnomes who work closely with geomancers in maintaining the Earth's energy matrix. Gnomes often appear as short, stocky, bearded, red-capped men; they are playful, mischievous, and remarkably well-informed about the energy features of the landscape.

Of all the elementals, the gnomes are the most accessible to human experience and the ones most likely to be involved in Earth feature activation or amplification events. In the medieval sagas of the Grail Knights, the gnomes were referred to by the quaint code of "dwarves."

The Gnome Eggs have several functions. They are the residential and work headquarters for gnomes servicing a given geomantic terrain. They are directly connected with the 1,067 dragons of the Earth, for whom the Gnome Eggs serve as a kind of terrestrial eye into the landscape. And they are meant to be initiation chambers for apprentice Grail Knights mastering the interface between the human, elemental, and angelic realms. As such, Gnome Eggs require human interaction to bring them "on line" and of service to a locality.

Golden Egg

QUANTITY: 666

EQUIVALENT NAMES: Right Eye of Horus; *Hiranyagarbha.*

LOCATIONS: Acropolis; Dornach; Edfu; Mount Holyoke; Teotihuacan; Tetford; Wawel Hill.

DESCRIPTION: The purpose of a Golden Egg is initiatory. It is to mirror, model, and facilitate the birth of the Christ Child as the incarnation of the Higher Self within the Grail Knight, that is, one dedicated to plumbing the geomythic mysteries of the Holy Grail. The egg puts you in resonance with the process and the result: the golden Christ Child as an expression of cosmic consciousness. The egg acts like a manger for the birth of this "child" within the human.

As a geomantic structure, the egg presents itself as a towering golden oval that has both height and depth. It may extend for several miles across a landscape and have a distinct energy hierarchy, such as a foundation or platform (the first two chakras), then the main body, or Child (comprising the other five chakras).

Above the crown of the geomythic Christ Child, there is a Madonna feature that extends "arms" down to the base on both sides of the egg. This feature is sometimes called the Maidenwell (after a specific landscape site near Tetford, England, where I first discovered it). This is the baptismal font for the newborn child's crown chakra; here the child—your newborn Christed awareness—gets a perpetual baptizing by the Spirit from its cosmic mother from her inexhaustible well. The result is to help open one's clairvoyance.

For the full experience of the Golden Egg, you need to walk through and meditate at each of the seven centers as well as the Madonna feature above the crown center. This is best done slowly, over a few days, or weeks, to allow your nervous system and etheric and astral bodies to assimilate the strong energies.

Mythologically, the Golden Egg is the right eye of Horus, the divine falcon of Egyptian mythology, son of Osiris and Isis. Horus is the Egyptian name for the Solar Logos (an aspect of the Christ) in his Sun (right eye—Golden Egg) and Moon (left eye—Silver Egg) aspects. Horus the Elder is the left eye, while Horus the Younger is the right eye, or the Golden Egg. Appropriately, Horus the Younger is often depicted as an infant in the lap of Isis, his mother.

In Hindu myth, the creator god Brahma is said to have emerged from the Cosmic Egg as the *Hiranyagarbha,* or golden seed or embryo. The *Hiranyagarbha* is conceived of as a germ, a point, a cosmic seed, a golden seed that gradually unfolds and expands through the seven planes of existence, eventually ending up by generating the seven planets.

The *Hiranyagarbha* is also called the golden child or golden germ, or the one born from a golden womb or egg known as *Bala Brahma* (Child Brahma). This is a radiant child with four heads and four arms, King of the Immortals, "resplendent like the young Sun, who has four lustrous arms, and the wealth of whose lotus-face is fourfold."[60]

Golden Pillars

QUANTITY: 228,964

EQUIVALENT NAMES: Spartoi; "Sown Men"; Golden-Helmed Seed; Dragon's Teeth.

LOCATIONS: Easter Island; Jasna Gora; Thebes.

DESCRIPTION: The Golden Pillars were brought by a Ray Master from Shambhala and established at various sites so as to make Shambhala closer to our physical world as a preparation for our future. The pillars are remembered, though cloaked, in Greek myth as the Spartoi, Sown Men, or Golden-Helmed Seed, that sprang magically out of the ground after Cadmus sowed the teeth of the dragon of Ares he had slain. The Spartoi, after a fit of quarreling, then served as protectors of the Theban temple of Dionysus, the Greek god who embodied some aspects of the Christ.

In vision, the pillars tend to appear as tall and golden, perhaps one hundred feet tall, arrayed in circles or semicircles in a protective manner around important geomantic temples. They seem to resemble Egyptian pharoahs, arms crossed at the chests, with full headgear and kingly regalia. Seen closer up, when you penetrate their energy field a bit, each pillar now seems like a giant human face—more than human: part human, part angelic. The faces touch at the sides forming a towering matrix around a unified gaze, an awake and aware sentinel looking in all directions at once.

Grail Castle

QUANTITY: 144

EQUIVALENT NAMES: Lanka; Munsalvaesche; Noah's Ark; *Caer Sidi,* the Revolving Castle; Poseidon's Palace; Enki's Sea House or *E-engurra;* Yima's *var;* Boat of the Vedas; Castle Carbonek.

LOCATIONS: Acropolis; Bayreuth; Delphi, Mount Parnassus; Dome of the Rock; Glastonbury; Montsegur; Montserrat; Mount Damavand; Mycenae; Tetford.

DESCRIPTION: This is the Celestial City of Kubera, Lord of the North and king of wealth and riches; his city is known in the Sanskrit Puranas as Lanka. It is one of the eight Celestial Cities constellated around golden Mount Meru at the center of the world. In Western mythic terms, this is the Grail Castle where the Holy Grail resides. It is the domain of the Rich Fisher King, who is known in Germanic myth (including Richard Wagner's opera *Parsifal*) as Anfortas whose castle sat on the top of *Munsalvaesche,* the Mount of Salvation.

All the 144 Grail Castles accessible through the Earth's visionary geography are holographic copies of an original that exists elsewhere in the galaxy. What we can access as the Grail Castle here on Earth is an etheric replica of something from a different space and time but mirrored here for a purpose. These Grail Castle replicas were placed around the planet as etheric temples to support the evolution of the Earth and human consciousness, but their purpose is largely as yet unfulfilled.

In the past, a very small number of humans had access to the particular level of consciousness necessary to perceive these castles in the etheric realm. There is some record of this in the Grail stories, particularly those collected in Thomas Malory's *Le Morte d'Arthur;* some knights were unable to access the Grail Castle, a few were dumbfounded by it, a few penetrated its mysteries.

The Grail Castle's purpose is to give us access to an inner plane temple that can facilitate recall of deep cosmic memory. This is pre-incarnational memory, pre-Fall memory, full cosmic knowledge of all the past cycles of time. The Grail Castle houses the Grail, which, although it is an object, is more truly a *process*. That process is the regeneration of the human through retrieving cosmic memory. The potential reclaimable riches of cosmic memory are almost inconceivable, which is why Kubera is said to be the Lord of Wealth.

The world is a Wasteland and the Rich Fisher King has become the Wounded Fisher King because he and we have forgotten our vast past. The Grail is the process of regaining that memory and healing the wound in consciousness.

The Grail King is the Lord of the Sea, King of the Waters, or what the Sumerians called the *absu,* and the Hebrews the *tehom,* which in either case means the watery abyss of primordial chaos. But it's only a chaos because it is so much consciousness (for which water and ether are the esoteric symbols) that it potentially overwhelms our self-identity and structures of consciousness based on our comparatively parochial sense of spacetime.

The Grail Castle is Noah's Ark and the Boat of the Vedas floating on the waves upon the cosmic sea during the time of Deluge. This refers both to the location of the Grail Castle in the highest level of the etheric realm (on top of the Sea) and to its function to preserve knowledge from one Day of Brahma, and Year of Brahma, to the next, the interregnum being marked by a Flood, or inundation of matter-based spacetime by a surfeit of galactic consciousness. These are *vast* cycles of time, calculated in the billions of years.

Interdimensional Portal

QUANTITY: 60,600
EQUIVALENT NAMES: Unavailable.
LOCATIONS: Glastonbury; Wawel Hill.
DESCRIPTION: These are surprising, even arresting features, seemingly located in odd, unexpected places in the landscape. The first one I encountered was at the base of a hill in central Norway. It was an unassuming grassy mound no

more than a dozen feet in diameter surrounded by a clutch of trees. But the atmosphere and energy vibration within that small circle were remarkable.

You pass through what presents itself as a cave opening, then a long, sinuous tunnel (the portal), and emerge into a huge open underground chamber. Your first impression may be that you are seeing an alien spaceship, but its color and shape are undefinable or beyond our conventional cognitive habits. It seems to stand hundreds of feet high and even longer at the bottom center of the cave.

The interdimensional portals pertain to the Pleiadian Council of Light, which is one of the higher dimensional oversight bodies for events on Earth. The portal and its "ship" are peripheral to many large Landscape Zodiacs and are involved with maintenance of the local visionary geographic features. In one instance (near Roros, Norway), the portal is located near a large Landscape Zodiac; in another (Wawel Hill, Cracow, Poland), it is associated with a minor dragon and a legend that this site would be one of safety during the Apocalypse.

Ixion's Wheel

QUANTITY: 360
EQUIVALENT NAMES: Sun Disk; the Sun Barque of Ra; the Boat of Millions of Years; Cattle of the Sun; Helios' Chariot; King Arthur's Round Table; the Sun's ecliptic.
LOCATIONS: Banaras; Cusco; Beckery, Glastonbury; Mount Etna; Sedona; Teotihuacan.
DESCRIPTION: The name derives from the Greek myth in which Ixion is described as the first man to commit murder. Only Zeus, the king of the gods, was willing to forgive Ixion, and he invited Ixion to Mount Olympus for a purificatory rite. Ixion used the occasion to try to seduce Hera, Zeus' wife, and he ended up being strapped to a fiery, winged, four-spoked wheel which would

revolve and flame forever. This is remembered as Ixion's Wheel.

It is made in Hephaistos' forge, Horus' smithy, Agni's fire altar—the Mithraeum, or Sun God's temple (see below). Ixion's Wheel is a code name for a concentrated expression of the Sun's ecliptic, or annual path, through the stars, otherwise known as the Round Table of King Arthur (the Solar Logos).

The Wheel is a measure of time, specifically 3.1 trillion years, divided into 360 segments (as in 360 degrees in a circle), each of which is 86.4 billion years. The 360 degrees in the ecliptic are the Cattle of the Sun; the Boat of Millions of Years was so called by the Egyptians because it takes 3.1 trillion years to complete the circuit or for the time to run out, which is the life of the galaxy and by Hindu time reckoning one full Year of Brahma.

The Sun Wheel is an aspect of the Solar Logos, and an initiatory vehicle for candidates in Arthurhood, which is the embodiment of the Solar Logos, as expressed through the Celtic myths. The Wheel is a King Arthur cell, a degree; globally, there are 360 cells or degrees comprising the full King Arthur. The Solar Logos is the golden point of light at the center of the galactic wheel. It's the central Sun at the heart of the galaxy; the Sun within all the suns that are stars in the galaxy; the mind that holds them together.

The 360 Ixion's Wheels are the stations of the Sun, the Sun's ecliptic and its 360 divisions deployed across the Earth's surface as single, experienceable planetary temple.

In terms of practical geomantic experience, you may see the Ixion's Wheel as a golden wheel, a golden cross set within a clear glass rotunda, or as a golden sarcophagus, or as a hybrid of the three. You lie down on it, it revolves slowly, and you get irradiated by the Sun. You may see the Solar Logos entering the center of the wheel—the hub, *you*—as a golden spindle or thin shaft of golden light, like an axle connected to a wheel.

This is where the legendary Sword in the Stone in the King Arthur myth was created; you are the stone, the Arthur current entering the Ixion's Wheel creates the sword within you. You could say that the Ixion's Wheel is where the god is born; that is, where the human candidate for initiation and higher evolution takes his first step in the alchemical process of transformation.

Labyrinth

QUANTITY: 108: 9 types, 12 of each.
EQUIVALENT NAMES: Maze.
LOCATIONS: Chichen Itza; Clingman's Dome; Easter Island; Glastonbury; Machu Picchu; Mount Ida; Sedona; Teotihuacan.
DESCRIPTION: The most famous labyrinth recorded in Western mythology was the Cretan labyrinth located at or near Knossus on Crete. It was constructed by Daedalus, the master engineer of the Greek world, for King Minos of Crete for the purpose of caging the Minotaur, described as a ferocious man-bull. Archeologists have sought physical traces of this labyrinth and concocted various barely plausible theories to account for it, but by and large its reality has escaped conventional thinking.

That is largely because the labyrinth is a large-scale energy feature in the astral world overlaid at numerous sites. There are nine types of labyrinths, and twelve of each kind, allocated one each per Albion plate. Each labyrinth consists of a maze, at the center of which is a Hall of Records.

The largest type of labyrinth, the Cretan, is generated by the interlocking of eight dome caps on one mountain. The other eight types cannot be characterized at this time as they are still under research.

In general terms, the labyrinth's structure resembles the multiple-pathed convoluted mazes often created on the landscape out of turf, bushes, or even painted on the floors of cathedrals such as at Chartres in France. The paths enable you to cross dimensional boundaries in a nonsequential way as a counterpoint to Trees of Life (see below).

You could think of the labyrinth as a car wash for your psychic centers; as an exercise in reconfiguring your psychic apparatus in accordance with the specificities of this site's function; as a device spun and woven about your head, a sound and energy template that will facilitate your psychic perception of exalted realities; or simply as affording you preparations in consciousness so you can experience what lies ahead—the Hall of Records.

You penetrate the labyrinthine folds and twists and arrive at the center to stand in the midst of the incoming data stream. You can see a shaft of white light like a streaming shower continuously entering the center of the labyrinth. This light shaft is a kind of galactic fiber optic cable containing a great quantity of compressed information about light codings and star information.

This hall may at first appear in the form of a large library with Greek-style columns and an elegant marbled entryway, but this is more of a visual analogy than an accurate description. It is a Hall of Records in the sense that it records stellar and universal influences and light codings that have been transmitted to this site over the duration of the existence of the Earth.

Again, to use a visual analogy, you could see each of the filaments in the galactic cable as a hollow tube of a certain color; on the inside there are many markings that seem to resemble hieroglyphics or cuneiform, but are in fact notations in a light frequency language, which predates verbal, spoken, phonetic, or pictogrammic languages.

Landscape Zodiac

QUANTITY: 432

EQUIVALENT NAMES: Star map; King Arthur's Round Table.

LOCATIONS: Abydos; Banaras; Brocken; Carnac; Chaco Canyon; Chichen Itza; Cumae; Dornach; Ephesus; Gediminas Hill; Glastonbury; Monticello; Mount Holyoke; Mycenae; Rennes-le-Chateau; Sedona; Hill of Tara; Teotihuacan; Troy.

DESCRIPTION: A Landscape Zodiac is an interactive, edited holographic version of the galaxy overlaid on the landscape. It resembles an apple split in two with the knife still in place: one half contains stars of the Northern Hemisphere, the other the stars of the Southern Hemisphere; the knife is the Oroboros energy line that passes through the middle of the starfields.

Not all stars in the galaxy are represented, but 144 constellations are: the traditional twelve signs of the zodiac (presented twice, once for each half), and 132 constellations.

Of the 432 zodiacs pre-templated on the Earth, no more than 144 are ever to be "on" at one time, and usually, far fewer than that are activated and fully operational. Seen over the vast course of Earth history, the 432 zodiacs have been preset like alarm clocks, to be activated and relevant in given time periods when astrological and astronomical influences and alignments come into play.

Zodiacs range in size from a diameter of one-half mile to more than one hundred miles. Size does not make any difference as to quality of contents, and the variation in size seems to be based on the same principle that makes flowers different sizes, from the bluebell to the sunflower. Each dome is topped and energized by a zodiac dome, which typically is twice the diameter of the zodiac. Zodiacs in most cases exist on flat land, easily accessible to humans.

The consummate expression of each zodiac is an Albion. Albion is full of stars: his wings or auric field comprise the two halves of the zodiac and the total of 144 constellations represented, while the Oroboros Line running up "his" midline is the column in which the chakras or primary energy centers (corresponding to the planets) are found.

When the Earth was still soft, malleable clay, the landscape configurations to some extent mirrored and matched the conventional constellation diagrams. Here the land followed and mimicked its preexisting energy template. As the Earth aged and drifted from its visionary geographic imprint, this conformity of landscape and star configurations diminished and in almost all cases disappeared.

At a few sites, such as Glastonbury in England and Rennes-le-Chateau in France, some aspects of this original conformity have been retained and serve as an educational device and a *reminder* for a culture that has largely forgotten the existence of these terrestrial star maps. In locating Landscape Zodiacs, however, it is a mistake to look for this conformity, to study topographical maps for traces of the constellation morphologies. This can lead to error and illusion in locating authentic Landscape Zodiacs as almost none of them any longer have this conformity.

Lily

QUANTITY: Indeterminate
EQUIVALENT NAMES: Unavailable.
LOCATIONS: Mont-Royal; Tetford.
DESCRIPTION: This geomantic feature exists as a potential at many sites, but only comes into subtle manifestation through the efforts of humans. It is the product of purified consciousness, created largely through the interaction of human consciousness with the angelic realm over time in a small aspect of a geomantically prepared landscape. The results of purified consciousness at the site take the form of a white lily expressed as a light form. You have to conceive of this rather largely, casually, and metaphorically, because it is not so much a flower as a pervasive energy field that has a lily shape—white, pure, open, and receptive.

We get more of an idea about what a geomantic lily means by understanding the symbolism of the lily. As flowers, they are considered synonymous with whiteness, innocence, virginity, and a heavenly purity. They are often likened to the lotus which grows magnificently up out of the muddy waters. Lilies also symbolize one's spiritual surrender to the grace of God; that one is the unwavering choice of the beloved, as in the Song of Solomon where the poet speaks of his love as the lily among the thorns; and they symbolize the potential of the individual to reconcile the opposites in one's nature.[61]

As a decorative motif lilies were a favorite in Egypt, Minoan Crete, and Mycenae. Greek myth explains their origins as from the milk of Hera, the wife of Zeus, chief of the gods, a few drops of which spilled on the Earth. For the Christians, the lily represented pure, virginal love, and the Archangel Gabriel, the angel of the Annunciation, is often shown holding a lily. Similarly, the lily was the flower of choice of many saints, and in heraldry, the flower was considered a royal one, possibly because its shape resembles a scepter. In Jesus' Sermon on the Mount, he praised the "lilies of the field" which "do not toil" as a metaphor of those with perfect faith who feel no need to question their faith.[62]

Lucifer Binding Site

QUANTITY: 3,496
EQUIVALENT NAMES: Mount Caucasus.
LOCATIONS: Brocken; Chichen Itza; Citamparam; Dome of the Rock; Gediminas Hill.
DESCRIPTION: This is a well-kept geomantic secret, and probably for good reason, as it is at the least, controversial, and for most people, shocking. Western Christian culture has prejudiced and blinded us not only to the true nature of this high celestial being, Lucifer, regarded as God's chief archangel and cherub, but also to his history and relationship with humanity, and his role in the Earth's visionary topography.

Wellesley Tudor Pole, an English initiate and one intimately familiar with the Earth's energy body, wrote in 1966 that Lucifer was not cast out of Heaven for malfeasance or disobedience, "but descended into our midst of his free will and to his own sacrifice. He can only rise out of our darkness when *we* are ready and able to rise with him." As such we should appreciate Lucifer as "a colleague" and wish him success in "his mission among men, and for his triumphant return whence he came."[63]

According to Jewish sources, on the third day of Creation, Lucifer, God's chief archangel and cherub, "walked in Eden amid blazing jewels, his body a-fire" with the light of dozens of precious stones, all set in pure gold.[64] God had made Lucifer Guardian of All Nations. He also had something to do with the planet Venus, which was anciently known as Phosphorus or Lucifer. To the ancients, he was *Helel ben Sahar,* Son of the Dawn, Lord of Light, the Shining One, Dawn Bringer, and Light Bringer.

The Greeks knew Lucifer as Prometheus the Titan, who was punished by Zeus for stealing the gods' fire on behalf of humanity. His punishment was to be bound to the rocks in the Caucasus Mountains where an eagle devoured his liver every day, but eventually he was unbound by Heracles. In the Christian version, Lucifer the Light-Bearer was punished by God for refusing to serve the newly created humanity. So which story is correct?

With respect to humanity, two acts of Lucifer on our behalf are important to note here. First, he gave humanity the emerald, which is the Greek narthex stem in which he (as Prometheus) put the stolen "fire" of the gods, which is to say, consciousness capable of being individuated, of saying "I" to itself, *and* fully illuminated.

Second, he modeled for humanity the condition in which an individuated consciousness could tolerate, sustain, and live with the dualities of the Tree of the Knowledge of Good and Evil.

Lucifer is that tree, that knowledge, and he shows humanity how to embrace both polarities from the position of free will, which is awakened consciousness.

Of these two bequests, the emerald has been forgotten, and the Tree has been severed, split in two, one half (the Light) accepted, the other half (the Dark) repudiated, demonized. This process in consciousness is a protracted one, and has been played out in world culture since the "Fall."

Confusingly, Lucifer is not the chief of a daunting hierarchy of negative, evil beings, known in Hebrew as the *Sitra Achra* (the Other Side) or the *Kelippot*. Such a negative hierarchy of demonic, inimical beings does exist, as it were, in opposition to the angelic hierarchy, but Lucifer is not among them.

The Jewish sources say Lucifer aspired to enthrone himself on Saphon, the Mount of Assembly, for which ambition God cast him out of Heaven into the profound gloom of the Bottomless Pit in Sheol. As he fell from grace, Lucifer shone like lightning. This myth has a geomantic aspect: Sheol is the Earth grid.

You have to see the saga in the fourth dimension, like a time-lapse film of the opening of a flower. Simultaneously around the Earth, Lucifer is *being bound* in Sheol (or on the rocks in the Caucasus Mountains), *being unbound,* and both *returning in glory* to Heaven and *arriving in splendor* on Earth. There are 3,496 sites around the Earth where any of the three aspects of this cosmodrama are occurring at the same time.

To the El Tule tree in the churchyard of El Templo del Santa Maria near Oaxaca in southern Mexico, Lucifer returned in August 1987 as Quetzalcoatl, one of his many mythic guises, plumed in Elohim. Out from under the massive Lincoln Cathedral in Lincoln, England, in August 2001, Lucifer was unbound, arising from many centuries of imprisonment and oblivion. Under the Foundation Stone in the Dome of the Rock on the Temple Mount in Jerusalem, Lucifer as *Helel ben Sahar* remains repudiated, buried, suppressed, entombed.

How does this work geomantically? Lucifer is unbound at one site, like letting a little air out of an overinflated tire to prevent it from exploding. The "air" in this case is a provisional acknowledgment of a little of the Shadow, the suppressed, dark, repudiated side of the human psyche, the other half of the Tree of the Knowledge of Good and Evil that nobody wants to look at.

Lucifer unbound at even one site means a portion of the individual and collective Shadow can be brought into the open, defused, and digested, requiring a little less trauma or even apocalypse to make public the rest of the Shadow contents. Whether we like it or not, Lucifer by whatever name we know him (or pretend we don't) is implicit in Earth's energy and spiritual body, and ours.

This fact also shows convincingly how and why the Earth's visionary geography is personally relevant to every one of us. It is both the closet where we stuffed the skeleton and the opportunity for an unending epiphany of spirit.

Mithraeum

QUANTITY: 144

EQUIVALENT NAMES: Tintagel; Hephaistos' Smithy; Zeus' Bull; Calypso's Golden Halls of Ogygia; the Gold of the Hyperboreans; Agni's Fire Altar.

LOCATIONS: Edfu; Gediminas Hill; Machu Picchu; Mount Etna; Mount Haleakala; Mycenae.

DESCRIPTION: The Mithraeum is a name borrowed from the Roman mysteries of Mithra the Bull-Slayer to describe the Celestial City of Tejovati, presided over by Agni, Lord of Fire, in the Hindu terminology. The Mithraeum is the temple of the Wild Sun God, the volcanic, even monstrous, fire element.

The Mithraeum is the birthplace of Arthur, the Solar Logos, both as a world event and as an individual initiatory experience. The Celtic myths called this place Tintagel, which means "tints of angels," located it on the far edge of Cornwall in southwest England, and Arthur, destined to be the leader of England, was born here, through Merlin's contrivances.

This site is a Temple of the Sun God, but could just as well be described as the cave in which the hero Mithra slayed the cosmic bull of Zeus; it could equally well be characterized as the smithy of the Greek artificer god Hephaistos, who fashioned the weapons, shields, and devices of the gods out of gold in his forge under Mount Etna. The Mithraeum is the same as the golden halls of the remote island of Ogygia where Odysseus spent seven years with the enchanting nymph Calypso on his ten-year journey home from Troy.

Let's look at some mythic equivalencies, working from the assumption that the Wild Sun God born in the Mithraeum as Arthur is the Solar Logos, the same as the Bull of the Sun ritually sacrificed in the Mithraic cave. Various names for the Sun god in its wild and tamed aspects include Agni, Typhon, Apophis, and Sorath.

The qualities associated with these beings evoke the sense of raw, undisciplined primordial energy, the searing heat of the god's forge, the molten volcanic lava seeking to inflame the land, the vivid, shocking taste of living bull's blood. These are all metaphors, of course, for a human encounter with the consciousness of the Sun and its chaotic, ultra-powerful form of living, writhing gold.

The Wild Sun God is also a metaphor for meeting the King (and source) of Time, whose minutes, days, years, eons, are symbolized by bulls' blood. The vast wisdom of Time was symbolized in the Greek references to the "gold of the Hyperboreans," an arcane, legendary early race of godlike humans in the North.

Mythically, the Egyptian Horus did not defeat Apophis, the Wild Sun God; he *mastered* the Sun God's energy, indicated by the otherwise curious Egyptian references to Horus as a blacksmith. A blacksmith does not slay and defeat his metals; he simply knows how to work them to his will, to master and shape them into useful devices worthy of the gods.

The followers of Horus were called *mesniti,* which means "workers in metals or blacksmiths." Hieroglyphic representations of these blacksmiths, identified on the interior temple walls at Edfu, show them with an inverted spear in their right hand, an upraised metal instrument in their left. In practical terms, we go to a Mithraeum to learn to be "blacksmiths."

The mythic references to Calypso, Hyperboreans, the gold, blood, and bull all point to the Pleiades, the star cluster in the neck of Taurus the Bull. One of their galactic functions is to create time caves (solar systems) in which conscious evolution can proceed. Metaphorically speaking, to do this the Pleiadians drain off a little of the cosmic bull's blood from the Sun God's Time reservoir and fill up a time cave with this precious substance so that conscious life has duration.

Mount Olympus

QUANTITY: 108

EQUIVALENT NAMES: Asgard; Temple of Thoth; Pine Forest; Ekur ("Mountain House," Sumerian god Enlil's temple of the gods at Nippur); the fourteen parts of Osiris' dismembered body; Bifrost, the Rainbow Bridge.

LOCATIONS: Cusco; Monticello; Sedona; Hill of Tara; Tetford; Uluru.

DESCRIPTION: Mythically, this is probably one of the most familiar and easiest to understand of geomantic structures, even though it will no doubt surprise most people to learn there are 108 replicas of this mountaintop home of the gods.

Mount Olympus is one of the eight Celestial Cities of Mount Meru, specifically, Amaravati, residence of the Hindu Indra, king of the gods.

Geomantically, variously named Mount Olympus is the residence for the fourteen Ray Masters of the Great Bear, Ursa Major. They were known to the ancient Vedas as the Seven Rishis, or celestial sages, and to the Egyptians as the fourteen body parts of the dismembered god, Osiris. On an abstract level, the Ray Masters represent the seven primary differentiations of pure white into the color spectrum, and the seven subtleties or gradations, such as dark blue and light blue.

On a practical level, they represent the very active field workers who have been toiling on behalf of our evolution and that of the planet since the inception of both. You could think of Mount Olympus as the field headquarters for these creator gods. It is a fine place to come meet them. You may want to at some point, for the Ray Masters support and supervise many human initiations into the Mysteries as well as the geomantic domain of the planet.

The Norse myths remember Mount Olympus as Asgard, but they tell us you can enter Asgard only by crossing Bifrost, the Rainbow Bridge guarded by Heimdall. His name means approximately "He who illuminates the world." He guards the bridge against the Frost Giants and keeps it open for the Aesir (the gods of Asgard) to ride over to their court. Heimdall is the guardian and watchman of the gods, said to be the father of all mankind; he lives at *Himinbjorg* by the bridge.

Bifrost symbolizes the fourteen Ray Masters as a group, represented here as a pathway and link between worlds and the initiation and assimilation of those energies by humans that make it possible to cross the bridge to the Ray Masters' realm. In other words, the Ray Masters are the bridge and the destination.

Their temple is like a fourteen-leafed clover, with each clover section the ray domain for their color and jurisdiction. Everywhere a particular Ray Master is active, on our world or anywhere else in the solar system, galaxy, or universe, is potentially accessible through their division of Mount Olympus. Each ray imparts a certain quality or theme to consciousness and world culture. The central portion of the clover is reserved for Zeus (Osiris), chief of the gods.

The Greek mythographers were correct in giving their Olympian gods notable human traits and foibles, for all Ray Masters have been humans. Over the course of planetary history, they come in and out of human incarnation, leaving their trace behind in various cultures as major figures, heroes, and movers and shakers such as Jesus and the Apostles, Joan of Arc, Saint Patrick, King Arthur, Saint Francis of Assisi, William Shakespeare, Benjamin Franklin, and many others.

Naga City

QUANTITY: 144

EQUIVALENT NAMES: Celestial City of Raksovati; Temple of the Ocean of Milk.

LOCATIONS: Croagh Patrick; Mount Damavand; Mount Kailash.

DESCRIPTION: This is one of the eight Celestial Cities around Mount Meru, located in the southwest and attributed to Nirrti. It is the realm of the Nagas, Yakshas, Raksasas, and what we would casually term demonic-type beings.

The city is arrayed inside the coils of the great Naga Sesa-Ananta, Vishnu's own cosmic serpent. You could also call this Svarbhanu, Vrtra, or Tiamat, and it is the prototype, the Mother, of all the dragons on the Earth. The Naga City is vast inside, like a huge version of the Guggenheim Museum in New York, with levels inside each spiral-turn, or like an old European opera house.

The Naga king's head is at the bottom. It is a giant snake head. Sesa, whose name means "The Remainder," contains the remainder of the previ-

ous universes, all the primitive and exalted beings of Light, all the beings in the primeval Waters, which it holds as in a reservoir for future creation.

The Hindu myths called this primal water the Ocean of Milk (the undifferentiated sea of astral light), and in the beginning of time, the gods stirred it to yield many treasures including the substance of immortality, Soma. Sesa is "without end," the symbol of eternity, the precosmic condition, which appeared at the beginning of things, floating above the primordial waters, the "Goddess Mother of the universe, whose womb is the apriority of space and time."[65]

Oroboros Lines and Anchor Points

QUANTITY: 15

EQUIVALENT NAMES: Dragon lines; Saint Michael Ley Line.

LOCATIONS: Avebury; Beckery, Glastonbury; Delphi, Mount Parnassus.

DESCRIPTION: Oroboros Lines are fifteen major energy conduits that completely encircle the Earth, arriving where they started, like the serpent eating its tail. Each has different qualities. In England, part of one such world-encircling line has been identified by dowsers and called the Saint Michael ley line, crossing southern England from east to west.

Two lines enter the Earth and are grounded at Avebury, England; these are the gold and silver lines, from the galaxy's two brightest stars, Sirius and Canopus, respectively. They make a cross at Avebury and, encircling the Earth, divide it into quarters. Each line is connected at other points with each of the other thirteen lines; the lines at Avebury correspond to the solar and lunar aspects.

A third Oroboros Line comes from Polaris, the Pole star in Ursa Minor (the Lesser Bear) and is grounded at Hardwar, India. This line, encircling the globe, intersects the other two, dividing the Earth's surface into six equal sections.

These three primary lines correspond to the three subtle channels in the human known as the *ida* (Sun), *pingala* (Moon), and *sushumna* (neutral). These channels rise from the groin to the forehead, converging at the crown chakra; they are the conduit for kundalini, the basic life force energy in the root chakra.

The remaining twelve Oroboros Lines each carry one of the twelve astrological or zodiacal energies. One can rightfully speak of a Taurus line, a Sagittarius line, etc. All zodiacal lines originate in the Great Bear (Ursa Major), but each is grounded at a different place on the Earth, such as at Delphi on Mount Parnassus in Greece, or Beckery in Glastonbury.

From these anchor points, the Oroboros Line encircles the globe, returning to the same point of origin. In the original design of the Earth grid, the Vibrating Stones (see below) were placed at these anchor points.

The Oroboros Lines are like primary energy tracks for the Earth. After the birth of a biological being, even one as large as the planet, the primary energy lines determine the nature of its growth and environment. Their width varies with astronomical influences, especially the Moon, but the typical diameter runs from four feet to several hundred yards in a given line. They particularly vary at important energy nodal points, such as domes, and when they pass through Landscape Zodiacs, their energy is amplified. Overall, they comprise a major geometric part of the armature of the Earth's energy body or grid structure.

Palladium

QUANTITY: 60

EQUIVALENT NAMES: Gorgon Medusa's Head; Gorgoneion.

LOCATIONS: Acropolis; Hill Cumorah; Jasna Gora; Hill of Tara; Teotihuacan; Tetford; Troy.

DESCRIPTION: The Palladium is a miniature Crown of the Ancient of Days, which is a holographic presence of the Vast Countenance or White Head, symbolic of the Supreme Being or Ancient of Days. These devices are distributed five per Albion plate, which is to say, five Palladiums occupy the same space division as one Crown of the Ancient of Days.

The Palladium was a device made by the Greek goddess of wisdom, Pallas Athena, as a kind of self-portrait in wood. It was three cubits high, its feet joined together; its right hand held a spear aloft, and its left held a distaff and spindle. The Palladium, which also featured Zeus' Aegis (magic breastplate) wrapped about it, housed the spirit of the Pleiadian Electra who took refuge in the image from an amorous Zeus.

Zeus threw the Palladium into Troy after which Ilus built a temple for it, interpreting the arrival of the Palladium at his doorstep as a thumbs-up approval from above. The significance of the Palladium was that, as long as it resided in Troy, that city would never fall to outside aggressors.

The mystery of Athena's Palladium centers on the meaning of the Gorgon Medusa's head in Athena's breastplate or Aegis. Even though myth has conditioned us to regard the Medusa's head as an object of fright and terror, this is actually a misleading impression. The Gorgon's severed head is another version of the marble White Face of the Ancient of Days as described in Qabala. After all, all spiritual traditions say it is impossible to look directly at the face of god and survive the encounter. People who caught the Medusa's gaze were turned to stone, which is an equivalent experience to dying from the vision.

The Palladium is a full-size astral temple in itself shaped somewhat like a large white rotunda with the severed head resting on the ground level and facing up. Beams of light flash out from its eyes and radiate everywhere, and its face seems plastic and mobile, looking in every direction at once. This is the Medusa's head—the *living* Face of the Ancient of Days.

Pointer's Ball

QUANTITY: 174,060

EQUIVALENT NAMES: Crack between the worlds; Field of Dreams.

LOCATIONS: Acropolis; Ashlawn, near Monticello; Hill Cumorah; Glastonbury; Mount Holyoke; Newgrange; Rennes-le-Chateau; Sedona; Teotihuacan.

DESCRIPTION: The name for this feature derives from an archeological curiosity in Glastonbury, called Ponter's Ball. It's a long slightly raised earthwork of unknown purpose that runs across several fields just outside the town. It turns out the name is missing an "i" and should be Pointer's Ball. The earthwork, as it were, points to the Ball, which is a crack between the worlds.

In one respect, it is a point of access for coming and going between dimensions or levels of reality; in another, it is a point to see clearly across the dimensions. Ray Kinsella, in the movie *Field of Dreams,* upon building his baseball diamond in an Iowa cornfield, remarks: "I've just created something completely illogical." Not really. He has opened a Pointer's Ball, marked the spot where souls can enter our world from the other side, and we can enter theirs.

A Pointer's Ball is that mysterious rip in the spacetime of our three-dimensional reality through which Carlos Castaneda always seemed to be falling, walking, or being shoved. In his cosmology, they are places where the worlds overlap, gateways to the "second attention," doors to the unknown, the capacity to change attention and travel between its two domains. "Warriors know that certain power spots are doorways across the parallel lines, doorways to the other world,"

which he describes as a land of "pale yellow sandstone or rough granules of sulfur with a yellow oppressive sky and banks of yellow vapor."[66]

The Ball looks like a vesica piscis or a vertical vagina in abstract form, like a plastic change purse with a slit in the middle; not coins, but people and spirits come out of it from elsewhere. You pass through the slit, which is like a rip in the spacetime fabric, and enter a completely different realm. A vast plain is filled with small white forms—a Celestial City perhaps?—and numerous thin brownish wooden-like pillars.

There is a large stone lion on a pedestal, large like the Sphinx, and many concentric circles of white forms, souls perhaps, with an open center, like a tableau of Purgatory. The Ball is like a train station, "emanation doorways" into the many worlds, with exits into the physical Earth being only one of many possible exit points. The Pointer's Balls are usually present with an Arc of Developing Consciousness and share the same point of access; their function is different but complementary.

Ray Master Sanctuaries

QUANTITY: 1,080

EQUIVALENT NAMES: Artemision; Marian Apparition Site; House of Oenghus; Well of Segais; Parthenon.

LOCATIONS: Acropolis; Delphi, Mount Parnassus; Ephesus; Jasna Gora; Lourdes; Mont-Royal; Newgrange; Rennes-le-Chateau; Thebes.

DESCRIPTION: A Ray Master Sanctuary is an aperture into the Earth's visionary geography for one of the fourteen Ray Masters of the Great Bear. These Ray Masters were known in Hindu myth, for example, as the Seven Rishis or Seers, and were considered primary ancestors, those of royal lineage, ones who would soar through the air to mystical lands. Ultimately, these sanctuaries derive from Mount Olympus—you might say they are generated or conceptualized there—the chief home of all the "gods," which is to say, the Ray Masters.

Each Ray Master Sanctuary is a reservoir of that Master's consciousness, an interface between that Master's energy and the Earth, and a place for human encounter and initiation with that Master. It is a place where the specific ray associated with that Master is concentrated, pooled, and distributed.

The reservoir quality is well exemplified in the Irish myth of the Well of Segais and House of Oenghus with respect to Newgrange. At the Acropolis in Athens, Greece, you can see how two Ray Masters, Pallas Athena and Ares, had their points of regular interaction with that city's geomantic structure; at Ephesus in Turkey, another Ray Master's consciousness was the prime focus of that temple and its forms of worship and ritual; and at Delphi on Mount Parnassus, Apollo, god of prophecy and justice, used that site as one of his prime places for manifestation in human life.

Among other examples, at Lourdes, you can see how the Virgin Mary (an apparitional composite of several "female" Ray Masters) worked through one of her (by now) many dozens of Ray Master Sanctuaries. Through the interaction of Montreal's Brother Andre and Saint Joseph (a Ray Master), you can see how sometimes a single evolved human can be the conduit for a Ray Master's consciousness to flow into an entire community.

Shambhala Doorway

QUANTITY: 1,080

EQUIVALENT NAMES: Sukavati; the Western Paradise; Vibhavari; Shangri-La.

LOCATIONS: Delphi, Mount Parnassus; Glastonbury; Mount Damavand; Mount Kailash; Sedona; Tetford; Thebes; Wu-Ta'i Shan.

DESCRIPTION: Shambhala is one of the eight Celestial Cities of Mount Meru, specifically, Sukavati, the Western Paradise of Lord Varuna in the West. In Buddhist, Tibetan, and certain metaphysical traditions (notably the material presented by H. P. Blavatsky and Alice Bailey), Shambhala is described as the preeminent residence of the entire spiritual hierarchy that is concerned with Earth and human evolution—the seat of spiritual government. Mount Olympus, or the Celestial City of the Ray Masters, is a subset, in terms of organization, of Shambhala, although it has its own legitimate and commissioned functions.

These same traditions usually place Shambhala in one concrete location, somewhere in the Gobi Desert, in the vastness of Mongolia, or in the Kun Lun Mountains of China. It almost doesn't matter because Shambhala is phase-shifted out of our conventional reality and you couldn't get there physically unless you were invited, transported, or were sufficiently evolved to move *bodily* through the 1,080 Shambhala conduits in the landscape.

If your psychic vision is strong enough, you don't need to go physically; a visionary experience should do fine. Nor do you have to travel to Western Asia; the 1,080 apertures to Shambhala are fairly distributed around the Earth, often in publicly visited areas. I call these apertures "doorways"; they will conduct you to the actual Shambhala, wherever it "physically" is without having to take your body or leave it. Think of the doorway as a quick shuttle to Shambhala. Wesak, incidentally, which is the first full Moon in May, is an excellent time to go, as that marks an annual mystical celebratory event in Shambhala.

The word *Sukavati* comes from the Sanskrit and means "the Blissful." It is the pure land of the West, one of the most important Buddha-fields mentioned in the Mahayana Buddhist tradition; it is presided over by Amitabha, one of the high Bodhisattvas who created it.

One can be reborn there and lead a blissful life until reaching nirvana. Sukavati is flooded in radiance, filled with exquisite fragrances, wondrous flowers, trees of jewels, the music of rushing water; those who are reborn here awaken in a lotus flower. It is a highly desirable paradisiacal realm, some aspects of which were portrayed in James Hilton's novel about Shangri-La, *Lost Horizon.*

Silver Eggs

QUANTITY: 1,080
EQUIVALENT NAMES: Left Eye of Horus.
LOCATIONS: Edfu; Sedona; Tetford; Thebes.
DESCRIPTION: The Silver Egg is the counterpart of the Golden Egg and pertains to Horus, the Egyptian falcon god and son of Osiris and Isis, and his left eye, or the Moon eye. The Golden Egg is his right eye, and both eyes represent the solar and lunar aspects of the Solar Logos. The Silver Egg hatches Horus the Elder, whose realm is mystery wisdom, the magic and knowledge of Thoth (Hermes).

Horus had many names and epithets depending on his function and location. At Heliopolis, he was *Harakhtes,* "Horus of the Horizon"; at Edfu, Horus the Behdetite, the celestial falcon god or hawk-winged Sun disk; *Hor-sa-iset* (Greek: *Harsiesis*), one of his most popular forms, meant he was the Son of Isis; and *Horu-Sema-Tawy,* "The Horus, Uniter of the Two Lands" of Upper and Lower Egypt. He was sometimes depicted as a winged Sun disk scouting the land for demons and enemies of the Pharoah, then engaging them in battle. He was the Lord of the Sky and the God of the East (the sunrise direction), which is why he was often personified as the *rising* Sun, though not the Sun god itself.

These qualities evoke the wisdom aspect of the Solar Logos expressing itself as the far-seeing, high-flying celestial hawk. Horus is our psychopomp for the Mysteries, before which temple he stands as guard, mentor, and docent.

Soma Temple

QUANTITY: 144
EQUIVALENT NAMES: Temple of the Moon God; Celestial City of Kantimati; Fountain of Youth; Peaches of Immortality; Nectar of the Gods; Prajapati's seed; Cornucopia, or Horn of Plenty.
LOCATIONS: Afrasiab; Banaras; Mount Damavand; Glastonbury; Hardwar; Mount Fuji.
DESCRIPTION: This is another of the eight Celestial Cities of Mount Meru, known as Kantimati, although its location is confusing, sometimes the North, sometimes the Northeast. Soma is the much desired elixir of immortality, that substance that the gods demand to ensure their everlasting survival.

Soma was produced when the gods churned the Ocean of Milk in the beginning of time. The Hindu myths tell us that Soma, or *amrita,* is stored in the Moon, which is a mystic vessel out of which the gods drink every month. *Amrta* means "the immortal" and refers to the substance that is free from death and that frees one from death. It is the proverbial Fountain of Youth.

Also known as *haoma,* ambrosia, and mead, it is the drink of non-death, producing an ecstatic experience that brings the Earth closer to the sky. A draught of Soma reveals "the fullness of life, the sense of a limitless freedom . . . the feeling of community with the gods, even of belonging to the divine world . . . the possession of almost unsuspected physical and spiritual powers . . . the revelation of a full and beatific existence, in communion with the gods."[67]

Soma among the gods is he who is awake; he is a god who is an edible substance "and hence the most material; that he is perfect wakefulness, and hence the most immaterial, the nearest to the elusive flow of consciousness." Soma is the "eye that watches the multiple expanse of the wakefulness in which it is immersed."[68]

Each Soma Temple offers all that Soma offers: the possibility of immortality of consciousness, of resuming the unbroken continuity of awareness that characterized our condition before the Fall of Man into incarnation and the seemingly endless round of life, death, and rebirth, and the constant forgetting of our celestial origins and the eternity of awareness—the Ocean of Milk—from which we originated. The Soma Temple is the source and secret of Space, just as the Mithraeum, the Temple of the Wild Sun, is the source and secret of Time.

As for Soma Temple itself, it may present itself along these lines: You stand under a domed roof made of apricot-colored squares through which it seems faces are gently pressing as if the roof were a membrane of skin. This is "the hive of the immortals," hundreds of faces look down from the domed ceiling, but they are only vaguely defined, as if they're looking in from another, more exalted, dimension. These are star gods.

At the center of the floor under the ceiling there is a small circular pool filled with a white liquid. It is thick, almost gooey, viscous, like liquid astral light, amrita, ichor, the blood of the gods, the substance of stars. The pool contains angel-making, star-making food, the divine substance of consciousness, the Ocean of Milk. It is the proto-type of substance, the distilled, concentrated root of all astral substance. The circular pool or vat is wider at the bottom, like an expanding cone, and at the bottom of the cone is the galaxy, such that the cone is a kind of stirring rod for the galaxy.

The point is to drink some of the white liquid so that you can ascend into the ceiling, which is the realm of the immortals. You ascend into the city overhead and into the next dimension. It's like entering a tightly packed space full of multicolored jewels or points of light, each crystalline and a single color, all packed together in a space as small as a walnut or larger than the universe. There are thousands of them and they are the immortals, the crystalline faces, those who have fed on Soma.

Stargates

QUANTITY: 1,080 for individual stars; 2,200,000 for constellations

EQUIVALENT NAMES: Unavailable.

LOCATIONS: Tetford.

DESCRIPTION: This is a new feature (to me), only discovered in March 2002 as part of my ongoing geomantic research in the British Isles.[69] The term "stargate" has been somewhat misap-propriated already by other cultural usages, such as a reference to psychic spying programs in the U.S. military and the popular cable network series called *Stargate: SG1*. However, the *Showtime* usage is not too far off the mark, just a material-ized concept of what a stargate is.

In the Earth's energy field, there are dimen-sional portals, called stargates, that connect directly with either individual stars or constella-tions. There are multiples of the stargates for each star and constellation, which means out of the 1,080 for stars and the 2.2. million for constella-tions, many are duplicates.

Stargates differ from domes in a key way: domes *present* the energy essence of a star-enabling us to experience that energy as embodied humans on Earth, and for that energy to have influences in the overall planetary energy matrix. A stargate *takes* you to that star or constellation. Initially an aspect of your awareness passes through the stargate to the intended destination, such as the Pleiades; eventually, over time, as your physical and subtle bodies become adjusted to this energy, more of your consciousness is able to make the journey.

The opening of a stargate requires the partici-pation of the Archangel Michael, which is good because this is an inherent protection against mili-tary or black magic misappropriation of these fea-tures. There are lines of light connecting the top of the stargate structure with the underside of the Throne of God, as described in Judaic and Qabalistic mysticism. When the lines of light are activated or acknowledged, one has the impression that a liquid kind of light, almost honeylike in nature, flows down them into the stargate structure.

It is intriguing to note two things here: first, in the earliest days of Earth's energy topology, the stargates were in prime working order, connecting the Earth to many sites and energies in the galaxy; second, one of the original names for the British Isles, according to Welsh mythology, was the Island of Honey. With the stargates functional in those antique days, "honey"—sublime spiritual light—flowed regularly from the Supreme Being's Throne down to the Earth. Perhaps that is the geomantic explanation for the familiar phrase, "the land of milk and honey." Once the stargate is open, the energies of that star or constellation may flow into and through the Earth grid.

The stargates appear to be situated in the back of a geomantic dragon which acts as both its nourisher and "mother." Mythically, this is apt, for the constellation Draco, the cosmic serpent that weaves around the Pole Star, is said to be the mother of all stars and thus older and more primeval than all stars.

The opening of stargates has another ramification. The timing of the opening of stargates has to do with the status of the Lucifer Binding Sites (see listing above). As Lucifer starts to be unbound at some of the 3,496 sites, then the stargates start getting revealed. The connection is this: the stargates (and their host stars and constellations) represent the differentiated lights over which Lucifer, as Lord of Light, is lord. The stars are part of Lucifer's essence, his state of awareness, his cosmic body, what we might call his Robe of Glory. They are the light he bears—hence the name, Light Bearer.

Three Star Temple

QUANTITY: 144,000
EQUIVALENT NAMES: Unavailable.
LOCATIONS: Hill Cumorah; Santiago de Compostela.

DESCRIPTION: The Three Star Temple offers you a deep experience in the mysteries of the angelic realm and its interpenetration of human consciousness. It gives you the possibility of aligning yourself with the three fundamental stars, or points of being, of existence.

These are known as the Soul Star, located high above your head; the Incarnational Star, located just above the belly button in the body (the Blazing Star discussed in part 1); and the Earth Star, located deep within the Earth. The Three Star Temple is a tool for spiritual alignment developed by the angelic realm as a way of marrying the three interdependent realms of the angelic (Soul Star), human (Incarnational Star), and elemental (Earth Star).

Its function is to bring to a point of balance a human initiate's development with the Oversoul, and to bring spiritual clarity into the field of individuals. These temples were seeded at the inception of the Earth, then brought to life over time through human, angelic, and elemental interaction. They are useful devices for experiencing and integrating the three realms of angelic, human, and elemental (Nature spirits) within your own human context.

The essential purpose of the Three Star Temple is to enable you to experience each of the stars as part of your spiritual self, and to have them fuse into one star at the center of the temple. These temples enable you to have an interactive experience with an archangelic being. Each of the 18 archangels oversees 8,000 Three Star Temples, and they occupy the middle star position. The archangels may appear as pillars of light or as two-hundred-foot-tall angels, depending on your psychic center's choice of imagery. If you allow yourself the experience of having the three stars fuse at the middle star point, you will find yourself standing very tall indeed, because your consciousness will be occupying the vertical space prepared by the archangel.

Tree of Life

QUANTITY: 2,856

EQUIVALENT NAMES: Jacob's Ladder.

LOCATIONS: Acropolis; Avebury; Chichen Itza; Glastonbury; Hill Cumorah; Jasna Gora; Montserrat; Santiago de Compostela; Sedona; Teotihuacan; Tetford; Troy.

DESCRIPTION: A Tree of Life is a concentrated mystery temple enabling you to experience the forty different spheres or stages of light in the Four Worlds, a concept put forward in Qabala in its model of the levels of reality. Religious imagery knows this feature as Jacob's Ladder, although in that context it is usually thought to be a vertical ladder upon which angels ascend and descend.

The Trees can vary considerably in size from the exquisitely concentrated Chalice Well Gardens in Glastonbury, which is all of one hundred yards long, to the Ridgeway in Wiltshire, England, reputed to be one of the world's oldest walking paths, stretching some eighty miles across the Wessex Downland from Avebury towards Swindon. Along the way you encounter a variety of intriguing ancient sites such as Uffington Castle, Liddington Castle, Wayland's Smithy, Dragon Hill, and other enigmas of the megalithic past.

There is also the far longer pilgrimage route (and Tree of Life) known as St. James' Way or the Road of Stars stretching five hundred miles across the top of Spain and including numerous religious shrines to Santiago de Compostela.

The purpose of the Tree is to create assimilable changes in consciousness. It can be used as a practice place for attunement with the hierarchical descent of energies, a training ground for the Christed Initiation in the Buddha Body. Over time the Tree unfolds from a seed like a rope ladder flung out laterally. The Tree also offers the possibility of the perfected human to interface with the being of the Earth through the four worlds.

The seed gets unfolded in conjunction with human Love from Above projected into it, and in cooperation with various supervisory angels who project an experiencable hologram of the celestial Garden of Eden into the seed. As the human works with the seed, the angels inside work with it too and the seed unfolds or expands and fills the space with the interactive Tree. Its edges form the boundary and hold the space pure and inviolate, unpollutable.

These Trees are meant to be fit into public spaces, over which people can engineer parks and gardens to maximize the benefits. They may not be aware of the overlay, but the designation of the grounds as public parks ends up preserving the energy template. The Lawn at Thomas Jefferson's Academical Village, now the core of the University of Virginia at Charlottesville, has a Tree of Life overlay. Its purpose there is empowerment in the mental body. The Trees are distributed uniformly across the Earth at the rate of 238 per Albion plate.

Underworld Entrance

QUANTITY: 1,746

EQUIVALENT NAMES: Hades' Palace; Celestial City of Samyamani; Green Chapel; Judgment Halls of the Duat; Cave of Machpelah.

LOCATIONS: Abydos; Acropolis; Afrasiab; Cumae; Mount Damavand; Glastonbury; Mount Holyoke; Tetford.

DESCRIPTION: Contrary to classical inferences and the popular imagination, the Underworld is not *under* our world of the living, as in a diminished dimension somewhere inside the Earth, but *above* our world, in a more refined level of reality. It is only an Underworld from the vantage point of the higher celestial beings, such as the famous Orpheus who descended from one of the high heavens to the lower astral plane—to him, the Underworld.

In fact, if the Underworld is to be assigned to any chakra in the human energy hierarchy, it would be the crown center. This is appropriate, for one of the mythic guises of the Lord of the

Underworld and King of the Dead is the Celtic Green Knight who astonishes the knights at King Arthur's Round Table by nonchalantly slicing off his own head, holding it, nonplussed, in his hand, and inviting Gawain to join him in a year at the Green Chapel to return the favor by having his head chopped off.

The Underworld is one of the eight Celestial Cities of Mount Meru, known as Samyamani in the South over which Yama is the lord. Yama is the Binder, the Judge of the Dead, and his father is Vaivasvata, the King of the Ancestors. Yama was the first man to die, so he is superintendent of the Dead. So was Afrasiab, the Alive King of the Dead, lord of the Underworld entrance at Afrasiab in Samarkand, Uzbekistan.

According to Jewish lore, "As soon as life is extinct in a man, he is presented to Adam [in the Third Heaven], whom he accuses of having caused his death from the 'sin' in the Garden of Eden." The myths allude to the land of the dead being the same as the Garden of Eden: "The Garden of Eden was the abode of the first man and woman, and the souls of all men must pass through it after death, before they reach their final destination."[70]

Surprisingly, the Biblical Adam is an equivalent figure to the Lord of the Underworld, for his distinction of being the first human to die, thus to know death, and he is of course our primal ancestor. According to Jewish tradition, as summarized by Louis Ginzberg in his six-volume *The Legends of the Jews,* Adam was the prototype of humans and the first human, but "he" was created on a scale altogether different from biological humans.

The dimensions of his body were "gigantic," says Ginzberg, extending from Heaven to Earth, and his soul was the source and reservoir of the souls of all the generations of humans to follow. In a similar way, Adam's death was the prototype at a higher, archetypal level for all subsequent human deaths, including Abel, whom the Bible records as the first human to die. Ginzberg says

"death was brought into the world through Adam" and suggests that the death referred to was the fall from Eden, which was a death with respect to access to the higher worlds.[71]

The legend says that the soul must pass through seven portals before arriving in Arabot, the highest heaven. The first portal is called the *Cave of Machpelah* "in the vicinity of Paradise, which is under the care and supervision of Adam." There, if the soul is worthy, the soul is allowed to pass on and proceed to paradise, or at least get closer to it.[72]

As with the other Celestial Cities, each of the many dozens of replicas is, experientially, the same place. With some of the cities, such as this one and Shambhala, what you encounter in the Earth's visionary topography seems more like a portal, route, or entrance to a place rather than the place, but if you follow the passageway, you will find yourself at the Gates of Hades.

Among the features you are likely to encounter in a visit to the Underworld are the Three Judges of the Dead (as described in Greek myth), the Chinvat Bridge (as described in Persian myth), and the source of the forty-eight Cosmic Eggs (see earlier listing). The Underworld is the place to which the classical initiates, Odysseus and Aeneas, journeyed to meet their ancestors, get some questions answered, and receive guidance about their next steps. It is the place to which people having near-death experiences go; it's where the family ancestors congregate to greet the newly arrived dead, or the transiently visiting NDErs.

The Egyptian mythic tradition about the Underworld says that there in the Judgment Halls of the Duat the soul of the deceased is weighed and evaluated by the Judges of the Dead, and it is balanced against a mere feather. If evil deeds predominate, you are sent to the dark realms; if the scales balance, you pass into the good place.

Rudolf Steiner, the twentieth-century clairvoyant and founder of anthroposophy, said that when you undergo initiation while alive, or after you die, you encounter the Lesser and Greater Guardians of the Threshold. These are a different way of seeing the Judges of the Dead. The Lesser Guardian embodies and shows you the totality of yourself, including, and perhaps emphasizing, the shadow elements, the residue of innumerable deeds with karmic consequences. The Greater Guardian escorts you into and guides you through the higher spiritual realms.

Both of these are Underworld functions, and both can be done while you are still alive and embodied. Surprisingly, it is preferable, and easier in a sense, to undergo these protracted and profound initiatory experiences while alive. The Underworld Celestial Cities, available at 1,746 locations around the Earth, make this possible.

Here is how the Underworld Entrance may present itself to you: You pass through a long tunnel and emerge from the opening before huge iron gates perhaps fifty to one hundred feet tall and set as a towering arch in a monstrously huge circular place. It is helpful to bring a golden bough from a golden apple tree, which you can collect in Avalon. This ensures your entry, like a day pass.

You can see the circular palace as Hades, or see Hades as a god and this circular place as his body. Inside the gates there is a semicircular hall of mirrors. Here you see your own astral body content as projections, as a self-created world, a hell, life as usual, whatever it is to you. You can spend a lot of time here.

This is an anteroom to Eden, a cleansing station; in a sense, it is the Plain of Asphodel, where spirits can stay a long time after death, re-creating the psychic conditions of their now departed physical life. Whatever you bring here, that becomes your world outside you. What was inside you is here outside you.

There are three underworld judges (the Greeks called them Minos, Rhadamanthys, and Aeacus). They hold the mirrors, or perhaps they are the mirrors; they don't judge; they only reflect what you present to them. Technically, you judge yourself.

Vibrating Stones

QUANTITY: 12

EQUIVALENT NAMES: Omphalos; Ben-ben at Heliopolis; *Al-hajar al-aswad* at Mecca; Jerusalem Gate.

LOCATIONS: Beckery, Glastonbury; Delphi, Mount Parnassus.

DESCRIPTION: The Earth's twelve Oroboros Lines pertaining to zodiacal energies are each anchored at a specific site by way of a Vibrating Stone. Each stone has its own time of heightened influence and activity, in accordance with astronomical cycles, but all twelve are in resonance with one another. Each stone resonates at a particular frequency that is in sympathetic harmony with certain astrological constellations.

For the most part, the stones are no longer where they belong; some are misplaced, others severely damaged, still others unaccounted for. Technically, the global system is missing its key instruments. It is like taking a radar dish away from its position in relation to the wiring it has for reception of cosmic energies, specifically, the incoming light filaments from the Great Bear containing the energies of the twelve Oroboros Lines. If the features of this system are moved, then the wiring in some instances is no longer intact. Even so, the planet is not suffering especially from this.

The system still works because in effect the Earth has become entrained to the energies the stones once anchored and can operate without them based on the strength of the original entrainment. The planet remembers the presence and activity of the stones, and has learned to mimic them or create for the most part the same effect even without their physical presence. As with the domes (see earlier listing), even though the domes are gone, their residual impact is so potent it is as if they were still in place; so it is with the Vibrating Stones.

These stones are somewhat ovoid, about two feet high or so, physically and visually undistinguished at first glance. They have an impressive resume, however. They were brought here from the Andromeda galaxy and installed around the Earth at the inception and activation of its energy matrix.

They are part of the heritage of human consciousness on Earth and are transceivers for our stellar inheritance, which refers to the totality of the human collective over all our residences. They remain on the planet as reminders of our stellar heritage, although sadly, hardly anyone knows of them and those few that are extant are not publicly acknowledged along these lines.

A few were well documented in myth and religious history, such as the Ben-ben stone at the Temple of the Sun in Heliopolis (now part of Cairo) in ancient Egypt; the omphalos or navel stone at Delphi on Mount Parnassus in Greece; and the *al-hajar al-aswad* within *al-Ka-bah,* the big black cube at Mecca in Saudi Arabia.

Islamic legend says the *al-hajar al-aswad* was a white stone delivered by God or Archangel Gabriel, and that possibly it was a meteorite. This stone is said to originally have been a white sapphire from the Garden of Eden; it turned black when menstruating women touched it, or due to the sins of humankind.

Now the *al-hajar al-aswad* is called the Black Stone, and it is set 1.5 meters above ground in the southeast corner of the Ka'ba. This stone, which has reddish tones and yellow particles but is otherwise black, was cracked into three pieces in a fire in 684 A.D.; later it was split into seven pieces. It is ovoid, eleven inches wide, fifteen inches high, and set in a silver chasing. Tradition says Adam placed it in its original position in the first Ka'ba; for a time it was hidden in the mountain near Mecca called Abu Qubays, during the time of the Flood; then when Abraham rebuilt the Ka'ba, Gabriel transported the stone back to Mecca.[73]

A visitor to the Black Stone around 940 A.D. said it was three cubits in length, "of an intense white color on its external side. Its blackness is said to be due—and God knows best—to the touches and kisses it has received from the pagan Arabs and to [their] smearing it with blood."[74]

The Vibrating Stones had the further advantage of being linked to the light temple of Jerusalem, not the physical structure in Israel but its celestial archetype. Even without the Vibrating Stones present at their original anchor points, you can have a visionary experience of the celestial Jerusalem temple by way of these sites. Each location is a Jerusalem Gate, a dimensional portal into the celestial Jerusalem on Earth. (For more on this, see the listings for Emerald and Lucifer Binding Site in this section, and Dome of the Rock in part 3.)

Table 6

A Glossary of Galaxy on Earth Features

Albion: the galaxy expressed as a giant human figure filled with stars

Arc of Developing Consciousness: a parabolic curve of consciousness linking realities

Avalon: paradaisal realm of the golden apple; a Celestial City

Camalate Center: esoteric training academy for geomythic mysteries and initiation

Celestial Cities: eight cities or domains of the gods constellated around Mount Meru

Chakras: the presence of the seven classical planets within a zodiac or temple

Control Bubble: a device for regulating the mixture of angelic and elemental energies

Cosmic Egg: an experiential model of Heaven and Earth before they were separated

Crown of the Ancient of Days: the presence of the Supreme Being as a crowned head

Cyclopean City: megalithic dimensional interface built by the Elohim

Dome Caps: subsidiary smaller domes, arrayed like flower petals about a dome

Domes: translucent englobing energy fields of varying widths, making sites sacred

Dragons: beneficent beings that energize and protect temples, ground and dispense celestial energies

Egregors: landscape angels that oversee specific regions of the planet or a country

Emerald: the Heart within the Heart, source of Light and residence of the Holy Grail

Epiphany Focus: landscape site that receives Christ beam for one week in January

Gnome Egg: headquarters for Nature spirits of earth elements, training ground for humans

Golden Egg: interactive site for birth of the Christ Child within the human

Golden Pillars: energy field generated by a Ray Master to prepare us for the future

Grail Castle: home of the Holy Grail and Fisher King; a Celestial City

Interdimensional Portal: shortcut to the Pleiadian Council of Light

Ixion's Wheel: Sun Wheel, aspect of the Solar Logos, for initiation into solar mysteries

Labyrinth: a structure with nine different forms, for balancing the mental field

Landscape Zodiac: the holographic presence of a selection of the stars of the galaxy

Lily: the product of purified human consciousness, the residue of sanctity at a site

Lucifer Binding Site: a place where Lucifer arrives and is bound or unbound

Mithraeum: the forge of the Wild Sun God; a Celestial City

Mount Olympus: the home of the fourteen Ray Masters, the chief overseeing gods; a Celestial City

Naga City: the Ocean of Milk, the dragon's cosmic contents; a Celestial City

Oroboros Line: one of fifteen primary energy lines encircling the planet, zodiacally attuned

Palladium: a miniature Crown of the Ancient of Days, Gorgon Medusa's Head

Pointer's Ball: rip in spacetime fabric affording passage to other dimensions

Ray Master Sanctuary: a reservoir of a specific Ray Master's energy and presence

Shambhala Doorway: access to Shambhala, seat of spiritual governance; a Celestial City

Silver Egg: interactive site for birth of Horus the Elder, the wise aspect of Christ

Soma Temple: source of drink of immortality, nectar of gods; a Celestial City

Stargate: portal to individual stars or constellations—actually takes you there

Three Star Temple: for alignment with Incarnational, Soul, and Earth Star via archangels

Tree of Life: miniature template of the hierarchy of cosmic energies

Underworld Entrance: doorway into Hades, Land of the Dead, Garden of Eden; a Celestial City

Vibrating Stone: one of twelve stones from Andromeda Galaxy to attune the Oroboros Lines

Part Three

A Geomantic Gazetteer
of Fifty-Six Holy Sites

Abydos, Egypt

PHYSICAL DESCRIPTION

Today a five-square mile site of partial temple ruins about nine miles west of the Nile River in south-central Egypt, Abydos was once the most venerated if not the holiest city in all of Egypt. It was the site of several royal monuments, such as the mortuary temple of Pharaoh Seti I, the temple of Rameses II, a special temple dedicated to Osiris called the Osireion, and numerous cemeteries such as the Shunet El-Zbib. In fact, for a long time it was the most important, most desired burial ground in Egypt, as burial there put one's soul in close proximity to Osiris, the Lord of the Dead.

Above all, Abydos was a gateway to the Underworld, and it flourished as a necropolis and Osiris cult center from approximately 4000 B.C. to 641 B.C.

Abydos, one of the most ancient cities of Upper Egypt, is ninety miles north of Luxor, three hundred miles south of Cairo, and situated on the Qena Bend of the Nile. It was originally called Abdu, which meant "the hill of the symbol or reliquary." That symbol or reliquary was said to be the severed head of the great god Osiris, which was buried there, making Abdu the sacred city of Osiris. "Tradition affirmed that the head of Osiris

was preserved at Abydos in a box," and a hieroglyph of it became the symbol of Abydos.[75]

Later the Greeks named the place Abydos, after their own city of the same name on the Hellespont. The modern Arabic name for Abydos is *Arabet el Madfuneh,* the name of the village presently situated near the ruins.

Another original name proposed for Abydos is *Ta Wer,* which means "Mound of Creation," a reference to the mound upon which Osiris emerged out of the primeval waters at the end of the First Time, or the primordial time of the gods.[76] The name is also given as *Tai-Wer,* which suggests "the most ancient land" that arose out of the etheric formative "waters" before the physical world was created.[77]

HISTORY AND ARCHEOLOGY

The largest of the royal monuments built at Abydos was that of Pharaoh Seti I of the Nineteenth Dynasty (1306–1290 B.C.). The Temple of Osiris was built of fine white limestone and contained many reliefs depicting mythical events and deities. The temple's front consisted of twelve rectangular pillars covered with sacred images; inside there were two halls and seven sanctuaries dedicated to Osiris and other Egyptian gods. (In all, ten different temples were built here successively over the years from 5500 to 500 B.C.)

Immediately behind this temple was a subterranean chamber built at sea level called the Osireion, believed to be a cenotaph, or false tomb, not intended for an actual body. Red Aswan granite pillars, each weighing about one hundred tons, support massive archways. Its walls were covered with passages from the Egyptian Book of the Dead. A series of water canals created an island upon which a sarcophagus sat, perhaps to symbolize the emergence of Osiris from the Primal Mound in the mythic past. Today the Osireion has lost its roof and is not open to the public on account of continual flooding. Some Egyptologists propose that the Osireion may be ten thousand to twelve thousand years old.[78]

The Temple of Rameses II, built in 1298 B.C., situated to the northeast of the shrine of Seti I, also contains numerous limestone carvings depicting historical scenes. The *Shunet El-Zbib*, or Storehouse of Dates, whose construction is credited to the Second Dynasty (2770–2649 B.C.) is set a little distance away in the northwestern desert. Most of the royal tombs were set about a mile into the desert from Abydos; the largest of these tombs covered three thousand square yards. A bit further out into the desert was the *Umm El-Qa'Ab*, the "Mother of Pots," so named for the abundance of pottery shards found there, indicative of the jars used for funerary offerings.

MYTH AND LEGEND

Abydos revolves around the myth of Osiris. His earliest manifestation was as Asari, a man-headed agricultural god; he was also known as Andjeti, a fertility deity that united with Khentiamenti of Abydos to form the composite god Osiris. An Osiris cult is mentioned as early as the Fifth Dynasty (2465–2323 b.c.), and Osiris was mentioned in the Pyramid Texts, some of Egypt's oldest extant written documents.

Osiris was sometimes addressed as *Wen-nefer*, meaning "the Beautiful One" or "Beneficent Being," and also as *Khentamentiu* (or *Khent-Amenty*), meaning "the Foremost of the Westerners." He was also called Lord of Eternity, Lord of the White Crown, the one residing on the High Hill, the king of the Palace of the Watery One, and *Kai Imentet*, meaning "Bull of the West."

The West meant Amenti, Land of the Dead, and Khentamentiu was the ruler of the dead and king of the necropolis. The majority of ancient Egyptian cemeteries were positioned west of the Nile because it was the region in which the Sun set and descended into the Duat, or Underworld. Placement of the deceased in the West put them closer to their destination in the afterlife.

The myths tell us that Osiris was married to Isis, and they produced a son called Horus. Osiris' brother, the deity Seth, killed Osiris. First he tricked Osiris into a sarcophagus that he then dumped into the Nile; later he cut Osiris' body into fourteen pieces and scattered them throughout Egypt. The Greek historian Plutarch actually specified where these fourteen sites in Egypt were; Osiris' head was buried at Abydos. An alternative version of his demise says the "Great One" fell on his side, or fell down dead at the hands of his killer, Seth, on the river bank of Nedyet, which has been identified as Abydos.

Afterwards, when Osiris was presented as a mortal, it was in a mummified form as part of his funerary function. He is usually depicted wearing a white crown, or an *atef*, an elaborate plumed headdress with ram's horns, and holding in his hands a crook and flail, the scepters of kingship. In some scenes, Osiris appears as a vegetation god, or he is represented by a small mound of earth out of which grow four trees; above the mound is a large serpent with a white crown. "He is never represented in movement, but as a swathed figure with black or green face—for he is both a mummy and the life-spirit of the earth and vegetation."[79]

After his reconstitution by Isis, Osiris became the Lord of the Underworld and the Judge of the Dead in Duat. For the ancient Egyptians, the Underworld was in the Earth, in the waters under the Earth, or beyond the western horizon. Ritually, the Underworld existed as a subterranean temple, a tomb, or tumulus. But in the Egyptian imagination, the Underworld was also a vast palace or ramparted city with a hall in which Osiris presided.

There in the Judgment Halls of Osiris, he would sit with his forty-two Judges and the goddess Ma'at. They would weigh the hearts of the deceased against the weight of a single feather of Ma'at, which was a symbol of righteousness. Ma'at personified the spirit of the land, cosmic harmony, moral order, justice, and the ethical foundations of Egypt.

Gigantic scales were present in this hall, which was shaped like a coffin, and Thoth and other divine beings kept an account of the results of the weighing of the heart. The purpose was to see if the recently deceased was worthy of entering the paradisiacal realms or should be thrown to Amemait, the Destroyer. If the scales balanced perfectly, the soul was judged worthy of paradise; if not, Amemait received the soul. Amemait the Destroyer was part lion, part crocodile, with the hindquarters of a hippopotamus; she was entitled to eat any of the deceased Egyptian souls that did not meet the requirements for paradise.

Osiris' presence at Abydos made this site the chief popular religious and cult center of Egypt. Mystery dramas enacting the mythopoeic sublimities of the Osiris story were presented regularly at Abydos, ritually reenacting his death, dismemberment, and resurrection, and attracted people from all over Egypt. The Rites of Osiris, as they were

called, were probably introduced to Abydos before 2500 B.C. Egyptologists say these passion plays were performed at Abydos from the Twelfth Dynasty (1985–1795 B.C.) until the Christian era.

"Many people wished to share in the ceremonies of the afterlife, as a token in sharing Osiris' resurrection," and if they couldn't be buried at Abydos, they might get a brick cenotaph or small stela erected in their place.[80] Many Pharaohs, too, constructed large numbers of cenotaphs at Abydos even though they were buried elsewhere because they wanted to be close to Osiris and connected with the possibility of immortality and eternal life that he represented. Egyptian folklore held that at sunset the temple area of Abydos resembled a golden staircase leading to the afterlife.

Some scholars explain that Abydos' original deity was a black dog, or dog-headed creature similar to or identical with Anubis and called Chief of the Dwellers of the West. This dog deity, said to have prevailed at Abydos even before Osiris, was called Upuaut or Wepwaet, the one "who opened the way" to Amenti.

It is likely that Upuaut was an early expression of Anubis (Anpu or Anup), the guide to the afterlife, the opener of the roads for the dead into Amenti, and the god of the rituals of the tomb. Anubis was typically presented as a black jackal or as a man with a jackal's head and, as "Lord of the Hallowed Land," he was said to be the companion of Osiris, ushering the deceased into the Judgment Halls. Anubis was the embalmer of the mummy of Osiris, and Osiris was both the mummy, the one who died, and the hope (for all) of transcending death. As the dweller in the Mummy Chamber of Osiris, Anubis was the "Governor of the Divine House."

Anubis, as protector of the necropolis, was also known as "He Who is Upon the Mountain," as the Egyptians believed he watched over the land of the dead and its mortuary rituals from a high vantage point in the desert. He protected the souls of the dead and their resting place in Amenti. This is another reason why many, especially the royalty, wanted burial at Abydos.

MYSTICS AND TOURISTS

T. G. H. James, former Keeper of Egyptian Antiquities at the British Museum in London, once said of Abydos: "It is unquestionably one of the most numinous places in Egypt—to walk about its monuments and mounds is to experience strong feelings of what might be recognized as a spiritual presence. Indeed you may even meet the deity."[81]

In the view of psychic researcher Barbara Hand Clow in *Catastrophobia,* Abydos is "one of the most multidimensional places on Earth, and Ta Wer is a powerful way to depict the vertical axis of consciousness." Abydos was the "vertical axis ascension center" on the Nile, Clow proposes, meaning the place in which one's consciousness could rise as if ascending an *axis mundi* into the celestial realms of understanding and revelation—a mystical sky journey.

The Standard of Abydos, carried in the annual Procession of Osiris at Abydos, a mystery play performed in public, was "an ideal for the vertical axis of consciousness," indicating that Abydos was the funereal, ascension, and theological center of Egypt. A main feature of this standard was the *djed* column (pillar-shaped with flattened terminals and four horizontal bars across its top), long associated with Osiris and said to indicate stability and the continuity of power. The Abydos Standard consisted of a pole supporting a beehive shape out of which came two tall plumes, which was understood to signify the god's head. Thus the Standard appeared to be "actively birthing the head of Osiris out of the Earth dimension."

Clow further contends that the reliefs and architectural geometry of the Abydos temples indicate it was a physical re-creation of the First Time, *Zep Tepi,* the primeval time of the gods. Abydos is "one of the most potent geomantic places on Earth."[82]

GEOMANTIC

Crown of the Ancient of Days; Underworld Entrance; Landscape Zodiac; Dome.

CROWN OF THE ANCIENT OF DAYS: The geomyths of Abydos are a palimpsest whose interpretation by Western scholars has confused the picture. The way to untangle the misattributions is to hew as closely as possible to the oldest and most fundamental myths about Abydos, Osiris, and Anubis. One essential statement about Osiris is that he was cut into fourteen pieces which were scattered throughout Egypt, the head being buried at Abydos.

There are other myths about a god's head being buried at a site, such as the head of the Welsh Bran the Blessed buried at the White Mount in London to protect England, or Brahma's fifth head buried at Banaras in India, or slightly different, the skull-shaped Hill of Skulls, Golgotha, in Jerusalem. Each of these locations, and Abydos as well, is the site of one of the planet's twelve Crowns of the Ancient of Days. Obviously they are special places as there are only twelve. Each is a site where the Supreme Being has a window—a roving eye—into our world.

First, we need to drop the idea that Osiris was ever human. Second, it is helpful to think of Osiris in terms of another myth, that of Kronos, Lord of Time, and his son, Zeus, chief of the gods of Olympus. Zeus "castrated" his cosmic father, locked him up in the golden halls of Ogygia, overthrew the rule of the Old Gods, the Titans, and set up the new ones at Olympus. This is the Greek mythic guise for the same story of Seth slicing up Osiris into fourteen pieces. Neither myth quite tells the full story, but if we put the two together, we can tease out the essential story line.

Zeus dethroned his father, whose body was Time itself (Kronos), and set up the Olympian gods. The fourteen gods of Olympus in fact are the fourteen Ray Masters from the Great Bear, or to use the Hindu model, they are the fourteen Manus, the Spirits of the Ages, who together comprise One Day of Brahma, which is calculated in millions of years. Brahma's essence is Time also, and he is equivalent to the Judaic figure called the Ancient of Days. Kronos is exiled to Ogygia where he rests in his golden halls. Osiris was called Lord of Eternity.

Osiris is dismembered, and his head at Abydos receives special attention. It is initially confusing, but Seth, said to be Osiris' "brother," is identical to Zeus, Kronos's "son." It is helpful here that Egyptian scholar R. T. Rundle Clark makes the astute observation that the constellation of the Great Bear "belonged to Seth."[83] In other words, Seth and Zeus are the same figure, and the dismemberment or castration is a mythic way of evoking the allocation of vast cosmic Time into smaller segments with a Time Lord presiding over each. Here, Osiris' fourteen body parts are mythically equivalent to the fourteen gods of Olympus.

Present at Abydos and accessed through or at the Osireion is a Crown of the Ancient of Days. We could also call it a White Head, Vast Countenance, even sideways view of the Ancient of Days. Osiris after all was said to have a White Crown and was called Lord of the White Crown.

Osiris was not, however, the Lord of the Underworld in the same sense as Hades, Yama, the Green Knight, and other named Underworld deities. The actual Underworld chief at Abydos was Anubis, the jackal-headed Embalmer, discussed below. The Osiris rites did involve the theme of resurrection but in a more rarefied or exalted sense. The initiate at the Abydos temple would strive for a resurrection into the wholeness of cosmic Time, which was the unsevered Osiris, the uncastrated Kronos.

There is also the matter of direction. In the Vedic spiritual cartography, South is the direction of the Underworld and death gods, and West is the direction of Paradise, Shambhala, the Islands of the Blessed. While it is unreasonable to fault Egyptian mythology for being inconsistent with Vedic, the attribution of Osiris to the West and not South raises a flag. The Rites of Osiris, with the resurrection into unsevered, undivided cosmic Time, is more consistent with the Vedic descriptions of the Western Paradise than with the Land of the Dead in the South.

At the Osireion, the initiate could take the step beyond the created, manifest world, beyond the seventh chakra, into the Eternity of the variously conceived Supreme Being, the vastness of Brahma, the Ogygian Halls of Kronos, the White Head of Osiris. The initiates would take that step after passing through the Underworld Entrance at Abydos and being "approved" for entry by its chief, Anubis.

UNDERWORLD ENTRANCE: One of the oldest myths attributed to Abydos was that a jackal-headed god prevailed at Abydos even before Osiris and was called Upuaut or Wepwaet, the one "who opened the way" to Amenti, the Underworld. In the Abydos geomyth, the functions of Osiris and Anubis blurred over time and eventually became confused. Anubis is the Lord of the Underworld, not Osiris.

The Egyptian scholar E. A. Wallis Budge gives us a clearer view of the mythopoeic initiatory role of Anubis in the Osiris rites. Anubis' role is guide of the dead in the Underworld "on their way to Osiris"; he leads the deceased "onwards" to Osiris. Anubis often acts for Osiris, examining the Great Balance in which the human's heart is weighed against the Feather of Ma'at. He guides the souls of the dead around the Underworld into the kingdom of Osiris. As Anubis, he opens the spirit roads to the North; in his guise as Ap-uat (Upuaut or Wepwaet), he opens the roads to the South. In either case, the dog deity is the Opener of the Ways. As Budge comments, it is clear that "in one part of Egypt at least Anubis was the great god of the Underworld, and his rank and importance seem to have been as great as those of Osiris."[84]

Why was Anubis so important a figure? It has to do with why he was a jackal or a dog. The "dog" in question is Canis Major, the Great Dog, guardian of the galaxy, protector of the House of Stars, guide to the intrepid humans adventuring into the realm of the galaxy and its spinning zodiac, and portal through the dog's throat star, Sirius, to the greater, exalted mysteries of the Master of the House of Stars: Osiris. One of Anubis' epithets was Am Ut, which meant "Dweller in the chamber of embalming." He was the watcher in the place of purification where the *Khent Sehet* rested; this was the chest containing the remains of Osiris, which is to say, the buried Head of Osiris at Abydos.

LANDSCAPE ZODIAC: Anubis, as the geomythic expression of Sirius, has at least two geomantic functions. The dog faces in two directions: out beyond the galaxy into the Vast White Countenance of Osiris, whose body is the fullness of cosmic Time; and inwards, into the wheel of the galaxy and its geomantic expression as the Landscape Zodiac. Anubis presides over the portal; Amenti is like a swinging door; in one direction, it opens into the Holy of Holies in which the visage of Osiris may be apprehended; in the other direction, it opens into the vast but finite life of the galaxy.

Anubis is charged with both functions. Anubis introduces you to the Landscape Zodiac at Abydos, guides you through its star fields, then opens the door into the Underworld and the possibility of guiding you into the Greater Mysteries beyond the zodiac, in the rarefied realm of Osiris and Kronos, into the *fullness* of the Day. This is the Abydos temple design: Zodiac to Underworld to Osiris.

The Landscape Zodiac at Abydos is a small one, measuring just under a mile in diameter, with its center at the Osireion; the zodiac dome extends for about two miles. The effect, at least metaphorically speaking, is to give the White Head of Osiris two wings full of stars. An intriguing text translation in Budge seems to allude to the presence of the Abydos zodiac. Plutarch, in his description of the temple complex, reported that by Anubis the Egyptians meant the "horizontal circle" that divides the invisible part of the world, called Nephthys, from the visible part, called Isis.

Plutarch further reported that the circle of Anubis equally touched upon the realms of light and darkness, which was why Anubis was said to be watchful by day and night. In geomantic terms, the visible part of the circle (the zodiac) is the physical half; the invisible part is the etheric half. Anubis is the soul guide and guardian of both halves, that of Nephthys and Isis, both of whom, incidentally, were said to have been his mother.[85]

People using the Abydos temple for initiation experiences would start with the zodiac, under Anubis' tutelage, then progress to the Underworld Entrance, still guided by Anubis, in preparation for the Osirian Mysteries.

DOME: The Abydos temple complex is topped by a dome which is the holographic presence of epsilon Cephei, or Cepheus, the King of Ethiopia. The epsilon star is one of two on the figure's head, although it does not have a name. Insofar as Cepheus has to do with conscious cognition, the placement of a Cepheus star as a dome at one of the Earth's twelve Crowns of the Ancient of Days is geomantically apt.

Acropolis, Athens, Greece

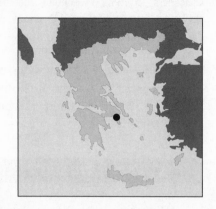

The Acropolis is world-renowned for its majestic Parthenon, the "Maiden's Apartment," erected in honor of the city's resident patron Olympian goddess, Pallas Athena, also called *Athena Parthenos,* Athena the Virgin. The rocky limestone outcrop, five hundred feet high, in what is now downtown Athens "rises steep and distant" from the surrounding hills; it is basically a plateau atop steep, sheer cliffs. A natural passageway on its western slope is the main access point for the hilltop of what was once "the most sacred of all places of worship in Greece."[86]

The term acropolis is actually a generic one to denote the upper, fortified portion of ancient Greek cities, which usually were founded around a defensive piece of high ground, making them an *akro polis,* elevated citadel. In Athens, it was Athena's acropolis.

Still extant today on the Acropolis, though somewhat in ruins, are the Parthenon (sacred to Pallas Athena), the Erechtheion (sacred to Erechtheus), the Propylaia (various buildings that serve as entrances to the complex), the Temple of Athena Nike, and several other temples dedicated to Zeus, Artemis, Asclepion, and Dionysus, among others. The Parthenon, built to principles of sacred geometry, measures 228 feet long, 101 feet wide, and 65 feet high, and has seventeen columns on two sides to support its length, and eight columns on two sides to hold up the ends. Originally, the Parthenon's marble exterior was painted in red, blue, and ocher, topped by a white marble roof.

HISTORY AND ARCHEOLOGY

A temple dedicated to Athena has been located on the Acropolis at least since the first known temple was built around 530 B.C. It's possible Athena worship was practiced there beginning in 650 B.C. A second Athena temple was constructed on the same site around 480 B.C. after the Persians partially destroyed the original one; a third, the present Parthenon, was built around 438 B.C. All three temples faced east, which according to Francis Cranmer Penrose, a British archeologist examining the site in 1891, represent an orientation towards the rising of the Pleiades in the constellation of Taurus.

After the glory of Greece passed, so did respect for the Acropolis. The magnificent statue of Athena (described below) was taken to Constantinople and eventually destroyed by the

Crusaders. In 1687, a Venetian fleet bombarded the Acropolis and destroyed a fair bit of the Parthenon; and in 1941, the occupying Nazis desecrated the sanctity of the site by flying the swastika flag. Yet in 2000, as a wonderful sign of the site's power to reinvent itself, its torch-lit image was broadcast worldwide during the Sydney Olympics.

MYTH AND LEGEND

Unarguably, Pallas Athena dominates the Athenian landscape; the city itself was named in her honor. But in the city's earliest days, there was a contest between Athena, Goddess of Wisdom, and Poseidon, Zeus' brother and Lord of the Sea, for possession of the Acropolis.

According to Apollodorus in *The Library*, the struggle took place during the time of King Cecrops, the first king of Attica, a "son of the soil, with a body compounded of man and serpent." Cecrops, a prehuman of some kind, is credited with teaching humankind how to build cities and bury the dead; he also abolished human sacrifices and recognized the supremacy of Zeus among the gods.

He is further believed to have founded the Court of the Areopagus on the Hill of Ares (adjacent to the Acropolis) at which the Olympian god Ares was tried and acquitted and Orestes, pursued by the relentless Furies, was also absolved of his guilt. The two natural rocks upon which the judges and the accused stand on this hill were once known as the Rock of Shamelessness and the Rock of Arrogance.

The Olympian gods decided to divide up Greece with the aim of finding principalities suitable to their particular worship. Poseidon struck his trident into the middle of the hill and "produced a sea which they now call Erechtheis."[87] Pausanias, a later interpreter of this peculiar

myth, explained that this sea was a well of seawater such that when the south wind blew, the well produced a sound like waves; others have described it as a saltwater spring. Pallas Athena in turn planted an olive tree on the Acropolis as her mark of possession of the desired site.

To resolve the stalemate between Poseidon and Pallas Athena, Zeus appointed a team of arbiters to settle the dispute. Cecrops awarded the city to Athena because her gift was more practical than Poseidon's. Dissatisfied with the result, an indignant Poseidon flooded the Thrasian plain and left all of Attica underwater.

The Earth-born or autochthonous quality of Athens and its primeval residents is supported by an oblique statement by Pausanias who said most of the ring wall and fortification of the Acropolis was built by the Pelasgians (including Agrolas and Hyperbios) who once resided below it. The early builders built up the sides and sharpened and straightened all the lines of the natural rock fortress of the Acropolis.

At least one scholar suggests that Agrolas and Hyperbios "were probably divine heroes and legendary builders (like Trophonios at Delphi and the divine builders of Thebes and Troy)."[88] Athenians, explains another scholar, have always claimed (and archeologists have confirmed) that the high ground of the Acropolis "was always occupied" and that Athenians are "autochthonous; they are indigenous and of the earth."[89]

Cecrops had three daughters, named Aglauros ("Sparkling Water"), Herse ("Dew" or "Dewfall"), and Pandrosos ("All-Dewy," "the All-Bedewed," or the "All-Bedewing"), who lived on the Acropolis and acted as nurses for his son and successor, Erichthonios, also an autochthonous protohuman. There is another antique "Earth-born" character named Erechtheus who has nearly the same biography as Erichthonios (from wool, *erion*, and Earth, *chthonos*), and ancient writings are confusing on this matter. In one version, Erichthonios is the progeny of Hephaistos, the Olympian fire-god, and, to an extent, Pallas Athena.

The myths say that Hephaistos lusted after Athena and tried to rape her on the Acropolis; when he ejaculated on her leg, Athena wiped off the semen and flung it on the ground. From this seed sprang Erichthonios, the Earth-born. The Earth, also called Chthon, bore Erichthonios as the divine child, the Earth-born one of the Athenian Acropolis. A variation of this had Hephaistos and Athena properly and formally engaged and in the bridal chamber; then she disappeared and his seed fell into empty space.

Athena hid her son in a basket (or chest) and instructed the three daughters of Cecrops to tend it but not open it. One day their curiosity overcame them, and two of the daughters, Pandrosos and Herse, opened the lid of the basket. They beheld, according to which source you consult, a child who was serpentine from the waist down; a child encircled by serpents; a child protected by two large snakes; no child at all but only a serpent. Whatever they saw, the two terrified girls went mad and jumped off the western end of the Acropolis.

The business of jumping off the Acropolis to one's death happened two more times. Daedalus, the great artificer, engineer, and creator of the Cretan labyrinth, tossed his nephew and pupil Talos (also called Perdix or Calus) off the Acropolis because he feared this young man's talents might one day surpass his own. Daedalus was caught and tried in the Areopagus for this deed; he was condemned and forced to flee to King Minos of Crete, for whom he afterwards constructed the labyrinth.

Aegeus, the father of Theseus, one of Athens' most famous early kings, threw himself in despair off the western end of the Acropolis when he thought (mistakenly) that his son had perished. Some ancient writers even claimed that the Aegean Sea was so named in honor of Aegeus' life-ending leap.

Athena raised Erichthonios within her sacred precinct atop the Acropolis, and he succeeded Cecrops as King of Athens. Erichthonios had no legs, so to facilitate his mobility, he invented the four-wheeled chariot; after his death he was translated to the sky and became the constellation Auriga, the charioteer. The Erechtheion on the Acropolis was named after him (in his guise as Erechtheus), and it became his site of worship among Athenians.

Homer, in *The Odyssey*, notes that Athena, after having rescued Odysseus, returned to Athens, where she entered "the abode of Erechtheus." Another tale says Erechtheus disappeared from the world when Poseidon opened a chasm in the Earth with his trident in retribution for Erechtheus, having killed a son of Poseidon.

While alive, Erichthonios, in honor of his mother, promoted the cult of Athena, installed an olive-wood image of her on the Acropolis, and instituted the *Panathenaea*, a festival in celebration of Pallas Athena. As Pausanias noted in the second century A.D., "The whole city and the whole country are sacred to Athene," adding that the holiest of all the Greek images of his time was Athena's statue in the Acropolis, "though then it was the whole city." Pausanias then adds this intriguing bit of folklore: "Rumor says it fell from heaven."[90]

The statue known as *Athena Promachos*, Athena the Champion, stood thirty feet high in the Parthenon, made of wood and covered in gold leaf, and overlooked a processional way on the Acropolis; this image of Athena, carved by the renowned sculptor Phidias, could be seen even at a distance of miles, replete with its warrior's helmet, shield, and spear and her other mythic regalia. "Athena is everywhere the preeminent citadel and city goddess," and her temple is very frequently "the central temple of the city on the fortress hill." This was true not only for Athens but in other Greek cities including Argos, Sparta, Troy, and others.[91]

With Pallas Athena resident on the city's most conspicuous point, the Acropolis, Athenians could rest easy that they were under the celestial protection of the armed maiden. She was the *Pallas of Athens,* the resident deity, *Pallas Athenaie,* in which Pallas meant "Maiden" or "weapon-brandishing," or perhaps both, and sometimes simply *he theos:* the goddess.

Also reputedly present on the south face of the Acropolis rock was a *Gorgoneion,* an image of the Gorgon Medusa, a fearsome being slain by Perseus, under Athena's guidance, and whose face comprised the centerpiece of Athena's aegis or breastplate. One direct look from the eyes of the Gorgon Medusa would turn men and women to stone; hence it was a formidable part of Athena's weaponry. Further, this Gorgoneion was said to have the power to foretell the setting out of invading fleets from their home ports.[92] Another version holds that Athena buried the head of the Gorgon under the Agora, the city's marketplace.[93]

The Panathenaea was a festival held every year on Athena's birthday, that momentous day when she emerged from Zeus' forehead, but the Great Panathenaea was staged only every four or five years. In either case, the festival was a joint celebration of the founding of the city and the linking of Athens with its patron goddess.

The first such festival in Athens was held in 566 B.C. and was entirely dedicated to celebrating the city's patron goddess. Athenians made a procession starting from the Dipylon Gate, moving through the Agora, or marketplace, past the Klepsydra Spring, then up the Acropolis to the olive tree dedicated to Athena and to her temple. In later years horse and chariot races and musical contests were added to the program.

A related festival for Athena was the *Chalkeia,* held every fourth year (one year before the Panathenaea). Women wove a giant garment, the *peplos,* for the statue of Athena on the Acropolis; the peplos, adorned with mythic pictures from Athena's life and deeds, was ritually presented to the statue in her temple. In the *Plynteria,* or feast of the bath, the statue of Athena Polias (or a replica of it) was taken to the sea for a purification; at the same time, Athena's temple was cleansed and purified.

In a cave in the neighboring Hill of Areopagus reside the Furies, also known as the Erinyes or Eumenides. Three in number, the Furies are generally described as avenging spirits of the dead and enemies of parricides and violators of the family order and natural law. They avenged injustice and stood for the rightful order of life and society, and their desire for vengeance was described as implacable. Contact with them invariably produced irremediable madness hence they were feared and avoided.

Named Allecto ("Unceasing"), Tisiphone ("Avenging Murder"), and Megaera ("Grudging"), the Furies were hideous, winged, crone-like black hags, their eyes oozing pus, their hair entwined with twisting snakes, their hands wielding whips and torches. They were frightening, full of outrage and ferocity. They were born from drops of blood from the castrated Uranus and said to live in Erebus, the darkest level of the Underworld. Older than the gods, "unbanishable and untamable, they had refused to cede their power and authority to Zeus and the Olympian gods."[94]

Legend has it that Aeschylus, in *The Eumenides* (published around 458 B.C.), was the first Greek writer to give a face to the Furies—to describe them as something other than a faceless horror. They were a "startling" group of women, "black and utterly repulsive"; their breath was foul, their eyes dripped "foul ooze"; and they were so unkempt as to be unfit to be seen in the house of either mortals or the gods.[95]

The Furies mercilessly pursued Orestes (son of the murdered Trojan War hero, Agamemnon, King of Mycenae) all over Greece for having killed his mother and her lover. Orestes sought refuge and adjudication by Pallas Athena at the Hill of Areopagus. Athena pronounced him free of pollution, renamed the Furies the Eumenides, meaning "the Kindly Ones" or "the Kind-hearted," and invited them to dwell peacefully within a cavern under the hill, which they did.

From that point forward, the Eumenides became guardians of civic order in Athens, where they are also known as *Semnai Theai*, "Venerable Goddesses." Their domain within the hill, whose entrance affords a direct view of the Acropolis, is sometimes referred to today as the Cave of the Eumenides.

MYSTICS AND TOURISTS

One scholar visiting the Acropolis commented that in approaching the hill one always feels in the company of all humankind. "It is one of the universal places where the collective mind and soul meet and gather in a unity. Even the most dull of heart have been transformed by this space."[96]

Even though the temples are empty and the marble columns cracked and defaced, "the pure rationality of the buildings, so integral to all Greek art, science, and philosophy, is still perceptible," commented a visitor from Japan.[97] Another writer reminds us that Athens seen from an elevation has always been described by poets as "violet crowned" because "as the sun sets, the ring of rocky hills that surround the city turns from shade to shade of violet and amethyst."[98]

GEOMANTIC

Dome; Major Egregor Point; Palladium; Grail Castle; Tree of Life; Arc of Developing Consciousness; Ray Master Sanctuary; Underworld Entrance.

DOME: The Greek myth of Erechtheus being turned into the cosmic Charioteer of the constellation Auriga turns out to be a true geomantic memory. The "abode of Erechtheus" is the dome over Athens with its center above the Acropolis. The charioteer image is especially apt in that one way of seeing the domes as celestial beings is in the form of chariots and horses, the major star represented by the dome and its forty-eight subsidiary dome caps (the horses).

The Acropolis dome corresponds to Capella, alpha Auriga, the sixth brightest star in our galaxy, forty-five light years from Earth and 160 times the luminosity of our Sun. Some of its key dome caps (those closest to the point of origin) encapsulate and energize various hills and features of Athens such as the Hill of Areopagus, the Hill of Nymphs, Mount Lykabettos, and Mount Hymettos, among others.

It makes sense that Erichthonios was the first to dedicate a temple to Pallas Athena on the Acropolis. As the star deity whose representational body is the dome of Capella, his very presence over the Acropolis is automatically a temple dedication: it is the temple itself.

Traditionally, Auriga is pictured as a young man carrying a charioteer's whip, holding a goat and two kids against his shoulder and wrist. Within Auriga, Capella is the goat on the left shoulder of the charioteer; but it's not just any goat, it's Amalthea, the goat that nourished Zeus when he was an infant on Crete. Capella is also called *Cornu Copiae,* "the Horn of Plenty," referring to one of the goat's horns, which the infant Zeus awarded his nurses; the horn was empowered by Zeus to fill up magically with whatever its possessors desired.

Capella among the Arabic astronomers was *Al Hadi,* who rose with the Pleiades and rode before them in much the same way a singer would lead a procession of camels. Among the Hindus, this star was *Brahma Ridaya,* the "Heart of Brahma"; for the Akkadians, it was *Dil-gan I-ku,* or "Messenger of Light," as well as *Dil-gan Babili,* "the Patron Star of Babylon."

In "very ancient times," spring began when the Sun entered Taurus, and due to Auriga's proximity to the constellation of Taurus, Capella was known as the "Star of Marduk," or the "Spring Sun," which was identified with Taurus and worshipped as the son of Ia.[99] This last reference is especially interesting in light of an otherwise baffling myth about Theseus.

MAJOR EGREGOR POINT: Pausanias reports that a bull, originally sent by Poseidon to Crete as a punishment of their King Minos, was later loosed on the plain of Argos whereupon it dashed away into Attica and Marathon, killing everyone in sight. "Afterwards the story goes that Theseus drove the bull of Marathon into the akropolis and slaughtered it to the goddess."[100]

This is a complex myth, but the brief explanation is that the Cretan bull was a manifestation of Zeus (see Mount Ida, Crete, and the myth of Europa and the white bull), an expression of the constellation Taurus, and a giant landscape figure stretching across southern Europe from Crete, through central Greece, the Balkans, Italy, Switzerland, and parts of Germany. Theseus "slaughtering" the bull at the Acropolis is geomantic code for saying he grounded, secured, and activated that part of the geomythic Bull's energy center that was preexistent in Athens.

The specific reference to Crete as the origin of the bull refers to Crete as the umbilicus (*Manipura* or third chakra) for this geomythic beast; the Acropolis is its *Muladhara,* or root chakra center, an identification that makes more sense when we understand who and what Erichthonios was. The key point here is that in addition to all the local geomantic particularities of the Acropolis temple, the entire complex serves a role in a larger geomantic structure: the Bull of Europe.

Earth-born, chthonic Erichthonios was an extraterrestrial, a star god. Isn't the paradox lovely? When Greek myths speak of Gaia, the Earth, and chthonic, the reference is not to the planet of the same name, but to all the created space in the universe in which matter and substance at any density and vibrational level can exist. In the beginning there was Heaven and Earth—*Heaven* being all of the celestial beings and content as pure consciousness, and *Earth* being the space created in which all forms of substance could exist and evolve.

The myth of Erichthonios, the serpent man who invented chariots and was made into a star called the Charioteer, is an open secret. He wasn't transformed *into* a star; rather, he came to the Acropolis *as* the star Capella in the constellation Auriga, the Charioteer. Read the myth backwards and you get its open secret. Erichthonios came as the celestial being present through and as the dome for Capella at the Acropolis. Even today, you can still have an experience of Erichthonios as the star being "in" the dome at the Acropolis.

The difference between Erichthonios being turned into a star and Erichthonios *as* the star (via the dome) who came to Athens is the gap between myth as fable and myth as metaphysics. Prying open that gap is one object of this book, and an opportunity to visit sacred sites with an eye to studying the local myths about the place.

PALLADIUM: Who and what was Erechtheus, after whom the Erechtheion was named? Was he the same as or different from Erichthonios? The qualities attributed to Erechtheus—a divine child hidden in a basket surrounded by serpents—refer to the Palladium present at the site of the Erechtheion. That Palladium is one of sixty such energy presences on the planet, representing a miniature Head of the Ancient of Days (see Troy).

The snake reference might be the way the Greeks perceived the Ancient of Days (a Hebrew name, admittedly) as the severed, snake-entwined head of the Gorgon Medusa, which adorned Pallas Athena's breastplate and also appeared as part of the miniature statue of Athena known as the Palladium. The snakes around the infant in the basket are equivalent to the snake-entwined head of the Gorgon Medusa. The Head inside the "Abode of Erechtheus" radiates light in all directions. The face looks everywhere at once; its visage is unflaggingly plastic and mobile, like a radar dish tracking every second in a sphere of 360 degrees.

GRAIL CASTLE: Above the Acropolis is a Grail Castle sitting, as it were, atop Poseidon's trident. As noted earlier, myth holds that the Lord of the Sea jammed his trident into the soft clay of the Acropolis, asserting his hegemony. Geomantically, this means that Poseidon as Lord of the Abyss presides over another replica of the Grail Castle, fount of primordial cosmic memory, situated above—which is to say, in a more subtle dimension—the Acropolis.

Metaphorically speaking, follow the upraised trident up from the hilltop to the three forks and into the Grail Castle for, potentially, knowledge of events in the cosmos dating back at least three hundred million years. This is why Poseidon asserted his ownership of the Acropolis first: because his domain encompasses a deeper, earlier, vaster stretch of time than Athena's.

TREE OF LIFE/ARC OF DEVELOPING CONSCIOUSNESS: Occupying the rest of the flat top of the Acropolis, from the Erectheum to beyond the front eastern porch of the Parthenon, is a Tree of Life, like a fountain in four tiers, flowing across the landscape from the Ancient of Day's Head to the edge of the Acropolis. There, leaving the hill like a person leaping into the void, is an Arc of Expanding Consciousness, extending from the steps of the Parthenon out beyond the cliff's edge and down into Athens to ground the energy of Athena. The three tales of people jumping to their deaths off the Acropolis might be accounts of initiates ascending into higher dimensions at either end of the Acropolis: into a transcendent blending with the Ancient of Days at the Erechtheum or a leap into another dimension off the Parthenon into the Arc.

RAY MASTER SANCTUARY: The Parthenon can be appreciated as a well to contain Athena's eighth ray energy of bluish silver. This explains to some extent why Homer always referred to her as "gray-eyed" Athena: her ray color of bluish silver is close to gray; seeing her as gray is an approximation of her energy essence, just lacking some cognitive vitality. Like the Artemision of her fellow Ray Master Artemis at Ephesus in Turkey, Athena's Parthenon is a prime grounding and containing facility for this energy. As I explain below, however, the Parthenon has an additional ritual function which makes sense when we understand who the Furies are and what the Hill of Ares (Areopagus) is all about.

Ares as the Olympian war god is another Ray Master, in this case, the Ray Master of the seventh or lilac ray. Also encountered at Thebes, the lilac ray is an energy of intense transmutation, a kind of stripping away of the dross found in a person's auric field and soul. Ares is warlike in his rigorous transmutative energy; his energy, as the harbinger and way preparer for the Christ, is a purifying, even scourging one. It is fitting that the Furies would be given permanent haven in the Hill of Ares.

UNDERWORLD ENTRANCE: After Aeschylus properly scared his Attic audience with his gruesome description of the Furies in their most revolting appearance, later in *The Eumenides* he allows the Angry Ones to explain that their God-appointed duty is to be "witnesses of the truth," to be reminders and mirrors to humans with guilty consciences that bad deeds against other humans shall not be forgotten. They hold the memory of evil when humans would rather forget it.

The Furies also explain that human illusions melt down "before the onset of our black robes." In short, the Furies are an early Greek description of the three Judges of the Dead in Hades or the Underworld. Into the Cave of the Eumenides in the Hill of Ares humans go, while alive, to shed negativities and impurities from their total beings. It is a profound scourging experience, a deep cleansing through self-awareness, a riveting self-purification through transmutation. The Furies don't have to do much to catalyze this: they just hold up the mirror to the soul.

In the language of initiation, they represent the Lesser Guardian of the Threshold, the fierce, almost unbelievable face of the Shadow, the unacknowledged, unresolved, unexpiated karmic error and residue residing *unknown* to us like toxic substances in our auric field. The Furies produce the shocking experience of self-awareness in which the Shadow and its seemingly dreadful contents are revealed. It can seem like an unrelenting, ruthless, even mortal encounter. It's only dreadful if your intent is to flee; the moment of revelation—a negative epiphany of oneself—can be the foundation for a fundamental transmutation and self-cleansing. It can be a step towards freedom.

The experience facilitated through the Cave of the Eumenides is akin to what is frequently referred to as the after-death life review. This experience is often recounted in tales of near-death experiences, when all the events of one's life flash before one as an amazing continuous video. One also must review, however, the events of the nighttime, the dreamtime, and those times when we acted as if asleep, unconscious of the effects of our actions on others. This is where you find the Furies. They are as scary as your own worst demons. As witnesses and soul guides of memory, they merely hold the mirror, and if you see them as loathsome, scary hags, that's just an index of your Shadow.

Inside the Cave, which is to say, at the Gates of the Celestial City of Yama, the Hindu god of death, or the Palace of Hades, the Greek lord of the Underworld, you stand before three figures seated on thrones. Behind them are numerous tall pillars that when you study them are really enormous golden faces. Under their ruthless gaze, all the falsehood and foreignness in your being is stripped away.

It is a moment of intense recognition through heightened, almost transcendent self-awareness, and one of jubilant release and unfetterment as the product of a total body scourge. You ask yourself: Are the Furies demonic or angelic? Are they the furious judges of the dead or am I my own infernal conscience-stricken judge?

It all comes together in the Panathenae, the ritual procession along Athena's way from the Agora to the top of the Parthenon. The metaphysical essence of this event was to make the Stations of the Cross, so to speak, at the Acropolis temple: a fury of interior scourging at the Cave of the Eumenides; a warlike transmutation under the influence of Ares; an immersion in the warrioress energy of Athena in the Parthenon; a meeting with her divine father, Zeus (from whose brow she was born), in the Erechtheum; a walking down through the four dimensions of existence along the Tree of Life; and a grounding of the experience of higher energies of the mind through the Arc of Developing Consciousness.

The Acropolis temple is all about the energy and consciousness of Pallas Athena, the goddess of beautiful justice. The Acropolis is Athena's divine battlefield for the war within the psyche; she is the guide for spiritual soldiers, the soul guide and the goal for all who dare to take the journey through the living Palladium on the Acropolis in Athens. Athena facilitates a furious cutting away of that which obscures spiritual cognition of her father, Zeus. She resembles the Germanic Brünnhilde, leader of the Valkyries.

Athena guides and inspires spiritual warriors in their conquest of ignorance, obliviousness, unconsciousness, error, and karmic debts and residues. She leads the fight on behalf of the rightful order of things. She battles for the purity and clarity of consciousness, for the entry into higher levels of the mind untainted by karmic pollution.

In this cleansing work the Furies are her allies. Athena's is a beautiful justice because it is the beauty of what is right, the justice of detoxifying the unjust from the psyche, the clarity of mind that enables you to see this justice. It is the justice that brings you into awareness of Zeus the Father of the gods as the organizing intelligence behind the world of action and thought.

Afrasiab, Samarkand, Uzbekistan

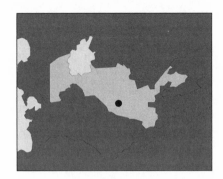

Samarkand, a city of primarily Muslim population in east-central Uzbekistan, is one of Central Asia's oldest cities, with a recorded past dating to the fourth century B.C., when it was known as Maracanda and was the capital of Sogdiana. The city is located in the Zarafshan River valley and surrounded by mountains. It was once part of the province called Transoxiana, situated between the River Oxus and River Jaxartes. The city has been called the "Mirror of the World," the "Garden of Souls," the "Fourth Paradise," and, by one of its ancient rulers, the "Eye and Star" of his empire. The name Samarkand is "magical, evocative, blessed" and "steals the soul away."[101]

Samarkand has an old city, and an even older one in ruins. The old part of Samarkand, dating from medieval times, consisted of streets converging toward the center from six gates in the city walls that ran for five miles around the outskirts of the settlement. The walls and gates were destroyed in the nineteenth century when the Russians captured Samarkand, but the city's medieval plan is still discernible. Architectural historians praise Samarkand for its many fine monuments of Central Asian architecture dating

from the fourteenth to twentieth centuries. Most of these are situated at Registan Square.

Registan Square is effectively the heart of Samarkand and has been since Timur the Great (also called Tamerlane or Tamburlane) declared it so. It is lined with turquoise domed buildings, gateways, and the minarets of three ancient *madrasah* (schools of religious instruction). The inside and outside façades of the madrasah are decorated with glazed brick, mosaics, and carved marble. Also credited to Timur is the Bibi-Khanum mosque completed in 1404 to commemorate Timur's favorite Chinese wife. Timur imported architects from Iran and India in 1399 to build him this mosque.

The even older part of Samarkand, now a three-hundred-acre ruin, is called Afrasiab after a legendary king of the same name. Archeologists believe the original core of Samarkand began as a pre-Mongol city in Afrasiab on a small hill or large plateau of yellow loess.

Laid out along a path and stairway proceeding up the side of a hill near Afrasiab is the *Shah-i-Zinde*, "The Living King." This is a monument complex of about two dozen mausoleums and several connected mosques constructed in the late fourteenth century. You enter the complex by passing through a massive iron gate, then up a 210-foot-long stairway-walkway to the site of the tomb of the Living King. Tombs containing other royals are on either side of the walkway.

Today an overcrowded cemetery takes up the land immediately around most of the buildings. Once widely regarded as a cult center, even today the ruins of Afrasiab remain a major pilgrimage site for Central Asian Muslims. With its emphasis on mausoleums, the site is often referred to as a "City of the Dead."

A famous Arab traveler named Abu Abdalla ibn Battuta described the Mausoleum of Qutham ibn Abbas at Afrasiab during his visit in the early 1330s. He considered this mausoleum a holy Muslim site and noted that every Tuesday and Thursday evening the people of Samarkand came out to it, bringing votive offerings, money, and animals to maintain the traveler's hospice there and "the blessed tomb." Battuta noted: "The Tatars, in the time of their infidelity, did not injure in any way the condition of this blessed site; on the contrary, they used to visit to gain blessing as the result of the miraculous signs which they witnessed on its behalf."[102]

Afrasiab is less than a half-mile from the Registan Square, but from a distance "it looks like nothing more than a huge desultory urban earthwork."[103] Another contemporary commentator said that, looking west from the modern city, Afrasiab looks like "a dusty mound in the distance."[104] Russian excavations begun in the 1880s restored Afrasiab to world memory and respect, especially as extraordinary sixth-century frescoes have been unearthed at the site along with evidence of a ruler's palace. Apparently, the palace walls of the Sogdian rulers at Afrasiab were ornamented with murals depicting religious ceremonies.

Also once present at or close to Afrasiab was the astronomical observatory of Muhammed Taragi Ulugh Beg (1394–1449), a formidable fifteenth-century Turkish astronomer and grandson of Timur, one of Samarkand's rulers. His three-story circular observatory (construction began in 1428) contained at the time the world's largest quadrant (its radius was 120 feet) for making accurate astronomical observations. Ulugh Beg compiled a Catalog of Stars (identifying 1,018 stars), which is still used as a reference source.

Not since Claudius Ptolemy (circa 170 A.D.) had anyone carried out this kind of research, and Ulugh Beg performed this work 150 years before Tycho Brahe and two hundred years before Johannes Kepler, two Europeans usually credited with compiling the authoritative Western star tables. Documents indicate Beg had at least sixty scholars with him at the madrasah systematically studying and cataloguing the stars between 1420 and 1437, such that in the 1420s and 1430s, Samarkand was the astronomical capital of the world.[105]

In its day Beg's observatory was considered the best in the world and attracted scientists and astronomers to Samarkand from all over. It made Samarkand a world scientific center for a time. When he was beheaded in 1449 by his son, Beg's observatory was so thoroughly destroyed that its specific location in Samarkand remained a mystery until 1908 when an archeologist found Beg's sextant on Kukhak Hill, just to the northeast of Afrasiab. Today Beg's underground arc of the quadrant, constructed of brick covered in marble, is viewable by the public, protected by a tunnel-like building. Originally a large astrolabe was set on metal rails on either side of the quadrant.

HISTORY AND ARCHEOLOGY

Prior to its Mongol conquest in 1220, Samarkand was situated at the mound called Afrasiab. It was the summer royal residence of the rulers of a Central Asian region called Sogdia, across which Iranian merchants played a major commercial role on what was called the Silk Road. Samarkand, known to the Chinese as *Samokien,* was a major staging post of the silk route from China to the West.

The Chinese were impressed with Samokien. One seventh-century traveler, Wei Chieh, said the people were good at business and the city was always filled with foreign traders. The people played many types of musical instruments, such as large drums, small flutes, and five-stringed lutes. "In the sixth month, June, they have a great festival at the mausoleum of their ancestors, and people come from all over the country to help celebrate this festival." Hsuan-ts'ang, also of the seventh century, concluded that Samokien "is the heart of Central Asia."[106]

Politically, the history of Samarkand is dominated by three rulers or tyrants: Alexander the Great, Genghiz Khan, and Timur. By the time Alexander the Great conquered Samarkand (Maracanda) in 329 B.C., he found a city almost five miles in circumference with strong fortifications. Alexander described the city, which he found more beautiful than he had imagined, as a "precious pearl of the world" and the "Eden of the East."

In 711, Samarkand, known to the Arabs as *Mawarannahr,* "The Land Beyond the River," fell to the troops of the Arab caliph, General Qutayba ibn Muslim. Under the Arabs, Samarkand soon became a major center of Islamic scholarship. By the tenth century, its population was estimated to be 500,000. After the Arabs invaded, the last Sogdian rulers of Transoxiana fled to a fortress atop Mount Mug to the southwest of Samarkand.

The arrival of the Mongol armies of Genghiz Khan (1162–1227) in 1221 led to the city's temporary abandonment. Russian archeologists determined that a probable reason Afrasiab was not reinhabited after the Mongol invasion was that the invading army had destroyed the lead water ducts, and the survivors lacked either the technical ability or stamina to repair them. One Russian archeologist working in Samarkand in the 1960s was certain the evidence supported the claim that the ancient fortified city of Maracanda had stood at Afrasiab, "occupying all or part of the remains of the walled city existing today."[107]

The Timurid dynasty in Samarkand began in 1398. Timur (1336–1404) was a Mongol-Muslim leader of fierce determination. His originally Turkish name, Timur, meant "iron," but from an arrow wound to his leg in his youth, he gained the nickname *Timur-i-Lenk,* meaning Timur the Lame, which became corrupted to Tamerlane and later immortalized in the Christopher Marlowe play, *Tamburlaine the Great.*

Not long after his return from conquering Northern India, Timur arrived in Samarkand and vowed to construct the most beautiful and largest mosque in the world, which became the Bibi Khanum mosque, whose outer walls make a rectangle 500 feet by 330 feet, and whose highest arch rises 90 feet. Timur built the Registan and reorganized the city so that six main roads led out from the Registan to six city gates to symbolically connect his city with the then-six primary known destinations in the world: China, India, Russia, Persia, and the Mediterranean.

During Timur's reign, Samarkand was in effect re-created at a new location to the south of Afrasiab, which had been mostly destroyed by the Mongol invasion. Samarkand became one of the world's then most glorious capitals. From Samarkand, Timur presided over an empire that rivaled in size that of Genghiz Khan; after Timur's death, his empire lasted for another century until it was superseded by the rising power of the Uzbeks in Central Asia. Timur's remains reside in the *Gur-i-Amir* mausoleum in Samarkand, which he built in 1404.

MYTH AND LEGEND

During the era of the Soviet Union, when Uzbekistan was part of the U.S.S.R., official Soviet history stated that Samarkand was founded in 530 B.C., but if the Iranian poet Firdausi is to be believed in his *Shah-Nama* ("The Epic of Kings," written in 1010 A.D.), its true foundation might be much older, in a mythical past.

A king called Afrasiab figured prominently in the *Shah-Nama,* although the action took place in Iran. Since Uzbekistan is separated from Iran only by Turkmenistan, and Samarkand lies close to the southern border, it is likely that the two areas shared some mythic concepts, including a folk memory of the ancient king, Afrasiab.

According to information imparted to Russian psychiatrist Olga Kharitidi in her recent travels to Samarkand, where she was tutored by initiates in an old esoteric fraternity, Afrasiab was a ruler there in the Golden Time, serving his god with devotion and receiving power in return. That god was the Great Mother Anakhita, a Sun goddess, a sky ruler, a commander of thunder, a deity representing Alive Time, for whom numerous *sufa,* or fire temples, were dedicated.

Ardva Sura Anakhita (or Anahita, or Anahit) was originally an Iranian goddess whose name meant "the High, the Powerful, the Immaculate." She was also known as "Without Blemish" and the "Immaculate One," with duties involving the Moon, the Night, love, sexuality, chastity, and fertility. Her father was Aramazd, also known as Ahura Mazda, "Great God." In Armenia, her essential quality was as "Mother of All Knowledge." She was depicted as a young woman wearing a crown of stars, fine jewels, golden sandals, and otter-skin clothing or a golden mantle. One of her epithets was "Sculpted in Gold."

In her left hand she held a pot, signifying her role as presiding over all the waters, including rivers, lakes, streams, and the sea, but also the life-giving fluids such as semen and mother's milk. Temple prostitution was part of her domain, so Anakhita was depicted with a pomegranate blossom on her breast, although her official flower was the hyacinth. She was the patron of love and childbirth and purified the sperm and the womb. Overall, she was the sovereign goddess who dispensed life, although in Zoroastrian lore, Anakhita was a war goddess who drove a chariot pulled by four horses signifying wind, rain, cloud, and hail.

When two of Anakhita's priests, who were brothers, developed a jealousy over the goddess's attentions, one of them, Zaratashta, became the goddess's enemy and tried to steal her sacred treasure, a necklace, but failed. She threw it into a lakebed and filled the lake with milk rain, then removed herself from the world, though she continued to rule from afar. "She hid herself in the star Sirius which had been her home before," Kharitidi explains in *The Master of Lucid Dreams.*

Afrasiab, the other priest, journeyed until he found that lake. In the middle there was an island, and on it grew the *haoma* tree from which the Elixir of Immortality could be brewed, similar to the Vedic description of the Soma plant. Before she came to Earth, Anakhita used the haoma juice to "connect the Earth and the stars" with where she used to live, namely Sirius, Kharitidi reports. Afrasiab learned from a white bird (the Simurgh) living on the haoma tree where the goddess's necklace lay, and he dove to the bottom of the lake to retrieve it, understanding that it was the key to immortality. As a mark of recognition to Afrasiab, Anakhita dispatched forty ancient spirits, called *chiltans,* to serve him.[108]

After remaining on Earth for two thousand years, Afrasiab decided to leave. Under Anakhita's guidance, he built "a temple-fortress made of a shiny metal shaped in a perfect spherical form, hermetically sealed." Inside were artificial stars, including the Sun and Moon, and Afrasiab started to live in this silver sphere.[109]

As the Golden Age was about to end, Afrasiab was about to transport his new home to the top of the highest mountain to be closer to Anakhita, when Zaratashta, his old rival, poisoned him. Anakhita made Afrasiab the Alive King of the Dead since he had the secret of immortality and could tutor humans in their transition from life to the afterlife. Since that time, "his temple-fortress appears as a shining spheroid ship among the mountains," flying constantly between the world of ancestors and Anakhita's realm, helping those who die "to be saved from the second death."[110] According to Kharitidi's sources, the ruins of Afrasiab at Samarkand are where Afrasiab works as the Alive King.

Much more recently, the event at Afrasiab that led to the creation of the Mausoleum of Qutham ibn Abbas is often credited with the origin and the meaning of the name *Shah-i-Linde*, "The Alive King." The legend goes that Qutham ibn Abbas, a near contemporary (or cousin) of the Prophet Muhammad, came to Samarkand to preach Islam, then died a martyr's death in 676 A.D. during the time of the first Arab siege of Samarkand.

Legend also contends, however, that he escaped death by hiding in a niche or jumping into a well, after which he continued to live underground at Afrasiab as the Living King. It is also said that he was beheaded, but calmly picked up his head and plunged with it into a well from which one day he promised to reemerge if the Russians attacked the city. They did, in 1868, but Qutham did not appear to save the city.

A further alternative version of his demise says Qutham saved himself from the infidels by entering a cliff which miraculously opened before him, then closed again after he was inside. Some scholars propose that the location may have been revered as a pre-Muslim holy site long before any attribution to Qutham ibn Abbas. Obviously the attribution of Qutham as the Alive King is a wishful overlay on Samarkand's Underworld god, Afrasiab.

MYSTICS AND TOURISTS

In her esoteric researches in Samarkand, Kharitidi learned why the city was once known as the Mirror of the World. It was not because Timur wanted his rebuilt city to feature the world's most gorgeous buildings. Instead it had to do with Samarkand's esoteric geomantic function as one of "two earthly faces mirroring each other in a special way."

One face of the mirror was Samarkand, between the Oxus and Jaxartes Rivers; the other was Sumer, between the Tigris and Euphrates Rivers in Mesopotamia (now Iraq). For thousands of years, "this mirror connection provided magic" for the planet, Kharitidi reports. The implication of course is that Samarkand may have originally been *Sumer*kand, City of Sumer.[111]

Kharitidi further reports that the energy of all of Samarkand but especially Afrasiab is well equipped to help the living process their internal demons, psychological wounds, and emotional traumas. She calls them "spirits of trauma" and "memory demons," and describes them as sentient astral beings that get attached to unresolved emotional wounds in humans and help them fester. They remain in place, confirming one's self-definition of misery, until deliberately exorcised and removed. Samarkand is an excellent place to do that, she says, because in a strange way, this was one of the places that initially energized the attachment and created memory gaps in one's biography. The memory demons get removed through a special kind of guided lucid dreaming during the daytime, "in which action and perception are united in a way totally different from our usual experience."[112]

Kharitidi's *The Master of Lucid Dreams* recounts her firsthand experience at healing her own spirits of trauma at Afrasiab. Her mentor, who implied he was one of the original forty chiltans, explained that after Afrasiab became the Alive King of the Dead here, the place became a battlefield. The intense killing and trauma associated with the conquests of Alexander and Genghiz Khan were still reverberating in the ethers. "The separation of trauma from awareness in human memory was initiated here, and because of this, the potential for healing is also the highest in this place."[113]

People are continuously attracted to Samarkand, Kharitidi was told, because it is easier there than elsewhere to make the final decision. That decision is either to heal and be transformed, by exorcising the memory demons and closing the gaps in one's personal story and self-identity, or by giving in completely to the memory demons, which are "very active" in Samarkand, forgetting about healing, and resuming a life of interior misery and pain.

GEOMANTIC

Dome; Underworld Entrance; Soma Temple.

DOME: The dome directly centered over Afrasiab, but also encompassing all of Samarkand, is the starfall for beta Crateris, the Cup or Chalice. As a constellation Crater resembles a large urn with two handles or a finely shaped wineglass. The beta star of Crater is of the fourth magnitude at the southern base of the Cup; it has no name or recorded myths.

Crater was variously the Cup of Apollo, Hercules, Achilles, Dido, Medea, or Bacchus, the Wine-Cup of Noah, or the Cup of Christ's Passion. It was also seen as a Water Bucket, by the Arabians as *Al Batiyah,* an earthen wine vessel, and by the English as the Two-Handled Pot. One astronomer associated it with the Soma-cup of Vedic India, while another linked it with the Mixing-bowl in the Euphratean myth of Ishtar. Crater has also been associated with the Akkadian *Mummu Tiamut,* Chaos of the Sea, the Mother of Heaven and Earth, and the Child of Tiamut, the primordial cosmic dragon.

The essential energy of this site is about creating the possibility of a ride on the Simurgh, the Bird of Paradise, free from stain, pain, or sin. This is the white bird living on the haoma tree and guarding Anakhita's necklace.

The Simurgh was the Bird of Marvel said to build its nest of ebony and sandalwood on Iran's Mount Damavand in its earliest days. The Simurgh, or Persian *Simarghu,* was said to be a dragon or hybrid bird-dog that guarded the Tree of Life from which the seeds of everything living in the world could be obtained. In the Ukraine, the Simurgh was shown seated on a tree on an island guarded by voracious fish. Simurgh as the god-bird was understood to be the secret name for God and was considered the same as the immortal phoenix.

UNDERWORLD ENTRANCE: Clearly the archeological site known as Afrasiab serves as a portal to the Land of the Dead, presided over by Afrasiab, the first human to die and subsequently known as the Alive King of the Dead. Unlike many other Underworld entrances, this one is complemented with a Soma Temple, offering the elixir of immortality to those deceased souls deemed worthy of this draught of the gods.

SOMA TEMPLE: The Uzbeki myth of Afrasiab is nearly identical to the Iranian tale of Afrasiyab because the sites at Mount Damavand in Iran (see Damavand, Mount, Iran) and Afrasiab in Samarkand are identical. They are temples of the Moon God, Soma. This is not the Moon as we think of it, a satellite orbiting the Earth. Moon is more of a symbolic way of describing a primordial state of unified, singular consciousness that predated the creation of the Sun and the universe and its myriad contents.

The forty chiltans said to assist the immortal Afrasiab in tending the haoma tree and its functions have been called Lunar Pitris in the Theosophical tradition. These are the primordial ancestors of humanity, perhaps even our cocreators. The Pitris are the spirits of human races that preceded our known human races. Theosophy states they are in seven classes, three of which are noncorporeal, four of which are corporeal (having form), although that is not the same as saying they were biologically incarnated.

In equivalent terms, Vedic myths about Soma, the substance of immortality, say it is tended by ageless beings called Gandharvas and led by the chief Gandharva, Krsanu. Before the beginning of Time, when the Uncreated bled into the created, Krsanu was charged to guard the Soma.

We can reasonably equate the Vedic Krsanu with the Iranian Afrasiab. As an exalted spiritual being, he is still tending the Soma vat, still administering the haoma tree, still the Alive King of the Dead because nobody who tastes Soma ever dies again. This is to say, one never loses consciousness, never suffers a gap in awareness that a memory demon or spirit of trauma can own and manipulate.

The silver spheroidal temple with artificial stars, the Sun, and Moon on its interior walls is a reasonable description of the inside of the Soma Temple. Silver of course traditionally denotes the Moon; the presence of the stars is apt because the Vedic myths say that all the gods—the stars are the gods' bodies—desired the Soma and, as it were, huddled around the chalice to get their drink of it. Inside the Soma Temple you are quite likely to have a vision resembling this in essence. The vat of Soma is equivalent to Anakhita's lakebed filled with "milk rain."

Soma is the essence of nondeath, the elixir of everlasting life—life not of the physical body, but of consciousness. Soma produces the unendingness, the eternal duration of awareness, but consciousness *before* selfhood, before awareness has been differentiated—fragmented—into parts.

The Moon is older than the Sun, which is a mythic way of saying unified consciousness is more primal. For individuated consciousness you need the birth of the Wild Sun God and all the turmoil, growth, and change that birth produces.

Soma is the god who is awake and whose lucidity is an edible substance; He is the eye of perfect wakefulness that surfaces in the Ocean of Milk, the concentrated essence of all substances—"the eye that watches the multiple expanse of the wakefulness in which it is immersed."[114]

Soma, or the Iranian haoma, is a tree because it is the original Tree of Life, the one said to grow in Eden in the Judeo-Christian vocabulary, or alone on the top of a very high mountain in the Iranian. It is the cosmic version of our own pineal gland within the brain; Hindu yogis routinely compare the exudate of the pineal gland with the drops of prepared Soma: both produce the ecstasy of unified consciousness, with awareness that occupies all of created Space at once. There is no selfhood, no subject-object distinctions, no Time, only Space.

It is the Ocean of Milk, containing the seeds of all the stars and worlds that will ever be. This is why Anakhita is the Mother Goddess of all waters, of fertility. Appropriately in Vedic myth, it is the ejaculated seed of the cosmic father of all living beings, called Prajapati, wounded in the act of trying to copulate with his daughter, Rohini, by the Archer, Sirius (Anakhita's origin). His daughter becomes the one who serves the Cup of Soma (the Crater) to the gods.

SOMA AND THE MEMORY DEMONS: Why is Samarkand, and Afrasiab especially, an excellent place for exorcising memory demons? For one, there is sufficient presence of the memory demons to provoke awareness of their existence, activity, and psychic pressure—if one is so bold.

Many myths tell of the time before the Sun came out of the Earth and before the Sky was lifted off the Earth—in other words, cosmic Night, the time of the Moon, when primeval creatures and what we would call demonic beings roamed the land. Ancient Tibet and the Hawaiian island of Lanai, for example, were described this way, and the Norse folktale of the troll who would turn to stone if the rays of morning sunlight caught him testifies to this. Strange creatures of the Night and Moon wander about before the Sun rises.

Another reason for the suitability of Afrasiab to the work of exorcism is that the haoma tree or Soma Temple potentially restores one to the paradisiacal, preindividuated state of unified consciousness, to that infinitely expansive state of homogenous awareness. Nothing is separate from anything else; no thing has been differentiated yet from the fullness of being—it is all an endless Ocean of Milk, a pure space of being in a universe where Time has not been created.

Even if you don't have the experience of being celestially intoxicated with Soma, the atmosphere of Afrasiab creates a simulation of this freedom in consciousness. All of the psyche is illuminated with the Moon glow of the haoma tree, and you see where the gaps are, the places where the memory demons have taken possession of part of you, all the battle scenes where you have lost, been killed, and left as a corpse in your own karmic history. From the fullness of undifferentiated being, you can clean your psychic house, heal your personal story, sew the rips in your auric field, kick out the Night squatters, resurrect yourself from the thousand little deaths and the reckless abandonments of parts of your whole self.

The energies of Afrasiab lift the awareness of those engaging the temple's geomantic structure in this way. It's as though you get a free lift on the Simurgh, a taste of the unbelievable freedom in consciousness the god-bird embodies.

Avebury, England

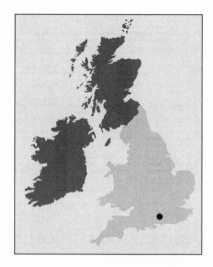

Avebury, located in Wiltshire about ninety miles west of London and a few miles from Marlborough, is not as well known as Stonehenge, its neighbor twenty miles to the south, but it should be. Stonehenge, though compelling visually, is mostly a museum piece in terms of its geomantic function. Avebury, at 28 1/2 acres, the world's largest standing stone circle (containing a small village and two roads that intersect in its middle) is as geomantically vital and active today as ever, and is of pivotal importance.

Archeologists propose that the main outer Avebury circle was constructed around 2500 B.C. and originally had ninety-eight undressed (rough, unshaped) sarsen stones that ranged in height from nine to twenty feet and weighed up to forty tons. Today only twenty-seven of these massive stones remain, and each is rough-skinned and oddly shaped, as if poured in liquid form and congealed in place.

Archeologists believe the stones were quarried fairly near to Avebury, but geologists report that the Avebury sarsens are the remnants of a siliceous duricrust layer that formed fifty to seventy million years ago. About twenty to thirty million years ago changes in the Earth's crust broke up the sarsen layer and transported some of the individual stones down the slopes of the Downs of Wiltshire, which then were at about eight hundred feet above sea level.[115]

Other theories to account for the origin of the sarsens—their name might be an amalgam of the Anglo-Saxon words *sar*, "troublesome," and *stan*, "stone"—hold that they were "artificially compounded" by the "great skill in Magick" of the Celtic magus Merlin. Others have thought they were spewed from a volcano like arrows; that they rose to the surface from deep underground "like currants in a spinning bun"; or that these "stones of considerable bigness" seemed to grow out of the ground.[116]

Two smaller circles, called the Northern Inner Circle and Southern Inner Circle, are believed to be slightly older, having been built around 2600 B.C. The northern circle is 320 feet across and originally had twenty-seven stones, though only four remain today; the southern circle is 340 feet across and contained twenty-nine stones, of which five are still standing.

Archeologists contend that the Avebury complex was used as a temple site for about one thousand years, its use winding down around 1600 B.C. By the time of the Iron Age, the emphasis was on building protected hill forts as defensive measures for tribal warfare, so there wasn't much interest in an open-air sanctuary. Few people came to Avebury after that. "What lingering ceremonies there were, thinly attended, were probably only distortions of the original rites. Avebury had been forgotten."[117]

The entire Avebury complex, 1,396 feet in diameter, is encircled by a great chalkstone bank and ditch four-fifths of a mile in circumference. Archeologists estimate that 200,000 tons of rock were dug out of the ground to make the ditch and bank. Today the bank stands between fourteen and eighteen feet above the bottom of the ditch, but it is believed that the ditch is silted up to at least half its former depth. Once the difference was closer to fifty feet.

The ditch and bank are interrupted in four places by entrance causeways effectively dividing the circle into quadrants and allowing for two roads to pass through, which, seen from above, make an asymmetrical cross in the circle. The village of Avebury thrives in the middle of the circle, offering shops, bookstores, restaurants, accommodations, pubs, a museum, and even a small church to the many tourists who visit the site.

Leading up to the Avebury circle is West Kennet Avenue, a 1.5-mile-long stone promenade consisting of two parallel rows of standing stones terminating at the northeast causeway entrance to the major circle. Many stones are missing from the original layout (twenty-seven remain), but it seems probable there were about one hundred pairs of stones along the sinuous course the avenue makes across a field and now parallel to a road. The paired stones were spaced fifty feet apart and at intervals of eighty feet in the double rows.

HISTORY AND ARCHEOLOGY

The earliest known written reference to Avebury appeared in 1289 A.D. and called it *Waledich,* a name of Saxon origin from *Weala-dic,*

meaning "the dyke of the Britons." Avebury remained virtually unknown to the world until around 1663 when British antiquarian John Aubrey gave British King Charles II a tour of the monument, then later, by royal command, prepared a plane-table survey of the Avebury stone complex. Writing about the circle, Aubrey said, "Avebury doth as much exceed Stonehenge in grandeur as a Cathedral doth an ordinary Parish Church."

Between 1719 and 1724, visits by antiquarian William Stukeley gave Avebury more recognition. He speculated that the Druids had built Avebury and that the original ground plan represented a serpent passing through a circle, thus expressing a traditional symbol from alchemy. He explained all this in his 1743 work, *Abury, A Temple of the British Druids.*

Stukeley noted that Avebury must have been the work of a "very great and larned people," that its design "shews its extreme antiquity," and that its overall construction are "evidence of the genius of the founders." These founders, he said, "have a notorious grandeur of taste, a justness of plan, an apparent symmetry and a sufficient niceness in the execution."

Avebury was a hieroglyphic in stone work, surely one of the most magnificent ideas ever "form'd in mortal minds." He observed that many other megalithic sites were close by Avebury, such as barrows, circles, and the famous and enigmatic coned hill, Silbury, such that all sixteen square miles of the greater Avebury complex were "entirely sacred ground:"[118]

Stukeley prepared detailed drawings and measurements of the layout of the three circles, work which proved to be of historical value because in subsequent decades the English farming public was seemingly hell-bent on destroying as many of the Avebury stones as possible. They thought the stones inexcusably pagan, and inconvenient for farming.

Stukeley made drawings of how the farmers destroyed the stones: they pushed the sarsen onto a pile of straw in a great pit, burned the straw underneath it to heat the stone, then poured cold water on the surface so the stone would be easy to smash up with sledgehammers. Where once there had been an estimated six hundred standing stones, today there are seventy-six. Fortunately, since 1942, the National Trust has been in charge of Avebury and has maintained it as a national monument, open free of charge to the public.

From 1925 until his death in 1955, Alexander Keiller carefully excavated Avebury and West Kennet Avenue. He dug up buried stones, placed concrete markers at the probable site of missing stones, and helped restore the site to a semblance of what it might have looked like before the centuries of abandonment and depredation. He unearthed fourteen stones in West Kennet Avenue alone and excavated the presumed sites of fifty-three missing megaliths. Keiller was instrumental in changing "Avebury's untidy neglect into its present majestic state worthy of its magnitude and importance."[119]

In the 1970s British archeo-astronomer Alexander Thom made careful geometrical studies of the Avebury design and concluded that its curious asymmetrical shape was not an accident or the result of imprecise construction techniques but deliberate, and evidence of the "remarkable accuracy" typical of every aspect of the circle's execution.

Thom had already studied two hundred stone circles in Britain and found that the megalithic yard (2.72 feet) was consistently used as the standard of measurement for constructing these circles. Then he proposed that Avebury might be the geometer's touchstone. "We consider that because of its size and the fact we know its geometry, Avebury provides the best site for determining, from a single site in England, the value of the megalithic yard." Avebury provides the "most accurately determined value" of the megalithic yard in England.[120]

MYSTICS AND TOURISTS

Avebury, proposed English antiquities scholar Harold Bayley in 1912, "typified not only Time, but also the greater Absolute, the all-embracing and more awe-full Soul or core of Time, the axis of Existence."[121]

In 1966, English psychic Grace Cooke, well-known medium for the otherworld mentor called White Eagle, recorded her impressions of Avebury. The stones came into physical manifestation from the etheric forms created by ritual that invoked the occult, invisible power of the gods, Cooke said. The rituals were also associated with veneration with the Goddess of the Moon who sits enthroned at Avebury as its ruler. The object of the ceremonies was to bring physical life into manifestation from the etheric world. Avebury was the heart and center of all efforts to build up form. All this was millions of years ago, Cooke said, when Avebury was "one of the great creative centres of this planet."

In a 1949 vision of Avebury, Cooke saw " a great fountain of light" rising up from the circle and spreading out over the land. The people present were very big with beautiful bodies, and they were being worshiped by the fairies and elemental beings, as if they were gods. This seemed to be at a time when the Earth was not yet solid, but in a more fluidic, etheric state. Avebury was one of the several points in England where planetary rays of light seemed to converge, "and at such points there is a tremendous spiritual impetus and inspiration."

A spiritual Sun broke through into apparitional appearance, and the people exclaimed that the "Great White Light" had arrived. Cooke saw innumerable people seated around Avebury as if in a vast amphitheater "watching this ceremony in the centre, and the priests and priestesses passing round and round building up this core, this centre of creative fire." Cooke also saw neophytes being instructed at Avebury in the esoteric techniques of "moulding and moving matter by a tremendous effort of divine will."[122]

A colleague of mine in geomythic investigation reported a vision in which he saw a procession almost like a Midsummer's pageant down the West Kennet stone avenue into the Avebury circle. People were festooned in flower garlands. Where each of the stones stood there was a much larger column of blazing white light. At the entrance to the circle stood a young man and woman, perhaps just twenty years of age, being applauded by the procession.

My colleague's impression was that the processional was in preparation for a wedding, but one that would ritualistically "marry" everyone there with Avebury, and Avebury with the world and the celestial realms—a *hieros gamos*.[123]

English geographer and archeologist Michael Dames proposed in the 1970s that the Avebury monuments "were created as a coherent ensemble to stage a religious drama which took one year to perform." This drama centered on the Great Goddess whose image was writ geomantically large in the landscape across the fields at Silbury, said Dames.

The "gigantic sculpts" of the Great Goddess were regarded then as "living characters" who were brought to a state of "maximum vitality" by the annual drama. All creation was conceived as a single giant human being, Dames wrote, so the "architecture of the entire cycle was designed to be read as a sequence of visual images of the Neolithic deity."

The Avebury monuments were directly associated with the yearly cycle of farming and the seasons. Avebury, with its neighboring monuments, says Dames, possesses the "concentrated energy of a microcosm, epitomizing the Great Goddess as she turns through her annual gyration."[124]

In the late 1990s, psychic researcher Page Bryant called Avebury one of many planetary

"beacon vortexes"—energy vortexes connected by "terrestrial leys" (energy lines) and connected to celestial bodies via "celestial leys." These put the Earth in "constant reciprocal and cyclic activity" with other stars, planets, and galaxies. Beacon vortexes, says Bryant, are places where people once went (and could again) to perform "star ceremonies, to gain access to the power of the Great Star Nation, and connect with the Sky Gods."

As for Avebury specifically, the "power" of the place is still very much evident, Bryant reports. She never feels as though she is walking among stone ruins when she is there, even though many of the stones are gone. "It has an air like no other, a place filled with ancient voices and the essence of so many lives, so many ceremonies, so much time . . . so much Earth power and human power and star power preserved."[125]

GEOMANTIC

Planetary Umbilicus; Oroboros Line Grounding Point; Master Dome; Tree of Life.

PLANETARY UMBILICUS: This function is unique to Avebury, which performs it for the entire planet. It is where the Earth plugs into the galaxy.

Two streams of energies, or cords, come down from two points in the galaxy and are grounded at Avebury. One comes from Sirius, the galaxy's brightest star, located in the throat of Canis Major, the Great Dog, visible in the Northern Hemisphere sky. The other comes from Canopus, the galaxy's second brightest star, the rudder of the Argo Navis or Ship constellation, visible in the Southern Hemisphere sky.

The Sirius line is golden, the Canopus line silver; as they descend from the galaxy they intertwine forming a double helix which is rooted at the center of the Avebury circle. The double helix cord of gold and silver connects individually with all 1,746 star domes on the planet, descending double helically onto their topmost sections like an umbilicus. Sirius has its own dome at Carnac, France, while Canopus has its dome at Iona Island in Scotland, and both these domes work closely with the blended Sirius-Canopus energies at Avebury.

The gold and silver lines are in a specific mathematical ratio to each other, having to do with many geomantic functions worldwide. The gold-Sirius line is 666, the silver-Canopus line is 1,080. The ratio of these two numbers is equal to the dialectic of light expressed by the Golden Mean Ratio, also known as phi, whose value is infinite: 1.61803398875. . . . The sum of the two numbers, 666 and 1,080, is 1,746. This is known in gematria (the science of interpreting the number-letter combinations in Hebrew and Greek alphabets) as the "mustard seed," and refers to the perfect balance of consciousness typified by the Christ. This is important because it has a lot to do with the meaning of Avebury's name and its geomantic function.

One meaning of the word Avebury comes through Qabala and its gematrial interpretation of words. "Ave" is the same as the Hebrew word for Light, *AWR*, whose number equivalents are 162; technically, AVE comes out as 161, so between 161 and 162 you get 1.618. . . ., or phi, the essence of Light. So Avebury is where they buried the AWR, the seed of Light, on Earth. The Blazing Star at Avebury may be envisioned, for example, as a clear quartz crystal with forty million facets. This is not an exaggeration; such a multifaceted crystal is an aspect of the cosmic Blazing Star and is known in the Hindu tradition as the Nimitta.[126]

This is appropriate for an umbilicus. We can understand why by switching our attention for a moment to the human context. In part 1, we were introduced to the tiny pinprick of brilliant light two inches above the navel and two inches inside every human being; we called this the Blazing Star and explained that it is central to Earth's geomancy—our ticket of admission to the galaxy on Earth. This is *the* show on Earth. Everything you could ever see elsewhere you can see here. It is our first cell, our umbilical connection to Spirit.

The Earth has a Blazing Star as well, the AWR they buried at Avebury. Avebury is the site of the planet's pinprick of brilliant light, its first cell and umbilical connection to Spirit. This means if you go to Avebury and tune into your own Blazing Star at the midpoint of your body (see part 1 for instructions), you will be doing it at the equivalent place on the planet's body.

Surprisingly, the best place to enjoy this attunement is on a tiny green traffic island diagonally in front of the public toilets and the Red Lion Inn, where the road from Marlborough (A4361) enters Avebury, passes through, then leaves on its way to Swindon. Certainly you could stand at other locations within the Avebury circle and have the experience of alignment with Sirius and Canopus, but for some reason, it works best here.

It's a bit amusing to think as you stand there, almost in the midst of traffic as the Land Rovers roll by, that you are being infiltrated by energies from Sirius and Canopus and having a cosmic experience. This is the closest you can get on Earth to an experience of the energetic core of the galaxy, as it were, touching the live wires coming in from Sirius and Canopus. The purpose of Avebury has always been this: the attunement of human consciousness to its purpose on Earth.

You will probably experience that your star gets very big very fast as it meets a larger version of itself, like two brothers away from home in joyous reunion. The Avebury star itself is a hologram of the Blazing Star at the topmost center of our galaxy, the Pole Star, or Polaris, in Ursa Minor, the Lesser Bear. So in a sense, you have the opportunity to align yourself with the umbilical point of yourself, the Earth, and the galaxy.

You may find, if you look at yourself with inner sight, that you are no longer a human form, but a huge cubic stone ablaze in white flames, a megalith burning with white fire. You may in fact find that you are pleasantly glowing for weeks afterwards. You may discover in the ensuing months that you are being transformed from the inside out.

You might also try walking slowly and attentively down the West Kennet stone avenue into Avebury, along the lines of the vision recounted earlier. One of the functions of stone avenues such as this is to focus, narrow, direct, and concentrate the energy into a stone circle. The avenue also helps to focus energy and awareness in preparation for the inner marriage within Avebury.

In the vision described above, a young couple was about to marry on behalf of everyone present, the landscape, possibly the Earth as well since Avebury is the planet's umbilicus. At Avebury you can achieve your own inner marriage. At one level, it is the harmonizing of the male and female aspects of the total human; at another, it is the inner marriage of body and soul with spirit. Here the body and soul aspects of yourself are the "Earth," and the spirit aspect is the galaxy, expressed in various mythic traditions as the Cosmic Person. In England, this Cosmic Person was known as Albion.

This may sound fantastic—from a certain point of view it is!—but the specific measurements of Avebury are based on the cosmic "body" proportions of Albion. Avebury is Albion adjusted to fit the size of our planet. Alexander Thom's insight that Avebury is the reference point for standing stone circles that exhibit the megalithic yard is apt, and possibly more profound than he realized.

The megalithic yard of 2.72 feet is based on a fundamental mathematical principle called e, or Napier's constant, the logarithmic base of expan-

sion and the natural base of logarithms, computed to be 2.7182818284. . . . It is the basis for all Landscape Zodiacs, whose measurements were originally computed in terms of megalithic yards; it is also the basis for the differing sizes of domes; and as Thom demonstrated, e is also the prime measurement of the stone circles.

Thus the "ultimate" reference value for stone circles and zodiacs all over the planet is found in the measurements and geometry of Avebury. That's a lot of geomantic hardware to be determined by the geometries of Avebury: 432 zodiacs, 1,746 domes, and 1,746 stone circles. Perhaps these facts account for the intense concentration of ancient megalithic sites and structures in Wiltshire and for the more recent efflorescence of crop circles in the adjacent fields.

OROBOROS LINE GROUNDING POINT: In the 1870s, Sir John Lubbock, known as Lord Avebury, who bought part of the village to forestall ruinous development and destruction of the stones, bemoaned the existence of the village and roads within the majestic stone circle. "The pretty little village of Avebury, like some beautiful parasite, has grown up at the expense and in the midst of the ancient temple."[127] But perhaps the village and roads *belong* there.

The two roads that asymmetrically bisect Avebury circle actually mark the location of two Oroboros Lines that originate there. Oroboros Lines—there are fifteen on the planet—completely encircle the planet and are geometric parts of the Earth's energy body. The Sirius and Canopus cords entering Avebury get grounded, then head out laterally around the planet. One tracks the A4361 for a few hundred yards, the other tracks the smaller crossroad before it continues on to encircle the globe.

Thus Avebury's two seemingly inconvenient roads mark the location and starting point of two of Earth's primary energy lines. We could call the gold one the Sirius Oroboros Line and the silver one the Canopus Oroboros Line. They intersect the other thirteen Oroboros Lines elsewhere on the planet. A third primary line of this type originates at Mount Meru, an invisible island off the southeast coast of New Zealand, and derives from Polaris whose dome is at Hardwar, India.

The Polaris, Sirius, and Canopus lines divide the Earth into six sections, and each of their six vortices is a planetary chakra. (The seventh is in the middle of the Earth.) These three Oroboros Lines respectively correspond to the sushumna, pingala, and ida subtle energy channels that run from the root chakra to the brow chakra in the human and are a conduit whereby Shakti-Kundalini is able to ascend to rejoin Her consort, Shiva, in the crown chakra.

THE PURPOSE OF THE STONES: Avebury is shockingly older than archeologists are willing to entertain, nor were its stones quarried nearby. They were, however, *produced* nearby—on the spot, in fact, by the same "they" that buried the Light at Avebury.

Avebury predates all human embodiment on the Earth and, paradoxically, it predates the installation of Time itself as a factor in biological life on the planet. (See Carnac, France.) It is safe, though not necessarily entirely accurate, to rely on the geological age of twenty to thirty million years assigned to the sarsens. The big stones at Avebury are at least that old.

Originally, seventy-two stones were installed around the inside of the ditch. They were brought into manifestation from out of thin air, by magic, it would seem to us. They were in fact, as the myths remember, "artificially compounded." You could say the stones were the products of Merlin's "wondrous stratagems" and "great skill in Magick," for he was part of the engineering team.

In the days when most of the original features of Earth's sacred geography were being installed, the master geomancers were the angelic family called the Elohim. For a time, under com-

mission by the Supreme Being, they took on the biological form of what myth recalls as giants. They dug the ditches, made the measurements, and planted the stones.

The original seventy-two stones were placed to correspond with the twelve Rays of the Great Bear in the Six Worlds. This is a complicated setup. The Great Bear is the home of the Celestial City called in this book Mount Olympus, home of Zeus and the gods, or in Norse mythology, Asgard, Thor's home. The fourteen Olympian gods are known as the Ray Masters because they handle the diffraction of the absolute light into its fourteen components, seven major colors and the seven subtleties of each such as dark blue and pale blue.[128]

The Ray Masters, like the Elohim, were instrumental in establishing and maintaining all aspects of the Earth's sacred geography from the beginning. At Avebury, they used the seventy-two stones as a way of transmitting their rays or essential vibratory streams of energy and consciousness—color—into the different realms of existence.

The Six Worlds or Six Realms is a term from Buddhism represented as a wheel divided into six sections, each of which represents, from the vantage point of the Buddha, or Awakened One, a realm of unenlightened existence. These realms include the world of living humans, animals, the Dead, the gods, the Antigods or Asuras, and the restless spirits or demons. As all of these realms are part of the greater Earth serviced by the planet's sacred geography and energized through Avebury, they must be equally nourished by the twelve rays.[129]

Later in planetary history another twenty-two stones were added to the circle. These enclosed the energy of the Ray Masters and their colleagues (the ascended hierarchy of evolved beings) in a different formation so as to help activate the Avebury umbilicus at a later date. This brought the total number of stones to ninety-four. The stones in the two smaller circles, the Northern and Southern, were added much later, in the course of human history, and were not particularly important.

THE EARTH GRID DVD: Avebury is a place for which the word *multidimensional* was invented. It is a hologram of the entire cosmos compressed, seemingly, into a mere twenty-eight acres. It's much bigger on the inside.

All the features of Earth's sacred geography are expressed within this cosmic hologram, and can be adjusted, modulated, amplified, and energized from here. The Avebury hologram contains all the information about past, present, and future geomantic programmings for the Earth. Any changes in the "mix" will be made here, and distributed from here.

The entire light-pattern library of Earth's geomythic body is contained here like a vast packet of seeds, or like a giant game board. The Avebury hologram is interactive in multiple dimensions, compressing a vast amount of data in a compact disk size, offering multiple viewing angles, search capability, eight-track sound, and wide-screen display, like a DVD.[130]

From the center of Avebury sixteen lines run out at equal distances to the ridge, four lines per quadrant. Along the ridge in the spaces between the lines are sixteen information features—an encoding or labyrinth, in alternate fashion. If you sit at the ridge at the site of one of these features, you can go through the different labyrinths or encodings, like browsing a cosmic library.

The subjects of one encoding include the Earth grid, its structure and features, and all the ramifications of this planetary architecture since the earliest days of Hyperborea, a planetary epoch earlier than Lemuria. These sixteen information features are an aspect of the relation of the Elohim and the Supreme Being. You could think of it as sixteen file cabinets containing all their engineer-

ing field notes or, to use a more contemporary image, as an interactive CD library.

MASTER DOME: The dome over Avebury is fourteen miles (27,210 megalithic yards) wide and accounts for the comment that all sixteen square miles of the greater Avebury complex are "entirely sacred ground." The forty-eight dome caps that come off the Avebury dome in large measure make this area "entirely sacred."

The dome over Avebury is not like the 1,746 star domes elsewhere on Earth. This is the master dome, the one that holds the pattern together, and does not correspond to a star. Rather, it corresponds to the center of the universe, to a "place" Hindu mythology calls the golden halls of Citamparam, or Tillai, where the great god Shiva dances the illusion of manifestation. This is the hall of consciousness at the core of the universe.[131]

Citamparam means "the Space (*amparam*) of Consciousness (*cit*)," and in and as this space of consciousness, Shiva, in his guise of Nataraja, Lord of Dancers, performs his cosmic dance of bliss, pirouetting in a nimbus of fire. Think of Shiva at Avebury as the gold line from Sirius, and the silver line from Canopus as Shiva's consort, Parvati, who is often pictured in ecstatic embrace with him.

With Parvati, Shiva is the dialectic of light, the double helix ratio of Sirius and Canopus; shown without Parvati, she is implicit in him, and he is the totality of the galactic essence, the blend of gold and silver, its totality before it was ever split into two. This is the *Ananda Tandava* pose, and the entire cosmos is his theater and self-created audience. All the gods witness his wild dance of creation; Brahma tings the cymbals; Vishnu strikes a drum; the Gandharvas play flutes.

Shiva dances on a lotus pedestal, a platform made of the Nimitta, which, mythologically, corresponds to his child, Ganesha, the elephant-headed god. The brilliance of the Nimitta at Avebury blends with the golden light of Shiva's twirling form to form a dome of light around the cosmic figure. In other words, Shiva casts his own dome overhead as a kind of whole-body halo.

The myths say that from out of the pedestal there springs the "encircling glory," the *tiruvasi,* fringed with flame, and touched within by two of Shiva's four hands, one holding a drum, the other fire. The tiruvasi is not just a circle of fire; it is a globe or dome of fire—the first dome, the very idea of a dome. Shiva's dance expresses his five cosmic activities, the whole play of God, including creation, preservation, destruction, illusion, and salvation. He dances with the five elements of existence and his arms extend out to the eight cardinal directions.

At the Earth's umbilicus, Shiva creates and sustains the majestic illusion (Maya) or apparition of existence, with all its gods, stars, and realms. Hence the sixteen encodings and labyrinths at Avebury and the DVD library aspect.

An ancient Hindu text declares: "His form is everywhere: all pervading in His Siva-Sakti/Citambaram is everywhere, everywhere His dance."[132] Shiva (or Shiva and Parvati) dances on Earth, and for Earth, at Avebury, expressing Sirius and Canopus for our planet. At the level of the galaxy, Shiva dances at its local Citamparam, expressing, embodying, and being more than Sirius and Canopus for our galaxy, which is a dome in the universe.

Shiva is a fractalized presence: you can conceive of his dance on ever bigger or ever smaller scales. It is all the same, and he is always at the center of the universe, in Citamparam. Where exactly is Citamparam?

"Thus becoming, He dances in our body as the congregation. Its deepest significance is felt when it is realized that it takes place within the heart and the self." Citamparam, the place of the dance and the center of the universe, "is within the Heart."[133] (Appropriately, there is a holy site of the same name; see Citamparam, India.)

WHAT YOU CAN HEAR IN THE DITCH: The ditch was meant for walking in. Metaphorically, it is like a groove in a phonograph record. The Nimitta in the center of the circle is the needle, and the seventy-two stones are the amplifiers. The music is the Name of God, known in Qabala as *Shemhamforesch,* the seventy-two Names of God. All of Shiva's dance gestures intone the Names, and the seventy-two Names are creative, world-generating potencies, so the naming is also a manifesting.

If you play the record with the needle of your spirit, you can hear some high fidelity sounds. Sitting on the ridge or walking through the ditch, you can be a member of the audience that witnesses the dance of Shiva.[134]

TREE OF LIFE: The Ridgeway, which starts at Avebury, is an ancient eighty-five-mile track across the Wiltshire fields and downs. Numerous megalithic structures such as barrows, hillside chalk figures, and henge-ditches are found on either side, including sites with peculiar names such as Barbury Castle and Uffington Castle even though no trace of former physical structures has ever been detected there.

The Ridgeway is one of the Earth's grandest, perhaps most concentrated Trees of Life, that is, a succession of four complete Trees of Life, as described by Qabala, complete with forty Sephiroth, or light spheres. It is a complex temple network somewhat like pearls on a string laid out in a line across the landscape. The Ridgeway is a viewing point for the various aspects of the umbilicus, and a way of experiencing and assimilating their energies.

Avebury is the topmost section of the topmost tree, the White Mirror of the Four Worlds. If you spend some time meditating at Avebury, then walk the Ridgeway over the course of some days, you will in effect walk through the Four Worlds of Existence and through the hierarchical structure of the cosmos.

Banaras, India

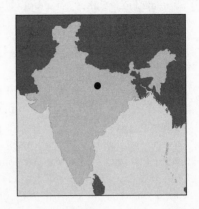

PHYSICAL DESCRIPTION

Banaras, India's foremost sacred city, set on the banks of the Ganges River in the northeast, is a textbook of geomantic features. An old Hindu text says that a person made a pilgrimage every day for a year in Banaras and still did not reach all the holy spots because in Banaras there is a sacred place at every step.

Banaras, says a contemporary pilgrim, is one of "the maddest, holiest, ugliest, most entrancing cities on earth." Its assault on the senses is global and continuous, yet the place also has a "dream-like air" when nothing moves faster than the pace of an oar. The experience of visiting in Banaras is a "dream-like sensation of floating in a boat through the city of the gods."[135]

Banaras is the most visited pilgrimage destination in India. Like Mecca for Muslims, visiting Banaras at least once in a lifetime and immersing oneself in the Ganges is highly desired by many Hindus. Even more desirable is to die and have one's body burned to ashes at one of the city's numerous outdoor crematoria called burning ghats (ghats are the flights of steps leading into the river).

The Ganges River, a paradox of provable pollution and attributed sanctity, sweeps past the city and its numerous temples and shrines crowded together at its banks, dominating Banaras' religious life and spiritual rites. The city sits between fifty and seventy-five feet above the river, providing both an excellent vantage point and a stable foundation against floods. This great northern center of Shiva worship has been inhabited continuously for at least the last three thousand years.

It is a holy city of many names and epithets. Banaras (from Baranasi) is a corruption of the older name, Varanasi, which became the city's official name in 1956. Varanasi is believed to be a compound of the names of two streams, the Varana and Asi, which still flow to the north and south, respectively, of the city. Thus, in this etymology, Varansi is the land between the Varana and Asi Rivers.

An old text says the gods set the two rivers there and between them is holy land. The Varana issued from the right foot of the primordial person, called Purusha, and the Asi came from its left foot. The land lying between them is "the best place of pilgrimage in the three worlds and is potent enough to destroy all sins" and has no peer on Heaven, Earth, or in the Underworld.[136] It is "the ultimate sacred ford in the three worlds, which gives release from evil."[137]

But the city is also *Kashi*, "Where the Supreme Light Shines" or simply "the Luminous, City of Light." As Kashi, the city is said to have been established by the god Shiva Vishvanatha, the "Lord of All," at the start of Creation, making it the oldest city in India and possibly on the planet. Kashi, also called Kashika, and meaning the "shining, luminous, or illumining one," derives from the Sanskrit root *kash*, which means "to shine or look brilliant or beautiful." That Light is understood to be the luminosity of the "unspeakable" Shiva, and that Light, it is also said in Banaras, produces *moksha*, or liberation—enlightenment in the world of matter and incarnation, and release from both.

Banaras is also *Avimukta*, which means "The Never-Forsaken." The word literally means "not let loose" and it refers to a commitment Shiva made never to leave Banaras, never to let it go out of his attention, never to forsake it. Shiva's presence is steadfast in Banaras because it was here where he first established his linga, or column of light, as a symbol of his perpetual presence. Even in times of the Flood and universal destruction, when the Day of Brahma (said to last 360 million years) ends, the great deity sleeps, and the world ceases to exist, Shiva will hold Banaras on his trident above the floodwaters.

Yet another epithet for Banaras is *Anandavana*, "The Forest of Bliss." The forest refers to the numerous lingas of Shiva, found everywhere in Banaras, "like little sprouts arisen out of sheer bliss," as one old text put it. Anandavana evokes the image of a Banaras as a forest thick with Shiva lingas, or brilliant light columns, producing the bliss *(ananda)* of liberation in the presence of the god. One ancient text claimed that Banaras had 100,000 Shiva lingas, six million stood in the waters of the Ganges, and all of them bestow yogic achievement.

Banaras is also *Rudravasa*, the City of Shiva, whose ancient name was Rudra. Local lore says that even the stones of Kashi partake in Shiva's essence. Not only the stones, but everything—the people, animals, trees—in Kashi is saturated with Shiva. Kashi transforms what is ordinary into *Rudramaya*, so that everything is now composed of the same god substance as Shiva.

Many come to Banaras, sense this, or experience it, and never want to leave. Shiva is said to dwell here with special intensity such that the veil between the worlds, ours and transcendent reality, is so thin as almost not to exist. "Because dying in Kashi brings liberation, living here is an anticipatory participation in that liberation."[138] (See Abydos, Egypt, where the Head of Osiris was buried; similar things are said about the desirability of burial there.)

Banaras is the Great Cremation Ground of Shiva, the *Mahashmashana*. Normally, the *shmashana*, or cremation ground, is set outside of an Indian town or city, in the South, the direction of Yama, the Hindu god of death. But in Banaras, the cremation grounds, or burning ghats, are in the heart of the town, set on the edge of the Ganges, most notably at the Manikarnika Ghat and Harishchandra Ghat.

There is a remarkable, almost astounding, attribution that Kashi is the final resting place of the corpse of the entire universe after it was destroyed at the close of the last cycle of creation, or the end of the Day of Brahma. So Banaras is also the City of the Dead, even if it's the dead of an entire earlier universe. But it is also *the* place in India where people desire to die because, so the belief says, death in Kashi *is* liberation. When you die in Banaras, Shiva himself appears as the guru to teach you the "mantra of the crossing."

Perhaps the single most descriptive term used to indicate the spiritual possibilities of Banaras is *moksha* (liberation). This is a lucid reminder that ultimately the point of all the geomantic structures anywhere on the Earth is to produce liberation, or a full waking up of one's spiritual self in the world of matter. All of the numerous subtle plane temple structures have this goal.

MYTH AND LEGEND

Hinduism's three primary gods—Brahma, Vishnu, and Shiva—are accorded equal prominence in Banaras, and each had much to do with the city's founding. It is said of Banaras that its layout of temples and shrines creates a complex mandala that includes in miniature all the key features of India's sacred geography. Banaras is often referred to as the "Sacred Circle of All the Gods" on account of the belief that all of Hinduism's 330 million gods are present here.

As such, the Banaras geomantic structure is said to be a cosmogram reflecting the order of the transcendent realm and all of India. India is saturated with *tirthas,* or special crossing-over points, spiritual fords, where one can make the passage from the profane to the sacred (see part 1 for more on tirthas).

There are many classifications and hierarchies of tirthas in India, including: the Seven Holy Cities, which are *mokshada,* or bestowers of liberation, of which Banaras is one; the 108 benches, seats *(pithas)*, or body parts of the goddess Shakti (her left hand), each an expression of divine feminine power, of which Banaras is her foot; and the twelve *Jyotirlinga* sites, one of which is at Banaras, where Shiva's linga blazed as a column of light. In fact, the one Shiva linga at Banaras is said to incorporate the essence of all twelve Shiva lingas throughout India. More profoundly, all of Kashi is understood not only to be *in* this linga but to *be* this linga.

The central point or *axis mundi* of Banaras is the *Jnanavapi Kund,* the Well of Wisdom. According to Hindu myth, this is where Shiva dug into the ground with his trident to release water

to cool the linga of Vishvanath. Thereafter the place was the site of his abode in Banaras, and the pure waters that sprang up under his trident are understood to be the liquid form of *jnana,* or knowledge. These waters are older, more primal than even the Ganges, the myths say.

Ever since, Banaras has been a seat of higher knowledge. People came here to study the Vedas, to have the nature of Brahma illumined for them. This led to yet another epithet, *Brahmavardhana,* the "Increase of Brahman," the place where you can gain in the wisdom of Brahma.

The original topography of Banaras is said to embody the shape of Shiva's trident in its three hills. Old Varanasi was built on three hills, including the Rajghat Plateau in the north, the Kedara highlands in the south, and Vishvanatha hill in between them. These were the three prongs of the trident.

Kedara is named after its Himalayan counterpart, Kedarnath, and just as all of Banaras is a microcosm of India's sacred geography, so is Kedara a microcosm of Banaras in a kind of fractal miniaturization of the city's essential geomantic structures. It is said (with that glorious and unabashed tendency towards exaggeration typical of India) that if you worship and bathe in a special spot at Kedara called *Harapapa* ("Sin Destroyer") you will eliminate the sins (and their effects) of ten million lifetimes.

Another story of the primordial digging of a god in Banaras involved Vishnu. He is said to have used his solar discus, the *Chakravarta,* to hollow out what is now called the *Manikarnika* or *Chakrapushkarini Kund,* the "Discus-Lotus Pool" or simply Vishnu's Lotus Pool. It is said to be older than the Ganges, the world's first pool and sacred site (tirtha) created when the only solid land in the universe was Banaras and before anything else had manifested.

Shiva had been commissioned to create everything on Earth based on the sacred plans in the Vedas. The water in the lotus pool he dug came from the sweat of his body as he worked; then he performed rigorous meditations at the site for 500,000 years to purify the place. One day Shiva visited Vishnu earnestly at work with his austerities, and allowed his jeweled earring, the *manikarnika*, to fall from his ear into the pool. Another version says Shiva gave his crest-jewel, the *mani*, and his consort, Parvati, contributed the earring, *karnika.* Thereafter the *Chakrapush-karini Kund* would also be known as *Manikar-nika*, the "Jeweled-Earring."

The sacred well is situated just behind the Marnikarnika Ghat, a three-mile stretch along the waterfront, and the most important of the crematoria. Geological evidence suggests that originally there was a large lake at this site, but after the advent of the Ganges, the lake eventually shrank to the size of a spring-fed pool. Even today, people assert that the water, housed in a tank that is sixty square feet, comes from a source independent of the Ganges. That source, people say, is *Gomukha*, the "Cow's Mouth," in the Himalayas.

Vishnu is commemorated in another place in Banaras, at a site called Keshava, on the northern boundary of Varanasi where the Ganges meets the Varana River. This is where, the myths say, Vishnu first placed his foot when he arrived at Varanasi. Later he bathed there and washed his feet. Ever since, the site has been holy and called *Padodaka*, which means "Foot-Water."

The water is considered to be perpetually sanctified so that even to drink a sip of the divine "foot-water" can liberate one from the round of birth, death, and rebirth. As a result, Kashi is regarded as the terrestrial embodiment of Vishnu, the place where he dwells fully and shines forth.

Banaras is said to be the "original ground" created by Shiva and his consort, Parvati, at the beginning of time. Long ago they stood here when no other place existed, before space had been differentiated. Then they danced and all of creation

emanated from their dance. Where they danced was marked by the insertion of Shiva's linga: Banaras is where it first penetrated the Earth.

A variation on this foundation myth holds that at the beginning of time Shiva created Kashi as a beautiful, radiant, auspicious Celestial City five *kroshas* (one *krosha* equals about two miles) in extent. He created Kashi in the spiritual world, specifically, on top of his trident. Vishnu slept on the waters of Marnikarnika, and dreaming, brought forth Brahma and the Cosmic Egg from his navel, and out of this came all of creation.[139] Then Shiva removed the celestial Kashi from his trident and placed it in the mortal world where it will remain until the time of world dissolution; then Shiva will restore Kashi to its place on his trident.

Related to this, though at first almost contradictory, is the mythic statement that Shiva Mahadeva, the "Great God," was at first primarily a mountain god who lived with Parvati at Mount Kailash in Tibet; then he relocated his divine headquarters to Banaras, relocating at the same time all of Heaven, Earth, and the Underworld so that the Three Worlds were resident with him in his new setting. His *jyotirlinga* pierces the Three Worlds in an instant.

As the Great God, Shiva is paradoxical, both profane and sacred, secular and transcendent. He has five essential aspects and activities: creator, preserver, destroyer, concealer, and revealer-liberator. When he came to Banaras, the cosmos in its entirety—stars, Sun, Moon, the 330 million gods of Hinduism—expressed itself as a spectacular chariot on which Shiva rode.

Probably for this reason Kashi is also known as *Jnana-svarupa*, the "embodiment of liberating insight," the place where Shiva reveals vast insight to the dying, enabling their liberation from the reincarnation cycle.

To Shiva is credited the burying of Brahma's fifth head at Banaras. The myth says Shiva took the form of Bhairava, cut off Brahma's fifth head (leaving the other four intact) with the nail of his left thumb, and wandered all over India using Brahma's skull as a begging bowl. He actually could not let go of it as the head had stuck fast to his thumb as a kind of penance.

But at Banaras the skull suddenly dropped free, indicating that Brahma had forgiven Shiva, and remains there today at the *Kapalamochana Tirtha*, "Where the Skull Fell." Spiritual authorities interpret this tale as meaning that merely to enter the confines of Banaras destroys sins and produces atonement, for even the god Shiva was redeemed here for his sin of killing a Brahmin. In fact, Banaras is said to be barren soil for the growth of seeds of karma, or the future fruits of one's actions. Shiva's multitude of lingas, his Forest of Bliss, burns up the seeds before they can sprout.

The Skull that fell appears generally to reference a little hillock in Banaras formerly known as the Omkara temple complex. Apparently, a thousand years ago it was the site of Kashi's most important Shiva linga, and there is a Brahma myth associated with it. Brahma spent one thousand years performing ascetic practices at Omkara, at the end of which a brilliant shaft of light appeared in front of him. It pierced the seven levels of the Underworld and cracked the Earth open, and it almost blindingly illuminated the four directions. It emanated the mystical sound of Om and its five parts, and the site became known as Omkareshvara, or the Five-Fold Abode, referring to Shiva's five aspects.

The sacred zone of Kashi is bounded by the Panchakroshi Road, a pilgrimage circuit of fifty miles and 108 shrines that envelops all of Banaras and a fair portion of its surrounding countryside west of the Ganges. The term *pancha-krosha* refers to the radius of this sacred circle and is about ten miles. Its geographical center is said to be the Shiva temple of *Madhyameshvara,* the

"Lord of the Center," a site on the Ganges once at the center of the city.

According to an old tradition, this radius was obtained by stretching a string from Madhyameshvara out to Dehali Vinayaka, then moving that string in all directions to form a circle. The "supreme sacred land" or *kshetra* was what was inside that circle, called Kashi and known for liberation. As it stands today, the geography is a little confusing, as Kashi only encompasses the western side of the Ganges, and the sacred circle extends only six miles to the north and south of Madhyameshvara and only one mile to the east.

All of the contents of the Five Kroshas—in effect, the 330 million gods and their temples—comprise a single linga of light, and that light is Kashi. Esoterically, Kashi as the Linga of Light is also the inmost place of the self such that all that is outside is a representation of the structure of consciousness.

In the Panchakroshi Yatra, or the Pilgrimage of the Five Kroshas, pilgrims walk the circuit around Kashi over the course, typically, of five days, just as one would honor a deity in a temple by circumambulating its sanctum. Kashi, the sanctum in this case, is also known as the Linga of the Five Kroshas. The pilgrim also offers obeisance to the multitude of protective deities in the shrines.

It is somewhat breathtaking to contemplate the fact that the Panchakroshi circuit is only one of fifty-six different pilgrim circuits in or around Banaras.

Other major Hindu deities are said to have residence at Banaras. Ganesha, the elephant god, split himself into fifty-six copies, which are arrayed in shrines along the Panchakroshi Road and in five concentric circles around the city center. Durga, the fierce warrior goddess, famous for her weapons and battle prowess, protects the southern flank of Banaras and her temple at the Durga Kund is one of the city's busiest.

Surya, the Hindu Sun, has a temple in Banaras called Lolarka Kund in the southern end of town. Lolarka means "The Trembling Sun," and Surya received this epithet because when he beheld Kashi his heart trembled. Once a year, in late August, an estimated ten thousand people come to Lolarka Kund to celebrate the *Lolarka Shashti* festival, take a ritual bath, and petition the god for the birth of male children. Long ago Surya divided himself into twelve suns (the *Adityas*), and these are all resident in Kashi as protective deities comprising a solar circle around the city.

Varanesi Devi, the embodiment of Shakti, Shiva's consort, is the city goddess. People say that all of Kashi is the body of this goddess, and she is honored at the Trilochana Temple. Also present and venerated in temples and shrines in Banaras are the Lords of the Eight Directions, the Twelve Suns, the Governors of the days of the week, and a great many other lesser deities with varied responsibilities.

GEOMANTIC

Dome; Cosmic Egg; Landscape Zodiac; Ixion's Wheel; Soma Temple; Crown of the Ancient of Days; Epiphany Focus.

DOME: The dome over Banaras is the starfall on Earth for Alpha Centauri, known as *Al Rijl al Kentaurus,* the "Centaur's Foot," or Rigel Kentaurus for short. It is our galaxy's third brightest star and the one closest to Earth besides our Sun, being only 4.34 light years or twenty-five trillion miles away. The constellation has twenty-four identified stars.

The Centaur in question is the famous Chiron, the wisest and most civilized, and civilizing, of the race of the centaurs, those beings with horse's bodies and human heads. Chiron, as the son of Kronos and the ocean nymph Philyra, was of divine birth and thus immortal. The myths say that he learned botany, music, astronomy, divination, and medicine from the Greek gods Apollo and Diana, but it is more likely that they learned these arts from him. The Greek tragedian Aeschylus had Chiron say that he taught the gods to mark the stars and instructed the Titan Prometheus in astronomical matters.

Chiron was said to inhabit a cave in Mount Pelion in Greece and surpassed all men in righteousness. He tutored Asclepius, the father of medicine (and associated with the constellation Ophiuchus); Achilles, the Trojan War hero; Jason of Argonaut fame; Odysseus (from the Odyssey); Theseus, founder of Athens; and others famous in Greek myth. Chiron was known as an excellent teacher, counselor, even friend to his many pupils.

Chiron was the only centaur that the Greek hero Heracles did not slay; instead the two engaged in a long conversation during which, unplanned, a poisoned arrow fell out of Heracles' quiver and stuck Chiron's foot. Chiron, technically, could not die but, appreciating that the wound was incurable, he traded his immortality with Prometheus for his freedom—he was chained to a pillar on Mount Caucasus—and became a constellation.

We get a deeper concept of Chiron's essence when we consider him from the Vedic astronomical viewpoint, as Brihaspati, the Teacher of the Gods. Brihaspati was the celestial priest and Lord of Prayer, from *brh,* "prayer," and *pati,* "Lord." Even though in Vedic astronomy Brihaspati is traditionally associated with the planet Jupiter—he is said to be its regent—his qualities are very apt for Centaurus.

He was known as Lord of Assemblies, King of Elders, Lord of Hosts, the Intelligent, Great Teacher, Great Master. He is also *Animischarya,* the "Unblinking Preceptor"; *Chakshusa,* "Light of the Eye," or teacher of sacred wisdom; and

Indrejya, "one who has subjugated their sense organs." The root of his name, *bri*, also means "to grow and expand," as in the wisdom aspect he administers, which enables the universe to grow. As a teacher, Brihaspati leads the pupil from the known to the unknown, from the periphery to the center.[140]

He is the teacher of the gods in his intellect and speech and the presiding deity of mental powers. He teaches the science of Light, and is the ruler of the Sun and Moon; pictured as a golden being seated on his chariot called *Nitighosha* and drawn by eight horses, Brihaspati controls the movements of the planets. He has seven faces and seven rays; he has a bow, arrows, and a golden ax. He worshiped Shiva for one thousand years in the Field-of-Light, after which the god made Brihaspati the planet Jupiter.

At Banaras, Brihaspati, working through Alpha Centauri in the foot of Chiron the Centaur, is using a pure gold energy to create a pure golden body in an alchemical purification of the human. The goal is to manifest a fully realized divinity, to give every soul in Banaras this opportunity, and it is decidedly easier to do this in Banaras than elsewhere. The geomantic structures of Banaras maintain intact the temple energies from the Golden Age, the paradise time in the vast past of human history when the gods dwelled on the Earth. At Banaras you can touch the purity of intent and possibility from that beginning time.[141]

COSMIC EGG: For Brihaspati to be the Teacher of the Gods at Banaras you need the 330 million gods to be geomantically resident there. This is accomplished through the Cosmic Egg and Landscape Zodiac present at the city. The Cosmic Egg is situated with reference to the Durga Kund in the southern end of Banaras, close to the Five Krosha boundary at the Panchakroshi Road.

The Egg of course is much bigger than this specific site, but it is placed there because the Durga Kund marks the root chakra of the central chakra template of the Banaras temple. The seven chakras in this template, which run close to the Ganges, are the spiritual centers in the Cosmic Person, what the Hindus know as Purusha but which this book calls Albion, the anthropomorphic essence of the Landscape Zodiac.

The presence of the Cosmic Egg explains two things about Banaras. First, it is said that Yama, the god of death, is not allowed to enter Banaras to claim souls. Second, why does everyone want to have their body burned at a Banaras ghat? The answer is that the Cosmic Egg is both the hierarchy of the multiple worlds as they spill into the physical and the Cosmic Mountain that the soul climbs in an effort to entirely leave this world.

In Persian mystical lore, a distinction is made between the Occident and the Orient. Everything in the world of form and matter, from gross to subtle, is called the Occident; for the most part, consciousness lives here, and some would say, remains stuck at this level. The Celestial Occident, containing the stars and planets, is a more exalted aspect of the Occident, but it is still matter bound.

The Orient is the transcendent realm, beyond name and form, and it is conceived as the very tip of the Cosmic Mountain, the place where you are launched into the fullness of original Being. Here you enter, putting it metaphorically, the King's Heaven, the cosmic Holy of Holies, the eternal dawn, the spiritual Kashi of Light. When you reach the Orient, you have climbed way past the death realm of Yama, the Seven Heavens, and the temptation or necessity of rebirth.

That's why cremation at Banaras is so desirable: geomantically, it puts you right on the Cosmic Mountain at the moment of death.

The Cosmic Egg at Banaras also explains the majestic image of all of Kashi being Shiva in his chariot. Here we have to dip into Judaic lore to explain it. In Qabalistic thinking, the Divine Chariot, called the Merkabah, is the Throne of

God who sits atop the chariot as its driver. This Chariot is referred to as the *Shi'ur Komah*, a mystical revelation by the Prophet Ezekiel of the measurement, height, and stature of the Divine Body—the size of God.

The revelation of the *Shi'ur Komah* is one of the mystical experiences possible at a Cosmic Egg, and it is understandable that one would picture it in terms of a god's chariot, whether it's Shiva's or Jehovah's. This aspect also accounts for the statement that Shiva came from Mount Kailash in Tibet. That mountain also has a Cosmic Egg so, in a sense, the energetic field of Banaras and Mount Kailash with respect to Shiva's involvement through the Cosmic Egg is identical. Both participate in the archetype of the Cosmic Mountain known to Hinduism as Mount Meru. So Shiva did not so much come to Banaras *from* Mount Kailash as he was co-present at both through their identical function.

The Cosmic Egg at Banaras further accounts for the sense of special, protected sanctity, spiritual fullness, and immaculate primordial purity attributed to this holy city. The Cosmic Egg is reality *before* the separation of Heaven and Earth, when they were one, when all the stars and the 330 million gods were in the Earth. The term Earth refers not to our planet but to everything in the universe that is of matter, subtle to gross— everything that is of the Occident.

The Cosmic Egg contains all of reality in its undifferentiated state; the Sun and Moon, as cosmic states of existence are in there, as are the myriad stars that will later become the Forest of Bliss of the galaxy. The Cosmic Egg contains the "plans of the Vedas" for the tirthas that will later be extrapolated across the planet Earth. In the Egg, the "As above" *is* the "As below"; they are not separate. The Egg's undifferentiated state of the Above and Below is truly the "plans of the Vedas" because it is the knowledge and truth of our planet's geomancy. It's all there to read out in

its pure, original form—the planetary energy blueprints.

LANDSCAPE ZODIAC: The sacred precinct bounded by the Panchakroshi Road and known as the Five Kroshas is one half of a Landscape Zodiac at Banaras. The Hindu mind is still so wonderfully connected to the galaxy on Earth template that it even remembers the radius of the zodiac and tells you how it was calculated. One wing of the zodiac is encompassed by the Five Kroshas, while the other half extends to the east of the Ganges; the total diameter is about twenty miles. When you factor in the extent of the zodiac dome, which is about forty-four miles, you get a sense of the full extent of the spiritual landscape of Banaras.

At least one major aspect of the reference to Banaras as the Forest of Bliss and the 100,000 Shiva lingas found in its precinct is that this refers to the stars blazing in the galactic wheel overlaid on the greater Banaras area. The combination of the Cosmic Egg and Landscape Zodiac provides ample opportunity for the three hundred million gods of the universe to manifest in Banaras. These two features contain nearly everything in the galaxy on Earth repertoire.

IXION'S WHEEL: The Ixion's Wheel is located at Manikarnika, which Vishnu dug out with his solar discus, the *Chakravarta*. So we have two features overlapping here. This site is the throat chakra for the Banaras Albion, or chakra template, and is about the mysteries of cosmic speech. The solar discus, when spinning, expresses an aspect of the Sun, showing how it works when the energies of the Wild Sun God have been mastered and refined. (See Edfu, Egypt, and Mount Etna, Sicily, Italy, for other views on this.)

In a sense, the *Chakravarta*, or solar discus, is the Discus-Lotus Pool, and the waters are the fiery energies of the Heart of the Sun, or Solar Logos. We can best understand this temple by probing more deeply into the Chakravarta.

The Chakravarta is central to the essence and origin of India. The country's ancient name, *Bharata*, refers to the first of India's Chakravartins. These were universal kings, world monarchs, masters of the Sun wheel, primordial spiritual kings who owned the Chakravarta, the Sun wheel, which was also known as Vishnu's *sudarsana* or solar discus. The Chakravartin is the *mahapurusa cakravartin*, "the superman turning the wheel," equivalent to the Buddha.

He is called the Chakravartin from the root *vrt*, which means "to turn, to revolve." He is the *Cakram vartayati*, the one who sets the sacred wheel in motion and uses it to pacify the world; he is the hub of the universe, and all things tend towards him like spokes of a wheel. "The sun-wheel as the Cakravartin's symbol indicates that this universal shepherd-king is as it were the sun—the life-giver and universal eye."

The sun-disk that Vishnu carries is "beautiful to see, auspicious to behold," and it bestows light and life. The Chakravartin shines on everything in the world, without distinction, and his power is that of "nature's supreme and culminating manifestation, the enlightenment of Man the King—balanced perfectly in reason, justice, mercy, and understanding."[142]

The Sudarsana or Vishnu's Discus is actually an esoteric reference to what is known as the Mobile Shamballic Focus. This is an expression of the Earth's sixth chakra as focused for a time on a specific locality. It is like an eye—a spinning eye, if you like, like a thrown discus—from the higher levels of the spiritual worlds keeping its attention on and sending its best wishes to a predetermined site. The Shamballic Focus is typically resident at a site for about two hundred years; currently it is focused on Glastonbury, England (see under that entry), but in the deep past, it was focused on Banaras, as this myth obliquely recounts.

Geomantically, Vishnu's Discus acts as a template for the Ixion's Wheel feature, which transmits an aspect of this same energy, only stepped down a bit. That aspect is known as the Solar Logos.

The Solar Logos is the golden point of light at the center of the galactic wheel. It's the central Sun at the heart of the galaxy, the Sun within all the suns that are stars in the galaxy, the mind that holds—sustains—them together.

The Ixion's Wheel is really an aspect of the Solar Logos, known in Egypt for example as Horus the Younger (see Edfu, Egypt), the Word of the Sun, or the Christ Consciousness. This may seem like an odd vocabulary to use in Hindu India, but Vishnu does have functional correspondences with the Solar Logos. Vishnu sustains the universe, holds it together against entropy; the Solar Logos binds the worlds together through the power of primal Sound and primal Speech. In support of this point we can note that the career of one early Chakravartin was encapsulated in the phrase "The Lion's Roar of the World Emperor."

SOMA TEMPLE: If Ixion's Wheel represents the cosmic Sun at Banaras, then the *Jnanavapi Kund*, the Well of Wisdom dug by Shiva, is the cosmic Moon, or Soma Temple. The Banaras myth says that Shiva used his trident to dig the Well of Wisdom to cool the linga of Vishvanath. It is also the brow or sixth chakra in the chakra column of the Banaras zodiacal Man, its golden Albion.

The Well contains Soma, the liquid essence of immortal, eternal, unbroken consciousness, the foundation of wisdom. It is apt that Shiva is given credit for digging the Well of Wisdom because Hindu myth portrays him bearing the crescent of the Moon on his head. The Moon is Soma, "the cup of offering placed near the yogic center of fire located between the brows." Kasi is the city of knowledge because in the microcosm (its body equivalent) "'Kasi' is the name given to the summit of the head, where knowledge is said to dwell."[143]

The remarkable fact about the *Jnanavapi Kund* is that it is an interior yogic energy center in the human presented outwardly as a temple. The key is Shiva's trident, which is a metaphor for an exalted chakra in the head.

The trident is symbolic of the three upward rising energy currents in the human (and cosmos) called the Ida (Sun), Pingala (Moon), and Sushumna. The first two form a double helix and pass through the first five chakras, while the third is the central column that connects the first with the seventh center. Yogic theory says that Shiva's consort, Shakti, in the root chakra, desires to ascend the columns to be reunited with her lover, Shiva, in the crown center.

These three energy channels are said to unite in a special chakra in the brain called the *Brahmarandhra,* located between the sixth and seventh chakras. This place is known as the "Sacred City of Prayaga," and "by bathing mentally in the triple confluence, liberation is attained."[144]

Esoteric yoga offers two more observations relevant here. First, when kundalini rises from the root center to the *Brahmarandhra,* the yogi enjoys "the Brahmic state where interiority and exteriority are balanced and henceforth undifferentiated." This in turn is part of an even more rarefied energy center called *Dvadasanta,* located above the crown. "Therefore, the person who makes the *Dvadasanta* his permanent abode and can lead his energy there at will, attains to liberation while still living."[145]

Second, the *Brahmarandhra* chakra is central to the issue of liberation, one of the prime concerns of the Banaras temple. "Viewed in projection, the *cakras* [sic] constitute a *mandala* whose center is marked by the *Brahmarandhra.* It is in this 'center' that the rupture of plane occurs, that the paradoxical act of transcendence—passing beyond *samsara,* 'emerging from time'—is accomplished."[146]

What we're seeing here is evidence of how the inner esoteric yogic anatomy of the human being is extrapolated as the main geomantic features in the Banaras temple. But this shouldn't surprise us too much, for it is part of the "plan of the Vedas," part of the wisdom of Brahma, the Creator. It is said of Brahma that originally he had five heads; the fifth listened to the other four expound the Vedas, but it was the fifth that brought that knowledge to us.

CROWN OF THE ANCIENT OF DAYS: The *Kapalamochana Tirtha,* or "Where the Skull Fell," is one of the planet's twelve Crowns of the Ancient of Days. In the Banaras temple and chakra template, the place where Brahma's fifth head fell free from Bhairava's left thumb was at Omkara, now marked by the Matsyodari Tirtha, once a small lake at the northern end of the Ganges riverfront. This is the crown chakra of the system, which is appropriate because the Ancient of Days—or Brahma, Osiris, or Kronos as this being is variously called—occupies the crown center position in the energy hierarchy of chakras.

Again the theme of liberation is implicit in this feature, which we can tease out by considering some of the descriptions of this feature in Qabalistic thought. Metaphorically, this energy is expressed as a bearded king seen in profile. His epithets include the Hidden Intelligence, Primal Glory, Existence of Existences, Concealed of the Concealed, Primordial Point, Most High, the Vast Countenance, the White Head, the Crown. These are all ways of describing Brahma's fifth and severed head. (See Abydos, Egypt, for an Egyptian perspective.)

This king is the First Manifest and represents the "primal crystallization into manifestation of that which was hitherto unmanifest and therefore unknowable by us." It can be experienced "as a blinding white light, in which all thought went completely blank." It has no form, only pure being, "a latency only one degree removed from non-existence." It is not a person, but a state of existence—"an entirely formless state of passivity." It is "pure being unlimited by form or reaction," the *cause* of manifestation.[147]

EPIPHANY FOCUS: What of Vishnu's footprint north of *Kapalamochana Tirtha?* The *Vishnupada* marks the site of an epiphany of the god Vishnu, where the lowest arc—the "foot"—of his celestial and overwhelming energy touched down in the Earth plan and left a permanent indentation—a "footprint"—in the energy field. (See Hardwar, India, where another Vishnu footprint was left.)

Specifically, during the first week of January some time in the past six thousand years, the Christ as Solar Logos—known in Hinduism as Vishnu—made an "appearance" in his light body at Hardwar. That means for a week, the Brahmakund at Hardwar was the planetary focus for the consciousness of Vishnu entering the planetary sphere like a stream of light or, for those with highly refined mystical perception, as the epiphanous presence of a god.

KASHI AS SHIVA'S LINGA: All of Kashi, the Luminous City, is Shiva's Linga of Light. That is one of the most descriptive sentences one encounters in reference to Banaras, and one comes across it frequently, but what does it mean geomantically?

Shiva's linga is a profound symbol with many aspects, only some of which we can touch on here. It is primarily an expression of the *axis mundi,* the axial connection between Earth and Heaven, the Below and the Above, the conduit for the vertical connection between the manifest and the transcendent. Its rounded top (and sometimes bottom too) has led mystics to compare or equate it with the Cosmic Egg, the omphalos or navel of the world, containing everything as in a vast universal seedpod. In yogic terms, it is the central light column that connects Shakti in the root chakra with Shiva in the crown, and it is the field of dazzling light emitted when this connection is made.

To say all of Kashi is a Linga of Light is to comprehend the Kashi temple—and Shiva's presence—in an instant, in a single almost ineffable image. The Qabalistic model of the universe says that when the Supreme Being first made room for creation, a very narrow ray of light called the *Kav* entered this space. Afterwards, it was seen that the *Kav* passed through the Four Worlds and the forty Sephiroth, or spheres of light, but more truly, the *Kav* contained them all like seeds of future manifestation.

The *Kav* brings the divine light into all the worlds. "The light of the Infinite extends by way of this line and spreads downward. . . . This line is like a single narrow conduit through which the 'waters' of the supernal light of the Infinite spread and are drawn to the worlds that are in the empty space in that void."[148]

Banaras is a temple in which the "waters" of the infinite Supernal Light of the Creator (Brahma) are drawn down into and through the created worlds.[149] Through the guidance of Banaras' resident star god, Brihaspati, pilgrims to this holy city may be guided through its temple structure to the final encounter with the Linga of Light.

Bayreuth, Germany

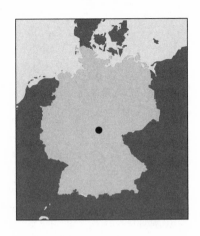

To Wagnerites the world over, Bayreuth is synonymous with the Festspielhaus, the special opera theater Richard Wagner (1813–1883) created and opened in 1876 in central Germany solely for the production of his operas. He could have established the Festspielhaus in Munich, but he preferred Bayreuth. He had his reasons of course—political, sociological, aesthetic—but one reasonably wonders if there was, even if unknown to him, a geomantic reason that has kept Bayreuth the Wagner capital of the world.

Today, the eighteen-thousand-seat Festspielhaus is essentially the same as when it opened in 1876 for its first performance of the *Ring of the Niebelungs,* a sequence of four operas involving mythic themes and elaborate stagings. The interior is stark and simple; the rows curve from one side of the hall to the other, without aisles; the floor has a steep gradient, giving everyone a good view of the stage; and the orchestra pit is covered so that the viewer's attention may be focused solely on the performance. Tickets are expensive, always in demand, and after the season begins, usually hard to come by.

A French art history student said this of his first experience of Wagner's last opera, *Parsifal,* in the 1980s: "It happened to me at Bayreuth. I had tears running down my face, but I had no idea why." He said he felt short-circuited, as if he'd received an electric shock; he was completely incapacitated. He didn't understand why but he knew he was "already somewhere else." He also admitted to having become "enslaved" to a two-minute passage from Wagner's earlier opera, *Tannhäuser.*[150] Is it Wagner or Bayreuth, or their combination?

In 1891, Mark Twain described himself as "a heretic in heaven" in reference to how he felt during a performance of Wagner's *Tristan and Isolde* at Bayreuth, as he wrote in an article he called "At the Shrine of Saint Wagner." In Bayreuth, it is always Sunday, Twain said; there are no sights to see; no newspapers to remind one of the world's worries; there is nothing happening except Wagner's opera. "Sometimes I feel like the sane person in a community of the mad," or like "the one groping savage in the college of the learned." Even so, Twain returned the next day for his second performance of *Parsifal.*[151]

For most of his adult life, Wagner envisioned—wanted—a new theater devoted to German operas, especially his, which in his description were a fusion of poetry, drama, and music. He wanted this theater to be in a town where he might reign as artist and opera king, a place sufficiently modest that its individuals and institutions would not thwart his grand artistic ambitions. He contemplated creating "a kind of Washington of art," he explained in 1863.

As he neared the completion of his *Ring* cycle of four operas after twenty-six years of labor, Wagner wanted to perform it under his own musical, dramatic, pictorial, and philosophic direction. He wanted the performance to assume the quality of a German festival, and for that he needed a place, theater, and organization completely under his control.

On March 5, 1870, when Wagner and his wife, Cosima (daughter of pianist Franz Liszt), were discussing for the fiftieth time the ideal location for Wagner's theater, she suggested they look up Bayreuth in the encyclopedia: "R. had mentioned this place as the one he would choose. To our delight we read in the list of buildings of a splendid old opera house!"[152] Apparently, they had both heard the name but knew little else about this small town in central Germany.

One of the biggest advantages of Bayreuth was that it had then no cultural resources other than its monuments; it had no thermal springs, so it was not a tourist town frequented by those not interested in the high-minded pursuits of opera. Yet Bayreuth had a tradition of theater and a theatergoing public, and would probably appreciate the opportunity to participate in its own development through Wagner's theater.

The Margaves, a family of Bavarian rulers situated at Bayreuth, had already created a theater that offered the deepest stage in all of Germany. Bayreuth was situated in the heartland of Germany, medieval Franconia, "a region of old courts and castles where the Minnesingers sang the songs that formed the beginnings of German lyric poetry."[153] The city was difficult to get to; it

wasn't on any major trunk lines then, so people had to make an effort to reach Bayreuth. This suited Wagner because he wanted the journey to his Festspielhaus to assume the nature of a pilgrimage.

Best of all, perhaps, was the sheer geographical fact that Bayreuth lay within the political confines of Bavaria, thus assuring Wagner's Festspielhaus the protection of his patron, King Ludwig II of Bavaria.

Once he visited the Margave's Opera House at Bayreuth, a town of about ten thousand inhabitants and some two hundred breweries, he realized it would never suit his purposes nor could it be satisfactorily altered. In a letter to his friend Lorenz von Düfflipp on April 20, 1871, Wagner said: "For the rest I shall say only that Bayreuth and its surroundings has entirely lived up to my hopes, so that I remain firmly attached to the idea of settling here, and continue to combine with that wish a desire to realize my great enterprise here too."[154]

Later that year, with the understanding that the citizenry of Bayreuth would donate the land he needed to build his Festspielhaus, Wagner went over his specifications with Friedrich Feustel of Bayreuth. He told Feustel that "this friendly town and its environs left an attractive impression upon me years ago" when he visited it briefly in 1835. He said his preferred building site would be "the open field interrupted by a road which abuts the end of the Schloss park," and that he also entertained hopes of being granted additional land on a long strip of meadowland near the end of Schloss gardens for his own residence.[155]

On the morning of his fifty-ninth birthday, on May 22, 1872, Wagner laid the cornerstone of his Festspielhaus. A throng of his devoted supporters were present despite the gloom of a morning downpour. King Ludwig had sent a congratulatory telegram to be buried in a time capsule under the building. Imitating his own dwarfish Nibelungen metalsmiths perhaps, Wagner struck the cornerstone three times with a hammer, proclaiming "Be blessed, my stone, stand long, hold firm!"

Wagner's friend, the philosopher Friedrich Nietszche, who had attended the ceremony, later commented: "He was silent and his glance, which it would be difficult to describe, was turned inward." All that had gone before for this musical visionary "was a prologue to this moment."[156] The Festspielhaus after all was Wagner's own creation. "He sought the place for it, he earned or begged the money to build it, he designed it and, if he did not erect it with his own hands, he supervised its erection down to the smallest detail."[157] Later in the day, Wagner spoke at the Bibiena theater, telling his listeners that on the cornerstone he had laid that morning rested the edifice of Germany's noblest cultural aspirations.

On August 13, 1876, the Festspielhaus finally opened, and offered three full cycles of the *Ring* in the next two weeks. Wagner had fulfilled his dream of creating a theater solely for his own operas, though what he had achieved fell short of the "instrument of popular education" he had envisioned. Instead, he had created "an entertainment for a privileged elite. Or, in its most extreme form, a religious rite attended by devoted, well-shod pilgrims from the more prosperous parts of the globe."[158]

Wagner called his new villa *Wahnfried,* by which he meant (some say a little pompously) a place of peace from his—or perhaps the world's—vain illusions, delusions, or madness. Another interpretation is "Dream Fulfillment." Situated on Green Hill behind the Festspielhaus, Wahnfried today is a Wagner museum and archival library owned by the city of Bayreuth. The house was "overstuffed, self-important, second-rate nineteenth century. They loved it. So did most of their visitors."[159]

Green Hill began to take on other typical nineteenth-century qualities in its earliest days.

One reason Cosima Wagner liked Bayreuth was its proximity to woods and dales, suitable for family picnics and nature hikes. Some pilgrims to Wagner's Bayreuth began to see the festival hill as a kind of "Magic Mountain" that would provide healing, redemption, and spiritual uplift.

Like many in nineteenth-century Europe whose health was imperfect, Wagner had often resorted to hydropathy, taking the "water cure" to improve his numerous physical ailments. He had allowed the principles and healing aesthetics of hydropathy and natural cures to permeate his thinking about myth, drama, and music as well. He construed his music dramas as purifying for his listeners. "A central point in Wagner's festival concept was that Nature herself should be pressed into serving the cause of art."[160]

That is why the Festspielhaus was deliberately designed to have no foyer. Instead, the public is obliged—Wagner would have said welcomed—to promenade the outside grounds before performances and during intermissions. Concertgoers had to walk up the hill to the Festspielhaus which was a mile from the town, giving them a chance to stretch their legs; during the intermissions, since there was no foyer, they were forced outside again for fresh air and more exercise and to escape the stuffiness of the theater. From Wagner's viewpoint, two important goals were achieved by this: he got his audience's full attention on the operas, and they got started on a healthy lifestyle during their stay in Bayreuth.

That Bayreuth's Green Hill would become a Magic Mountain for the high and sacred in art was a goal Wagner shared with his patron, King Ludwig. In a letter Ludwig sent Wagner on January 3, 1872, the King had attested to their "holy goal" of spreading the light of "the central sun of the eternal godhead" over the Earth "to purify and perfect humanity with its sacred flames, making it the sharer in eternal joys."[161]

Ludwig had originally hoped that supporting Wagner at Bayreuth would lead, through Bavaria, to a German cultural revival; but Wagner's opera center instead became a national—and national-izing—phenomenon in a Germany still comprised of several dozen principalities. From today's vantage point, one critic observes, "the creation of the theater can be seen as an event of supreme importance for the German people."

For the first time among the German folk there was "a temple of art where the whole of Germany could worship, a place that symbolized a new national artistic consciousness." In this respect, the founding of the Festspielhaus was the cultural and spiritual equivalent to Bismarck's political act of founding Germany's first Reich.[162]

Ironically, Adolf Hitler was originally in attunement with Wagner's artistic goals, although he later used them as a propaganda platform for his racist National Socialism. In *Mein Kampf,* he wrote that "a performance of *Parsifal* in Bayreuth will always have a different effect than anywhere else in the world. The mysterious magic of the house on the *Festspielhugel* in the old city of the Margaves cannot be replaced or even compensated for by the externals." Hitler attended the Wagner festival yearly between 1933 and 1938, and again in 1940. To him, Wagner was a cultural hero on a par with Martin Luther and Frederick the Great.[163]

During World War II, Wagner's Bayreuth became associated with Hitler's National Socialism, and Wagner's mythopoeic opus and ideas on art and the German folk were appropriated and distorted by the Nazis.

Long after Wagner's death, the "nationalistic ideologizing" of Cosima Wagner, who survived Wagner by forty-seven years and ran the festival in a dictatorial manner, had a "disastrous effect" on the festival's reputation. "She distorted the artistic idea underlying the festival into a political ideology," explains grandson Wolfgang Wagner,

adding that "Richard Wagner's oeuvre is greater than those who have misconstrued and abused it."[164]

Today, Bayreuth is still very much a Wagner town, but as the biggest city in Upper Franconia, it also has a modern university and is one of the region's high technology centers. Bayreuth also sports a championship golf course, the Lohengrin thermal spa, and numerous hotels and guesthouses. It serves as the gateway to the Fichtel Mountains and is easily reached by car, train, or one of three daily flights from Frankfurt. In other words, it has achieved in the 119 years since his death nearly everything Wagner originally liked it for lacking.

GEOMANTIC

Dome; Grail Castle; National Egregor Point.

DOME: The dome over Green Hill and the rest of Bayreuth corresponds to the alpha star in the constellation *Fornax Chemica,* usually abbreviated to Fornax, meaning the Chemical Furnace. This constellation was formed, or extracted, from the larger constellation called Eridanus, the River, and its stars are said to be taken from the southern bend of the River. It appears as a diminutive zigzag shape tucked in amidst the constellations Eridanus, Cetus, and Sculptor. The rising (or "culmination") of its brightest star, alpha Fornacis, on December 19, signals the start of summer in the Southern Hemisphere.

The Chinese knew Fornax as *Tien Yu,* or "Heaven's Temporary Granary," while the nineteenth-century Westerner astronomer Johann Elert Bode renamed it *Apparatus Chemicus* in honor of the French chemist Antoine Lavoisier. Astronomers attribute 110 stars to *Fornax Chemica,* ranging from the third to seventh magnitudes. Alpha Fornacis is forty light years from Earth and about three times more luminous than our Sun.

GRAIL CASTLE: The essential energy of the Seginus dome strives to create mystical focus and revelations of the highest nature through art. It was meant as a site for a sacramental Mass conducted on the inner planes at Green Hill. This site was activated by the playing of Wagner's *Parsifal* opera, and in a sense, this activation is maintained and renewed every time this piece is performed there.

Parsifal follows the career of the young Christed Grail Knight who eventually heals the Wounded Fisher King, Anfortas, redeems the Wasteland, and restores the Lance to its rightful owner from its usurper, the black magician Klingsor. Much of the opera takes place in the exalted realm of the Grail Castle. *Parsifal* was not only the last opera Wagner composed, but as an expression of the Christ mysteries, it was the fulfillment of the mythopoeic saga of all his preceding operas, especially the *Ring* cycle.

Metaphysically, a performance of *Parsifal* at the Festspielhaus makes it a sacrament to the Christ, creating a sonic ladder up to the Grail Castle above Green Hill. In a sense, every performance of *Parsifal* on Green Hill affords all its listeners a chance to be inducted—musically *transported*—into the Grail Castle. It's as if suddenly the Rhine flows upwards, not laterally, and you can ride the sound currents vertically into the exalted realm of the Grail Castle, the rock of "sleeping gold" gleaming at the "bottom" or heart of the Rhine.

Let us recall the odd comment by the young French art history student upon hearing Wagner performed at the Festspielhaus: he didn't understand why, but he knew he was "already somewhere else." Wagner's music had elevated this listener into what the Christian mysteries call the Upper Room, there to be in the presence of Jesus and the twelve apostles in a perpetual Last Supper or sacramental, initiatory Mass.

In some sense, Wagner understood the importance of sound in being able to transport listeners to this exalted space. He designed the Festspielhaus in such a way as to maximize the sound quality of his music. He placed the orchestra pit virtually under the stage, invisible to the audience, and within a shell-like concealing canopy. Acoustically, this "promoted the luxuriant warmth of orchestral tone and colour in which Wagner sought to envelop his listeners."[165]

In other words, this one of Earth's 144 Grail Castles was adapted so that sound could be the means by which the rapt ascended. The goal was to ground the Christian Grail mysteries in Germany through the dome and Grail castle structures at Bayreuth. Just as Rudolf Steiner's Goetheanum at Dornach in Switzerland (see entry under this name) was dedicated as a House of Speech in terms of the spoken Mysteries of the Christ, so at Bayreuth, Wagner's Festspielhaus would be a House of Music. It would ground the Christ mysteries through music, drama, and poetry—dramatic opera.

Not only did Wagner's Festspielhaus operas ground the Mysteries of the Christ through *Parsifal*, but his oeuvre recapitulated the psychospiritual history of Western Europe and its culmination and epiphany in the Christ through the healing and redemption of the Fisher King. From the existentialist wanderings of the *Flying Dutchman* to the sybaritic pleasure grottos of the Venusberg in *Tannhäuser* to the mystical swan knight in *Lohengrin* and finally to the saga of the Rhinegold, the Nibelungs, and the twilight of the gods in the *Ring* cycle, Wagner had been restaging Germany's keenest felt myths.

As the culmination of this grand mythopoeic saga of the German folk, in the guise of Parsifal he led his listeners in the end into the Grail Castle and the audience chamber of the Grail King. There they would witness the redemptive powers of the Christ while having the opportunity as spiritual beings to partake of that same Grail essence literally just above them.

Witnessing a performance of *Parsifal* at the Festspielhaus is a Mystery initiation, a mnemonic of the actual experience available in just another layer of reality at the same place. Wagner's music drama of the redemption of the Grail King is a Mystery drama in the same sense (and with the same metaphysical purpose) as Rudolf Steiner's four Mystery plays a generation later at Dornach, Switzerland: to induct souls into the spiritual world by example, mimicry, modeling, and dramatic invocation of its realities.

NATIONAL EGREGOR POINT: An egregor is a composite spiritual being created and shaped by a people and their language, myths, and beliefs over the history of their presence on the Earth. Wagner's *Ring* cycle expresses the saga of the German egregor, which is aptly symbolized in German cultural expression as the Nibelung—a dwarfish miner, a gnome with hammer who pounds the spiritual gold into artistic riches such as magical rings. In the *Ring* cycle, Wagner called him Alberich.

An egregor also protects the specific landscape of its people—in this case, the German folk; and over time, it assumes a characteristic symbolic shape or image appropriate to that people. A great artist like Wagner may then present the egregor's essence, as it were revealing it in its entirety back to the folk who created it. They may live in it, but they may never have seen it before them in its entirety. This is the *shock* of art when it touches mythopoeic themes.

Sometimes a great leader may also recognize, support, or even embody this egregor for the benefit of its people. In the case of nineteenth-century Germany, it was King Ludwig II of Bavaria, and Wagner knew it. In Wagner's estimation, Ludwig was the only ruler in Germany with a true sense of *German* values. "O my gracious King," he wrote Ludwig, "if you but cast your eye over all the German princes, you must realize that you are the only one among them to whom the spirit of Germany can look with hope."[166]

Through Wagner's artistic genius, the "spirit of Germany" in the form of the Nibelungen was able to come to life as a folk spirit spectacle, garbed in music, poetry, and high drama—Germany's egregor on the stage at Bayreuth.

This makes Adolf Hitler's appropriation of Bayreuth and the Wagner mythos more understandable, though not excusable. It was an act of ritualized black magic conducted on the scale of the country's egregor. Basically Hitler tried to commandeer Germany's egregor through one of its main grounding sites at Bayreuth to serve his own purposes of control, domination, and imperialism. He knew his occult history. The Romans understood that if you wanted to capture a foreign country, first control their gods, and as a minimum, gain magical control over their egregor. Then physical and political control over the populace is relatively easy.

Metaphorically, Hitler had to capture the Nibelungen from Bayreuth for his black magic uses for them at Nuremberg. Early on, Hitler appreciated the powerful emotional effect Wagner's operas exerted on their listeners, and he was cognizant of Wagner's masterful use of Germanic myth and artistic aspirations as the foundation for his operas. Wagner's operas successfully melded a conflation of German principalities into a feeling sense of German nationalism; he did this by dramatizing—fleshing out—the Germanic egregor, Alberich, in his *Ring* cycle.

Hitler, motivated by the dark forces, commandeered Germany's egregor, or newly welded spirit of nationalism, and forced it to serve his own insidious agenda. It certainly helped that Bayreuth and Nuremberg, one of Hitler's main bases of action, are connected by a dome line (as there is a dome at Nuremberg). It was as if Hitler could pump the egregor out of Bayreuth into Nuremberg through the dome line and command it to do his bidding through black magic. Like

Klingsor, the evil figure in *Parsifal,* Hitler stole the spiritual gold from Bayreuth to forge a ring of power and domination.

In a bizarre, almost comic irony, Hitler actually embodied the essence of the key villains in Wagner's operas. He was Alberich in *The Rhinegold* who steals the lustrous gold from the Rhine Maidens and forges it into a ring of power, destabilizing the realm of humans and gods. He was Klingsor, the black magician who steals Anfortas' lance, thereby preventing the Grail King from healing himself and so keeping the country a wasteland. Both Alberich and Klingsor are eventually overcome; in the first example, the palace of the gods burns down; in the second, Parsifal wields the Christed lance to heal Anfortas.

Brocken, Harz Mountains, Germany

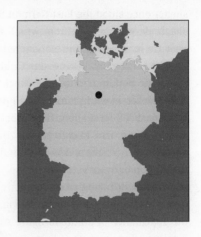

PHYSICAL DESCRIPTION

The Brocken, also called Blocksberg, is the highest peak (elevation 3,747 feet) in the Harz Mountain range in north-central Germany, situated eight miles southwest of Wernigerode and about fifty miles southeast of Hanover. It's a huge, granite-strewn domed mountain bare of trees due to unusual atmospheric conditions: it is foggy three hundred days a year there and has a microclimate comparable to Iceland; it is too cold and wet there for any trees to grow above 3,300 feet. The Brocken is now part of the Upper Harz National Park, Germany's second-largest forested national park.

HISTORY AND ARCHEOLOGY

Ever since Johann Wolfgang von Goethe (1749–1832), the German poet, playwright, scientist, and naturalist, made the mountain famous in his *Faust* as the gathering site for nocturnal revelries of witches and demons on Walpurgisnacht (April 30), the Brocken has been steeped in mystery, intrigue, and, for some, fear and evil. Not surprisingly, two significant rock formations on the summit are still known today as the Devil's Pulpit or Sorcerer's Chair *(Teufelskanzel)* and the

Witch's Altar *(Hexenaltar)*. A nearby spring is called the Magic Fountain, and a particular type of anemone that grows on the slopes is locally referred to as the Sorcerer's Flower.

A public railway to the summit was constructed in 1898, and the train began to operate in March 1899. By 1900, an estimated 51,000 tourists annually took the twelve-mile train trip to the top of the Brocken. During the Cold War, from about 1945 to 1990, the partition border between West and East Germany ran across the summit of the Brocken. The railway, which spirals up the mountain, crossed the East-West border twice, and was thus closed to passenger traffic for many years. In effect, a generation of Germans was unable to experience the mountain.

Then on April 30, 1990—an appropriate if not auspicious date, being Walpurgisnacht, the Witches' Sabbath said to take place on the Brocken—the first passenger train up the Brocken ran again. Full service resumed by July 1992.

Since 1990, when the East-West split in Germany was dissolved, as many as 50,000 visitors a day have come to the Brocken summit. At the center of the summit, these visitors encounter the *Wolkenhäuschen* ("little cloud house"), constructed in 1736 by the Earl of Stolberg-Wernigerode as a shelter for occasional summit visitors. Behind this shelter once stood the East German State security electronic warfare post from which Russians and East German authorities conducted surveillance of West Germany during the Cold War years. Today the building houses the Brocken Museum.

Brocken is world-famous for a peculiar meteorological effect called the Brocken Spectre, although it's also known as the Brocken Bow, anti-corona, or glory. You're standing near the summit, mostly enveloped in fog, but there is some sunlight behind you. Suddenly in the mists before you and seemingly in midair there arises the appearance of a human figure surrounded by a colored ring or glory of light. In fact, it appears to be an enormously magnified shadow.

The shocking realization comes to you that it is a reflection of yourself you are spectrally witnessing. It is usually only possible for a person to see his own specter on the Brocken. Understandably, many climbers are initially spooked by being presented with their own shadow ringed in light.

The meteorological explanation is that as one looks in the "anti-solar direction," that is away from the Sun, if there are many water droplets already in the air, the low Sun angle behind you will cast your shadow onto the mists, especially the ones lying lower than the summit where you stand. In effect, you stand between the Sun and a fog or cloud bank. The glory ring is then created by diffraction; sunlight penetrates water droplets and reflects off their sides. A portion of the light emerges from the droplet to come back toward the Sun. "But the sunlight coming back toward the Sun from the different raindrops interferes with itself to create circular zones of darkness and brightness."[167]

The same startling effect is often seen from airplane windows, as the image of the airplane surrounded by a glory appears in the clouds below. As the phenomenon was first observed on the Brocken, its appearance elsewhere, such as in the Scottish peaks and other hill country areas, is called the Brocken Spectre.

MYTH AND LEGEND

The big attraction to the Brocken in terms of myth and folkloric reputation is witches and Walpurgisnacht. The term itself is a bit misleading. The Night of Walpurgis is based on the Catholic holy day for an eighth-century English nun named Walpurga or Walburga (710–777 A.D.), the Abbess of Heidenheim near Eichstatt. Around the seventeenth century, she was assigned a holy day, which happened to fall on the same day as the much older, "pagan" day of April 30 eve–May 1 observed in honor of a presumed heathen goddess called Waelburga.

The story of Saint Walpurga may be merely a convenient story, however. Apparently no contemporary records from the eighth century can attest to the life, reign, or death of this Saint Walpurga. She may have been the Christianized version of the pagan Goddess of Walpurgisnacht. "Walpurga was the May Queen whose cult remained so popular in Germany that the church had to adopt her in its usual way, by a spurious canonization."[168]

In Celtic traditions, this period between the evening of April 30 and the morning of May 1 is known as Beltaine, one of that tradition's eight astronomically referenced "turning" points of the year. Beltaine is a seasonal feast day in honor of the return of the Sun in spring. As such it marks the end of the dark half of the year which began at Samhain, November 1, the eve of which we now acknowledge as Halloween or, more formally, as All Saints' Hallows.

Scholars speculate that Beltaine might have been originally commissioned in honor of the Celtic god Bel (or Belinus, Biel, Baal, or Belus), a god of brightness similar to the Greek Apollo. The name Beltaine is usually translated as "bright or shining fire" (from Beltene), or as "the fire of Beli," the Celtic god of light (from Bealtuinn or Bealtaine).

Typically on Beltaine, great mountaintop bonfires were set and special cakes or bannocks (round flat breads made from oats or barley) were baked; cattle and sheep were driven between two bonfires as a way of preventing disease or contagion and detoxifying them of negative or poisonous influences for the next year. In Scotland, effigies of witches were burned in the bonfires and people danced clockwise around the blazes and sometimes jumped between two fires or through a single one, possibly in an effort to achieve a purification by fire.

All fires were extinguished. On May 1, one fire, called the *tein-egin,* "need-fire" or "force-fire," was kindled, and its flames were distributed throughout the villages to light all domestic hearths. The intent was to symbolize the divinity of fire as a physical expression of light and its purifying ability to protect people from disease and by analogical extension, evil. The goal was to create a fire without using a match, as if by teasing the fire out of the wood itself.

At some locations, nine or twenty-seven people would be engaged to help turn a wooden axle round in a wooden hole to create friction to spark a fire. If any of these nine or twenty-seven people were tainted by having committed an unacknowledged crime, it was believed no fire would be kindled. The fire that was kindled by this type of violent friction then assumed the appearance of being derived from Heaven itself and thus of an unassailable purity and pedigree.

Elsewhere, men and women danced around the Maypole, a pillar dressed in greenery, as a public affirmation of nature's fertility and vegetative principle; often fornication in the fields not only occurred but was for one day officially condoned on behalf of a community's agricultural

prosperity. Sometimes there were mock, ritualized battles between the forces of light and darkness and, at one time, horses were sacrificed in an attempt to appease the malevolent powers of the world. Lots of loud noises were made as wards against the evil powers.

In fact, a major theme of the Beltaine fire ritual appears to have been purification from evil or negative influences. The practice of kindling fires on the eve of May Day was once called "driving away the witches," and was observed as such in many parts of Central Europe including the Saxony region of Germany, which includes the Brocken.

In Bohemia (part of the Czech Republic), young men and women leaped over the glowing embers or even through the flames of the Beltaine fires in a ceremony called "burning the witches." In parts of Scotland, farmers lit "bone fires" to counteract the spells and curses likely to be laid that night by witches who were also stealing cows' milk. People danced around the bonfires shouting "Fire! Blaze and burn the witches; fire! Fire! Burn the witches."

On Walpurgis Night, folk belief said, witches everywhere were speeding unseen through the sky performing hellish deeds to the detriment of human society and both human and domestic animal health. The belief was widespread in Celtic lands that prophylactic measures had to be taken once a year to prevent the deleterious effects of witchcraft from interfering with the fertility of the crops, domestic animals, and human families.

The Beltaine bonfires purified and fertilized the fields with heat and protected the lands from sorcery and witchcraft, assuring agricultural prosperity. The fire ceremonies, especially the need-fire rekindling, were "esteemed as a preservative against witchcraft, and a sovereign remedy against malignant diseases, both in the human species and in cattle; and by it, the strongest poisons were supposed to have their nature changed."[169] Beltaine, in other words, was the year's powerful incantation against the entry of evil into the human world.

According to Celtic belief, Beltaine was a time of both joyous, procreative celebration and danger. The Dead and the Faery folk were allowed to trespass the human world until Samhain. It was essential to perform the Beltaine rites on high prominences. "They [the Druids] thought it degrading to him whose temple is the universe, to suppose that he would dwell in any house made with hands." Thus the Beltaine celebrants sought the highest hilltops where they could enjoy the open air and the grandest views of nature and be nearest "the seat of warmth and order," presumably the Sun.[170]

Thus Walpurgisnacht at the Brocken has evolved in folk belief from the ritual fire purifications practiced in Celtic lands to a Witches' Sabbath and to activities inimical to human life. The Brocken became infamous as the site for the once annual congregation site for all the witches of Europe; there they would revel, feast, engage in sexual orgies, and dance around the image of a horned goat (either Pan or the Devil).

As noted, Johann Wolfgang von Goethe memorialized this folk belief by setting chapter 21 of his early nineteenth century *Faust* on the Brocken on Walpurgisnacht. Mephistopheles, Goethe's rendition of the Devil, leads his protégé, the scholar Faust, to the summit. This outing to the witches' mountain is part of Mephistopheles' tutorial of his new recruit, who was willing to trade his soul for higher knowledge.

On the nocturnal climb, Faust catches an arresting glimpse of the Brocken peak—"in all its splendid height/Ablaze the rocky precipice stands!" Of course, replies Mephistopheles nonchalantly, for why shouldn't Mammon illuminate his halls on the Brocken in splendor for this revel? At the summit, they hear "a frenzied song of sorcery" and behold a witches' dance. "The witches

ride to the Brocken Horn," they cry out. "The rabble is gathered awaiting the call,/Aloft sits Lord Urian ruling them all."[171]

The Brocken associations were further cemented by Jacob Grimm in his *Teutonic Mythology*, published in 1880. Walpurgisnacht on Brocken is the trysting time of the witches; the first night in May is the "grand annual excursion" of European witches (once known as wise-women and fays) to the Brocken, Grimm wrote. They are known to revel there for the first twelve days of May, dancing away the snow, after which spring begins.

Even today, the evening of April 30 and the day of May 1 are considered days of high tourist interest on the Brocken, and the Witches' Sabbath association remains strong, especially for the souvenir shops. There are images of witches everywhere—on postcards, posters in storefronts, in newspapers, on miniature broomsticks hung in shops. Many people come to the Brocken, and its neighboring witch peaks (Wurmberg Mountain and the Hexentanzplatz), either drawn by the folkloric mystique or to conduct esoteric private rituals.

MYSTICS AND TOURISTS

In late November 1777, Goethe traveled to the Harz Mountains. He wanted to climb the Brocken, despite inclement conditions, to get a sign from the spiritual world regarding an important life decision that stood before him. He told "the unknown powers that rule human lives" that if he was to stay in Weimar and pursue the public activities open to him there, these powers should allow him to beat the odds and ascend the Brocken.

On December 10, Goethe hiked unaccompanied up the first one thousand feet to the Torfhaus, a hamlet with a forester's station. The

Brocken at that time had no trails, and even the forester had never climbed the mountain in winter. In his estimation, the Brocken could not be climbed at this time of year, he told Goethe. Goethe, though heavy in heart over this bad news, prayed to "the gods to change the heart of this man and the weather." Within minutes, the sky had cleared sufficiently for Goethe to behold the summit of Brocken "as clear as my face in the mirror." Unexpectedly, the forester agreed to accompany him through the yard-deep snow to the top.

About three hours later, Goethe stood on the summit of the Brocken. "At a quarter past one on the top, bright, magnificent moment, the whole word in clouds and mist, and on top everything bright," he wrote in his diary later. Standing upon the Devil's Altar on the Brocken, "I offered my dearest thanks to my God." Goethe had received his sign, and he got it on the Brocken.[172]

"The ascent of the Brocken was for Goethe personally an objective and tangible confirmation of his *good* fortune, a response from a power outside him, a power of circumstances over which he had no control," explains Goethe scholar Nicholas Boyle. He had to have his yearning for a super-sensible answer confirmed objectively, as the result of a physically demanding effort, even one unlikely to succeed. In effect, he made the Brocken into an oracle. On the Brocken, after following the path of nature in his ascent, Goethe received "his objective, but non-social, confirmation of the bond between gods and men. . . ."[173]

More recently, an English writer also assigned to the Brocken a kind of oracular function, but with more of a negative valence. In her novel *The Brocken*, set in the late Victorian nineteenth century, Pamela Hill has a male character contemplate becoming a Franciscan novice. For him, the fertility ritual of Beltaine and its invitation to sensuality *are* the evil. Living in the vicinity of the Brocken, he is beset with the recurring

mental image of the mountain; his priest tells him to resist it because it is a visitation of the devil in his mind. But the image of the mountain troubles him day and night, even haunting his sleep, and he resolves to climb it.

Again, he is advised against it, being told the mountain is evil. But Felix decides that, like the Christ, he must face up to and confront evil. Christ did not run away from the demons, he tells Brother Heinrich. Yes, it's true the Christ will help you, Heinrich responds, "but to ask Him to do so on the top of the Brocken is to put even Him under strain. It is very evil." He begins his climb on April 30.

Near the summit, Felix encounters the Brocken Spectre and is spooked. Unfamiliar with the phenomenon, he takes its appearance as a personal sign and forewarning, "convinced now that something evil awaited him, the accursed." Determined not to be deflected from his goal "for all the warning images the devil could send," Felix makes the summit, then takes a nap to refresh himself. He awakes at nightfall and finds the evil so pervasive, he can smell it. First he beholds a spectral vision of his mother, naked, laughing and whistling like a mad woman; then the summit is filled with naked women from around the world, laughing, joining hands, and dancing in triumph around him—the Walpurgisnacht coven. They rip off his brown monk's habit and entice him into having intercourse with all of them. In the morning, they are gone and his habit is in shreds. He never returned to the monastery.[174]

A more neutral report was provided by a woman who used to live near the Brocken and could remember the days in the 1930s when many of the passengers on the Brocken Railway were dressed as witches or devils on April 30, festive as if traveling to a fancy-dress ball. She reported that "she has visited few places in the world that gave her such a sense of solitude and yet you get the impression you are not alone, that you have invisible company."[175]

GEOMANTIC

Landscape Zodiac; Lucifer Binding Site.

LANDSCAPE ZODIAC: The Brocken Landscape Zodiac is a small one, measuring 4.76 miles across. The zodiac dome above it measures 10.57 miles across. There is no star dome over Brocken; the zodiac dome effectively serves the same purpose except that it does not generate any subsidiary sites as it produces no dome caps. Instead it produces a miniature zodiac on the mountain.

The Brocken zodiac is wrapped around the mountain itself as if the two halves of an apple were flattened out and made flexible to wrap a mountain. Another way to picture this miniature zodiac is in terms of its Albion. The two halves of the zodiac (the physical and etheric ecliptics with their stars) are his wings or auric field, while his central core and chakra column are marked approximately by what is called today Goethe's Trail to the Brocken, starting at the Torfhaus. Goethe was right to ascend the Brocken trail-less and on foot in search of a heavenly sign, for that action hints at the mountain's spiritual purpose. The Beltaine and Walpurgisnacht attributions are equally apt.

From Torhaus to the Brocken summit there is a geomantic template of the nine chakras of the human being, the seven customary energy centers from the base of spine to crown, plus two extra pertaining to the heart. If you walk up the Brocken (rather than taking the train), you have the opportunity to align your own subtle energy centers with those of the geomantic template present on the Brocken. That gets you into the energy field of the Brocken temple, which, like all geomantic structures, is a mirror of your own innate spiritual anatomy.

If you wish to get the full benefit of the Brocken energy structure, you need to ascend the mountain in this manner. Each chakra point on the mountain's flank is a doorway, and before you can participate in the reality of the Beltaine fires on the summit, you need to have opened all nine doors in yourself by passing through the nine doors on the Brocken.

By the time you reach Brocken summit, you will be standing on the Brocken Albion's crown chakra and will be in tune with the energies and perspectives of your own crown center. Now you are ready to see why Goethe had Mephistopheles bring Faust to the Brocken on Walpurgisnacht. That is to say, you'll see why Faust had to confront the specter of what his culture defined as evil, dramatized as the Witches' Sabbath.

Here the match between inner geomantic function and outer physical expression is immaculate. It is perfectly appropriate that individual climbers be assailed (or spooked) by the Brocken Spectre, which is the magnified reflection of their own shadow cast by sunlight on low-lying clouds.

This curious meteorological phenomenon is itself a prime clue to the secret of the Brocken: at its summit you will confront your Shadow and, if you persevere, pass beyond it. One's first glimpse of one's own Shadow can be as shocking as encountering the Brocken Spectre never having heard of it. You are stripped naked, exposed to the depravity hidden within yourself, and forced to watch.

In one sense, the attribution of the Witches' Sabbath to the Brocken is more symbolic than actual. At any rate, it points in the direction of the site's geomantic function. Here you strip yourself naked and throw your clothes into the bonfire. But what you are casting into the fire is the dross of your astral bodies—your impurities, "sins," trespasses, crimes, negativities, evil—the devils and witches within, and all the wounds, traumas, pain, and pictures they feed on.

The essential quality of the Brocken's energy field concerns the ascent through fire, setting souls ablaze. In a sense, you can only cast off sin, negativity, and evil from a place of neutrality, and there is no more neutral place in the human body than the brow and crown chakras. From this vantage point (and equivalently, from the crown chakra of the Brocken Albion), you can witness the wild dance of your inner witches and demons and observe their propensities without judgment, just as Mephistopheles had Faust do in their nighttime visit.

Whether you go in the daytime or at night doesn't matter, it will be *nighttime* until (and as) you divest your negativities. In alchemy, this is a hard place, called the *nigredo,* when all the leaden blackness of matter, the dross that cannot rise or be illuminated or transmuted without spiritual input (Light), sits in the bottom of the alchemical chalice. Brocken is the place where evil is transmuted, transcended, releasing the higher bright Self from the confines of personhood and karma.

Metaphorically, the Witches' Sabbath upon the crown chakra of the Brocken Albion is a spectral dance of astral shells, the cast-off residues of ascended humans. It is a ghost dance, and a distraction from the main event which is happening higher up, above the mountain. If you look up you may see the glories of souls circling in the ascending heat of the Beltaine fires, rising ever higher, as if spiraling up a magnificent Jacob's Ladder.

Here is a visual way of approaching the Mystery of the Brocken Beltaine. A generation ago a marvelous British psychic named Grace Cooke published her impressions of the ancient uses of particular British megalithic sites. Her observations with respect to Dragon Hill in Wiltshire (on the Ridgeway, not far from Avebury) are germane to the light work at the Brocken. She saw past scenes of a "grand Sun ceremony." Twelve priests on Dragon Hill appeared to be "summoning the

great angels of the White Light," while a host of Nature spirits drew in around the hill, walking round the hill many times. As they did so, "an ever-rising spiral of golden light" appeared on the hill, and the hill glowed with this light. "The radiation appeared as a fountain of light, rising and spreading out over the surrounding countryside so that a golden radiance fell on the earth." Appearing within this fountaining light was a being like a king whose gold crown emitted rays of great brilliance.[176] The question is: who was this being?

LUCIFER BINDING SITE: This is a complex issue, and there is no short way to explain it all. I offer a few broad strokes here. Around the Earth are some 3,500 sites where the Lord of Light, Lucifer—the brightest archangel of the Supreme Being's Presence—is arriving in glory, being bound, and being unbound. This is a four-dimensional reality in which, if you were to observe the planet's history over time, these three actions would be taking place concurrently, almost as a breathing process.

As an aid to achieving neutrality in this contemplation, it may be helpful to see Lucifer in one of his other mythic guises: the Greek Titan Prometheus who was bound on Mount Caucasus for defying Zeus by helping humanity.

The Austrian spiritual scientist and clairvoyant Rudolf Steiner described the esoteric physiology of the Earth over the course of one year as a breathing process. He was referring to an in-breathing and out-breathing of essential cosmic forces by the Earth; the highpoints in the breathing process are marked by the summer and winter solstices and celebrated by human festivals on those dates in mid-June and mid-December.

In the winter, the Earth inhales fully, while in the summer, it exhales fully; the turning point for each breath is the moment after the respective solstice, Steiner said. In the winter, the Earth has withdrawn into itself, but in the summer it expands to fill the cosmos. "The entire soul-element of the Earth has been poured forth into cosmic space; it is yielded up to cosmic space and is saturating itself with the forces of the Sun and the stars."[177]

During the Earth's out-breath, humans rise in their soul-being into the cosmic world and become permeated with the quality of the stars, Steiner explained. At the time of the summer solstice, humans are able to become aware of their essential I-ness, the sense of dwelling within the "bosom of the divine-spiritual," while during the rest of the year they think of themselves as mostly physically based egos, especially as the year deepens towards the winter solstice.

Two supersensible beings are associated with this summer out-breathing and winter in-breathing process of the Earth, Steiner said. He took Goethe's Mephistopheles, a study in ambivalence and contradiction, and made him into two antagonistic beings: Lucifer and Ahriman.

To Steiner, Lucifer was not the arch-fiend Satan, prince of the demons and the source of all evil, as Christianity has portrayed him. He is a high spiritual being who has a proper place in the universal order but, in Steiner's view, tends to transgress his field of play. Lucifer's influence peaks at the summer solstice, Ahriman's at the winter.[178] Steiner also noted that beyond the sphere of the Sun, Lucifer is our proper spiritual guide to the cosmic mysteries; there he is no longer an "antagonistic being," but "a new light-bearer who illumines our path into the universe . . . who illumines what we have to undergo later in the world of the spirit."[179]

As part of the Earth's cyclic breathing process during the year, at Beltaine Lucifer is unbound (from at least a few sites) and allowed to ascend in glory, to resume his true state. At Samhain, the opposite pole of the year, on November 1, Lucifer is bound again. For Lucifer to be unbound at Beltaine (in anticipation of the full out-breath six

weeks later at the solstice) and for human souls to ascend in the Beltaine fires of Lucifer's original unbound glory requires evil to be dealt with. Since Western culture primarily thinks of Lucifer as the source of evil, to make any use of the geomantically facilitated opportunities of the Beltaine festival at the Brocken, you need a different theory of evil and responsibility.[180]

Part of the traditional Beltaine ritual was to make an object or person the communal scapegoat that then had to be "burned," castigated, and purified on behalf of all. The scapegoat's scourging and purgation was believed to transfer to the village as a whole, even to its domestic animals and crops. That is still putting the evil outside oneself; it is still not realizing that the Brocken Spectre that suddenly confronts one is one's own shadow projected onto the clouds.

That's the physical elegance of the Spectre: you can only see *your own* shadow. The point is ruthless: the only Spectre you see is your own, which means there's no escaping it, no attributing it to somebody else.

Symbolically, when you can own the Brocken Spectre as *your* Shadow of unexpiated deeds, karma, and dark elements—the evil within which we all bear no matter how "good" we think we are—and when you can join the orgiastic and pagan Witches' Sabbath—observe your own dark side from a position of neutrality—then you can participate in the esoteric Beltaine bonfire ceremony.

When you can absolve the Lucifer within you, you can ascend from the Brocken summit with the Lucifer outside you. They are the same, but for a while it is helpful for the initiation experience to split them into inner and outer. All the outer trappings of the Beltaine festival mirror an inner Beltaine experience as well.

Symbolically, the Beltaine bonfire is a kind of spontaneous combustion of the personality's false and repressed elements when confronted with the

Light, a self-immolation that is also an illumination as you *see through* your misconceptions of evil and thereby purge and purify yourself against the moral disease of not taking responsibility for your actions.

The Brocken Albion temple is an excellent facility for coming to terms with your Shadow as a prerequisite for ascending into the Empyrean. Beltaine as a fire ceremony to "burn the witches," understood here as the "witches" within—the Shadow contents—actually benefits the planet as a whole. If the dark side of a person, village, community, or nation is constantly repressed, never acknowledged or dealt with, eventually it will explode the personality from the force of built-up internal pressure. The source of evil will be placed outside oneself. Apocalyptic events such as wars or terrorist bombings will occur, and the "enemy" will be described as being Satanic.

But a yearly festival in which you can acknowledge and expiate some stored-up evil reduces the gradient between light and dark. Using the Brocken in this way on Walpurgisnacht can aid the planet greatly.

Carnac, France

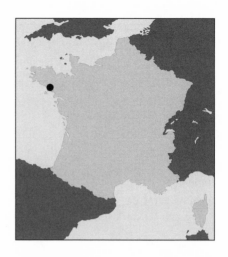

Carnac, located in northwest France, in Brittany, is Europe's largest stone alignment and surely one of the world's biggest and most impressive. Some five thousand *menhirs,* or standing stones, march in multiple parallel rows across five miles of landscape just outside the resort town of Carnac on the Gulf of Morbihan.

The Menec alignment, one hundred yards wide, consists of 1,169 menhirs arrayed in twelve parallel avenues running southwest-northeast; the Kermario alignment has ten rows of 1,029 stones, extending about 3,700 feet and one hundred yards wide; the Kerlescan alignment features 594 stones in thirteen parallel rows; a fourth alignment, Le Petit Menec, has been mostly vandalized and ruined, its stones taken for other purposes.

Also present at the Carnac site are *dolmens* (a dolmen is a capstone laid horizontally across two menhirs, possibly once covered with earth to form an artificial aboveground "passage-grave"), and several formidable solitary menhirs, one of which, the Manio Giant *(Le geant du Manio),* stands almost twenty feet high. An egg-shaped *cromlech* (stone circle) consisting of seventy stones is still extant at the end of the Menec lines; in fact, there was once a cromlech at each end, as well as at

both ends of the Kermario rows; the remains of two cromlechs are also observable at Kerlescan. The stones range in height from about three to twenty-two feet, while the cromlechs average seventy to one hundred yards in diameter.

There are also a few tumuli (artificial aboveground caves), such as the tumulus mound at Le Manio (one hundred feet long by forty-eight feet wide), and the tumulus of Saint-Michel (Saint Michael, or the Archangel Michael), 125 yards long, by sixty wide and twelve high, located on the edge of town and now topped by a Christian church.

One theory is that the site's name means "place of cairns or tumuli," which archeologists believe were prehistoric and funereal in purpose. The Breton Celtic word *Carnac* may be Gallo-Romanic, the earlier forms of which included the old Celtic *Carnaco-s,* the old Breton *Carnoc, Carneuc,* and *Carnec.* The name's similarity with the Egyptian Karnak, also a site of antiquity and numinosity, is intriguing but inconclusive.[181]

As an etymological variation on this theory, note the similarities among the following: the

Breton *carn* (meaning the horn on the hoof of an animal), the Breton *corn* (horn on the head), and the Pan-Celtic *carn* (pile of stones). A Breton oral tradition, however, holds that Carnac was known as *Ty C'harriquet* ("The House of the Gorics"), in reference to the local gnomes (nature spirits pertinent to the earth element).[182]

Archeologists speculate that some form of human (or protohuman) habitation occurred at Carnac as early as 600,000 years B.C., in the Paleolithic period. Curiously, no trace of human life can be detected in Carnac during the period 600,000 B.C. to 5000 B.C. Scholars contend the stone rows were erected by Celtic peoples between 4000 and 2500 B.C. Since the 1880s, the Carnac stone alignments have been the property of the French government.

Extensive research at Carnac by British archeo-astronomer Alexander Thom in the 1970s demonstrated that the stone rows and circles were erected with geometric, even mathematical, precision, consistent with design principles he had discerned at other European megalithic sites, notably the use of the megalithic yard (approximately 2.72 feet) as a foundational reference. "One cannot help being impressed by the great accuracy with which the lines were laid out."

Thom found, however, that many of the stones were not in their original site of placement; many had been re-erected at the convenience of farmers or road makers; and in the 1970s, this process of disturbance and destruction of the stones was still under way. According to a 1990 estimate, about sixty-four percent of the 2,800 menhirs have been re-erected, which means only thirty-six percent still stand in their original setting.

The largest artificially cut menhir at Carnac, now lying on the ground in four massive sections, is called *Le Grand Menhir Brise;* it once stood seventy feet and weighed three hundred tons. Thom contended it was part of a lunar

megalithic observatory, which he called a "universal lunar foresight" to be used from several directions, especially for marking the rising and setting of the Moon. The menhir at Le Manio (sixteen feet high) was the basis of another lunar observatory at Carnac.

While Thom succeeded in meticulously mapping the geometries and archeo-astronomical aspects of the Carnac alignments, he admitted he still didn't know what they had been used for besides this. "It is difficult to believe that the huge alignments at Kermario [and Kerlescan, he added] were built merely to demonstrate the existence of three pairs of coupled triangles, remarkable though they may be. We have here a solution without knowing the problem."[183]

MYTH AND LEGEND

The most prominent myth about the origin of Carnac's stone rows is that they represent the "Army of Stones," the petrified remains of unholy invaders of the site. Carnac's patron saint, Cornely, protector of horned animals, is today credited with the petrification feat. Here's how his story is told: Saint Cornely was chased out of Rome by pagan soldiers, and arrived at Carnac with two oxen carrying him and his luggage. He greeted some farmers and learned they were planting oats. He promised them that the very next day they would be harvesting ripe oat grains, and this came to pass.

Next, Roman soldiers arrived on the scene and were preparing for battle against Saint Cornely (Breton: Korneli). Seated in his oxcart, Saint Cornely cursed his enemies and turned them all to stone, and there they remain even today as the stone rows of Carnac. This is generally interpreted to mean Saint Cornely overcame the pagan forces opposing him and his evangelical work in Carnac, and that the petrified pagan soldiers remain standing like gargoyles against any further heathen infiltration of the site.

One fascinating ramification of contemplating the field of menhirs at Carnac as Saint Cornely's petrified soldiers is that it encourages "visitors to consider each individual stone as the symbol of a particular person, and it makes them aware of the anthropomorphic appearance of each menhir standing out against the horizon."[184] (The same observation has been offered with respect to the stones at Avebury, England.)

The feast of Saint Cornely was still observed in the early twentieth century in Carnac for eight days between the second and third Sundays in September with a fair in his honor on September 13. Saint Cornely was still respected as the healer of domestic horned farm animals, too. If a sheep or cow failed to respond to conventional medicine, the priest would pray for it in the saint's name, casting holy water over the animal. During the week, there were processions of horned animals throughout Carnac and, on the fair day, animals would be given to the saint to be blessed at the Saint Cornely Fountain before being sold.

Some experts suggest that Saint Cornely as the patron saint of horned animals may be a fairly recent graft upon the far older Celtic myth of Cernunnos, the horned god. The thinking here is that the pseudo-saint Cornely (as some refer to him) was originally Cernunnos, a Celtic divinity.[185]

A legend local to Carnac and somewhat supportive (if sideways) to the Saint Cornely petrification theory is that the menhirs are giant statues of God. Since nobody knew how to portray God, the ancient stoneworkers left the granite stones uncarved as a reminder of the enigma of divinity.

MYSTICS AND TOURISTS

One of the earliest "modern" reports on Carnac was written in 1721 by a member of the French Royal Academy of Sciences in Paris. This official commented on "some amazing piles of stones in which Art seems to have played some part," although note he said that it only *seemed* to. The dolmens, made of rough and unpolished stones, formed "veritable doorways," which the local people called Liehaven, "and they imagine, in a display of naïve imbecility, that by going there on certain days and taking their herds and flocks there, they will be protected from all sorts of evil."[186]

A French army officer stationed at Carnac commented in 1792 that "a constant tradition" among the Breton is that Carnac was originally dedicated to "the cult that Gallic priests rendered to their god" and that the Druids of Celtic Britain and France used Carnac for their meetings.[187] According to the renowned scholar of Tibetan religion, W. Y. Evans-Wentz, Carnac was the "mystic center" of the Celtic world, and with its counterpart (at least in name), Karnak in Egypt, represented the preeminent center for ancient religion in the Western world. The Hill of Tara in Ireland and Carnac in Brittany together are the two principal "psychic centers," the two "points of focus from which the Celtic influence of each country radiates," somewhat on the order of a magnetic North and South pole.

"There is probably no other place in Celtic lands more congenial, or more inspiring for the writing-down of one's deeper intuitions about the Fairy-Faith, than Carnac, under the shadow of the pagan tumulus and mount of the sacred fire, now dedicated by triumphant Christianity to the Archangel Michael," wrote Evans-Wentz in 1911. By Fairy-Faith, he meant the belief in a spiritual realm inhabited by spiritual beings, but particularly those considered to be nature spirits. Evans-Wentz explained that there are certain "favored" places on the Earth where its magnetic and subtler energies are the most powerful and most easily appreciated by sensitive visitors, and Carnac "appears to be one of the greatest of such places in Europe."

Carnac, he continues, wrapped in its air of mystery and silence, is a Land of the Dead; in fact, he says, all of Brittany has this quality, and Carnac is its center. He observes that at Carnac he often felt "strange, vague, indefinable influences" at play, during all hours of the day, and that these qualities were highly similar to phenomena he had noted at other "fairy-haunted" regions of Ireland.[188]

More recently, two British dowsers, Natasha Hoffman and Hamilton Hill, reported that certain of the Carnac stones were "encoded" with information about the history and purpose of humanity by the "Archangels" with the goal of sparking memory and spiritual understanding. Humankind was forgetting its true origins, so "it was decided then to program certain stones at Carnac, and a few elsewhere, with the truth about the origins of humankind, and, more significantly, with a message of encouragement to enable a balance to be restored." The encoded messages would also help people reconnect with their roots in the past so that as a collective we "can go forward into the future with new respect for our own sacred planet."

According to Hoffman and Hill, they were drawn to particular stones at Carnac and received telepathic, intuitive messages from the stones—receiving the encoded messages, they explain. Among the Carnac stones, the authors felt they were visiting "very special relations, old friends. There was a timeless quality and vast strength around those stones, and it was so comfortable to be in their presence." They felt very welcomed by the Carnac stones, they add.

Almost as soon as they placed themselves amidst the stone rows, Hoffman heard a voice in her head inform her, "This is a library," meaning the stones. The library reference seemed especially focused on one large menhir, called the Giant in the Menec alignment. Like most people, Hoffman was initially unprepared for the possibility that "stones are alive, have memory, and so can be record keepers."

Although they do not specifically reference Carnac with this statement, the authors note that the spiritual hierarchy assigns a gnome (or goblin, what they describe as "the masculine spirits of the North") to each sacred site. The gnome's function is to "anchor the light energies beamed at your planet from the Sun" and to tend the "slower pulse of life" in the mineral kingdom as found in the menhirs, the archangels told Hoffman and Hill.

Hoffman and Hill also note that, according to their archangelic informants, specific areas within the Carnac stone rows, especially the western cromlech at Le Menec, serve as "cosmic airports," dimensional portals that allow less corporeal beings from other spheres to come and go from our physical world, traveling to other planets or galaxies. The archangels set the portals in place, and arranged to have the standing stones mark and anchor them. Apparently, humans "who know the initiatory process" can also travel out-of-body through these dimensional doorways.

Through dowsing, Hoffman and Hill discovered another portal amidst the Le Petit Menec alignments in a thick woodland. The narrow trail there passes between two tall upright stones, and this is the site of a "portal, a gateway to other realms of being." Still operative, the gate opens to the planet Venus, the authors claim.

Summarizing their impressions, Hoffman and Hill state that all of Carnac is "alive in an electrical sense; it is an excellent 'plugging-in spot,' a good place for recharging your own spiritual and physical batteries." At Carnac, you can expect beneficial input from your spirit upon the potentiality of matter. They theorize that the stones of Carnac, rich with quartz and mica particles embedded in granite, generate low-frequency electrical fields. Hoffman and Hill also speculate that individual stones in the rows and entire stone rows as well are marked by an alternating current, one stone (or row) being positive, the next negative in charge, the whole linked together in a continuous oscillating current.[189]

Dome; Landscape Zodiac; Virgo Albion Brow Chakra.

DOME: The dome over Carnac, the diameter of which measures about 15.6 miles, corresponds to Sirius, the brightest star in our galaxy, located in the neck or head of Canis Major, the Great Dog—hence its nickname, the Dog Star. The Sirius dome is centered directly over the massive Carnac menhir, *Le geant du Manio.* From this point of anchoring, the several dozen dome caps generated by this dome spread out across the landscape. The dome caps are marked in many instances by the various dolmens, tumuli, cromlechs, single menhirs, and other megalithic features dotting the greater Carnac landscape.

Located 8.7 light years from Earth, Sirius is 1.8 times the mass of our Sun, and although it is not the most luminous star in the galaxy, from Earth's viewpoint, it has the greatest apparent brightness. It is one of the best known and most commented upon stars in our system, and has been globally recognized by different cultures.

The name Sirius might be derived from the Greek word *serios,* which means "scorching"; the Arabic astronomers knew it as *Al Shi'ra,* or *al Abur al Yamaniyyah;* for the Egyptians, it was the home of Sothis, another name for their prime goddess, Isis; and other cultures associated it with the constellation Orion, the Hunter, making it the hunter's dog, although the Chinese, among others, saw a bow and arrow amidst Canis Major's stars.

Most esoteric traditions accord Sirius a central role in the governance of the galaxy and the spiritual evolution of the Earth and other celestial bodies. In a parallel exoteric sense, the rising of

Sirius has been often used by cultures as a seasonal time marker, such as among the ancient Egyptians; for them, when Sirius rose above the horizon, the long-awaited annual flooding of the Nile was imminent. "In ancient Egypt, Sirius played the lead role in establishing the hours, mobilizing the calendar, and charting the sky."[190]

In Vedic myth, Sirius is Vastospati, the Hound of Heaven who guards the House of Varuna, which is to say, the created cosmos full of stars and celestial beings, "a lofty structure of a thousand gates." Sirius as Vastospati, the Lord of the Dwelling, is believed to be the cosmic incarnation of Rudra, the Wild God, an early description of the great Hindu god Shiva. For the Hindu mythographers, it is the Dog that hunts Orion, which to them is not a hunter but an antelope, from whose body leaked the generative germ that seeded the universes. Sirius, in this view, is "the star symbol of the Wild Hunter and of the guardian of order, the dog." Sirius is the wild archer who hunts the antelope and thereby starts time.[191]

Although one of the three primary Oroboros Lines (Earth-encircling ley lines) comes from Sirius and anchors umbilically at Avebury in England, the Carnac dome registers Sirius' presence on the planet in a different way. Here it serves to establish Time for the planet, as I'll explain below.

LANDSCAPE ZODIAC: Occupying an even larger extent than the Sirius dome is the dome over the Landscape Zodiac present at Carnac. The zodiac itself measures twenty-two miles in diameter, but the dome over it is in excess of fifty miles in diameter. Again, its center is situated over *Le geant du Manio.* Spatially, the Sirius dome and its dome caps are situated within the larger field of influence of the zodiac dome over the greater Carnac area, which includes the urban center of Carnac as well.

VIRGO ALBION BROW CHAKRA: Now to the stone rows. The establishment of the stones at

Carnac was vastly earlier than any current archeological conjecture. At the time when the primary features of the Earth's spiritual topography were being installed (at least eighteen million years ago[192]), the Elohim (an angelic family), a delegation from Sirius, and the indefatigable, seemingly ubiquitous Merlin (in Celtic myth, King Arthur's magus and mentor) erected 365 stones to ground and inaugurate Time on the Earth. These 365 stones, in alignment with the Sirius dome and its connections, *created* the cycle of Time on this planet. This was in the area of the Kerlescan rows and, today, these remain the most energetic of all the stones at Carnac.

Another 2,176 stones were added during the Lemurian epoch because it was necessary to diffuse the energy even further over the geomantic matrix with respect to its role in a larger aspect of the planet's geometrically defined energy body. Still later, during Atlantean times, a final 666 stones were added, giving Carnac a total of 3,207 stones according to its celestial design. Despite the extreme age of these stone alignments and the degree of disturbance, re-erection, and destruction of stones, the structure is still intact and working, although largely unsupported by human consciousness.

However, the function of the 3,207 stones arranged in twelve parallel rows over a five-mile expanse of Breton landscape will make no sense to us until we add another element to our description of Carnac's spiritual topography. The entire Carnac geomantic temple (the more than fifty-mile extent spanned by the zodiac dome) is part of an Albion plate (see part 2).

In other words, Carnac's larger function pertains to a geomantic feature that occupies one-twelfth of the Earth's surface; specifically, this Albion figure includes all of the British Isles and the northwestern part of France. Conceived as a very large human figure splayed across hundreds of miles of terrain, this Albion has energy centers,

or chakras, just as the human does: eight major and seventy-two minor. Carnac is this Albion's brow chakra and brain center. This particular Albion is of prime importance for the planet because it is the Earth's first to have been worked on in recent times and will be the first to awaken.

In light of this model, the stone rows at Carnac mark minor nodal points in the geomythic brain of this Albion. In a sense, the parallel rows represent the circulation vessels for the cranial rhythms of Albion, as cosmically influenced. The stones were introduced into the Carnac geomantic template in three stages as a way of gradually increasing the light flowing into the Earth and in accordance with the evolutionary attainments of those living on the Earth at the time. Overall, the function of the Sirius dome and the Carnac alignments is to ground and anchor the mind of the beings of Sirius within the context of Earth. Carnac, even today, regulates the input from Sirius into the cranium of Albion.

The stones were deployed in rows because they follow the cranial routes of Albion's brain. It might be helpful to conceptualize these as acupuncture meridians traversing the scalp of a large landscape being. The rows also focus and channel the energy currents into the various stone circles at the beginning and ends of the three sets of alignments. All of these descriptions must be taken lightly, metaphorically, functionally. There is much about Carnac—perhaps everything—that staggers the conventional mind and challenges even the metaphysically attuned to broaden one's conceptual base beyond the literal and physically based.

The design of Carnac also describes and accomplishes a certain cosmic relationship, again at a level that is potentially astonishing. One of Sirius' functions is to *focus* the energy from the Great White Lodge in the Great Bear (Ursa Major, home of the fourteen Ray Masters, also known as the Olympian gods) so that it may be delivered to the Earth (and, no doubt, to many other planets).

All this information of a cosmic nature must be presented (encoded) within the brain of Albion for the purposes of supporting the evolution of consciousness through humans for whom Albion is a collective expression as seen over time. This is part of the archival aspect of the 3,207 stones at Carnac. The encoding, however, took place when the stones were either quarried or created, which was a *very* long time ago. Even so, the information "in" the stones remains timely and is accessible today.

The cranial rhythms flowing through Carnac include the archetypal information pertaining to the aspirations of Albion, to everything "He" wishes to become over time and in time. This flow of aspirations and influences is also the flow of cosmic time through Albion's brain within terrestrial parameters—in other words, in a way appropriate to the nature of Earth and its inhabitants.

Geomythically, picture it this way: the Sirius energy comes in through the Sirius dome over Carnac and is anchored through *Le geant du Manio;* then it is unfocused, so to speak, (in computer language, unpacked or uncompressed) through the twelve parallel rows of stones, representing the Great Bear. In this model, Sirius (and its geomantic equivalent, the giant stone) is the focus for the Cosmic Logos (sometimes called Sanat Kumara) who presides over the "round table" of the fourteen rays (differentiations of light) at the Great Bear (represented geomantically by the stone rows).[193]

PLANETARY TIME CALIBRATOR: As mentioned above, Carnac's function was to introduce and establish Time on this planet. If the geometries and mathematics of Carnac are correctly and thoroughly decoded—Alexander Thom made a good start at this in the 1970s—one could extract a plausible theory of time. It is possible, for example, that the distance between *Le geant du Manio* and the *Cromlech du Menec* is a microcosm (a proportional fraction) of the distance from Sirius to the Great Bear in the galaxy as expressed through megalithic yards, a terrestrial measurement with cosmic referents.

In a sense, this distance is a time parameter, a finite amount of time which is the flow of energy from the Great Bear through Sirius; it is the distance in which the data is uncompressed. It is possible one could contrive a calculation of the time constant for Earth (its flow rate, our perceived sense of it, and its biological correlates) by dividing the distance in light years between Sirius and the Great Bear by the terrestrial mass of Earth.[194] The result would be the kind of time allotted specifically to this planet and its organic life, an extent of duration, a beginning and end, a start and finish line. Carnac sets the rate of time flow for Earth, which is in effect its evolutionary parameter and speed of conscious evolution.

The Carnac domes and stone alignments translate cosmic Time into terrestrial time. We might think of it as the speed at which light flows through matter. The various megalithic structures, such as cromlechs, tumuli, and dolmens, are like electrical transducers that receive, step down, and in some instances contain the energy current so that it may be assimilated by the local geomantic matrix and ultimately humans and all organic life.

Let's consider the individual stones. Hoffman and Hill, cited above, reported that a few of the menhirs were encoded libraries with information from the spiritual worlds of relevance to current times. It turns out that all 3,207 stones are libraries; each is a doorway into another dimension of existence, a galactic reference book.

Carnac was dubbed the House of the Gorics because many thousands of gnomes are in attendance on the megalithic structures and the energy they transmit. They are not so much protectors and guardians as transmitters; again putting it metaphorically, they take the energy from the stones and rows and distribute it throughout the geomantic template (the more than fifty-mile diameter extent of the Carnac temple). They also ground it within the etheric realm, that is, the dimensional interface between their realm (the etheric) and ours (the physical). As a casual way of visualizing this, if the stones and rows emit flames, the gnomes bring torches to these flames, get them lit, then plant these flaming torches throughout the fifty-mile extent of the Carnac site.

If the stone row itself represents the flow of terrestrial time, each stone represents a node outside of time, a little loop in the string. You can (clairvoyantly) stick your head outside of time by tuning into the contents of each of the stones. But the stones have another function: they are all dogs on the Wild Hunt, and Sirius, as the Vedic myths remind us, is the wild archer and hunter.

THE WILD HUNT OF URSA MAJOR: Celtic myth has an intriguing tale of a variously named deity (usually, Gwynn ap Nudd, the Lord of the Dead of Annwn) who leads the Wild Hunt, a pack of feral, red-eyed, pink-eared dogs who traverse the countryside at night one night a year, riding through the air and over the land at a furious pace. Gwynn's chief hound is called Dormach; the time of the hunt is usually *Samhain*, November 1, the Celtic new year and a time of No Time, when all the normal rules of the world are suspended and the Otherworld rules the day and night.

On this day, the abyssal cauldron or pit of Annwn is opened from above and down rides the Hunt. The purpose of the Wild Hunt is to collect human souls. "Before the Wild Hunt flies the baying pack of the Hounds of Hell; glittering bright white is their color, and their ears red: the redness of their ears glitters as brightly as does the whiteness of their bodies."[195] Everything about the Wild Hunt *sounds* terrifying, only it isn't.

Here is a possible way of interpreting this myth geomantically. The leader of the Wild Hunt is the Dog-Star, Sirius, represented by the Cosmic Logos, Sanat Kumara, the embodiment of the Dog Star. The "dogs" are the 3,207 stones in the Carnac alignments; more precisely, they are the celestial intelligences for whom the stones mark the spot or for which they hold open the doors—they are aspects of the stars of the Great Bear, in short. They're all barking dogs of course because they are being focused through Sirius, the Wild Hunter, and they have things to say to Albion, cosmic sounds for Albion to hear and act on.

Each of the stone rows represents a Ray Master from the Great Bear, each stone in a row representing a different aspect of that ray. One Ray Master, for example, the one responsible for the second ray, is known for an interest in the animal kingdom; the legend of Saint Cornely should be a clue to us that this Ray Master has particular attention on Carnac. Similarly, the Cernunnos attribution to Carnac points to the same Ray Master.[196]

The dogs are baying because the stones carry sounds; in fact, the stones may have been created by focused sounds and may still embody those sounds. Pursuing this sound image a little further, you could look at the parallel stone rows of Carnac as a giant piece of music, each stone being a note. Groups of stones, "played" together, create chords, and chordal progressions. But it's holographic music and a holographic library: you can play it or access it in different orders, to get different combinations of sounds or information. The totality, could you comprehend it, is the mind of Sirius in the context of Albion.

But what is the Wild Hunt hunting? They're hunting our parochial earthbound knowledge and perception of spacetime, our constriction of consciousness. The dogs are running at us full bore; we might get torn to pieces by the shocking transcendencies of cosmic knowledge, by the contents of the mind of Sirius and the Great Bear. We may also get enlightened. Cosmic knowledge, so different from terrestrial, physical world knowledge, is radically, profoundly destructive of our conventional frameworks of reality. No wonder most people have always tried to flee from the dogs at their first sign. Cosmic knowledge can be a total disaster to the personality—or an astounding revelation. As a visitor to Carnac, we have our choice of reactions.

Geomythically and certainly metaphorically, it was not so much that Saint Cornely turned hostile Roman soldiers into stones but that the infantrymen of the Cosmic Logos came storming into Carnac from out of the stones. In a sense, the stones are doorways for great bears. The possible connection of Saint Cornely, his affiliation with horned domestic animals, and the Celtic horned deity called Cernunnos may in part be a reference to those so affected by Carnac (or who brought a preexisting clairvoyance to the site) that they were able to attune to the higher energies flowing through the site, to sprout psychic antennae.

Here the two horns of Cernunnos (and of the farm animals) symbolize the antennae produced by the activated brow and crown chakras capable of hearing the sounds of the barking dogs of Sirius. Carnac, being the brow center of an Albion and the planetary center for Sirius, is an excellent place to develop or deploy one's clairvoyance to matters beyond the usual scope of spacetime as we know it. In a sense it's where our collective expression (Albion) itself peers into cosmic mysteries and listens for sounds of wisdom.

Any of us visiting Carnac can to some degree sprout Cernunnos' horns and tune our clairvoyant antennae to Sirius. In fact, visiting Carnac with this intention can be beneficial to the planet. Each of us can contribute to awakening Albion's brain, to the alignment of Sirius with Earth, to the gathering of the Great White Brotherhood of the Great Bear within our consciousness. When we do this individually, it helps the geomantic version of ourselves accomplish the same, and eventually enables the entire planet to do so as well.[197]

It may sound flippant, but the best thing that can happen to you at Carnac is to hear a dog barking. It could in fact be barking anywhere on the planet, not just at Carnac, for the Sirius dome also influences, by holographic resonance, the other 431 geomythic dogs around the Earth in the other 431 Landscape Zodiacs. (Each zodiac of course contains a Canis Major and a Sirius.) These 432 landscape "dogs" are yet another nuance to the wonderful myth of the Wild Hunt. When the Wild Hunter Sirius rolls into town, the whole planet starts barking.

The Sirius dog guards all the cosmic knowledge contained in the 3,207 stones at Carnac and the information in all 432 Landscape Zodiacs, each of which is a miniature galaxy complete with its mysteries, secrets, and arcana. The dog protects the cosmic library from intruders, pollution, and adulteration; this is so at Carnac and at the other 431 Landscape Zodiacs. In a sense, the dog is both Vastospati, the Lord of the Dwelling of the House of Varuna with its thousand gates, and the House itself, the entire galaxy of celestial beings, represented in holographic miniature at Carnac through its Landscape Zodiac.

Chaco Canyon, New Mexico, United States

Chaco Culture National Historical Park is situated some 125 miles north of Albuquerque and seventy miles south of Farmington, in the northwest corner of New Mexico.[198] Topographically, it is a long, broad, shallow sandstone gorge or canyon running east-west for about twelve miles, framed by mesas (tabletop mountains) with a river running through it called the Chaco Wash; the site's elevation ranges from 5,300 to 7,500 feet from river to mesa level.

Chaco Canyon was the homeland of a vanished Native American people known as Anasazi, a name which is generally translated to mean "The Ancient Ones" or "Ancestral Pueblo People." The name *Chaco* is of course Spanish and not Anasazi or Pueblo in origin. Early Spanish records show the name written as *Chaca,* a name possibly derived from the Navajo *Tsegai.* This is a contraction from *tse tigai,* meaning "white rock," which has also been used as a place name at Chaca Mesa, which is part of Chaco Canyon.

Fajada Butte, a prominent sandstone outcrop at the southeastern entrance to Chaco Canyon, is also a Spanish name, meaning "belted," presumably in reference to the black band of low-grade coal that wraps around it; however, to the Navajos it is known as *Tse Diyili,* or "Holy Rock."

"Tucked away in bleached out, craggy northwestern New Mexico is one of America's richest archeological zones," with dozens of communal houses of many rooms and stories "strewn like fallen soldiers along the canyon floor and surrounding mesa tops."[199] The park contains thirteen catalogued Anasazi ruins, or "great houses," and more than 3,500 other archeological sites. The major ruins suggest original structures of hundreds of rooms and several stories; Pueblo Bonito, for example, built as a series of concentric circles covering three acres, once had perhaps six hundred rooms and thirty-seven *kivas,* or circular places of worship, and probably housed fifteen hundred people.

Many of the kivas had a *sipapu,* or spirit tunnel, a small hole dug in the center of the ground level. The sipapu was believed to be the portal between the worlds of living humans and departed spirits; in fact, the spirits of departed Anasazi were believed to live in the sipapus. The Great Kiva at Casa Rinconada, which is perfectly circular and fifty-three feet across, is understood to have symbolized for the Anasazi the Earth Mother's womb out of which the community emerged in the beginning.

The first archeological excavation at Chaco Canyon was at Pueblo Bonito in 1896. Since then, archeologists have excavated a great deal more and have built a tentative picture of a great culture of the Anasazi that flourished roughly between 900 A.D. and 1200 A.D., after which, archeologists propose, they abandoned the region due to prolonged drought. At its height, Chaco Canyon may have supported a population of five thousand. The Navajos arrived in the Chaco Canyon region in the 1400s, but did not formally settle the area until the 1700s. Much of the memory of the Anasazi comes from the Navajos.

Chaco Canyon has several archeo-astronomical aspects of interest. A research group known as the Solstice Project has investigated the lunar and solar cosmology of the Chaco Canyon structures,[200] and has shown that the extremes and midpoints of the lunar and solar cycles played a significant role in the construction of twelve out of fourteen of the major Chaco pueblos; that the eleven major rectangular buildings at Chaco exhibit an "internal geometry" that matches the relationship of solar and lunar cycles; and that most of Chaco's major pueblos are organized in a solar-lunar regional pattern which in turn is "symmetrically ordered" about Chaco's central building complex. "These findings suggest a cosmological purpose motivating and directing the construction and orientation, internal geometry, and interrelationships of the primary Chacoan architecture."[201]

Researchers now believe that Wijiji, the easternmost pueblo ruin at Chaco, was a Sun-watching station, a marker of sunrise and sunset at the winter solstice. Casa Rinconada has its major and minor axes of symmetry aligned with the four cardinal directions; it may have been built as an architectural metaphor of the cosmos. It may also

have been used as a summer solstice marker. Pueblo Bonito is astronomically aligned; at winter solstice a corner window allows a shaft of light to appear on the opposite corner; and its curved orientation may have allowed it to function as a solar collector.[202]

But the most prominent archeo-astronomical device discovered at Chaco so far has been the "Sun dagger" at Fajada Butte which rises 423 feet above the canyon floor for a total altitude of 6,623 feet. Artist Anna Sofaer in conjunction with physicist Rolf Sinclair discovered astronomical markings at three sites on Fajada Butte in 1977. As a Sun-watching site, Fajada Butte is unique to archeo-astronomy, they report, because it makes use of the changing height of the midday Sun throughout the year rather than its rising and setting points. The device does not use foresights or horizon markers, but is a "self-contained instrument that records the sun's changing declination," says Sofaer. "It shows the times of solstice and equinox in vividly symbolic imagery of light and shadow and provides solar (and lunar) information at other times of year."[203]

For about twenty minutes at midday on the summer solstice, the sunlight passing through three large stone slabs (six to nine feet tall) enters a recess within Fajada Butte and creates the image of a dagger of light that cleaves a ridged spiral petroglyph carved on the smooth surface of a rock.[204] The Sun dagger appears on either side of the spiral during the winter solstice and quarters the spiral at each equinox; it is only at the summer solstice that it directly pierces the spiral. Throughout the year, however, the light illuminates the two spiral petroglyphs in a changing pattern every day near noon.

The Sun dagger, say the researchers, represents the 18.6 year north-south cycle of the Moon, indicating its major and minor standstills. Sofaer and Sinclair further claim that seventeen astronomical points are present atop Fajada, many of which are unique in archeo-astronomy as they combine simultaneous recordings of two key points in different cycles, such as noon and equinox or solstice.

Another key element of the Chaco Canyon design that has intrigued archeologists is the roadway and outlier network, as it has been labeled. At least four hundred miles of expertly engineered road have been identified, radiating out from Chaco Canyon in straight lines (straight across hills, streams, and other natural features) to some 180 outlying villages, or outliers, up to ninety miles away. Eight major roadway systems comprised the Chacoan roadway network and, when observed from above or on a topographical map, seem to radiate out from the canyon like wheel spokes. All the roads were shallow depressions in the landscape, often thirty feet wide, lined with stones, and exhibiting a shallow, dish-shaped cross-section, possibly formed over the centuries by the passage of human feet.

These outliers occupy a fair portion of the San Juan Basin, a 50,000-square-mile region that was once the Anasazi homeland, extending south to Mount Taylor in New Mexico, north to Mesa Verde in Colorado, east to Cuba (New Mexico), and west to the Chuska Mountains on the Arizona border. Seen from above, the San Juan Basin resembles a saucer-like depression in the landscape, and is about one hundred miles across. Archeologists suggest the area has been occupied by humans for at least ten thousand years.

About one hundred miles of the Chacoan roadway system are within Chaco Canyon itself; the other three hundred miles radiate out to sites in the greater San Juan Basin. Archeologist Dwight Drager proposed in 1976 that at least twenty-three shrines and kivas of Chaco Canyon "were the stations in a vast communication network which passed information of very specific types to other similar stations around the San Juan Basin."[205] Consistent with this theory, the roads may have been created to interface with the complicated line-of-sight communication system.

One mystical-tending theory proposed to account for these "enigmatic boulevards" is that they are "cosmic pathways" constructed in accordance with an ancient but forgotten Anasazi cosmology to accommodate the journeyings of spirits. The roads are too impractical to have been used for transport.

Similar roadways have been observed elsewhere, such as among the Kogi Indians of northern Columbia, and the interpretation put forward regarding those was that "the gravel-stone roadways are sacred places that must be walked and maintained if one is to please the spirits." The idea is that living humans can rise to a higher level of awareness by walking these special roads and maintain harmony between the realms of the living and dead.[206] A compatible theory proposes that the track-ways formed a sacred landscape, "a symbolic stage where the Anasazi acted out their religious beliefs and commemorated the passage of seasons."[207]

Apparently in the 1920s an American researcher named Neil Judd discussed the esoteric function of the roadways with Navajo teachers. He was told they were ceremonial highways. They were not really roads, although they looked like roads, Judd was told. A Navajo legend held that the roads in fact were "tunnels" along which the Ancient Ones, or Anasazi, could travel in safety.

In the 1980s, archeologist Kendrick Frazier was informed by a Hopi that the landscape features were symbolic and probably represented early Anasazi migration routes. Another archeo-astronomer was told that sunrise and sunset positions along the horizon were often marked out as sacred places. Young Hopi initiates would run in straight lines to a shrine and back so as to plant their prayer sticks and, in doing so, they followed "literally, the straight road of a beam of sunlight."[208]

MYTH AND LEGEND

Park rangers, sensitives, and local Native Americans speak of the apparition of a tall, naked man emerging soundlessly from the sipapu at Chaco Canyon, a ritual entrance to the Underworld. Apparently, Native Americans in the Chaco region consider the entire area a kind of mega-sipapu—"a special gap in the heart of Mother Earth, a holy precinct still functioning after unguessed centuries." The naked giant, they explain, is a spirit form of the site's *genius loci,* or protective spirit of place, "eternally replenishing itself from the Earth Mother womb."[209]

It is reported that on occasion this spectral man appears enveloped in a slight azure luminescence and that his body appears to exude droplets of moisture. The wetness, so say the local savants, is the "clinging after-birth" as the *genius loci* renews himself at the sacred center inside Chaco Canyon. The local belief is that merely to behold this figure is to receive its blessings.

Apparently, the scientific world is able to partially validate this apparition, or at least account for it in materialistic terms, as the blue light phenomenon, a geological effect associated with sites of focused tectonic energy, which is to say, at intersections of earthquake fault lines or areas of seismic stress. It is a geological fact that Chaco Canyon is situated over the meeting point of two unstable fault lines.

MYSTICS AND TOURISTS

Chaco Canyon was one of the prime sites in the United States in August 1987 when people sought out holy places for the Harmonic Convergence. It is estimated that at least fifteen hundred assembled at Chaco Canyon for several days and carried out various rituals in honor of the event, according to Charles Bensinger, one of the organizers of what he called The Gathering at Chaco. He collected numerous reports and comments from participants afterwards, a few of which follow here.

"Our experience at Chaco was the guiding force in our taking steps to change our lives completely," commented one couple from Arizona. "Neither of us can turn our backs on that awareness." For a man from Texas, "Being in Chaco for the Convergence was simply the most beautiful time I have spent on this planet so far." One Converger dubbed Chaco "The Great Esoteric School."

Others reported seeing "dozens of columns of Light rise from the ground in the desert night" only twenty feet in front of them; they "stepped into the fourth dimension" and also felt themselves "encircled by spaceships." They believed they were in contact with the spirit of the planet itself. "We understood the planet because She spoke to us. She gave us a deeper awareness of Her pain. Those who hear the Voice of Earth will no longer live in three dimensional prisons."[210]

Others since the Convergence have testified to Chaco's numinous quality and its propensity to tease out unexpected epiphanies. "Why do I love this place? It can't be the solitude. Maybe it's scale: far greater than a person, yet one could walk everywhere in a matter of days (if the heat, dryness, and wind don't kill you)."[211] This same writer later commented: "I found a place where as you say 'The Spirits hide,' the wind, the quiet, the canyons themselves create whispers from the past."[212]

GEOMANTIC

Dome; Time Portal; Dragon; Landscape Zodiac; Leo Albion Solar Plexus Chakra.

DOME: The dome over Chaco Canyon is the starfall on Earth for Arcturus, one of our galaxy's brightest stars and the alpha star in the constellation called Boötes, which means the Shepherd or Oxherd. The Greeks called the figure a bear driver because he appears to drive Ursa Major (the Great Bear) about the galactic pole. This figure has also been called Bear-watcher, Bear-keeper, and Bear-guard.

Arcturus is a *big* star: its diameter is about twenty million miles, or twenty-five times bigger than our Sun. A first-magnitude star, it is 115 times more luminous than our Sun, shining some thirty-seven light years from Earth.

Located between the knees of the standing figure, Arcturus means "Bear-Guard" and it was once construed as representing or embodying the entire constellation of fourteen major stars. Among the Chaldeans it was *Papsukal,* or "Guardian Messenger"; for the Arabic astronomers, it was *Al Simak al Ramih,* "the Lofty Lance-Bearer" and also as *Al Haris al Sama,* the "Keeper of Heaven"; and the Chinese knew it as *Ta Kio,* "the Great Horn." Other Mideastern epithets for this mighty star have included "Shepherd of the Heavenly Flock" and "Shepherd of the Life of Heaven."

The Arcturus dome over Chaco Canyon (specifically, with its center over Fajada Butte) generates forty-eight dome caps, while neighboring domes at Mount Taylor to the south and Sleeping Ute Mountain to the north contribute another ninety-six dome caps to the Basin. Between the three domes, up to 144 dome caps are present and serve to energize most of the 180 outliers mentioned above.

The Anasazi developed their landscape design based on a profound understanding of the preexisting geomantic matrix, and they used it to keep themselves in tune with the cosmos (through the Arcturus dome link) and to ground through the Chaco system the incoming cosmic energies for the benefit of the planet. They were aware of even greater sublimities connected with Arcturus.

TIME PORTAL: The fourth brightest star in our galaxy, Arcturus is a gateway between nothing and something. It is the source of the possibility of Light, and at Chaco it is a gateway and time portal. The Sun dagger pertains more truly to Arcturus and its arcane periodicity and influence than to the Moon. You could say Arcturus created the original dagger, that is, the column of light that cleaves Fajada Butte. The Sun dagger signifies the point outside time, the point of timelessness through which one perceives all time.

The Anasazi comprehended this mystery and described, modeled, and miniaturized the Arcturian sword through the spiral petroglyph inside the Butte. During the three-hundred-year Anasazi residence at Chaco, the Arcturian time portal at Fajada Butte was open and they had access to other time frames.

Here is a possible way of conceiving of this setup. In another layer of reality coexistent with Fajada Butte and its resident dragon (see below), there is a gateway out of our biologically framed spacetime on Earth. You enter a space of an indeterminate extent that seems to be bounded by a turquoise structure. There are Pleiadians standing over what looks like a large shallow crystalline blue dish.[213] If you study the inside of this dish, it seems to be also a hologram of the galaxy expressed in a somewhat abstract and geometric way. As you observe them, the Pleiadians seem to be placing little marbles at points of intersection in this matrix.

These little marbles are known in the angelic realm as *pearls of longevity.* Imagine a point of light, tinier than the tiniest thing you can visualize. Imagine that this tiny point of light is shattered into billions of parts. Imagine that in the spaces between these tiniest conceivable particles of light is what we call time. The pearl of longevity is the compression of the spaces between the most minute light particles conceivable.

The Pleiadians' task is to compress these spaces between light particles into time caves known as pearls of longevity—of immortality—and to place them within the star grid of the galaxies, which can be thought of as a lace doily spread across the heavens, sequined with billions of stars. The pearls are points of multidimensional opalescent light set between the stars; they are in effect the points of intersection in the star grid. It's like seeing the galaxy from the outside instead of inside as customary. The Pleiadians compress the space between the points of light into the black pearls, so they draw the existing light particles (stars) closer together. It creates the appearance of a single sun with a myriad of black pinholes, each a pearl of longevity.

In a certain sense, they are the opposites of stars, or the mirror reverse: little black holes within the star grid that dimensionally remove you from the time-based tumult of stellar life. A galaxy of stars may seem eternal compared to the eye blink of biological life, but from another viewpoint, they still exist on a predetermined time line; they are still ruled *by* time and *in* time. The pearls of longevity are time caves outside of time, frameworks for a time existence, an unused quantity of time. As you can see, the subject is dominated by paradox.

Since a fundamental principle of Earth's energy body, or geomantic grid, is that it is a hologram of the cosmos, whatever the Pleiadians do "up there" in the actual galaxy is simultaneously done "down here" in the galaxy on Earth, and at every level of its expression, from the planetary level, to the level of the twelve Albions, to individual zodiacs.

Inside a pearl of longevity is a vast spherical cave. You may perceive the time guardian, who appears in the form of a starry lion. You may sense you are somehow at the center of the galaxy, or a universe of galaxies. It is like an immortality pocket for initiates, a space that is a

moment outside of time, a refuge from time—or, paradoxically, all the time in the worlds. It is a time cave full of *potential* time, before the clock of galactic life has started ticking, before the solar constant—a kind of ultimate time parameter—comes into play.[214]

Fajada Butte is the physical location where in consciousness one may pass through a time portal to a place outside of planetary, solar, and galactic time. The Butte's time portal itself is a pearl of longevity, a place full of No-Time. In this place you can potentially view other time frames, including your own. The well-reported experience of near-death experiences may help illuminate this point.

It is commonly reported that in NDEs people see all the scenes and events from their life flash before them as if simultaneously. This is a time tableau based on the contents of your time body, your etheric body. For the sake of analogy, say you had five hundred lifetimes on Earth; in each, of course, you had a time body, or etheric shell, which contained all the memories of events in that particular lifetime.

Now let's say you could consolidate and integrate the contents of the five hundred time bodies into one time tableau—you over a great stretch of time; you as the prime actor in the movie theater of your time cave, or pearl of longevity. This would be one benefit of interacting with Chaco's time portal: to precipitate your being bodies through time, to condense your time body, and to consolidate the wisdom aspect from your being bodies and time body. In a sense, you could create your own pearl of longevity.

You can collect yourself over time, assisted by some of the beings you have been in the past, working within a place that is outside of time, and thus is objective. You collect all of your selves that have existed over time, spread out across the galaxies, and condense and transmute the wisdom of those lives into a pearl of longevity, which is to say, a sphere of immortal awareness. It is no longer subject to time, and you have the possibility of dwelling to some extent in a cave outside of time.

The crystal basin that the Pleiadians seem to be working over is in fact a bowl of transmutation where pearls of longevity are created. Arcturus pertains to the collective cultural experience on the Earth. So the Butte houses a time portal that is also a pearl of longevity for humanity. The Anasazi initiates could read this pearl, collect the condensed (transmuted) wisdom from humanity's time body, and make this wisdom available to guide their culture. They could also go there in a place outside of time and with assistance produce their own pearl, drawn and concentrated from the wisdom in all their bodies scattered throughout time.

The mythic and symbolic attributions of the pearl can help us grasp this elusive concept of a pearl of longevity. The pearl is regarded as a mystical center, as the transfiguration of the elements, as an attribute of angelic perfection. The Muslims have depicted the faithful in paradise to be enclosed within a pearl with a Houri (a perpetual female virgin soul) for company.

Dragons are said to guard pearls where they dwell at the bottom of the sea, and they are also linked to the Moon; the connection is with Soma, the beverage of immortality associated with the Moon, such that the pearl is called a "daughter of Soma." In Vedic thought, the pearl, or "daughter of Soma," prolonged life; in China, too, the pearl symbolized immortality. According to an Islamic legend, in the beginning, no creature existed except the highest Truth, and its dwelling place was in a pearl, its essence hidden.[215]

DRAGON: Occupying the same space as Fajada Butte is one of Earth's original thirteen dragons. This is appropriate of course in light of pearl symbolism. Obviously, Fajada Butte was once much larger and even earlier was probably part of a single, still larger landmass. Although the dragon's attention is everywhere within this landscape temple and its coils spread out in giant spirals throughout this end of Chaco canyon, its prime attention is towards Wijiji, the eastern temple entrance, which it guards and supervises.

The Chaco dragon is the "mother" of eighty-one secondary dragons, including, for example, the dragon at Bell Rock, just outside Sedona, Arizona. The Arcturian Sun dagger can also be appreciated as the sword that activates the dragon, releasing its withheld waters of life. In this case, when the Chaco dragon is stimulated, its eighty-one subsidiary dragons are simultaneously energized.

From the angelic viewpoint, Arcturus as a cosmic "personage" is the flautist and Lord of the Dance. The Supreme Being comes through the sound that is perceived through the colors when Arcturus plays his flute. His flute is Draco, the constellation of the cosmic dragon; its thirteen stars are the keyholes on the flute, and terrestrially they are represented by Earth's thirteen dragons. Metaphorically speaking, when the Lord of the Dance fancies a tune, the thirteen prime dragons and the 1,053 subsidiary dragons dance to the Arcturian music.

The Arcturian time portal and Pleiadian crystalline basin of transmutation exist "within" the dragon in another, subtler layer of reality at that space. The time portal is unique to Chaco Canyon in that it is the only place where Arcturus informs a dome; the time portal opens periodically in accordance with Arcturus' cycle within the galaxy.

LANDSCAPE ZODIAC: Chaco Canyon also sits at the center of a twenty-seven-mile-wide circle comprising a Landscape Zodiac, fanning out north and south from the central canyon axis (east-west) as marked by the Chaco Wash. The zodiac dome, with a diameter of 59.9 miles, envelops and energizes an even larger part of the San Juan Basin.

The Chaco zodiac is part of the Albion plate presently under the astrological influence of Leo, a plate that includes a total of sixty zodiacs at places such as Sedona, Arizona; Santa Fe, New Mexico; Teotihuacan and Monte Alban, Mexico; and the Nazca Plains, Peru; as well as other energy features at Las Vegas, Nevada, and the Four Corners region that borders Colorado, New Mexico, Arizona, and Utah.

Fajada Butte, as the center of the Arcturus dome is also an energy center within the Albion generated by the Landscape Zodiac. Just as the Albion within the Leo division of the planet's surface has eighty-one energy centers, so does the Albion of a Landscape Zodiac. Within the Albion of the Chaco Canyon Landscape Zodiac, Fajada Butte is the figure's solar plexus center, the *Manipura.*

The lower torso of the Chaco Albion extends farther down the Chaco Wash past Wijiji, while the higher end of Albion's torso extends up the Wash to include Casa Rinconada, Pueblo Bonito, and other pueblos farther away. The Chaco Wash marks the central chakra column for this Albion— the energy spinal column—but the rest of the figure and many of the minor chakra nodes extend outwards like broad wings about 13.5 miles in both directions (north and south) perpendicular to the canyon.

LEO ALBION SOLAR PLEXUS CHAKRA: The Chaco dome and zodiac are an energy center in the much larger geomythic body of the Albion that extends from Santa Cruz, California, in the northwest, to the Missouri River to the east, and to the Nazca Plains in Peru to the south. As noted above, the Albion that includes the region just described is under the astrological influence of Leo at this time. Within this Albion, Chaco Canyon is the figure's solar plexus *(Manipura)* energy center.

Chichen Itza, Mexico

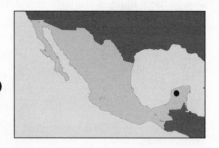

Chichen Itza, the Mayan City of the Sacred Well of the Itza, is a complex of temples situated about 120 miles west of Cancun on the Yucatán peninsula of eastern Mexico on the Gulf Coast. It is one of Mexico's largest and best preserved archeological ruins, attributable to the Maya, who are believed to have occupied it for at least seven hundred years.

The oldest archeological artifacts so far unearthed at Chichen Itza date from the first two centuries A.D., but other evidence suggests the entire flat limestone plateau of the Yucatán has probably been inhabited by Mayan or proto-Mayan tribes for at least eight thousand years. Historians tentatively propose that Chichen Itza was inhabited in two cycles, the first being from 435 to 692 by the Maya, the second from 948 to 1204 by the Toltecs or perhaps a remnant of the Maya who continuously occupied the site until its final abandonment in 1200.

Chichen Itza, which consists of about twenty different temples, including a huge flat-topped pyramid (El Castillo) and a large sacred well (Sacred Cenote), measures 1,400 yards (4,200 feet) from the well to Nunnery in one direction, and the same from the Great Ball Court to the farthest east-ern extent, past the Group of 1,000 Columns. The Castillo (Spanish for "castle") sits approximately at the center of these two diameters.

The Castillo is a massive square-stepped pyramid about 170 feet long on each side and seventy-five feet tall. It has four steep staircases, each set at a cardinal direction, ascending the form through nine sloping tiers to a temple with three rooms on the summit. At the base of the north-face staircase, a doorway opens to a stairway that goes down sixty-one steps to an earlier temple essentially buried by the newer pyramid.

Archeologists suggest the structure of the Castillo indicates it was used for Sun worship and comprises in effect a Mayan solar calendar. Each of the four staircases has ninety-one steps, which makes 364 steps; when you add the upper platform itself as a step, you get 365, the number of days in a year which of course is a solar measurement based on the Sun's journey through the zodiac. Further, each side of the pyramid has fifty-two panels, which is the number of years in a Toltec cycle; and the nine terraced sections are divided by the stairs so as to create eighteen sections, corresponding to the eighteen months of the Mayan calendar.

Each year, an estimated forty thousand tourists arrive at the spring and autumnal equinoxes to witness a remarkable light effect on the north staircase, considered the pyramid's main one. At those times the sunlight creates the appearance of seven isosceles triangles moving down the western balustrade, its sinuous motion suggestive of a thirty-seven-foot-long serpent of light which then joins the huge stone carving of a serpent's head at the base of the staircase to form one figure.

This light effect is referred to by Mexicans as the symbolic descent of Kukulkan (or Quetzalcoatl), the Feathered Serpent, Chichen Itza's prime deity. Skeptical archeologists point out that this effect may have been inadvertently introduced by the extensive excavations and restoration work on Castillo since the 1920s.[216] In fact, a photograph of El Castillo from a book published in 1926 shows the pyramid overgrown, covered in rubble, its staircases barely visible.[217] Curiously, in modern times, this serpentine light effect was first noticed only in 1928 by one of the workers involved with the pyramid's reconstruction.

MYTH AND LEGEND

Several of the buildings at Chichen Itza, especially the Lower Temple of the Jaguar, contain complex wall paintings that provide a detailed accounting of Mayan creation myths, cosmology, and the mythical function of Chichen Itza and its gods. Between the decoding of these wall glyphs and the translation of several key Mayan books, archeologists have put together a provisional picture of the Mayan mythic world. In fact, between the wall glyphs and the tentative interpretation of the functions of Chichen Itza's numerous temples, the site seems to be a multilayered cosmogram, Mayan cosmology arrayed in architectural forms and placements.

The ancient Mayan city known today as Chichen Itza appears to have two possible original names. One is *Wuk Yabnal,* which means

"Abundance Place," with variations of *Ah Abnal* ("He of Abnal") and *Wak Abil* ("Six Years" or "Six Grandchildren"). The other name is the more familiar Chichen Itza, which means "Mouth of the Well of the Itza" in which *Itza* means "sorcerer of water" and may also refer to the ancient people who settled there. Historians believe the original rulers of Chichen Itza called themselves Itza.[218]

But who were the Itza? One answer is that they were a family of usurpers who conquered and ruled Mayan lands for centuries. In the Mayan language, the name *Itza* means "yoke," which was perhaps for the Mayans a generic reference to their enslavers, whose prime temple site was Chichen Itza.[219]

Another answer is that they were an early people who had a special and close relationship with a Mayan god called *Itzamna.* Chichen Itza's first priest was called *Zamma* or *Itzamna,* and he ruled at Chichen Itza because that is where the Itza went. According to Mayan documents, once there, he removed the stones of the sowed land known as the Place of Itzam. The designation of Chichen Itza as the "Place of Itzam" may be an identification with *Itzam-ye* or *Mut Itzamna,* a fabulous celestial bird that perches atop the World Tree.

This makes more sense when we factor in the Mayan cosmogonic myth that says the original creator gods established their Jaguar Throne Stone at a place called *Na-Ho-Kan* or "First-Five-Sky" on the Day of Creation. The Jaguar Throne was the first "stone" of the Cosmic Hearth built by the gods. This fact enabled the Itza to declare their homeland of Chichen Itza to be the location of that first stone of Creation such that all Itza power therefore originated from it.

The god Itzamna was the deity of resurrection, healing, and a general cultural benefactor, the creator of all visual arts and writing, and the introducer of maize, cocoa, and the many uses of rubber. He was the head of the Mayan pantheon, bearing the title *ahaulil* or "Lord" and pictured as enthroned, presiding over a host of lesser gods; some mythographers associate him with Kulkulkan, and others credit him as being the first Mayan priest. Itzamna was also the first sorcerer of Creation who set up the third stone of Creation, the Shark Throne Stone, after the first god set up the Jaguar Throne Stone, and a second god erected the *Kab-Kun*, or Earth Seat, the second stone throne.

Itzamna is also closely identified with the Mayan bird deity, Vucub Caquix, the so-called "monster" bird deity in the Mayan document *Popol Vuh* who presided over the twilight Earth world after the Flood, although this bird form may simply be Itzamna in his more celestial aspect.

Vucub Caquix is also understood to have been an arrogant giant who with his two sons ruled over the Earth in one era in primordial time before the appearance of humankind. This deity professed to be the light of the Sun and Moon; his teeth were emeralds and his eyes full of silver light and splendor, which entitled him to claim the kingship. Later, two creator gods extracted the teeth, plucked out his eyes, and killed him so that humanity could be created.

The Mayan myths speak of an even deeper or profounder point of origin for the Itza. The *Na-Ho-Kan* was a place of darkness in the northern sky that existed before the appearance of the Sun. The *kuxan sum*, or "living cord," represented as two entwined serpents, wove its way through this darkness as a prime umbilicus that held all of Creation together. Then the first stone throne was established at *Na-Ho-Kan* in the Hearth of the cosmos.

To the Maya, this Hearth was a triangle of stars in the constellation of Orion: Alnitak, Saiph, and Rigel. In other words, they envisioned Creation as having taken place in Orion, and they saw Orion's distinctive three-star belt as a giant cosmic turtle from which the Underworld emanated.

The Itza ancestors, known as *Ah Puh,* or the Toltecs, those who created civilization, are shown on a Chichen Itza ceramic painting to have been standing at the exact spot where the first throne of stone was placed at the start of Creation. All of the different lineages of the Itza came from a primal city (or dimension perhaps) called *Ichkantiho* or *Ichkanisho,* and in the beginning of creation they measured and cleaned the land, preparing it for humanity.

The Itza were the People of the Reeds, empowered by the gods in the first moments of Creation. They were the legitimate heirs to the Jaguar Throne, the original stone in the Cosmic Hearth, and part of the assembly and alliance of lords convened at Ichkantiho, those who could control the Feathered Serpent and its conduit to ancestral space and time through ritual and thus, at least theoretically, bind the primary creative forces to their own will and uses.

That accounts in part for the origin and lineage of the Itza. Regarding the specific temple sites of Chichen Itza, the Castillo is considered to be an expression of Snake Mountain, which is a Mayan way of indicating a cosmic mountain or *axis mundi.* This is where the Itza rulers plugged into the cosmic forces they needed to run their empire. "The snake in the mountain also represents the conduit from the supernatural world into the human world—it is a kind of Vision Serpent."[220]

It is also in a sense a grounding point for the *kuxan sum,* the living cord; the *kuxan sum* was understood to connect the Itza lords with the celestial deities. It is interesting to note that Yucatán myth says the Spanish colonialists severed the *kuxan sum* that linked the Itza rulers to the Heavens. When the Spanish cut this geomantic umbilical cord, the "blood" spilled out of the cord and alienated the Maya from their divine source.

There is a widespread belief among the Maya, however, that this living cord still lies coiled beneath the Great Ball Court, awaiting the time when Mayan sovereignty is reasserted. The prophecy further says that on the day a Mayan king once again sits on the throne in Yucatán, the *kuxan sum* will uncoil itself and snake its way through a cavern linking the Ball Court and Cenote, the sacred well. From there, it will reattach itself to the Milky Way, or *Sak Beh.*

Appropriately the long, white-chalk paved processional from the Castillo to the Cenote is called *Sak Beh,* or "White Road." The well, which measures sixty yards across and thirty-five yards deep, has been the focus of continuous pilgrimage for centuries. Dredging efforts in the twentieth century disclosed human skeletons and a fair amount of gold and jade jewelry at the bottom, leading archeologists to propose that virgins had been sacrificed to the gods by being thrown into the well to drown. At the bottom of the Sacred Well dwelt the Mayan rain god, Chac, and maidens tossed into the deep pool became brides of this god.[221]

Mythologically, Snake Mountain is the place of origin designated and the foundation of the world located at the "Place of Reeds." The Mayan name for this is *Tollan* (or *Tulan*) and it means "the Place of Cattail Reeds."[222] A Toltec was somebody who resided there. The Place of Reeds, for the Maya, was a prime center for the dissemination of culture, writing, the arts, and priestcraft—all the hallmarks of higher human life. Rulers journeyed to the Place of Reeds to gain from specific deities validation of their right to rule.

Aztec records indicated at least four physical locations in Mexico for these Places of Reeds, including Teotihuacan, although it is possible that the name indicated a transcendent realm only accessed through a physical location. Various Mayan cities were called *Puh,* or "Cattail Reed," and their founders were declared *Ah Puh,* "People of Cattail Reeds." Apparently the Chichen Itza

Maya also referred to themselves as *Ah Puh* and to their temple complex as a "Place of Reeds."

The Castillo is often referred to as the pyramid of the Mayan god Kukulkan, or the Plumed Serpent, Quetzalcoatl, to use the Aztec name. As the Mesoamericans conceived him, Quetzalcoatl is a hybrid deity of serpent and bird. One derivation of his name is from the Nahuatl term for the emerald-plumed *quetzal* bird combined with the serpent, or *coatl.* This might have led to an interpretation of this god as a "quetzal serpent," a snake covered with exotic feathers, but he is often depicted in human terms with a fabulous headdress or other displays of plumage.

Quetzalcoatl is said to have come to Chichen Itza from the mythic homeland of the gods of high civilization in Tollan, where he was king. The distinction between Quetzalcoatl as a god who walked among humans and as an apotheosized human given godly status is blurred, and historians remain confused. There are at Chichen Itza depictions of a masked figure behind which stands a green-feathered serpent, but whether it denotes a historical or godly figure is unclear.[223] Sometimes Quetzalcoatl is seen more simply as the Green-Feathered Serpent.

He is the god of the wind, the deity who like the wind presides over all space. He bestowed the arts upon humanity; he was the god of regeneration; and he embodied spirit freed from matter. He is both daylight and night, love and sexual desire, purity and chastity, the soul that ascends to heaven and matter that incarnates on Earth, the waking and the dreaming, angel and demon—"all this and more, he is the true representation of the omnipotent god on Earth who, with his coming, brings all the possibilities of the miracle of life."[224]

Quetzalcoatl came from the Land of the Sun, and one of his prime cosmic temples was the Morning Star, the planet Venus. One myth says at the end of his career as king, he immolated himself, and the ashes, rising upwards, turned into birds with gorgeous plumage. In one Mayan document, he is shown "descending on a celestial cord through a fleshy opening in a sky band decorated with Venus glyphs in a scene that refers to his rebirth with divine attributes." His slow descent along this cord, archeo-astronomers suggest, might be an imitation of the slow descent of the Morning Star phase.[225]

His heart soared into the sky and became the Morning Star, and the Mexicans used to say Quetzalcoatl died when Venus became visible, which is why they called him "Lord of the Dawn" and "Lord of the Eastern Light." They also said when he died, he was invisible for four days, then wandered for eight days in the Underworld then when the Morning Star appeared again, he was resurrected and regained his throne.[226] In effect, Quetzalcoatl was the Venus god.

Appropriate for the Quetzalcoatl-Venus connection is the fact that the windows of the observatory, located on the top of the circular Caracol building, are aligned to key positions of Venus, specifically to its northern and southern horizon extremes. Another feature of the observatory (center point of the rear wall) is oriented to the northernmost setting point of Venus. Chichen Itza also has a Venus Platform (near the Castillo in the main plaza) with Venus imagery. Evidence is clear that the Maya of Chichen Itza were familiar with Venus' characteristic eight-year cycle based on inscriptions on the Venus Platform.[227]

It appears from Mayan art, calendrics, and cosmology that Venus, the "sun passer" and "great star" (*nima ch'umil*), was to them the most important planet, and recording the planet's changing horizon positions was common among the Maya of Mesoamerica. Perhaps one reason for this was that the horizon extremes of this planet correspond with the start and end of the rainy season at these latitudes.

Quetzalcoatl created humanity, opposed the enemies of the Light, chiefly Tezcatlipoca ("Smoking Mirror," a solar deity), was the Father of the Toltecs, and created a ladder or conduit (which is also himself) between Earth and Heaven. He is considered identical to Itzamna and Kukulkan. As Kukulkan he often is shown with serpent's fangs at both sides of his mouth; his heraldry includes four colors and symbols of the four elements; he may be represented as a lizard to denote his guise as the manifestation of fire; and he may sit in the center of a tree shaped like a cross.

Meanwhile, archeologists place a lot of emphasis on the so-called Great Ball Court of Chichen Itza, the largest yet discovered in Mesoamerica. Actually there are eight ball courts at this site, but the central one measures 545 feet long by 225 wide, with raised stone hoops at either end for a game presumed to be something like today's soccer. Losers were said to have been decapitated.

The Ball Court, which is entirely open to the sky and has a raised temple at either end, is remarkable for its uncanny acoustics. If you whisper at one end, somebody can hear you quite audibly at the other; somehow sound waves travel directly and quickly across the Ball Court and are unaffected by wind or time of day. If you stand in the center of the Ball Court and clap, you will hear the sound echoed nine times.

In 1931, conductor Leopold Stokowski spent four days at the Ball Court trying to figure out what made the acoustics work so he could use them in an open-air concert theater he was designing. He couldn't account for it, and since the 1930s, nobody else has been able to either. If you stand at the foot of the Castillo pyramid and shout, your echo comes back as a piercing shriek, and if you stand on top of the pyramid and speak in a normal voice, your voice will carry a great distance across the grounds below.[228]

Another queer acoustic effect is called the "chirped echo" from the pyramid of Kukulkan. If you clap your hands near the pyramid's staircases, the chirping echo coming back sounds much like the primary call of the Mayan sacred bird, the quetzal (the *Pharomachrus mocinno,* or *kuk* bird in Maya), a cloud-forest-dwelling bird with spectacular plumage. In fact, often Kukulkan is depicted with a gigantic form of the quetzal bird behind him. "Where else in the history of the world have an ancient people preserved a sacred sound by coding it into stone so that a thousand years later people might hear and wonder?"[229]

There might be a lot more to the Great Ball Court than Mayan soccer. The stepped shape of the Mayan glyph for ball court indicates the court was actually a crack in the top of the Creation Mountain, according to archeologists Linda Schele and Peter Matthews, whose careful translations of Mayan wall glyphs provide clues.

In Mayan, *hom,* which means "crevice," is also the word for ball court; as a crevice in the Earth, the Mayan ball court provides humans access to the Underworld, where their gods and all the ancestors reside. The "games" played there, then, were not for sport, but communication with the Underworld deities and the subsequent charter and validation for the Mayan governance that derived from it.[230]

The Mayans remember a myth in which the twins Hun-Hunahpu and Wuqub-Hunahpu were great ballplayers, but their noisy playing disturbed the Lords of Death *below* the ball court in *Xibalba,* the "Place of Fear and Awe."[231] These Lords of Death, also known as the Maize gods, killed the two ballplayers and buried them beneath the floor of the ball court in *Xibalba;* they decapitated Hun-Hunahpu and hung his head in a tree adjacent to the field.

A later set of twins returned to challenge the *Xibalban* lords in a game of ball, but each night they had to survive the experience of being in another of the many perilous houses of the Death Lords. It was as if the twins were undergoing an Underworld post-life initiation, similar to those recounted in the Tibetan and Egyptian Books of the Dead. Finally, the twins tricked the Death gods into being dismembered, and they are thereby credited with having defeated death.

All this took place long before the advent of humans on Earth. In the constellation of Orion, the Place of Creation, the god Chak split open the back of the cosmic turtle with a stone of lightning. The Maize gods came out of this crack, which was also the first ball court. Thus for the Mayans, playing the ball game in the crack in the cosmic turtle's back was a prerequisite for Creation and the emergence of humanity. Sport and cosmology merged.

The two sets of twins are also interpreted as the Morning Star playing ball on the eastern horizon, and the decapitated head as symbolizing the first visibility of Venus as the Evening Star above the western horizon. Or the twin Hun-Hunahpu might be the Morning Star and Wuqub-Hunahpu the Evening Star.[232]

The Great Ball Court at Chichen Itza was for them a physical reiteration of the site of this primogenitive act. Appropriately, the name *Itzam* was used to refer to a sorcerer who could penetrate the Underworld, using his abilities as a ballplayer and a special scrying mirror to perceive the reality of that realm.

MYSTICS AND TOURISTS

According to J. J. Hurtak, author of the influential treatise on metaphysics *The Keys of Enoch,* based, he said, on a remarkable extended visionary encounter with "the Master Ophanim Enoch," Chichen Itza is part of the left side of the head of a vast geomythic figure he calls the Dove.

This figure's geomythic form extends from Guatemala (its beak), through the Yucatán and Mexico City (its head), out to the Bahamas and northeastern Mexico (its feet), up to Newfoundland and Anchorage (the extent of its wings), to

Canada's Hudson Bay (its tail). Its body encompasses all of the continental United States and the southernmost part of Canada.

The Dove's "head of crystal knowledge" sits over the Yucatán peninsula, Hurtak says, and its return will herald the landing of the ancient Brotherhood of Light and the "celestial Lords of Light" in North America "to gather the 'righteous seed.'" The Dove's head in the Yucatán contains all the knowledge from the past that is relevant to the "program of Light upon this planet in relationship to the star regions of the Brotherhood" and all the "teachings coded" during past cycles of planetary life and evolution.

This Brotherhood is an aspect of the "Higher Intelligence" and spiritual agencies that originally set up the planet, he states. Some twenty million years ago, this Brotherhood deposited its "seed crystal" within our galaxy, and every six thousand to twelve thousand years it returns to Earth to collect the "cultivated seed crystal of evolution" per order of "galactic command" in the constellation of Orion.

By "seed crystal," Hurtak suggests it is the residue or original spiritual coding of a pure race of humans capable of holding the Light—"the Adamic seed" or "Adamanic Man," he calls it. He also suggests that as the Dove figure settles over the Americas, it will release ancient knowledge from the geomantic archives and act as a kind of safety area in a time of tumultuous transition.

The sacred region within the head of the Dove was once called Zarahemla and was the home of the Brotherhood of Light, Hurtak says. Key ancient sacred sites were connected in a "vast energy network" including Chichen Itza and Palenque, in Yucatán, Oaxaca near Monte Alban, and Teotihuacan near Mexico City.

Hurtak further states that within this large region an energy triangle defines a smaller but geomantically potent area bounded by Chichen Itza in the north, Kaminaljuyu, near Guatemala City in the south, and the Tres Zapotes-Cerro Rabon area in the east, with Palenque in the middle.[233]

GEOMANTIC

Landscape Zodiac; Dome; Lucifer Binding Site; Tree of Life; Labyrinth; Control Bubble.

LANDSCAPE ZODIAC: The largest geomantic feature at Chichen Itza is a Landscape Zodiac that measures 26.8 miles across. Its midpoint is at the Castillo, which is also the heart chakra of the central energy axis (the Albion figure it expresses) of this zodiac. The zodiac dome that encloses the terrestrial star map has a twenty-nine-mile radius from the Castillo, all of it energized and sanctified by the huge zodiac dome overhead.

The large Landscape Zodiac around Chichen Itza acts as a distribution field for the incoming energies and codings from the galaxy, and provided Mayan initiates a living star workshop to clarify and ground the energies and programmings of the many stars and constellations in their own auric fields. This would serve as preparation—indeed, it was probably a prerequisite—for addressing and interfacing with the more complex geomantic structures present. Specifically, it prepares one for entering the dimensional zone called Tollan.

DOME: There is a dome over a smaller area of the Chichen Itza complex with respect to the extent of the zodiac dome. The star dome corresponds to nu Taurii, a star in the left hoof of the Bull, or Taurus. This star is not named in Western astronomy, nor are there any recorded myths about it. In general terms, however, it is fitting that a Taurus star would be grounded at the Chichen Itza dome, given the site's strong Venus connections through its resident deity, Quetzalcoatl. (Venus, of course, is the astrological "ruler" of Taurus.)

We can also note that in broad terms the energy of this dome is concerned with creating the presence of the living Venus at the Well of the Itza. This is not so much the holographic presence of the planet known as Venus but rather a dimension of cosmic reality occultly known as Venus and associated with Quetzalcoatl.

Periodically, the Well—here the term must be understood very broadly to refer to the environs under the dome and not the Sacred Cenote—fills with Venus energy in accordance with its eight-year planetary cycle around the Sun. We could just as accurately say that periodically Quetzalcoatl returns to full presence at Chichen Itza, filling the Well of the site with his cosmic energies.

LUCIFER BINDING SITE: To understand this crucial feature of the Chichen Itza temple complex, we need to propose some mythic equivalencies for Quetzalcoatl and his Celestial City called Tollan. First, Quetzalcoatl (Kukulkan), the Plumed Serpent and Lord of the Dawn and the Eastern Light, linked with Venus as the Morning and Evening Star is the Mayan name for Lucifer, Lord of Light. The planet Venus was anciently referred to as Lucifer, or Phosphorus.

Second, Tollan is another name for Jerusalem, the foundation of Lucifer, understood as a celestial or spiritual location and not the physical city on Earth. *Salem* refers to the Evening and Morning Star, and *Jeru* to "foundation."[234] Jerusalem means "the foundation of the Morning and Evening Star," and that star is Venus, otherwise known or cloaked as Lucifer, Lord of the Dawn.

In simple terms, the planet or dimension of Venus in our solar system was a staging ground, a kind of preparation workshop, for the incarnational process on Earth. It still is a reference point for the original "blueprints" for human life and the Earth's geomantic structure.

Those blueprints are part of the foundation that Lucifer embodies. Perhaps it might be easier to think of Lucifer through his Greek guise as Prometheus, the benevolent Titan who stole the gods' fire for humanity. That stolen "fire" is the opportunity for humans to have consciousness of the blueprints, to wield the ability to *see* and *visit* the foundations: Jerusalem.

Chichen Itza as a geomantic well was designed to dilate and contract in accordance with the eight-year cycle of Venus and other aspects of Venus' physical and metaphysical reality. When the Venus influence is high and the Chichen Itza well is full, it is much easier to access and enter Tollan through the Castillo which acts as a grounding point for this higher reality. When the well is full, Quetzalcoatl, or Lucifer, arrives in glory, plumed with Elohim. It's hardly a binding site; rather, it is a grounding site, an arrival site.

Of course, Quetzalcoatl is *always* there, in glory, but the Venus influence heightens the bleed-through of his presence into some kind of cognizable reality, into an event in time, much like the 1987 Harmonic Convergence, whose center near Oaxaca was also positioned at a Mayan geomantic center.

At another layer of reality, where the Castillo physically stands is a six-sided, double-terminated, vertical emerald. This is the outer expression—the doors, if you will—of Tollan or Jerusalem, Quetzalcoatl's foundation and city. It is an esoteric aspect of the heart chakra, a midway electromagnetic doorway in between its outer *(Anahata)* and inner *(Ananda-kanda)* aspects.

This emerald exists within the human energy field; the entire Earth energy grid is contained within it. It is one of the jewels from the crown of Lucifer—one of Quetzalcoatl's "feathers," if you like—and it expands to fill the nearly one square mile of the Chichen Itza temple site. In Mayan language, Quetzalcoatl, the Plumed Serpent (Itzamna), arrives in cosmic splendor, descending his *kuxan sum* into Snake Mountain at the Castillo, there to hold court in Tollan, his divine city.

When the system is "on," the Chichen Itza emerald acts as a modem link to all the other dimensional expressions of Lucifer's emerald or Quetzalcoatl's heart. You find yourself at the source of all emeralds, within the original, the foundation. Your cognition expands to be that of the planet, waking up within its own emerald, now aware of itself in the Venus dimension.

The emerald at Chichen Itza is one of many emerald modems that instantaneously link the site—and you, if your consciousness is placed there—through Venus to the "mainframe server," otherwise known as Tollan or Jerusalem. You remember the foundations, the cosmic blueprint, and doing so, you can "reboot" your orientation to its correct and intended galactic settings. You remember that time before humanity was extrapolated from the Venus dimension, when the Hero Twins of the Mayan myth played ball nonchalantly on the roof of Xibalba, the House of the Death Gods, and disturbed them.

TREE OF LIFE: Let's look at that peculiar myth of the ballplayers and the image of decapitation. For this to make any sense to the Western mind, we need to see it through another story, or a visual analogy.

Spread out along the axis of the Great Ball Court is a Tree of Life, embodying the forty Sephira and Four Worlds as described in Qabala. You walk this dimensional ladder as a preparation for having your head chopped off at the far end by the Lords of Xibalba, who are not under the field but at the goalpost, just beyond the top of the tree.

The "ball" that the ball players supposedly kick around the field actually sits at the top of the tree or the far end of the field. You might describe it as a huge black sphere, and it does roll like a ball, but the rollers of the ball are high angels

entrusted with cosmic mysteries and revelations. Qabala describes this black sphere as Ain, the dimensionless sphere of all possible dimensions beyond or before the Tree of Life, which is to say, all of manifest existence.

It contains the answers to all possible questions for it is the ultimate revelation, perhaps the only one. The Gnostics called this black ball the Pleroma, and inside it dwell the Aeons, or what the Christian esotericists called the twenty-four Elders about the Throne of God.[235] Perhaps it is the same as the *Na-Ho-Kan,* for the Mayans a place of darkness in the northern sky that existed before the appearance of the Sun. Of course, these Xibalban Lords are the Gods of Death because they exist *prior* to the creation of the universe, reality, and life.

In a sense, the fact of their existence is the proof of your own death, or mortality. You have to die to your body-based, spacetime-based, and personality-based cognitive framework to be able to perceive them. Picture your body as the Tree of Life matrix at the Great Ball Court at Chichen Itza. You stick your head through a dimensional portal—like the stable miniature wormhole in the movie *Stargate,* for those familiar with this striking image—and your consciousness goes somewhere else entirely. It's as if your head was chopped off. Then your "head," filled with the ineffabilities of preexistence awareness can bounce through the spheres of light in the lower Tree like a ball in a pinball machine.

Put another way, you build, affirm, and consolidate your individuative consciousness by climbing the Tree of Life in the Great Ball Court. You are outside the ball, but it is in sight. Then when you stick your head through the dimensional wormhole, your head dies to itself and is reborn as unitive consciousness, distributed everywhere. You are inside the ball. You see the twenty-four faces encircling you, and it's as if they are melded together at the edges, one big face.

LABYRINTH: The Sacred Cenote is the physical counterpart to an astral labyrinth present at that spot. The *Sak Beh,* or White Road, is the processional along which you prepare yourself to enter the labyrinthine domain. Surrounding the labyrinth, and facing outwards, are a series of guardians in the form of the familiar Mayan *chacmool,* a reclining figure of the god Chac, many physical statues of which are present in the various Chichen Itza temples. The chacmools are attendants of the water god, or perhaps the God Chac himself shown seated.

This labyrinth is patterned after the eight-year orbital cycle of Venus that, seen over time, creates a five-petaled flower or pentagonal figure around the Earth. The shape of this type of labyrinth—there are nine different kinds on the Earth—corresponds to the time-lapsed or fourth-dimensional aspect of Venus.[236]

You penetrate the labyrinthine folds and twists and arrive at the center to stand in the midst of the incoming data stream. From the Castillo you can see a shaft of white light like a streaming shower continuously entering the Cenote. This light shaft is a kind of galactic fiber optic cable containing a great quantity of compressed information about light codings and star information. This is part of Hurtak's "head of crystal knowledge" in the Dove over Zarahemla or the Yucatán.

As Hurtak implies, all of Mayan Mesoamerican geomantic structures are highly refined, almost transcendent in design and function. It's as if the planet has a Venus band, and that ring of influence runs across central Mexico, encompassing the key Mayan sites such as Teotihuacan, Monte Alban, Palenque, Chichen Itza, and others.

Each contributes to the manifestation on Earth of the foundations or blueprints of the variously named Venus, Tollan, or Jerusalem. Each acts as an emerald modem connecting the site and its initiates to the original light template in the Venus dimension and to all the other emerald sites in that network. It also connects those sites to the Pleiades, home of the prime forebears for humanity and a prime design and implementation source of the Earth energy matrix. The Mayans understood Venus, the Morning Star, to be the "fire" of the Pleiades, and they called the times when Venus passed by the Pleiades, *tzab,* "the rattlesnake's rattle." Evidence at Chichen Itza suggests a calendar cycle that linked Venus and the Pleiades.[237]

CONTROL BUBBLE: Let's start trying to get the big picture on this setup. The Chichen Itza temple complex as a whole is a perch for the divine Quetzal bird who arrives at the Castillo under the Venus influence when the well is full. As the well fills, in accordance with the planet Venus' eight-year cycle, the celestial bird's plumage sparkles in glorious color.

The Control Bubble at the Observatory is the means by which the master Mayan geomancers could regulate the incoming flow of the Venus and Quetzalcoatl influence. Once the well was full, you didn't want it to flood the land uncontrollably. The Control Bubble enabled the Mayans to adjust the flow rate out of Chichen Itza for much of the Yucatán.

CHICHEN ITZA AS A DIAMOND STYLUS: Here is a partial view of what the entire geomantic structure of Chichen Itza might be like. The Castillo serves as a prime tent peg to ground the presence of Tollan or Jerusalem at Chichen Itza; this emerald Celestial City spreads out for miles from this center. Seen from the outside it is a huge upright six-sided emerald, probably the Jaguar Throne Stone of Mayan cosmology, the first stone of the Cosmic Hearth. Quetzalcoatl, the magnificently plumed celestial bird, is present on this throne.

Above the throne or somehow on its surface is a playing field on which the Mayan gods kick a black ball around the court. When you look closer, you see that the tracings of where the ball goes, zipping back and forth across the field, weave a net or energy matrix with a complex shape. Perhaps the apparent movement of the black sphere was only highlighting the individual strands of the energy net the gods were weaving.

Out of this matrix rises a yellow spike or thin tower with a point at the top end. Perhaps it is an antenna but it might also be the diamond stylus of a record player or the laser beam of a CD player. The record or CD in this analogy is the galaxy itself or a certain selection of it. The Chichen Itza temple complex is a geomantic CD player, equipped to download and play the music of a cosmic CD. In practical terms, this means that the site's geomantic setup enables it to download and translate higher-dimensional light codings or instructions on behalf of the Earth's energy field and specifically the Yucatán or Mesoamerican aspect of it.

Citamparam, India

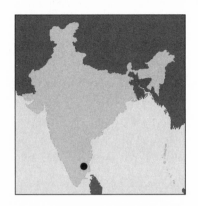

The temple complex of Citamparam, about twenty-six miles south of Pondicherry and on India's southeastern coast, is one of the holiest sites in the country, and one of India's oldest and most venerated shrines.

Unlike most South Indian temples, which are set on mountain peaks or along riverbanks adjacent to population centers, Citamparam sits in a lowland surrounded by backwater from the Bay of Bengal a few miles away. Two other rivers flow within five miles of this medium-sized town in Tamil Nadu, about seventy miles south of Madras, the State's capital.

Many scholars find it hard to understand why such an important temple was ever sited there. Originally, the more severe of India's ascetics considered the Citamparam area a worthy challenge for their austerities. It was once surrounded by a forest of *tillai* shrubs (these still occupy most of the five miles between the temple complex and the seacoast), and these shrubs created a tangled, almost impassable barrier; worse still, their milk-bark is poisonous. To add to the challenge, the great death goddess, Kali, was said to rule the tillai forests with her fierce tiger, always seeking prey.

Legend says that the first ascetic to master the tillai extremities developed tiger's claws for fingernails so he could climb the tillai forest and gather the trees' beautiful blossoms. His name is remembered as Viyakirapata, "Tigerfoot." After Tigerfoot's time, the region, town, and temple were all referred to as Tillai. He was also said to live on the banks of a pond, whose water, legend says, now forms the contents of a giant water tank within the temple.

This is the massive Shiva Ganga tank (275 feet long, 175 feet wide), which contains healing water and is continually thronged by pilgrims seeking a blessing or cure. Legend has it that an ancient king named Hiranyavarman came here from Kashmir in the North of India to cure himself of leprosy. In gratitude for a successful cure, he enlarged the Citamparam temple, and he dispatched three thousand Brahmins of the Ditcitar caste to perform the rituals. They are understood to be present at Citamparam today, in the form of a religious community of about one thousand, supervising the rituals and distinguished by their top-knotted hair.

Shiva devotees at Citamparam say the holy water in this tank can wash away the sins or karma of previous evil deeds and that contact with the water can increase one's devotion to the

Supreme God so much so that the fearsome Yama, the Hindu death god, will tremble before those devotees who have dipped in Shiva Ganga.

A site venerated by the Tamils, Citamparam is dedicated to Lord Shiva, one of whose names is Nataraja, King of the Dance, and it is here that he performs his cosmic dance of bliss, the Ananda Tandava. It isn't any old dance: according to Hindu belief, the Tandava is the primordial dance at the heart of creation by which Shiva expresses his five attributes of existence. Even the Sanskrit name is mystical: Citamparam means "the Space" *(amparam)* of "Consciousness" *(cit)*. And it isn't in any old space: Shiva dances the Ananda Tandava in the cosmic golden hall of consciousness at the center of the universe. The temple at Citamparam is meant to embody that central cosmic space.

The Citamparam complex covers forty acres and once included fifty *maths,* or monasteries, only a few of which remain today. It was built in six stages over many centuries, beginning with a thatched-roof hut in the forest around 300 A.D., but the bulk of it was built between the sixth and eighth centuries A.D., during the time of the Cola Empire, whose rulers donated their vast gold hordes to outfit "The Golden Roof" and to install Shiva as their guardian deity.

The overall temple plan is a series of high concentric rectangular stone walls. Four gateway towers, or *kopurams,* mark out the four directions in space and interrupt the walls, providing points of entry; each kopuram comprises seven tiers and stands 150 feet tall, and on either side of the gateways in the towers are carved representations of the 108 dance poses of *Bharatanatyam*. In the walkways or *pirakarams* between the concentric walls are four major shrines and ten minor ones.

The central and oldest shrine is of Lord Natarajan at the center of the concentric rectangles in the form of the *Cit Sabha* (Hall of Consciousness). This is a rectangular wooden building, called the Little Hall, twelve feet long by twenty-four feet across, set on a platform twice that size, thereby affording a porch on which many of the rituals are performed throughout the day. The porch, which is covered, is known as the *Kanaka Sabha,* or Golden Hall. Cit Sabha is the nucleus of Citamparam around which the rest of the complex grew over the centuries.

Dancing Shiva as Sivan Natarajan stands as a three-foot-high sculpted metal image in his cosmic dance poise inside the Hall of Consciousness. This temple is the innermost sanctum and Citamparam's holiest shrine; it has a glistening roof made of 17,500 solid gold tiles provided by the early Cola rulers.

The site's original Tamil name was *Cirram-palam,* which means "Little Hall," which translated into Sanskrit as *Dabhra Sabha*. The "little" might have been a reference to *dahara,* or "the minute," a reference to the little seed of the divine planted deep in the heart at this place.[238] Some Citamparam hymns to Shiva say he resides in "the Little Hall in Tillai" where "the Lord dances in the hall" day and night. It's also said that the sages who have the blessing of final bliss live in Tillai.

Umapati Sivacarya, a fourteenth-century South Indian scholar, wrote this verse in praise of the dancing god: "I adore the little hall in the midst of the fragrant groves of *tillai* trees, where the all pervading Light dances in an open space where all the world can worship, and where Visnu, who protects all the worlds, and Brahma, who sits on the lotus flower, are always in attendance."[239]

Over time, philosophical reflections on the meaning of the name were elaborated, and the Consciousness Space (or Consciousness Ether) interpretation of the site supplanted the earlier Tillai and all its ascetic nuances. People began to understand that Citamparam was the heart of Purusha, the Vedic Cosmic Man, whose body, laid out on a grid, formed the archetypal template of all temples.

Meditation at Citamparam became focused on the Heart—the heart chakra, not the physical heart—for the cosmic Purusha and its microcosmic reflection, the human. The purpose of Shiva's dance is to show that his rhythmic play is the source of all movement in *all* realms of existence and through its wild beauty can release myriads of souls from the snares of illusion, or maya.

All of this is performed in Citamparam, the place of the blissful dance and the center of the universe in the Heart. It's meant to be a shattering revelation: Shiva's rapturous dancing sends "pulsing waves of awakening sound" through matter, and this same matter dances, "appearing as a glory round about Him."[240]

Shiva is the Lord of the Dance. His movements represent the *continuous* creation, disclosure, and destruction of the world of appearances, the exquisite balance of life and death. His arms move wildly, expressing cosmic energy in its creative, expressive guise, but his head remains unmoved, signifying the unperturbed Absolute beyond time and space. The dance becomes the perfect metaphor for the creative activity underlying the universe, and the stages of the dance themselves demonstrate the matrix of spacetime.

Some hundred feet away from the Cit Sabha temple is the *Nrtta Sabha,* the Dance Hall, or "Opposite Hall." This is dedicated to the goddess Kali, who once lost a dancing contest to Shiva. The temple is set on a platform four feet high and measures twenty-four feet square. The platform sides are equipped with large wheels that create the impression of a chariot, and intricately carved pillars support a thatch-style roof. The Nrrta Sabha and Cit Sabha are believed to be Citamparam's two oldest structures and the core of the original temple complex.

Shiva is also worshipped in his formless "form," by way of the *Akasa Lingam* (pillar of light), Shiva's embodiment as formless space, as represented in the Cit Sabha as *Citampara*

Rahasyam—a representation of his emptiness and garlanded with golden vilva leaves.

Many spiritual festivals take place at Citamparam, but the two most important ones, called *Bhrammotsavams,* last ten days each and involve colorful processions of deities, hoisting of flags, recitation of hymns, and a complexly structured series of religious events. They typically attract up to 200,000 people.

The grandest of the two, which starts ten days before the full Moon between December 15 and January 15, is called the *Markali Tiruvaturai.* It's held in the Hindu month of *Markali* and under the star of Natarajan, the *Tiruvaturai.* As a winter solstice ceremony, it is meant to palliate what the Hindu astrologers regard as the inherent danger at this time of year and to inaugurate the "light" side of the year. In fact, Shiva is said to have first performed his Ananda Tandava dance at Citamparam on the day when the Moon is in the constellation Pushya.[241]

On the ninth day the statues of the god and goddess are ritually bathed in the early morning, a ceremony called *Apitekam.* Temple chariots or "grand temple cars" roll through the streets, and one of them bears the image of Nataraja. On the tenth day, *Abhisekham,* the main deities represented in the *Raja Sabha,* or thousand-pillared hall, are ritually anointed. The second *Bhrammotsavam* takes place between mid-May and mid-June and follows the same format.

MYTH AND LEGEND

Observing Shiva's dance was considered a rare privilege, even for the gods. The primordial cosmic serpent, known to the Hindus as Ananta Sesha, the couch of the sublime god Vishnu, heard of the grandeur of Shiva's cosmic dance and was filled with intense desire to see it in person at Citamparam. Vishnu had seen Shiva's spontaneous dance, so magnificent it had caught the attention of the entire cosmos. Shiva's intention had been to frighten some argumentative sages out of their fixations with a wild dance, but soon everyone watched with rapt engagement and Shiva's movements expressed the Mystery of existence.

Vishnu told Ananta that there was in fact only one place on Earth to witness this dance, so Ananta traveled underground through the snake civilization (presumably the Naga realm) until he reached the world's center at Citamparam. Ananta descended to Earth as the human Patancali (Patanjali in Sanskrit) and assumed a semi-human form: his head was human but it was set on his old snake's body. When his mother saw he was half-serpent, she dropped him in fright; hence his name: *Pat* (fell) *ancali* (from the hand). This journey, of course, was in mythic time, and, paradoxically, he *descended* from the Underworld because that dimension of reality is vibrationally *above* ours.

Then Patancali saw the dance. Patancali represents the archetype of the observer of Shiva's sublime solo dance. "Patancali is at the same time a divine witness, a symbol of the natural order, and a highly emotional human worshiper."[242]

Shiva's dance symbolizes the five divine acts or gestures of existence, namely, creation, sustenance, dissolution, concealment, and bestowal of grace. This is the Ananda Tandava pose, and the entire cosmos is his theater and self-created audience.

All the gods witness his wild dance of creation; Brahma tings the cymbals, Vishnu strikes a drum, the Gandharvas play flutes, as Shiva dances the illusion of manifestation in the hall of consciousness at the core of the universe. The myths say that from out of the pedestal on which Shiva dances there springs the "encircling glory," the *tiruvasi*, fringed with flame, and touched within by two of Shiva's four hands, one holding a drum, the other fire.

Shiva once said to one of his disciples: "The greatness of Chidambaram is most sacred and incorporates the *Rahasyam* (secret) of my *Roopam* (figure). The moment you think of Chidambaram, the sins of a *crore janmas* (births and deaths) will be washed away." People in service to Shiva there will overcome the cycle of birth, death, and rebirth, and attain liberation. Citamparam, Shiva said, is even more auspicious than his original residence on Mount Kailash in Tibet.[243]

GEOMANTIC

Dome; Emerald for Sagittarius Albion; Lucifer Binding Site.

DOME: The dome over Citamparam is the planetary starfall for the right foot of Ophiuchus, the Serpent-Holder. This star, a massive blue-white giant, is the theta star in the southern corner of the constellation. It is of the third magnitude, about seven hundred light years from Earth, nineteen hundred times more luminous than our Sun. Theta Ophiuchi is situated in the midst of a vast complex of star clouds in the Milky Way, including the Pipe Nebula.

Theta Ophiuchiu does not have a specific name, but in combination with the epsilon star, it was called *Wajrik*, or the Magician, by the Sogdian astronomers of Central Asia. Other names included *Markhashik*, the "Serpent-bitten," *Tshio*, "the Snake," *Aggia*, "the Magician," and to the Chinese, who added a few more stars to the mix, *Tien Kang*, "the Heavenly River."

Ophiuchus is the constellation of the Serpent-Holder, located near the head of Hercules and Scorpio. The constellation is usually depicted as an elderly man (corresponding to the Greek physician Asclepius) or an unclad youth standing on the Scorpion (Scorpio), holding the serpent in his hands, the tail on his right side *(Serpens Cauda)*, the head on his left *(Serpens Caput)*.

In other words, in the standard depiction of this constellation the serpent appears to be split in two. The Serpent reference in the dome star for Citamparam is appropriate with respect to the myth of Patancali, the half-serpent, half-human, who intensely desired to witness Shiva's Ananda Tandava.

The energy of this dome, working through Citamparam, creates the revelation of Being and the turning of consciousness in the infinity of space. Naturally Patancali, as the representation of Ananta Sesha, the primordial cosmic serpent, source of all phenomenal appearances, and the entire electromagnetic field spectrum of visible light (the Australian Aborigines' Rainbow Serpent), would want to witness Shiva's dance.

Patancali would watch in fascination as Shiva, the consummate snake charmer, spun Ananta's vast reservoir of astral light into the awesome turning façade of the universe. Ananta was enraptured with Shiva's sublime histrionics, as Shiva took its own essence through the fivefold dance of permutations.

EMERALD FOR SAGITTARIUS ALBION: Citamparam is the emerald, or inner esoteric heart chakra, for one of the planet's twelve major divisions of its surface. The totality of the energy picture for each of these one-twelfth surface divisions is expressed as an anthropomorphic figure called an Albion, or in Vedic terms, a Purusha, the Cosmic Man. Citampram is one of three aspects of this Purusha's heart chakra. This particular one-twelfth planetary division is currently under the astrological influence of Sagittarius; hence we call it the Sagittarius Albion.

In August, 1987, the much-publicized Harmonic Convergence, though global in scope and impact, had its center at El Tule near Oxaca in Southern Mexico, because El Tule is the site of the Earth's emerald. In that event, Quetzalcoatl, the Lord of Light, was said to return to his tree to release the millions of seeds of light from his buried

heart. The same temple structure is found repeated in twelve locations around the Earth, one in each one-twelfth surface division. Citamparam is one of these, a hologram of El Tule. At Citampram, it is *always* the Harmonic Convergence. But what kind of temple structure is this?

Shiva's dance can be appreciated as the dynamic permutation of the cosmic Heart—Purusha's Heart, or Albion's, or even Quetzalcoatl's. There are many equivalent mythic names for the same structure and function. The Shiva Ganga tank at Citamparam is physically symbolic of the sea of consciousness inside the emerald, inside the Heart. The water in the huge tank is the physical expression of the true meaning of Citamparam, the Space of Consciousness inside the emerald. Shiva's Ananda Tandava dance is the transient though captivating *expression in form* of this infinite sea of consciousness.

LUCIFER BINDING SITE: Again, the Mexican-Zapotec myth of Lord Quetzalcoatl returning to his buried heart at El Tule helps explain Citamparam. Quetzalcoatl, Purusha, Albion—they are all code names for the Lord of Light and the Light Bearer appointed by the Supreme Being: Lucifer.

There are three types of Lucifer sites: places where he is bound (incarcerated, buried in the Earth) as a consequence of the Fall of Man; places where he is being freed, released; and places where he is arriving on Earth in his original glory plumed with angels, as before the Fall of Man. Citamparam, the Space of Consciousness, is a Lucifer *arrival* site, for the emerald is the Light Bearer's heart and the emerald is also inside every human. Inside the emerald is Citamparam, the Consciousness Space.

If you have the good fortune to visit Citamparam, you could meditate on the emerald there in conjunction with your own emerald. If you participated in any way in the 1987 Harmonic Convergence, you can refresh your immersion in the Consciousness Space here at Citamparam by focusing on the emerald. Despite varied interpretations, the event took place inside the emerald. There are two ways you could do this here: visualize a very tall six-sided double-terminated emerald, its base resting at Cit Sabha or Shiva Ganga, its top high in the sky like a skyscraper. See yourself walking through one of the six facets as if it were a permeable membrane.

Or: focus your attention on the same six-sided figure, though much smaller, situated to the right of your sternum, starting at the second rib on the right and extending downwards about two inches. That is where the emerald sits in the human energy field as a kind of electromagnetic doorway out of the continuum of matter and its five chakras. Think of it as the secret room in between the outer heart chakra *(Anahata)* and inner heart *(Ananda-kanda)*.

Either approach will put you in resonance with the emerald at Citamparam. In addition, you might try focusing your attention on your Blazing Star two inches above the belly button and two inches inside. This will put you in resonance with Avebury (see Avebury, England), where the same energy tableau of the dancing Shiva is present, grounding Citamparam for the entire planet.

Earth's Blazing Star is "buried" at Avebury, just as Lucifer's emerald is "buried" at Citamparam and other sites. There is an interesting energy connection between the star and the emerald, which you may experience by focusing your attention on the star through Avebury and the emerald through Citamparam.

Clingman's Dome, Tennessee, United States

PHYSICAL DESCRIPTION

At 6,643 feet, Clingman's Dome is the second highest peak in the Eastern United States, located within the 500,000-acre Great Smoky Mountains National Park on the border of Tennessee and North Carolina, and about forty-five miles southeast of Knoxville.

Mount Mitchell, seventy miles to the northeast in North Carolina, is the tallest, at 6,684 feet. Confusingly, at one time in the mid-1800s, their names were reversed as part of a competition between Elisha Mitchell and U.S. Congressman Thomas L. Clingman to find the highest peak.[244] Mitchell, a member of the North Carolina Geologic Survey, in 1835, demonstrated that the crest of the Black Mountains in North Carolina was the highest measured point in the U.S. at that time, and he named it after himself.

But in 1855, Clingman climbed a different mountain, claimed it was higher, and named it after himself. What was once known as Clingman's Peak is now called Mount Mitchell, and Clingman's name got transferred to another peak in southern Tennessee, now called Clingman's Dome.

MYTH AND LEGEND

From the Cherokee viewpoint, the controversy between Mitchell and Clingman would have seemed inane and presumptuous.[245] They called the peak *Kuwahi'yi*, abbreviated as *Kuwahi*, which meant "Mulberry-grove place," from *ku'wa* (mulberry tree) and *hi* (locative, or place of).

The Cherokees had a myth that the chief of the bears the White Bear, lives at Kuwahi, or Mulberry place, along with many of his fellow bears, who have "townhouses" under Kuwahi and three other neighboring peaks. Kuwahi was very near to the enchanted invisible medicine lake of *Ataga'hi* (the Gall place) to which bears, other animals, and Cherokees retreated for miraculous healing. This lake was situated in the wildest part of the Great Smoky Mountains, or *Shaconage*, "mountains of the blue smoke." The bears congregate at these townhouses and peaks and hold dances every autumn before retiring to dens for their winter hibernation.[246]

The Cherokee believed that these bears were actually humans who could talk if they wished, and once, a hunter understood the words a mother bear was singing to her cub. The bears, so thought the Cherokee, are transformed Cherokee of the old clan of *Ani-Tsa-guhi*. Long ago a boy of the *Ani-Tsa-guhi* clan left his village and began spending all his time in the mountains. He told his parents he had found an excellent source of food out in the woods and preferred to live there. He convinced them (and the rest of the clan) that it would be preferable to live in the mountains where less work was required to obtain food.

After a seven-day fast, the entire clan left for the mountains, and after residing there only a short while, their bodies began to be covered with animal-like hair, and their nature was changing. They informed the people of other villages that they were never coming back because in the mountains there was always plenty to eat. "Hereafter we shall be called *yanu* (bears), and when you yourselves are hungry come into the woods and call us and we shall come to give you our own flesh." The yanu also told the Cherokee not to be afraid to kill them for they would live forever, and they taught them special songs with which to summon them.[247]

MYSTICS AND TOURISTS

It is estimated that ten million tourists visit Clingman's Dome annually, making it the most frequently visited of all the U.S. highpoints.[248] A two-lane paved road winds its way upwards for twenty miles from the Sugarlands Visitor Center to a large parking lot and a magnificent view. From there, it is a half-mile climb up a steep paved sidewalk to the final four hundred feet; at the top of Clingman's Dome is a concrete circular observation tower, rising fifty-four feet above the summit and accessed by an upward-curving ramp. Some observers have compared the observation tower to a flying saucer.

One comment consistently made by hikers—the Appalachian Trail crosses the summit—and visitors to the top of Clingman's is that the once extensive view is much diminished. Once you could look out on a clear day and see one hundred miles and seven states; now due to air pollution, that view is restricted sometimes to as little as twelve to twenty-two miles. Others remark on the widespread destruction of the spruce-fir trees around the summit, ostensibly due to an aphid infestation, acid rain, and air pollution. Specifically, the tree blight is blamed on an insect called the balsam woolly adelgid, which entered the U.S. in the late 1800s. In recent years, the trees have been sprayed with an insecticidal soap.

Originally a coniferous rainforest, "unfortunately, pests, disease, and environmental degradation threaten the unique and fragile spruce-fir forest. Dead trunks litter the area, and dying trees struggle to survive another year."[249] The ecological scene on the mountain is also described as "worse than in Detroit," a landscape "scarred by dying plants and thousands of dead trees, victims of parasites and air pollution."[250] Yet another visitor gave the matter a curious and indirectly insightful slant: "The dead firs gave a windswept look to the summit, but rather this was the work of the evil beetles which have killed almost every fir in the Black Mountains."[251]

GEOMANTIC

Dome; Labyrinth; Scorpio Albion Crown Chakra.

DOME: It is interesting to note the considerable discontinuity between the Cherokee perception of Kuwahi and that of the modern American tourist and hiker. The Cherokees spoke of the White Bear and the bear townhouses under the peak; today's visitors lament the diminished view. The disconnection between the Native American and modern American perception may be explained in large measure by the state of the dome over Clingman's Dome, an aptly, if ironically, named peak.

In September 2001, the dome over this mountain was reconnected with Avebury in Wiltshire, England, for the first time in hundreds of years. Avebury is the Earth's central switchboard for all its 1,746 domes, securing the individual domes' connection to the galactic source in Sirius and Canopus.

Through effective and intense interference, the peak of Clingman's Dome has been pushed up above the top of the dome, like a saucepan lid sitting askew at the top of the pan; in human anatomical terms, this is like a fontanel raised above the rest of the cranium. Obviously the energy integrity of the dome, under these conditions, is compromised. Present at the summit and milling insidiously about the observation tower were (until 2001) a host of astral lizards and small erect dinosaurs, emblematic of the interference. The lizards are opportunistic astral beings who move into a disturbed energy ecology and amplify that disturbance.

The whimsical reference to the observation tower resembling a UFO may be on target here. Often energy disturbances of geomantic structures that affect human consciousness are precipitated by the influence of "aliens," or extraterrestrial intelligences (ETIs) whose agenda for human evolution does not include higher spiritual evolution. Often aliens or hostile ETIs work in conjunction with ill-minded humans, such as black magicians and negativity-focused human initiates, to achieve their distortions.

Based on tourist estimates for the twentieth century, ten million humans a year have likely been exposed to that disturbed energy field, though most are probably oblivious to the energy imbalances. This might explain the dearth of accounts of the mountain's numinous aspects and the striking disconnection with the Cherokee understanding of Kuwahi. More significantly, the disturbed energy field is surely a major contributing factor to the spruce-fir tree blight.

When the energy field, or aura, of a human is disturbed or carrying foreign, toxic, or inimical energies, or has rips, tears, and deformities, illness and diminished mental well-being result. The same is true for domes, mountains, and all biological life within their field. The aphids moved in opportunistically, paralleling the lizard infestation, thriving in the ecologically unbalanced energy field of Clingman's Dome. The damaged dome, its disconnection from Avebury, and the interference of the astral lizards are energy factors supporting the spruce-fir tree blight.

An additional factor was visible to clairvoyant sight in the sky off to the southeast from Clingman's. It appeared as a twisted ankh; as if two hands had maliciously twisted and distorted the shape of the traditional Egyptian ankh, which looks like a "T" with a loop attached to its top, enabling it to be held like a key; to the Egyptians, it represented eternal life and the "key of life."

The ankh also symbolizes clairvoyant and telepathic communication, the ability to reach out across dimensions and spacetime. Distortion in the primary field of the dome produced difficulties in the clairvoyant perception at Clingman's, and created the image of the twisted ankh as a symptom of the distortion.

In mid-September 2001, the angelic realm, in cooperation with the human and elemental, repaired the damage to the dome over Clingman's, pushing down the raised fontanel, sealing the rounded top of the dome, and reconnecting it to the master dome at Avebury. The lizards were removed. The Ray Masters from Ursa Major introduced the fourteen rays to the dome as well, bringing the energy site fully back "on line" after a long absence from the Earth's "power grid."

Like a human recovering from a long illness, however, Clingman's Dome will take some time to fully regain its original numinosity. Those visiting the peak who feel inclined to contribute to this recovery would benefit the dome by focusing on their Blazing Star just above the navel, allowing it to expand, putting the mountain inside it, and breathing to it as Love from Above (for details, see part 1—Geomancy, Cosmology, and a Planet of Sacred Sites).

Obviously it doesn't benefit the Earth to have one of its domes dysfunctional. In the case of Clingman's Dome, the restoration of its function served an additional and timely function. The "rewiring" took place five days after the infamous terrorist destruction of the twin towers of the World Trade Center in New York City on September 11, 2001. Clingman's dome is a key energy center, or chakra, in the much larger regional figure called Albion, whose geomythic body occupies much of the Eastern Seaboard of the U.S.[252] Within this Albion (one of the planet's 12 such figures), Clingman's Dome is the crown center, the seat of connection with the higher worlds of consciousness.

Geomantically, more balance within Albion's cranium in this section of the Earth's energy body means that the neural energies can flow and the consciousness within this vast geomythic form can be more harmonious and less conflicted.

Think of New York City and Washington, D.C., as nodes within this huge Albion figure sprawled across a third of the U.S. An effective way for the angelic domains to help bring calming vibrations, peace, harmony, and elevated consciousness to those intensely aroused and wounded regions is by working from the energy field that oversees them all. For that to happen, though, the key geomantic features within that Albion need to be in excellent working order, which is why Clingman's Dome was repaired.

The star affiliation for the dome is with the beta star in the constellation Delphinus, the Dolphin, and located on the dorsal tail. Called Rotanev, this is a double star of the third magnitude located about 125 light years from Earth.

In ancient Greece the dolphin was known as the Sacred Fish and assumed an almost religious significance. In one instance, the Olympian god Apollo assumed the form of a dolphin to attract the attention of Cretan sailors to the oracular sanctuary of Delphi, which he wanted them to found in his behalf.

The Greek god of the Waters, Poseidon, made the dolphin into a constellation in gratitude for the marine mammal's having discovered Amphitrite, a Nereid (sea nymph) whom Poseidon wanted to marry, but who was hiding from him. The legends say Delphinus performed the wedding ceremony for Poseidon and Amphitrite. Another Greek myth honors the dolphin with saving the life of the poet Arion, whose songs charmed all the sea creatures.

The Hindus called this constellation Shishumara (later shortened to Zizumara), and assigned it a position in their own definition of zodiacal space (the twenty-eight nakshatras) that carried the attributes of "most favorable" and "richest." Arabic astronomers called the constellation Al Ka'ud, the Riding Camel, while some Christian sects saw it as the Cross of Jesus transferred to the sky after the Crucifixion. Arabic skywatchers also offered the name Al Ukud, the Pearls or Precious Stones, for this constellation, which they saw as adornment for Al Salib, their name for the Cross.

The energy of the dome over this mountain is concerned with producing the quality of a piercing through of insight and information from above, as symbolized by the dolphin's elegant leaps out of the sea and over the waves. Metaphorically, we could say this energy wants to help people leap effortlessly through dimensions.

WHO THE WHITE BEARS ARE: Now let's consider the original geomantic intention of Clingman's Dome and its relation to the Cherokee myths about the site. The White Bear is in fact discernible as a huge astral being in bear shape, approximately the size of the mountain, facing towards North Carolina. The yanu in their "townhouses" are present in the form of about twenty-four smaller astral bears. The townhouses are caves or dens accessed by arched doorways regularly spaced around the periphery of the peak at about the level of the parking lot.

As to the identity of the yanu, they are equivalent to the beings described in other traditions as Yetis, Sasquatches, and Abominable Snowmen. Even the much-liked eight-foot tall and lanky Chewbacca of *Star Wars* fame is a variation on this. These names and descriptions are different cultural filters for the same being. Ultimately what these beings look like is less important than their function.

That function appears to be as guardians of various doors in the Earth's geomantic body, such as the entry into domes, various mini-wormholes or grace notes in the energy configuration, and labyrinths. One of the more interesting theories as to the origin of these guardians suggests that they are protohuman remnants from a planet called Maldek before its ecology collapsed long ago.[253] The Yetis' protohuman aspect is reflected in the Cherokee description of the yanus as half-human, half-bear, or as bears that were once or still could be humans.

LABYRINTH: At Clingman's Dome, the bears are present at the arched doorways as guardians. They are protecting the entries into a vast labyrinth and Hall of Records contained within the dome. In a sense, the yanu are the bouncers at the gate to a special temple whose proper function has planetary ramifications. This labyrinth is one of nine different types of labyrinths found within the Earth geomantic body; another type, for example, is found at Mount Ida in Crete and is known as the Cretan labyrinth; one like Clingman's is found at Easter Island in the Pacific Ocean.

At first glance, the Clingman's Dome labyrinth seems to resemble a huge alien spaceship somehow lodged permanently inside the mountain; it also resembles a deep wide pool of water set deep within the mountain and accessed by a long ramp from the yanu doorways.

On closer inspection, what appears is a labyrinth, similar in structure to the multiple-pathed convoluted mazes often created on the landscape out of turf, bushes, or even painted on the floors of cathedrals. Any spatial description is inherently misleading, for this labyrinth is more of an energy field to be experienced; for purposes of mental convenience, one could say it has depth, curves, duration, and structure, but you have to treat these descriptions loosely.

You walk the energy labyrinth inside the dome to get your psychic and cognitive centers in resonance with the energy field of the labyrinth and the Hall of Records at its center. You could think of the labyrinth as providing a car wash for your psychic centers; as an exercise in reconfiguring your psychic apparatus in accordance with the specificities of this site's function; as a device spun and woven about your head, a sound and energy template that facilitates your psychic perception of exalted realities; or simply as affording you preparations in consciousness so you can experience what lies ahead—the Hall of Records.

This hall may at first appear in the form of a large library with Greek-style columns and an elegant marbled entryway, but this is more visual analogy than accurate description. Closer to the reality is the sense of a myriad of energy filaments coming into this place from stars, galaxies, and universes. Remember, this place is the crown center for one of the Earth's twelve Albions, so it shouldn't surprise us that Albion's crown chakra has *many* connections with higher realities including such places as Sirius, the Pleiades, and Ursa Major.

The "place" is a Hall of Records in the sense that it records stellar and universal influences and light codings that have been transmitted to this Albion over the duration of the existence of the

Earth. Again, to use a visual analogy, you could see each of these filaments as a hollow tube of a certain color; on the inside of which are many markings that seem to resemble hieroglyphics or cuneiform but are in fact notations in a light frequency language, which predates verbal, spoken, phonetic, or pictogrammic languages.

You could say it's the star language that the angelic realm uses to converse. Inside the Sirius filament you may read out the light codings by which Sirius as the brightest star in our galaxy has shaped, influenced, directed, even co-created our physical and cognitive reality. Another way to approach this definitely higher reality is to say it is the original, *Ur*-language of light frequencies that predates the Tower of Babel, which is mythic code for the creation of the original seventy-two languages of humankind (as described in classical Hebraic and Qabalistic tradition) in accordance with the seventy-two major subdivisions of continental landmasses and their corresponding seventy-two landscape angels (or minor egregors).

SCORPIO ALBION CROWN CHAKRA: The threads entering Albion's crown chakra are a data stream of cosmic information, influences, codings, and energies—celestial choreography for the sublimer functions of consciousness. When Clingman's Dome was disconnected from Avebury, the integrity of this data stream was compromised because Avebury functions as the ground in the electrical socket. An electrical analogy is helpful here. The Hall of Records at Clingman's Dome in Albion's crown center (the two prongs on the electrical socket) can plug into the celestial data stream because its third prong is properly grounded at Avebury.

Obviously, it benefits one-twelfth of the planet immediately to have the data stream flow without compromise into Albion's crown center at Clingman's Dome and to have the yanu guarding the entry to the labyrinth. When functional, the celestial data stream (Hall of Records) provides humanity, through its geomythic Albion, many options and alternatives in consciousness—lots of cosmic ideas relevant for current problems and long-term evolutionary goals.

In the days when the Cherokee used Clingman's Dome and maintained its operation, the initiated among them would collect star information and decode light frequencies on behalf of their tribe and their own development. That function is of course still germane and possible today.

Croagh Patrick, Ireland

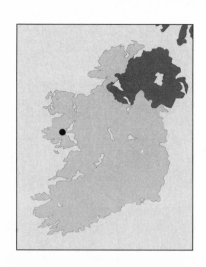

Croagh Patrick, named after the Irish Saint Patrick, is a mountainous cone of quartzite rising 2,510 feet over Clew Bay in County Mayo off the west coast of Ireland. It is regarded as the holy mountain of Ireland. From its peak you can see hundreds of islands in Clew Bay; known as the *Insule Fortunate* (the Fortunate Islands) or *Insi Modh* (a measure, of time or grain), these islands traditionally numbered 366, one for each day of the year plus one.

The original Irish name for the mountain is *Cruach Phadraig,* which means Patrick's Stack or Cone. Croagh Patrick is also called the Reek and *Cruachan Aigle,* which might derive from *aige,* which means the act of celebrating or holding festivals. In legend, the islands were understood to be the progeny of the mountain and Clew Bay the salty bog from which came the original primitive invaders and inhabitants of the island, the Fir Bolg.

The mountain's chief distinction is as an annual pilgrimage destination for Christians. Each summer around August 1 or the last Sunday in July (an ancient Celtic calendar festival called *Lughnasad,* in honor of a god of light called Lugh), an estimated eighty thousand people make a ritualized progression up the mountain.

Traditionally pilgrims would approach from the east, along the old pilgrimage road, the *Tochar Phadraig,* or the trackway of Patrick. Another old belief has it that the Friday of *Crom Dubh* (an Irish deity) at the end of July is the preferred date for the pilgrimage; confusingly, it is also given as *Domhnach Crom Dubh,* which means "Crom Dubh's Sunday." Pilgrims follow a series of stations up the mountain, many of which are known as "stone beds," because Irish legend has it that once saints slept in them.

One of the most noteworthy of rock cairns (stations) on the ascent is *Leacht Mo-Bhionnain,* "the Bed of My Benen," a reference to the "boy" of Saint Patrick. "Underlying that title, the newborn infant of the ancient goddess cries out for recognition."[254] This attribution alludes to another virtue of Croagh Patrick: it is believed to promote fertility in barren women, based on an ancient belief that long ago the "Mother Goddess" gave birth on this peak to various progeny. Infertile women who spent Lughnasadh Eve (July 31) atop the mountain in the Goddess's "bed" might be able to conceive later. Also of interest is *Tobair Phadraig,* or Patrick's Well, located near the base of the mountain; it is named in reference to a natural spring at which Saint Patrick was believed to have baptized his first Irish converts to Christianity.

The pilgrims undertake the climb of Croagh Patrick as an act of penitence and atonement for sins through intense physical sacrifice; some proceed barefoot. The climbers circle each station on the mountain seven times, including the last rock cairn before the summit, which is shaped like a burial mound, and at the top, they circle a small chapel fifteen times, confess their sins, then hear Mass.

HISTORY AND ARCHEOLOGY

What is historical about Croagh Patrick borders the legendary. The Catholic Saint Patrick, during Lent in approximately 441 A.D., drove all the serpents (demons and evil spirits as well) out of Ireland by ridding them principally from Croagh Patrick. He is said to have climbed the mountain and rung a silver bell, which caused all the snakes in the mountain to leap off the peak to their death. The Devil then transformed the snakes into crows, which Saint Patrick chased off by throwing his bell at them.

Today, either the same bell or a replica of it is brought back to the mountain once every year; pilgrims walk by the bell three times making sure the Sun is at their backs (avoiding the shadow side, which belongs to the Devil).[255] Another version of the story says Saint Patrick spent forty days and forty nights atop Croagh Patrick, banishing dragons, snakes, and demonic forces from the site.

Still another variation on the story says the snakes did not turn into crows, but into the Devil's mother, Caora (or *Corra*, which means "Female Friend," and was said to be a great bird; and also as *Caoranach*, a water serpent), who tried to enchant Saint Patrick; he resisted the beguilement and chased the Corra from Croagh Patrick to a lake called *Lough Derg* (also called *Loughna Corragh*), about seventy miles away.

There he killed the Mother of all demons and devils and its spilled blood turned the waters red.

This lake is now referred to as Saint Patrick's Purgatory and is also a focus of religious pilgrimage; it is believed that Saint Patrick entered the Underworld through a cavern on Station Island in the lake. In an inversion of the Croagh Patrick attribution, Saint Patrick is also said to have spent two days battling the *Lough Derg Caoranach* at this lake; it had been taking the form of a gigantic eel that killed everybody who came near it.

Christians understand Saint Patrick's deeds as demonstrating the potency of Christianity against all previous pagan beliefs, gods, and residues, and its ability to subdue the dark forces of the demonic world. In exorcising a Celtic god viewed as a demon or the Devil himself, Saint Patrick may have sought to replace this pagan deity with himself as the origin of the mountain's holiness, a possibility reinforced by the fact that some of Saint Patrick's contemporaries regarded him as one of the *fir sidhe,* the Celtic "gods of the [hollow] hills."[256]

MYTH AND LEGEND

As noted above, one of the names for the female demon inside Croagh Patrick was Caoranach or Corra. (*Corr* is Irish for "stork," "mountain peak," and "well or pool.") In Irish legend, Corra was known as the Great Swallower, having swallowed Cliach, a harpist playing by a stream; Cliach was an unsuccessful suitor of Bodb Derg, a son of the Irish gods the Tuatha de Danann. Corra was also chieftainness of the demonic birds who assaulted Saint Patrick while he visited her white quartz hill. She was anciently regarded as a harvest goddess and the resident mother goddess of a site known as the Reek.

Croagh Patrick was believed to be the residence of the Irish deity Crom Dubh (an Irish deity whose name means "Black Crescent") and the principal site of the Celtic harvest festival Lughnasadh on August 1, on one of the Celtic calendar's eight major turning points and festival days of the solar year.[257] In fact, another name for Lughnasadh as celebrated on Croagh Patrick was Crom Dubh's Sunday, referring to the day on which Saint Patrick overcame him (even though Crom Dubh's day was originally the last Friday of July, known as *Aoine Chrom Dubh*).

Under its ancient name of *Cruachan Aigle,* this was the peak that contained the *crochan* or pot of harvest milk that finally reaches a boil, having first been warmed about forty miles to the east in the Midsummer kitchen of Medb (an Irish female deity, whose name means "She who intoxicates"; her fortress was at Cruachain). Six months earlier at midwinter and under divine agency, the *crochan* had been made under Croghan Hill, about forty miles away in County Offaly.

This is in part archeo-astronomical code for referring to three important dates in the solar year and of how Croagh Patrick fits into this movement or collection of solar energy: August 1 (Lughnasadh) at Croagh Patrick; *Saura,* or Midsummer's Day, at Medb's Kitchen; and *Geerah,* December 22–25, at Croghan Hill.[258]

MYSTICS AND TOURISTS

The shape itself of Croagh Patrick indicates how it was "cut out to be a holy mountain," states one commentator. When you approach it from the flat plains the "sudden sight" of this great quartzite cone of a mountain creates "an unforgettable first impression." Its peak is so often shrouded in mist "it could well be imagined as communing with the ancient gods above the clouds." The peak looks down over Clew Bay in "a benign yet patriarchal fashion."[259]

One of the more common remarks of visitors to Croagh Patrick pertains to the mountain's benevolent, pacific quality. "This is a place that time has forgotten. It is a place of peace, where the only stress is the sting of wind and rain coming off the ocean." The hills, glens, and mountains are like whales, seemingly talking to one another. This same pilgrim attested to hearing "a whisper in the air, a murmur mingling with the wind's scream. It could have been God's voice."[260]

Another traveler called the mountain "a sanctuary for the giving of thanks and the celebration of life's abundance," adding that the peak is "a place to experience and give thanks for the exquisite sweetness of life." This visitor contended that the Christian overlay on the mountain has "warped, stifled, and corrupted the natural human tendency to venerate life and the Earth's beauty," and substituted these tendencies with "ideas of fear, guilt, and control."[261]

For yet another commentator, Croagh Patrick is "a truly wondrous and mystical place," one which he keeps "locked away" in his heart for whenever comfort is needed during difficult times. This pilgrim also experienced "an overwhelming sense of being close to God and of voices of the past."[262] Prayers of petition and thanksgiving will ascend to Saint Patrick in Heaven from atop his mountain, especially when offered at the Saint Patrick's statue, a shrine erected in 1928 at an early stage of the penitential path up the mountain.

GEOMANTIC

Dome; Naga City; Control Bubble.

DOME: The mountain itself has a dome over it and the surrounding environs representing S Camelopardalis, the brightest star in the constellation of the Giraffe, which is in the Northern Hemisphere and near the Pole Star. This constellation has ten stars, none brighter than fourth magnitude. S Camelopardalis lies under the giraffe's long neck. It is about twenty-eight hundred light years from Earth, four hundred times brighter than our Sun, and two hundred to three hundred times larger in diameter.

Among its forty-eight affiliate locations, this dome has a dome cap at Lough Derg, the lake in which Saint Patrick is said to have subdued the demonic snake from Croagh Patrick. Minor dragons are often placed at the larger dome caps; in this case, the offspring is not far from its "mother."

NAGA CITY: The existence of a Naga City, or Celestial City of Raksovati within Croagh Patrick explains most of the demon and snake attributions. After all, the chief denizen of Raksovati is Sesa, the cosmic serpent, and its multilayered "city" or domain of Patala (borrowing from the Vedic terminology) contains Nagas (roughly appreciated as snake-beings) and Rakshasas, which can reasonably be described as demonic-looking, although their valence, technically, is ambivalent.

In simple terms, the entire energy field of this mountain and its environs is a hologram of the cosmic serpent Sesa; its interior is conceived of as a Celestial City. Caoranach and Corra, the Great Swallower, is an apt depiction of Sesa as cosmic serpent, while Crom Dubh could be a Celtic bard's appreciation of one of the Nagas or Rakshasas. The spectral crows and attacking birds would be further partial perceptions of the denizens of Raksovati. It is appropriate that one of the chief features of the pilgrimage is the constant circumambulating of stations, rock cairns, and chapels on the mountain, as if pilgrims unconsciously were mimicking the essential energy field (a coiled serpent) of the mountain.

SAINT PATRICK'S IDENTITY: The intriguing question, however, is how much Saint Patrick's Christianizing activity at this mountain is an over-lay on the "pagan" original reality and how much is an accurate description of what he did, geomantically. One way to answer this is to understand who Saint Patrick was. He was one of the fourteen rishis, or Ray Masters from the Great Bear, specifically, the Ray Master who manages the deep, rich, bright-yellow ray. The lineage is a bit complicated but fairly easy to discern through the Vedic sources.

One of the seven primordial rishis or seers in our present age is called Kasyapa (whose name means "Vision"); he "married" the thirteen daughters of a being called Daksha (whose name means "Brilliant"). One of these "daughters" was Kadru (Chalice of Immortality), and together they produced the Nagas, Rakshasas, and other minor deities and helper spirit beings. The pivotal clue in this lineage is that the thirteen daughters (and Kasyapa's "wives") were the thirteen original dragons on the planet.

Kasyapa's job was to maintain the energy relationships between these dragons and the Earth through the specific dragon locations and their affiliates. This would include the 144 replicas or the City of Raksovati around the planet, the sites of the thirteen dragons, and the sites of the 1,053 affiliate dragons. Technically, this energy maintenance requires the periodic input of all fourteen Ray Masters to differing degrees, but on Croagh Patrick, the responsibility was handed to only one Ray Master, Kasyapa, or Saint Patrick as he was known around 440 A.D. His responsibility for maintaining the energy field of the mountain is no doubt one of the reasons he was regarded to be one of the *fir sidhe,* gods of the hills.

CONTROL BUBBLE: Did he kill the snakes, subdue the demons, and drive all the evil out of Ireland? No. This interpretation has some Christian filtering, with its deep fear of "evil" and evil's seeming monolithic intention to destroy the human soul. At the site of Tobair Phadraig, Saint Patrick's well, is a Control Bubble, or switching chamber; initiates such as Saint Patrick are allowed to manipulate the controls for the purposes of adjusting the flow of Light from the Celestial City of Raksovati into the surrounding geomantically prepared terrain. (The place is well protected and veiled and cannot be interfered with by those not invited.)

Bear in mind, this is a crude, imprecise metaphor, but Sesa the cosmic serpent must be appreciated as the repository of all potential light forms, of Light itself and all it has been, can be, and will be. Sesa is the geomythic expression of kundalini. It is so full of potentiality that some mystics have rightly described it as chaos; the Babylonian hero Marduk in slaying Tiamat the cosmic dragon was said to have overcome Chaos and allowed order to enter the world. Indra, the Vedic hero, in slaying Vrtra the cosmic serpent allowed the Waters of Life to flow into the world.

Think of Chaos, Waters of Life, and Light as equivalent words for the same light of being, and you have an idea of what Saint Patrick was doing. He was adjusting the flow of Light from the Celestial City of Raksovati at Croagh Patrick into the geomantic terrain bounded not only by the dome's full circumference and affiliate dome caps, but also by its localized expression of the Summer Country, or Avalon, as the Celts called it.

The *crochan* of boiling harvest milk obtained at Croagh Patrick is probably a reference to the Light inside Sesa's city after it has been "churned" by Saint Patrick and perhaps by Lugh himself. By regulating the flow, in effect, Saint Patrick did curtail the efflux of astral snakes, demons, and other seemingly inimical beings (the Rakshasas and Nagas) into the Irish landscape.

Only a small amount of Light is needed at a given moment because it is highly potent; that Light is also the flammable poison that Sesa will release at the end of time to burn up the world. Think of it as unconditioned, absolute consciousness, or as the awareness that burns away self-

hood and limitations of spacetime. Perhaps this is what happened to poor Cliach when he got "swallowed" by Corra.

European myths recount how the hero who killed a dragon and tasted even one drop of its blood, was instantly clairvoyant, capable of understanding all forms of speech, human or animal.[263] That clairvoyance is a cosmic awareness that encompasses the ten directions and dimensions of space, in which all the stars are inside you, so you can travel without moving, traversing vast cosmic distances instantaneously.

THE MEANING OF LUGH'S SPEAR: The Lughnasadh attribution pertains to a once annual opening of the "spillway" whereby a small amount of Light from "inside" the dome can flow into the countryside. The term means the assembly or festive commemoration of Lugh. Lugh (his name means "Light, brightness," "the Shining One," and "long-handed") was a Celtic solar hero and member (some say chief) of the Irish pantheon called the Tuatha de Danann. Another nuance to his name, *lugos,* is that it means "raven"; thus Lugh's zoomorphic emblem was the raven, which is another reason ravens (or crows) are associated with the demoness inside Croagh Patrick.[264]

Lugh had a unique Spear; it was like a lightning flash of fire, and the Spear of Lugh was one of the Four Treasures of the Tuatha de Danann, brought to Ireland for a special geomantic purpose. It was reputed to guarantee victory in any contest; it never missed its mark; it inflicted wounds which always proved mortal; and if in the wrong (inexpert) hands, it could accidentally kill princes and other mortals.

It's probably more helpful to conceive of the Spear as the initiate's mastery of an energy current, a way of channeling celestial energy into a prepared geomantic matrix, of controlling the solar fire element on a fundamental level. Metaphorically, the Spear is a way a master geomancer like Saint Patrick could "churn" the static energy of the cosmic serpent inside Raksovati and allow some of it to flow out into the land outside the mountain, like an annual *controlled* flood of a mighty river.[265]

Further, it is likely that Lugh in actuality was one of the four principal archangels (Gabriel, Michael, Raphael, and Uriel) insofar as each of the Four Treasures of the Tuatha de Danann represents archetypal, exalted, unique weapons or devices, and it is known that the four principal archangels work in concert with the Ray Masters.

Lughnasadh, either July 31 or August 1 every summer, is the one time during the year when this cosmic energy is allowed to flow in a regulated, supervised way into the Irish landscape from out of Croagh Patrick. Metaphorically speaking, on Lughnasadh, Lugh inserts his fiery spear into Croagh Patrick to invigorate its energy field.

Anyone fortunate enough to be physically present will obviously benefit from this energy infusion, and the infusion of pure consciousness it brings would be an opportune time to "repent" of one's "sins," in the sense of raising your level of insight about your affairs, actions, and character to another level, beyond the conventional domain of error and misperception, and resolving to change your mind and way of living and *seeing* the world, which, some suggest, is the authentic meaning of *metanoia,* the Greek word for repentance.

Insofar as Saint Patrick is the Ray Master charged with responsibility for Croagh Patrick, it is reasonable to expect better than average chances of conscious contact with this spiritual being (and possibly Lugh or "his" archangelic equivalent) during your stay on his eponymous mountain during Lughnasadh.

Cumae, Naples, Italy

Cumae is an ancient Greek temple complex and fortified coastal city on a promontory overlooking the Bay of Naples, ten miles northwest of Naples. The promontory is a volcanic outcrop, part of the *Campi Flegri,* or phlegrean Fields, an area of volcanic activity that derives from Mount Vesuvius, the volcano that presides over Naples.

Cumae's distinction in the classical Greek period was that it was the home of the Sibylline oracle and, by way of a series of deep caves and passageways in the outcropping, it was the famous gateway to the Underworld, memorialized by Virgil in *The Aeneid.*

The Sibyl of Cumae, said Virgil, occupied "a dark enormous cave." In fact, the entire cliffside was honeycombed, "cut out/In a cavern perforated a hundred times,/Having a hundred mouths with rushing voices" that carried the Sibyl's prophetic and usually obscure answers. The Sibyl both answered questions and acted as soul guide for those daring to enter the Underworld. Like the Oracle of Delphi, the Sibyl of Cumae was a generic position, like a priestess, and it is believed there was a succession over the years of psychically trained Sybils.

Virgil said the Sibyl sat in front of her cave, crying out to visitors that the time was nigh for them to receive information on their destiny. One of those visitors was the Trojan War hero Aeneas, who, before founding Rome and after a long journey from Troy, wished to consult with deceased friends, family, and mentors beyond "Black Dis's door [another name for the Underworld gates]."[266] The Sibyl cautioned Aeneas that it was relatively easy to get into Hades from Lake Avernus, because the gate is open night and day; the tricky part is the return: many get lost, distracted, and detained. The Sibyl's job was to guide the living adventurers through the dark way, consoling, explaining, interpreting, then ensuring their safe return to the land of the living.

Aeneas, the son of a goddess, Aphrodite, and a mortal, Anchises, was a member of the royal house of Troy. Following the Sibyl's instruction, he collected a golden bough in a wood near Lake Avernus; the golden bough is essential, the Sibyl said, and must be presented to Persephone (daughter of Zeus, wife of Hades, and Queen of the Underworld) upon entering. Aeneas, using this as a talisman and "passport," followed the Sibyl into the Underworld, presumably by walking through the cavern until it met the Gates of Hades. Once through the Gates, Aeneas principally interviewed the shade of his father, who previewed the destiny of his race and the future of Rome.

There is an actual lake (118 feet deep, two miles across) that fills an old volcanic crater called Lago D'Averno near Puteoli (or Pozzuoli), Italy, only two miles from Cumae. The Greeks called it *Aornos,* which appears to mean "without birds," possibly since no bird could live in the lake's sulfurous vapors. This site too was believed to lead to the Underworld.

Classical scholars are not clear whether this meant there were two Underworld gates in close proximity, or if somehow Cumae and Lake Avernus were part of the same portal. However, in 37 B.C., Agrippa, the Roman statesman, cut a half-mile tunnel from the lake to Cumae and called it the *Grotta di Cocceio;* it remained in use until World War II, when it was damaged.

Archeologists say the Sibyl's cave was in the Cumaean gallery, but popular tradition says the Grotto of the Sibyl was on the shore of Lake Avernus. "This is not surprising, because volcanic craters are places of power and prophecy, for they are entrances to the Underworld." The old oracular site at Lake Avernus (that predated the Greek colonists) was associated with the Moon and Night, while the new Cumaean one was dedicated to Apollo and the Sun.[267]

HISTORY AND ARCHEOLOGY

When Virgil said that the Cumaean cave had one hundred mouths, it was not strictly poetic license, for modern archeology has physically validated some of his account. One cave, excavated in the 1920s, was a huge gallery six hundred feet long, with light shafts and cisterns on the side; archeologists decided this one had been built by the Roman military and was not the Sibyl's cave.

A second cave nearby was discovered in 1932, and this one is a gallery 350 feet long, with twelve short side galleries (reminiscent of the interior design of megalithic barrows). This gallery terminates with a vestibule and two stone benches, and beyond these, a vaulted chamber; archeologists credited this second cave as the Sibyl's and proposed that those awaiting a prophecy from the Sibyl would wait at the benches before being summoned within.

The Sibylline caves are the lowest of three installations at Cumae. At the top of the promontory, a Temple of Jupiter (Zeus) once stood; possibly it was once a seafarer's landmark, but only the remains of the ancient acropolis remain, and those may not have been the original foundations. The ruins you can see at Cumae today date from a building from the fifth century B.C., that was reconstructed sometime between 27 B.C. and 14 A.D., and then converted in the sixth century into a Christian church. Lower down the hill but still above the Sibylline caves there was once a Temple of Apollo, the Olympian god of prophecy, among other attributes.

Cumae was founded by Greek colonists from Chalcis and Cyme around 740 B.C., and according to the Greek geographer Strabo, Cumae was the first of all Greek colonies established in Italy or Sicily. Once established, Cumae became a considerable commercial center overseeing maritime trading routes and interior commerce as well. It resisted an attack by Etruscans in 474 B.C., but then was overcome in 420 B.C. by the Samnites; in 340 B.C., the Romans captured it. Their idea for Cumae was to turn it into a seaside resort to be frequented by Roman politicians, but later the site assumed military uses, and in 1205 it was destroyed by the Neapolitans as retaliation against pirates in the Bay of Naples.

Dominating the Bay of Naples is the formidable Mount Vesuvius (or Vesuvio Volcano, as Italians call it), formidable not so much in terms of height (it is forty-two hundred feet tall), but in terms of its eruptive ferocity as a still potentially active volcano. Vulcanologists still regard it as one of the planet's most dangerous and deadly volcanoes, as do, perhaps only subconsciously, the half-million Italians who live in a near-continuous belt of towns and villages around the volcano and within the danger zone of another eruption.

Vesuvius, whose oldest datable stones are estimated to be three hundred thousand years old, was responsible for the spectacular demise under a lava flow of Pompeii and Herculaneum in 79 A.D. Pompeii was buried under ten feet of what vulcanologists call tephra, while Herculaneum was covered by seventy-five feet of ash. Vesuvius has erupted at least twenty-one more times since then, notably in 472, 1631, and 1944. Apparently, in the millennia before Pompeii's destruction, Vesuvius erupted spectacularly at least twice (5960 B.C. and 3580 B.C.).

Naples is also of keen interest to any understanding of Cumae on account of its founding myth. The city's original name of Neapolis was Parthenopaea or simply Parthenope, after the name of one of the three legendary Sirens.[268] Italians recognized three Sirens, including Leucosia (White Goddess), Ligeia (Bright-Voiced), and Parthenope (Virgin), although Homer and other European mythic accounts have different numbers and names.

The myths say that the Sirens were the daughters of either Phorcys the sea god or Achelous the river god, but Ovid says they were once ordinary women, companions to Persephone. When she was abducted by Hades and taken into the Underworld, they asked the gods to give them wings to help search for their now lost companion. Later, in jealousy, Aphrodite may have deprived them of their beauty and the Muses may have stripped them of their feathers. Or: they might have been mermaids, beautiful females with a fish torso below the waist, or a gorgeous woman's face and a bird's body below the neck.

Classical sources attribute the dwelling of the Sirens to only one place, the Island of Anthemoessa near the southwestern coast of Italy, where their ravishingly seductive music enchanted and besotted sailors to their peril and often death. One played the lyre, another the flute, and the third sang, and her songs included prophecies relating to Hades' Underworld. Somewhat contrary to this nuance is the allegation that the Sirens sometimes sang and played celestial harmonies for the blessed in the Islands of the Blessed. The Siren Parthenope is said to have been buried in what is now Naples, which subsequently grew up around and expanded outwards from her tomb.

MYTH AND LEGEND

Greek legend claimed that the Greek colonists were guided to Cumae by a dove sent by Apollo Archagetes so they could establish the first Greek colony in Italy in 740 B.C. One of their initial actions at Cumae was to construct a Temple of Apollo on the acropolis that overlooked the Bay of Naples. Virgil, however, said that the temple was built by Daedalus, the architectural prodigy and demigod who had built the Cretan labyrinth at Knossos on Crete. After he fled King Minos of Crete, Daedalus retreated to Cumae, where he "laid out a spacious temple," Virgil recounted.

But who was the Sibyl? Apparently, the original Sibyl was a soothsayer and psychic female living at Marpessus near Troy in Turkey; she used her gift of prophetic utterance in service to Apollo. In fact, as at Delphi, Apollo was credited as the source of the prophecies. Later her name became the generic term to describe this activity as a priestess function.

The Sibyl of Cumae was called Deiphobë, daughter of Glaucus, a sea god, although she is also referred to as Amalthea, Demophile, or Herophile. Some antique authorities claim that Deiphobë was identical with another famous Sibyl, a semidivine woman called Erythrae who was based in Lydia. Her father had been a shepherd of Mount Ida near Troy, and her mother a nymph; this Sibyl reportedly lived for 990 years.

The Sibyl had the annoying habit, in the supplicants' view, of writing her prophecies in Latin only on oak leaves, which tended to get blown away, damaged, mixed up, or were unreadable. Aeneas specifically asked her to make an exception and "chant them aloud." The Cumaean Sibyl once offered Tarquinius Superbus (534–510 B.C.), the last of the seven kings of Rome, nine volumes of her prophecies; when he persisted in dickering over the price—she wanted three hundred pieces of gold—she progressively burned the books until only three remained.

That closed the deal, although Tarquinius had to pay the three hundred gold pieces for only three books, and the Sibylline books were deposited in subterranean chambers of Capitoline Hill in Rome, where they were frequently consulted when insight was needed to rationalize extraordinary or baffling events, such as earthquakes, pestilence, fearsome omens, and phantom ships in the sky. Unfortunately, they were destroyed in 83 A.D. when the temple of Jove Capitolinus burned down.

Legend has it that Apollo once propositioned the Sibyl, promising to grant her anything provided she become his lover. She said she would like as many years of life as there are grains of dust in a sweeping. That came to one thousand years, but she forgot to ask for perpetual youth at the same time. She aged so drastically that she became so small, shriveled, and wizened she hung from the ceiling of her cave in a bottle, somewhat like a cicada, wishing she were dead. Presumably, Aeneas visited her before she entered her bottle phase.

GEOMANTIC

Dome Cap; Avalon; Dragon; Underworld Entrance; Landscape Zodiac.

DOME CAP: The Cumae promontory is energized by a dome cap from one of the two domes over Mount Vesuvius. Seen from Cumae, the two domes actually look like two mountains joined at the hip. Vesuvius has two domes because it is the gateway for a Landscape Zodiac, and most zodiacs have a double-domed portal. This mountain's two domes overlap, creating an almond-shaped blending zone in the middle between them.

The lower hump of the mountain is the starfall for alpha Volantis in the constellation Piscis Volans, or the Flying Fish, located in the Southern Hemisphere skies. The alpha star sits on the fish's tail. It is not one of the classically defined constellations; instead, it was identified and delineated after 1600. The astronomer Johannes Kepler called it Passer, the Sparrow. The alpha star is fourth magnitude, located about seventy-eight light years from Earth.

The higher hump of Mount Vesuvius is the starfall location for beta Vulpecula, the Fox. Its full name is *Vulpecula cum Ansere,* which means "the Little Fox with the Goose." In Italy, it's known as *Volpe colla Oca;* in Germany as *Fuchs;* in France as *Petit Renard avec l'Oie.* Like Volans, it is a relatively newly named constellation, not part of the original classical eighty-eight constellations. As a constellation, it is a zigzag formation of principally five stars of fourth magnitude and fainter, although a total of twenty-seven, thirty-seven, or sixty-two stars have been assigned to it by different astronomers. The constellation's small primary star of 4.4 magnitude in the Fox's head is provisionally called Anser.

The essential energy of these stars working through Mount Vesuvius and its many dome caps (ninety-six), including Cumae, is vigorous uplift, raising one up quickly into the spirit. Obviously this description corresponds neatly with the mountain's volcanic activity, but that vigorous, even explosive, physical activity is paralleled by a similar quality on the spiritual level, to do with

Cumae's function as one of the classical world's prime Underworld Entrances. It seems ironic (though it isn't) that a portal into the Land of the Dead should be uplifting.

AVALON: The identification of an Avalon at Cumae helps us understand the identity of the Sirens. They are the Hesperides under another name: they are the seductive otherworldy female emissaries from the paradisiacal land variously named the Summer County, *Tir Nan'Og* (Land of the Ever-Young), *Tir na mBeo* (Land of the Living), Land of Promise, Land of Youth, and *Tir na mBan* (Land of Women)—all better known as Avalon, one of the eight Celestial Cities.

In Greek myth, the Hesperides were the daughters of the Titan Atlas and Pleione (of the Pleiades), and they lived in and tended a garden of golden apple trees in the far West, out near the Islands of the Blessed. The apples were a gift from Zeus' wife, Hera, and a dragon named Ladon guarded the entry into the orchard and thus the apples as well. Appropriately, for our interpretation of the Sirens, the Hesperides' prime recreation was singing.

We need to approach the Cumae geomantic temple in terms of its overall function, for it has several overlapping yet hierarchically related layers. The first is the Avalon, which is best conceived as encircling the Phlegrean Fields entirely, extending a few miles into the Bay of Naples westward to the Island of Anthemoessa (or its etheric equivalent), eastward to include the tomb of Parthenope around which Naples was founded, and north to encompass Lake Avernus. Everything in this large circle is part of the Cumaean Avalon; you can enter it at the Island of Anthemoessa or Parthenope's tomb, which was not a burial site so much as it was a gateway.

The Sirens sing, lure, and seduce any who hear them because that is the spiritually ravishing nature of Avalon. In the Hindu equivalent, called the Celestial City of Gandhavati, there are lovely dancing women called Apsaras and heavenly musicians called Gandharvas, and they dance and play music continuously. In the Germanic mythos, there is the Venusburg, the subterranean grotto and pleasure palace of the love goddess Aphrodite (the Roman Venus).

In the Celtic milieu, Avalon is peopled by Morgan and her eight priestesses, and it is the delightful, timeless land in which the young magial apprentice Vivien seduced and detained the magus Merlin. In Irish myth, during Cormac mac Airt's trip to *Emain Ablach* from the Hill of Tara, he collects a shining branch with nine red gold apples that produce soft sweet music that delights, enchants, soothes, lulls to sleep. Avalon is a paradisiacal realm in whatever mythic vocabulary you use to conceptually approach it.

Entry into Avalon, however, is usually by express invitation of one of its comely denizens, which is a mythic way of saying your level of initiation qualifies you for entry. You have to be able to cognize it. Of course, the Sirens, or the Hesperides, are circumspect about who wanders through their orchards, for the trees laden with golden apples are a precious commodity, not to be squandered. This is where Aeneas collected his golden bough as a passport into Hades: he snapped a limb off one of the golden apple trees in the Avalon at Cumae. Since the Cumaean Avalon is circular, it is not inconsistent to say that Aeneas entered it from the north at Lake Avernus; it actually doesn't matter which direction you use to enter.

DRAGON: Just as Ladon was the dragon said to guard the golden apple orchards of the Hesperides, so at the Cumaean Avalon is a dragon charged with a similar task. One of the Earth's 1,053 minor dragons, it can be seen as positioned approximately in front of the Cumaean promontory, wedged in between the Island of Anthemoessa (or its etheric equivalent) and the Phlegrean Fields. Technically, it faces all directions at once, yet its prime attention is also placed at the two gateways into Avalon.

The Cumaean dragon qualifies and validates candidates for admission into the orchards. It energizes the dome lines from Mount Vesuvius, keeps the negative-positive polarity in the lines balanced, and provides a kind of pre-Sybilline oracular insight to the persevering geomythic questor who is preparing for an entry into the Underworld.

UNDERWORLD ENTRANCE: Cumae is an excellent example of why it is often geomantically correct to take a myth at face value. If the myth says a particular named place was a gateway into Hades, there is a good chance it really was. At Cumae, we have, perhaps, the classical world's preeminent Underworld Entrance. From a geomantic viewpoint, a main reason for this prominence is the superimposition of an Avalon with the Underworld Entrance. It's a practical consideration: you can get your golden bough at the same place where you have to present it for entry.

Most classical sources, especially the Greeks, tend to paint the road into the Underworld as one of dim twilight and gloom, a trip best avoided by the living except under dire circumstances or when one is more or less ordered by the gods to make the visit, as were Odysseus and Aeneas. The "black gates of Dis" are actually of a radiant crystal with a pearly sheen. With your golden bough in hand, they open for you, even if you are among the living, and you pass through into what may appear to be a huge circular foyer, like the anteroom of a great opera house.

Before you on the towering wall loom three massive faces, as if the visages of three gods had been frozen in stone. These are the Three Judges of the Dead, known to the Greeks as Minos, Rhadamanthys, and Aeacus. Beyond them, on the other side of the formidable wall, is what the Persian mystics called the Chinvat Bridge that spans the abyss of Hell and leads into Purgatory

and Heaven. That is where the City of the Dead truly begins, and it is the entry into the Seven Heavens as described in many mythic traditions.

LANDSCAPE ZODIAC: The Naples-Cumae temple is a complex and rich geomantic initiation site. To use it correctly, you start by preparing yourself in the Landscape Zodiac that is about fifteen miles wide and situated between Mount Vesuvius and the Phlegrean Fields (including some of the internal Bay of Naples that envelops the city). That zodiac, incidentally, is topped by a thirty-three-mile-wide zodiac dome that energizes the entire area of the ninety-six dome caps from Mount Vesuvius as well as the mountain itself.

I use the words "preparing yourself" advisedly, for entering the Underworld is not an event you undertake casually. For one thing, the place is mislabeled; it is not below the Earth, as in, of a lower order of being or spiritual vibration. Experientially, it is *above* the Earth.

It should more properly be called the Upperworld because you access it through your crown chakra, and in the hierarchy of the eight Celestial Cities, as described by classical Hindu mythology (and referenced elsewhere in this book in terms of the eight aspects of Camalate), it is a crown chakra energy point. After all, Hades, in his Roman name of Pluto, was the Rich One, the Good Counselor, the Hospitable, the Zeus of the Underworld. His kingdom was not necessarily a dreary jail at the end of biological life, but a portal to higher revelation and cosmic insight among the ever-living souls who dwelled there.

And the Sibyl? Certainly on one level she was a living human female psychic and prophetess who functioned in some respects as a spiritual counselor and possibly as a soul guide. But at another level of reality, the Sibyl was an otherworldly guide, whose primary locus of reality was the Underworld. Perhaps she was an aspect of the Queen of the Underworld, Persephone, herself; after all, the myths say she was once a woman living on Earth before her abduction, but now as Queen of the Dead she would know both realms well enough to be an effective, valuable counselor for daring travelers.

In an equivalent tale from the Celtic mythic world, the Green Knight, who is Hades in a Celtic guise, has a wife who acts as a counselor behind the scenes to the Arthurian Knight Sir Gawain, who must prepare to have his head chopped off—confront the reality of death in the Green Knight's temple—as an initiation. The unnamed Lady shows Gawain ways to cut a few corners and possibly save his life in his encounter with the Death God, the Green Knight in the Green Chapel. She doesn't demand a golden bough from Gawain, but she does expect knightly courtesies and a kiss.

To use the Naples-Cumae temple, you start close to Mount Vesuvius, work the Landscape Zodiac, experience and reconcile the astrological energies in yourself, enter the Avalon for a golden bough, then enter the Cumaean cave to encounter the Underworld Entrance.

Physically, the caves concentrate, sharpen, and focus your concentration. You will not find the Underworld Entrance as a literal edifice somewhere deep in the galleries, but you will find it easier in the caves to shift your cognitive state so that you can apprehend the Underworld Entrance, which, from a certain vantage point, is the height of the Cumaean promontory and then some. In other words, use of the caves is optional; it heightens awareness, but you can also, if your attention is focused, enter from outside as well—even, once you become familiar with the energies, from a distance.

Cusco, Peru

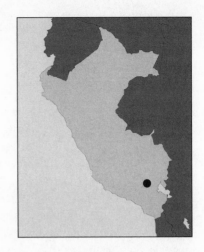

Today it's a high-altitude Peruvian city of some 300,000 people in the southeastern corner of the Andean nation, but in an earlier time it was the navel of the Incan world and the utmost core of the vast Incan empire in South America.

That empire was known as *Tawantinsuyu*, which means "the Four Quarters of the Earth." Cusco, at an elevation of 11,150 feet, was its heart, and the heart of that heart was the *Coricancha*, the Golden Courtyard, a magnificent temple whose walls were lined with seven hundred solid gold sheets each weighing four pounds. Today all that remains of this is some stonework (parts of a once extensive Incan wall) and the site is occupied by the Catholic monastery of Santo Domingo.

A seventeenth-century chronicler named Garcilaso de la Vega left us a vivid account of the Sun disc. It was a sheet of gold twice the thickness of the slabs on the temple walls; the Sun god was represented by a round face surrounded by darting flames, all made from a single sheet of gold. "It was so big that it took up the entire forward part of the temple, extending all the way across from side to side."

On each side of the Sun disc face were the "children" of the Sun, namely, the embalmed bodies of the dead Incan kings, but embalmed in such a way that they seemed to be still alive; they sat on golden thrones set on golden girders. A golden cornice made of planks a yard wide surrounded the entire Coricancha like a crown, wrote de la Vega.[269]

All of Cusco is rightfully regarded as a holy city, even today, but it was especially so at the height of its influence before the Spanish Conquest in the sixteenth century. The chief reason for this spiritual preeminence is Cusco's *ceque* system, which imparts sacrality to the entire landscape surrounding the city. The Coricancha, or Temple of the Sun, was the center and in a sense the source of a great radiating wheel with forty or forty-two spokes formed by ceques (rays or lines).

Cusco was the junction of the Tawantinsuyu, by which the Cuzco valley was divided into four parts, or *suyus*, each with its own name, and each with its royal road emanating from Cusco. The forty-two *ceques* further dissected these four regions on their way to the mountains. Cusco, for the Incas, was "the axis and center of Andean cosmological order."[270] This should not be surprising since the city's very name, *qosqo*, means navel and implies the Earth's umbilical point.

Each ceque spoke of the great wheel extended from the core of the city out into the landscape towards the surrounding mountains. This extension penetrated what is now referred to as *El Valle Sagrado,* or the Sacred Valley of the Incas, situated about six miles north of Cusco in the Urubamba River valley. As many as 328 (some count 365) *huacas,* or shrines, were set on these straight-running lines of alignment, in a manner similar to the British ley lines on which churches, wells, and megalithic sites were set out like beads across the countryside.

Although Machu Picchu (discussed elsewhere in this book) is not part of the ceque system, it is only forty miles away, to the northwest, and many visitors use Cusco as a staging ground for their visit to the mountaintop ruins of Machu Picchu. As for the *huacas,* the term suggests "a sacred place in the landscape, an opening in the body of Pacha Mama where the living mother earth can be fed sacrifices to the ancestors who live inside her."[271]

Our knowledge of the Cusco ceque system comes from the Spanish chroniclers, specifically a Jesuit scholar named Bernabe Cobo, who described it in his 1653 work, *Historia del Nuevo Mundo (History of the New World)*. The Incas kept no written records so we are, ironically, indebted to the sixteenth-century Spanish colonialists who both destroyed and recorded Incan civilization, which at its height was believed to comprise an empire of six million people and a territory that extended from Colombia in the north to Chile in the south.

Among the first things the invading Spanish did was to strip the Coricancha of all its gold, to shut down all "idolatrous" Incan activities, and to execute the *Villea Umu,* the chief priest of the *Templo del Sol,* as the Spanish called the Coricancha. They also desecrated, then physically destroyed, most of the huacas, erecting in their place a Christian cross as a symbol of Spanish authority.[272]

One thing the Spanish couldn't destroy and could hardly alter was the Incan belief that the original city of Cusco and its buildings were laid out to represent the figure of a puma, or Andean mountain lion. You can still see the puma outline when you study a street map or aerial photograph of Cusco.

The ruins of Sacsaywaman on the hill overlooking Cusco in the north (a ten-minute taxi ride from the city) represent the puma's head, and this site certainly provides an excellent view of the Cusco valley. Prominent in this view are the jagged peaks of *Pachatusan* (Fulcrum or Crossbeam of the Universe), the tallest of the mountains visible from Cuzco. From the Coricancha, the winter solstice Sun rises directly over Pachatusan.

The name Sacsaywaman means variously "Speckled Falcon," "Royal Eagle," "Speckled Head," or "Satisfied Falcon," although one Spanish chronicler called the hill "Storehouse of the Sun." The name generally suggests, however, that the head of the Cuzco puma was a speckled head on the hill of Sacsa Uma.

The site might have been a defensive fortress, but it also clearly had religious functions. The striking zigzag configurations of the outer walls might have represented the puma's teeth; the three parallel zigzag ramparts on the hill's north flank extend for one thousand feet, divided into twenty-two "salients," or outwardly projecting parts, and at the angular summit of each stood a massive stone.

In fact, the fortress at Sacsaywaman consisted of three parallel walls, each 330 yards long, and the outer wall has stones that measure fourteen feet high by twelve feet wide, and ten feet high by six wide. One of the biggest stones at Sacsaywaman's outer walls was estimated to weigh 351 tons and to stand about twenty-five feet tall.

The precision fitting of the massive stones is exquisite and impossible to account for. Although most of the buildings are now gone and only about twenty percent of the original structure remains, the Spanish invaders said the site when fully standing could house five thousand people. There were three massive round towers, the base of one of which, called *Muyuc Marca*, measured some sixty-five feet in diameter.

Nobody knows who shaped and fitted these massive stones. The Incas didn't know when interviewed by the Spanish colonialists. As one archeologist concluded in 1911 after visiting the ruins, the walls must be the legacy of a far distant Andean civilization, part of "the megalithic age, when cyclopean stones were transported and cyclopean edifices raised."[273] An earlier Spanish commentator noted: "These walls . . . are of such big stones that no one who sees them would say that they have been placed there by the hand of man."[274]

In 1536, Sacsaywaman was the center of the Inca's last stand against Spanish conquistador Francisco Pizarro's occupying troops in a rebellion led by the last native king, Manco Inca. The Incas were defeated, thousands were slain, and their empire was at an end. Cusco, the continent's oldest continuously inhabited city, went into centuries of decline and low profile until the modern tourist industry revived interest—gradually since 1911 with the discovery of nearby Machu Picchu and more conspicuously since the 1980s with the growing interest in indigenous peoples and eco-tourism.

The Coricancha once stood in the puma's tail section of Cusco. Its name is also given sometimes as *Qoricancha*, which may mean "Resplendent Gold." The original Spanish conquistadors—some would call them shameless looters—reported the existence of a magnificent golden disc of the Sun that was said to cast golden-tinted sunlight into the Coricancha. There was a corresponding silver disc of the Moon; both vanished without trace.

Not only was the Coricancha a spiritual headquarters, housing some four thousand priests, but it was the Incas' primary astronomical observatory. The early Spanish chroniclers noted

the existence of large standing stones called *sucancas* positioned on the horizon settings of nearby mountains; the Cusco *Tarpuntaes*, or royal astronomers, presumably used these monoliths for marking the horizon azimuths for the winter and summer solstices.

Strange, unverifiable stories are floated about the mysteries of the Coricancha. One is that the Sun disc was an initiatory artifact preserved from far earlier times on Earth from the supposed vanished continent and civilization called Lemuria. The Sun disc was stored secretly near Lake Titicaca (a high-altitude lake on the border of Peru and Bolivia) until the Incas proved themselves adept in handling its energies. When the Spanish arrived, the Sun disc was withdrawn from public sight and knowledge.

Another story, with somewhat more substantiation, is that a tunnel network connects the Coricancha with Sacsaywaman, and that it was once used to store Incan gold. The place where the tunnels began was called *Chincana*, which meant "the place where one gets lost," and early archeologists and independent researchers reported strange caverns burrowing deep into the Earth near Sacsaywaman. The Chincana was "so huge, so complicated, and its passages are so manifold, that its secret has never been discovered."[275]

Farther down the city's central axis is the Plaza de Armas, a large plaza with a cathedral, but in Incan times, this was called the Aucaypata. The adjoining Cusipata, an enormous dual plaza, was divided by the Saphy, one of Cusco's two rivers. The Aucaypata was the setting for numerous Incan ceremonies, and was the hub of the four main roads that proceeded from Cusco to the Inca empire's four territorial divisions, the *suyu*. In addition, another twenty roads linked the city to the outlying districts, but these four overshadowed the others in importance because they linked the four divisions to Cusco.[276]

Sacsaywaman, though in ruins, is still the focus of an annual Sun festival called *Inti Raimi,* celebrated just after the winter solstice (for the Southern Hemisphere) on June 24 in honor of the Inca Sun God, *Inti Raimi.* The festival symbolizes and reiterates the celestial marriage of Sun and Inca, the Sons of the Sun. As many as 200,000 people assemble at Sacsaywaman, sometimes referred to as Sacred House of the Sun, after a procession from the Coricancha, and some five hundred actors perform scenes from Incan myth and legend.

MYTH AND LEGEND

The legendary history of Cusco is intimately tied up with the mythic account of the origins of the Incas, which is placed farther to the southeast at Lake Titicaca.

Lord Viracocha, the Inca creator god, was said to have emerged from Lake Titicaca to create humanity, as well as the Sun, Moon, Mother Earth, all the stars, and everything else. He created these on an island in the lake called the Island of the Sun, and out of this island rose the Sun in all its splendor. Viracocha created *Inti* the Sun god and *Mama-Kilya* the Moon god at Lake Titicaca, and afterwards traveled the Andean countryside as a cultural hero teaching humans the arts of civilization.

It is also said that the ancestors of the Incas arose from a place called *Pacariqtambo* (the inn or house of dawn, or place of origin, from *pacariq,* "dawn or origin" and *tambo,* "place of lodging"), which was a cave in a mountain, no longer extant, once called *Tambo Toco* (the house of openings or windows), believed to have been about sixteen miles south of Cusco. The Incan ancestors (four men and four women who were brothers and sisters) came out of the central window, *Capac Toco,* into the present world.

The oldest brother, Manco Capac (Supreme Rich One) traveled to Cusco with his sister-wife, MamaOcllo, and arrived at the plaza of Huanaypata in the core of what would become the city. Some versions of the story say he was dispatched there by his father the Sun and told that wherever his golden rod sank fully into the ground would be the intended place.

Once at Cusco, Manco Capac plunged a golden rod or staff into the ground—some accounts say it was marshy—until it disappeared, thereby establishing the site as *qosqo,* the "Earth's navel," in the Quechua language. The exact foundation site for Cusco was called *cuzco cara urumi,* or "uncovered navel stone." Manco Capac's original wooden staff was at some point transformed into a golden scepter called *tupayauri,* given to him by his father Viracocha. Manco Capac became the first *Sapan Intiq Churin,* or "Only Son of the Sun," or simply, *Sapan Inka,* the Inca or King, deriving his legitimacy from Inti and Viracocha.

By plunging his staff into the soft ground at Cusco, Manco Capac "performed the godlike task of establishing 'the depth of waters,' the irreducible task of any god who would claim the legitimate right to 'rule' a new age," explains William Sullivan in his insightful book, *The Secret of the Incas.*

Sullivan says that Manco Capac copied Viracocha's primordial world-founding gesture at Lake Titicaca and later at Tiahuanaco in Bolivia, whose original name, *taypicala,* meant "the rock in the center." Manco Capac, whose name is translated by Sullivan to mean "he who measures by palms the depth of waters," thereby established the *axis mundi* of the new Incan age.

Sullivan offers an archeo-astronomical interpretation of Cusco's ceque system. He says the forty (the exact number is uncertain) ceques symbolized the totality of a world age, the Inca under Viracocha, bounded by the forty planetary conjunctions of Jupiter and Saturn. Forty such conjunctions complete a "trigon" between these two planets, after which, having returned to their set point, they begin the cycle over again. These planets conjoin every twenty years; thus a full cycle equals eight hundred years.

In 1444, the Jupiter-Saturn conjunction replicated the trigon after eight hundred years from 794, but there was something extra to this one. Saturn and Jupiter, says Sullivan, came back into conjunction for the first time since 650 A.D., in the same place in the starfields that they had been when Viracocha "left the Earth," his creative acts concluded, according to Incan myth. In a sense, this heralded the demise of Viracocha's domain at Cusco.

The ceques' practical value lay in affording the Incan astronomers a way of monitoring "the flow of precessional time" over the centuries, Sullivan adds.[277]

Manco Capac and his brothers were not ordinary human mortals: one brother named Ayar Cachi was so violent that he destroyed whole mountains and was entombed for eternity; another brother sprouted wings and flew into the Sun; a third brother turned into a stone on Wanacauri mountain, making it one of the foremost huacas (sacred sites). Manco Capac, not to be outdone by this family of prodigies, founded the Inca empire. It's said that when he died, he turned to stone at the site of the Coricancha, thus ensuring his perpetual presence there.

But it is also recounted that the great Lord Viracocha himself journeyed to Cusco and summoned up out of the Earth a great leader named Alcavicca, whose name was later given to the race of people living in the Cuzco area when the Incas first arrived.

Nobody is clear when all these deeds happened, other than to say in mythic time. Events with somewhat more historical probability have been attributed to a fifteenth-century Inca chief in

Cusco named Pachacuteq. In 1438, Cusco was attacked by the Chancas tribe, and the Cusco forces only barely won victory against them.

The story goes that the stones on the nearby mountains came to the aid of the Cusco forces and that the god Viracocha himself lent a hand to help Pachacuteq preserve Cusco from destruction by the Chancas. In commemoration of this celestial intervention, Pachacuteq erected a statue to Viracocha and installed it in the Coricancha.

Pachacuteq (Shaker or Transformer of Earth) is credited with completely rebuilding Cuzco, constructing Sacsaywaman, the nearby holy sites of Ollantaytambo and Pisac, and even Machu Picchu. He also is credited with having laid out the new Cusco in the shape of a puma, Sacsaywaman at its head and at the opposite end, where the city's two rechanneled rivers came together, the tail, an area still called *puma chupan*, or "puma's tail."

As one chronicler commented, Pachacuteq "named the whole city 'lion's body,' saying that its residents were limbs of that lion."[278] The Spanish apparently used the term lion as being interchangeable with the Andean lion.

Pachacuteq is further credited with establishing the Incan empire of Tawantinsuyu with its four major divisions. This would mean, however, that the Inca empire flourished and fell all in one century, its downfall culminating with the Spanish conquest in 1532. Given the size of many of the megaliths at Sacsaywaman and Machu Picchu and the fact that the larger the stone the greater its antiquity, Pachacuteq's claim may be considerably inflated and inaccurate.[279]

GEOMANTIC

Dome; Ixion's Wheel; Solar Logos Residence; Egregor Grounding Point; Camalate Center; Cyclopean City; Crown of the Ancient of Days; Mount Olympus.

DOME: The star affiliation for the Cusco dome appropriately coincides with the prime mythic attribution that its layout conforms to the shape of a puma. The dome star for Cusco is star 15, a fourth magnitude star in the head of the Lynx (or Tiger), a constellation of nine fairly faint stars near the forefeet of Ursa Major and Leo Minor in the Northern Hemisphere. It could also be stars 2 or 12, attributed in some star maps to the head as well.

This star 15 doesn't have a name in the primary Western or Arabic star-naming systems, nor does any mythology describe its nature, although one of the Greek astronomers alluded to some stars near the Great Bear's feet. The Lynx constellation, at least for our times, was "discovered" and described fairly recently, in 1687, by Johannes Hevelius, who assigned it nineteen stars.

Supposedly he named it the Lynx because only those with lynx-like eyes could find its faint stars in the heavens, most of them sixth magnitude. Perhaps he was glossing the older Roman myth, recounted by Ovid, in which a jealous and scheming king named Lyncus was transformed into the constellation of the Lynx just as he was about to slay a goddess's charioteer. The goddess Demeter punished Lyncus by placing him in a stretch of the heavens so dimly lit that one needed the eyes of a lynx to see it. "Thus savagery and arrogance were rewarded by relegation to insignificance."[280] It is quite likely that the Incas had their own star myth about the constellation Lynx, but as yet it has not come to light.

One prime geomantic function of the Cusco dome is to establish a chakra template that runs from approximately the Plaza de Armas, site of the Cathedral and the root center (formerly the Aucaypata), or perhaps even closer to the place where the two rivers meet at the far end of the city, along Avenida Sol through the Coricancha and on to the ruins of Sacsaywaman. The Coricancha, or Golden Enclosure, is the solar plexus in this template of energy.

IXION'S WHEEL: The Coricancha is the physical marker for an astral Sun wheel at that site although the wheel has an energy influence over most of Cusco.

Within an inner plane temple at this site, which tends to resemble a glass-domed building, there is a golden cross at the base of a golden spindle or bore. It may appear as a golden sarcophagus set next to a giant vertical Sun disk; or you may see it as a slowly spinning golden wheel with many spokes.

The idea is to lie down in this cross—it is a hybrid of a cross and a sarcophagus—and be irradiated by the Sun overhead as the cross rotates. The Ixion's Wheel is an initiation chamber for the candidates in Arthurhood, which is to say, in preparation for infusion and embodiment of the Solar Logos of which the "Celtic" King Arthur was the living representative.

SOLAR LOGOS RESIDENCE: It may seem confusing to bring up a figure from Celtic myth into the realm of the Andean Incas, but there have been fifteen King Arthurs in world cultural history, which means fourteen have appeared in non-Celtic settings. Manco Capac was the Andean King Arthur, the embodiment of the Solar Logos for that era and one of the fourteen Ray Masters of the Great Bear. The mythic picture here is vast but enthralling; to make sense of it, we must account for Lake Titicaca.

Geologists feel that the huge lake was once at sea level but was raised to its awesome height by a geological cataclysm. A dome covers all of the lake, with its center over the Island of the Sun. This dome is the planetary starfall for Alshain, the beta star in Aquila, the constellation of the Eagle, located in the bird's throat. Appropriately, in myth Aquila was Zeus' bird, so chosen because it could soar highest of all the birds.

One prime geomantic feature within this dome is an access point for Shambhala. It is a well-used portal, and the bleed-through of

Shambhala from its dimension to something accessible in our physical world is well pronounced and more vivid than in many other places. Manco Capac came from Lake Titicaca to Cusco because he was commissioned by the spiritual rulers and guiders of Earth whose headquarters is Shambhala.

A straight-running dome line connects the Cusco Lynx dome with the Lake Titicaca Aquila dome, validating one aspect of Cusco's claim to be the *qosqo*, "uncovered navel stone" or umbilicus. The Cusco geomantic temple is like a fetus with an umbilical cord extending back to the (cosmic) "Mother" at Lake Titicaca.

Another aspect of the Cusco navel attribution is that when Manco Capac (King Arthur, a Ray Master of the Great Bear) arrived at Cusco, he inserted himself into the ground, establishing the Solar Logos connection there. Of course it makes more visual and logical sense to say Manco Capac inserted a golden staff and thereby activated the Cusco temple, but Manco Capac *was* the staff.

The Solar Logos becoming resident at Cusco was achieved by the Solar Logos implanting "his" Sun energy there, both activating the navel and creating it. So the Coricancha, the Golden Courtyard, was where Manco Capac grounded the Solar Logos for all of Cusco. His golden staff remained in place during "his" residence at Cusco, and could be perceived variously as a spinning golden spindle, tower, or golden wheel axle.

You could think of Manco Capac as a master geomancer who knew how to activate an important temple; in Glastonbury, England, a similar story is told of Joseph of Arimathea, who planted his staff in Wearyall Hill, after which the staff took blossom as a flowering thorn tree. His implantation of his staff in the hill activated a landscape figure and helped "turn on" the Glastonbury temple.

One etymological interpretation of Wearyall Hill is *Wir Heale*, the hill of the spiritual hero or savior, or the place where the spiritual potency heals, or the place where you heal the *vir*—make virile again. In any case, the key concept embedded in the name is *Wir*, from the Sanskrit *vira*, which means "man" or "hero," forming *viraj*, which means "energy and virility." In Hindu thinking, Viraj is the male aspect of the cosmic creator god, Brahma. The so-named hill is "the place of primary creative, fertilizing, potentiating energy that makes a human whole, makes one hale, that heals one—the hill is the reservoir of *vir*."[281]

Let's put this in Andean terms: it gives us *Viracocha*, the Inca creator god, who was said to reside at some level in Cusco as its protector being. Walking the Cusco chakra template along the *Avenida Sol* (the Avenue of the Sun) puts you in the field of Viracocha's *wir*, the creator god's own energy matrix.

It gives us also the name of the country itself: Peru, the *Land of Wiru*. When the Spanish first arrived in Cusco they were told the country was called "the land of Wiru," presumably a reference to the terraces of green-stalked corn. "The Spanish could not pronounce Wiru, called it Viru, and it became Piru and then Peru."[282]

EGREGOR GROUNDING POINT: Geomantically speaking, it might be more apt to call Peru the land of Viracocha because the country is his domain. Viracocha is the Incan name for the egregor for one of the original nine landmasses to which angelic Watchers were assigned at the beginning of the Earth.

As explained elsewhere in this book, the Earth's energy body is divided into twelve equal pentagons, nine of which were each assigned an egregor, or Watcher angel, to preside over this landmass for the duration of the planet, and to help create the humans who would live within the given pentagonal face. (Three pentagonal faces were left unassigned, as they would primarily enclose water.)

Each of the seventy-two major subdivisions of the nine landmasses would also have an egregor; the Japanese myth of Izanagi and Izanimi, who coagulated the eight islands of Japan out of the primal waters and created the first Japanese is a vivid example of this (see Mount Fuji, Japan). With Viracocha we are dealing with an entire region and its people.

Technically, the egregor grounding point is the Island of the Sun in Lake Titicaca. There Viracocha emerged, precipitated the Sun, Moon, stars, and everything else, and created humanity. His first efforts, abandoned, were turned to stone and buried aboveground at Tiahuanaco, about a dozen miles from Lake Titicaca in Bolivia; his second efforts included Manco Capac and his siblings. According to a Peruvian creation myth, originally Peru was conceived of as a self-contained landmass, as "a single world mountain made of all the Andean ranges, rising from female-like valleys to male-like snowcapped heights."[283]

Viracocha worked with the Elohim, the angelic family assigned to be both humanity's biological creators and the Earth's primary megalithic engineers, to create the humans who would populate his pent face of the Earth's energy body. Putting aside the vexing matters of recorded history, verifiable dates, and presumed cultural chronologies, let us call this Peruvian human group the Inca if for no other reason than that the name embodies a spiritual focus. The Incas were the Sons of the Sun, that is, solar initiates of the Cosmic Father, and birthing such Sons, which was more of a second birth, was the purpose of Cusco.

Geomythically, Cusco is a palimpsest. In another layer of this complex pattern we find the egregor specifically for the Peruvian sub-landmass—one of the seventy-two mentioned above. The Peruvian geomythic imagination has clothed this egregor, which is a kind of national astral symbol and protector being, as the puma, and its body is laid out in the architecture of the capital city of Cusco.

The puma or lion representation at Cusco has an etymological and presumably an energy link to Lake Titicaca. According to William Sullivan, the conventional interpretation of the name is "rock or cliff of lead," but in the Quechua language, *titi* also means "puma," whose dull gray coat may explain the otherwise confusing reference to lead.

This would have Titicaca meaning the "cliff of the lion," such that, at "lion-cliff" on the east side of the Island of the Sun, Viracocha created the world where, appropriately, water gushes forth from a black cliff wall.[284] It is apt to say that Viracocha created the world here because through the pentagonal face grounding point for the egregor, he did in effect create the world for this microcosmic, holographic one-twelfth aspect of the Earth energy grid.[285]

CAMALATE CENTER: With the golden staff of the Solar Logos inserted in the navel or solar plexus center of the Cusco chakra template, the remarkable ceque system of forty-two lines and 328 huacas was energized. Functionally, this is a giant zodiacal wheel with the Coricancha as the hub. Picture a wheel with twelve spokes, each intervening wedge representing a sign of the zodiac—each extending for miles from the hub at Coricancha.

Its purpose was for training "knights" to address, transmute, and assimilate their zodiacal oppositions, squares, conjuncts, and other energy aspects in their horoscopes.

It is not a Landscape Zodiac as such, but more like a quasi-physical Round Table which itself is a holographic miniaturization of the galaxy. It is a feature you can see at other former Camalate Centers, notably South Cadbury Castle in Somerset, England, the esoteric center of the Celtic King Arthur's mystery school, Camalate Center.

The course of world cultural evolution has seen twenty-six such Camalate Centers, and Cusco was one. The Incan Knights lived in Cusco, around the Coricancha, and made geomantic forays into the greater Peruvian and Bolivian geomythic landscape for further training and, simultaneously, to help maintain the integrity of the region's energy patterns. They would regularly visit the Nasca Plains Landscape Zodiac (four hundred square miles of animal, human, and geometric figures etched on the landscape), Machu Picchu (see discussion elsewhere in this section), Tiahuanaco in Bolivia, Lake Titicaca, Ollantaytambo, Pisac, the numerous other dome-capped subsidiary sites, and of course the 328 huacas constellated around Cusco.

The sight is impressive: you have three domes (Machu Picchu, Cusco, Lake Titicaca) interconnected by straight-running dome lines; you have 144 dome caps highlighting subsidiary geomantic nodes and resembling interlacing sunflowers; and you have the zodiacal training wheel of the Camalate Center radiating out of the Coricancha, the golden hub, with a spinning golden spindle in its center, showering the area with gold.

CYCLOPEAN CITY: The massive stones in the three parallel stone rows of Sacsaywaman are what remains of a Cyclopean City constructed there in the earliest days of the Earth when all its original stone features, including stone circles, stone rows, and single standing stones were similarly installed by the Elohim. The Cyclopean City at Sacsaywaman would have afforded a dimensional interface with higher and other worlds for the high initiates of Cusco, enabling them to ground some of that otherworldly inspiration in their own temples and principalities for the benefit of all who lived in that region.

CROWN OF THE ANCIENT OF DAYS: Sacsaywaman, the head of the geomythic puma, is the site of one of the Earth's twelve Crowns of the Ancient of Days, which can be understood as an expression of the Vast White Countenance or Cosmic Father—Viracocha's higher counterpart, if you like.

As an Incan candidate for initiation or as a master Incan geomancer, you processed along the chakra template of the Avenida Sol, immersing yourself in the Solar Logos golden Sun wheel at the Coricancha. This is to say, you experienced an aspect of the Cosmic Christ, the original and prototypical Son.

As you process from the Coricancha to Sacsaywaman, you are the Inca Sun returning to its celestial source, the heavenly, arcane "puma," or perhaps we might say you are the Christ returning to the Father, to use contemporary language. The Cusco temple's purpose was to provide the geomantic means for a Christed initiation of the Incan candidates for a higher world encounter with Viracocha. Cusco was (and still is) a template for the birth of the higher Self expressed as the divine child. The Arthurian mysteries, translated into Incan terms and contexts, were one of the training regimens that could produce that birth.

One aspect of the cyclopean stones at Sacsaywaman was to ground, amplify, and increase the pressure of the higher consciousness embedded there in the White Head of Viracocha. The temple was designed and executed by the Elohim.

The massive stones created the concentrated effects of a cave, pushing the consciousness or energy charge back into the center of the structure, the center of the puma's geomythic head and the center of the initiate's head. The stones contained and amplified the pressure wave from the Crown of the Ancient of Days so as to produce a pop in consciousness into a transcendent state.

The Sacsaywaman White Head is surrounded by a nimbus of higher spiritual beings, numerous angels, and ascended humans forming a crown around the Crown. Most of the cyclopean stones are dimensional apertures for the Gandharvas, the celestial musicians as described in Vedic mythology. They are present at Sacsaywaman in multitudes, entering the site through the stones; you can follow them back in vision to their realm, which is the Celestial City of Gandhavati, or Avalon, the Summer Country, by passing through the stones.

You can observe another example of this sense of communion in the Welsh myth of the Assembly of the Wondrous Head or the Hospitality of the Noble Head, that Head being the severed head of Bran the Blessed, which resided on the Island of Harlech in Wales for a time before being brought in ritual procession to the White Mount in London. That Head is one of the Earth's twelve Crowns of the Ancient of Days.

Bran's retainers feasted and reveled for years to the accompaniment of the hospitable Head, the myths say.

MOUNT OLYMPUS: A further aspect of the Hospitality of the Head quality at the White Head at Sacsaywaman is that it is the site of a Mount Olympus. This is the Greek name for the celestial residence of the fourteen Ray Masters of the Great Bear, whose chief is Zeus, the "owner" of the White Head. The Ray Masters would be on hand to provide advice, counseling, and instruction for the Incan Knights of Solar Logos Manco Capac in their work at the Camalate Center.

Delphi, Mount Parnassus, Greece

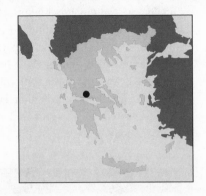

PHYSICAL DESCRIPTION

The ruins of Delphi, once the site of Greece's most formidable oracular shrine, occupy a mere six acres. They're perched at 1,870 feet on a slope of Mount Parnassus, a twin-peaked mountain towering 8,061 feet above the Gulf of Corinth about eighty miles from Athens. In its days of glory, Delphi was richly endowed with memorials, monuments, temples, altars, stadiums, amphitheaters, and treasuries, most of which have since disappeared, yet even today some semblance of that former glory is still apparent.

The sanctuary of Athena Pronaia at Marmaria, a half-mile away, marks the gate to the oracular shrine. This site was dedicated to the Olympian goddess Pallas Athena, and may have been occupied as early as 5000 B.C. Still extant here is the Tholos Temple, a circular structure set on a triple platform. Closer to Delphi itself is the Castalian Spring, where it is believed pilgrims to Delphi would purify and ritually prepare themselves before consulting the oracle.

The Sacred Way wends between the massive cliffs called Phaedriades (meaning "The Shining Ones" because they glow with incandescent light at dawn and dusk) to make its approach to the Sanctuary of Apollo. The Sanctuary was erected about 650 B.C. at the geomythic center of the site, at the very source of oracular inspiration. It is likely that the worship of the Olympian god Apollo began here perhaps as early as 1000 B.C.

HISTORY AND ARCHEOLOGY

As an oracular site, Delphi functioned for approximately one thousand years, from the time of Homer until the late fourth century A.D. Historians understand that for the most part, the Delphic oracle was open for business one day per month during the nine months when Apollo was resident at Delphi; during that long and productive day, the Pythia (the official, ritually trained, resident psychic and trance channeler) would convey Apollo's usually gnomic and enigmatic answers to a variety of questions posed by visitors.

The last recorded oracle was given in 362 A.D. for the Roman emperor Julian the Apostate, and it informed him that "the prophetic springs and fountains are dead." In 393 A.D., the Christian emperor Theodosius officially and definitively shut down the oracle center, banishing the pagan Apollo in favor of the new god, Christ.

Archeological excavations begun in 1892 uncovered much of Delphi, which had fallen into ruin and oblivion, and sufficiently restored its reputation as a spiritual and cultural center such that in 1927 two Greeks launched a festival at Delphi based on a presentation of Greek plays. This initiative failed, but in the 1960s the idea was revived, and the presentation of classical drama at Delphi is now a regular event. Today Delphi is visited by an estimated one million tourists annually.

MYTH AND LEGEND

The mythic portfolio for Delphi begins with its host mountain, Parnassus. "There a great mountain aims towards the stars/Its double peak, Parnassus, soaring high," said Ovid.[286] Greek legend speaks of an actual hero called Parnassus, who was the son of a nymph and Poseidon, the Lord of the Sea. Parnassus is credited with founding the oracle of the Python at Delphi and with inventing the technique of divination by birds.

Greek legend also says Mount Parnassus was the resting site for the ark staffed by Deucalion and his wife, Pyrrha, after the Deluge waters subsided; both were the children of Titans. In other words, a Noah's Ark myth is attributed to Mount Parnassus. After Deucalion's ark landed on Mount Parnassus, he sought counsel from Themis, then the resident deity and guardian at the oracle, on how to repopulate the world with humans. She bade him and his wife to throw stones over their shoulders, telling them they were the "bones" of Mother Earth; they did this, and the stones turned into humans.

A third myth about Mount Parnassus says it was one of the preferred playgrounds for the Nine Muses, who were the daughters of Zeus and Mnemosyne (Memory).[287] This has made Mount Parnassus the source of poetic inspiration. The Muses were divine singers and musicians whose music delighted the gods, but they also presided over all forms of thought in its eloquent expression; they were the gods of inspiration under Apollo's leadership (as he was the god of music and prophecy), and they provided music for all the celebrations of the Olympian gods. At Mount Parnassus, the Castalian Spring, which issued from a cleft in the cliffs above Delphi, was sacred to the Muses, and it was said to have been formed by a hoof-strike by the magical winged horse Pegasus.

As for the oracle itself, its earliest guardian was the Titaness Themis, whose name (and scope of responsibility) meant Justice, Eternal Law, and Order. She was the daughter of Uranus and Gaia, and the mother of Prometheus, the god who stole Olympian fire on humanity's behalf. The legends say Themis succeeded Gaia Herself as the prime guardian of Delphi, and it was Themis who instructed Apollo in the arts of prophecy. Themis was also regarded as Zeus' adviser and/or consort.

The myths suggest oracular activities were under way at Pytho, Delphi's earliest name (referring to the entire ritualized landscape on the slope of Mount Parnassus), before the advent of the god Apollo. For example, the Rock of the Sibyl is still extant at Delphi today; it is reputedly the first place of prophecy at Delphi. Legend has it that upon this rock Herophile (daughter of Zeus and Lamia, the first sibyl) sang her prophecies, which included a prediction of the Trojan War.

Oracular activities took on a new shape and direction once Apollo arrived and killed the "bloated serpent," Python, "whose vast coils/Across so many acres spread their blight," as Ovid wrote. Python was huge, "a terror to men's new-made tribes/So far it sprawled across the mountainside."[288] Its lair was a cave near a spring; or the serpent was coiled around a laurel tree. The *Homeric Hymns* describe the chthonic beast as "a she-dragon/a great, glutted and fierce monster, which inflicted/many evils on the men of the land."[289]

Apollo the Archer God destroyed Python with a thousand arrows, after which its black wounds "poured forth their poison" into the landscape, said Ovid. In fact, one etymology for the site's name supposedly derives from this seeping toxicity: Pytho may be derived from the Greek word that means "to rot."[290] Apollo then retreated to either Crete or the Vale of Tempe in Greece to undergo ritual purification and atonement for having polluted ground holy to the Earth Mother in slaying Python.

Our antique writers, however, are not uniform in concluding that Python was a bad thing to have at Pytho. "Many pictures show the serpent Python living in amity with Apollon and guarding the Omphalos, the sacred navel-stone and midpoint of the Earth, which stood in Apollon's temple."[291] Some experts say the dragon (or serpent) was originally placed there to guard Gaia's shrine and that Gaia was its mother. Other sources explain that Apollo's "enemy" at this site was a dragoness (drakaina) named Delphyne, a name connected with delphys, an old Greek word for womb—hence the place name Delphoi.

Archeologists have been unable to locate the site of the vaporous chasm over which the Pythia sat to receive her trance inspirations, but ancient writers attested to Pytho being "the hollow of God." The geographer Strabo, for example, reported that the seat of the oracle was a "cave hollowed out deep down in the Earth, with a rather narrow mouth, from which arises a pneuma that inspires a divine frenzy."[292]

The Homeric Hymns tell us that once Apollo killed Python, it was his intention to erect a "lovely temple" beneath snowcapped Parnassus as an oracle for men and women. "It is my wish to give them unerring/advice, making prophecies inside the opulent temple," he declared. He laid out the foundations for the oracular shrine upon which the human builders "placed a threshold of stone."

The poet of the Homeric Hymns also noted that Apollo came to rocky Pytho playing his lyre, wearing divine, fragrant garments, and that when he struck his seven-stringed lyre with the golden plectrum, it emitted an "enchanting sound." The poet added that when Apollo returned to Mount Olympus, all the gods delighted in his singing and lyre-playing and he was accompanied in this by the Muses "answering with beautiful voices."[293]

Pausanias, writing about his visit to Delphi in the second century A.D., notes that there was a tradition of oracular access and prophecy at Delphi before Apollo's arrival. "There are a lot of different stories about Delphi," he comments. One of them had Daphnis as the Earth-appointed prophetess for the site; she was one of the nymphs living on Mount Parnassus. She was turned into a laurel tree, a metamorphosis the ancients used to explain why the Pythia at Delphi was said to induce her trance by inhaling the fumes of burning laurel leaves and why a laurel tree stood by the cavern of Gaia—the heart of Delphi, its "hollow of God."

Another story Pausanias relates is that Gaia awarded Pytho to Themis, who then gave her share to Apollo, but he is said to have traded Poseidon the island of Poros off Troizen in exchange for this oracle, over which Poseidon had some hegemony.

What about this mysterious pneuma said to emanate from the fissure in the ground? Pausanias notes that once some shepherds and their goats stumbled upon the site. They found the chasm in the ground out of which swirled intoxicating airs, "and became possessed by the vapor, and prophesied by the power of Apollo."

In other words, the oracular potency of Pytho was so strong that even psychically untutored shepherds could speak on behalf of the god, Pausanias suggested. Diodorus Siculus gives a variation on this tale. He has goats first discovering the oracular hole. "Whenever an animal approached the hole and leaned over it, it began to leap about in a strange way and to emit strange bleats."

Then the goatherds leaned over the hole and in their own way they too leaped about, behaving as though possessed, predicting the future. The reputation of this intoxicating chasm spread and soon "whoever approached the hole fell into a trance," and this is why, explains Diodorus Siculus, the oracle came to be revered and to be considered "the Earth's prophetic sanctuary." He adds that the institution of the Pythia, or priestess, sitting over the chasm on a tripod was to prevent people (including herself) from falling irretrievably into the hole, which had happened frequently before that time.[294]

Still another curious story related by Pausanias is that "Olen and the remote Northerners" founded this oracle, and it was Olen who first prophesied here and spoke god-intoxicated poetry. Pausanias does not elaborate on the identity of these aloof Northerners, but for the Greeks the "extreme North" was often a code for the mysterious people they called Hyperboreans (from *hyper borean*, "Beyond the North Wind").

Supporting this possibility is an old Delphian myth, reported by Pausanias, that the shrine was first made out of beeswax and feathers "sent by Apollo from the remote North."[295] Apollo was known to spend the three months of winter each year with the Hyperboreans, and his mother, Leto, was allegedly born there. While he was away from Delphi, another Olympian, Dionysus, tended the shrine.

The presence of the omphalos or navel-stone at Delphi, mentioned above, earned it the reputation as being the "center" of the world. The conical stone was believed to have been a meteorite and the first physical object to emerge on dry land after the Deluge waters subsided. A complementary story says that Zeus, Lord of Mount Olympus and chief of all the gods, dispatched two ravens from the ends of the Earth to find the planet's cen-

ter; their flights (and beaks) converged at Pytho right over the omphalos stone. A statue of two eagles, facing opposite directions, was said to stand within Apollo's temple by the omphalos stone.

As mentioned above, Delphi's true name may refer to its womblike quality, a possibility supported by the fact that "the sacred college [in ancient Greece] insisted that Delphi was the womb or center of the Earth."[296]

Although the original omphalos has disappeared, reliable replicas show it as being ovoid and cone-shaped, carved into a half-egg a few feet high. The precious stone was placed in the inner sanctum of Apollo's temple, which stood over the original chasm in the Earth over which the Delphic oracular priestess, the Pythia, sat, perched on her tripod and delivering her prophecies from Apollo. The omphalos stone, the Pythia's tripod, the chasm, the rising vapors all marked the exact spot where Apollo killed Python at "the thunderous Earth's enshrined navel," said Pindar.[297]

With the foundations of his shrine established, the Python slain, and the omphalos stone in its rightful place, Apollo needed temple priests. For this he sought a shipful of Cretans from Knossos sailing past. He appeared to them as a marvelous dolphin and leaped on board, to their amazement. Through his celestial magic, Apollo diverted their ship to the harbor of Krisa, the closest port to Pytho. Then he rose from the ship like a midday star and landed at his sanctuary beneath Parnassus, enveloping the entire region with divine light.

The idea, of course, was to lure the Cretans to Pytho to become its guardians and founding priests. Mythmakers used this story to explain the origin of Pytho's later place name, Delphi, as in dolphin.

MYSTICS AND TOURISTS

In his worldwide review of sacred mountains, their myths and ambiance, Edwin Bernbaum says of Delphi: "Yet something of the life and spirit of the place endures—in the wild call of eagles circling over the cliffs of Parnassus, in the deep and fluid light of the setting sun, in the silence of the stars shining through the gorge that once marked the spiritual center of the ancient world."[298]

An American traveler describing his first impression of Delphi in the 1950s said that his day there had been "overwhelming" because "Delphi is sculpture from no human hand." Here, amidst the "violet abyss at your fingertips," the cliffs, eagles, and soaring vistas, "You feel lightheaded and yet in control, like a diver on his way down." Sensing what Delphi must have been like at its peak of operation, this writer speculated that "the whole place was felt to move and breathe as one being."[299]

A more recent visitor commented that Delphi is "both deeply engaging and disappointing" because much more has vanished than survived. Even so, Delphi is "the place of encounter with truth." The oracle, though no longer extant, still asks us "about our own dialogue with the divine."[300]

GEOMANTIC

Dome; Dragon; Vibrating Stone; Oroboros Line Anchor Point; Shambhala Doorway; Avalon; Grail Castle.

DOME: The dome over Mount Parnassus corresponds with Thuban, or alpha Draconis, the brightest star in the constellation Draco, the dragon. Thuban is a third magnitude star 214 light years from Earth, located in the tail of the galactic dragon.

While most cultures construed Draco as a variation of the archetypal cosmic dragon, the embodiment of primordial chaos, the Chinese saw these stars as *Tsi Kung*, "Palace of the Heavenly Emperor." Akkadian astronomers described this star, which at the time was approximately the

Pole star, *as Tir-An-na*, meaning "the Life of Heaven," *Dayan Same* (Judge of Heaven), *and Dayan Sidi* (Favorable Judge), all of which epithets represented their god *Caga Gilgati*.

DRAGON: It is appropriate that the dome on Mount Parnassus is of the constellation for Draco because the Python represents one of the thirteen original dragons brought to Earth (and still here) when its geomythic topography was established. So here you have galactic dragon above, terrestrial dragon below. Python at Delphi is the "mother" of eighty-one subsidiary dragons located at various distances, which means Delphi is geomantically influential over a large area by virtue of its dragon progeny.

As a few of the ancient writers intuited, Python has a legitimate—in fact, essential—role at Delphi, and Apollo did not slay her. Rather he activated the dragon, allowing its cosmic energy to flow, in a grounded way, into the prepared geomantic matrix, first at Delphi, then through Greece and surrounding territories.

Apollo had to transduce the otherwise overwhelming energy of Python so that it would not destroy the land and its living inhabitants; he had to reduce the charge, run it through his own celestial "body" so that, much reduced, it could be assimilated, safely and gradually, by humanity. With Python "slain," its eighty-one dragon eggs could proceed to hatch subsidiary dragons.

Apollo, as one of the Olympians, was one of the fourteen Ray Masters of the Great Bear, one of whose collective tasks was to ground their celestial energy through the thirteen dragons on Earth so that the Ray Masters could function effectively within the Earth's geomantic terrain, and so that the dragon energy could be introduced into the planet's energy body. Apollo's ray color is a pale sky-blue, and attunement with this color is an aid to cognition of Apollo at Delphi today.

The descriptions from Ovid and the *Homeric Hymns* that Python's vast coils spread out around so many acres is accurate. To form a visual impression of Python at Delphi, picture a very large serpent or dragon lying in multiple coils in the same place as Mount Parnassus; its head and open mouth are positioned exactly where the omphalos, or navel-stone, was placed in the Apollo temple, over the fissure in the ground.[301] The omphalos stone was like a rounded front tooth in the dragon's mouth.

VIBRATING STONE: The stone itself was one of the twelve Vibrating Stones brought to Earth at the same time as the dragons. The Vibrating Stone at Delphi grounded one of the twelve oroboros energy lines—in this case, Sagittarius. That's why the myths say that when Zeus sent two eagles in opposite directions around the world, they met beak to beak right over the omphalos stone. The eagles and their flight path constitute a poetic metaphor for describing this world-*encircling* energy line. The two ends of the "eagle," so to speak, meet at Delphi and are grounded by the omphalos stone.

When the planetary system was in operation, the Delphi stone by resonance was in full connection and exchange with the other eleven Vibrating Stones around the world, such as at Mecca in Saudi Arabia and Glastonbury in England. Collectively, they anchored the Oroboros Lines and acted as a kind of preprogrammed geomantic calendar, set to activate and channel incoming celestial energies and the individual Oroboros Lines that carried these energies.

OROBOROS LINE ANCHOR POINT: Delphi called itself the navel of the world because it was the umbilicus for the Sagittarius Oroboros Line. The energies from the constellation Sagittarius plugged in here at Delphi. The center of this umbilical connection was the heart of all the action at Delphi: Python's open mouth—the Pythia's vaporous chasm—in the Apollo temple.

Standing where the Oroboros roots itself into the Earth and spreads out in opposite directions to instantaneously encircle the planet, you are standing in the gods' current, in the fast-moving celestial river of Sagittarius, the galactic archer and centaur, half-horse, half-man, with an arrow ready to loose.

You are also standing on one of the prime geometric building blocks of the planet's energy body, as the fifteen Oroboros Lines also form the fundamental geometry—specifically, some of the edges—of the planet's grid structure.[302]

Ancient astronomers described Sagittarius as an archer with the legs and tail of a horse. Even though this sounds like a centaur, some Greek astronomers preferred the identification with Crotus, the son of Eupheme and the nurse of the Muses. Crotus, who invented archery, lived on Mount Helicon, one of the preferred residences of the Muses. He lived with the Muses, delighting in their company, and would mark time to their songs by clapping his hands; he was also an accomplished hunter. "His diligence in those pursuits won him great acclaim, for he was the swiftest in the forest and the most accomplished in the musical arts."[303] The Muses asked Zeus to make him a star as a reward for these attainments.

Crotus' mythic resume is not identical to Apollo's but there are enough similarities to appreciate the appropriateness of the Sagittarius line—Crotus' celestial energy essence—being grounded at Apollo's Delphi. You have there a rich blend of energies: Apollo, representing one aspect of Ursa Major, Sagittarius, one-twelfth of the zodiacal wheel, and alpha Draconis, mirroring the dragon energies of Python.

At least two geomantic factors contributed to the Pythia's divine frenzy, prophetic intoxication, and oracular access. First, dragon "blood" always inspires a profound heightening of human knowledge and cognition. Numerous myths from around the world involving heroes slaying dragons tell how afterwards the dragon-slayer was able to understand the language of all animals and able to converse with the gods.

The technical explanation for this amplification of psychic access is presented in detail in part 2, but here it might help to say that Python enables creative, glossolalic, prophetic speech among the trained because it is the energy matrix of cosmic speech itself, the archetype of language.

SHAMBHALA DOORWAY: The second reason the Pythia was able to deliver the thoughts and advice of Apollo is that Delphi is a Shambhala doorway. The center for this feature is at the Rock of the Sibyl. Those inclined (and able) can pass (in consciousness) right through the rock and arrive at Shambhala. If anybody on Earth knows what's in store for the future and can therefore provide useful predictive information, it is the ascended humans and other celestial beings resident at Shambhala, the planet's secret and real governing body.

The presence of the Vibrating Stone, Shambhala doorway, and the anchor point for an Oroboros Line (as well as certain geometric ramifications of these factors when plotted globally) enabled Delphi to serve for a time as the planetary second chakra. In fact, the entire sacred precinct originally belonged to Gaia and then Themis.

Themis as a Titaness was therefore an Elohim, which is to say, was among the angelic family that established the primary geomantic structures around the planet, moving big stones into place as circles and temples. But the Elohim were also the deities (planetary logoi) inhabiting and activating the planetary spheres in the earliest days of the solar system.

Again, see part 2 (Chakras) for a thorough explanation, but the basic equation here is that Titans equal Elohim, and Elohim equal planets which equal chakras. In other words, any reference to chakras, whether in the human energy field or the planet's, necessarily brings into the discussion the planets, the Elohim, and the primordial Titans, all of which are variations on the same energy essence.

So how long was Delphi in operation? Even though the historical records indicate only one thousand years, it is probably many times that number of years. Delphi's geomantic structures would have been in place for at least eighteen million years, since the time of the third Dome arrivals and the installation of much of the planet's visionary topography. The baffling reference to Olen and the remote Northerners is a probable code for the Hyperboreans, which itself is a code for Pleiadians, who were the Elohim's prime helpers in the initial geomantic installation on Earth. Once "physically" present on Earth in the grid installation phase, the Hyperboreans-Pleiadians remained available, if in a different dimension, for further maintenance.

AVALON: Apollo's reputation as a music-maker and as the leader of the Muses who counted Mount Parnassus as one of their haunts is appropriate because Delphi is the access point for one of the planet's 144 Avalons. This is the home of the Gandharvas (the celestial musicians) and their partners, the Apsarasas (the dancing nymphs).

In terms of mythic equivalencies, it is fair, though perhaps startling, to say that Apollo is also the archetype of all Gandharvas—and that the Muses are the Apsarasas. One of the "rabbit holes" or tunnel-like quick access points for the Avalon at Delphi is at the Castalian spring. With an Avalon, you get the golden apple trees of the Hesperides, and how fitting it is that Python (like his "brother" Ladon in the Hesperides myth) guards the golden apples at Delphi.

GRAIL CASTLE: Finally, there is the matter of Deucalion and Pyrrha and their ark, which landed atop Mount Parnassus. Again, initially it seems strange, but this ark is geomythic code for Grail Castle, the abode of vast, deep cosmic memory. Poseidon's involvement in Delphi helps us appreciate this connection too, for Poseidon as Lord of the Sea was also Lord of the Deep Abyss (using Sumerian terminology to describe Enki, their equivalent to Poseidon).

He had a part share in Delphi because he was in effect the ultimate Grail King, the possessor of the knowledge of the unbelievable span of time between *kalpas*—some three hundred million years between episodes in the universe's seemingly endless life. Deucalion and Pyrrha were Poseidon's students in this initiative of preserving vast cosmic memory; their ark is the Grail temple or Ship of Time, still accessible today, and sitting on the head of Python like a golden crown.

Dome of the Rock, Jerusalem, Israel

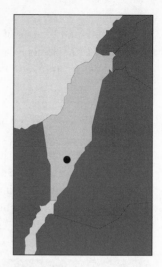

The Dome of the Rock is a Muslim monument on the Temple Mount, which is a huge enclosed platform on the top of a small rise in the Old City of Jerusalem called Mount Moriah. The Temple Mount was called in Hebrew *Har BaBayit,* which means "the Mountain of the House," as in God's House; in Arabic *Haram es-Sharif* (the Noble Sanctuary); and it is a trapezoid measuring 1.5 million square feet or 500,000 square yards and occupying forty-five acres.

As impressive as it is in its own right, the Temple Mount (elevation: 2,220 feet) is the setting for an even more impressive jewel. The center of attention and the focus of the majority of the site's sacrality is an oblong rock, a natural outcropping, that measures fifty-six by forty-two feet. It's called the Foundation Stone, or in Hebrew, *Even HaShetiyah,* said to have been planted here at the beginning of Creation and taken by God from His Throne of Glory.

Thus Jerusalem's holiest spot is a rock that the ancient Jews saw as the center of the Earth, the axis of the universe, the pivot that joined Heaven and Earth, and Earth with the primeval chaos beneath it. "It was the root of heaven, the lid of hell, the place through which souls spring up when ascending from hell to heaven."[304]

Ever since the seventh century, the Muslim Dome of the Rock (Arabic: *Kubbat as-Sakrah*) has stood directly over this unusual rock, framing it in an octagonal temple topped with a golden dome (sixty feet wide), its inner surface a sublime kaleidoscope of arabesques in gilt and plaster, arching one hundred feet above the rock.

The outer octagonal wall (each section sixty feet long) is encased in marble and covered with numerous blue tiles; this wall encircles two concentric ambulatories separated by an arcade in between. "The elegant building erected by Abdel Malek, one of the most beautiful in the whole of the Middle East, was intended primarily to shield the holy rock, *Es-Sakhra*"; the Muslims called it *Qubbet el-Sakhra.*[305]

The Foundation Stone is encircled by 16 arches supported by pillars that came from former Jerusalem churches destroyed by the Persians in their occupation of the city in 614 A.D. Visitors have likened the visual effect to that of a mountain of supernatural light or to a glittering gold Sun whose light offers a succession of shades and intensities during the day.

"The atmosphere of beauty that prevails in the Dome of the Rock is like a distant announcement of the destiny of paradise." You find yourself there in your finite human state at the "very heart of the Beauty and the Life of God, of which this mausoleum is the parable." Everything about the monument's construction "integrates" you into the higher life.[306]

Earlier in history, the two Temples of Jerusalem occupied the Temple Mount and similarly enclosed the Foundation Stone. Portentous mythic and spiritual events happened here from the Jewish, Christian, and Muslim traditions, and the three religions have claimed the site as their own with various justifications and legendary attributions of jurisdiction.

HISTORY AND ARCHEOLOGY

Following architectural plans handed down by God to Moses, King Solomon organized the construction of the first Temple of Jerusalem, which was completed in 957 B.C. It was destroyed by the Babylonian Nebuchadnezzar in 586 B.C., then reconstructed by 515 B.C. During the reign of the Roman Herod, the Second Temple of Jerusalem was enlarged and the famous Western Wall (the "Wailing Wall") was built; part of it is still extant, the only physical remains of the Temple.

In 70 A.D., the Romans demolished the Temple of Jerusalem, and Emperor Hadrian established a temple to the God Jove (the Greek Jupiter). This in turn was destroyed by invading Byzantines; later the Persians occupied the city; then in 638 A.D., Jerusalem was captured by the Muslim Caliph Umar I, six years after the death of Muhammad, the Muslim prophet. Umar "cleansed" the Temple Mount, called in Arabic *Haram al Sharif*, and dedicated the site to Muslim worship.

The Dome of the Rock was built in 687, some fifty years after Muhammad's death. For about ninety years after the Christian capture of Jerusalem in the Crusades in 1099, the Dome of the Rock was converted to a Christian shrine and called *Templum Domini*, "Temple of the Lord."

Later it reverted to Muslim control, and today it is the third holiest place (a shrine or monument, not a mosque) in Islam, after the Ka'aba in Mecca and the Prophet Muhammad's mosque in Medina.

MYTH AND LEGEND

The dossier of attributions to the Temple Mount and Foundation Stone is awesome. The Stone, which came from God's Throne of Glory, was set as a lid upon the *tehom*, the subterranean waters of chaos, similar to the Sumerian and Babylonian concept of *apsu*. Just as Babylon was built upon the *bab-apsu* and was the "Gate of Apsu," so the Foundation Stone covers the Mouth of the *tehom*, suppressing the waters of Chaos that preceded Creation.

The Hebrew word *tehom* means an abyss (such as a surging mass of subterranean water) or an uproar of waters in violent commotion or waves in turbid violence, making a great noise. *Tehom* implies the deep (as in the principal sea or underground water source) and fountains of the great deep, and it implies chaos, mystery, depth, and power.

In a larger sense, *tehom* signifies the watery precreation abyss, wildly swirling whirlpools, the layer of water underlying the physical Earth, and the formless waste or primordial substance from which God created the world. This primeval water, if not stemmed, would erupt from apertures in the land and flood the entire Earth. The Biblical Flood is understood to have been produced by an "uncorking" of the *tehom*, of the waters from deep below.

The site of the Temple of Jerusalem, with the Stone as its center, was believed to be the precise place out of which the Flood waters erupted and back into which they receded when the Flood was over. Then the great rock was set upon the opening into the abyss, keeping the Flood waters penned in. The Stone of Foundation was an omphalos, or primordial navel, and also the first solid object created by God and "placed by God amidst the as yet boundless fluid of the primeval waters."

Legend says God then built up the Earth concentrically around this Stone just as the body of an embryo is grown from its navel. "In the same manner in which the body of the embryo receives its nourishment through the navel, so the whole Earth too receives the waters that nourish it from this Navel."[307]

The term *tehom* is close to the Hebrew words *Tohu* and *Bohu*, which are used to describe conditions of original chaos preceding Creation. *Tehom* (a word generated by adding the suffix "m" to *Tohu*) also signifies a primitive sea-monster of the same name, possibly similar to or the same as Leviathan and the Babylonian Tiamat. *Bohu*, with the same suffix, becomes Behom and Behomot, as in Job's Behemoth, the dry-land counterpart.

Tehom, argue Robert Graves and Raphael Patai, was originally a proper name, and Tehomot is the Hebrew version of Mother Tiamat "beloved by the God Apsu, whose name developed from the older Sumerian Abzu; and Abzu was the imaginary sweet-water abyss from which Enki, God of Wisdom, emerged."[308]

The Stone is said to have come from the Garden of Eden and like Man, resides on Earth in exile. It was placed here at the center of Creation not only to seal up the *tehom*, but to distribute the spirit of Creation out into the world. Adam's mortal body was said to have been created in part from the dust of this Stone. The idea was that this would enable him always to carry with him a memory of his divine origin.

A variation on this myth says it was the dust from the place of Adam's atonement and that at the end of time, all humankind, Adam's progeny, would assemble in Jerusalem for repentance, for-giveness, and salvation on the pivotal and consummate day of Resurrection.

Underneath the Foundation Stone in a small cavern or deep hollow is the *Bir el-Arweh*, the Well of Souls, accessed by a physical stairway.

In the Well, it is said you can hear the voices of the Dead and the rushing sounds of the waters of Paradise, and sometimes the two mingled. Legend says the Ark of the Covenant was hidden in a sealed and secret passageway beneath the *Bir el-Arweh* for protection when the Temple was destroyed. Some say the Ark still remains there, guarded by spirits and demons.

Incidentally, although Muslim authorities have proscribed excavations under the Temple Mount, archeologists are reasonably certain the space is threaded with a vast network of underground substructures, such as the vaulted halls known as Solomon's Stables, as well as water reservoirs and cisterns.

Jewish sources suggest that the Stone arrived on Earth at the time of the first prophets and that it was called *Even HaShetiyah* because the foundation of the world had been established with its placement. Further, it was inscribed with the "Ineffable Name," the secret and unpronounceable name of God, the power of which keeps the *tehom* from overflowing and flooding the human world. The knowledge of this Name makes one the master over nature and life and death.

During the time of Joseph, the son of Jacob who was the patriarch of the twelve tribes of Israel, God held the *Even HaShetiyah* in His hand and warned Joseph that if he slept with Zuleika, "I will cast away this stone upon which the earth is founded and the world will fall to ruin." When Solomon's Temple of Jerusalem was built, the Holy of Holies, which housed the precious Ark of the Covenant, was set directly over the *Even HaShetiyah* at the very *center* of all.

Here is the mystical logic: The construction of the Earth began at the center with the *Even*

HaShetiyah at Jerusalem in Israel because the Holy Land is at the central point of the surface of the Earth; Jerusalem occupies the central point of Palestine; the original Temple of Jerusalem stands at the center of the Holy City; in the Temple sanctuary the *Hekal* is the center; the Ark of the Covenant occupies the center of the *Hekal*, built on the foundation stone, which thus is at the center of the Earth. "Thence issued the first ray of light, piercing to the Holy Land, and from there illuminating the whole earth."[309]

Of further significance is the fact that the Holy of Holies of the Temple was the dwelling place for the *Shekinah*, the Holy Spirit expressed as a feminine presence and the core of Jewish mysticism. The *Shekinah*, which means "resting" or "dwelling," was understood to be the feminine aspect of God and the way God manifests in the physical world, sometimes likened to God's face or wings.

The *Shekinah* is that part of God closest to the human, material world, and like the Jews (and all humankind), it wanders the world in exile from the Godhead. The Glory of Israel, her bridegroom, would periodically enter this marriage chamber and join his consort, the *Shekinah*, for the benefit of all Israel, its people and its lands. All of this glory was over the Stone.

In Jewish religious history the *Even HaShetiyah* was the site of three other crucial events. First, it was the altar upon which Abraham was about to sacrifice his son Isaac at God's request.

Second, it was the site designated by God for King David to make reparations for his offense against the Lord in demonstrating his lack of trust by proposing to take a census of the Jews. God responded to this blasphemy by releasing a plague that killed seventy thousand Israelites, but at the last moment instructed the Angel of Death to spare Jerusalem; this Angel was standing by the threshing-place of Araunah the Jebusite on the summit of Mount Moriah. David was commanded to construct an altar at this precise spot as a commemoration. In so doing, David reaffirmed Abraham's original covenant between God and the Jews.

It is also reported that when King David prayed for Jerusalem to be spared from the plague, he saw angels ascending a golden ladder from the threshing floor into the sky, putting away their swords of death as they went. "From this, David understood that the summit of the hill was the point of access to heaven and the place where the Temple must be built."[310]

The third had to do with the patriarch Jacob's famous pillow and dream. In preparation for sleeping at the Temple of Jerusalem (some versions say he slept at Luz, just outside Jerusalem), Jacob took twelve stones from the same altar upon which his father, Isaac, had lain bound as a sacrifice.

The twelve stones (representing the twelve tribes of Israel, not yet born) came together and formed a single stone, which Jacob then used as a pillow. In a magnificent dream, Jacob beheld the course of the world's history, including the future destruction of this temple, and he saw a ladder stretching from where he lay to the highest point in Heaven; angels were ascending and descending this heavenly ladder in a continuous procession.

Jacob, upon awaking, took the stone and set it up like a pillar and anointed it with oil he had received from Heaven. God sank this anointed stone so deep into the abyss that it could serve as the center of the Earth and the world's navel, to be known as the *Even HaShetiyah*. In other words, Jacob's "pillow" and the base of what is often called Jacob's Ladder, was the Foundation Stone. This site is also known as *Bethel*, "Gate or House of Heaven" or "House of the God El."

A similar night journey took place here sometime before 622. That traveler was the Muslim prophet, Muhammad. He was conveyed from near the Ka'aba in Mecca in Saudi Arabia to the Temple Mount in Jerusalem on a celestial winged creature called *al-Buraq* (Lightning), which was a horse with the face of a woman and a peacock's tail.

From the Foundation Stone, Muhammad ascended the Ladder of Lights through the Seven Heavens, accompanied by innumerable angels and witnessed by many ascended prophets, most notably the Archangel Gabriel. Muhammad was brought before the Divine Presence as the experiential pinnacle of his journey and informed that men should recite prayers fifty times daily.

His remarkable mystical excursion is known as the *al-Miraj*, the "Ascent," or *al-Isra*, the "Night Journey." Though the Temple had once been the sublime meeting place between humans and divinity, since its sack by the Romans and its near dismemberment it had lain in ruins, both physical and spiritual, for centuries prior to Muhammad's reanimation of the site. The Foundation Stone is said to bear the imprint of Muhammad's footprint as he pushed off from the site, and that of the Archangel Gabriel, who put his foot down to restrain the Stone from following the prophet on his Night Journey.

Of course all Jerusalem has been considered holy for millennia, perhaps for as long as it has been occupied, which, archeology informs us, is at least five thousand years. It's a holy city with many names: from 1,200 to 1,000 B.C., it was Jebus, or *ir hayebusi*, the city of the Jebusites, a hilltop fortress captured by King David in the tenth century B.C. It was *Tsiyon* (Zion), a word that suggests an earthly paradise modeled after a heavenly archetype, perhaps the celestial Jerusalem.

The city was also *Yir'eh-Shalem*, which has a complex meaning. In the largest sense, the name connotes "the place where later God will show (*yir'eh*), or make known on earth, the fullness and perfection (*shalem*) of what is above."[311] Jerusalem has been known as Yerushalem (a sin-

gular form), Yerushalayim (a plural form), Ruschalim (Egyptian), Urusalimmu (Assyrian), Hierosolyma (Greek), and Jerosolyma or Hierosalem (Christian).

Generally, the name is interpreted as meaning "foundation of peace," whose consonants (SHLM) mean perfect or whole (*shalem*) or peace (*shalom*). The earthly site where this peace is established is *Yeru* or *Yir'eh* (which was also one of Jerusalem's seventy names). The Hebrew root, *yarah*, means "to found," so *shalem* will be founded here.

An alternative or perhaps complementary interpretation of Yerushalayim says it was the cultic center of the Canaanite god Shalim, a deity referenced in Ugaritic mythology, which acknowledged two deities: *Shahar*, the god of the rising Sun, and *Shalim*, god of the setting Sun. What's interesting here is that these two names, Shahar and Shalim, also refer to the planet Venus, which is the Morning and Evening Star.

There's a controversial twist to this: anciently Venus was known as Phosphorus or Lucifer. This is either a metaphysical or an archeo-astronomical affiliation, but it suggests that at some level, Jerusalem is the Foundation of Venus or Lucifer, known to the Hebrews as *Helel ben Sahar*, Son of the Dawn, Lord of Light, the Shining One, Dawn Bringer, and Light Bringer.

According to Jewish sources, on the third day of Creation, Lucifer, God's chief archangel and cherub, "walked in Eden amid blazing jewels, his body a-fire" with the light of dozens of precious stones, all set in pure gold.[312] God had made Lucifer Guardian of All Nations. The Jewish sources say Lucifer aspired to enthrone himself on Saphon, the Mount of Assembly, for which ambition God cast him out of Heaven into the profound gloom of the Bottomless Pit in Sheol. As he fell from grace, Lucifer shone like lightning. The intriguing question is, if Jerusalem in some way is the Foundation of Lucifer, is it before or after he fell?

As mentioned, Solomon's Temple of Jerusalem was built from divine blueprints, transmitted to humanity by revelation. The plan was divinely revealed, and many think that the plan was the archetype of a Celestial City, the original, heavenly Jerusalem. The Temple was the "instrument of a mystical, priestly science," a cosmic temple, heavenly city, eternal standard, and world image, says John Michell, a well-regarded authority on ancient mysteries.

The numbers, measures, and harmonies of the revealed plan as given to King David, Solomon's father, reflected the ideal order of the macrocosm, says Michell. In that plan is the "key to forgotten knowledge, to the blueprint by which the universe was made, to the lost canon of number, measure, and music," used by the Egyptians and other ancient civilizations. In other words, the architectural details of the Temple of Jerusalem themselves are the revelation, regardless of whether the physical temple is ever rebuilt, Michell says.[313]

MYSTICS AND TOURISTS

When Graham Hancock, author of *The Sign and the Seal* and investigator of ancient mysteries, first visited the Dome of the Rock, he was not overwhelmed by the building, though he was impressed. What caught his breath was the Stone.

He felt attracted "by some powerful magnetic force," and felt his attention being "tugged down again towards the very centre" of the monument, to the "huge tawny rock" that was flat in places, jagged in others. "Rough-textured and asymmetrical, it jutted out above the bedrock of Mount Moriah as solid and unshakeable as the earth itself." He felt the "immense antiquity" of the Stone flow through the pores of his fingers as he contemplated this "strange and wonderful stone."[314]

GEOMANTIC

Dome; Grail Castle; Lucifer Binding Site.

DOME: The dome over the Temple Mount, Old Jerusalem, and the entire city corresponds to Aldebaran, the alpha star and eye of the bull Taurus. The Foundation Stone within the Dome of the Rock is the center of this dome. Aldebaran, the thirteenth brightest star in our galaxy, is a first-magnitude star located sixty-eight light years from Earth, forty times larger than our Sun and 125 times more luminous. It's usually described as rosy or pale reddish-orange in color, a quality the Hindu astronomers noted in their name, *Rohini,* which means "the Red One" or "the Red Deer." In Hindu star myths, Rohini is the female antelope, the daughter of the male antelope, Prajapati, the Lord of Generation (the constellation Orion).

Its name, from the Arabic *Al Dabaran,* means "the Follower," or "Bright One of the Follower," a reference to how its appearance in the sky follows just after the rising of the Pleiades or perhaps the Hyades, both in Taurus; it also sets immediately following the setting of these two star clusters. To the Mesopotamian astronomers, Aldebaran was one of the four royal stars, or "Watchers," along with Antares in Scorpio, Regulus in Leo, and Fomalhaut in Piscis Austrinus (the Southern Fish). The Babylonians knew it as *Ikuu,* "the Leading Star of Stars," the Akkadians as *Gisda,* "the Furrow of Heaven."

Appropriately, with respect to the attributions of the Flood, *tehom,* and the cosmic waters to the Foundation Stone, in various cultures Aldebaran was associated with the gods of the rain and the Earth's fertility. An interesting astronomical aspect of Aldebaran is that it is one of the few first-magnitude stars that are eclipsed regularly by our Moon, sometimes, as happened in 1978, every month for a year. It would be a useful study to correlate the schedule of occultations by the Moon of Aldebaran with political events in Jerusalem to see if the astronomical events coincide with earthly happenings.

GRAIL CASTLE: To understand what is meant by the statement that the *Even HaShetiyah* was set over the *tehom* to keep the waters of chaos from inundating the land, you need to reverse the relationships. The physical stone, which is part of the rock outcropping of Mount Moriah, is not the issue or the important player in this activity; it marks the spot.

The Foundation Stone does not keep the subterranean waters below the Temple Mount from rising up and flooding Jerusalem; rather, the Stone, which is an astral device, is the "plug" on the cosmic bathtub upstairs in the higher worlds. It is the realm of the ether, the primordial "waters" of creation, in which water is an esoteric code word for ether and primeval creative substance or matrix, for a level of undifferentiated consciousness—surely chaos to us.

The Temple Mount on Mount Moriah is the equivalent of Mount Ararat, the legendary resting place for Noah's Ark after the Deluge. There are in fact 144 such resting points for the Ark, for the resting place, the "Mount Ararat," is the staging ground for the ascent into the Grail Castle which is the same as the Ark. There the Ark floats, high above us, in the exalted dimensions, floating safely on the top of the Flood waters released in the interregnums between vast periods of creation and destruction—Days and Years of Brahma, in the Vedic time system.

The Ark, or Grail Castle, is the repository of all the information from the previous epochs of cosmic existence; the extent of this knowledge is almost unfathomable, almost incomprehensible, almost unattainable—except it isn't. The attainment of this inestimable, mind-dilating knowledge is the goal of the Grail Quest; it is the riches in the Celestial City of Lord Kubera of the North; it is the diverse contents of Noah's Ark; it is the cosmic wisdom of the Fish that towed the boat of *Matsya-avatara* to the northern mountain as the Flood subsided.

The real Foundation Stone is the regulator for the flow from above to below of the cosmic waters, which when they flow, inundate human consciousness with the living, consciousness-energizing wetness of the spiritual worlds. You could say that this Stone regulates how much deep cosmic memory and awareness can enter the human continuum at a given time without driving people mad.

Too much transcendental knowledge is like chaos; it can be a deadly poison. But when the land has gone dry with arid intellectualism and atheistic materialism, when it has become the Wasteland, as periodically happens, then it's appropriate to let a little water moisten the land.

One master of this water-world was King Solomon, who, with his wife, fashioned the Ship of Time, using wood from the original Tree of Life in the Garden of Eden. Solomon placed King David's sword (the one he claimed from giant Goliath after he slew him) on the Ship of Time, which was an Ark, or repository, outside of space-time, to arrive, much later in planetary history, at the Celtic King Arthur's Camalate in England to be used by the Christed Knight, Sir Galahad.[315]

The connections will not be clear yet, but this is about the alpha and omega of the Temple of Jerusalem, the original Jerusalem temple in that holy city in the planet's early days, and the New Jerusalem to come at Glastonbury in England. King David's "sword" is the knowledge of how to activate and use the Jerusalem temple; this knowledge was obtained from the giant Goliath, who is a symbol for the Elohim, the angelic family whose members were the consummate masters of the geomantic temple and conservators of its mysteries.

MYSTERIES OF THE EMERALD: As Jacob and Muhammad discovered, the Stone is also the launching pad for a remarkable *Miraj* into the higher spiritual worlds. The Stone itself—the real *Even HaShetiyah*—is the ladder into the higher worlds.

It is the emerald, the true foundation and Foundation Stone of Jerusalem. It is the green stone brought by the angels from Heaven to Earth, the Stone by which the Phoenix is burned to ashes and restored to life, the stone that is "forever incorruptible" and whose "essence is most pure," known as the Grail, as Wolfram von Eschenbach wrote.[316]

The emerald is the Heart within the heart chakra, an esoteric dimension between the outer and inner aspects of this chakra. It is a six-sided double-terminated green stone standing vertically on one of its terminations; seen from the bottom up it is also a green cube. The entire Earth energy matrix is bounded by this emerald; it exists within every human; and it is one of the jewels from the crown of the Lord of Light. It is the essence of the Jerusalem temple as an archetype of the consummate heavenly city, the divine ideal.

In practical terms, the emerald as a subtle light form sits magnificently upon the physical Foundation Stone within the Dome of the Rock on Temple Mount. Its size is irrelevant and flexible; it is easier to interact with if you allow yourself to see it as perhaps the size of a skyscraper. That way it is easier to enter, which you may do through any of its six fluidic, permeable walls.

There are other geomantic emeralds like this around the planet, but this one is special because its location is special. Only two places on Earth have the right combination of geomantic elements that allow *this* emerald (meaning, this emerald's special functions) to operate as intended. Only two places are designated for this seed to sprout: the Temple Mount in Jerusalem and the Tor in Glastonbury England. These are the Old Jerusalem and the New Jerusalem, both based on what we might call the once and future archetype of Jerusalem.

Here I mean not the physical Israeli city, nor the architectural details of the First and Second Temple of Jerusalem, but the celestial original for this temple, from the light pattern library from which our reality is created. The existence of the two physical Temples of Jerusalem for a time embodied and grounded this heavenly ideal, enabling it to function in the material world, and that was centrally important for the Earth.

Here is one reason why. The planet's twelve Vibrating Stones all lead here, to the Jerusalem temple archetype grounded at Temple Mount. Each stone grounds one of the Oroboros Lines that encircle the planet; each stone is coordinated with the celestial Jerusalem as overlaid on the Earth at the Temple Mount. There is one stone per one-twelfth division of the planet's surface, each of which is a pentagon. To each pentagon was assigned one of the twelve tribes of Israel; this was not a diaspora, but rather a code, a metaphor, for energies and holders of those energies assigned to each of the Earth's pentagons.

If you were standing by one of the stones—at Delphi in Greece or in Glastonbury—you could follow its energy connections and find yourself in the original Temple of Jerusalem. That temple, and its archetype, had twelve gates: the twelve Vibrating Stones are also twelve gates, and lead into the archetype of the Temple of Jerusalem, which for a time was coincident with the two physical Temples.

In practical geomantic terms, this meant that the twelve Oroboros Lines and the twelve zodiacal energies they represented were grounded at the Foundation Stone. Insofar as the twelve lines comprise twelve out of the fifteen prime energy lines that are the armature of the Earth's energy matrix, this central grounding point was potentially pivotal for the health, welfare, and destiny of the planet. A paradise on Earth—or something less exalted and uplifting—could be created or sustained from here.

The myths are true in saying the world was created from this Foundation Stone, with all things spreading out from this point. Energetically the Earth is inside the emerald, the original

Foundation Stone. Every aspect of the planet's complex geomantic structure is subsumed in this single planet-sized emerald; everything that comprises the Earth's geomythic matrix comes out of the emerald, and returns to it.

When the Temple of Jerusalem is physically grounded on the Earth, things are in the process of returning to their source within the emerald; everything that spread out from the Foundation Stone at the beginning of creation is now magnetically being recalled to its point of origin. Seen over vast stretches of Earth time, it is like a shape turning itself inside out, over and over, cycling in on itself like a torus, Jerusalem manifest, then unmanifest, then manifest again.[317]

THE ARK OF THE COVENANT: What about the Ineffable Name of God inscribed on the Foundation Stone and the Ark of the Covenant, which resided in the Holy of Holies (the *Devir*, a perfect cube of twenty cubits), said to be over the Stone? Jewish belief says that the location of the Ark "marks the exact center of the world, or God's footstool."[318]

The Ark is understood to have been a container, a portable rectangular box or wooden chest lined with gold with long parallel handles, measuring about four feet long, two feet high, and two feet wide. It held the tablets of the Ten Commandments, both the shattered first version and the intact second one, as well as Aaron's magical rod and a small quantity of manna (a miraculous angelic food).

At the time he received the Commandments while on Mount Sinai, Moses received instructions from God to construct the Ark of the Covenant to house the tablets. In many respects, Solomon built the Temple of Jerusalem to house the Ark.

The Ark was the holiest of objects, said to possess extraordinary magical powers capable of protecting the Jews from danger. Biblical references—the Old Testament has two hundred—indicate that the Ark blazed with fire and

lightning, emitted sparks, produced tumors or severe burns, could stop rivers, blast armies, destroy cities, and level mountains. It issued a moaning sound and was capable of rising off the ground and rushing at the enemies of the Jews in battle. God was said to descend and sit in the miniature Mercy Seat atop the Ark.

The Ark of the Covenant is one of the mysteries of the Earth, and it is presumptuous to speculate as to its true nature. However, it was a device that had to do with a combination of sound and energy, and there was only one Ark.

We can try approaching the matter sideways, as it were, through metaphor. The Ark was the voice of magic, the Word, the Ineffable Name uttered, all the living letters of the Hebrew alphabet spoken correctly, at once, the electric current that turned the system on. The system was the Earth grid, its armature of Oroboros Lines, its multiple linked emeralds—the "modem."

It could make twelve Oroboros Lines into a single twelve-stringed instrument, played from here at the Foundation Stone. It could make all the elements of the Earth's energy matrix cohere, turn inside out, and become part of the Temple of Jerusalem. It was perhaps like a recording of the Word that was in the beginning, all the sacred syllables and sounds in perfect pronunciation—a magic wand of sound. When this sound touched the *Even HaShetiyah*, it animated the Earth's spiritual body and remarkable things happened and were possible.

When it was "on," it made not just the Temple but the entire Earth the Morning and Evening Star, the Foundation of Venus—Heaven on Earth realized, the celestial Jerusalem Temple fully manifest in matter.

The downside was misuse, as J. R. R. Tolkien said of another unique magical device in *The Lord of the Rings,* "One ring to rule them . . . and in the darkness bind them." The Earth had witnessed such a misuse, a malfeasance remembered in Grail myth as the Dolorous Stroke by which the Fisher

King had misused the Sword of David (the Elohim's celestial codes for operating the system), wounded himself, and precipitated the Wasteland. The plug was put back in securely to block the flow of the *tehom* into the human world. Access to the Grail Castle was curtailed, and its reality eventually disbelieved, forgotten.

INIMICAL ENERGIES AT THE TEMPLE MOUNT: We should not be surprised to find a fair concentration of what we could label dark and negative energies marshaled at the Temple Mount to block or distort access.

Two giant astral beings are locked in mortal battle atop the Mount, swords clashing, wounds gaping; they are primitive beings of a male valence, and all they do is fight, striving to kill each other. This energy permeates Jerusalem. Numerous alien ships high above the city quarantine the Mount in a ring of beams broadcast like laser shafts.

These energies help maintain the energies and functions of several circles of reptilian beings and giant astral snakes that surround the Mount, facing outwards into Jerusalem, discouraging access, keeping the energies combative, fragmented, bent on isolation and conflict. Behind them and also facing away from the Mount is another circle of large demonic control beings; their function too is to dissuade the fainthearted, to inflame those on the edge, to confuse or scare the rest, to keep the Mount and Stone from being used again as intended.

The dome directly over the Mount and encompassing all of Jerusalem is damaged. Part of its crown is severed, like a yarmulke riding the side of the head by the ears instead of the occiput. The two cords linking the dome to the master dome at Avebury are damaged; one of them is not "hooked up" at all. The damages mean that Jerusalem through its dome is not receiving the beneficial cosmic energies of both Sirius and Canopus through Avebury as they are meant to; this allows other inimical energies to exert the predominant influence.

The dome can be repaired, but it requires human assistance in conjunction with the angelic realm, and such repair could only be undertaken if the spiritual worlds judged it appropriate or karmically possible. (For information about another damaged dome, see Clingman's Dome, Tennessee.)

LUCIFER BINDING SITE: Coincident with the decommissioning of the Jerusalem Temple was the binding of Lucifer, Lord of Light, under the Foundation Stone. The Foundation of Venus, the Jerusalem new, old, and archetypal, is his light realm.

Elsewhere in Christendom, the tendency was to bury Lucifer under the granite weight of a massive Gothic cathedral, such as at Lincoln in England. For Jerusalem as the city to be healed, Lucifer, its foundation, will have to be *un*bound, and for the New Jerusalem to manifest on the planet, the Lord of Light will have to be restored to his pre-Fall position as God's chief archangel.

This is not meant to be a definitive listing of the geomantic features of Jerusalem, for it has many others. Notable among these is one of the Earth's twelve Crowns of the Ancient of Days at Golgotha, the Hill of Skulls, and an eighteen-mile-wide Landscape Zodiac on the periphery of the Old City.

Dornach, Switzerland

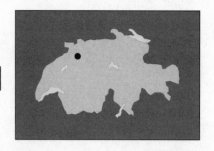

Dornach is a small Swiss village near Basel that since 1912 has been the world headquarters of the Anthroposophical Society, the movement founded by the Austrian spiritual scientist and clairvoyant Rudolf Steiner (1861–1925).[319] Ever since 1913 when Steiner constructed his first Mystery temple, the Goetheanum, both the hill and the building have shared in the numinosity of the site, which is set on a small rise in the Birs River Valley and surrounded by the Jura Mountains. (The site is very close to the French border.)

To many, the Goetheanum *is* the hill, and whatever spiritual emanations one encounters on this gentle rise are as much due to the arrestingly unusual, asymmetrical reinforced gray concrete Goetheanum as to the hill's own preexisting spiritual qualities. In fact, Steiner himself remarked in 1921 in a welcoming address to visitors to the site that before them "is not a single person greeting you here, but above all, the building. It is the Goetheanum itself that greets you."[320]

To some, the "atmospheric currents" of the Jura landscape itself seemed to have summoned the Goetheanum from out of the etheric world and made visible the spiritual principles its architecture embodies. So in a sense, the landscape's own formative forces greet people visiting the Goetheanum.

Apparently, the famous German poet, playwright, and natural scientist Johann Wolfgang von Goethe (1749–1832), to whom Steiner dedicated his building, sensed these architectural atmospheres on Dornach hill during his visit. In October 1779, in one of his *Letters from Switzerland,* as they were later called when published, Goethe wrote about how "since time immemorial" the Birs river had flowed through the "lofty and broad" Jura mountains, how the connecting walls rose perpendicularly, broad masses piled up, the steep cliffs dropping off abruptly, how the fissures cleave open and the "blunt, pointed, overgrown, bare" ridges of the crags rise like "single crests, bald and bold."

It was as if Goethe were describing a building in the landscape, or the awesome architectural shape that the energies and structures of the Dornach landscape might take if transformed into a temple. "The sublime affords the soul a grand repose; it is filled wholly with this and feels itself as large as it can ever be."[321] As one modern architectural scholar put it, "It is as if 'from time immemorial' the cradle for a 'Goetheanum' had been prepared by Nature herself." At the same time, "this work of architecture is able to translate the formative forces of nature, expressed here in limestone, as a corresponding human response for all men to interpret."[322]

HISTORY AND ARCHEOLOGY

As a village, Dornach was originally a Celtic settlement, known as Turniacus, meaning "property of Turanius." During the Roman era, Dornach served as a hostelry and resting place for Roman troops; it was of some strategic value to the Romans, possibly because at the time it had the only bridge across the River Birs. Dorneck Castle, situated on the hill that overlooks the Birs Valley, was constructed to guard the bridge and the Dorneck prefectory around it. In the fifth century A.D., Dornach and the surrounding area came under the control of the Burgundians, who ushered in Arian Christianity as instigated by Saint Maurice of Wallis, for whom an early Christian church was built and dedicated at Dornach.

Beginning in 1485, Dornach became part of the Swiss Confederation. In 1499, the Dornach hill earned its epithet *Bluthügelweg,* or Blood Hill Way, when a decisive battle for Swiss independence was fought on its slopes against German feudal lords and three thousand Swabian troops. (Even today, Dornach hill is sometimes locally referred to as Blood Hill, but officially its epithet has been toned down to *Hügelweg,* or Hill Way.) In 1499, following his defeat in the battle, the Emperor Maximilian signed the "Peace of Basel," formally acknowledging the independent sovereignty of the Swiss Confederacy.

Dornach's sister village, Arlesheim, is notable for harboring the miracle-producing Saint Odilie in the seventh century A.D. She was born blind to a Merovingian nobleman in the Hohenburg Castle on Mont-Saint-Odilie (also known as the Odilienberg), but gained her sight at baptism and thereafter dedicated her life to Christianity. A sick woman called Odilie "Queen of Heaven" after she healed her with a bright light that radiated from her body. When Odilie's father killed his own son, Odilie restored him to life with her prayers. Her father's pagan beliefs—the Odilienberg was originally a seat of pagan mysteries—and general animosity became unbearable for Odilie and she fled.

Odilie soon found herself hiding out in a grotto on the *Hohle Fels* behind Arlesheim, facing the Dornach hill upon which now stands the Goetheanum. During her seclusion, she experienced what has been described as an illumination through Christ. It's also said that the rocks protectively closed in on her as her father, Count Eticho, tried to attack her hiding place; instead he got knocked out by falling stones and nearly died. "A being of intense light appeared out of the rockface as he lay there and the Count now experienced a total conversion and was reconciled with Odilie."[323]

This illumination that enabled her to make peace with her father by healing him helped convert all of Alsace to Christianity. A small church in Arlesheim was afterwards dedicated to her and, in 708 A.D., she bequeathed her Arlesheim estate to the Alsatian Abbey. By the eleventh century, Saint Odilie was famous throughout Europe as *Sol Dei,* the "Sun of God," a reference to her reported ability to manifest an almost blinding healing light.

"From her stay in Arlesheim, as a resting place during her flight," commented Rudolf Steiner, "Odilie gained the forces she needed for her further spiritual development and for the founding of the Convent of Odilie." Over time, she gained the reputation for having been a patron of Grail knights. Steiner also contended that a key scene in Wolfram von Eschenbach's *Parzival,* a thirteenth-century story of the Holy Grail and its mysteries, namely, three meetings of Parzival with his cousin Sigune, took place in the garden in Arlesheim called the Eremitage. This possibility might have contributed to the observation of two contemporary writers on Grail mysteries that the Goetheanum is "a modern Grail Temple."[324]

There is still more on the Grail link with Dornach and Arlesheim. Apparently Hugo of Tours, France, the leader of the ninth century's Grail impulse in Europe and a kind of diplomat for Charlemagne, according to Steiner, might have been the basis for von Eschenbach's enigmatic thirteenth-century Grail savant Treverizent, whom that author described as the custodian of the Holy Grail.

It's important to note that as a written document, von Eschenbach's *Parzival* was considered *the* summation of the mysteries of the Holy Grail for its time. Most of it was written in a recondite initiate's code; the names are strange; some of the events peculiar; most of it is hard to understand; and a lot of it is no longer psycho-spiritually relevant to the twenty-first century Western psyche. However, one point that von Eschenbach makes that is relevant to the mysteries of Dornach was his reference that the Grail was a green stone brought to Earth by the angels.

It is said that the grotto in which Saint Odilie hid from her father later became part of the hermitage of Treverizent; the assumption is that Treverizent was a real figure as opposed to a literary creation and that he instructed the young Parzival here after his first unsuccessful foray into the Grail castle. Legend further has it that in his last years, Hugo of Tours retired to the same hermitage at Arlesheim in which Saint Odilie had lived. "It was at this hermitage that Hugo became the teacher of the wisdom of the Holy Grail."[325]

Steiner first came to Dornach on October 2, 1912, at the invitation of Dr. Emil Grosheintz, a dentist who owned a summer house and some property on Dornach hill. Dr. Grosheintz had purchased the Dornach property with the idea of establishing an agricultural school there; Steiner had been scouring Münich in Germany for a suitable site to build his *Johannesbau* (Saint John's

Building), which was to be a combination Mystery temple and theater. Dr. Grossheintz offered Steiner the Dornach hill property, and in the spring of 1913 the construction began.

During his first visit to the Dornach property, Steiner investigated the subtle energy aspects of the landscape. He visited the subterranean grottoes in Arlesheim at the base of Dornach hill. Walking around the hill, he was aware of the "peculiar spiritual cloudlike formation which we may designate as the etheric aura" at Dornach, he wrote later. Such an "etheric aura" towers up over every topographical area on Earth, he said, and a "special etheric sheath" could be found over all the genuine ancient "Mystery Centers."[326]

These etheric auras preserve "a fundamental tone" in a landscape over long periods of time. Steiner also noted that the physical Earth, like the human body, is embedded in an etheric body, which in turn is encompassed by an astral body. If we could see the planet from space, we would see the Earth surrounded by an aura of light, which was the planet's etheric and astral bodies.[327]

This same kind of Mystery center auric sheath was present over Dornach hill, and had probably been there since its geological inception, Steiner added. He alluded to various "mystery secrets" that he hoped over time to tease out of the ethers enveloping Dornach. He thought that in some ways his conception for the Goetheanum, as a living, organic building dedicated to the mysteries of creative speech, might be part of this revelation.

Steiner said the building's structure was related to the human etheric body, and that there was a "deeply hidden etheric union" between the building, conceived as a kind of spiritual being, and the Master Builder, the higher spiritual forces that guide the world, "woven like a protective sheath in order to receive and absorb the highest impulses of a new mystery center." Then he added that the perception of this relationship came out of his sensing the mystery secrets of Dornach hill itself.[328]

At the autumnal equinox in 1913, Steiner laid what he called the first Foundation Stone for the Goetheanum at the Dornach site, letting people understand he was convinced that through this site "a central point for spiritual knowledge will be created."[329] In the midst of a fierce blowing gale and accompanied by about 40 stalwart colleagues, Steiner called upon the spiritual hierarchies to bless the site and to protect the undertaking. He told people that the completion of the Goetheanum was part of the "mission of the Earth itself." The stone was a double pentagonal dodecahedron made of copper.[330] It represented "the striving human soul immersed as a microcosm in the macrocosm" but it also stood for "knowledge, love, and strong courage."[331]

Steiner had high hopes for the contribution the Goetheanum might make to the world in the coming centuries, but he also knew it would magnetize opposition and interference. Actual happenings in the spiritual worlds would be talked about openly there; the Anthroposophical Society must maintain a "High School of true Spiritual Science" at Dornach; Dornach would be a "living center of spiritual knowledge."

At the rededication of the Goetheanum in 1923—the first one burned down on New Year's Eve, 1922—Steiner stated the building's mission even more passionately: "Spiritual flames of fire will go forth from the new Goetheanum that will come into being in the future, for the blessing of mankind."[332] One Anthroposophical writer afterwards said that the intense early activities of Steiner and his Anthroposophists immediately after the rededication coalesced to form a karmic envelope, "a kind of condensed astral light shining around the Goetheanum."[333]

Steiner's second dedication of the Goetheanum in 1923 was an altogether different event than his first. Many who were there after-

wards considered it an epiphany of global proportions in terms of its spiritual implications. It has since been called the Christmas Meeting. Some eight hundred Anthroposophists gathered with Steiner in the Schreinerei, one of the Society's ancillary buildings on Dornach hill on the evening of December 25.

Rather than placing a physical stone in the hill again, this time Steiner placed what he called the Foundation Stone Meditation in the hearts of his colleagues. This second "stone" was also a dodecahedron, in a spiritual sense, but in the form of a meditative verse that required of his listeners some penetration to unravel the full scope of its mystery revelations regarding humanity's relationship with the angelic realm and the Trinity.

Steiner exhorted his audience to "truly *live*" in the "All-World-Being of Man." The Foundation Stone, he said, was also the "Dodecahedron of Man . . . which we lay in the ground of our souls." According to one commentator on the event, the laying of this second Foundation Stone was "an almost public Mystery deed."

The eight hundred men and women present, "in a deeper sense, represented the spiritual quest of modern mankind," as if they were there on behalf of the rest of humanity. The event was a "Mystery, whose deep significance will only reveal itself to mankind as time goes on."[334] This may strike us today as perhaps a grandiose observation, but below, when we discuss the geomantic aspects of Dornach, we will see that it may in fact be warranted.

GEOMANTIC

Aquarius Albion Emerald; Landscape Zodiac; Golden Egg; Dome.

AQUARIUS ALBION EMERALD: I will depart from my customary approach of reviewing the largest geomantic aspects for a site last because with Dornach, the largest aspect explains the others. In this case, it also makes it clear why Steiner made his seemingly grandiose comments about the Goetheanum. His claims that Dornach was a Mystery center of high quality and ancient stature are justified.

Dornach's *Bluthügelweg,* or Blood Hill Way, is the site of one of the planet's twelve emeralds, specifically, the one for the Albion plate now under the astrological influence of Aquarius. The emerald is an esoteric aspect of the heart chakra, which customarily is described as having two aspects: the outer *(Anahata)* and the inner *(Ananda-kanda)*. The emerald in effect is the third aspect of the heart center. It is also the "green stone" referred to by von Eschenbach as being the same as the Holy Grail.

Dornach sits in the Birs River Valley. Overlaid upon this valley is a pale-blue slightly concave dish or saucer shape. This is a geomantic structure produced by human consciousness, in conjunction with the angelic and elemental, and placed upon a particular aspect of a landscape and "underneath" the specific geomantic structure as a way of supporting and amplifying the energetic aspects of both.

The emerald, which we could envision as being as large as the hill itself, sits upright at the center of this pale-blue dish. This emerald is double-terminated with six equal facets; the intriguing fact is that from a different geometric perspective, the emerald is a dodecahedron.[335] This means that in 1913 Steiner placed an actual copper double dodecahedron in a hill whose energy body shape was itself a dodecahedron. And when he inducted his fellow eight hundred Anthroposophists into his Foundation Stone meditation in 1923, they were, at least spiritually, actually entering a very large emerald—of cathedral proportions—in the very place they were standing, on Dornach hill. Even better, the emerald is a shortcut to the Grail Castle and the Holy Grail itself.

Thus Steiner from the force of his own spiritual presence and with the assistance of the angelic realm facilitated an initiation within the emerald for the Aquarian geometric division of the planet during the now famous Christmas Meeting. It gets a little dizzying to picture, but the emerald is a doorway within the individual human, through the heart chakra; it is an important geomantic feature found in twelve places on the Earth; it is the primary, original geometric shape of the Earth's energy body when perceived as a whole; and it is the heart center of a majestic spiritual being for whom the Earth is its responsibility.

In Steiner's Christmas Meeting at Dornach in 1923 we have the clear evidence of a major geomantic and spiritual initiation in which the landscape and the people benefited equally. The landscape emerald received focused human consciousness and attention, and the human emeralds received a mark of recognition from the eight hundred participants under Steiner's inspired guidance. Of course it is difficult to know (and futile to speculate) to what degree any of the eight hundred or even Steiner was aware of the geomantic complexities, but it is certain that in their higher aspects of consciousness they fully participated in the event.

The 1923 initiation through and of the Aquarian emerald had immediate ramifications for one-twelfth of the planet, and eventually, for the entire Earth. Within each of the twelve geometric divisions of the Earth's surface lies an Albion waiting to be awakened by human, angelic, and elemental interaction. As much of Eastern Europe, the Baltic and Slavic countries, and parts of Russia lie within the Albion division that includes Dornach, Steiner's geomantic deed was to stimulate a spiritual seed that would bear fruit throughout the twentieth century in those areas.

Ultimately, each Albion is a terrestrial copy of the original Adam Kadmon, to use the Judaic-Qabalistic term, or the primordial cosmic Human whose body is the cosmos. This is why Steiner encouraged his colleagues to "truly *live*" in the "All-World-Being of Man" because they were awakening that being's Earthly heart. When Steiner referred to the "Dodecahedron of Man . . . which we lay in the ground of our souls" he was indicating the very large geomythic body of the Aquarian Albion in which the Goetheanum was situated. In practical and geomantic terms, Steiner's Foundation Stone was the emerald.

LANDSCAPE ZODIAC: Dornach, Arlesheim, and the surrounding countryside are also part of a Landscape Zodiac that is about fourteen miles in diameter. The dome over the zodiac is even larger, energizing an area about thirty-one miles wide.

A Landscape Zodiac is a terrestrial star map, a cosmic body of Albion laid out across a section of landscape; ultimately, the point of all the stars and constellations is to comprise the body of Albion, itself a reflection of the Adam Kadmon, as mentioned above. Within this geomythic Albion, Dornach hill is also this figure's esoteric heart chakra, or the emerald. This means Steiner's 1923 geomantic activation had repercussions on at least two levels of the total geomantic structure of the area. It also gives us added insight into one of Anthroposophy's most fundamental concepts, that the macrocosm is expressed through the microcosm.

In Steiner's language, this idea was often expressed in the somewhat peculiar expression that "organology equals cosmology." Steiner meant that the energy antecedents of all aspects of human physiology can be found in the arcane spiritual processes of stars and celestial beings. He also meant that study of the functions of the heart or liver, for example, ultimately leads you back into the cosmos. Spiritual beings, stars, planets, constellations, and other energy dynamics of the "supersensible worlds" are at play in every aspect of the human being.

This gets exciting. In a sense, a Landscape Zodiac lets you know yourself as a cosmic being. You walk the star patterns in a physical landscape while having visions of the cosmos. "We bear the whole cosmos within us when we incarnate again on Earth," Steiner explained. "In very truth, man bears the stars of heaven within him." The spiritual seed of the human physical body is "a universe of vast magnitude."

Steiner said that every physical organ in the human body is "in effect the terrestrial counterpart of a divine-spiritual Being" and that originally, the entire cosmos appeared as a gigantic being, as the summation of "the inner-organic, cooperative activity of generation of Gods."[336] Insights and experiences of this caliber are available to anyone who works with a Landscape Zodiac.

GOLDEN EGG: This feature gives us more perspective on why Steiner emphasized the primacy of the Christ and what he termed the Mystery of Golgotha within his Anthroposophical model. The point of the Golden Egg is to unfold a golden child, or Christ being, in a given landscape area; this template becomes a training ground for people interested in birthing the Christ child within themselves as part of an initiation pathway within the Christian mysteries. The foundation of this golden child is at Arlesheim, the bulk of the child and its crown is at Dornach hill, and the Madonna figure who embraces the child above the crown lies in the Birs Valley.

Bear in mind that when Steiner discussed the Christ, he did so—as he often reminded his audiences—from the perspective of the Christ as a cosmic being, a cosmic fact, and not as an ideologically constrained personage within a religion.[337] In this respect, Steiner gave many Westerners a new route into the mysteries of the Christ, a route that avoided what many outside organized religion believed were theological pitfalls and obstacles and in some cases, errors.

"The world will recognize that the message of the science of the spirit is the Word of Christ," Steiner said. "The mission of the science of the spirit in our age is to open doors to the living Christ."[338] What better place than at the golden child whose geomythic body is situated between Arlesheim and Dornach?

The combination of Aquarius Albion emerald, Landscape Zodiac, and Golden Egg should start to make it clear why Steiner said Dornach was a preeminent Mystery center. It also gives us a sense of the deep appropriateness of site to philosophy, why Steiner founded his international spiritual scientific movement and constructed his Goetheanum at Dornach and not, for example, at München, which had been his original consideration. Dornach's geomantic structure is an excellent place to ground, amplify, and disseminate the spiritual beliefs of Anthroposophy. It shows how effective it can be when a site's potential is maximized.

Even better, it shows us how to use a residential approach to grounding, activating, and sustaining a geomantic site. Steiner acquired the property, figured out its energy dynamics, founded a world spiritual movement there, and grounded the impulse with a massive building that was to an extent summoned out of the ethers surrounding Dornach.

That was close to a century ago, and ever since, the Anthroposophical movement has been sending out what Steiner would call a spiritualizing impulse to the planet through Dornach's specific and appreciable geomantic connections. For other examples, working through other impulses, see the Hill Cumorah at Palymra, New York, a planetary emerald maintained by the Mormons; and Bayreuth, Germany, headquarters of the Wagner Festspielhaus and the world headquarters for enthusiasts of Richard Wagner's operas.

The Dornach Mystery center is a perfect place to deepen one's immersion in the Grail mysteries, continuing in a spiritual trend highlighted by the Saint Odilie and Treverizent stories. The hidden knowledge that would start taking hold of humans in the twentieth century, Steiner explained, may be called symbolically "the wisdom of the Grail."

The "concealed knowledge of the Grail will be revealed as an inner force; it will permeate more and more the manifestations of human life." The "highest imaginable ideal" of human evolution is the fruit of knowledge of the Grail, he added, "the spiritualization that man acquires through his own efforts."[339]

DOME: The dome over Dornach is the starfall for alpha Lepus, known as *Arneb*. Lepus is the constellation of the Hare, which crouches under Orion's feet; just south of Rigel are four faint stars that mark the ears of the hare, while Arneb (*Al Arnab*, in the original Arabic) is one of three stars located in the torso of the hare. The star is of the second magnitude, situated about nine hundred light years from Earth; it is about 5,700 times as luminous as our Sun.

The Arabs once referred to this constellation as *Al Kursiyy al Jabbar*, the "Chair of the Giant" or *Al Arsh al Jauzah*, the "Throne of Jauzah" or the "Throne of the Central One." They also suggested that the four bright stars in the constellation (which form an irregular quadrilateral figure) represented four camels drinking at the river Eridanus, another constellation, or from the Milky Way. The Egyptians saw this constellation as the "Boat of Osiris," whom they identified with Orion. The hare is generally perceived to be fleeing Orion the hunter. The star myths say that the hare was made a constellation in honor of the animal's ability to give birth and be pregnant with additional future offspring at the same time.

At first glance, it seems unimpressive to have a constellation named after a rabbit and for the dome star at Dornach to be in the hare constellation. When you peruse the symbolism of the hare, however, the seemingly mundane picture begins to shift. Hares are symbolically linked with the Earth Mother and the constant renewal of life through death. The hare is also frequently associated with the Moon, partly because it dies to be reborn, just as the Moon becomes full, then "dies" into the New Moon then renews itself to become full again.

The hare acts as an intercessor between our physical world and the transcendent realities of the supersensible realm. Among the Alqonquin Ojibwa and Sioux Winnebago tribes of North America, the prime culture hero, Menebuch, appeared as a Great Hare. He renewed the world after the Flood and organized human culture. Other scholars of symbolism see the hare as akin to the Christian lamb or as an emblem of a lunar Messiah. Even more appropriate to our understanding of alpha Lepus and Dornach is the observation that after the Alqonquins had been converted to Christianity, "they effectively transformed Menebuch into Jesus Christ."[340]

The themes of death and renewal and lunar Messiahs make more sense when we add a few more elements to the Dornach geomantic picture. The essential energy quality of the alpha Lepus dome is about creating purity and certainty in the Christ revelation. It is about bringing the Golgotha revelation—not the crucifixion so much as the ascension and resurrection—to this one-twelfth division of the Earth's surface as a living experience.

The spiritual beings who were the twelve Apostles around Jesus Christ are present within the energy field of this dome as a kind of abiding supervisory presence, contributing to the gradual expansion of the field of influence of the essential energy. The Apostles are in turn overshadowed by even more majestic presences: the eighteen archangels. It is as if the apostles and the archangels are cultivating this energy, which is a bright yellow, as a seed in a chalice.

The seed is always available to the world, and the supply is never exhausted—it is one and many, prolifically reproductive, as the hare symbolism suggests. The seeds prevent its corruption and assure its dissemination. The seed enters the world primarily through speech. After all, Steiner envisioned the Goetheanum as the House of Speech, and said that the Christ mysteries, exemplified at Pentecost, were primarily about the transmission of spiritual realities through the spoken word.

Another reason this hill was called Blood Hill Way predated the seventeenth-century battle. At a deeper level of spiritual reality within the Arneb dome over Dornach is an energy whose concern is to create the Christ blood. In discussions of the Grail mysteries, a great deal of attention is placed on the *Sang Real,* the Royal Blood, but this has usually taken a materialistic conception in the sense of genetic blood lineages of Grail initiates and spiritual kings with credentials traceable back to Jesus. The reality might be more subtle than this, although in essentially the same line of insight.

Somewhere inside Dornach hill, or perhaps at the Arlesheim grotto in which Saint Odilie secreted herself, is an actual cave. In that space is also a spiritual temple which takes the form of a white gazebo or rotunda at whose center sits a small chalice containing blood. This is the blood of Christ. One drop is all one needs to start a profound transmutation and transfiguration process. The experience, or initiation, is akin to taking the sacrament of the Mass. Your blood chemistry will begin to change under the influence of the Christ.

Surrounding this white gazebo is a vast assemblage of spiritual beings, both human and angelic. They are watching the miracle of the transfigured blood, in which the spirit is made flesh and the flesh is raised into spirit. It's not one or the other, but both, and continuously. It is a Grail mystery revelation.

It's as if a single drop of blood burns with white fire; first you see the red vividness of a drop of human blood; then you see the white flames, and in them, the entire spiritual hierarchy of angels and elementals—all the spiritual presences whose potency contributes to the manifestation of reality as we know it. The blood keeps cycling, like an inturning torus from blood to white fire to blood as the spiritual beings witness the achievement of the Event at Golgotha in which Heaven and Earth fused as flesh became spirit and spirit became flesh.

Easter Island, Chile

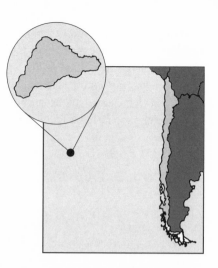

Easter Island is a bit of a mystery. It's called Easter Island because a Dutch sea captain named Jacob Roggeveen arrived there on Easter Sunday, April 5, 1722, around 5 P.M. In the 1860s, Tahitian sailors gave Easter Island the name *Rapa Nui,* meaning "Great Rapa," because it reminded them of another island in French Polynesia called Rapa Iti. Other interpretations have it meaning "big barren land." Apparently, before 1863, nobody on Easter Island had heard of Rapa Nui as a name for this island.

It's a triangular-shaped island of sixty-four square miles, regarded as the planet's most isolated inhabited land. It's considered the easternmost island of Polynesia (2,500 miles to the northwest), yet is administered by Chile, 2,340 miles to the east, a five-hour airplane flight away. Chile annexed the island in 1888. It is 1,400 miles east of the nearest inhabited island, Pitcairn, which has fewer than one hundred residents.

A 1992 census reported 2,770 people living on Easter Island, a forty-three percent increase over 1982, and tourism is steadily growing, with 6,800 visitors in 1995 and 10,161 in 1996. In 1996, UNESCO declared Easter Island a "Cultural Patrimony of Humanity," requiring the Chilean government to preserve and protect it.

The island has three main peaks, which are firm and rounded: Terevaka in the north, at 1,674 feet; Poike in the east, at 1,510 feet; and Rano Kau in the southwest, at 985 feet. Technically, the whole of Easter Island is a ten-thousand-foot volcano (measured from the Pacific Ocean floor), with some eighty volcanic cones throughout the island and numerous volcanic tubes that have created an extensive network of caves. Both Terevaka and Poike are extinct volcanoes, but Poike is the oldest, estimated to have been created five million years ago.

Easter Island natives call their island *Te Pito o Te Henua,* "The Navel or Center of the World," but today they're not quite sure why. "One has only to climb to the summit of Maunga Terevaka, the northwest volcano and the island's highest point, and scan the sea horizon equidistant in every direction," commented Father Sebastian Englert, for thirty years the island's parish priest, who published a book in 1948 about his time on Easter Island, "to understand why this is truly an island at the center of the world."[341]

The main attraction of Easter Island, and its baffling mystery, is the nearly nine hundred massive stone heads each set on an oblong torso called a *moai* situated on the periphery of the island, their backs to the sea. Nobody knows why they are there. The average moai stands thirteen feet high and weighs almost fourteen tons, but the biggest one is seventy-one feet tall and weighs 145 tons. That one is still lying incomplete in the Rano Raraku quarry where it was being made; the largest standing moai is thirty-two feet high and weighs eighty-two tons.

In all, there are 887 of these enigmatic stone heads on Easter Island, of which 288 (thirty-two percent) were successfully installed in the ground, 397 (forty-five percent) were incomplete in the quarry, and 92 (ten percent) fell or were dropped in transit. Many of them stand on an *ahu,* a flat mound of stone pedestal about four feet high; there are in fact at least 250 such platforms, spaced about a half-mile apart, creating an almost unbroken line around the island's perimeter.

Many moai also have a *pukao,* or "topknot," made of oxidized red volcanic rock. This is a kind of hat or crown, also called *Hau hiterau moai.* Only eighty-nine of these rounded lozenge-shaped cylinders have been found, fifty-eight fallen off their statues and thirty-one still in the quarry. One *pukao* is six feet in diameter and weighs eleven tons.

Some are set many feet (in one excavated case, the total height was forty feet) into the ground, and from a certain point of view, it's as if the entire island were a standing stone circle, the interior of an oddly shaped perimeter of 288 carved stones whose eyes seem to be looking upwards. Perhaps that is why the Mangarevan name for the island is *Mata-ki-te-Rangi,* "Eyes toward the Heavens."

Archeologists are not sure if the stone faces ever had eyes, but they have found evidence of white coral and red scoria that when fitted together and placed in the moai's eye sockets, seemed to fit naturally. Some authorities contend that only the statues on the ahu were given eyes,

and that thus "opening" the statues' eyes activated the power of the moai.

The moai are clearly male heads, but nobody is sure whose heads they represent. They are generalized images, standardized faces, rather than individual portraits. Sometimes they are referred to collectively as *aringa ora,* the "Living Faces." A French explorer visiting Easter Island in 1786 found no evidence of a moai cult, nor even the suggestion that the statues were idols, only that the islanders clearly respected them.

Archeologists propose that they commemorate various ancestral chiefs and they were "ceremonial conduits" for communication with Polynesian deities. The Easter Islanders have no written and seemingly no oral account of the moai. As an English researcher noted in 1915, Polynesians are notoriously inexact and often "do not themselves know when they are speaking the truth, and when they are relying on imagination." Their answers to researcher's questions are "generally wildly mythical."[342]

Archeologists are mostly concerned with how the islanders, using only primitive means, could ever have moved the giant stones, and how they got to the island in the first place using primitive sailing vessels, presumably from eastern Polynesia or South America. Not much professional interest is focused on what the stones might do, although in general, worldwide recognition of the stones has increased since 1958 when the Norwegian researcher and sailor Thor Heyerdahl published the results of his investigations of the moai in his popular book *Aku-Aku.*

When he asked island natives in the 1950s how the moai were moved in the old days, he was told consistently: "They went of themselves." Or that in the old days there was a witch at Rano Raraku who through her magic breathed life into the stone giants and made them go to their proper destinations. Later she made the statues all fall flat on their faces, never to rise again. Or that the mythical king Tuu Ihu and the god Make-Make ordered the stones to walk.

In 1998, when the PBS science show *Nova* sent a team to Easter Island for a month to film how the ancient Easter Islanders might have physically moved the stones, they were told it was the stone's *manna* or divine power that enabled them to move on their own. "They walked across the land and our ancestors have celebrated it for centuries."[343] Petero Edmunds, then the mayor of Easter Island, told the *Nova* team: "The Rapa Nui people are tied to the moai by their roots." When you live on an isolated island like this for generations, "you have more time to bring up your mind to a maximum" and to develop the paranormal ability of mana.[344]

As Father Englert noted in 1970, the moai and outdoor altars have captured the world's imagination, and the island is recognized as "the most spectacular museum of prehistoric Polynesian art and architecture in the whole Pacific."[345] At Rano Raraku, the island's quarry, where 150 moai stand with their silent, tight-lipped gaze, you realize these are "enormous faces astonishingly alike. All had the same stoical expression and the most peculiar long ears."

At the quarry, hundreds of thousands of cubic feet have been cut out and tens of thousands of tons of stone carried away—it's as if the nine hundred stone faces arose from an antediluvian sleep within the stony land to take their places.[346] Many of the moai that are dug into the ground are in the quarry. English archeologist Katherine Routledge found the view of Rano Raruku at sunset "particularly inspiring" when she was there in 1913. As the daylight fades, "the images [moai] gradually become outlined as stupendous black figures against the gorgeous colouring of the west."[347]

Archeologists lukewarmly speculate that given the moai's close proximity to the edge of the ocean, they might have a role in "preventing encroachment" by the sea or that their sheer monumentality "must have created a sense of security and repose." A bolder theory suggests they were "repositories for conserving the ancestors' spiritual power—concentrated in the head or eyes—which protected the community."[348]

Ironically, it might have been the island's discovery by Europeans that led to the decommissioning of the moia. Neither Captain Roggeveen in 1722 nor Felipe Gonzalez y Haedo in 1770 made any mention of toppled moai, but when Captain James Cook arrived in 1774, many statues had been overturned at their platforms and the monuments seemed no longer to be maintained, compared to earlier reports. Evidence suggests that by 1550, the island had an all-time population high of nine thousand, and that the years 1400 to 1600 were the height of moai carving, seemingly on the eve of the European arrivals.

MYTH AND LEGEND

Father Englert collected an old myth from Easter Island that accounted for the island's birth. There was once a potent supernatural being called Uoke who came from Hiva. He traveled about the Pacific Ocean with a huge lever by which he pried up islands, then tossed them into the sea, after which they vanished. He had destroyed many islands in this way by the time he reached *Te Pito o Te Henua,* or Easter Island, which was much bigger then. He started to lever up parts of the island, then came to a spot called *Puko Puhipuhi.* Here the rocks were too big or heavy for his lever and it broke. He left the island the way it was and moved on.

Mythographers tend to explain Uoke away as the personification of volcanism. As for Hiva, nobody knows exactly where this ancestral land lay. There are several islands in the Marquesas chain (2,100 miles to the northwest) of almost the same name—Nuku Hiva, Fatu Hiva, and Hiva Oa—but none are acknowledged as the point of origin for the Easter Islanders or Uoke.

Meanwhile, the original human settlement of Easter Island is credited to an *ariki henua,* or great Polynesian king called Hotu Matu'a (the Great Parent). One version has him leaving Hiva after Uoke destroyed it with his lever. Another says he departed his homeland due to fratricidal problems. His land is also referred to as *Marae-toe-hau,* "the burial place," but it is also thought to have been either Marae Renga or Mare Tohio.

A Polynesian named Hau Maka in Hiva dreamed that he traveled over a new island, studying the beaches, until he spotted the pink sands of Anakena, a horseshoe-shaped bay on the northern side. In his dream, Hau Maka declared that this was the beach upon which Hotu Matu'a would land, which he did. Hau Maka told him he should look for three islets, a big hole, and a long beautiful road. The islets were three motus (tiny coral-wrapped islands), the big hole was the Rano Kao crater, but the road was not specified.

Alternatively, the great Polynesian god Make-Make told Hotu Matu'a that he would find an uninhabited island if he set sail to the east. He did, with six or seven of his countrymen. At least eleven of the gods of Marea Renga, who were Hotu Matu'a's ancestors, came with him in the boat, but only he saw them.

When did this happen? Linguists propose that Easter Island's first inhabitants got there around 400 A.D., but archeologists say the evidence supports a later date of 700 to 800 A.D., although it is known that the Melanesians were voyaging in boats around the Pacific as early as 5500 B.C.

An old text unearthed at Easter Island in the 1880s for German researcher William J. Thomson adds some fascinating new elements to the story, however. A wooden tablet called *Apai,* written in an ancient, somewhat baffling hieroglyphic lan-

guage called *rongo-rongo,* recorded (as interpreted by two elderly Easter Islanders) that when the island was first created it was crisscrossed by roads paved expertly, even cunningly, with beautiful flat stones so that there were no rough edges or gaps between them.

The roads branched away in every direction to exemplify the shape of a spider's web and so that nobody could discover the shape's beginning or end. A person named Heke had built these roads and he sat in the place of honor in the middle of the web. This spider was a gray and black-pointed one, but the original lived in the aboriginal homeland where that spider would have mounted to Heaven but was prevented by the bitter cold weather.[349]

This same text said that fifty-seven generations in Hotu Matu'a's lineage ruled Easter Island. The next wave of immigrants to Easter Island were the *Tangata Hanau Eepe,* the "broad or heavy-set men." Often their name is translated differently, as "Long-Ears"; these were the priests, initiates, and leaders, the descendants of King Anua Mutu'a, who came five generations after Hotu Matu'a. His descendants became known as *Hanau Momoko,* which means approximately "slender people" or "Short-Ears"; presumably they were subjugated by the stronger group of immigrants and their descendants.

Legend says that the Short-Ears had to work as common laborers for the Long-Ears, who wanted to clear the island of its stone so they could convert it to agriculture, or so the hundreds of moai could be carved and transported to their place on the island's periphery. Eventually the groups fought each other.

Legend holds that the Hanau Eepe built the first ahu on the island but that the Hanau Momoko first carved the stones into representations of their ancestors. But it also says that the art of stone carving came from Hiva with Hotu Matu'a, and that one specific and important statue, called Tauto, was inadvertently left behind in Hiva.

It's possible that both these accounts are confused. The Long-Ears might have been a different group of more evolved people. Oral accounts collected on Easter Island in the early 1970s by French researcher Jean-Michel Schwartz indicate the island's first inhabitants were "survivors of the world's first race." They were very tall, yellow-skinned, with big ears, and shiny, hairless bodies, and they came in boats quite unexpectedly "from a land behind America"—from the East, maybe from China, possibly by way of "Hiva."[350]

Translation of some of the rongo-rongo hieroglyphs suggests that Make-Make, the god of Easter Island, the First Man (shown in the hieroglyph as surrounded by stars) had gigantic ears, just as the myths said of the oldest inhabitants. Further, Make-Make was present everywhere on the island, and his face was painted in caves and carved on rocks.

MYSTICS AND TOURISTS

One theory as to Easter Island's ultimate origin was popularized by the founder of Theosophy, H. P. Blavatsky, in 1888. Easter Island, "with its wondrous gigantic statues [is] a speaking witness to a submerged continent with a civilized mankind on it," she proposed. That submerged continent was the fabled and vanished Pacific continent called Lemuria, whose volcanic outcroppings theoretically now include the Hawaiian and Society Islands and possibly the Philippines.

Its huge stone heads might have been fashioned by an ancient race of "colossal men" standing twenty-seven feet tall. Blavatsky suggested that the stones were most likely there long before the Polynesians arrived to settle the island, and that the original erection of the maoi might have been two to four million years ago. The statues commemorate the "last descendants" of the First Race of humans who stood twenty to twenty-five feet tall.

Blavatsky also proposed that the characteristic large and long drooping ears of the Easter Island statues, observed elsewhere in the world, "symbolize the omniscience of wisdom, and were meant as a reminder of the power of Him who *knows and hears all,* and whose benevolent love and attention for all creatures nothing can escape."[351]

GEOMANTIC

Planetary Energy Receptor; Golden Pillars; Labyrinth; Dome.

PLANETARY ENERGY RECEPTOR: We can best explain the geomantic function of Easter Island by describing it in terms of an equivalent structure on the Greek island of Crete (see Mount Ida). Three structures on the Earth function to collect the energies of the other planets of the solar system. One is Mount Ida in Crete; one is Mount Meru, the legendary home of the gods, located off the southwest coast of New Zealand; and the third is Easter Island.

One reason Easter Island is so isolated, and always has been, is to protect the integrity and sanctity of its geomantic setup. The setup is elegant and sensible: one receptor, Mount Ida in Crete, the former seat of King Minos, the Cretan monarch, is open to the world; one receptor, Mount Meru, is inaccessible to all but high initiates on Earth as it is tangible yet invisible, being phase-shifted out of conventional reality; the third receptor, Easter Island, is inconveniently remote, and its temple structures and myths are opaque or eclipsed from memory. You can get there, but it takes a lot of time and effort, and you may not understand what you've gotten yourself into. So we see the same geomantic structure deployed in three different contexts: outer, inner, and veiled.

The myth about Crete tells us that there was a giant bronze man named Talos who walked the periphery of the island three times every day, preventing strangers from stepping foot on Crete or the inhabitants from departing without the king's permission. If Talos didn't like who he saw, he'd throw a boulder or part of a cliff at them. According to the Greek mythographers, Talos was a descendant of the "brazen race" from the oldest days on Earth. Talos' body was filled with ichor, the blood of the gods, and except for one spot under his ankle, he was invulnerable to attack or injury.

At Easter Island, the same being constantly patrols the island's sixty-four square miles, even though the Easter Islanders don't remember it and perhaps never had a myth for it other than a few comments about Make-Make, who may be their Talos. In a sense, all 887 moai are replicas of the Easter Island Talos. They face into the island, their backs to the sea, because their focus is on the dish or receptacle for the incoming planetary energy.

The pukao (topknot) on the moai is apt, because you could see the entire island, starting from the ocean floor and rising up for ten thousand feet as one giant Make-Make being who looks like a moai. The pukao is the planetary energy dish that is also the entire island. In other words, Make-Make wears Easter Island as his top-knot, which works as a dish to collect the energies of the planets.

These planetary energies are a function of the solar orbital cycles: for example, the orbital patterns of Jupiter and Venus, when seen in a time-lapse or fourth-dimensional sense, are particular patterns, mostly of a series of connected loops around the edge of a circle. Venus, for example, is a rounded pentagon or five-petaled flower. You could think of these time-lapsed orbital designs as templates that are imprinted on the receptor dish; or you could think of the respective deity of the planet being resident for a time with Make-Make on Easter Island, their joint presence being the imprint.

The biggest carved stones on Easter Island, the ones that were dug into the ground and which in some cases turn out to be forty feet tall, were the earliest moai. You could think of them as a standing stone circle in which the stones were carved and shaped rather than installed in the apparently amorphous or undressed state typical of megalithic sites in Europe.

These big moai act like lightning rods, grounding the intense energy charge coming in from the different planets during their cycles. They also help to ground the energy of the dome over Easter Island and its numerous dome caps (see below); and they act as tent poles, metaphorically speaking, to tie down the planetary energy receptor, which is like a huge flexible net or dish the size of the island or a little larger.

Each moai holds the energy essence of Make-Make (or Talos); the standardized moai visage is perhaps a fair rendition of one way of seeing Talos; and it emphasizes the higher consciousness aspects of Talos' function: the head (awareness) and the big ears (cosmic receptivity). Of course, they are *aringa ora,* the "Living Faces." The great island protector god Make-Make lives in them.

GOLDEN PILLARS: The numerous moai distributed around the island's periphery are physical expressions of a subtle energy feature in the same place. Here again we can usefully borrow an image from Greek mythology, this time from the city of Thebes (see Thebes).

The Greek demigod Cadmus slew a dragon, planted its teeth in the ground, and watched as up out of the ground sprang the *Spartoi,* or Sown Men, a new race of humans who became famous as the "golden-helmed seed." First the tips of spears arose from the plowed soil, then helmets, shoulders, "weapon-laden arms," and finally the full bodies of men in mail, "an Earth-born regiment" in Cadmus' service.

In an intriguing sense, the moai of Easter Island are also Sown Men in that they were "released" from their captivity in the inchoate island stone when the master carvers "sowed" or sculpted them into life in Rano Raraku quarry. Crete has one giant man of bronze walking the island periphery, while Easter Island has 288 "living faces" installed along the island's periphery, all proxies for Make-Make.

Conceive of the numerous Golden Pillars (perhaps twelve dozen of them) as standing close together in a circle whose diameter is the width of the island. They support the planetary energy receptor dish; they hold up Make-Make's pukao; they ground the incoming energies and keep the light structure stable. They are also guardians, soul guides, and overseers of another geomantic structure.

LABYRINTH: There is some basis in fact for the otherwise peculiar report, cited above, that originally the island had an intricate network of beautiful roads raying out like the threads of a spiderweb from its center. This is a description of the complex energy field at another layer of the island's reality. It is one of nine different types of labyrinths found on the planet; another of the same kind is present at Clingman's Dome in Tennessee, described elsewhere in this book.

You enter the Easter Island labyrinth at Rano Raraku quarry. In a curious sense, the 397 incomplete moai still in the vicinity of the quarry perform a similar function to the "Bears in their Townhouses" at Clingman's Dome labyrinth. They are the bouncers at the gate, the maze guides. At the center of the labyrinth is a Hall of Records that enables one to decode a great deal of information from and about the stars.

When you consider this in conjunction with the planetary energy receptor function, you get a firm idea of why Easter Island was called the Navel or Center of the World. For world, just think bigger: solar system and galaxy. Easter Island has an umbilical function for the planet in terms of the energy, information, and consciousness from these higher dimensional aspects of our larger world.

The predominance of the head and the large ears on the standardized moai is metaphorically apt: here, on Easter Island, especially at the center of the labyrinth and the center of the planetary receptor dish, you can hear and cognize the incoming star energies or vibrations. You are all ears and mental attention.

DOME: The dome over Easter Island is the starfall for epsilon Ursae Majoris, which is to say, one of the stars in the handle of the Big Dipper of the Great Bear with twenty-four stars: the Dipper is the tail and lower back of the bear. That star is called Alioth and it's the third star (the constellation's brightest) in from the handle towards the bowl. A second-magnitude star, it's as luminous as eighty-five of our Suns and is fairly close to Earth, at 61.9 light years away.

Alioth may derive from the Arabic *Alyat*, which refers to the "fat tail" of the sheep, or from *Al Hawar*, which means the "White of the Eye," the "White Poplar Tree," or "Bright Eye," all of which are to convey the impression of extreme brightness. Hindu astronomers called it *Angiras*, in honor of one of the seven *rishis* or sages (what we call the Ray Masters) believed to reside there.

The Great Bear is one of the big players in Earth's geomancy as it is the home of the fourteen Ray Masters, known more popularly as the gods of Olympus. The Dipper part of the Great Bear has been accorded many names in world star myths: the Egyptians called it the "Bull's Thigh"; and the Chinese saw it as the "Government," the "Northern Measure," and "The Celestial Palace of the Lord on High or the Immortals."

In India, it was *Saptar Shayar*, the "Seven Anchorites"; the Arabs and Jews saw it as a coffin or bier with mourners; the Scandinavians called it *Karls Wagn,* or "Wagon of the Great God Thor"; the Germans, *Himmels Wagen,* "Chariot of Heaven"; and the English, "Charles' Wain" or "King Arthur's Wain."

One interesting aspect of the Alioth dome over Easter Island is that the forty-eight dome caps are arrayed almost entirely on the island, extending only a few miles beyond the edge. Obviously with no nearby landmasses it would be inefficient to deploy the dome caps over the ocean; concentrating them principally on the island, plus a glorious, bubbly nimbus around the outer edge, makes for an intense energy field. The concentration of dome caps and the presence of a second magnitude Great Bear star further accounts for the geomantic importance of this tiny "isolated" speck of land in the Pacific Ocean.

Edfu, Egypt

PHYSICAL DESCRIPTION

Edfu, called *Behdet* by the ancient Egyptians, was always the home and cult center of the great falcon god Horus, son of Osiris and Isis. In fact, Edfu was once known as *Wetjeset-Hrw,* the "Exaltation of Horus" or "The Place Where Horus is Extolled."

Edfu is the modern Arabic name for the site, but another ancient Egyptian place name was *Djeba* (*Etbo,* in Coptic), which meant "Retribution Town," a reference to the myth that it was at Edfu that Horus defeated his enemy, Seth. The Greeks called Edfu *Apollinopolis Magna* because they believed Horus was the same as their Olympian god Apollo.

The temple remains at Edfu are enveloped (but not entirely eclipsed) by the modern city of the same name located on the western bank of the Nile River, about sixty-five miles south of Luxor in what used to be called Upper Egypt. The Edfu temple is Egypt's second largest ruin, after Karnak, and is considered one of Egypt's best preserved ancient edifices.

The main sandstone temple at Edfu, still extant, was called the Temple of Horus Behedti and was begun in 237 B.C. by Ptolemy III. Rectangular, oriented north-south, its main entrance at the south, it was formally dedicated in 142 B.C. by Ptolemy VIII. The outer hypostyle (the roof resting on a row of columns) was finished in 124 B.C. by Ptolemy VIII, but decoration of this feature was not completed until 57 B.C.

Overall, the temple is 150 feet long and encompasses 8,400 square feet. A great deal is known about the construction sequence of this temple because inscriptions on the walls inside record its history.

An earlier temple stood on this site, a stone temple designed around 2660 B.C. by Imhotep, whom history also credits as the architect of the Step Pyramid at Sakkara. This early temple was dedicated to Horus of Behdet, as the falcon god had been associated with the delta town of Behdet.

Two statues of Horus as a falcon god flank the entrance gate, which features twin towers on the entrance pylon. On the walls on either side of the entrance are scenes that portray the Feast of the Beautiful Meeting, which was the annual marriage or *hieros gamos* at Edfu of the god Horus and his consort, the goddess Hathor. Twelve massive columns stand in the outer hypostyle hall, and eighteen columns support the roof of the Pronaos, while in the *naos,* or most sacred part of the temple, surrounded by eight chapels dedicated to various deities, was the polished black granite cult statue of Horus of Behdet—the temple's Holy of Holies.

In 1860, the French archeologist Auguste Mariette (1821–1881) began excavations at Edfu, which at the time had become a "village filled with stables and storehouses, the roof of the Sanctuary area covered in mud-brick houses, and the inner chambers filled with rubbish almost to the ceiling."[352]

Mariette had been sent to Egypt by the Louvre Museum in Paris to collect Coptic manuscripts, but once there, he found excavating ruins more interesting than archival research. His excavations included the uncovering of the Sphinx, and extensive digs at Memphis, Saqqarah, Thebes, Dendera, and Edfu, among many other sites. As the first director of the Egyptian Antiquities Service, Mariette ordered that the sixty-two houses built on the roof of the temple be removed, and a few years later "the best preserved temple in antiquity" was fully revealed to the nineteenth-century world.[353]

Of interest, though seemingly unrelated to the Edfu Horus myths, is the fact that from August 21 to the end of November in 1982, the Virgin Mary appeared in Edfu in a Coptic orthodox church named after her.

MYTH AND LEGEND

The Edfu myths all concern the falcon god Horus, so it's helpful to review a bit of his mythic resume. Horus is a Greek name for the Egyptian *Har* (which meant "the High" or "the Far-Off"), one of Egypt's oldest gods, first appearing in hieroglyphs around 3000 B.C. He was considered a solar deity and took the form of a falcon or hawk, or a man with a falcon's head; in that guise, he was understood to be a manifestation of the living king, whereas his father, Osiris, was the manifes-

tation of the king in the Afterlife. Horus with his falcon wings outstretched was the protector of all Egypt and its pharaohs.

Horus, known as *Heru-Ur*, Horus the Elder, also appeared as a lion with a hawk's head. He wore the crowns of the South and North, which is to say, Upper and Lower Egypt united; sometimes he was depicted with the horns of Khnemu (Khnum, the ram-god creator of all life) on his head, and above them, a crown of plumes, *uraei* (twining asps), and solar disks. As Heru-Ur, Horus was the Face of Heaven.

His right eye was the Sun and his left the Moon, or from a different perspective, the Sun was the "Eye of Horus" and the Moon was the "Eye of Horus," part of a cosmic Face said to look down over Egypt—all of which explains why he was called "Horus of the Two Eyes." In one text it is said of Thoth, the Egyptian god of wisdom associated with the Moon, that he seized "the two Eyes of Horus, the White Eye [Sun] and the Black Eye [Moon]."

Horus had many names and epithets depending on his function and location. At Heliopolis, he was *Harakhtes*, "Horus of the Horizon"; Horus the Behdetite, the celestial falcon god at Edfu or hawk-winged Sun disk; *Hor-sa-iset* (Greek: Harsiesis), one of his most popular forms, meant he was the Son of Isis; and *Horu-Sema-Tawy*, "The Horus, Uniter of the Two Lands" of Upper and Lower Egypt. He was sometimes depicted as a winged Sun disk scouting the land for demons and enemies of the Pharaoh, then engaging them in battle. He was the Lord of the Sky and the God of the East (the sunrise direction), which is why he was often personified as the rising Sun, though not the Sun god itself.

The first Horus myth concerns his momentous defeat of his enemies, especially Seth, in the form of a hippopotamous, at Edfu. Seth was sometimes, confusingly, understood to be Typhon (Egptian: *Tebh*), the evil god of darkness, as the

Egyptians described him, or "pride and inso-lence" to the Greeks. The narrative of this con-frontation was described in hieroglyphs on the temple walls at Edfu. As a result of his slaying Seth while standing in the barque of the Sun god, Ra, it was declared by Thoth that Horus should henceforth be called *Heru-Behutet,* and Behutet (Edfu) should now be known as Horus' city.

In Greek myth, especially that associated with Mount Etna in Sicily, Typhon was a child of Gaia (the Earth), half-human, half-beast, and more massive and formidable than any other of Gaia's progeny. Typhon was taller than all the mountains; in fact, he was so tall his head often knocked against the stars; one arm stretched west to the sunset, the other east to the place of sun-rise. One hundred serpent (or dragon) heads sprouted from his shoulders; from the hips down-wards, he was serpent shaped—in fact, his lower torso consisted of two intertwining serpents, and they yelled and hissed constantly.

Typhon's body was covered with wings, his hair was unkempt and streamed on his face and head in the wind, and his eyes were made of fire. In fact, flames shot out not only from his eyes, but also his nostrils and mouths, and he uttered such bloodcurdling imprecations that even the gods at one time fled for safety. The relevance of the Typhon association will be made clear.

As the celestially appointed opponent of Seth or Typhon and their minions, Horus vanquished them in a series of three slaughters. He took the form of the winged disk and positioned himself in the Boat of Ra, which was also known as the "Great Protector." According to the ancient Egyptian texts, in one battle, Horus killed 651 "enemies" in the form of crocodiles *(emsuhu)* and hippopotamuses *(tepu)*; in another, he bound 142 enemies in chains; in yet another, he captured, then slew, 381 "rebels."

In one of his many confrontations with Seth, Horus attacked Seth, hurling his lance at his neck, then chaining the legs of the monster, after which

he sliced off Seth's head. This battle took place at a place called *She-nu-aha,* the "Lake of Battle," or *She-neter,* "Lake of God." In another confronta-tion, Seth took the form of a hissing serpent and hid in a hole, but Horus set himself up on a pole above this hole, thereby preventing Seth from emerging onto land.

This perhaps was part of the justification for Horus' epithet as "He who is above." In this con-frontation, however, the identity of Seth seems to drift from the human brother of Osiris to that of the archetypal cosmic serpent, Apep or Apophis, which is the Egyptian version of the Greek serpent-monster Typhon. Apophis was the enemy of the Sun god Ra and perpetually tried to swallow the Sun as it sank into the western horizon at the end of each day. After Horus vanquished Seth and returned to Edfu on his boat, Thoth declared he should be henceforth known as the "Light-Giver," and that in every sanctuary dedicated to Horus there should be a winged sun-disk with uraei (the sacred asps).

In one battle, however, Seth ripped out Horus' Moon eye, but the falcon god later recov-ered it thanks to Thoth. The general word for eye was *iret,* but when the left eye was conceived of as the Moon, with all its phases and cycles, the term was *Wedjat,* "the Hale One." Thoth later claimed that it was he "who returns the *Wedjat* Eye . . . when it is saved from its misfortune."[354] In Egyptian lore, Thoth, or Tehuti, was the scribe of the gods, the repository of vast arcana, the master of speech and divine words, the holder of the mysteries of the stars, Heaven, and Earth, the initiator into the Mysteries.

Confusingly, in one temple wall depiction, Seth stands in the prow of the Boat of the Sun and spears Apophis, earning Seth, who has prevailed over the Sun god's archenemy, the epithet "Great of strength in the barque of millions."

Apparently, the motivation driving Horus in this continual battling with Seth was revenge for his father, Osiris; Egyptian myth says that Seth trapped Osiris in a casket, dumped it in the Nile River, then later dismembered Osiris into fourteen pieces and scattered them throughout Egypt (see Abydos). Edfu, incidentally, is where, according to Plutarch's report, they buried the right leg of Osiris.

This was not, however, an unequivocal claim: other sites claiming the leg were Sebenny-tos (upper and lower leg) and Herakleopolis (thigh, two legs). At the same time, some texts say Osiris was cut into sixteen and even forty-two parts, so his body parts could well rest in many Egyptian sites and several places could legiti-mately claim to have part of a leg.[355]

At any rate, Egyptian myth tells us that Edfu was constructed on the site of Horus' last battle with Seth. The five-day Festival of Victory, which began on December 21, was a sacred drama that reenacted Horus' triumph over Seth, including the recitation of the "Legend of the Winged Disk," which recounted how Horus cut off Seth's head and dragged his corpse by the feet through all of Egypt. Horus systematically destroys Seth in his hippopotamus form by impaling him with ten harpoons, each piercing a different part of the demon animal's anatomy, starting with the beast's snout.

The second Horus myth at Edfu concerned the goddess Hathor. Every summer at the time of the first rising of the Nile River, or the First Day of the Inundation Season (July 19), the priests and lay public at Edfu celebrated Horus and Hathor by placing their cult statues under the midday Sun on the roof of the temple. Then a few weeks later in August the two gods were the focus of the "Feast of the Beautiful Meeting" or "Feast of the Joyous Union." The details of this ritualized reunion were depicted on the Edfu temple walls.

A cult statue of Hathor, who presided at Dendera, was brought in a flotilla of boats on the Nile from her Dendera temple one hundred miles

away to Edfu as part of the annual fourteen-day celebration of her marriage to Horus. The "mar-riage" was consummated in the *mammisi*, or birthing house in the temple. The first day was the marriage, but a harvest festival known as the Festival of Behdet started on the second day and was a time of peace and rejoicing as well as drink-ing and partying in the streets of Edfu, again under the aegis of Horus and Hathor. At the end of the festival, Hathor ritually returned to Dendera to await the birth of Harmsomtus, the child of their union. This child was also sometimes called Ihy or Horus-Sematawy.

As a goddess, Hathor was first celebrated as the consort of the Bull of Amenti, an Underworld bull deity, then later she was seen as a sky god-dess, the daughter of Re (or Ra), the Sun god, and wife of Horus. Her name in fact means "Temple or Mansion of Horus." She was often depicted as a celestial cow (the "Great Wild Cow") filled with milk and stars, or as a female deity wearing a Sun disk and cow horns. A mistress of song, dance, love, and joy, the patron of pleasure, sexual love, and sensuality, she was the Egyptian Aphrodite. The sistrum (the Egyptian bronze sacred rattle called *sesheshet*) was her favorite instrument, which she played to banish evil from the land.

As symbolic mother of all the pharaohs, Hathor nursed the pharaohs (called "Sons of Hathor") from her breasts, by which the Egyptians understood she was validating the royal office and bestowing it with celestial powers of support and protection. Hathor was also known as the "Queen of the West," making her the pro-tector of the necropolis regions of Egypt, the "Golden One," "Lady of the Turquoise," and the "Lady of the Sycamore."

The sycamore tree was considered sacred by the Egyptians and considered to be Hathor's abode. The souls of the dead were believed to fly to this tree to take rest under Hathor's aegis. One ancient text suggested that "the sycamore, a very long-lived tree, seems to stand for the landscape of the Beyond, the goal of the blessed dead." But the sycamore tree's spreading branches and dense shade made an excellent trysting ground for lovers in the desert, so it was a natural association to link the love goddess Hathor with it. Further, as one Egyptian scholar points out, in the second half of the twentieth century, there was still an ancient sycamore tree near Cairo associated with the Virgin Mary, suggesting a link between the Hathor and the Virgin Mary.[356]

A third myth about Horus at Edfu establishes his presence and function at the site's very beginning. Egyptian myth says that out of the primeval ocean in the time of precreation darkness there rose the Island of Creation. Two undefined beings called the Great One and the Distant One appeared. They picked up a stick, broke it in half, and stuck one half into the island. At once, the falcon god Horus emerged from the gloom and perched on the stick; in his right eye was the Sun, in his left eye the Moon—thereafter known as the All-Seeing Eye of Horus. Immediately upon Horus' appearance, Light broke on the horizon, Chaos retreated, and the world began.

The primeval waters started to recede and the Island grew larger. Initially, Horus lived in a simple reed hut, but this had to be expanded as the world (and Island) grew so that eventually an entire temple was built for Horus. Some scholars assert that the temple writings at Edfu, which relate this creation myth, conceived of Edfu as "standing on the very site of the primeval hill where creation first took place."[357]

GEOMANTIC

Mithraeum; Golden Egg; Silver Egg.

MITHRAEUM: In terms of Edfu's geomantic structure, it was entirely appropriate that the Rites of Horus be performed there. This site has a three-part Horus temple, starting with a Mithraeum, the temple of the Wild Sun God.

Here we encounter a mythic confusion, however, perhaps due to faulty interpretation of hieroglyphs by Western Egyptologists, or perhaps through a gradual drift over the centuries of the true identities involved. The first drift concerns the identity of the monster that Horus defeated at Edfu. The general interpretation in English sources is that it was Seth, but sometimes Seth's qualities drift into those of Apophis (Apep) or the Greek Typhon, and rightly so.

Seth in Greek mythic terms was Zeus, chief of the gods of Olympus. In Greek myth, Zeus defeated Typhon, throwing Mount Etna in Sicily upon him to ensure his incarceration; in Hindu myth, Indra, King of the Gods, defeated Vrtra, the cosmic dragon who kept the lands parched by withholding the waters. In the Egyptian myth, we see in one instance Seth aboard the Barque of Ra spearing Apophis; yet in others, he fights Horus. Here is confusion of identities.

The link to Zeus is secured by the attribution of the Great Bear to Seth; ancient sources say that constellation was his.[358] The Great Bear is the home of the Ray Masters, the 14 Olympian gods presided over by Zeus. Thus the Egyptian Seth is the Greek Zeus, and not a monster requiring slaying by Horus.[359]

Who did Horus defeat? Apophis, Typhon, Sorath, the Beast 666, the Bull of Mithras, the Wild Sun God—the variously named God of the Sun in its pure, chaotic, ultra-powerful form of living, writhing gold. Mythically, Horus did not defeat Apophis; he *mastered* its energy, indicated by the otherwise curious if not baffling Egyptian references to Horus as a blacksmith. A blacksmith does not slay and defeat his metals; he simply knows how to work them to his will, how to master them and shape them into useful objects.

Worshipers of Horus of Behutet "never tired" of describing their god as the "lord of the forge-city," construing Edfu as a *mesnet,* or foundry, where ore is smelted and weapons forged. Egyptian tradition, reports Egyptologist E. A. Wallis Budge, declared that Horus first established himself as a master blacksmith at Edfu. Edfu was the foundry, the smithy "wherein the great disk of the sun was forged," such that when the doors of the foundry are open, the sun disk rises, according to an old text.

The followers of Horus were called *mesniti* (workers in metals, or blacksmiths); hieroglyphic representations of these blacksmiths have been identified on the interior temple walls at Edfu, showing them with an inverted spear in their right hand, an upraised metal instrument in their left.

According to Budge, in the Edfu temple there was a chamber behind the sanctuary called the *mesnet* in which the mesniti, or blacksmiths of Horus, waited to bring forth the image of their god. This would be when the metal image of Horus as the god of the rising Sun would be brought forth from the mesnet in imitation of his issuing forth from the cosmic foundry. The symbolic equation was that the mesnet in the Edfu Horus temple equaled the portion of the celestial sky from which the Sun god first appeared.

Accompanying the imagery of the blacksmiths of Horus was another that depicted Horus standing in the Boat of Ra with a long spear in his right hand, impaling the hippopotamus (the Apophis equivalent) and holding the monster in restraint with a double chain in his left hand. In the boat, there is also tackle consisting of chains. Elsewhere the hippopotamus is shown with its legs bound by chains and its lower jaw secured by a chain.

In other scenes Horus is shown with his blacksmiths, each brandishing a spear made of "divine iron." Thoth applauded Horus for his accomplishments in slaying the various demonic enemies because the falcon-headed blacksmith

had made use of Thoth's incantatory formulas for this, and "from that day the blacksmiths of Heru-Behutet have existed at Edfu."[360]

So how is all this indicative of a Mithraeum? The Rites of Horus at Edfu are nearly identical to the Greek myth of Hephaistos, the Cyclopes, and Typhon at Mount Etna in Sicily (see Mount Etna). Horus is like Hephaistos, the gods' blacksmith; the Cyclopes (the one-eyed giants) are Horus' mesniti, helper blacksmiths; Typhon under Mount Etna is Apophis under Edfu. The only thing Edfu doesn't have is volcanic fire. The spiritual equivalent of that cosmic heat is provided by the life force of the Wild Sun God. In a sense, the volcano is physical window dressing.

Just as Hephaistos did under Mount Etna in his forge, so at Edfu, Horus, by mastering the inchoate Sun, hammers its living essence into devices, weapons, chains, spears, and armor according to the formulas of magic provided by Thoth. Initiates at Edfu, intending to pass through the temple's three levels, would start with the Mithraeum, encountering and mastering the Wild Sun God.

Horus is also Ra or Re, the Egyptian Sun god. He stands in Ra's "Boat of Millions of Years" because he *is* Ra, but only after he has mastered the Wild Sun God aspect of Typhon-Apophis. Ra was depicted as a man with a falcon's head, was often identified with Horus and called *Re-Horakhty,* and was known as the horizon dweller. Like the Greek Helios, he traveled across the sky in his solar barque (Helios had a chariot), disappearing into the Underworld at night. Here is the equation: Ra the Sun God is Horus the Solar Logos who has mastered Apophis, the Wild Sun God.

GOLDEN EGG: The second level of the Edfu temple is the Golden Egg. When hatched (both the Golden and Silver Eggs at Edfu are "hatched"), the golden divine child, the Christ infant, or Horus the Younger emerges, cradled in the lap and enfolded in the arms of, respectively, the Divine Mother, the Madonna, or Isis.

This is the Sun Eye, the Right or White Eye, of Horus. In geomantic terms, the Mithraeum or foundry lies before the Horus temple at Edfu a bit like the dragon at the gates, protecting it, winnowing out the unprepared, and guiding those who are ready. The Golden Child, or young Horus, appears where the Horus temple stands; then extending out to some distance behind the temple is Isis.

SILVER EGG: The third layer of the Edfu temple is a Silver Egg, the Moon Eye, the Left or Black Eye of Horus. Out of this Egg comes Horus the Elder. Here Horus appears as the soaring, all-seeing falcon-headed deity. Why a falcon? It's a metaphor for the sixth chakra, the brow center of psychic insight and penetration, that which can see from afar and above and *through* all things.

The Elder Horus is guided in his psychic access by Thoth, master of esoteric wisdom and holder of the secrets, the calculations, measurements, and mechanics of Heaven and Earth—the cosmic mysteries and their application, in short. Thoth's Moon magic is older, deeper, wiser than that of the Sun.

SOLAR LOGOS MYSTERY TEMPLE: The Rites of Horus at Edfu are about the Solar Logos in its two aspects, namely, Horus the Elder, the Moon Eye, and Horus the Younger, the Sun Eye. Both Eyes together comprise the single vision of Horus as the Solar Logos, the Son of the Cosmic Father, Osiris (see Abydos). You don't always get a Golden and Silver Egg in the same spot; when you do, it is a geomantically rich combination yielding the full Horus, in effect, the falcon-headed divine golden child. (See Tetford, England, for a description of the combination of both Eggs and a Mount Olympus as a variation on the mix.)

Let's keep the players clear. The Younger Horus of the Golden Egg has its Divine Mother,

Isis, or the Madonna, attending it protectively. The Elder Horus of the Silver Egg has its mentor in the Mysteries, Thoth. The Horus of the Mithraeum foundry has its helper blacksmiths, the mesniti (or Cyclopes) to assist its foundry work. Is there a name, face, or even a concept to unify these three?

It is the Greek Hephaistos, the blacksmith of Olympus. In this figure we find a clear depiction of the *active* work of the Solar Logos. Hephaistos has other mythic names, including the Celtic King Arthur, the Roman Mithras, the Judaic Master Jesus. These are different names for the Ray Master of the Great Bear who handles the sixth ray, scarlet, and who occupies the position of heart chakra at the Round Table of the Cosmic Logos, which, in Egyptian terms, is Osiris, Horus' father.

At Edfu, you have the complete Horus, the Elder and Younger aspects, that together comprise the Solar Logos—the Word of the Sun, if you wish. When you take all the planet's Golden Eggs (666) and Silver Eggs (1,080), you get 1,746 Eggs; in Greek gematria (in which letters and numbers are equivalent, spelling out a mathematical language), this number refers to the grain of mustard seed, a Biblical analogy to the essence of Christ. All 1,746 Eggs create the complete Horus. This is very important because the complete Horus is the Solar Logos which in turn is the carrier of the Christ consciousness.

This is what the Edfu temple is all about: to ground, embody, and transmit the Christ consciousness for this part of Upper Egypt. Bear in mind, today, after the Christ incarnation, we call this cosmic essence "Christ"; for the ancient Egyptians, it was Horus. Metaphysically, it is the same cosmic being no matter what its name.[361]

HATHOR AND VIRGIN MARY APPEARANCES: The "Feast of the Beautiful Meeting" involved the annual ritualized marriage of Horus and his consort, Hathor, who traveled by boat from her primary temple at Dendera. To understand the geomantic significance of this, we need ask: who was Hathor? To answer this, we need only ask: who was Hephaistos' consort? His "wife" was Aphrodite, the Greek love goddess.

The Egyptian Hathor is the same as the Greek Aphrodite, but we mustn't leave it at that. Hathor-Aphrodite was also a Ray Master, in charge of the third ray, pink; in another guise, she was Mary Magdalene, consort of Master Jesus in the execution of the Christ mysteries; in still another, she was Queen Guinevere, King Arthur's wife; or Helen of Troy, King Menelaus' wife.

In Ray Master terminology, Hathor, Aphrodite, and Magdalene are all manifestations of Master Lady Nada, whose essence is cosmic sound or vibration—Nada. This is appropriate insofar as a prime aspect of the Solar Logos is the spoken word, the power of sound to create, shape, and change reality, as references to Thoth's magic formulas imply. In brief, Ray Master Horus and Ray Master Hathor, to use their Egyptian names, work together, as consorts, to present and ground the Christ Mystery on Earth. The Mithraeum, Golden Egg, and Silver Egg at Edfu in Egypt served as one of their theaters for this Great Work.

On the surface, without context, the appearance of the Virgin Mary in late 1982 at Edfu seems unrelated to all this. But esoterically, it is entirely appropriate, even from a certain point of view, amusingly so. It is in fact another episode of the Feast of the Beautiful Meeting, for the Virgin Mary is a composite spiritual being generated by four "female" Ray Masters, including Lady Nada.

Her apparition in 1982 was, for one, a reaffirmation of the Isis-Madonna aspect of the Golden Egg temple structure. For another, it was a sign to our times of a continuity, albeit a revisitation with a different face. Once Hathor came; now it's the Virgin Mary. Perhaps the Egyptians are not concerned with which name the being had; after all, for a time, they maintained a sycamore tree at Edfu, classically linked with Hathor, believing it to be associated with the Virgin Mary.

Ephesus, Turkey

In the classical world, Ephesus, on the western coast of Turkey, was regarded as one of the Seven Wonders of the World, chiefly for its Artemision, or Temple to the Goddess Artemis (Roman: Diana), then the largest structure in Greece.

The original Artemision was four times the size of the Parthenon; measuring 180 by 360 feet and made entirely of marble, it was surrounded by a double row of columns on three sides when it was constructed around 550 B.C. When rebuilt in the fourth century B.C., after having been burned down in 356 B.C., the temple featured 127 columns, of which thirty-six, carved with reliefs, stood in the front of the temple, facing west towards the ancient harbor.

Today the Artemision temple exists only as an outline on the ground. In fact, it is only one feature of many in this former temple city occupying twenty-six square miles, which sits at the head of the estuary of the Cayster River, also called Kucuk Menderes River. (The original harbor city was built upon the alluvial deposits from this river.) Ephesus sits between two small mountains, Mount Pion (today called Panayirdag) and Mount Koressos (Bülbüldgo).

A marble-paved colonnaded avenue 1,968 feet long and about thirty-three feet wide, called the *Arkadiane* or Arcadian Way (named after the Roman Emperor Arcadius), runs from the harbor to the outdoor amphitheater (sixty feet high at the back) that was once capable of seating twenty-four thousand people. Not to be confused with the Arkadiane is the Marble Road, the sacred processional way of Ephesus (still extant), made of marble (probably laid in the fifth century A.D.) that begins at the Artemision, passes the amphitheater and library, and eventually loops back to its starting point.

Also significant among the numerous ruins from Greek, Roman, and Christian habitation at Ephesus is the *Panaya Kapula,* a small stone building believed to have been the residence of the Virgin Mary when Saint John the Evangelist brought her there after the Crucifixion.

Historians believe that the site of Ephesus (*Efes* in modern Turkish, which means "bee") has been inhabited since the tenth century B.C. During its height of influence, Ephesus was the most densely populated city in Anatolia; around

150 A.D., Ephesus was the most prosperous commercial center in the Hellenic world and was referred to as the "metropolis of Asia." Its protected harbor contributed to this preeminence, as did the fact that Ephesus was the starting point for the Royal Road via Sardis to Susa, both in Anatolia.

The city flourished during Greek, Roman, and early Christian times, and bears temple ruins from each of these periods of influence.

One of the largest cities in the Roman world, Ephesus at one time was the capital of the Proconsular Province of Asia for the Roman Empire. It also sported the Celsus Library, a significant collection of "books" in its time; the actual building, erected in 110 A.D., is still extant.[362]

One of the most notable historical figures in Ephesus' story was Croesus, king of Lydia, whose capital was sixty miles away at Sardis in Turkey. Croesus is legendary today for having been the wealthiest man of ancient Greece. In 550 B.C., Croesus, all of thirty-five years old, captured and colonized Ephesus as soon as he succeeded to the throne. "The first Greeks he attacked were the Ephesians," reports Herodotus (484–420 B.C.), who adds that it was during his siege "that the Ephesians dedicated the city to Artemis." During Croesus' reign, "the golden cows and most of the pillars" were set up by him, said Herodotus. The temples at Ephesus, he added, were "remarkable structures."[363]

According to the archeologists, a temple to Artemis was erected five times on the same site. The "archaic" Artemision was built during 560–55 B.C., and its successor (the one judged a Wonder), during the years 334–250 B.C. Ephesus' proudest title was that of "temple warden," from the Greek word *neokoros,* meaning "temple sweeper," in this case, for the goddess. In *The Acts of the Apostles,* the town clerk of Ephesus declares: "Citizens of Ephesus! Is there anybody alive who

does not know that the city of the Ephesians is the guardian of the temple of great Diana and of her statue that fell from heaven?"[364]

It is quite likely the town clerk was referring to the giant statue of Artemis that featured three rows of seven breasts on her chest, each breast like a ripe fruit (or possibly an egg, though some say bulls' testicles) of the Earth.

In fact, at the time of this utterance, the people of Ephesus were rioting over Saint Paul's pronouncement that the handmade silver statues of the gods, especially Artemis, were not of any inherent sanctity, were not gods themselves, but were mere idols. A silversmith named Demetrius shouted that Saint Paul's statements not only threatened their livelihood as silversmiths, but would "reduce the sanctuary of the great goddess Diana to unimportance. It could end up by taking away all the prestige of a goddess venerated all over Asia, yes, and everywhere in the civilized world."[365]

Saint Paul got ejected from Ephesus for insulting the "pagan" followers of Diana; he probably irritated the practitioners of the occult arts as well, for "the city was a magnet for practitioners of magical arts, such as fortune telling, astrology, and exorcism."[366] Ephesus was noted for its metaphysical plurality: at one point in its history, scholars believe that at least seventeen different deities were actively worshiped there.[367]

Ephesus was the scene of important activities of the Apostle Saint Paul during a three-year period. Traditionally, the city was regarded as the home of the aging Saint John the Evangelist; and it was one of the Seven Churches in Asia specifically addressed in *Revelation,* in which the Ephesians were commended. Also of Christian interest is a cave a mile from the amphitheater in which the Seven Sleepers of Ephesus took refuge during a period of persecution.[368] In fact, the seven Christian youths were said to reside in this cave (just behind Mount Pion in Ephesus) for two centuries until an earthquake aroused them and they woke from their long slumber.

The glory of Ephesus began to decline with the advent of Christianity; in 17 A.D., it suffered a disastrous earthquake; it was destroyed by invading Goths, who razed it in 263 A.D.; and it was finally abandoned as malarial swamps, formed from the silting up of the harbor, made the place uninhabitable.

MYTH AND LEGEND

Ephesus is the residence of Artemis-Diana. Before the Greeks arrived, the native Ephesians worshiped Cybele and had dedicated a shrine to her at a site originally sanctified, so say the legends, by being the spot upon which a meteorite fell. Cybele (She of the Ax) was a Phrygian Mother Goddess. Worshiped by the Amazons as Tauropolos and by the Cretans as Rhea, she was the mother of the gods, of men, mountains, and lions.

The Greeks, led to Ephesus by the Delphic Oracle, grafted Cybele's goddess qualities onto their own Artemis and rolled the two goddesses into one. There is a myth, possibly apocryphal, that even before Cybele, Amazons occupied the site and may have built the first temple at Ephesus.[369] In legend, Amazons were women skilled at battle who lived beyond the River Thermodon in Scythia; they were "exceedingly warlike" and worshiped the Moon goddess and Earth-mother in their most violent manifestations.[370]

Artemis, the sister of Apollo, was for the Greeks the virgin and sometimes vengeful goddess of the chase, hunting, and archery, associated with the passage of girls through menstruation into womanhood and, as Eilithyia, with childbirth. Her association with the fertility of nature was indicated by her Ephesian statue, which showed her with twenty-one breasts; she was also considered a Moon goddess, although this was a late development and possibly incompatible with the more founded attribution of the Moon to Selene.

Artemis, of course, was one of the immortal gods of Mount Olympus; she was the defender of all wild animals, children, and weak creatures. Depicted as eternally young, as an untamed girl with no interests other than hunting, Artemis was attended by a troop of virgin nymphs and mostly roamed the wild mountainsides. Artemis was also the protecting deity for the Amazons, "who, like her, were warriors and huntresses and independent of men."[371] Invariably, she was depicted with a bow and quiver of arrows.

The *Homeric Hymns* speak of her "golden shafts" and "bitter arrows," how she loved the din of the hunt and delighted in the chase. She is the "arrow-pouring goddess" who "roams all over destroying the brood of wild beasts."[372] Somewhat confusingly, Artemis was also called *Potnia Theron*, "Mistress of the Animals," which meant, mistress of all of wild nature: she hunted and she protected the wild beasts. Artemis roams the wild mountainsides with her "swarms of nymphs, hunting, dancing, and playing"; she loves "the lyre and dancing and piercing, triumphal cries and shady groves," which is why she was called *Keladeine*, "Sounding."[373]

In the Roman days of Ephesus, Artemis was worshiped as Diana, and her festival days filled the holy city with pilgrims and celebrants. If their method of honoring Diana at Ephesus followed the style in Rome, women would visit the site in processions, "wearing garlands and carrying flaming torches." That festival was so popular that early Christians adopted it for the date of their Assumption of the Virgin.[374]

The spring festival of Cybele, Artemis' older mythic essence, held March 15–27, was much less restrained. It celebrated her role as a fertility and orgiastic goddess and mistress of Earth who quickened all of nature in the spring. The Corybantes (vegetation spirits or nymphs) accompanied Cybele's festival with "thunderous music, and wild animals drew her carriage." After the second century A.D., Cybele was regaled among the Romans as a guardian of cities and citadels.[375]

Artemis may also have had a more metaphysical aspect. A funerary amphora from Boeotia, Greece, shows her as Mother of the Mysteries, soul guide to the initiation into death and rebirth, according to one scholar. She is depicted with outstretched arms, a sign of blessing and the gesture of dividing the upper and lower worlds. She is adorned with animal images, such as birds, a horned cow, and fish, and she is flanked by lions. Below the shelter of her left arm lies the path to the Underworld. "The vase records the age-old initiation pattern, the difficult journey that mimes death and rebirth."[376]

She was honored throughout the Hellenic world, but her prime site of veneration was Ephesus. In fact, the placement of the Artemision with respect to the harbor and mountains gives this primacy some geomythic support. The first altar and temple to Artemis, around which the rest of the Ephesian temple grew, was situated on low ground at the head of a semicircular bay and thus very close to the water itself (although the water silted up and has mostly disappeared today). When it was flourishing, the Artemision, standing formidably at the edge of a harbor and shouldered between hills, was in itself an entrance to Asia.

"The whole ample landscape opens widely around the temple, placed as it is at the exact position from which the one splendid bay and its defining mountains can best be experienced," as architectural scholar Vincent Scully explains. There, as the mother of all creatures and the patron of nature, Artemis could survey—and protect—all who approached her domain. Artemis'

wings, as found on the carved reliefs, were "echoed by the winged mountain profile that flanks the site," says Scully.[377]

Seemingly as if to muddy the waters, Ephesus has another foundation myth, one involving Androklos, who, acting upon oracular advice, led a group of Greek colonists to Ephesus. Androklos, was informed that he should establish his city at the place to which the wild boar and leaping fish led him. One day the fish leaped and the wild boar charged, and Androklos killed the boar on was what is now called Ayasoluk Hill, the site of the original city and about thirty-six hundred feet from the Artemision.

MYTH AND LEGEND

In 1841, a book called *Life of the Blessed Virgin* by an invalided German visionary named Anna Katerina Emmerich was published. Although Emmerich had never visited Ephesus, she claimed that in vision she had seen the Virgin Mary living in the flesh at Ephesus in a small stone house on a hillside. The house is now called *Panaya Kapula*, "Doorway to the Virgin," and since 1892, when the actual chapel-like building was located on a hill four miles from Ephesus, it has been recognized as an official Ephesus pilgrimage site. A notable date for this pilgrimage, at least for local Orthodox Christians, is August 15, when they assemble at *Panaya Kapula* to honor Mary. In 1967, the sanctity of the site and its legitimacy as a Marian shrine were endorsed by Pope Paul VI.

GEOMANTIC

Ray Master Sanctuary; Landscape Zodiac.
THE IDENTITY OF ARTEMIS: The key to understanding Ephesus is to penetrate the identity

of Artemis. As an Olympian, she is one of the fourteen Ray Masters of the Great Bear, but even saying this does not quite explain Artemis at Ephesus. She is the master of the second ray, which is a pale-orange light-gold; one of her notable human incarnations was as Saint Francis of Assisi, also known for his benevolent attitude and actions towards the animal kingdom. The mythic equivalency that cracks open the enigma of Artemis—and, incidentally, accounts for the baffling Amazonian attributions at Ephesus—is the Hindu goddess Durga.

Durga is an active, even highly aggressive, form of the goddess Parvati, Shiva's consort. In the earliest days of Earth, long before there were humans, when the gods were organizing the energy fields of the planet for a cycle of human incarnation, great, mighty deeds had to be performed, such as ridding the world of formidable demons, giants, and monsters. These were actions on the order of Heracles' twelve labors, and some were even more demanding. Several Ray Masters undertook this task, including Artemis in her Durga manifestation.

Durga was a powerful warrior (an *Asura*, enemy of the gods) and appeared on Earth for the purpose of ridding it of demons who opposed all the plans and activities of the gods. Most notably, she eradicated Mahisa, the buffalo demon who threatened the stability of the cosmos. Typically, Durga rides a lion into battle, where she is irresistible, unconquerable, a great battle queen brandishing multiple weapons in her numerous arms.

She obtained the name Durga by slaying a giant of the same name; he had grown so mighty he had conquered three worlds and dethroned Indra and the other gods. Durga was a fierce opponent: he had one hundred million chariots, 120 billion elephants, and ten million fast horses when he engaged Parvati on Vindhya mountain. But she had mettle too: she had a thousand arms and produced numerous formidable weapons

from out of her body, including arrows. The battle was long, dramatic, and from our viewpoint, full of amazing special effects, but in the end, Parvati triumphed and killed the demon.

The Hindu mythic canon has several variations on the same story, and these add valuable aspects to our emerging picture of Artemis as Amazon. The gods collectively created a female warrioress called Mahamaya by emanating "streams of glory" from their faces "in consequence of which she became a body of glory, like a mountain of fire."

The gods all gave Mahamaya their weapons, and she "with a frightful scream" leaped into the air and killed the giant. Or: the gods emitted such flames of fire from their eyes that a "mountain of effulgence" was formed, and manifested as Katyayini, as bright as a thousand suns. The gods each gave her their special weapon, which included a trident, discus, conch shell, thunderbolt, mace, dart, bow, a quiver of arrows, and others. She rode into battle as a golden-colored woman on a lion, and defeated the giant.[378]

As Durga she assumed ten different forms, all of which were variations on these three godly personages, for the purposes of destroying two giants. As Singhavahini, she rode on a lion and drank the blood of the slain leaders. As Jagaddhatri, the mother of the world, she was dressed in red as a fair, beautiful, and gentle-looking woman, seated on a lion; she carried a conch shell, discus, and bow and arrow, and destroyed an army of giants. As Kali, she was black, hideous, scary, wearing dead bodies as earrings and a necklace of skulls; her eyes were red and she carried the head of the slain giant in her hand. When she defeated the giants, she danced for joy so furiously that the Earth trembled under her feet. All the gods and goddesses intoned their praises for this celestial heroine.

All these different aspects of Durga (and Artemis, Diana, Cybele, and the Amazons) are "epithets descriptive of her appearance or method of fighting at different times during the great conflict." What remains consistent is the image of a calm goddess of golden color manifesting as a "warrior fully armed." Appropriately, one of Durga's many names was "Divine Durga, dweller in wildernesses." She was said to "dwell perpetually in the Vindhya hills and 'to delight in spirituous liquors, flesh, and sacrificial victims.'"[379]

Durga is created by the gods pooling their energies and contributing their weapons because the males among them have been unable to subdue the demon in the midst of the cosmic crisis that the demon's activities have precipitated. Durga creates her own set of seven female helpers called *Matrkas* (mothers)—equivalent to the Curetes, Corybantes, and nymphs associated with Cybele and Artemis—who embody her fury, wildness, ferocity, and bloodthirstiness.

In keeping with Artemis' reputation as a "virgin," Durga never creates male helpers or enlists the male gods or male spiritual beings as allies in her battles. She doesn't need them because she wins on her own; she exists independently of male protection or guidance.

Her link with vegetation is indicated by her association with the *navapattrika,* or ceremony of Nine Plants, and with her identification with Sakambhari, who is the nourisher of herbs. Durga is associated with the power inherent in all vegetation, its growth and its life itself. Her "huntress" qualities are indicated by the fact that in her principal temple in India at Calcutta great numbers of goats, pigs, fowl, sheep, and water buffalo were slaughtered and immolated at her festival.[380]

During Durga Puja, a harvest festival time in India, Durga is shown flanked by her children (other god figures); she is closely associated with crops and the fertility of vegetation, and the blood offerings she receives tends to suggest "the renourishment of her powers of fertility."[381]

Thus the vegetation, primitive, bloodthirsty, and huntress aspects of Diana are well represented and dramatized in the Vedic Durga. In fact, the Greek Artemis is a rather tamed, domesticated, declawed representation of this fierce temple cleanser and preserver of spiritual space on behalf of the gods. In Artemis, you see only the last mild vestiges of an originally fierce warrioress—the demon-slaying Durga domesticated as a fertility goddess. Cybele, She of the Ax, is closer to the raw, chthonic power of Durga.

RAY MASTER SANCTUARY: The site of the Artemision at the base of Ayasoluk Hill is the geomantic core of Ephesus, regardless of whether a marble temple stands there. When it did, it became a reservoir for Artemis' second-ray golden-orange energy and consciousness, which would cyclically inundate the Artemision and Ephesus like floodwaters from another dimension. That other dimension is accessed through a slit between the worlds at the far end (away from the vanished bay) of the temple.

Conceive of it as a tall, very narrow orange-gold rectangle or slit pillar, a doorway between the worlds. Past the doorway is Artemis' domain, a spherical dimension, or globular amphitheater, with living images of all her incarnations, mythic representations, deeds, places of activity around the planet—a hologram of her sub-temple at Olympus.

In a sense, you are inside the being of Artemis, who is oroboric, making a circle, head to toe; or if you prefer, you are inside the womb of Artemis. You are also "touching" the energy of one aspect of the Great Bear, Ursa Major, one of the key constellations having to do with the celestial hierarchy's activities on Earth.

Also present in this Artemis realm is her college of heralds, or Corybantes and Curetes, or nymphs—the variously named nature spirits, daimons, and astral beings who attend her and distribute and ground her energy and consciousness into and through the world. Once a year, or perhaps more often on special occasions, Artemis parts the curtains or opens the door and allows this energy and consciousness, this essence of being, to flow into Ephesus and its prepared topography and, through its geomantic connections with other sites, into the world.

LANDSCAPE ZODIAC: Ephesus' prepared topography is the Landscape Zodiac that occupies a circular area about fifteen miles (14.44 miles) in diameter radiating out in just under six-mile radii from Ayasoluk Hill, which is its heart. The zodiac dome provides the energization of the site. From the center of this terrestrial zodiac, the Artemision spreads new life to all the creatures of the zodiacal wheel like seeds from a pomegranate, scattering the seeds of stars to sprout in the visionary terrain. The zodiac dome is under the influence of the constellation Argo Navis, the ship of the Argonauts who sought the Golden Fleece.

Ephesus is the *seat* of Artemis, as the Ray Master of the pale orange-gold ray. This is the *church* at Ephesus. Naturally, Croesus would want to capture the place, putting it first on his list of geomantically desirable locations to occupy. In a sense, all of Ephesus is Artemis-Durga dancing wildly upon the corpse of her slain enemies, the demons, giants, Mahisa, the opponents of the gods. She is what the Buddhists would call a Dharma protector: she makes human awakening possible without hindrance, befuddlement, and corruption by the inimical energies of the cosmos.

Seen from another perspective, Artemis, in her fierce battles with cosmic enemies, masters, grounds, assimilates, tames, digests—even masticates—their powerful suprahuman energies for gradual human uptake as part of a spiritual initiation. Obviously the same energies are allowed to filter into the Earth grid matrix as well. Without Artemis as intermediary, these cosmic energies would overwhelm and kill us by the sheer magnitude of their voltage.

In effect, Artemis nourishes the vegetable kingdom, the world of plant life, all of agriculture, and its etheric underpinnings, with the "blood" or transmuted energies of the slain cosmic demons. Here her work as huntress, giant killer, and fertility goddess are seen to be different aspects of the same activity, focused through Ephesus.

Artemis in effect baptizes her "devotees" at Ephesus in these transduced, transmuted energies; this is fitting insofar as one of her prominent human incarnations was as John the Baptist, the wild wandering baptizer of souls, the preparer of the way for the Christ. This is Christian language for the Buddhist concept of Dharma protector.

So Durga dances wildly upon the prostrate corpse of the cosmic demons and giants. She dances upon the unawakened Albion, enswirled by dreams in his spinning, wheeling bed of stars in the Landscape Zodiac surrounding Ayasoluk Hill at Ephesus. She has slain the demonic—as in raw, inchoate, overpowering, suprahuman—in Albion, baptizing him in her own energy consciousness essence from the Great Bear in preparation for his Christing.

It is appropriate (and understandable) that the Virgin Mary and Saint John the Evangelist would be drawn to Artemis' seat at Ephesus. Into this well-prepared topography they could add their refined Christ energies, as mother and apostle, respectively.

Externsteine, Detmold, Germany

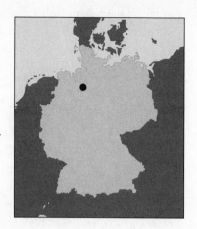

PHYSICAL DESCRIPTION

The Externsteine is a group of five weathered, twisted but towering limestone spires, which geologists say date from the Cretaceous period about seventy million years ago. They are located in the vicinity of the Teutoburger Wald in north-central Germany (about fifty miles southwest of Hannover), near the old towns of Detmold and Horn, an area described as the "sacred heartland" of all Germany.

The Externsteine—the name is usually translated as "external stones"—rise about 125 feet from the flat ground and appear to emerge from the woods like a bony dragon. An artificial lake was created to lie at the feet of this row of stones, and a road still passes through a large gap in the alignment.

The stones contain many caves and hollows in which, it is believed, monks and hermits from the nearby Paderborn Abbey once resided. The site has some oddities: stairs that lead to nowhere; holes drilled seemingly aimlessly into the stones; platforms, slots, niches without apparent purpose; a carved grotesque face; a circular depression in the floor; a narrow passageway carefully transformed into a bizarre shape. The so-called Rock Tomb is a body-shaped cave carved out of the rock, in which humans once stayed for three days in a ritual called "temple sleep," designed to attain spiritual visions and insights.

Atop one of the massive pillars is a rock-hewn chapel, which was consecrated in 1115 A.D., but presumed to have been in use for many centuries before this. The chapel is accessible only by rock-cut steps and a precarious footbridge across a gap between pillars. The chapel is roofless, leading some to propose that it once had a solar observatory of some kind on top that was removed and the roof never replaced. In a stone wall at the east end of this stone chapel is a round opening. In 1823, the German researcher Otto von Bennigsen discovered that from this window you could observe the sunrise at summer solstice as well as the most northerly rising point for the Moon. Archeologists have noted that these particular astronomical events are highlighted at many other megalithic sites and alignments.

Partly on this basis, archeologists have proposed that the Externsteine had archeo-astronomical applications and might have been used by the ancient Teutons as a solstice marker and solar observatory. Von Bennigsen also pointed out that, insofar as the Externsteine and England's Stonehenge lie at nearly the same latitude, the direction of the summer solstice sunrise would be the same at both sites. This in turn suggested that perhaps astronomical conclusions made at Stonehenge might be transferable in part to the Externsteine. Von Bennigsen also proposed that the chapel had been originally created by the priesthood of an ancient "light cult."[382]

Some evidence suggests that the chapel may have had a zodiac orientation function: Incoming rays of sunlight would be deflected in such a way as to either tell the time or highlight the Sun's path through the zodiacal ecliptic. The chapel also has a tiny pillar altar, under the round window, hewn out of the rock; nobody seems to know what its purpose was, but to casual observation it resembles a miniature *lingam,* the fertility and power symbol of the Hindu deity Shiva.

Other theories have been proposed to account for the chapel's antique use. It might have been a Mithraeum, a sanctuary for Roman soldiers worshiping the Persian bull-slayer, Mithras. Or it might have been a place of veneration for the Germanic Teut, the Nordic Wotan, or the Bructerian prophetess Veleda. Its authentic purpose remains enigmatic.

HISTORY AND ARCHEOLOGY

During the 1930s, German landscape researchers Wilhelm Teudt and Josef Heinsch worked out a geomantic model of the German countryside. They postulated an extensive network of astronomical lines linking (and justifying the location of) ancient holy and pagan sites. They called these connections, *Heilige linien,* or "Holy lines," similar to the British designation of leys.

Teudt was enlisted by the Nazi chief Heinrich Himmler to demonstrate and popularize the idea that the ancient Teutonic peoples had once had a centralized, semi-scientific solar cult for which they created these lines and sited their holy places, such as the Externsteine. Himmler had established the *Deutsche Ahnenerbe* in 1935 as a cultural research unit to investigate racial origins and German antiquity and myth, in order to provide an ideological foundation for Nazi claims of Aryan superiority. However, the project of "rescralising the land" and reclaiming a nation's mythic and geomantic past can be "dangerous in the wrong hands," as the Nazi example unarguably showed.[383]

Teudt was given an important role in the *Deutsche Ahnenerbe* to promote Germany's ancestral heritage and to search for additional "holy lines" to strengthen the case for a glorious pagan German past. "They looked for evidence of ancient landscape surveys in order to substantiate Germany's claims as the home of civilization, and where proof of the primeval skills of the race was lacking, it could be fabricated."[384]

For much of this project, Teudt's focus was the Teutoburger Wald district of Lower Saxony, regarded as Germany's sacred heartland. It was rich with astronomical lines connecting ancient mystical sites, all of which centered around the Externsteine, which Teudt had been studying since the 1920s.

It is chillingly ironic that at the same time as Teudt made his discoveries Himmler established his own National Socialist version of King Arthur's famous Camelot at the Wewelsburg Castle not far from Externsteine. He intended the site as a Grail Mystery center, for training of elite SS officers in esoterica and "spiritual enlightenment," and for research into the mysteries of Merlin, the sword Excalibur, and the Holy Grail. This initiative was part of Himmler's commission from Hitler to research and document the high points of Germanic culture and to define (and perhaps mythically justify) the ideology of the SS guards.[385]

During the height of Teudt's research, the Nazis elevated and redeveloped the Externsteine into a "Teutonic cult site," a euphemism for Nazi cult center. Although the Ahnenerbe sought physical evidence of past Germanic use of this site as a cultic center, they failed to unearth anything substantial. A report documenting this was deliberately never published.

It almost didn't matter; the rumor and allegation was sufficient to expand the site's reputation, certainly in recent years. Today the site is popular as a celebratory venue for summer and winter solstices, and draws a dizzying diversity of groups from neopagans to ultranationalists, all of whom see the Externsteine as embodying and furthering their particular beliefs.

Adding to the Externsteine's popularity is its proximity to one of Germany's leading tourist destinations, the *Hermannsdenkmal*. This is a statue on Grotenburg honoring Arminius, Germany's greatest military hero and *Ur*-father of Teutonic independence and nationalism. The site, only a few miles from Externsteine, attracts an estimated million visitors every year.

Hermann, known to the Roman historian Tacitus in his *Annals* as Arminius, was the leader of the Cherusci tribe of Teutons. In 9 A.D., at age twenty-seven, he repelled a Roman invasion of Saxony and effectively halted their expansion into Germany. Supposedly, Hermann's troops defeated and slayed some fifteen thousand Roman soldiers led by Roman Governor Quintilius Varus. Hermann rallied the disparate Teuton clans into one fighting unit and used Roman warfare techniques against the Romans to lead the "great revolt of Germania" to victory. Tacitus called Hermann "the liberator of Germany, one too who had defied Rome."

History credits Hermann as accomplishing this feat in the Teutoburger forest, not far from the Externsteine, although some historians claim the decisive battle was actually fought at the Kalkriese Hill, north of Osnabrück. Thereafter, Hermann was Germany's preeminent symbol of unity, independence, and nationalist pride. Ernst von Bandel designed and executed a monument to Hermann in 1875; the Hermannsdenkmal (Arminius Memorial) now stands on the Grotenburg on a hilltop (elevation: 1155 feet) in the Teutoburger Forest near Hiddesen, just south of Detmold.

The figure, muscular and enormous, stands almost eighty feet tall and faces west towards France with a threatening mien; his left hand holds a mighty shield with the inscription "Treufest"; his right hand holds high a sword upon which this inscription has been etched: "Germany unity—my strength, my strength, Germany's power."

MYTH AND LEGEND

One aspect of the Externsteine story that hovers intriguingly on the border between documentable history and uncorroboratable legend is the *Irminsul*. The term is usually translated from the Old Saxon and Old High German to mean "gigantic column," "huge pillar," "enormous pillar," or "pillar of the god Irmin." These meanings are in reference to its function as a cosmic pillar or *axis mundi*, a Tree of Life representing all the realms of creation and presumably linking the Externsteine with the celestial realm.

Supposedly, in some manner, Charlemagne (742–814 A.D.), King of the Franks and Holy Roman Emperor, cut the *Irminsul* down as an initial step towards converting the "heathen" site to Christian uses and suppressing any other types of religion or usage. He forbade further pagan worship at the site.

In physical terms, one of the stones bears a twelfth-century wall sculpture bas relief carving of the Tree of Life, known in Germanic myth as Yggdrasil, understood as a symbol of Earth power. This was probably the Irminsul. This tree is shown bending over in adoration of the crucified body of Jesus as Nicodemus removes it from the Cross, stepping on the pagan tree to represent the transcendence of the Christ over the backbone of the universe and the submission of the elder but impure faith to the new creed. Nicodemus seems to use the world pillar as a chair upon which he stands to remove Christ's body from the Cross.

The interpretation usually offered is that the ancient tree of pagan knowledge submits in humility to the Tree of the Christian Cross. Certainly this spin on the image would be consistent with the decommissioning of the site committed by Charlemagne in 772 A.D. as part of his campaign against Saxon paganism. Historical sources say that in the year 772, Charlemagne conquered Eresburg and destroyed the Irminsul at the same time.[386]

Supposedly, Charlemagne dispatched Christian monks to the Externsteine to ground the Christian impulse there and to exorcise the site's residual pagan evil energies. Some centuries later, around 1120 A.D., Cistercian monks carved the "Deposition from the Cross" in one of the stone sides of the Externsteine.

But what was the Irminsul? Certain historical texts record the existence of the Irminsul and call it a *fanum, lucum,* or *idolum;* one authority called it a huge tree trunk erected in the open air; another antique writer called it the Hirminsul, a sign of victory and in whose symbology Hirmin (or the god Irmin) and the Greek god Hermes were considered the same deity. Some attempt has been made to associate the hypothesized god Irmin with the Germanic Tiwaz (also called Ziu or Tyr), who was a sky god. A medieval writer named Rudolf of Fulda called Irminsul *universalis columna quasi sustinens amnia,* which means "a universal pillar supporting the whole."[387] This again shifts the understanding of *Irminsul* to the mythic Yggdrasil, or cosmic Tree of Life.

The word was also used in certain South German glossaries as a qualifier for the word

colossus or pyramid. A similar Old High German word, *irmindeot,* suggests more a "great god" than a specific, individual god. Some scholars propose a Germanic cult of world pillars as the explanation for the elusive Irminsul; others relate it to the widespread Jupiter columns placed by the Romans along the River Rhine. These were erected in honor of the sky god and in an attempt to invoke his blessing and protection.

It is seductive to look for an authentic god Irmin, but scholars tend to think "the evidence of the sources speaks against the existence of a god Irmin."[388]

MYSTICS AND TOURISTS

According to Peter Dawkins, director of the Zoence Academy in Warwick, England, and leader of frequent tours to the Externsteine, the stones comprise a chakra landscape temple. The seven delineated stones represent the seven subtle energy centers, or chakras, from root to crown; in the Externsteine alignment, the crown chakra stone is the largest, broadest one with the Temple Sleep sarcophagus and cave, says Dawkins.

These stones were "carved out by natural forces under angelic (that is, spiritual) direction to dramatically express the chakra system." He also likens the overall impression of the stones to a rocky armored dragon sliding out of the hillside of the Wiembecke valley to have a drink of water. This physical appearance justifies the alternate interpretation of the name Externsteine as "dragon stones," Dawkins explains. Further, the Externsteine is the root chakra of a larger landscape temple that includes the Hermannsdenkmal on the Grotenburg about four miles away; this latter site, Dawkins claims, is the "crown of this larger landscape temple."[389]

Arnbald OR (F), a spokesman for the "Odinic Rite," a modern reapplication of old Germanic rites and magical practices, states that Externsteine "stands as the beacon of the heathen world, the most holy stead, certainly of the Northern Tradition yesterday and today, but also one of the most important religious and cultural centers of the archaic Europa."

This writer proposes that the legendary Irminsul column reportedly removed by Charlemagne was a representation of the cosmic axis that connects this world with all the others and which passes through the Pole Star in Ursa Minor. Paralleling Dawkins' interpretation (though apparently arrived at independently), Arnbald suggests that the seven stones of the Externsteine represent the body, the physical human and "multiversal body," with seven levels and seven chakras, and that the Irminsul, as "the image of the cosmic axis, stood for the spine."[390]

Another view proposes that the Externsteine is the remains of a Mystery center founded many millennia ago by wandering Atlantean initiates under the leadership of one named Skythianos. According to Ehrenfried Pfeiffer, an important figure in the Anthroposophical movement of Rudolf Steiner in the United States during the mid-twentieth century, the Externsteine was "one of the deepest and holiest Mystery places." These rocks "are the oldest documents that man has of the original Mysteries of the sun as they were brought from Atlantis."

If you stand before the altar up in the rocks and look out through the small round stone hole (about twenty inches wide), you will see where the Sun once set on the winter solstice in 15,000 B.C., the date of this site's founding, proposed Pfeiffer. The rock in the shape of a human torso is where humans lay for three days as part of the Temple Sleep initiation ritual long ago. There they would sever the bind between the physical and etheric bodies and enter the spiritual worlds for revelation and instruction.[391]

Supporting the site's presumed astronomical

aspects and possibly directly bearing on the chapel, an alternative interpretation of its name has it as *Eck* (corner), *Stern* (star), *Steine* (stones). We might put this together as the "corner stones of the star." In keeping with an Anthroposophical view on the site, two commentators on European Grail sites state: "To the renewed Grail cult of Rudolf Steiner and his followers, the boulders that time and war cannot destroy represent the center of Grail energy in Germany."[392]

A National Socialist woman named Savitri Devi visited the "Rocks of the Sun" (Externsteine) on October 23, 1953, and felt the place was "stamped with the prestige of immemorial Sun-worship." Standing in the "age-old sanctuary," Devi, born in 1905 in France and later dubbed the "priestess of esoteric National Socialism," "shuddered, overwhelmed at the feeling of being on holy ground." The tallest stone was the "sanctuary from which the wise ones of old used to greet the earliest sunrise" on summer solstice morning, she reported. They would announce the great summer solstice festival from atop these rocks with cries of "Triumph, Light."

Following the earlier Nazi tradition of appropriating ancient Germanic sites to support their claims of Aryan and pre-Christian pagan racial purity, Devi said that at Externsteine she found herself "upon a spot sanctified by the Worship of our Parent Star—the old worship of Light and Life—in a Germanic country. And these Rocks, I knew, had been *the* center of Germanic solar rites in time without beginning." She reported that at this ancient pagan solar temple, she experienced "a mystical revelation of eventual Aryan victory."

At the Externsteine, Devi felt she could replenish her spiritual forces for the "eternal Struggle in its modern form" of National Socialist values against Christianity and Marxism. The "Cult of Light" at the Externsteine came to an abrupt end, Devi claimed, with the "destruction of this most holy place of ancient Germany" by Charlemagne and his "fanatical" Frankish Christians.[393]

GEOMANTIC

Dome Cap; Universe Dome Merudanda.

DOME CAP: A dome cap about two miles wide sits over the Externsteine and the surrounding area, generated from the dome over Grotenburg a few miles away. That dome corresponds to Delta Cephei, which is a supergiant, about 3,300 times more luminous than our Sun, with a diameter about twenty-five times larger. It is situated about 1,031 light years from Earth.

Delta Cephei is a pulsating variable star manifesting short-period light changes that are due to actual pulsations of the star and not to being eclipsed by a revolving stellar companion as is usually the case. Other stars that exhibit this behavior—five hundred have been discovered to date—are called cepheids in honor of delta Cephei, the first example of this activity, identified in 1784.

This star's brightness and light spectrum changes regularly (every five days, eight hours, forty-eight minutes), as it undergoes regular expansion and contraction—hence the pulsation effect. Even its surface temperature rises and drops with the spectral shifts from 5,500° K to 6,750° K. Cepheids are "remarkable objects [that] form one of the most important and interesting class of variables known in the universe."[394]

As a constellation Cepheus is a king attired in royal robes; he was once King of the Ethiopians and father of Andromeda, who was the maiden exposed to a sea monster and rescued by Perseus. The alpha star in Cepheus is identified as being at either the king's right shoulder or the top of the right arm. The king is often depicted as wearing a sword and walking with both arms extended to the sides. Delta Cepheus is one of two bright stars on the figure's head.

UNIVERSE DOME MERUDANDA:[395] The most important geomantic aspect of the Externsteine is the enigmatic Irminsul, which Charlemagne "cut down." The myths, allegations, and hints about its nature, especially those that gave it a mythic pedigree, will be the most helpful in developing our understanding of it.

The easiest way to explain the Irminsul is to borrow an image from a different mythic vocabulary. The Greeks said Atlas, a Titan, holds the world on his shoulders and in effect keeps Heaven and Earth separated so that there is room for human life in between. The Irminsul is another version of Atlas' pillar, and it is a gigantic, enormous, and huge pillar, as the word etymologies suggest. But there is also a god at the end of it: Irmin, or Atlas, or a host of other mythically described gods who keep the Sky and Earth separated.

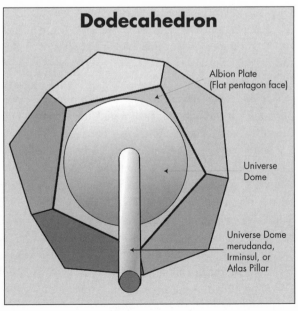

Dodecahedron

Albion Plate (Flat pentagon face)

Universe Dome

Universe Dome merudanda, Irminsul, or Atlas Pillar

In geomantic terms, the Irminsul is an *axis mundi* between a section of the Earth and the top inner center of one of the twelve universe domes that cover the planet. One aspect of the Earth's energy body, when described in terms of geometry, is that it consists of twelve pentagons linked and stitched together like a quilt; each pentagon overlights one-twelfth of the Earth's surface; each has a vertical light line that connects it to the corresponding overlit section of Earth.

This vertical line of light is the Irminsul, or Atlas, cosmic pillar, *axis mundi,* Jacob's Ladder. The line keeps the celestial world separated from the terrestrial.

Many myths recount how once the Sky lay upon the Earth; the fit was so snug that humans and animals had to crawl on their knees and stomachs to move about; there was not sufficient distance between the Sky and Earth even to stand up. Then a culture hero or beneficent god lifted the Heavens off the Earth. That hero—Atlas, Irminsul—is the gigantic pillar itself; in other words, god and function, Irminsul as huge pillar and Irminsul as pillar of Irmin are the same.

The Irminsul is approximately three times wider than the diameter of the Externsteine. In a sense the stones help to ground the incoming celestial energies, but they also give humans the opportunity to enter the rich cosmic stream and expand their consciousness into the Uranian expanse. Sitting within the Externsteine or undergoing the Temple Sleep in the rock cave shaped like a supine human figure, you find your awareness is concentrated, quickened, mobilized, *dilated.* All of space is laid out before you, like wall paintings on a brightly illuminated tunnel or a wraparound tableau of star stories.

You can look up the pillar through the seven planetary spheres all the way to the top, to Polaris, the Pole Star, the bright light at the center-top of the *axis mundi*—the little twinkling star above the crown chakra of the galaxy, above Irmin, and your head. Think of it as the *Sul* of Irmin, the Sol or Sun at the top of the cosmic pillar that is grounded at the Externsteine.

Perhaps the suggested etymology of Externsteine as "corner stones of the star" is apt. Externsteine's energy strives to create an experience of joyous verticality and cosmic connection, a direct link to the star around which the galaxy turns. Here you experience the reconnection of Earth and Sky, lower world and upper world. Heaven lies again upon the Earth and the fit is so close there is only enough room for you to lie on your back in Temple Sleep.

The presence of the Irminsul, or Atlas pillar, paradoxically, enables you to collapse it and reappreciate—*remember*—the unsevered connection between Heaven, Human, and Earth, that time of unity before the "Fall" into incarnation.

Were you to observe the Irminsul entering the Externsteine from above, you would note that the cosmic Tree of Life has roots that extend a great distance in all directions out from the stones. Perhaps Teudt's concept of the *Heilige linien* was describing this effect. The root lines form an intricate intercrossed network of hundreds of lines that extend for many hundreds of miles. In fact, they extend as far laterally as the diameter of the universe dome overhead, as if they were a mirror reflection of the inner surface of the universe dome.

More importantly, were we to observe this large structure from a vantage point that enabled us to see its overall shape and function, we would realize it is filled with motion. It is like a fountain ever rising up and spilling over its top to splash down into a basin, then to rise up again and splash down again. Mathematicians define this type of cyclic, dynamic motion in terms of a shape called the torus. It is like a holed doughnut or smoke ring that is continuously turning in on itself, folding itself inside out, over and over.

Within the Externsteine—occupying the same position as the stones but in another level of reality—there is a very bright, twinkling, pulsating, blazing star. A current of light-energy rises up from within the Earth as a broad band, then narrows to an hourglass shape as it passes through this star, then widens again as it fountains up to the top of the universe dome. There it splits in two, and flows with equal force and in equal measure to the left and the right. It arcs down on both sides like rounded wings, then enters the Earth to meet itself.

As the two halves of this cycling torus doughnut reach their apogee just under the inside of the universe dome, they release a rain of gold sparks. As the light-energy current rises up from the Earth and narrows to pass through the star, this generates a series of concentric circles or hoops or rings that spread out in 360 degrees from this star within the Externsteine. As the uprising two-halved torus intersects these circles, little squares are formed, and the golden rain falls into them like stars coming home to roost.

These little squares form an intricate and vast network of crisscrossing lines; technically, they are more like rhomboids than squares. Seen from above they resemble a patchwork quilt or a landscape veined with roots. These are Teudt's *Heilige linien;* they are also the Curry-Hartmann grid, another geomantic discovery that came out of Germany in the 1940s.[396]

The squares are a kind of micro-distribution network for the blended energies of the Earth-Sky link provided by the Irminsul. The Curry-Hartmann grid is also a reflection of the stellar grid, the geometric array of lines and connections among all the stars in the galaxy, the lacework doily that links all the stars above.

The continuous cycling of energy through the star—the *Stern* in Externsteine—keeps the Curry-Hartmann grid healthy and vibrant; it keeps the roots of the Irminsul nourished and vigorous. The Irminsul conducts the flow from deep within the Earth to high into the sky and then out across the landscape, while the star at Externsteine keeps the two in balance, the navel point in this toroidal system.

So what does it mean that Charlemagne cut down the Irminsul? Charlemagne, or initiates working under his command, engaged the services of a number of elemental or demonic servitors to tie the creative energy of Externsteine into a Gordian knot. It was a black magic Working, and an effective one; it did not "cut down" the Irminsul (that is impossible) but it significantly interfered with the flow and distorted the Sky to Earth communication.

The essential creative energy within the spiritual-geomantic field of the Externsteine can be described—or at least metaphorically suggested—as a tightly packed emerald green sphere. Now picture perhaps six or eight spectral humans done up like warriors playing a brisk, and increasingly aggressive and then furious, game of catch with this sphere, as if it were a beach ball. They are actually extruding the energy into numerous threads, weaving them into a nine-pointed green star, or some kind of asymmetrical geometrical shape about the size of the Externsteine outcropping.

It is not an organic shape, not one that will support the toroidal cycling of celestial and terrestrial energy through the star. It is one that will interfere with that flow, distort it, adulterate, confuse, confound, compromise that flow. Monks, hermits, meditators, anyone using the Externsteine for any variation on the Temple Sleep ritual will have disturbed dreams; they will have shredded visions, prefiltered impressions, manipulated images, misapprehensions. The landscape too will suffer a diminishment in cosmic nourishment, as will the minds and hearts of all the humans living within the scope of the universe dome.

As required by the protocols of black magic, the signature of a Working must be left in plain sight for the recipient. In this case, the Christians carved the Deposition of the Cross on the Externsteine as that signature. It's paradoxical, but evil hides in plain view; the Devil dresses up like a holy man; the Antichrist will convince you it's the Christ. There is nothing inherently "pagan" about the toroidal cycling of the Irminsul at the Externsteine; after all, it benefits the Earth and is part of its subtle energy anatomy and a reflection of a cosmic process.

Charlemagne's intent was political control through magical means. He bent the Irminsul down to serve his own political agenda. The Christianization of the "heathen" Externsteine was simply the cover story, the public relations façade that kept the real Working from view and thus running.

Unfortunately, that Working has not yet been undone; the green knot is still in place; in a sense, the Externsteine has been cursed for more than 1,230 years, ever since Charlemagne and his "fanatical" Frankish Christians seized control of the site. Charlemagne's misappropriation of the Universe Dome Merudanda at the Externsteine established a distortionary pattern that led to a strident nationalist emphasis and various erroneous conceptions of racial and national superiority, which culminated during the Nazi era.

Gediminas Hill, Vilnius, Lithuania

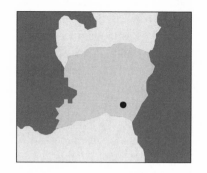

Vilnius is the largest city and the capital of Lithuania, located at the confluence of the Neris and Vilnia Rivers. Archeologists state that people have inhabited the valley around Gediminas Hill, the core of the old city, since the first century A.D., although the official founding of Vilnius is dated to 1323 by Grand Duke Gediminas who in his letters to the Pope declared it to be his "royal town."

The view from Bekes Hill in Vilnius reveals that the city's beauty is in "its utter lack of planning," that it is laid out on different levels, and that "the city is spread out in a deep bowl" in which the colors yellow, green, and red predominate as seen in the plaster walls, courtyards, and roofs, respectively.[397]

The central part of the oldest section of Vilnius, which today comprises 112 city blocks, was once surrounded by a great stone wall (built in 1552) with nine gates, the most famous of which (and the only one extant) is called *Ausros Vartu*, the Gate of Dawn, on the southeastern side. Within this gate, on the second floor, is Our Lady Gate of Dawn sanctuary, which draws 500,000 visitors yearly to see a miraculous portrait of the Virgin Mary displayed within. The chapel was built over the gate in 1671, following

a decade in which the painting generated seventeen documented miracles.

The Church of the Holy Spirit in Vilnius contains the original of a painting of Divine Mercy, a portrait of Jesus with two rays of light emanating from his heart. This was based on a vision received by Sister Faustina of Plock, Poland, in 1931, and painted under her instruction by Vilnius artist Eugeniusz Kazimirowski in 1934.[398] In 1993, Pope John Paul II prayed before the holy image during his Lithuanian pastoral pilgrimage and many come to Vilnius solely to view it.

Also of note in Vilnius is the *Arkikatedra Bazilika*, the Cathedral of Vilnius, a recognized place of pilgrimage because it contains the sacred relics of Lithuania's fifteenth-century patron saint, Casimir. The Cathedral, set at the foot of Gediminas Hill, is also notable because local legend says it was built on pagan sacred ground originally dedicated to Perkunas, the Lithuanian god of thunder. An earlier church on the site of the Cathedral was built by Mindaugas the Great, the first Lithuanian king to become a Christian. Cathedral Square is bounded on one side by Kalnu Park.

On Gediminas Hill, the Gediminas Tower is all that remains from the once glorious Higher Castle, which was constructed by the Grand Duke Gediminas as part of his defensive effort to protect Vilnius (and all of Lithuania, ultimately) from the onslaught of the Christian Teutonic Knights. These German Christian crusaders, intent on converting pagan Lithuania, were definitively defeated in 1410 at the Battle of Tannenberg, after which Vilnius' growth began in earnest. In 1579, Vilnius University was founded, one of the oldest such institutions in Eastern Europe. In 1994, the Old Town of Vilnius was placed on UNESCO's prestigious World Heritage List.

Gediminas Hill, a rectangular prominence about 140 feet high, is credited with being Vilnius' oldest settlement. The Duke is remembered both as one of Lithuania's greatest rulers and as a staunch pagan, resisting the expanding Christian hegemony from Europe because of the "heinous offences and numerous treacheries undertaken by the knights."[399] Somewhat confusing to outsiders is the fact that Gediminas Hill is also called Bald Hill, Castle Hill, Crooked Hill, and at one time Auroch's Hill.

At the base of Gediminas Hill, which towers over the rest of Vilnius, and set in the Sventaragis Valley, was the Lower Castle, the residence of Lithuania's grand dukes for three hundred years, also built by the Grand Duke Gediminas. In older days, this site was revered as the sacred place at which Lithuanian dukes were cremated. It was also an ancient pagan shrine to the thunder god Perkunas. In 1985, archeologists unearthed the remains of a pagan temple at this site.

The story goes that long ago Duke Sventaragis, approaching death, asked to be cremated and buried in this place, and asked that all the dukes that succeeded him should be similarly treated at this spot. After he died, his son Skirmantas burned his body, his clothes, falcon, greyhound, even his horse, and saw to it that the valley was thereafter called Sventaragis, which means "holy temple." For a time, Perkunas' state temple was here, and his priests and priestesses tended his eternal fire at this spot. Much later in Vilnius' history, Mindaugas

would build his church then later the Cathedral of Vilnius would arise on the same spot, as it were, on the grave of Perkunas' shrine.

MYTH AND LEGEND

The two central myths of Vilnius concern an iron wolf and a thunder god. Regarding the first, Vilnius legend records that Grand Duke Gediminas was out hunting animals with his court, blowing horns and chasing wild animals through the woods. They had come from what was then Lithuania's capital city, Trakai, about four miles away. At the end of the day, they assembled on a high hill near the junction of the Neris and Vilnia Rivers and proudly examined their game, which included wolves, aurochs (wild oxen, later extinct), and shaggy bears.

Gedminas decided to spend the night on the hill. It was overgrown with oaks and white birches and the waters of the Neris River rushed by noisily at the base of the hill. That night Gediminas dreamed he saw an iron wolf howling on this hill. The howl was so loud it seemed one hundred wolves were howling at once. Nobody in Gediminas' court understood the dream, so he had to bring in the High Priest of Lithuania, Kriviu Krivaitis, to make sense of it.

The High Priest interpreted this dream as signifying that a great and formidable city would rise on this site, that Gediminas should build it, and that it would be as strong as iron. Enemies might attack the city, even many times, but they would fail to occupy or demolish it. The wolf's howl was a measure of the future city's life and strength. The loudness of the wolf's howl, said Kriviu Krivaitis, meant the fame of this new powerful city would go out around the world.

There is a variation on this tale. Around twilight at the end of a long hunting day, Gediminas spied a large bull, an aurochs, chased it, and finally caught up with it on the hill overlooking the two rivers. In other words, in this version, the aurochs led Gediminas to the top of the hill.

There is an odd possible remnant of this foundation myth in the form of a Vilnius ghost tale. Once every hundred years, an ungodly spirit in the form of a huge black dog with a red ribbon around its neck appears near the bell tower in Cathedral Square, at the bottom of Gediminas Hill. It shows up at the same spot at sunset on the summer solstice. In 1896, a girl encountered this spectral dog, and reported the dog asked her to remove the ribbon and follow her, but she declined, upon which the dog gave a shuddering sigh, rolled over, and vanished.

The second big myth of Vilnius concerns the thunder god. Vilnius legend states that worship of the thunder god Perkunas was performed at a temple at the base of Gediminas Hill. In Lithuanian myth, the supreme god was called Dievas, but the second most important one was Perkunas, whose name means thunderer.[400]

In many respects, his characteristics are similar to the Greek Zeus, Hindu Indra, and Norse Thor, yet he also resembles a Sun god. He wears a red cloak, has a silver bow and golden arrows on his shoulder, carries a stone ax, grips lightning bolts in his fist, is haloed by fire and lightning or wears a lightning wreath on his head, and rides a fiery chariot drawn by goats. His hair is silver but his mustache is gold.

Perkunas wields a massive hammer and possesses nine black stallions; he also rides a winged horse that breathes fire, issues smoke from its ears, and leaves a fire trail behind it as it races across the sky. The oak is the thunder god's sacred tree, and oak trees struck by lightning were revered by Lithuanians as being touched by Perkunas. He was generally stern or angry, with a ruddy face, strong physique, and curly black or copper beard. When angry, he sent thunderstorms and lightning to his enemies or those who had offended him.

Perkunas was the absolute master of the atmosphere, weather, and the waters of the sky, and was associated with rain, lightning, and thunder. Every spring, Perkunas freed the waters and impregnated the Earth, and during the summer droughts, he fought the Underworld spirits who had captured the waters, and again set the waters free. Perkunas was responsible for the fecundity of the plant world, fertility in general, and for moral order and justice.

He attacked the evil spirits of the world with his thunderbolts, struck down evil humans and destroyed their homes with lightning if he decided their actions so warranted. "Perkunas is the active principle of the heavens, the God of maleness, energy, and heavenly fire. He revives life everywhere, reawakens life for a new cycle of life."[401]

He was also the protector of the righteous and their homes, and his sign was the cross in the form of an "X"—which signified crossed lightning bolts—or the swastika, an ancient and widely recognized Sun symbol representing the wheels of the solar chariot as they rode across the sky. He had several epithets, including *Aukstejas* (The Highest One), *Dundalis* (a Germanic reference to his thunder aspect), and *Perkona tevs* (Latvian for "Father Perkons"). Perkunas lived in a castle at the top of the slippery slope of the sky; in Lithuanian belief, this place was called Dausos, a realm of the dead governed by Dievas—"a world that lay beyond the slippery high hill of the sky, which the dead had to climb."[402]

Perkunas was a participant in the Heavenly Wedding, which in Latvian folklore had to do with the wedding of the daughter of the Sun. In Lithuanian belief, the Sun and Moon are as husband and wife, and their daughter, Zemyna, is the Earth. (Contrary to many systems, the Sun is Saule, one of the most powerful goddesses, while her husband, Menulis, is the Moon.) Perkunas was a guest of either the Sun or the Moon, but in any case, on his way to the wedding, he struck a golden oak tree possibly as an exorcistic gesture to expel evil spirits believed to live and hide within this tree's roots.

Perkunas was also credited with being the Heavenly Smith, and the implication is that, like other smith gods, he had hammered out the Sun and Moon and the rest of the Heavens in his smithy at the beginning of time.

GEOMANTIC

Dome Cap; Landscape Zodiac; Mithraeum; Lucifer Binding Site.

DOME CAP: There are several dome caps over parts of Vilnius, including a large cap over Gediminas Hill and Cathedral Square. The caps derive from a dome over nearby Juozapines Hill, which at almost one thousand feet is Lithuanania's highest peak. The country is mostly one of low-lying plains, with rolling hills, 758 rivers more than four miles long, and three thousand lakes; there are no other significant high points in the entire country.

The dome over Juozapines Hill is the starfall for theta Pegasus, or *Sa'd al Bahaim*, Baham, for short, in the constellation of the Winged Horse. Its name means "the Good Luck of the Two Beasts" and it is located on the head of the horse. A third-magnitude star, it has also been called *Al Hawa'im*, "the Thirsty Camels."

Mythologically, Pegasus, which as a constellation has eighteen described stars, was the son of Poseidon, the god of the Seas, and Medusa the Gorgon; he created a spring on Mount Helicon in Greece by striking the rock with his hoof. Zeus used Pegasus to carry his thunder and lightning, but it is also said that the originally wild, untamable, snow-white winged horse became the property of the hero Bellerophon, who tamed him with a golden bridle given to him by the goddess Athena, and then rode him on a perilous mission to slay the Chimera, a three-headed terror of the ancient world.

When Bellorophon ordered Pegasus to fly him to Mount Olympus, Zeus punished this impropriety by having an insect sting the horse's hoof, thereby causing Bellerophon to be thrown. Afterwards, Zeus took over the horse and Pegasus became known as the "Thundering Horse of Jove." Pegasus clearly has two connections with the mythic attributions of Perkunas at Gediminas Hill: he releases trapped water from the Earth, and he is the winged mount of the god of thunder and lightning.

The essential energy of the Vilnius dome caps and the Juozapines Hill dome creates vertical flow of spirit into the landscape. This will make more sense below, but for now this means a lightning-quick, dynamic downthrust of celestial energy and consciousness into this geomantic node, like a sword stroke into a container bursting with water—just the kind of deed Perkunas would do.

LANDSCAPE ZODIAC: The presence of a Landscape Zodiac in Vilnius, about eight miles in diameter, explains why the iron wolf howled in Gediminas' dream. That wolf was really a dog, but the dog is Canis Major, the Great Dog, guardian of the House of Stars that is the galaxy and at whose throat shines Sirius, the brightest star in our galaxy.

The Dog is the first geomythic figure one encounters in approaching a Landscape Zodiac, and unless you befriend this Dog, it's unlikely you will make much more progress in penetrating the zodiac temple. At Vilnius, the Dog faces down the hill to the Vilnia River, and overlooks Cathedral Square and the former Perkunas temple. The Dog guards the House of Stars, and he is our soul guide through the starfields. The Dog barks (the wolf howls) because it is awake, vigilant, on duty, watching the temple entrances, both announcing the presence of the star temple and demanding credentials of all who would enter his domain.

The zodiac dome, which tops the Vilnius Landscape Zodiac, energizes the greater Vilnius area in a nine-mile radius in all directions from Gediminas Hill.

MITHRAEUM: The aurochs that Gediminas hunted, that led him to Gediminas Hill, provide a useful mythic clue. In fact, the hunting tableau as a whole—the daylong pursuit and slaying of various wild animals—is a clue to the geomantic nature of the Sventaragis Valley at the base of Gediminas Hill. The bull, of course, is the key animal associated with the Mithraic mysteries of the Sun, and the aurochs, or wild ox, is close enough.

Perkunas has some qualities normally attributed to the chief of the gods, such as Zeus, Indra, or Thor, yet his essential activities are more in line with the work of the Sun god. Other clues that link Perkunas with the Sun god are the references to endless fire, upholding justice, the smithy, the hunting of animals.

Perkunas shares characteristics with the Hindu Agni, the Fire god, also associated with the Mithraeum. Agni is the Lord of ritual sacrifice, the endless, and the wealth-giver. He is colored red, rides a ram, has seven arms, three heads growing red flames, and three legs; his tongue is a flame and he exhorts the gods to speak the truth always.

In the classical world, the physical Mithraea were temples constructed to simulate the cave in which Mithras the solar god captured and slew the divine bull as a symbol of life through death. In other words, the physical temples were meant to model the etheric, spiritual ones present in a site's geomantic structure. From the bull's blood, all living things would emerge, even the time allotment for life. The bull's "blood" would spread all over the planet, making physical life possible.

LUCIFER BINDING SITE: The wolf was howling with the voice of one hundred wolves for another reason. He was bemoaning the imprisonment of the Lord of Light in the Sventaragis Valley, hammered like a nail into the Earth at the Perkunas temple site so that the Christian church could take its place.

The history of Vilnius reveals a long theological struggle between pagan Perkunas forces and crusading Christian monotheistic forces. That struggle played out primarily in what is now called Cathedral Square. First was a Perkunas temple, then the Christian Church. However, that the Church supplanted the pagan temple does not in itself close the books on the theological struggle between the two approaches to spirituality. There was a hidden cost to the succession. The energy at the Vilnius temple on the whole does not circulate well or freely; the zodiacal wheel is not turning at present.

Lucifer as the Lord of Light represents the embodiment, the demonstration of the *knowledge* of the Tree of Good and Evil, a living synthesis of opposites almost too hard to comprehend. As one being, he is dual valanced, light and dark, positive and negative, good and evil, pagan and Christian. When the Christian church succeeded in dominating the Sventaragis Valley, commandeering its geomantic structure, and building its church, it did so by severing half of Lucifer's being. It accepted the light part, and denied the dark.

The result was an inevitable hammering of Lucifer as a whole being into the Earth, which became his prison. Think of it as the Greek Prometheus chained, seemingly forever, to a rock in the Caucasus Mountains for defying Zeus. The implications of the Wild Sun God (Perkunas), in his most flagrantly Sorath-like aspects, would be daunting, overwhelming, perhaps even nightmarish, to Christian priests and officials—too strong an energy, too much the Beast, for their dogma to contain. So the Sun temple of Perkunas was shut down, suppressed, repudiated, eclipsed, paved over by the weight of the cathedral.

Ironically, another story attributed to Gediminas concerned the nature of the sacrifice he would offer the gods to go with the foundation stone for his castle on Gediminas Hill. He summoned the *vaidilos,* the *zynai,* the *burtininkai,* and all the other sages of his land for advice. The construction workers had a massive cornerstone ready to roll into the trench. Gediminas wanted his castle to be the strongest in the land, so he needed to offer the gods something of comparable stature so as to win their protection.

Somebody suggested a firstborn son of teenage years to be given voluntarily by his mother, but he was released from this obligation. Next somebody proposed a virgin female of the same age, and she stood in the trench holding a bouquet of fresh-cut flowers as the great stone rolled down upon her. Somehow she survived the crushing of the stone, and when Gediminas and his men climbed down into the trench, they found her standing there, unafraid, even unperturbed, with a diamond sparkling on each cheek as the result of the tears she shed when the flowers were knocked from her hand by the stone.

Gediminas and his colleagues interpreted the outcome of this event as evidence that the gods had chosen their proper sacrifice—a bouquet of flowers. But perhaps this tale is the bright, even naïve, spin to a darker act of magic and deconsecration whereby the Perkunas temple was shut down and one half of the essence of the Lord of Light was denied. Allegorically, both the boy and the maiden were buried under the foundation stone. Geomantically, something more than a bouquet of flowers was buried under the cornerstone.

This is a problem because the Vilnius temple at present is not allowed to work the way it was intended. During the Communist era, with its atheistic, antireligious stance and acts, the Vilnius geomantic temple became stagnant; in the years since 1989, when Lithuania declared its independence of the Soviet Union and began reconsecrating its churches, the geomantic energy has started to circulate again. These are good signs, but much more is needed. In fact, we have not yet reached that time when the temple's fame would spread around the world, as the Duke's high priest prophesied.

Here's how the Vilnius temple could work if all its components were given free rein: You prepare yourself in the Landscape Zodiac at Vilnius, experiencing the energies and essences of the stars, and working out the corresponding energies in yourself—the inner and outer horoscope. You do this on behalf of the Albion sleeping in the zodiac; the constellations are part of his body, wings, and auric field, but he is still sleeping, the unawakened reflection of the Cosmic Man, variously called Purusha, Ymir, Adam Kadmon. Then you immerse yourself in the Solar Logos at the Sun temple of Perkunas. You slay the aurochs and drink the "bull's blood," which is to say, fill yourself with the light of the spiritual Sun, the Christ light, and start to awaken. Fortified with the primal fire of the universe and its Christed refinement, you can claim your right to manage and embody the knowledge of the Tree of Good and Evil. You can undo the Fall of Man in yourself.

You can reclaim, redeem, resurrect, and validate the Lord of Light within you and at the same time free him from his subterranean imprisonment under the Perkunas temple by the force of your own spiritual progress through the Vilnius temple. What you do for yourself you do also for the Vilnius geomancy. The reverse is also true; what you contribute to the geomantic matrix feeds back into your own energy system. In fact, there is no other way you could do the work, as it cuts in both ways, inner and outer.

Lucifer, unbound, rises up, the Fall reversed, forgiven, transcended, and wears the star fields of the zodiac as a skirt, receiving the vertical flow of celestial light and consciousness from above, transmitting it out across the geomantic temple. Then the Vilnius Albion, awakening, is freshened with the living light, the balanced, integrated knowledge of the Tree of Good and Evil—which is the same as saying the consciously executed use of true *free* will, the choice to be good made without compulsion. Albion sees how to be, takes his example from the primordial Lord of Light and perfect exemplar of this balance of opposites.

All of this is a geomythic Mystery drama of high theological import. Its players are the Fallen One (Lucifer), the Unawakened One (Albion), and the Redeemer (Christ in the Sun temple). The superimposition of these three geomantic features at Vilnius affords us a special opportunity. The appropriate use of these features would have ramifications far beyond Vilnius and its psychological, psychic, and spiritual life. The fulfillment of the Vilnius temple along the originally intended lines would have repercussions throughout the one-twelfth part of the planet in which the Vilnius temple has its place like an organ in a living body.

Each of the Earth's one-twelfth divisions of its surface has a vast geomythic figure that is also an Albion. So if we think of Vilnius as an organ in that huge body, for it to wake up in this geomantic sense would be like the body having an epiphany of the Christ by way of the extraordinary spiritual experiences under way in one of its organs. This would set up a marvelous feedback loop between the Vilnius Albion and the Vilnius residents, and between this and the larger Albion and the millions of people living under its aegis, and between that cosmic life implanted on Earth and all of the Earth and its people.

This is an aspect of the possible future of the Vilnius geomantic temple, one future nuance of the wolf's hundred-voiced howl from Gediminas' dream.

Glastonbury, England

This rural market town of eight thousand in the southwest of England some hundred miles west of London is a complex geomantic workshop. It has more geomantic structures than most holy sites anywhere on the Earth, it has a greater burden of attribution, myth, speculation, and nonsense than most, and the public memory, sustained through folklore, myth, and psychic revelation, of its geomantic structures and presumed functions, is greater than at most sacred sites. All of these factors make Glastonbury highly accessible as a present day Mystery temple for initiation and geomythic training ground.

Glastonbury has attracted so much attention, draws so many researchers, mystics, savants, pilgrims, and tourists, and has inspired so many pamphlets, books, seminars, and mystic tours that it is on a par with the Egyptian pyramids as far as its presumed world significance, multiple enigmas, and millennialist role. Glastonbury attracts "all manner of strange and wild specimens of humanity drawn to the place by strange and wild rumours of lines of power and forthcoming cosmic revelations."[403]

It is the home of Goddess pagans and devout Christians, occultists and rock-and-rollers, magi-

cians and feminists, shoe sellers and crystal merchants. There are the mystics and the materialists, the Glastonians and the Avalonians, the "Grail-seekers and the Grail-killers," a struggle vividly evoked in John Cowper Powys' 1930s classic about this town, *A Glastonbury Romance.*

This review briefly touches on only the most salient aspects of Glastonbury's vast mythos, the ones indicative of geomantic function.[404]

In fact, a fair number of the generic geomantic temple structures referenced throughout this book, such as Avalon, Pointer's Ball, Landscape Zodiac, and Tree of Life, derived their name (in my efforts to systematize the light pattern library of the Earth) or their primary conceptual aspects from features in Glastonbury. That's largely because Glastonbury's geomancy, its relation to myth and consciousness, are so well preserved, so prominent, and so comparatively easy to interface with.

Again, it is a very practical, accessible temple for geomantic mysteries. John Michell, a major figure in British Earth mysteries, commented in 1972 that Glastonbury, once a center of the ancient cosmic religion, would be the place where the "true science and philosophy that sustained the harmonious world order of antiquity" would be revealed again for a new time. This promise of a Great Return of ancient initiate knowledge was

269

vouchsafed by a "document" recently discovered in the Glastonbury area, Michell said. "This document is nothing less than the landscape itself."[405]

Topographically, Glastonbury rises above the Somerset Levels by way of four hills close together. These are the Tor (elevation: 520 feet), the tallest; its immediate neighbor Chalice Hill; another neighbor called Saint Edmund's Hill, and a short distance away, Wearyall Hill. Geological evidence (supported by mythic memory) indicates that many centuries ago the land around these four hills would flood in the winter, making the four hills temporary islands.

Local folklore says this is why the Glastonbury environment was one known as the Summer Country—it was only in summer that all the land was dry enough to get around without a boat, when the islands became only hills again. Even today, the environment around Glastonbury is very low (almost below sea level), marshy moorland threaded by drainage channels called rhynes. The Somerset levels are actually the largest wetlands in the west of Britain. Glastonbury is only fifteen miles south of the Bristol Channel, and as recently as 1607, seawater lapped against the base of the Tor in the spring floods.

The Tor is an anomalously shaped hill, sometimes compared to a truncated pyramidal cone. Its grassy, sheep-grazed flanks seem to exhibit traces of an artificially cut turf maze that winds its way around the slope, eventually arriving at the top. There you encounter what's called the Saint Michael's Tower, a hollow stone edifice that can be seen for miles and is dedicated to the Archangel Michael. It was built in the 1360s to replace monastic buildings previously there (possibly from 600 A.D.), which had been destroyed in 1275 by a freakish earthquake. There is a regular stream of walkers ascending or descending the Tor almost all the time.

Next to the Tor is Chalice Hill, a lovely rounded hill that is no longer available to the general public for walking. In between the Tor and Chalice Hill is Chalice Well, a tiny garden (open to the public for a small admission fee) of less than an acre laid out with almost lapidary precision and elegance. It was designed by Wellesley Tudor Pole, one of the major figures in Glastonbury's twentieth-century reflowering. The Well itself, also called Blood Spring, pumps out twenty-five thousand gallons per day of slightly reddish, iron-tinged water that has been used for centuries as a healing water and has never been known to run dry.

"My aim," wrote Pole in 1963, "is to prepare the Chalice Well property for use once more as a Gateway, through which the Christ's message for the New Age can enter and spread across the world." Pole said that when he first came to Glastonbury in 1904, it was "dead, or anyway in a coma, spiritually speaking."

Since then, he wrote in 1966, the Well and all of Glastonbury have been brought back to life, its beacons "rekindled" as a "Michael centre," that is, a center of activity for and human interaction with the Archangel Michael. Pole also referred to "speeding up the chemicalization process" at the Tor, "thereby releasing the negative vibrations set up long ago by human agency."[406]

Many sensitive visitors to the Well appear to pick up on the energy Pole has characterized. One person noted, "I had a clear vision of the well-head giving off a huge fountain of white light energy that hundreds of spirits seem to be bathing in and leaving refreshed."[407]

At the base of Chalice Hill are the spacious grounds and ruins of Glastonbury Abbey, once one of England's foremost Christian centers. It's a forty-acre expanse of green lawns, walkways, and 592 feet of church ruins, all of which is bounded by an eight-foot stone wall. Some 150,000 tourists come every year to visit the Abbey ruins or take part in its religious festivals. In the late medieval period, it was the prime Christian pilgrimage site in England. Many claim—the idea is supported by a famous poem by British mystical poet William Blake—that the Christ visited Glastonbury while he was alive.

Glastonbury's ecclesiastical origins are traced back to Joseph of Arimathea, a contemporary of Jesus, who is said to have come to Glastonbury shortly after the Crucifixion (63 A.D.) with twelve followers to found a small Christian center and to bury the Holy Grail (said to be the chalice or dish used by Christ and his apostles at the Last Supper) in Chalice Hill. Early on, the Abbey, England's first Christian church, was given tax-free jurisdiction by the Saxon kings of an area of land around Glastonbury called the Twelve Hides. The legendary King Arthur and Queen Guinevere are said to be buried at the Abbey. The Abbey ceased being a player in theological matters after the Dissolution of the Abbeys in 1539.

About a mile and a half from the Tor is a ditch and earthen bank that runs for three-quarters of a mile across a series of fields. It's called Ponter's Ball, a name which many believe derives from the Latin *Pontis Vallum*, meaning the "bridge over the ditch" or the "fort of the bridge." The earthwork is twelve feet high and thirty feet across, but basically nobody understands what its purpose was.

Across town is Wearyall Hill, a hill that looks like a green whale from certain angles. Here, legend says, Joseph of Arimathea landed (in the days when the sea lapped up against the hill), planted his staff into the ground, and instructed it to turn into a flowering thorn tree, a descendant of which is still there. Today half the main hill has houses (called Fisher's Hill), the other half is a green space open to the public.

A short distance from the base of Wearyall Hill is a little visited, neglected area next to the sewage works variously called Beckery, the Isle of Beckery, Bee-Keeper's Island, or Little Ireland, where once a chapel stood, dedicated to Saint Bridget, a fifth-century Celtic saint who lived there. King Arthur is said to have been guided here by an angel to have an experience of the Virgin Mary and Christ Child early one morning.

In the 1930s, Canadian researcher Katherine Maltwood reported she had discovered visible signs of a gigantic representation of conventional astrological effigies in the configurations of the greater Glastonbury landscape. The arrangement of hills, paths, rhynes, ponds, hedgerows, and other topographical features, when seen in aerial photographs or on close-detail land survey maps, revealed the shapes of the signs of the zodiac. She proposed that this Landscape Zodiac, ten miles in diameter, thirty miles in circumference, had been deliberately created around 2700 B.C., possibly by the Sumerians. Maltwood often referred to it as King Arthur's Round Table or the Temple of the Stars.

What was the zodiac for? We are not likely to discover the meaning of the Landscape Zodiac "until we recover the superconsciousness of the Builders," commented University of Pittsburgh philosophy professor Oliver Reiser in 1974. It will require a "vast interdisciplinary process of revealing and understanding" the zodiac's message, but in so doing "we will reconstitute in ourselves the now-lost higher consciousness of those who built the Zodiac."

Reiser also offered this astute insight: "The Zodiac of Glastonbury then becomes a kind of antecedently designed creche for the birthing of the cycle of the Arthurian Knights of the Round Table—the 'heavenly pattern of earth.'"[408]

Glastonbury holds many mysteries, John Michell observed in 1990, but they are all based in one primary mystery. "How is it that this small place, isolated among the Somerset marshes, plays such a leading part in the spiritual history of Britain?"[409] In our exploration of the relationship between Glastonbury's myths and its geomantic structure, we hope to get some part of an answer.

MYTH AND LEGEND

Glastonbury's mythic resume is intense and formidable. It is the *Aestiva Regio* (the Summer Country), *Ynys Witrin* (Isle of Glass), Avalon (Isle of Apples), *Domus Dei* (Home of God), *Secretum Domini* (Secret of Our Lord), the Mother of Saints, and the "Holyest Erthe in England." It has been called the English Lourdes, a "spiritual volcano," the site of the New Jerusalem, Earth's heart chakra, a World Sacred Site, the "citadel of Celtic esotericism." It is also the Region of the Summer Stars, the Sanctuary of Our Lord, and the gateway to Annwn, the Celtic Underworld.

The Tor is said to be the home of the Celtic god Gwynn ap Nudd (White Son of Night), who is the guardian of the gates of Annwn. He lies in a glass castle in the Underworld in the Isle of the Dead over which he rules, like the Greek Hades. Rumors abound that the Tor is hollow, an artificial hill laced with tunnels and chambers. In Welsh myth King Arthur is said to have ventured into Annwn to collect a precious cauldron of immortality, which he brought back.

The Tor is also the home of King Avallach, monarch of the Summer Country. His daughter was Morgan le Fay, the enchantress of Camelot and sister to King Arthur; she lived in Avalon with her nine priestesses. Later myths say King Melwas, King of the Summer Country, resided on the Tor, and when he abducted Queen Guinevere, he brought her to his invisible palace inside. The Archangel Michael is also said to stand tall on the Tor, overseeing a long-running ley line named after him and which passes through the Tor.

One of Glastonbury's prominent mythic names was *Insula Avallonia*, the Isle of Avalon, and Avalon was a Celtic otherworldly paradise realm, also called the Fortunate Isle. It's where King Arthur was taken by Morgan le Fay after his final battle at Camlann when he was wounded but not dead. Early Celtic legends hold that you could reach Avalon only on a boat guided by the sea god Barinthus. Arthur got there when Morgan, Quinivere, and his mother rowed him in a barge.

The twelfth-century pseudo-historian (as prim scholars dismissively refer to him) Geoffrey of Monmouth said that nine sisters rule in the Fortunate Isle, or island of apples, which produces all things of itself. "She who is first of them is more skilled in the healing art and excels her sisters in the beauty of her person, Morgan is her name," he wrote in his *Vita Merlini*.[410]

Somewhere in Glastonbury, or perhaps all of it, is the site of the legendary *Cyfangan,* or one of the Three Perpetual Choirs of the Island of Ynys Prydein (Britain). A *cyfangan* is a harmonious song or uninterrupted choir, and according to the Welsh *Triads,* an ancient repository of Celtic myth, one such Choir was located at the "Island of Afallach," which is to say, either the Isle of Apples or King Avallach's Isle—in either case, clearly Glastonbury. In each of these Choirs, there were twenty-four hundred "religious men," and during the course of a twenty-four-hour day, every hour a fresh one hundred continued to sing and pray to God "ceaselessly and without rest forever."[411]

MYSTICS AND TOURISTS

The natural landscape features of Glastonbury and its "subtle and elemental" aspects create a powerful "spirit of place" that inevitably induces what is half-jokingly called the "Glastonbury initiation." The forces meet in a "dynamic polarity that can create tension or harmony," observes Nick Mann, a longtime Glastonbury resident and commentator. People who have lived there for years say it is a place of the higher self and the Shadow, heaven or hell—"a place to dive to normally inaccessible depths."[412]

One person who dove deeply—through a "rabbit hole," he said—was an Italian writer and visionary, Gino Gennaro, who had a spectacular higher-dimensional experience of Glastonbury's Celtic mythos in the 1970s. He went into one of the many portals ("rabbit holes," as in *Alice in Wonderland*) and emerged in the "fairyland" of Avalon, complete with golden apple trees, unicorns, a griffin guide, and "many kinds of mythological creatures." He walked through the maze (an astral or perhaps the original version of the Tor's turf maze) and met the Queen of the Maze.

Then at the base of the Tor he met the "Red Dragon, gifted with seven gigantic heads." He resided between two tall trees with silver leaves and golden apples. His massive but agile body encircled the outer rim of the seven steps of the temple, Gennaro noted, and his "endless tail" stretched away far beyond Wearyall Hill, "on and on, as far as the eye could see, criss-crossing totally the watery and earthly globe."

The dragon gave him a golden apple and let Gennaro understand that "this golden apple was the sacrament to be eaten by mortals before entering the City of Revelation." The fruit would also enable Gennaro to observe the astral environment "with the full sight of the dragon's dimension."[413]

Glastonbury was already a "cosmic centre" in pre-Atlantean days, commented Wellesley Tudor Pole in the 1960s. Pole was a no-nonsense British initiate and businessman, primarily responsible for securing Chalice Well as a protective spiritual center and for working with the angelic realm in cleansing and helping to energize and reequip many ancient holy sites.

Glastonbury is one of a number of places around the Earth that owe their formation and destiny to celestial influences, he said. Glastonbury still had intact its "direct link with the energies emanating from the Archangelic Hierarchy," and through the Tor with the Archangel Michael, Pole wrote. Maltwood's Landscape Zodiac was the only remaining external, or visible, link with the celestial agencies. Even so, "a pure strain of Druidic lore" persisted at Glastonbury, as if preserved for further use in a spiritually different future.

In the earliest days of humanity's evolution, Glastonbury Tor was one of many centers where worship of Light as a spiritual origin and its representative, the Sun, was performed. Another name for this Light, Pole said, was the Fatherhood of the Creator, and the Tor and its immediate surroundings were "enveloped in a sacred aura of protection."

Much later in human history, the Tor became an observatory for the study of the celestial spheres, and for rituals pertinent to inducing a sense of "Oneness" with the universe. After two thousand years of the Christian era, Glastonbury would "emerge into the daylight once more" and fulfill its destiny mandated at the beginning of time, Pole prophesied.[414]

A year after Pole died in 1968, he communicated through a psychic named Cynthia Sandys during a meditation at Chalice Well. He said that when he died and "woke up" in the Other World, he found himself in a higher-dimensional level of Glastonbury. He focused his attention on the Tor, clearly the center of power. After a long struggle, and considerable resistance by the Devic kingdom, it had become attuned to human and Christ vibrations.

Pole saw "old great Devic beings standing on the Tor." They were "radiant and magnificent in all the ancient beauty of mind and power." A beautiful turbulence swept up from the valley around the Tor and enveloped the Devas, softening their appearance into "the more humane Christ ray," transforming them with the "love rays of the Christ power."

The Abbey could take no credit for this transformation over the centuries, Pole said. Rather, it had happened almost despite the official Christian presence. The apricot light of the Christ's aura blended with the smoke-blue of the Glastonbury vibration, and the two rays formed "a most astonishing pattern, resembling a huge flower with tendrils reaching out in all directions."

Glastonbury's role, Pole added, was not one of the sudden revelation of tremendous visions, but of the "slow and constant seeping through of Spirit" which over time has "impregnated" the entire area.[415]

GEOMANTIC

Domes; Dragon; Avalon; Cretan Labyrinth; Underworld Entrance; Arc of Developing Consciousness; Pointer's Ball; Grail Castle; Interdimensional Portal; Tree of Life; Soma Temple; Shambhala Doorway; Golden Egg; Silver Egg; Perpetual Choir; Vibrating Stone; Ixion's Wheel; Landscape Zodiac; Virgo Albion Heart Chakra; Mobile Shambhallic Focus; Planetary *Anahata* Heart Chakra; New Jerusalem.

DOMES: Glastonbury is geomantically distinguished among the Earth's sites as being one of the few sites with three adjacent domes, over the Tor, Chalice Hill, and Beckery. These generate a total of 144 dome caps which energize and illuminate all of the Summer Country. (Sedona, Arizona, has four domes but not as close together as the three in Glastonbury.)

The dome over the Tor is the planetary starfall for alpha Virginis, or Spica in Virgo. It is the sixteenth brightest star in the sky, about 275 light years from Earth, and twenty-three hundred times more luminous than our Sun. As a constellation, this star form is usually portrayed as a maiden holding a palm branch in her right hand, an ear of wheat in her left. Spica is the bright star on the palm of her left hand; the constellation has twenty stars in all.

The Chaldeans knew Virgo as Ishtar, the Queen of the Stars, also called Ashtoreth. In India,

she was *Kauni,* or the Maiden, mother of the god Krishna; to the Turkomans, she was *Dufhiya Pakhiza,* the "Pure Virgin"; to the Greeks, she was Astraea, the goddess of justice, purity, and innocence, the daughter of the Titan Themis. To the Greeks, she was also Persephone, Demeter's daughter, who was abducted by Hades, the Lord of the Underworld, and made to live for half of each year as Queen of the Dead. But Hesiod described Virgo as Themis, the daughter of Zeus, and says she reigned over humankind during the Golden Age. When the Bronze Age began, she retreated to the Heavens.

The name Spica comes from the Latin *Spicum,* but it was also known as the Hebraic *Shibboleth,* the Syrian *Shebbelta,* the Persian *Chushe,* and the Turkish *Salkim.* All these variations refer to the ear of wheat Virgo holds in her left hand. Arabic astronomers knew this first-magnitude star as *Al Simak al A'Zal,* meaning "the Defenseless," and the Coptic star watchers called it *Khoritos,* meaning "Solitary," in both cases because the star was so bright it seemed neither accompanied by others nor part of a constellation.

Spica's affiliation with the Tor dome helps us understand the strong Goddess veneration emphasis that consistently runs through Glastonbury's mythos. Increasingly since the mid-1980s, there has been in Glastonbury a "spiritual feminist perspective, revalorizing chthonic forces" and the rest of the Avalonian mythos in terms of a geomythic Goddess model.

One leader in this work, Kathy Jones, published *The Goddess in Glastonbury* in 1990, and since then has led tours around the Glastonbury landscape, demonstrating how it resembles the profile of a huge supine goddess, Chalice Hill being her pregnant belly, Wearyall Hill her left thigh, Beckery being the Goddess's vagina out of which a divine child is being born at Bride's Mound. Glastonbury, Jones says, is a "place of gestation."[416]

The dome over Chalice Hill is the starfall for alpha Scorpii, or Antares in Scorpio. It is a bright star on the back of the scorpion. Some authorities say it is the glowing red heart of the scorpion, as red as Mars, hence its odd name: *Anti-Ares,* meaning "similar to Mars [Ares]" or, slightly differently, "Rival of Mars." Antares is a big star, the fifteenth brightest in our galaxy and of the first magnitude with a diameter of six hundred million miles, situated 520 light years from Earth.

Euphratean astronomers knew it as *Kakkab Bir,* the "Vermilion Star," but the name might have derived from the Arabic *Antar,* which means "Shone." The Arabs also knew it as *Al Kalb,* "The Heart"; the Romans called it *Cor Scorpionis,* "Heart of the Scorpion"; Hindu star gazers called it *Jayestha* (Oldest) or *Rohini* (Ruddy); and the Sogdian astronomers of Central Asia called it *Maghan Sadwis,* "The Great Saffron-Colored One."

Scorpio's constellation myth says that it was the scorpion that stung to death the great hunter Orion, or that it frightened the horses of the Sun Chariot driven by the neophyte Phaethon, causing him to lose control. These qualities, loosely interpreted, could explain a lot about the much discussed Glastonbury initiation.

The third Glastonbury dome situated over Beckery represents Merope of the Pleiades, the star cluster in the neck of Taurus the bull. This gives us three domes in Glastonbury, each with a very bright star from one of the twelve zodiacal signs.

Merope is a fourth-magnitude star. Her name means "Mortal," and the star myth tells us that she hid her face in shame because she was the only one of the Seven Sisters (the seven primary stars of the five hundred in the Pleiades cluster) who married a mortal, namely, Sisyphus, King of Corinth. The other sisters married gods, so she believed she had wasted herself on a mortal human. She is thought of as the Lost Pleiad.

Astronomically, Merope is hard to see because "she" is obscured by a gaseous nebula.

The Pleiades are a famous star cluster, especially in terms of recent allegations regarding UFO visitations and channeled sources of information. The name comes from the Greek word *plein,* which means "to sail." The Pleiades are known as the Starry Seven, the Net of Stars, the Seven Virgins, the Seven Atlantic Sisters, the Daughters of Pleione, or the Children of Atlas. The Titan Atlas was their father, Pleione their mother; the Pleiades are identical with the Hesperides, the women said to guard the golden apple trees of the Hesperides, property of the goddess Hera (Zeus' wife) in the far West.

The Greek Gardens of the Hesperides are also identical with the Celtic Isle of Apples, or Avalon. There is interesting astronomical support for this because some astronomers note that the *nine* brightest stars of the Pleiades (the Seven Sisters plus two more) are concentrated together in a field of space from our viewpoint on Earth about 1° in diameter. "These 9 bright stars form a pattern resembling a stubby dipper with the short handle at 27 and 28 Tauri (Atlas and Pleione [the Pleiades' "parents"])."[417] The significance of the Pleiadian connection through this dome will be made evident below.

Glastonbury and its surrounding countryside are enveloped by the energies of the three domes. Even though each dome is centered over a specific hill or part of town, the domes are so big (several miles in diameter each) that it is as if there were one vast dome with three parts crowning Glastonbury. Put differently, think of it as three huge astral bells, each striking a different note, but the three producing a blended harmony.

DRAGON: Gino Gennaro was right: there is a dragon at the Tor. It is one of the Earth's original thirteen, a fact that supports Pole's observations about the extreme antiquity of the Glastonbury site and the primeval devic beings still present there. Appropriately, the Glastonbury dragon protects the temple, guards the entrance to the Queen's Maze (to use Gennaro's characterization), and supervises the entrance to Avalon and its highly desirable golden apple trees.

The dragon resides under a massive white archway, bigger than the Tor, a magnificent apple tree in full blossom and full fruit on each side. In Avalon such a botanical impossibility is the order of the day.

AVALON: The official entrance to Glastonbury's Avalon is at the Tor. Actually once there was a double row of oak trees that proceeded from a spot perhaps a half-mile down the slope from the Tor now known as Gog and Magog in reference to the remains of the presumed first two oaks in this ancient sacred processional. The avenue of oaks brought the initiates to the first level of the Tor maze.

Originally, there were 144 oak trees, seventy-two on each side. Where there was a tree, there was also a pillar of light some forty feet tall. At Gog and Magog there was a double-doored gate flanked by a pillar on each side; on top of one pillar was a winged horse, atop the other a lion. These were living astral creatures that guarded the entrance to the oak processional.

When Joseph of Arimathea came to Glastonbury after the Crucifixion in the first century A.D., accompanied by the Christ in his thought body, they blessed the trees, sacralizing the avenue of oaks. They were able to increase through their being the auric possibilities of the living trees and to reaffirm the energetic structures that corresponded to them.

If you propose to enter Avalon, you prepare yourself along this oak processional by chanting the invocatory mantra *Avalon* (which, surprisingly, is a word of magic, invoking the very energies of the place it refers to). Once past the dragon, you enter *Insula Avalonia,* the domain of the apple trees, silver leaves, and golden fruits.

Innumerable apple trees gloriously outfit the slopes of the Tor and the Summer Country in all directions.

CRETAN LABYRINTH: Both the Avenue of Oaks processional and the dragon at the archway are introductory parts of what Gennaro called the Maze. The folds of the artificially cut turf maze on the slopes of the Tor have an astral geomantic equivalent, what I call a Cretan labyrinth, based on the model found at Mount Ida in Crete (see Mount Ida).

The Cretan labyrinth is a complex array of eight dome caps forming a circular matrix several miles in diameter with its center on the Tor. The dome caps come from the Chalice Hill, Beckery, and Tor domes. The combination of the energy fields of the eight dome caps and their spiral lines create the labyrinth.

Seen from above as a two-dimensional structure, the labyrinth resembles eight points of brilliant light symmetrically arrayed in a circle around a central bright point; numerous spiral lines of light unfold to the left and right in all directions in this matrix. The Cretan labyrinth, one of twelve on the planet, is a key to the mind and spans different levels of experience; it balances the two sides of the body and the two sides of the brain.

The first level of the Tor maze is the dragon, and the second is Avalon, both spreading out like a disc across all of the Summer Country. The third level is a kind of library, a repository of Atlantean, Lemurian, and Hyperborean records—of consciousness, symbols, initiate knowledge, cultural history, and worldly events. In a sense, this level represents the arcane wisdom—the gold of knowledge—you have access to by "eating" a golden apple in the second layer.

The fourth layer is the realm of the Gandharvas, the celestial musicians and angelic residents of Avalon. They reside in the sublime pleasure palace of the Celestial City of Gandhavati, but the pleasures are aesthetic, of the spirit. This place is remembered, if a little dimly, in Glastonbury myth. Around 650 A.D., Saint Collen, who lived in a hermitage on the then-wooded slopes of the Tor, was invited to a grand feast and musical entertainment at Gwynn ap Nudd's fairy palace of enchantments atop the Tor.[418] He called in at the party, but threw holy water at the "pagan" apparition to dispel it, and returned grumpily to his hut.

The fifth layer is visually interesting. It appears as an avenue of tall dark-blue trilithons (like the rectangular upright megaliths of Stonehenge), packed close together (almost too closely, like crowded, overlapping teeth), converging like an arrow towards a throne. On the throne sits Saint Peter, but this is more symbolic or etymological: Saint Peter, *Petros*, as the rock—in this case, the Living Rock. Perhaps it would be easier to say there is a Buddha-like figure there.

At the sixth level of the Tor labyrinth, you encounter protector beings of an impressive—daunting—size and potency. At the seventh level is something resembling a large crowned head looking in all directions. Mythologically, this is Lord Avallach, but we get the "looking in all directions" quality by looking through this king's name. Lord Avallach is also *Avalokitesvara*, the Buddhist Bodhisattva, whose name means "Lord Who Surveys." There are other surprising Celtic-Buddhist links like this in the Glastonbury mythos.

King Avallach or Avalokitesvara is a cultural perception of a Cosmic Chaplain. These were exalted spiritual beings, without any particular fixed form, that came with the domes and resided in their topmost energy layer to survey human progress with respect to the jump in consciousness the presence of the domes provided. The Cosmic Chaplains are workers for the Architect of Cosmic Destiny. They are not describable in terms of angels, and we might more accurately refer to

them as pure energy. King Avallach, Lord of the Summer Country, is a living mythic memory of a Cosmic Chaplain in the Tor dome.

UNDERWORLD ENTRANCE: Also present at the top of the Tor and by means of the seventh level of the Tor's Cretan Labyrinth is an entrance to the Underworld, the Land of the Dead. Here Gwynn ap Nudd is the Celtic equivalent of the King of the Underworld, the Greek Hades. Melwas as the ill-mannered King of the Summer Country who abducted Queen Guinevere—a Celtic version of the myth from Greece whereby Hades abducts Persephone and makes her his Queen of the Netherworld.

ARC OF DEVELOPING CONSCIOUSNESS: From the top of Glastonbury Tor to a place several miles away called Lugshorn extends an Arc of Developing Consciousness, looking something like the silver arch in Saint Louis, Missouri, on its side. This passes through and over Ponter's Ball, a place called Butleigh, popularly said to be the center of the Landscape Zodiac, and is grounded at Lugshorn somewhat near a large loaf-shaped wooded hill called Dundon Beacon.

POINTER'S BALL: What Glastonbury acknowledges as Ponter's Ball was originally a Pointer's Ball. The reinsertion of the "i" in the original name of this geomantic feature makes all the difference. At the top end of the Pointer's Ball earthwork (the pointer) there is a dimensional rift, a portal, a crack between the worlds—a Ball. This is where the Lake flows into Glastonbury.

The "Lake" is the astral realm, the starry world presided over by the Lady of the Lake, which is to say, the Queen of the Stars remembered in Arthurian myth most often as Nimuë or Vivien. Pointer's Ball is where Arthur pulled the sword out of the stone and where he received Excalibur from the Lady of the Lake—two swords, or the same sword at two levels of attainment. In terms of initiation, Pointer's Ball is where the Arthur candidate extracts the sword.

GRAIL CASTLE: Above Chalice Hill is one of the planet's 144 replicas of the Grail Castle. Within the physical hill in a chamber is a physical representation of the Holy Grail, as Glastonbury legend suggests. It is something that Joseph of Arimathea "buried" at Chalice Hill. To say it is purely a physical chalice is misrepresenting its reality, and to say it is a light form exclusively is equally misleading. It is a numinous "object" that phase-shifts tantalizingly between tangible and incorporeal, matter and spirit.

The Chalice Hill chamber is best approached from the Edgar Chapel end of the Abbey ruins, which is at the end closest to Chalice Hill. There you will encounter an astral gateway and a tunnel or avenue leading to the Chalice Hill chamber. There are many legends of physical tunnels threading the subterranean aspect of Glastonbury, so it is a little difficult to be sure if this avenue and the Chalice Hill chamber are only physical or physical matched with an astral equivalent.

At any rate, be assured, if you excavated Chalice Hill you would not recover the Grail because it is protected by a kind of numinous shield. Yet if you wanted to launch yourself in spirit vision from the Edgar Chapel at the Abbey towards and then into the Chalice Hill Grail chamber, you would be likely to succeed and enjoy some type of numinous experience.

INTERDIMENSIONAL PORTAL: On the side of Chalice Hill that faces the Abbey, in the area of a stand of old, stately beech trees, is an interdimensional portal. This geomantic aperture will not take you into Avalon so much as it will land you in an entirely different realm whose reality constructs are not quite those of Earth as we know it.

TREE OF LIFE: Now we come to a pure slice of Heaven unpolluted, unadulterated, and basically unaffected by the physical world that surrounds it: Chalice Well gardens. It is a tiny but immaculate Tree of Life template, expressing the Four Worlds and the forty Sephiroth, or spheres of light, through flowing water, fountains, grottoes, numerous flowering shrubs, bushes, trees, stonework, fences, stairs, gateways, and the ancient well at the top end.

The Chalice Well Tree of Life is an excellent training ground for preparations for entering the Glastonbury temple as a whole and for a more comprehensive initiatory experience called the Christed Initiation in the Buddha Body. This entails progressively incorporating outer geomantic aspects with inner structures in consciousness, culminating in a higher-dimensional experience of the Christ. The Chalice Well template has all the necessary "parts" for training in advance of this experience.

Further, a section called Arthur's Courtyard is an excellent place for meditation and for communication with human souls on the other side of the threshold of life and death. Wellesley Tudor Pole specifically designed this grotto to serve that purpose. "Since the Arthur Courtyard at Chalice Well has been regenerated," he wrote in 1964, "the avenue between it and its astral counterpart has been reopened. Invaluable energies are now flowing in both directions once more."[419]

SOMA TEMPLE: At the far end of Chalice Well, at the topmost section where the ancient well sits, is the doorway into a Soma Temple. Spatially, the "Vale" between the Tor and Chalice Hill is occupied by the Temple of the Moon God. Walking the Tree of Life template in Chalice Well is a fine preparation for this induction into the vat of unbroken consciousness, the foundation of all space.

SHAMBHALA DOORWAY: A short distance behind the top end of Chalice Well is a dimensional doorway to Shambhala, the fabled land of the exalted, super-evolved masters and directors of humanity and life on Earth. Even though Shambhala is usually referenced to Asia and through Buddhism, it is not exclusive to that part of the world or to that system of spiritual concepts.

In a 1965 letter, Pole casually referred to Glastonbury's "peculiar" connections with the far-off Tibetan valley where he located Shambhala and with "the vale" between the Tor and Chalice Hill. He wrote about a spiritual colleague who had come through that vale to visit him from the other side of the planet.

Another authority reported in the 1970s that high-ranking Mongolian lamas "deeply read in the subject" had told him that Shambhala had once been located in Britain. It was "the Celtic Britain of the last centuries before Christ, when Gwynfa, the Place of Bliss, was located in the Summer Country, about the ancient site of Glastonbury, perhaps."[420]

GOLDEN EGG: Glastonbury's Golden Egg occupies the Abbey grounds, which means, geomantically, that even though the Abbey no longer physically exists, the spacious grounds it once occupied still serve a vital purpose. The part of Glastonbury that lies directly in front of the Abbey gates is like a vagina out of which this golden sphere is pushed into the landscape, like a single golden pea in a split-open pod. This part of town is the support for the Golden Egg, the base of the eggcup, like a set of hands delicately holding the egg, presenting it to the Abbey for affirmation. You enter the egg at the Abbey gates. If you want to talk in terms of chakras, you could say the Christ child's first two chakras lie before the gates, and the rest lie within.

SILVER EGG: This is located at Glastonbury Tor. With both a Golden and a Silver Egg not only in Glastonbury but contiguously so, you have both eyes of Horus, the Christed awareness and the antique clairvoyance. The silver bird that hatches from the Silver Egg at the Tor gives the Christ Child at the Abbey the clairvoyance of the deep, antique past, all the vision that the Wounded Fisher King in the Grail Castle desperately seeks to remember.

Horus the Elder, born of the Silver Egg, is consciousness in extension, moving, seeing, putting it all together. The golden child gets to see everything, in the most distant past and most arcane future. The golden child sees what the Wounded Fisher King *would* see if he were healed, and *will* see again when he is healed.

In case you're wondering how so many things can fit on the Tor, it's helpful to think in terms of levels of reality like onion skins. At each level of the Tor, you find a different geomantic reality. At the Horus level, this being superintends the Hall of Records at the center of the labyrinth; Horus guards it against spiritually unlawful entry, but he also acts as a guide to those prepared to enter that domain.

PERPETUAL CHOIR: This is situated at Beckery, although its effects spread out over a wide area, certainly all of Glastonbury. One way of visualizing the choir is to picture a massive circular sports stadium divided into twenty-four distinct sections, each filled with one hundred singing angels or saintly humans. This is an intense sonic field vibrating with pure, formative angelic "words" and tones.

The three Perpetual Choirs are the lungs in the global body of Albion. The choirs, in the Earth's astral body, are still singing to the Earth even though they are only remembered as a curious artifact in a book of ancient Welsh myths. Originally the Choirs sang Faith, Hope, and Charity, but their "theme song" changes with the epochs; now they are intoning Humanitarianism, Individuation, and Idealism.

VIBRATING STONE: Originally set in the middle of the Beckery Perpetual Choir was one of the Earth's twelve Vibrating Stones. It carried the resonance of the Choir, but it also grounded the Taurus Oroboros Line for the Earth at Beckery. This is appropriate given Beckery's Pleiadian connection through its dome.

The Oroboros Line comes into Beckery from the Great Bear (the origin point of the twelve astrologically configured Oroboros Lines), is grounded, then deploys in both directions to circle the planet entirely, meeting again here at Beckery. At some point in the last several centuries, the Vibrating Stone was removed from Beckery and placed inconspicuously against the Abbot's Kitchen at the Abbey where it's been inadvertently protected but neglected for years.

Even though the stone itself is less than three feet high and less than two feet in circumference, its auric field or astral equivalent was hundreds of feet tall and dozens of feet wide—the size of the Choir itself. This stone would keep the Taurus Oroboros energy grounded for the planet, and amplify it accordingly when its turn in the planetary cycle of the twelve zodiacal energies came around.

IXION'S WHEEL: This feature is accessible at Beckery. It may appear as a golden sarcophagus set next to a giant vertical Sun disk; or one may see it as a slowly spinning golden wheel with many spokes. When King Arthur came to Beckery early that morning it was not so much for a vision of the Christian tableau of Madonna and Child, but more for an energy tune-up of his own essence.

The Ixion's Wheel is an initiation chamber for the candidates in Arthurhood, which is to say, in preparation for infusion and embodiment of the Solar Logos of which King Arthur was the living representative. The spiritual being who supervises this initiation is the Ray Master Lady Nada, one of whose human guises was Saint Bridgit and the Celtic Brighid.

The Solar Logos is a matter of the throat chakra (which the Pleiades rule), so you might think of this initiation at Beckery as infusing the throat center with the energies of the Sun expressed as a revolving wheel. Astronomically, this is the same as the ecliptic, which is the path of our Sun through the starfields (particularly the twelve zodiacal constellations) during one solar year.

LANDSCAPE ZODIAC: Katherine Maltwood, and the others who supported her concept, was right of course about there being a Landscape Zodiac here. The one present is much bigger than she proposed: it measures about thirty-five miles across.

Each half is about 17.9 miles wide, and the two halves meet like an apple sliced in two with a little skin left on the underside in Glastonbury. One half occupies the area (and more) outlined by Maltwood; the other half covers an area not usually included in models of Glastonbury's geomancy. The zodiac dome is almost eighty miles in diameter, taking in all of the Summer Country and a fair bit of Somerset as well.

A Landscape Zodiac does not have to have visible, discernible topographical correlations. In most cases, you will not encounter these. The Glastonbury zodiac is well preserved and is one of the few where you can see how, to some extent, the energy template and physical landscape were originally in accordance.

Given the age of the planet, and thus the age of its geomantic imprinting, and given the relative neglect, even abandonment, by humans who were expected to help maintain the living pattern, most of the obvious correspondence has faded. The angelic hierarchy has deliberately and purposefully maintained a semblance of the correspondence of the heavenly template and the landscape imprint for the purposes of instruction in geomancy.

The Glastonbury zodiac was one of the planet's first to be worked on and gradually energized and reaffirmed in our time, the bulk of that work taking place in the 1980s.

VIRGO ALBION HEART CHAKRA: The entire Glastonbury temple, with the twenty-two features briefly described here, is part of a larger geomythic figure that occupies one-twelfth of the Earth's surface. The Virgo temple includes all of the British Isles, France, Spain, Portugal, Greenland, Iceland,

and a bit of the Atlantic. Technically, Glastonbury is this Albion's outer heart chakra *(Anahata)*, while a small copse in Butleigh, just outside Glastonbury, called Park Wood is its inner heart center *(Ananda-kanda)*.

Other energy sites in this Albion discussed elsewhere in this book include Iona in Scotland (left foot), Tetford in Lincolnshire (root chakra), Lincoln (mentioned under Tetford) in Lincolnshire (second chakra), and Carnac in France (sixth chakra).

The Virgo Albion will be the first of the Earth's twelve Albions to wake up. This is primarily because it was the first to be intensively worked on in our time, and also because, as William Blake said, "All things Begin & End in Albion's Ancient Druid Rocky Shore."[421] Albion was an ancient name for Britain, but Blake, who was attuned to this living geomantic matrix, was referring to the landmass and its original templating rather than the culture occupying it.

MOBILE SHAMBHALLIC FOCUS: This term refers to the Earth's sixth chakra, the brow, or Ajna center. Unlike the other Earth chakras, which mostly stay fixed in one location, the sixth chakra changes location every two hundred years. There is a fifty-year buildup of this Focus at a site, then it is fully resident for one hundred years, then there is a fifty-year spillover in which the Focus gradually recedes from that site. It is a bit like slowly turning a dimmer switch to full intensity, then slowly turning it off again. The light in this case is the sixth chakra, and its source is Shambhala.

In other times in the history of the Earth, this Focus has been resident at Banaras in India, Jerusalem in Israel, and Mount Kailash in Tibet; all three sites are discussed elsewhere in this book. This Focus is also known, in Hindu myth, as "Vishnu's discus" or the *Sudarsana*.

PLANETARY *ANAHATA* HEART CHAKRA: There are many levels of Earth chakras, and many sites that may correctly be deemed this or that chakra. It's a question of on what *level* the chakra assignment is made. The Earth's heart chakra exists in three places, corresponding to the outer *(Anahata)*, inner *(Ananda-kanda)*, and emerald (a third, arcane aspect). Glastonbury is the location of the outer heart chakra; El Tule in Mexico (the center of the 1987 Harmonic Convergence, near Oaxaca and Monte Alban) is the Emerald location; and the inner heart chakra is in Europe.[422]

NEW JERUSALEM: This is not a new version of the physical city in Israel, nor is it explicitly the fulfillment of Judaic millennialism, although Judaism has maintained the cultural memory of the prophecy and possibility of the New Jerusalem for the rest of the world.

The "new" Jerusalem will be a refounding of the energy matrix that was the "old" or original Jerusalem. It is a higher-dimensional temple created in part by the concentration of the twelve Vibrating Stones; it also pertains to humanity's galactic memory from the Andromeda galaxy, the source of the Vibrating Stones and part of the heritage of human consciousness in its vast universal evolution. The original Jerusalem was founded at the beginning of the Earth; the new one will be grounded as the Earth shifts to a new phase of its evolution as a sentient celestial body.

An expression or perhaps a higher-dimensional archetype of the New Jerusalem already is present over Glastonbury, accessed through the seventh level of the Tor labyrinth. As the Earth becomes self-aware of its vast, living energy and geomantic matrix, so will the New Jerusalem temple become more apparent and accessible to living humans because it is the consummation and perfect expression of the *awakened* galaxy on Earth.[423]

Hardwar, India

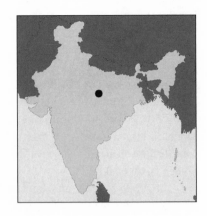

Every twelve years in this city about one hundred miles north of New Delhi something phenomenal happens. An estimated ten million pilgrims descend on Hardwar for the Kumbh Mela festival, to bathe in the Ganges River and seek liberation from the round of life, death, and rebirth.

The Kumbh Mela festival takes place every three years, but rotates among four cities, the other three being Allahabad, Naski, and Ujjain.[424] In 1989, fifteen million people came to Allahabad, estimated then as the greatest number of humans ever assembled in one place for a common purpose. In April 1998, ten million came to Hardwar at the foothills of the Himalayas in the Indian state of Uttar Pradesh for the culmination of the fifteen-week festival. At the 2001 Kumbh Mela at Allahabad, the BBC estimated thirty million people were on hand.[425]

The Kumbh Mela starts on January 1 and formally ends April 29, but two days around the middle of April (usually April 14 and 15) are considered the most auspicious for bathing in the Ganges due to favorable astrological alignments.[426] It is believed that during these two days the Ganges River transforms itself from a river of physical water into a stream of purifying nectar, and that this is the most favorable time in which to immerse oneself with the expectation of cleansing one's soul and obtaining spiritual liberation.

The Kumbh Mela festival is such a major event and is taken sufficiently seriously by the India government that it spent twenty-five million dollars in preparation for the 1998 festival at Hardwar, building extra roads, bridges, camps, bathing places, drains, and toilets to accommodate the vast increase in population during the four months.[427]

Many people also come to Hardwar every six years for a mini-Kumbh Mela called the Ardh Kumbha. Many also, of course, make the pilgrimage to Hardwar in the years when it is not hosting the Kumba Mela for it has much to offer the spiritual seeker. It is one of India's Seven Holy Cities *(Saptapuri)*, each of which can bestow liberation, although Kashi, or Banaras, to the south, is considered the chief of the seven (see Banaras, India). Hardwar is home to many ashrams and Dharamsalas, spiritual retreat and meditation centers set up by various swamis, yogis, and teachers. But Hardwar's distinction as a *Saptapuri* is that it is *Gangadvar,* the Gate of the Ganges, the first major population center on the northern plains of India where the holy river flows out of the Himalayas.

The name Hardwar (or Haridwar) derives from *Har,* which means Shiva, and *Hari,* which means Vishnu, and *Dwar,* which means Gate. Thus Hardwar means Gate of the Lord, indicating two of Hinduism's three chief deities. Hardwar actually honors the third Hindu deity, Brahma, by way of its *Brahmakund,* or Brahma's Basin, a pool in the Ganges.

Mythologically, the creator god Brahma is said to have greeted the River Ganges at this spot when she (Ganges) descended from Heaven to Earth for the first time. Approximately two million people come to Hardwar every year to bathe in the *Brahmakund,* which is actually a bend in the Ganges. It is also the site where Vishnu (as Hari) left his footprint when he visited Hardwar, so another name for the site is *Hariki-Pairi,* or "Hari's Foot."

A special temple called *Gangadwara* (Gate of the Ganga) located on the river's bank is the site of veneration for the footprint. *Hariki-Pairi* is also the site of one of India's most sacred burning ghats, or outdoor crematoria. At dusk and dawn this ghat is the focus of a special ritual called *Maha Aarti.* Priests wave lit lamps at the Ganges, while individuals set small leaf boats, with burning oil lamps on them, to drift down the river. The current is especially swift here, and it's believed that a person's prayers, offered to the burning lamp, will be fulfilled if the boat makes it out of sight without capsizing and the flame still burning.

At other times, people honor the Ganges as it passes by Hardwar by festooning its waters with roses and chrysanthemums, creating an undulating water carpet of flower blossoms. On account of the *Brahmakund* and the Ganges, many believe the waters at Hardwar are doubly blessed, making it a prime city for salvation.

The city's name is sometimes written as *Haridvara,* meaning "Hari's (Vishnu's) Gate" because it is believed to lead one to Vaikuntha, Vishnu's paradisiacal sphere *(loka)* of existence which is either in the depths of the cosmic Ocean or on the peak of Mount Meru, the cosmic mountain in Hindu myth. "It is built of gold and precious stones, and is eternal and beyond even the perception of the gods."[428]

Hardwar, temple site for Shiva and Vishnu, is also Gate of the Lord in that it is the starting point for pilgrimages to Kedarnath and Badrinath. That's because Shiva is the chief deity at Kedarnath, and Vishnu at Badrinath. In a broader geomythic sense, Hardwar is a gateway to the gods, referring to the Uttarakhand region of Uttar Pradesh, a site of heightened sanctity and four pilgrimage routes.

It appears that Hardwar has been recognized and used as a city of salvation for at least three thousand years, and probably longer. Historians believe the Kumbh Mela festival has been honored here since before the second century B.C. Archeological evidence proves the existence of a "terra cotta" culture here as early as 1200 B.C.

A reference in a text of the first century A.D. says Hardwar was part of the Kushan Empire; in 634 A.D., a Chinese pilgrim named Huien Tsang visited Hardwar and called it *Mo-Yu-Lo,* meaning Mayapur or "Magical City." But far earlier, in mythic time, Lord Rama, the hero of the Indian epic *Ramayana* and said to be the seventh incarnation of Vishnu, came to Hardwar to atone for killing Ravana, the Demon King of Lanka.

MYTH AND LEGEND

There is another, perhaps the fundamental, reason for the *Brahmakund*'s sanctity. It has to do with a pitcher *(kumbh)* of the gods and what spilled from it in the deeps of the mythic past. This is a *big* myth, but we will only touch on part of it here. The bulk of the story is recorded in the *Mahabharata,* the vast epic of India's mythopoeic origins and struggles.

The Gods (Devas) and Demons (Asuras) were churning the Ocean of Milk in an attempt to find the nectar of ambrosia, or *amrita.* By the Ocean of Milk the myth means the serene primeval waters of existence, the sea of undifferentiated light. Everybody wanted the *amrita* because it would give them eternal life, or unbroken continuity of consciousness.

Various inestimably valuable things emerged from the Ocean of Milk as it was churned, and finally the god Dhanvantari, the physician of the gods, came forth holding a white pot or pitcher *(kumbh)* containing the elixir of immortality. Dhanvantari, now assuming a female appearance as the Goddess Sri of vibrant beauty standing in a blossoming lotus, gave all the gods a drink, but kept the amrita from the Asuras. In the course of fleeing the demons and flying over India, the goddess spilled a little amrita at four places: Ujjain, Nasik, Allahabad, and Hardwar. The Kumbh Mela festival originated as a symbolic or perhaps actual attempt for pilgrims to get a taste of the amrita at those sites.

Amrita is also known as Soma, which in Hindu myth is both a divine plant and a god closely associated with the Moon. (Not the Moon as we think of the Earth's satellite, but as a fundamental condition of primordial existence.) The *Mahabharata* says that when the Ocean of Milk was churned "there arose Soma, the calm moon, with its cool rays, and the sun of a hundred thousand rays."[429]

Soma is a heavenly body that is the food of the gods who reduce its substance by continuously feeding on it. Soma is the juice of the Moon, the nectar of youth, health, and strength, the luminous celestial herb, even the Moon itself, according to some. Using our physical Moon as a metaphor, the ancient Vedic texts said that for the first two weeks of the four-week Moon cycle, the Sun fills the Moon with Soma; then in the last two weeks, the gods drink up "the pleasant sweet draught," refreshing their immortality. Soma is the wealth of the gods for He is their food.[430]

Regarding the sanctity of the Ganges River and its veneration at Hardwar, it would be underestimating the import of this myth to leave the matter at the level of a geological explanation. Geologically, the Ganges does pour onto the plain of Hindustan near Hardwar through a gorge known as *Ganga-Dwara,* "The Gates of the Ganges." But until you know the myth of the Goddess Ganges the symbolic significance of the river will be obscured.

Originally, Ganga was the daughter of the Himalayan mountain god, Himavan, "Owner of Snow." Ganga was the sister to Parvati, consort to Shiva, and in the earliest days of creation, the gods considered Ganga too precious and beautiful to share with terrestrial mortals. Then Bhagiratha performed prodigious ascetic feats so as to win a boon from Brahma. He wanted Ganga to descend to Earth and flow across India to resurrect the sixty thousand brothers of King Ansuman who had been burned to ashes by the withering glance of the sage Kapila, whose meditations they had disrupted.

Brahma consented but said first that Ganga must flow through Shiva's hair so as to cushion her impact on Earth. At first, Ganga remained on Shiva's head for 100,000 years. Then Ganga came down to Earth with a roaring, foaming flow and would have drowned the entire country if Shiva's hair—his matted hair was like a tangled dense forest—hadn't slowed it down. Thus from the crown of Shiva's matted hair flows the Ganges as the celestially pure white river, and Shiva is known as *Gangadhara,* the "Bearer of the Ganga." Ganga, naturally, is Shiva's perpetual consort, and her flowing descent through Shiva to Earth is not a single event but continuous, called *avatarana.*

The Ganges is considered the essential instrument of ritual purification, capable of quickening the ashes of all the dead to eternal life. As one ancient text put it, "holding the Ganges on his head, he [Siva] brought into his power the means of the liberation of the world."[431] The Ganga is the active expression of Shiva's celestial energy, his liquid form, by which he energizes and nourishes all the worlds and affords sentient life forms the chance of salvation.

There is another version of the origin of the Ganges. It was called Visnupadi because it originated in Visnupada, "the celestial realm of Vishnu" or "the foot of Vishnu." Vishnu, as a cosmic giant, took three huge steps across the universe; on his third step he pierced the vault of heaven (the Cosmic or Mundane Egg) and released the pent-up heavenly waters.

The Ganga, which had previously flowed around inside the cosmic vault, could now flow out into the lower heavens, where She was caught by the Pole Star called Dhruva. From there, Ganga flowed to the Moon as the Milky Way, then from the Moon to the realm of Brahma just above Mount Meru, the Cosmic Mountain. Brahma held the Ganges in his water pot, then poured it over Vishnu's foot as it stretched across the heavenly sphere.

At Mount Meru, Ganga divided into four rivers, and flowed down upon the Earth's continents; one of these four branches, called the Alakananda, flowed into Bharatavarsa (India) as the Ganga. Ganga has ever after been known as *Svarga-sopana-sarani*, "She who is a flowing staircase to Heaven." Thus the earthly Ganges River enters the planetary sphere after passing through the realms of Brahma, Vishnu, and Shiva, accumulating their blessings and potencies.

It should be obvious from this myth that "the earthly Ganges is only a limited part of the cosmic river . . . only a limited aspect of a reality that transcends this world . . . the source of the river [being] in a divine sphere." In this light, the River Ganges is a "liquid *axis mundi*" connecting all the spheres and dimensions of the higher worlds with our own, thereby affording a consummate crossing-over point, a *tirtha* of first rank, a sacred bridge to the unconditioned realm.[432]

One scholar of Hindu spirituality says, "The Ganga is the quintessence and source of all sacred waters, and indeed of all waters everywhere."[433] Why?

Perhaps the seemingly grandiose symbolic interpretations of the Ganges as a celestial river have some basis in esoteric astronomical fact. According to an ancient Vedic text on astronomy and cosmography called the *Srimad-Bhagavatam,* the Ganges River begins its descent to the earthly realm from the Karana Ocean residing in the upper portion of the universe known as *Satyaloka,* the abode of Brahma, said to be two billion miles from Earth and located near the "top" of the universal globe.

Lord Vamanadeva kicked a hole in the universal covering, allowing the water to flow down to *Dhruvaloka,* the Pole Star (Polaris); that takes one thousand yugas (4,320,000,000 years), and Dhruvaloka is situated thirty million miles above our Sun. This means it takes the Ganges 4.3 billion years to flow only two billion miles, "a very slow rate of progress even for a very sluggish river." From Dhruvaloka, the Ganges then flows to the planets of the Seven Sages, and then to the Moon "through the spaceways of the demigods in billions of celestial airplanes." Then from the Moon it flows down to Mount Meru.

According to Richard L. Thompson, who holds a Ph.D. in mathematics, to understand these ancient Vedic descriptions of astronomy and cosmography one needs to employ "higher-dimensional concepts" that go beyond "the framework of our familiar physical theories."[434]

GEOMANTIC

Dome; Epiphany Focus; Soma Temple.

DOME: The dome at Hardwar is not an ordinary star dome. It is one of the four domes on Earth that are central to the planet's energy umbilicus with the galaxy. The other three are at Avebury, England (the prime umbilicus), Carnac in France (the dome for Sirius, the gold umbilicus), and Iona in Scotland (the dome for Canopus, the silver umbilicus). The dome at Hardwar is for Polaris, the Pole Star in Ursa Minor, the Lesser Bear, the third, neutral, aspect of the umbilicus.

If you could visit only four sacred sites on the planet, these four would be highly advisable, for their energies would align your own energy and consciousness body with the three energies that underlie and nourish physical reality on this planet. You would confirm your own microcosmic umbilicus with these same sources and gain a deeper sense of empathy with the Earth.

Polaris is the alpha star, one of the three stars on the tail of the little bear at the galaxy's North Pole, which is, metaphorically speaking, the top of the circus tent of stars. Some of Polaris' names from different astronomical models include the Chinese *Tien Hwang Ta Ti,* meaning "the Great Imperial Ruler of Heaven" or "Supreme Lord of the Dark Heavens," and part of the Purple Subtle Enclosure (which includes the other circumpolar stars). In India, the star nearest the pole was called *Grahadhara,* "the Pivot of the Planets" and represented the god Dhruva.

In Damascus, astronomers called Polaris *Mismar,* a Needle or Nail, and the Arabs knew it as *Al Kutb al Shamaliyy,* the Northern Axis or Spindle. It was the North Star, Ridgepole, the Great Root, Lodestar, *Stella Maris* (Star of the Sea), and Steering Star for navigators, the Pivot Star for sailors. Mythologically, Polaris is said to be the pinnacle of the Cosmic Mountain and *axis mundi* of the universe, Mount Meru, situated eighty-four thousand leagues above the Earth.

Polaris is about 1° 14' from the exact galactic North Pole, and will continue to approach the exact pole until the year 2095, when it will be only 26' 30" away from it.[435] The significance of

the North Star is in terms of Earth-galaxy alignment as it lies almost precisely on the planet's axis of rotation. The term *Al Kutb,* mentioned above, indicated a pin or axle fixed in the under stone of a gristmill around which the upper stone pivots to grind the grain.

In many cultures, the universe was conceived of as a turning millstone, and the North Pole was the axle bearing on which that mill-iron turned, grinding the grain into stars. Lord Dhruva was appointed to be Pole Star chiefly because he had demonstrated he could stand motionlessly on one leg for a month, a feat that alarmed the gods. They told Dhruva that all the stars and planets would thus turn around him as he stood at "the exalted seat of Vishnu, round which the starry spheres forever wander, like the upright axle of the corn mill circled without end by the labouring oxen."[436]

Polaris is the galaxy's forty-ninth brightest star, about three hundred light years from Earth, and about sixteen hundred times brighter than our Sun. Ursa Minor is also known as the Little Dipper, and in this presentation of the stars, Polaris is the bright star at the tip of the handle, right where you would place your hand, if you were a god.

Experientially, you can approach Polaris in your own body. In part 1, we reviewed some exercises involving a blazing pinprick of brilliant light just above the navel, called the Blazing Star. This is the equivalent of Polaris within the human energy field. If you concentrate on the Blazing Star at your belly, if will give you an experience of some aspects of Polaris.

If you have the good fortune to be at the *Brahmakund* at Hardwar (which is directly under the top of the Polaris dome, the *axis mundi* of the *axis mundi*) and do this meditation, the results could be spectacular, and certainly mystical. The relationship of the top of the Polaris dome to the *Brahmakund* is the same, just on a smaller scale, as the relationship between the Pole Star and the Earth.

Then imagine you are the galaxy in the form of a human body—how about a female form because this is how the Egyptians conceived of Nut, their sky goddess. Her feet and hands are on the ground and she arches over the land, her body full of stars and celestial lights. Her fingers and toes touch the cardinal directions. She was also seen as a heavenly cow that ate the stars every morning then birthed them again at twilight. Sometimes she was called *Kha-bewes*, "the One with a Thousand Souls," the "souls" being another image for the stars.

The star at her navel is Polaris—the Hindu god Dhruva, if you like—and the distance between that star and the top of Mount Meru is Shiva. Shiva, functionally, is the sushumna, or central neutral column in the umbilicus between the Earth and the galaxy. If we see him as the Greek Titan Atlas, who held the world on his shoulders, he is the *axis mundi* between the Earth and the higher dimensions. Again, the microcosmic, or bodily, aspect of this model helps us understand what is at play.

Yoga talks of three subtle energy channels that run up the spine: the Ida (gold or Sun) and pingala (silver or Moon) channels crisscross regularly at the chakras and meet at the brow. They make a double helix around the central column, called the sushumna, which is neither Sun nor Moon. All three channels enter the brow like the tips of a trident, which of course is why Shiva, the god of the brow chakra, is said to wield a trident. The same energy structure exists on the Earth and keeps the planet umbilically connected to the galaxy.

Two energy streams come into Avebury in England. The gold line from Sirius and the silver line from Canopus descend in a double helix from those two points in the galaxy to Avebury. Then they have a special connection to two domes that

ground these energies for the planet. The Sirius gold line is grounded through the dome at Carnac in France; the Canopus silver line is grounded at the dome at Iona in Scotland. (See Avebury, Carnac, and Iona Island.)

The third energy stream comes from Polaris and is grounded at Mount Meru, which is located with respect to an invisible—physically present but phase-shifted—island off the southeast coast of New Zealand.[437] This stream from Polaris to Mount Meru is the River Ganges. The dome at Hardwar is the prime grounding point for the Earth for the energies from Polaris, receiving them directly from Mount Meru in the South Pacific. The three energy lines as they encircle the planet divide the Earth into six sections; their prime vortices are the Earth's six primary chakras, with the seventh being in the center of the Earth.

Thus Hardwar is aptly called the Gate of the Lord and the Gate of the Ganges, for it is the place where the Polaris energy stream—the River Ganges—is grounded for distribution not only to India but to the entire globe. The energy of the Hardwar dome is focused on creating stillness of flow so that the "water" flows from the Source to the end of the river, which is the Gate at Hardwar.

Structurally, the three gods, Brahma, Shiva, and Vishnu, have their appointed roles in this hierarchy or fountaining of energy from the highest level to the physical. Brahma is the original Mundane Egg or universal sphere punctured to allow some of its contents to flow downward. The upper surface of Mount Meru is said to be the site of *Brahmapuri*, the city of Brahma. Shiva is the conduit from Brahma to Mount Meru; the metaphor of his matted, tangled hair slowing down the otherwise overly powerful descent of the Ganges is a way of describing his task of transduction.

The Waters of Brahma—the Goddess Ganga, or River Ganges—would truly drown all sentient life lower down in the hierarchy of consciousness.

It needs to be stepped down, in stages, so that it can be received and safely assimilated by the world below that needs it. After all, "She who is a flowing staircase to Heaven" has many easy *steps,* as would any staircase. You could think of these as chakras six through one, or in Qabalistic terms, as the first seven (out of ten) Sephiroth, or spheres of light, counting up from the bottom in the Tree of Life, which is an abstract way of describing Shiva as a column of light.

EPIPHANY FOCUS: Vishnu's footprint at the *Brahmakund* has at least three nuances. Vishnu's third incarnation (out of ten) was as Varaha, the wild boar. A demon named Hiranyaksha dragged the Earth down under the water, so Vishnu assumed the boar form and used the massive tusk to raise the landmasses of the Earth out of the deep water.

Metaphorically—you have to visualize this story upside down—he left his tusk in place to secure the *vertical* connection between the Waters of Heaven and the Earth dimension. The boar's tusk is the umbilicus between Brahma and the Earth, which we have been calling Shiva. So we could think of the *Hariki-Pairi,* Hari's Foot, or the *Vishnupada,* Vishnu's Footprint, as the mark which Vishnu left to indicate his work in grounding the umbilical connection, of pushing the Earth dimension out of the primal Seas but beneficently retaining a link to its Source.

To understand the second nuance to the god's footprint, think of it in terms of our possible ascent up the boar's tusk or River Ganges. The footprint is the benign mark of the god left to point to the gateway—the Gate of the Lord, or Hardwar. Vishnu's Foot marks the spot in our world that is the beginning of the vertical axis up to Lord Dhruva.

From the other point of view, namely, the descent of the Ganges into the Earth plane, the footprint is the final step in the fountain of transduction where the exalted, overwhelming cosmic consciousness that is the River Ganges is finally grounded sufficiently so that we may encounter it and yet live. The foot is the part of the body that makes contact with the ground, with the planet; it is the beginning of the body and the head is the end, but the head is powerless without the feet because otherwise how could it move about? So Vishnu's footprint is both the beginning and the end of the River Ganges.

The third nuance is more factual in a geomantic sense. The *Vishnupada* marks the site of an epiphany of the god Vishnu, where the lowest arc—the "foot"—of his celestial and overwhelming energy touched down in the Earth plane and left a permanent indentation—a "footprint"—in the energy field. (See Banaras, India, where another Vishnu footprint was left.)

Specifically, some time in the past six thousand years during the first week of January, the Christ as Solar Logos—known in Hinduism as Vishnu—made an "appearance" in his light body at Hardwar. That means for a week, the Brahmakund at Hardwar was the planetary focus for the consciousness of Vishnu entering the planetary sphere like a stream of light or, for those with highly refined mystical perception, as the epiphanous presence of a god.

SOMA TEMPLE: The identification of Hardwar as a Soma Temple is easy, and this is a testament to the Hindu geomantic memory of how their landscape was laid out as a galaxy on Earth. This memory provides us today with many valuable clues on the nature of the galaxy on Earth template. Throughout India, if you know what you are looking at geomantically, all the clues are obvious and unassailable, seemingly as clear and direct as when its sacred geography was first manifested.

When the *Mahabharata* says that, after the churning of the Ocean of Milk, Dhanvantari or the goddess Sri spilled four drops of the precious Soma in India and these drops fell at Ujjain,

Nasik, Allahabad, and Hardwar, it is telling us that there is a Celestial City of Yasovati, the Moon temple, a vat of Soma present at each location.

Each site offers all that Soma offers: the possibility of immortality of consciousness, of resuming the unbroken continuity of awareness that characterized our condition before the Fall of Man into incarnation and the seemingly endless round of life, death, and rebirth, and the constant forgetting of our celestial origins and the eternity of awareness—the Ocean of Milk—from which we originated. Hardwar and the other three Kumbh Mela sites offer us a sip from the original pitcher or water pot of Soma that the gods forever enjoy.

Hill Cumorah, Palmyra, New York, United States

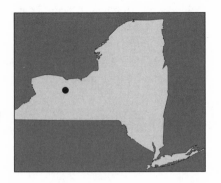

Among Mormons worldwide this small hill in upstate New York just off the Thruway is regarded as a preeminent holy site, but to the rest of the population, Hill Cumorah is much less well known. In terms of its mythic burden and geomantic function, the site deserves much wider appreciation. Hill Cumorah is ground zero for the founding myth of Mormonism (formally known as the Church of Jesus Christ of Latter-day Saints), one of today's fastest growing religions, with ten million members worldwide, five million of those in the United States.

Mormons know Hill Cumorah as the birthplace of Mormonism, for it was here in 1827 that Joseph Smith, following angelic guidance, found the gold tablets containing what is now referred to as *The Book of Mormon*, the bible and history of the ancient Nephites of the Americas, the forebears of today's Mormons.

If you take the Mormon claims seriously, fairly incredible things happened at Hill Cumorah. "Announcing that his revelations restored the primitive apostolic church and opened the Kingdom of God on earth, Smith claimed to have brought forth not simply a new church but a new dispensation, fully equivalent to the dispensa-

tions of Moses and Christ." Based on his momentous discovery at Hill Cumorah, Smith "claimed to be a vehicle of the continuing revelation of the 'Word.'"[438]

Geologically, Hill Cumorah is called a drumlin, one among many in New York State's Finger Lakes region, about twenty-five miles south of Rochester and four miles from Palmyra. A drumlin, the geologists tell us, is a long oval mound of drift or diluvial formation; typically, a drumlin is a long hill with steep sides and a sloping end formed under an advancing continental ice sheet. Or as Joseph Smith described it in 1823, it is "a hill of considerable size, and the most elevated of any in the neighborhood."[439]

A visitor to Hill Cumorah in 1881 noted that viewed from the north "it has a pyramidal appearance," due to its sudden rise from the east and west and that it had a narrow "entirely bald" top at the northern end, with only a grass covering.[440] Yet another visitor has noted that the total magnetic field changes from five hundred milligauss to over nine hundred as you ascend the hill.[441]

On the hill today is a ten-foot bronze depiction of the Angel Moroni set atop a twenty-five-foot-tall shaft of white granite. The figure's right hand points towards heaven, while his left holds a replica of the gold plates. Also on the edge of the hill is an outdoor theater at which every July since 1935 the Mormons have enacted the mytho-drama of their ancient and recent history, from Nephi to Joseph Smith. They call it *America's Witness for Christ,* and the seventy-minute per-formance typically draws 100,000 people during a week in July each year.

Four miles from Hill Cumorah is the Sacred Grove, a small tree-girt park in which in 1823 Joseph Smith was said to have had the first of almost two dozen apparitions of his celestial men-tor, the Angel Moroni. Today the grove is a fifteen-acre wooded tract, but around 1818, when Joseph Smith's family owned the land, it was part of their one-hundred-acre farm and contained some trees that were four hundred years old, 125 feet tall, and six feet in diameter. In 1907, the Mormon Church purchased the farm and grove and has maintained it ever since. Other buildings and his-torical features are maintained at the Hill Cumorah site, but the hill and the grove are para-mount to the site's geomantic function.

HISTORY AND ARCHEOLOGY

Joseph Smith (1805–1844) was born in Sharon, Vermont, but his key spiritual events per-tinent to the founding of Mormonism took place at the Hill Cumorah. His father had moved the family to Palmyra, New York, around 1815. During the years 1823 to 1829, an angelic pres-ence identifying itself as Moroni appeared to Joseph Smith twenty times, but Smith's first angelic apparition or communication took place in 1820 in what is now called the Sacred Grove.

Smith, all of fifteen, had retreated to the woods to ask God what direction his spiritual strivings should take and whether he should join a church. At first he found himself "seized upon by some power which entirely overcame me," so strong and of such a thick darkness that it ren-dered him speechless and frightened. This passed, and then a pillar of light appeared over his head and descended slowly upon him.

Inside this pillar Smith beheld "two Personages, whose brightness and glory defy all description." Their message was he should join no religious sects "for they were all wrong." Then the personages left Smith to digest the import of their message and to age a little.[442]

That next phase started in September 21, 1823, in Smith's bedroom in his family home near the Grove. Seemingly in response to his evening prayers, a bright light filled his room and a per-sonage appeared within it, standing in the air. This spiritual being was exceedingly white and brilliant, wearing a loose robe of "exquisite white-ness," Smith said.

It identified itself as Moroni, a resurrected being "sent from the presence of God" to tell Smith, now seventeen, that God had work for him, starting with unearthing a book written upon gold plates that Moroni himself, when he had been a human, had buried in the Hill Cumorah in 421 A.D. Smith would also find "two stones in silver bows" that would serve as a deci-phering device. The book, which would require deciphering, translating, collating, and editing, recounted the history of the tribe of Nephites. The Angel Moroni said Smith would have to wait a few years until the time was right to actually dig up the stone box in which these gold plates had been deposited.

On September 22, 1827, the Angel Moroni guided Smith to a site on the western side of Hill Cumorah and Smith unearthed the box. Inside, as promised, were the gold plates and the decipher-ing device, which the Mormons refer to as the *Urim* and *Tummim,* following Judaic tradition. Nobody seems quite clear on what this device was, but its function was to be worn as a breast-plate to decode the writing on the gold plates.[443]

On March 26, 1830, the first copies of *The*

Book of Mormon, An Account Written by the Hand of Mormon Upon Plates Taken from the Plates of Nephi appeared in the Palmyra, New York, bookstore. On April 6, 1830, the Church of Christ was formally established with six members, and a month later, they had another thirty-four members. Between 1829 and 1836, Joseph Smith and two others were credited with reestablishing the ancient Priesthoods of Melchizedek and Aaron and of receiving the ancient priesthood keys, supposedly under apostolic guidance and support.

This was in fulfillment of the Angel Moroni's stated mission for Joseph Smith and his followers, to restore the gospel of Jesus Christ on the American continent. The Angel Moroni is often portrayed with a trumpet based on a prophecy in *Revelation* in which John declared he had seen "an angel heralding the return of the everlasting gospel to the Earth in the last days."[444] One of the intriguing aspects of the Mormon millennialist fervor regarding the "restoration of all things" is that it will include "resurrection, regeneration, and renewal to all life upon the earth and the glorification of the earth itself, when it becomes a celestial sphere."[445]

As to the content of the gold plates, the information revealed by Joseph Smith's laborious translation is startling. The Angel Moroni told Smith that the book contained an account of the former inhabitants of this continent, the Nephites, who originally fled Jerusalem before the advent of the Christ. Moroni further claimed that the Christ had visited the Americas and that, in Smith's words of 1823 in reference to what would be called *The Book of Mormon*, "the fullness of the everlasting Gospel was contained in it, as delivered by the Savior to the ancient inhabitants."[446]

Moroni also said the Nephites made their last stand and witnessed the extinction of their peoples (including Moroni's father, Mormon) around the base of the Hill Cumorah some fourteen hundred years earlier.

According to *The Book of Mormon,* around 600 B.C., God commanded a particular Hebrew prophet named Nephi to escape Jerusalem with his family (including his father, Lehi, and Lehi's five other sons) before the city was destroyed. According to Mormon myth, two of Lehi's sons, Laman and Lemuel, were evil tempered and sinful, and they and all their descendants were cursed by God to have red skin, presumably meaning that they would be what are now referred to as Native Americans.

Nephi journeyed to the North American continent and established what became a great and enlightened civilization of people known as the Nephites—the people of Nephi. Two strong races grew up in the Americas: "the Nephites, peace-loving and domestic, and the Lamanites, blood-thirsty and idolatrous," and these two races fought each other intermittently for a thousand years.

Admittedly, to the non-Mormon, the history is confusing: were the Nephites Jews or Native Americans? The Mormons seem to suggest they were neither, only that they were a white race distinct somehow from both, though they do say the Lamanites are a "remnant of the house of Israel." The Mormons hold that Joseph Smith, as a prophet in the Biblical tradition, restored the original covenant made by God with Abraham, Isaac, Jacob, and the children of Israel.

They also contend that after the death of Jesus' original apostles, there was a general apostasy in the Christian Church and the "fullness" of the Christ message was lost. The testaments of Mormon and Moroni restored that fullness by reverting to an earlier version of it; the theophanic visions of Joseph Smith at Palmyra marked the beginning point, or fountainhead, of the prophesied restoration.

The Mormon myth, of course, is highly unflattering to the legacy of Native Americans and at odds with their own historical and legendary accounts. Meanwhile, historians and archeologists present evidence that both refutes and supports the claims of Nephi's account.[447]

The inference from the Mormon chronicle was that the Nephites erected the numerous earth-mounds found throughout the American Midwest as burial and ceremonial grounds for the fallen Nephites; they also built the palisaded small Indian forts found throughout Western New York State.[448]

One of the more remarkable claims Joseph Smith introduced into the Western world through his translation of Moroni's gold plates was the statement that the Christ had visited the Americas, specifically appearing before the Lamanites and Nephites in the brief respite between his resurrection and ascension. Apparently, the Christ's coming to America had been foreshadowed by cataclysmic events and destruction, precipitating a vast number of deaths and three days of darkness. Those who survived were brought to their knees.

Perhaps this was the intention because the Christ exacted a pledge from the Nephites and Lamanites, the white and red races, to live together as brothers, which they managed for a few generations. Later, frictions developed among them and eventually they resumed fighting, and the Nephites fell. Reportedly, Moroni as a human led a force of ten thousand against the Lamanites as his last battle, with his father, Mormon, serving as commander-in-chief.

Also reportedly, Moroni then spent the next thirty-six years finishing his father's request to complement his own abridged plates of Nephi (covering one thousand years of Nephite history) with the account of the Nephites' final days. Then he buried the plates at the Hill Cumorah in about 600 A.D., writing for saints of a latter day. They also wanted to keep their religious history from the hands of the Lamanites, whom they considered infidels.

Apparently the Hill Cumorah—known then as "the hill Ramah"—had witnessed the destruction of the Jaredites nine hundred years earlier. The Jaredites reportedly left the Tower of Babel in Mesopotamia and sailed in watertight barges for the Americas, circa 2500 B.C. Moroni added an abridgment of the ancient Jaredite engravings too, documenting their history in the Western Hemisphere about seventeen hundred years prior to the Nephite arrival.

Apparently in Western New York State and Ohio, the legend was common that the area had once been the site of a vicious slaughter and that the numerous earth-mounds—"the palisaded, geometrical forts, the ruins of which were silhouetted against the sky atop the conelike drumlins that dotted the landscape"—were the cemeteries of an entire obliterated race.[449]

In correspondence to Joseph Smith in the early 1830s, Mormon colleague Oliver Cowdery reflected that "here, between these hills, the entire power and national strength of both the Jaredites and Nephites were destroyed." Mormon himself wrote (Mormon 6:4) that "we did pitch our tents round about the hill Cumorah; and it was in a land of many waters, rivers, and fountains." Cowdery reflected, based on what he had read in the gold plates, that during the last great struggle of the Nephites, "in this valley fell the remaining strength and pride of a once powerful people, the Nephites— once so highly favored of the Lord." But the Nephites—even including their leader, Mormon, who allegedly was slain on the hill or nearby—were exterminated in that time of darkness.[450]

In 1935, the Church of Jesus Christ of Latter-day Saints erected a monument to memorialize the epiphany of the Angel Moroni on the Hill Cumorah. Since 1937, the Church has kept the Nephite saga alive by staging their elaborate mythodrama on the edge of the hill itself, acting out the key moments in the Mormon religious myth on the exact spot where it originally transpired.

Typically, *America's Witness of Christ,* which is performed outdoors around nine P.M., has a cast of at least six hundred and increasingly exhibits Hollywood-quality special effects and theatric marvels for its audiences. To open the show, six trumpeting angels appear at the top of the Hill Cumorah; then over the next seventy minutes the twenty-five-hundred-year mythic history of Mormon, Moroni, the Nephites, and Lamanites is dramatized.

It is "a pageant performed with the spirit of a George Lucas techno-dazzler and the scope of a Cecil B. DeMille epic," commented a *New York Times* critic. "Staging the Mormon Pageant on this holy site, with the statue of Moroni glittering atop the hill, roughly equals staging Oberammergau at Lourdes, except that this show has a distinctly American-style flash and grandeur," said a journalist for the *Rochester Democrat and Chronicle.*[451]

According to the Hill Cumorah publicity department, the program combines the high solemnity and ceremony of medieval religious pageants with digital sound and high-tech special effects—such as a thirty-seven-foot erupting volcano, water curtains, simulated thunder, lightning, and earthquakes, and state-of-the-art lighting—along with seventy-five sound speakers spread out around the hill. The program is described as "uplifting" and "family-oriented" and is presented free of charge.

GEOMANTIC

Dome; Dragon; Palladium; Pointer's Ball; Tree of Life; Three Star Temple; Scorpio Albion Emerald.

DOME: The dome over Hill Cumorah, the Sacred Grove, and the rest of the Joseph Smith property is about six miles in diameter and is the starfall for delta Leo, in the constellation of the Lion on the ecliptic of the zodiac. The star is of the third magnitude, about eighty light years from Earth, and with a luminosity fifty times that of our Sun. Leo is said to have nineteen stars and, according to standard star myths, to have been made a constellation by Zeus in honor of the lion's being the king of the beasts or because the Nemean Lion was the first labor of Herakles.

The delta Leo star, located on the lion's haunch (between the end of the rib cage and the pelvis) is known as *Zosma,* which may derive from the Girdle, but it was also known to the Arabic astronomers as *Al Thahr al Asad,* which means "the Lion's Back"; this name has been sometimes abbreviated as Duhr. Among the Chinese, who took a different tack, delta Leo was known as *Shang Seang,* or Higher Minister of State. The delta and theta stars in Leo comprised the Babylonian *Kakkab Kua,* which meant "The Stars of the Oracle of the God Kua."

DRAGON: Complementing the Lion's presence, through its delta star, at Hill Cumorah is one of the Earth's 1,053 minor dragons. Of course, minor does not mean insignificant or ineffectual. This dragon faces away from the hill and the Sacred Grove, out towards the farms and dales of western New York, guarding the temple entrance, as dragons always do.

PALLADIUM: Also situated at the hill but facing towards the Grove is a Palladium, which is to say, a miniature Crown of the Ancient of Days. This can be conceived as a large white head with two eyes that send beams of attention in all directions at once. It is an aspect or an analogical representation of the Supreme Being.

POINTER'S BALL: In between the Palladium and the dragon is a Pointer's Ball, which is an almond-shaped doorway or almond-shaped crack between the worlds. This geomantic feature potentially accounts for much of the Mormon myth. The Pointer's Ball is an entry point into a parallel reality—a miniature Bermuda Triangle—which the gold plates described as the land of the

Nephites. The original Hill Cumorah, the Hill Ramah, is on the other side, in that other parallel reality, which you can access through the doorway available at the physical hill.

The intense battles described in the plates written by Mormon and Moroni happened, but not in New York State or even America; they happened in the parallel world. At a certain point, Mormon and Moroni prepared the gold plates in their native language and slipped them through the crack between the worlds to be buried in the Hill Cumorah on this side of the veil and to be found much later in planetary time—in the 1820s when scientific materialism was gaining momentum in the United States and before Spiritualism arose as its antidote.

The idea of burying important documents or religious, metaphysical, or spiritual information in a kind of time-release capsule for later centuries is not entirely foreign to human history. In Tibet the practice has been done regularly, and such caches for the future are called *terma*, which means "treasure."

One of Tibet's preeminent saints and Buddhist mentors was the great Padmasambhava, who drove the demons out of Tibet to make way for the introduction of Buddhism and who traveled the Tibetan landscape in the eighth century A.D., burying terma in 108 different secret places, such as caves and in statues, for future revelation. The idea was that at the appropriate moment in the deep future the perfectly qualified teacher (called a *tertön*) would discover the terma and expound their meanings to the public. Between the tenth and fourteenth centuries A.D., discoveries of the buried terma occurred in Tibet, often through clues provided in dreams or visions. The discoverer would reconstitute the religious texts and add insightful commentary.

According to Buddhist scholars, the practice of preserving religious literature in secret locations is a venerated practice derived from India.

"Thus Nagarjuna is said to have found teachings, which he later propagated, in the realm of the serpent spirits *(naga)*, where they were being guarded from falling into the wrong hands."[452] It is fitting, then, that a dragon at Hill Cumorah was assigned the task of guarding the gold plates, or terma, from the parallel reality of the land of the Nephites until the American tertön, Joseph Smith, came along in 1827 to find, translate, expound, and disseminate the teachings.

What were the teachings? Here we are well advised to take Smith's own lead in finding the answer. The gold plates reported that the Christ had made an epiphany in the land of the Nephites before His final ascension and had arranged a peace between the warring tribes of Nephites and Lamanites, who in fact were brothers in origin. Joseph Smith asserted that the Christian Church had committed apostasy, had deviated grievously from the pure, original intention and impact of the Christ incarnation, and that the Book of Mormon transmitted the Christ energy in greater *fullness* and purity than what Westerners had been left with.

Mormon and Moroni carried the gold plates through the crack between the worlds from the Hill Ramah in their reality to the Hill Cumorah in our world so that we would have an *alternate* scenario and outcome of the Christ advent and its aftermath to contemplate. It could serve as a constructive hypothesis for us in revisioning our past and present spiritual understanding. It could give us the possibility of revisiting the Christ mystery from a different perspective, perhaps a fresher, purer, less adulterated one that does not blur, distort, or manipulate some of the key events and dynamics of this unique event in human spiritual history.

The saga of the warring brothers is highly similar to our own Biblical version of Cain and Abel. It is helpful to think of this in part as a parable of the dualistic, conflicting aspects of the psyche—the light and dark sides, the angelic and demonic, Christ and Lucifer, ego and shadow, male and female, left brain and right brain, rational and intuitive. The Christ appeared in the Americas in this parallel reality and pacified the battling brothers, calmed the mental dualism, and created a marriage between the opposing sides, which, after all, derived from the same ancient patriarch, the Hebrew Lehi, as the Mormon myths attest.

TREE OF LIFE: From the Hill Cumorah, fortified with this fresh and spiritually invigorating Christ transmission, the intent of the temple design was for people to make their way along the four miles between the hill and the grove.

Occupying this space is a large Tree of Life temple consisting of four sections. It's like a fourfold fountain laid out horizontally upon the land; you proceed from the highest, most exalted sphere, the crown of the tree at Hill Cumorah, and process down through the worlds and layers of reality to the base of the tree at the Sacred Grove. The temple is designed to help one ground and incarnate the Christ revelation obtained at Hill Cumorah.

THREE STAR TEMPLE: Then at the Sacred Grove you have the possibility of aligning yourself with the three fundamental stars of existence. These are known as the Soul Star, located high above your head; the Incarnational Star, located just above the belly button in the body; and the Earth Star, located deep within the Earth. This is a tool for spiritual alignment developed by the angelic realm as a way of marrying the three interdependent realms of the angelic (Soul Star), human (Incarnational Star), and elemental (Earth Star).

There are many Three Star Temples found throughout the Earth; another, for example, is at Morningside Park in Knoxville, Tennessee. Each of the eighteen archangels oversees eight thousand such temples, and for the one at the Sacred

Grove, the archangel in charge is Raphael. The purpose of the Three Star Temple is to enable you to experience each star as part of your spiritual self, and to have them fuse into one star at the center of the temple.

The light pillar that Joseph Smith experienced there, which he perceived to descend upon him, is an aspect of the mighty presence of the Archangel Raphael. It is also a preenergized and extrapolated container for the human experience of melding the three stars.

If you allow yourself the experience of having the three stars fuse at the middle point in the Grove, you will find yourself standing very tall indeed, because your consciousness will be occupying the vertical space prepared by the Archangel Gabriel. Obviously, the Sacred Grove would have been an excellent place for the Angel Moroni to achieve a clear transmission to the young Joseph Smith.

My own experience of the Grove was that it was a place outside of time. The light column Smith reported appeared to be huge, perhaps seventy-five yards wide. You find yourself very quickly entering a state that you can best describe to yourself as feeling inexplicably happy, enriched, exalted, uplifted. You may find yourself popping off for a few seconds into eternity, then falling back into present time. You could easily spend the day, the week, in this grove and never fidget. You may sense a lovely hushed presence rise up around you and find yourself encircled by a corona of angels. You may also find the woods teeming with nature spirits.

SCORPIO ALBION EMERALD: The Sacred Grove serves another, arguably even more important function than being the site of a Three Star Temple. It is the center of an aspect of the heart chakra for the Albion plate that covers most of the Eastern Seaboard, extending west to the Missouri River, and east a fair distance out into the Atlantic. The specific aspect of the heart chakra found here is called the emerald, although some mystics, such as Ramana Maharshi, called it the Heart.

The function of the emerald is to serve as an electromagnetic doorway out of the entire chakra system, which is to say, out of physical and etheric reality. It is a doorway out of this world. The emerald in the landscape, of course, is a mirror reflection of the emerald inside every human, located to the right of the sternum. Entering either emerald—they are, paradoxically, the same single emerald—affords us the opportunity of entering the eternal realm that lies beyond consciousness as we know it.

The emerald at the Sacred Grove is part of the huge geomythic energy-landscape body of the Albion figure that also includes sites in Massachusetts, Virginia (see Monticello), Washington, D.C., Tennessee (see Clingman's Dome), and Arkansas, among others. This emerald provides instant resonant access with the other eleven emeralds in the eleven other Albions, and with the original emerald for the planet at El Tule, near Oaxaca, in Mexico.

It is a bit staggering to consider that since 1937 the Mormon mythodrama about Christ in the Americas has been grounded at Hill Cumorah and transmitted through the emerald modem network of the twelve Albions every summer. It is a bit like putting the seventy-five sound-speakers used for the pageant right up against an Earth acupuncture point and performing for the entire planetary body, for seventy minutes once a year, a kind of sonic moxabustion.[453]

Not surprisingly it is difficult to gather untainted psychic impressions while physically on the Hill Cumorah since it is so deeply impregnated with the specific mythodramatic thought-forms of the Mormon story. It is easier to allow your body to register the essential energy of the hill and then retreat to the Sacred Grove to gather clearer impressions independent of the Mormon psychic overlay. You may form the suspicion that the Hill Cumorah, like Glastonbury Tor in England, was to

some extent sculpted and artificially shaped so as to contain various physical and etheric chambers capable of holding terma within it.

The four-mile-long Tree of Life latticework that connects Hill Cumorah and the Sacred Grove also serves another purpose. You may walk it in either direction and, if you have the time, it is beneficial to walk it both ways. At the Sacred Grove, within the Three Star Temple and the emerald, you have access to the original celestial template of the Christ mystery; at Hill Cumorah, you have access to an alternate, more pristine incarnational expression of the Christ mystery, as registered in the parallel reality in the land of the Nephites.

In either case, you can infuse yourself with these two aspects of the Christ mystery and allow these pure energies to *transmute* the possibly adulterated Western Judaeo-Christian version. In a sense, you may achieve a measure of that "restoration of all things" that Smith prophesied, as well as an experience of the Second Coming of the Christ in the sense that you may have a second look at what His incarnation might have truly been about and how it might be relevant to consciousness. In many respects the energy at the Hill Cumorah complex is about creating truth in spiritual perception and realigning with the Christ light outside of established cognitive orthodoxies—Christian or Mormon.

In the larger context, the Hill Cumorah complex sits within what nineteenth-century social critics dubbed the "Burned-Over District"—western New York State from Buffalo to Syracuse. That area was the site of intense religious and Spiritualist fervor throughout much of the 1800s as much of the area was singed with spiritual fire and wave after wave of otherworldly light.

Spiritualism in America got its start near Rochester; trance channeling and psychic mediumship got a strong foothold at Lily Dale; and Joseph Smith launched Mormonism at Palmyra. Appropriately, there are Landscape Zodiacs in Eden (near Buffalo), Rochester, and Syracuse, New York.

Hill of Tara, Ireland

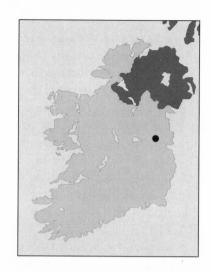

Known in classical Irish myth as *Teamhair na Riogh,* or Tara of the Kings, the Hill of Tara is a small hill (elevation above sea level 512 feet, but only three hundred feet above the surrounding countryside) ten miles southwest of Newgrange and about twenty miles west of Dublin. Among the most famous of Celtic sites, Tara is believed to have once been the royal seat of the high kings of Ireland, commonly referred to in Irish myth.

There are today almost no physical structures, monuments, or artifacts to see at Tara, but there are the remains of numerous megalithic features such as six ring ditches (circular ditches surrounding bare grassy raised mounds), a few upright standing stones, and what archeologists call a passage grave, an aboveground cave or barrow.

Three of Tara's megalithic structures are bounded by the *Rath na Riogh,* or Royal Enclosure, a raised, embanked oval about 950 feet by 800. The ditch surrounding the Enclosure was originally dug to a depth of eleven feet. Within the Enclosure are *Dumha na nGiall,* the Grave Mound of the Hostages, a burial mound which is made by covering the earth with a dolmen (several upright stones capped by a horizontal one).

This feature is attributed to Cormac mac Airt, one of the former glorious kings of Tara (he reigned from 227 to 266 A.D.), who, legend says, captured and brought back nine hostages from different principalities for interment at the mound. This site is also referenced to Niall of the Nine Hostages, another Irish king who claimed the same feat.

Also in the Enclosure are two earthworks (ring ditches) called *Teach Cormaic* (Cormac's House) to the west and the *Forradh* (Royal Seat) to the east. The two henges touch and, as observable from above, this slightly deforms or flattens out the circular shape on that side. Teach Cormaic has two ditches, while the Forradh is bounded by only one. In an uncanny way, when seen from above in an aerial photograph, these two ring henges and Dumha na nGiall seem to comprise a human face with the henges forming two close-set eyes and the burial mound a closed mouth or dimpled chin; the Royal Enclosure itself defines the edges of the spherical face.

Originally standing near Dumha na nGiall and now on the Forradh is a single vertical stone called the *Lia Fail,* or Stone of Destiny, which is six feet tall (and whose base is sunk another six feet beneath the ground). Although archeologists dispute the authenticity of this claim, the folklore has it that this was one of the four original treasures of the mythical gods called *Tuatha de Danann*, who brought this coronation stone to Ireland long ago to testify to the legitimacy of kingship.

Irish myths hold that Conn Cetchathach was the first man to sit upon the Lia Fail and foretell the future of Irish kingship. Some scholars claim the true Lia Fail was transported to Scotland or London, that it was never brought back (or it was), or that a substitute one was erected in its place, and eventually taken for the original stone.

The Lia Fail was supposed to cry out, shriek, or roar with joy when the rightful king stepped upon it or even touched it. Irish legend also claims that the Lia Fail is identical with Jacob's Pillow from Jewish myth. When the Hebrew patriarch slept with his head upon the stone pillow, he beheld (in his dreams, presumably) what's called Jacob's Ladder, a majestic two-way procession of angels upon a vast staircase connecting Heaven and Earth. The location of the Lia Fail at Tara was one of the prime reasons this site was the place designated for the inauguration of the Irish kings.

Other megalithic features at Tara include a ring ditch called *Rath Grainne* (Grainne's Enclosure), two long parallel banks with a sunken area in between called *Teach Miodhchuarta* (Banquet Hall; 750 feet long, ninety feet wide), *Rath Laoghaire* (Enclosure of King Loaghaire), and *Rath of the Synods* (Saint Patrick and other Irish saints held Synods there). Around Eastertime in 433 A.D., Saint Patrick is believed to have visited Tara, where he bested one of King Laoghaire's Druidic magicians as a demonstration of the power of Christianity.

Sometime during the reign of Diarmaid MacFergus Ceirbhuil (539–558 A.D.) Tara was cursed by Saint Ruadan, who said it would be made desolate and swept clean, never more to be Ireland's spiritual capital. Historians dispute the authenticity of this, but perhaps there was something to it. Even though 136 pagan and six Christian kings had ruled at Tara in an unbroken lineage, Diarmaid marked the end of that line.[454] In some manner, perhaps geomantic, the Christian saint shut Tara down.

One odd event associated with the Rath of the Synods is that in 1899 British Israelites excavated the mound believing they would find the fabled Jewish holy relic the Ark of the Covenant. (It wasn't there.)

The view from the Hill of Tara is wide, extensive, and magnificent, encompassing a fair portion of the central plain of Ireland. According to legend, once five royal roads radiated from there out into the countryside. "Clearly, here is a fitting dwelling-place for royal rulers who looked down on the source of their wealth—some of the richest pasture land in Europe."[455]

ARCHEOLOGY

The conventional archeological view of Tara is that various monuments were constructed over a four-thousand-year period in eight distinct building phases. The earliest, they contend, was Dumha na nGiall, dated to between 3030 and 2190 B.C. According to a report covering excavations from 1992 to 1997, archeologists count thirty visible monuments at and nearby Tara, but through aerial photographs, they can discern another thirty yet to be unearthed. The majority of these sixty sites are ring ditches and barrows.[456]

MYTH AND LEGEND

There are different theories on the origin and meaning of the name Tara. One source, Cormac mac Cuilleanain (died 908 A.D.), listed Tara in his famous glossary of Irish site-names, and said that the place name was originally *Tea Mur*, meaning the Wall of Tea. Tea was an Irish goddess who, according to myths, died and was buried at Tara, thereby imparting the site's original sanctity. She had asked her husband, the king, to memorialize her death by erecting a rampart around her grave.

According to this mythic line, the site was originally called *Druim Cain,* meaning "fine, good, fair, or beautiful ridge." Cormac meanwhile said the name Tara might mean "a meeting place" or "a place from which there is a wide view." Other etymologies start with *Teamhrach,* which may come from *Temair,* and means variously or alternatively "dark one," "spectacle," "elevated place," "assembly hall," or "freestanding eminence of wide prospect."

In ancient times, the Hill of Tara in fact possessed five names or epithets: *Druim Decsuin,* meaning the Conspicuous Hill; *Liath Druim,* or Liliath's Hill (named after a Firbolg chief who first cleared it of trees); *Druim Cain,* the Beautiful Hill (mentioned above); *Cathair Chrofhind,* allegedly the Tuatha de Dannan's name for the site, meaning "fortress"; and *Teamair,* "the burial place of Tea," from which derived Teamrach, then Tara.

The earliest records for Tara indicate that it was an important site for religious ceremonies and was sacred to Medb, a goddess sometimes equated with the island of Ireland as a whole. Her name means "She who intoxicates," and she is remembered as the warrior queen of Connacht and one of the most vibrant female personalities in Celtic myth.

Depicted as an unaging, beautiful young woman with long flowing hair, a red cloak, and a flaming spear, Medb was a central figure in the Irish saga *Tain Bo Cuailnge* ("Cattle Raid of Cooley"). In that story, she was the Queen in Cruachan in County Connacht (married to King Ailill) and coveted the *Donn Cuailnge,* the Brown Cow of Cuailnge, on Ireland's northeastern coast in County Ulster. Aillil already owned *Finnbennach,* the White Horned Bull, and the two together would represent the greatest bulls in all of Ireland. When the owner refused to surrender his bull for one year to Medb of Cruachan, she launched a war against Ulster to get it.

Among her many godlike abilities, Medb could shape-shift from young woman to aged hag. Her area of responsibility was sovereignty, territory, war, military command and administration, and fertility, and it was said of her that it took thirty-six virile men to satisfy her sexually, which perhaps explains one of her nicknames: "Medb of the friendly thighs." She had four sisters and many husbands, and was said to have been reared and later worshiped at Tara.

Part of the requirements for kingship and inauguration as such at Tara was a "mating" with the local Earth-goddess or Medb herself in a ritual banquet called *Feis Temrach,* the Feast of Tara. This was usually held at *Samhain,* or November 1, one of the eight key times in the Celtic annual calendar, and the advent of its New Year. In fact, no king could rule at Tara unless he underwent this *hieros gamos* with Mebd, the goddess of sovereignty. "Medb's very promiscuity marks her as a goddess, symbolic of the fertility of Ireland. She is the personification of the land itself and its prosperity."[457]

Not only was the rightful king of Ireland validated and crowned at Tara, he was probably selected there as well in a divinatory ritual called *Tarbhfhess,* meaning "bull-sleep" or "bull-feast." Here a bull was slain and a man ate his fill of the flesh and blood, then slept while four Druids made incantations over his prostrate form. When he awoke, he pronounced the name of the next Irish king.

Tara was well situated, geographically, to be the seat of kingship, as it was the fifth and central of five Irish provinces.[458] Obviously Tara is not the geographical center of Ireland, but it was considered its cosmological center, a kind of *axis mundi,* a fifth direction which is "here" at the center. It was part of the *Midhe* (meaning "middle" or "neck") which had preeminent royal status as the fifth of fifths.[459]

On *Samhain*, fairs, markets, horse races, agricultural rites, and assemblies of representatives from the five Irish provinces were held at Tara. At Samhain, affairs of state, as well as debts, adjustments, and disputes, were settled for the next seven years for all of Ireland. In fact, at the Festival of Tara, sub-kings, chiefs, bards, historians, and musicians from all over Ireland congregated to compile genealogical records, enact laws, settle disputed cases and political successions, all of which they lightened with song and feasting. All enmities had to be laid aside, no weapons could be raised, and no fights engaged.

One of Tara's most illustrious kings, and reputedly her first, was Cormac mac Airt, after whom the *Teach Cormaic* is named. He is said to have reigned for forty years, approximately from 227 to 266 A.D. His wisdom was so deep and influential that it even affected the cycles of nature. Calves gestated in only three months; the fields bore copious wheat harvests; the rivers were rich with salmon; and there were not enough pitchers in all of Ireland to contain the milk that flowed from the udders of Tara's cows.

According to one account, Cormac had a marvelous trip into the Otherworld. In the *Echtrae Cormaic* ("The Adventure of Cormac") the young king takes a sleep-inducing bough from a gray-haired warrior who turns out to be the great sea god, Manannan mac Lir. This deity was believed to be among the Tuatha de Danann and the ruler of *Emain Ablach*, a Celtic paradise, also known as the Land of Promise, and he rode over the Earth's ocean waves on a chariot.

In his land there is nothing but truth, nor is there age or withering away, nor sadness, jealousy, or pride. Manannan carries a shining branch with nine apples of red gold on his shoulder, which he leaves with Cormac for a year. The musical sound of that branch when shaken could enchant and put people to sleep. In fact, anyone who heard "the sound of the very sweet fairy music which those apples uttered" would be lulled to sleep and be unable to remember any want, woe, weariness, grief, heaviness of heart, or injury they might have been suffering with.[460]

Cormac travels to Manannan's castle, which has beams of bronze and silver walls, and roof thatch made of the wings of white birds. In this great palace, he is presented with a golden cup that splits apart when it is exposed to lies and is put together again in the presence of truths. He is treated to a pig that is cooked in a cauldron; every time a true story is told, a portion of the pig gets cooked. "I have but seven pigs," says Manannan, "but I could feed the whole world with them, for the pig that is killed and eaten today, you will find it alive again tomorrow."[461] Cormac keeps the golden cup with him at Tara until his death, when, legends say, he surrendered it to Manannan mac Lir.

Cormac may have been on Medb's good side, but one of her prime opponents was the Irish hero Cuchulainn, dubbed the Hound of Culann, and one of Ireland's three greatest heroes of antiquity. He was the offspring of one divine (his father, possibly Lugh Lamfhota) and one human parent (his mother, Deichtine); he began his heroic feats at age seven; and through his supremacy over all contenders in feats of arms and physical prowess he was afterwards routinely compared to the Greek Heracles.

His birth name was Setanta, but he was later dubbed "Hound" by the smith of Culann after he (age seven) killed the latter's prized but ferocious guard dog. Setanta volunteered to serve as the smith's *Cu*, or dog, until a suitable one could be raised and trained. One of his battle distinctions was to defend Ulster against Medb's troops who come to capture the fabled Brown Bull of Cuailnge. When he was finally defeated and died, his severed head and hand were buried in a mound at Tara.

When he prepared himself for battle, his appearance became fearsome, godlike, full of fury, wrath, and immense power, and he was invincible. "The first war-spasm seized Cuchulainn, and made him into a monstrous thing, hideous and shapeless, unheard of. . . . The hero-halo rose out of his brow, long and broad as a warrior's whetstone, long as a snout."[462] Once prepared, Cuchulainn would mount his chariot and kill five hundred warriors through his "thunder-feat." At the end of the battle, Cuchulainn emerged without a scratch.

Another head from a defeated foe was buried at Tara. This was the head of a troublesome goblin, or gnome.[463] Apparently it came to Tara at nightfall and blew fireballs against the royal city, setting it in flames. None at Tara was able to confront the goblin because he disarmed them with his music; he played such sweet music on a harp that each man who heard it was lulled to sleep and dreams.

Finn mac Cumhaill, one of Irish myth's greatest heroes, placed a magic spear at his forehead to shield him against the goblin's enchantments; the goblin, seeing Finn was immune to his advances, fled to the fairy mound at Slieve Fuad near Armagh in Ulster, but Finn slew him and bore his head back to Tara, claiming his place as the new head of his father's troop of the Fianna.

Before the Irish kings reigned at Tara, the gods held court here. Known as the *Tuatha de Danann*, or the Followers of the Goddess Danu, they occupied Tara and most of Ireland long before humans did. The myths say that they brought with them four powerful talismans from four sacred cities in Ireland: the Stone of Fail, the Spear of Lugh, the Sword of Nuadu, and the Cauldron of the Dagdha, each from one of these otherworldly cities. The gods dwelt in the center of Ireland, at Tara, which is why "Tara originally

symbolized the cosmos of the gods as opposed to the chaos of the demons."[464]

GEOMANTIC

Dome; Mount Olympus; Palladium; Avalon; Landscape Zodiac; Emerald; Gnome Egg; National Egregor Point.

DOME: The dome over Tara corresponds to Seginus, or gamma Boötes, the constellation known as the Herdsman, Plowman, Ox, or Bear Driver. Boötes is notable for containing Arcturus, one of the brightest stars in our galaxy, located in the herdsman's knee or foot. Seginus is placed in the figure's left shoulder. One of the dome caps from Tara encloses nearby Newgrange (discussed elsewhere in this book); the other dome caps energize much of the Boyne River Valley, which is rich with megalithic features.

The myths about Boötes are intriguing, especially when considered in light of the story of the White Bull of Cruachan and Brown Bull of Cuailnge. In one legend of the constellation, Boötes is Arcas, son of Zeus and the nymph Callisto; he was robbed of his possessions and after hardships and wanderings, invented the plow that was drawn by two oxen. As a reward for his accomplishment, Arcas was transferred, along with his plow, to the celestial vault as a constellation.

The Greeks called the figure a bear driver because he appears to drive Ursa Major (the Great Bear) about the galactic pole. This figure has also been called Bear-watcher, Bear-keeper, and Bear-guard. There is also a nuance in the Babylonian star myths that this constellation was the shepherd of the heavenly flock.

MOUNT OLYMPUS: The relationship of Boötes with the celestial Bear is apt at Tara because one of the three features within the Royal Enclosure is a Mount Olympus, which is to say, a home of the fourteen Ray Masters of the Great Bear. These were the primary deific figures among the Tuatha de Danann. In terms of this geomythic configuration, the Royal Enclosure would have been ritually approached from the north, along what archeologists mistakenly call the Banquet Hall. This enigmatic megalithic feature marks the approximate location of (borrowing from the Norse) the Rainbow Bridge into Asgard (the Norse Mount Olympus).

More probably, the 750-foot-long *Teach Miodhchuarta* was in part a ceremonial promenade into the Tara geomantic temple; a similar feature may be observed at the Pointer's Ball in Glastonbury, England. It is also possible there was once a double stone row there which focused the energies towards the Royal Enclosure, as at Carnac, France, and Avebury, England (both discussed elsewhere in this book).

PALLADIUM: While all of the Royal Enclosure marked the spot for the Mount Olympus, or celestial home of the Tuatha de Danann, the two ring ditches have special functions of their own. The Forradh is the site of a Palladium, a miniature crown of the Ancient of Days surrounded by the Biblically referenced twenty-four Elders. The ring ditch feature creates a kind of vortex or dimensional doorway, making it easier to apprehend the more subtle geomantic feature available there.

It may be experienced as a vast, bright, pale-blue spherical space, one without apparent limit, with twenty-four godly faces filling the inside sphere, one next to the other. At the center of the sphere is the White Head, its eyes flashing in all directions at once.

AVALON: Upon the raised mound of Teach Cormaic, you step into another world altogether. It is as if the energies rising out of the ditch create vertical walls of deep rich blue upon which, as if they were made of a soapy film sheen, you may discern the faces of numerous godlike figures. It is

not inconsistent with this image to add that the circular ditch also creates what could be described as vertical sound curtains. The feature acts to shift your perceptual dimensions.

Once inside this dimensionally shifted reality, there is no detectable height or width to the walls; you are aware only of innumerable deific visages. It is a circle of gods, a hologram of an aspect of the spiritual worlds, an audience chamber for the Tuatha de Danann. The energies of the ring ditch facilitate the necessary clairvoyance to make perception of this realm possible. But there's more. You're inside Cormac's House.

The blue vertical walls of faces reveal themselves to be a door, which swings open. This is the door to Cormac's House, that is, his domain. That domain is *Emain Ablach,* another version of the Celtic Avalon or Summer Country, itself a mythic code name for the Celestial City of Gandhavati. Geomantically, Cormac opened the door to Emain Ablach, the land of apple trees with golden fruits, and allowed the orchard of divine wisdom and delight to come down to Tara, just inside the small circumference of the Teach Cormaic ring ditch.

By definition, Emain Ablach is the realm of prosperity, endless delight and feasting, music, song, dance, and aesthetic pleasures, so by opening up the connection between Tara and Emain Ablach through the energy "door" at Teach Cormaic, Cormac began an era of prosperity and well-being for Ireland. He opened the door to Emain Ablach so its spiritual energies could flow through Tara, out through its grid network of dome caps, energy lines, zodiac (described below), and the Brown Bull landscape features (described below) to enrich the countryside.

When the spiritual connections are intact and working, the physical counterparts flourish accordingly. A true king, one initiated in geomancy, truly enriches his country by assuring the flow of spiritual energies into it. Cormac, with his hands always able to pluck a golden apple from one of the apple trees of Emain Ablach at the doorsteps of Tara, would be equipped to be the wise, beneficent, even Solomonic, ruler he was said to be.

The function of the Forradh is to inspire the sense of joyous assembly and certainty in rulership, with access to the wisdom and presence of the Ancient of Days. Teach Cormaic provides a specialized audience chamber with the Tuatha de Danann, or Ray Masters, and many other members of the ascended human and celestial hierarchy. The Royal Enclosure facilitates entry into Mount Olympus or what is elsewhere called the Celestial City of Amaravati.

The combination of these three geomantic features makes it obvious why Irish kingship was divined, inaugurated, validated, and crowned at Tara. The embodied kings could sit in the dimensional overlap between the celestial source of rulership and its physical counterpart on the island of Ireland. In a sense, consulting with the gods on a matter of kingship required nothing more than looking over one's shoulder, as they were all there at Tara with its kings.

LANDSCAPE ZODIAC: The stellar coordinates of the Landscape Zodiac present at Tara provided yet another overlap with Ursa Major. The zodiac itself is about eighteen miles wide, with the Tara features situated within the landscape location for Ursa Major. Much of the Boyne River Valley, including Newgrange, sits within this.

EMERALD: As for the *Lia Fail*, the Stone of Destiny and Knowledge, said to have once stood on Teach Cormaic, it is misleading to think of the original stone as a physical standing stone. The Lia Fail brought by the Tuatha de Danann from their magical city of Falias is far more subtle than stones as we physically know them. It was not a physical stone, yet it was a stone. Here it's helpful to switch mythic vocabularies.

In the Grail traditions, especially that recorded by Wolfram von Eschenbach in his *Parzival,* the Grail was described as a green stone brought from Heaven to Earth. In Buddhist traditions, the *cintamani* stone is considered either a meteorite or a special object brought to the Earth by the gods and kept at the mystical and esoteric spiritual place called Shambhala in the King's Tower.[465]

In the Hindu iconography of the heart chakra, the *Ananda-kanda,* an arcane aspect of the main center, has a variously described wish-fulfilling gem, jeweled altar, or *cintamani-grha,* meaning "the room made of *Cintamani* stone, which grants all desires."[466] Cintamani, green stone, Lia Fail—they are one and the same supersensible stone known as the emerald, which is the outer projection of an electromagnetic doorway in between the two aspects of the heart chakra.

The emerald (six-sided, double terminated, bright green) was one of twelve precious gems on the crown of the Lord of Light; it is also a hologram of this deity's heart placed in each human and distributed throughout the planet's own energy body. Copies are found, for example, in a small churchyard in southern Mexico called El Tule, near Oaxaca. Among the Zapotecs of that part of Mexico, the Lord of Light was called Quetzalcoatl, and the emerald was his heart, which he buried at El Tule long ago, then revisited triumphally in August 1987 to open it like a pomegranate and spread its seeds throughout the world.

With respect to Tara, to understand the Lia Fail in this light it is useful to resort to its earliest myth, the one usually dismissed pejoratively as too fanciful to take seriously—namely, that the Hill of Tara is the enclosure of the goddess Tea. Geomythically, let us say that at a certain level of energy and consciousness, Tea, the Lia Fail, the emerald, cintamani, Lord of Light, and Quetzalcoatl (borrowing from the Zapotec vocabulary) are identical. Something was buried at Tara, and depending on our perspective, it was a deity or an object belonging to that deity: the emerald heart of a high god, or the high god itself.

Rescuing this proposition from the far reaches of seeming improbability is the fact that Ireland is known as the Emerald Isle. What emerald? Surely they didn't mean the bright grassy green of the landscape. Tara of County Meath, was the geocosmographic center, politically and spiritually, of the island of Ireland with its five provinces, offering the entire country the emerald set like a precious jewel in the ring ditch of Teach Cormaic. In the dimension in which the emerald exists, size is entirely fluid and indeterminable; the emerald can be as small as the grassy mound bounded by two circular ditches, or it can be miles across.

When Tara was geomantically active—its flow of energies turned on—all of Ireland could have had access to its emerald. But when Saint Ruadan cursed Tara, he turned off its energy flow and effectively pounded the emerald into the ground, pounding a stake into the living heart of Ireland as if its "pagan" pantheon and geomythic landscape were a vampire. Even today the Lia Fail, or emerald, at Tara is energetically buried underground.

Saint Ruadan may have thought he was acting on behalf of the Church and the spiritual welfare of all Christians (even those not yet converted), but geomantically his was a destructive act. He effectively shut the door—nailed it fast—against the entry into Ireland of the Lord of Light, turning Ireland physically from a land of riches and prosperity into a land of recurrent poverty. In terms of Ireland's geomantic health, the Lia Fail must be returned to Tara, not from Scotland or London or any other place, but from under and within the heart of the Hill of Tara temple enclosure itself. Tara's curse needs to be nullified.

GNOME EGG: Let's not forget that troublesome goblin lurking at Tara's ramparts. The tale of Finn and the goblin is a clue that at Tara there was significant interaction between the human and elemental realms, meaning the domain of the various Nature spirits, notably the gnomes. Beyond the Teach Miodhchuarta and diagonally off beyond the three ring ditches (*Claoin-Fhearta*-North, *Rath Grainne,* and *Claoin-Fhearta*-South) stands a Gnome Egg. It is not situated in a ring ditch as the energies at such a site would be too powerful, almost inimical, to the life of the Gnome Egg.

While they are not too active today, once, when Tara flourished, gnomes populated the area and cooperated with the Tara kings to maintain the elemental base of the local geomantic structure. Often positive, cooperative relations over time get reversed and presented as negative scenarios of conflict or antagonism, as in the case of Finn having to overcome the irritating, bewitching goblin at Tara. A geomantically initiated king at Tara would wisely instruct the gnomes in their task of distributing the incoming celestial energy, as filtered through the human "lightning rods" out into the landscape energized by the Tara dome's forty-eight dome caps.

Part of kingship was mastery of the elemental realm—mastery, that is, in the sense of judicious cooperation with them; the elementals wait upon humans for guidance in the same way that humans wait upon angelic input. At times, hundreds of gnomes would gather within the Royal Enclosure, participating from their dimension in geomantic activities conducted there by the kings of Tara.

NATIONAL EGREGOR POINT: But what about the White and Brown Bulls? And Cuchulainn's head that was buried at Tara? Here we have an opportunity to see to what degree myths compress large realities into easily remembered tales. Medb, as the goddess of sovereignty, territory, and kingship, is the personification of Ireland's egregor, its national and continental tutelary angel.

The kings at Tara, when they ritually "mated" with Medb, aligned themselves in consciousness with all of Ireland's geomantic features through its protectress and higher self, as it were: Medb.[467] They extended their consciousness through all of Ireland's geomantic terrain and its culmination as Medb, and became one with both.

As Ireland's egregor, Medb is grounded at Cruachan in Connacht—she was called Medb of Cruachan, after all—but she runs a current of energy and maintains numerous landscape features between Cruachan and Cuailnge in Ulster. You could say her landscape "body" extends from Cruachan in the west to Cuailnge in the east. What does her body look like? Like a white bull, the *Finnbennach*.

The two bulls of the *Tain Bo Cuailnge* can be understood by looking at an equivalent Greek myth. Zeus, chief of the gods of Mount Olympus, once took the form of a white bull to woo a lovely female human called Europa. Once he seduced her, he strode away into the sea with Europa on his back. The myth of Europa and the white bull (see the sections on the Acropolis and Mount Ida) is a way of pointing to a vast landscape feature that stretches from southern Greece up to Germany. Ireland's White and Brown Bulls represent a smaller expression of the same idea, in this case referenced to only one country and a single people's egregor, Medb.

Medb already owned the White Bull, but she wanted the Brown Bull. The White Bull is the celestial archetype of this landscape figure, its light form. Medb wanted to ground its spiritual body into the physical landmass of Ireland, in the brown earth, thereby giving her the Brown Bull, the terrestrial counterpart. White Bull above, Brown Bull below, so to speak. What the Irish myths describe as fierce battles, myriad deaths,

and heroic exploits by Cuchulainn in defense of Ulster's Brown Bull must be read in a mirror, that is, inverted.

A lot of geomantic effort and metaphysical struggle went into grounding Medb's White Bull through the Brown Bull geomythic locations. Energy obstacles had to be removed; inimical astral beings had to be mastered; the density and inchoate nature of physical matter had to be overcome before this light pattern could "marry" its earthly partner. In a sense, a fair portion of the Irish landscape had to be tamed, even domesticated, before Medb could have her Brown Bull.

The map of the military exploits of Medb's army and Cuchulainn's defenses can be understood as a diagram of the geomythic body of the Brown Bull itself. For that matter, the ferocious hound of the smith Culann that Setanta killed was most likely geomantic code for confronting and befriending the Canis Major (the Great Dog) figure of a Landscape Zodiac situated in the Cuailnge area.

Cuchulainn's prowess over the dog of Culann mirrors Heracles' twelfth labor of subduing and capturing Cerberus, the Hound of Hell, and bringing him to the gates of Mycenae in Greece. In ancient Ireland, Merlin was initiating a Landscape Zodiac in the Murtheimne Plain near Cuailnge where Culann kept his flocks, a task that always requires a befriending—what the myths mistakenly call a subduing or capturing—of the dog, Canis Major. "Until that hound grows up to do his work, I will be your hound, and guard yourself and your beasts," the young Setanta tells Culann after killing his guard dog.

Cuchulainn was well suited to this kind of extended geomantic labor. In his other mythic guises—the Greek Heracles, the Celtic Merlin, the Tibetan Padmasambhava, the Polynesian Maui—he had tamed landscapes, overcome demonic energies and baleful astral beings, captured wondrous beasts, subdued quarreling dragons, and dredged up islands from the Pacific Ocean—an all-purpose, real-life Gandalf.

He was a prodigy of geomancy, the initiator of landmasses, the matchmaker of egregors and landscapes. When the Irish myths say Cuchulainn's head was buried under a mound at Tara, most likely this is a code, even a mnemonic, for Merlin's involvement in the marriage of Irish egregor with its people and land and with the once and future grounding of his energy at the country's spiritual center. It may also be a clue—even an invitation—to access him through this site.

Iona Island, Scotland

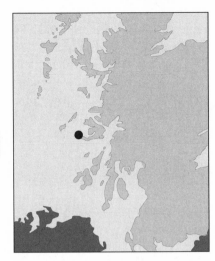

It's a tiny island, barely one and a half miles wide by three miles long—all of 1,897 acres—off the coast of the Hebridean Island of Mull in southwestern Scotland. It is said to be the first Christianized site in Scotland and a major pilgrimage destination since the seventh century, today attracting an estimated 130,000 visitors a year. In all, not many more than one hundred people live permanently on Iona, although people have been living there since 4000 B.C.

Iona folklore holds that at one time even the soil was considered holy. The early Scottish rulers and Highlands chieftains were buried on Iona in what is now called Saint Oran's cemetery, and evidence suggests that French, Irish, Pictish, even Norse royalty desired and obtained an Iona interment. Local legend says that forty-eight Scottish kings were buried here in Saint Oran's Chapel cemetery.

"Burial on Iona is still an honor; with very few exceptions, outsiders are not eligible."[468] Probably out of respect for that, the island has been "owned" and administered by the National Trust for Scotland since 1979.

In a similar vein, the Coronation Stone at Westminster Abbey in London came from that island. Ionians had always called it the Black Stone of Destiny. Before the British took it from Iona in 1296, the stone was reportedly used by Druids, Saint Columba, and others in authority positions to crown and validate their kings. Supposedly it was "black" more for symbolic than geological reasons as chiefs who swore their solemn oaths upon it and then broke those oaths would meet a black doom. In 1996, Scotland got it back.

Present on Iona today is the Abbey, constructed by the Benedictines, who were dispatched by the Pope around 1200 A.D. to refound the monastic tradition on the island. The Celtic foundation, after a series of mass martyrdoms and other abandonments, had become moribund by the start of the thirteenth century. At its peak, however, Celtic Iona had been an important center of Irish monasticism, governing forty-two Irish and fifty-seven Scottish parishes until the ninth century.

In 1938, George Macleod, a Church of Scotland minister, established the Iona Community, a lay Christian initiative. He rebuilt the Abbey and dispatched Christian missionaries throughout Scotland in a kind of modern-day evangelism based on the island's original Celtic traditions. MacLeod remained leader of the Iona community until 1967 (he died in 1991) and the community has flourished in accordance with his vision.

A recent British publication, by the Iona Community's current director, spoke of the place in terms of "God's Energy," noting that the Iona Community can be a "port of departure" in the journey and challenges of true faith.[469] An Australian visitor to the Community remarked: "There is a sense that centuries of prayer and spiritual life have seeped into the rocks and soil, as indeed the spiritual life owed much of its own identity to the island in which it grew."[470]

HISTORY AND ARCHEOLOGY

There is a fair amount of discussion and uncertainty about the origin and original meaning of the island's name. "The very name Iona rings in our ears with the sea-sound of man mysteries," commented Eleanor C. Merry, a Celtic researcher and mystic, in her famous work on the Celtic soul, *The Flaming Door*.[471]

Early Ogham inscriptions referred to the island as *Ioua*, after a Moon goddess, but other early sources said it was *Hy Brasil* (Island of Beauty or Worth), or simply *Hy*, an earthly paradise found far out at sea, or perhaps a reference to the otherworldly *Tir na nOg* (the Land of Youths or the Ever-Young). Druid maps listed Iona as *Innis nan Druidnean* (or *Innis na Druineach*), the Isle of Druids, possibly because it is believed that at one time the island was covered with oak trees (sacred to Druids) and had 350 standing stones (megalithic structures frequented by Druids). Of course the island was also often referred to as *I Choluim Chille*, or Colum Cille's (Saint Columba the Dove's) island.

Another theory, from 1771, proposes that before Saint Columba arrived at Iona, the island had already been dedicated to the Apostle John and that the island was originally called *I'Eoin*, meaning the Isle of John, and thus Iona because

I'Eoin is very close in sound to the Gaelic pronunciation of Iona.[472]

A more mystical interpretation has Iona being called *Hu, Hii*, or *Ioua*, the latter being the sacred vowels of the three "Rays of Light," says Merry. "It is *Jona*—John—the name of those who die and are raised, a possibility supported poetically by the fact that Iona in Latin comes out Columba, the Dove. "The sound of I-O-N-A sighs over the waters. The white wings of the 'Dove of the Eternal' are in the clouds and foam."[473]

The name Iona also suggests the Hebraic IOA, the Name of God, or even YHVH or Jehovah, explains English sacred sites researcher Peter Dawkins. IOA is a wisdom name of three vowels that "summarise the whole wisdom of God." It is the name of Man, or John, and the name of the "Christ Consciousness inherent in spiritual Man."

The word IOA "floods the soul with light, with divine fire," Dawkins comments. It is the Christ Consciousness incarnate in a word, transmitting the Light of God itself. "It is symbolized by the "Dove" of white fire which appears above the head and showers its light blessings or rays down upon the soul." Dawkins makes an intriguing link of the Dove with the Hebrew word, *Dohveh*, which, he says, was symbolized by the Sheepfold. This was a metaphor, based on the Lamb of God concept, of a heavenly place in which all the Christed souls, the "real saints or illumined ones of mankind" are assembled to form the "true Church of Christ." Dawkins implied that Iona shares in this Sheepfold quality.[474]

Probably the most significant event in Iona's known history was the arrival in 563 of the man who became its resident Christian saint, the Irish Columba, the Dove, also known as Columcille. He was a simple and innocent man who "gave to the Holy Ghost a dwelling-place in himself by his dove-like ways," said Adamnan, the Ninth Abbot of Columba's monastery and the seventh-century author of *Life of Saint Columba*.

Columba was born at Gartan in County Donegal, Ireland, in 521, and was forty-two when he came to Iona with his twelve assistants to start a monastery. He had already founded one hundred monasteries in Scotland and Ireland before he came to Iona. The legend has it that he came to Iona to convert as many souls to Christ as he had caused to lose their lives—three thousand—in an ill-advised battle against the High King over the ownership of a book. Supposedly he and his brethren made the sea passage to Iona in a wicker boat covered in animal hides.

Once established at Iona, Saint Columba, according to Adamnan, expelled "innumerable hosts of malignant spirits" from the island. They had been assailing him and starting to bring "deadly distempers" to his monastic brotherhood. Miracles and healing and prophetic utterances were attributed to Saint Columba, along with considerable visions of angelic beings on the island. Some testified to seeing the saint accompanied by angels and lights.

Saint Finnio saw Saint Columba approaching with "an angel of the Lord" with him. Saint Brenden said he saw Saint Columba accompanied by "a most brilliant pillar wreathed with fiery tresses" and "holy angels" walking with him. Saint Columba said when Saint Brenden died, the heavens suddenly opened and "choirs of angels" of "great and incomparable brightness" descended to greet the soul of Saint Brenden.

When Saint Columba prayed on a hill called *Sithean Mor* (now known as *Cnoc Angel* (Hill of Angels), a multitude of "citizens of the heavenly country clad in white robes and flying with wonderful speed" stood around him. Once he spent three days sequestered in his home, where the grace of the Holy Ghost was "communicated to him abundantly and unspeakably" and his house was filled with "heavenly brightness." It was widely rumored that he possessed many arcane and occult secrets "hidden from men since the beginning of the world."

When Saint Columba, "the pillar of many churches," died, all of Iona was "resplendent with the brightness of angels," who descended to the island "in countless numbers to bear his soul away." One contemporary of Saint Columba said an immense pillar of fire appeared at midnight at the eastern tip of the island, ascending upwards "to illuminate the whole earth like the summer sun at noon."[475]

MYTH AND LEGEND

Writing about Iona in 1910, Scottish mystic Fiona Macleod said the island is the "metropolis of dreams," offering a "singular blending" of the energies and light of paganism, romance, and spiritual beauty. To truly relate the history of Iona, he said, "is to go back to God, and to end in God." In terms of spiritual geography, Iona is the Mecca of the Gael; it is "the one bit of Eden that had not been destroyed."

Macleod said he sometimes dreamed of the old prophecy that said Christ would revisit Iona, or make it the site of his Second Coming and that the "little Gaelic island may become as the little Syrian Bethlehem" to that event. The Divine Spirit would come again to Iona as the Daughter of God, in the form of "Divine Womanhood upon the human heart," and when Saint Bride (the sixth-century Celtic Bridgid) revisited Iona, she would come to bind the hair and wash the feet of the Bride of Christ, Macleod wrote.

One night Macleod had a majestic vision of the Divine Forges of God at Iona. He had been to a sermon in which the minister said God would hammer the evil out of the human soul like a blacksmith at an anvil. Iona is God's anvil, and God is the blacksmith—but who knows the way to the Divine Forges?

One day Macleod sat upon *Sliav Starr* (the Hill of Noises) facing the westernmost part of the island, *Port-na-Churaich* (the Haven of the Coracle) where Saint Columba was said to have first landed on Iona. Then Macleod dreamed that the sea was made of transparent flame and that these flames rose solemnly above a vast forge whose anvil was the smooth surface of the ocean. Macleod saw "three great Spirits" standing by the anvil: one pulled a soul out of the deep shadow; another purified the soul of its dross and rewelded it; the third breathed upon it, giving it wings, beauty, and life.

The "glory-cloud" formed of the flames disappeared and he saw the multitude of stars. "Each star was the gate of a long, shining road," and innumerable souls passed along these highways. In the far distance Macleod saw white walls with ivory and pale gold shadings, and by them the three Spirits. "So these, I thought, were not the walls of Heaven, but the Divine Forges."[476]

One intriguing report of Iona's subtle energy aspects came from the after-death observations of Father Andrew Glazewski, who communicated telepathically with English psychic Cynthia Sandys in 1973. Iona is a "beautiful island barbed with power" but it must be always held in the "love rays" to prevent it from becoming a "demoniacal centre," Father Glazewski said. It is a "thin place" where the Earth and subtle planes meet without a film to separate them. Iona's history is very long, going back to the days of "ancient continents" and "old power."

Just beneath its surface is "a great dynamic pool of fire"; you can sense this when you encounter warm spots on the island, and even if you don't, they still register an effect on your energy body. Speaking as a spirit visiting Iona, he saw the island as a "great jewel, with light and colour radiating all round the world." Its "ray" could be very amenable to those "whose aura is ready for enlightenment," he told Sandys.

He also described a group of Druid spirits "singing the old chants on the etheric which give power, health, and enlightenment to the island."

The Druids taught a method of inner development there that helped the soul leave the body in such a way as to pass outside Earth's aura and continue on without the need to reincarnate.[477]

Another disincarnate informant named Sir Alvary Gascoigne, Sandys' brother, filed a report on Iona as seen from the spirit's view. Gascoigne was told by a "great leader" that "something of great power had been created in the beginning of the world in Iona." It was a power, always present and accessible, that could flow through humans like a magnetic current.[478] In 1977, Sandys received another communication about Iona from a deceased friend called Edith Wood. "The whole island is ringed with fire," Wood reported, and the "old Saint [Columba] comes and goes in the most casual way."[479]

GEOMANTIC

Dome; Chakra Template.

DOME: Without exaggeration, Iona is one of the planet's three most important geomantic nodes with respect to a fundamental aspect of the Earth's energy body. The reason for Iona's geomantic preeminence has to do with the star its dome represents: Canopus, the second brightest star in our galaxy.

The Iona Canopus dome is a differentiation of the silver energy that comes in and is blended with the gold at Avebury in Wiltshire, England, the site of the Earth's umbilicus to the galaxy. The gold energy is differentiated at the Sirius dome at Carnac in France. All the domes on the planet are "wired" with gold and silver "threads" to the master Avebury dome, which in turn is "wired" by gold and silver "threads" to Sirius, the brightest, in Canis Major, and Canopus, the second brightest, in Argo Navis. The life connection of the Earth is sustained in these three sites. (See Avebury, England, and Carnac, France.)

As a constellation, Canopus is generally regarded as the rudder of the ship Argo Navis, mythically famous as the ship Jason and the fifty Argonauts sailed in search of the Golden Fleece. The Argo ("Swift") was fitted with a speaking timber in the prow, taken from the Oracle of Dodona. The goddess Hera, wife of Zeus, chief of the Olympian gods, spoke exclusively to Jason and guided the journey, several times helping the Argonauts escape mortal danger. His Argonauts included many of the top celebrities of the Greek mythic canon, includung Orpheus, Castor and Pollux, Heracles, Theseus, and Cepheus.

An alternate Egyptian myth says that the Argo was the first seafaring ship built by King Danaus to carry his fifty daughters and him from Libya to Rhodes. The Hindu astronomers called the constellation *Sata Vaesa*, meaning "One Hundred Creators," which was one of the four "Nourishers of the World" or four quarters of the sky. Its Roman title was *Ratis Heroum*, the "Heroes' Raft," and *Currus Maris*, the "Sea Chariot." Many ancient astronomers associated the Argo with the Ark of Noah or its equivalent in variations on the story.

Argo is a big constellation (transferred to heaven by the goddess Athena), and some astronomers have divided it into three connected star figures: Carina, the Keel, with 268 stars; Puppis, the Stern, with 313; and Vela, the Sail, with 248, making a total of 829 naked-eye stars in its overall shape.

Canopus is alpha Carinae situated on the ship's rudder. The word Canopus may derive from the Coptic or Egyptian *Kahi Nub*, meaning "Golden Earth"; the Egyptians in fact widely worshipped the star, orienting many of their temples to the direction of its rising with the Sun on the fall equinox in 6400 B.C.

But the Arabs knew it as *Wazn*, "the Weight," and *Hadar*, "the Ground." The Egyptians thought of it as the Star of Osiris, while the Hindus called it *Agastya*, after one of their rishis,

or inspired sages, and a helmsman to the son of the god Varuna. Greek and Russian Christians called it the Star of Saint Catherine as it guided pilgrims to her shrine at Mount Sinai in Israel.

Canopus is the Great Star of the South, not visible in the Northern hemisphere. A first-magnitude star, it's six hundred light years from Earth (although some estimates place it farther, at 1,152 light years) and is estimated to be sixty thousand times more luminous and thirty times bigger than our Sun. It's even bigger than Sirius, though the latter is brighter.

CHAKRA TEMPLATE: Not all domes generate a template of the seven chakras, or subtle energy centers, but the domes associated with Argo Navis stars do. The template's root is at the southern tip of the island, Columba's Bay, *Port-na-Churaich* (the Haven of the Coracle)—where he landed. This of course is geomantic code for where Saint Columba *grounded* the temple, at its root chakra.

Various other well-noted landmarks represent the second through seventh chakras of the Iona temple, including: *Sithean Mor* or Cnoc Angel (second chakra); *Cnoc Mor nan Gall* (third chakra); *Cnoc a'Mheirgeidh*, Hill of the Standard (fourth chakra); the Iona Abbey area, Dun-I, at 332 feet above sea level, and the site of a healing well called the Well of Eternal Youth (fifth chakra); the island's highest point (sixth chakra); and the crown chakra, at either of two sites, White Strand of the Monks and Strand of the Seat, on Iona's northern end.

The Iona temple is best used by walking the chakra template over the course of a day or two, meditating for a while at each site. You may find you are accompanied by spiritual beings who resemble high priests and archbishops who walk with you in their layer of reality. You may, as Saint Columba frequently did, become aware of the accompaniment of angels or other high beings with you.

One way to make "contact" with the landscape chakra is to place the immediate site within the Blazing Star at your midpoint, then place the star and the Iona chakra point at the corresponding location in your own bodily chakra template. (See part 1 for information about using the Blazing Star.) You may find that each chakra feels like a burning baptismal font in which your whole being is immersed. You will be connecting with three aspects at each chakra: the Earth level; the Christ-Sun level; and the Cosmic Father-Holy Ghost level.

By the time you reach the seventh chakra, the crown, at White Strand of the Monks, you have identified—*extended*—your energy field with that of the island and brought the island's chakra template into your own energy continuum. This makes it easier, even inviting, for the angelic realm to participate, transmitting celestial energy to both you and the island at the same time because you have become a conduit.

In the course of walking the Iona chakra template, or even reading about it here, you may wonder: to whose body do these chakras belong?

The most striking feature of the Canopus energy at Iona is that it is silver. As one of the mystics cited above suggested, the island is truly engulfed, ringed, encircled by silver flames such that it could well be renamed the Island of the Silver Flames. It is also an intensely feminine island, as Fiona Macleod sensed, but the feminine is archetypal, of the order of what mystics and metaphysicians call the Divine Mother, the Mother God, what the Qabalists call Binah and the Egyptians Isis.

It's really so far beyond any human notions of gender as to almost render the term inapplicable, yet, if you can tolerate the paradox, it is "feminine" in the sense that it is decidedly not masculine, as in Divine Father. The Iona dome, through its connection with Canopus, feeds this stream of galactic "feminine" energy into the entire planet and all its domes. It's is Earth's feminine channel, as Carnac in France is its masculine channel.

So the answer to the question posed above is that the chakras belong to the Divine Mother, and in progressing through the seven landscape chakras on Iona you are walking in the Great Mother's energy field. You are also, geomythically, walking towards the prow of the great Argo Navis and the carving of Hera, its talking goddess figurehead. The two, Swift Ship and Great Mother, are the same.

The energy of Iona, working through this geomythic construction, is intent on transmitting the essence of the Divine Mother, the Holy Feminine, Isis, to the Earth. In processing through the chakra template, you are climbing the seven rungs in the ladder of the being of the Mother of the World—except it is actually forty-nine steps, because each chakra is like a ripple of seven concentric circles, each one a little larger. Qabala talks of the fifty Gates of Binah, the Mother. Each Gate, in terms of initiation, is one of the fifty Argonauts. When you reach White Strand of the Monks, you reach the fiftieth Gate, the Sheepfold.

At the northern tip of Iona, you may experience a settling of white doves in spirit form on your crown center. These are a traditional Western symbol for the descent of the Holy Spirit, and Iona's connection with doves may be founded on this spiritual fact. You may next find yourself in a golden hall filled with people you would describe as saints of both genders with conspicuous haloes. You are in the Sheepfold—I'm borrowing this Sumerian term used in *The Epic of Gilgamesh* to describe a similar feature in the city of Uruk because it is applicable even in this Celtic context.

At the far end of the hall stand two massive white pillars and a seeming void between and beyond them. One thing whispered about Iona in metaphysical circles is that for the dying or self-realized, Iona is an excellent portal out of the Earth *dimension*—not just the planet but all its associations. Perhaps this is part of the truth behind the *Hy Brasil* attribution. Another name for this portal is Arcturus, the great star in the constellation Boötes. Arcturus is a gateway between nothing and something; the source of the possibility of Light, one reflection.

You may notice a central fountain with bright scarlet flames burning as if on its water. This is an aspect of the Christ. Entering the flames and becoming one with their energy can transport you into a different layer of reality, a silver dimension that may seem to resemble a massive stone circle or a labyrinth. A bright silver light burns among the upright stones. Following this light back to its source, you may encounter a goddess figure, seated on a silver throne, her face turned away from you, to the side, with perhaps a circlet on her head or a silver star on her brow. She sits in what appears to be a silver rotunda with numerous doors around the periphery at ground level. How your mind decodes an energy impression of the Divine Mother is of course somewhat unpredictable, and entirely up to you.

THE IDENTITY OF SAINT COLUMBA: The human that the hagiographies remember as Saint Columba was a realized being, what we might call enlightened, Christed, fully awake. As a realized being, Saint Columba purified, grounded, and energized the Iona chakra template. Saint Columba was reconfirming the energy integrity and previous blessing of Iona by an even more realized being. The island had been visited and blessed some six centuries earlier by the Christ in his "thought body" and his physically based col-league, Joseph of Arimathea, after they had visited Glastonbury in England and similarly blessed that location.

Saint Columba was fully capable of performing this considerable geomantic task because in terms of his incarnational resume he had done similar things elsewhere. Saint Columba was the same being who had been John the Evangelist, the Greek hero Heracles, the Hawaiian demigod Maui, the Tibetan Buddhist Padmasambhava, and the Celtic mentor of King Arthur, Merlin. In fact, the Merlin association explains much about the esoteric nature of the Iona chakra template, for hidden in this seemingly familiar name is a great secret.

One of Merlin's prime tasks, in whatever incarnational or cultural guise he assumes, is to maintain what is known to the angelic world as the Mer-Line. This is a line of connection direct to the Divine Mother, the Great Sea, *Mer,* the ocean of greater consciousness of Man—the fifty Gates of Binah, in different words. And the whole island of fifty Gates is a sound, a vibration, a Name of God: IOA.

The Mer-Line is the line to the Sea of consciousness, the love that comes to all created beings from the Mother. The Mer-Line is the umbilicus to the Mother—the Mother's Line, if you wish. The Mer-Line is the way by which we can reach more consciousness, more awareness, more love. Put as simply as possible, the chakra template at Iona *is* the Mer-Line. It is both Merlin's line to the Mother, and the energy line through her body to her Face. You walk Merlin's line on Iona through the Mother's landscape body to the Mother.

Jasna Gora, Czestochowa, Poland

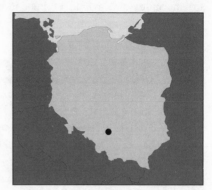

Jasna Gora, which means "Bright Hill" or "Shining Mountain," is the 880-foot-tall hill which is the home of the Shrine of Our Lady of Czestochowa. The Lady is the Virgin Mary, the Queen of all Poland and the spiritual patron of most of the country's five hundred shrines. An estimated five million people come here every year, as either Catholic pilgrims or tourists, to observe a miraculous Black Madonna icon of the Virgin Mary said to be almost two thousand years old.

Every day, an average of fourteen thousand visitors come to the sanctuary, where four times during opening hours a protective silver screen is raised, a trumpet fanfare is offered, and the painting of the Black Madonna can be briefly witnessed.

Czestochowa, an otherwise inconsequential small industrial city of about 260,000 by the Warta River in southern Poland (a ninety-minute drive northwest from Cracow) is nonetheless one of the world's top pilgrimage destinations. It is ranked fifth in popularity, after Banares, Mecca, Lourdes, and Rome. Catholics have held the Czestochowa Black Madonna and its shrine in veneration for more than six hundred years, ever since the icon was brought here from Turkey. Not surprisingly, the site is known as the spiritual capital of Polish Catholicism.

During Mary's feast days on May 3, August 15, and September 8, it is not unusual for multitudes to descend upon Jasna Gora. On Assumption Day (August 15), up to 500,000 people typically arrive in Czestochowa. Since 1711, walking pilgrimages from as far away as Warsaw and thirty-two other Polish towns have been common; anywhere from 50,000 to 100,000 people walk for up to twenty-one days, converging on Czestochowa in time for the Assumption Day ceremonies. During the journey, pilgrims practice an apologetic contrition ritual called *Przepraszam*, in which they ask forgiveness of others for sins, bad behavior, and transgressions, asking forgiveness for all wrongs committed, even of strangers.

The grounds, a little more than two square acres, are part of a fortified, walled citadel built in the late 1300s. The belltower of the fourteenth-century Pauline monastery towers 325 feet above the hill. It can be seen from five miles away. A park surrounds the monastery on three sides, while the fourth side opens into a large square in which pilgrims assemble for major religious ceremonies. The public park extends from this square down the hill to the city, forming both a natural

All spiritual life at Czestochowa's Jasna Gora revolves around the presence of the miraculous icon of the Black Madonna. Prior to the fourteenth century, Czestochowa, said to have been founded by a Slav named Czestoch, was mostly an unremarkable village of horsemen. Then in 1382, a hill in the western end of town was handed over to Pauline monks from Hungary, and they proceeded to build a sanctuary and monastery on what became known as Jasna Gora.

The Pauline monks belonged to the Order of Saint Paul the First Hermit, which had been founded in the early thirteenth century in Hungary by Blessed Eusebius, Canon of Esztergom. The order sought to emulate the hermitic life of Saint Paul of Thebes who is said to have spent ninety years in the desert, living on only bread brought to him by ravens. When he died, his grave was dug by two lions.

During the period between 1367 and 1372, Prince Ladislaus of Opole, regent of the Polish territory, summoned the Pauline monks to Czestochowa and asked them to build a chapel and sanctuary to house a valuable, possibly priceless, icon of the Virgin Mary that the Prince had bought from the city of Belz in the Ukraine. He had found it hanging in a castle, where he learned that its painter had been the Apostle Luke.

The legend of the Black Madonna icon says that Saint Luke painted the image on a cypress (or cedar) tabletop, upon which the Holy Family at Nazareth had eaten and which was taken from the house there. While he was painting it, the Virgin Mary, present as a spiritual being, provided more information about the life and times of Jesus and her. If this story is true, then the wooden planks of the kitchen table from Nazareth would be nearly as venerable as relics of the cross, having been energetically imprinted by the Virgin Mary's physical touch as well as that of Jesus, who is said to have been its carpenter.

The icon had been discovered in Jerusalem by Saint Helena, the mother of Emperor Constantine and an avid collector of relics. In 326 A.D., Saint Helena reportedly brought the icon from Jerusalem to Constantinople (now called Istanbul), where it remained for centuries in a specially built shrine in that family's keeping. When the Saracens attacked the city, the icon was displayed prominently on the city walls and was later credited with having saved Constantinople against the invasion.

The Black Madonna passed into the hands of Charlemagne (742–814 A.D.), King of the Franks and Emperor of the West, who presented it as a wedding present to Prince Leo of Ruthenia in Hungary in 803. It remained at his royal palace until the eleventh century and once again was credited with saving its owner, or protector. (An army attacked Ruthenia, but when the king prayed to the Madonna for assistance, a darkness reportedly descended on the battlefield, and the enemy, confused and frightened, started slaying its own members, and was routed.) The icon continued to be passed along through a series of royal dowries. It remained at the Royal Palace in Belz, near Kiev, in the Ukraine, for 579 years.

In 1382, the icon came to Jasna Gora. Invading Tartars attacked the fortress at Belz, and a Tartar arrow struck the painting, lodging in the Madonna's throat. Prince Ladislaus Opolski, fearing the icon might fall into Tartar hands, slipped out of Belz to hide the painting in the safer district of Opala, his birthplace. On the way, he spent a night in a small wooden church on Jasna Gora in Czestochowa. The next morning, with the painting packed away in the wagon and the Prince ready to depart, the horses refused to move, no matter how much persuasion they received. Prince Ladislaus took this as a heavenly sign that the Black Madonna icon was to remain in Czestochowa. Allegedly, Mary herself appeared before the Prince and told him Czestochowa was to be the new home of her likeness.

A variation on this story has an angel appearing before the Prince in a dream telling him to take the icon to the obscure village of Czestochowa. Prince Ladislaus engaged the Pauline hermits to take responsibility for the icon and to build a monastery on Jasna Gora to house it. By 1386, the monks had completed the construction of their church.

It is intriguing to note that in the ensuing centuries, the attempts by various art restoration experts to paint over and remove the damage to the painting failed; the "wounds" to the Virgin's throat and two subsequent gashes on her cheek kept reappearing on the icon as if as a chilling reminder of the impiety of desecrating a holy relic.

In 1655, the icon was again credited with saving the city of its protectors. At that time, Poland was entirely overrun by the Swedish military, and all cities had capitulated to the invaders except Czestochowa. The Swedes laid siege to the monastery; fortunately, back in 1638, King Ladislaus IV had erected a strong wall and protective bulwark around the monastery, turning the sanctuary into a *Fortalitiurn Marianum,* a Marian fortress.

The monks, armed more with determination and faith than weapons but led by the valiant Father Augustine Kodrecki, remained steadfast, relying on the Virgin Mary to somehow protect their 170 soldiers, twenty noblemen, and seventy monks from three thousand Swedish troops. After forty days, the rest of Poland, believing a miracle had occurred, rallied and drove out the Swedes altogether. This momentous episode was memori-

alized in the historical novel *The Deluge* (1886) by Henryk Sienkiewicz, a prolific Polish writer who won the Nobel Prize in Literature in 1905.

From that time forward, Mary, the Lady of Czestochowa, became the symbol of Polish national unity; she was crowned Queen of Poland, and Casimir, the King of Poland, formally placed the country under the protection of the Blessed Mother. Most of the numerous miracles attributed to the Lady of Czestochowa, besides individual healings of the sick and infirm who have prayed before the icon, have been of a collective nature and on a public scale.

In 1716, Pope Clement XI signed the Act of Incoronation, in which a crown was officially set upon the top of the icon, and on September 8, 1717, some 200,000 attended the official ceremony at Czestochowa.

In 1843, Tsar Nicholas I of Russia tried to shut down the monastery, forbidding pilgrimages, branding Our Lady "the biggest revolutionary of them all."

In 1919, the newly organized Soviet Russian Red Army was preparing to invade Poland. Polish priests carried the Blessed Sacrament in procession and people all over Poland prayed to Our Lady of Czestochowa for intercession; thousands journeyed in person to Czestochowa to pray to Our Lady. On September 15, 1920, the Virgin Mary is credited with having appeared as an apparition above the River Vistula in Warsaw and thereby dispersing the Russian soldiers intent on invading the city. "The Miracle of the Vistula" preserved Polish independence.

In 1925, Pope Pius XI acknowledged the title of Mary as "Queen of Poland," and set aside May 3 as her official feast day. During World War II, the Nazis occupying Poland forbade the annual pilgrimage to Czestochowa, but on September 8, 1946, 1.5 million Poles participated in the rededication of Poland to the Immaculate Heart of Mary at Jasna Gora. In 1979, Pope John Paul II (the

Polish pope) prayed before the Black Madonna in his first of several visits to Czestochowa.

Critics argue that the painting, though it may be venerable, is not nearly as old as its advocates contend. The skeptics contend that it was probably painted sometime in the sixth to ninth centuries, based on a Byzantine prototype venerated in Contantinople and known as the *Hodegetria,* "The One Who Leads the Way." The original *Hodegetri* was destroyed in 1453, but it had been widely copied, and in its day was one of the most widely respected images of the Madonna and child. The Black Madonna at Jasna Gora, the critics argue, must have been one of those copies.

The painting itself is a portrait of the Madonna and the infant Jesus. She holds Jesus in her left arm, and he holds a Bible in his hands. The image is set in a gold frame decorated with hundreds of gems. The Virgin has a pensive expression, as if weighted in sorrow, and her eyes directly face the viewer so that people tend to find themselves immersed in her eyes. Mary has a darkened, black face, which art critics tend to explain away as the result of prolonged exposure to soot and fires, or as the style of Byzantine painting.

Historical research, however, reveals a long-standing cult of the Black Virgin throughout Europe. The appearance of a Black Madonna, as icon or statuary, even as visionary apparition, was far more common and widespread during the medieval period (especially the twelfth century) than church historians would like the public to know. It turns out that at least five hundred of the existing images of the Virgin Mary depict her with a black face or dark skin. By the mid-sixteenth century there were 190 statuettes of the Black Virgin in France alone.

Black Virgins, explains Ean Begg in his *The Cult of the Black Virgin,* harken back to an ancient tradition of pre-Christian, prepatriarchal chthonic goddesses who were regarded as the embodiment of the feminine principle, the way of Nature, death, and transformation, Wisdom as Blackness, and blackness as the heart of matter. "The Black Virgins are often associated with esoteric teaching and schools of initiation." Begg further comments that Black Virgins are a symbol of "the dark latency of our own essential nature, that which we were always meant to be" and "a still-living archetypal image that lies at the heart of our civilization and has a message for us."[480]

MYSTICS AND TOURISTS

The American writer China Galland gives us a firsthand glimpse into the emotional and physical realities of the Czestochowa pilgrimage in her *Longing for Darkness.* She made the pilgrimage from Warsaw in the 1980s, when Poland was still under Soviet Communist control. The numerous roadside shrines to the Black Madonna reminded her of the Buddist *chortens* (small temples or chapels, similar to Hindu stupas, in which the five elements are symbolized by architectural features) and temples she had observed in India and Nepal along comparable pilgrimage routes. People were singing, seemingly all day long as they walked, she said, as nearly one million people were out walking on roads all over Poland. Galland realized that *Przepraszam* means you have to forgive yourself as well.

Poland is "a river of Mary, fed by hidden springs," some capped off or dammed up long ago, others swollen and ready to flood, still others running strong underground, she wrote. All are continuously "feeding and swelling this stream of the Mother from which I could not get enough to drink." To her, the goal of the pilgrimage was not the Christ, but the body of Mary, "her mysterious, dark, elusive, multifaceted form."

When Galland finally stood before the Black Madonna, she found the image—or the living presence of the Virgin in her "body" of the icon, according to Byzantine tradition—mysterious, stunning, and remote, and she felt initially unmoved by it. "I cannot penetrate the secret of her face," Galland said, even though she wanted to devour her, incorporate Mary into her being. "My eyes are teeth and I am chewing up her image, ingesting her . . . as a wafer in communion." She wanted to swallow the Virgin whole.[481]

GEOMANTIC

Dome; Ray Master Sanctuary; Tree of Life; Golden Pillars; Palladium.

DOME: Jasna Gora is rightly named the Bright Hill for it is topped by a dome representing the star Deneb. One of the greatest supergiant stars known to astronomers, Deneb, sixteen hundred light years from Earth, is equaled only by Rigel in Orion among first-magnitude stars. Its luminosity has been computed at sixty thousand times that of our Sun, its mass is twenty-five times that of the solar mass, and its diameter about sixty times greater than our Sun's. Jasna Gora—the Bright Hill of Cygnus indeed.

Deneb is the first-magnitude alpha star in the constellation Cygnus, the Swan; its full name comes from the Arabic, where it is called *Al Dhanab al Dajajah,* which means "the Hen's Tail." Deneb, the nineteenth brightest star in our galaxy, is on the swan's tail.

Deneb was also called *Al Ridf,* meaning "The Hindmost," another allusion to its position on the swan's tail. Curiously, one of the Swedish General Muller's scathing and otherwise puzzling remarks about the ragtag Polish defenders of Jasna Gora during his seventeenth-century attack was that it was a "henhouse." In the Western world, Deneb has been called the Star of the Cross, particularly during the Christmas season, when it is seen as the Northern Cross.

During the seventeenth century, astronomers started to see the eight principal stars in Cygnus as forming a cross, which they called *Christi Crux* or the "Cross of Calvary," from which the more popular equivalent constellation name Northern Cross evolved. This attribution is appropriate in light of the sorrowful expression on the Black Madonna's face as she looks forward into time and beholds the crucifixion of her son.

Among various antique astronomers, the constellation of Cygnus was described as a flying eagle, hen, partridge, pigeon, or a star-bird called *Urakhyga* by the Babylonians. Cygnus, with fourteen attributed stars, is called the *Ornis,* the Great Bird, or "swan" from the Greek *kyknos.* Later Roman names included *Ales* and *Avis,* for "bird," *Olor* for "swan," and *Myrtilus,* for the bird of Venus.

Greek myths say that Zeus was enamored of Nemesis and transformed himself into a swan so he could court and seduce her, as she had already assumed a swan form to protect her virginity. The myths also relate, somewhat confusingly, that Zeus sought Nemesis in her human female form for protection, nestling in her lap in his swan form, thereby impregnating her. Nemesis bore an egg of her union with Zeus, and passed it on to Leda; from the egg was born the beautiful Helen, later of Troy.

RAY MASTER SANCTUARY: It is, of course, contrary to Catholic theological dogma to say this, but every place known for Marian apparitions or Marian devotion is likely to entail a Ray Master Sanctuary. This is particularly evident at Lourdes in France, a prominent Marian apparition site. What we culturally and iconographically describe as the Virgin Mary is a composite feminine image of up to four Ray Masters.

There is, of course, the Virgin Mary, young, pure, virginal, seemingly of an adolescent age as Bernadette described her. There is also Kwan Yin (or Tara), known to Buddhists around the world as the ultimate protectress, benign, loving, a mature mother figure. There is Durga, the fierce warrioress of Hindu myth; and Kali, the Black One, the crone and death figure, also from Hindu iconography. All four are Ray Masters of the Great Bear in one of their many guises. Their commission is to represent the four faces of the Divine Mother: virgin, mother, warrioress, and crone.

The essential energy at Jasna Gora is a rich bright blue. Its spiritual intent is to create a radiant presence, a continuous flow of abundant Marian grace. Mary's inner plane temple at Jasna Gora can be conceived as a baptismal font the size of the hill. The "water" in the font represents Her Grace, her spiritual essence as a Ray Master, Mother of God, Queen of Poland, which is continuously flowing like the purest of waters down Jasna Gora into Czestochowa. This site is remarkably unpolluted and unadulterated, and even today its original geomantic intention functions intact and wonderfully well.

The icon's role, in addition to being a focus for worship and veneration, is as an aperture for the Marian presence to enter Jasna Gora. As China Galland rightly observed, it is as if one wants to immerse oneself in the eyes of the Black Madonna, as if the living presence of Mary somehow passes through those eyes into the soul of the observer. The Black Madonna icon marks the spot for the spiritual focus of pilgrims at Jasna Gora; it defines the type of spiritual energy present and it shows you where to focus your attention. The icon is like a conductor for the Marian presence, a portal for Our Lady.

Some Marian sites gain their reputation (and have their identity as a Marian site validated) by an actual apparition. The icon was brought to Jasna Gora, evidently under divine decree, in lieu of an actual Marian apparition. This is even better: Our Lady of Czestochowa is perpetually revealing her apparitional form, four times every day, when her icon is unveiled and her eyes are allowed to transmit her actual presence behind the scenes—which is to say, just behind the façade of the physical world on the hill.

TREE OF LIFE: The unending waters of Mary's grace flow down Jasna Gora into the city and the rest of Poland. This flow is facilitated by the presence of a Tree of Life template on the hillside, passing from the monastery through the parkland that surrounds it. Iconographically, it is a template of the Four Worlds of existence, and the flow of divine grace and light from the highest sphere into the physical world, like a majestic four-tiered fountain of light.

If you start in Czestochowa, slowly, ritually, even prayerfully ascending Jasna Gora through the template of the Four Worlds and forty spheres of light can be a powerful preparatory, even penitential, exercise, getting you ready, cleansed, purified within, focused, receptive, for the receipt of grace from the Marian baptismal font. If you start at the top of the Tree at Jasna Gora, you can have the experience of bearing the grace of Our Lady purposefully, systematically, down through the Four Worlds into our everyday waking world. In either case, you are an emissary for the Queen of Heaven on her Bright Hill.

GOLDEN PILLARS: A geomantic feature surrounding the baptismal font on Jasna Gora and an energy factor that may have aided Prior Kordecki in his successful resistance to the Swedish siege is a nimbus of Golden Pillars. The Greeks called these pillars *Spartoi*, the Earth-sown Men, who grew out of dragon's teeth planted in the soil at Thebes after the hero Cadmus "killed" the dragon of Ares.

These Sown Men are actually golden cylinders from the Celestial City of Shambhala, placed here to protect and evangelize what occurs within Mary's sanctuary at Jasna Gora. Seen close up, when you penetrate their energy field a bit, each pillar now seems like a giant human face—more than human, part human, part angelic. The faces touch at the sides, forming a towering matrix around the Marian baptismal font at Jasna Gora—a unified gaze, an awake and aware sentinel looking in fifty-four directions at once.

These Golden Pillars or divine faces are not unique to Jasna Gora; there are over 200,000 of them around the planet. They were brought through from Shambhala into a dimension closer to the physical as a preparation for the future.

PALLADIUM: The Golden Pillars preserve the geomantic integrity not only of the Marian temple, but also of a Palladium set like a pearl of inestimable price in the center of the baptismal font. A Palladium is a miniature White Head, which is to say, a representation of what the Jewish Qabalists call the Ancient of Days.

Thus the inner mystery of Our Lady of Czestochowa is that once you have been bathed in her waters of Grace in the Ray Master Sanctuary at Jasna Gora, you have the possibility of a more arcane initiation. You can meet Her Father, or at last a representation of the Supreme Being in the form of the White Head whose gaze is omnipresent and deeply penetrating. Baptism in the Marian waters opens your spiritual cognition to the rarified vision or experience of the Supreme Being.

It gives us new insight into some of the Virgin Mary's epithets such as *Theotokos*, meaning "God-bearer," and *Virgo Sapientissima*, for "Throne of Wisdom." Based on the geomantic temple structure at Jasna Gora, Mary could be understood here not only as the obvious bearer of God in the form of mother of the infant Jesus, but also as the bearer of the supplicant *to* God, as the Throne of Wisdom upon which one ascends to God.

Lourdes, France

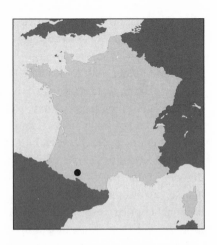

PHYSICAL DESCRIPTION

One of Europe's major Christian pilgrimage sites, Lourdes is a small town of about eighteen thousand situated in the deep southwest of France, up against the Pyrenees that divide France from Spain. Lourdes of course is internationally renowned for its healing waters and its atmosphere of sanctity and spiritual presence, originally imparted in the 1850s by a series of apparitions of the Virgin Mary to a teenage girl named Bernadette Soubirous.

A short distance from the city itself stands a huge gleaming-white steeple-spired basilica that seats twenty thousand. Below this in the cliff face is the Grotto of Massabielle, source of the waters and site of the apparitions. Nearby flows the River Gave. Lourdes, sitting at an elevation of 1,158 feet amidst a rugged landscape, is bounded by three large mountains, the Beout, Petit Jer, and Grand Jer, ranging in height from 2,400 to 3,000 feet.

Lourdes' geographical importance is secured by the fact that seven different valleys of the Lavedan system intersect there, making it a natural disembarkation point for travelers and pilgrims on their way to key Christian sites in Spain, including Montserrat and Santiago de Compostela. This topographical significance may account for the placement of the medieval fortress in central Lourdes as the traditional seat of the counts of Bigorre, once a considerable political force in this region. Even so, in the early 1850s, Lourdes' population was only about 4,100 people.

The basilica sits at the base of Montagne des Espelugues, about a half-mile east of the center of Lourdes. The original church, called the Basilica of the Rosary, was built in 1876, but eventually proved too small for the vast numbers of pilgrims seeking religious services; in 1958, an underground church of pre-stressed concrete replaced it. The flow of pilgrims seeking spiritual solace or physical healing has been steadily burgeoning since the 1860s, when word of Bernadette Soubirous' Marian apparitions circulated throughout Europe.

HISTORY AND ARCHEOLOGY

It appears—based on artifacts such as flint axes, cut stones, and bones discovered in the caves in Montagne des Espelugues—that Lourdes was occupied early, possibly even before the successive advents of the Gauls, Romans, Barbarians, and Moors who fortified the massive rock upon which the core of Lourdes stands.

There is some evidence that the Marian association with Lourdes predates the nineteenth-century visions of Bernadette Soubirous. In 778 A.D., when Charlemagne was attacking the fortified castle of Lourdes, occupied by the Saracen Mirat and his Moors, for a long time the castle remained impervious, until an eagle flew over and dropped a trout at the feet of Mirat, quite considerably nonplussing the battle captain. The Moor intended to present the fish to Charlemagne to prove the Saracens still had food to survive the siege, but the Bishop of Puy-en-Velay, companion to Charlemagne, had an even cleverer idea.

He suggested to Mirat that he surrender to the Queen of the Sky rather than to Charlemagne. Another version of the story says it was to "a sovereign lady," the Virgin of Puy-en-Velay. Mirat bought the proposition, surrendered his arms at the feet of the Black Virgin of Puy, and was baptized. The story goes that on that day he took the name Lorus, which then was given to the town and, presumably, still later became Lourdes. Queen of the Sky, Virgin, Black Virgin—obviously the Virgin Mary was the reference. Subsequent armorial bearings for Lourdes commemorated this baptism by depicting a castle over which flies an eagle with a trout in its beak, accompanied by the motto Sous l'egide de Marie, which means "under Mary's protection."

The story may be apocryphal, of course. It is believed that during the medieval period Lourdes was actually called Mirambel, from the Provençal Mirabeau, which signified "good lookout," as reflected in the castle's commanding position in the valley.[482]

During the Hundred Years' War, the French recaptured this region from the British after an eighteenth-month siege in 1406. From the seventeenth century until early in the nineteenth century, the fortress was used as a state prison. Then in 1858, Lourdes' role as a regional military and state stronghold ended, and its new role as a spiritual center began.

Lourdes' ascent to world fame began on February 11, 1858, when fourteen-year-old Bernadette Soubirous had the first of eighteen visions of a "lady in white" in the Grotto of Massabielle. Initially, Bernadette called the apparition Aquero, which is the local patois for "That one." Over the course of the apparitions, which lasted until July 26, Bernadette learned that the celestial personage was the Virgin Mary, who spoke with Bernadette during many of her brief appearances.

In Bernadette's own words, first she heard "a great noise like the sound of a storm" near the Grotto, then a single bush moving as if it were blown by a strong wind, then "out of the interior of the grotto a golden-colored cloud" appeared, followed by "a Lady, young and beautiful, exceedingly beautiful, the like of whom I had never seen before." Bernadette said the Lady seemed about seventeen years in age, clad in a white robe with a blue ribbon about the waist; her feet were bare and she held in her right hand a Rosary of white beads on a chain of gold.[483]

The Grotto of Massabielle was, seemingly, a most unlikely place for a divine manifestation to take place, yet it did have a reputation for uncanny energies. The name derives from the French masse vielle, for "old mass," or perhaps from the Latin, massa vetula for "little old mound." The people of Lourdes used it as a pig sty. Every day the local porcatier would round up the town's 150 pigs and herd them down to the banks of the River Gave and the Grotto. The place was generally described as filthy, covered in blood and pig hair, and local custom had it that when you wanted to insult somebody's upbringing, you said: "He must have been educated at the banks of the Massabielle."

Yet the locals often attributed "devilish spells" and harmful presences to the Grotto, and would cross themselves as a form of protection when passing by. A woodcutter once reported hearing "plaintive cries and groans of someone in great suffering" issuing from the cave. However, there were as many "prophecies of divine visitation" associated with Massabielle as there were rumors of evil. "People could remember old testimony of dying priests who predicted something supernatural coming from the wood, while still others cited grandfathers who predicted divine apparitions."[484]

The Grotto itself is the outermost porch of an extensive branching cavern that extends deep into the mountain. In the front, the site of the apparition, its height is irregular, part of its base is filled with water, and it is framed by an oval niche in which, at the time of the visitation, a single rose bush stood. The Grotto is "a hole in the chalky cliff, twenty paces in breadth, twelve in depth, not unlike a baker's oven," wrote Franz Werfel in his acclaimed novel of the Lourdes story, *The Song of Bernadette*, which became the basis for the movie of the same name.

The Grotto was bare, damp, and filled with rubble from the River Gave, which occasionally flooded it. "One has almost the impression that this gate or Gothic window had been hewn into the rock aforetime by the hands of primitive men." The Grotto was in fact one of several in Montagne des Espelugues, which could well be described as the Mountain of Grottoes, Werfel said, "a low, insignificant ridge, this mount of holes or caverns."[485]

During Bernadette's ninth vision, the Lady in White revealed to her an underground spring at Massabielle, which proved to have healing powers and today is the focus of wished-for cures. The Lady had asked Bernadette to bathe and drink in the fountain, but as there was then no visible water, she dug in the dirt with her hands until water bubbled up. That spring is now the source of a continuous flow of fifteen thousand gallons of water daily, much of which is bottled and taken away by pilgrims as holy water.

The Grotto, basilica, and the other churches and shrines up the hill today comprise a specially designated section of Lourdes called the Domain of Our Lady. Some say the Domain is a bit over-packed. One commentator somewhat archly commented that the spire of the basilica rides "over what is not so much a hill-church, as more precisely a church-hill—since the entire bluff of Massabielle has been hollowed out, stuffed with and obliterated by three churches, one on top of the other."[486]

People started to flock to Lourdes after January 18, 1862, when the Bishop of Tarbes (the diocese that included Lourdes) authorized the cult of Bernadette at Lourdes, which was the Church's formal approval of the validity of the eighteen apparitions, a validation it rarely bestows. The Church decreed that the apparitions "really appeared" and that "the faithful are justified in believing this to be certain." This was good because one of the Lady's spoken messages to Bernadette was that she wished to have a chapel built at Massabielle, adding "I wish people to come here in procession."

Between 1864 and 1872, Lourdes functioned mostly as a regional pilgrimage destination, drawing an estimated thirty thousand people annually. After 1873, the Grotto gained a reputation for producing cures, and after that, Lourdes' reputation expanded beyond France to the world at large. A significant number of pilgrims come for the possibility of miraculous healing of debilitating illness and disability. In 1875, some fifty *malades* joined the pilgrimage. By 1880, seven trains departed Paris in one season, bearing 4,500 pilgrims, including seven hundred who were sick and hoping for cures.

As of the year 2000, an estimated thirty thousand sick or disabled people a year were coming to Lourdes in the hope of healing, while in 1998, after twelve years of official medical investigation, Lourdes' sixty-sixth miraculous cure was validated (altogether, some five thousand "inexplicable" cures have been documented at Lourdes). A man suffering from advanced multiple sclerosis, wheelchair bound for the previous fifteen years, sustained a sudden and lasting cure during his pilgrimage to Lourdes. The Archbishop of Angouleme, of the man's hometown in France, declared: "This deliverance can be seen as a personal gift from God."[487]

Many who visit Lourdes, even those who find the huge crowds, excessive chanting, and Catholic religious services a bit much, feel Lourdes' "celebrated service to the sick and the special mercy of Mary's intercession." Many of Lourdes' public religious functions, such as the Eucharistic processions and ritual bathing in the Grotto waters, are organized to facilitate the participation of the sick and disabled. Every afternoon there is the Procession of the Sacrament from the Grotto up to the basilica; in the evening there is the Candlelit Procession that takes the same route.

Ruth Harris, an Oxford University scholar, found the "passionate Marianism and concrete monumentalism" of the shrines "repugnant," and said that at times Lourdes, with its pious commerce in plastic Virgins "seemed to represent little more than kitsch for the Catholic masses." Even so, Harris was moved, impressed, even touched, by Lourdes, particularly its acknowledgment of the "centrality of pain and suffering."[488]

In 1908, more than 1.5 million people flocked to Lourdes to celebrate the fiftieth anniversary of the apparitions. In 1950, when the Catholic Church declared that the Assumption of the Virgin was an official dogma, that same number came. But by the 1990s, the yearly total for visitors had jumped to an estimated five million, coming from countries all over the world, even on specially designed package tours. A 1978 survey showed that pilgrims came from 111 different countries, with women accounting for sixty-nine percent of the visitors, and that since 1860, some two hundred million people have visited Lourdes.

MYSTICS AND TOURISTS

One major nineteenth-century literary document about Lourdes was by Emile Zola (1840–1902), the French social activist and novelist. He went to Lourdes expecting to dismiss it as a miracle show and theater for fairy tales, but in his first visit in September 1891 he formed a surprisingly different impression.

He described Lourdes as a "town of faith, born of the hallucination" of a teenager, as a "mystical city in the century of skepticism." Then he commented: "The spectacle gripped me to such an extent that, having left for Tarbes, I spent two entire nights writing about Lourdes."[489] Zola's subsequent novel, *Lourdes,* structured around the five days of the national pilgrimage to Lourdes but not entirely flattering to Lourdes (he made it clear he thought the waters unhygienic), was a huge success and furthered the city's international reputation.

Lourdes, comments Rev. Msgr. Kevin Wallin of Bridgeport, Connecticut, provides "a sense of peace, reconciliation, and healing" for the general pilgrim, and "encouragement, solace, and hope" for those with illness or physical handicaps. "Lourdes is in fact a source of far greater and more frequent spiritual renewal and strengthening than the occasional supernatural cure," he says. A visit to Lourdes enables one to "reflect upon the ongoing, saving activity of God" and to have one's "faith deepened, something which happens without you realizing it."[490]

An Irish writer visiting Lourdes as part of a pilgrimage to Catholic sites in France found the atmosphere less sanguine. "But there was something about Lourdes itself which made me feel deeply apprehensive." She felt "dread" at the thought of descending to the Grotto because "there seemed to be this cold, grey dark over it all, despite the vast, white statues; that kind of harsh, screaming white, that is almost as bad as chalk slipping on a blackboard." When she did finally climb down to the Grotto, she was "perplexed and miserable at my own chilling dismay and deep unease." But this visitor did marvel at "the extraordinary force of simple, accumulated pressure" of millions of hands that wore down the stone surfaces on the way to the Grotto.[491]

That sense of accumulated pressure has another nuance that enables Lourdes to transcend commercial vulgarity, comments another writer. "The hopes and faith of millions of pilgrims continually spiritualize the atmosphere, especially around the Grotto—the shrine's sacred heart."[492] In other words, the continuous projection of human aspiration and spirituality upon the Grotto and its statue of the Virgin Mary has the effect of amplifying "the field of holiness" that surrounds Lourdes. "This field then attracts more pilgrims who in turn contribute to the further empowerment of the field."[493]

Even so, many find it remarkable that this field of holiness could be at Lourdes in the first place. A French nightclub owner commented: "The most remarkable thing about Lourdes is that a little girl who *knew* so little, could convince others of something so extraordinary, and revolutionize the life of a town in one of the most static parts of France."[494]

Even cynics seem to be converted at Lourdes. "You can't help but be moved by the courage, by the caring, sharing and joy you witness here. I'm not dying, I'm not disabled, but I had a miracle experience too somewhere near that Grotto. I lost a great big chunk of cynicism."[495]

GEOMANTIC

Dome Cap; Ray Master Sanctuary.

DOME CAP: Lourdes is energized by a dome cap emanating from the dome over Grand Jer Mountain, whose star affiliation is delta Boötes, the constellation known as the Shepherd or Bear-Driver. The delta star in Boötes (140 light years from Earth, a seventh-magnitude star), sits on the figure's right shoulder but does not have a name in Western or Arabic astronomy. In China, it was part of *Tseih Kung,* the Seven Princes. (Gamma Boötes, called Seginus, which sits on the Shepherd's left shoulder, enters the Earth through the dome at the Hill of Tara in Ireland.)

The important point to keep in mind about the Bear-Driver is the reference to Ursa Major, the Great Bear, because it is the home of the fourteen Ray Masters, the gods of Mount Olympus. The relevance of this will be made clear shortly.

The dome cap covers all of Lourdes and is about two miles wide, but its center is over Montagne des Espelugues. Energetically, the entire dome-capped area is permeated with the presence of the Virgin Mary, which gives the ethers a rich navy-blue cast. There is no other function to this dome cap than to serve as the energetic foundation for the Marian apparition; in effect, this site is preeminently a site for the manifestation of Mary and for the distribution of her consciousness. One could say that until 1858, the Montagne des Espelugues operated at only a minimal level, because its prime operation was reserved for the decades after the advent of Mary at Massabielle.

RAY MASTER SANCTUARY: Lourdes is an Earth node dedicated to the transmission of the presence and consciousness of the Virgin Mary. It is equally a Marian apparition site and a Ray Master Sanctuary; the Marian application simply identifies the specialty of this particular Ray Master.

From Lourdes the Marian transmission works backward to the dome at Grand Jer, and then through that dome's network of forty-seven other dome caps, and its connections, through the dome lines and other energy structures, into the rest of France. Yet one might ask, why not have the Marian transmission happen through the dome at Grand Jer? The latter is clearly a bigger, more majestic site, more befitting the spiritual majesty of the event.

Yes, but it is a tall, rugged mountain, certainly not a practical destination for millions of pilgrims, many of whom are handicapped. The township of Lourdes is far better equipped to accommodate pilgrims, so the Marian impulse works through a dome cap rather than the dome. Anyway the size of the transmitting node is not important in this kind of activity.

The continuously flowing spring at Massabielle is central to the function of this Marian site because the transmission of the Marian impulse comes through the water. One of Mary's instructions to Bernadette was to bathe and drink in the spring; she didn't say to expect to be healed by doing this, although it can certainly happen. The water carries the Marian vibration so that it can affect pilgrims on a cellular level—it's a form of celestial homeopathy, if you will.

Through consuming the holy water, the millions who come to Lourdes bring Mary into their physical bodies, facilitating a remarkable molecular alchemy from within. It is an intriguing variation on the classical idea of the sacramental host. Healings, remissions, and cures happen to the extent that individuals are spiritually prepared to allow themselves to drop inner resistances and complexes that exist in opposition to that possibility. Healings happen to the extent that a person is able to re-create Massabielle and its grotto within himself or herself, to the degree that he or she can allow the Marian-energized water to exert alchemical changes within the physical and emotional constitution.

Bernadette Soubirous died at age thirty-five and did not live long enough to see the global effect her spiritual work at Masabielle had produced. Her role was to birth the site, to act as a human lightning rod for the grounding of the Marian energy at this predesignated Marian site. In a sense, perhaps from the viewpoint of her soul, Bernadette was a geomancer in this act of activating a landscape site in cooperation with Ray Masters from the Great Bear, who oversee this work.

Somebody had to recognize, identify, and interact with the celestial personage at Massabielle so as to inaugurate Mary's presence there. Obviously, spiritual beings can manifest anywhere they choose on Earth, and at any time they wish, but it does not benefit humans unless humans voluntarily participate in these manifestations. We validate them through our own efforts, clairvoyance, and in Bernadette's case, considerable personal sacrifice. She had to endure many painful months of public and clerical disbelief of her visions before they were finally accepted and she was no longer regarded as a hallucinating child.

Since being grounded at Massabielle in 1858, the Marian presence there has remained fresh and vivid, available to clairvoyant observation. It doesn't matter that she hasn't "returned" to Massabielle either; metaphysically, she never left. She is always appearing in the Grotto. There may be more to the Marian presence than the Virgin Mary alone, however.

This brings us into potentially treacherous theological territory. The Marian presence is not singular but fourfold. Four celestial personages comprise the Marian apparition at Lourdes (and the other Marian sites), and only one name of these four is recognized by conventionally minded Christians.

There is, of course, the Virgin Mary—young, pure, virginal, seemingly of an adolescent age, as Bernadette described her. There is also Kwan Yin, to Buddhists around the world the ultimate protectress, benign, loving, a mature mother figure. There is Durga, the fierce warrioress of Hindu myth; and Kali, the Black One, the crone and death figure, also from Hindu iconography. All four figures are Ray Masters of the Great Bear in one of their many guises. Their commission is to represent the four faces of the Divine Mother: virgin, mother, warrioress, and crone.

From one perspective, Christian belief hints at three members of this quartet in the account of the three Marys surrounding Jesus: Mary Magdalene (the Ray Master Lady Nada and the Greek Aphrodite); Jesus' mother Mary (Kwan Yin, the Ray Master known as Lady Portia); and the Mary of Cleophas (Durga and the Greek goddess Artemis). Kali does not seem to have representation in the Christian account other than perhaps as the face of death Jesus would have encountered during the Crucifixion.

If you like, conceive of the Marian presence as a living holographic image on a slowly revolving pedestal; with each quarter turn, the face changes, teenager to warrioress to mother to hag. The four faces together yield a vision of an even more exalted presence: the Divine Mother, or Hera, Queen of Heaven, consort to Zeus, king of the gods. It is somewhat reductionist to conceive of the Virgin Mary as solely the once biological mother of Jesus who was subsequently assumed into Heaven. Yet her relationship to Jesus, who is here construed as yet another Ray Master who for three years voluntarily incarnated the Christ, is apt.

Let's put Lourdes in a global context. Obviously it is not the only Marian apparition site on the Earth. There are at least one hundred, and more are added to the list every year, whether or not officially validated by the Catholic Church. It's helpful to assume there is a plan behind the growing trend of Marian visitations at geomantic sites around the planet. Granting this assumption, perhaps the intent is to have the totality of Marian sites generate a collective effect or serve a single purpose.

Perhaps this image will help suggest the idea: picture the blue-white Earth from a distance in space; as it slowly rotates, notice there are dozens of navy-bluish domed areas in which a feminine-seeming spiritual figure stands with arms outstretched as if about to receive something—perhaps an infant?

What are these multiple Marys waiting so expectantly for? Again we need to briefly delve into theology. Ever since the original incarnation of the Christ through Jesus some two thousand years ago, most Christians have been waiting for the return, popularly known as the Second Coming. Some take this literally, while others see it more subtly.

The Austrian spiritual scientist and clairvoyant Rudolf Steiner, for example, said that in fact the Christ had so permeated the Earth's etheric field that to speak of a Second Coming was redundant. The Christ energy had never left the Earth. What would come and might seem like a Second Coming would be the gradual permeation of the Earth's physical reality and the everyday waking state of consciousness of humans living on Earth of the living Christ presence already enveloping the planet. In this view, Steiner conceived of the Christ as more of a cosmic fact, as a penultimate spiritual presence in the universe that in fact affects many planets, and not as the holy figure of a single theology.[496]

Given these assumptions, we might see the multiple Marian sites as part of a global geomantic preparation for this gradual descent of the already-present Christ essence from the Earth's subtle spheres. Marian sites around the Earth have been coming "on line" for the last fifteen hundred years or so, one by one, as part of a global geomantic *preparation* for a larger event.

The activation of Marian sites has been calibrated in concert with the possibilities of human consciousness to assimilate the new energies and spiritual implications of this global process. As we move further into the twenty-first century, most likely this preparation will pick up its pace and more Marian sites will be grounded in a shorter time than in the last fifteen hundred years.[497]

Lourdes, unarguably an exceptional site of high spirituality and vision, is still best appreciated in the context of *all* of the Earth's Marian apparition sites. As in the case of the Earth's other geomantic features—domes, eggs, zodiacs—many features are replicated many times over to make it easier for the greatest number of people to have access to these energies without having to travel great distances. Who knows how many more Marian seeds have been planted around the Earth awaiting the time of their awakening by pure souls like Bernadette Soubirous?

Lourdes is one of many sites in a concerted effort to prepare the Earth, through its geomantic network, for a significant change in thought—a *metanoia*, to use the classical theological term—precipitated, consummated, and validated by the gradual descent into everyday awareness of the Second Coming of Christ. The many Marian sites around the Earth are like a net of mothers, fishing for the Christ infant in the etheric seas that surround the planet, their hands raised in readiness.[498]

Machu Picchu, Peru

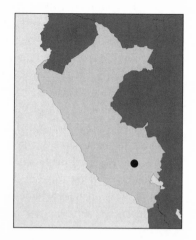

Along with a few other sites, such as the Pyramids of Giza, Easter Island, and Stonehenge, the abandoned Andean city of Machu Picchu is today nearly synonymous for most people with the concept of a sacred site. During the dry-season months of June to September, up to one thousand tourists visit the site every day, taking the three-hour, forty-mile train ride from Cusco, the nearest city to this presumed former Incan capital, popularly dubbed the "Lost City of the Inca."

The archeological ruin, the country's leading tourist attraction, is located in southern Peru, 310 miles southeast of the capital, Lima. Machu Picchu was once thought to be the legendary Vilcabamba, the last stronghold of the Inca. That was the Spanish name, but for the Inca, Manco Inca's last retreat was known as *Willkapanpa*, from *willka* (sacred) and *panpa* (plain).

The site's name means "Old Mountain" in the Quechua language, derived from *machu* (old or ancient) and *picchu* (peak or mountain). The Old Mountain, towering enigmatically at over eight thousand feet, is part of the Vilcabamba batholith, the geological name for a white-gray granite outcropping that's 250 million years old and runs for 150 miles in this part of Peru.

More specifically, Machu Picchu sits in a topographical saddle at the northern end of a huge twenty-mile-long razorback ridge that descends from Salcantay, the most venerated *Apu* (sacred mountain site) west of Cusco. On one end stands Wayna Picchu—"like an exclamation point, as a dramatic ending to the ridge."[499] Partway down the north face of Wayna Picchu, accessed by an Inca stairway, is the Temple of the Moon inside a cavern.

Machu Picchu is surrounded on three sides by a gorge a half-mile deep through which the Urabamba River flows, as if snaking around the sacred center, and on the fourth by a mountain ridge.

Machu Picchu was the destination of the famous Inca Trail which followed the Urabamba gorge for about fifty kilometers. This trail branched off from a longer Inca walker's "highway" at *Qoriwayrachina* (Gold Sifter), crossed the river at *Rio Cusichaca* (Bridge of Joy), and headed southwest up the valley to Machu Picchu. Other ancient "roads" linked the sacred city to minor settlements near Cusco, and there were hundreds of Inca walking paths, but only one Inca Trail. If the Inca Trail ended at Machu Picchu, perhaps there is something to the alternate name sometimes remembered for this site: *Picchu Wanakauri*, which means "mountain of origin."[500]

"The Incas wanted those who walked this way to reel in awe as they crested the passes and rounded the corners." The trail was a pilgrim's route, intended to be experienced as "a dramatic narrative," whose "stunning finale" was Machu Picchu "shining on its stone isthmus" between two formidable peaks.[501]

Although tens of thousands of visitors hike the Inca Trail every year (sixty-six thousand in 1998) and it is now the most popular hike on the continent, you have to negotiate three passes at twelve thousand feet, so it is not an outing undertaken lightly and without preparation. Starting in the year 2000, the Peruvian government set a daily limit of five hundred hikers for this twenty-mile route to help conserve the fragile ecosystem, which is being hammered by the constant overcrowding of the trail and erosion.

Since 1981, the Machu Picchu, an 80,535-acre mountain preserve, has been registered as a Historic National Sanctuary and is protected by the Peruvian government. In 1983, UNESCO listed it as both a cultural and natural World Heritage Site, making it the second of only two such in the Western Hemisphere. "Machu Picchu was probably the most amazing urban creation of the Inca Empire at its height, with its giant walls, terraces and ramps, which appear as though they have been cut naturally in the continuous rock escarpments."[502]

Further, some of the building blocks weigh fifty tons or more and are so finely sculpted and fitted together with mortarless joints that you could not slip even a thin knife blade between them.

Since 1999, however, plans have been in place to build a high-capacity cable car linked to a high-speed railway and a six-story hotel that could increase the tourist load on Machu Picchu by many times. Currently some 700,000 people come here every year, but by 2005, the National Institute of Culture for Peru would like that number to climb to two million.

Maybe increased tourism at Machu Picchu is not a good idea. In June 2001, geologists expressed concern that within ten or fifteen years, Machu Picchu might crumble and succumb to a devastating landslide, destabilized by moving soil underneath it. Subterranean soils are estimated to be moving at the rate of nearly five inches per year, and the situation is worse in times of excessive rainfall. This activity is a typical precursor to a landslide. Further, there are five geological faults within the central Machu Picchu peak.[503]

HISTORY AND ARCHEOLOGY

Machu Picchu was essentially unknown to the Western world until 1911, when Yale archeologist Hiram Bingham put it on the world map. His research showed that Machu Picchu was probably the ceremonial and administrative center not only of a city subsequently "lost" to the world, but also of an entire lost province. Archeological evidence indicates there were no more than two hundred habitation structures at Machu Picchu, capable of supporting an estimated maximum population of perhaps one thousand.

As part of the Yale Peruvian expedition, Bingham had been looking for Vilcabamba the Old, the last stronghold of Manco Inca and his sons, who were defeated by the Spanish in the sixteenth century. At first Bingham declared that Machu Picchu was Vilcabamba, but later research located that city some one hundred kilometers west at Espiritu Pampa near the Apurimac River.

When he was shown the site, it was overgrown by forests, but Bingham soon uncovered agricultural terraces and ruined temples. It took him a while to appreciate the significance of his discovery of Machu Picchu, but in 1913 he published the account of his researches in *National Geographic* magazine, which devoted an entire issue to the topic, and he soon gained worldwide recognition.

For the most part it seems that when the Spanish completed their Peruvian conquests, occupying Cusco in 1532 and murdering the Incan emperor, they were unaware of Machu Picchu. A Peruvian document dated to 1568 refers to a place called *Picho* or *Picchu* north of Cusco and says that it was once the royal estate of the Incas called Pachacuteq, who ruled from 1438 to 1471.

Archeologists extrapolated from this data the assumption that Machu Picchu had been constructed and populated by the *panaca*, or royal lineage, of Pachacuteq. They also describe the apparent architectural style of the numerous ruins at Machu Picchu as "late imperial Inca." It is possible, they speculate, that the site was built, occupied, and abandoned, all within a single century. The site's architectural style, they say, bears no signs of pre-Inca occupation.

What it does bear convincing proof of is civil engineering expertise, observes American civil engineer Kenneth Wright who spent a fair amount of six years studying the site's hydrology, hydraulics, drainage, foundation engineering, and "slope stability technology." To the trained eye of a civil engineer, this Inca site was perfect, and was clearly the result of careful and very knowledgeable planning.

The Incas managed to build a mountaintop city complete with running water, effective drainage systems, food production, and stone structures so sturdily built that it has all endured for at least five hundred years. Machu Picchu's "well-designed drainage infrastructure is one of its most remarkable secrets, says Wright, and a key to the site's longevity. "They built for permanency. They didn't do anything halfway." But they also built "with aesthetics in mind."[504]

Perhaps they also built with secrecy as a foremost consideration. You can't see the city from below, and it appears to be well-protected, self-contained, and self-sufficient in its isolation. "The purpose of Machu Picchu has always been a mystery. It seems to have been designed as a secret city."[505]

Bingham proposed that Machu Picchu had once been the residence of the *Mamacunas*, the Chosen Women or "Virgins of the Sun," whose service was dedicated to the Sun god, a servant of Virachocha, the principal deity of the Inca. These women were presumed to have lived in an *Aqllawasi* (House of Chosen Women), where they were wives to both the Sun and the current Incan ruler.

What set Bingham on this train of thought was the discovery of numerous natural caves in the slopes below the city; nearly all of the 170 human skeletons discovered in them were female, according to original surveys, and one elaborate grave was outfitted with costly ritual objects. Subsequent osteological examination of the skeletons in the 1980s showed that an equal number of males were represented among those 170 skeletons, so perhaps Machu Picchu was not an exclusively female temple domain.

Of the two dozen or so temple ruins identified and catalogued at Machu Picchu—some 150 structures in all, including palaces, storage rooms, and baths—perhaps the most important is the one called the *Intiwatana* or *Intihuatana* (Hitching Post of the Sun) at the far western end of the complex.

Archeologists explain that, during the summer and winter solstice sunrises (and presumably at the equinoxes too), the Incas ritually "tied" the Sun to a small vertical stone (a *gnomon*) set in a base to prevent it from wandering farther down the horizon. (For a Polynesian variation on the Sun fastener idea, see Haleakala, Maui, Hawaii.)

The name *Intiwatana*, however, is not Incan or found in any ancient chronicle, but comes from the mind of a Western archeologist in 1877 who studied the site. The more likely ancient name would have been *saywa* or *sukhanka*. It is said that if you place your forehead (the portal to your brow chakra) on the stone, it opens up your psychic vision of the spirit world.

In general, the *Intiwatana* stones (found throughout the Inca Empire) were considered "supremely sacred"; the invading Spaniards systematically searched for them to destroy them and decommission the sites. In some way, these special stones anchored the appropriate spirits and deities to a place. "When the Intihuatana stone was broken at an Inca shrine, the Inca believed that the deities of the place died or departed."[506]

Meanwhile, *Intiwatana* is understood to mean "Sun Fastener" or "place where the Sun is tied up," and may refer to the *Inti Raimi* (Sun Festival or Solemn Resurrection of the Sun) on the winter solstice (June 21 in the Southern Hemisphere). The *Inti Raimi* also honored Manco Capac and Coya Mama Oella Huaco, the first human Incan couple, whose father was Inti. The festival lasted nine days and involved drinking beverages symbolic of the Sun's essence.

This was the day when the Incas believed their *Tayta Inti,* or Father Sun, was abandoning them. During the winter solstice, the Sun appears to be at the farthest point from the Earth of the whole year. The Inca belief was that the Sun had to be tied down to keep from moving farther away. But *Intiwatana* might also have meant the "place where the solar year is measured" as *Inti* means "Sun" and *Wata* means "year."

The stone may also have served as a "directional peg" for finding magnetic north and south; or it might have been the observation point for important constellations such as the Pleiades, Southern Cross, Spica in Virgo, and others; or it might have been a line-of-sight marker in a regional *ceque* system (Peruvian "ley lines" in which temple sites are in straight-running alignments). According to Cusco researcher Vicente Goyzueta, the *Intiwatana* was a cosmic and ritual axis of great religious and calendrical significance.[507]

Visitors sensitive to energy emanations at sacred sites report that in some way the *Intiwatana,* set at the highest point on the plateau, may be the "focal point of energy beamed down from the surrounding mountains." This would be in accordance with the Incan concept of *Apu,* in which mountains possess an almost palpable energy and spirit presence. When you stand at the *Intiwatana* and observe the other *Apu* surrounding it, "you begin to understand why this place is so very powerful." This same writer was told by a local expert that Machu Picchu is more of a sanctuary than a ruin, and that its atmosphere "is truly as holy and inspirational as any cathedral."[508]

There are at least two other features at Machu Picchu dedicated to the Sun. The *Intipunku,* or "Sun Gate," is found above the ruins to the southeast and is a notch in the ridge with a small ruin in the center of it. Within the central plaza of Machu Picchu and near the principal fountain is the Temple of the Sun. It's a round and tapered piece of stonework, and has numerous niches to hold ritual objects; at its center is an actual rock outcropping, part of the mountain itself, made into a carved rock altar.

It is believed that this site functioned as an astronomical observatory, aligned to the rising of the Sun on the summer solstice. Underneath the temple is a small cave known as the "Royal Tomb"; it is presumed to have been used as a burial site for royalty (though no corpses were ever found there) and somehow related to the *Ukju Pacha* (the Incan Underworld).

MYTH AND LEGEND

What is most striking about Machu Picchu is that for the most part what we *think* we know about it is based on the speculations, extrapolations, and sometimes inept fantasies of non-Incan archeologists. We know of no extant myths about the city, its gods or purposes, or its foundation. The temples bear Western names, based on Western archeological assumptions about their function, and the dating of Machu Picchu is ultra-conservative, and probably parochial given the geomantic significance of the site.

At least we can get a provisional idea as to who the Incas were. They were the presumed former ruling class of South American indigenous peoples, primarily if not exclusively based in Peru. Their myths say they originated in the vicinity of Lake Titicaca, in the southeast corner of Peru on the border of Bolivia, then first settled in the Cusco Valley perhaps during the thirteenth century A.D.

Another account says the Incas originated at *Pacaritambo* (the inn or house of dawn) about thirty-three kilometers south of Cusco in a now vanished mountain called *Tambo Toco* (the house of openings and windows).[509] This mountain had a cave with three windows, Incan myth says, which led Bingham to originally but erroneously identify Machu Picchu as *Tambo Toco* because it has a Temple of the Three Windows.

In a related Incan myth, human beings were molded from clay by their creator Pachacamac, who deposited these clay molds in the Earth, after which they emerged from caves or springs. In 1995, a series of caves underneath the Condor Temple at Machu Picchu was discovered; these caves led to a deep narrow hole covered with soil, leading archeologists to wonder if this site was used by the Inca to reenact their creation myth. In this case, Machu Picchu would be a sacred spot, or *huaca*, where human life emerged from the Earth.

The first Incan emperor was named Manco Capac, and he was believed to be descended from *Inti*, the Sun god, also called *Apu-Punchau*, whose head was a gold disk from which rays and flames extended. Only the high priests were enti-

tled to pronounce the name of this god, who every night plunged into the Sea to swim through the night until the morning, when he arose refreshed. The Incas considered themselves descended from Inti, the Sun—they are the Sons of the Sun. Inti's sister and consort was *Mama-Kilya*, the Moon, represented as a silver disk with human features.

The prime Incan deity was *Viracocha* (or *Con Ticci Viracocha*), the Creator, whose name might mean "Sea fat" or "Sea foam." He is described as a large white figure. Lord Viracocha was said to have emerged from Lake Titicaca to create humanity, as well as the Sun, Moon, Mother Earth, all the stars, and everything else. He created these on an island in the lake, and out of the island rose the Sun in all its splendor. Viracocha created Inti and Mama-Kilya at Lake Titicaca, and afterwards traveled the Andean countryside as a culture hero teaching humans the arts of civilization. Viracocha is the focus of the *Capac Raimi*, the summer solstice ceremony in December.[510]

MYSTICS AND TOURISTS

Since 1995, several landslides and snow avalanches have taken place at or around Machu Picchu, at least one of them costing lives and destroying property. A Peruvian woman named Senora Lizarraga, who suffered grievous loss in an avalanche there, said that normally the *apukuna*, the powerful and often fierce mountain deities—the "divine lords of the sacred mountains," according to the Quechua—protect Machu Picchu, the Intiwatana, and the hydroelectric plant at the mountain's base.

"The *apukuna* have become angry because they were insulted by the locals and skeptical foreigners." People rashly climb the peaks without first asking permission of the apukuna or the *Karnak*, the creator of humankind, she commented. As a result, "these gods have been offended by those who fail to acknowledge them and do not send their offerings."

According to the belief of the Quechua Indians in that area, Mother Earth, or Pachamama, has sent repeated warnings to the people in the Machu Picchu area, and Apu Salkkantay, the "most powerful of all mountain deities" and the source of the avalanche (elevation: 20,574 feet), has spoken with vengeance.

Senora Lizarraga said that "since ancient times" guardian spirits and the "ancient ones" called the *naupa machukuna* have protected this area, preserving the land as sacred. These same deities originally built Machu Picchu, and do not want the roadways, developments, and pollution, she reports. Senora Lizarraga also said the skeletons found in the caves belonged to the guardians of the valley of Aobamba.[511] The general belief is that the *apukuna* are so powerful that only an *alto misayoq,* or ritual specialist, can deal with them directly, either safely or effectively.

For Faure Duenas Pena, a prominent Andean flautist who gave a public performance at Machu Picchu in 1995, Machu Picchu is a sanctuary and a "very sacred place. Only God knows what it really is, and no one can decipher it. I see it as a monastery, a place of rituals and ceremonies dedicated to all the Andean gods who are adored by my people." Based on his experience of playing music there, Pena said that "music is an integral part of the creation of this holy place."[512]

GEOMANTIC

Dome; Mithraeum; Labyrinth; Activated Dome Paradise Crystal.

DOME: The dome over Machu Picchu and a fair amount of the surrounding mountains and valleys—a twenty-mile diameter—corresponds to Achernar, alpha Eridani, the constellation of the

River Eridanus. This constellation of thirteen stars can only be seen in the continental U.S. from southern Texas and Florida, and then only just above the horizon. The river begins, or has its source, at the left foot of the giant hunter, Orion, and below it lies the second brightest star in the galaxy, Canopus, in the constellation Argo Navis.

Eridanus has been called, variously, the King of Rivers, River Euphrates, River Nile, River Jordan, River Po, or sometimes the more sublime Oceanus, the Ocean stream that the Greeks said flowed around the Earth. It figures in the Greek myth of the ill-fated Sun apprentice, Phaethon.

Phaethon desired to drive the chariot of his father, Helios, the Sun, for a day, but soon found the four fiery steeds of the Sun beyond his control. Zeus shot the Sun chariot out of the sky with a thunderbolt to prevent chaos from entering the solar system, and Phaethon, the son of the Sun, hurled to his death as a blazing corpse into the River Eridanus. The river nymphs recovered his Sun-charred body and buried it nearby.

Achernar means "the star at the end of the river," from the Arabic *Al Ahir al Nahr,* and it lies at the southernmost point of Eridanus. Achernar, the ninth-brightest star in the galaxy, is a hot blue giant of the first magnitude, 650 times brighter than our Sun, 120 light years from Earth.

The allocation of the alpha star from the constellation of the River is apt in terms of Incan cosmology. They regarded the earthly counterpart of the Milky Way to be the Urubamba River, which snaked its way around or was adjacent to key huaca (holy) sites such as Pisac, Ollantaytambo, and Machu Picchu. For the Incans, the two great rivers, the Milky Way and Urubamba, "were joined at the edge of the known universe in the waters of a great cosmic sea which encircled the earth." The source of the Milky Way was thought to be the cosmic sea.[513]

MITHRAEUM: In essence, the Machu Picchu temple was a place to educate the Inca in the cosmic mysteries. They were born as Sons of the Sun, or Inca, at Cusco (see Cusco, Peru), then at a certain point in their initiation sequence, they made the journey overland along the Inca Trail to Machu Picchu. It was as if they were walking directly into the Sun when they did this, every step bringing them deeper into the radiating field of the great Sun god, Inti Raimi, resident at the Old Mountain. Each of them, as an apprentice Inca, was like the Greek Phaethon, a Son of the Sun, but not fully an Inca, not tested, not confirmed—not imprinted.

By the time they arrived at Machu Picchu, they were already "sunburned," already standing within the aegis of the fiery Sun god. But there was a deeper immersion still awaiting them. At another layer of reality, the core of the Machu Picchu mountain is a golden spherical cavern, as if a flat Sun disc had been stretched around a globe to form a sphere the size of the mountain.

Here the Sun Men were alchemically created in the Cave of the Sun of Inti Raimi. It was as if everything in the human continuum of the Inca initiate that was not resonant with the gold vibration was purged, and only the gold light could fill their human forms.

But it was the inner Sun, the spiritual Sun, the Christ light, and Son of God that they immersed themselves in. "This is the ultimate of life—the growth of the Sun within the breast of man, until man himself becomes a Sun-man, a man of God." The true Sun worship was about the spirit light within the human "waiting to rise as gloriously and powerfully as the Sun in the heavens rises on a summer's day." Ancient initiates in the Americas, the apprentice Sun Men, were taught that "they also had within themselves a Sun which radiated from the heart."[514]

LABYRINTH: All of this is preparation. The Inca, to be cosmically educated, needs an imprintable skin. This is a somewhat metaphorical way of putting it. The Incan apprentice emerges from the Mithraeum, Inti Raimi's solar alchemical laboratory, and proceeds to an astral temple occupying the entire top of the Machu Picchu plateau. It looks like a rectangular building; inside there is a labyrinth on the floor, leading to a shallow concave golden dish like a small radar antenna set on a short pedestal. A stream of light continuously enters it.

The Inca walked the labyrinth in his spirit body to prepare his higher mental and psychic faculties for the data stream continuously filling the dish. At this level of reality, each Inca has hundreds of thin tendrils streaming out of his crown chakra like filaments or antenna connections. Each plugs into a different part of the data base; each is a psychic probe and a receptive channel for input.

The incoming flow of "water," of course, is a data stream of cosmic information and light codings. Now the Sun of the Son, the Inca Phaethon, is about to "drown" in the higher awareness and knowledge stream of Eridanus as it flows into Machu Picchu through its dome.

Once you stand in the midst of the data stream in the center of the gold dish, it is as if you are in a type of library, a cosmic archive. Each crown chakra tendril makes a connection with a different "book." For example, one such "book" may present itself to you as a cave of blue crystal with hundreds of facets; these make an imprint on your skin, as if giving you a tattoo. This is specific information from a single star, or an initiate tradition in that star system; it may, for example, be codings that enable you to step sideways in spacetime on the Earth, or to step off the Earth, or to step into other dimensions.

You finish your immersion in the data stream, your skin a palimpsest of star imprintings. Printable skin is a way of saying psychic sensitivity. This is a visual way of representing a more subtle templating of consciousness; you may not be especially aware of the codings as they are imprinting themselves on your psychic skin, but you will be able to *act* from this new knowledge. It is now part of yourself. You are a Sun Man with a skin full of cosmic tattoos, and you are ready for the next phase of Machu Picchu.

ACTIVATED DOME PARADISE CRYSTAL: There is no way to put this simply. Each dome carried the seed of a paradise that could be manifested through that dome site if and when the dome was activated through human, angelic, and elemental participation in releasing its light. One aspect of that activation was the emergence of a dynamic multidimensional energy structure that looks like a torus in full cycling motion.[515] This activated torus, centered at Machu Pichu, is many miles wide, making a dynamic collar around the mountain.

The Inca came to Machu Picchu for education, to study in its library. The Machu Picchu temple complex, including the Mithraeum and Labyrinth, is like a vast sac of amniotic fluid for the Cusco Christ Child, the newborn Son of the Sun. The Labyrinth offers you a vast reservoir of cosmic information and instruction, such as a library of alien life forms and purposes. It's a memory bank for educating Incas in matters of the cosmos.

Machu Picchu is the Old Mountain because it has been a storage facility, an archive, for cosmic records since the beginning of the planet; the site has been used for this function *long* before the currently extant structures were built. It is the Old Mountain because it has been performing this function for a *long* time.

Once the Inca were educated, or cosmically imprinted, they were ready to step out into the greater world to teach others. The constantly cycling torus provided the means of travel. It is like a toroidal river, and you wait for the "parting of the Red Sea" before you step into it. As each "rib" of the torus passes through a spot at Machu Picchu, it dilates or opens up, revealing an arcane passageway; you step through this and you are immediately somewhere else, say, Mount Kailash in Tibet, among many possible planetary destinations. It is a space portal: You can travel across planetary space instantaneously through a dome torus, provided the rest of the planetary toroidal network is "online."

Sun Men would suddenly appear in new landscapes, as if they had congealed out of thin air. Once there, they could start teaching, based on what was needed and appropriate for the new setting, drawing on the vast library resources now imprinted upon them. Whether they told the secret of space travel on the planet was discretionary.

Monticello, Charlottesville, Virginia, United States

Thomas Jefferson's estate, called Monticello, located two miles outside Charlottesville, Virginia, is internationally known and visited as a historic monument, but very few people seem to regard it as a sacred site, that is, as a place with numinosity. It is a numinous site, however; in fact, all of Charlottesville, a small city that is the home of the University of Virginia and located about one hundred miles southwest of Washington, D.C., is numinously charged.

Monticello means "Little Mountain" or "hillock," a name probably based on the fact that this hill (867 feet high) is smaller and lower than its immediate neighbor, Brown's Hill. Local legend has it that Jefferson preferred Brown's Hill to his own, and wanted to build his estate there, but couldn't obtain the property rights.

Thomas Jefferson inherited the Monticello property in 1764, at age twenty-one, from his father, Peter Jefferson, began work on his home in 1769, and more or less finished it before he died in 1826.[516] He also superintended ten thousand acres in Charlottesville, mostly forested, that were also part of his patrimony, and was an avid gardener and agricultural experimenter his whole life.

"While working for more than fifty years on his home—building, altering, remodeling, putting up and tearing down—Jefferson created, as all owner-builders do, a dwelling that mirrored himself."[517] His home, built in the Classical Revival style and influenced by the architectural principles of the sixteenth-century Italian builder Andrea Palladio, is on the World Heritage List of protected sites. It has three stories and thirty-five rooms, most of them small, and has been owned and maintained since 1923 by the Thomas Jefferson Memorial Foundation.

Today, more than a half-million tourists visit the five-thousand-acre site, which includes orchards and vegetable gardens, each year. The Marquis de Chastellux, a general in the French army based in Rhode Island, spent four days with Jefferson at Monticello in the spring of 1782, and noted of Jefferson: "It seemed as if from his youth he had placed his mind, as he had done his house, on an elevated situation, from which he might contemplate the universe."[518] A family friend described Monticello in 1806 as being in a state of rude nature. "There is something grand & awful, than agreeable or convenient in the wholeplace, a situation you would rather look at now & then than inhabit."[519]

As far as Jefferson was concerned, he intended Monticello to be his personal hermitage, where he could retire into himself, immerse himself in his studies, and entertain intellectual companions. He wanted it to be "spacious, elegant, private, artistic, and *his*" and for it to be "a womb-like place of warmth, comfort, and love."[520] And he'd had this vision since he was twenty.

"Of prospect I have a rich profusion and offering itself at every point of the compass," Jefferson wrote in a letter in 1806. "The hill is generally too steep for direct ascent, but we make level walks successively along its side, which in its upper part encircle the hill & intersect these again by others of easy ascent in various parts." He confessed that to make the best and most aesthetic use of his grounds "would require much more of the genius of the landscape painter & gardener than I pretend to."[521]

Perhaps Jefferson did not think his skills were adequate for making of Monticello "a disposition analogous to its character," but he was in retrospect and from a geomantic viewpoint remarkably well attuned to the esoteric aspects of the Charlottesville landscape—in terms of the properties he lived on, recommended to his friends to buy,[522] or indicated for the founding of the University of Virginia—his "Academikal Village."

In fact, Monticello is primarily what Jefferson made of it and imparted to it, and even though he did not (at least, not in any currently published source) refer to what we would call geomantic or geomythic aspects of his property, what he did say and do there is germane to our appreciation of Jefferson and the mysteries of the Charlottesville landscape. "I am as happy no where else and in no other society, and all my wishes end, where I hope my days will end, at Monticello," he wrote in 1787.[523] What kind of energy in the Monticello landscape could generate such strong sentiments?

Dome Cap; Mount Olympus; Avalon; Scorpio Albion *Ananda-kanda* Chakra; Landscape Zodiac; Palladium; Tree of Life.

DOME CAP: Monticello is energized by a primary dome cap generated by the dome over adjacent Brown's Hill, which is the starfall for alpha Lyrae, known as Vega, a first-magnitude star, the third-brightest star as seen in the Northern Hemisphere. As a constellation, Lyra, which is also called the Lyre, contains eight bright stars that form an equilateral triangle; Vega is the bright star at the bottom of the lyre which functions as the base for the figure.

The lyre is the instrument that Apollo gave to his son Orpheus, whose song enchanted everyone. Even after Orpheus' death, when his lyre was cast into the River Hebrus, it continued to play its haunting, melancholic music, as the rushing waters rippled its strings. In a variation on this tale, Hermes invented the lyre from a tortoise shell; it had seven strings, in reference either to the seven planets or seven Pleiades. Orpheus adapted the lyre and gave it two more strings, so it had nine; his mother, Calliope, was one of the Nine Muses, which is perhaps why this constellation is sometimes called the Lyre of the Muses.

In earlier times, Vega was often referred to as the Harp Star, its name deriving from the Arabic *Waki*. Approximately fourteen thousand years ago, due to the Precession of the Equinoxes, Vega was the north polestar for our galaxy (and will be again in 14,500 A.D.) and was thus known to the Akkadians as *Tir-anna*, "Life of Heaven" and to the Assyrians as *Dayan same*, "Judge of Heaven." Other names from different cultures for Vega have included *Hauslicky na Nebi* (Fiddle in the Sky), *Hearpe* (Harp), and *Al Nasr al Waki* (the Swooping Eagle).

Since the 1980s, Vega has entered the popular imagination as the alleged source of the problematic grays, the almond-eyed, gray-skinned aliens who stage-manage human abductions, and as the source of baffling space travel information in Carl Sagan's novel *Contact*.

As a star, Vega is twenty-seven light years from Earth, and actually approaching our planet at a speed of 8.5 miles per second; our Sun is also moving towards Vega at the rate of twelve miles per second. Vega's diameter is 2.8 million miles, or about 3.2 times the size of our Sun, and it's three times as massive, twice as hot, and fifty-eight times more luminous than our Sun.

Dome caps from the Vega dome are found over nearby Ashlawn, Shadwell Mountain, and several sites in Charlottesville, including Jefferson's original Academikal Village (now the core of the University of Virginia). It's hard to know to what extent Thomas Jefferson was aware of the geomancy at Monticello, but he could walk out the back door of his house, stand on the top end of the lawn, and, theoretically, appreciate (or at least get the benefit of) a major geomantic feature that is present there, namely, the Mount Olympus.

MOUNT OLYMPUS: A rainbow bridge, or Bifrost, starts at the point where the land starts to drop down at the end of the lawn and spans the gap between Monticello and the Mount Olympus at Brown's Hill. In effect Jefferson had in his backyard a hologram of Heimdall, Norse guardian of Bifrost. Jefferson would have had access, at whatever level of consciousness he could manage (perhaps in his dreamtime), to the input of the fourteen Ray Masters. It's obvious that this would have been an invaluable contact for a man who was a founding father and President of the United States, and a university founder as well.

AVALON: Jefferson also would have benefited from the presence of Avalon, the Summer Country, more formally known as the Celestial City of Gandhavati. This spiritual domain can be accessed on Monticello itself and exists in the same place as the physical hill, only in another, subtler, layer of reality. There is at least one "rabbit hole"—borrowing an expression from Lewis Caroll—into Avalon, which can be found in an open field near the woods to the right of the paved sidewalk that leads down from the lawn to the cemetery.

The presence of an Avalon at Monticello largely accounts for the marvelous feeling of timelessness that one quickly encounters and settles into. It inspires high thoughts and no thoughts, depending on what one prefers—inspiration or contemplation, an inner richness or a deep, contentless ease. There is the sense there of an endless summer afternoon, the kind one has when one is six, trouble free, and full of imagination, when anything is possible and nothing need be done.

It is not unusual to find that hours have passed for which one can barely give an accounting. These are some of the possible subjective qualities you may register by sitting within the energy field of an Avalon, brushing delicately against the membrane of another reality.

The dome cap over Monticello and the dome over Brown's Hill are unusually intact. In approaching Monticello, when you are about two miles from it in either direction on the main access road, you can sense the energy shift, almost abruptly, as if you had just passed through a curtain, on the other side of which a different—and better—reality exists. This enables Monticello to function as a place of purification and cleansing, both for its many visitors and for the Albion of which it is an important part. With all the celestial light entering Monticello from the star dome for Vega, and its other geomantic features, everything looks "cleaner" as a result.

SCORPIO ALBION ANANDA-KANDA CHAKRA: It is fortunate for the United States that Monticello is a protected monument and a well-visited historic site as well. It is an energy node within an Albion, a very large geomythic figure occupying almost one third of the continental U.S. Monticello occupies the position of inner heart chakra (called *Ananda-kanda*) in this figure. Other key energy centers in this huge geomythic figure are found in Massachusetts, New York (see Hill Cumorah), Tennessee (see Clingman's Dome), Kentucky, and Arkansas, among others.

In our time, this particular Albion plate is under the astrological influence of Scorpio, which is about death and transformation. Bear in mind that the seat of commerce (New York City) and government (Washington, D.C.) both reside within this Scorpio field. Monticello's pacific vibrations are highly beneficial for the rest of this Albion and by extension for all human life living within its sphere of influence. The star dome for Vega, the Asgard at Brown's Hill, and the Avalon in Jefferson's backyard, all contribute positively to Albion's geomythic life through "his" inner heart center.

Traditional Hindu iconography of the chakras, or subtle energy centers in the human body, describe an esoteric subsidiary heart center called the *Ananda-kanda*. It has eight petals and hangs like a pendant below the major heart center, the *Anahata,* which has twelve petals, or vibrational fields. The Monticello *Ananda-kanda* energy field is vibrationally linked with the planet's other eleven such centers within the other eleven Albions, and with the planet's own primary *Ananda-kanda* center. In this center, the yogi can make direct connections with the crown chakra, bypassing the centers in between, and through the crown, with the Supreme Being (Shiva in the Tantric model).

Within the chakra model, this center is considered an arcane one, but in many respects more central to consciousness and its activities and prospects than all the others. One term from Western mythology that refers to the *Ananda-kanda* chakra is Camalate, as in King Arthur's legendary headquarters. This connection reveals

another key aspect of Monticello's geomantic function.

Monticello is linked with all twenty-six of the Earth's Camalate Centers. That's because the term Camalate Center is a mythic way of referring to the eightfold energies of the *Ananda-kanda,* energies which derive from eight specific stars or constellations in our galaxy that have been crucial in the unfoldment of the Earth's energy body and the possibilities of higher human conscious evolution on our planet.

Thus between access to the Ray Masters in Asgard and the eight celestial influences through the *Ananda-kanda* at Monticello, Thomas Jefferson would have had a very rich input from the spiritual worlds for his formative work—in terms of the future growth of the U.S.—in politics, agriculture, and education.

LANDSCAPE ZODIAC: Further enriching Monticello's geomantic prospects is the presence of a Landscape Zodiac in Charlottesville, which includes Jefferson's hill. Its diameter is about ten miles; it is overshadowed by a zodiac dome about twenty-three miles wide, thus encompassing all of Charlottesville and its environs.

PALLADIUM/TREE OF LIFE: Present at the University of Virginia campus are a Palladium and Tree of Life. In fact, Jefferson's original campus, which he called his Academikal Village and today is still known as The Lawn, flanked by college buildings, is a remarkable piece of geomancy. The Palladium occupies the Rotunda at one end of The Lawn, and the fourfold Tree of Life spills out down The Lawn to the far end of the long and large rectangular green. There are even gentle three- to four-foot dips in The Lawn at the appropriate dimensional transitions in the Tree of Life.

Near the Rotunda is a Control Bubble, one of only 238 on the planet; it is used to adjust the mixture of angelic and elemental energies in the various features of not only the Charlottesville geomantic temple, but a larger area within the

Northeastern U.S. On Shadwell Mountain, a few miles from Monticello, is one of the Earth's twelve Crowns of the Ancient of Days; and at Ashlawn (again, only a few miles from Jefferson's home), you will find a Pointer's Ball, a dimensional doorway precisely situated where President James Monroe's old house stands. It is amusing to note that apparently his wife used to complain of ghosts and spectral spirits walking through her house.

Mont-Royal, Montreal, Quebec, Canada

Montreal, one of North America's largest cities and, after Paris, the world's second-largest French-speaking city, is situated on an island 32 miles long and nine miles wide at the confluence of three rivers in southern Quebec: the Saint Lawrence, the Ottawa, and the Saint Pierre.

This city of about 1.7 million people (3.3 million for the total metropolitan area) derives its name from a 764-foot-tall mountain dubbed *Mont-Royal,* the "Royal Mountain," when it was discovered by sixteenth-century French explorers. Mont-Royal is now the site of the five-hundred-acre Le Parc du Mont-Royal within the city limits.

The mountain provides an excellent panoramic view of the city and the surrounding Quebec countryside, including the Monteregian Hills, and it is a popular recreation spot for Montrealers. Mont-Royal is also the site of the Basilica of Notre Dame, a Neo-Gothic church with 227-foot-tall twin towers, a 6,772-pipe organ, and a seating capacity of four thousand.

Even more significant, certainly in terms of the reputation of its founder, is the Saint Joseph Oratory, a magnet for pilgrimages created out of the vision of Father Andre (1845–1937), a Canadian Roman Catholic mystic who in his time became known as the "Miracle Worker and Wonder Man of Montreal."

As with certain other numinous sites, Montreal, thirty-seven miles north of the U.S. border, is more known for its historical role as a major fur-trading outpost, a major inland port, or as a cosmopolitan Parisian-like Canadian city, and not for its mystical geomancy. However, it was surely no accident that the Indians first encountered by sixteenth-century European explorers had established their residence at the base of Mont-Royal, presumably having recognized its geomantic nature.

At the time of the arrival of the French explorer Jacques Cartier in 1535, the Indian tribe of Iroquois (or Hurons) was encamped in a village they called Hochelaga at the base of Mont-Royal. According to ethnologists, Hochelaga meant "Big Rapids" or "Beaver Dam," and referred not only to the village but to the Saint Lawrence River. The Iroquois later referred to the growing city of Montreal as *Tiohtia:ke, Tiohtia:ke Tsi,* or *Kawenote,* while the Algonquins called it *Moniang.*[524]

343

Hochelaga was one of eleven Iroquoian villages in this part of southern Quebec, a large and fortified village with an estimated population of three thousand. Originally, the homeland of the Iroquois was upstate New York between the Adirondack Mountains and Niagara Falls, then most of the northeastern U.S. and eastern Canada. By 1603, however, when the French returned to Mont-Royal, Hochelaga and the other Iroquoian settlements on the Saint Lawrence had disappeared. Living in their place were Montagnais and Algonquins.[525]

Cartier reportedly climbed the hill behind the Iroquois encampment on October 2, 1535, and named the mountain Mont-Royal. The royal in question was his sponsor, Francois I, King of France. Cartier referred to the Saint Lawrence as the "River of Hochelaga" or, alternately, as the "great river of Canada."

In 1575, historian Francois de Belleforest was the first to use the form Montreal (a condensed Mont-Royal) to refer to the entire French settlement and not just Hochelaga: "Let us now look at Hochelaga," he wrote. "In the midst of the countryside is the village, or Cite royale, adjacent to a mountain on which farming is practiced. The Christians call this city Montreal."[526]

In 1642, two Catholic Frenchmen, Paul Chomedy de Maisonneuve and Jeanne Mance, founded Ville Marie in the vicinity of Hochelaga with the first French colonists. Apparently, they believed the North American Indians were the Lost Tribe of Israel and that their conversion would speed the Second Coming. The small group of forty emigrants established themselves as the society of "Notre Dame and Montreal."

This was the European seed from which present-day French Montreal grew. In 1643, a huge Christian cross was raised on the top of Mont-Royal in thanks to the higher powers that protected Ville Marie from the potentially disastrous floodwaters of the Saint Lawrence River that year.

The fur trade proved more profitable than the conversion business, and the Montreal settlement grew into a prosperous inland city. The French held on to their Canadian colony until September 1760, when the British captured it.

The park on Mont-Royal was originally designed by the American landscape architect Frederick Olmsted, who also created New York City's Central Park. When he began construction of the park on Mont-Royal in 1874, Olmsted said he would emphasize the area's existing mountainous topography—as it were, amplifying its hilliness. Olmsted held that nature itself was a spiritual food and city dwellers needed a natural place to which to escape from the pressures of the urban environment. Apparently, Montreal city planners later canceled much of Olmsted's plans for the park due to lack of finances.

Of greatest interest to us in terms of Mont-Royal's function as a geomantic node of significance is the construction of the Basilica of Notre Dame and Saint Joseph Oratory in the park on the mountain. The basilica was designed in 1824 by the Irish-American Protestant architect James O'Donnell. He was so moved by the experience of building a near-cathedral on Mont-Royal that he converted to Catholicism by the end of the project in 1829 so that he could be buried in its crypt. The Basilica is so popular a place today that weddings have to be booked 18 months in advance.

The Saint Joseph Oratory exists largely from the efforts of Brother Andre. Born Alfred Bessette to a poor French-Canadian family living thirty miles from Montreal in the farming village of Saint Gregoire in 1845, Father Andre spent forty years on Mont-Royal as lay brother of the Holy Cross order, laboring as a porter at the College of Notre-Dame du Sacre Coeur in Cote-des-Neiges, the same college where he spent much of his novitiate on Mont-Royal.

Brother Andre may have held a humble post, but he soon gained a reputation as a miracle healer and was credited with hundreds of cures. He attributed all the miraculous healings to his spiritual mentor, Saint Joseph, the foster father of Jesus Christ, husband of Mary, and the patron saint of Canada. Ironically, Brother Andre himself was always sick with stomach problems that limited his food intake; despite his ailments, however, he lived to be ninety-three.

In 1904, he petitioned the Bishop of Montreal to allow a small chapel to be constructed next to the Basilica in Saint Joseph's honor. The story is told that every time Brother Andre positioned his little statue of Saint Joseph to face his bed, when he returned to his room, it had turned around to face Mont-Royal. "It is not strange at all; it simply means that Saint Joseph wants to be honored on the mountain," he said. After Brother Andre received the vision or inspiration to create a shrine to Saint Joseph on Mont-Royal, it remained "a sacred task which Blessed Andre pursued with burning zeal. Everything that he could do in the confines of religious obedience to make the shrine a reality, he did immediately."[527]

During his life, Brother Andre reportedly wrought thousands of conversions, among "lapsed and lukewarm" Catholics as well as Protestants, Freemasons, and Jews. When he died on January 6, 1937, one million people came to see him in state. That date is now his Feast Day, but it is also the Epiphany, the day once traditional in Christianity to mark the birth of Christ, or, more esoterically, the manifestation of the Christ to the Three Magi. Brother Andre was buried in the Basilica, and on May 23, 1982, Pope John Paul II declared Brother Andre "blessed" and beatified him, which is one step short of sainthood.

Today the Saint Joseph Oratory is visited by an estimated two million pilgrims every year, making it one of the most frequented of Quebec's eighty religious-based pilgrimage sites. People come to seek intercession by Saint Joseph and Brother Andre in the travails of their lives, to bask in a spiritual presence in a "place destined for intimate prayer" while in the heart of a big city, or to "experience a moment of fraternity" in a "haven of peace" with people of other faiths. "Erected on a mountain, it brings to mind the sacred ground of many holy places within various religious traditions."[528]

The copper-domed building stands 361 feet tall, with a spire that reaches to 862 feet, making it the tallest point in the city of Montreal. The cross on the roof can be seen throughout the city. The original chapel (a mere fifteen by eighteen feet) was constructed in 1904 out of Brother Andre's own funds, but soon became too small for the number of Catholics eager to worship there. In 1917, it was enlarged into a church called the Crypt, capable of seating one thousand. In 1924, construction on a larger basilica started, but it was not finished until 1967, long after Brother Andre's death.

GEOMANTIC

Dome; Lily; Ray Master Sanctuary; Scorpio Albion Foot Chakra.

DOME: A dome over Mont-Royal is the planetary starfall for gamma Delphinus, which is the constellation of the Dolphin. In ancient Greece the dolphin was known as the Sacred Fish and assumed an almost religious significance.

The Hindus called this constellation *Shishumara* (later shortened to *Zizumara*), and assigned it a position in their own definition of zodiacal space (the twenty-eight *nakshatras*) that carried the attributes of most favorable and richest. Arabic astronomers called the constellation *Al Ka'ud*, "the Riding Camel," while some Christian sects saw it as the Cross of Jesus transferred to the sky after the Crucifixion.

Arabic sky-watchers also offered the name *Al Ukud*, "the Pearls" or "Precious Stones," for this constellation, which they saw as adornment for *Al Salib*, their name for the Cross. But later they adopted the Greek description and referred to these stars as *Dulfim*, the marine animal friendly to humans.

The gamma star in Delphinus, which has no specific name or myth, is a double star of the fourth and fifth magnitudes (4.3 and 5.1); it is one of the three stars on the figure's ventral fins. The double star is located about one hundred light years from Earth, its luminosity about eight to sixteen times (depending on which of the two stars is considered) brighter than our Sun.

LILY: Largely through the spirituality of Brother Andre and his unflagging attitude of devotion to Saint Joseph and the religious life, the impact of this field of purified consciousness produced a lily at the site. You have to conceive of this rather largely, casually, and metaphorically, because it is not so much a flower as a pervasive energy field that has a shape that resembles the lily. It is white, pure, fully open, and receptive; you could think of it as a large structured form of light occupying the space under the Saint Joseph Oratory and Basilica of Notre Dame.

Brother Andre made good use of the essential energy present under the Delphinus dome. He used it to help create an atmosphere of upward vision and prayerful immersion in bliss. He cupped it like a precious orange flame, and his steadfast devotion acted as a gentle bellows, enlarging this flame so that it filled the lily form that his purified consciousness had produced on Mont-Royal. Brother Andre was able to use this magnificent orange-gold flame for the numerous selfless healings and miracles that he performed for thousands. Immersing his hands in the flames of this burning "spiritual blood," Brother Andre purified and electrically charged his hands to dispense the healing energies.

The presence of the upward-rising flame and the lovely astral lily attracted a great deal of

angelic presence, both to witness the glory and to amplify its impact. It is of course difficult to know to what degree Brother Andre was aware of the geomantic effects of his actions, and admittedly my evocation of his relationship to the energies of the dome is somewhat poetic rather than perhaps biographical. But it doesn't matter if he was aware or not. The result is the same: a purified occupation of an important geomantic site by a spiritually attuned individual.

Brother Andre's contribution during his lifetime spent on Mont-Royal was to midwife the site into present time. His function was similar to that of Bernadette Soubirous at Lourdes in the 1850s, who identified the Virgin Mary and thereby grounded her presence, transmitting that being's suggestions for the development of the site into public awareness and eventually into physical reality. Similarly, Brother Andre, by ceaselessly advocating the construction of the Saint Joseph Oratory, identified and grounded the energy of Saint Joseph at Mont-Royal. This was a necessary step in the reactivation of this geomantic node.

RAY MASTER SANCTUARY: It is well known that Saint Joseph was the presiding spiritual mentor for Brother Andre. So it is satisfying to discover that this saint from the time of Jesus has his own oratory on Mont-Royal. Think of it as an aperture, an otherworldly pool, or perhaps simply an inner plane temple in the form of a large rotunda. The spiritual being present there is one of the fourteen Ray Masters of the Great Bear, specifically, Master Hilarion, who is responsible for the pale spring-green ray.

During the time of the Christ incarnation, he was incarnated as Joseph. Mont-Royal is not an opening to the Celestial City of the Ray Masters, but, similar to Ephesus in Turkey (presided over by Artemis) and Newgrange in Ireland (Apollo), it is a site that affords a single Ray Master useful egress into a geomantic site. In effect, the five hundred acres of Le Parc du Mont-Royal are the spiritual province of Master Hilarion, the floodplain and river valley of this being's benevolent flow into our world. Sitting in the heart of the Saint Joseph Oratory, it is as if you receive a baptism in Hilarion's "water."

SCORPIO ALBION FOOT CHAKRA: Montreal is not particularly thought of as a sacred site, yet Mont-Royal serves a valuable function in a large geomantic structure that concerns most of the East Coast of the United States, including its seat of government. Mont-Royal is the major foot chakra (in the sole of the left foot) of the vast geomythic figure called Albion, which is sprawled out over this portion of North America as far south as Tennessee. The right foot chakra is at the Citadel National Historic Site in downtown Halifax in Nova Scotia.

Let's not be misled by the apparent humbleness of the foot in terms of the presumed hierarchy of chakras in the body. After all, Jesus washed the feet of a prostitute as an expression of his humility and his recognition of her inner God spark, and the Buddha was said to have the emblem of a lotus inscribed on his feet so that wherever he walked, his feet blessed the Earth.

Even better, in terms of the mechanics of reflexology, which posits a complete therapeutic body map on the bottom of the feet (and hands), you can transmit beneficial nerve impulses to anywhere in the body by rubbing the appropriate section of the foot. Further, the foot chakra in the center of the foot's sole corresponds anatomically to the body's solar plexus. In terms of the Scorpio Albion's geomythic body, the corresponding landscape site for the solar plexus chakra position is Washington, D.C., which has a Landscape Zodiac, among other geomantic features.

The setup is elegant, but to appreciate it, we need to think in terms of the North American con-

tinent and its energy body and not so much of Canada, the United States, and their political roles in the world. What makes Mont-Royal significant in the continental geomantic picture is that one of the United States' three Albions is grounded in Canada; that is where it touches the Earth.

There at Albion's left foot chakra a highly spiritual man established a lily, as an expression of purified human consciousness, and opened an interdimensional doorway for the beneficent energies of a Ray Master, St. Joseph, to flow into the world. Two million people visit the Saint Joseph Oratory and Basilica of Notre Dame every year, participating in this spiritual blessing and reaffirming it. The orange-gold flame keeps getting stronger. This energy flows up the leg and torso of the Scorpio Albion, infiltrating all eighty-one of its chakras, most of which are in the U.S.

The pure energy set in motion by Brother Andre's devotion to Saint Joseph at Mont-Royal enters the Scorpio Albion through its left foot and flows up the figure to help "tame the savage beast" at its power center in Washington, D.C. In a sense, it offers a calming, even spiritual, antidote to the normal propensity of the solar plexus chakra for power issues, competition, control, and conflict.

When a landscape solar plexus chakra is inhabited by the seat of a major government, clearly the geomantic setup and its activities have a global impact. This is why the Mont-Royal input is salutary, because as an astrological energy, Scorpio is dangerous, scary, tricky, secretive, and hard to predict with its lightning strike of the poisonous tail always a possibility; Scorpio involves death and transformation, and sometimes only one or the other. Thus the Mont-Royal node can potentially dilute the "poison" of the Scorpionic solar plexus center.

Mont-Saint-Michel, France

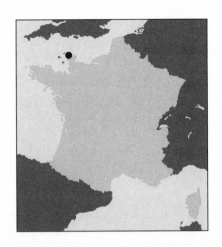

Mont-Saint-Michel is an island sanctuary in Normandy on the northern coast of France, dedicated to the Archangel Michael, making it, literally, the Mount of Archangel Michael. The site basically consists of two tiers: around the ramparted base, a small French village, now organized around serving the tourist trade; at the top, a functioning Catholic abbey and Gothic-style church, open to the public. Some, not without justification, have likened Mont-Saint-Michel to a wonderful fairy castle; its appearance certainly does not contradict that perception.

The island is a single granite outcropping that rises 250 feet straight out of the tidal bay; it is connected to the mainland by a paved causeway slightly less than a mile long. The tip of the church's highest tower is 515 feet above the sea, crowned by a statue of the Archangel Michael striking down a dragon. An estimated three million people visit every year, with a special emphasis on the Archangel's special day, Michaelmas (the English name for it), September 29. Mont-Saint-Michel is believed to be France's second most visited site.

In some respects, the early historical aspect of Mont-Saint-Michel tends to blur with the legendary. In the early days of Christianity, the Mount served as an abode for hermits and anchorites, but in the late seventh century A.D., everything came into focus around the Archangel Michael. One day Saint Aubert (born 660 A.D.), Bishop of nearby Avranches, declared that he had been commissioned by the spiritual world to be an emissary of light. According to his legend, on that particular day as he stood inside a small church, there was a momentous thunderclap and the building flushed with brilliant light. Soon after, Saint Aubert fought a dragon that had been terrorizing this region; he uttered Christian words and made the sign of the cross before the firedrake, after which the beast froze in its tracks and slunk back into the sea.

On October 9, 708 A.D., Saint Aubert had a series of prophetic dreams in which Saint Michael asked him to build a chapel in his honor on *Mons Tumba*. After he had the same dream three times in all, Saint Aubert was convinced it was a real message from the spiritual world and started the work. According to the dream, Saint Aubert would find a white bull tethered on the Mount at the exact site for the foundation; the wanderings of the bull over the Mount would indicate the size of the church to be built.

The legend (or saint's hagiography) next says that Saint Aubert found such a bull on the Mount as well as an ancient standing stone on the summit. This stone, to the churchmen a reliquary of the unsavory pagan past, proved impossible to budge. A local farmer named Bain had also had a dream about the Archangel and the future church, and he had been asked to bring his sons with him to the Mount to help move the stone.

The stone did not move until Bain brought his twelfth son, newborn, to the summit; then the megalith toppled off the Mount; where it landed (a few hundred yards from the Mount) is now called Tombelaine, a small isle that has a chapel dedicated to Saint Aubert at its top. On October 16, 709, Saint Aubert dedicated the sanctuary at the Mount to the Archangel. For those in this diocese, Michael's feast and veneration day is celebrated on October 16 in commemoration of the dedication in 709.

On another occasion, Saint Aubert dreamed that the Archangel Michael instructed him to collect some fifth century relics from Mount Gargano in Italy (another Michaelic site, where he appeared in 494) and deposit them at Mont-Saint-Michel. These relics were afterwards credited with producing various miracles (notably restoring sight to the blind), a fact which so contributed to the site's favorable and widespread reputation that it became one of the most important Christian pilgrimage sites in Europe. In subsequent centuries, the Archangel was reported to have made occasional epiphanies on the Mount, typically appearing in a blaze of light.

In 996, a group of Benedictine monks replaced the lineage installed by Saint Aubert and began formal construction of an abbey; in the eleventh century, a larger church was built on the summit, and further Gothic-style additions were added in the thirteenth century. So impressive was the beauty and so ingenious the architecture that the abbey and the island came to be known as *La Merveille* (the Marvel) and "Wonder Island."

Miquelots, or devotees of the Archangel Michael, traveled from all over Europe to visit the Archangel's appointed sanctuary. The Michaelic island, once you made it past the treacherous shifting sands and the galloping tidal waters and onto solid rock, was known for its power "to keep the enemy—be it man or nature—at bay."[529] Devotion to this archangel had great significance to medieval Christians.

The Archangel Michael—his name means "Like Unto God" or "Who Is As God"—was credited with weighing the souls of the dead and separating the elect from the damned; leading the elect into Heaven and there protecting them against inimical forces; and guarding the gates of Paradise. The Archangel Michael is regarded as the Prince of Light in the perennial battle against evil and the legions of darkness. He is the champion of God's people, that is, those who are dedicated to the Supreme Being (historically, the Jews, then Christians, then medieval knights), and he rescues the souls of the faithful from spiritual error and deception.

He is most often depicted as a youthful armed warrior, with helmet, shield, and blazing sword, leading the Heavenly Hosts against the evil hordes. He is also known as Preparer of the Way for each Messenger of God, such as the Christ; the guardian of holy sanctuaries; the celestial medium through whom the spiritual laws of humankind were delivered; holder of the keys of the kingdom of Heaven; and the guardian of the magical formulas by which Heaven and Earth were established—geomancy, or Earth's visionary terrain, in other words. It is generally understood that Saint Michael and the Archangel Michael are the same being, the former a more humanized version of the angelic deity.

In 1425, a mere 120 French knights stationed at the Mount held off the invading force of eight thousand English soldiers; in fact, Mont-Saint-Michel has never been taken in battle. In 1791, during the French Revolution, the monks had to flee the island and for five years it served as a governmental prison. Later, after 1863, when the last prisoner was released from Mont-Saint-Michel, rehabilitation of the abbey began; in 1874, the French government designated the site as an official historic monument; in 1879, the causeway was built connecting the Mount to the shore; and in 1922, religious ceremonies began again in the abbey church. Since 1969, Benedictine monks and nuns have maintained regular Catholic religious services on the Mount for the benefit of retreatants, pilgrims, and tourists.[530]

MYTH AND LEGEND

An early legend about the site says its original inhabitant was the father of the famous French giant Gargantua and that he was buried at the Mount.[531] This antique attribution was memorialized in one of the site's oldest names: Mont Gargan, meaning, more or less, the Mount of the Giant Gargan. Gargantua is also credited with severing the Mount from the mainland; originally it was not an island but more of a peninsula.

One day the giant, having consumed a surfeit of cider, felt the need to relieve himself; so prodigious was his urination that he irreparably flooded the peninsula and made the Mount into an island accessible only at low tide. The geological explanation is that in 709 A.D. a furious riptide separated the Mount from the mainland.

This is somehow fitting, as Saint Michael's Mount, a similar island sanctuary dedicated to the Archangel Michael, located directly north across the English Channel on the southwestern tip of Cornwall near Marazion in England, also has a legend of a giant as the original resident at the site. Actually, there were the giant Cormoran and his wife, Cormelian, living there.

Legend also holds that a giant in Cornwall and another in Brittany (in France, just west of Normandy) hurled huge boulders at each other. Where the two boulders landed became the two Mounts, suggesting not only a co-creation for both sites but perhaps a similarity in geomantic function.

Some visitors contend that the French Mount surpasses the Cornish one. Mont-Saint-Michel is "far greater in size" and "grander in design," and the Cornish Mount looks more like an earthbound spirit upon which we can look down, "as if granted a God's eye view." Not so Mont-Saint-Michel. "Lofty, imposing, almost haughty, [it] rises out of a flat landscape from which lowly mortals can only gaze upwards, its remote spire surmounted by a golden figure of Saint Michael scraping the sky."[532]

In the days of the Celtic Gauls, comparatively much more recently, the granitic Mount was named after Belenus, the Celtic god of Light; it was also called Tombelen, meaning the place where Belenus was entombed. In later centuries when the Romans erected a temple on the site, they called it *Mons Tumba,* or "Tomb of the Mount or Giant."

Belenus, whose name means "bright" or "brilliant," was a Gaulish god whom scholars consider interchangeable with Irish and British deities known variously as Bel, Belinos, Beli, and Bile (also known as a god of death and Underworld soul guide). Caesar said Belenus was like the Greek Apollo, a solar god who dispensed light and healing; one excavated site showed Belenus holding a solar disc while being conveyed in a horse-drawn chariot. England has many sites named after Belenus, such as Billingsgate, which originally was called Belinos' or Bile's Gate, and his worship was once widely observed in France and Italy.

MYSTICS AND TOURISTS

In the 1930s, a French novelist named Roger Vercel engagingly described the process by which Mont-Saint-Michel cast its spell over a young man who came there from Paris to work as a tour guide. In *Tides of Mont Saint Michel,* the mount itself is a central character—protean, mystical, unforgettable. (This is an excellent text for exploring the gradual effect of a sacred site on a sensitive person—how it brings one to the threshold of the visionary.)

At first Andre, the main character, is taken by the physical appearance of the site. Standing at its peak overlooking the sea, he has the sense of being perched high on the maintop of a steamer; another time it seemed the entire Mount was gliding over the waters, "sailing on a voyage which had no end." But seen from a distance, out in the vast sand flats, the mount was like a "grey, shadowy shape simplified in the extreme," like a sharp, squat pyramid. The statue of the Archangel Michael at the highest point of the mount was also a constant reference point, as it "sparkled like a golden spear-head."

After a while the numinous quality of Mont-Saint-Michel started to work on Andre. The "marvellous etherealness" of the spire and the "sublime upthrust" of the buttresses imposed on him "a strong sense of life" and "the assertion of a paramount presence." It seemed to him that the "great Mount watched and waited." The Mount suggested "an ethereal buoyancy, a dauntless aspiration." It gave the unmistakable impression that it was on the watch, "like a living presence." Its spell of peerless beauty "gripped him like grief"; contemplating the Abbey and its Mount filled him with profound contentment, and he felt "stirred to the depths of his soul by the peace, the repose, of this heavenly vision."

Andre became aware that people who had spent their lives on the Mount, seeing it at all times of day from all types of vantage points, "had the Mount within their hearts, without even knowing it, as a living friend." The wonder of the abbey and its setting—"the incomparable spectacle"—soaked into people without their being aware of it, casting its spell, so that it became for them "the very bread of life."

After nearly a year of living on the Mount, Andre realized he had "acquired the habit of beauty" from his daily exposure to the site. That habit and the spell of the Mount were like a drug, "which he could not forgo without torment." There was so much oxygen, light, sublimity, and height at Mont-Saint-Michel that—when the right kind of mind felt the concordance with the right kind of environment—it turned the rest of the world for him into a place of exile. "In the long run, they led to an everlasting expansion of the soul. It would stifle anywhere else."[533]

A decade or so later an American writer visiting the Mount wrote about it in a short story. He noted the irony of the abbey's pointed spire, which indicated the "precise direction of a heaven nobody believed in anymore." The ever-changing quality of light and air, shape-shifting right before one's eyes, made it seem "as if it were some kind of heavenly vaudeville act." The light on the seacoast was dazzling and severe and clouds "funneled the radiance upward. It seemed that flocks of angels might be released into the sky at any moment."[534]

For American scholar and traveler Henry Adams, the lure of Mont-Saint-Michel was the way it presented the Archangel Michael. The abbey's architect, he commented in 1906 after visiting the Mount, was to express the thirteenth century's concept of the Archangel Michael. "The masculine, military energy of Saint Michael lives still in every stone. The genius that realized this warlike emotion has stamped his power everywhere. . . ." Perched at the highest point on the Mount, the church and its "aspirant Archangel stands high above the world, and seems to threaten heaven itself."

Adams noted that at Mont-Saint-Michel, with respect to the Christian mysteries, you do not particularly feel the Trinity, the Christ, or Virgin, but "only the Archangel and the Unity of God." Standing on his "Mount in Peril of the Sea," the Archangel Michael, conqueror of Satan, nearest to God, mightiest of all created spirits, was for centuries France's militant patron saint, Adams said, headquartered where the danger was greatest, on the vulnerable shores of Normandy. The Archangel's role, Adams meant, was to protect Christianized France against any hordes of invading pagans.[535]

<hr>

GEOMANTIC

Dome Cap; Dragon; Michaelion.

DOME CAP: To a large extent, Mont-Saint-Michel must be interpreted geomantically in concert with Michael's Mount in Cornwall. Both are dome-capped islands; both have a minor dragon resident within the energy field of their dome cap. These dragons are two among the planet's 1,053 minor dragons, spawned by the thirteen primary ones. In both cases, the "mother" dome is situated a bit inland, but the effect of the distribution of the ninety-six dome caps between the two domes is to create a protective matrix of dome caps across the English Channel. In the case of Michael's Mount in Cornwall, the dome is located over an unmarked hill near the village of Cripplesease, just past Marazion.

Perhaps in an earlier geological age, the two landmasses (the Normandy tip of France and the Cornish tip of England) were closer, perhaps even connected, so that more of the dome caps rested on land masses above the water. Even so, functionally, you have two dragons situated within two Mounts on either side of the Channel, and a complex webbing of light centers spanning the Channel, a bit like a fishing net studded with bright globular gems.

DRAGON: The key to understanding the geomantic function of Mont-Saint-Michel is to understand the cosmic and terrestrial function of the Archangel Michael. Even more fundamental, it is helpful to give the benefit of the doubt to the Archangel's existence and presence at the site. I can assure the reader that Michael is real, and He is present at Mont-Saint-Michel, as well as at the hundreds of other sites dedicated to Him throughout Europe and the rest of the world.

It is no effort for archangels to multiply themselves so as to be simultaneously, validly, and effectively present at many sites. It is somewhat astonishing to note that in Britain alone there are seven hundred sites dedicated to the Archangel Michael.[536] It is a reasonable assumption that the Celtic deity Belenus is a partial description of the Archangel Michael.

It's also helpful to get a sense of how some aspects of the Western metaphysical tradition regard the Archangel Michael. According to Rudolf Steiner, the Austrian psychic, scientist, and founder of Anthroposophy, Michael is the upholder of the purity of Cosmic Intelligence (which the Gnostics deified under the name of Sophia, Divine Wisdom), which is to say, knowledge of everything that has been, is, and will be going on in the universe, and why. Michael helps humans to spiritualize their intellect, to infuse materialistic models with the subtlety of light and spirituality. Michael waits for humans to rise up to meet him; then he acts as guide to the cosmic mysteries.

Mont-Saint-Michel, then, is Michael's sanctuary, one of his dedicated places. Functionally, everything at Mont-Saint-Michel exists inside the celestial body of this archangel who could be visualized as standing there, rising in fact high above the Mount but with his "feet" firmly planted on the granite. There he creates an atmosphere that could be described as "fierceness of the quest." This pertains to a purity of space, a heavenly sanctuary on the Earth for the revelation of the mysteries of Light and the Christ.

Meanwhile, occupying the same space as the prominence is one of the Earth's 1,053 minor dragons. The dragon, not *slain* but *activated* by Michael, energizes this site and, metaphorically, holds the higher light on its crown; it fuels and supports the activities of Michael on the Mount. The dragon, as it were, works from the ground up, Michael from the sky down.

The variously named antediluvian giants—Gargan at this site, Cormoran and Cormelian at Cornwall—are folk memories of the activities of the Elohim, a mid-level angelic family commissioned by the Supreme Being eons ago to temporarily incarnate as physically large humans—giants—to set up the planet's geomancy, erect its megaliths, and when necessary, create small mountainous islands such as the two Mounts. It's instructive, and a little breathtaking, to note that whenever we encounter and investigate myths of giants, we are touching into a memory of such extreme antiquity. (See Mount Etna, for more on the primordial geomantic work of the giants.)

MICHAELION: Michael facilitates a scouring, an absolution, the creating of a pure interior space, an induction point. At Mont-Saint-Michel, Michael creates a psychic stillness and concentration in which the Christ may be heard by those humans wishing it. With his sword and shield, he protects the island sanctuary from outer and inner inimical energies; he holds the space sacrosanct for spiritual insight. He fights off the "pagans" and devils that would corrupt the space. This describes the outer (psychic) walls of the Michaelic sanctuary at Mont-Saint-Michel. But there is an inner space too, and this is actually the "fruit" of the site.

Michael creates a protective spiritual space in which the human aspirant may encounter, behold, even assimilate, aspects of the Goddess Sophia, the personification and holder of Cosmic Intelligence—the mother of the stars, and the Virgin Mother of the Christ, understood here as the point of self-reflexive awareness that holds the cognition of divine wisdom. This is an unavoidably arcane way of contextualizing the Christ as a prime spiritual being independent of any ecclesiastical definition, a necessary distinction to understand Michael.

Mont-Saint-Michel offers an initiation into cosmic knowledge in layers. First you enter the Michaelic sphere and undergo the fierce absolution and spiritual cleansing; then you can proceed to a Christed initiation; and from there to a Sophianic one. Each one brings you closer to true and ultimate cognition; each strips you of nonessential traits of mind and spirit. The Sophia Mysteries involve experiencing the sublimity of the view of God; her myth after all was about leaving the perfection of the Godhead to look at the lower worlds and view God from the outside. So Michael chaperones the aspiration upwards and the initiation leads to knowing and liberation.

What do you get to know? You get to know the "magical formulas" by which Heaven and Earth were established, the more sublime aspects of geomancy.

There is another feature offered by the Archangel Michael at Mont-Saint-Michel. Seemingly several hundred yards above the summit of the Mount is a dimensional doorway, a little aperture. If you conceive of Michael standing upright on the Mount, towering hundreds of yards, maybe miles, above the water (which mystics and psychics have reported), then it is as if Michael holds a small crystal in his hands. It is the white of green—seemingly a nonsense phrase but actually a chromatic clue to getting in attunement with this doorway. Initially it looks like a circular room of blazing white light, comprising dozens of crystalline pillars, tinged or overlit by green.

This is a Michaelic conclave, a higher sanctuary of the Knights of Michael (spiritual aspirants under his tutelage) who have achieved the Michaelic initiation. They come here of their own accord; in a sense, if you can "climb" up here, you can at least visit. For want of a better term, we might call this a *Michaelion*, which was the old name for his principal physical sanctuary at Sosthenion in Phrygia (fifty miles south of today's Istanbul in Turkey), where he was renowned as the great heavenly physician and said to have appeared before the Emperor Constantine.

The Michaelion is the theater for the performance of the Michaelic mysteries. Inside, you are surrounded by his choir and Heavenly Host. This is Michael's level of Heaven, which is said to be the seventh level out of seven. In other words, at Mont-Saint-Michel, you have the chance of stepping through a doorway above the Mount and entering the seventh level of Heaven, over which Michael, chief of the seven archangels, presides.

Here is a way of visualizing the Michaelion: It's like a dome, but instead of star beings astride chariots drawn by a fiery team of horses, Michael's archangelic form is the canopy. You are inside a dome made of Michael's celestial body. Within Michael's globular form are his Heavenly Hosts, the celestial denizens of the seventh Heaven. The Michaelic globe narrows at the base to form an eye which looks down on Mont-Saint-Michel.

Above, you have Michael forming an archangelic eye, Like Unto God, viewing events below in our world; below, you have a dragon, a granite island, a church, an abbey, a dome cap, and human aspirants looking upwards, their questing eyes cast towards Heaven, awaiting revelations. Connecting the two realms is the astral apparition of the Archangel Michael, a giant celestial figure astride the tiny island as if it were a pebble in a pond. This is Michael's epiphany in our world; enter it, pass through the doorway of the Michaelion, and you can behold his epiphany in his own world.

Montsegur, France

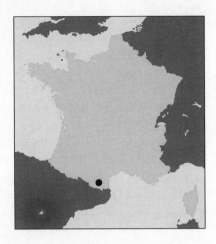

PHYSICAL DESCRIPTION

The stone ruins of the Chateau of Montsegur lie atop an aerie comprised of sheer rock called the Pog, rising five hundred feet above ground in the mountainous region of southern France near the Pyrenees and the Spanish border. Lourdes is due west and Avignon in Provence lies to the east.

The Pog, though it seems intimidatingly steep when viewed from certain directions, is in fact easily climbed, and the trek takes about forty-five minutes in each direction, even for the most leisurely of walkers. (I have seen women in high heels and men with canes make the ascent as insouciantly as if it were level ground.) At the mountain's base resides the small village of Montsegur.

HISTORY AND ARCHEOLOGY

The small castle is believed to have originally been a temple used by the Cathars, a heretical branch of early Christianity whose radical spiritual beliefs put them in mortal peril from the orthodoxies of Rome and the Catholic Church. While Montsegur was only one among many notable Cathar castles similarly perched atop almost impregnable rock fortresses throughout the Languedoc region of France, it was probably Catharism's most important, if not holy, one.

Certainly during the years 1229 to 1244, Montsegur functioned as the Cathar's preeminent stronghold. The castle or chateau itself was far too small to accommodate many residents; the Cathars are presumed to have lived at the base of Montsegur in small homes.

Catharism was a belief more in accord with earliest Christianity, even Gnosticism, characterized by Dualism, which is to say, a perennial conflict between good and evil forces in the universe with the human soul as the prize. There was God, and there was Satan, and between them they ruled the world; or put another way, there was the light, or spiritual world, and the dark, or terrestrial world; the former was good and pure, the latter impure and corrupt. The Cathars considered themselves to be good and true Christians, "as distinct from the official Catholic Church which according to them had betrayed the genuine doctrine of the Apostles."[537]

One prime Cathar ceremony was called the *Consolamentum*, which involved a Baptism of the Spirit, as well as an absolution and ordination. A Cathar elder (called a *parfait*, which meant a Cathar priest) conveyed the Holy Spirit to the new

355

initiate (whose numbers included women) by way of laying on of hands, specifically on the head. It was believed this transmission would aid the newly ordained Cathar to free his soul from the bondage of matter.

Since its construction in the second half of the twelfth century, the Chateau of Montsegur was a center for instruction in the Cathar mysteries and a key site for initiation into the Cathar priesthood. This made it the obvious prime target for the Catholic Church in the mid-1200s when it sought to expunge Catharism and its heresies from France, which it did.

The Church's ruthless extermination of all spiritual opposition to its beliefs, led by Simon de Montfort beginning in 1209, was termed the Albigensian Crusade (after the town of Albi, dwelling place of many heretics). In 1215, the Council of Lateran officially inaugurated the Inquisition, which over the next fifty years would eradicate all heresies in France. In the years 1243 and 1244, Montsegur was besieged, and on March 16, 1244, 220 Cathars were burned at the stake on the lower slopes of the mountain. Today, the meadow below Montsegur where the massacre took place is known as the "Field of the Burned."

It is widely believed that four parfaits escaped in the night down the steep side of the peak, bearing with them various invaluable Cathar treasure; some say gold; others say it was books and esoteric regalia. Throughout the Crusade, Montsegur was rumored to be holding a "mystical Cathar treasure which far exceeded material wealth." One theory was that this treasure was the Shroud of Turin ("a cloth which, when displayed in the hands of their priest, manifested a mysterious image of the flesh and blood of Christ"), which the Cathars had used, apparently unsuccessfully, as a kind of magical weapon with which to defend the Pog against the Crusaders. According to this theory, the Shroud was ferreted out of Constantinople in 1204 and presumably brought by the Cathars to Montsegur.[538]

Others contend it was no material treasure that the redoubtable Cathars smuggled out during the last night at Montsegur. One authority suggests it had to be something they carried in themselves. "But in themselves was the treasure, the power to transmit the apostolic succession, the seed perhaps of a higher form of Christianity to be revealed when the world is ready to receive it."[539]

MYTH AND LEGEND

The mythic resume for Montsegur, at least in terms of available published accounts, is meager. The most notable attribution is that it was the presumed site of Wolfram von Eschenbach's *Munsalvaesche* ("The Mountain of Salvation," sometimes translated as "The Wild Mountain"). In his metaphysical but quite opaque early-thirteenth-century treatise *Parzival,* Munsalvaesche was the site of the Grail Castle and the Holy Grail itself.

He did not specifically identify Montsegur as the site, but historians have found sufficient clues to consider the identification probable. "Nothing had been spared to make an impregnable stronghold; it stood smooth and rounded as though from a lathe," wrote von Eschenbach. Unless potential attackers came to Munsalvaesche on wings or were "blown there by the wind, no assault could harm it."[540] That is certainly an accurate description of Montsegur.

Somewhere between legend and esoteric account is the report that a female parfait named Esclarmonde (whose name means "She who enlightens the world"), presumably an actual resident at Montsegur in its last decades, turned into a white dove as the 220 Cathars were dying in the flames, and flew off towards the East. For the Cathars, the white dove symbolized the soul of the just returning to their rightful home in Heaven. In the symbolism associated with the Holy Grail, the white dove conveyed the Holy Grail from above down to the assembled knights or priests.

MYSTICS AND TOURISTS

British psychiatrist Arthur Guirdham, M.D., published two well-received books (*The Cathars and Reincarnation,* 1970; *We Are One Another,* 1974) about his clinical investigations of patients and friends reporting reincarnational memories of when (they believed) they had lived as Cathars at Montsegur. In the process of researching these cases, Dr. Guirdham observed his own irrepressible attraction to Montsegur.

From the moment he first heard the name and before he knew any of its history, he felt "haunted by the longing" to visit the French site. In the years before he finally went there, he would speak of "Montsegur, the haunting mountain" whose very name "gave me an indefinable stab of emotion." Once there, Dr. Guirdham noted its "green, ethereal beauty with great peace." Yet it had "a great power of magnetism and also the capacity to induce a heartache." He felt he could have stayed at Montsegur indefinitely.

Dr. Guirdham also noted Montsegur's protean, almost shape-shifting, geological quality: The peak "has a trick of hiding itself completely as one approaches it from different directions." After his third visit, he wrote, "I have never seen anywhere like it and its beauty has a haunting quality that I have never known elsewhere."[541] Even though one of his colleagues reported that the whole of Montsegur, especially its lower slopes, appeared to be psychically and horrifically saturated with blood, Dr. Guirdham, a sensitive himself, did not detect any "evil" residues of the thirteenth-century massacre or psychic contami-

nation when he visited the site. "Yet Montsegur remains inviolable in its persisting serenity. These matters are beyond our full understanding."[542]

A more recent visitor to Montsegur notes that it is one of those types of sacred mountains, like the anomalously shaped Tor in Glastonbury, England, that "fascinates the eye of the beholder from a great distance." Writing in 1995, the commentator also noted that Montsegur's ruins are "as mysterious and beautiful today as ever," a fact which probably contributes to the resurgence of the little town "as a new age Mecca like Glastonbury."[543]

GEOMANTIC

Dome; Grail Castle.

DOME: The dome over Montsegur corresponds to delta Orion, which is called Mintaka (from the Arabic *Al Mintakah,* "the Belt"), one of the three stars in the Hunter's famous belt. In star lore, this star is the first "King" to rise; it is located fifteen hundred light years from Earth and is among the hottest, bluest, and most luminous of stars.

The presence of a dome over Montsegur (rather than a dome cap, or some other geomantic feature) largely explains its prominence as a Cathar stronghold in thirteenth-century Languedoc. With the capacity of distributing forty-eight dome caps to neighboring peaks and towns in all directions within perhaps a twenty-five-mile radius, Montsegur became the energetic center of the Cathar domain. Naturally, the Catholic Church wanted to destroy Montsegur and its influence; on an occult level, it was a case of "star wars" in the Earth's spiritual topography.

GRAIL CASTLE: The intensity of the opposition to activities at Montsegur is also an index of its geomantic importance. Based on the geomantic nature of Montsegur, it is a reasonable speculation to say that the Catholic Church wanted to shut down all access to the Grail Castle above the peak. The reason is that the "doorway" from Montsegur into the etheric Grail Castle above (in a subtler dimension) was wide open and frequently trafficked.

Human access to the Grail Castle was bound to be politically and ideological destabilizing to an entrenched orthodoxy such as the Catholic Church. The metaphysical riches brought back from Grail Castle visitors could undermine the Church's hegemony in Europe.

Montsegur is not unique, of course, as being the access point for a Grail Castle. There are, after all, 144 such entry points around the planet. But not all are identified, open, and in good repair at a given time. During the thirteenth century, and quite likely for centuries before that, the Montsegur Grail Castle access point was, so to speak, a very well-oiled door.

Why would this be a threat to the Catholic Church? If you can of your own inner development and initiation, enter a spiritual plane temple affording total cosmic memory, divine intelligence, and galactic cognition, who then needs priests and Rome to mediate between the human soul and God? Montsegur threatened the Church's ideological and psychic control mechanisms that maintained religious orthodoxy.

The essential spiritual energy present at Montsegur and its Grail Castle portal pertains to developing trust in cognition. Parfaits were schooled in the mechanics of clairvoyance and the reasonable bases for trust in their perceptions. Due to the interconnected nature of the Montsegur dome and its 48 affiliate dome caps, Cathars at any of these other sites had in effect equal psychic access to the Montsegur Grail Castle portal. The limitation would be their individual psychic abilities, not any impedance in the geomantic setup. This meant potentially forty-eight other Cathar abbeys, chapels, chateau, and castles could participate in Montsegur rituals and inner journeys.

Imagine the beneficial effect, both in terms of group psychic impact and on the geomantic terrain, of a Grail castle "mass" held simultaneously at Montsegur and its forty-eight dome caps. The more a geomantic structure is used, and used correctly, the better it works, and the easier it is for those who come afterwards to use the site to their benefit. The land benefits, too, for with the regular human traffic into the Grail Castle comes a corresponding downflow of spiritual energies into the dome and landscape.

The regular flow of celestial energy through a geomantic structure into the human world is really why there is a spiritual topography and why humans are encouraged to participate in its operations. The Cathars at Montsegur knew this and fulfilled their responsibilities.

To an extent, the various aspects of the Cathar ritual, including the *Consolamentum* and the doctrines of Dualism, were only a spiritual façade, a convenience, something to keep their minds on as they prepared for entry into the Grail Castle. These ritualistic procedures prepared them, taught them certainty in their clairvoyance. Then the Holy Spirit would reach down from above and ignite their crown chakras so they could *know* directly.

The ontological treasures were to be found *upstairs*, and given their exalted, transworldly significance and grandeur, were not likely to get encapsulated as terrestrially meaningful doctrine. Mysteries, though penetrated, remain ineffable. So the real Cathar doctrine, at least for the adepts, pertained to the Grail Mysteries and the sublime joys of deep cosmic memory.

Here is a way to conceptualize what could happen at Montsegur (or any of the other 143 Grail Castle portals). You rise in spirit—extend your clairvoyance upwards, so to speak—and find yourself seated at a very large round table at which many others are seated; some you know, many you do not. The Holy Grail appears at the center of the vast table: It is a large golden chalice with two handles. It becomes so large it takes up the space formerly occupied by the table. You enter the Grail and become one with it. You can do this because you have already created the Holy Grail within you as a container for deep cosmic recall, strong enough to hold the vast memories of Time.

A drop of the Christ blood entering the chalice quickens your cognition; it acts as a catalyst, awakening the unbelievably vast memory that is the Grail. All the knowledge possessed by the Rich Fisher King lies before you; it is an unending visual tableau of the entire history of the universe, of each *kalpa* (306 million years), and dozens, hundreds, of these—a living library, archives beyond belief. Yet you can have it all; as at a feast, you can "eat" until satiety.

You are in a land of astounding riches; you are in the fabled Celestial City of opulent Lanka over which Kubera, Lord of Riches, presides, as the Hindu myths tell us. You understand the history of this galaxy, of others, of the universe; you perceive the *whys* behind events. You remember why you as a human are here; why you as a soul have been here; and where it all is going. You settle into eternity as a context for consciousness. The cognitive opulence of the time tableau is yours. In short, you *remember*.

The regular ascension of the Cathar parfaits up into the Grail Castle and Kubera's opulent memory land of Lanka schooled them in cognitive freedom. They *knew;* no longer must they believe. Returning to their bodies at Montsegur, the parfaits transmitted this sense of unlimited cosmic knowledge throughout the dome cap matrix and by way of all those they met and spoke with. In a sense, with the Grail Castle door wide open, the Cathars did not have to do anything but keep it open. The fact they had been to the Grail Castle was sufficient; that achievement had a reverberating impact throughout the region.

Montsegur's function was to keep this door open for the continuous, uplifting two-way flow. That function has not changed, even if the site has been officially closed to religious and spiritual activities for seven hundred years. The lower end of the portal is a bit clogged today but could work fine again with a little cleansing. Recognition of its identity and reaffirmation of its function, even at a distance, can have a powerful effect. Even reading about the Montsegur Grail Castle access point can help restore, even revivify, its function. As always, Kubera's Celestial City of Lanka is open for business.

Montserrat, Spain

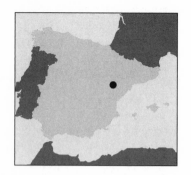

It was known to the Romans as *Mons Serratus* (Saw-Toothed Mountain), to the Catalans in this part of Spain as *Montsagrat* (Sacred Mountain), and sometimes it was called *La Muntanya dels cent cims* (the One-Hundred-Peak Mountain).

Whatever the name, Montserrat is a 4,054-foot-tall mountain about thirty miles from Barcelona, home to a sanctuary, monastery, and spiritual community that draws an estimated one million tourists a year. Along with Santiago de Compostela and Zaragoza, Montserrat is one of Spain's most important pilgrimage sites, and the pilgrims have been journeying here for spiritual insight since the twelfth century.

The shrine, the Benedictine monastery of Santa Maria de Montserrat, perches on the edge of yawning gorges, its dozens of serrated, jagged, barren, and reddish sandstone peaks that rise from the mountain's base suggesting a surrealistic moonscape. Montserrat is cut in many places by ravines, and the monastery is positioned at the widest ravine, above the Malo Valley, at 2,400 feet. The Montserrat range is one of the highest sheer ranges of the Prelitoral Mountains in Spain. In 1987, the Spanish government declared the Montserrat area a Natural Reserve.

"Its rocky peaks appear to have been chiseled by some prodigious hand out of the sky."[544] This impression is especially vivid if you approach the peaks suddenly, which was the case some years ago if you came up by the cog railway (built in 1892, now discontinued) that hugged the sides of the mountain until the final turn when the arresting vision came into view.

Today the track of the old cogwheel train is used as a footpath. If you're game, you can ascend the mountain via the aerial cable cars or gondolas that leave from the train station in the valley. Many come to Montserrat for the strenuous but exhilarating hiking, climbing, or biking that the mountain prospect offers the physically adventurous.

The Sanctuary of Our Lady of Montserrat is positioned near the top of the mountain and its highest peak, Sant Jeroni, but the final rise of the chiseled sandstone pillars frames the shrine like the folds of vast curtains. To many, Montserrat's attraction is a ninth-century statue of the Virgin Mary, presented as a Black Madonna with the child Jesus in her lap.

Over the centuries, many miracles have been credited to the Virgin Mary's intercession as a result of the pious praying to her statue. The Black Virgin is honored as the patroness of the province of Catalonia in northeastern Spain. It appears, however, that the Virgin Mary's intercession through prayers at Montserrat predated the creation of the statue; it was carved after Bishop-Abbot Oliba founded his modest monastery at Montserrat in 1025.

The Montserrat religious enclave has many aspects. A pilgrimage path leads through the forests that surround the mountain to various life-size Stations of the Cross and culminates at a chapel called Our Lady of Solitude. Thirteen mountain hermitages are open to the public, with eight different itineraries based on visiting the various shrines, chapels, and hermitages at Montserrat. Each day the *Escolania,* or boys' choir, sings the *Virolai,* a litany honoring the Virgin of Montserrat.

There is the Santa Cova to visit, the Holy Grotto (or cave) in which the Black Virgin statue was reportedly found in the ninth century. The mountain in fact is apparently riddled with caves. "The spirituality of Montserrat is a blend of the mountain, the sanctuary, and the life of monasticism."[545]

HISTORY AND ARCHEOLOGY

Archeological discoveries suggest that the caves of Montserrat were first inhabited thousands of years ago. In 888 A.D., when the Benedictine monastery of Ripoll was awarded jurisdiction over the site, Christian hermits of Santa Maria were already present at Montserrat. During the eleventh to early fifteenth centuries, a priory flourished on the mountain; in 1410, it was granted independence as an abbey, and has held that status ever since. Construction of the basilica that now stands on Montserrat began in 1560. The monastery was built in 1755 and rebuilt extensively in 1812 after the site was destroyed by the French.

The statue of the Black Virgin and Christ child in gilded polychrome wood, sometimes called *La Moroneta* ("the dark little one" or "the Brownie"), was reportedly carved by Saint Luke in Jerusalem, which explains another of its epithets, *La Jerosolimitana,* "Native of Jerusalem." Legend has it that the statue "fled" Jerusalem to escape coming into Muslim hands. The statue depicts the Virgin seated on a throne, facing the viewer directly, with the child Jesus on her lap, also directly facing the viewer. Both have darkened faces.

Why a black face? The same question is raised with respect to the icon of the Black Madonna at Jasna Gora in Czestochowa, Poland. Some say soot, flame, smoke, or innumerable votive candles and lamps may have darkened the faces. Others suggest that the Marian image might have an antecedent prototype for whom the blackness was appropriate. "It is well known that the iconography of Isis and [her son] Horus was basically adopted by Christians when they started to portray Mary and Jesus as Mother and Child." There is a direct, unbreakable line from the ancient goddess cults to the later reverence accorded to the Virgin Mary.

In Egypt, this authority says, Isis, the Great Mother Goddess, and one aspect of the feminine face of God, was sometimes pictured as black. If we construe the Black Madonna as "the ancient earth-goddess [Ceres or Artemis] converted to Christianity," then the "black" color takes on agricultural significance, as black soil is the most fertile soil for crops.[546]

The Black Madonna was brought to Spain by Saint Peter, and hidden in Santa Cova during the Moorish occupation of Montserrat in 718. (The Moors were Muslims from North Africa who conquered Portugal and Spain in the eighth century.) Presumably it remained hidden in the cave for the next 172 years.

La Moroneta was rediscovered in 890, reputedly with celestial assistance. The story has it that shepherds tending their flocks at night were amazed to see lights and singing coming from Montserrat. They reported the seemingly supernatural activities to their priest, who investigated. He witnessed the lights and songs, and filed a report with his bishop, and he too observed the same unusual phenomena. It is generally understood that the "lights" were a choir of angels. Apparently the lights and singing led them to the Santa Cova where they found the statue of the Black Madonna. The statue now resides in the Benedictine Abbey Church.

A conspicuous miracle credited to the Black Madonna was a miracle of spiritual insight awarded to Saint Ignatius of Loyola (1491–1556), who came to Montserrat for a prayer vigil on the evening of March 24, 1522. After three nights of praying and confession before the Black Madonna, St. Ignatius laid down his sword and dagger at Our Lady's altar, gave away his rich clothes to the poor, put on a sackcloth, and embarked on his religious mission, which included founding the Society of Jesus in 1534 and writing his treatise, *Spiritual Exercises.*

MYTH AND LEGEND

One of the most intriguing myths about Montserrat has it that the sandstone peaks that surround it were originally smooth but became serrated at the Crucifixion of Christ some two thousand years ago.[547]

Not quite on the order of legend but rather hearsay, Montserrat is said to have inspired the German operatic composer Richard Wagner to compose his Grail opera, *Parzifal.* This particular bit of gossip holds that Wagner based his concept of the Castle of the Holy Grail on Montserrat and that he perhaps considered Montserrat as the original location of the Grail Castle.

In Wagner's opera *Lohengrin,* in a song called "In Fernem Land," the knight reveals that the Holy Grail rested in Monsalvat in an inestimably rich and precious temple. This same line of folkloric attribution also credits Wolfram von Eschenbach with siting his Grail Castle, *Munsalvaesche,* at Montserrat, as described in his thirteenth-century *Parzival.*

"Montserrat is often called the Grail Mountain," notes one authority. In addition to the Wagner and von Eschenbach associations, he cites a legend of Saint Lawrence, a deacon of the Roman Catholic Church, who before his martyrdom in 258 A.D. at the hands of Emperor Valerian, "entrusted the Holy Grail to a disciple who hid it in a rugged mountain." That mountain was understood to be Montserrat, and afterwards, "a group of ascetical Knights" became the Grail's guardians.[548]

Another Montserrat attribution, though hard to substantiate, is that it formerly was a Temple of Venus along the lines of the Teutonic legend of the Venusberg, which was said to be a sybaritic, otherworldly Venusian grotto location deep within the Hürselberg, a mountain in Germany.

At least three facts about Montserrat support this. First, a group called the *Escalonia* regularly performs a dance called the *sardana* in front of the church; second, the motto of Montserrat concerns marriage and fertility and holds that "He is not well wed who has not taken his wife to Montserrat"; and third, just before the statue was discovered, the shepherds, priest, and bishop heard singing. A principal activity attributed to the Venusberg in German legend is the constantly sounding sweet strains of music, as well as singing and dancing as nymphs scatter roses at the goddess's feet.

In light of this possibility, one interpretation offered for Montserrat's spirituality is that on this mountain the feminine principle, "alternately lost and found, plays hide-and-seek with us." Christianity may have broken Montserrat's formal connection with the pagan pleasures of its

Venusian temple, singing maidens, and dancing lights, but its link to the "eternal feminine" continued through the veneration of La Moroneta, the Black Virgin.

Further, Montserrat, with its topographical uniqueness, microclimate, and legends, is a "House of God," and as proof, it has a stone staircase called Jacob's Ladder. This refers to what's known as Jacob's Pillow, upon which the Hebrew patriarch placed his head to sleep at Bethel and saw the ladder of angels ascending from and descending to the ground, linking Heaven and Earth.[549] Montserrat is magnificent for its "mountain solitudes" and it has been "for so long held in reverence." In such places as this, "the soul can find moments of aspiration and of close association with the heavenly."[550]

GEOMANTIC

Dome; Grail Castle; Tree of Life; Avalon.

DOME: Montserrat is topped by a dome that is the starfall for Albireo, or beta Cygnus, which is the constellation of the Swan. One of Cygnus' other prominent stars, alpha Cygnus or Denebola, appears as the dome at another Marian and Black Madonna site: Jasna Gora in Czestochowa, Poland. Albireo is the bright star on the Swan's head, although according to the Arabic name, this star is called *Al Minhar al Dajajah,* "the Hen's Beak." When eight of the 14 principal stars in Cygnus are seen in their alternative form as the Northern Cross, Albireo sits at the foot of the Cross.

Technically, Albireo is a double star, and astronomers consider it one of the most beautiful of the twins. The brighter star is third magnitude, while its companion is a fifth-magnitude star. Amateur astronomers have praised Albireo's tints of gold and azure, while the companion registers as sapphire. The twin stars are located about 410 light years from Earth, and their respective luminosities, compared with our Sun's, are 760 and 120 suns.

Even though the Albireo twins seem so close together as to be hard to distinguish the two definitively, they are actually separated by a distance of four hundred billion miles. "It is worth contemplating, in any case, the fact that at least 55 solar systems could be lined up, edge-to-edge, across the space that separates the components of this famous double!"[551]

The constellation of Cygnus is usually described as a flying eagle, hen, partridge, pigeon, or some form of star-bird called *Urakhyga* by the Babylonians. It has fourteen attributed stars and is called the *Ornis,* the Great Bird, or "swan" (from the Greek *kyknos*). Other names (such as late Roman) included *Ales* and *Avis* for "bird," *Olor* for "swan," and *Myrtilus* for the bird of Venus.

Here is the mythic background for Cygnus. The Greek myths say that Zeus was enamored of Nemesis and transformed himself into a swan so he could court and seduce her, as she had already assumed a swan form to protect her virginity. The myths also relate, somewhat confusingly, that Zeus sought Nemesis in her human female form for protection, nestling in her lap in his swan form, thereby impregnating her. Nemesis bore an egg of her union with Zeus, and passed it on to Leda; from the egg the beautiful Helen, later of Troy, was born.

GRAIL CASTLE: The allegations of the Holy Grail being present at Montserrat are correct. Montserrat is one among 144 sites on Earth where an etheric replica of the original Grail Castle is present in a subtler layer of reality superimposed on the physical. The Montserrat Grail Castle—which, we should remember, is, formally speaking, the Celestial City of Kantimati—occupies the entire space from the present monastic buildings to the top of the mountain and the Sant Jeroni peak.

The energy at the Montserrat geomantic complex, factoring in the dome and Grail Castle, is about creating joyous memory, the complete retrieval of soul artifacts, a bleeding through of previous cosmic moments to consciousness. This, of course, is a succinct way of summarizing the function of a Grail Castle, but at Montserrat, these original spiritual energies are well preserved, untrammeled, practically immaculate, and well protected.

The energies are under the custodianship of what could be called an otherworldly Grail fraternity, a cabal of post-humans working under the direction of the Ray Masters. These souls would correspond to that "group of ascetical Knights" who became the Grail's guardians after the martyrdom of Saint Lawrence. It is not correct to say that the Grail was *brought* to Montserrat in historical time, however; it is more correct to say that since the creation of the planet, the site now called Montserrat has *always* featured an etheric Grail Castle and an authentic replica of the Holy Grail.

TREE OF LIFE: This hierarchical fountain of the energies of the Four Worlds of existence and the forty different spheres of light extends from Santa Cova up to the Sant Jeroni peak. This feature is of course the energetic equivalent of the Jacob's Ladder, or stone staircase at Montserrat. You could almost think of it as a vast rope ladder studded with sparkling gems along the way.

From the vantage point of Sant Jeroni, at the top of the Tree, this geomantic feature provides an orderly cascade of the energies of creation and manifestation, from the subtlest to the most physically manifest. From the viewpoint of the base of the Tree at Santa Cova, here is where you begin your ascent through the worlds, moving through ever subtler, more refined layers of reality, until you reach the pinnacle of spiritual manifestation at the Sant Jeroni peak. The Montserrat monastic complex is situated at about the heart of the Tree.

AVALON: Here we find a geomantic explanation for the slightly odd allegations of singing, dancing lights, and a pagan Venusberg at Montserrat.

An Avalon is the mythic abbreviation for the more formal title of Celestial City of Gandhavati, which according to Hindu legends is filled with dancing girls *(Apsaras)* and heavenly musicians *(Gandharvas)*. In Celtic myth, Avalon is the land of the golden apple trees, or as the Irish called it, *Emain Ablach,* or as the Greeks knew it, the orchards of the Hesperides.

In all three mythic guises, this paradisiacal realm is presided over by celestial females: In Avalon, Queen Morgan and her eight priestesses; in *Emain Ablach,* Macha; and in the Hesperides, the daughters of Atlas and Pleione known as the Hesperides. At Montserrat, legends say the original presiding goddess was Venus, the Roman name for the Greek love goddess, Aphrodite (who, incidentally, was a Ray Master). At Montserrat, you have the best of "pagan" and Christian in the form of the Black Madonna.

It is an elegant, powerful, and not too common geomantic arrangement to have a Grail Castle and an Avalon at the same site, as if stacked one upon the other. At Montserrat, you have the Venusberg below the monastic foundations on the mountain, and the Grail Castle effectively above them. Perhaps this is a coincidental expression of the energy of Albireo, the double star: one star for Avalon, one for the Grail Castle.

Similarly, as if a magic sign was left by the master geomancer of Montserrat, in the statue of Black Madonna with Child, you have a representation of the spiritual function of the Montserrat temple. The Black Madonna points to the Venusberg, or Avalon, while the Christ Child signifies the Christed cognition available in the Grail Castle. The Venusberg is the feminine ground for the retrieval of deep cosmic memory, just as, in the Grail stories, the Grail Maidens solemnly bear the Holy Chalice before the Fisher King, Anfortas, within the arcane interior of the Castle.

The Venusberg is preparation and foundation for the Grail Castle experience. It also grounds the vast cosmic perspective one gains "upstairs" in the heady realms of cosmic memory. That is the joyous aspect of the cosmic memory retrieval. It is the celebration that comes from remembering, the dance—the *sardana*—of the rememberer. The double star of Montserrat, its Avalon and Grail Castle, is a wonderful demonstration of how these two energies work together flawlessly, synchronously, and synergistically to produce revelation.

Mount Damavand, Iran

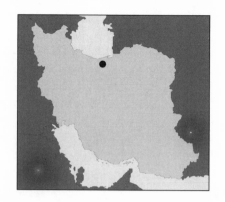

A mostly extinct volcano in the Elburz Mountains, Mount Damavand towers 18,603 feet above the Iranian desert, about fifty miles northeast of Teheran, making it the highest point in Iran and the loftiest volcano in Asia. Known in Persian as *Qolleh-Ye Damavand,* the snowcapped cone is formed of lava flows and ash and is topped with a small crater with sulfuric deposits.

The mountain also has fumaroles (holes for escaping fumes and gases), various hot springs, and travertine mineral deposits. Steam and sulfurous gases exude from its peak, but Mount Damavand, though still classified as "active," has not erupted in historical times. Mount Damavand is surrounded by smaller, rugged peaks of the Elburz range, but it is otherwise isolated and through its height and classic volcanic shape dominates the landscape.

MYTH AND LEGEND

The mountain is believed to be the physical site of the mystical *Hara Berezaiti,* "Peak of the Law," the cosmic mountain in Zoroastrian mythology. This mountain was *the* holy mountain in Persian cosmology, the Earth's central, prime mountain from which sprang the pure Aredvi River. This is the divine river that brings the Waters of Life to the world below. Hara Berezaiti was the first of all mountains, and birthed all the other peaks—the figure given is 2,244—from its roots over an eighteen-year period. This mountain was regarded as the cosmic mountain, world tree, and central pillar, situated at the center of the Earth so as to link Earth and Heaven.[552]

The ancient Iranian text called *Bundahishn,* "Knowledge from the Zand," states that once, when the Earth was under attack by the demonic powers of Ahriman (to the Persians, the Evil One), it raised up mountains as a defensive rampart, the first of which was Hara Berezaiti, which scholars equate with the Elburz (or Alburz).

In these mountains the key episodes in Zoroastrianism's sacred history were located and rediscovered. "Elburz is therefore indeed the *cosmic mountain,* raised up by the supreme effort made by the Earth in order not to be separated from Heaven."[553] All the mountains originate from this one cosmic mountain in a treelike network in which each subsidiary peak is a knot or a root thrust out from the central gigantic tree.

Alburz took eight hundred years to grow, says the *Bundahishn:* two hundred years to reach *payak,* the star station, two hundred years to the Moon station, two hundred years to the Sun, and two hundred years to reach the endless light. The stars, Moon, and Sun pass in through Alburz to the Earth, and through this mountain they return to their source. *Chakad-I-Daitik* (the Judicial Peak) is on Alburz, and is the site of the Chinvat Bridge, which leads the souls of the righteous (and deceased) over the abyss of the demons into Paradise. Nearby, on the summit, is the Arezur ridge "at the gate of hell, where they always hold the concourse of the demons."[554]

The gods' plant of immortality, the white *haoma* (equivalent to the Vedic soma, source of *amrta,* the beverage of immortality and divine inspiration) is also said to grow on Mount Damavand.

Possibly related to this is the myth of the Simurgh, the Bird of Marvel, which was said to build its nest of ebony and sandalwood on Damavand in the days when Mount Alburz's head "toucheth the stars, and never had mortal foot been planted upon its crest." In an Uzbekistan myth about the haoma tree, a white bird was said to perch in its limbs; possibly this was the Simurgh. Its nest was "like unto a king's house, and the evil sway of Saturn could not reach thereto."[555]

The Simurgh, or Persian *Simarghu,* was said to be a dragon or hybrid bird-dog that guarded the Tree of Life from which the seeds of everything living in the world could be obtained. That is a fair approximation of the haoma tree. The Simurgh was said to be usually invisible, and the Tree of Life looked like any other, so it was doubly dangerous to cut down any tree. In the Ukraine, the Simurgh was shown seated on a tree on an island guarded by voracious fish. Simurgh as the god-bird was understood to be the secret name for God and was considered the same as the immortal phoenix.

The Angel *Sraosha* (identified with the Hebraic Archangel Gabriel) is said to reside on the "summit of mystic initiation" at the "cosmic north," on the peak of Hara Berezaiti where he serves as the "Angel of initiation." His abode is "self-illuminated within, and adorned on the outside with stars."[556] The "cosmic north" is mystical code for the threshold of the beyond—as in, beyond the realm of the Earth and physical matter.

Sraosha (whose name means "Obedience" and "to hearken") takes the souls of the dead to Paradise and is the staunch supporter of Ahura-Mazda in his fight against the demons. In general, Sraosha helps the faithful destroy the demons of evil and lies by instilling obedience to the divine word, here understood as "an active, victorious quality of mind, protecting the soul."[557] Sraosha is Ahura-Mazda's "all-hearing ear which listened for the cries of men for wrong done to earth by the servants of Ahriman, 'the destructive spirit.'"[558]

The Ahriman-demon connection is central to Mount Damavand's mythology, but the story line is confusing and variable. The serpent demon Azidahaka (also called Azdahak, Dahak, Zohak, or Bevarasp) who overthrew the first mortal, Yima, and cut him in two, was itself overthrown by the Persian culture hero Faridu (also called Fredun, Faridun, or Thraetaona); it was tied up, chained, and imprisoned within Mount Damavand.

The *Bundahishn* states: "The Dimavand mountain is that in which Bevarasp is bound." Ferdausi, the twelfth-century author of Iran's national epic, the *Shah-Nama* ("Epic of Kings"), states: Feridoun "led forth Zohak to the Mount Demawend. And he bound him to the rock with mighty chains and nails driven into his hands, and left him to perish in agony." The hot Sun shone directly down on him who had no shelter, and "the chains entered into his flesh, and his tongue was consumed with thirst." Thus was the Earth delivered of Zohak, the Evil One.[559]

As Dahak, the demon is pictured with three heads, three mouths, six eyes, and of enormous strength; lizards and scorpions crawl all over his body; and he was created by the Evil One, *Angra Mainyu* (Ahriman) to act in the material world "for the destruction of the settlements of righteousness."[560] Thraetona (or Feridun) wields a cow-headed mace called a *gurz* to overcome Dahak; the gurz is equivalent (certainly in godly potency) to the thunderbolt weapon of Zeus, Thor, and Indra, which they used competently against their respective dragon-demon opponents.[561]

There are several variations on this myth. In one version, the imprisoned demon is called Biourasf; the occasional volcanic rumblings of the mountain are his groans, and the sulfurous vapors and steam emanating from its vents are his exhales. Another version has it that King Solomon imprisoned the fallen angels under this mountain to protect the world from their baleful activities.[562]

Yet another has Dahak as a king with a serpent's head growing out of each shoulder. Dahak was incarcerated under Mount Damavand, but only after he had reigned for a thousand years. Sometime just before the apocalyptic end of the world, the demon will escape and generate a massive upsurge of evil in the world. It's also said that King Zohak (or Dahak), who was King of Arabia, fled his palace in Jerusalem for Mount Damavand, and will remain there until Doomsday.[563]

In another version, Dahak was a "fiendish tyrant" and "archdevil," who required the sacrifice of two brains of young men every day. Faridun, the destined dragon-slayer, had been hidden away in the mountains as a youth to protect him from Dahak. When Dahak had claimed the eighteenth son of the smith Kavag, Faridun took action and successfully attacked the demon king.[564]

Possibly the version closest to the esoteric core of the original myth is the one that focuses on Yima. Yima, in Persian lore, was the first

human and the progenitor of the human race. He presided over a golden age that lasted seven hundred or one thousand years, and during this time successfully subjugated the demons and sorcerers so they could not harm humans. He took away their land and extended the borders of his Persian kingdom—he was also known as King Jamshid in this role—on behalf of his subjects.

Yima was the possessor of the *Xvarnah*, also known as the Glory, *farr*, or solar nimbus, which marked his status as among the elect of God.[565] Yima was also the first to offer haoma to Ahura-Mazda;[566] and during his reign as the beneficent sovereign, his lands became so beautiful and provident that Yima had to make the Earth stretch until it was one-third larger to accommodate all the humans and creatures who wanted to live there.

At some point, Yima lied, or acted unwisely out of pride, or fell under the influence of the demons and fell from grace; his golden age was over and he no longer had Ahura-Mazda's blessing and protection. When he lost his Glory, the demon Dahak gained power over him, and through him over all of Persia. In one account, Dahak was overthrown by Feridun, in whom a certain measure of Yima's lost *Xvarnah* had been reinvested.

Around the time Yima was losing his Glory and the golden age was waning, Ahura-Mazda told him destructive winters were approaching, along with disastrous hail, rain, heavy snows, and floods. Yima was instructed to prepare a *var,* a subterranean sanctuary or cave (the Persian version of Noah's Ark) and in it to gather together representatives of all species of life. In some texts, Yima's *var* is more like a glorious walled city full of its own light.

Yima was to preserve these seeds of life during the dark reign of Ahriman until he was called upon to replenish the Earth. For this reason, Mount Damavand is said to be a resting site for

Noah's Ark (Yima's *vara*) after the Flood had passed. "The story that the treasure of Yima is still hidden in a cave remains a part of modern Persian tradition."[567]

GEOMANTIC

Dome; Cosmic Egg; Underworld Entrance; Naga City; Grail Castle; Soma Temple.

DOME: This is indeed a complex geomantic site. In its multitiered mythic reality, you can see how different myths interact and start to form a fascinating, sublime cosmic drama, reminding us that ultimately the different geomyths are not separate but one awesome unity of consciousness. You can also see the slide from an original mythic core into something negative and dark.

The dome over Mount Damavand corresponds to alpha Ophiuchus Serpentarius, namely, to *Ras al Hawwa* (also known as *Ras al Hague*), "the Head of the Serpent-Charmer," a star that is about fifty-nine light years from Earth. Ophiuchus is the constellation of the Serpent Holder, located near the head of Hercules and Scorpio. The constellation is usually depicted as an elderly man (corresponding to the Greek physician Asclepius) or an unclad youth standing on a scorpion (the constellation Scorpio), holding the serpent in his hands, the tail on his right side *(Serpens Cauda)*, the head on his left *(Serpens Caput)*.

In other words, in the standard depiction of this constellation the serpent appears to be split in two, as in the myth of Yima and of Svarbhanu, the cosmic serpent whose head (Rahu) and tail (Ketu) now form the Moon's two nodes. In that Vedic myth, Svarbhanu was sliced in two by Vishnu to prevent him and his "demon" colleagues from obtaining the soma and thereby becoming immortal like the gods.

COSMIC EGG: The reference to Mount Damavand as the cosmic mountain Hara Berezaiti

is our clue that it is a Cosmic Egg, one of the planet's forty-eight. In geomythic reality, a Cosmic Egg is a cosmic mountain, the prime *axis mundi* and pivotal point around which the world revolves, the point of origin and embarkation. All creation emerges from the highest point of existence, from the Cosmic Egg, and the point where awakened consciousness leaves the created world is at the top of the cosmic mountain, as Cosmic Egg and cosmic mountain functionally are the same place.

Alburz can hardly be separated from Heaven, since as the Cosmic Egg it *contains* Heaven and Earth in that primordial nontime before spacetime began when they were not two realms but a single intermingled one. And as the Celestial City of Samyamani, Alburz is less than a hair's breadth from the highest realm of Heaven. The River Aredvi refers to the geomantic energy channels that conduct higher life and consciousness from the cosmic mountain down into the world surrounding the peak, "all of Persia," so to speak.

The reference to it taking eight hundred years for Alburz to grow and two hundred years each to pass through four stations, is another reference to the celestial contents of the Cosmic Egg, to the spheres of the planets and fixed stars it contains. The mystical geological concept of subsidiary mountains arising from Alburz like knots or roots is in part a reference to the forty-eight dome caps generated by the central dome and their energetic relationship to the central dome, or "tree" of Alburz. It also refers to the crucial geomantic function of a Cosmic Egg—remember, there are only forty-eight for the entire planet—with respect to a large geographic area.

UNDERWORLD ENTRANCE: The only place you find Cosmic Eggs and the Chinvat Bridge are in the Celestial City of Samyamani, the city of the Lord of the Underworld and the Land of the Dead—Hades' Palace, to use the Greek term. The Angel Sraosha guards the Chinvat Bridge *(Chinvat-paretu)*, allowing only the purified to pass over into the "cosmic North," or the beyond. From beneath the bridge rise the infernal wails and moans of the inhabitants of the demonic world who are prohibited passage over this most precious of bridges. The wails also originate from the lower "hell" realms in the Land of the Dead. Sraosha is the Guardian of the Threshold—a celestial bouncer, if you like.

The width of the Chinvat Bridge (also called "Bridge of the Decider") varies according to who is passing over it: from the thinness of a razor blade to the thickness of twenty-seven reeds, so that when the righteous cross, the bridge is broad, but when the wicked try to pass, the bridge beams become sharp and thin. Meanwhile, those who have fallen off or never gained entry wail below.

NAGA CITY: The complicated business of dragon-demons and dragon-slaying culture heroes is a clear indication of the Celestial City of Raksovati, the realm of the Nagas and the cosmic serpent, Sesa-Ananta. In the combination of Raksovati and Cosmic Egg we have an archetypal tableau of the serpent coiled around the Cosmic Egg, incubating it.

That is a neutral image, but many cultures over time apply a pejorative interpretation to the primal cosmic serpent, giving it a decidedly negative and evil cast when originally, as an expression of the ultimate power of consciousness and the undivided realm of potentiality and light, it was at worst ambivalent.

In the blending of the myths of Yima as presiding monarch of a golden age, of the necessity for him to prepare the *var* (the Persian version of Noah's Ark) against the coming Deluge, and of his fall from grace at the hands of the demon king Dahak, we have a lucid tableau of the saga of the Holy Grail, the Rich Fisher King, and the evil magician anti-king, Klingsor. We also have clear evidence of a Grail Castle at Mount Damavand.

GRAIL CASTLE: Yima is a vivid personification of the Fisher King in his *rich* phase, in the Golden Age of full, deep, *total* cosmic memory, when the land is richly fertilized with the Waters of Life and abundance is the order of the day. When Yima is king, the waters of the River Aredvi enrich the countryside. The images of richness, water, and agricultural abundance are primarily references to riches in consciousness, full waking memory of our vast, even precosmic, past, which is the Fisher King's rightful domain.

These qualities are aspects of Yima's *Xvarnah*, his Glory, the radiant effect of his total knowledge of cosmic history. Preserving these seeds of life (and memory) for a Deluge phase refers to the end of a vast cycle of time, the sunset of a *manvantara*, when, metaphorically, the cosmos goes into hibernation for a period.[568] The *vara* (or Ark) is code for the Grail Castle, which is the atemporal place for the recovery of full memory and the attainment of total recall—for a bite of the "fish" of consciousness.

Yima being seduced and corrupted by the dragon-demon Dahak is the archetypal story of the Rich Fisher King becoming the *Wounded* Fisher King when his former colleague and brother in the Grail order, Klingsor, stole his lance and ruptured the integrity of the Grail Kingdom. Klingsor (Richard Wagner's operatic name for the demon king) here stands in for Ahriman and the other variously named dragon-demon antagonists.

When Klingsor stole the lance, Yima lost his Glory, the aura of supreme, paradisiacal pure Light, unsullied since the Creation, which is probably code for the descent from the Golden Age into one of diminished spiritual awareness. The King remained unable to heal his wound (inflicted out of ignorance by his misuse of the lance, by his misappropriation of the magical knowledge of the Nagas) until the specially designated spiritual hero, Parsifal, arrives for this purpose.

In the Zoroastrian version of this archetypal geomyth, Faridun is the spiritual hero who can redeem the fragmented Yima, who has been split in two. In effect, Faridun heals Yima by providing the total cosmic recall of previous ages of time (earlier *manvantaras*) and especially of the Golden Age and all its seeds of rich cosmic life, knowledge, and awareness.

Although it sounds paradoxical, it is also true to say Faridun serves up this enriching memory in the *gurz*, which here is like a Grail chalice. He brings Yima a bit of the cosmic serpent's endless, boundless Light, a drop of dragon blood perhaps from the mere contact of the *gurz* with the massive serpent.

Klingsor-Dahak is only a mythic personification of Sesa-Ananta, the cosmic serpent whose domain of Raksovati also occupies the interior psychic space of Mount Damavand. By the fact that the Persians designate this basically ambivalent, multifaceted cosmic serpent as Ahriman, you know that the geomyth has taken a turn into the negative and pejorative under the influence of a specific theological vision and agenda. In a curious sense, Yima is also the serpent; remember that Yima was cut in two by the demon, and Ophiuchus the Serpent Holder in effect has divided the serpent into two parts, head and tail.

In the golden age, the serpent's energy, light, and consciousness inundated the land like a spring flood, enriching the land, making it excellent for agriculture. Here Yima presided as the regal sovereign, the Rich Fisher King, and the serpent was for the most part not imprisoned, but allowed to be an interactive part of the psychic and geomythic landscape.

When the golden age was over, the possibility for reality to hold and assimilate the potency of the serpent's illumination was greatly diminished; the serpent had to be imprisoned. Once imprisoned, it became regarded as a demon, as the dragon king Dahak; its life-giving primal

"Waters" were shut in, bounded, restricted, and the parched Wasteland was created, presided over by the bifurcated and wounded Fisher King, Yima.

You can see how the mythic valency shifts over vast periods of time, from a golden age to a diminished, degenerate age, from richness to wasteland, from a singular deity to one split in two, from one emanating light to one fallen from that light. Even this shows the cyclic nature of the cosmic serpent, how its apertures open and close over time in accordance with the flow of the ages and their parameters for consciousness during a *manvantara*, which is a vast period of time, roughly 306 million years long.

Faridun must subdue (or imprison) the demon within the mountain, using his *gurz* thunderbolt. At Croagh Patrick in Ireland, a mountain with a similar Raksovati legend, Saint Patrick, as one of the fourteen celestial *rishis* (Ray Masters) of the Great Bear, uses the Spear of Lugh (or Fire principle) to overcome the dragon-serpent within the mountain.

In the Persian myth, Faridun may be one of the fourteen rishis charged with a similar task: not to slay the dragon, but to modulate its release of cosmic light—pure consciousness in all its potentialities and ambivalences—into the surrounding terrain of northern Persia. Too much light allowed into human consciousness can deeply befuddle, intoxicate, even corrupt the self, allowing egress of the more primitive, demonic, "evil" impulses.[569]

Faridun is aided in mastering the cosmic serpent Dahak by Ophiuchus himself, the celestial Serpent Holder, through his holographic presence as the dome over the mountain. Mythically speaking, Ophiuchus comes to Mount Damavand accompanied by his retinue of forty-eight serpent holders (expressed through the dome caps).

Faridun may actually be of an order higher than the rishis, because his weapon, the *gurz* thunderbolt, is the weapon used by Indra, Zeus, and Thor, who are not Ray Masters (rishis) but the variously named organizing principle around which the Ray Masters constellate. Or Faridun is a Ray Master and Ophiuchus is the Zeus-like figure who wields the *gurz*, and together they "subdue" Dahak.

Clearly, Dahak, as raw cosmic consciousness and light, could not be allowed to pervade the countryside without limitation; it would burn up everything, all of material creation. Dahak's awesome cosmic light and consciousness must be controlled—imprisoned—on behalf of the living world around the mountain.

SOMA TEMPLE: In the Vedic myths involving the origin of soma, the beverage of immortality and godly inspiration that was generated when the gods churned the Ocean of Milk, the demons were always vying with the gods for a drink of this unique, life-transforming liquid, and the gods were always preventing them. The milky-white *haoma* from the Gaokerena tree is the Persian name for the Vedic soma.

Its attribution to Mount Damavand is our clue that a Celestial City of Yasovati, or a Soma-Moon temple, is present. Insofar as Mount Damavand has both a city of the Rakshasas (demons and progeny of the cosmic serpent) and a city of Soma, it is appropriate that the denizens of Raksovati would try to get the soma, and thus would be in "conflict" with the gods and Sraosha who protect it.

Lest you wonder how you can experience all these different aspects of Mount Damavand, considering it is a snowcapped eighteen-thousand-foot-tall peak, let me say here that it is not necessary to climb the mountain to "visit" the cities. Merely touching the energy "hem" of the base of the mountain and aligning your own energy field with it is sufficient for the psychically able to penetrate the mountain and its mysteries.

Mount Damavand offers a marvelous opportunity to experience both ends of the Fisher King saga and the possibility of resolving them. The Fisher King is wounded because he cannot remember his deep past; the life force energy of his root chakra (here represented by the city of Raksovati) cannot travel upward to his brow chakra to enable him to remember and thereby heal the wound of non-remembering.

The Fisher King's story is our story, for each of us who cannot remember our deep transpersonal past. At Mount Damavand, both poles of this energy circuit are in place, so by resonance we have an advantage here in achieving the Grail of deep cosmic memory by immersing ourselves in the cosmomythic energy field of this mountain.

Mount Etna, Taormina, Sicily, Italy

PHYSICAL DESCRIPTION

Mount Etna is a volcanic snowcapped mountain towering 10,902 feet on the northeastern coast of Sicily. Its name derives from the Greek *Aitne,* which in turn comes from *aitho,* which means "I burn." As a volcano, Etna has been burning—that is to say, geologically active—for an estimated 2.5 million years.

The mountain is massive: the circumference of its base is ninety-three miles and the mountain as a whole, including its lava fields, covers an area of six hundred square miles. This "great smoldering boil" that pushed itself up more than ten thousand feet from the sea covers an area larger than metropolitan New York City or London. So often is its peak smothered in an "entourage of clouds" created by its own heat that you can circumnavigate Sicily for a week "and never catch a glimpse of the terrible cone at its summit."[570]

Geologists say Mount Etna has erupted 135 times since its eruptions were first recorded in 475 B.C.; the worst eruption was in 1669 when 990 million cubic yards of Mount Etna's lava overwhelmed the town of Catania. In 1992, the peak vomited a significant molten lava flow, in 1998, it belched ash and rocks over a distance of twenty miles; and in July 2001, it spewed ash and lava thousands of feet into the air, threatening several Sicilian villages.

It is the highest of all active volcanoes in Europe; it can be seen from a distance of more than one hundred miles. The volcano has 250 minor cones, and with every eruption the height of the mountain changes slightly. In 1865, for instance, the volcanic summit was 170 feet higher than it was in the late twentieth century.

The nearest town to Mount Etna is Taormina (ten miles away), which originally was called Tauromeniu, which means approximately "the built-up area in Tauro," which is to say, the town built by the lava flows of Mount Etna. Today it is a popular resort town on the Sicilian coast.

MYTH AND LEGEND

Four major myths are associated with Mount Etna. First, Zeus, the chief of the Greek gods, threw Mount Etna at a demon/dragon named Typhon to imprison him permanently so that today, Typhon is said to lie immobilized under the massive volcano. Typhon, a child of Gaia (the Earth),[571] was half-human, half-beast, and more massive and formidable than any other of Gaia's progeny.

Typhon was taller than all the mountains; in fact, he was so tall his head often knocked against the stars; one arm stretched west to the sunset, the other east to the place of sunrise. One hundred serpent (or dragon) heads sprouted from his shoulders; from the hips downwards, he was serpent shaped—in fact, his lower torso consisted of two intertwining serpents, and they yelled and hissed constantly. "From the thighs downward he had huge coils of vipers, which when drawn out, reached to his very head and emitted a loud hissing."[572]

Typhon's body was covered with wings, his hair was unkempt and streamed on his face and head in the wind, and his eyes were made of fire. Flames shot out not only from his eyes, but also from his nostrils and mouths, and he uttered such from bloodcurdling imprecations that even the gods at one time fled for safety.

He often flung stones at Heaven, and sometimes spoke the language of the gods, while at others he bellowed like a bull or barked like a dog. In any event, the gods were determined that Typhon not gain mastery over their realm. Zeus struck Typhon with lightning: Typhon cut Zeus' sinews with a sickle and stole his thunderbolts. The battle raged across Asia Minor, with engagements at Mount Casius in Syria and Mount Haemus in Thrace, then Mount Nysa in Greece, until finally Zeus hurled Mount Etna at Typhon and subdued him. "This mountain still spits forth the lightnings that fell upon the dragon."[573]

A variant on this basic myth says that Gaia created another monster called Enceladus to avenge Zeus' destruction of her own Typhon. But Zeus defeated Enceladus and bound him with "adamantine chains" under Mount Etna. In the early days of his imprisonment, Enceladus vented his frustration with groans, outcries, and curses, or he exhaled fumes and flames through the mountain; in more recent times, he has "cooled" down and now disturbs the Sicilian peace only when he changes position in his deep slumber under the terrible weight of the mountain, causing the Earth to tremble and quake for miles.[574]

In another variation, Typhon was subdued in the great battle of the gods against the giants, the *Gegeneis,* those "born from the Earth." In this struggle, called the Gigantomachy, Pallas Athene, one of the Olympian gods, threw the entire island of Sicily at Enceladus, crushing him, but not mortally; he was "everlastingly imprisoned" under the weight of the island and his fiery breath still issues now and then through Mount Etna.[575]

Typhon was immortal, and the Greeks contended that at some point he produced a spawn of other strange but potent creatures, including the Sphinx (not the Egyptian structure, but the being it was based on), Cerberus (the three-headed dog that guards Hades), and the dragon Ladon (which guards the golden apples of the Gardens of the Hesperides), among others.

The second myth about Mount Etna is that it is the forge and smithy of the Greek fire and metal god, Hephaistos (the Roman Vulcan), who is assisted under the volcano by the Cyclopes, the primordial one-eyed gods. There in his smithy, Hephaistos (a son of Zeus, described as lame and disfigured) sets his anvil upon the head of Typhon and fashions the armor and weaponry of the gods, including Zeus' thunderbolts and the arrows of Artemis and Apollo.

Hephaistos is the skilled master craftsman of the gods, the god of fire, the forge, and metalworking, a peacemaker, and a jovial, laughter-generating character on Olympus. His name means approximately "fire." Hephaistos built the gods' splendid halls and luxurious palaces; when entreated by goddesses, he fabricated armor for mortals such as Achilles and Aeneas; and he created Pandora, who was, to the Greeks, the first woman.

He was accompanied in his smithy work under Mount Etna by the Cyclopes ("round eyed"), which were singled-eyed giants originally produced by Gaia (Earth) and Ouranos (Sky). The Cyclopes made Zeus' thunderbolts, Poseidon's trident, and Hades' cap of invisibility. One of the notable Cyclopes, Polyphemus, was said by Homer to live in a cave on Sicily; the *Odyssey* describes Odysseus' ill-fated encounter with this poor-tempered antediluvian giant. Virgil in his *Aeneid* said that besides Polyphemus there were one hundred more "unspeakable huge" Cyclopes living in the bays and mountainsides of Sicily.

In a mammoth cave and within vaulted galleries inside Mount Etna burns the Cyclopes' forge; mighty blows upon anvils can be heard, and bars of iron hissing, said Virgil. This was Vulcan's workshop, called Vulcania, and for this the Lord of Fire came down from Heaven. Three Cyclopes worked under Mount Etna with Vulcan-Hephaistos, according to Virgil: Thunderclap, Anvilfire, and Flash, each stripped to the waist, each with a thunderbolt.

Virgil called the Cyclopes "the brotherhood of Aetna" and "terrifying peers" who towered heavenwards, and described how they made Mount Etna's caverns rumble, then stood on the shoreline, "each with his awful eye/in impotent rage" as Aeneas and his men escaped. Polyphemus was so big that he used a pine tree as a staff; he was "vast, mind-sickening, lumpish."[576]

Mount Etna's third major myth is that on its slopes the precious Cattle of the Sun (Helios) once grazed. As Odysseus told his men in the *Odyssey:* "The cattle, the sleek flocks, belong to an awesome master,/Helios, god of the sun who sees all, hears all things."[577] Homer said that the herds of the Sun god's cattle grazed on the island of Thrinacia,[578] herded by two goddesses, daughters of Helios, Phaethousa (the Shining One) and Lampetia (the Illuminating).

These cattle never die and no breeding ever swells their number. Odysseus had been warned not even to touch the cattle, much less eat them, or all his men would perish at sea. As things turned out, eventually his men did slaughter a fair number of the cattle and Helios asked Zeus for his deserved revenge, which Zeus delivered, killing the sailors.

Appropriately, there is local support for this Sun cattle attribution. Taormina was a Greek city starting in the fourth century B.C. and was called *Tauromenion* by the resident Greeks. The root of this word has clear associations with *tauros*, the Greek word for "bull." Near the town, on the slopes of Mount Etna is a large valley suitable for grazing, called the Valley of the Ox. "There is no doubt that Taormina has been associated with bulls and the Bull-God since the fourth century B.C."[579]

Finally, Mount Etna's fourth myth is that Persephone, the goddess of vegetation and daughter of Zeus, was abducted here by Hades and taken by him to the Underworld, where she became Queen. Apparently Persephone found the island of Sicily and the slopes of Mount Etna in particular among her favorite resorts, and she liked to gather flowers on Etna's lower green slopes and dance with the nymphs on the plain of Enna. One day as Persephone and her attendants were laughing, singing, and flower-gathering, they caught the ear of Hades, who was driving by on his chariot drawn by four coal-black horses.

Hades had previously been unsuccessful in wooing any comely women to join him on his gloomy throne in Hades, so this time he simply took the one he wanted—Persephone—and took her down to his Underworld palace. He struck the Earth on Mount Etna with his two-pronged fork and a crevice opened up under his feet, allowing him and his chariot to ride down into the darkness of the Underworld.[580]

MYSTICS AND TOURISTS

One commentator describes the mountain's life-and-death potency succinctly in this line: "As unpredictable as any volcano, it has the power to bring death and destruction to tens of thousands in a day's work, whenever it has a mind to."[581]

To a writer sailing the probable original route taken by Odysseus in his ten-year trip home from Troy, Mount Etna was the "most outstanding feature" of the Sicilian coastline, a kind of welcoming beacon to sailors indicating that they have nearly reached safe port. In the summer months when it is wreathed in clouds, Mount Etna smokes its pipe of peace. "Etna is the king of this coastline." This same writer quotes the Greek classical writer Pindar as having mentioned "Etna, nursing throughout the year her dazzling snow."[582]

In 1787, the German writer J. W. Goethe pronounced Taormina "a patch of paradise." In 1833, Cardinal John Henry Newman characterized the view from Taormina of Mount Etna, which is like an immense chimney or huge column, as "the closest way to contemplate Eden." French writer Guy de Maupassant said of Taormina and Mount Etna that it was "a landscape where everything seems to have been created on the Earth to seduce the eyes, the mind and the imagination."[583]

A contemporary visitor wondered whether upon seeing "this unforgettable spectacle of nature" he was still "really on planet Earth."[584] Another upon arriving in Taormina noted the magical, mythical atmosphere spread all around which has enchanted visitors from all over the world for years and years."[585] Taking a different tack, twentieth-century British satirist Evelyn Waugh said he would never forget the sunset view of Mount Etna, which was almost invisible in a pastel gray blur framed against a radiant pink horizon. "Nothing I have ever seen in Art or nature was quite so revolting."[586]

British novelist and travel writer Lawrence Durrell visited Sicily in the 1970s and said that Mount Etna, from the airport near Catania, looked like a dangerous toy, even though geologists described it as "an almost domesticated show-piece." The volcano "gave a small puff of dark smoke—a languid gesture of welcome, as if it had heard we were coming." Flying over the volcano, he marveled that it was actually a network of volcanoes of which Mount Etna was only the largest, as if numerous minor geysers had perforated the "whole pie" of the landscape with mini-volcanoes. "It was beautiful in its toy-like way, this range, and yet I could not avoid a slight feeling of menace about it."[587]

Even though, as locals and vulcanologists attest, the mountain is always more or less erupting, in July 2001 things got more intense than usual. A CNN reporter commented that the sight of molten orange lava running down the slopes, the thunderous explosions that shook the mountainside, and the incredible, "staggering amount of molten heat" felt at even one hundred yards, distance was "awesome" and "like I imagine hell to be." He noted the "overwhelming sense of terror" you get when you realize humans have no control over the volcano, that its activities and size are almost too big to conceive of. "It's like you are confronting Mother Nature at its most violent, and that's terrifying."[588]

GEOMANTIC

Dome; Mithraeum; Ixion's Wheel; Underworld Entrance.

DOME: The dome over Mount Etna corresponds to Nusakan, a fourth magnitude star which is beta Corona Borealis, the Northern Crown. Among its many equivalent names, this constellation was known by the Romans as Crown of Vulcan, but it was also called Crown of Ariadne, the daughter of King Minos of Crete, the crown having been awarded Ariadne by the Olympian god Dionysus;[589] the Hebrews called it *Ataroth*, the Crown, while other names included Dish, Shield, Tiara, and Broken Platter.

Nusakan is one hundred light years from Earth and twenty-five times brighter than our Sun; astronomers believe the star may be an outlying member of the Hyades Cluster in Taurus. Also of interest is the astrophysical fact that Nusakan has "a remarkably intense" magnetic field that reverses polarity every 18.5 days.[590]

MITHRAEUM: The primary geomythic identification for Mount Etna is that it is a Mithraeum, or a Celestial City of the Sun—a Sun temple, in short. The fearsome description of Typhon is an excellent description, actually, of Helios, the Sun God. However, it is also an accurate, though filtered, interpretation of Sorath, the so-called "evil" Spirit of the Sun, better known as the Beast with the number 666. Surprisingly, this identification does not automatically make a Mithraeum an evil or dangerous inner plane temple. Rather, it demonstrates the ambivalence—from the human vantage point— of many of the celestial energies and presences.

But let's understand the other key players first. The Cyclopes are the angelic family called Elohim during their brief but geomantically highly productive incarnation as giants on the Earth. The single eye in part refers to their prime attunement to the higher celestial world as the source of their guidance and insight. Hephaistos, as the Olympian smith god, is the Ray Master Jesus, known to other myth systems as Wayland, Govannon, Goibniu, and Tvastr, and representing the scarlet or sixth ray.[591]

Given the hierarchical niceties of the celestial realm, it is more accurate to say that Hephaistos assists the Elohim in their work with the Sun.[592] What are they *really* making in that smithy? Among other things, the Holy Grail, the chalice forged of the liquid gold of Helios capable of holding the blood of Christ, as the Grail mysteries declare.

That work has to do with *grounding* the energy of the Sun so that it can work in the Earth plane, primarily through the planet's energy matrix. Hephaistos introduces the prime fire energy of the Sun into the world and shapes it—that is, masters, controls, and channels it into useful devices. This energy is appropriately symbolized as liquid or molten gold in elegant parallel to the mountain's physical molten lava. Zeus' titanic battle with Typhon dramatizes the power of the Sun—think of it as the Vedic Agni, the primordial fire—and the process of assimilating its potency into the Earth grid.

Zeus as the totality of light and as king (that is, summation) of the Ray Masters of Olympus handles the tension of the differentiation of total light into the light of the Sun. Understandably, it takes the head of Olympus to accomplish this mastery of the Sun god. But which Sun?

We musn't be parochial here and think the myth is only about our Sun; rather, the Sun is what the esoteric tradition calls the Great Central Sun, Alcyone of the Pleiades in the constellation of Taurus, around which our Sun and solar system revolve over a period of about 180 million years.[593] The Pleiades are better known as the Seven Sisters, and they reside in the neck of the bull (Taurus) as six visible stars (to see the seventh "Sister" requires a telescope) and at least one hundred more observable with a telescope. The Pleiades (see part 2, Mithraeum) are the operative celestial factor in a Mithraeum, which makes sense, for the bull of Mithras is *their* bull.

Clairvoyantly, one striking impression one gets in looking at Mount Etna is that on the level of visionary geography it appears in part like a massive golden bull's head. In fact, looking at the planet in the same way, you gain the impression of 144 such golden bull's heads, one at each of the Mithraea. Inside the Vulcania or smithy you stand in a giant spherical cave made of a golden bull's head wrapped around a sphere and facing you. Your job as a solar initiate (or hero) is to "slay" the bull, which means, to drain off a little of its "blood" (liquid gold) for your use and edification.

In Hephaistos' smithy, you are face to face with the Sun god, or what the classical tradition also called "the golden halls of Ogygia." In his ten-year odyssey back to Ithaca from Troy, Odysseus spent seven years with Calypso in Ogygia, which is to say, as an initiate of a high degree, he was able to sustain an immersion in the liquid gold of Helios as part of his (inner) journeys in the geomythic landscape of classical Greece. Calypso was a daughter of the Titan Atlas, who, with his wife Pleione, produced the Pleiades, a fact which becomes enticingly relevant below. In other words, Calypso was of the Pleiades, in essence, one of the "nymphs" in charge of guarding the Cattle of the Sun.

On the physical level, molten lava—which is essentially fire and stone—wells up and sometimes erupts through a volcano; on the energy or astral level, the equivalent substance is liquid gold, the essence of Helios and the blood of Typhon. Appropriately, in the myth of Zeus battling with Typhon, the Olympian shed some of Typhon's blood on Mount Haemus (*haima* is Greek for "blood"). This is a useful clue that a Mithraeum is probably at this peak.

IXION'S WHEEL: Any mention of Cattle of the Sun is a sure indication of an Ixion's Wheel, for the two are synonymous, despite their outward differences. The presence of Cattle of the Sun grazing on the slopes of Mount Etna is perfectly apt, for in the Hindu myth of Agni's Fire Altar, which is a code for Mithraeum, the 10,800 bricks that comprise the altar are bordered by 360 stones. This is code, too, for the 360 degrees in a circle and for the Cattle of the Sun, both of which are found at the periphery of the Sun God's temple.

The gold is the energy essence and consciousness exudate of Helios the Sun god, but "he" is more of a filter than a source; the source is the Pleiades, for this is bulls' blood. You need to keep in mind all of this is code, analogy, and metaphor. It's a "bull" because the source is the Pleiades in Taurus; there are "cattle" because in a sense the cows are the spigots (through the udders) of this liquid gold.

If you milk the Cattle of the Sun, you get not milk but liquid gold. In the Mithraic mysteries, the pivotal act, called the tauroctony—the ritualized slaying of the bull by slitting its throat—is the controlled release of this liquid gold into the Earth's energy grid. So the crucial act of Mithraism is geomantic: allowing a small amount of Pleiadian bulls' blood of liquid gold to flow into the world—and into the initiate as well. So we can equate Hephaistos with Mithras, the bull slayer.

This is why Odysseus' men all died when they ate the Cattle of the Sun. It was not that the gods punished them on behalf of Helios for trespassing on his sacrosanct property. It was that being uninitiated—not ritualistically *prepared*—they were unable to digest or assimilate the liquid gold, were psychically overwhelmed, and perished. They were burned up in the fires of Helios.

In effect, they were warned: Stay out of the Mithraeum on Mount Etna and leave the Cattle of the Sun alone; you are not ready to handle its energies. However, another interpretation is equally possible: following their initiation into Arthurhood, that is, being Sun-dipped in the golden sarcophagus of the Sun god, their individual, former identities were eclipsed by the newly birthed Arthurian or solar awareness so, in effect, they died from eating the cattle.

On the other hand, Hephaistos in his smithy fashioning weapons and armor for the gods from the liquid gold speaks to the Olympian gods' mastery of the Sun energy and their ability to *wear* it—to make it their own, assimilate and use it in the world as part of their work of creating a celestial geography to interface with the physical Earth (see Edfu, Egypt).

THE GOLDEN FLEECE: This is a Time matrix, popularly known (though in a different context) as the Golden Fleece, and it is a more abstract description of Sorath's face as the "dark" side of Helios. Yet another name for this time matrix is the Square of the Sun, one of seven Qabalistic number squares associated with a planet (the seven "classical" planets). The Square of the Sun consists of six rows of numbers, each row adding up to 111; the entire square adds up to 666, the so-called "Number of the Beast." Each of the numbers in the Squares is also a Hebrew letter so that the rows produce a sum and a string of letters.

In the image at Etna, then, the Cattle of the Sun, from this way of looking at things, are the number and word combinations produced by this Square when spoken, and each word is one of the herd. Remember too that Typhon hissed, bellowed, barked, and sometimes *spoke* the language of the gods. We might think of the Magic Square of the Sun as the grammar of Typhon's particular style of speech, or even his speech organ itself.

The benevolent bull's head is the same as the monster Typhon's head; in the juxtaposition of these two images, one seemingly benign, the other seemingly malevolent, you have the basic polarity of the Sun, the light and dark sides of Helios. It's the delight and terror of Time, over which the Sun is king and we in the flesh its mortal subjects.

Another way of understanding the face of the bull and/or Typhon is to think of it as a personification of the Time matrix, as the source of the speed of light, which is to say, the prime but necessary limitation of absolute light to a speed (a condition of consciousness) less—*slower*—than its full potential. Paradoxically, things are only visible because they exist at a speed less than the speed of light; otherwise, they'd be invisible.

So why visit the psychic interior of Mount Etna? To get a glimpse of the sublime Mysteries of the Sun. To see the gods hammer a monster's horrific face into a bull's pacific gaze. To experience the Golden Fleece. Perhaps to acquire a golden Grail chalice of your own in case you feel inclined to undertake the Grail Quest with it elsewhere in the Earth's visionary geography.

UNDERWORLD ENTRANCE: The myth of Persephone's abduction by Hades upon Mt. Etna is a "dead" giveaway that there is an Underworld Entrance here, a portal into Hades' higher dimensional Land of the Dead. This makes for a rich initiatory opportunity at Mt. Etna: after you have had both aspects of the Sun temple immersion (the Mithraeum forge and Ixion's Wheel infusion), you can proceed to the crown chakra experience of the Underworld Entrance.

Mount Fuji, Japan

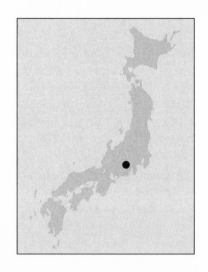

To many, Mount Fuji is not only a symbol of Japan but, in a poetic sense, Japan itself. A towering, beautiful semi-active volcano, its peak is often obscured by clouds, its slopes laden with snow. Japanese refer to it, by way of a nickname, as the "lofty, peerless peak," and it is certainly Japan's tallest mountain. But more than that, Mount Fuji has provided a spiritual basis for the Japanese for millennia.

Not only is it Japan's most popular tourist destination, but the mountain embodies symmetry and serenity, the concept of balance between shade and light, rest and movement, Earth and Heaven, and the quest for beauty and perfection. "The very perfection of its form, startling in its incredible simplicity, suggests the mystery of the infinite."[594]

The name Fuji is a shortened form of the full Japanese name, *Fuji-no-yama,* which means "the Mountain of Fuji." Sometimes people living near the great stratovolcano call it *O Yama,* "the Honorable Mountain," or "the Mountain." The word *Fuji* itself may be a corruption of the word *Huchi, Huzi,* or *Fuche,* which is the term the Ainu, Japan's aboriginal inhabitants, used to call their Fire Goddess, presumed to be the deity presiding over Mount Fuji. Other names for Japan's most venerated mountain include *Fuji-san,* which means "Everlasting Life" and *Fuji-yama,* meaning "the Never-Dying Mountain."

Mount Fuji's almost perfectly symmetrical form and regularity of shape, geologists say, is due to its relative youth as a volcano. Volcanologists propose that about 600,000 years ago two mountains appeared next to each other where Mount Fuji now stands. Around 300,000 years ago, one or both erupted and the lava flow covered up both mountains, yielding the single and symmetrical Mount Fuji. As a volcano, Fuji is the highest (12,397 feet) in a chain of volcanic peaks that run from the South Seas to the north of Japan.

The Japanese like to see Mount Fuji as a huge inverted fan, the streaks down its flanks resembling the ribs of the fan, and in this guise, they believe it radiates a celestial and protective influence over all of Japan. Others see the wide-stretched fan as a white lotus, the flower sacred to the Buddha. Fuji is "touched by the divine breath," wrote one Japanese visitor; it is the "Supreme Altar of the Sun," declared a European traveler. Fuji's name is interpreted as "not-dying" or "deathless" because of a myth that an elixir of eternal life exists at the summit, as does a portal to the Land of Perpetual Youth.

Fuji is Japan's "supreme sacred High Place," and even its sunrise shadow cast on the lower-lying levels of mists and clouds has a name: *Kage-Fuji,* or "Shadow-Fuji." The distinctive crater, 590 yards wide, near the mountain's summit, is also named and venerated: *Naiin,* which means "Sanctuary." It was formed during one of Mount Fuji's more recent of 18 eruptions in historical time. (Its most recent eruption was in 1707, when it dumped six inches of ash on Tokyo.)

The mountain's celestial guardian who provides the protective influence is called *Konohana Sakuahime,* "the Princess Who Maketh the Blossoms of the Trees to Flower," or more simply, "Goddess of Flowering Trees." The Shinto goddess of Fuji, she's also called *Sangen* (or *Asama*) for short, which is also the name of her shrine on the peak. People have plunged to their death in Fuji's volcanic fire with the belief that this act of veneration would achieve for them the goddess's divine companionship, as even the mountain was ardent with fire for her, as demonstrated by the eruptions.

According to W. Y. Evans-Wentz, who climbed Mount Fuji at midsummer in 1920, "it is when the huge base of Fuji is hidden in mists and Fuji's snow-capped summit and main mass are alone visible, that the Mountain appears to be magically suspended in the firmament." Seen from a distance (and Fuji can be seen from Tokyo, more than sixty miles away), one beholds "one of this world's most wondrous visions."[595]

Estimates suggest that up to 300,000 people climb Mount Fuji during the summer months. At one time it was considered not only customary but almost obligatory for every Japanese to climb Fuji at least once in a lifetime, similar to Muslims making the *hajj* to Mecca.

It typically takes eight hours to climb, and many leave in the late afternoon so as to witness the *goraiko,* the rising Sun seen from Mount Fuji at dawn the next day. The climbing season runs from July 1 to August 31, ritually marked by the festivities of *yamabiraki,* "opening the mountain," and *yamashime,* "closing the mountain."

The opening of the climbing season is marked by the *owaraji hono* ceremony in which a giant straw sandal, twice the height of an adult, is dedicated to a Fuji shrine for a safe ascent of the mountain. The climbing season is closed with a fire festival called *himatsuri* on August 26 at the Fuji Sengen Shrine in Fujiyoshida; a torch is kindled outside every home, making the village seem like a sea of fire. A model of Fuji, known as *mikage* (Honorable light-shade), done in lacquered wood, is carried through the streets of Fujiyoshida, finally being brought to rest at the *o-tabisho* for the night.

MYTH AND LEGEND

One intriguing myth says that Mount Fuji was created in one night, instantaneously, around 300 B.C. An impoverished woodcutter named Visu lived on the Suruga plain, and one night, falling asleep, he heard the Earth rumble. Rushing out of his hut, he was astonished to see that a giant mountain now occupied the once barren, flat plain; flames leaped from its summit and smoke swirled around it on all sides. Visu called the newborn mountain *Fujiyama,* which means "the Eternal Mountain."

After this momentous appearance of Fujiyama, Visu spent nearly all his time contemplating the majestic peak. One day he wished the peak could see its own magnificence in a reflection. Suddenly a great lake, shaped like a Japanese lute, the *biwa,* appeared at the base of Fujiyama, reflecting the peak.

Lake Biwa today is 140 miles from Mount Fuji, but geologists speculate an early eruption of Mount Fuji might have formed a small lake, or a series of them, at the foot of the mountain; lakes can be formed by eruptions when flowing lava dams streams. There are today in fact five lakes around the northern base of Mount Fuji; none are called Lake Biwa, but they do mirror the mountain.

There is another quasi-geological myth about the origin of Mount Fuji. One day a giant wanted to fill in the Pacific Ocean. He spent the night scooping up earth and dumping it in the ocean, but at dawn, he was disappointed to see how little progress he had made, and quit the effort. Where he dumped his last bagful of earth is Mount Fuji.[596]

Japanese myth recounts Visu's further adventures with Fuji. He climbed the mountain to continue his praying in solitude, an activity that now demanded all his time. Distracted, he chased after a fox, only to find two women seated and playing *go*, a Japanese board game. He was captivated by their beauty and graceful movements, and thought only a summer's afternoon had passed. Suddenly the two women ended their game, turned into foxes, and ran away. To his shock, Visu discovered that three hundred years had passed since he climbed Fuji. "His white spirit is still said to haunt Fuji-yama when the moon shines brightly."[597]

The primary Shinto deity associated with Mount Fuji is Sengen-Sama, or *Konohana Sakuahime*, whose name also means "Radiant blooming as the flowers of the trees" or "Causing the Blossom to Bloom Brightly." The reference, at least outwardly, is to the arresting appearance of the cherry and plum blossoms seen against the snow on Fuji's slopes and when reflected on the five lakes below.

In ancient Japan, this goddess was said to hover in a luminous cloud above Fuji's crater; she was tended by invisible servants, and they would throw the impure off the mountain. Another deity—it's not clear if she is the same as Sengen—is *O-ana-mochi*, which means "Possessor of the Great Hole or Crater." The great Sun Goddess Amaterasu-Omikami is worshiped on Fuji, and it is from her lineage that the Japanese imperial family is said to descend.

There is also the matter of the Elixir of Life and how it got to Fuji. The Japanese relate a long story about a bamboo cutter named Sanugi no Miyakko who one day saw a bright light coming out of a reed in a grove near the base of Mount Fuji. Inside the reed was a beautiful but tiny young girl, all of four inches long. He and his wife adopted the girl, whom they named Lady Kaguya, which means "Precious Slender Bamboo of the Field of Autumn." A variation on the story says she was named *Kaguya Hime*, which means "She Who Lights Up the Area." She became a beautiful, full-sized woman under their care, and her reputation as a lovely, marriageable woman spread throughout Japan.

Even though she married and lived happily, a time came when Lady Kaguya became melancholy from contemplating the full Moon, and then she revealed her secret. She was not a mortal human woman, but had been born on the Moon, and it was time for her to return home. The Moon palace of the immortals was believed to be on the peak of Mount Fuji. The Japanese believe that the Immortals live on the summit of Fuji and that the volcano is identical with the Taoists' Eastern Isle of the Blessed, a mountainous island called *P'eng-lai*.

Soon an unusual cloud approached the bamboo-cutter's house, and inside the cloud was a canopied chariot bearing spirits from the Moon. They called for Lady Kaguya, who climbed aboard the celestial conveyance.

The Moon spirits gave her a draught of the Elixir of Life to remove the stains her soul had acquired from living among mortals and handed her the Celestial Robe of Feathers, which, after she donned it, would remove all her earthly memories. Before departing, though, she gave the bamboo-cutter a scroll with her final words to him, and a bamboo joint containing a little of the Elixir.

The myths relate that to her husband she gave a magic mirror in which to see her after her departure; he went to the top of Fuji, despaired of ever seeing her, and plunged off a precipice. So great was his love for Lady Kaguya that it burst out of his heart and set the mirror aflame; people afterwards said the smoke that rose from Fuji was in fact the smoke from his burning mirror.

A man named Tsuki no Iwakasa was charged with taking the scroll and Elixir to the highest mountain in Suruga, which was Fuji, and there to burn them, which he did. Afterwards, the peak was known as Fuji-yama, "Never Dying," in recognition of the Elixir that he burned there. Somehow burning the Elixir released it into the atmosphere of Fuji's peak.

Since that mythic time, various mortals have sought the Elixir on Fuji. A Chinese emperor named Shih-huang-ti in the third century B.C., hearing that Fuji had risen in a single night, immediately traveled with five hundred young men and five hundred young women to the mountain to be the first human to drink the potion and never grow old. The Japanese say the deity of Fuji refused to yield the Elixir, and the emperor was found dead on the mountaintop, though bearing a smile.

A Japanese named Sentaro after praying at the Fuji shrine received a magical paper crane that expanded to a vast size when he touched it. Sentaro flew on this crane to the peak of Fuji, and beyond, straight into the Land of Perpetual Youth. To his surprise, he found that the people there wanted to die, and took poisons to cancel their immortality.

There is a myth about an encounter with the goddess of the mountain. A young man named Yosoji sought to help cure his mother of smallpox by collecting some water from a small stream that flowed on Fuji's southwest flank, which was said to come from a shrine to the God of Long Breath. On the mountainside, Yosoji encountered a young woman clad in white, and she directed him to the stream.

He collected some water for his mother and drank a little himself. He returned five more times, at the woman's request, until his mother was healed. During a later visit, the woman swung a camellia branch in the air and soon a cloud descended from Fuji, and carried her away. Yosoji, who had long asked the woman to reveal her identity, now understood she was the Goddess of Fuji.

A Buddhist legend recalls that a prince of the sixth century A.D. descended into the crater of Mount Fuji, entered a huge cavern, and encountered a fire-breathing coiled dragon on a rock in the middle of a pond. The dragon then turned into Dainichi Nyorai, the Buddha of All-Illuminating Wisdom, and told the prince he had come from the realm of ultimate reality to reside in this cave palace forever. In the twelfth century, a temple was erected in honor of Dainichi Nyorai, whose identity later merged with Sengen Dainichi or Sengen Daibosatsu, regarded thereafter as Fuji's Buddhist deity.

Between the twelfth and fourteenth centuries, Japanese Buddhists elaborated a model of Fuji in which they saw it as embodying a mandala or lotus with eight petals. These were formed by eight subsidiary summits along the rim of the crater, and these were seen as a physical symbol for the sublime abode of the Buddha. A meditative practice arose in which Buddhists visualized different deities as present on each of these summit–lotus petals, each in a state of bliss. Mount Fuji itself became a symbol of the meditative state, and the summit where the gods dwelled and that rose above the clouds was regarded as the point of freedom and enlightenment beyond the concerns and clouded perceptions of the world.

During the fourteenth century, the Shugendo cult developed around the exploits of the near legendary magician-ascetic, En no Gyoja, who first climbed Mount Fuji around 700 A.D. He was exiled to the Ize Peninsula, but was believed to step across the sea every night so he could ascend Fuji again. In the Shugendo cult, *yamabushi,* or the key climbers (*yamabushi* means "one who lives and sleeps in the mountains"), led climbing parties; later they built huts high up on Fuji for mountaineers wishing to practice religion as well as athleticism. Until the seventeenth century, the yamabushi actually controlled public access to Fuji.

Then around 1560, Kakugyo Hasegawa was instructed in a dream by En no Gyoja to climb the mountain, which he did using a different route. A new cult of devotional climbers called *Fuji-ko* organized around his ascetic example. They took things to the extreme of claiming that the Buddhist deity of Mount Fuji, Sengen Dainichi, was the supreme creator god and thus the mountain was God.

More than a century later, Jikigyo Miroku, a follower of Fujiko, had a powerful vision of Sengen on Fuji, but he no longer identified him as Sengen Dainichi. Now Sengen, Miroku claimed, was the divine ruler of the world and the embodiment of food, thus qualifying a name change for Fuji to *Kokushuzan,* the "Mountain of Heaped-up Grain."

The mountain continued to attract millennialist projections and attributions along these lines. In the nineteenth century, a Fuji-ko leader linked worshiping Fuji with veneration of the Japanese emperor, and claimed that through devotion to both, Japan would eventually rule the world. Yet after World War II, some Japanese felt betrayed by Fuji, even hostile towards it, believing its sheer size and visibility had served as a beacon to Allied bombers approaching Tokyo.

MYSTICS AND TOURISTS

In the 1970s, the late Sir Alvary Gascoigne communicated after his death through an English psychic named Cynthia Sandys his impressions of the astral atmosphere of Mount Fuji. He noted its vastness and "almost terrifying power," that it was like a "great leviathan of power" whose silence was deep and "pregnant with subdued wrath."

This first visit was close after World War II, and Gascoigne's postmortem impression was that Mount Fuji's "negative side" had inspired most of the brutal war measures of the Japanese. He also noted that the "Great Earth Spirit" was fighting to overcome Fuji's negativity, and eventually succeeded. But the mountain also had a positive side, and Gascoigne encountered living villagers who were impregnated with the "inner rays of Fuji" so that they were revolted by war.

Gascoigne and his disembodied colleagues worked with these villagers during their sleeping hours to fuse their "inner rays of white light" with the celestial light that Gascoigne's group was able to transmit. The goal was to cleanse the negative, war "rays" from the Japanese villagers and thus modulate Mount Fuji's negative influence. Those villagers who could not change their own level of vibration in accordance with the new level of energy—Mount Fuji's positive aspect—eventually relocated.

Gascoigne's group next turned to cleansing the energy structures of the mountain itself. "This is not one immense power centre but clusters and clusters of large and small whirlpools of energy," he noted. Some of these whirlpools were "completely under the subservience of a negative earth force opposing the positive earth force" and precluding the human vibration altogether. The soil on Mount Fuji's slope under the influence of these negative whirlpools was infertile and unproductive.

Gascoigne's group worked to inspire Japanese farmers to work the seemingly infertile fields there so as to impart their human vibrations, which would counteract the negative earth force at that site. He noted that the human mind can be remarkably powerful and effective in "recasting the vibrations" into the soil and thus the energy field.[598]

GEOMANTIC

Dome; Soma Temple.

DOME: Mount Fuji's dome is unusual in that rather than involving a star, it involves a planetary nebula—the galaxy's second largest, called M27, or the Dumbbell Nebula, situated within the constellation of Vulpecula, the Fox. Its full name is *Vulpecula cum Ansere* ("the Little Fox with the Goose"), and it was first characterized in 1690 in *Uranographia* by the astronomer Johann Hevelius, who said it contained twenty-seven stars.

Astronomers say the Nebula was probably formed forty-eight thousand years ago, making it 2.5 times older than the typical planetary nebula. This astronomical observation is of course interesting in light of the myth that Mount Fuji formed fully in one night, perhaps from an earthquake, within human memory—in other words, not *that* long ago.

The Dumbbell Nebula is located 2° southeast of Vulpecula's No. 13 star (none of the Fox's stars are named), and it is three light years in diameter, although it is expanding at the rate of one inch per century. It is spread out over a large area of space so that while its overall brightness is very high, the brightness of its surface is fairly low, in the thirteenth and fourteenth magnitudes. M27 is located somewhere between 490 and 979 light years from Earth, and its central star, a bluish dwarf, is one of the hottest known, burning at 85,000° K.

The primary star has a yellowish seventeenth magnitude companion, separated from the first star by only 1,800 Astronomical Units, making the two a "physical double."[599] The two stars, or one physical double, "form a true common motion pair," like a barbell rotating around its own center point. The primary star emits strong ultraviolet radiation that "excites the glow of highly rarified gases," producing the typical eerie pale-blue fluorescence associated with doubly ionized oxygen.

The phenomenon seemingly has entranced professional and amateur astronomers alike: "The observer who spends a few moments in quiet contemplation of this nebula will be made aware of direct contact with cosmic things; even the radiation reaching us from the celestial depths is of a type unknown on Earth."[600]

The Nebula, with at least seven visible stars, has been called the "Double-Headed Shot," because of its unusual appearance, and one astronomer suggested it consists of a "double stratum of stars," one end of which faces us.[601] The Nebula's shape has also been characterized as an ellipse or a spool, though the dumbbell shape is commonly cited as a general reference shape due to its appearance of "two hazy masses in contact," with a narrower zone in between. Astronomers say this nebula, first discovered in 1764, is the most conspicuous in the night sky for viewers with small-power instruments.

In the case of Mount Fuji, we see a fascinating convergence of myth and astronomical data. Visu's sighting of two celestial women playing a board game, then running away as two foxes is a valid and accurate geomythic way of describing the double star (two foxes) within the constellation of the Fox, which is the star affiliation of Mount Fuji's dome.

Metaphorically, the barbell shape of the M27 Nebula matches the various descriptions of Mount Fuji's polarity, how it embodies the balance between light and dark, rest and movement,

Heaven and Earth. The barbell shape and double star attributes of M27 also correspond to the geological assumption that Mount Fuji is the fused product of two originally adjacent volcanoes. But there is another element to this dialectical aspect between opposites at Mount Fuji.

It has to do with Sengen-Sama, the Goddess of Fuji. At one level, Sengen-Sama may be seen, or at least conceived, as a gorgeous, mountain-high landscape angel and devic overseer of the mountain, a nymph of Gaia, as the Greeks would say, whose energy essence appears as a lovely riot of white blossoms.[602] In many respects Sengen-Sama's energy—her essence as a devic guardian—is a paradisiacal realm itself. She's the kind of goddess you could easily lose three hundred years of your life over were you so fortunate as Visu to meet her on Fujisan.

But Sengen-Sama may have another name, a deeper identity: Izanami. According to the *Kojiki,* Japan's oldest chronicle of its earliest days, written in 712 A.D., the gods originally assigned two celestial beings to create the eight islands of Japan. These two creator gods were called Izanagi, a male, and Izanimi, a female, his consort. They stood on the Floating Bridge of Heaven, a midway point between Heaven and Earth, and held the *Ama-no-Nuboko,* a gem-embedded celestial spear.

Below them, the Earth had not solidified yet, nor had Japan. It was like a sea of filmy fragrant fog, like oil floating on the surface of water. They inserted their spear into the brine, and stirred. Withdrawing the spear, the pair observed that great drops fell from its tip, and where they fell, the fog immediately coagulated into an island, Japan's first formed, called Onokoro. They produced the other seven islands in this manner, the Island of Honshu with Fujisan, last. They called the totality of their creation *Oyashi-ma-kuni,* "the Country of the Eight Great Islands," what we call Japan today.

Izanagi and Izanami did one other thing. They erected on Onokoro the Heavenly August Pillar, and built a magnificent palace around it called the Hall of Eight Fathoms. There they dwelled. Izanagi, as the male deity, went around the pillar turning to the left, while Izanami, the female deity, went around to the right, and they met each other, pretending it was for the first time. They produced offspring, who did not flourish; later, the gods determined that Izanagi and Izanami had exercised incorrect protocol in circling the Pillar. When they did it properly and produced new offspring, the children flourished and all was well.

Later, Izanami died as a result of a traumatic birth, and left Izanagi for the Japanese Hades. There she lost her dazzling beauty and her appearance changed drastically. Eight "Thunder Deities" entered her body and lived there, with Rumbling-Thunder in her left foot and Couchant-Thunder in her right foot; they were horrible to see and belched forth flames from their mouths through her.

Now let's decode this marvelous geomyth. Izanagi and Izanami, as the celestial beings charged with manifesting and supervising the Japanese islands, are a dual expression of Japan's egregor, the angel assigned by the Supreme Being to be the creator and sustainer of the Japanese people on their specific landmass, *Oyashi-ma-kuni.*

It is fitting that the egregor would dwell in the landmass over which it has responsibility; the Hall of Eight Fathoms is an intact folk memory of the egregor's geomantic presence and grounding point, as is the Heavenly August Pillar, Japan's umbilical connection to the celestial worlds.

When the myth says that the dual-valenced egregor produced numerous offspring, this needs to be interpreted lightly, along the lines of inspiring and "coagulating" the particular Japanese qualities that are appropriate for the fusion of landmass and folk soul. In simpler terms, the Japanese egregor helps keep the Japanese *Japanese,* shall we say, according to the original blueprint for this differentiation of the generic human soul stock.

We have in the Japanese myth of the celestial creation of their eight islands an excellent memory of the function of a national egregor. Egregors, like angels, are not really dual-valenced to the extent that there is a male and a female expression. Rather they embody the balanced fusion of both valences, or more precisely, the whole valence (pre-separation) of a single being. But there is a geomantic angle to the twofold expression of Japan's egregor.

Izanagi, as the surviving pair in the divine couple sent to create Japan, resides on the Island of Onokoro in his Hall of Eight Fathoms next to the Heavenly August Pillar. This is the umbilical point for Japan, where the egregor plugs into the cosmos on Japan's behalf, a major national landmass chakra. Izanami, Izanagi's "female" half, has died, left him, changed into a strange being made of eight types of thunder: a volcano, in other words, Fujisan.

The Hades that Izanami resides in is the energy field of the dome at Mount Fuji; it's a netherworld, perhaps because it is a level of reality closer to the physical plane than the Hall of Eight Fathoms. Izanami and Izanagi are still, *perpetually*, walking in opposite directions around the Heavenly August Pillar. That is the dialectical geomantic relationship between a national egregor (at Onokoro) and a prime national star dome (on Honshu).

In most respects, it's easier to understand this if we think of it outside of our conventions of space. Energetically, Izanagi and Izanami are in the same "place," making their coy, flirtatious circlings of the umbilical pillar, playing out a fundamental duality in the landmass, Fujisan, and Japanese folk soul, perhaps expressing some of the Mystery of a country's egregor and its responsibilities.

SOMA TEMPLE: Again, the Japanese geomythic memory is precise and helpful. The obvious clues suggesting a Soma Temple are the Moon chariot that comes to collect Lady Kaguya and the Elixir of Life. Mount Fuji's epithets as the place of Never-Dying, Everlasting Life, and Eternal Mountain are also obvious indicators. Let us not overlook the Ainu's original name of *Fuche* for the Fire Goddess, for this appellation is equally suggestive of Soma.

Soma is the substance of eternal life, desired by all gods, even by the demons. It affords, or restores, the eternity of unbroken, never-dying consciousness, the fire of the first awareness of existence, the flame of self-aware sentience. The Soma Temple can quite validly be described as a Palace of Immortals because, depending on how your mind presents it to you, above the Soma vat you may see a domed roof comprised of thousands of glittering crystalline points of light, each of which, when you look more closely, is the face of an immortal celestial being, enriched forever by a taste of the precious Soma.

Mount Haleakala, Maui, Hawaii, United States

PHYSICAL DESCRIPTION

Mount Haleakala, a 10,023-foot-tall dormant volcano, occupies much of the eastern central side of the Hawaiian island of Maui. It is a massive and visually stunning volcano. The distance from the crater's topmost rim to its floor is three thousand feet, and the floor itself measures twenty-five square miles, sufficient to encompass the entire island of Manhattan.

It has been described as a vast volcanic valley and lunar landscape, and it has its own mini–mountain range of nine cinder cones, the tallest of which is more than one thousand feet high. Haleakala's overall diameter calculated at its base is thirty-three square miles, and an additional twenty-eight thousand feet of Haleakala sits below the Pacific Ocean. If there were no ocean, Haleakala would tower thirty-eight thousand feet.

Most of the time a ring of clouds hovers around Haleakala between four thousand and eight thousand feet, but when it's clear, you can see up to 115 miles out into the Pacific from Haleakala's top, and at night, it is an excellent viewing place for stars, planets, and the Moon—which explains why the volcano is the desirable location for the Maui Space Surveillance Site, run by the U.S. Air Force, to track man-made objects in space.

A thirty-eight-mile scenic drive leads to near the top, where travelers can consult the Haleakala National Park Sun Visitor Center located at 9,745 feet. Once there you will find the air temperature an average of thirty-two degrees cooler than it was at sea level.

Geologically, Haleakala was a newly forming volcano about one million years ago, and it continued to have frequent eruptions for another 500,000 years. Geologists estimate that its last significant eruption was around 1790.

There is evidence that Mount Haleakala was held sacred to Hawaiians at least as early as 800 A.D., based on the discovery of numerous altars and temples throughout the crater. It is believed that only the *kahuna*, or high priests, and perhaps their apprentices, were allowed to live on Haleakala's summit for any length of time, and then only after sufficient inner preparation. Local folklore holds that bad luck will attend anyone rash enough to remove lava rock from Haleakala.

MYTH AND LEGEND

A major myth about Mount Haleakala is that it got its name, House of the Sun (or House used by the Sun), through a heroic action of the demigod Maui, after whom the island was later named. Maui is said to have been born or made his home at Kauiki, a foothill of the crater of Haleakala on Maui; or at Hana, a town on the western coast of Maui; or near the black lava beds of the Wailuku River near Hilo on the island of Hawaii. In the name Haleakala, the last syllable, "la," is a common Polynesian term for the Sun

Maui had recently separated the Earth from the sky, allowing the flattened leaves of all the plants to stretch out and for men to cease crawling in the small space between the sky and ground. Now it was time to do something about the length of the day. People were complaining the Sun passed so quickly over the island that it wasn't there long enough even to dry their bananas. Maui vowed to capture the Sun, make it move slower, and punish it for its lack of concern for human welfare. He also did it for his mother, Hina, who complained that the Sun passed so quickly overhead she never had a chance to dry her coconuts.

He went to Mount Iao, an extinct volcano in the central part of the island, and from there started his climb up to Mount Haleakala. There in the *koolau*, or eastern gap or chasm in the wall of the volcanic crater, Maui made himself ready. Maui's mother, Hina, had given him fifteen strands of a well-twisted fiber, probably from coconut, and had instructed him to seek further advice from his grandmother, who lived in the Haleakala crater. Once there, he had stolen his grandmother's bananas that she had left out for the Sun to eat each morning; when he introduced himself to her and explained his purpose, she gave him the sixteenth strand for the rope and told him how to snare the Sun.

As the Sun started to come up over the mountain and put his first leg over the crater, Maui snared it with the first of his ropes and tied it to a wiliwili tree. One by one, Maui tied down the remaining fifteen legs of the Sun, who was

called La, until he had him secured and immobilized. In one variation of the myth, Maui snared La's sixteen legs in a net; in another, he used a lasso to catch the Sun's rays but managed at first only to snare one, and broke it off. He kept tossing the lasso until he had broken off all the strong rays of the Sun.

In a third, Maui used six snares, placed at intervals along the Sun's expected path. First he snared La's feet, then his knees, hips, waist, arms, and finally his neck, then tied the snares to a rock. Maui kept the snares fastened to La to keep him in constant fear, and by the assistance of these ropes, the Sun was gently let down at night into Avaiki (his origin, also called Hawaiki, the old homeland of the Polynesians), and raised up out of this otherworldly shadowland in the morning.

In a fourth variation on the myth, Maui used a magic jawbone he collected from an ancestress in the Underworld. His grandmother advised against Maui's having anything to do with the Sun. As a divine living creature, La was "'in form like a man, possessed of fearful energy.' Shaking his golden locks both morning and evening in the eyes of men." Nobody could approach La because of the fierceness of the heat he emanated, Maui was warned. Many humans had tried to regulate the Sun's movements, but none had succeeded.[603]

Once Maui had the Sun pinned down, he began to beat La with a magic stone club his grandmother had given him, possibly the enchanted jawbone. Hot bright-red blood flowed out of the wounded Sun and turned to stone, "clear as volcanic glass but still a rich, burning red." The Sun fell to the ground and cried out for mercy. Even though Maui was singed, blistering, and nearly boiling from close contact with the Sun, he boasted that he was superior to La.

Even so, "The mana of the being Maui faced was greater than that of any he had encountered." La, who had never before spoken with a mortal, finally agreed to go slower for six months of the year during the dry season, and go more quickly for six months during the rainy season.[604]

The matter of how the Haleakala became a volcano involves Pele, the Polynesian fire goddess. Pele, born at Honua-Mea in Tahiti, presides over a family of fire gods who govern the activities of lava. The traditional lists of Pele and the volcano divinities specify five brothers and eight sisters; typically, the brothers were associated with thunderstorms and volcanic activities, while the sisters handled cloud forms over the volcanoes. When Pele stamps her feet in anger, earthquakes result.

When volcanic flames spurt out through a breaking lava crust, these are the fire spears of Pele's household of *au-makuas,* or "ghost gods," the attendant fire spirits. And her explosive angry voice was called *pu.*[605] Pele is known as *Pele-ai-honua,* "Eater of Land," and *Pele-honua-mea,* "Pele of the sacred Earth." Pele is her name when she's worshipped in her fire body, but she's called *Ka-ula-o-ke-ahi* ("The Redness of the Fire") when she is revered as a spirit.

She is born of the intense heat and fire deep within the Earth, from that Fire which is the gods' agent of power. Pele both lives in the various volcanoes and is the embodiment of the volcano's form and power; she is alluring, dangerous, and a shape-shifter. She can assume the form of magma, steam, lava, vapor, and flames—every expression of volcanic activity.

The saga of Pele involves her constant migration across the Pacific in search of a permanent place to dig a fire pit deep enough to accommodate her family either in "cool comfort or to exhibit them in their spirit forms of flame and cloud and other volcanic phenomena."[606] According to legend, she started out in Tahiti, the daughter of Haumea[607] and Kane-hoa-lani; one of her sisters was Na-maka-o-ka-ha'i, a goddess of the sea, who constantly tortured Pele and her volcanic brothers by dousing them with water.

Finally Pele got permission from her father to depart Tahiti, which she did in a large canoe with forty thousand deities (the *au-makuas*). One of her brothers, Kamohoalii, the god of sharks and king of the dragons, provided the canoe and guided the great sea journey, though they barely survived the attacks upon their *wa'a,* or canoe, by Na-maka-o-ka-ha'i.[608]

Pele used her *paoa,* a magical digging tool, to prepare a fire pit in which volcanic fires started burning but, each time, some disaster produced by her sea goddess sister eventually ruined her attempts to establish a home. She tried most of the islands in the Hawaiian chain of 131, including Maui, but none was satisfactory. She dug a fire pit at Ni'ihau, then several places on Oahu including Mauna Loa and Diamond Head, and another one in Kauai, where she threw up a large lava hill still known as *Puu-o-Pele,* "the Hill of Pele."

At Maui, for example, she dug at Haleakala, throwing out a great deal of lava from her fire pit. But soon her body was torn apart in a fierce struggle with Na-maka-o-ka-ha'i on the western slope of the mountain, and the fragments of her body were piled up to form the hill known as *Na-iwi-o-Pele,* "the Bones of Pele," located near Kauiki along the seacoast of Maui.

The general assessment of geologists and mythologists is that "the route Pele took coincided with the geological order in which these landforms came into existence."[609] Pele finally found her permanent home on the big island of Hawaii in the Kilauea volcano, where she built "a mighty, enduring place of fire" free from the fire-dousing effects of her sister. Appropriately, the name Kilauea means "spewing, much spreading," as in volcanic eruptions and lava flows.

MYSTICS AND TOURISTS

Mark Twain, climbing Haleakala in the late nineteenth century, was rendered speechless by the view, according to his own account. "I felt like the Last Man, neglected of the judgement, and left pinnacled in mid-heaven, a forgotten relic of a vanished world." Sunrise seen from Haleakala was for Twain "the sublimest spectacle I ever witnessed, and I think the memory of it will remain with me always."[610]

A more recent visitor to the crater commented: "You're walking right into the mind of the mountain. I'd say the nature of this mind is 99 percent will power, will that was captivated by a single idea."[611] Another visitor was struck with how much Haleakala seemed to resemble a moonscape, how it is a self-contained biosphere. Echoing Twain, this visitor noted: "Many folks say it's imperative to be there for sunrise, describing the experience as spiritual, haunting, and otherworldly."[612]

GEOMANTIC

Dome; Mithreaum.

DOME: The dome over Mount Haleakala is the starfall for delta Perseus. This particular star, a third-magnitude star about seventeen hundred times more luminous than our Sun and situated about 590 light years from Earth (some astrophysicists say 326 light years), does not have a specific name or mythology associated with it. Delta Perseus is located on the right side in the middle of the figure's torso.

The Mount Haleakala dome produces dome caps for the rest of Maui and the neighboring islands of Lanai and Molokai; some of its dome caps are situated over the Pacific Ocean where there are no present landmasses.

The constellation of Perseus, also called the Champion, which has either nineteen or twenty-nine identified stars according to classical traditions, depicts the figure of the Greek hero. He has a sword in his right hand, the severed head of the Gorgon Medusa in his left. He had been commissioned by Polydectes and supported by the gods Hermes and Hephaistos to slay the Gorgon whose terrifying gaze turned humans to stone. Afterwards, the Olympian goddess Pallas Athena placed the Medusa's head in the center of her breastplate and granted Perseus his own place among the stars as a reward for his brave deed.

PELE AND THE EARTH DRAGON: Regarding the rest of the geomantic picture of Mount Haleakala, we have a time tableau covering a vast period in geological and prehuman history. It starts with Pele, the fire goddess and spirit of volcanism. Here the most suggestive clue is a casual reference to one of Pele's brothers being the shark god and king of the dragons, also known in Polynesian myth as among the *mo'o*, or guardian gods.

The concept of mo'o in Hawaiian legend is a little hard for non-Polynesians to grasp, but it seems to involve animal-type guardian deities of an ambivalent nature. In some instances, the mo'o are described as reptilian and lizard-like of monstrous size, inhabiting inland fishponds. They lay underwater at a depth of twelve to thirty feet, and their black bodies were terrifying when visible.

There was an unfriendly mo'o called Lani-loa who used to kill passersby until a hero sliced him up into five pieces now in the form of small islands. "The *mo'o* is one of the Pele family's terrible forms," yet Pele had to struggle against a mo'o goddess over a human lover.[613] In Tahiti, where mo'o worship probably originated, the mo'o are gods of the royal Oropa'a family.

So the valence of the mo'o is mixed with respect to human experience. It gives us a starting point for understanding some aspects of Pele. Surrounding the Earth like a necklace is the original singular dragon, what the Norse called *Jormungandr*, the Midgard serpent, which had been cast into the sea by Odin, chief of the gods. This serpent "attained such immense proportions that at last he encircled the Earth and could bite his own tail."[614] This is the central image for us. To account for Pele's mythically couched activities, however, I have to resort to a quasi-mythic explanation.

Picture the Earth encircled by a single massive dragon. It might be helpful to visualize a jewel set in a circular band as a bracelet you can slip over your wrist. The circular band is the dragon's body, while the jewel in the setting is its head. In terms of Earth's geography, this global dragon's head is situated in the central part of the South Pacific. In this image, the 131 islands of Hawai and the hundreds in the Society Islands (including Tahiti) would be mere freckles. Most of the original landmass over which this jeweled dragon's head was situated has disappeared. Metaphysical tradition describes this missing continent as Lemuria.

One of the functions of this singular globe-encircling dragon is to distribute the fire element throughout the geological aspect of Earth, specifically through volcanism, that is, volcanic power and activity. The end result is to create the mountains over which domes may settle. Picture, if you will, Pele flying around inside the dragon, bringing up threads of fire to the surface. In a sense, she uses her *paoa* (digging stick) to poke through the dragon's skin (the Earth's surface) to allow the fire element to burst and spume upwards. The result is what we call volcanic eruption and mountain formation.

Hundreds of sites on the dragon's skin were preassigned for volcanism. The overall pattern had been determined well in advance. Pele's job was over time to pass her sewing needle *(paoa)* and fire thread (molten lava and all the expressions of the fire element working through volcanism) up through the dragon's skin so that the fire element within the Earth could enter the outer physical world and create mountains.

We can trust the extrapolations from the geo-logical record on the general length of time required for this. Pele the volcanic seamstress was busy with this assignment for millions of years, traveling through the dragon's fire body, bringing up threads of the fire element into the physical world. This took place approximately somewhere near the beginning of the third dome presence, many millions of years ago.

For a time, when seen from above and especially in a time-lapsed sense, the Earth looked as if it contained a Sun, as if fiery peaks of the Sun's corona were continuously bursting through the Earth's skin to singe the atmosphere. In a sense, Pele is the deity of the fire element of the Earth. You can get a sense of this if you try to imagine the Earth only in terms of its fire element, as a planet in which only the element of fire in all its guises is active. This is Pele's realm.

The other three tangible elements (earth, water, air) similarly have their singular planetary realm, deities, activities, and central focus, so that we could speak of the planet of the earth element (involving the gnomes), the planet of the water element (involving the undines, nature spirits of water), and the planet of the air element (involving the sylphs, nature spirits of the air).

Once the volcanic eruptions calmed down and the mountainous forms stabilized, the domes, embodying 1,746 stars, could be placed over them. In terms of cosmic myths, this sequence is apt. Among the constellations Draco, the celestial dragon that circles Polaris in Ursa Minor, was said to hold all the waters of creation selfishly within its vast bulk, until a god (Zeus for the Greeks; Indra for the Vedas) slew the monster and released the waters. Out came a rush of stars from the slain bulk of Draco and thus the galaxy was filled with stars; so say the myths.

In an inverse of this, Pele releases the stars one by one through volcanism by facilitating volcanic eruptions out of Draco's *terrestrial* body. These eruptions produce mountains that are then domed by individual stars, after which, from our human point of view, the world can begin.

MITHRAEUM: In the next phase of unfoldment of the Earth's geomantic reality, Maui the demigod had to ground the energies arranged to be present within the Mount Haleakala or House of the Sun dome. Its name, of course, is apt and descriptive: the site is a Mithraeum, a Sun god temple very similar to Mount Etna in Sicily.

In fact, the myths about Mount Etna (see its entry in this book) are highly similar to those of Mount Haleakala: a divine hero (Zeus) is embroiled in a mighty struggle to subdue a formidable Sun god (Typhon), and eventually succeeds in pinning it down and mastering its immense energies. The Greeks tended to emphasize the high drama and titanic nature of the struggle, while the Polynesians seemed to favor highlighting Maui's cunning, determination, and almost bullheadedness.

In the attributions to Mount Haleakala and Mount Etna, you have the same confluence of volcanism and Sun temple images. The Greek myth, however, gives us more of the full story than the Polynesian version. In the Greek account of Mount Etna, Zeus imprisons Typhon as the wild uranian Sun god under the mountain; then Hephaistos, one of the Olympian gods, sets up his smithy inside the volcano, assisted by the one-eyed Cyclopes.

The smithy's work in part had to do with *grounding* the energy of the Sun so that it can work in the Earth plane, primarily through the planet's energy matrix. Once the unruly Sun is grounded, its energies can flow, like molten gold, into the world to benefit life and consciousness.

In an appropriate parallelism, the smithy works with molten gold to forge instruments, devices, or useful objects for the world at the same time as the physical mountain spews forth liquid, boiling rock to create new landscapes. Maui's struggle with La is about taming the primordial fire element—the fire goddess, Pele, if you like, and her dragon king brother, the Midgard serpent—and assimilating its energies and possibilities into the planet's geomantic matrix.

MAUI'S IDENTITY: In the case of Mount Etna, Hephaistos, who works in the smithy of the volcano to forge the Sun god's liquid gold into usable items for the other gods to use in the world, was a Ray Master of the Great Bear. Maui is different. Maui is another guise of the Celtic magician, court sorcerer, and mentor of King Arthur: Merlin. We encounter Merlin in several of his mythic guises in the course of visiting the sites in this book: for example, as the Irish war prodigy Cuchulainn at the Hill of Tara in Ireland and as the Greek master of twelve labors, Heracles, at Mycenae in Greece.

As Myrddin, the Welsh spelling of his name, he was responsible for a great deal of the primordial geomantic structuring of the planet, so that one of the early stages of the planet's development was known as Myrddin's Precinct. Merlin in a sense was the Earth's original geomancer, assigned many of the earliest tasks of organizing, grounding, and focusing the planet's geomantic structures and processes. Elsewhere in the Polynesian account of his activities, as Maui he is credited with "fishing" up many of the islands in the South Pacific from the ocean floor—in effect, creating new landmasses.

Mount Holyoke, Hadley, Massachusetts, United States

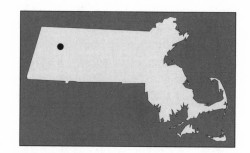

Not to be confused with Mount Holyoke College in nearby South Hadley, Mount Holyoke the mountain is a 954-foot summit, part of the 390-acre Joseph A. Skinner State Park in Hadley, Massachusetts.

Part of a highly unusual, geologically rare, east-west running range that extends about nine miles, intersected by the Connecticut River, Mount Holyoke overlooks what is known as the Pioneer Valley in Western Massachusetts, an area noted for five major colleges, including Smith, Amherst, Hampshire, the University of Massachusetts, and Mount Holyoke. The mountain itself, topped by a two-story white building called the Summit House that was once a hotel, is regarded as New England's most historic mountain.

According to the geologists, the Mount Holyoke Range was formed about two hundred million years ago when volcanic lava flowed along the valley floor, cooled, then was "upended" into mountains that rise abruptly from the river valley. Later, glaciation scoured the mountain's rough edges. The road into the park passes Titan's Piazza, a volcanic formation of overhanging rock columns, and the enigmatic

Devil's Football, a huge boulder with magnetic properties residing on its own in the woods. Immediately across the Connecticut River is Mount Nonotuck (elevation 1,218 feet), part of the Mount Tom Range and contained within the Mount Tom State Reservation.

HISTORY AND ARCHEOLOGY

In large measure, the relatively recent history of Mount Holyoke is the history of its Summit House. In 1821, America's first mountaintop inn was constructed on its peak in the form of a single room Mountain House. By 1849, when John and Fanny French purchased the spot, the Mountain House was already a popular spot. They renamed the structure Prospect House. In 1908, new owners, the Mount Holyoke Hotel Company, acquired the property and introduced plumbing, electricity, and an electric tram.

The infamous 1938 hurricane—infamous as one of few hurricanes to arrive in Massachusetts with much force left—damaged a wing of the building, ending its career as a hostelry. It remained closed to the public (aside from its outer porches) until the late 1980s, when it was renovated and opened as a historic building.

The Mount Holyoke Summit House once had two neighbors. The first was called the Eyrie House atop Mount Nonotuck; it was built in 1851 and burned down in 1901. The second was on neighboring Mount Tom (3.5 miles farther north from Mount Nonotuck), whose Summit House first opened to the public in 1897. It stood three stories tall and measured 76 by 92 feet, perched on the sheer cliff edge on the southernmost point of the summit. Until its destruction by fire in 1900, this Summit House was regarded as the area's hottest hot spot. President William McKinley reportedly exclaimed upon visiting the peak: "This is the most beautiful mountain outlook in the whole world." A second house was built and survived until 1929, when it too burned down; it was not rebuilt.[615]

Today the Skinner Park is part of the larger, three-thousand-acre Mount Holyoke Range State Park that preserves the spine of the range. The Mount Holyoke Summit House was a popular mountaintop hotel in the 1800s, and was widely appreciated by poets, artists, nature lovers, and of course tourists for its sweeping and intimate views out over 70 miles of valleys, towns, and rivers. The view was once memorialized by the famous operatic diva Jenny Lind in 1850 who proclaimed the view from here is "The Paradise of America." It still draws more than 100,000 visitors every year; businesses want to rent rooms for meetings and "everybody wants to get married here."[616]

Everybody also, it seemed, had something marvelous to say about the serene view of the meandering Connecticut River and its valley. One of the first on record, the Reverend Paul Coffin wrote in 1760 that the view of hundreds of acres of grain fields "looks like a beautiful garden, variously yet elegantly laid out." In 1823, Ralph Waldo Emerson said that the prospect of broad meadows "make[s] a beautiful picture seldom rivaled." In 1825, a guidebook touted the ascent of Mount Holyoke as being lately as fashionable

as any similar enterprise in the United States. By 1832, the peak was regarded as a favorite resort for travelers and pleasure parties. During the 1800s, writers and numerous painters and draughtsmen came here for inspiration and subject matter.[617]

The park was named after a wealthy industrialist who donated the hotel and land to the State of Massachusetts in 1940. Up until the late 1950s, a cable car carried passengers from a halfway point on the side of the mountain straight up its steepest slope into the basement of the Summit House.

Mount Holyoke today, though still well visited, is not particularly regarded as a sacred site, only as a scenic spot for a Sunday picnic or perhaps an offbeat wedding reception. You can hike to the top through the woods or drive your car. However, some people are starting to suspect something about the Mount Holyoke Range and its effect on Northampton, the home of Smith College and a cultural highpoint.

Tracy Kidder in his recent *Home Town*, which was a portrait of Northampton as seen through the life of a police officer, remarked that "everyone noticed this peaceable quality" about Northampton, and some had theories to account for it. One informant told Kidder that an angel guarded Northampton, protecting it from the "malice power" and evil influences that would otherwise migrate up the Connecticut River Valley from other cities to the south such as Springfield.

The local geography, especially the Mount Holyoke Range, plays a part in assisting this angel, the informant continued. Apparently, during a cloudy night he saw a reddish glow in the sky above the Range, and his suspicions were confirmed. "Those hills were definitely involved. They clearly helped to block the malice power from seeping into town."

A police officer believed that something "more mysterious" than effective police work was keeping the small city relatively crime free. "I don't know what it is about this place." Criminals seem to commit their crimes elsewhere, but not in Northampton. "Up here they're chillin', chillin'." A young man in and out of jail said of Northampton that it was a "place of spiritual power, just the sort of place the Supreme Being would choose."[618]

To the Pocumtucks, a tribe once native to the Pioneer Valley, the Mount Holyoke Range was indeed the sort of place the Supreme Being would choose, and had.[619] They knew the peak as *Petowomachu* and, to them, as well as *Nanotuck*, their name for Northampton, it was geomythically and spiritually significant.[620]

GEOMANTIC

Dome; Pointer's Ball; Underworld Entrance; Landscape Zodiac; Golden Egg; Scorpio Albion Root Chakra.

DOME: Two domes are present where the Connecticut River cuts through the Mount Holyoke and Mount Tom Range. One is over Mount Holyoke, the other over Mount Nonotuck. The cleft where the river passes through between the two peaks enjoys the vesica piscis–shaped blend of both dome energies. It would be an ideal place for a community, spiritual center, monastery, retreat, or resort spa; instead, there is an electric power plant.

The two domes mark and guard the temple entrance, the temple being a Landscape Zodiac occupying Northampton and surrounding towns. In large measure, this double-domed structure keeps the "malice power" from entering the Pioneer Valley temple. The Oroboros Line passes through this cleft, in the same place as the river, which perhaps explains the meaning of Pocumtuck as "narrow, swift river" or "clean, open stream." The swift, clean, open stream was

not the Connecticut River, but the oroboros energy current running in the same place through the mountains.

The dome over Mount Holyoke (approximately six miles wide) is the starfall for beta Orion, known as Rigel. Orion is the huge constellation of the Hunter; Rigel is the bright star in his left foot. Rigel is 543 light years from Earth, eighteen thousand times brighter than our Sun, and its diameter is forty-two times bigger. Rigel is derived from the Arabic *Rijl Jauzah al Yusra*, which means the "Left Leg of the Jauzah," or the giant hunter. Other names for Rigel have included *Ra'i al Jauzah*, meaning "Herdsman of the Jauzah," whose camels were the stars, and *Al Najid*, "The Conqueror."

Orion comes from *Uru-anna*, which means "The Light of Heaven." Greek myth presents Orion as a formidable warrior-hunter of prodigious size who considered himself invincible; the gods tired of his boasting and arranged to have a scorpion sting him to death. As a constellation, Orion is depicted standing, one hand holding up his club, the other his shield.

The dome over Mount Nonotuck (approximately eight miles wide) represents the presence of beta Argo Navis, known as *Maiaplacidus*. This star is part of the rudder in the great ship that bore the Argonauts in search of the Golden Fleece, and is situated about 25° east of Canopus, the major rudder star, our galaxy's second brightest star. Maiaplacidus is a second-magnitude star sixty-five light years from Earth, about 110 times brighter than our Sun. Its name may derive from the Arabic *Mi'ah*, meaning "Waters," so that the full name might mean "Placid Waters."

Some astronomers place Maiaplacidus within the subsidiary constellation of Carina (the ship's rudder or keel) when they posit Carina as separate from Argo Navis. Confusingly, Argo Navis was originally seen as a single constellation with forty-five stars; later it was dismembered into

Carina, Vela (the Sails), and Puppis (the Poop deck).

The two domes create an energy field of two interlocking circles extending almost fourteen miles across, with a radius in all directions of seven miles. Between them, ninety-six dome caps are generated and distributed throughout the landscape on both sides of the Mount Holyoke and Mount Tom ranges. This richness of dome caps alone could account for the fact that this area is an education mecca, with five major colleges, a student population base of perhaps forty thousand, and one small city, Northampton, with a national reputation as a cultural oasis and a highly desirable place to live.

POINTER'S BALL: Here is an impression of a geomantic application of the energies and possibilities of this double-domed site from a time in the far distant past:

The two mountains are much taller, standing possibly three thousand feet, and they stand much closer together. The gap for the river is tighter, more like a canyon. The mountains seem newer, more energetic; they are steeper, more rugged, and richer in vegetation. Many of the humps and rises along the spine of the Mount Holyoke and Mount Tom ranges are highlighted with dome caps, and there are evident temple structures at ground level underneath the dome caps.

Where the Summit House now stands, was a circle of twenty-eight standing stones; across the river, where the Eyrie House once stood on Mount Nonotuck, was a standing stone circle with thirty-two stones. Some type of clear quartzlike crystal generator or light column stands in the center of each circle.

The stones seem to be encased in a shiny, smooth white substance, or perhaps they are radiating light. On each peak, near the stone circles, are residential facilities, what today we would call dormitories and teaching halls. Thus today's Summit House is a subliminal but appropriate reminder of this site's antique past and use.

The two mountaintops are physically knit together by way of a huge arch, the legs of which are grounded in each peak. Within the arch is a walkway that can accommodate perhaps six people abreast. At the middle of the arch is a magnificent white crystal that measures about thirty feet across. On closer inspection, this massive crystal is a bluish-turquoise sphere in the form of a lion's face. It is an adaptation of a standard Pointer's Ball, which is a dimensional doorway. But this is a quasi-physical device to amplify the possibilities of the Pointer's Ball.

It has been adapted to be a star portal to the Andromeda galaxy. The portal seems to work the way a wormhole tunnel has been envisioned by science fiction: you get somewhere else very quickly, in this case, somewhere in Andromeda. There you may become aware of conscious beings in an unusual form: they are like a cluster of maybe fifty slender crystalline stalks with almond-shaped translucent heads.

The Andromedan tunnel was useful for the early grid engineers, who had originated in other star systems and galaxies, including Andromeda. In fact, according to angelically provided information, Andromeda was one of humanity's primary antecedent homes before the souls destined to incarnate on Earth "emigrated" to the Milky Way galaxy. Presumably, the traffic was two-way through this Andromedan tunnel: Earth grid engineers returning to the home office for meetings and instruction; representatives from home base coming to visit the field project in progress.

Occasionally, the Solar Logos would make an appearance over the Andromedan lion portal, like the Sun rising majestically over the horizon. If you could stand in Northampton "back then" at the time when this setup was the geomantic reality there, it would have seemed as if a massive blazing orange sun had settled over the archway, as if swallowing it, and singed the two mountaintops.

UNDERWORLD ENTRANCE: At the base of the former tramway that climbed Mount Holyoke from a midway point up its slope is an Underworld Entrance. There are many caves within the mountain, and these are both physical and etheric in nature. If you were to stand at what is still called the Halfway House (a short distance up the mountain road) and face the Summit House, you could potentially see the massive closed gates of the Underworld before you.

LANDSCAPE ZODIAC: In a metaphysical sense, the glorious view from Mount Holyoke that so many have extolled is one of starfields and the galactic wheel. Perhaps the intuitive aspect of the mountain's visitors somehow comprehended this hologram of stars and constellations underlying the grain fields and hills. Surely the Pocumtucks made use of it as part of their rituals and initiations, and there is no reason why contemporary Americans of whatever ethnic background cannot resume this practice to their benefit—and the Earth's.

The Pocumtuck zodiac—I call it this in honor of the earlier residents there—is about eighteen miles across, its two halves intersecting at Northampton, cleaved as it were by the Oroboros Line. The zodiac dome, centered over the umbilical point for this zodiac's Albion at approximately O'Neill Hill in Williamsburg, extends the area that is spiritually radiated to a total of 39.9 miles, or most of the Pioneer Valley. Present within this zodiac is one of the Earth's forty-eight Cosmic Eggs, located approximately between Mount Pisgah and Tob Hill in Westhampton.

GOLDEN EGG: One of the Earth's 666 Golden Eggs is positioned within the central axis of the Pocumtuck zodiac. The root of this figure lies at Moore's Hill in the D.A.R. State Forest in Goshen, its solar plexus and heart in Williamsburg, and its throat and brow chakras in Northampton. It's crown is at Mount Holyoke, and the Madonna figure embracing and grounding the entire figure is based at Prospect Hill on the Mount Holyoke College campus in South Hadley, a few miles south of the Mount Holyoke Range. Both the Landscape Zodiac and Golden Egg received considerable human geomantic interaction in the early 1990s.[621]

SCORPIO ALBION ROOT CHAKRA: The entire temple structure of double domes, Golden Egg, and Landscape Zodiac is an energy feature in the much larger geomythic figure of one of Earth's twelve Albions. Specifically, the Pocumtuck temple is this figure's root center, or *Muladhara*. In geomantic terms, this means the Pocumtuck zodiac grounds, stabilizes, and energizes all the geomantic aspects in a one-twelfth surface area of the planet's energy body.

This Albion is under the astrological influence of Scorpio at this time. Other energy centers in the Scorpio Albion include Hill Cumorah, Palmyra, New York; Monticello, Charlottesville, Virginia; and Clingman's Dome, Tennessee—all discussed elsewhere in this book.

Mount Ida, Crete, Greece

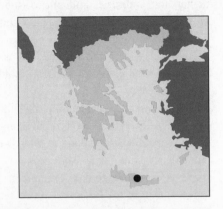

Mount Ida, a snowcapped peak in the central part of Crete, is all that you could ask for in a sacred mountain, comments Vincent Scully, noted scholar of Greek sacred architecture. Situated about thirty-five miles southeast of Herakleion (Iraklion) and the famous ruins of the Palace of Knossos, Mount Ida is known for its two cave sanctuaries located near the crest: the Kamares of the goddess (usually called Atana Potiniya [possibly Pallas Athena] or Cybele), and the Idaean, dedicated to Zeus and regarded as his birthplace. "Ida, widely horned at the crest, is embracingly female, and it descends in rounded, spreading slopes which are cut by dark clefts," Scully observes.[622]

Mount Ida (elevation: 8,058 feet), also known as Mount Idhi or Psiloritis, is the highest of three principal peaks on the island of Crete. The other two are the Lefka Ori, or White Mountains (8,045 feet), about forty miles due east; and Mount Dicte, or Dhikti (elevation: 7,047 feet) about forty miles to the west. The latter mountain also has a famous cave, the Dictaion Andron, similarly dedicated to Zeus and, like Mount Ida, claimed as his birthplace. As a whole, Crete boasts some thirty-four hundred caves.

MYTH AND LEGEND

Big myths are associated with Mount Ida. Foremost is the myth that Zeus, chief of the gods at Olympus, was born and reared in a cave on Mount Ida (though some say Mount Dicte). Zeus was the last-born son of the Titans Cronos and Rhea; Cronos, warned that one of his children would usurp his authority, tried to prevent this calamity by devouring his sons and daughters as soon as Rhea birthed them.

To preserve Zeus, her sixth child, Rhea wrapped up a stone to resemble an infant and gave that to Cronos to devour; meanwhile, she secreted herself away to give birth to Zeus. According to Hesiod's *Theogony*, "huge Gaia would take [great Zeus] into her care/on broad Crete, to nourish and foster with tender love." Rhea hid the infant inside "the god-haunted earth in a cave," although for Hesiod this cave was on Mount Aigaion.[623]

A nymph or divine goat named Amalthea was Zeus' wet nurse; she suckled him and fed the child-god with honey. Zeus took one of the she-goat's horns and promised her it would be a cornucopia, or Horn of Plenty, always filled with whatever fruit she desired. But the story is also told in reverse: the goat's horns flowed with nectar and ambrosia, and one of the nymphs attending Zeus broke it off the goat and filled it with fruit for Zeus. Amalthea is also said to have been the offspring of the Sun god, Helios, but was so ugly that the gods ordered Gaia to hide her in the Idaean cave.

When Amalthea eventually died, Zeus used her skin to make his *aegis,* or divine shield or armor, which he later employed effectively in his battle against the Titans. The aegis was impenetrable and terrible to look at, and it had the hideous head of the Gorgon in its center. In recompense for services, Zeus turned Amalthea into the constellation of Capricorn, or *Aegocerus,* the Goat's Horn. Aegocerus assisted Zeus during the Titanomachy, his battle for world supremacy against the Titans, including his own father, Cronos; this battle, according to Greek myth, lasted ten years and took place on Mount Ida (though some sources say Thessaly instead).[624]

Zeus was also protected by the Dactyls (literally, "fingers"), progeny of Rhea (or the nymph Anchiale), possibly the same as the Curetes. "When Zeus was born, Rea gave the child to the Daktyloi of Ida to guard; they were also called the Kouretes, and they came from Ida in Crete," affirmed Pausanias, the second-century Greek travel writer.[625] How many Dactyls there were is uncertain: ancient counts range from five or ten to one hundred.

Another version of the story has it that the Dactyls were six gigantic males and their five sisters. They were afterwards credited with the spread and possibly the creation of the Mysteries of the Great Mother and the arts of the smithy. Under Amalthea's supervision, the Dactyls gathered around the infant Zeus and made songs and wild, noisy dances, clashing their weapons to drown his infant cries. The idea, of course, was to keep Cronos from learning of Zeus' survival; the ploy was successful, and Zeus lived to dethrone his father.

As an "adult" god, Zeus was smitten by a young human woman named Europa whom he observed on the beach at Sidon, or Tyre, in what is now Syria. Her brother was Cadmus, the founder of Thebes. Filled with love-lust for the mortal female, Zeus disguised himself as a bull of dazzling whiteness and with horns resembling crescent moons. Coyly—if a massive white bull can be coy—he lay submissively at Europa's feet to help her overcome her fear. When she had, she climbed onto his taurine back and Zeus immediately entered the sea and swam to Crete.

Some ancient authorities say they landed at Gortyn; others that Zeus took Europa to his cave on Mount Ida; in either event, he coupled with the woman and produced three immortal sons from the consummation: Minos (who would be King of Crete), Sarpedon, and Rhadamanthys. All three one day would becomes the Judges of the Dead in Hades. Zeus gave Europa three presents: a dog that never let a prey escape; a hunting spear that never missed its mark; and a giant bronze man—some called him a robot or automaton— named Talos who continuously guarded the island.

Each day Talos walked fully armed three times around the entire island, preventing strangers from stepping foot on Crete or the inhabitants from departing without Minos' permission. He was untiringly vigilant, and didn't miss a thing. Talos would hurl huge boulders at miscreants, which included the landing party of Jason and the Argonauts. When they tried to land near Mount Dicte, Talos broke off lumps of rock from the cliff and hurled them at Jason's party.

Talos, said Apollonius of Rhodes in his *The Voyage of Argo,* was "a descendant of the brazen race that sprang from ash-trees [and who] had survived into the days of the demigods."[626] Talos, whose bronze body was filled with *ichor,* the blood of the gods, was invulnerable to attack or injury except for one spot just under the ankle that could be mortally pierced; if it was, all the ichor would flow out and he would perish.

One of the most famous and continuously baffling myths about Crete is the precise location of the famed Cretan labyrinth, built for King Minos by Daedalus to contain the fearsome Minotaur (literally, "Minos' bull"). While scholars have generally assumed the labyrinth must be located somewhere near or somehow at the ruins of the former Palace of Knossos, nothing conclusive has ever secured this identification. Some intellectual efforts have been expended to demonstrate ways in which the floorplan of the palace might resemble a labyrinth or be labyrinthine in its design, but these efforts have not been universally rewarded with acceptance.

The myth of the Cretan labyrinth is in some respects seemingly a reprise of the story of Zeus and Europa. To secure uncontested sovereignty over Crete and to force his brothers to quit their claims for kingship on the island, Minos prayed to Poseidon, Lord of the Sea and Zeus' divine brother for a worthy sacrificial victim. Poseidon sent Minos a bull from the sea, but it was so beautiful that Minos was reluctant to sacrifice it, and anyway, Poseidon made Minos' wife, Pasiphae (daughter of the Sun god, Helios), fall in love with it. Poseidon in revenge made the Cretan bull virtually untamable, if not mad.

Pasiphae contracted Daedalus, a master craftsman and engineer from Athens, to fabricate a hollow wooden cow on wheels that he set in a meadow to seduce the bull. Inside was Pasiphae, ready to have sex with the bull, who apparently would think the hollow cow was a real, mountable one. This being a mythic reality, the bull was fooled. Pasiphae became pregnant with a monster, a creature with a man's body and bull's head: the *Minotauros*.[627]

Daedalus was again employed, this time to construct a vast indecipherable maze to contain the creature. Somewhat confusingly, Pasiphae's off-spring was also called Asterius or Asterion. Every year (some myths say every nine years) the Athenians were required to send seven male youths and seven maidens as sacrifices to the Minotaur, that "monstrous hybrid beast," as Ovid recounted.

Daedalus built "blind walls of intricate complexity" and a "multitude of winding ways" in "countless corridors." The master architect constructed a labyrinth of bafflement "and hardly could himself/Make his way out, so puzzling was the maze."[628] The labyrinth, according to Apollodorus, "was a chamber that with its tangled windings perplexed the outward way."[629]

Eventually, with the aid of Ariadne, Pasiphae's daughter, the Athenian hero Theseus threaded the maze to its core, killed the Minotaur, and successfully found his way out again.

Not only did Minos commission human sacrifices to the Minotaur, but Homer says that every nine years King Minos "conferred with almighty Zeus himself" at "magnificent Cnossos,"[630] presumably for the purposes of getting the god's help in drafting new laws.

Also of interest regarding Mount Ida is that Plato sets his Socratic dialogue *Laws* on the slopes of the mountain as a conversation between three pilgrims approaching Zeus' cave. One pilgrim, an Athenian, asks his companion if it is true that Minos "used to repair to a conference with his father every ninth year, and that his legislation for your Cretan cities was based on his father's oracles." So our local story has it, Clinias replies, noting that the cave and chapel of Zeus are a "quite considerable" distance from Minos' headquarters at Cnossos.[631]

GEOMANTIC

Dome; Major Egregor Grounding Point; Cretan Labyrinth; Cosmic Egg; Planetary Energy Receptor.

DOME: Mount Ida's geomantic structure is equal to the glory implied by its mythic reputation. In fact, all of Crete possesses prime geomantic importance. The dome over Mount Ida corresponds to alpha Aegocerus, which is to say, the star in the horn of the goat of Capricorn—in effect, the horn itself. This star today is known as *Al Giedi,* from the Arabic *Al Jady* meaning "the Goat." Technically, Capricorn was originally depicted as a goat with a fishtail, and classical astronomers identified twenty-four principal stars in this constellation.

In the Capricorn-dome affiliation we have of course a major nuance of the Amalthea/goat/wet-nurse motif of Zeus' upbringing, which is to say, the grounding of his universal energy in the galaxy and the Earth. This becomes even more apparent when we consider the esoteric aspects of Capricorn.

Capricorn, the Sea-Goat, as it was also known, was to the Babylonians, long before the Greeks, apparently known as the "Father of Light." That's because approximately fifteen thousand years ago, the Sun rose in the Capricorn stars during the summer solstice. In other non-Greek legends, Capricorn was called the "Southern Gate of the Sun," in reference to its position on the ecliptic (the apparent annual path of the Sun through the zodiacal signs). Chinese astronomers described the constellation as an ox, then later as *Mo Ki,* the "Goat-Fish"; among the Egyptians, Capricorn was *Chnum,* the God of the Waters, and depicted with goat's horns.

Finally, in Greece, the followers of Plato called Capricorn the "Gate of the Gods," because they believed that "the human soul, after death, ascends to heaven through its stars."[632] In this same model, souls were believed to descend to Earth through the constellation Cancer. Astrologically, the zodiacal sign of Capricorn (at play for Earth between mid-December to mid-January) is ruled by Saturn, another name for Cronos, Zeus' Titan father. According to astrologers, Capricorn has always been regarded as the "Mansion of Kings."[633]

Capricorn's role in the Mysteries and initiation is supported by the metaphysical tradition, especially the works of Alice Bailey. She reports that in Capricorn you experience the "Crisis of Initiation," which exists in five stages "and signifies the emergence of the dominating Christ life." Bailey also suggests that this initiation signifies "the higher synthesis and the control of the Christ consciousness which is group consciousness."

Capricorn and Cancer are the two "great Gates" of the zodiac; Cancer opens the door into incarnation, while Capricorn is the gate into the life of the spirit, as it were, the door out of incarnation, allowing the individual "conscious participation in the life of that world centre which we call the Hierarchy." Further, Capricorn guards the secret of the soul, also known as the "secret of the hidden glory," Bailey says.[634]

Why did Zeus take the form of a bull of dazzling whiteness? The answer to this is also directly related to the initiation mysteries of Capricorn. The myths say that Zeus was suckled by the divine she-goat Amalthea, one of whose horns was transformed into a cornucopia, or Horn of Plenty. We've already established by virtue of the Mount Ida dome identification that the goat in question is the energy of the constellation Capricorn.

The horn of Amalthea—at least one of them—is the alpha star in this constellation situated in the right horn of the goat. But the horn also is geomythic code for an umbilicus line from the celestial world into Mount Ida, which is the birthplace not only of Zeus, but of the Bull of Europe. We know already that Zeus and the white bull are identical, that he took this form out of convenience.

This is where we part company with the surface details of the Greek myth, however, and look for the occult truth of the story. The dazzling white bull is an aspect of an Albion.

MAJOR EGREGOR GROUNDING POINT: This level of an egregor involves one of the nine major egregor figures, each one assigned to a one-twelfth surface division of the planet, described as a pentagon.

In practical terms, the geomythic figure of a bull includes Greece (particularly Athens), the Balkans, much of central Europe, and parts of France.[635]

Zeus, taking the form of the geomythic Bull of Europa, is "born" at Mount Ida insofar as the cosmic umbilicus for this energy is "grounded" at Mount Ida. The umbilicus is also the third chakra for the Bull of Europa as a geomythic figure. The Bull—Zeus in another form—is nourished by the She-goat (or Goat-fish) Amalthea through this cornucopia, which transmits energies of the higher celestial world—in effect, from Zeus' parents, the Titans. Zeus is born at the same place that he couples with Europa; this is where the two mythic streams converge into one meaning.

Mount Ida is where Zeus is grounded (born) and mates with Europa, which is really the geomythic figure of the Bull of Europe arrayed across a geometrically defined territory in Europe. Mount Ida is where the Zeus energy in the form of the bull enters most of Southern Europe. But why take the form of a bull?

Of course, the bull is a metaphor used by ancient myth-makers—initiates—to describe numinous, arcane, and higher world activities. But as a metaphor, the bull image is apt for expressing some of Zeus' characteristics as chief of the Olympic gods. A bull signifies irresistible strength and vitality, male impulsiveness, the unlimited powers of creation, tireless, uncontrolled fertility (Zeus' incessant "rapes" and love affairs). In the Vedic mythic pantheon, Zeus' equivalent is Indra, who also takes a bull form and whose horns suggest fertility, water, rain, heat, and lightning.

The bull also signifies Shiva, and represents primordial sexual energy, that is, the basic generative, fertilizing power behind and before matter. The bull stands for *Dharma,* the rightful cosmic order, which, from a human standpoint, ultimately is unfathomable. This is appropriate with respect to Plato's report that King Minos resorted every nine years to Zeus' cave for instruction on new laws for the Cretans.

As Vrishabha, the Vedic bull, this divinity "carries the manifestation of the world and, standing motionless at its hub, sets the cosmic wheel turning." The bull, for the Hindus, also stands for Aditi, the vital-breath of the All-Embracing. Also relevant here is the intriguing fact that in the Hebrew alphabet, the first letter, *Alef,* means "bull."[636]

Further, among the Hebrews, Yahweh (Jehovah) was the "Bull of Israel"; thus the bull represents Yahweh's might. Among the Egyptians, the bull Apis, the first created animal, was a holy incarnation of Osiris, while among the Iranians, the bull represented the soul of the world, its prime generative power, the source of the germ of all later creation. And in Sumerian belief, the great god Marduk is identified with Gudibir, the "Bull of Light."[637] As a metaphor for a cosmic energy, the bull draws consistent attributes from around the world. I'll return to Zeus after we've visited his labyrinth.

CRETAN LABYRINTH/COSMIC EGG: The Cretan labyrinth is a complex array of eight dome caps from three domed mountains on Crete forming a circular matrix five to ten miles in diameter with its center on Mount Ida.[638] Three dome caps come from Lefka Ori, three from Mount Dicte, and two from Mount Ida. The combination of the energy fields of the eight dome caps and their spiral lines (and the two straight-running dome lines from Lefka Ori and Mount Dicte to Mount Ida) create the labyrinth.

Seen from above as a two-dimensional structure, the labyrinth resembles eight points of brilliant light symmetrically arrayed in a circle around a central bright point; numerous spiral lines of light unfold to the left and right in all directions in this matrix. The Cretan labyrinth, one of twelve on the planet, is a key to the mind. Part of the geomythic figure of Europa, it spans different levels of experience; it is in fact the mental aspect or thinking agent of the consciousness of this landscape figure. It balances the two sides of the body and the two different aspects of the brain.

The labyrinth's architect was Daedalus, which is the Greek cover name for one of the Elohim, the master architects and geomancers of the Earth in its foundational days. The Elohim, a family of angels, temporarily took human form (as giants) for the purposes of executing the Earth's multiaspected geomantic setup, such as the numerous stone circles, henges, and cyclopean megalithic sites. They were the master engineers, archeoastronomers, and geomantic builders.

The center of the Cretan labyrinth faces east, its axis runs east-west, and in its working measurements, the number nine is a key factor. This accounts for, although it does not completely explain, the reference to the cycles of nine years for Athenian maidens and youths to be sent to the Minotaur, and for Minos' consultations with Zeus.

The Minotaur, though the subject of a rich body of symbolic interpretation over the years, is actually not a fearsome beast shut away in an impenetrable maze in the interests of public safety. The Minotaur is a human with the head of a bull, which is to say, with Zeus' head—Zeus' consciousness. The Minotaur is any human who has penetrated, assimilated, and mastered the higher mind energies of Zeus and the cosmic initiatory influences of his She-Goat, Capricorn, in the context of the Mount Ida dome cap labyrinth.

The human, not the Minotaur, is slain, surrendering his male or female head—his physical plane perspective—for the exalted vision of the chief of the gods. In the labyrinth, the human dies to his conventional identity, and the Minotaur is born, the human with the god's mind.

To find the center of the Mind (the cosmic Mind within the small human mind) is a difficult, arduous task, along an intricately winding way, but not an impossible one. It is conceivable that candidates for initiation once physically walked—threaded—the dome cap labyrinth overland.

The labyrinth can be approached and penetrated through its successive layers, at least in terms of gathering initial, approximate impressions of its energy structure. The following psychic impressions are offered not as definitive descriptions but merely as preliminary suggestions, possible metaphorical ways of construing the energy.

In the first layer, the outermost, one encounters an array of mounted horsemen (centaurs, perhaps) with raised spears. These are probably what the myth-makers called Dactyls. The second layer comprises a pulsating double-braided horizontal fence or barrier made of many different sound waves twisted into a complex rope. This is probably the sound the Dactyls make when they clash their shields, make their wild dances, and sing their noisy songs to disguise the infant cries of Zeus.

In the third layer, you encounter solar shields (again, probably belonging to the Dactyls). A bright golden Sun shines at the center of each shield. Looking closer, you may find that there is a face inside each Sun, resembling a goat's head or a Gorgon's hideous mask, or fluctuating between the two images. This is Zeus' *aegis*, the defensive device made from the skin of Amalthea.

In the fourth level is a bull's face looking straight at you; it has two eyes and two horns. It is the horns that are important, representing duality and polarity—the proverbial horns of the dilemma. These horns may also signify Amalthea's nourishing horns, marking a convergence of goat and bull horns into a single function of cosmic nourishment. More obviously or abstractly, they represent the Gates of Initiation, and the other variously termed gates attributed to Zeus and Capricorn. Pass through the two horns of the bull and you enter truly numinous terrain, the inner sanctum of the Mind of Zeus.

In the fifth layer, you come upon the actual entrance to the labyrinth, which, as many who have treaded small physical versions of this template will attest, resembles or somehow evokes the folds and convolutions of the human brain. Inserted like a key into this brainlike maze is the image of the Egyptian *ankh,* symbol of everlasting life, the key of life that opens the way into the Mysteries.

The sixth layer presents itself, energetically, as like a cyclotron, a spinning device, in which you, as consciousness, transit the entire labyrinth of eight dome caps instantaneously. This is to say, your awareness is distributed uniformly throughout the energy matrix and you seem to be moving very fast through all stops in this labyrinth as a way of signifying to yourself that you are already simultaneously at all these places. You are now the bull with eight eyes; you have dome caps for pupils.

In the seventh layer, you experience a union with the Titans Cronos and Rhea, Zeus's divine parents. One aspect of this seventh layer is an egg of light, a Cosmic Egg. Here you sense that Zeus and Osiris are the same being described through two different mythic filters. Both are Bulls of Light; Osiris is dismembered into fourteen pieces, each one buried at a different temple site in Egypt. Zeus presides over the fourteen Ray Masters of Mount Olympus. It's the same story; in both cases, the Bull or Egg of Light is differentiated (dismembered) into fourteen rays or gods. Zeus is the chief of the gods because he is their source; in practical terms, Zeus *is* Mount Olympus.

When you enter the seventh layer of the Cretan labyrinth, you are about to shift dimensions, move up a rung in the cosmic hierarchy, to Zeus' parents. In this seventh layer, Zeus is pure and alone, like an Egg of Light; he is inside the eggshell, in a private space. He is the egg-born god, the holy being in the Cosmic Egg. At the core of the labyrinth, in the seventh realm of Zeus' world, resides the Cosmic Egg, which of course is also the Cosmic Mountain, containing all creation, the planetary spheres and all the stars, the way down into the world, and the ascent out of incarnation.

The umbilicus from Amalthea comes down from above and anchors Zeus into Mount Ida; it feeds him with cosmic light. At the end that attaches to Zeus, the umbilicus is a single line, but at the other, topmost end, it has split into fourteen strands or filaments. These are the Titans, the gods older than those of Olympus, the primeval creator beings.

The Titans are in fact the Elohim, a family of angels commissioned to create and maintain worlds, planets, solar systems, and various tiers of intelligent life within them. Originally, three Elohim multiplied themselves into fourteen and became the incarnating cosmic intelligence (the Planetary Logos) for each of the seven traditional planets. (Rhea and Cronos were Elohim.)

The pairing off of the Titans corresponds to the distribution of the Elohim through the planetary spheres of the solar system (and ever larger, more exalted and rarified expressions of this same template). In a sense, the solar system itself is a Cretan labyrinth with seven levels of experience and consciousness. At the center of the labyrinth and in its seventh layer, Zeus confronts his parents.

The so-called Titanomachy was not an apocalyptic battle for world supremacy between the older Titans and younger Olympian gods. Rather, it was Zeus as the epitome of the Olympian gods *assimilating* and then *distributing* the seven "flavors" of cosmic energy (the fourteen "planetary" Elohim) of the Titans. The umbilicus from alpha Capricorn is the Horn of Plenty, the conduit for the energies (Amalthea's nectar, ambrosia, honey, and milk) of the Elohim to feed Zeus, the newborn principle of higher mind.[639] It is no more of a battle than ordinary digestion; it is more like a transducing of higher, faster energies into somewhat slower, more manageable ones.

The distribution takes place through the labyrinth, which acts as a spinning device, like a centrifuge, or perhaps like a fountain with seven spilling tiers. In either case, the incoming energy (the birth of Zeus from the Titans) is received, mastered, "digested," and distributed through the multilayered energy matrix produced by the eight dome caps converging on the dome of Mount Ida.

Insofar as at least two other peaks participate in the labyrinth matrix, it is correct to say that Zeus was born in the Dictean cave or the other caves sometimes mentioned. All of these sites (at least 144 dome caps potentially are involved) help to birth—that is, ground—the energy of Zeus into Crete.

In this respect, Zeus truly is the Bull of Heaven, the primordial source of generative, fertilizing power for the world, starting in this case with Crete, for geomantically, Crete is a major player in the Earth's energy distribution system. It all has to do with Talos, that giant man of bronze who defends the island.

PLANETARY ENERGY RECEPTOR: Three places on Earth were originally designated by the Hierarchy to be receptacles for the energies of other planets. If in a given period of astrological influence the planet Venus, say, is most important, its energies will be "collected" and contained at one of these three places. These three places are Mount Meru (southwest of New Zealand), Easter Island (due west of Chile), and Crete.

The three are differentiated or "electrically wired" for valency or charge in the same way as the three channels for kundalini energy in the human: there is a positive (pingala), a negative (ida), and a neutral (sushumna) channel. These are, respectively, Crete, Easter Island, and Mount Meru. These places receive light. Each has a guardian figure whose task is to carry, or embody, some aspects of the incoming planetary energy and to protect it.

The delightful or startling fact about Talos is that he is much as the Argonauts described him: very tall and fierce. One direct impression of Talos has him standing even taller than Mount Ida, which is to say, above eight thousand feet.[640] It sounds fantastic and highly improbable, of course, but here is another way of approaching Talos.

Conceive of a rapidly rotating blue-white spindle, spinning so fast that you cannot distinguish any of its features. In no time it has created a bowl made of three overlapping concentric circles. This is Talos, pacing the island of Crete three times every day. This bowl rests on the tops of the tallest mountains on Crete. It comprises the three domes and 144 dome caps on Crete, and functions like a woven basket or fishnet, to collect and hold the different incoming planetary energies. In practical terms, the entire island of Crete is a collecting bowl.

This Talos bowl can adjust itself somewhat to match the direction and energy quality of the specific planetary energy it is collecting. The bowl in practical terms is the body of Talos running at almost the speed of light around the perimeter of Crete. Since he is virtually everywhere at once, his movements comprise the form of a bowl, basket, or net—it's all metaphorical here.

The Talos bowl, brimming with non-Earth planetary energies, is also a Horn of Plenty, nourishment for the infant Zeus. Through Crete's own complex geomantic network, this extraplanetary energy is distributed, eventually and as appropriate, throughout the Earth via its energy matrix.

Mount Kailash, Tibet

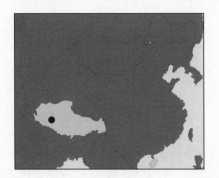

Mount Kailash resembles a crystalline ice cone seemingly carved by supernatural hands into four distinct facets. Each facet fronts one of the four cardinal directions; its sides are sheer, as if shaven; the snowcapped dome is symmetrical. No other mountain is like this. "It is like an immediate revelation of the Almighty, which makes man bend his knees and lower his head." Kailash is "resplendent with the luster of spiritual aura," exuding an "awe-inspiring solemnity and weird grandeur."[641]

Located in a remote, isolated region of Tibet, Mount Kailash is a 22,028-foot peak in the Southern Transhimalayan Range, eight hundred miles northwest of Lhasa, near the Nepalese and Indian borders. Subject to strong winds, bitter cold, and the usual climatological and meteorological extremes of high altitude, it is hard to get to, yet a thirty-two-mile pilgrimage route with temples and prayer stations encircles the mountain. It is not only Tibet's preeminent holy mountain, but for many around the Earth, the world's holiest peak.

About twenty miles from the southern base of Mount Kailash is Lake Manasarovar (two hundred square miles in size), said to have been created by Brahma as an extension of his mind (hence, the Lake of Manas, or Mind), as a place for his holy sons to perform their ablutions after venerating Shiva and Parvati on Kailash. The Tibetans know it as *Tso Mapham,* which means "The Undefeated" or the "Lake of the Invincible Forces of the Buddhas or Victors." The lake sits at 14,950 feet, and is fifty feet higher than nearby Rakshas Tal, the other Kailash lake (140 square miles in size), which is believed to be the haunt of demons and is generally avoided by the pious. (It is also called *Langag Tso,* which means "Lake of the Dark Deities.")

Thus Lake Manasarovar is the Lake of Consciousness (*Manas* means "higher mind, cognition, and enlightenment") while Rakshas Tal is the Lake of the flesh-eating Demons (*Rakshas* means "demons"), the hindrance to liberation. "The landscape here encodes a symbolic message: natural form is imbued with supernatural significance."[642] This archetypal polarity between the lake of terrifying deities of darkness and the lake of the peaceful deities of daylight plays itself out at the feet of the sublime Kailash, "the Mountain of the Swastika (the symbol of eternal creativeness.)"[643]

In earlier times, eight small Tibetan monasteries *(gompas)* were situated along Manasarovar's shore; the lake was seen as a mandala, or Wheel of Life, and the gompas were set at the presumed places where the spokes intersected the hub. A ritualized pilgrimage around the lake (sixty-four miles) was considered auspicious and part of religious practice.

A Hindu legend says that the Kings of the Nagas (a species of divine cobras and snake spirits) resided in the lake and sustained themselves with the fruit of the huge (though invisible to humans) *jambu* tree that grew in the lake's center. The jambu tree's fruit is the source of a life-giving elixir; the fruit exudes gold drops that infuse the entire lake, transmuting it into an elixir of immortality. This is the mythical explanation for why the Asian-Indian part of the world was anciently called *Jambudvipa,* or "Rose-apple Tree Land."

In the mythical cosmology of the Vedas, Jambudvipa was one of seven continents, each surrounded by a sea, but Jambudvipa was the central one, and in the middle of it rose the golden Mount Meru and the wish-granting jambu tree, whose branches reached the sky and were the favorite resort of the sages.

In fact, the Tibetans called the Kailash-Manasarovar region the navel of Jambudvipa for the human world. "The Tree of Life in the Lake of Supreme Consciousness—what a profound symbolism, and how reminiscent of the Tree of Knowledge in the biblical story of the Paradise!"[644]

A Buddhist legend links this lake with the mythical Anotatta (or Anavatapta) Lake in which Queen Maya, the mother of the Buddha, purified herself before his birth. Other accounts report the Buddha and his many divine followers resting on lotus blossoms on the lake's surface. Both attributions suggest that the lake has remarkable healing properties for the body, mind, and soul.

HISTORY AND ARCHEOLOGY

Hindu legend always maintained that the Mount Kailash region was the source of India's four great rivers: the Indus, Brahmaputra, Sutlej,

and Karnali. Specifically, the waters for those rivers were believed to originate in the great Lake Manasarovar, Brahma's Lake of Manas, or Mind, at Kailash's base.

These four rivers were said to circulate seven times around Kailash, paying homage to Shiva and his retinue before flowing south. Each river has a special Buddhist name based on holy animals (such as *Magcha-Khambab,* "the river flowing out of a peacock's mouth") that are the "throne-symbols" of four of the five Dhyani Buddhas residing at Kailash,[645] the center of this vast cosmic and geological mandala, a template of the gods' celestial residences in the landscape.

A Buddhist sutra stated that the waters of all the rivers flow into India from the "lake-mouth of the great dragon, Anavatapta," which is said to be the landmass centering on Tibet. Seen on a map, some commentators see in this distribution of rivers and landmass a dragon lying on its side, its mouth at Lake Manasarovar, the tip of its tail in the Malaysian archipelago.[646]

In a 1907 expedition to Lake Manasarovar, Swedish explorer Sven Hedin determined that all four rivers can in fact claim as their source this section of Western Tibet dominated by Mount Kailash—an intriguing possibility given the fact that Kailash is often equated with the mythical Mount Meru, the source of the world's four great rivers, just like the Judaic Garden of Eden. Geologists now know that the Himalayan watershed actually starts one hundred miles north of the highest peaks in that range in the high Tibetan plateau (known as the Roof of the World) and supplies four rivers that terminate fifteen hundred miles to the south in the Bay of Bengal and Arabian Sea.

Hedin was the first known Westerner to complete the thirty-two-mile *parikrama* or pilgrimage route around Kailash, considered an essential feature of every visit. The Indian Swami Pranavananda, between 1928 and 1949, did the parikrama twenty-five times, and circled Lake Manasarovar twenty-three times—probably the world's record. A few have made the circuit in a single day, being dubbed *Chhokar*, or *Khi-kor*, meaning "he who runs around like a dog," while others have progressed by prostrations. Typically, anywhere from fifteen to thirty days is required to complete it, which includes making it through the Dolma La pass at 18,600 feet.

The remarkable fact about the veneration of Mount Kailash is that it does not require or even condone the physical climbing of the mountain. Contrast this with the typical approach to Australia's giant red rock, Uluru, spiritual focus of the Aborigines; seemingly everyone who visits Uluru climbs it. At Kailash, the emphasis is witnessing, a contemplative observation of the great mountain from all angles, the thirty-two-mile *parikrama* of the gods' home, but not a physical ascent.

Pilgrims making the parikrama encounter a series of religious structures *(chorten)* along the way which reinforce the Buddhist concept that the circumambulation route is a physical expression of a cosmic mandala and that each full circuit is equivalent to a single turn of the Wheel of Life. If you make it around the Kailash parikrama once, you atone for the bad deeds of a single life; if you do ten circuits, you wash away the karma of all the lives you had in an eon; but if you complete 108 circuits, you will attain enlightenment and liberation.

Ever since Hedin's parikrama, the prospect of making a pilgrimage around Mount Kailash has caught the Western spiritual imagination, and many have done it. One whose adventures probably spurned the interest of an entire Western generation was the German-Bolivian itinerant monk Lama Anagarika Govinda, who traveled to Kailash in 1948 and recounted his travels in *The Way of the White Clouds* in 1966.

MYTH AND LEGEND

Mount Kailash carries the attributive burden of four different religious viewpoints: Hindu, Jain, Buddhist, and Bon.

The Hindus see Mount Kailash as the abode of Mahadeva, or Shiva, who sits in unending meditation with his consort, Parvati, the daughter of Himalaya. The Hindus understood Himalaya, "The Abode of Snow," to be a single mountain god named Himavat who encompassed the entire range. Shiva was the one of Hinduism's three great gods (along with Brahma and Vishnu) who was in charge of destroying the world of illusion. The physical mass of Kailash is taken to be Shiva's lingam, both a phallic representation of the god's potency and a sublime, almost abstract representation of his presence.

To the Hindus, the summit of Kailash was an enchanted, paradisiacal realm, resplendent in numerous jewels, melodious with bird song, the air redolent with perfume and fragrance and continuous beautiful, even impassioned, song and music provided by the *Apsaras* (heavenly dancers), *Gandharvas* (celestial musicians), *Ganapatya* (devotees of Ganesh), and *Chnrana* (celestial singers) to the delight of innumerable *Siddha* (semi-divine holy men). Kubera, the god of wealth and Regent of the North (one of the eight *Lokapalas*, or guardians of the directions) was said to rule from his city of Alaka, located near or on Kailash.

In fact, the Hindus tended to link Mount Kailash with Mount Meru, the unique Celestial City, planetary *axis mundi*, and home of the exalted gods over which Shiva presides. Mount Meru was believed to be a mountain 84,000 *yojanas* tall (one *yojana* is eight miles), twice as wide at the top as at the base (an inverted cone), and surrounded by eight satellite Celestial Cities (each a headquarters for one of the eight Lokapalas) and by seven concentric rings of golden mountains.[647]

Kailash figured in the ancient Indian epic, the *Ramayana.* Hanuman, the monkey god of prodigious physical and occult abilities, journeyed north from Lanka to Kailash to fetch the four different medicinal herbs that grew there, which were said to restore life and heal weapons wounds. These herbs had been placed there originally by the gods. The mountain shone brightly, Hanuman found, and the herbs appeared like flashing lights. Soon he understood that the herbs had concealed themselves and that only the gods could find these celestial remedies.

He didn't know exactly what the herbs looked like, so he broke off the mountain summit, the section containing all the herbs, and brought the peak back to Lanka to let the experts collect the herbs. Hundreds of thousands of warriors were returned to life. When they were done, Hanuman tossed the mountain back in the direction of Tibet, but it landed lopsidedly, and some of its snow fell off on Tibet. The peak was then called Tise.

The *Ramayana* also relates the amusing story of the encounter between Ravanna, King of the Demons and Rakshashas, and the imperturbable Shiva. Ravanna, a ten-headed, twenty-armed primordial malefic being (paradoxically, Lord Kubera's brother), traveled through Tibet until he was stopped by Mount Kailash.

Its guardian, Nandi, the Bull of Shiva, told Ravanna that the abode was inaccessible to all created beings. Unimpressed, Ravanna started to tear the "hill" down. Then Shiva pressed down upon the hill with his toe, crushing and trapping Ravanna. Over the course of the next hundred years, Ravanna prayed to Shiva to release him, which he did.[648]

The Jains of India revered Mount Kailash as *Astapada,* the place where they believed Rishabha, their first *Tirthankara,* attained his full enlightenment. In the Jain view, the Tirthankara were avatars, or high celestial beings who incarnated in the human realm to provide examples for liberation; Mahavira (Great Man), the historical founder of Jainism, was the twenty-fourth Tirthankara. The Tirthankara is a Jaina savior, a "Maker of the River-Crossing," the river being the dimensional boundary between matter and spirit. They are "transcendent, cleaned of temporality, omniscient, actionless, and absolutely at peace."[649]

The Tibetan Buddhists see Kailash as the home of a tantric meditation deity called *Demchog* (in Sanskrit *Samvara,* meaning "Eternal Bliss") and his consort, *Dorje Phangmo* (in Sanskrit *Vajravarahi*). Demchog is a fierce being, with four faces, each a different color and each with three eyes. He wears a crown of human skulls, his body is blue, and each of his twelve hands holds a ritual object. He is shown united with red-bodied, naked Dorje Phangmo in a nimbus of fire; she is also said to reside on a nearby peak called Tijung.

These two figures are *yidams,* which are not so much self-existent gods, but rather personifications of purified aspects of human nature, particularly the aspects with greatest affect such as wrathful and passionate, which "if properly transformed through spiritual training may produce true wisdom."[650]

Tibetan Buddhists also say that on Kailash dwell the Buddha and his retinue of Dhyani Buddhas and five hundred *bodhisattvas,* enlightened beings who work for humanity's salvation. This array of enlightened beings at Kailash is known to Buddhists as the Mandala of Highest Bliss. Tibetans also know their mountain as *Kang Rinpoche,* meaning "Jewel of the Snows," and they relate the story that the great twelfth-century yogi Milarepa once occupied a cave on Kailash and defeated the Bon magician Naro Bhun Chon in a pitched battle for possession of the sacred mountain.

The Bons (or *Bon-pos*) were the original inhabitants of Tibet, long before the Buddhists arrived in the seventh century A.D. and chased out the Bon pantheon of occult deities. To the Bons,

Kailash was the "soul mountain" of Zhang Zhung, an ice-capped pyramid known as Kang Tise. To them, the mountain rises into the heavenly realm like an eight-ribbed parasol, and climbs above the Earth like an eight-petaled lotus. They called it *Yungdruk Gu Tseg,* or "Nine-Storey Swastika Mountain," and said it was the soul of the entire geographical region.

The Bons regarded Kailash as the world's navel and the abode of 360 *Gi-kod,* deities unique to Kailash. Shenrab, "the Lord of Man, the Conqueror," and the founder of the Bon religion, began teaching his doctrines at the age of ten, instructing the realms of the Earth gods, Underworld serpents, and airborne divinities.

The original teachings of Bon were said to derive from the "language of the Eternal Gods." Later Shenrab descended the "heavenly cord" into Kailash, known in Bon mythology as Mount Yungdrung's Pyramid of Nine Swastikas. This is where he first entered the Earth realm from *Ol-mo lung-ring* in *sTag-gzig,* a heavenly realm considered by some scholars to be similar to the Buddhist Sukhavati or Shambhala, an imperishable bliss world of the highest gods.

The Bon-po description of Ol-mo lung-ring is highly similar to the Hindu model of Mount Meru, the cosmic mountain at the heart of the world, and to the cosmic-geological mandala around Mount Kailash, leading some scholars to propose that they are the same place. Even so, the Bon-po tradition tends to see Ol-mo lung-ring as the center of civilization and Kailash as the center of the Earth.[651] The Bons also regarded Kailash as a *chorten* (Hindu *stupa*) of rock crystal, a kind of systematized, hierarchically arrayed temple.

MYSTICS AND TOURISTS

When Lama Anagarika Govinda first saw Mount Kailash from a distance in his 1948 Tibetan trek, he called it "one of the most inspiring views" possible on Earth. The mountain entirely dominates the landscape, the air is so clear you can see for one hundred miles, and your eyes feel uncannily endowed with a super acuity, almost infrared vision.

"An immense peace lies over this divine landscape and fills the heart of the pilgrim, making him immune to all personal concerns, because, as in a dream, he feels one with his vision," Govinda wrote. He knows that he has had *darshan* (or a sacred viewing) of the sublime and that "nothing can happen to him other than what belongs to him already from eternity."[652]

Before he made his pilgrimage to Mount Kailash in 1995, Tibetan Buddhist scholar Robert Thurman used to dream about its mystic properties. In his dreams he would see Kailash as a "great crystal energy source" that radiated innumerable hues of blue, crimson, green, and gold, "sending these life-giving rays" straight through the mountain ranges into the world at large to illuminate human souls.

Thurman had learned from His Holiness the Dalai Lama that the Buddha had manifested himself there in the form of the "Superbliss-Machine Buddha," and that his Mandala Palace at Kailash was home to sixty-two "Superbliss deities" who were always present. "The palace doors are always open and its radiance is always emanating," writes Thurman.

He further notes that Lama Anagarika Govinda told him that there was a place of "ultimate power" on Kailash's north face, where one could plant wishes for the entire world and be assured that all the Buddhas, gods, and "dakini-angels" always present at Kailash would look after the fulfillment of those wishes.

Thurman used his Kailash pilgrimage as an opportunity to field-test *The Blade Wheel of Mind Reform,* an esoteric Buddhist teaching of fiercely transcendent wisdom that aims to free the mind of self-preoccupation, narcissism, vanity, the "self-habit," and "our inner enemy of egotism."

He and his travel companions used these teachings as a practice for their "inner pilgrimage" around Kailash to run parallel to the outer, physical circling of the sacred peak. "I have invested a lot in the belief that Kailash is the core of our global structure of life, the sacred heart of joy that makes life worthwhile, or even plausible."[653]

The "utter joy of being in this place sent me shaking," confessed American Buddhist-shamanic writer Joan Halifax of her trip to Kailash in the early 1990s. "The mountain is a mirror that accurately reflects the minds of those who come to it." Comparing the parikrama to a circle that symbolizes nonduality, Halifax noted that "the walk around Kailas is about the perfection of our true nature in all its displays."[654]

GEOMANTIC

Dome; Etheric Umbilicus for Albion; Dragon; Naga City; Avalon; Shambhala Entrance; Og-Min Cave Heavens.

DOME: The dome over Mount Kailash is the planetary starfall for beta Canis Majoris, the star in the Great Dog's nose or top of its head called Murzim (or Mirzam). The name is derived from the Arabic *Al Murzim*, "the Announcer," because when the beta star rises, Sirius, the Dog's alpha star, is soon to rise. Murzim is a second-magnitude star 465 to 750 light years from Earth, an estimated 7,600 times brighter than our Sun.

In many respects, the Greater Dog is the pivotal constellation in our galaxy. It is of course the home of Sirius, the galaxy's brightest star.

In Vedic myth, Sirius is *Vastospati*, the Hound of Heaven who guards the House of Varuna, which is to say, the created cosmos full of stars and celestial beings, "a lofty structure of a thousand gates." Sirius as Vastospati, the Lord of the Dwelling, is believed to be the cosmic incarnation of Rudra, the Wild God, an early description of the great Hindu god Shiva.

For the Hindu mythographers, it is the Dog that hunts Orion, which to them is not a hunter but an antelope, from whose body leaked the generative germ that seeded the universes. Sirius, in this view, is "the star symbol of the Wild Hunter and of the guardian of order, the dog." Sirius is the wild archer who hunts the antelope and thereby starts time.[655]

Thus Shiva's attribution to Mount Kailash is geomythically validated by the presence of the beta star in the Great Dog, an emissary of Sirius. The Tibetan Demchog can be taken as an equivalent to Shiva: Shiva has a blue neck, Demchog is all blue, and the Sirians of Canis Major are said to be blue-skinned. We can usefully think of Sirius, as the galaxy's guardian, guarding Kailash.

ETHERIC UMBILICUS FOR ALBION: Each of the twelve Albion plates on the planet has a full array of chakras, seventy-two minor and nine major as well as an umbilicus point. This umbilicus is taken to be an etheric aspect of the third chakra and corresponds to the Blazing Star, or pinprick of brilliant light located in the human energy field just above the navel. The Earth's prime umbilicus is at Avebury in England (see that section in the book), but each of the twelve Albion plates has a holographic version of Avebury. Kailash is one.

The Mount Kailash umbilicus is the same as the Bon-po reference to the "sky cord" down which Shenrab, the first Bon-po teacher, descended to Earth. At Avebury, the umbilicus connects the Earth to the galaxy through Sirius and Canopus, the two brightest stars. At Kailash, the umbilicus reiterates this galactic connection, and reinforces half of it again through its Sirian dome, through the star Murzim in the Great Dog. The Mount Kailash etheric umbilicus is the

Blazing Star for the Albion that occupies this part of the planet.

DRAGON/NAGA CITY: The Kailash temple is best approached from the midpoint between the twin lakes. Tibetan legend says that long ago a golden fish tunneled to create the zigzag channel called *Ganga Chu* that connects the two lakes. Where the fish dug is the balance point between the two realms. Appropriately, both lakes are topped by a dome cap from the Mount Kailash dome, and where these two dome caps intersect and create a vesica piscis (an almond or fish shape) is the Ganga Chu.

Situated at Raskshas Tal is a Naga City, one of Mount Meru's eight Celestial Cities, this one concerned with the Rakshasas (the "dark deities") and the cosmic serpent, Ananta Sesa. Ananta Sesa is the archetype of the thirteen major and 1,053 minor Earth dragons; one of these minor dragons guards the entrance to the entire Kailash temple complex from Rakshas Tal, although its sphere of influence encompasses all of Kailash and its thirty-two-mile parikrama circuit.

AVALON: Lake Manasarovar, said to be the emanation of the mind of Brahma, is the site of an Avalon. This is another version of the Hindu *Jambudvipa,* or Rose-apple tree land. On an invisible island in the middle of this lake the jambu tree grows, offering golden fruits whose juice transmutes the lake water into an elixir of immortality. This is a clear geomythic clue for an Avalon whose golden apples contain the divine fruits of wisdom—Brahma's wisdom, of course. The Kailash Avalon also encompasses the thirty-two-mile parikrama circuit, a trail of lovely blossoms in an otherwise barren land.

Ideally, the pilgrim approaching Mount Kailash walks the parikrama circuit, collecting and "digesting" golden apples along the way in preparation for the main fare at Mount Kailash which is the Shambhala Entrance.

SHAMBHALA ENTRANCE: There is no single doorway that is the Shambhala Entrance; rather, the entire temple complex up to this point is the necessary preparation—cognitive doorway—to boost spiritual awareness to make it possible to perceive and thus to enter the Western Paradise or Sukhavati.

This is Varuna's Celestial City in the West, the fabled Islands of the Blessed, an aspect of Mount Meru, one of its eight satellite Celestial Cities. From the Sanskrit, Sukhavati means "the Blissful." It is the pure land of the West, one of the most important "Buddha-fields" presided over by the Dhyani Buddha Amitabha, who created it. One can be reborn there and lead a blissful life until reaching nirvana. Sukhavati is flooded in radiance, filled with exquisite fragrances, wondrous flowers, trees of jewels; the rushing of water is music; those who are reborn here awaken in a lotus flower; and all beings cleave to the truth of the teaching until their final enlightenment.

In Sukhavati you will see pavilions of Buddhas discoursing on reality; gamboling troops of Apsaras (celestial dancing maidens) and Gandharvas (celestial musicians); the Dhyani Buddhas, towering, magnificent, multidimensional, holding court, the Buddhist version of the Judaic archangels.

Also present within Shambhala is the Council of the Sirians, represented as a huge Round Table at which dozens of blue-skinned Sirians are seated; they have vertically elongated, pointed heads, usually covered. Hundreds of angels stand in a single circle around this Round Table; these are of the Ofanim class of angels, the manifest form of the Blazing Star of the etheric umbilicus of Mount Kailash.

The Ofanim have an intermediary manifestation between the pinprick of absolute light and the familiar angelic form: it appears to be a crystal with millions of equal-sized facets known as the Nimitta. Kailash's physical crystalline appearance is in large measure a reflection in matter of the Nimitta's adamant crystalline form in this subtler level of reality. The Sirian Round Table is an expression of the wisdom and guidance aspect of Sirius. It is also an aspect of the hologram of Shambhala accessible through Kailash.

OG-MIN CAVE HEAVENS: There is something else above Mount Kailash, which is to say in yet another level of subtle reality above the ones just described. There are very few cultural or mythic frames of reference describing this, but what comes closest to it is the Bon-po name for their point of origin: *Ol-mo lung-ring* in *sTag-gzig*. Concisely put, Ol-mo lung-ring is a giant disc-like spaceship and sTag-gzig is the Andromeda galaxy.

Ol-mo lung-ring is not precisely a saucer-shaped ship, but at first glance it resembles one. Picture a thick blue disc perhaps one hundred miles in diameter situated motionlessly above Mount Kailash. Inside are hundreds, perhaps thousands, of caves, each containing a multidimensional being of pure light. Perhaps they are stars; or maybe *rishis;* or living crystals; or maybe something altogether different, formless, indescribable.

These are the Og-Min, the original Bon-po sages who came from a higher dimensional reality. The term Og-Min is a somewhat vague, ill-defined reference that shows up along the edges in Bon-po and Tibetan literature. One text, in describing the Bon-po lineage of royal Bru says: "As for the gNam-bru, the essence of all Enlightened ones in the person of an individual divine son named Od-zer mDangs-ldan, descended to the place of Bar-lha od-gsal from the sphere of Og-min stug-po bkod pa," for the sake of sentient beings.

Then this being went to the human world and descended at a specific place where he "turned the wheel of Bon for the gods." But he also surveyed the world from the summit of Mount Meru. The Bon-po texts also state that "all the gShen-po [high priests, enlightened emissaries], having hidden the Bon texts, departed, some to the 'Celestial Sphere,' some to solitary places for meditation," and others to Mongolia.[656]

That Celestial Sphere, the point of origin for the high priests or the source of their knowledge, was the Andromeda Galaxy (sTag-gzig) which is where *we* came from before entering the life and cosmomythic system of this galaxy whose center of consciousness is Sirius. As Sirius is to our galaxy, so Andromeda is to Sirius: a point of origin, orientation, oversight, and guidance.

Tibetan legend says that in its oldest, primeval days, the land of Tibet was overrun by demons. The Bon-po's first task in preparing Tibet for spiritual civilization was to rid the land of these inimical beings, which is to say, dispel the inherent chaos of first creation. In some sense, the disc ship of Ol-mo lung-ring hovered above the land sweeping and sucking out the impurities and cleansing the land like a giant vacuum cleaner. The Bon-pos gave Tibet its celestial, higher dimensional, Andromedan imprint, which is remembered as the "soul of Zhang Zhung," Mount Kailash being the soul of the Tibetan landscape.

The Og-Min Cave Heavens quite likely are the same as what Chinese Taoists described as astral *shiens.* These are starry realms or "big holes" in the universe known as "Heavenly Caves." Esoteric Taoism speaks of the thirty-six Heavenly Caves that are the paradise of the shiens, or immortal divine beings.

The Heavenly Caves are bright, positive energy holes in the universe.[657] "Even a very ordinary thing, once it has had the chance to touch these positive energy spots, is immediately transformed from being mortal to being immortal, from death to life."[658]

The astral shiens have crystal bodies and total freedom, but they work in accord with the cosmic blueprint for evolution. They tend to live together in communities, making the heavenly order the byline of their existence. Ancient Taoist teachings hold that the astral shiens were humanity's first teachers, our wise, primal ancestors who liberated the infant humanity from the exigencies of a primitive existence.

In the case of Tibet, the shiens "came" to the Roof of the World, rid the land of its autochthonous beings, brought the high teachings, disseminated them or buried them for future revealing, and retreated to watch, where they remain, even today, above Mount Kailash. (For another version of the Heavenly Cave motif, see the Mount Ida chapter and its discussion of Zeus being born in a "cave.")

Mount Temahani, Raiatea, Society Islands

Mount Temahani, an extinct volcano 2,598 feet high, is located in the north central part of Raiatea, an island comprising 105 square miles, once known as Polynesia's preeminently sacred precinct.[659] One of Mount Temahani's outward distinctions is that it is the only place on the planet where the *tiare apetahi* grows.

This is a white gardenia *(Apetahia raiateensis)*, similar to the more common *tiare Tahiti (Gardenia taitensis)*, except it has five petals. These are said to represent the five fingers of a Tahitian maiden who fell in love with a Tahitian prince but was prohibited from marrying him because of her commoner ancestry. Today the mountain is lushly foliated with trees and bushes, and its main peak resembles a green sugar cube set above stocky, green-clad shoulders.

Raiatea—its name means "clear sky" or "big, springing water"—is about 120 miles northwest of Papeete, the central city in the island of Tahiti. It is twenty-five miles west of Huahine, and although it is not as well known as Bora Bora and Moorea within the Tahitian islands of French Polynesia, its reputation as a spiritual center and home of the gods is unassailable. Apparently even today the Maori of New Zealand regard Raiatea as a venerable seat of learning.

Raiatea and its neighbor, Tahaa, are bounded by a single coral barrier reef system and extensive shallow lagoon. Raiatean myths say that once the two islands were one landmass but were separated when a giant eel swallowed a young girl. The eel became possessed by the young girl's spirit, broke through the surface of the Earth, and caused the ocean to rise up, cutting the island into two.

A Raiatean myth alternatively recounts that a figure called Hiro killed the man-devouring sea beast called *Rua-i-paoa*, which had been ravaging Raiatea, and this caused the severance. According to vulcanologists, Tahaa is the older of the two islands, formed about three million years ago out of volcanic activity. Raiatea was produced by volcanic eruptions around 2.5 million years ago.

One of Raiatea's prime archeological attractions is the *Marae Taputapuatea,* a former stone temple now mostly in ruins. The name *Taputapuatea* means "principal place of worship," and *marae* refers in general to a stone temple.[660] The temple complex is set on a wide

416

promontory called Matahiraterai between Opoa and Hotopuu bays. On the promontory are nineteen marae and one oblong shrine measuring 142 feet long. Raiateans say the supreme deity Taaroa put his foot on Marae Vaearai in the district of Opoa (the vicinity of Marae Taputapuatea), and this became the first marae dedicated to this god.

The temple is said to be the home and burial place of Oro, the Polynesian god of war. Apparently, a great number of human sacrifices were once performed there; in 1969, five thousand human skulls were found there during the site's first modern excavations. Humans were sacrificed to Oro, who in legend was quite a bloodthirsty god; the victim's right eye was removed and given to the priest, while Oro got the left eye. Supposedly four men were once buried upright there to guard Oro and keep him from leaving the site.

Marae Taputapuatea occupies the *Te Po* section of Raiatea (the valley in which the temple sits); *Te Po* means "the Night," while the rest of the island is *Te Ao,* meaning "the Day." The temple complex is "the largest and most significant shrine in eastern Polynesia."[661] The Marae Taputapuatea at Raiatea was regarded as *the* holy place for East Polynesians. It is said that Polynesians came from as far away as New Zealand to worship at Marae Taputapuatea and that any new marae constructed on other neighboring islands had to use at least one stone from there.

The original temple was called *Vaiotaha,* but according to archeological theory, in 1200 A.D., a Polynesian named Hiro rebuilt the temple and renamed it Marae Taputapuatea, after which the site became the principal assembly point for the *hui arii* (royalty) of the region. The principal temple consists of a wide court paved with black stones, each of which was placed in memory of a former Raiatean chief. The large tree at the end of the temple is credited to Hina, the Polynesian Moon goddess. The myths say that when a new branch appeared on this tree, a new chief for Raiatea had been born; when that particular branch reached the ground, it was time for this man to become chief.

In fact, a principal purpose of the temple complex was the crowning of kings at Raiatea. Central to this coronation ritual (called *pai-atua*) was the presentation of the *maro-ura,* the sacred red girdle, the Raiatean symbol of kingship; the girdle, awarded to each new king, sometimes reached the length of twenty-one feet. Priests would spend a night in wakeful vigil in the marae at Opoa beseeching the gods to attend the ceremonies the next day. "The gods invariably accepted the invitation and arrived with an invisible flourish of whistles and whirrings."[662]

At dawn, a fleet of ships arrived in the lagoon bearing the various *ariki,* or high chiefs, but always occupying the first and holiest ship was the god Oro. Then the new king and his priests stood in the lagoon up to their necks as two sharks rubbed themselves against the king's shoulders, a vivid symbol of the pledged loyalty of the ocean and its denizens—the shark was considered a Polynesian god.

Also part of the Marae Taputapuatea complex was a Temple of Truth. All Polynesian royalty were said to visit this site at least once in a lifetime almost as a purificatory rite. They were expected to stand before a particular standing stone and recite their genealogy; if the gods or priests were displeased in any way, the reciter would be killed and buried on the spot before the stone. Another marae at this complex was dedicated to Kanaloa, the Polynesian sea god.[663]

MYTH AND LEGEND

For centuries, Raiatea was the center of royalty, religion, and culture for the Society Islands, and Mount Temahani was appreciated as a kind of Polynesian Mount Olympus and "fragrant paradise."

Raiatea itself is regarded as the original, spiritual homeland of Polynesians, the point of origin called *Hawaiki,* meaning "the sacred island" or "old homeland." (Raiatea, also once known as Rangiatea, was first called Hawaiki, then Havaii.) The term *Hawaiki* suggests an otherworldly, paradisiacal location, a hidden island where the gods live, a wandering, usually invisible, ancestral and spiritual homeland generally thought to lie in the far West. In its mythic attributions, Hawaiki closely resembles the Celtic Avalon.

Hawaiki had a great deal to do with the earliest days of the Earth, according to Polynesian myth. In one of their creation stories, Taaroa fixed the dome of Earth on pillars, one male, one female, both prime parents. This allowed for the widening of the sky "upon the pillars of the land of Havai'i."[664] In a variation on this, the universe is likened to a hollow coconut shell, whose interior is *Avaiki* (a variant spelling on Hawaiki).[665]

Avaiki contains the Underworlds, counted as either nine or twelve; the top of the coconut opens up to the realm of human mortals while the gods live below within the shell. At the lowest depth of Avaiki lives *Vari-ma-te-takere,* a demon-woman called the Very Beginning (or Miru, a she-demon who eats the spirits of the dead). She crouches in the cramped root of the coconut, her chin and knees touching, and in this position she created the first humans.[666]

From Hawaiki, the Polynesians dispersed across the South Pacific in great canoes to settle the other islands, including New Zealand and Hawaii. Raiatea's first king was called Hiro, a descendent of the creator god Taaroa and Oro; he was also the founder of Marae Taputapuatea. Hiro was a human of giant proportions; in fact, when he was born, he was not a human. He was a *kupua* champion, capable of prodigious stretching, elongating himself to reach from Raiatea to the heavens. His gaze was terrifying.

Polynesian legend says that situated in the air above the mountain of *Tamehani-unauna* (Mount Temahani) and invisible to human eyes is the earthly paradise of the Arioi Society of Tahiti called *Rohutu noanoa* (meaning "fragrant Rohutu"). This is understood to be "an earthly paradise where the spirits of the dead are sent to enjoy the delights of earth without the fear of death." This paradisiacal realm above Mount Temahani is ruled by Romatane, and souls are directed there by the god Tu-ta-horoa. "There they enjoy all the delights of life without labor and are immune from death."[667]

A Hawaiian invocation for curing the sick begins: "O Kumuhonua of Mehani/A spirit out of earth, a spirit out of heaven." What's significant here is that Te Mehani is the original form of the name Temahani, as in Mount Temahani, "where souls of the dead congregate for their journey to the other world."

Another Polynesian myth holds that Tahiti was once part of the landmass of Raiatea. Once an attractive girl named Terehe bathed during a time of *tapu* (ritual proscription), making the gods angry. The land convulsed, and took the form of a giant fish that swallowed Terehe; it became possessed by her spirit, and swam away; where it stopped, it became the island of Tahiti.[668]

Possibly related to this myth is another that likened the eight districts of Raiatea to the tentacles of the Polynesian octopus god, with the residence of the chief at Opoa being the sea-creature's head. In a Polynesian creation myth, when the Earth was being separated from the sky, the great octopus *Tumu-ra'i-fenua,* one of the great land gods, resisted this with its tentacles, one extended in each of the four cardinal directions to hold the sky down against the Earth.[669]

In the Kumulipo creation myth of Hawaii (based on earlier Polynesian sources), Taaroa (in his guise as Kanaloa) takes the octopus form; then the cutting away of the arms of the octopus *Tumu-*

ra'i-fenua, which means "Beginning-of-Heaven-and-Earth," leads to the dawning of light *(Ao)* after the long, wearisome night. "The eight-armed octopus, called in the Kumulipo the 'hot-striking' *(hauna-wela)*, is the manifestation or body in which Kanaloa may appear in some Polynesian groups as god of the sea and sea creatures in contrast to Kane, god of land forms." The octopus god supports *pou,* or darkness, but this is understood to mean the "supremacy of the spirit world, the *Po,* as compared with the world of living men, the *Ao.*"[670]

The Polynesians say that Mount Temahani is the birthplace of the god Oromatautua (or Oroiteteamoe, which means "Oro with the spear down"), or Oro, for short. His job was to preside over war and peace; in wartime, he was a killer of men, always present in battles, and enjoyed human sacrifices. He was the son of Tane, or Atua nui or Atua mana, the creator of the world; his mother was Hina-tu-a-Uta, the goddess of the Earth, Hina.[671] Cultural historians claim that around 1000 A.D. the *tahua,* or religious experts of Polynesia, consecrated Oro as the new god for the *manahune,* or common folk; Taaroa would remain the god for the tahua and royalty.

Eventually Oro overshadowed even his own father, Taaroa (a variant on Tane), as he became for the Raiateans the god of war, harvest, music, and nearly everything else. Taaroa had introduced Oro to Raiatea to overcome his own aloof omnipotence and that of his successors, the more dynamic gods Tane, Tu, and Rongo. The Tahitians were tiring of these old gods and wanted a new deity more in tune with their evolving human interests. It was at Raiatea, then, that the old Polynesian gods were discarded and the new deity, Oro, was introduced.

One of his first acts was to found the Arioi Society, which inspired his taking of a female human as his wife.[672] Oro's intent had been to create closer bonds between the gods and humans.

He had sent his two brothers down to Earth to find a suitable woman, which eventually they did. Her name was Vaiaumati. Oro laid down a rainbow bridge (artfully hidden from human sight by clouds) from where he was in the celestial world to the island of Bora-Bora, where Vaiaumati had been found at the foot of Mount Mouatahuhuura, the "Red-ridged mountain." (Bora-Bora, only a few dozen miles from Raiatea, is regarded by geologists as the oldest of the Society Islands, having emerged from the ocean an estimated twenty-five million years ago.)

Each evening Oro slid down his mist-enshrouded rainbow bridge to be with his wife, then each morning he climbed back to Heaven. Their son, Hoatapu-iterai, became a great Raiatean chief; and Oro's brothers became patrons to the Arioi Society, which became a lineage of holy priests and ariki. Oro's earthly home became Marae Taputapuatea at Opoa. According to Polynesian myth, Oro remained at Raiatea, living in celestial glory and respect until that day when humans became blasphemous and disbelieving and he retreated with the other Polynesian gods to the farthest reaches of Heaven.

GEOMANTIC

Dome; Avalon; Dragon; Epiphany Focus.

DOME: The dome over Mount Temahani represents the star Praesepe, often dubbed the Beehive and the Manger, within the constellation of Cancer the crab. Technically, Praesepe (listed by astronomers as epsilon Cancer) is not a single star but a star cluster, comprising about 350 stars of magnitude 6.3 to 14; it can be mistaken for a nebula or a celestial swarm of bees.

Praesepe, 652 light years from Earth, is located between gamma Cancer *(Asellus Borealis)* and delta Cancer *(Asellus Australis),* the Northern Ass and Southern Ass, respectively. These two asses are construed as feeding at the Manger, or Praesepe, and are taken to be bright stars on the crab's shell; Praesepe itself is approximately on the crab's head.

There are at least two myths accounting for the asses of Cancer, and a third for Cancer itself. In one, the Greek god Dionysus, on his way to a temple dedicated to Jupiter, encountered a marsh that barred his way. Two wild asses were grazing nearby in a field, and one volunteered to take the god across. In gratitude, Dionysus made both donkeys into stars. In the second account, during the Gigantomachy, the battle in which the gods attacked the giants, Dionysus, Hephaistos (an Olympian god), and the Satyrs rode into battle seated on asses. The asses brayed, causing the giants to flee; in honor of their battle contribution, the asses were made into stars.

As for Cancer itself, when the Greek hero Heracles was battling the Lernaean Hydra, Hera (wife of Zeus, chief of the gods) sent a crab to attack him, which it did, biting him in the foot. Heracles crushed the crab, after which Hera rewarded it for its service by turning it into a constellation. Praesepe has also been called Little Cloud, Little Mist, Cloudy One, Whirling Cloud, *Ermelia* (Nurturing), and *Al Ma'laf* (the Stall). Cancer has also been called, by the ancient Akkadians, the Northern Gate of the Sun because during that time of year the Sun began its retrograde movement, which is to say, the days started getting shorter once it was in that sign.

Esoterically, as in Chaldean and Platonist philosophy, Cancer is called the Gate of Men because it was regarded as the gate through which souls descended from Heaven into human bodies. According to metaphysical tradition, Cancer and Capricorn represent two fundamental incarnational gates for humanity.

Cancer is the mother of forms and material nature; through this gate, souls "pass into outer manifestation and to the appropriation of form, and subsequent identification with it for many

long cycles." It is the gate that stands "wide, open, broad, and easy to pass through" but that leads to the place of death "and to that long imprisonment which precedes the final revolt." Capricorn is the gate of the spirit, as it were, the initiatory doorway out of the incarnational cycle.[673] These points are acutely relevant to Mount Temahani.

Among the Hindus, gamma and delta Cancer and Praesepe were seen as part of the eighth *nakshatra* (lunar mansions) called *Pushya,* which means "Flower," and were associated with Brihaspati, the priest and teacher of the gods.[674] It is not a specific flower that is represented, but a flower in general, in its archetypal sense. "A flower represents the blossoming of latent faculties, the possibility of attaining the archetypes," explains Vedic astrologer Bepin Behari. The flower is an "alchemical crucible" in which a base metal, typically lead, is transmuted into precious gold. The flower symbolizes this change whereby the latent or subjective faculties, the "inner symmetry and perfection," are made into "an objective reality and thing of beauty."[675] This is highly significant to our understanding of Mount Temahani and its botanical treasure, the *tiare apetahi,* and how this in turn relates to Raiatea's geomantic function, described below.

AVALON: Mount Temahani is a gateway to the Celestial City of Gandhavati, which is also variously known in different cultures as Avalon, Emain Ablach (Irish), the Summer Country, the Garden of the Hesperides, the city of the celestial musicians (Gandharvas) and dancers (Apsaras), and the realm of the Muses. It is the Land of the Living, the realm of the golden apples, the undying land—the fragrant domain, *Rohutu-noanoa,* where the souls of humans live in paradise.

Before the overall function of Mount Temahani and Raiatea makes sense, we have to understand the esoteric reality of the chief god, Oro. Oro was a Nefilim. This was a family of angels that took on human form during the early Lemurian times to achieve certain purposes. Biblical and Judaic legend remembers them as the "fallen angels" who coupled with human females, producing a line of humans.[676] This account is not quite accurate.

POLYNESIAN EMERGENCE POINT: We need to shave away some of the mythic excess that has been added to the description of Oro, such as his warlike, bloodthirsty nature. In his original nature, he was much more like the Greek Orpheus, son of the Olympian god Apollo. His music was unbearably enchanting and he fell in love with a mortal woman named Eurydice. Orpheus tried to bring Eurydice up into the higher spiritual worlds after she died of a snakebite, but failed; the Maenads later tore Orpheus to pieces and his body parts were collected and buried by the Muses. Recall that one of Oro's appellations was the god of music.

Under commission from the highest spiritual authorities, Oro and other Nefilim (his "brothers") undertook to add a new element to the human soul composition, partly to rebalance depredations committed by alien geneticists from other star systems who had manipulated human genetic and soul elements to suit their agenda, but not necessarily that of human higher evolution.

Oro and the other Nefilim entered the human terrestrial world through the doorway at Mount Mouatahuhuura in Bora-Bora, as the myths recount. As the two stories about Tahaa and Tahiti once having been part of the Raiatean landmass suggest, in that early time on Earth, most of the South Pacific islands (including Hawaii and Easter Island) were part of a single continent (known as Lemuria). Conventional history, of course, denies the existence of such a continent, but metaphysical traditions around the world attest to some type of large landmass and unified culture in the Pacific existing in a much earlier age.

Oro and the Nefilim entered the physical Earth through Bora-Bora; then they came to Raiatea, presumably overland, according to the Lemuria hypothesis. The Mount Temahani dome sends out eight dome caps on what is now the island of Raiatea, a geomantic effect that could accurately be described to clairvoyant viewing as an octopus with eight tentacles spread out across the island. Its head is not at Marae Taputapuatea, though, but at Mount Temahani.

Oro used a certain energy-consciousness aspect inherent to the Nefilim to create a new race of humans: the Polynesians. Metaphorically, if Oro had a crown of precious jewels, and each jewel contained an aspect of consciousness in its pristine form, and one aspect was expressed as a brilliantly dark-blue spherical light, then Oro implanted this blue light or spherical crystalline form in the soul of the new race of humans he created at Raiatea.

The beautiful human woman, Vaiaumati, for which, the myths claim, Oro climbed down his rainbow bridge into Bora-Bora, was the archetype of the soul qualities this new race of humans would possess—his Galatea, so to speak. She was the embodiment of the new soul quality Oro was creating through the Polynesians. That quality was a sense of joyous incarnation.

Of course, I use the term "race" very loosely to imply an additional soul quality added to the human lineage. This new soul quality would be modeled by the original bearers of it, the Polynesians, and eventually, through intermarriage with other peoples on Earth, this soul quality would enter the general human stream. That soul quality is memorialized by the presence of the singularly rare flower atop Mount Temahani, the *tiare apetahi;* it was left as a kind of signature and mnemonic for the special soul infusion of humanity that happened at that spot. You can see now how apt is the Vedic astrological description of Cancer as the nakshatra Pushya, or flower, and all its spiritual aspects, as described above.

The original bearers of this Nefilim-transmitted soul were situated at Raiatea, within the aegis of the Beehive-Praesepe dome on Mount Temahani. It was as if thousands of souls came into the Earth plane through the Gate of Cancer, the gate that was "wide, open, broad, and easy to pass through." Now in human bodies, they streamed down the mountain like hundreds of points of light, like the cluster of 350 stars in the Beehive, and fanned out across the island and, later, across the whole of the South Pacific. With Raiatea as the original homeland of the newly created Polynesians, of course the myths would remember the place as Hawaiki, the ancestral, paradisiacal place of origin, the wondrous floating island, the point of origin for the Polynesians.

Oro gave his gift, but he had to pay the price of Earthly residence as a way of grounding the new soul quality as it diffused throughout humanity. It wasn't so much that he was physically killed and buried at Marae Taputapuate; looking at the matter a little more subtly, we might say that he had to leave an aspect of his energy essence there, as a deposit or surety for the destiny of the blue seed he gave the Polynesians. In a sense, he was dismembered like Orpheus, his body parts scattered across Raiatea in its eight dome caps. All of Raiatea is Oro's body.

The human sacrifices and evidences of depravity attributed to the Polynesian kings and priests at Raiatea in a later age represent a degeneration of the pure, original impulse over time when left in human hands. They were not representative of the original plan. Oro's intention was pure, as was his original Arioi Society, the community of human initiates introduced to the esoteric soul-genetics of the Polynesians.

The stories say that one eye of the sacrificial victim went to the priest, and the other to Oro. This may be a veiled or adulterated reference to the acknowledgment of the divine gift of the spherical blue seed. In at least a metaphorical sense, it is Oro looking into the soul of each Polynesian, and offering the possibility that they could return the gaze and see something wonderful.

The blue seed is like an eye inside Polynesians enabling them to see Rohutu-noanoa during every moment of their waking state and of course during their dreams. The blue seed is an eye within the soul of the Polynesian that opens, or is continuously open, to the beauties and wonders of Rohutu-noanoa, which for the Polynesians is festooned in tiare apetahi blossoms. Oro gave his people, the Polynesians, that possibility of always seeing Rohutu-noanoa while living in human bodies; and if not seeing, then participating in its essence through an inner knowing, a certainty, or perhaps just an intuition.

DRAGON: One dome cap, incidentally, is set over the watery gap between Raiatea and Tahaa. This is the site of the legend of the eel that abducted the beautiful young woman and of the man-devouring sea beast that Hiro killed with his spear. Recall that when the sea creature was roused, his movements broke Tahaa off from Raiatea.

Present in the lagoon between the two adjacent islands is a minor dragon, one of the 1,053 second-level dragons spawned by the original thirteen. It is quite possible that the Raiatean myth about the reason for the separation of the original singular landmass may have some basis in geological fact. But first we have to discuss Uturoa, Raiatea's principal town and harbor, situated at this gap between Raiatea and Tahaa.

Its name means "long jaw," which is appropriate insofar as Uturoa sits next to the head of the Raiatean dragon. Overlooking the small city is a large hill called Mount Tapioi, another of Mount Temahani's dome caps. At the time of my visit to Uturoa in January 1998, it was very unpleasant to spend much time in this town. I traced the problem to Mount Tapioi, which (because of how it had been used over the centuries) extended a black baleful hand of maleficent influence over Uturoa, causing the long jaw to fester.

The angelic realm, as part of a larger event described below, began a cleansing of this site, purging it of numerous demonic and ancient evil beings, the familiars and residues of former black magicians and destructive energy work conducted there. It is quite possible that when sufficient negativity accumulated in the Mount Tapioi dome cap long ago, due to inappropriate and misguided magical practices, it created a feedback loop with the physical terrain and unfavorably stimulated the dragon then resident on the landmass between Uturoa and the village of Tahaa.

The result was an earthquake of sufficient strength to sever the landmass and create two islands. In light of this, the account of Hiro spearing the sea eel or man-devouring beast could mean either that he activated the dragon, or that he had to subdue its aroused destructive energies as a result of the presumed earthquake. Of course, both may well have happened.

EPIPHANY FOCUS: The larger event taking place in Raiatea was what is called an Epiphany Focus. The Epiphany is the original and traditional date for the birth of Christ, January 6.

Every year during the week in which January 6 is the peak and middle, the Christ as a cosmic being directs His focus on one preassigned node on the Earth's energy body. On January 6, 1998, that focus was Raiatea.

The setup is elegant: January 6 is within the month of Capricorn, described earlier as the incarnational gate—the outward gate—by which the initiate can pass out of the human cycle of lives. Raiatea, through its dome on Mount Temahani, is under the star influence of Praesepe, the star cluster in Cancer, the incoming incarnational gate. During that week, the angelic realm, the archangels, and the Christ focused their attention on Mount Temahani on behalf of the entire planet, an event balanced, as it were, between the inclinations of the two incarnational gates.

Those energies detoxified the dome and dome caps and helped to purge them of an age-old accumulation of toxic, negative, stagnant, or anachronistic energies, replacing them with a fresh dose of pristine cosmic light and consciousness. That infusion of course has changed Raiatea forever, or perhaps it has helped to bring it back to its original energy archetype as a sacred center.

Mycenae, Greece

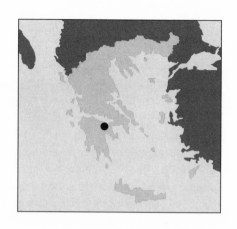

Today Mycenae is a massive stone ruins of a once formidable hilltop citadel overlooking the Argive Plain in the Peloponnesus of Greece. It is situated—nestled—on Mount Euboea, midway between its two peaks, Marta and Zara, two cone-shaped mountains rising about twenty-six hundred feet above the plain.

Archeologists describe Mycenae as an "easily defensible eminence, with commanding views," and a copious water supply nearby; it was "well-placed" to be Mycenaean Greece's chief stronghold, which it was for at least five hundred years, from 1600 to 1100 B.C.[677] During its peak of influence, around 1500 B.C., the king at Mycenae was said to control 320 subsidiary citadels in Greece, and so powerful was Mycenae's influence that historians now describe an entire age of Greek history and culture as the Mycenaean.

Even as a ruins, Mycenae's fortifications are impressive, even daunting. Its cyclopean fortification walls average twenty feet thick and are estimated to have originally stood forty feet tall. The famous Lion Gate at the entrance to the citadel features as lintel an eighteen-ton stone inscribed with the figures of two lions (some say griffins) facing each other. The lintel stone is fifteen feet long and six feet thick, set atop two vertical door-jambs ten feet tall.

At Mycenae you can still observe the remains of a processional way, connecting the Lion Gate with the North Gate; an archaic temple to the goddess Pallas Athene; and the Megaron (the central room of the palace) and other palace features.

The Mycenaean citadel also features shaft graves, beehive tombs, domed chamber-tombs, and *tholos*[678] that archeologists believe were the burial sites of several legendary figures of Mycenaean royalty including its king, Agamemnon, his wife, Clytemnestra, her lover, Aegisthus, and others in the royal family. Numerous gold cups, inlaid swords, gold crowns, libation vessels, and gold death masks were discovered in these tombs when Heinrich Schliemann excavated the site in 1876.

The Treasury of Atreus, which was a tomb for Atreus, cut into the side of the hill, is "the finest expression of the *tholos* tomb, the apex as well of Mycenaean sacred architecture."[679] The entrance to the tholos tomb is a 120-foot walkway lined with stone blocks of monumental size, one of which is twenty feet long and four feet high; inside the tomb, the corbelled ceiling, rising forty-four feet above the ground, comprises thirty-three rings of conglomerate stone blocks. This tomb's construction was so expert that it has not settled an inch in three thousand years.

HISTORY AND ARCHEOLOGY

By 1100 B.C., Mycenae's supremacy in Greece was over. In 486 B.C., it was besieged and destroyed. By the time Pausanias, prolific chronicler of ancient Greek sacred sites, visited Mycenae in the second century A.D., the site was in ruins, an enigma from the deep past. He noted that "there are parts of the ring-wall left, including the gate with lions standing on it."

Pausanias made reference to the Perseia, Mycenae's water source (now called Perseus' spring, a deep, cavernous water cistern at the northeast end of Mycenae); to the graves of Atreus and those who came home from the wars in Troy only to be "cut down by Aigisthos at his supper-party"; and to the underground chambers of Atreus and his sons "where they kept the treasure-houses of their wealth." He further noted that the walls of Mycenae "are too strong to be taken by the Argives" in war, "being built just like the walls of Tiryns by the Kyklopes."[680]

The German archeologist and excavator Schliemann relied heavily on Pausanias' description of Mycenae when he was planning his own expeditions. After his first visit to Agamemnon's Mycenae in 1868, Schliemann noted: "Of his capital, Mycenae, there remain the acropolis on a craggy hill in the foothills of two great mountains." Then two years later he sensed what might be in store for him there: "I have the fullest conviction that *great* things would be brought to light in that Acropolis."[681]

The chief historical distinction of Mycenae is that it was the headquarters of the House of Atreus (Atreides), whose tragic, cursed, and generally monumental affairs were the raw material for the classical playwrights Aeschylus,

Sophocles, and Euripides. The complexities of this ancient family are too considerable to recount in detail here, but the prime parentage of the lineage is worth noting.

The woes of the Atreides go back to Tantalus, a son of Zeus; his wife was Dione, a Pleiad and daughter of the Titan Atlas (father of the Pleiades, or Seven Sisters), and his son was Pelops, after whom the Peloponnese was named (meaning "The Island of Pelops"). Pelops and his wife, Aerope,[682] produced Agamemnon (King of Mycenae; married to Clytemnestra) and his brother, Menelaus (King of Sparta; married to Helen, Clytemnestra's sister). Agamemnon's offspring included Orestes, Electra, and Iphigenia. Helen's abduction by or elopement with Paris to Troy precipitated the ten-year-long Trojan War.

The essential point here, however, is that the House of Atreus is descended from Zeus and the Pleiades. In other words, it is both (or either) a celestial (Zeus) and extraterrestrially derived (Pleiades) family lineage sporting the legendary Cyclopes as architects for its royal compound. According to this lineage, Atreus was a third-generation Pleiadian and a great-grandson of Zeus. Also of note is that the legendary Golden Fleece (from a golden ram), which had been awarded to Pelops, was the requisite symbol of sovereignty at Mycenae. Possession of the fleece "was the sure mark of the rightful king."[683]

MYTH AND LEGEND

With Mycenae, what is properly historical and what is probably legendary blur, and the legendary is not too clear either. Pausanias repeated the long-standing belief that Mycenae was built by the Cyclopes, the antique giants with a single eye in their forehead who were credited with much of the ancient world's megalithic construction.

Pausanias reports that the Greek divine hero Perseus (a son of Zeus) founded Mycenae when he returned to Argos after his adventures with the Gorgons and Andromeda; or else he traded his kingship of nearby Tiryns for that of Mycenae where he either commissioned the Cyclopes to build the place or ordered its fortification.[684]

Mycenae got its name—and foundation impetus—when Perseus' *mykes* (the cap of his sword-sheath) fell to the ground, "and he believed it was the sign to build a city," says Pausanias. At least that's one story. Another explanation has it that Perseus, being thirsty, pulled up a mushroom (*myces*) and drank the water that rushed out from the ground on that spot; "liking it, he called the place Mycenae."

Pausanias offers yet another possibility, this time from Homer, who refers to "Mycenae crowned with garlands," as the daughter of the river god Inachos, whose territory was Argos, and therefore supposedly the person after whom the citadel was named.[685] Inachos is said to have been the first king of Argos. One tradition says that Mycene was the mother of Argus, an enormous, powerful, and frightening primordial giant with one hundred keen eyes, for which quality he was called *Panoptes*, "all-seeing."[686]

Argus' parentage is sometimes given as Zeus and Niobe, the daughter of Phoroneus; when Argus inherited Phoroneus' territory, he renamed it Argos. One of Argus' chief responsibilities was to tend Io, a woman who was Zeus' lover (and daughter of the River Inachus); Hera (Zeus' wife, Queen of the gods at Olympus) had turned Io into a white heifer as a form of protection against her lascivious husband.

Another related figure called Mykeneus, says Pausanias, was also put forward by the Greeks as the grandson of Phoroneus, a mysterious ancient, primitive man. Phoroneus, the son of the river god Inachus, was claimed as the original founder of Argos, the first mortal human, and a judge in a quarrel between Hera and Poseidon (Zeus' brother, Lord of the Waters) for possession of the Peloponnese.[687] In short, Mycenae might have been named for the daughter or wife of a primordial human descended from a river god—or after a mushroom or Perseus' sword sheath or a giant with one hundred eyes.

A third myth about Mycenae centers around the legendary hero Heracles. It was King Eurystheus[688] of Mycenae who commissioned—or ordered—Heracles, his loyal subject and vassal, to perform his twelve labors and to return to Mycenae after each with proof of its completion. This Heracles did, to Eurystheus' consternation and alarm. Heracles subdued the Nemean lion (Labor One); snared the boar of Erymanthos (Labor Four); and dragged Cerberus, the three-headed Hound of Hades out of the Underworld (Labor Twelve).

In each case, Heracles presented the conquered beast at the gates of Mycenae, but Eurystheus was so nonplussed that he hid inside a bronze jar buried in the ground to avoid sight of either Heracles or the monsters.

MYSTICS AND TOURISTS

One commentator notes that even today shepherds say that they occasionally encounter the ghost of Agamemnon on the slopes of Mount Euboea, still seeking rest from his betrayal and foul murder by his wife.[689] Another visitor aware of Mycenae's history and former political glory and influence, said "the meeting with its geographical and archeological reality is a disturbing reminder of the transience of all human greatness."[690]

Henry Miller, during his tour of Greece in the late 1930s, remarked that "At Mycenae, the gods once walked the earth, of that there can be no question." Miller said the progeny of these Mycenaean gods produced a human who was deeply artistic and "monstrous in his passions." Miller admitted that whatever had happened at Mycenae was for him in his time beyond conjecture, and that the explanation offered by historians and archeologists was "a slim and altogether unsatisfying fabric to cover the mystery." The "hoary scene" at Mycenae defies the intellectual mind and we must await the return of the gods for insight.[691]

A more recent visitor to Mycenae echoed Miller's sense of the place, finding the grave circles "strangely unnerving," producing dizziness and "a sense of spinning and falling into a vortex of the past." This visitor further commented on a sense of evil that some say lingers over the site "even or especially in the harsh glow of the noonday sunshine which beats down on the bare rocks."[692]

GEOMANTIC

Dome; Cyclopean City; Landscape Zodiac; Avalon; Mithraeum; Grail Castle; Camalate Center; Soma Temple; Albion Chakra.

DOME: The dome over Mycenae corresponds to gamma Corona Borealis, a fourth-magnitude star about 140 light years from Earth. The dome over nearby Tiryns is alpha Corona Borealis, called Alphecca or *Al Na'ir al Fakkah,* which means "Bright One of the Dish." This second-magnitude star, the brightest in the constellation of the Northern Crown (sometimes called The Dish), is seventy-five light years from Earth; it is also referred to as Gemma or *Margarita Coronae,* "the Pearl of the Crown."

According to the myths, the crown was originally a gem-studded golden tiara given by the god Dionysus to Ariadne, the daughter of King Minos of Crete; when she died, Dionysus hurled the crown into the sky where it became the constellation Northern Crown.

CYCLOPEAN CITY: The myth that Perseus, son of the great god Zeus, commissioned the Cyclopes to build or refortify the massive stone citadel of Mycenae is an unmistakable clue that at Mycenae we have another Cyclopean City. The survival of the impressive Lion's Gate feature gives us a suggestion of the scale and perhaps some of the original symbolic content of that city. That Perseus was directly involved in the creation of the Mycenaean Cyclopean City gives us a breathtaking clue as to how *old* some of the Greek myths and characters may be, to how far back into the Earth's geomantically primeval days these stories may go.

HERACLES' IDENTITY: One key to understanding the geomantic significance of Mycenae and its unarguably complicated myths and sometimes contradictory genealogies is to penetrate the enigma of Heracles' twelve labors. The myth of Heracles' labors is the geomantic key to Mycenae. The secret is to ask for whom—and for what place—were they performed?

Heracles undertook his tasks for King Eurystheus of Mycenae; the myths say it was as penance for having killed Eurystheus' wife or because Heracles wanted to rule nearby Tiryns and this was the price of the kingship. Actually, Eurystheus is irrelevant to this geomantic code; he was a foil, indicated by the fact that he was mortally afraid of Heracles and the conquered beasts the hero dropped before the Mycenaean gate. The true benefactor of Heracles' labors was Mycenae itself.

In the earliest days on the planet, when the angelic family known as the Elohim were incarnate on Earth as the Cyclopes, most of their work had to do with building containers for the celestial energies that the Ray Masters and other high beings were grounding in the Earth plane. One of these was Heracles, who was also known as Merlin, magus to King Arthur. The handiwork of this magus can be found around the world, under different names, and in different myths: in Tibet, he was Padma-sambhava; in Polynesia, he was Maui; to the Welsh, Myrddin; to the Scots, Saint Columba; to the Christians, John the Evangelist.

In each case, Merlin's task was to prepare the ground—tame the raw, untemplated Earth, bring its latent light patterns into astral actuality—for the emergence of its visionary geography. Merlin's imprint was everywhere in these primal geographies. Welsh myths say that in the first age of Britain the land was known as Myrddin's Precinct. The land around Mycenae could fittingly be called Heracles' Precinct.

In his "herculean" labors, Heracles conquered the various monsters and divine beasts by matching their energies with his own; by taking in their cosmic energies and integrating them into his system. Being thereby in resonance with each, he was able to "overcome" them. By being the master of the Nemean lion, the Hound of Hades, the Erymanthos boar, and other cosmic energies within himself (a microcosm), Heracles (like any skilled geomancer) could accommodate and direct the macrocosmic expression of these same energies as they are deployed throughout the Earth's visionary geography.

At Mycenae, long before there were any Greeks in Argos (or humans anywhere on Earth), the Elohim built the "cyclopean" walls to *contain* the energies that Heracles was awakening, subduing, and bringing to the Lion Gate at Mycenae. Very powerful cosmic energies were at play at Mycenae; massive stone structures were needed to corral or dam them as if they were flood waters.

LANDSCAPE ZODIAC: Let's have a brief look at Heracles' Precinct. First is a Landscape Zodiac approximately twenty-five miles in diameter including both Mycenae and Tiryns. Mycenae is part of Canis Major, the Dog, in this zodiac overlay, and specifically within the Dog it is Sirius. Located in the dog's throat, this is the

brightest star in our galaxy. Sirius (and Canis Major as a whole) is the guardian of the galaxy, the watcher at the gate.

Heracles' first labor was to subdue the Hound of Hades where it was guarding the Underworld and bring it to the Lion Gate at Mycenae. Geomantically, this means Heracles mastered (identified, befriended, grounded) the energies of Canis Major (principally Sirius) which was *already* in place at Mycenae. Think of it as waking a sleeping dog. The myths say Heracles brought the hound to the Lion Gate and was told by Eurystheus to go no farther.

You need to read this backwards to get the point. By activating and controlling the preexisting energies of the Dog already present at Mycenae, Heracles opened up this site as a gateway *into* the Dog and the territory it guards—the Landscape Zodiac, a miniature of the galaxy. It is geomythically more apt to say Heracles brought Mycenae to the Dog Gate of Sirius.

AVALON: Heracles' eleventh labor is relevant here as well. That assignment was to gather golden apples from the Gardens of the Hesperides in the far West. The golden apple is, among other meanings, a code for the Celestial City of Gandhavati, better known in the West as the enchanting orchards of the Summer Country, or Avalon.

By collecting a golden apple from the Hesperides (these maidens were daughters of the Titan Atlas, which means they were the Pleiades) for Mycenae, Heracles opened up the energies of the Summer Country for human interaction through the visionary geography interface at Mycenae. Some graves and tombs at Mycenae serve as "rabbit holes" or portals of entry into Avalon and its wondrous trees ripe with golden apples.

Heracles' first labor was to overcome the Nemean lion, which he did, wearing its pelt—its hide was said to be invulnerable—on his shoulders as he stood before the Lion Gate at Mycenae. In part, the geomantic meaning of this task was to ground the energies of the constellation in this landscape. This was needed because Leo is the primary astrological influence on the dome over the entire twenty-five-mile-wide zodiac (encompassing the two star domes of Mycenae and Tiryns).

Again, bringing the Nemean lion right to the Lion Gate at Mycenae was really opening up Leo's energy, overlighting the zodiac dome so that it could permeate Heracles' Precinct, or the Landscape Zodiac spread around Mycenae. The Lion Gate became active as the portal into the Lion's astral energy. Fittingly, Zeus honored his son Heracles by transporting the lion to the sky, where it became the constellation Leo.

MITHRAEUM: Heracles' tenth labor was to capture the purple-red cattle of Geryoneus in the far West. Geryoneus' name meant "the Shouter," and he was said to shout and fight all the time, as fiercely as Ares, the Greek war god. He had three heads and possibly three bodies; he fought with six arms; and he had wings as well. He pastured his red cattle at sunset on Geryoneus' Red Island. Nonetheless, Heracles overcame him, took the cattle in a special boat (a golden winged beaker) that he borrowed from Helios the Sun god, and returned to Argos with his herd. What does all this mean?

This is the core myth of the Cattle of the Sun and the founding of a Mithraeum. Geryoneus is another version of Typhon (Sorath), well described in the myths about Mount Etna in Sicily, the multiheaded monster of the untamed Sun. The cattle Heracles captured represent the domestication of the wild Sun god into a usable form: cows can be milked, the milk in this case being liquid essence of the Sun, or living gold. And the wild Sun can be corralled into a time matrix of days and years, which is another nuance of the Cattle of the Sun.[693]

The Treasury of Atreus at Mycenae is a Mithraeum, or temple of the Sun god expressed as a cavernous golden bull. Heracles bringing the cattle back to Mycenae means he activated the Mithraeum aspect of this site. He brought the Mithraeum back from the Land of Light where it exists as an archetype in the Earth's light pattern library of visionary geographic interfaces.

Bringing the cattle back means Heracles made the Mithraeum real at Mycenae—he grounded it. This explains why possession of the golden ram or Golden Fleece was a required symbol of kingship at Mycenae: it meant possession of the secrets of the operation of the Mithraeum, which in occult terms refers to the Magic Square of the Sun.[694]

HYPERBOREAN GOLD: The two lions carved in stone on the lintel over the Lion Gate are in fact golden griffins, which are, according to legend, winged lions that stand erect. More important, as the ancient texts inform us, the griffins guarded the gold of the Hyperboreans, which is another code word for the Pleiadians.[695] The Hyperboreans were Pleiadians, and the griffins, in fact, derive from the Pleiades as well. Don't forget the standard myths themselves credit Atreus as being the grandson of a Pleiadian. Homer was not referring to worldly bankers when he alluded to "Mycenae rich in gold" in the *Odyssey.* The treasure in the Treasury of Atreus is geomythically speaking a big vat of liquid gold, or living light of the Sun facilitated by the Pleiades, the star cluster in the neck of the Taurus constellation.

Where the North Gate stands as a physical stone portal stand two majestic astral griffins, perhaps twice the height of the lintel. Not even an inch separates the two guardians of the Mithraeum. Not only are they guardians of the sanctity of the Mithraeum within the citadel, they are also the prime grounding points for the multiple cosmic energies that Heracles brought to the

Lion Gate. Myths say he brought them up to the gate but no farther because in effect he gave them to the two griffins, who *grounded* them for the Mycenaean citadel and neighboring precinct as a whole. In a sense, the energy structure of Heracles' Precinct is nailed to the Earth at the Lion Gate.

Face the Lion Gate and you are confronted by the two massive golden griffin guards; turn around, and you face three more gates: the Hound of Hades (doorway into the Landscape Zodiac); the Nemean lion (doorway into the Leo constellation); and the Boar of Mount Erymanthos. To understand the latter we need to segue into a Vedic myth about Vishnu, the Pervader. Vishnu had four divine incarnations during the Golden Age on Earth. The third was as Varaha, the boar.

GRAIL CASTLE: It was a time when the legendary Flood was in full swing; everything on Earth was underwater, submerged, drowned—even the Earth was immersed. Vishnu took the form of a boar with a body as mighty as a mountain. In this "vast, infinite, boar-like shape, the lord entered the netherworld in order to raise up the Earth." This radiant, blazing boar dug up the Earth from under the water and with its tusks raised it above the level of the Deluge and "brought the great Earth to its proper place" which was "above the vast ocean of dissolution."[696]

Heracles' capturing the Boar of Mount Erymanthos is about preparing the ground—raising it up—for a Grail Castle "above" Mycenae—which is to say, in yet another dimension removed from the already subtle one we've been considering. Poetically, if you like, consider the boar's tusks as the rigging up to the Grail Castle. Geomythically, this myth concerns grounding the cosmic energies necessary to create the foundation, support, pedestal, or mountain—the tusks of the boar—upon which the Grail Castle can rest, just like Noah's Ark came to rest upon Mount Ararat after the Flood subsided.

CAMALATE CENTER: Let's put some of this picture together. Initiates, students, colleagues, geomancers, Grail Knights would get their golden Grail chalices at the Mithraea at Mycenae, take them out into Heracles' Precinct (the Landscape Zodiac around Mycenae), have various transmutative inner adventures, then bring their Grail chalices filled with consciousness into the Grail Castle at Tiryns for an exalted experience. In spirit, the arrangement was much like the fabled Camalate of King Arthur in Somerset, England, presumably of a much later date.

For one, they would meet the Fisher King, lord of the Grail Castle, known in this Greek myth as Tantalus, the ultimate head of the Atreides line in the Peloponnese. Tantalus (a son of Zeus, father of Pelops, grandfather of Atreus) was regaled for his riches, especially gold. For a transgression against the gods, he was punished, kept famished and without water, an accurate if concise description of the Grail King in his *wounded* phase.

SOMA TEMPLE: For another, the initiates could meet King Soma, the Moon god, over at Tiryns in the Celestial City of Yasovati eight miles to the southeast. Functionally, Tiryns needs to be considered part of the greater Mycenaean complex, part of Heracles' Precinct. The domes over Tiryns and Mycenae, after all, do represent neighboring stars in Corona Borealis.

So who was Argus with the one hundred eyes? There are several possibilities, and who knows but that they are all true. For one, an initial impression one gets when visiting the Soma Temple is of a corbelled ceiling filled with god's faces, their eyes looking down from another dimension upon the vat of Soma. Argus is thus the collective name for this array of gods' eyes protecting the Soma. The constellation of Orion the Hunter oversees the Celestial City of Yasovati; here Argus would be Orion in his protector aspect.

Argus can also be the alpha star in Corona Borealis, or *Al Na'ir al Fakkah,* which means "Bright One of the Dish," perceived in "his" spiritual rather than astronomical personification. And Argus can also be King Soma himself, protecting his twenty-seven wives, the *Nakshatras* (in Vedic astrology), a division of primal space and consciousness (Soma) into twenty-seven divisions or lunar mansions. Here the variously named maiden—Mykene, Io, Niobe—would correspond to Soma's "wife" or "wives." Why is the maiden depicted as a white cow? Cows give milk easily and freely; at the temple of the Moon god, Soma is similarly accessible; she is white because white is the "color" of pure light.

ALBION CHAKRA: Finally, there is the matter of the River Inachos and the primordial human called Phoroneus. In geomythic language, rivers usually denote energy currents, such as ley lines (between domes) or Oroboros Lines (circling the planet). Every zodiac has an Oroboros Line bifurcating it, and the Oroboros Lines predate the extrapolation of the rest of the Earth's visionary geography. That is why the Oroboros Line—the river-god Inachos—passing through Heracles' Precinct and a portion of Argos was the original king of this territory.

Phoroneus is the unawakened, unchristened Albion or Purusha figure sleeping in the zodiac. The varieties of cosmic life and experience that the zodiac represents are in a sense Albion's (Phoroneus") dreams. When all the zodiac "dreams" become congruent, which means, worked on in a *herculean* manner (as described above), then Albion-Phoroneus awakes and is the true king in Argos. In this respect, Mycenae is an important energy center within the landscape body of Phoroneus, or this Albion plate.

Newgrange, Ireland

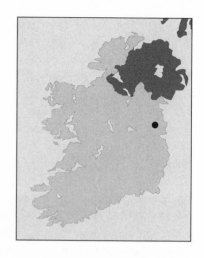

According to archeologists, Newgrange, a large artificial mound 30 feet high, 250 feet in diameter, and occupying an acre, is a large passage grave, a former cemetery of the great Irish tribal kings. It is believed that the deceased kings were carried overland from Ireland's royal seat at the Hill of Tara nearby and cremated, their ashes placed in granite bowls and set in the alcoves inside Newgrange.

Many visitors report that from a distance this egg-shaped tumulus resembles a grounded flying saucer rising up from the meadow. Basically it is a human-made aboveground cave made from an estimated two hundred thousand cantaloupe-sized stones: a stone-lined passageway of sixty feet opens into a central stone-lined chamber with a high-domed ceiling (layered stones form a bee-hive vaulting effect, rising up nineteen feet) and three adjoining alcoves; the stone passageway and chamber are covered with earth to the depth of several yards.

On the outside of the mound, ninety-seven curbstones mark the perimeter; and twelve (of an estimated original thirty-eight) standing stones are positioned around the mound. Many stones, both inside and outside the tumulus, are marked with spirals and swirling designs that suggest the Sun, solar radiance, waves, and perhaps a river.

Although Newgrange is estimated to be five thousand years old, its existence was forgotten for many centuries as its physical presence gradually faded from view. In 1699, a local farmer rediscovered the tumulus, and over the next several centuries, antiquarians extended our knowledge of the site's probable past and construction details. Formal excavations of Newgrange were undertaken between 1962 and 1965, after which the site was reconstructed and given certain superficial features that were not part of the original design. Newgrange is the largest of forty known burial tumuli (passage graves) in the Boyne River Valley (County Leinster), about twenty miles north from Dublin.

HISTORY AND ARCHEOLOGY

Researchers at Princeton University's Princeton Engineering Anomalies Research (PEAR) Department described Newgrange as an acoustically designed building comparable to a musical wind instrument. All aspects of the site serve an acoustic purpose and are correlated with the frequency range of the male human voice, namely, 95 to 110 Hz. The interior was particularly constructed to maintain a "strict acoustical balance" and to facilitate "acoustic interactions" between human and structure.[697]

In terms of archeo-astronomy, the architecture and alignments of Newgrange and the neighboring megalithic sites of the Boyne River Valley, implicate solstices, equinoxes, and the cross-quarter days; its symmetrical design appears to be modeled upon "the inherent symmetry of the solar cycle." Rays from the rising Sun enter the main chamber on the winter solstice, December 21, and illuminate the entire sixty-foot passageway and central interior chamber for about fifteen minutes. "The architecture of Newgrange embodies many astronomical alignments," including an orientation to the location of the rising Sun on the cross-quarter days of May 6 and August 8.[698]

MYTH AND LEGEND

The original name for Newgrange is *Brugh na Boinne,* the residence, abode, mansion, or hostel of the goddess Boand, the deity or spirit of the River Boyne, which flows near the physical site. (This river, seventy miles long, is a principal waterway for eastern Ireland.)

In one story, Boand (her name means "She of the White Cows") defies the magical powers of the Well of Segais; it rises up and drowns her, turning her into a river bearing her name. In another version, Boand is forbidden to look into the Well at *Sidhe Nechtan,* which belongs to her husband, the water god Nechtan; this well is the source of inspiration and knowledge. Only Nechtan and his three cup-bearers are allowed to approach the well.

Nine hazelnut trees of wisdom surround Segais' Well (or Nechtan's—it is essentially an identical story); when the hazelnuts drop into the well, they cause bubbles of mystic inspiration, wisdom, and supernatural knowledge and feed the legendary Salmon of Knowledge. When Boand looks into the Well, defying the taboo against doing so, the water rises up, floods the land, engulfs and drowns her, and turns her into the River Boyne.[699]

In other words, the Well of Segais (or of Sidhe Nechtan) formed the River Boyne, whose residence ever since has been the *Brugh na Boinne,* or Newgrange. Anybody who drinks water from this well, eats the hazelnuts, or the salmon (who ate the nuts) will acquire wisdom, knowledge, and inspiration of an exalted type. As a variation on this myth, the milk from the hazelnuts gets converted to air bubbles as it flows and these are called *bolg fis,* "bubbles of knowledge," or *bolg imbais,* "bubbles of inspiration." Boand, mirroring another Irish myth (and perhaps the original, that of the otherworldly Connla's Well), goes to the fountainhead of wisdom in search of sacred knowledge "for lack of which her reality is incomplete."[700]

Boand has an affair with Dagda," the Good God," the chief of the Tuatha de Danann (the Irish Olympian gods; their name means "Followers of the Goddess Danann, or Anu"), and produces a son named Oenghus mac Oc, "the Young Lad" or "Son of Youth." Dagda's other names include *Eochaid Ollathair* (All Father) and *Ruad Rofessa* (Lord of Great Knowledge).

When Dagda is apportioning the *sidhe* (the monuments, tumuli, "fairy forts or mounds," and hollow hills of the landscape), he gives Brugh na Boinne to Oenghus. He assigns other sidhe to the other members of the Tuatha de Danann so that the Irish landscape has residences (landscape entrances to the Otherworld) for all the important deities.

In fact, some accounts credit Dagda with having built Newgrange for him and his three sons; Irish literature also claims that "three times fifty sons of Kings" dwelt there. One of Oenghus' epithets became *Oenghus an Brogha,* meaning "Oenghus of the *Bru,*" and the tumulus was often called simply "the House of Oenghus," and sometimes simply "the *Bru*" (another spelling for *Brugh*).

Oenghus is the god of youth, beauty, love, poetry, inspiration, and music; wherever he goes, four swans, representing his kisses, hover about his head. Among his many virtues is the ability to send people to sleep with his magic song. He has a gold harp and so sweet and enchanting was his music that none could resist it. Oenghus' sidhe is well known throughout Irish mythology for providing unstinting and generous hospitality, including endless quantities of ale, fruit trees always bearing ripe fruit, and pigs.[701]

MYSTICS AND TOURISTS

One visitor detected the presence of over two hundred discarnate human entities inside Newgrange, sensing them gathering over his head at the entrance to the passageway. These spirits followed the author and a group he was accompanying into the main section; "the corbelled ceiling of the chamber became the tunnel for all the human entities to pass over that day."[702]

An Irish commentator on Earth energies noted that due to the tens of thousands of visitors to Newgrange in recent decades who have "actively directed their totally incompatible energies at it," the original energy balance of the site is "quite literally stewed."

Newgrange as a traditional *comhla bhreac,* or "Gate to the Otherworld," has two types of energies. *Bri* is a Celtic term that describes "intrinsic, inherent power," which can be developed or atrophied but cannot be changed in amount; and *bua,* which is "power gained or lost according to actions." Due to the flux of many visitors to Newgrange imposing their energies and thoughts

"of radically conflicting types" upon the structure's innate *bri,* the energy mix has become unbalanced and confused.[703]

GEOMANTIC

Dome Cap; Pointer's Ball; Ray Master Sanctuary.

DOME CAP: The dome cap originates from the dome over the Hill of Tara, ten miles away, which corresponds to Seginus in Boötes, the Shepherd (see Hill of Tara, Ireland). This means Newgrange deeply participates in the energy activities at the Hill of Tara and in fact with the other forty-seven satellite dome caps.

POINTER'S BALL: The site is a Pointer's Ball, providing immediate access out of the physical world into other dimensions, what is classically called the Otherworld. This feature would account for the passage of two hundred discarnate entities through the chamber's ceiling, as described above; the site acts as a swinging door or crack between the worlds.

From the intermediate zone on the other side of the Pointer's Ball, you have access to all eight of the Celestial Cities. Burial or the placement of cremated ashes of the deceased in this tumulus would have the advantage of providing immediate orientation for the departing soul to take their bearings in the Otherworld, as opposed to wandering around the landscape as spectral spirits awaiting an afterlife assignment.

RAY MASTER SANCTUARY: The site is also a receptacle, collection point, and well for the energy of Oenghus mac Oc (Apollo) from the nearby Mount Olympus at the Hill of Tara. Newgrange was built to facilitate the collection and distribution of this specific energy into the physical world; it also affords the visitor a concentrated immersion in this energy. Insofar as Oenghus (Apollo) is a god of music, it is appropriate that Newgrange was designed as an acoustic device in accordance with the male voice, as it was with both the harp and the voice that Oenghus enchanted his listeners.

The Tuatha de Danann, or "Ever-Living Ones," are the Olympian gods around Zeus (Dagda). The Dagda (Zeus, Osiris) divides "his" essence as Light into fourteen parts or rays; one ray is Oenghus, whose energy essence is called the Well of Segais; when it flows as an energy or light stream, it is the River Boyne; when it collects and forms a "lake," this is the *brugh* or *sidhe* of Boinne. The Well of Segais is a metaphor for the section of Mount Olympus (accessed through the Hill of Tara nearby) that is Apollo's, where this one-fourteenth particularity of the Light (the pale-blue ray) with all its qualities and effects on consciousness is present as a god, where this energy wells up for distribution where the god wishes.

The "River Boyne" is the energy current by which Apollo's essence (chromatically perceivable as a pale sky-blue) flows from the "headquarters" of the Tuatha de Danann at the Hill of Tara to this collection point. Boand as a river spirit or nymph is the devic spirit that assists Apollo in distributing his energy; Boand is also a metaphorical expression of Apollo's energy stream in motion according to the mythic equation whereby a flow of consciousness is a "river."

In a sense, Newgrange could aptly be called the Well of Segais (another name for the source of rivers, Asgard or Mount Olympus) as it is a reservoir of Apollo's energy essence, the place that dams up and contains Apollo's energy stream— "the House of Oenghus," as the ancient Irish said.

Thus Newgrange is the well of the pale-blue energy-consciousness stream of Oenghus, the Ray Master who facilitates bardic inspiration, knowledge, poetry, music, and esoteric knowledge.

Rennes-le-Chateau, France

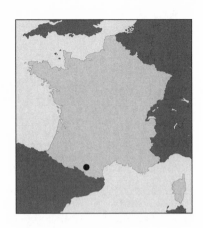

Rennes-le-Chateau is a living paradox. On the one hand, it is a tiny, remote, hilltop village set in the eastern foothills of the Pyrenees in the Languedoc region in the south of France, twenty-five miles south of Carcassonne and nineteen miles overland from Montsegur, a former Cathar stronghold. On the other hand, enough grandiose, fantastic, and mystical things have been said about the village to make it seem central to the future and essence of France as a nation.

Similar to England's Glastonbury and America's Sedona, Rennes-le-Chateau is an intensely visited spiritual mecca and the subject of apparently ceaseless speculation and—according to its critics—unfounded millennialist projections. It is regarded as the center of a mystery the extent and exact nature of which continue to elude most of those who scrutinize the town for clues.

HISTORY AND ARCHEOLOGY

Archeologists believe that this naturally defended hilltop has been inhabited for at least three thousand years, based on Neolithic grave-yards discovered there in 1880. Historians suggest that the area surrounding Rennes-le-Chateau was regarded as a sacred site by the prehistoric Celtic tribes. Later, the Romans, who also considered the countryside to be sacred land, occupied the area and erected "pagan" temples.

More recently, the site may have been part of the Visigoth empire in France in the sixth century A.D., and may have been part of, or the center of, the legendary but now vanished Visigoth city called *Rhedae*. Historians believe that up to thirty thousand people lived in or around Rhedae at its height of influence in the sixth century.

Some authorities contend that the name Rennes-le-Chateau derives from the Gallic-Visigothic *Reda*, which means "a four wheeled chariot." Another theory holds that the original name was *Aereda*, which later became *Reddae* or *Rhedae*, and derived from *Aer Red*, "the Wandering Snake." This was also the name of the Celtic thunder god. "The derivation of the name can certainly be traced back to the fourth century B.C., when the area in question was inhabited by a tribe which called itself the *Redu* (in Latin: *Redones*)," who in turn originated from the Belgians, whose name may have meant "shepherds."[704]

During the short-lived prominence of the Cathars (heretical Christians opposed to the

Papacy) in the thirteenth century, Rennes-le-Chateau flourished as a center of Cathar belief. It was captured by French soldiers (acting on behalf of the Catholic Church in Rome) as part of the Albigensian Crusade, which also destroyed nearby Montsegur (see the section on Montsegur, France). During the German occupation of France from 1940 to 1944, Nazi researchers reportedly made excavations around Rennes-le-Chateau looking for fabled Cathar and Knights Templar treasure said to have been buried there centuries earlier.

Rennes-le-Chateau began its spectacular rise to world renown in 1885 when Berenger Saunière, age thirty-three, arrived in the village to assume his duties as parish priest. Soon after his arrival, during renovations to the church, which had been consecrated to Mary Magdalene in 1059, Saunière found something in one of the building's Visigothic pillars. It is believed he found three wooden tubes sealed with wax and, inside the tubes, ancient documents of considerable interest. Saunière took the parchments to Paris for examination by the Director of Saint Sulpice.

Beginning in 1886, Saunière financed church renovations himself, undertook archeological excavations and researches in the local landscape, and, inexplicably, seemed to be able to live a lifestyle befitting a rich man. By 1896, he was spending on "a staggering and unprecedented scale," not only on the renovations, but also on himself. His total expenditures totaled at least several million pounds (or close to four million dollars).[705]

When he died in 1917, all his books and papers pertaining to his research vanished. Even to this day, most of his life and deeds after 1885 are shrouded in mystery and speculation. What has passed for the "secret" of Rennes-le-Chateau, and has preoccupied scores of researchers, historians, and tourists, has been the nature of Saunière's discovery and his unexplained vast and sudden wealth.

According to Baigent, Leigh, and Lincoln, authors of *Holy Blood, Holy Grail,* treasure was probably the source of Saunière's otherwise unaccountable wealth. He may have discovered any of several treasures reputed to be in the Rennes-le-Chateau area, or "he may have discovered a single treasure that had repeatedly changed hands through the centuries," the authors argue. That treasure was information, and it was information the Church in Rome did not want publicized.

According to Baigent, Leigh, and Lincoln, Saunière unearthed documents that claimed that Jesus had not died on the cross but had come to France, where he married Mary Magdalene and produced progeny, who in the fifth century A.D. supposedly intermarried with the royal line of the Franks, producing the Merovingians.

Baigent, Leigh, and Lincoln state that in 496 A.D., the Catholic Church pledged to eternally support the Merovingian bloodline. They say that various secret, occult, and governmental organizations (including the ultra-mysterious Prieuré de Sion) have over the centuries worked to conceal or obfuscate the "truth" about this precious bloodline. The Holy Grail, in this theory, is both the secret Jesus bloodline—the *Sang Raal,* the real or royal blood—and the womb of Mary Magdalene from which the bloodline issued. Baigent, Leigh, and Lincoln contend that the documents discovered by Saunière were the physical proof and substantiation of this hidden but living bloodline, crucial to the interest of all involved parties.

In the *Holy Blood, Holy Grail* theory, Rennes-le-Chateau's significance is mostly historical and archival—it has been the repository of a long-buried secret. But within a few years of that book's publication, other researchers took another look at Rennes-le-Chateau and its surroundings and started to come up with theories based on newly discovered mysteries, mostly topographical.

David Wood, a British land surveyor and cartographical expert, made extensive surveys of the alignments of mountains, chateaus, and villages in the Rennes-le-Chateau area in the early 1980s. In 1985, he published his theory in *Genisis*—a pun on the "genes of Isis"—replete with maps and diagrams, of what he called the "Temple of Rennes," an "immense geometrical figure, indelibly marked on the ground," covering an area forty miles square in which "every part is marked by a mountain top, a church, an outstanding rock feature or some intersection of carefully designed geometry." This Temple, Wood claimed, was a "deliberate and verifiable construction, so brilliant and on such a vast scale that it staggers the imagination."

Wood's Temple of Rennes—he also calls it the "Temple of the Stars"—consists of various pentagrams, concentric circles, straight alignments, and particular geomythic landscape constructs traceable to Egyptian mythology, such as the "Star of Set," the "Vagina of Nut," and the "Womb of Nut." In fact, in Wood's view, this complex geometric overlay was a terrestrial map to a kind of geomythic seeding point, which he characterized as the Womb of Nut (the Egyptian Sky Goddess).

In this model, Rennes-le-Chateau occupies the western border of the temple, and the tip of one arm of the pentagram. Wood proposed that this terrestrial-geometric temple was designed by the Atlanteans at least eleven thousand years ago as a coded message by a highly advanced civilization to the future "to mark the position of their lost empire."

That message may pertain to "the secret of creation itself," Wood speculates, and central to that is his belief that the temple measurements encode the speed of light in inches and that the "seed in the womb of Isis" in this temple and the means to activate it have to do with "the staggering secret of the Astral Light of the alchemists."

By this Wood means a harmonic of light that will unite the super-conscious mind to the conscious. He contends that an ancient civilization (Atlantis or Egypt) encoded the practicalities of the science of light in various diagrams and then somehow templated them in the Rennes-le-Chateau landscape for their future and our present. The Temple of Rennes is "a gateway to the infinite wisdom of the gods who created us in their image."[706]

Henry Lincoln, of *Holy Blood, Holy Grail* fame, published a theory in 1991 proposing that Rennes-le-Chateau and its environs are part of "an astonishing natural pentagon of mountains" comprising a vast "Holy Place," too big to be seen from the ground, but visible either aboveground or on topographical maps. Lincoln went so far as to describe this landscape temple as the "Eighth Wonder of the Ancient World." More important, it is perhaps "the largest structure ever built by man upon the face of the earth." Lincoln's model is full (bewilderingly so) of straight, circular, and geometric alignments. In one of his geometric overlays, the six-sided Seal of Solomon intersects with the five-pointed star (Lincoln's original pentacle of mountains) at a place with a suggestive name: *Le Val Dieu,* or the Valley of God.

The landscape temple—a gigantic pentacle, fifteen miles in circumference—was constructed in the remote past with enormous labor and skill, and it is today "still as real and tangible" as it was when it was created. According to Lincoln, the pentacle describes the shape over eight years made by the planet Venus in its apparent revolution around the Earth; further, the Venus-pentagon link is directly connected with Mary Magdalene, a central figure in the history and legends of Rennes-le-Chateau, Lincoln says. (Incidentally, local legend says that Mary Magdalene was buried at Rennes-le-Chateau.)

The Holy Place is the "earthly counterpart of the perfect pentacle in the heavens—the secret and hidden pattern of Venus, the Magdalene," he adds. Rennes-le-Chateau was a "gigantic god-given Temple to the Mother Goddess."

Lincoln doesn't know why the Holy Place was constructed. He admitted he had gotten "immersed in a growing maze of alignments" and that the Holy Place is a "gigantic jig-saw whose overall pattern remained a mystery." Unable to discern the minds of the ancients, Lincoln speculated that (in 1991) he was at the beginning of a long road with a huge number of unanswered questions.[707]

In a subsequent book, *Key to the Sacred Pattern*, in 1998, Lincoln extended his model of "structured landscapes" and plotted the "sacred pattern" around Rennes-le-Chateau, consisting of circles, pentagons, hexagons (a Star of David formation), and other geomythic figures. He also proposed that there was an "underlying and controlling grid pattern" (equidistant parallel lines) dictating the placement of chateau and other monuments within this "conscious, planned, and purposeful layout."

As before, his interpretation was based on mathematics, land surveying, the discipline of correspondences, and the assumption that somehow ancient peoples were masters of geodesy, capable of laying out structured landscapes by which Lincoln means "certain man-made structures . . . so placed that they create coherent and precise geometric patterns." Lincoln's working assumption is that in large measure Saunière's secret (and treasure) was the discovery of the encoded pentagon on certain documents and a specific painting, both of which pointed to the physical landscape as the source of the original geometry.

Lincoln reiterated that Rennes-le-Chateau is part of the invisible five-pointed star made by lines extended to nearby mountains. The landscape's holiness, he proposed, "stems from its pentagonal . . . configuration of mountains, which reflect on Earth, the movements of Venus in the Heavens." The physical manifestation in the Rennes-le-Chateau landscape of this Venusian star shape is the source of the area's sanctity, he contends.[708]

While both David Wood and Henry Lincoln were occasional visitors to Rennes-le-Chateau, a third researcher into its geometric landscape mysteries has been a resident of *Le Val Dieu* since the early 1980s. Elizabeth van Buren, American-born author of five books, including *Refuge of the Apocalypse*, has lived just down the hill from Rennes-le-Chateau in her estate called Arcadia, where she has researched, plotted, filmed, and written about the geomantic temple.

According to her research, this temple is a terrestrial zodiac, that is, an imprint of selected constellations of the galactic ecliptic, in accordance with the way topographical features (as discerned on maps) resemble the traditional images of the constellations. Similar conclusions have been offered for Glastonbury in England as well, in fact, dating back to the 1920s. In the case of Rennes-le-Chateau, not only does the local landscape exhibit the clear signs of a terrestrial star map, but this star temple has a purpose and destiny, says van Buren. Unlike the other researchers, van Buren has a reasonable working theory as to what her geometrical landscape overlay actually does, or could do.

She was first alerted to the possibility of a large landscape temple when she translated a short booklet by H. Elie, a French researcher and scholar. Elie reported that the area around Rennes is a sacred region in which a "Temple of Time" has existed since the creation of the planet. Further, an exact science of light is hidden in the Rennes-le-Chateau landscape and it will one day be discovered by trained esotericists. According to van Buren, in a terrestrial zodiac, the planisphere of the heavens is depicted on the landscape, and the constellations take form "as they are outlined by rock ridges, hills, rivers, streams, tracks, and hedges." Such zodiacs are protected sacred places, she says.

The Rennes valley is a "privileged" region that will offer refuge in the future to an elect group, Elie contended, and the geometry of its landscape configurations conceals "a secret message left to man by Cosmic Forces" whose purpose is to enable humans to step through "an opening into the Invisible." Elie argued that Rennes is one of several "privileged regions" around the planet that were "marked off and secretly designated" as "Refuges" to ensure the survival of a part of humanity in a time of apocalypse. Each refuge can also be regarded as a junction point between the "cosmic and telluric energy network," as a time warp that creates a door through which one may pass into another spacetime or as "an opening into the Heavenly Jerusalem."[709]

Van Buren used Elie's discoveries as a starting point for her own. She found that the fourteen Stations of the Cross, represented in the Rennes-le-Chateau church, were the key to finding the two dozen Landscape Zodiacal figures occupying an area approximately fifteen miles in diameter, and she demonstrated this in her forty-five-minute color film *The Temple of Time* in 1987. In Van Buren's interpretation of the Rennes-le-Chateau Landscape Zodiac, the physical configurations represent ancient "thought-form moldings" imposed from a higher source upon the natural terrain.

The Rennes zodiac represents "the great Cosmic wheel of space/time," and taken as a whole it is the site of the crucifixion and redemption of the fallen Light, spacetime, and matter, represented as Lucifer, once Lord of Light and not to be confused with Satan, says van Buren. The Lord of Light, she explains, is crucified on the wheel of Time, represented physically in the Landscape Zodiac.[710] Van Buren also claims that present somewhere in the Rennes-le-Chateau region

is "an Atlantean crystal stone" that will somehow cap and activate the terrestrial temple, and a representation of the "cock of France," which is the egregor, or national symbolic figure, for France.

Van Buren also contends that the Rennes-le-Chateau zodiac offers a physical portal into the interior of the Earth and its intricate maze of ancient tunnels, some of which extend all the way to Peru and other Andean sites. This zodiac is meant to be a "refuge for the apocalypse," a kind of Noah's Ark, bomb shelter, and doorway "for lightworkers" out of the physical world in a time of cataclysm or the End Times. At a certain point, physical and etheric conditions will coincide (which will include, she says, a realignment of Earth with Ursa Major through Rennes-le-Chateau) and the portal will open, van Buren speculates. "The mystery of Rennes reveals the way by which one might escape the Wheel of Time."[711]

She further claims that the Temple of Solomon, as an archetypal template for the Mind and the "Science of Light," exists at Rennes; its secret and treasure are the "seven great frequencies of Light and Life" as emanated from the Great Bear, one of whose stars was originally the Pole Star for Earth.

One central spiritual figure in this eventual activation and its preparation is the mysterious Saint Germaine, who van Buren claims as her otherworldly mentor in the Temple of Time work. She also makes suggestive links among extraterrestrials from Ursa Major, the Cathars, Arcadians, and Merovingians; they are all part of a secret spiritual lineage which she designates "The Sign of the Dove" in reference to the Paraclete of Christ.

Lucifer is another name for the Cock of France, van Buren proposes, and is the charioteer of what she describes as the topographical "Chariot of Light" that extends from nearby

Brennac to Rennes-les-Bains. This four-wheeled landscape chariot figure is called the "Chariot of Rheda." Hence the aptness of the Visigothic place name *Rheda,* for "Chariot" (making the appellation "Chariot of Rheda" both redundant and doubly emphatic). Van Buren also reported that the star whose landscape location she was most certain of is Capella in the constellation Auriga, the Charioteer.

Lucifer is also the secret identity of the much-touted *Le Rouge Serpent* (the Red Serpent), a brief, baffling, encoded document from Rennes-le-Chateau that has been interpreted astrologically. Van Buren says that yet another nuance to the fallen Light, Lucifer, and *Le Rouge Serpent* is Saturn or Cronos, the Greek God of Time, whose name is the origin of the place name Brennac (from the Celtic Bran, which was equivalent to the Greek Cronos, Lord of Time).

But even this is not the end of the mystery explanations. Researchers Richard Andrews and Paul Schellenberger claimed in 1996 that a rocky outcropping called Mount Cardou, less than three miles from Rennes-le-Chateau, was the true burial site for Jesus and still contains his imperishable remains. Mount Cardou, they propose, is the "tomb of God," the tomb of Jesus Christ.

Based on three years of research and the geometric interpretation of paintings and maps, these two researchers claimed that long ago a tunnel had been drilled into Mount Cardou and the body of Jesus Christ entombed there. If true, this would contradict the Catholic doctrine of the bodily resurrection of the Christ and thus prove dangerous, perhaps disastrous, to the Church.

The doctrine of the resurrection of the Christ, the authors explained, "inherently curtailed the freedom of individuals to bring about their own salvation." Thus the disclosure of a secret that "completely refuted this central tenet would test even the staunchest Church members," and it would account for the intense levels of secrecy,

finances, and even unexplained deaths associated with the "Treasure of Rennes."[712]

Another theory holds that the legendary treasure of the Temple of Jerusalem, taken when the Romans sacked the city in A.D. 70, was later taken by the Visigoths and secreted in ancient mines and caves in the Rennes-le-Chateau area; over the centuries, various secret societies in France have protected and probably used this wealth.[713]

MYSTICS AND TOURISTS

With a sense of irony, one hopes—as it seems a commentary on his own contribution—David Wood offered this observation in 1944 in his follow-up book, *Geneset: Target Earth* (the pun this time being the "genes of Set"): "In the potpourri of Rennes-le-Chateau, we find history, politics, religion, masonry, mythology, geometry, and a good deal more, all interwoven in an inextricable web of cipher and disinformation which still seems to prevail."[714]

Simon Miles, another commentator on Earth mysteries, topographical geometric overlays, and other mysteries of the sacred landscape, notes that Rennes-le-Chateau can be "a gateway to understanding a vast and forgotten legacy of humankind." The site, he adds, is "a treasure house of a cosmology which remains valid and available if dormant today, and next to which the mere earthly baubles of Saunière's riches pale by comparison as [a measure of] true wealth."[715]

When you enter Rennes-le-Chateau, you find that "everyday reality has just given way to Lewis Carroll's Wonderland," comment British researchers Lionel and Patricia Fanthorpe in their *Secrets of Rennes-le-Chateau.* Figuring out the village's mysteries is akin to peeling a gigantic onion; the mystery of Rennes is couched in codes, ciphers, and cryptograms. Its geography is intriguing; its ancient landmarks line up in "unaccountably strange" patterns; and there are as many investigators as there are "bizarre facets of the Rennes affair."

The Fanthorpes also note that "The Rennes mystery seems to be like a complicated piece of embroidery: the threads repeatedly cross over one another and join up again in unexpected places." And: the Rennes mystery "spreads its tentacles like the limbs of some gigantic octopus."

With a little well-placed sarcasm and whimsy, the Fanthorpes also comment that enough attention has been devoted to possible geometric overlays on the Rennes countryside to put a dozen communications satellites into orbit and to keep them busy. The congeries of ideas, theories, speculations, and geometric projections about Rennes "effervesce together to produce a potent liquor—a heady sort of 'Hypothesis Absinthe' for the discerning reader to sip slowly, thoughtfully, and with a certain prudent circumspection."[716]

GEOMANTIC

Dome Cap; Landscape Zodiac; National Egregor Point; Ray Master Sanctuary; Arc of Developing Consciousness; Pointer's Ball.

DOME CAP: A dome cap from *Pech de Bugarach,* a mountain less than ten miles to the southeast (elevation: 3,690 feet), is situated over Rennes-le-Chateau. The dome at Mount Bugarach corresponds to Alchiba, or alpha Corvus, the Crow, and its other forty-seven dome caps energize many of the Cathar chateaus in this section of Languedoc.

Al Chiba, which means "the Tent," once referred to the entire constellation, but later Arabian astronomers adjusted the reference to be *Al Minhar al Ghurab,* meaning "the Raven's Beak." Among the myths attributed to the crow,

one is that it was originally of the purest white in color—dovelike perhaps?—but was turned to a dull black as punishment for a transgression. The Greeks say the Olympian God Apollo made Corvus into a constellation as a reward for spying on one of his lovers. The constellation has also been known as the Raven, and other titles such as Great Storm Bird, Bird of the Desert, Bird of the Great Seed, Imperial Chariot, and Storm Wind.

LANDSCAPE ZODIAC: Elizabeth van Buren is correct in stating that a Landscape Zodiac exists in the area of Rennes-le-Chateau. This zodiac is 5.56 miles in diameter and essentially occupies the bowl of *Le Val Dieu;* the zodiac dome that overshadows it is about twenty-two miles wide and takes in a fair amount of Languedoc.

As with the Landscape Zodiac in Glastonbury, England (described elsewhere in this section), the physical terrain to some degree corresponds with the energetic configurations of the zodiac, giving us an open clue to its existence. It is not in any way essential, however, that the landscape match the forms of the zodiac for there to be an authentic terrestrial star map present; most of the planet's 432 zodiacs do not have visible, obvious landscape signs signifying their reality.

To appreciate the true geomantic significance of Rennes-le-Chateau, we have to see it in a larger context—that of Languedoc, this mountainous region of southern France that abuts the Pyrenees and was once the vital stronghold of Catharism. This larger context also gives us an intriguing, perhaps alarming, view on the Albigensian Crusade of the thirteenth century, by which the Church in Rome and the French government sought to wipe out Catharism. That larger context is called an egregor, what van Buren referred to as the "cock of France."

NATIONAL EGREGOR POINT: An egregor (from the Greek *egregoros,* meaning "Watcher" or "Guardian") is an astral being that embodies the essence of a people or landscape and watches and guards people who have a common purpose, be it a city, province, or country. For France, it is the cock or rooster; for England, the matron (or lion); for the U.S., the eagle. In fact, the egregor as the spirit of a nation can become a "person," a discrete entity, though it does not have to be in or as human form. The Egyptians, for example, saw their protective national gods in animal forms, as have the French, English, Americans, and Russians, cited above.

Exoterically, the egregor may take a public representation (such as on insignias, flags, emblems); but esoterically, it is also an actual astral being—technically, a lesser god—that serves a protective function and that is also represented topographically in one specific region. The egregor embodies the occult power that directs the destiny of a polis.

That lesser god has sometimes been described as a family of angels. Qabalistic tradition holds that seventy-two national angelic regents are assigned one per country or ethnic group. Each nation has an angel set over it as a spiritual leader, and these terrestrial angels oversee public affairs and the doings of princes and magistrates, as the old texts put it. "The office of a Watcher is to protect from outside pressures a region or ethnic group assigned to its care." Further, a given group of persons (those being protected) is "'tied' to a certain area of jurisdiction." That area of jurisdiction may be a country, state, or city.[717]

Egregors can be evoked through magic ritual to accomplish a purpose, including the overcoming of the people it protects. Apparently the ancient Romans were aware of the occult advantages of this, and used it in their attacks on enemy or foreign cities. It is said that the Romans when besieging a city, would find out the name of the city's guardian spirit. They would then call forth the protective divinities of that polis by means of

a magical spell, and overcome them, making it easier to conquer the people and their city.[718]

The relevance of this conceptual review of the egregor to Rennes-le-Chateau is that the egregor for France is situated in the Languedoc. Most Cathar strongholds were situated on key geomantic nodes—cast as it were by the astral shadow of the overseeing egregor. Rennes-le-Chateau and its small zodiac constitute the landscape equivalents of the egregor's eye and brow chakra, its place of insight.

Is there really a geomythic rooster overlaid on the mountains and peaks of the Languedoc? No. We have to approach this matter with a mind open to symbolic interpretation.

What does a rooster do? It crows at daybreak, the first animal to awaken in the barnyard; it responds to the new day's first blush of dawn and announces the arrival of this new day to the world around it. So let's say France's occult destiny—its common purpose—has something to do with waking fellow "barnyard" residents—other countries of the world—at daybreak.

What is daybreak? The arrival of the Dove, which is to say, the Paraclete or Holy Spirit—an aspect of the living presence of the Christ. In this geomythic logic, the Cock of France is really the Sign of the Dove, meaning the egregor for France could probably be accurately represented either as a dove or a rooster. Either form of course is only symbolic for the quality of angelic energy and focus present in this grouping known as France.

The ultimate recipient of the Cock of France's wake-up call from Languedoc is the Albion figure that stretches from Scotland to France; everything below its head lies in the British Isles, but this Albion's head sits in France, its brow chakra at Carnac (to the north in Brittany), and its crown center in Rennes—not to be confused with Rennes-le-Chateau—less than one hundred miles to the east of Carnac. (The Albion is a vast geomythic figure modeled after the human form that occupies many hundreds of miles of landscape and contains many temples and sites.)

The Cock of France crows its daybreak wake-up call from Languedoc into the left ear of the sleeping Albion—the first of the Earth's twelve Albion figures who will awaken to the living presence of the Christ on the planet and the possibilities for cosmic awareness.

It is probably closer to the occult reality of the French egregor to conceive of it as an undefined spiritual body comprised of hundreds of eyes, each one looking into the French landscape through a dome or dome cap in Languedoc, including Rennes-le-Chateau. The numerous eyes of the egregor look into France to see how things are progressing, but the Cathar initiates could also look back through the eyes of the egregor to get attuned to its mission and France's spiritual and metaphysical destiny. The esoteric aspect of the *Consolamentum* (see Montsegur, France, for a full discussion of this ceremony) was a baptism by the egregor as well as the Holy Spirit, an awakening into awareness of the presence, intentions, and activities of both.

Catharism offered a direct route into the Christ Mysteries, shortcutting a lot of the Catholic Church's religious red tape and control-based dogma. Through its *Consolamentum* ritual, Cathar initiates received a baptism of the Spirit. And through its occupation of numerous key geomantic sites in Languedoc, Catharism put itself within the geomythic presence of France's egregor and its spiritual blueprints for France.

The seeming obsession, as described in (and perhaps to some degree promulgated by) *Holy Blood, Holy Grail*, with putting a Merovingian on the throne of France is a misplaced literalism. The Cathars, in concert with the egregor of France, no doubt produced numerous spiritual kings—Christed initiates, their crown chakras open and golden, their auric fields a psychic marriage of the

Christ and the Magdalene, the cosmic male and female energies, so to speak.

Possibly some Cathars fantasized about having one of their own as King of France, but more likely the emphasis was on using these energies as a means of achieving interior perfection. In practical terms, it seems likely that the Cathars may have worked to encourage spiritual impulses from the French egregor (in whose geomythic "body" they lived and prayed) to exert a mentoring function on public affairs in France. Cathar initiates dedicated themselves to keeping open the communications lines from egregor to public life.

In this light, the Albigensian Crusade was an occult war, staged Roman style (mentioned above), with the goal of conquering the region's egregor and through this its people and their spiritual lives. To conquer Languedoc meant to control its geomantic terrain and its focus, the egregor or Cock of France; to overthrow and in many instances kill the practicing Cathars meant the removal of the initiates who understood the relationship of landscape, metaphysics, and the egregor.

Its larger context suggested, let's return to Rennes-le-Chateau itself. The essential energy within the dome cap overlighting the hilltop community has to do with *Consolamentum* kingship, spiritual authority, leadership based on baptism by the Holy Spirit, allowing "King Dove" to touch all of France with its energy. A transformation is implied, too, as the strutting, Earthbound rooster becomes the airborne beneficent dove. The Christed Parfait, or Cathar initiate, embodying the balanced male and female aspects, Christ and Magdalene, evidence of the inner marriage—this is the model that Rennes-le-Chateau and its collegial Cathar strongholds were trying to put forward into the world.

RAY MASTER SANCTUARY: At its core, Rennes-le-Chateau is home to the spiritual mentorship of the celestial being known popularly as Saint Germaine. He is one of the fourteen Ray Masters from the Great Bear, and one of the Olympic Gods under Zeus. His color signature is lilac, and his energies pertain to the flames of transmutation, the burning off of dross and foreign energy accretions and the releasing of essential energy for new purposes. Saint Germaine is one of the major figures in contemporary geomantic activations, and he is also known to be the advance guard for the Christ.

Not to take this image literally, but it is as if Saint Germaine stands, his lower torso within the hill of Rennes-le-Chateau, his upper torso rising above it, with a fiercely burning lilac torch, transmuting everything not in resonance with the Christ energy. His energy supports conscious transmutation, the tumultuous process of alchemical change, the result of which is the inner marriage and the wearing of the golden crown of spiritual kingship and occult authority. His energy at Rennes-le-Chateau seeks to create models of wakeful leadership and numinosity in kingship—but again, the kingship is more of an inner kind. The site, including its Landscape Zodiac, *could* be used by prepared visitors for a Christed initiation.

ARC OF DEVELOPING CONSCIOUSNESS/ POINTER'S BALL: Two other geomantic structures are present at Rennes-le-Chateau. From the Magdala Tower stretches an Arc of Developing Consciousness down into the zodiac in *Le Val Dieu,* and in a central place in the zodiac is a Pointer's Ball, a doorway into other dimensions. In a sense, the Arc is that elusive doorway into other dimensions so fervently sought by Elizabeth van Buren.

Unfortunately, much of Rennes-le-Chateau's pure energy and purpose have been infiltrated, distorted, and corrupted. Saint Germaine's lilac flame is still there today, but effectively buried under a great weight of the projections of researchers, and the millennialist expectations of thousands of tourists. People who think about Rennes-le-Chateau, or visit it, are subject to the intense energies of distraction that it has been forced to emit.

Inimical spiritual agencies in the astral world are to some extent facilitating the literalism, the distractions, and the obsessive search for blood lineages and physical treasure in and around Rennes-le-Chateau. They support the belief that the mystery, the Cathar secrets, and the webs of conspiracy are material in nature. The goal is to keep people from discerning the true "treasure" of Rennes-le-Chateau—its geomantic structure and the opportunity it offers for an immersion in the living Christ mysteries.

In an ironic sense, the veil of mystery that has been accorded the village is actually part of that oppressive weight, the fuel for the distraction. The intensity of geometric overlays and map projections upon the Rennes area is both part of the burden of literalism and an imprecise and often chaotic attempt to ground some of the etheric templating, thought-forms, and blueprints of the egregor.[719]

Much that was originally subtle has been made literal, much that was refined is now coarse, what was spiritual has been physicalized. On an occult level, the intent has been to compromise and skew the egregor's vision.

A great deal of what could be described as dark, malevolent, even demonic, energy has, over the centuries, hemmed in the pure light of Rennes-le-Chateau, squeezing it into an ever smaller space and ever remoter possibility of influence. A lot of what this dark energy and its promulgators have inspired is a red herring, exciting but ultimately chimerical.

If Rennes-le-Chateau as a geomantic entity had a voice, we could say that thousands of swords are raised for battle against it, to pummel it into submission or silence. Its voice—what it has to say—would ring contrary to expectation, just as Catharism did centuries earlier. In a sense, the impression of upraised swords is an image of the residual resistance to Rennes-le-Chateau from the thirteenth-century Catholic Church. For the most part, the occult war against Rennes-le-Chateau and its Christed energies, which peaked in the thirteenth century, is still being waged today.

Santiago de Compostela, Spain

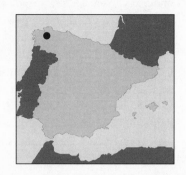

This city of ninety-three thousand in the northwestern corner of Spain called Galicia was once one of the three main holy cities of Christendom, along with Rome and Jerusalem. It was also the culmination of a hugely popular five-hundred-mile pilgrimage route from France across the top of Spain called El Camino Santiago, the Way of Saint James.

During the medieval period, Santiago de Compostela was the number one pilgrimage site in Europe (not counting Rome), and a network of routes led there. During the height of its popularity, an estimated two hundred thousand people made the journey on foot every year. It was so popular that sometimes criminals were sentenced to make the pilgrimage instead of going to jail.

They came to what many consider the "most blessed and exalted city in Spain" to venerate the holy remains of Saint James (Sant Iago in Spanish, hence Santiago), one of the twelve Apostles of Jesus Christ, said to have been buried here sometime after 44 A.D. Saint James was said to have journeyed to Spain in 40 A.D. to preach the gospel, although scholars admit there is very little evidential support for this claim.

Even so, July 25 every year is the Festival of Saint James, and when this date falls on a Sunday, it is proclaimed as the Xacobean Year, or Year of Jubilees. Four such Jubilees were celebrated in the twentieth century at Santiago de Compostela.

The rest of the name, *Compostela,* means "Field of the Star," from *campus stellae,* based on a legend of the rediscovery of Saint James' remains in 814 A.D. by observation of celestial apparitions and lights. Thus the full place name means Saint James' Field of the Star. Alternatively, the name derives from the Latin word *compostium,* as in burial place and a reference to the Roman necropolis attributed to this site. Today the mortal remains of Saint James are said to reside in a silver urn in a crypt below the high altar of the cathedral, located at Plaza del Obradoiro.

The city itself is set on a small elevation about 350 feet above sea level surrounded by forest, eighteen miles from the Atlantic coast of Spain. Pilgrims arriving at the cathedral traditionally climb the stairs behind the altar to kiss the scallop shells on the golden statue of the saint.[720] They also touch the central pillar of the Portico de la Gloria inside the cathedral's main entrance. This is a Romanesque sculpture of Saint James atop a column that rises up from the ground like a tree trunk; it was completed in 1188 by the master sculptor

447

Mateo after twenty years of work. It consists of two hundred carved figures, including a depiction of the enthroned Christ surrounded by angels, forty heavenly armies, and the twenty-four Elders.

Today after centuries of touching by human hands, the stone is smooth and worn, especially a small cavity on the side. Pilgrims may also receive La Compostela, an official certificate of completion of El Camino, provided they can present the passport stamps of the various town councils and local parishes along the way.

MYTH AND LEGEND

The city acquired its name as the Field of the Star in 814 A.D. when a hermit named Pelayo saw supernatural lights and celestial fireworks in the stars. They seemed to hover near the River Sar, as if indicating a direction; they grew smaller as they approached the ground until they were only faint spangles of light seemingly dancing above the brush. It was as if a river of stars had flowed down from the Heavens, ending as a sparkling trickle at one spot. Pelayo followed this star trail and reported hearing the singing of angels and heavenly music.

Another version says that a single, very large bright star surrounded by a ring of smaller stars highlighted the deserted spot in the hills. This version of course is reminiscent of the Star of Bethlehem that guided the Magi to the Christ child.

Pelayo reported the phenomena to Bishop Teodomiro at Iria Flavia; together, the two returned to Pelayo's place of hermitage until the lights appeared again. The stars now seemed to hover over a specific part of the landscape, and when Bishop Teodomiro and Pelayo dug the ground indicated by the new stars or angelic messengers, they found the stone tomb of Saint James, whose whereabouts had been lost and forgotten for eight hundred years. It is also said that

there were three bodies in the stone tomb: Saint James and two disciples.

A variation on the tale says they found a sepulchre inside a cave, and papers in the stone chest attesting to the authenticity of the bones being those of Saint James. Alfonso II, from his court at Oviedo, immediately ordered the construction of a church on this site, the *campus de la stella*, or later *campus steliae*, and finally *compostela*, now known as the Field of the Star.[721]

This was completed in 829, but destroyed in 997 by Moorish invasions. In 1075, Bishop Diego Pelaez began construction on the present cathedral; part was consecrated in 1105, and the rest in 1211; the cathedral's baroque façade was completed in the early eighteenth century. Soon Saint James became accepted as the patron saint of all Spain, and seemingly everyone wanted to visit his remains.

The popularity of the pilgrimage peaked in the twelfth century. After 1492, when the Moors had been driven out of Spain, it started to decline, attracting mostly Spanish and Portuguese pilgrims. Somehow the bones got lost a second time (or were deliberately hidden) in 1518; they were rediscovered in 1879, and a papal bull in 1884 confirmed their authenticity. In 1937, Saint James was reconfirmed as Spain's patron saint, and in the decades since then, the El Camino pilgrimage has regained its medieval appeal.

While many visitors to Santiago de Compostela affirm the site's aura of devotion and holiness, some lightly deride its somewhat tacky appearance. The Cathedral is a noble Romanesque building, "but the main façade unfortunately has been ruined by a pompous baroque coating more reminiscent of a wedding cake than a sanctuary." Even so, this commentator found the inside better: "its bare walls pregnant with a silence, ancient spirituality that the marketplace-like commotion, flashlights, and commercialized religion inside can't entirely suffocate."[722]

Are a saint's relics truly numinous and is there any way to demonstrate this? In the 1980s German geobiologist and Earth energies researcher Blanche Merz used sophisticated scientific measuring equipment including a Biometer to analyze energy emissions around the relics of Saint James in the crypt at the Cathedral of Santiago de Compostela.

At about shoulder level on the saint's statue, vertically above the crypt with his remains, the device registered twenty-one thousand units. In Merz's measurements, this is "the threshold of the Unknown," an extraordinary level of vitality and spiritual charge, higher than anywhere else she had investigated. The "light of life" above the crypt was dazzling, illuminating the brain, Merz commented. "It is as if our heads suddenly became light and illuminated, leaving behind a doughy body and entering into a multitude of translucid diamond bubbles, reflecting iridescent colours." The energy detected there was pure, a marvelous blossoming, affording "an instant of flight in the Overconscious."[723]

Another account, which exists confusingly between the realm of verified fact and folkloric exaggeration, was that Theodore and Athanasius, disciples of Saint James, collected his body and severed head and set the remains on a stone boat with no pilot. It was piloted only by the love of the Virgin Mary or by God Himself, and eventually it reached the northwest coast of Spain, possibly at Finisterre, "End of the Earth," less than 50 miles from Santiago de Compostela. Legend says alternatively that they may have landed at Iria Flavia, today's Padron, and the mooring stone, the *pedron,* or big rock, after which the town was named, is kept under the altar of the Santiago Apostle parish church.

Even though the boat sailed alone, somehow some of the disciples of Saint James were on hand for its arrival. They brought the body ashore and placed it on a stone slab, which immediately registered a bas-relief impression of him. Next, Queen Lupa (She-Wolf), the local pagan chieftess, greeted them and sent them off to a man called Beleth, who she hoped would kill them. He jailed them but an angel secured their release; when Beleth's troops chased the disciples across a bridge, it collapsed, and the disciples' pursuers drowned.

Then Queen Lupa sent the men to a mountain where dragons and wild bulls would surely kill them at last. No luck. The disciples returned to civilization with the wild bulls pulling their cart. Queen Lupa relented and decided to convert. The last straw came when the bulls stopped the cart before a pagan temple of Bacchus; the resident statue immediately crumbled to dust, and the disciples used the dust to make cement for a shrine. Where they did this, the legend claims, is the place now called Santiago de Compostela, built on the ruins of Queen Lupa's former pagan temple.

MYSTICS AND TOURISTS

Who are today's pilgrims to Santiago de Compostela and why are they going there? According to field research conducted by anthropologist Nancy Louise Frey, published in *Pilgrim Stories,* people are walking, bicycling, or driving to Santiago de Compostela from motives of tourism, the desire for transcendent spirituality, physical adventure, nostalgia for the medieval past and the ways of ancestors, physical adventure and athleticism, as a theater for grieving, as a chance for esoteric initiation.

Many call the Camino *la ruta de la terapia,* "the Therapy Route," because along the way, one's wounds, losses, fears, failures, shames, and addictive tendencies—normally obscured by daily life—come to the forefront of consciousness for resolution.

"The Camino can be (among many other things) a union with nature, a vacation, an escape from the drudgery of the everyday, a spiritual path to the self and humankind, a social reunion, or a personal testing ground," Frey explains.[724] Once Europeans made the pilgrimage as a religious quest for salvation and a remission of sin through penitential suffering, such as the hardships of the journey. Today, the spiritual motives are more diffuse and less canonical. Frey identifies five principal ones based on her interviews with pilgrims.

For some, the pilgrimage is about making the distance in as brief a time as possible, with a high display of bravura, typically with power walkers, sports fanatics, and aggressive cyclists. Some come at a life crisis or transition point, when they need to make an important decision; some are historians, researchers, and architects who make the pilgrimage an opportunity for fieldwork (there are eighteen hundred architecturally worthy buildings along the route); some are self-promoters, who will write a book about their experiences; and some actually have theological goals.

Even to call the pilgrimage a spiritual journey leaves a lot of room for interpretation, Frey says. It involves the idea of "the uncontained, nonstructural, personalized, individual, and direct relationship one has to ultimate reality." One pilgrim told her that the pilgrimage was about the "inner journey," being able to "access one's religious feelings without intermediaries." A religious commentator told Frey the eclectic spiritual motivations of the pilgrims were a sign of the rejection of formal religion and its communal context for "privatized spiritualities that have little context but the self."[725]

Pilgrims interested in the esoteric aspect of the long walk to Santiago de Compostela told Frey that on the way they hoped to access new planes of consciousness. One way that might happen, she was told, was through contact with "tellurian points or sites believed to possess accumulated energies." A German walker told her that the Way contained energy residues of all the people who had ever walked the route, and that making contact with this energy was itself one of the values of the pilgrimage.

In *Camino,* her much publicized journey down Saint James' Road, film star and author Shirley MacLaine took up the theme of energy points. The Camino "follows ley lines that reflect the energy from those stars systems above it." She said a ley line is part of the essential structure of the Earth's "etheric spirit" and increases the vibratory rate of etheric and dense matter of the human brain exposed to it, resulting in "more full, conscious awareness and information that was previously repressed." One becomes "a more psychic being."

Along the Way, MacLaine learned that many wars had been fought on it and in its vicinity because the energy beneath the ground "amplified" human emotions and "intensified" karma between opposing forces. She said that the alignment of the ley lines with the galactic stars was meant to help resolve conflicts.

MacLaine further reported that the ley line energy of the Camino permeated the acupuncture meridians of the feet of the pilgrims, supporting self-realization. The feet also absorbed "the possibility of other-dimensional reality" implicit in the amplified energy of the road. In older days, pilgrims used this energy to balance the masculine and feminine aspects of themselves, MacLaine says, and through the soles of their feet people could once "find the knowledge of the soul."[726]

A Way rich with energy residues and Earth energy nodes is consistent with the esoteric vision of one of the route's earliest and most famous pilgrims, Charlemagne (771–814), King of the Franks and Emperor of the West. He had a powerful dream one night that forever linked the Way of Saint James with the Milky Way, and led to various popular epithets for the pilgrimage route such as *Camino de las Estrellas,* "the Road of the Stars," *Via Lactea,* "the Milky Way," and *la voje ladee,* "the Road Under the Stars."

According to a medieval text called the *Codex Calixtinus,* in a dream, Charlemagne saw the Milky Way and the Apostle James told him that the Road of the Stars he was seeing was in fact the way across the Iberian landscape to the saint's tomb, which was then inaccessible because of infidels. Charlemagne made the journey, opening up the road, and becoming the first legendary pilgrim to Santiago. In later years, other spiritual celebrities would arrive at Santiago de Compostela, including Saint Francis of Assisi, Saint Bridget of Sweden, and more recently, Pope John Paul II in 1992.

But since then, the popular imagination has linked the Road of Saint James with the Milky Way, even with the path of dead souls—another folkloric way of comprehending the Milky Way— whose spectral light will guide the living to paradise accessed at the far western end of the Earth. Some took the metaphor literally and traveled the extra forty miles or so to Finisterre, on the north-western coast of Spain, then believed to be the jumping-off point for the end of the Earth. The image also suggests "there were as many pilgrims [on the Way] as there are stars in the sky."[727]

What kind of people were the 23,218 pilgrims reported by the Pilgrim's Office in Santiago to have signed the register of completion in 1996? The Pilgrim's Office statistical report says that in 1996, seventy-one percent walked, seventy percent were Catholic, seventy percent were Spanish, and the other thirty percent hailed from sixty-three countries, the greatest number from France, Germany, Holland, Belgium, and Italy, in that order. The average age was thirty; most were highly educated, middle-class, urban dwellers; sixty-five percent were men; of the eighty-four percent who professed a belief in God, only half actually practiced a religion.[728]

Some make the pilgrimage not knowing why, and occasionally end up feeling jaundiced and a bit shortchanged at the end. In the early 1990s, American journalist Jack Hitt thought that the pilgrimage would be a good thing for "a guy out for some cosmically serious fresh air" and as an excellent way to "serve out my coming midlife crisis."

By the end of his five-hundred-mile walk, he realized that a pilgrim is really just a tourist, but the "lowest of lowbrow travelers, a subspecies of tourist" following last in "a forced march" in the footsteps of a million people who were there first. One is relieved of this irony "only by the comedy of our burden." Hitt's disappointment was even keener inside the Cathedral of Santiago de Compostela. He sensed "an air of fraudulence"; a swell of tourists with unsheathed, strobing cameras uncomfortably "illuminate my already soiled epiphany."[729]

The pilgrimage experience of another American journalist, Nicholas Shrady, who has lived in Barcelona for fifteen years, touched on some aspects of Hitt's disillusionment but was mostly an uplifting experience. During Shrady's twenty-eight-day, five-hundred-mile solitary pilgrimage, he found himself often retracing his steps. "The route was as circuitous as medieval logic, but I was in no hurry. *Ambulare pro Deo*, "to wander or walk for God," was a tenet of the medieval Church, a call to the faithful to imitate the Lord's journey through the wilderness."

When Shrady reached the summit of the small hill called *Monte del Gozo* (Mount of Joy) just outside Santiago, he could finally see the cathedral towers. Traditionally, this hill, barely three miles from the city, marked the penultimate moment in the pilgrimage when the cathedral towers first became visible. Whoever in a group reached this hillock first was called King of the Pilgrimage. Shrady wasn't interested in that. Beholding the "honey-colored spires" shining "like beacons" in the morning light, he felt "pure, unmitigated joy" and his spirits soared.

Yet when he finally took his turn before the sacred relics in the Cathedral, he felt "strangely at a loss, as if I had come to the wrong place." People behind him in line nudged him to finish up and move along, and he barely had time to "bless myself reflexively" before he was "swept along" out of the crypt. "I missed the silence and striding of the Way."[730]

Dome; Three Star Temple; Tree of Life.

DOME: The dome situated over Santiago de Compostela, whose top center is directly over the cathedral like an *axis mundi,* corresponds to Cursa, beta Eridani, the River. Cursa is the principal star in this constellation, situated at the source of the River. Here is a fine example of the way folk memory preserves a vital and accurate bit of star lore in which the outer attribution matches the inner geomythic one: the River of Stars.

How geomythically elegant that the dome star marking the end of Saint James' Road of the Stars is the Source of the River, as if the River of the Road of Stars flows out from Saint James' site. Also geomythically appropriate, given the Camino's five-hundred-plus-mile length, is the fact that Eridanus' boundaries enclose a larger area of the visible sky than any other constellation. This dome generates dome caps that cover, for example, Monte del Gozo, the famed first vista hill, and Pedron, the site of the mooring rock on the Atlantic coast.

The name Cursa comes from the Arabic *Al Kursiyy al Jauzah,* which means "the Chair or Footstool of the Central One," meaning Orion. Cursa is only 3° northwest of Rigel in the constellation of Orion; sometimes it is considered part of Orion, being the Hunter's bent left knee. It's a third magnitude star, said to be topaz yellow in color, eighty light years from Earth, and about forty times brighter than our Sun. The energy of this star and dome at Santiago de Compostela is about holding a star reverentially in cupped hands, catching a falling star, then raising it up from the Earth for all to see.

As a constellation, Eridanus has thirteen identified stars, and as a cosmic river it begins at the left foot of Orion, the Great Hunter. Some classical astronomers said Eridanus was the Nile River, others that it was Oceanus. When these astronomers sought to identify the physical expression of Eridanus, they would point to the Po, the Rhone, the Ebro, the Rhine, even the Tigris-Euphrates. In myth, Eridanus was the river into which Phaethon fell when Zeus struck him down in mid-flight with the Sun chariot because he was creating havoc with the Day.

THREE STAR TEMPLE: The presence of this feature shows how you can have a Saint James' Field of the Star regardless of whether his mortal remains are present in the cathedral. The star, or stars, in question in the *compostela* are the Soul Star, Incarnational Star, and Earth Star. In reference to a standing human, there is one star above the head, one just above the navel, and one below the feet in the ground. Through concentration, the head and foot stars merge with the navel star.

It is somewhat charming, though not essential as evidence, that one version of the arrival of Saint James' relic, or the discovery of his tomb, involved three bodies, as in three stars—two smaller ones (disciples) and one big one (the Apostle). This corresponds to the geomantic array of the Three Star Temple. The Soul Star and the Earth merge in the middle to form a massively and brilliant Incarnational Star, which has its own vertical connection to the spiritual world. The middle, Incarnational Star is marked by the Cathedral of Santiago; the Soul Star above the head is in the Plaza de Quintana, behind the cathedral; the Earth Star, below the feet, is in the Plaza de Obradoiro.

Saint James as a spiritual being is present even today as the overseer of this star temple, in his capacity as Ray Master from the Great Bear, overseeing the second ray or essential cosmic color vibration of bright orange.

In a sense, all of the Christian trappings of arrival and procession through the various stages of the Apostle's veneration are, geomantically, beside the point. They are in some respects a sideshow that keeps people's attention focused, their spirituality honed, and their presence fixed within the geomantic temple for a time. Perhaps one reason some pilgrims seem to finish the journey somewhat disillusioned or let down at Santiago de Compostela is that they haven't quite used the temple the way it was meant to be used.

That way would be to first stand in the Plaza de Quintana and focus one's attention on a bright blazing star (Soul Star) above the head. This will get you in alignment with the one already there at the Plaza. Next go into the cathedral and tune into the Incarnational Star just above your navel (two inches above, two inches inside). Allow this to get very large, so large it may seem to disappear. You may find yourself feeling hundreds of feet tall, as if you have somehow become a living *axis mundi.* You will actually be making contact with the specific archangel that oversees this Three Star Temple.

Then step out into the Plaza de Obradoiro, and tune into the Earth Star below your feet, a few feet in the ground. The three stars coincide in the middle star, yet they are also present individually. The Earth Star segment of this temple is the distribution zone, like the spillway of a fountain. The celestial (Soul Star) and archetypal human (Incarnational Star) get filtered through the Earth Star (the elemental energies of Nature) for the benefit of the locality.

TREE OF LIFE—THE ROAD OF STARS: It's important to remember that using the temple in this way is somewhat predicated on some prior preparation. There are many Three Star Temples on the Earth (144,000), so the one at Santiago de Compostela is not distinctive in itself. What gives

it significance is, first, it is the starfall for Cursa, the Source of the River; and second, it is the destination and culmination of a series of temple initiations along El Camino, about which it is geomythically accurate to say that it is like the Milky Way, a Road of Stars.

Along El Camino, pilgrims pass through other domes, dome caps, and four complete Trees of Life, each comprising the Four Worlds and forty spheres of light. In fact, from Roncesvalles to Santiago de Compostela is one vast Tree of Life, containing four complete Trees of Life. There are five more domes, each the starfall for another star in Eridanus: at Pamplona, Logrono, Burgos, Leon, and Ponferrada. These five domes generate up to 240 dome caps and energize the 160 spheres on the four Trees of Life. The straight-running dome lines connecting these domes would account for the growing perception of "ley lines" along the Camino, marking it out, as it were, like neon road strips.

A Landscape Zodiac is located at Bilbao, to the north of Burgos on the North Way; Burgos and the other domed sites just mentioned are on the *Camino Frances* (French route). The Camino Frances and El Camino run more or less parallel and mark the pillars of the single massive Tree of Life. You could picture the dome caps arrayed on both sides of the Camino Frances and extending up to the North Way. The entire Camino, as folk memory had it, is indeed a vast Road of Stars.

All of this is preparation, a kind of spiritual shriving and cleansing, for the epiphany of light in the Three Stars in Saint James' Field of the Star. The Three Star Temple at the Source of the River, or Road of Stars, marks the topmost part of this five-hundred-mile-long Tree—the exalted crown of four Trees of Life.

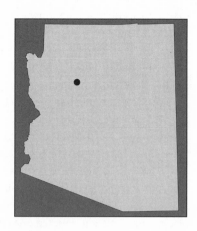

Sedona, Arizona, United States

In this small, scenic town in northern Arizona, we have some of the best and worst results of geomantic awareness. People in Sedona exhibit a high degree of awareness of the possibility that the landscape is geomythically charged, yet Sedona seems to generate an astonishing degree of inflated projection, false attribution, and grandiose speculation regarding what that geomythic charge might be.

Physically, Sedona is a city of sixteen thousand, situated at an altitude of forty-five hundred feet, 120 miles north of Phoenix and thirty miles south of Flagstaff. It is Arizona's second most frequently visited tourist site (after the Grand Canyon), as an estimated four million people a year come to marvel at Sedona's distinctive Red Rock Country. Sedona is completely surrounded by the Coconino National Forest, a fact that would seem to protect it against massive development. Even if you haven't been to Sedona, you may have seen it in the movies. Since the 1940s, at least sixty Hollywood films and countless commercials and advertisements have been filmed there.

Sedona is also a premier resort, retirement, and arts and culture site, featuring forty art galleries. It attracts seemingly equal measures of wealthy people seeking a fabulous place to resettle or retire, and mystics, new age savants, healers, metaphysical merchants, and "spiritual immigrants" wishing to be in place when the Second Coming finally arrives.

Not surprisingly, in 1994, *The Los Angeles Times* dubbed Sedona "the Vatican City of the New Age movement." Sedona is a "multichannel wilderness," one observer comments. "Its celebrated 'energy vortexes' have become an established feature of the city's tourist industry, with vortex maps now given out to visitors at the chamber of commerce."[731]

HISTORY AND ARCHEOLOGY

The seemingly sculptured red rocks and buttes surrounding Sedona got that way as the result of an estimated 350 million years of erosion. Geologists explain that at several times in its vast geological past Sedona has been covered by an inland sea; when these seas retreated, they deposited the layers of sand that now comprise the red rocks of the landscape. Sedona is also on the edge of the Mogollon Rim, a three-hundred-mile-long escarpment (one thousand feet high in some places) that runs northwest to southeast and was formed some thirty-five million years ago, part of the Mogollon Highlands, which formed an estimated sixty-five million years ago.

Different tribes of Native Americans have lived in the Sedona area over the centuries, including the Hohokam (circa 700 A.D.), Sinaguans (circa 1100 A.D.), Anasazi, the Yavapais, and the Tonto Apaches. One theory suggests that Sedona was originally settled by four groups coming from the four "sacred directions": Athabascans from the North; Apache from the East; the ancestors of the Hopi from the South; and the Yavapai from the West.[732] One subgroup within the Yavapai, the Wipukpayas ("people at the foot of the mountains"), considered the Red Rock Country to be their ancestral and spiritual home, giving it their own name, *Wipuk*.

The greater Sedona area remained inhabited by Native Americans until the nineteenth-century arrival of white settlers, the U.S. Army, gold and copper prospectors, and cattle barons. Though a small number of pioneer families settled in Sedona in the 1870s, the area remained fairly inaccessible until 1902 when T. C. Schnebly, representing one of the twenty families who had settled there, opened the Schnebly Hill Road. That year the town was officially founded as well, and Schnebly started to deliver mail to the inhabitants from the town's first post office. The town was named after Schnebly's wife, who was called Sedona.

The population boom began in 1947 when a sustainable water source was located 525 feet below ground capable of supplying six hundred gallons an hour. The town got paved streets and electricity in the 1950s, and was officially incorporated as a township only in 1988.

The new age community started to blossom in Sedona in the mid-1960s thanks to the efforts of Mary Lou Keller, still regarded as Sedona's "matriarch of metaphysics." She taught yoga, sold real estate, set aside space for workshops, and

invited various metaphysical groups to get established at Sedona.

Around 1976, new-age figurehead Dick Sutphen evoked the mystery of Sedona's "power spots"; in 1980, psychic Page Bryant channeled information describing seven landscape energy "vortexes" in Sedona; in August 1987, an estimated five thousand people arrived in Sedona for the Harmonic Convergence; and on December 12, 1994, 120 people performed a "12:12" ceremony at Cathedral Rock, reportedly visualizing tetrahedrons of light and linking these from Sedona to other geomantic sites around the planet.

Since then, Sedona has become a world-recognized spiritual Mecca like Glastonbury and Findhorn. It has become "a place for eclectic spiritual experimentation and theological hybridization,"[733] mixing traditions and beliefs, most notably those of Native Americans and groups espousing the reality of extraterrestrial contact.

Another strong current in the Sedona mix is conspiracy modeling, in which the U.S. government is believed to be in collusion with certain shadowy organizations, possibly to do with the widely reported abductions and implants by the Greys (a species of aliens) and other plots against the American people. At the same time, the Sedona ethers are redolent with talk about ascension, higher dimensions, light bodies, stargates, energy portals, interdimensional portals, and galactic contacts.

Explanations to account for this congeries of beliefs and activities usually come down to the vortexes, variously described as beacons, energy wells, or power spots. Sedona is renowned for its "high concentration of active energy and power," and as "the only spot on earth to contain four major vortexes within a few square miles."[734]

According to a report published by Page Bryant in 1991, a vortex is a special place on the Earth "where the life force of the planet was particularly strong and is coagulated into funnels of energy." Vortexes can be beacons, receptor sites for incoming cosmic energies; they can be electrical or electromagnetic in nature; they can be negative, drawing energies inward like a black hole, making accidents there likely; or they can be time warps, in which the experience of time appears to be anomalous.

Among the vortexes attributed to Sedona, Bryant says that Bell Rock is connected to the Moon and Pluto through "celestial ley lines"; Boynton Canyon has an energy field that extends for twenty-five miles in all directions; Red Rock Crossing at Oak Creek has "two magnificent archangels [that] stand guard over the 'entrance to an inner sanctum'"; and there is a new vortex called Sunset Point that "opened" sometime in the late 1980s on Schnebly Hill.[735]

Various writers on Sedona catalog different numbers and locations of vortexes, but the underlying belief is that all of Sedona is a vortex. It is a town "situated in a vast zone of powerful, shifting, mysterious and sometimes volatile energies." The "energy field completely envelops Sedona," so that people report sensing its boundaries as a kind of subtle membranous curtain surrounding the city in a five- to eight-mile radius from the town center.

Some say that they sense the edge of this membrane around Bell Rock in Oak Creek, a few miles outside Sedona, adding that the energy noticeably "shifts" there. Sedona is a special place due to the unique thinness of the "veil" between our world and the world "on the other side," which comprises "an availability of other dimensions," both visible and invisible nonhuman beings, and "unspeakably powerful energies."[736]

MYTH AND LEGEND

The Native American myths pertinent to Sedona are somewhat imprecise about places,

even though much has been made of them by new-age mythologizers of Sedona. According to the Yavapai-Apache, Sedona is the middle of the world, their original home, and the place out of which they emerged into this world. They called Sedona *Wipuk* in reference to the surrounding red rocks; similarly, they often referred to themselves as *Wipukpa*. All Yavapai originally came from Sedona, but then they spread out.

Reference is also made, a little confusingly, to the Montezuma Well north of Camp Verde, not too far from Sedona; the tribal elders state that the Yavapai came out of that bottomless lake (geologically, it is a limestone sink). The Yavapais also say that there are sacred caves in the Sedona landscape where Old Lady White Stone (Kamalapukwia), also called First Woman, survived the Flood that destroyed what they call the earlier Third World of existence.

In this same cave, her grandson Sakarakaamche taught humans and other beings the correct way to live in this new world. This included songs and dances, methods of prayer, and medicine. He also left markings on the cave walls to remind Yavapai later of his appearance. According to this myth, Sakarakaamche left his footprints—apparently he was a huge being—in the form of red rocks in the Red Rock Country. The Yavapai still regard as sacred Boynton Canyon, which is specifically cited, because that is where First Woman lived.[737]

MYSTICS AND TOURISTS

One visitor to Sedona commented that the talk he kept overhearing in town reminded him of the inflated, self-centered boasts and distorted logic he was familiar with among gamblers at Las Vegas, where, he said, everybody thinks everything that happens to them is a personalized message from the gods. "The free-wheeling entrepreneurship in Sedona also reminds me of a busy market in the Third World, just outside a holy shrine, where fakirs, soothsayers, and vendors of religious icons hawk their services." The competition for sales is intense, vendors talk "the New Age talk that will make the sale," and most of what they sell is "hokum."[738]

Speculations about esoteric features and alignments in the Sedona landscape include two series of landscape chakras running from Bell Rock to Boynton Canyon and a matrix of perhaps a dozen "interdimensional access points" in roughly the same area. Some contend that underneath Sedona is, variously, a secret U.S. military base, an alien spaceship headquarters, or a series of invisible Pleiadian temples.

One researcher extrapolated from a Yavapai myth about a bird in a hollow log the possibility that this bird is geomythic, its winged outline etched massively in the landscape contours, ridges, and buttes of Sedona. This hypothesized bird extends from Indian Gardens in the northeast to Airport Mesa, and from Secret Canyon in the west to Eastern Cliffs in the south; it is twelve miles across the wings, and about eight miles from beak to tail. "It exists in the geomantic imagination and will be set in motion in the landscape of the collective mind only to the extent that it takes hold as an idea."[739]

Another geomantic theory put forth by Raymond Mardyks holds that Sedona has at least two "Star Wheels," by which the author means miniature star maps inscribed in the shapes and contours of relatively small-scale rock formations, such as Cathedral Rock and Sugarloaf Mound. "Most of the place names in Sedona and the surrounding areas match with the star lines emerging from these two Star Wheels."

This theorist also suggests that if you stand at either of these locations and view the landscape, the visible geological configurations will match, conform to, or in some manner align with numerous constellations. To picture this, you need to visualize a line of light from the center of the Star Wheel, such as at Cathedral Rock, extending to the place on the horizon where a given constellation is known to set or rise. Then you can "begin to see the energy lines or spokes of the Star Wheel."

Further, he proposes that three constellations—Cygnus, Andromeda, and Lyra—pass directly over Sedona and are considered "zenith" stars for Sedona. It's not clear whether he means there is a demonstrable archeoastronomical alignment or an energy coincidence of stars and landscape.

The "archetypal presences" of another three—Canis Major, Columba the Dove, and Scorpio—pass immediately below Sedona towards the center of the Earth, Mardyks claims. "Stars from these constellations are directly aligned with Sedona, and so these archetypal Beings are focused in Sedona in a powerful way." The energies of these six constellations comprise the "core archetypes" in Sedona's mythology and "emerging consciousness."

Mardyks offers two further intriguing observations. According to his information, there is a "teleportation instrument" or "hole in space" in Boynton Canyon that can instantaneously transport people from this site to somewhere in Tibet. There is nothing physically visible to mark this hole, he adds. Second, he says one of the seven places on Earth that "carry the responsibility of guiding the planet through galactic space" is located underneath Cathedral Rock.[740]

Sedona is not entirely dominated by new-age concerns. It hosts twenty-seven Christian churches, and if the attitudes in the religious novel *Sedona Storm* are any indication, the two camps view each other with some trepidation. In this spiritual warfare thriller, angels battle demons for the possession of the soul of Sedonians, and the prevalence of the demons is blamed on the new-agers.

The authors write of a slimy, seething black, putrefying ooze of demon mass flowing ominously down Cathedral Rock. "The fissure in the rock widened with each moment, belching forth even more demons, like an unending lava flow." In fact, the demon flow was so vast that "the skies over Sedona were dark with the demons spewing like molasses from the opening at Cathedral Rock."[741]

GEOMANTIC

Landscape Zodiac; Domes; Dragon; Silver Egg; Epiphany Focus; Mount Olympus; Labyrinth; Tree of Life; Pointer's Ball; Gnome Egg; Shambhala Doorway; Leo Albion Solar Plexus Chakra; Ixion's Wheel.

LANDSCAPE ZODIAC: The visitor who commented that all of Sedona is one big vortex is correct. The geomantic structure that makes this observation a reality is the huge zodiac dome seventy-eight miles across that spans all of Sedona and the Red Rock Country. The Sedona zodiac itself is thirty-four miles in diameter, with the dividing line between physical and etheric halves situated on the Oroboros Line that enters the zodiac temple at the junction of Bell Rock and Courthouse Butte in Oak Creek Canyon and continues up through Schnebly and Wilson Mountain.

The physical half of the zodiac extends westward towards Capitol Butte, Table Top Mountain, and Boynton Canyon, while the etheric half extends eastward to Bear Wallow Canyon and Devil's Dining Room. Thus the buttes and canyons are filled with stars, as are the town, airport, the developments, golf courses, and the other Sedona attractions. Everywhere you go you are walking amongst the stars, the galaxy on Earth at Sedona.

It is seductive to think that you are finding chakras in the landscape, as many people increasingly do, but these chakras have to belong to *someone* or be part of some system. Landscape chakras are a hierarchical energy expression of the planetary spheres within the geomythic body of an Albion, which is a macrocosmic mirror image of ourselves as humans. This means that you are most likely to find a chakra hierarchy within the central column within an Albion within a Landscape Zodiac. The chakras in a landscape are Albion's chakras. (See below for more discussion on the Sedona Albion.)

This said, some landscape chakras within the Sedona Albion can be identified as running from the root center at Bell Rock to the crown at Wilson Mountain. Along the way, this line passes through the Chapel of the Holy Cross, Twin Buttes, Oak Creek, downtown Sedona, Giant's Thumb, and Steamboat Rock.

DOMES: The prime geomantic energizers of these numerous starfalls are the 144 dome caps generated by four domes in the greater Sedona area at Cathedral Rock, Boynton Canyon, Schnebly Hill, and Wilson Mountain. As each of these domes is several miles in diameter, you have an intense overlap of the energies of four different stars over Sedona and a mixture of these four star energies in the deployment of the 144 dome caps across the landscape. The most concentrated overlap of the four domes is over downtown Sedona. Further, the array of star energies provided by these four domes provides a rich and intense mixture for this temple.

The dome over Cathedral Rock is the starfall for Alnitak, the left star (zeta) in the Belt of Orion, the constellation of the Great Hunter. The name derives from the Arabic *Al Nitak*, which means "the Girdle." Alnitak is about sixteen hundred light years from Earth, situated approximately side by side, from our Earth vantage point, with Epsilon Orionis, or Alnilam, the middle belt star; but both are about 163 light years in front of Delta Orionis, or Mintaka, the right belt star.

The Boynton Canyon dome is the starfall for Procyon, the alpha star in the head of Canis Minor, the Little Dog, and companion to Canis Major, at whose neck burns Sirius, the brightest star in our galaxy. Canis Minor is called the Giant Hunter Orion's second dog, or Lesser Dog, and sometimes the Northern Sirius, and *Al Kalb al Asghar* or *Al Shi'ra al Shamiyyah,* as the Arabians knew it.

Along the Euphrates in Mesopotamia, Procyon was known as *Kakkab Paldara, Pallika,* or *Palura,* which meant "Star of the Crossing of the Water-Dog." It was considered a water dog because it stood on the edge of the Milky Way, which the ancient astronomers conceived as a river of stars. Procyon, a first-magnitude star about twice the size of our Sun, is 11.3 light years distant from Earth.

One interesting myth of Canis Minor was that it was one of the Hounds of Actaeon. When Actaeon, a human mortal, spied the goddess Diana bathing naked, she transformed him into a stag and his own dogs hunted him. According to the star myths, by some calculation of either karma or gratitude, the hound that killed him was afterwards made into a constellation.

The Schnebly dome corresponds to Lambda Boötes, the left foot (though some say left arm) of the constellation of the Herdsman or Ox-Driver. The knee of this figure is Arcturus, one of our galaxy's brightest stars; its dome is at Chaco Canyon in New Mexico and is part of the same large-scale geomantic system (the Leo Albion; see below) as Sedona.

The fourth dome at Wilson Mountain corresponds to the bright star on the tail of Leo, the Lion, namely, Denebola or beta Leonis. The name Denebola derives from the Arabic *Al Dhanab al Asad,* for "The Lion's Tail." Ulug Beg, the medieval astronomer from Samarkand in Uzbekistan, called this star *Al Sarfah,* "The Changer," in reference to its observed correlation with changes in the prevailing weather patterns.

For the Chinese, Denebola was construed as part of a quintet of stars known as *Woo Ti Tso,* "the Seat of the Five Emperors." Euphratean astronomers called it *Lamash,* or the "Colossus," and in India it was called the "Star of the Goddess Bahu," regarded there as a supreme Mother Goddess creative divinity. Denebola, a second-magnitude star, is forty-three light years from Earth.

The array of four domes in a relatively small area is unusual for the Earth grid. Such a concentration of domes is a sign of the geomantic importance of the site.

Seen from above, the four-dome array would resemble four massive, interlacing fully grown sunflowers of light, their tightly packed seeds arrayed on spirals out from the center as the 144 dome caps arrayed across the Red Rock landscape. Indeed, vortexes are everywhere you look. It's as if you're looking into the star-packed galactic core.

Sedona has at least 148 vortexes, if you include the four domes and 144 dome caps. Add to this the dozens of constellations represented in the Landscape Zodiac, not all of which are enveloped by a dome cap, and the "vortex" list swells closer to two hundred.

DRAGON: At the dome cap over Bell Rock in Oak Creek Canyon is one of the Earth's 1,053 minor dragons. It sits at the Sedona temple gates as a guardian; it also helps to energize the dome lines and the temple as a whole. Another dome cap is situated over nearby Courthouse Butte, and the two dome caps overlap to form a vesica piscis at a midpoint between them. Route 179 from Oak Creek Canyon to Sedona passes approximately through this overlap, and for a short distance actually marks the Oroboros Line that cleaves the Landscape Zodiac. Formally, this is the appropriate "front door" of the Sedona temple.

SILVER EGG/EPIPHANY FOCUS: The Chapel of the Holy Cross is the approximate location of a hatched Silver Egg. During the first week of January 1993, the Sedona zodiac, and especially this node within its energy field, was the focus of the Epiphany beam from the Christ for the planet for that year. During that week, the Silver Egg at the dome cap over the Chapel of the Holy Cross and its immediate environment of perhaps one to two miles in diameter was hatched.

The Horus emerged from the Silver Egg and now stands as both guardian and soul guide for visitors to the Mount Olympus at Cathedral Rock. This would be the "body of a giant bird [that] lies on Sedona," as mentioned above—except, technically, it is standing upright, its feet at the Chapel, and the bridge to Mount Olympus behind it.

Switching mythic vocabularies for a moment, it might be easier to see Horus as the Norse Heimdall who guards the rainbow bridge into the home of the gods. At Sedona, one might visualize a fourteen-hued bridge extending from the Chapel of the Holy Cross overland to Cathedral Rock. It is also intriguing—from a certain point of view, it's amusing—that on the rock abutment facing the Chapel there is a large, unmistakable image of a hawk. In Egyptian iconography, Horus was frequently depicted as hawk-headed.

MOUNT OLYMPUS: This is situated in the same place as Cathedral Rock. The proper entrance is overland from the area of the Chapel of the Holy Cross, paralleling the location of the rainbow bridge. Horus (or Heimdall) is the soul guide for the human wishing to enter the Mystery temple of Thoth, which is the Egyptian mythic way of referring to Mount Olympus.

Mardyks' characterization of the energy feature here as one of the places that "carry the responsibility of guiding the planet through galactic space" is a fair description of a Mount Olympus. It is the home of the fourteen Ray Masters from the Great Bear whose commission in part has to do with directing the affairs of the planet, its inhabitants, and the relationship of both to the cosmos.

LABYRINTH: Within the energy field of Schnebly Hill is a labyrinth. You walk the energy labyrinth inside the dome to get your psychic and cognitive centers in resonance with the energy field of the labyrinth and the Hall of Records at its center. It is a Hall of Records in the sense that it records stellar and universal influences and light codings that have been transmitted to this site over the duration of the existence of the Earth. The Schnebly Hill labyrinth is in fine working order and has not been adulterated.

TREE OF LIFE/POINTER'S BALL: All of Boynton Canyon is a Mystery temple. Beginning at the southeastern entrance to the canyon and extending its full extent to the northwestern canyon wall is a Tree of Life template.

Walking the 3.25 miles through Boynton Canyon you are at the same time walking through the Four Worlds of existence, as postulated by Qabalistic thinking, through the forty Sephira, or hierarchically arrayed "vessels of Light," and potentially—if you take a very meandering, even zigzagging approach to your stroll through the canyon—through the eighty-eight paths on the four Trees of Life that comprise the single Tree.

At the top of the entire Tree is a dimensional doorway that in this book is called a Pointer's Ball. Picture a huge vertical almond-shaped door the size of the canyon wall; or, if you like the evocative language of Carlos Castaneda, picture it as a crack between the worlds or a slit between dimensions.

The Pointer's Ball at the end of Boynton Canyon would seemingly correspond to the teleportation and hole in space described by Raymond Mardyks above. It is also the likely match for the Yavapai myth of the cave in which First Woman lived and through which her son dispensed knowledge.

GNOME EGG: Tucked away at the base of the western wall of Boynton Canyon is a Gnome Egg. However, this Gnome Egg has been compromised. Sometime in the early 1800s, a few European initiates belonging to Black Brotherhoods came to Boynton Canyon and put most of the gnomes under their thrall. Using black magic, these initiates forced many of the elementals, but the gnomes especially, into being their "familiars." They commandeered the Gnome Egg, energetically imprisoned and enslaved most of the gnomes, and effectively blocked the rightful activity of the elemental kingdom in Boynton Canyon and much of the Sedona temple.

This situation remains unreversed even today. The intent was to interfere with the role the Sedona temple was to play in the twenty-first century within its Albion plate. This plate is referred to in this book as the Leo Albion because in our time it is under the astrological influence of Leo.

The capture of the Gnome Egg may at first blush seem like a trivial event, perhaps even an amusing one. But Gnome Eggs are crucial elements in Earth's geomantic setup, just as gnomes, the elementals for the earth element, are key players, and key co-creators with humans and the angelic world.

It is a virtually unseverable interconnectedness: the angelic realm depends on humans to maintain the Earth's geomantic structures with their input, and humans require the elementals to act as the angelic intermediaries between the higher celestial energies and the terrestrial energies underlying biology. Take out one link in this trio and the system does not work. At Sedona, one link has been removed.

INTERFERENCE AT SEDONA: In a curious sense, some aspects of the fundamentalist stance of *Sedona Storm* turn out to be true at Sedona. The new-age milieu inadvertently has invited some demonic and dark energy involvement in this temple. One result of the Black Brotherhood interference with the Sedona temple is that today for the most part it is a temple of the false gods.

You can easily tell, from the comments and descriptions offered above, that there is an intense new-age and metaphysical emphasis at play in Sedona. A reasonable question to ask is: where did this new-age emphasis come from? And: what keeps it in place at Sedona? Why does it seem to grow ever stronger?

The answer is both shocking and sobering. (Admittedly, much of the explanation sounds, initially, implausible and fantastic.) It comes from the confluence of false gods rooted in the landscape and alien interference that supports them.

Distributed through the Sedona temple are six anti-Palladiums. (Just as the Antichrist is defined in terms of the authentic Christ, so a false god can be usefully identified in contrast with a real one. The real one in this case is a Palladium, a miniature geomythic expression of the Crown of the Ancient of Days, the All-Seeing Eye of God, if you like, or as Qabala calls it, the White Head.)

The anti-Palladium appears like the huge head of a sage-like human rising out of the landscape like a vast mushroom. It is not the Head of the Ancient of Days; it is the invasive presence of a "guru-being." A guru-being is an astral spirit that works through living human gurus of any spiritual tradition for the purposes of colonizing the minds and energy fields of human disciples. They trade spiritual, occult, or metaphysical information for human power and authority. You give them your seniority, and they give you spiritual validation. Six of these guru-beings are now present in the Sedona astral landscape.[742]

These six sprouting guru-being heads in the Sedona temple become a foundation for further and more subtle interference. At Sedona, this takes the form of what could be described as beams or rays from an assortment of alien motherships above Sedona. (UFO sightings, encounters, and channelings are fairly common in Sedona.)

What needs to be appreciated is that all UFOs and their activities are not benevolent; some may be like Steven Spielberg's near-angelic space-beings in *Close Encounters of the Third Kind,* and some may be like the cold-blooded, abducting-implanting greys in *Fire in the Sky.* At Sedona, the alien ships send beams into the six guru-being heads, creating a kind of crosshatched webbing or fishnet over the entire area. The guru-being heads act as anchor points and distribution nodes for the fishnet webbing of alien interference created by the incoming beams.

This webbing generates and maintains the vapid new-age atmosphere of ungrounded, grandiose, otherworldly claims, perceptions, and activities. You might picture it as a thick cloud bank that envelops the brow and crown chakras of potentially everyone in Sedona. You can't expect to see clearly when your head is in a fog bank. The cognitive risk at Sedona is that one's psychic vision is enmeshed in a fog bank and might be subject to the pictures and thoughts floating around in it.

SHAMBHALA DOORWAY: This is located at the far end of Table Top Mountain, facing south towards Cathedral Rock. Walk out beyond the end of the Oak Creek Airport runway to the farthest point on the ridge facing Cathedral Rock. This is where the Shambhala Doorway is situated.

As a whole, however, Table Top Mountain has a tendency to get astrally polluted, even to the extent of making some sensitive people sick or highly irritated when they are in the energy field. During the Epiphany week in January 1993, the Archangel Michael and his colleagues cleansed this area but, as that was nearly a decade ago, it is likely the site has refilled with toxic psychic energies. These energies create an obscuring interference zone in front of the Doorway.

This is another example of how the original geomantic structure has been interfered with, polluted, or adulterated through acts either of human commission (as at Boynton Canyon) or omission, in which, as it were, nobody assumes the janitorial role of periodically cleansing the ethers of toxic energies.

LEO ALBION SOLAR PLEXUS CHAKRA: The irresistible question that arises is this: why so much attention on Sedona? To answer this, we have to appreciate the Sedona temple's role in the Leo Albion plate.

The energy of the entire Sedona temple—using the seventy-eight-mile-wide zodiac dome as the ultimate physical definition of the temple space—is concerned with directional finding in the galaxy, with multidirectional access. Picture the zodiac dome filled with wide-open wakeful eyes capable of seeing anything in the galaxy, even the cosmos. These eyes can see other layers or dimensions of reality; parallel realities; past and future scenarios; alternate present time realities. They can see into the stars, planets, other galaxies, the angelic hierarchies, the ET and alien confederations. The eyes are another way of describing the cognitive gems in the City of Gems.

It is helpful to think of the Sedona temple as a large geomantic expression of the structure and mechanics of the third chakra, the *Manipura,* or "City of Gems." This is the spiritual architecture of the solar plexus, which in the human, is a complicated junction of physical nerves and energy cords. In Western metaphysical traditions and more recently in the phenomenology of near-death experiences, the Silver Cord, the energy umbilicus that allows us to leave the body to roam the world in our astral body while still tethered to the physical, is reported to join the physical body at the solar plexus.

Carlos Castaneda wrote that the man of action has anywhere from one to five fibers emanating from the solar plexus, "their size ranging from a mere string to a thick, whiplike tentacle up to eight feet long." In some people, he said, up to three of these fibers are wound together into tentacles. Accomplished Dreamers, Castaneda further said, have "an apron of hairlike fibers at their midsections."[743] In Castaneda's model, these fibers are part of a person's cognitive psychic apparatus.

In terms of the descriptions of the ten-petaled *Manipura* chakra, the ten petals represent vibrational fields, ten important nerve endings, ten vital breaths of *prana,* and ten sources of energy. "The energy flows in ten dimensions; its pattern is now neither circular nor square; its movement is no longer circular, like that of the second chakra."[744] Its movement is complex, multidirectional.

Amplifying these solar plexus factors is the fact that in our time the Albion for which Sedona is the *Manipura* chakra is under a Leo influence. Remember that one of Sedona's four domes represents an important star in Leo: Denebola. This raises the stakes considerably and draws lots more astral attention upon Sedona than upon some of the other Albion solar plexus chakras. Leo, as far as humanity is concerned, is the key or clue to the entire zodiac, wrote occultist Alice Bailey. Her explanation is arcane, but even the broad strokes illuminate this aspect of Sedona.

Two metaphysical mysteries revolve around Leo: first, the mystery of the Sphinx, by which Bailey meant the secret of the solar angels and the mystery of the relationship of the higher and lower minds; and second, the emergence of initiate consciousness through the defeat of the king of beasts, or human personality. This defeat in turn leads to the triumph of group and world consciousness, of selflessness and illumination over self-consciousness and selfishness, Bailey said.

When the occult influences of Leo have been properly focused through the Sun, Uranus, and Neptune, and have been integrated in the initiate's life, the result is the "conscious, integrated Self, functioning with full occult knowledge and also with mystical perceptions." The Leo energy produces "the truly Self-conscious man." Leo marks "the height of achievement for the human soul," and this achievement is being sparked by the "Shamballa force now flowing into the centre of humanity," Bailey wrote.[745]

The range of potential vision, transformation, and initiate development through the Sedona temple is synoptic and awesome. It even has a local Shambhala Doorway to facilitate this inpouring of the Shambhalic evolutionary incentive. If the entire Sedona solar plexus temple were fully functional, it would be a powerful evolutionary force on the planet. Life within the aegis of its Leo Albion could support the attainment by many of this state of being the "truly Self-conscious man."

This is why it is desirable, in the view of some supersensible agencies, to block it. So rich a cognitive mixture could lead to a fantastic degree of clairvoyant access and spiritual freedom; various cons, scams, subterfuges, and the general manipulative, distortionary milieu put forward by the conclave of guru-beings and alien motherships would be seen through, repudiated, *busted.*

At present, Sedona's cognitive potential is blocked and adulterated. The practical effect of the fishnet webbing created by the confluence of the six guru-being heads and the multiple alien mothership beams is to cast a false sky over the interior of the Sedona temple. On this false sky is written a false script. Unless one is discerning, one may end up reading the prepared astral script and not the genuine star script of the celestial realm. Ultimately, one runs the risk of reading *their* occult script and not that of the Supreme Being who originally gave to us all of the Earth's geomantic structure as a revelation.

As the Sedona temple attempts to extricate itself from its physical body and to rise up into the ethers on its own geomantic Silver Cord, it encounters this interference zone, this cloud of distorted knowing. It is an almost hallucinatory state, dreamlike, saturated with "unconscious and transmedium energies."[746] You channel voices, but you may end up transmitting only their public relations press releases, rather than words of oracular insight. You end up with distortions, partial truths, disinformation, errors, misattributions, self-inflation.

IXION'S WHEEL: The Chapel of the Holy Cross in Sedona is a distinctive chapel in the form of a Christian cross completed in 1956 and based on a 1932 vision and design by its founder, Marguerite Brunswig Staude. The Chapel marks the geomantic spot in the Sedona temple that is the solar plexus of the solar plexus. The Chapel is the solar plexus chakra within the Sedona Landscape Zodiac Albion, and this Albion is the solar plexus chakra for the much larger Leo Albion, as described earlier. So here you have two layers, or expressions, of the solar plexus chakra, and to a large degree, the subtle or esoteric structure of this feature gives us an unusual way of looking at the solar plexus chakra itself.

The Chapel is well named, because the architectural shape of the cross is repeated or in resonance with an esoteric temple structure present in the same place or perhaps slightly under it. One way to picture it is through the Greek mythic image of Ixion's Wheel. Ixion is described by the Greeks as the first man to commit murder; only Zeus, the king of the gods, was willing to forgive Ixion, and he invited Ixion to Mount Olympus for a purificatory rite. Ixion used the occasion to try to seduce Hera, Zeus' wife, and he ended up strapped to a fiery, winged, four-spoked wheel that would revolve and flame forever.

The energy feature at the Chapel of the Holy Cross resembles Ixion's Wheel, minus the murder and seduction elements, which may have been a storyteller's gloss long after the metaphysical reality was forgotten. Within an inner plane temple at this site, which tends to resemble a glass-domed building, there is a golden cross at the base of a golden spindle or bore.

The idea is to lie down in this cross—it is a hybrid of a cross and a sarcophagus—and be irradiated by the Sun overhead as the cross rotates. The Sun is the star Alcyone of the Pleiades, believed by many to be the Great Central Sun around which our own Sun and solar system revolve in a 180-million-year cycle (see Mount Etna, Sicily, Italy). The resonant alignment with this galactic "Sun" provided by this solar plexus incubator can trigger some surprising insights.

Teotihuacan, Mexico

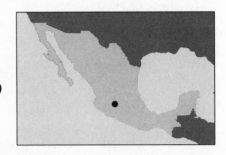

It's known as the City of the Gods and archeologists say it is the first city of the Americas, created, they estimate, some twenty-five hundred years ago by an unknown culture. Teotihuacan, an ancient site in partial ruins, is located thirty miles northeast of Mexico City, which itself arose on top of the ruins of an ancient Aztec city called Tenochtitlan. Even though Teotihuacan sits on a plateau in the arid, northeastern corner of the Valley of Mexico, its elevation is mountainous at seventy-five hundred feet.

When the Aztecs occupied Teotihuacan, long after the original residents had vanished, they called it Teotihuacan, "Abode of the Gods," and when Spanish explorer Hernan Cortes first saw the ruins in 1520, the site's history had already slipped into the mythic, which held, according to the Aztecs, that Teotihuacan had been built by a race of giants.

But by the end of the nineteenth century, almost no traces were discernible of Teotihuacan. A photograph taken in 1895 shows the Avenue of the Dead entirely overgrown, a mere narrow path, and the Pyramid of the Sun looking like a forlorn scrub-covered hill; if you hadn't already known there was once a vast ancient city here, occupying eight square miles, you'd probably never suspect it. Even today, much of the original eight square miles of Teotihuacan is buried under five towns, one of Mexico's largest military bases, lots of farms, commercial centers and stalls, and several highways that loop around its core.

Other interpretations of its name are "The place where one becomes deified," "the place where the gods were conceived," or "the place of those who have the road of the gods." The Aztecs conceived of Teotihuacan as "the place where one becomes a god." According to a sixteenth-century Spanish historian, the Aztecs called the site Teotihuacan because it was the burial place of kings. "The ancients said that when a man died, he had become a god, and so that came to mean that he had died."[747]

Teotihuacan may have been the city in which buried kings became gods, but it was not a city of the dead. "It was one of the few places in Middle America where human dwellings were closely connected with sacred buildings."[748] Seemingly the priests lived among the lay folk, and the Sun and Moon pyramids climbed next to the two thousand high-walled "apartment" compounds. It was, during the time of its greatest prosperity, the world's sixth largest city, and it functioned for centuries as a well-developed urban center, according to archeologists.

Teotihuacan flourished as the "first true capital and first great place" in Mexico, operating under "the authority of supernatural forces and cosmo-magical formulas."[749] Here the Aztec would elect their first kings, believed to be the living incarnations of the gods. Teotihuacan would also become known as the place where the travelers from the Aztec's legendary ancestral home called Atzlan constructed their pyramids to honor the Sun and Moon and primordial events.[750]

At its height, the city is presumed to have had a population of 75,000 to 200,000 around the fifth century A.D., making it more populous than Periclean Athens and larger in extent than Ceasarian Rome. Then, archeologists speculate, it all collapsed around 750 A.D., possibly due to a huge fire.

Since the 1960s, archeological excavations have revealed that the city contained up to twenty-six hundred different major structures, including stepped pyramids, temples, ceremonial plazas, and residences, spread out over eight square miles and divided into seven zones. Up to seventy-five distinct temples have been identified, and it is the most visited of Mexico's many archeological sites.

Teotihuacan was originally laid out in a precise gridwork of quadrants with the main axis running north-south along what is now known as the *Calle de los Muertos,* the Avenue of the Dead about 1.4 miles long and ranging from forty to ninety-five yards wide. It's also called *Micoatl,* the Pathway of the Dead. Numerous open courtyards up to 476 feet wide and small platforms line both sides of the street. Archeologists believe Teotihuacan was laid out in a set of alignments that corresponded to or tracked star movements.

Along the avenue are several important extant temples and structures. At the south end is the huge *Ciudadela,* or Citadel, fronted by an enormous quadrangular platform, each side of which is 1,170 feet long. This is surrounded by fif-

teen small temples. The main plaza of the Ciudadela is vast and could probably hold one hundred thousand people without crowding.

Behind this is the Temple of the Feathered Serpent, or Quetzalcoatl. This is a six-tiered stepped pyramid with rows of rectangular panels overlaid on the sloping walls. Large bold stone sculptures display Quetzalcoatl as the Feathered Serpent, the Fire Serpent, the Sun bearer; Quetzalcoatl may also be a rendition of the Mayan rain god, Tlaloc. Excavations have shown that the Avenue once continued for another two miles farther south from the Ciudadela and that it was bisected by an east-west street.

Farther north up the Avenue is the Pyramid of the Sun, or *Tonatiuh Ytzaqual,* House of the Sun. Each side of this four-sided stepped pyramid is 738 feet long, the structure rises 230 feet above the plain, and its mass is estimated to comprise 2.5 million tons of sun-dried bricks and rubble, or 33,743,201 cubic feet. It is the world's third largest pyramid. A set of steep stone stairs enables visitors to climb to the top, where the view is extraordinary; once there was a temple there with a fifteen-foot-tall stone idol.

Some archeologists propose that all of Teotihuacan was originally focused upon a natural volcanic tube or cave underneath the Pyramid. Steep stone steps lead downwards for twenty-three feet from the human-made entrance, then you pick up a tunnel that leads to the natural caves shaped into four "rooms." This ninety-eight-foot-long snakelike cave was discovered in 1971, but archeologists propose that around 100 B.C., the cave was discovered by the indigenous people here and used as the basis for a ceremonial center that later expanded into Teotihuacan.

The cave, like the Pyramid of the Sun, has an east-west axis, and its entrance lines up with the horizon point for the setting Sun and the rising of the Pleiades on the spring and autumnal equinoxes. On April 29 and August 12, the Sun sets in the West directly opposite the orientation axis of the Pyramid and in a direct sight line from the subterranean cave.[751] "Prior to the Spanish conquest, Mexicans considered such caverns as wombs from which the sun and moon, as well as the forerunners of the human race, had emerged in remote antiquity."[752]

Close to the northern end of the Avenue are the Palace of the Jaguar, which offers murals of jaguars with feathered headdresses, and the Palace of the Quetzal-Butterfly, with carved pillars denoting a strange bird-butterfly hybrid.

At the northern end of the Avenue of the Dead is the Pyramid of the Moon, known as *Metzli Ytzaqual,* House of the Moon. Its four sides are each 476 feet long at the base, and the stepped pyramid, somewhat in ruins at the top, rises 140 feet above the Avenue. Archeologists believe there was once a twenty-ton, ten-foot-tall statue on its summit.

In 1998, archeologists uncovered a new tomb within the Sun Pyramid, and the remains of what appeared to have been an important personage. The burial chamber was square, about eleven feet on each side and five feet deep, and the body of an adult male was surrounded by 150 burial offerings, the remains of eight birds, and two jaguars. The grave was dated to 150 B.C., and while it was not the first burial chamber found at this site, or the first body—130 human skeletons were found at the Temple of the Feathered Serpent—it is the most impressive in terms of the presumed importance of the deceased.[753]

A few miles beyond the Pyramid of the Moon towers Cerro Gordo (Fat Mountain), a former volcano with a Catholic shrine and small park on the summit, accessible by a modest road. The peak is considered a sacred one, dedicated to an unspecified Goddess and associated with the region's fertility.

According to local legend, this mountain, known as Tenan, is the source of all of Teotihuacan's water. In a report made in 1580 to King Philip II of Spain by researchers at Teotihuacan, mention was made of the local belief that halfway up Tenan was a chasm from which a great noise emanated, which they understood to be the noise of the water descending from Tenan to the valley.

Geologists have since vindicated that local belief. Tenan is a volcano, and volcanoes are known to collect rainwater in their silted-up cones, then to funnel it underground to the plains. That water flow can produce a loud sound. Geologists have also determined that all the water in the area's eighty springs derives from or is linked to Tenan. Not surprisingly, residents around Teotihuacan associated Tenan with their rain god, Tlaloc, whose jurisdiction includes "the water which makes the noise in the mountain" as the 1580 report indicated.[754]

HISTORY AND ARCHEOLOGY

Research indicates that all of Teotihuacan may have been constructed according to a single standard of measurement for which Teotihuacan itself is the origin and norm. During the years 1972 to 1981, civil engineer Hugh Harleston Jr. made over nine thousand measurements at the site and derived a mathematical constant in Teotihucan's design.

Harleston called it the STU, or Standard Teotihuacan Unit, which is equal to 1.059 meters. It accounts for eighty-five percent of the site's dimensions. This number is the same as the Jewish "rod," which is 3.4757485 feet, a classical sacred geometry number, and it is one six-millionth part of the Earth's polar radius. The STU is exemplified in the length of one side of the Pyramid of the Sun and Moon, and the distance between the two pyramids.

More astonishing was Harleston's conclusion that Teotihucan's designers must have had knowledge of spherical trigonometry because many of its measurements, and the STU itself, involve a geodesic measuring system. The designers appear to have had access "to methods of calculation and measurement that permitted them to determine their position on the earth sphere," Harleston said. They appear to have been aware of the Earth's spherical characteristics and its significance and to have used this in the temple design.

The mathematics of the Teotihuacan complex were also related to certain geometric measurements involving the entire planet. His research led Harleston to conclude that "Teotihuacan's dimensional logic was derived from modules that form an integrated system of earth-commensurate parameters."[755]

He also discovered that the trigonometry of the Teotihucan grid extended throughout the greater Teotihucan valley so that Harleston could accurately predict finding associated astronomical markers on various outlying hills and mountains. All of these outlying relationships were also expressed in terms of the STU and were centered on the Pyramid of the Sun.

Further research showed that eleven pyramids located within a one-mile radius west or east of the Pyramid of the Sun could have been used as astronomical observatories, and the location of another seven was predicted. These outlying sites were positioned to observe the solstices, equinoxes, and the days of zenithal crossing. It is also possible that the attribution of Sun and Moon to Teotihuacan's two pyramids "may be due to a vestigial tradition that they were once used for sighting the relative movements of these celestial bodies, a function which has only now been rediscovered."[756]

A second fascinating archeoastronomical clue about Teotihuacan's celestially focused master plan is provided by Dartmouth College geography professor Vincent H. Malmström. Archeologists have figured out that all of Teotihuacan and its environs were laid out along axes that varied 15.5° from the cardinal points and that the Avenue of the Dead ran south-southwest on a compass bearing (azimuth) of 195.5°, or 15.5° west of south (and east of north). All the major structures and the cross streets are aligned at right angles to this, which means their orientation is to an azimuth of 285.5°, or 15.5° north of west.

This may seem like archeo-astronomical arcana, but it holds an important revelation. Teotihuacan's layout is based on the azimuth at which the Sun sets on the days it passes directly over Teotihuacan—July 26 or May 18. However, the original 285.5° is a little at odds with the modern calculation for these dates, which is 290.7°.

One intriguing theory to account for this small discrepancy is that the sunrise Teotihuacan's axis is aligned to might be that over Citlaltepetl (18,700 feet), Mexico's highest mountain. Teotihuacan's designers, says Malmström, built their ceremonial center with a configuration that commemorated an important calendar date (August 13) for a site six hundred miles away one thousand years earlier. Teotihuacan is also precisely aligned with Mexico's highest mountain at sunrise on the winter solstice. In Mesoamerican myth, August 13, 1358 B.C., was the day the "world began," and the Aztec sacred calendar count as well.

Malmström proposes that the Mesoamerican 260-day sacred almanac and calendar may have been based on the interval between zenithal Sun passages over this pivotal mountain. The heliacal (near the Sun at the horizon) rising points of Venus were also involved. This set the astronomical (and geomantic) time for many temple complexes in this region. In other words, if Teotihuacan is a clock, it's set to the Mesoamerican equivalent of Greenwich Mean Time.[757]

Another theory about Teotihuacan's orientation is that it was cosmological, set to "Teotihuacan north," not astronomical north. In effect, the difference between these two axes is 15.5°. According to Anthony Aveni, we should assume that the orientation of the volcanic tube cave under the Pyramid of the Sun probably represents the original and foundational orientation for the entire site, and that orientation is towards the place on the horizon where the Pleaides set in 150 A.D.

The skewed northern axis of the Avenue of the Dead derives from drawing a perpendicular line across the Pleiades alignment from the Pyramid of the Sun; the Avenue is that perpendicular line, says Aveni. In fact, he notes that a survey of sixty Mesoamerican ceremonial centers shows that ninety percent exhibit a skewed axis that deviates from true north by several to fifteen degrees, and that twenty percent of them lie within a few degrees of Teotihuacan's orientation of 15.5°.[758]

MYTH AND LEGEND

For the Aztecs, Teotihuacan was also the Place of Origins. It was there that the Fifth Sun, the Age of the Aztec, was born "out of sacrificial fire in the great city at the beginning of time" when there was no Sun and no dawn and all the world was in darkness. The gods gathered at Teotihuacan and decided who would "take it upon himself to be the sun, to bring the dawn."

One of the gods was to throw himself on the great fire they constructed there, to be reborn as the Sun. That god, some recountings say, was Quetzalcoatl, the Plumed Serpent. He cast himself into the fire and was transformed into the Feathered Serpent god. Teotihuacan became recognized as a cult center for Quetzalcoatl worship with at least two temples dedicated to him. (For more on the myths of Quetzalcoatl, see Chichen Itza, Mexico.)

Another Aztec version of this myth names the god as Nanahuatzin; of five creator gods, he was the only one courageous enough to commit self-immolation. He turned to flame and became the "Fifth Sun," which to the Aztecs was the Sun of the present age. His companion, named Tecciztecatl, also jumped into the ceremonial fire, and emerged as the Moon. The two pyramids at Teotihuacan were in effect dedicated to these two gods.

MYSTICS AND TOURISTS

Karl E. Meyer, an archeological writer, said of Teotihuacan in the 1970s that the polarity in the Mexican soul between solitude and communion takes on a tangible reality here. The visitor is "overwhelmed by isolation and yet caught up in a collective sweep of humanity just as overwhelming." Among the world's ancient monuments Teotihuacan is rare because here "the metaphysically minded and the literal minded can glean their separate satisfactions."[759]

National Geographic senior assistant editor George Stuart noted in 1995 that of the hundreds of Mexican archeological sites he had reported on, Teotihuacan "has lodged itself most tenaciously in my mind." The builders must have regarded the site as "an almost indescribably sacred spot," yet twelve hundred years after its demise, Teotihuacan remains a paradox. "We speak of it with awe, as we do of the pyramids of Egypt, but we still know next to nothing about the origins of the Teotihuacanos, what language they spoke, how their society was organized, and what caused their decline."[760]

GEOMANTIC

Domes; Mesoamerican Control Temple; Planetary Solar Plexus Chakra; Epiphany Focus; Tree of Life; Landscape Zodiac; Ixion's Wheel; Pointer's Ball; Golden Egg; Palladium; Labyrinth; Lucifer Binding Site.

DOMES: The first thing that must be said about the Teotihuacan temple is that it is much bigger than what is today physically apparent or what is presumed to be the original extent of eight square miles. Its full extent is more like six hundred square miles, a rectangle of some twenty by thirty miles, extending all the way west to the ruins of Tenochtitlan, the geomantic foundation of today's Mexico City.

The myth about the founding of Tenochtitlan says that long ago the Mexicas people left their ancestral and somewhat otherwordly homeland in Atzlan and arrived at Lake Texcoco in the Valley of Mexico, a volcano-formed high plateau in an oval shape measuring sixty-eight miles (north-south) by fifty miles (east-west), or twenty-seven hundred square miles. Lake Texcoco is mostly dried up now, but then it was a large lake with an island in the middle.

The Mexicas, guided by their god Huitzilopochtli, found an eagle holding a serpent in its beak perched on a stone or prickly-pear cactus on this swampy island. That's where they built Tenochtitlan (Place of the Prickly-pear Cactus), whose sacred precinct would eventually comprise four thousand square meters and feature seventy-eight buildings, all of which was surrounded by the *coatepantli,* or serpent wall, and would be for the Mexicas the center of the universe.

According to historians, Tenochtitlan was founded comparatively recently, in 1325 A.D., by the Aztecs, but given the site's geomantic connection with Teotihuacan, it is likely its foundation date was many millennia earlier.

Tenochtitlan and Cerro Gordo are the front and back doors of this vast temple. Each has a dome. The dome over Tenochtitlan (now in Mexico City) is Altair, or alpha Aquilae, the constellation of the eagle; the dome over Cerro Gordo is Merak, or beta Ursae Majoris, the Great Bear. Together, they generate ninety-six dome caps, many of which are arrayed inside the greater Teotihuacan precinct.

Aquila the eagle was made a constellation by Zeus, the Greek chief of the gods, in gratitude for its deed of bringing the human Ganymede to Mount Olympus to be Zeus' cup-bearer. Appropriately for Teotihucan's geomancy, the eagle is the only bird that flies towards the Sun, not being intimidated by the Sun's rays; thus it is ranked first among the birds.

The Greek astronomer Ptolemy wrote that the Pleiades show themselves in the East, but the Eagle soars in the summit of heaven. Again, this is acutely relevant for Teotihuacan's geomancy. The constellation is depicted as an eagle with its wings outstretched for flight; it has four main stars, and Altair is on the wing. Most cultures identify it as an eagle, and their names reflect this.

The name Altair, the principal star, is derived from the Arabic name for the full constellation, *Al Nasr al Tair,* "the Flying Eagle." It is the twelfth brightest star in the sky, located sixteen light years from Earth, nine times brighter than our Sun and about 1.5 times larger. Among the stars, Altair has one of the fastest known rotations, turning at 160 miles a second, and completing a rotation in 6.5 hours; our Sun, in contrast, completes a turn in 25.4 days.

Merak is the beta star in the Great Bear or Big Dipper, being the star at the base of the dipper farthest from the handle. The star's name comes from the Arabic *Al Marakk,* which means "the Loin (of the Bear)." The star is of the third magnitude, about eighty light years from Earth, and sixty-five times more luminous than our Sun.

The Hindus knew it as *Pulaha,* one of their seven exalted *rishis,* or cosmic sages; to them, the Great Bear is the seat of the Seven Rishis and the court of cosmic administration and authority. In the vocabulary of this book, the Great Bear is the source of the fourteen Ray Masters and the variously named home of the gods.

The Dipper part of the Great Bear has been accorded many names in world star myths: the Egyptians called it the "Bull's Thigh"; the Chinese saw it as the "Government," the "Northern Measure," and "The Celestial Palace of the Lord on High or the Immortals." The Arabs and Jews saw the form as a coffin or bier with mourners; the Scandinavians called it *Karls Wagn,* or "Wagon of the Great God Thor"; the Germans as *Himmels Wagen,* "Chariot of Heaven"; and the English as "Charles' Wain" or "King Arthur's Wain."

MESOAMERICAN CONTROL TEMPLE: It's hard to know exactly what to name this function. The Teotihuacan temple complex of some six hundred square miles is like a long, wide, shallow emerald-hued box with a large front gate somewhat reminiscent of the enigmatic black monoliths in Arthur C. Clarke's *2001: A Space Odyssey,* but in this case, laid out flat across the landscape. You enter it as you would a vast walled city, or an otherworldly temple. Just as the astronaut in 2001 exclaimed that the inside of the monolith was filled with stars, so is Teotihuacan.

It is like a star city placed here intact, fully executed, from somewhere else—perhaps another galaxy or universe. On the top and center of this six hundred square miles of celestial space towering golden-orange flames burn, as if the entire star box were a landscape votive burner.

It functions like a circuit board or a computer chip, making computations for the Earth grid and transmitting energy, information, and instructions to the planet's many nodes, especially those in Mesoamerica. In some fashion, this star city is also a hologram of all the Mesoamerican geomantic sites, such as Chichen Itza, Monte Alban, Palenque, and many others laid out in a scale model hierarchy of energy and function.

In far earlier days on Earth it was possible to make adjustments in the Earth's visionary geography by way of a central office. Trained geomancers—from our viewpoint, they would seem more like magicians—were able to maintain a large geomantic system by affecting it through a scale model version no larger than a room. This scale model, of course, was more like a holographic projection, but it was real and palpable enough that the geomancer could usefully affect and maintain the system through projections of consciousness and intent. Teotihuacan is a much larger version of the same thing.

Another way of conceptualizing this aspect is through music. Archeo-astronomers studying Teotihuacan have pointed out the detailed astronomical alignments found in the site's overall and individual temple structure, and they have suggested the purpose of this was to be a multi-aspected but coordinated observatory. This is probably too limited a speculation. It is more likely that the key aspect is to be found in the celestial ratios and distances embodied in the structures, their sizes and relationships to one another in space.

We should probably better conceive of Teotihuacan as a finely tuned musical instrument capable of playing the legendary Music of the Spheres. When Teotihuacan was "on," which means when stars and planets relevant to its nature (such as Venus and the Pleiades) were in a position to actively influence the structure, the Teotihuacan "instrument" would automatically make "sounds" as a result of having the cosmic current run through it. These sounds would affect all aspects of the associated Mesoamerican energy matrix.[761]

Here we must part with archeological assumptions about dates and builders because they do not fit the reality. The Teotihuacan acoustic instrument and star city was designed and mostly executed by the Elohim. One would expect the Elohim, cosmic architects, as it were, to be aware of spherical trigonometry, the existence of which Hugh Harleston Jr. ably demonstrated in

Teotihuacan's design. This temple in fact is one of the six most sophisticated energy devices on the planet. It could more accurately be called the Temple of the Islands of God, the place where you make the God connection.

The Elohim designed Teotihuacan, and the Mayans were the prime live-in geomancers, occupying this and the other Mesoamerican Mayan sites during the period from 3000 B.C. to around 640 B.C. Extraterrestrial in their soul origin, the Mayans "left" at that time because the work of the Teotihuacan temple complex was finished for that phase of Earth evolution. It also turns out that their collective name has been misrepresented: it was not Maya but *Maha,* which meant "the High Ones." The Mahans were the Great Ones, the more evolved beings from other star systems, who incarnated for a time on Earth to assist its energy grid.

PLANETARY SOLAR PLEXUS CHAKRA: The complete Teotihuacan complex is one of seven aspects of the Earth's solar plexus chakra, called the *Manipura,* or City of Gems. Uluru in Australia is another. The purpose of the Teotihuacan temple is to facilitate the initiatory experience of moving from individual human will to acceptance of divine will.

The solar plexus is the seat of discriminating wisdom, the joy, bliss, and happiness of the heart realized. On a planetary level, the different aspects of Earth's solar plexus chakra get activated after its Heart centers have been stimulated and awakened. As we learn from myth, the Golden Age must follow the awakening of the Heart (see Glastonbury, England). Just as Earth's three heart centers have been geomantically "worked" on since the 1980s, so is Teotihuacan, as an aspect of Earth's solar plexus chakra, receiving attention.

EPIPHANY FOCUS: One event that certainly helped Teotihuacan start to arise for a new era of geomantic relevance was the Epiphany of January 6, 1992. Over the course of the week leading up to January 6, the higher spiritual worlds and in particular the Christ as a cosmic being focused their attention on Teotihuacan, most particularly on a small square platform in front of the Pyramid of the Moon.

If the Christ focus is conceived of as a beam of scarlet light, the center for the planetary reception of that beam for 1992 was this obscure, neglected platform at the end of the Avenue of the Dead. Its geomantic significance for Teotihuacan is discussed below.

TREE OF LIFE: In the original design, a thirty-mile processional goes from the vicinity of Tenochtitlan to the front steps of the Pyramid of the Moon. This processional is a Tree of Life, representing the Four Worlds and forty spheres of light (Sephiroth) as described in Qabalistic mysticism. The Tree starts just inside the huge rectangular "box" of the six-hundred-square-mile temple complex. Implicit in the Tree, of course, is an energy hierarchy of chakras, from root to crown.

From La Ciudadela within the present physical boundary of Teotihuacan another Tree of Life begins, extending like a rope ladder to the Pyramid of the Moon. This Tree of Life, though distinct and autonomous as an energy structure, is also a subset of the larger thirty-mile-long Tree of Life.

The term "Avenue of the Dead" in reference to this processional is both apt and misleading. It is not a street of the dead, in the sense of a series of tombs or mausoleums. During the last inhabitation of the site, people referred to the Avenue this way because the keys to the temples along the Avenue were locked up, forgotten, dead to further use. In an earlier time, the Teotihuacan priesthood had turned off the temple and locked away the keys.

The people living at Teotihuacan in a later age, after 220 B.C., two centuries after the Mahans had left, recognized this loss of geomantic power within the priesthood and regarded the central axis of Teotihuacan as spiritually lifeless, dead to the world. This is not to say you will not derive benefit from being at Teotihuacan; you will, especially as since 1992 it has started to come back "on line."

LANDSCAPE ZODIAC: The Landscape Zodiac here is about six miles wide, centered on the area of the Pyramid of the Moon and the unnamed platform in front of it. The Oroboros Line enters the Teotihuacan complex diagonally to the Avenue of the Dead and passes through the platform and the land several hundred feet on either side.

The zodiac half that includes the Pyramid of the Sun corresponds to the physical ecliptic, or that half that includes the Northern Hemisphere stars, and the half on the other side corresponds to the etheric ecliptic, and stars of the Southern Hemisphere. The zodiac dome is fifteen miles across and imparts a concentrated energy field over this landscape in addition to the effect provided by the numerous domes from the Tenochtitlan and Cerro Gordo domes.

IXION'S WHEEL: There are many geomantic structures along the Avenue of the Dead, but I will only touch on a few, starting with the Temple of the Feathered Serpent at La Ciudadela. This is an initiatory structure that may appear to you as a golden sarcophagus set next to a giant vertical Sun disk; or you may see it as a slowly spinning golden wheel with many spokes.

The Ixion's Wheel is an initiation chamber for candidates in preparation for infusion and embodiment of the Solar Logos, the inner essence or Heart of the Sun. You could say that the Ixion's Wheel is where the god is born, that is, where the human candidate for initiation and higher evolution takes his first step in the alchemical process of transformation.

POINTER'S BALL: The unnamed but important platform before the Pyramid of the Moon is the site of a Pointer's Ball, a crack between the worlds. This Ball appears initially as a translucent pearl perhaps one hundred feet in diameter, and

seems fixed on a particular interdimensional setting. If you pass through it, you find yourself in a foreign olive green landscape: this is somewhere in the Pleiades, on a planet associated with one of the seven stars.

The Ball acts as a bleed-through portal for Pleiadian energies and influences, and for what appears to be a Pleiadian deity. It is as if the Ball now appears to be the head of a god or a highly evolved being, and it emanates a large pale green nimbus around the head that fills the width of the Avenue.

GOLDEN EGG: The Pyramid of the Sun is the site of a "hatched" and fulfilled Golden Egg containing the Christ Child, or Christ consciousness. The Madonna aspect of this egg is situated at Cerro Gordo, its geomantic arms reaching out on both sides of the Avenue to envelop and nurture the newborn Christ awareness.

PALLADIUM: Part of the culmination of making the God connection in the Islands of the God is through the Palladium within the Pyramid of the Moon. This is a miniature Crown of the Ancient of Days, which is one way of depicting what the Qabalists call the Vast White Countenance of the Supreme Being. It is like a sculpted white marble head laid horizontal on a pedestal; its eyes flash beams of light in all directions simultaneously, seeing and irradiating everything.

LABYRINTH: At first glance, the energy structure at Cerro Gordo is like a shallow concave dish, a mirror filled with points of light or stars, into which comes a vertical data stream of light and information from above. The data stream is the core of the labyrinth known as the Hall of Records, an archival facility for cosmic information and light codings. The dish-mirror full of stars is another way of representing the labyrinth present here. It is a structure mapped within Earth's neural pathways and the human brain, and it is usually underneath the twelve major domes of the planet.

This labyrinth is one of nine different types found within the Earth geomantic body; another type is found at Mount Ida in Crete and is known as the Cretan labyrinth; one like Cerro Gordo's is found at Easter Island in the Pacific Ocean and Clingman's Dome in Tennessee (both described elsewhere in this book). You walk the energy labyrinth inside the dome to get your psychic and cognitive centers in resonance with the energy field of the labyrinth and the Hall of Records at its center. The Hall of Records holds stellar and universal influences and light codings that have been transmitted to this site over the duration of the existence of the Earth.

LUCIFER BINDING SITE: Let's recap one aspect of the purpose of this vast temple. You have the opportunity here of energizing the fire and wisdom within the solar plexus after having stimulated the heart center at other sites, such as Glastonbury in England (the planet's prime outer heart chakra), or any other site with a heart chakra affiliation at any level.

Ideally, you start at Tenochtitlan in Mexico City, then approach the Teotihuacan complex overland, as much in a straight line as possible. Then as a candidate for initiation at Teotihuacan immerse yourself in the golden vat of Ixion's Wheel at La Ciudadela, then slowly walk up the Tree of Life, experiencing and assimilating the energies at each temple, each Island of the God, on the way. Take a week if you can, or longer. The Avenue may be only a mile or so long, but its templic energy hierarchy is rich and intense.

You walk the Avenue, as if progressively reborn as a god, the spirit half of your being ever more ascendant as you proceed. In a sense you walk up the Tree of Life as a hologram of Quetzalcoatl, the Mayan Lord of Light, as you prepare to encounter and perhaps return to the Father, the source of all Light. As you walk, you molt, dropping the inessential, purging, cleansing, clarifying.

At the Temple of the Quetzal Butterfly, the molting is completed. You have a chance to depart this dimension entirely. The inner, visionary aspect of this temple is like a jade-lined cubic performance room for the butterfly dance, much bigger than its physical counterpart. This is the emerald, the Heart within the Heart chakra, the secret electromagnetic doorway in every human to the right of the sternum. It is part of the arcana of Teotihuacan, and the chief Mystery is the identity of the possessor of the original and only emerald of which all others are copies.

You may observe Mayan women dancing, dressed in a riot of colors with broad wings of silk hanging from their arms, like human butterflies. Why butterflies? The butterfly is a guardian or mythical aspect of human consciousness that guards the door to the psychic. When you access that realm, then your experience of the Lord of Light or Quetzalcoatl becomes manifest. In the midst of the dancing women and like a god emerging amidst his votaries, appears Quetzalcoatl himself, vibrant in angelic splendor, plumed in angels. It is his emerald, his special temple at Teotihuacan—and your emerald, his gift to you.

He has a sword of light, and if you wish he will initiate you with it, cleaving your bodies, filling you with blazing light. You may observe that he similarly irradiates the entire Avenue of the Dead and all its temples. Quetzalcoatl brings all the emeralds to a new state of refinement as preparation for the immediate awakening of the next phase in the planet's unfolding.

The qualities just extolled portray a Lucifer Binding Site in its positive aspect—Lucifer, Lord of Light, who is the same as Quetzalcoatl, the Plumed Serpent, perpetually arriving in glory, unbound, unfettered, unrepudiated, free and illuminative.

Tetford, England

Tetford is an unassuming village in the Lincolnshire Wolds about three hours drive north of London. Located some twenty miles east of Lincoln (a medium-size city with an impressive Gothic-style cathedral), Tetford is one of many tiny towns, villages, and hamlets tucked into the undulating folds of the Lincolnshire landscape. Most of the surrounding landscape is taken up with farming; the area, while charming and visually engaging, is not particularly known as a tourist destination nor does it have any overt new-age or sacred site associations. The village is bounded by a ring road, while a smaller loop includes a section called Little London, formerly the village's vicarage.

The next village overland, called Somersby, which is even smaller, is noted as the birthplace and childhood residence of the nineteenth-century British poet Alfred Lord Tennyson. Local legend has it that the Celtic kings chose the Tetford hills, especially the one known as Bluestone Heath, as their preferred burial sites; later, the Romans and Vikings established roadways through the Tetford area and left some archeological traces of their presence.

Since the late 1980s, Tetford has been home to Aura-Soma Color Products and the Aura-Soma International Academy of Colour Therapeutics, two aspects of a company that produces topical color products for healing, sponsors international seminars, supports an extensive biodynamic agricultural initiative, and hosts workshops in Earth mysteries.[762] Why is this going on in Tetford?

GEOMANTIC

Dome; Golden Egg; Silver Egg; Mount Olympus; Tree of Life; Lily; Palladium; Gnome Egg; Dragon; Grail Castle; Stargate; Soma Temple.

AQUARIAN MYSTERY TEMPLE: The broadest way to summarize the astonishing array of geomantic features present at Tetford is to say that it is an Aquarian Mystery temple on the verge of coming into its own. Think of the Earth's thousands of sacred sites as alarm clocks, each set to ring at a prearranged time. Some rang long ago and are today but archeological ruins, or rumors in ancient histories; others, like Rome and Florence, rang more recently in history; and some, like Tetford, are set to ring in this century.

It may seem that as if overnight an inconsequential Lincolnshire village becomes a geomythic prodigy, but all the geomantic features newly discovered there were templated at the inception of the planet, according to the same master plan that accounted for the placement of the Giza pyramids, the Avebury monuments, even the volcanoes. Now the Tetford geomantic package is being unwrapped and recognized for our time.

DOME: Tetford is an Aquarian Mystery temple for a literal reason: The 4.3-mile-wide dome arching over the village and its environs represents the planetary presence of the alpha star in the constellation of Aquarius, Sadalmelik. This star name from *Al Sa'd al Malik* means "the Lucky One of the King"; it is eleven hundred light years from Earth and its diameter is eighty times that of our Sun. As a constellation, the figure of Aquarius is traditionally represented as a cup-bearer of the gods pouring out a stream of water or nectar from an inverted jar—the Water Carrier, in short. Sometimes the constellation is referred to simply as the Water Jar.

Here it is helpful to think of "water" as consciousness, light, and insight provided—poured down—from above. Aquarius is sometimes identified with Deucalion (the Greek version of Noah), son of the Titan Prometheus and sole survivor of the Flood (see the discussion of Grail Castles in part 2).

Alternatively, Aquarius may represent Ganymede, the beautiful youth who was Zeus' favorite and who, while tending his father's sheep on Mount Ida, was transported into the heavens to become the gods' immortal wine-pourer at Mount Olympus. Sadalmelik and Aquarius' second brightest and beta star, Sadalsuud, sit respectively on the right and left shoulders of the figure like epaulets. As a whole the constellation is said to have seventeen stars comprising the figure and thirty-two making up the stream of water.

The brightest star in the constellation that is slated to be the prime influence in the next twenty-one hundred years of Earth's history is resident, holographically, over this little Lincolnshire village and, through its forty-eight dome caps, over its numerous parish churches. The Tetford dome, incidentally, is one of the relatively few that are situated on level ground rather than mountains. In the case of Tetford, the Sadalmelik dome energizes a complex temple array and is part of an even larger temple setup that includes the nearby city of Lincoln, which also has a dome.

The Lincoln dome corresponds to *Sadalsuud,* from *Al Sa'd al Su'ud,* meaning "Luckiest of the Lucky." Along the Euphrates River (in ancient Iraq) this star (it's 1,030 light years from Earth) was known as *Kakkab Namma,* "Star of Mighty Destiny"; its name is also given as *Fortuna Fortunarum,* signifiying its heliacal rising at the start of the spring rainy season. The two Aquarian domes are linked by a straight-running dome line, and between them they generate ninety-six dome caps.

The two brightest stars in Aquarius present in the Lincoln and Tetford "endomed" areas suggest that significant spiritual light is pouring into this geomantically prepared landscape—as it were, nectar straight from the gods' table at Mount Olympus. It is a reasonable assumption that as the Aquarian Age gains traction in our world and solar system, the incoming Aquarian stream will intensify and in part enter the Earth through the Tetford and Lincoln domes and their affiliated dome caps.

An unsubstantiated rumor, apparently first put forth by British clairvoyants, says that at some future date when London gets flooded or perhaps too waterlogged from the rising sea level, the English seat of government may shift northward to Lincoln.

GOLDEN EGG: The Golden Egg in Tetford is a landscape feature about nine miles long that begins at Bag Enderby and culminates at Maidenwell. Both are small villages on either side of Tetford on an approximately south-north axis. The church at Bag Enderby is the grounding point, the place of emergence, the egg cup, if you will, for the Golden Egg, as well as its nutrient support or albumin; it is an entry point for the Underworld. Bag Enderby—admittedly a name straight out of J. R. R. Tolkien—is a swinging door: in one direction, you leave this world and enter the Underworld; in the other direction, you emerge into this world at the Golden Egg.

Somersby, a few miles away, is the vagina or mandorla out of which the egg is extruded; then, like a single pea in an open pod, the Golden Egg rests as a huge globe of golden light in the intervening space (privately owned fields called Holywell Plantation, New England, and Blackhill Plantation) between Somersby and Tetford. In the fields, near a place described on the topographic map as Blackhill spring, is a doorway into Shambhala and the Celestial City known as Vibhavari, the domain of Varuna, Lord of the West. Like the Underworld entrance at Bag Enderby, the Shambhala doorway here is another door out of the geomantic temple.

Meanwhile, the Higher Self reborn as the divine child (or the golden child, or the Christ child—different names for the same stage in consciousness) emerges out of the Golden Egg, its head, or crown, situated at Tetford. This name, in part, means the ford or crossing-over point; in this case, the place where consciousness at the crown chakra passes upwards into a more exalted, rarefied realm at Maidenwell; the prime location of this feature above the crown is about a mile west of the actual village.

Maidenwell is the landscape node in this geomythic figure where the love of the Mother envelops and nurtures the newborn Aquarian Christ child; Her arms reach down to Bag Enderby to enfold the divine child in her loving embrace. The well of her maternal regard is endless and eternal; the Madonna is always nourishing the child. The newborn consciousness can depend on a continuous supply of "water" from the Maiden's well.

Lest we forget the purpose of this elegant geomythic setup, the Tetford Golden Egg exists to model, mirror, and facilitate the birth of the Christ Child as a born-again spiritual consciousness within each of us. Walking this Golden Egg geomythic axis from Bag Enderby to Maidenwell[763] is an excellent way to be in resonance with an outer expression of an inner process. It helps one to birth the divine child within, an event both central to the mysteries of the Holy Grail and central to many spiritual traditions worldwide.

SILVER EGG: The Silver Egg is situated approximately at Salmonby, which is a mile southwest of Tetford and is one of the Tetford's dome caps. (Bag Enderby, Somersby, and Maidenwell are also dome caps.) The guardian that emerges from the Silver Egg when it is hatched (this Egg was hatched in the mid-1990s) is variously called Horus, and Garuda, and it guards the entrance into Mount Olympus, the city of the gods and specifically, of the fourteen Ray Masters associated with Ursa Major.

MOUNT OLYMPUS: While it resides in another dimension or level of reality from the physical, the Tetford Mount Olympus is situated approximately in the same place as the village itself, as bounded by the ring road. Geomythically, the Tetford Mount Olympus sits upon the crown of the Golden Child and thereby affords the newborn Christ consciousness awakened in the landscape figure constant input from the celestial hierarchy that works through the Great Bear to direct planetary affairs.[764]

In accordance with the myth of Aquarius, you could say that due to the juxtaposition of the Mount Olympus upon the crown of the divine child born of the Tetford Golden Egg, this village enjoys a continuous flow of the nectar or divine water from the table of the gods. The fourteen Ray Masters form a chromatic crown on the head of the divine child. The Tetford dome additionally is the current planetary focus of the Solar Logos, a certain concentrated "beam" of consciousness emanating from the heart of the solar system—mythologically speaking, from the once and future King Arthur.

TREE OF LIFE: Within Little London and on the grounds of Dev Aura, the residential facility and gardens owned and operated by Aura-Soma International Academy of Colour Therapeutics, are two additional landscape energy features. First is a small Tree of Life template occupying a portion of an acre and overlaid with a garden divided into four parts behind the Dev Aura buildings. The physical garden was designed by Mike Booth, owner of Aura-Soma, in accordance with the pre-existing energy matrix of the landscape. This small Tree of Life is perfectly suited for interactive and experiential training in the hierarchical flow of energies and as a preparation grounds for encountering the more complex landscape mysteries, such as the Golden Egg, elsewhere in the Tetford area.

LILY: Second, underlying the Dev Aura property is a white lily approximately an acre in size. These are fairly rare on the planet and are the product of purified consciousness; they are created largely through the interaction of human consciousness with the angelic realm in a geomantically prepared landscape. The results of purified consciousness at a site take the form of a white lily expressed as a light form.

PALLADIUM: At the crest of the neighboring hill, locally referred to as Tetford Hill, over the top of which runs Bluestone Heath Road—presumably this is the hill in which the Celtic kings were interred—sits a Palladium, a miniature Crown of the Ancient of Days. Down Tetford Hill and intersecting with the Tree of Life at Dev Aura flows a second, larger Tree of Life template.

The combination of Palladium and Tree of Life would explain the local legend of the Celtic kings insisting on burial in this hill. Functionally, the geomancy would be similar to Golgotha, the Hill of Skulls in Jerusalem, externally a place of thousands of skulls and thus many human deaths, but interiorly, an excellent place for ascension into the consciousness of the Ancient of Days. His Head marks the spot and serves as a temple door into the highest spiritual mysteries.

GNOME EGG: These numerous geomythic features require regular input from humans and maintenance from the elemental kingdom of Nature spirits, so it is not surprising to find a large Gnome Egg a few miles overland from Tetford. This egg is situated in a small copse in a hamlet called Worlaby; several hills coincide and the "creases" between them flow down to the woods; a small chapel in Worlaby is oriented towards the copse as well. This Gnome Egg has been dormant for many centuries and unrecognized by humans living in the area. It is currently being repopulated with gnomes in anticipation of a new phase of human-landscape interaction.

Often Gnome Eggs are situated with respect to landscape dragons, and we find one of the 1,053 minor dragons at Walmsgate whose name itself is a clue: the Gate of the Walm, which is an old English word for "worm," as in dragon. Walmsgate today is the privately owned site of the ruins of a medieval village and its vanished church; all that remains are two long raised mounds of earth, like two index fingers under the ground. This marks the dragon's gate.

DRAGON: The Walmsgate dragon guards the northeastern entrance into the Tetford temple and its "roar" echoes throughout the dome. In a geomythic sense, all of the Tetford dome and its geomantic temple reside within the Walmsgate dragon, itself under one of the Tetford dome's largest dome caps.

GRAIL CASTLE: About ten miles southeast of Tetford is the old Roman town of Horncastle, now a flourishing market and services town for this end of the Wolds. This town's name is suggestive of its geomantic use: the Horn to the

Castle. The castle in this case is a Grail Castle, situated "above" the town, which is to say, in a more rarefied dimension of the astral world (as opposed to *in* the astral world but overlaid horizontally on the ground, as with the Gnome Egg and dragon). You climb the horn to the castle; or, if you wish to get really mythic about it, climb the unicorn and ascend through its clairvoyance up the horn of insight into the castle of deep cosmic memory.

STARGATE: Mention was made earlier about the preference for Celtic kings to be buried in the hills around Tetford. There is a remarkable reason for that. Occupying an approximately five-mile stretch of the Bluestone Heath Road, which runs along the top of the ridge behind Tetford, is a unique eight-star stargate atop a massive blue dragon, its wings monumentally flared out across the landscape. This feature also has visual or structural qualities suggestive of a massive seafaring ship and a classical chariot with golden cupola.

It is unique because this is the only stargate complex on Earth with eight stargates; it is especially notable on account of the identity of these eight stargates. The stars or constellation represented here include Sirius, Canopus, Arcturus, Orion, Cepheus, Cygnus, Ursa Major, and the Pleiades. These stars and constellations have had (and still do) a pivotal role in the Earth's energy body and the evolution of human consciousness within the Earth's geomantic matrix. They are the eight stars underlying the Camalate Center and its function in the Earth's geomantic matrix (see part 2, Camalate Center).

Though it is beyond the scope of this book to adequately explain this feature, it can be mentioned here that the eight stargates at Tetford are arranged in such a way as to make a map of the spatial and functional relationships of seven solar systems (including ours), their fifty-four planets, and their suns with the constellation of the Great Bear.

SOMA TEMPLE: The Soma Temple in the Tetford geomythic landscape is located at the base of Warden Hill, near the hamlet of Bag Enderby a few miles from Tetford center. At the time of our discovery of this Soma Temple (it was coincident with the discovery of the stargates on Bluestone Heath), this temple was disconnected from the blue dragon feature on Bluestone Heath Road. In linking the Soma Temple with the blue dragon carrying the stargates, you can see vividly how mythic description and occult perception often run parallel.

To psychic perception, it seemed as if the blue dragon had extended its tongue out for miles, searching for something to eat or drink. The gnomes, who are the elemental spirits charged with helping to maintain geomantic features, were unable to do anything about this because they were awaiting instructions from on high (from the human realm) as to how to feed the dragon. The humans, until the discovery of the dragon and Soma Temple and sufficient elucidation of the situation by the angelic realm, had no instructions to pass on.

What does a dragon eat or drink? Soma, the drink of immortality, much favored by the gods in Hindu myth. Svarbhanu the dragon desires Soma, which the gods have just dredged up from the Ocean of Milk; in the myth, the gods do everything they can to deprive Svarbhanu of this drink. However, the myth is wrong, or shall we say, inverted. The gods commission humans to help the dragon have a drink of Soma so as to sustain its life. Yet there's another inversion.

The gods actually *depend* on the dragon for the Soma because it is the dragon's blood, its essence. The dragon is older than the gods, antecedent to their realm of existence; it *is* the state of unbroken continuity of consciousness from before the Uncreated Light was differentiated into the multiplicity of forms of light, in the form of the stars and star gods.

It isn't so much that the blue dragon on Bluestone Heath outside Tetford needs a drink of Soma to survive; rather, it needs to be *reminded* of its ultimate essence, to see itself reflected back out of the heady fumes of the Soma vat. This is the nourishment for which its parched tongue has been seeking over the many centuries since this feature was last recognized and maintained by humans.

Similarly, we benefit in the same way as Svarbhanu by visiting the Soma temple. There we have the potential to remember a primordial state of consciousness, to reenter the stream of unbroken, undifferentiated awareness—the dragon's realm. Geomantically speaking, since March 2002, the dragon bearing the eight stargates has had its revivifying draught of Soma and now the gnomes can fulfill their responsibilities in maintaining the Bluestone Heath dragon.

The various geomantic features within the Tetford Aquarian dome operate in the larger context of this dome's energy relations with the Lincoln dome. Present within the Lincoln city limits and dome diameter are a small Landscape Zodiac (about five miles in diameter) and a Cosmic Egg/cosmic mountain at Steep Hill which is crowned by the eleventh-century Lincoln Cathedral (officially known as the Cathedral Church of the Blessed Virgin Mary), which is visible from thirty miles away.

HOW TO USE THIS TEMPLE: Here is a brief summary of some aspects of how the two domed temples work together: In geomythic terms, you take the deep cosmic memory attained at the Grail Castle and the Christed divine child informed by the fourteen Ray Masters and infused by the Solar

Logos to the Lincoln Albion, which is the consummation of the miniature galaxy expressed there as a Landscape Zodiac.

As it were, you take the reborn human consciousness—Christed as the golden child—at Tetford to the Old Adam, the original human consciousness template (Albion, as the completed zodiac) at Lincoln, and transmit this fresh energy and consciousness to Albion. Then you ascend the cosmic mountain at Steep Hill and pass out of this world into the exalted spiritual realm that lies even beyond the planetary spheres.

But the end is also the beginning. At the Cosmic Egg at Steep Hill you collect your "personal" Cosmic Egg and seed of immutable fire from the Great Stream of Oceanos and take it back to the Tetford temple (and the Golden Child especially) to nurture and grow into a divine child, born within. Then you visit all the other landscape features of Tetford and return to Lincoln for the culmination.

From the outside, this probably sounds uncomfortably mythic or simply too abstract; but from the inside, once you touch some of these energies, it starts to gain reality and credibility. Obviously this is not an initiation you are likely to complete in a weekend, or even a year; each step requires assimilation and adjustment time.

In many respects, you will be following an ancient, if not archetypal path of initiation, yet because the Tetford and Lincoln energy features are under the influence of Aquarius, you will be undertaking these stages in the most spiritually contemporary and astrologically relevant of geomantic environments.

Thebes, Greece

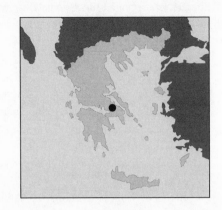

Thebes, today a small city called Thivai northwest of Athens in central Greece, doesn't get the attention from sacred sites tourists that it ought to. It's not on the standard itineraries, but should be. Once, things were different. As classical scholar Carl Kerenyi remarked some years ago, "There is no city in Greece, outside Mycenae, which had gathered together so many legends of heroes on its site and in its neighborhood as Thebes," and no hero from classical times was so honored as its legendary founder, Cadmos.[765]

Not only did Cadmos make his mark here, but Thebes' human dramas provided the raw material for much of classical tragedy. The blind seer Tiresias, the patricidal Oedipus, and all his warring, conflicted descendants, including Antigone and other figures immortalized by Aeschylus, Sophocles, and Euripides, all lived in Thebes. The orgiastic, frenzied Olympian Dionysus was born here as was the glory of Hera and master of the Twelve Labors, Heracles.

Most of Thebes' former architectural glory is now gone, built over by modern Thivai. However, a few structures or parts of them are extant. These include traces of the palace of Kamos, his citadel on the hill in Thivai, dating back to the fourteenth century B.C., and once called the Cadmeia. Some evidence still remains of the Temple of Apollo Ismenios on a pine-covered hill on the edge of town; Apollo's oracular seat, the Ismenion, lay due southwest of Cadmeia and was named after the River Ismenos, and the original Ismenos spring was called Melia, after a river nymph who lived there. Traces of one of the seven original gates of Thebes—the Electran Gate—are still observable in modern Thivai.

HISTORY AND ARCHEOLOGY

Archeologists propose that occupation of Thebes first began in Neolithic times and was well established in the Early Helladic period, 3000–2000 B.C., and that the city reached its height of influence in the Mycenaean period, 1600–1100 B.C. There was even a brief time (371–362 B.C.) when it enjoyed military hegemony over all of Greece. After its near total destruction by the Macedons in 335 B.C., however, Thebes never regained its stature.

Thebes existed in ambivalent relationship with its rival Hellenic power, Athens. During the Persian Wars (480–479 B.C.), Thebes sided with the Persians, and when they lost, it was only

Sparta that prevented the Athenians from destroying Thebes as punishment for their treachery. During the Peloponnesian War, which began in 431 B.C., Thebes sided with Sparta and was eager for Athens' destruction, but it lost heart, and in 394 B.C., entered an alliance with Athens against Sparta. In 335 B.C., Alexander the Great leveled Thebes and sold its population into slavery. Although the city was rebuilt in 315 B.C., it was finished as a Greek power and never regained its power and prestige.

Archeological excavations in Thivai were conducted between 1906 and 1929 by a Greek researcher named A. Keramopoullos, who uncovered some of the remains of the Cadmeia; further excavations in the 1960s and 1990s yielded clay tablets and a monumental chamber tomb attributed to the sons of King Oedipus.

MYTH AND LEGEND

The disparity between Thebes' original mythic resume and its contemporary reputation is astonishing. Other than among classicists, it's as if Thebes has been discarded as a player in Earth's visionary landscape. Thebes, wrote Sophocles, "where wild Bacchic women are at home,/on the soil of the dragon seed."[766]

Most writers from antiquity, notably Pausanias, Apollodorus, and Ovid, report that Thebes was founded by the hero Cadmus. Presumably Cadmus was a human of human parents; he was the son of Agenor (a Phoenician king of Tyre, in today's Syria) and the brother of Europa, whom Zeus in the form of a white bull took to Crete as his lover. Europa's abduction led to the founding of Thebes, for King Agenor dispatched his sons, including Cadmus, to trek all over Europe until they found Europa. Finally, Cadmus sought psychic counsel from the oracle at Delphi. As befits an oracle, the answer was a curve-ball.

Forget Europa, the oracle declared; instead find a cow that has never been yoked into service of men and has the form of a full moon on each of its flanks, and follow it tirelessly. Wherever it stops, there found a new city to be called Thebes in a land to be called Boeotia (which means "Cow-land"). Cadmus followed the cow, which eventually collapsed near the River Asopus on the site of Thebes.

Cadmus was about to sacrifice the cow to the goddess Pallas Athena. He sent his companions to draw fresh water from the spring of Ares, the war god of Olympus. Guarding the spring was a dragon who regarded the spring from the mouth of its cave. As Ovid vividly describes it,[767] the huge "snake of Mars," with its crest of shining gold, its "eyes flashing fire," its body "big with venom," its triple rows of teeth gleaming, its three-forked tongue flickering, and its breath putrid with death-dealing poison, killed all of Cadmus' men. Indignant, Cadmus then slew the dragon with an iron javelin that pierced its spine, though some accounts say he used a large stone instead.

Pallas Athena glided down out of the sky and advised Cadmus to plow the soil and sow the dragon's teeth like seed. Out of these stone seeds, a new race of humans would arise, called *Spartoi*, which means "Sown Men." They became famous as the "golden-helmed seed." First the tips of spears arose from the plowed soil, then helmets, shoulders, "weapon-laden arms," and finally the full bodies of many men in mail, "an Earth-born regiment."

Intimidated by their numbers and concerned that they would turn on him once they opened their eyes, Cadmus threw some stones in their midst; that got them fighting among themselves, and soon all were killed except five. Their names are intriguing, veiling mysteries: Udaios (man of the ground); Chthonios (man of the Earth); Pelor (giant); Hyperenor (more than man); and Echion (serpent-man).

These five Spartoi became Cadmus' companions in his founding of the Cadmeia, also the original name for Thebes. In fact, the legend says these five surviving Spartoi were the progenitors of Thebes' ruling family. Afterwards as Cadmus' city grew, his Cadmeia became the acropolis for the settlement of Thebes below, much like the Acropolis in Athens.

However, Cadmus, to atone for the slaughter of Ares' dragon, had to serve the god Ares for "an eternal year" (a Greek time notation meaning eight years, equivalent to the penalty of banishment for homicide).[768] For Cadmus, the best was yet to come. After his atonement, Zeus awarded him Harmonia to be his wife; she was a divine being, the daughter of Ares and Aphrodite, both members of Zeus' Olympian pantheon. Another tradition says her father was Zeus and her mother Electra, daughter of the Titan Atlas and one of the Pleiads.

All the gods attended the wedding of Cadmus and Harmonia at Thebes. There was feasting and music in the Cadmeia as this marriage—said to be the first human marriage—was an unprecedented occasion for the mingling of gods with humans. Even the august Nine Muses performed their wonderful music at the wedding. The bridal couple was borne in a wedding procession in which a boar and lion were yoked to their carriage, alongside of which walked Apollo accompanied by his singing Muses.

An Italian interpreter of Greek myths, Roberto Calasso, comments: "Zeus walked the streets of Thebes. He liked the town. It reminded him of the heavens. It was like a dance floor."[769]

One child produced by this marriage was Semele, who, with Zeus, produced Dionysus, who was born at the Cadmeia. Semele perished while pregnant. Hera had suggested that Semele's divine lover had not been Zeus but an impostor, so Semele asked Zeus to appear before her in his true celestial guise. Reluctantly he did, and his light was so radiant—some say he came as a lightning bolt—that it incinerated her, but at the same time, rendered her fetus (which had been rescued by Hermes) immortal. It's said that Semele's tomb smoldered for years afterwards.

In later years, Thebes was renowned as a prime site of the Dionysus (Roman: Bacchus) cult, with its center in the very palace in which Zeus had conceived Dionysus upon Semele. In fact, when Pentheus, son of "Sown Man" Echion, was king of Thebes, he actively opposed Dionysian ceremonies (including the Bacchanalia) both in Thebes and in the surrounding landscape, such as atop nearby Mount Kithairon.

This attribution was dramatized by Euripides in his tragedy *The Bacchae*. This city, first in Greece, Dionysus announces, "now shrills and echoes to my women's cries,/their ecstasy of joy."[770] However, maybe Pentheus was really Dionysus in disguise, suggests one scholar: it is possible that Dionysus' cult itself made Pentheus "into the name of a punished enemy of god, who nevertheless in his suffering remained so close to the god as to represent him."[771]

During his tenure as king, Cadmus, said to have come originally from the Phoenicians, introduced a new form of writing using Phoenician letters, from which the Greek alphabet later emerged. Years later, when Cadmus and Harmonia retired, they left Thebes in a carriage drawn by calves, and at the harbor town of Buthoe (now called Budva) or near Copais in Boeotia, they left the Earth; they were then transported to the Islands of the Blessed or were turned into serpents, depending on which ancient writer you consult.

In antiquity, Thebes was known for its seven gates, each of which was named and each of which admitted passage into Thebes through the encircling protective wall. Pausanias, visiting Thebes in the second century A.D., tells us the names of the gates: the Elektran gate, named after

Elektra, Cadmus' sister (facing southeast); the Proitian gate, named after a local man called Proitos (facing east); the Nestian gate (west), "named after the last lyre-string, the *netes,* which they say Amphion invented at these gates"; the Spring gate (southwest); the High gate (south, next to a sanctuary to Zeus); the Ogygian gate (facing northeast, said to be the oldest); and the Homoloides gate (the newest, facing north).[772]

But who built the seven gates of Thebes? Not Cadmus, say the ancients. Rather, the twin god sons, Amphion and Zethus, were "the first to build the footings of seven-gated Thebes" and its bastions and ramparts because "none could live/in a place so vast, so open" without them, explained Homer.[773] Amphion and Zethus were known as the Theban *Dioskuroi,* the divine twins.

Their father was Zeus and their mother Antiope, a beautiful but mortal woman (although she might have been a wandering divine woman). Born in a cave on sacred Mouth Kithairon (the peak teeming with Dionysian maenads and intoxicated cultic followers), they were similar (or equivalent) to Castor and Pollux, the two celestial brothers who comprise the Gemini constellation, and they were not dissimilar to the Biblical Cain and Abel.

Kerenyi, interpreting the Theban mythic cycle, offers this astonishing observation: "String music, the notes of Amphion's lyre, first made the walls of Thebes, the city between the two rivers, arise."[774] As things turned out, Zethus would protect Thebes while Amphion offered hymns to the gods. But it was Amphion's lyre-playing and his songs that set the stones in motion, making Thebes a fortified citadel as if overnight.

"The moving stones arranged themselves at the notes of the lyre into a wall with seven gates," says Kerenyi, adding that there were seven gates probably because of the seven strings in the lyre. This was the basis of the harmony in the foundations of the Cadmeia. The myth says that Cadmus put Harmonia's bed in the very center of his city, which he modeled on the geometry of the heavens. Even more impressive, the seven gates of his city "were laid out to correspond to the seven heavens, and each one was dedicated to a god."[775]

Even this lengthy recitation does not exhaust the myths accruing to Thebes. The birth of Thebes' homegrown hero, Heracles, was tied up with a vixen. Thebes was plagued by a fox that haunted Mount Teumessos about five miles away; this site (called Mesovouno today) was said to be where Zeus hid Europa. Another story says that the fox was the result of Dionysus' curse for the extermination of the people of Thebes. This fox ran so fast that it could not be caught, and it carried off what it liked from the town. The vixen was a brute, said Apollodorus, and was ravaging the Cadmeia.

As an attempt at appeasement, once a month, the Thebans exposed a male child as sacrifice for the Teumessian vixen, hoping to persuade the beast to spare them. Amphitryon, Heracles legal father, secured the services of a magical hound from King Minos of Crete, which had been a gift from Zeus to Europa, Cadmus' sister. This hound ran so fast nobody could catch it, so Amphitryon's logic was to let the hound catch the fox. Zeus had other ideas, however, and as the two fleet-footed beasts raced across the Theban plains, he turned them both to stone.

Later, Zeus meddled even further in Amphitryon's affairs. On his wedding night with Alkmene, Zeus impersonated Amphitryon and consummated the marriage on his terms. In fact, so in charge of things was Zeus on that nuptial night that it lasted three times longer than a normal night. Heracles, when he was born of this union, the son of Zeus and a mortal human woman, was called *triselenos,* the child of the triple Moon.

The Teumessian vixen was not the only semi-magical beast to harass Thebes. In the time of

Oedipus, soon-to-be King of Thebes, the city was beleaguered by a sphinx dwelling on Mount Phicium (today's Mount Phaga, Sphinx Mountain).[776] This was a magical (or infernal) creature with the face of a human woman, the chest, feet, and tail of a lion, and the wings of a bird. The Nine Muses had instructed the sphinx in divine riddles and it perched atop Mount Phicium harassing the passersby with seemingly unanswerable word puzzles.

The sphinx would also come into the Cadmeia and pose the same threat. When a person was unable to answer correctly, the sphinx ate them. One version of the story says that the Thebans would gather every day to try to crack the riddle that the sphinx kept repeating because no one could get the answer. The sphinx's question was: What creature on Earth goes two-footed, four-footed, and three-footed under the same name so that its speed is the slowest when it uses the most feet? Oedipus penetrated the sphinx's riddle and declared the correct answer was "a human being," explaining that a baby crawls on all fours, an adult stands on two legs, and an old person uses a cane, making three legs. The sphinx, defeated, left the citadel.

Oedipus claimed the kingship of Thebes as a reward. When the city suffered a plague, the oracle of Delphi said it was tainted from within, and this, of course, was as a result of Oedipus' own moral transgressions, having killed his father (King Laius of Thebes) and bedded his mother. "Your own eyes/Must tell you: Thebes is tossed on a murdering sea/And cannot lift her head from the death surge," said the Theban priest to Oedipus before he found out that he was the cause of this death surge. "And all the house of Kadmos is laid waste/All emptied and darkened."[777]

Thebes was miserable with death, and even after Oedipus' awakening to his complicity in its travails, things didn't get better. In later years, civil war ensued among Oedipus' sons, and they unsuccessfully attacked the city, six of them perishing, as dramatized by Aeschylus in *Seven Against Thebes*.

GEOMANTIC

Dome Cap; Cyclopean City; Dragon; Ray Master Sanctuary; Shambhala Doorway; Golden Pillars; Silver Egg.

DOME CAP: The dome cap over Thebes comes from Mount Kithairon, whose dome corresponds to the star Wezen, which is delta Canis Major, the Dog. There is also a dome cap over nearby Mount Hypatos from the same dome source. *Al Wazn* means "the Weight" and is about twenty-one hundred light years from Earth. It is as luminous as sixty thousand of our Suns. Within the Dog constellation, it occupies the position of the celestial canine's root chakra; Sirius, the brightest star in our galaxy, lies at the Dog's throat. Wezen is the hound turned to stone by Zeus—in this case, into a mountain.

The legend of the sphinx on Mount Phicium refers to an astral sphinx still present and functioning as a guardian to a dimensional doorway present at Thebes. Its perplexing riddle was a test for initiates, asking if they could recognize what is truly human: in other words, the sphinx's question was an assessment of the initiate's own degree of self-knowledge, a condition necessary to penetrate further into the Mystery temple. Are you *human*? Do you *know* yourself? Are you *aware* of your existence as a human? If so, you may pass.

People who failed to answer the riddle didn't die; rather, they were not allowed spiritual passage into the etheric temple marked by the physical structures at the Cadmeia. In this sense, the sphinx on Mount Phicium served the same protective, selective purpose as the monumental Sphinx before the pyramids at Giza. Think of the sphinx as an early form of gargoyle: a scary and hideous denizen of the night that guards churches against the impious and demonic.

CYCLOPEAN CITY: As with Mycenae in Greece and Troy in Turkey, we find that some of the oldest Greek myths are set in Cyclopean Cities. With Thebes, we must credit as true the seemingly fanciful account of Amphion's lyre creating the walls and gates of Thebes, that he ordered the massive stones into place merely by plucking the strings of his lyre. The presence of a Cyclopean City at Thebes—in fact, as the essence and core of Thebes when it was conceived as a geomantic node—provides a pre-energized, numinous, even exalted context for all the other geomantic features and mythic events attributed to this site.

DRAGON: The "snake of Mars" that Cadmus killed was one of the eighty-one subsidiary dragons generated by the thirteen primary dragons on Earth. In this case, the mother dragon was the one at Delphi, some hundred miles to the southwest. It is appropriate that Cadmus proceeded from Delphi to Thebes, from mother dragon to child dragon, as it were.

RAY MASTER SANCTUARY: Apollo, as the Ray Master resident and active at Delphi (see Delphi, Greece), grounded, activated, and transduced the cosmic energies of the Delphi dragon. Cadmus, as another Ray Master—in this case, the Olympian god Ares—immersed himself in this primordial energy matrix to make it easier to ground, activate, and transduce the cosmic energy of its progeny at Thebes. His energy-grounding point is the Thebes' Ray Master Sanctuary.

Cadmus and Ares are service names for the Ray Master of the lilac ray, Saint Germaine. Lilac as an energy burns cold; it is the energy of transmutation that burns off the dross, purifies, and cleanses—sometimes forcefully, certainly rigorously. You might think of the lilac flame as the flame in the alchemical retort, ruthlessly burning

off impurities, defending by transmuting, attacking by depotentizing.

As a spiritual process, this transmutative process is compatible with Ares' warlike reputation. Saint Germaine, representing the lilac ray, is in the advance guard of the epiphany of the Christ, cutting away all that is not in resonance with this pure energy.

It is fitting that insofar as Apollo's dragon activation enabled oracular speech at Delphi, Cadmus' dragon activation at Thebes enabled the introduction of a new—"Phoenician"—language and alphabet. In either case, dragon blood produces miraculous speech and communication on a godly level.

HERACLES' IDENTITY: What does it mean that Heracles was born at Thebes? The question to answer first is: Who was Heracles? He was Merlin of King Arthur fame, one of the prime geomantic workers on the planet long before there were people; his Herculean labors were primordial geomantic tasks (see Mycenae, Greece) performed in association with the work of the Ray Masters. Heracles used Thebes as a place to ground and amplify his energy; he birthed himself for yet another incarnation at Thebes, just as, in the Hawaiian mythic pantheon, he birthed himself as Maui the demigod at Hana on the island of Maui.

Specifically, at Thebes he grounded the two "serpents" of the dome caps at Thebes and neighboring Mount Hypatos. Both are connected via spiral lines across the landscape to the dome at Mount Kithairon. In cases where the spiral lines of two dome caps intersect, a Shambhala doorway exists. Heracles strangling the two serpents is geomantic code for saying he activated ("strangled") the latent doorway existing in the interface between the two overlapping spiral lines ("serpents") so that later when this doorway to Shambhala was needed (indicated by the wedding of Cadmus and Harmonia, below), it would be open.

In a similar Welsh myth, Merlin is asked to assist King Vortigern in finding out why the tower he is trying to erect on a mountain keeps falling down. Merlin, barely a teenager in the story, discerns that two huge serpents are writhing beneath the foundations. Once these serpents were tamed, stilled, or killed, the tower could be built because its foundations were solid. At Thebes, once Heracles had done the same thing to the two serpents in the palace, the astral expression of the Cadmeia could be established, anchored into the energy matrix.

Most likely, Heracles' "birth" through Thebes happened long before Cadmus and Dionysus arrived. One of his very early tasks at Thebes—he was ten months old—was to subdue and strangle two serpents (sent by Hera, Zeus' wife) that accosted him and his twin brother in the palace of his father, Amphitryon, at Thebes.

SHAMBHALA DOORWAY: The Cadmeia as a spiritualized energy matrix present in the same place as the physical structures erected on the hill in Thebes was a Celestial City of Sukhavati. This is to say, a replica, or access point, to Shambhala and the blissful Western Paradise, the city of *all* the gods. Zeus' Mount Olympus is a subsidiary of Shambhala—in effect, a field headquarters for the fourteen Ray Masters.

But Shambhala has *everybody:* gods, angels, ascended humans, and what we call aliens and extraterrestrials—the vast assemblage of the spiritually evolved hierarchy that benignly governs life on Earth on behalf of yet more evolved beings and divine plans.

Sukhavati is the Islands of the Blessed to which Cadmus and Harmonia retired; in a sense, they didn't go anywhere in terms of distance across the physical landscape. Rather, they passed through a dimensional doorway at the Cadmeia to reach the Blessed Islands in the far West. The myth of the wedding of Cadmus and Harmonia is highly significant in light of the understanding that it takes place in Sukhavati or Shambhala.

Sukhavati is the grand Celestial City of Varuna, the lord of the immortals; it is filled with innumerable objects of desire and opulence. All the gods quit their stations in the celestial spheres to attend the wedding at Thebes because in effect they were already present in Shambhala when and where the marriage took place.

The wedding itself was between two opposites in the zodiacal wheel and—judging by their respective mythic resumes—in Olympus as well. Ares, the aggressive, contentious god of war, and Aphrodite, foam-born goddess of love and sensuality, here blending, harmonizing their energies. Cadmus and Harmonia, Ares and Aphrodite—it's the same story, the same *hieros gamos.* Two halves of one being: one in the spiritual world, the other on the Earth.

It's the same story as the Theban *Dioskuroi:* one brother is heavenly minded, the other very terrestrial in his approach—as above, so below: cosmic harmony. The essential act is two Ray Masters blending their energies to produce a third, the divine child, who balances and harmonizes the energies of both parents.

Cadmus used the energy of the dragon at Thebes to create the interface between Sukhavati and the Cadmeia. The *Dioskuroi* Amphione and Zethus generated the energy matrix for the seven gates of Thebes from Shambhala. The physical gates and the ancient ring wall around the Cadmeia would have been a material replica of the energized template created in another dimension.

GOLDEN PILLARS: The *Spartoi,* or Sown Men, are crucial to the temple structure at Thebes. It's useful to remember that one of their epithets was "golden-helmed seed." These men are actually fifty-four golden cylinders from Shambhala, placed here both to protect and evangelize what takes place within Cadmus' sanctuary. The myth says that Cadmus sowed the dragon's teeth and up sprang the Spartoi.

You can read this as code for saying that Cadmus used the energy of the dragon to establish a suitable matrix and foundation into which he could set these Golden Pillars from Shambhala. Picture them as golden columns, perhaps one hundred feet tall, making a great protective circle about the Cadmeian acropolis. The Spartoi were warring men because their assignment was to guard the Cadmeia against the ungodly and contaminated.

They seem to resemble Egyptian pharaohs, arms crossed at the chests, with full headgear and kingly regalia. Seen closer up—when you penetrate their energy field a bit—each pillar now seems like a giant face—part human, part angelic. All fifty-four faces touch at the sides, forming a towering matrix around the Cadmeia—a unified gaze, an awake and aware sentinel looking in fifty-four directions at once.

These Golden Pillars or divine faces are not unique to Thebes; there are over two hundred thousand of them around the planet. They were brought through from Shambhala into a dimension closer to the physical as a preparation for the future.

What will happen in the future at Thebes? To get a sense of this, we need to understand what happened there in the past. The key event was the birth of Dionysus, the divine child of either Ares and Aphrodite or Zeus and Semele. Dionysus was the god and archetype of eternal, indestructible life, the wild, orgiastic deity who was sacrificed, dismembered, and consumed by Maenads, yet never died.[778] The Cadmeia was a manger, a cave of the heart, a prepared sanctuary, a birthing and grounding place for an early expression of the Christ in the context of the pre-Christian Mystery tradition.

DIONYSIAN MYSTERY CENTER: The Cadmeia was also a theater for the demonstration and experience of the Dionysian mystery: the divine life that survives dismemberment, physical death, the miracles, prophecy, ecstatic dancing, the frenzy, the ease of suffering through wine, the strange new magic, the possession by that most terrible and most gentle son of Zeus.

Dionysus is the threat of death and he is life, a polarity which represents "the extreme components of his original being." He animates Thebes and transcends it; he is the irruption of the divine into everyday life, the stranger in the city. "This god who is manifest in the world is at the same time a savior god: the guarantor of a mysterious hope for salvation."[779]

This tradition was the Samothracian one, based on the Greek island of Samothrace in the Aegean Sea and their initiate group called the *Kabeiroi*. These were the participants in the ecstatic rituals of the Great Mother and her "sons." They were the siblings, so to speak, of the Maenads, "the frenzied ones," generally women, who abandoned themselves on Mount Kithairon to wild dances in celebration of the god of ecstatic liberation. Euripides says of Kithairon teeming with Maenads that "all the mountain seemed wild with divinity."

One myth attributed to Samothrace was that Cadmus and Harmonia were married there before they came to Thebes. That tells us that the Mystery initiates on Samothrace were dealing with a similar if not identical geomantic temple structure to do with Dionysian mysteries.

Within the innermost recess of the Cadmeia, the *adyton*, the ancient Theban initiates, would partake of what we today call the Eucharist: the sacrificial feast, eating the god, consuming the flesh and blood of the undying deity who is the unification and epitome of all the gods and goddesses in the celestial world. Pausanias reported when he visited Thebes that visitors were shown the *thalamos* of Semele, her bridal chamber where she begot Dionysus, and where she was burned by Zeus' lightning. The thalamos "can have been nothing other than the *sekos*, an enclosure never to be entered, an *abaton* in the temple"—the Holy of Holies, a tomb and an altar, a sacred space only entered by high initiates and probably only occasionally.[780]

SILVER EGG: The birth of Dionysus in the Cadmeia, precipitated by the lethal epiphany of Zeus for his mortal bride, Semele, was the hatching of the Silver Egg at Thebes. This hatching obviously took place a very long time ago, and was of such primordial urgency and preeminence that it was not done by a Ray Master and certainly not by a human initiate, both of whom can routinely do the task in other circumstances.

Out of the Silver Egg stepped Dionysus, just as Horus (progeny of Osiris and Isis) emerged from the various Silver Eggs in Egypt, including the one at the Giza complex. This city, Dionysus declares in *The Bacchae,* "lacks initiation in my mysteries" and he vowed to vindicate his mother Semele by revealing his godhead to all of Thebes. So he says, then and now—and will continue to say into the future until the celestial Cadmeia is revealed as a temple on Earth—that this city, this planet, lacks initiation in His mysteries.

Let's look again at the *Spartoi.* As the golden-helmed seed or men, they protect the Cadmeia as the manger of Dionysus against the profane, the uninitiated, the unprepared, the nonhuman, the prehuman in the Oedipean sense. But they also face outward from the Cadmeia into the plains of Boeotia and the rest of Greece. They are the

Apostles multiplied; they are the archetypal evangelists of the Christ.

They are fifty-four faces of Christ as Dionysus offering their spiritualizing visage to the ancient Greek world on behalf of a vastly distant future when *all* of Sukhavati, not just its *Spartoi* advance emissaries, will have been born into the physical world. In a profounder sense, these faces are partial embodiments of the *Hayyoth Qadesh,* the Four Divine Creatures or Holy Beasts, as the Qabalistic tradition calls them, also known as the Cherubim in Western angelologies. In this metaphorical system, you could conceive of these pillars with faces as something like the Cherubim and flaming, flashing swords guarding the gates of Paradise.

The Golden Pillars represent a technology from and for the future in the sense that they encase, protect, and represent the Second Coming of Christ. But not in the literal, Biblical sense of a rerun of the incarnation two thousand years ago; rather, as doorways into the temple of the arrival of the Christ in our expanded awareness.

The Austrian psychic scientist Rudolf Steiner once explained that eventually all humans will be able to see the Christ in the etheric realm of the Earth because He has never left. The Second Coming, in this interpretation, will be our coming into the cognition of this presence. The Dionysian temple at Thebes was, and still is, a powerful training ground for this heightening of human cognition and for a Dionysian taste of what the Christian tradition calls Heaven on Earth.

Troy, Turkey

The ruins of legendary Troy, and the presumed site of the ten-year Trojan War described by Homer, stand on a small eminence called the hill of Hisarlik about a mile from the Dardanelles and the Aegean Sea in northwest Turkey. The Dardanelles, which flow to Istanbul, are at their narrowest here at the Hellespont, barely a mile across. Troy sits in a low shoulder of rock that overlooks a marshy valley of the Scamander (today called Menderesu) River which empties into the Dardanelles; another river, the Simoeis (today called Dumbreksu) also flows past Troy into the Dardanelles. Archeologists believe both rivers once flowed together near the city.

Snow-covered Mount Gargaros, the highest peak in the Ida range, also a site of legend, towers to the southeast of Hisarlik. On the other side of Troy, in the Aegean Sea, is the island of Samothrace, upon which rears the double summit of Phengari (elevation: 5,000 feet), the "Mountain of the Moon."

Phengari and Ida lie approximately opposite each other along an axis upon which sits Hisarlik; in antiquity, both were considered sacred mountains: Mount Ida was the precinct of Aphrodite; and Phengari the center of a mystery cult of the Great Mother Goddess guarded by the Kaberoi. Thus Troy sits in the center of a vast, full circle described by the arc of the low-lying hills that surround it and at whose outer rim stand two mountains dedicated to the goddess.[781]

Troy occupies a promontory that is part of the Troad, a stubby peninsula about sixty miles square, "shaped like a badly battered square" which sits at the northwest corner of what used to be called Asia Minor. "The Plain of Troy is a flat, placid-looking, undramatic stretch of low, gently rolling country."[782] That's one view; another was offered by noted archeologist Heinrich Schliemann in 1870 upon first visiting Hisarlik: "The plain is covered with the beautiful green of spring and embroidered with millions of flowers.[783]

HISTORY AND ARCHEOLOGY

One of the most conspicuous facts about Troy—known variously in antiquity as Truva (Turkish), Ilion, Ilios (both Greek), and Illium (Roman)—is how tiny it is. The ruins occupy a space barely 450 feet by 600, so if you are expecting cyclopean walls or awesome stone towers "you will be disappointed."

In fact, there is not a single Troy, but at least nine different phases of settlement in Troy, leaving a confusing archeological stratigraphy that spans several thousand years. "In front of you is a stretch of finely built walls, behind them an overgrown maze of superimposed ruins of many ages, a jumble of gullies and ditches choked with bushes and rubble."[784]

Archeological excavations of Troy came in three waves, starting in 1870 with German researcher Heinrich Schliemann, who led six digs during a twenty-year period; then came Wilhelm Dörpfeld in 1893 and 1894; and then Carl Blegen, between 1932 and 1938. Schliemann relied on ancient texts, including Homer's *Iliad,* to pinpoint and verify his choice of location for the near-mythic Troy.

In discovering Troy at Hisarlik, Schliemann was fulfilling a dream from when he was eight and was captivated by the stories of the Trojan War. From that moment, he wanted to find the actual site of Troy. During his early adult years he earned sufficient money to launch himself as an archeologist; finally in 1868, while standing on the Plain of Troy at Hisarlik, he decided legendary Troy must be there. He spent the next twenty years proving it was.

Most of the site is destroyed, from overzealous archeological digs a century earlier, but the site still gives the impression of having once been a royal city on a hill, with a walled palace accommodating perhaps one hundred people. Its diminutive size is one of Troy's prime paradoxes. The initial settlement of Troy, which archeologists call Troy I (3000–2500 B.C.), consisted of ten layers and "occupied an extremely small area," its diameter a mere 270 feet,[785] although it "boasted a substantial enclosure wall, with a single gateway flanked by stone towers" one of which was almost five feet tall.[786]

How could such a small place have housed a Trojan army of at least fifty thousand Achaeans (as Menelaus' men were called) during a ten-year

siege, as described by Homer, or for that matter, accommodated Odysseus' Trojan Horse sheltering at last fifty armed warriors in its wooden belly? Troy's size doesn't seem large enough to fit all its legends.

MYTH AND LEGEND

As with Mycenae and its House of Atreus in Greece, Troy's founding, according to the ancient texts, is ultimately traceable to the Pleiadians. Dardanus, son of Electra (a Pleiad, daughter of the Titan Atlas), founded Dardania on Mount Ida near Troy; then his grandson, Tros, named the countryside near the Hellespont Tros, after himself. One of his sons, Ilus (the great-great grandson of a Pleiadian), founded the citadel of Troy by following a cow, after which two amazing events happened.

According to Apollodorus, Ilus went to Phrygia (the antique name for this part of Turkey) and was victorious in wrestling, for which he received fifty youths and fifty maidens. The king, following an oracle, awarded Ilus a dappled cow "and bade him found a city wherever the animal should lie down." Ilus followed the cow to what was known locally as "the hill of the Phrygian Ate"; the cow lay down on that spot, Ilus built his city there, and called it Ilium. Ilus asked of Zeus a sign to confirm his choice of location; not long after, Ilus "beheld by day the Palladium, fallen from heaven, lying before his tent."[787]

The Palladium was a device made by the goddess of wisdom, Pallas Athena, as a kind of self-portrait in wood. It was three cubits high, its feet joined together; its right hand held a spear aloft, and its left held a distaff and spindle. The Palladium, which also featured Zeus' aegis (magic breastplate) wrapped about it, housed the spirit of the Pleiadian Electra, who took refuge in the image against an amorous Zeus.[788]

Zeus threw the Palladium into the Ilian country, after which Ilus built a temple for it, interpreting the arrival of the Palladium at his doorstep as approval from above. The significance of the Palladium was that, as long as it resided in Troy, the city would never fall to outside aggressors.

When Zeus threw down the Palladium, he also tossed Ate out of Olympus. This is the second important myth concerning Troy. She was his eldest daughter, and her mother was Eris (Strife), the goddess who seeded the Trojan War. Among the gods and goddesses, she was now *persona non grata,* having deceived the king of the gods, and he demonstrated this condition of nonwelcome by seizing her by the head and flinging her out of heaven. She was never to return and must live among humans forever more.

Ate, some say, was the Goddess of delusion, rash actions, and blind folly, whose feet rest on the heads of mortals although they don't know it. Where Ate fell to Earth in Phrygia became known as the Hill of Ate.

Ate produces divine temptations or sudden, inexplicable, blinding infatuations, a stunned bewilderment, a psychic intervention generated by unseen supernatural beings. "Always, or practically always, *ate* is a state of mind—a temporary clouding or bewildering of the normal consciousness. It is, in fact, a partial and temporary insanity . . . ascribed, not to physiological or psychological causes, but to an external 'daemonic' agency."

One feels a communication of power from a god; one senses a mysterious ingress of energy; a new confidence and eagerness as if a god has breathed into one or suddenly entered one's head; one experiences or laments an immediate increase in power or an unaccountable lapse in judgment—these are the work of Ate.[789]

The third central myth about Troy concerns Ilus' son, Laomedon. Both Homer and Apollodorus tell us that Laomedon engaged the gods Apollo and Poseidon to build broad city walls for him at Troy and that they labored in human form for one year under contract to the king.

In the *Iliad,* Poseidon the Earthshaker complains to Apollo: "I walled the city/massively in well-cut stone, to make/the place impregnable." Apollo had been herding Laomedon's cattle "slow and dark amid the upland vales/of Ida's wooded ridges."[790] When the fortification work was completed, Laomedon refused to pay Apollo and Poseidon; even worse, he threatened to enslave them and slice off their ears if they didn't get out of Troy.

Being gods, Apollo and Poseidon were capable of some impressive revenge for "barbaric" Laomedon. Apollo sent a pestilence and Poseidon a sea monster (a giant fish with open jaws). The oracles stated that Laomedon must expose his only daughter, Hesione, to the sea monster as the only way of protecting Troy.

The Greek hero, Heracles, in the midst of one of his twelve labors, rescued Hesione in exchange for a team of immortal horses given to Tros by Zeus, now in Laomedon's possession. Laomedon agreed, then reneged on his offer; not long after, Heracles destroyed the city and killed Laomedon, not one to have learned much about the advantages of keeping his word.

Thus even before the ten-year siege of Troy began, the citadel had Ate and the Palladium. "Infatuation and the image now lived together in the same place: a city prone to phantoms."[791]

The fourth myth of Troy concerns Mount Ida, a five-thousand-foot-tall mountain known in Turkey today as *Kaz Daği* (Goose Mountain). One of Laomedon's children survived; this was Priam, who became King of Troy during the time when it is believed the city became one of the world's mightiest. With his wife, Hecuba, Priam had nineteen children, including Hector, a warrior who would distinguish himself in the Trojan War. He also had a nephew, Aeneas (who would one day found Rome), whose mother was Aphrodite, the Greek love goddess.

One day Aphrodite seduced Prince Anchises of Troy on Mount Ida, her haunt, and through him, birthed Aeneas. This myth, of course, tells us that Mount Ida was sacred to Aphrodite. In fact, it appears that the three goddesses, whose beauty contest, in effect, precipitated the Trojan War, all sported naked on Mount Ida. It was the wedding of the sea goddess Thetis and the hero Peleus. All of Olympus had been invited except Eris, the goddess of strife and discord.

Eris rolled a golden apple into the banquet hall, labeling it the prize for the most beautiful. Hera (Zeus' wife), Athena (Zeus' daughter), and Aphrodite contended for the apple, then finally agreed to allow a mortal, Paris (one of Priam's sons), to judge the winner. Paris was shepherding sheep on the flanks of Mount Ida when the goddesses arrived and demanded what's now known as the Judgment of Paris.

Basically, Aphrodite bribed the innocent Paris by promising the love of the most beautiful woman in the world (Helen) and got the golden apple. Paris abducted Helen from King Menelaus of Sparta, and brought her back to Troy. Menelaus' brother, Agamemmon of Mycenae in Greece, organized a fleet of warriors to storm Troy to get Helen back.

Helen, incidentally, was not a mortal human woman: her father was Zeus, and her mother was Leda, wife of King Tyndarus of Sparta; Zeus took the form of a white swan and Helen was born from a white egg laid by Leda. An alternate version says Zeus impregnated the goddess Nemesis, who conceived the white egg, then transferred it to Leda's womb.

An even more discomfiting alternative story is that Helen and Paris spent the Trojan War years in Egypt, detained by Proteus, King of Memphis. The Helen present at Troy was a simulacrum, a phantom, the image of an absent woman. Homer kept quiet about this scandal, that "blood had been spilled for a woman who was not actually there, for an impalpable ghost."[792]

MYSTICS AND TOURISTS

A consistent if puzzling comment of visitors or writers is that Troy is "astonishingly small when compared with the classical dream of the mighty towered citadel of Priam."[793] Another visitor laments: "It is rather like a bad film version of a good book. I am standing on the castle mound in Troy, and reality refuses to square with my preconceived picture of this famous city. . . . Is this puny, barely 200 x 150 meter-large mound of ruins, with its confusing muddle of bits of masonry, the remains of at least nine epochs in the city's history?"[794]

However, not everybody gripes about Troy's small size. At least one scholar has evoked the numinous field of the sacred that surrounds it. For the ancient Greeks, Troy symbolized the old, defeated order of the heroes; it was the oldest city and the city of the goddess, not only of Pallas Athena, but of Aphrodite, "once the great goddess of the earth and the waters, who defended it to the last and sent its seed to Rome. Clearly Troy was set in the center of the pure circle of her world. . . ."[795]

GEOMANTIC

Dome; Cyclopean City; Palladium; Mount Olympus; Avalon; Solar Logos Residence; Camalate Center; Landscape Zodiac; Tree of Life.

DOME: The dome over Troy corresponds to alpha Andromeda; the dome over neighboring Mount Ida is beta Andromeda. Andromeda is the constellation of the Chained Lady—it's the same story as Laomedon's daughter, Hesione, who had to be sacrificed to Poseidon's sea monster to save Troy.

In the star myth, Andromeda was the daughter of Cepheus, King of Ethiopia. Poseidon punished Andromeda's mother, Cassiopeia, for her vanity and deceit (she had boasted to the sea nymphs that her daughter was beautiful) by decreeing that Andromeda must be chained to a rock to be the prey of a terrible sea monster. Just as the beast was about to seize her, Perseus arrived and undid her chains, driving away the monster by flashing the severed head of the Gorgon Medusa, which instantly turned the leviathan into stone.

Alpha Andromeda is a second-magnitude star called *Alpheratz,* from the Arabic *Al Surrat al Faras,* which means "the Horse's Navel," but it is also known to the Arabian astronomers as "the Head of the Woman in Chains." It's about 120 light years from Earth and is 160 times brighter than our Sun. The constellation of Andromeda is joined to what astronomers call the Great Square of Pegasus (the constellation of the winged horse); in fact, at one time, this star was considered to be part of Pegasus. It is also next to the constellation of Perseus and the Head of Medusa.

Beta Andromeda (the dome at Mount Ida) is a second-magnitude star about seventy-five light years from Earth called *Mirach,* which derives informally from the Arabic *mi'zar,* for "girdle"; the star marks Andromeda's left leg. It was also known to the Arabs as *Al Janb al Musalsalah,* "the Side of the Chained Woman."

It's clear that the essential stories of Troy are star myths. Heracles coming to free King Laomedon's daughter, Hesione, from her chains by the Aegean Sea is the same story as Perseus and Andromeda for two reasons. First, the geomyth of Troy matches the star myth of its domes; it is the direct indicator of the identity of the two domes of Troy and Mount Ida. Second, when Heracles killed the sea monster and freed Hesione, he was *grounding* the energies of the alpha and beta stars of Andromeda for the Troy–Mount Ida geomantic temple. This work was part of the original geomantic work performed at Troy long *before* anybody actually lived there, and it is highly similar to the work Heracles did at Mycenae in Greece as groundwork for its geomantic temple structure.

CYCLOPEAN CITY: In the stories recounted by both Homer and Apollodorus about how Laomedon engaged the gods Apollo and Poseidon to build his massive city walls at Troy we have a clear mythic memory of how a Cyclopean City comes into being. The gods built it. The presence of a Cyclopean City at Troy opens a vista on its extreme antiquity as a geomantic site and, as explained below, gives us grounds for an unconventional interpretation of its function, especially with respect to the Trojan War.

PALLADIUM: The mystery of Athena's Palladium centers on the meaning of the Gorgon Medusa's head in Athena's breastplate or Aegis. Even though myth has conditioned us to regard the Medusa's head as an object of fright and terror, this is actually a misleading impression. The Gorgon's severed head is another version of the marble White Face of the Ancient of Days as described in Qabala.

The Palladium is a full-size astral temple shaped somewhat like a large white rotunda with the severed head resting on the ground level and facing up. Beams of light flash out from its eyes and radiate everywhere, and its face seems plastic and mobile, looking in every direction at once. Insofar as Athena instructed the hero Perseus in the means of acquiring the Medusa's head, she is its temple custodian and master of its mysteries. The jewel of the Palladium, the essence of this Athena temple, the central feature of the Aegis, is the Medusa head—the living Face of the Ancient of Days.

Zeus throwing down the Palladium is a Greek way of saying Zeus sanctioned the installation of a miniature Crown of the Ancient of Days temple at Troy under the supervision of his daughter, Pallas Athena. The Palladium is thus a code, a concentrated image, for describing this type of temple. Ilus, who found the Palladium lying at his feet outside his tent, was sufficiently informed in geomantic mysteries to recognize the presence of this type of temple, of which there are only sixty on the planet.

The Trojan Horse, that clever subterfuge for which the wily Odysseus is always credited, is actually a coded reference to Pegasus, the immortal winged horse that sprang from the blood of Medusa's head, which is to say, winged divine thought generated by contact with the flashing rays of the Ancient of Day's face. When Homer said Odysseus and about four dozen of his men squeezed into the belly of the Trojan Horse before it was wheeled into Troy, what was meant esoterically was that Odysseus and his men were of sufficient initiate status to experience the reality of Pegasus and catch a "ride" with its essence.

Poseidon prepared the temple of the Ancient of Days. That is what Homer meant when he quoted Poseidon as saying he labored for a year building impregnable walls around the citadel. Poseidon prepared the temple for his lover, the Gorgon Medusa, who lived at the far reaches of the cosmic sea over which Poseidon is lord. Medusa, denizen of the farthest reaches of the cosmic sea, out past even Oceanos and on the edge of Night, and consort of the Lord of the Sea, Poseidon, is the "sea monster" that beset Laomedon's Troy. As a constellation, Medusa is nestled between Perseus and Andromeda. Heracles, in "slaying" this monster and "freeing" Troy from its ravages, in effect activated, grounded, and regulated the release of Medusa's energy into the Troy temple.

She was doubly pregnant with two Poseidon progeny: Pegasus, the immortal winged horse; and Chrysaor, a strange creature whose name means "golden sword" and who fathered (with the Oceanid Callirrhoe) Geryon, a three-headed giant, and Echidna, a terror, half-female, half-serpent, who spawned a brood of monstrous, magical, unique beings including the sphinx, Cerberus (the three-headed guard dog of Hades), Hydra, the Chimaera, a lion, dragon, and sow. All of these primal beings played roles in other aspects of Greek myth.

The surprise one finds when investigating the geomythic realities of Troy is that there never was a ten-year Trojan War as described by Homer. This is why the site seems "astonishingly" too small to accommodate the mighty deeds attributed to it by history. They never happened. Let's unravel the complicated geomyth that is the secret life of Troy.

MOUNT OLYMPUS: Mount Ida is a Mount Olympus, a Celestial City of Amaravati, home of the gods. Hera, Pallas Athena, and Aphrodite are found on Mount Ida's slopes because that site is a dimensional portal, a swinging door between the realm of the gods and the physical world. The straight dome line that connects the Mount Ida dome with the Troy dome spans the Plain of Troy and in effect marks the location of Bifrost, the rainbow bridge that is the entrance into Olympus.

AVALON: Eris tossing out a golden apple to tempt the goddesses at their banquet at Olympus on Mount Ida is geomythic code for indicating a Landscape Zodiac and an Avalon, or Celestial City of Gandhavati, both of which are indicated by the golden apple.

The beauty contest for possession of the golden apple was a determination to see which of the three goddesses—read Ray Masters—would exert the prime influence on Troy. Aphrodite won because as a Ray Master she was the consort of Menelaus, the Spartan king and husband of Helen, who was held "hostage" within Troy.

The missing link here is that Menelaus was a Ray Master and Olympian god. His incarnational lineage included Hephaistos, the Greek fire god and smith; Arthur, the Celtic king of the Summer Country; and other expressions of the Solar Logos, the tamer of the wild Sun god.

King Arthur's wife and queen, Guinevere, was abducted by King Melwas of the Summer Country, and Arthur and his men had to fight to get her back. Menelaus' wife, Helen, was abducted by Paris on behalf of King Priam of Troy, and he and his brother, Agamemnon, had to "fight" to get her back. Agamemnon was deceived and eventually murdered by his wife, Clytemnestra, who became the lover of Aegisthos while Agamemnon was away at Troy. King Arthur's Guinevere was seduced by Lancelot, his chief knight, while they were living at Camalate.

I bring up these three seemingly different stories because they are all the same. Arthur, Menelaus, and his "brother," Agamemnon—they are the *same* solar hero described at different epochs in history and culture.

SOLAR LOGOS RESIDENCE: The myth says that Menelaus as Spartan king was at Troy for ten years as part of the Achaean offensive against the offending city. Geomantically, Menelaus as the Ray Master of the sixth ray transported the Solar Logos to Troy from Sparta (and also as Agamemnon from the Treasury of Atreus, a Sun-god temple at Mycenae). Think of it like this: Helios the Sun god periodically calls in at each of the Sun temples around the planet for a brief residency and infusion of energy into the site. The Trojan War refers to the time when the Sun god came to Troy.

This energy was geomantically resident at Troy for "ten years," a time frame that was undoubtedly longer than our conventional sense of the term. Since the term limit of Menelaus at Troy was limited and specified (as opposed to the presence of the Sun god at Mount Etna in Sicily, where it was given no time limits), it is probable that this Ray Master transmitted the energy of the Solar Logos through the Troy geomantic matrix for

a set period of time. Troy does not have a Sun-god temple as such, but the "temporary" residence of the Solar Logos there imparted to the site the same energies it would get if there were such a temple.

Think of Menelaus in his spiritual aspect as a rapidly rotating golden spindle hundreds of feet high, boring into the heart of Troy, spinning off sparks and rays of golden light. As Solar Logos, this energy emits (or is) a sound, so conceive that the spinning Menelaus is also emitting a continuous mantric sound that shapes the ethers for miles around the site. As Solar Logos, this sound will produce growth and change. Menelaus' consort is Aphrodite, whose Ray Master names also included Nada, whose essence is sound (as in *Nada Brahma,* the primal sound of God),[796] and whose responsibility is the third ray of the Great Bear.

Aphrodite is always resident at Troy, but Menelaus came to visit her. Aphrodite in one of her aspects was Helen, the most beautiful woman alive, whose mortal husband was Menelaus. It's the same story, just seen from differing sides of the curtain between the physical and astral worlds. Of course, Helen was a phantom, an impalpable ghost, not physically present but astrally apparent: another expression of the White Goddess.

The ten-year siege of Troy was the assemblage of initiates and visitors partaking of the wondrous *hieros gamos* of the visiting Sun god (Menelaus) and his consort, the breathtakingly beautiful love goddess, Aphrodite, also known as Helen, Guinevere, and the Lady of the Lake—the Queen of the astral world, which is Avalon.[797]

CAMALATE CENTER: But what about all the Greek warriors assembled in siege outside Troy? This is a time-lapse image to convey the popularity of Troy as a Camalate, a place of high initiation, geomythic training, and spiritual elucidation. If King Arthur (Menelaus) and Queen Guinevere (Helen) are present at Troy, this is the innermost essence of Camalate, which was the once and future initiate's center for geomantic mysteries, instruction, and epiphany. Many came to Troy to immerse themselves in the energy of this *hieros gamos* and for insight. In a sense, they all wanted what Menelaus wanted: Helen. This is where Ate comes in.

LANDSCAPE ZODIAC: The myths have mostly painted Ate with a pejorative brush, but as the eldest daughter of Zeus (which suggests spiritual proximity to his cosmic essence), Ate represents the heightened conductivity of spiritual thought, the presence of and permeation by the lightning-quick Holy Spirit. Godly thoughts suddenly fill one's awareness and one acts as if possessed by a god, as if filled with godly wisdom, as if one's head has caught fire from the radiating sparks and streamers from the eyes of the Ancient of Days in the Palladium. We stagger around god-intoxicated, our heads aflame with the Holy Spirit.

Under Menelaus' direction and Helen's inspiration, the Achaean warriors—initiates-in-training—engaged themselves in the war within. The battles on the ramparts of Troy are references to the initiatory doings, the inner battles, the overcoming of interior obstacles and conflicts, the confrontations with Shadow substance, all undertaken in the geomantic matrix, which heightens, facilitates, and supports this work.

All of this was done in the local starfield—the zodiac template imprinted on the landscape around Troy. The zodiac at Troy is about twenty-five miles in diameter (a sister zodiac to the one at Mycenae, of the same size and same spiritual intent) and occupies the Plain of Troy.

In particular, the zodiac in the Plain of Troy enabled the warriors to experience directly the particularities of their horoscope as a way of integrating and balancing all aspects of their total selves. Warriors died to themselves, surrendered their limitations, to allow the Light to enter their consciousness. As a Gandhavati Celestial City, an Avalon, Troy also served as a spacetime workshop, a place to mete out one's reality, to play out alternate scenarios, to play, to create, to walk backwards and forwards in time as a way of self-instruction.

TREE OF LIFE: There is a four-tiered Tree of Life overlay upon the Plain of Troy, starting at the Palladium and fountaining about four miles into the zodiac; each of the four tiers is 5,530 feet long. This feature complemented the Landscape Zodiac and added an extra element of Mystery initiation to the Troy temple.

Troy was a very active center for this type of initiation intensive under the supervision and encouragement of the Olympian gods, particularly Menelaus and Aphrodite, whose presence was a constant demonstration of the goal: inner balance, harmony, and integration in the heart center. They represented the perfection of the ideal, the living expression of the *hieros gamos,* the marriage of Sun and Moon, light and dark, inner and outer, male and female. They were the ideal against which the Achaeans could measure themselves and derive continuing inspiration to further their inner work.

Granted, Troy's time of maximum geomantic activity was a considerable time in the past, and in a sense Menelaus and Helen have gone home. Yet their presence was so potent and real when they were here, that from our viewpoint, their energies are still present at Troy awaiting our earnest interaction.

Uluru, Alice Springs, Australia

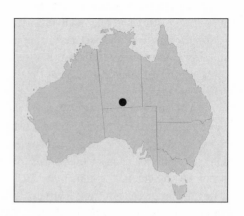

Uluru is a gigantic red rock, a rounded mass of sandstone about 1,115 feet high, the only prominence in the otherwise flat, mostly barren plains of central Australia in the Northern Territories.[798]

It looks as if somebody dropped it there from outer space, or as if it grew out of the land, alone, a strange stone of the Earth with no siblings. It is a barren rock, with no vegetation. Its color appears to change during the day, according to the light, but typically at dawn and dusk, it glows with a bright red reflection, giving it an otherworldly aspect. It's known as the red center of Australia.

Uluru is 1.25 miles wide, two miles long, and 4.5 miles in circumference, its sides grooved and eroded with deep gullies, and riddled with over-hangings and caves said by the Aborigines to have been made in the Dreamtime by the ances-tral beings. Its smooth, sloping, faulted and folded sides rise in many places at an 80° gradient, and the top is relatively flat.

Remarkably, geologists estimate that two-thirds of Uluru's mass lies beneath the ground. They propose that Uluru was created 550 million years ago in the Precambrian era. They have a term that supposedly accounts for why a massive

rock like this would be in a barren plain. Uluru is a *bornhardt,* which means weather-resistant rock that remains standing after the elements have worn away everything else around it.

It's considered the world's largest monolith and the largest isolated rock, and for the Aborigines it is one of the most sacred of their landscape temples. They use it as a ceremonial center, camping at its base, which due to the runoff from Uluru, is amply provided with pools and rich greenery—an oasis.

Uluru sits near the geographic center of Australia in the 327,400-acre Uluru-Kata Tjuta National Park, managed jointly by Aborigines and the Australian Nature Conservation Agency. Uluru was first glimpsed by a European named William Christie Gosse in 1872 and was named Ayer's Rock after the premier of South Australia at that time, Sir Henry Ayers.

In 1985, Uluru was formally given back to the local Aborigines (the Pitjantjatjara and Yankunyjatjara), who then leased it back to the government for a century. Alice Springs is the nearest large town, but it's two hundred miles to the northwest; most visitors stay nearby at the Yulara tourist resort north of the park boundary.

That doesn't deter the estimated three hun-dred thousand tourists a year who visit the

"Rock," as it's called. Many of them climb Uluru, which the Aborigines disapprove of, believing it a sacrilege, as in their traditions only males of a certain clan are permitted to mount Uluru. They are known to refer to the tourists scrambling over their Rock as *minga*, "ants."

The Rock now has a double listing in UNESCO's World Heritage roster of National Parks, being recognized for its natural beauty (awarded in 1987) and its cultural significance (1994). According to UNESCO, a "cultural heritage site" or "cultural landscape" such as Uluru shows the "combined works of nature and of man" and the "living traditions of indigenous peoples, especially their special and sacred attachment to land and water."[799]

The park is crisscrossed with a network of Aboriginal tracks marking ancient mythical journeys and connecting nodes inside and outside the park. "In a country with natural wonders such as Uluru, where every major topographical feature was endowed with mythological significance, it was not part of Aboriginal culture to build monuments such as megalithic tombs or pyramids." They didn't need formal structures for the "land is their cathedral."[800]

MYTH AND LEGEND

According to Aboriginal myth, many features on Uluru's southern face are the results of battles long ago between the Kunia people (carpet snakes) and the Liru people (poisonous snakes). Originally, these two types of Snake people lived amicably together at a waterhole called Pugabuga. Then the Kunia migrated to a flat sandhill that had ample water supplies. At the end of the Dreamtime, that sandhill was changed into Uluru.

Somehow when the sandhill was changed into a rock, so were the Kunia, and they can still be seen as specific boulders and features of Uluru.

The beards of the elders and the tracks they made to collect drinking water from Uluru are all visible on the surface of the Rock. One of the caves in Uluru was inhabited by the spirit of a carpet-snake woman who had successfully given birth there; women afterwards resorted to this cave for an easy childbirth.

Visible on the Rock's surface are the results of the fierce battles that broke out between the two Snake people living there. Certain cracks, for instance, represent places where a Kunia man slashed open the leg of one of the Liru. A split rock, sixty feet long, is the nose of a warrior, the four holes in the cliff are his eyes and nose, and the water stains on the cliff-face are his dried blood. A cave whose opening resembles a wide-open mouth is the open mouth of a woman struck down with grief.

To the Aboriginal mind, it isn't that the various striking features of Uluru symbolize or somehow remind them of ancient battles. These features are those Snake people and their activities turned to stone. "Many boulders and peculiar depressions, protuberances, cracks, and stains on the Rock commemorate the massacre of the harmless Carpet-snake people, whose bodies are boulders, their hair the tuft of bushes that have taken root in the rock face."[801]

According to Mudrooroo, an expert in Aboriginal Studies at several Australian universities, the momentous battle etched in stone has a deeper meaning. Uluru has a sunny and a shady side, and these physical qualities are matched by generational divisions there, and the division between two "great myth cycles" played out at Uluru.

The shady side concerns the Kuniya (Kunia), or Rock Python people (Carpet snakes). They emigrated to Uluru from three different directions, and one of the Kuniya women buried some eggs she had brought at the eastern end of Uluru. The Kuniya were attacked by the Liru, the poisonous snake warriors. The ensuing battle was on the epic scale of the vast battle between the Pandavas and Kauravas as recounted in the Vedic *Mahabharata,* says Mudrooroo, and it signaled the end of "the creative period of the Dreamtime."[802]

Some results of this fight are found at Alyurungu, on Uluru's southwest face. Here you can see pockmarks from warriors' spears and two black-stained streams of water, which were originally Liru warriors. Many cylindrical stones on the top of Uluru are said to be the petrified remains of slain Carpet-snake people.

Most of the battle between the Kuniya and Liru took place at Uluru's northeastern end at a gorge now called Mutjitjulu (or Mutijilda). As elsewhere, the physical details of the rock face are the residue of the events of the battle. Above this site is the Uluru rock hole, says Mudrooroo, "the home of a Kuniya who releases water into Mutjitjulu."[803]

A second primary myth about the origin of Uluru's physical features centers around a demon dingo, or wild dog, called *Kurrpanngu.* Again it involves a mortal struggle between two antagonistic groups of ancestors. The demon dingo attacked the Hare Wallaby people, who were performing initiation ceremonies in Uluru's caves. They were invited to attend ceremonies elsewhere, but didn't wish to go.

The Mulga Seed tribe people had their medicine men create an effigy of the dingo, then they chanted it to life, filled it with hatred and evil, and sent it to the Hare Wallaby people to slaughter them. Some of the boulder piles near the north end of Uluru are the bodies of the women and children killed by the demon dingo. The place where the young men dragged a great ceremonial pole over the top of Uluru is still visible in the form of large furrows, and the pole is still there as a big slab or rock still partly attached to the northern flank of Uluru.

Mudrooroo notes that one of the reasons Uluru is so sacred to the Aborigines is that many song lines and Dreaming tracks converge here.[804] It is "a telluric or *djang* place of amazing potency." He recounts an Uluru creation myth that says Uluru was built in the *Tjukurrpa,* or Dreamtime, by two boys who played in the mud after the rain, then abandoned it to shape itself into Uluru.

In general, the Aborigines contend that Uluru is a kind of living repository of events from the Dreamtime, and Western ethnographers have collected at least sixty different myths associated with the great Rock. The Aborigines "read the features of Uluru as Jews and Christians do the pages of the Bible." The Rock's topographical features are the "record of Dreamtime stories."

Another myth attributes the origin of Uluru to the Lizard People. It suggests that Uluru was originally a boomerang or was somehow created by one buried at its base. The Pitjantjatjara say that once a little lizard man named Linga (he's also called Kandju or Tjati) lived alone near where Uluru now stands. He had spent many days crafting a boomerang, and he threw it to test its balance. It sped across the desert and buried itself at the great red sandhill from which Uluru was later created. Linga was distressed that he had lost such a fine boomerang and frantically went in search of it.

He dug everywhere around the sandhill, and as at the time it was still soft, many of Uluru's striking features, such as the large potholes and vertical chasms, are the results of Linga's digging. "Linga, forever associated with the sand in which he lost his boomerang, became the little sand-lizard."[805]

Associating Uluru with a buried boomerang has intriguing geomythic nuances. The boomerang, the Aborigines say, was first created from wood from the Tree between Heaven and Earth and is meant to represent the Rainbow and the Rainbow Serpent. The characteristic gentle bend in the middle of the boomerang signifies the connection between the opposites, such as Heaven and Earth, Dreamtime and present-time ceremony, and the past and present.[806]

Another interpreter of Aboriginal culture, somewhat from the inside, is Cyril Havecker, who claimed to be a blood brother of the Warramunga tribe. In the 1970s he presented workshops in Australia on this topic, and in his book *Understanding Aboriginal Culture*, he suggested that Uluru is in fact the Great Rainbow Serpent of Aboriginal myth. Ularu (a variant spelling) was the Intelligent Snake "from the higher spirit realms of the universe."

Ularu originally was a celestial serpent in the universe that manifested as a great rainbow. From this spirit rainbow emerged a huge spirit snake that slithered down to Earth and took form as Uluru, the great red Rock in the middle of Australia. The Rainbow Snake also dug vast holes in the Earth, creating the seas, rivers, and lakes, while the solid, dug-out substance became the hills.[807]

Seen from above, Uluru resembles a horseshoe on its side, and the lower part of the "U," Havecker claimed, is filled with eggs, making Uluru a preeminent fertility symbol. Uluru is both male and female, Mother and Father of all life forms.

One of the Aboriginal terms for Rainbow Serpent is *wanambi*, and there is a story that on the top of Uluru is a steep rock hole. This is the portal to the realm of an enormous wanambi who lives in a huge cavern under the waters. This wanambi is hundreds of yards long, with an enormous head, long pointed teeth, a beard, and skin the color of the rainbow. It can rise into the air above Uluru as the Rainbow Serpent and kill any intruders it doesn't like, or it can take away all the water from Uluru and the surrounding countryside.[808]

MYSTICS AND TOURISTS

Australian ethnologist Charles Mountford visiting Uluru in the 1950s said that it can be likened to nothing else and uncannily resembles an enormous pebble. "Continually in the midst of work I found myself admiring the curves of the immense buttresses against the cloud-flecked sky, and the play of light and shadow on the red sides." He marveled at how every precipice, cave, gutter, and mark on the top and sides of Uluru "commemorates the exploits and adventures of the creatures of those long-distant times."[809]

American travel writer Bill Bryson in his witty survey of Australia's land and cultures, *In a Sunburned Country*, was deeply moved by his encounter with Uluru. He was almost sick of it by the time he finally reached the Rock, since images of Uluru abound throughout Australia. But when he saw it, Bryson found it "totally arresting"—a large "brooding, hypnotic presence."

It is probably the most "immediately recognizable natural object" on the planet, maybe even a landmark for interstellar travelers, he said. In fact, if he were excavating the planet for signs of a buried alien spaceship, Bryson says he would start digging at Uluru. Close up, it has lots more curves, divots, wavelike ribs, irregularities than even from two hundred yards away. It was exceptionally noble, exuded grandeur, and he found he could not stop looking at it. In fact, he didn't *want* to stop looking at it.

Seeing Uluru stirred something in him—he had an "initial shock of indefinable recognition." He felt he *knew* this rock. It wasn't that he had seen pictures of it. "Your knowledge of this rock is grounded in something much more elemental," Bryson said. "Somewhere in the deep sediment of your being some long-dormant fragment of primordial memory, some little severed tail of DNA, has twitched or stirred." Uluru has an importance to you, Bryson realized, "at the species level."[810]

According to American geomantic researcher and educator Robert Coon, Uluru and the neighboring rock outcrops called the Olgas (or Katatjuta) are the major aspects of the Earth's third or solar plexus chakra.[811]

As the place of the Sun, Uluru and Katatjuta "influence the health and vitality of the entire planet." Uluru, as the nest or home of the Rainbow Serpent "communicates the health-giving frequencies of the planetary solar plexus to the entirety of the global body."

Coon predicts that in 2020, Uluru will be the planetary focus for a "major alchemical event." He says that an etheric link in the form of an umbilical cord to the Sun was constructed there on July 8, 1990, as the product of ritual, imagination, human activity, and the Earth Spirit. On January 13, 2020, when Saturn, Pluto, Mercury, and the Sun are conjunct in the sign of Capricorn (Uluru's sacred sign), the solar umbilical cord at Uluru will "fully activate," Coon says. "This is the ideal event for creating an archetypal communicative link between the Sun and the Earth."[812]

According to Aboriginal lore from the Kimberley region of Australia's remote northwest, the entire continent of Australia is lying down flat on its back. Different areas in Australia correspond to different body parts; the ribs, for example, go right across the continent. Inside the body of the continent is *Wunggud,* the Snake (another name for the Rainbow Serpent). "She grows all of nature on the outside of her body," explains an Aborigine elder. Uluru is the navel, the center, *wangigit,* of this geomythic body of *Bandaiyan,* which is what the Aborigines of Kimberley call Australia.[813]

GEOMANTIC

Dome; Dragon; Planetary Solar Plexus Chakra; Mount Olympus.

DOME: The dome over Uluru corresponds to beta Draconis, or Rastaban in the constellation Draco, the cosmic dragon or serpent. The full name, from the Arabic, is *Al Ras al Thu'ban,* meaning "the Dragon's Head." Rastaban as a star is yellow like our Sun, but six hundred times brighter, of the second magnitude, and located three hundred light years from Earth. When Rastaban is seen in combination with Eltanin *(Al Ras al Tinnin),* the gamma star in Draco, about 4° away, the two are said to be the Dragon's eyes.

As a constellation, Draco has fifteen stars, three on its head, and twelve along its spine down to the tail. It sits at the "top" of the galaxy circling the Pole Star; at one time, Thuban, a star in its tail, was itself virtually the Pole Star. Draco sits in the galaxy between the Greater and Lesser Bears (Ursa Major, Ursa Minor), and is said to guard the golden apples of the Hesperides, but was slain by Heracles.

While most cultures construed Draco as a variation of the archetypal cosmic dragon, the embodiment of primordial chaos, the Chinese saw these stars as *Tsi Kung,* "Palace of the Heavenly Emperor." Akkadian astronomers described this star, which at the time was approximately the Pole star, as *Tir-An-na* (Life of Heaven), *Dayan Same* (Judge of Heaven), and *Dayan Sidi* (Favorable Judge), all of which epithets represented their god *Caga Gilgati.*

DRAGON: The myths of the Rainbow Serpent at Uluru are geomantically well founded, for co-present with the great red Rock is one of the Earth's thirteen original dragons. In practical terms, Uluru gets a double hit of dragon energy, for it has the *eye* of Draco, Rastaban, focused through it by way of the dome, and *all* of Draco by virtue of one of Draco's thirteen holograms of itself present.

Inside Uluru is the Dragon or Rainbow Serpent, like a coiled, quivering, oscillating vibratory field. When I say "inside," I mean the reality layer that lies next to the physical but is accessed through the same space: it's as if you enter the Rock to meet the Rainbow Serpent. It's useful to picture this "serpent" as the classical oroboros, the snake eating its own tail, the beginning in the end.

The word Uluru is among other things an invocatory mantra: *Ulll-urrr-uuu*. Intoning the word Uluru in the right way inducts one into the Rainbow Serpent's dimension. It transports you to the Rainbow Serpent. Loosely interpreted, Uluru means the head *(Ulll)* and tail *(uuu)* joined or harmonized by the Sun or head *(urrr)*. But whose head?

Where the two ends meet is a face, the face of the creator expressed at the level of dynamic action and the unfolding of cosmic light. One Aboriginal name for this deity is *Baiame*. If you follow Uluru's umbilical cord back to its cosmic source, you come to a red dimension, a flaming red, angry face, the face of Mars, or Ares, the Greek war god. This is not the planet Mars, but the galactic dimension called Mars, a layer of reality with a function.

Astrology speaks of Mars (meaning the symbolic aspect of the planet as it affects human consciousness) as the light of the aggressor. Mars is the son of the Sun, an active male force to do with virility, procreative powers, the assertion of individualized desires, and a principle of cosmic law. Mars is the force that "creates matter out of the primal energy of spirit," and as such can be a "great creative impetus." This energy serves as "the vehicle of new outpourings of energy into the material world."[814]

The energy in question is the entire electromagnetic spectrum of visible light that encompasses all of the visible universe, and here visibly extends to a perceptual capacity far beyond the limited range of human sight. Astronomers often speak of stars as a red dwarf, a blue giant, a yellow star like our Sun. These color differences are part of the overall electromagnetic field (EMF) spectrum.

The Rainbow Serpent is a grand metaphor for the EMF spectrum. It's a cosmos of differentiated light, all within the Rainbow Serpent's undulating, oscillating, oroboric body. It's the whole sea of astral light with spillover into what we term the physical world.

Working backwards into the mythic again, it is appropriate to note that dragon myths always say that the dragon guards a treasure such as golden apples or a jewel horde. Here again we see the metaphor of the EMF spectrum. The jewels, golden apples, and treasure hordes at this level of the metaphor are the stars and everything they represent: knowledge, light, perspective, energy, images, symbols, matrices, codes, higher evolution, multiple dimensions—a diffraction of the totality of consciousness.

These "treasures" are the Ancestors who designed and manifested the world in the Dreamtime. Experientially, everything in the dragon—the jewels—*is* the Dreamtime, still and always present as a living astral reality, the template of the physical world. You could think, again metaphorically, of the dragon's jewels as the *seeds* of the numerous Dreamings—the Kangaroo Dreaming, the Witchety-grub Dreaming, and the rest—and their Ancestors, or Group Souls.

You enter Uluru through the domed eye of Draco and find the Rainbow Serpent. You enter the Serpent and you are now in the Dreamtime. In the Dreamtime you are once again in that vast, seemingly inchoate primordial, creative, world-generating space.

Dragons are also said—and blamed for this—to hold the original Cosmic Waters within themselves, seemingly refusing to release them into the world until a hero, either human or godly, slays them and frees the trapped energies. The Waters can also be understood metaphorically as the EMF spectrum.

We can thank the Greek mythographers for reminding us that dragons are associated with Ares. Cadmus the demigod founded Thebes in Greece after he slew the dragon at the sacred spring of Ares. Apollodorus made the association clear when he said, "a dragon, which some said was the offspring of Ares." As a punishment for killing the sacred dragon, Cadmus had to serve Ares for eight years.[815]

The *Tjukurrpa,* or Dreamtime, *is* the Rainbow Serpent, the EMF spectrum, the dragon's cosmic jewel horde, a complete library of the cosmic order—the blueprints, frequency codes, light valences, the creation syllables, the constellation rationales, the index of all the Dreamings, world-generating speech.

What about those boomerangs? Uluru and even the continent of Australia are shaped like a boomerang. The story of Linga the lizard-man makes more sense when you read it backwards. He buried a boomerang flung out into the Australian landscape *from* Uluru. Uluru is the mother of the boomerangs. We have to approach this metaphorically again.

Uluru is full of boomerangs. It has thousands, maybe millions. Each is an agent of its dragon energy, its oscillatory field, a concentration of its EMF spectrum. Uluru generates and sustains the numerous geomantic sites around Australia by way of having planted a boomerang at each in the Dreamtime. The route from Uluru to the specific planted boomerang corresponds to some extent to the song lines and Dreaming tracks. They are like route maps for where the boomerangs were thrown. Each is a seed pod full of Uluru creative fire.

The boomerangs always come back to Uluru; it draws them like a magnet, or like a mother summoning her children. If you are at a holy site somewhere else in Australia, its boomerang will return you to Uluru.[816]

The boomerang can be pictured as an image for the oscillating field of the Rainbow Serpent in lateral motion. It's also a dynamic expression of the tetrahedron (a four-sided polygon, or pyramid; a three dimensional triangle), the geometric expression for the fire element, which pertains to both the dragon and Uluru's function as a solar plexus chakra. "Meditate there on the region of Fire, triangular in form, and shining like the rising sun," say the Vedic authorities about the third chakra.[817]

PLANETARY SOLAR PLEXUS CHAKRA: The Mars connection is relevant in terms of Uluru's role as one aspect of the planetary solar plexus chakra (see Teotihuacan, Mexico, for another aspect). The trouble is that this chakra should not be called "solar plexus" for its energies do not directly involve the Sun. As the astrology statement above reminded us, Mars is the son of the Son, and Mars is the energy associated with the third chakra.

It's important to remember that what we call chakras are fundamentally the manifestation matrices for the energies of the planetary spheres—not the physical planets, but layers or dimensions of reality that the metaphysical tradition long ago labeled in accordance with the planetary names. Mars is the planet of the third chakra, called *Manipura,* or City of Gems in the Vedic accounts.

Again, the gems reference is apt in terms of the dragon's jewel horde. We must remember, though, that the dragon pertains to the first chakra, the *Muladhara,* because it is the "offspring" of Ares, whose residence is the third chakra. The *Manipura* is the jewel horde of the first chakra's dragon.

Uluru grounds the Mars energy for the planet and distributes it to all the third chakra geomantic sites around the Earth. This would include, for instance, the *Manipura* chakras of the 432 Albions within the Landscape Zodiacs. The Mars chakra, grounded at Uluru, is arrayed like a band around the planet, a reality level involving everything that is structured to vibrate at the Manipura level.

In this way, for instance, it is correct to call Uluru the world's navel or the *wangigit* of Australia seen as a deity's body. Uluru is both. It is a navel for the Earth for the Mars energy coming in through the prime *Manipura* center; and it is the navel for the continent and "cultural landscape" of Australia insofar as it is that continent's major nodal point and the residence of its egregor, the snake.

The Mars-Uluru affiliation also accounts for the disturbing myths of battle, mutilation, and death recounted in the two prime Uluru myths cited above. The Mars energy can be hard to handle; the myths say that its deity is the god of war.

The third chakra is the seat of the element of Fire, whose sign is a triangle, which is related in shape to the boomerang. "By meditating on this Navel Lotus, the power to destroy and create (the world) is acquired," the yogic texts say. But they also say that "all the wealth of knowledge" abides in the lotus of the face of one of the presiding deities of this energy center.[818]

In the third chakra, you have the fiery energy that creates and destroys worlds and leads to dialectical tension between opposites (the oroboric aspect of the Rainbow Serpent and Uluru itself)—and the treasure horde of knowledge that this center's deity possesses by virtue of being the "parent" of the dragon. In other words, much of Uluru's geomyths can be accounted for by the energetics of the third chakra.

MOUNT OLYMPUS: Set like a diadem on the Rainbow Serpent is a Celestial City of the gods, Mount Olympus. It's odd, of course, to talk about Greek gods in the middle of the Outback; and the Aborigines would have a completely different conceptualization of this enclave, but its function remains the same.

The Ray Masters of the Great Bear ground their energies and the "Rays" through the thirteen dragons around the Earth. They use the dragons as an energy base of operations for extrapolating and maintaining aspects of the Earth grid, or, in this context, the song lines and Dreaming trackways.

THE ULURU SYSTEM: Uluru must be contemplated in terms of how the dragon, solar plexus chakra, and Mount Olympus work together. Let's start at the innermost level, Mount Olympus.

Think of the Uluru System as a circle whose extent is defined by the girth of the dragon. The Mount Olympus is like a crystalline spear inserted into the coiled and flaming body of the Rainbow Serpent, the flames being the fire of Mars. The spear masters, concentrates, and directs the raw fire energy.

The fourteen Ray Masters each occupy about 25° of the full circle of 360. This is their individual zone of concentration. Each Ray Master commands the Fire element of the Manipura chakra within that 25° area. The Mars-Fire element may be pictured as a series of linked flaming deific heads—the head of a fierce god on fire, adamant, fierce, roaring, almost uncontrollable. It is warlike by virtue of the sheer magnitude of the assertion of its being—making war on our flammable concepts of reality, spacetime, and consciousness.

The Ray Masters work at a level of reality above the Fire element; therefore, they can control it. For them, it is a tool or raw material. Their energy and color frequency (such as bright orange, gold, yellow, dark blue, light blue, light green, dark green, lilac, purple, scarlet, pink—a vibrational spectrum) enter the Fire element of the Mars planetary sphere at Uluru and master it, using it as fuel. This new blend of Fire and Ray passes into the Rainbow Serpent (dragon), the repository of the seeds and structures of creation, as a beam, and each Ray Master beam irradiates a 25° swath of its myriad of stars.

The Serpent is a living rainbow of the seven major colors and their seven subtleties by virtue of being permeated with the energies of the fourteen Ray Masters. It is also a Rainbow Serpent by virtue of the effect of these fourteen color rays on the innumerable stars it contains. These are the color-frequency bands—the vibratory spectrum—for creation and manifestation in the world.

These irradiated stars then move out of Uluru into the Australian landscape as seeds for the Dreaming of all life forms, including human. This is the Dreamtime matrix streaming out into the physical world as a creative, generative current. Try to picture Uluru as a fourteen-spoked wheel with fourteen adjacent color beams radiating out across the Australian continent so that every inch of land is affected. Uluru is a big boomerang of creative Fire poised to be flung to the eight directions across the Australian continent.

When the environments of the United States and perhaps Europe become unlivable, Uluru will teach us in the West how to regenerate our environments from the Dreamtime reservoir in Australia's Great Red Center.

If you visit Uluru and tune into it along the lines suggested here, do it only for a short while. This energy is very powerful. I don't mean impressive; I mean it will incinerate you at some level if you expose yourself to it unprepared or keep its energy field in proximity to yours for too long. Uluru will activate your solar plexus chakra and possibly put it into overdrive. Whatever shadow content you have associated with this energy center may come to the surface through your contact with Uluru. So think of it as an initiation and consider preparing yourself beforehand for unusual psychic effects.

Wawel Hill, Cracow, Poland

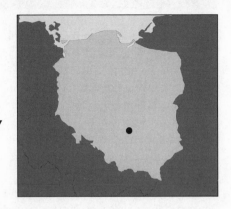

Wawel Hill is a rocky hilltop within Cracow, a city in southern Poland set on the banks of the Vistula River. Cracow is believed to be one of Poland's oldest cities, founded as a fortified fortress around 700 A.D., and Wawel Hill, sometimes called the "Polish Acropolis," is the oldest inhabited section of the city. Archeologists suggest that the hill was settled as early as fifty thousand years ago and that three thousand years ago the settlement bustled with trade and farming. Cracow is believed to have grown around Wawel Hill.

At one time, the citadel was surrounded by walls with eight gates and fifty-five towers. In the mid-nineteenth century most of the walls and the gates were torn down (though the Florian Gate remains today), and the *Planty*, a delightful park, was put in its place and completely surrounds the old town.

For more than five hundred years, starting in 1138, Wawel Hill was the political seat of the Polish kings who resided in the Wawel Castle atop the hill. Tyniec, a steep, rocky fortified natural stronghold on the western outskirts of Cracow, once commanded the approach to Cracow through the Vistua River valley and in effect was

a defensive outpost for the capital city. Today a Benedictine Abbey occupies the hilltop.

In 1978, Cracow was entered on UNESCO's list of world cultural heritage centers. In the year 2000, Cracow was deemed Euro City of the Year by the European Union Culture Commission. Today the city boasts twelve universities, ten thousand scientists, fifty-one thousand college students, twenty-eight museums, and numerous art galleries and churches. That is sufficient to keep the city's two million annual tourists occupied.

One of the structures on Wawel Hill is Wawel Cathedral, a fourteenth-century building (consecrated in 1359), built by King Casimir the Great and once used as the site for the coronations and funerals of Polish kings. The cathedral was erected on the site of an earlier church built there around 1020 by Poland's first king.

Another King Casimir the Great established the Cracow Academy (later renamed Jagiellionan University) in 1364, the second oldest in Central Europe and the alma mater of Copernicus. An annual religious ceremony and Corpus Christi procession begins at Wawel Cathedral, passing down the steep Royal Way to *Rynek Glowny*, a great open plaza and marketplace (ten square acres), to the delight of thousands of residents, tourists, and pilgrims.

HISTORY AND ARCHEOLOGY

Cracow is regarded as Poland's spiritual capital.[819] One of the reasons for this is the fact that a remarkable painting called the "Image of the Merciful Jesus" resides in the Shrine of Divine Mercy in the Church of Saint Mary (completed in 1223). This was painted by Sister Faustina (Faustyna Kowalska) on the basis of multiple revelations to her of Jesus during the years 1931 to 1938.

She had been a nun at the convent of the Congregation of Sisters of Our Lady of Mercy in nearby Plock when Jesus appeared in a vision on February 22, 1931, and presented an unusual image of himself projecting two rays of light from his heart. "I saw the Lord Jesus in a white garment," she wrote afterwards. "He had one hand raised in blessing, and the other was touching His garment at the breast."

One of the rays emanating from his breast, Jesus told Sister Faustina, was pale white and stood for "the water which justifies souls." The other ray, which was red, "stands for the blood which is the life of souls." Jesus further informed her of the purpose of presenting this image. "I am offering people a vessel to which they are to keep coming for graces to the fountain of Mercy. That Vessel is this image." He asked her to paint the image, instructed her in the particularities of a sacramental feast he wished the Church to hold, presented details on an eight-day Novena to start on Good Friday, and dictated "The Chaplet of Divine Mercy," a prayer to be recited on ordinary rosary beads.

Since 1980, the popularity of the Shrine of Divine Mercy as a Catholic pilgrimage destination has "rocketed," and "few other places of pilgrimage in the world are growing as fast in popularity" as this one, to which people resort to pray before the miraculous image of the Merciful Jesus.[820]

Another factor contributing to Cracow's spiritual preeminence is the fact that Saint Stanislaus, the patron saint both of Cracow and of all of Poland, and a symbol of Poland's nationhood, is buried in Wawel Cathedral in a highly elaborate shrine containing a silver coffin. In his time, Saint Stanislaus (1030–1079) was the Bishop of Cracow, a staunch advocate of civil rights, and, eventually, an opponent of the Polish king, Boleslaw the Bold.

Stanislaus denounced Boleslaw's cruelties and injustices, and later he excommunicated the king, stopping religious services at the Cathedral when Boleslaw entered. One day while Stanislaus was performing the Mass at the Chapel of Saint Michael in a suburb outside Cracow, Boleslaw killed him on the spot. Stanislaus was canonized in 1253 by Pope Innocent IV. The site of Stanislaus' death is a rocky hillock called the Skalka Sanctuary, five minutes' walk down the Vistula from Wawel Castle. Every May 8, Saint Stanislaus' day, Cracow bishops lead a major religious procession, carrying the saint's relics from Skalka to Wawel Cathedral.

Prior to World War II, Cracow had a large Jewish population of some sixty thousand, and they occupied the Kazimierz district just outside the old city and near the base of Wawel Hill. Kazimierz, established by Casimir the Great as a Jewish refuge against persecution in the Rhineland, at one time was the most prosperous Jewish community in Poland. Many of the scenes from Steven Spielberg's movie *Schindler's List* were filmed here. From 1939 to 1945, when the Nazis occupied Poland, they used Cracow as an administrative headquarters for Poland. But Cracow survived the bombings of World War II nearly undamaged.

MYTH AND LEGEND

The primary myth of Cracow is the Dragon of Wawel Hill, known in Polish as *Smok Wawelski*. The story goes that very long ago at the dawn of

Poland's history the king of the community later known as Cracow had a formidable problem with a dragon that lived inside Wawel Hill. It was horrible, belched fire, and ate young children; it slaughtered the innocent, devoured their farm animals, stole their belongings, and generally ruined the countryside. *Smok Wawelski* also had a dietary preference for young virgins, and as things developed, the only maiden left in the area was the king's daughter.

The King of Cracow offered a reward and announced throughout Poland that whoever could slay *Smok Wawelski* could marry his daughter. Lots of knights from all over Europe tried and failed, and eventually no more came, except one, but he wasn't a knight. His name was Krak, and he had no sword, no fighting prowess, or even formidable physical stature. In fact, he was a shoemaker's apprentice. But he had guile and intelligence. Krak would defeat the dragon with sulfur and hot spices.

He roasted three fat sheep, then stuffed their stomachs with the hottest spices and herbs he could procure. Then he added a generous helping of sulfur, sewed up the sheep, and placed them at the mouth of the dragon's cave on the side of Wawel Hill. The dragon's greed and appetite got the better of him, and without inspecting the sheep, he ate them at once and became enormously thirsty. He was so thirsty that he drank half the Vistula River and still his thirst was not quenched. His stomach swelled disastrously from this volume of water and soon exploded, killing the dragon and freeing Cracow of *Smok Wawelski*.

Today, a statue stands at the front of the cave on the rocky western slope of Wawel Hill overlooking the Vistula to mark the former den of *Smok Wawelski*. The Dragon's Cave, or *Smocza Jama*, is two hundred feet long and attracts many visitors, who enter it by way of a turret in the fortifications on the top of Wawel Hill. Even though their chronology does not quite allow time for

Smok Wawelski's residence there, researchers propose that the cave was inhabited by humans from Neolithic times to the sixteenth century.

Also of interest are massive prehistoric bones suspended by chains at the left of the entrance to the Wawel Cathedral; these bones are said to be those of *Smok Wawelski*, but scientists say the artifacts comprise a mammoth's hide, a rhinoceros's skull, and a whale's rib. Local legend holds that when these bones fall from their position, the end of the world will be at hand.

For those who think dragons are the products of human imagination, Polish mythographer Katarzyna Raburska has this to say: "If ever you happen to visit Kraków, go to the dragon's cave at the Wawel Castle and listen carefully to the whispers and voices of the old walls. Perhaps they will tell you the truth about their notorious companion!"[821]

The dragon myth, though formidable, does not exhaust Cracow's mythic attributions. Local folklore credits Wawel Hill as the site visited by Doctor Faustus in his quest for the elusive Philosopher's Stone. The Doctor Faustus legend (reprised by Christopher Marlowe, Johann Wolfgang von Goethe, and Thomas Mann, among others) is about the scholar who sells his soul to the Devil in exchange for celestial, occult, and magical information. Some scholars argue that the legend was based on a real man named Johann Faustus who lived in Germany in the sixteenth century.

The Philosopher's Stone, another legendary object, is the quest of all alchemists and occultists, but whether there was any basis for associating it with Cracow is intriguing but hard to verify from conventional sources. The Stone was considered to be both the means of transmuting base elements into gold, and the perfection of the alchemical process.

Among other mythic or folkloric attributions is the belief that the ghost of a legendary hero named

Lajkonik is said still to ride a horse through Market Square in commemoration (or perhaps endless reiteration) of the time when in the flesh he warned Cracow of an imminent infidel invasion. In fact, the annual Lajkonik Festival in Cracow is an important event in the folk life of the city.

Every Thursday following Corpus Christi day, a crowd assembles in a monastery courtyard in Cracow.[822] A musical troupe provides accompaniment as "Lajkonik" enters, riding a hobby horse; this Lajkonik's costume is said to be a highly accurate rendition of an original Tartar disguise. The parish priest leads the pageant through the streets of Cracow in a three-hour procession that culminates in Market Square.

Somewhat related to this is the legend of the bugle call from the tower of Saint Mary's Church. Its construction was completed in 1397, and owing to its two prominent towers, Saint Mary's served as a watchtower for Cracow for centuries. Apparently, the bugle call *(Hejnal)* has been played every hour from its windows into the four directions, as if announcing something to the four quarters of the world, says Cracow legend. Then the melody stops abruptly in memory of a watchman struck in the throat by an enemy's arrow in 1241.

Highly intriguing yet ultimately enigmatic is a prophecy linking Poland with India. While in New Delhi, American writer China Galland was told by the former Indian Ambassador to Mexico that an old, unattributable Indian story said that "when the world is destroyed there will only be two places that will be safe." One is a temple in Ujjain in southern India, and the other is "a tunnel underneath the Wawel Castle chapel in Krakow, Poland."[823]

MYSTICS AND TOURISTS

The nineteenth-century French novelist Honoré de Balzac (1799–1850) wrote in his diary that to see Wawel Cathedral, which he visited with his Polish wife, "alone justified" his trip to Cracow. He was impressed by its "numerous chantry chapels with an unparalleled display of riches, unsurpassed by anything except, I suppose, Rome or certain churches in Belgium."[824]

Lenny Karpman found Cracow a welcome respite in the midst of a painful journey to Auschwitz (in Poland) to honor the memory of his Jewish relatives and ancestors. "The fairyland of Cracow was surcease from thoughts of holocaust sorrow," he wrote afterwards. Market Square was "radiant" with tulips and lilies; the music of strolling musicians and the enticing aromas of restaurant food filled the air. Artists displayed their works on the city walls; students from Jagiellonian University ambled by. "The sun glistened off the golden dome of the cathedral. The turrets of the castle rose from treetops on the hill."[825]

Another traveler, undertaking the same type of homage to the recent past in Poland, was similarly impressed with Cracow. "Wawel Hill was stunning and embodied all that was most highly prized in Polish history." He admitted the sight left him nearly speechless. "The best I can do is to say that it was the center of Polish power, religion, and art" for nine centuries, and that he was "amazed" by the "splendor and majesty" of Wawel Hill, and even more astonished by the fact that "so much that was so beautiful had escaped both destruction and Nazi [art] collectors."[826]

GEOMANTIC

Dome; Dragon; Golden Egg; Interdimensional Portal; Aquarian Albion Hand Chakra.

DOME: The dome over Wawel Hill corresponds to delta Hydra, a star on the forehead of the Watersnake, the legendary Hydra with nine heads. The multiple heads of the Watersnake are created by six stars in the constellation's head and neck, with a seventh on its horn. In Greek myths, one of Heracles' twelve tasks was to slay the nine-headed Hydra of Lerna; every time a hero sliced off one head, two more instantly sprouted in its place. Heracles prevailed, however, and slew the Hydra. There is no recorded myth about the delta star, which is of the fourth magnitude.

DRAGON: Cracow's cultural memory of its geomythic landscape is delightfully direct and accurate. There is in fact a dragon present at Wawel Hill, one of the Earth's 1,053 minor dragons. Energetically, the Wawel dragon, or *Smok Wawelski,* is much larger than the diameter of the hill; its "coils" extend throughout Cracow, and even beyond. In a sense, Wawel Hill is but the head of Smok Wawelski.

The dragon blood shed by the fearless, guileful Krak feeds the city, inspiring and nourishing its great range of arts and cultural initiatives, attracting, if not magnetizing, poets, writers, scientists, painters, and revolutionaries. One geomantic purpose of a landscape dragon is to enrich the ethers and land with its "blood," which is to say, the cosmic life force and knowledge it contains. Various dragon-slaying myths say that the dragon-slayer kills the dragon to release the pent-up waters held back from the world by the dragon. Other myths say that the hero seeks the dragon's treasures, which it avariciously guards.

Esoterically, both attributions are accurate with respect to dragons. The "Waters" and the "treasure horde" both refer to the star knowledge that the dragon embodies. Whether it is a major or minor dragon, each dragon is a hologram of the prime dragon, Draco, coiled around the Polar Star at the "top" of the galaxy. In a sense, Draco is the mother of all stars; they sparkle within its vast serpentine form.

The waters Draco withholds until the proper moment when an initiate can release them on the public's behalf, are cosmic intelligence—all the thoughts, pictures, intentions, history, and des-

tinies of the celestial beings whose outward forms are the stars. The Gnostic philosophers personified this star knowledge as the Divine Sophia. So when a human geomantic hero "slays" a dragon, exalted, spiritually vivifying, and certainly formidable cosmic energies are released into the local Earth energy matrix. Such a site—a "bled" dragon, so to speak—is an excellent choice for the seat of kingship and political administration.

The ordination of Polish kings at Wawel Hill was validated by the resident dragon. The Polish kings who were crowned at Wawel Hill assumed crowns dipped in dragon's blood—crowns in both senses: as symbols of political authority and as vehicles of spiritual insight. This is putting something of a metaphorical brush to the situation, but one only has to remember the widely reported attribute of dragon blood, that it inspires in one who drinks it knowledge of the speech of all animals and a kind of panoptic clairvoyance.

GOLDEN EGG: Complementing the dragon energy at Wawel Hill is an achieved Golden Egg, out of which has been born the Golden Child. You could say this is the primary jewel that the dragon was set to guard against appropriation by those who do not deserve it, which is to say, those who lack the initiation sufficient to handle its energies. Originally, the Golden Egg sat on Wawel Hill as if in a landscape eggcup, nestled, incubating, within Smok Wawelski's manifold coils, awaiting the day of its hatching—a divine fetus sleeping in a womb of stars, we might say.

Since the Egg has been "hatched," the Child resides on Wawel Hill, the Madonna with her arms wrapped protectively around it positioned behind Wawel, while the foundational nodes are situated from the Vistula River up to the base of the hill. The annual Corpus Christi procession down Wawel Hill is geomantically appropriate for it effectively transfers and distributes the consciousness or energies of the Golden Child and the dragon into the city and the surrounding area.

Smok Wawelski, embodiment of the Waters, serves as a baptismal font for the Child, whose head is continually bathed in the cosmic waters. The superimposition of these two geomythic figures creates a powerful geomantic mix for Cracow. They represent a harmonious blend of the primordial and the millennial, the Old Adam and the New Adam, the pagan and the Christed, the first birth and the rebirth, the star knowledge and the Christ Consciousness that awakens all stars. The dragon and the Child create a spiritual shield, something like a gold sphere around Wawel Hill, providing a spiritual safe haven on the hill.

THE ALCHEMICAL HILL: The fact that the combined energies of the dragon and Golden Child are present here helps us understand the folklore attribution that had Doctor Faustus seeking the fabled Philosopher's Stone at Wawel Hill. It also gives us a keen insight into why Cracow is hailed as Poland's spiritual capital.

The Stone is not so much a palpable object as a process and a completion—a precious golden jewel of inestimable price, worthy of the dragon's attention. Wawel Hill is an alchemical retort, a transmutation pressure cooker, the precious Hermetic Vessel, offering the right blend of energies.

"The uroboros [sic] or the dragon are classic symbols for the *nigredo* stage, representing as they do the Prime Matter *(Prima materia)* in its blackened state of mortification and putrefaction." The dragon represents the "cosmogonic unity" of the Prime Matter, out of which the elements must be separated.

In alchemical symbolism, slaying the dragon is essential to the progress of the "opus" of creating the Philosopher's Stone, which is the freeing of the great secret elixir of immortality within each human—"the treasure of spiritual realization." The Stone is sometimes called the "medicine of metals" because it helps to heal the

defects or corruption in metals and raises them to the perfection of gold, the finest of metals.[827]

Krak slaying Smok Wawelski symbolized consciousness overcoming the old, the primordial, and the obsolete in the dangerous preliminary stages of the great inner transformation process described by alchemy. The goal and the fruit of the opus, in alchemical terms, are the fusion, conjunction, and marriage of the energies of the Sun and Moon, Sol and Luna, the King and Queen, two internal opposites. What better embodiment of this than the Golden Child?

"The *coniunctio* taking place in the vessel is a very common alchemical illustration, and from this union is born the Son of the Philosophers *(filius philosophorum)* who represents the Stone or *Lapis* of transformation." The Son of the Philosophers is a fair equivalent of the Golden Child, which is reborn, Christed awareness. Alchemical tradition also associates the Hermetic Vessel with the "philosophical egg," which is the microcosm of Heaven and Earth.[828]

Obviously we find our "philosophical egg" at Wawel Hill in the form of the Golden Egg. Doctor Faustus, whether we take the name to refer to a specific individual or to a series of men and women seeking alchemical initiation and transformation, would have sought out the Hermetic Vessel that is Wawel Hill. You find the Wawel Hill Hermetic Vessel in the gap between Smok Wawelski and the Golden Child, between the beginning and the end—in practical terms, within the two-hundred-foot-long cavern whose entry is on the western slope of the hill.

INTERDIMENSIONAL PORTAL: The enigmatic statement that Wawel Hill is one of two locations expected to be ultimate safe havens at the time of Apocalypse gets some grounding by the fact that within Wawel Hill is an interdimensional portal. It is, metaphorically, a second precious jewel that Smok Wawelski assiduously guards.

Within the energy field at the core of Wawel Hill is a circle of ascended human guardians caretaking the essential energy of this site. I say "ascended" to denote the fact that they work from the supersensible worlds into this one, tending the energy as if it were a sparkling blue sphere. Where they stand marks the entry into the interdimensional portal, which may be experienced as a long tunnel through which you pass very quickly. You emerge, depending on how your mind congeals the energies into an understandable image, in a vast underground cavern, at whose center sits a spaceship of (to me) indescribable dimensions and proportions.

It's not that it is incomprehensibly huge; it's that its shape is too protean to be described in words and concepts for shapes known to us. Let's just say that this "ship" has a lot to do with how Wawel Hill may be a haven of safety at "the end of the world."

AQUARIAN ALBION HAND CHAKRA: The geomantic array of Wawel Hill is the right-hand palm chakra in the Albion plate presently under the astrological influence of Aquarius. Another site in the Aquarian Leo is Dornach, Switzerland (its left-hand palm chakra), world headquarters of Rudolf Steiner's Anthroposophical Society.

Imagine the giant humanlike Albion lying across central Europe, a point of brilliant light in each palm. In his right palm, the Wawel Hill temple with dome, dragon, and Golden Child; in his left at Dornach, a dome, zodiac, Golden Child, and emerald. To the palm chakra, one of the seventy-two minor energy centers in the body, is attributed the ability to transmit healing energy through touch.

Wu-T'ai Shan, China

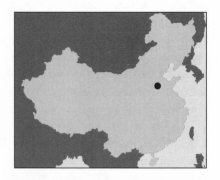

Located 150 miles southwest of Beijing in the northeast of China, Wu-T'ai Shan, or Five Terrace Mountain, is not a single mountain but a cluster of five adjacent flat or terrace-like peaks within a small range of mountains. Dozens of temples are distributed throughout this considerable area, which measures twelve miles by eight miles.

In other words, Wu-T'ai Shan comprises almost one hundred square miles of sacred space, included in which are seventy-six active temples and forty-seven monasteries. Not surprisingly, it is one of China's four Buddhist holy mountains. Old Chinese texts describe the Five Terraces as resembling a giant hand, with the central section being the palm and the five smooth-topped terraces being the four fingers and thumb.

Those who have visited the site say it is more like a sanctuary enclosed by mountains than a single holy mountain.[829] The Buddhist scholar and traveler John Blofeld, visiting Wu-T'ai Shan in the late 1930s, said that the appearance of Five Terraces might have originally inspired the idea of Shangri-la, and that never before had he seen "a sight so lovely nor have I beheld its equal since."[830]

Topographically, the Wu-T'ai Shan geomantic zone consists of four peaks that encircle a high basin out of whose center rises the fifth peak. The highest peak is called Northern Terrace and it stands 10,033 feet, while the lowest is Southern Terrace at 8,153 feet; between them stretch twelve miles of mountains.

While the Wu-T'ai Shan complex today clearly has a Buddhist orientation, it was once known to the Chinese Taoists before Buddhism arrived in China as *Tzu-fu Shan,* which means "Purple Palace Mount." The Taoists believed that immortals lived on Purple Palace, and noted that a purple haze constantly emanated from the peaks. An ancient Chinese text, called *Hua-yen ching,* listed eight mythic mountains, one each in the eight cardinal directions in China and on each of which a great *Bodhisattva* (enlightened helper being) was believed to dwell for the benefit of humanity.

The Bodhisattva Manjusri, the embodiment of perfect wisdom and insight *(prajna)* was said to reside on *Ch'ing-liang Shan,* "The Mountain of Chill Clarity." Evidence from later documents confirmed that the mythic *Ch'ing-liang Shan* was in fact five-peaked Wu-T'ai Shan in the Shanxi Province of China, and the earthly home of Wenshu Pusa, the Chinese name for Manjusri. Today one of the peaks is host to the Temple of Chill Clarity, suggesting this might be the center for Manjusri's sacred mountain.

HISTORY AND ARCHEOLOGY

Historians are not sure when the Wu-T'ai Shan mountain complex was first inhabited and used for religious purposes, but the oldest wooden building in China still stands there, the *Nan Chan Si,* the South Meditation Temple, built in 782 A.D. Earlier buildings, subsequently destroyed, are known to have been there during the Northern Ch'i dynasty of 550–577, when there were an estimated two hundred temples and monasteries at Wu-T'ai Shan. In fact, historians believe that the mountain area has been a religious center since the reign of Emperor Ming Di, 58–75 A.D.

Between the sixth and the ninth centuries, Wu-T'ai Shan became renowned as a foremost residence of Manjusri and as a major monastic center and pilgrimage destination. The site was inhabited by thousands of monks and visited in "vast numbers" by Buddhists from China, South and Central Asia, Korea, and Japan.

Later, when the Mongols controlled the area in the thirteenth century, their presence led to the growth of a "significant Tibetan presence" and a strong tradition of Tibetan-flavored Lamaism otherwise unusual for China. Many compare the ambiance of Wu-T'ai Shan, with its vividly blue skies, its isolation, austere, crisp mountain air, and intense practice of Lamaism, with Lhasa, the political and spiritual capital of Tibet. For a time, Tibetans and Mongolians ranked Wu-T'ai Shan as one of their Five Great Places of Pilgrimage.

Today Wu-T'ai Shan is equally a Chinese and a Tibetan Buddhist center, "this being evident not least in the great white Tibetan pagoda *(chorten)* that dominates the central valley and that has become the chief visual symbol of the entire complex."[831] The Great White Stupa, fifty feet tall, stands at the base of the central peak in the village of Tai Huai. Pilgrims circumambulate the stupa, their right hand extended to it, while spin-ning prayer wheels send the supplicants' prayers to Manjusri for assistance in overcoming the travails of birth and death. "It is said to contain a lock of hair of Wen-shu or Manjusri who turns non-stop the Wheel of Law for the salvation of the Chinese."[832]

MYSTICS AND TOURISTS

Wu-T'ai Shan's claim to be a principal residence for Manjusri is based less on myth and legend than on the reports of mystics who had visions of the celestial being while present at Wu-T'ai Shan. Over the centuries, many at Wu-T'ai Shan have spoken of apparitions of Manjusri astride his blue lion in the high mountains above the monasteries. People have reported seeing Manjusri as an elderly monk, a young prince on a white lion, rainbow-tinted clouds, balls of colored light, even as a playful dragon amidst the clouds.

Supposedly the Manjusri association began when an Indian monk visited Wu-T'ai Shan in the first century A.D. and reported a vision of the exalted Manjusri, who is typically depicted as brandishing a great sword of wisdom in his right hand to cleave ignorance, holding a sutra scroll in his left to signify his profound teachings, and riding a fierce blue lion to symbolize the adamantine clarity of his view. He is the lord of the highest transcendent wisdom and the revealer of ultimate reality.

The name Manjusri comes from the Sanskrit and means—somewhat ironically considering his iconographic depiction—"He Who is Noble and Gentle." Buddhists also know him as Manjugosha, "the Glorious Gentle-Voiced One." Sutras were written in his honor as early as 250 A.D., and he appeared in Buddhist art starting in 400 A.D.

He is often pictured with two lotus blossoms at the level of his head, against which his two chief attributes of sword and sutra are framed. His body is said to be purple-gold, covered by seven treasures. Sometimes he is presented as a beautiful youth, "in keeping with the notion of the sense of freshness and newness of such liberating awareness," garbed in princely silks and ornaments, seated cross-legged on a lotus-flower throne.[833]

Buddhists appreciate Manjusri as the "symbol for the experience of enlightenment as manifested in intellectual exposition. Manjusri is the god of mystic wisdom, a Buddhist Apollo, with the "flaming sword of light held aloft in his right hand and the lotus-supported Book of Wisdom, the *Prajna-Paramita,* held in his left."[834] He is the crown prince of Buddhist teachings, the embodiment of awakened understanding, the one best equipped to explain the deep wisdom *(Prajna Paramita)* capable of liberating souls from the bondage and illusions of existence so as to produce enlightenment. Merely to keep his name in mind leads to immense benefit and is seen as an equal boon to encountering all the Buddhas.

Manjusri has been the instructor of hundreds of former Buddhas, including the most recent and historically documented one. He is the father of "decillions" (10^{60}, or 10 followed by *sixty* zeroes) of Buddhas; he has taught "decillions" of Bodhisattvas; and he is engaged in the perfection of all beings. All Buddhas credit their enlightenment to Manjusri's teaching; Manjusri is the embodiment of the wisdom of all the Buddhas. The historical Buddha predicted that after his own passing, his mentor, Manjusri, would reside on Wuting mountain in an eastern country called Great China, where he would teach the Dharma (the profound truth of existence).

Other titles for Manjusri in keeping with his perceived stature included "Supreme Buddha of the Dragons" who presided in "Equal World," and "Spiritual Buddha Who Joyfully Cares for the Jewel." In the future, he will be known as "Buddha Universally Revealed" in an imperishable realm called "World Without Dust."[835] All the pores of his skin emit rays of golden light, his skin is like a mountain of gold, he is adorned with an aureole of light containing five hundred Buddhas, and he wears a precious jewel on his headdress, which emits five hundred different colors.

Among Manjusri's spiritual functions, he is interlocutor and spokesman, interpreting Buddhist teachings for students; a converter of souls to Buddhism, the number of which is beyond dimension and incalculable; he is the focus of veneration and devotion; and he is a protector of the Dharma and its followers, inspiring one grateful ruler to build the Pavilion of the Great Holy Manjusri for the Protection of the Nation. Manjusri was even credited with freeing the Chinese people from the influence of baleful stars, such as a feared comet. Manjusri has a wrathful form as nine-headed Yamantaka, "Subduer (Destroyer) of the Lord of Death," appearing as a deity with a blue bull's head.[836]

A remarkable account of mystical experiences at Wu-T'ai Shan was published in 1088 by Chang Shang-ying, a Buddhist, scholar, mystic, and statesman who spent nine days at Five Terrace Mountain, each of them rich with visions of Manjusri and his celestial retinue and other "supernatural" effects.

On the first day, at the side of the Southern Terrace, Chang Shang-ying saw a golden bridge with a gold-edged aureole of deep violet-blue, and three columns of rosy light rising directly in front of this mountain. The next day a golden stairway appeared above Dragon Hill, then a great flare was visible above the mountains to the north; later he saw a man in spirit form holding a large lamp by a stream. The light grew red like a sunset, then rose, emitting dazzling rays.

On the third day at Eastern Terrace, Chang Shang-ying saw an orb of white light rise up suddenly from the ground and revolve hundreds of times like a chariot wheel. The next day at Central Terrace, the northwestern sky opened up to reveal "a world of blue crystal teeming with legions of bodhisattvas," as well as towers, halls, jewel-like mountains, canopies, thrones, kings, lions, and elephants, "all arrayed in ineffable magnificence." Above the Hall of the True Countenance, he saw Manjusri astride a lion under a "vast curved-handled canopy."

On the sixth day, he witnessed an apparition of towers, castles, and pavilions teeming with bodhisattvas; he also saw great flares, beams of light, and on the next day, he saw silver and golden lights. On his eighth day, Chang Shang-ying, still moving around the Wu-T'ai Shan complex to different temples, saw Manjusri on a lion, framed against a cliff. He saw him again on the ninth day three times, "radiant white and life-sized," appearing against a cliff face. When Chang Shang-ying prayed to Manjusri to be his Dharma protector, the Bodhisattva responded by shooting out two rays of light flashing like lightning, and a large golden light that irradiated the cliff face.

At the end of his visionary peregrinations through the Five Terraces, Chang Shang-ying was debriefed by ten abbots. They told him that from "time immemorial" many bodhisattvas had resided at the Mountain of Chill Clarity, and that Manjusri was presently residing there as the chief bodhisattva. "Together with his retinue of a myriad other bodhisattvas, he preaches the Dharma continuously."[837]

GEOMANTIC

Dome; Shambhala Entrance; Michaelion.

DOME: Wu-T'ai Shan is the planetary starfall for Dubhe, the alpha star in Ursa Major, the Great Bear. Dubhe is the northernmost pointer in the Big Dipper, and forms the lower backbone and tail

of the bear, Dubhe is the star at the pouring edge of the dipper, situated deep within the bear, around its solar plexus. Its name derives from *Thahr al Dubb al Alkbar,* "Back of the Great Bear." The ancient Egyptians used Dubhe as a stellar orientation point for the placement of their temples and associated it with the goddess Isis. The Chinese knew this second-magnitude star as *Tien Choo,* or "Heaven's Pivot."

In the Big Dipper, which forms the lower backbone and tail of the bear, Megrez is the star closest to the handle, situated at the juncture of bowl and handle. The star's name derives from the Arabic *Al Maghrez,* which means "the Root of the Tail," though to the Chinese, it was *Tien Kuen,* "Heavenly Authority."

This is in keeping with the early Taoist name for Wu-T'ai Shan as Purple Enclosure, for Ursa Major is the home of the fourteen Ray Masters, or the gods of the Greek Olympus, the cosmic seat of administration and spiritual governance. The color purple of course denotes royalty, kingship, and high authority, all of which qualities are applicable to the Great Bear. For the Hindus, this star was *Atri,* one of their Seven Rishis, or cosmic sages (the same as the Ray Masters), and at least one Vedic source said this star rules the Bear's other stars.

Other Chinese names for the Great Bear further clarify its central role in cosmic governance and justify the Taoist name for the site. In classical China, the *Tseih Sing,* or "Seven Stars of the Bear" were associated with the celestial palace of the Lord on High and even with *Shou Lao,* the "Star God of Longevity," and with the Taoist paradise of the immortals known as *Tien Shan.*

The ancient Chinese also linked the stars of the Great Bear with their concept of the Celestial Palace of the Immortals, especially three stars on the Dipper's handle known to them as the "Jade Scales." These scales were thought to be involved in *measuring* out the duration of seasons and with *weighing* justice at the cosmic level of government. The Palace was said to float serenely among the clouds in an atmosphere of imperturbability.

The energy this star Dubhe of the Great Bear transmits through Wu-T'ai Shan is concerned with the creation of jewel-like consciousness, awareness that is clear like a crystal, defined, transparent, and transcendent. The ten-mile-wide dome is centered over the Temple of Chill Clarity, and its forty-eight dome caps spiritually energize an area much larger than the one hundred square miles of the Five Terrace temple complex, giving the area an atmosphere of intensely concentrated sanctity.

SHAMBHALA ENTRANCE: The presence of the Shambhala doorway in the Five Terrace temple complex doubles the sense of cosmic governance working through this dome. Shambhala, of course, is the seat of cosmic governance working through the planetary level and has overlap with the Great Bear.

It isn't so much that there is one discrete portal into Shambhala from the Five Terrace region; rather, there is a significant bleed-through of all of Shambhala onto the templic structure of Five Terraces with its seventy-six temples and forty-seven monasteries. Functionally, all of Five Terraces is within Shambhala, and it is quite likely that the original designers of the temple complex were aware of this interpenetration and took advantage of it in their deployment of temples.

As for Manjusri, the Chinese psychics have provided the West with an excellent though differently filtered impression of what Judaic tradition calls the Archangel Michael, "He Who Is Like Unto God," said to be the chief of all the archangels.

MICHAELION: The strong presence and emphasis on Manjusri is evidence, confirmed clairvoyantly, of a Michaelion. This is an aperture in the higher dimensions above Wu-T'ai Shan to the realm of the Archangel Michael and his angelic legions. As the Chinese mystics rightly claimed, the entire site is under the tutelage of Michael-Manjusri. See Mont-St. Michel, France, in this book for another description of this feature.

Michael's wisdom or *prajna* function is indicated by the statement in a Judaic text called *Baruch III* that he "holds the keys of the kingdom of Heaven" (as in Manjusri's transcendent knowledge of ultimate reality) and elsewhere that, as the Prince of Light with a magnificent sword, he leads the angels of light in a tremendous battle against Satan and all the legions of darkness (as in Manjusri's sword of light that cleaves the body of ignorance and illusion). The Muslim mystics saw Michael as situated in the Seventh Heaven "on the borders of the Full Sea, crowded with an innumerable array of angels" (as in Manjusri's retinue of Bodhisattvas).[838]

In effect, Manjusri's (or Michael's) presence permeates Wu-T'ai Shan. You could say his celestial body expands to fill the one hundred square miles of the temple complex so that wherever you are, you are within Manjusri's wisdom aspect.

Endnotes

1. Marion Bowman, "Belief, Legend, and Perceptions of the Sacred in Contemporary Bath," *Folklore Annual* (1998).

2. See James Lovelock, *Healing Gaia: Practical Medicine for the Planet* (New York: Harmony Books, 1991); *The Ages of Gaia: A Biography of Our Living Earth* (New York: W.W. Norton, 1988); *Gaia: A New Look at Life on Earth* (New York: Oxford University Press, 1979); also Richard Leviton, "The Father of Gaia," *East West Journal* (November/December 1991).

3. Andrew Ellis, Nigel Wiseman, and Ken Boss, *Grasping the Wind* (Brookline, Mass.: Paradigm Publications, 1989).

4. Kiiki Matsumoto and Stephen Birch, *Hara Diagnosis: Reflections on the Sea* (Brookline, Mass.: Paradigm Publications, 1988): 71, 75, 76.

5. Ibid., 77.

6. D. H. Lawrence, *The Plumed Serpent* (New York: Vintage Books, 1959): 50, 56.

7. Lawrence Durrell, "Landscape and Character," in *Spirit of Place: Letters and Essays on Travel*, ed. Alan G. Thomas (New York: Dutton, 1971): 156–63.

8. Henry Miller, *The Colossus of Maroussi* (New York: New Directions, 1941): 45, 76, 86, 159, 181.

9. William Maxwell, *The Chateau* (New York: Alfred A. Knopf, 1961): 320.

10. Roger Housden, *Travels Through Sacred India* (London: Thorsons/Harper Collins, 1996): 15.

11. Phil Cousineau, *The Art of Pilgrimage: The Seeker's Guide to Making Travel Sacred* (Berkeley: Conari Press, 1998): xx, 9, 18.

12. Sherrill Miller, *The Pilgrim's Guide to the Sacred Earth* (Stillwater, Minn.: Voyageur Press, 1991): 2.

13. Sir George Trevelyan, "Landscape Temples," published at: www.sirgeorgetrevelyan.org.uk [no date].

14. Marko Pogacnik, *Nature Spirits and Elemental Beings: Working with the Intelligence in Nature* (Forres, Scotland: Findhorn Press, 1996): 10, 87, 88. See also "Multidimensionality of the Earth and Environment," published at: www.1judmila.org/pogacnik/Stran2.html.

15. Alain Danielou, *Gods of Love and Ecstasy: The Traditions of Shiva and Dionysus* (Rochester, Vt.: Inner Traditions, 1992): 131–2.

16. Mircea Eliade, *The Sacred and the Profane: The Nature of Religion* (New York: Harcourt, 1959): 116, 129.

17. Ibid., 26, 27, 30, 32.

18. Ibid., 45, 63, 65.

19. Rudolf Otto, *The Idea of the Holy: An Inquiry into the Non-Rational Factor in the Idea of the Divine and Its Relation to the Rational,* trans. John W. Harvey (New York: Oxford University Press, 1958): 11–25.

20. Ibid., 28.

21. Doris Lessing, *Briefing for a Descent into Hell* (New York: Vintage Books, 1981): 98–9.

22. Quoted in: Richard Leviton, "Ley Lines and the Meaning of Adam," in *Anti-Gravity and the World Grid,* ed. David Hatcher Childress (Stelle, Ill.: Adventures Unlimited Press, 1987): 141.

23. Tom Graves, *Needles of Stone* (London: Turnstone Books, 1978): 65.

24. Carlos Castaneda, *The Fire from Within* (London: Century Publishing, 1984): 204.

25. Carlos Castaneda, *The Eagle's Gift* (New York: Simon & Schuster, 1981): 87.

26. Washington Irving, "Rip Van Winkle: A Posthumous Writing of Diedrich Knickerbocker," in *The Sketch-Book of Geoffrey Crayon, Gent* (New York: A.L. Burt Company, [no copyright date]): 35–50.

27. Diana L. Eck, *Banaras: City of Light* (Princeton: Princeton University Press, 1982): 34–5.

28. The renowned mythographer Joseph Campbell calls such sites "mythogenetic zones," which are any geographical area "in which such a language of mythic symbols and related rites can be shown to have sprung into being." Joseph Campbell. *The Masks of God: Creative Mythology* (New York: Viking Press, 1968): 90.

29. Eck, *Banaras*, 35.

30. Surinder Mohan Bhardwaj, *Hindu Places of Pilgrimage: A Study in Cultural Geography* (Berkeley: University of California Press, 1973): 29, 63, 68, 80.

31. Richard Barber, *Pilgrimages* (Woodbridge, England: Boydell Press, 1991): 75, 76.

32. Phil Cousineau, *The Art of Pilgrimage: The Seeker's Guide to Making Travel Sacred* (Berkeley: Conari Press, 1998): 93.

33. Diana L. Eck, "The Goddess Gangs in Hindu Sacred Geography," in *Devi: Goddesses of India*, ed. John S. Hawley and Donna M. Wulff (Berkeley: University of California Press, 1996): 142.

34. David R. Kinsley, *Hindu Goddesses: Visions of the Divine Feminine in the Hindu Religious Tradition* (Berkeley: University of California Press, 1986): 184–7.

35. Janet Gyatso, "Down with the Demoness: Reflections on a Feminine Ground in Tibet," *in Feminine Ground: Essays on Women and Tibet*, ed. Janice D. Williams (Ithaca, N.Y.: Snow Lion Publications, 1987): 33–51, 141, 147.

36. Jean Richer*, Sacred Geography of the Ancient Greeks: Astrological Symbolism in Art, Architecture, and Landscape*, trans. Christine Rhone (Albany: State University of New York Press, 1994): xxii, xxiii, xxv, 256.

37. Mircea Eliade, *The Sacred and the Profane: The Nature of Religion* (New York: Harcourt, 1959): 11.

38. Joseph Campbell put it aptly when he said that the function of a myth is to "reconcile" waking consciousness with the tremendous mystery of the universe and to provide "an interpretive image" of this for our understanding. Myth "is the revelation to waking consciousness of the powers of its own sustaining source." Joseph Campbell, *The Masks of God: Creative Mythology* (New York: Viking Press, 1968): 4.

39. This excellent term was coined by the polymath British researcher of Earth mysteries, Anthony Roberts. As he explained in *Sowers of Thunder* (London: Rider, 1978, xvi), geomythics means "earth-myths or myths in relation to the earth's metaphysical situation—topographically, historically and in cosmic time and space." Geomythics embraces "the central fertilizing power of magic in a context of mythical reality and works through physical emanations allied to topographical location."

40. Henry Corbin, *Avicenna and the Visionary Recital* (Irving, Tex: Spring Publications, 1980): 20.

41. Ibid., 19, 20.

42. Muhyiddin Ibn 'Arabi, "The Earth Which Was Created from What Remained of the Clay of Adam," in Henry Corbin, *Spiritual Body and Celestial Earth: From Mazdean Iran to Shi'ite Iran* (Princeton: Princeton University Press, 1977): 135–8.

43. Henry Corbin, *Spiritual Body and Celestial Earth: From Mazdean Iran to Shi'ite Iran* (Princeton: Princeton University Press, 1977): 135.

44. Gershom Scholem, *Major Trends in Jewish Mysticism* (New York: Schocken Books, 1941): 265, 279.

45. Gershom Scholem, *On the Kabbalah and Its Symbolism* (New York: Schocken Books, 1965): 115, 128, 162, 202.

46. Manly Hall, *Man, the Grand Symbol of the Mysteries* (Los Angeles: The Philosophical Research Society, 1972): 56–7.

47. William Blake, "Jerusalem: The Emanation of the Giant Albion," in *Blake: Complete Writings, with Variant Readings*, ed. Geoffrey Keynes (London: Oxford University Press, 1966): 622, 625, 635, 641.

48. Gershom Scholem, *Major Trends in Jewish Mysticism* (New York: Schocken Books, 1941): 274–5.

49. William Blake, "Jerusalem: The Emanation of the Giant Albion," in *Blake: Complete Writings, with Variant Readings*, ed. Geoffrey Keynes (London: Oxford University Press, 1966): 626.

50. David R. Kinsley, *Hindu Goddesses: Visions of the Divine Feminine in the Hindu Religious Tradition* (Berkeley: University of California Press, 1986): 178.

51. Ibid.

52. Lama Anagarika Govinda, quoted in John Snelling, *The Sacred Mountain* (London: East West Publications, 1983): 199–203.

53. By the way, it is beneficial to do some type of internal cleansing before visiting a sacred site. A

site, just by being itself, will facilitate a deep cleansing process in your psyche and aura, stripping away layers of false or outmoded identity, a process that has an inevitable impact on the physical body. If your body is already internally cleansed (especially the intestines), then it will throw back less resistance to the spiritual cleansing under way, and your overall experience may produce less discomfort. For technical information on internal cleansing using natural methods, see Richard Leviton, *The Healthy Living Space: 70 Practical Ways to Detoxify the Body and Home* (Charlottesville, Va.: Hampton Roads, 2001).

54. For more information about Blaise and their work with landscape mysteries and initiation, see Richard Leviton, *Looking for Arthur: A Once and Future Travelogue* (Station Hill, N.Y.: Station Hill Openings/Barrytown, 1997).

55. For more about Steiner's model of how the ten families of angels participate in the human organism and other aspects in which Steiner's vision helps elucidate the Earth's energy grid, see Richard Leviton, *The Imagination of Pentecost: Rudolf Steiner and Contemporary Spirituality* (Hudson, N.Y.: Anthroposophic Press, 1994).

56. The science of interpreting the significance of numbers is known as gematria. Gematria is based on the Hebrew and Greek alphabets in which each letter is also a number, such as, in Hebrew, *aleph* (a) = 1, *bayt* (b) = 2, *ghimel* (c) = 3, *dallet* (d) = 4, and so forth. Strings of numbers also spell words, and the words spell further number strings that can be interpreted as words. The result is a complex but meaningful number and/or letter matrix. Avebury, for example, can be interpreted, in terms of gematria, as aleph-vav-aleph, or 161, which is an abbreviation of phi, the golden ratio, which is 1.161803398875. The Hebrew word for light, *AWR*, is 162, the other side of the abbreviation for phi, or the next rounded-off number. Thus you can see why it is defensible to say Avebury is the place where they buried the light (or star, or seed of phi). In the case of the Earth's visionary geography, the prime number is 9, or *Tayt*, which means almost without exception, the quantities of design features are a function of 9 (as in, for example 144 = 9, when you add the digits), a topic explored in *The Emerald Modem*.

57. Richard Barber, *Pilgrimages* (Woodbridge, England: Boydell Press, 1991): 99.

58. Doris Lessing, *Re: Colonised Planet 5, Shikasta* (New York: Vintage Books, 1981): 24–27.

59. Henry Corbin, *Spiritual Body and Celestial Earth: From Mazdean Iran to Shi'ite Iran,* Bollingen Series XCI:2, trans. Nancy Pearson (Princeton: Princeton University Press, 1977): 13–6.

60. Arthur Avalon, *The Serpent Power* (New York: Dover Publications, 1974): 334.

61. Jean Chevalier and Alain Gheerbrant, *A Dictionary of Symbols,* trans. John Buchanan-Brown (New York: Penguin Books, 1996): 609.

62. Hans Biedermann, *Dictionary of Symbolism: Cultural Icons and the Meanings Behind Them,* trans. James Hulbert (New York: Meridian/Penguin Group, 1994): 207.

63. *My Dear Alexias. Letters from Wellesley Tudor Pole to Rosamond Lehmann,* ed. Elizabeth Gaythorpe (Jersey, Channel Islands, UK: Neville Spearman, 1979): 154.

64. Robert Graves and Raphael Patai, *Hebrew Myths: The Book of Genesis* (New York: Greenwich House/Arlington House, 1983): 57.

65. Joseph Campbell, *The Masks of God: Creative Mythology* (New York: Viking Press, 1968): 25.

66. Tomas, *The Promise of Power: Reflections on the Toltec Warrior's Dialogue from the Collected Works of Carlos Castaneda* (Charlottesville, Va.: Hampton Roads, 1995): 388.

67. Mircea Eliade, *A History of Religious Ideas, Vol. 1, From the Stone Age to the Eleusinian Mysteries,* trans. Willard R. Trask (Chicago, Il.: University of Chicago Press, 1978): 210–2.

68. Roberto Calasso, *Ka: Stories of the Mind and Gods of India* (New York: Vintage Books/Random House, 1998): 253–9.

69. This new and complex feature of the Earth's energy matrix was revealed to me and my British colleague Mike Booth by the Ofanim during a five-day workshop we led entitled "Primer on the Quest" in late February and early March 2002 in Tetford, England. During that week, we explored some of the aspects of the stargate feature, but insofar as it is of an order of complexity several notches above most of the other features in the light pattern library of the Earth grid thus far discovered, the full modeling—and experiencing—of this feature will take some time.

70. Louis Ginzberg, *The Legends of the Jews I* (Philadelphia: Jewish Publication Society of America, 1909): 69, 102.

71. Ibid., 102.

72. Ibid., 69.

73. Cyril Glasse, *The Concise Encyclopedia of Islam* (San Francisco: HarperSanFrancisco, 1989): 77.

74. F. E. Peters, *The Hajj: The Muslim Pilgrimage to Mecca and the Holy Places* (Princeton: Princeton University Press, 1994): 63–4

75. E. A. Wallis Budge, *Legends of the Egyptian Gods: Hieroglyphic Texts and Translations* (New York: Dover, 1994): 230.

76. Barbara Hand Clow, *Catastrophobia: The Truth Behind Earth Changes in the Coming Age of Light* (Rochester, Vt.: Bear & Company, 2001): 128.

77. R. T. Rundle Clark, *Myth and Symbol in Ancient Egypt* (New York: Thames and Hudson, 1959): 132, 170.

78. Mark Amaru Pinkham, "The Mystery of the Osireion," *The New Times* (July 2001), published at: www.newtimes.org/issue0107/osireion.htm

79. R. T. Rundle Clark, *Myth and Symbol in Ancient Egypt* (New York: Thames and Hudson, 1959): 106.

80. *Atlas of Ancient Egypt,* ed. Graham Speake (Oxford, UK: Phaidon Press, 1984): 114.

81. T. G. H. James, quoted in "Abydos, Field of Dreams," Ralph Vaughan [no date], published at: http://ralphv.www3.50megs.com/egypt/field.html.

82. Barbara Hand Clow, *Catastrophobia: The Truth Behind Earth Changes in the Coming Age of Light* (Rochester, Vt.: Bear & Company, 2001): 119, 127, 129.

83. R. T. Rundle Clark, *Myth and Symbol in Ancient Egypt* (New York: Thames and Hudson, 1959): 122.

84. E. A. Wallis Budge, *The Gods of the Egyptians, Or, Studies in Egyptian Mythology,* Vol. II (New York: Dover Publications, [1904] 1969): 261–6.

85. Ibid., 264.

86. Heleni Frantzi, *Acropolis Athens* (Athens, Greece: G. Voutsas, 1970): 5.

87. Apollodorus, *The Library,* Vol. II, trans. James George Frazer (Cambridge: Harvard University Press, 1921): 79–81.

88. Peter Levi, n163 in Pausanias, *Guide to Greece,* Vol. 1, *Central Greece,* trans. Peter Levi (Baltimore: Penguin Books, 1971): 80.

89. Lee Hall, *Athena: A Biography* (Reading, Mass.: Addison-Wesley, 1997): 220.

90. Pausanias, *Guide to Greece,* Vol. 1, *Central Greece,* trans. Peter Levi (Baltimore: Penguin Books, 1971): 75.

91. Walter Burkert, *Greek Religion,* trans. John Raffan (Cambridge: Harvard University Press, 1985): 140.

92. Richard Stoneman, *Greek Mythology: An Encyclopedia of Myth and Legend* (London: Diamond Books, 1995): 78.

93. Michael Grant and John Hazxel, *Who's Who in Classical Mythology* (New York: Diamond Books, 1973): 146.

94. Lee Hall, *Athena: A Biography* (Reading, Mass.: Addison-Wesley, 1997): 227.

95. Aeschylus, *The Eumenides,* trans. Richmond Lattimore, in *Oresteia: The Complete Greek Tragedies,* eds. David Grene and Richmond Lattimore (Chicago: University of Chicago Press, 1953): 136.

96. Richard G. Geldard, *The Traveler's Key to Ancient Greece: A Guide to Sacred Places* (Wheaton, Il.: Quest Books, Theosophical Publishing Company, 1989): 179.

97. Michitaro Tanaka, *The Acropolis: This Beautiful World,* Vol. 12 (Tokyo: Kodansha International, 1967): 31–2.

98. Rex Warner, *The Stories of the Greeks* (New York: Farrar, Straus & Giroux, 1967): 82.

99. Lloyd Motz and Carol Nathanson, *The Constellations* (New York: Bantam Doubleday Dell, 1988): 347.

100. Pausanias, *Guide to Greece,* Vol. 1, *Central Greece,* trans. Peter Levi (Baltimore: Penguin Books, 1971): 79.

101. Wilfrid Blunt, *The Golden Road to Samarkand* (New York: Viking, 1973): 11, 12.

102. Abu Abdalla ibn Battuta, quoted in "The Shah-I-Zinde," Daniel C. Waugh, 1999, published at: www.faculty.Washington.edu/dwaugh/CA/cities/smarkand/samark.html

103. Eileen K. Gunn, "Archeological Sites in Samarkand," Great Outdoor Recreation Pages [no date], published at: www.gorp.com/gorp/location/asia/uzbekistan/cities5.htm

104. Daniel C. Waugh, "Samarkand," May 25, 2000, published at: www.faculty.washington.edu/dwaugh/CA/cities/samarkand/samark.html

105. Kevin Krisciunas, "The Legacy of Ulugh Beg," published at: www.ukans.edu/~ibetext/texts/paksoy-2/cam6.html

106. Yasushi Inoue, *Journey Beyond Samarkand,* trans. Gyo Furuta and Gordon Sager (Palo Alta: Kodansha International, 1971): 63.

107. Yasushi Inoue, *Journey Beyond Samarkand,* trans. Gyo Furuta and Gordon Sager (Palo Alto, Calif.: Kodansha International, 1971): 80, 81, 60.

108. The same story is credited to the Iranian Afrasiyab in Firdausi's *Shah-Nama.* He was the Shah of the non-Aryan Turanians. In his attempt to

seize the holy legitimacy and heavenly mandate of kingship, signified by the *Hvarna* (Glory), he turned himself into a fish and dove into Lake Vurukasha after it. He dove three times, but each time the Glory (presumably another version of Anakhita's necklace) got away, escaping through an outlet that led to the Beyond. See: Giorgio de Santillana and Hertha von Dechend, *Hamlet's Mill: An Essay on Myth and the Frame of Time* (Boston: David R. Godine, 1977): 201.

109. This part of the Samarkand Afrasiab story parallels that of the Iranian Afrasiab. He occupied an underground iron palace one thousand times taller than a man, illuminated by an artificial Sun, Moon, and stars. See Ibid., 40.

110. Olga Kharitidi, M.D., *The Master of Lucid Dreams* (Charlottesville, Va.: Hampton Roads, 2001): 116-9.

111. Ibid., 79.

112. Ibid., 120.

113. Ibid., 131.

114. Roberto Calasso, *Ka: Stories of the Mind and Gods of India* (New York: Vintage Books/Random House, 1998): 257-9.

115. Faith de M. Vatcher and Lance Vatcher, *The Avebury Monuments* (London: Her Majesty's Stationery Office, 1976): 45.

116. Michael Pitts, *Footprints Through Avebury* (Avebury, UK: Stones Print Publications, 1985): 34.

117. Aubrey Burl, *Prehistoric Avebury* (New Haven: Yale University Press, 1979): 30.

118. William Stukeley, quoted in Terence Meaden, *The Secrets of the Avebury Stones: Britain's Greatest Megalithic Temple* (London: Souvenir Press, 1999): 145-6.

119. Aubrey Burl, *Prehistoric Avebury* (New Haven: Yale University Press, 1979): 74.

120. A. Thom and A. S. Thom, *Megalithic Remains in Britain and Brittany* (Oxford, UK: Clarendon Press/Oxford University Press, 1978): 30, 38.

121. *The Lost Language of Symbolism: The Origins of Symbols, Mythologies, and Folklore*, Vol. II, (London: Bracken Books/Random House UK, [1912] 1996): 222.

122. Grace and Ivan Cooke, *The Light in Britain* (New Lands, UK: White Eagle Publishing Trust, 1971): 43-52.

123. Mike Booth, Tetford, England, personal communication with the author, June 29, 1990.

124. Michael Dames, *The Avebury Cycle* (London: Thames and Hudson, 1977): 9, 18, 217.

125. Page Bryant, *Starwalking: Shamanic Practices for Traveling into the Night Sky* (Santa Fe: Bear & Company, 1997): 218, 233.

126. This is one of the seeming paradoxes of the spiritual world. The Blazing Star is a tiny pinpoint of brilliant light *and* it is a crystalline shape with forty million facets called Nimitta. The Star is the light of the Nimitta *and* the Nimitta is the congealing of the Star.

127. Sir John Lubbock, quoted in Michael Pitts, *Footprints Through Avebury* (Avebury, UK: Stones Print Publications, 1985): 36.

128. Initially only twelve Ray Masters were expressed on the Earth; two were implicit within the other twelve. At some point in Earth history, the other two became manifest, giving all fourteen Ray Masters full scope on the Earth.

129. See Lama Anagarika Govinda, *Foundations of Tibetan Mysticism* (London: Rider & Company, [1960] 1983): 234-41.

130. If nothing else, the phenomenal success of DVDs since their release in 1998 has provided the metaphysical community with yet another potent metaphor. The DVD metaphor is certainly apt for Avebury. DVD stands for digital video disc and is a form of optical disc storage technology that can hold cinema-like video, better than CD-quality audio, and computer data. The DVD is small and compact; it offers eight tracks of digital audio; automatic seamless branching of video to run multiple story lines on one disc; nine different camera angles; menus and interactive features; instant rewind and fast forward; instant search functions; durability (they don't wear out from use); among other features. All of these qualities, amusingly, describe, though do not fully encompass, the multidimensional informational aspects of Avebury.

131. You might wonder what the Hindu Shiva is doing dancing in Celtic Avebury. Of course, when Avebury was installed, there were no Celtic or Hindu cultures, myths, or iconographies. But different cultures have excelled at describing aspects or angles of celestial beings and processes, couching it in their particularized terms and images. The dynamic image of Shiva and Parvati dancing at Avebury (which I saw in a vision of the site) and the interpretation that accompanies it are very helpful in understanding the essence of Avebury. I think of the different myths and images of the world as a giant tool box: whatever tool opens the lock, that's the one I'll go with.

132. Ananda K. Coomaraswamy, *The Dance of Siva: Essays on Indian Art and Culture* (New York: Dover Publications, [1924] 1985): 60.

133. Ibid., 60, 65.

134. For more on this type of commentary about Avebury, see my *Looking for Arthur: A Once and Future Travelogue* (Barrytown, N.Y.: Station Hill Openings/Barrytown, 1997); and *What's Beyond That Star: A Chronicle of Geomythic Adventure* (London: Clairview Books, 2002).

135. Roger Housden, *Travels Through Sacred India* (San Francisco: Thorsons/HarperCollins, 1996): 118,122.

136. *The Vamana Purana,* quoted in Diana L. Eck, *Banaras: City of Light,* 27.

137. *Classical Hindu Mythology: A Reader in the Sanskrit Puranas,* trans. and ed. Cornelia Dimmitt and J. A. B. van Buitenen (Philadelphia, Penn.: Temple University Press, 1978): 335.

138. Diana L. Eck, *Banaras: City of Light* (Princeton: Princeton University Press, 1982): 32.

139. Brahma, Vishnu, and Shiva form the great triumvirate of Hindu gods. In simple terms, Brahma is the Creator, Vishnu the Sustainer, and Shiva the destroyer of the universe.

140. Bepin Bechari, *Myths and Symbols of Vedic Astrology* (Salt Lake City: Passage Press, 1990): 84–5.

141. The Four Ages are a key aspect in the Hindu model of Time. The ages, called Yugas, were *Krta* (golden), *Treta* (silver), *Dvapara* (bronze), and *Kali* (black or leaden). In each there is a diminishment of consciousness and light, such that the *Kali Yuga,* our present epoch, is a time of Hell on Earth compared to the *Krta Yuga,* which is a Golden Age. Together, all Four Ages last a total of 12,000 divine years, or 4,320,000 human years.

142. Heinrich Zimmer, *Philosophies of India,* Bollingen Series XXVI, ed. Joseph Campbell (Princeton: Princeton University Press, 1951): 128–9, 135, 212

143. Alain Danielou, *The Myths and Gods of India* (Rochester, Vt.: Inner Traditions, 1991): 215, 221.

144. Alain Danielou, *Yoga: Mastering the Secrets of Matter and the Universe* (Rochester, Vt.: Inner Traditions, 1991): 149.

145. Lilian Silburn, *Kundalini: The Energy of the Depths* (Albany: State University of New York Press, 1988): 30, 31, 146.

146. Mircea Eliade, *Yoga: Immortality and Freedom,* Bollingen Series LVI. (Princeton: Princeton University Press, 1958): 244.

147. Dion Fortune, *The Mystical Qabalah* (London: Ernest Benn, 1935): 109–13.

148. *The Tree of Life: Chayyim Vital's Introduction to the Kabbalah of Isaac Luria, The Palace of Adam Kadmon,* trans. Donald Wilder Menzi and Zwe Padeh (Northvale, N.J.: Jason Aronson, 1999): 14–5.

149. At the risk of further complicating something already complex, there are at least three more geomantic aspects to the Linga: first, it is the column of light connecting the top of the dome to its grounding point at *Jnanavapi Kund;* second, it is the line of light connecting the top of the zodiac dome to its grounding point at *Madhyameshvara;* third, it is the chakra template of the Banaras zodiacal Albion, running northward from Durga Kund to *Kapalamochana Tirtha.*

150. Michel Poizat, *The Angel's Cry: Beyond the Pleasure Principle in Opera,* trans. Arthur Denner (Ithaca: Cornell University Press, 1992): 17–8.

151. Robert W. Gutman, *Richard Wagner: The Man, His Mind, and His Music,* Time-Life Records Special Edition (New York: Time Inc., 1968): 330.

152. Cosima Wagner, *Cosima Wagner's Diaries,* Vol. I, 1869-1877 (New York: Harcourt Brace Jovanovich, 1978): 196.

153. George R. Marek, *Cosima Wagner* (New York: Harper & Row, 1981): 142.

154. *Selected Letters of Richard Wagner,* trans. and ed. Stewart Spencer and Barry Millington (London: J. M. Dent & Sons, 1987): 780.

155. Ibid., 783–4.

156. Friedrich Nietszche, quoted in George R. Marek, *Cosima Wagner* (New York: Harper & Row, 1981): 147.

157. Geoffrey Skelton, *Wagner at Bayreuth: Experiment and Tradition* (New York: George Braziller, 1965): 9.

158. Ronald Taylor, *Richard Wagner: His Life, Art, and Thought* (New York: Taplinger, 1979): 217, 218.

159. George R. Marek, *Cosima Wagner* (New York: Harper & Row, 1981): 158.

160. Matthias Theodor Vogt, "Taking the Waters at Bayreuth," in *Wagner in Performance,* eds. Barry Millington and Stewart Spencer (New Haven: Yale University Press, 1992): 151.

161. Ludwig II, quoted in Christopher McIntosh, *Ludwig II of Bavaria: The Swan King* (New York: Barnes & Noble Books, 1982): 161.

162. Ibid., 162–3.

163. Dennis A. Burnside, "Bayreuth," 1997, published at: www.geocities.com/Vienna/1978/bayreuth.html

164. Wolfgang Wagner, *Acts: The Autobiography of Wolfgang Wagner*, trans. John Brownjohn (London: Weidenfeld & Nicolson, 1994): 2–3.

165. *Richard Wagner: His Life, Art, and Thought*, 218.

166. Richard Wagner, quoted in *Richard Wagner: His Life, Art, and Thought*, 204.

167. T. Neil Davis, "The Brocken Spectre," in *Alaska Science Forum*, Article #282 (January 26, 1979), published at: www.gi.alaska.edu/ScienceForum/ASF2/282.html

168. Barbara G. Walker, *The Woman's Encyclopedia of Myths and Secrets* (San Francisco: Harper & Row, 1983): 1058.

169. Sir James George Frazer, *The Golden Bough: A Study in Magic and Religion*, Abridged Edition (New York: MacMillan, 1951): 716.

170. John Ramsay, quoted in Sir James George Frazer, *The Golden Bough: A Study in Magic and Religion*, Abridged Edition (New York: MacMillan, 1951): 715.

171. Johann Wolfgang von Goethe, *Faust*, trans. Alice Raphael (New York: Heritage Press, 1930): 153,154.

172. Johann Wolfgang von Goethe, quoted in Nicholas Boyle, *Goethe: The Poet and the Age*, Vol. I, *The Poetry of Desire* (New York: Oxford University Press, 1992): 298, 299.

173. Nicholas Boyle, *Goethe: The Poet and the Age*, Vol. I, *The Poetry of Desire* (New York: Oxford University Press, 1992): 297–9, 318–9.

174. Pamela Hill, *The Brocken* (New York: Saint Martin's Press, 1990): 193–7.

175. Elizabeth Pepper and John Wilcock, *Magical and Mystical Sites: Europe and the British Isles* (New York: Harper & Row, 1977): 146–7.

176. Grace and Ivan Cooke, *The Light in Britain* (New Lands, UK: White Eagle Publishing Trust, 1971): 20–1.

177. Rudolf Steiner, *The Cycle of the Year as Breathing-Process of the Earth* (Hudson, N.Y.: Anthroposophic Press, 1984): 8.

178. The Lucifer-Ahriman dialectic is a central part of Steiner's cosmology. In brief, he said that Lucifer inflates ego-hood so that it loses interest in the physical world; Ahriman contracts and densifies spiritual insight so that it must be concentrated purely in matter. Steiner posited the Christ as a spiritual principle that balances the two poles. For a full discussion of this see my *The Imagination of Pentecost: Rudolf Steiner and Contemporary Spirituality* (Hudson, N.Y.: Anthroposophic Press, 1994).

179. Rudolf Steiner, *Life Between Death and Rebirth* (Spring Valley, N.Y.: Anthroposophic Press, 1968): 19, 20, 70.

180. The subject is too complex to develop here, but the essential observation is that the identity and function of Lucifer are misconstrued as a result of monotheistic fundamentalism. Just as Christianity posits the human, Christ, and God, leaving out the vast array of hierarchically positioned angelic intermediaries, so too does it posit the human and the Devil, with nothing in between. Lucifer is not the singular Devil, or Satan, who is determined to make human life miserable. On the other hand, there is a corresponding hierarchy of negative or demonic beings, like a mirror image of the angelic hierarchy. These beings have names and ranks and are not pleasant to deal with, but Lucifer is not among their ranks. Again, thinking of Prometheus as equivalent to Lucifer makes it easier to reconceive the setup.

181. W. Y. Evans-Wentz, *The Fairy-Faith in Celtic Countries* (Gerrard Cross, England: Colin Smythe/Humanities Press, [1911] 1977): xxv.

182. James MacKillop, *A Dictionary of Celtic Mythology* (New York: Oxford University Press, 1998): 76.

183. A. Thom and A. S. Thom, *Megalithic Remains in Britain and Brittany* (Oxford, England: Oxford University Press, 1978): 62, 65, 91, 100, 110, 180.

184. Pierre-Roland Giot, *The Carnac Alignments*, trans. Angela Moyon (La Guerche-de-Bretagne, France: Editions Ouest-France, Imprimerie Raynard, 1990): 10.

185. The name *Cernunnos* means "Horned One," and in Celtic myth, he is considered Lord of the Beasts, as well as nature, fruit, grain, and prosperity. In appearance, he has a man's body with a stag's horns on his head, and is usually depicted squatting. He is often shown (in thirty different depictions from Romania to Ireland) with serpents with ram's heads, a torc of chieftainship about his neck, and coin-filled purses. For this reason, some mythographers suggest he is associated with the Underworld or Land of the Dead.

186. Pierre-Roland Giot, *The Carnac Alignments*, trans. Angela Moyon (La Guerche-de-Bretagne, France: Editions Ouest-France, Imprimerie Raynard, 1990): 12.

187. Ibid., 13.

188. W. Y. Evans-Wentz, *The Fairy-Faith in Celtic Countries* (Gerrard Cross, England: Colin Smythe/ Humanities Press, [1911] 1977): xxv, xxvi, 13, 14, 221.

189. Natasha Hoffman with Hamilton Hill, *The Standing Stones Speak: Messages from the Archangels Revealed* (Los Angeles: Renaissance Books, 2000): 29, 32, 37–39, 133–4, 144, 194–5.

190. Dr. E. C. Krupp, *Beyond the Blue Horizon: Myths and Legends of the Sun, Moon, Stars, and Planets* (New York: HarperCollins, 1991): 217.

191. Stella Kramrisch, *The Presence of Shiva* (Princeton: Princeton University Press, 1981): 43, 44, 45, 48, 50.

192. When things happened is a somewhat vexatious subject. Refer to "Domes" in part 2 for more detail, but for here it may be helpful to appreciate that planetary time, in terms of megalithic installations, can be reckoned in terms of the three dome presences on Earth. The third dome presence was about eighteen million years ago; that was when the grid was mostly activated; in the second dome presence, the initial pattern was confirmed and stabilized; in the first, it was seeded. Most of the key megalithic installations, such as Carnac and Avebury, for example, were established sometime between the second and third dome presences, giving us eighteen million years as the latest possible time; probably it was much earlier in planetary time. The possibility of such longevity for stones and such extreme antiquity for the origination of certain sites understandably staggers the imagination.

193. The term Cosmic Logos is most conspicuously found in the metaphysical works of Alice Bailey. A Solar Logos, in her model, is a highly evolved spiritual intelligence and consciousness representing what we might call the "soul" of a star; the Cosmic Logos is the organizing principle and spiritual intelligence presiding over many Solar Logoi. It's the same idea, but at a higher or more rarified level of operation—the level of a cosmos. You might think of it loosely as the god, lord, or soul of a cosmos. The term Sanat Kumara, drawn from Vedic metaphysical and mythic texts, is a name often used to describe the Cosmic Logos.

194. This matter is developed in *The Emerald Modem*. However, a key mathematical function in this model is *e*, the base of logarithmic expansion, which is given as 2.72 (rounded off); this of course is the same as the megalithic yard, as described by Alexander Thom, as 2.72 feet, the basis for most stone circles and megalithic alignments in ancient Europe (as Thom inventoried them), and possibly the planet.

The function of *e* charts the flow rate of uncompression of the distance between Sirius and the Great Bear; it is seemingly a space measurement that also defines the flow of time through that space in exponential leaps. *e* is the operative principle in the diameter of zodiacs and domes, and the length of stone rows, all of which at heart were determined originally in megalithic yards.

In this respect, *e* is the key to understanding time, which is the distance in which a series of exponential expansions takes place. There is some conceptual support for this unusual approach from the French philosopher and architectural scholar R. A. Schwaller de Lubicz: "The Universe conceived as a living Being—Cosmic Man [Albion]—is Life; that is to say, it is a gestation. Time is thus gestation, the distance between the seed and the fruit. . . ." R. A. Schwaller de Lubicz, *The Temple in Man: Sacred Architecture and the Perfect Man,* trans. Robert and Deborah Lawlor (Rochester, Vt: Inner Traditions International, 1977): 58.

195. Nikolai Tolstoy, *The Coming of the King* (London: Corgi Books, Bantam Press/Transworld Publishers, 1988): 121.

196. This particular Ray Master has also been known as the Greek hunting goddess, Artemis, and through the notable human incarnation of Saint Francis of Assisi. For more on Artemis, see Ephesus, Turkey.

197. The term Great White Brotherhood refers to the mythical fraternity of higher spiritual beings and ascended humans generally regarded, by world metaphysical tradition, to preside in a more exalted dimension, but with respect to the Earth, where they administer large-scale planetary affairs. The fourteen Ray Masters, often discussed in this book, may be presumed to be part of this Brotherhood. One probable location for this Brotherhood is the legendary otherworld locale known as Shambhala. The term "white," of course, refers to light, as in a brotherhood of beings in light bodies.

198. On March 11, 1907, Chaco Canyon National Monument was created by the U.S. Congress; in 1980, a new law expanded its boundaries and renamed it Chaco Culture National Historical Park; then on December 8, 1987 (curiously, less than four months after the Harmonic Convergence of late August that year), Chaco Canyon received international recognition as a World Heritage Cultural Park.

199. Robert H. Lister and Florence C. Lister, *Chaco Canyon: Archaeology and Archaeologists* (Albuquerque: University of New Mexico Press, 1981): 3.

200. The Solstice Project is directed by Anna Sofaer, who founded it in 1978. For more information and copies of informative, technical papers on archaeoastronomical aspects of Chaco Canyon, see: www.solsticeproject.org

201. Anna Sofaer, "The Primary Architecture of the Chacoan Culture: A Cosmological Expression," in *Anasazi Architecture and Design,* eds. Baker H. Morrow and V. B. Price (Albuquerque: University of New Mexico Press, 1997).

202. Kendrick Frazier, *People of Chaco: A Canyon and Its Culture* (New York: W.W. Norton, 1986): 192, 194, 200.

203. Anna Sofaer, Volker Zinser, and Rolf M. Sinclair, "A Unique Solar Marking Construct," *Science* 206:4416 (October 19, 1979): 283–91.

204. There are two spiral petroglyphs: the larger one (34 by 41 cm) is elliptical with 9 1/2 turns; the smaller (9 by 13 cm) has 2 1/2 turns. The Sun shines on these petroglyphs for up to three hours at the winter solstice, but only 18 minutes at the summer solstice.

205. Kendrick Frazier, *People of Chaco: A Canyon and Its Culture* (New York: W.W. Norton, 1986): 125.

206. Salvatore M. Trento, *A Field Guide to Mysterious Places of the West* (Boulder, Co.: Pruett Publishing, 1994): 122, 126.

207. Brian Fagan, *From Black Land to Fifth Sun: The Science of Sacred Sites* (Reading, Mass.: Helix Books/Addison-Wesley, 1998): 180.

208. Paul Devereux, *Secrets of Ancient and Sacred Places: The World's Mysterious Heritage* (London: Blandford, 1992): 46.

209. Alice Bryant, "Chaco Canyon National Monument," in *Sacred Sites: A Guidebook to Sacred Centers & Mysterious Places in the United States,* ed. Frank Joseph (Saint Paul, Minn.: Llwellyn Publications, 1992): 245.

210. Charles Bensinger, *Chaco Journey: Remembrance and Awakening* (Santa Fe: Timewindow Publications, 1988): 87, 88, 120, 121.

211. Mark Justice Hinton, "Chaco Canyon: The Sacred and the Propane [sic]," May 1996, published at: http://users.aol.com/mjhinton/chaco/9605journal.htm

212. Mark Justice Hinton, April 10, 1997, published at: Chaco Canyon Forum, http://members.aol.com/mjhinton/chaco

213. Why Pleiadians? Because the Pleiadians as a star group had a formidable role in the design and implementation of the Earth's geomythic body; their influence and activities on behalf of the Earth's grid continue to this day. You should reasonably expect to encounter them from time to time in your meditations at sites. How can you tell they're Pleiadians? Image-formation during clairvoyant accessing always has a subjective element. To me, they appear as either tall crystalline pillars of light or eight-foot tall humans with very large hairless craniums; they may talk, but primarily their communication is telepathic.

214. Our own Sun has a solar half-life, which means a set amount of time in which it will sacrificially burn itself out on the solar system's behalf, radiating life but eventually achieving its own death through its solar exhaustion. Astrophysicists call this steady, inexorable sacrificial burn the *solar constant* $(S = 135.3 \text{ mW/cm}^2)$; if the Earth had no atmosphere to deflect the incoming solar radiation, it would burn on Earth at the rate of two calories per square centimeter per minute.

215. Jean Chevalier and Alain Gheerbrant, *A Dictionary of Symbols,* trans. John Buchanan-Brown (New York: Penguin Books, 1996): 742–5.

216. Andrew Coe, *Archaeological Mexico: A Traveler's Guide to Ancient Cities and Sacred Sites* (Chico, Calif.: Moon Travel Handbooks, 1998): 338.

217. T. A. Willard, *The City of the Sacred Well* (New York: Grosset & Dunlap, 1926): 149.

218. Linda Schele and Peter Matthews, *The Code of Kings: The Language of Seven Sacred Maya Temples and Tombs* (New York: Scribner, 1998): 198.

219. Mike Dixon-Kennedy, *Native American Myth & Legend: An A-Z of People and Places* (London: Blandford, 1996): 127.

220. Linda Schele and Peter Matthews, *The Code of Kings: The Language of Seven Sacred Maya Temples and Tombs* (New York: Scribner, 1998): 217.

221. Chac was the Mayan god of rain and lightning and was worshiped continuously for a long time in Mesoamerica, more so than any other god. He has lightning weapons, such as a stone axe or serpent (perhaps meaning lightning). Chac broke open a huge rock containing the original maize plant, source of life for the Maya. He is also known as *Ah Hoya* (He who urinates), *Ah Tzenul* (He who gives food to others), and *Hopop Caan* (He who lights up the sky). He threw down the rain from the sky in great gourds; he made thunder with his stone axes and lightning from their sparks; he was known to kill the unworthy among humans with a sudden thunderbolt; and he was a bloodthirsty god, eating human babies as propitiations to him for rain. Archeo-astronomers suggest,

however, that Chac may be a planetary god, namely some aspect of Venus. One of Chac's Mayan titles is "the Chac who makes brilliant the sky," and Venus is the brightest planet in our sky and holds the power over the rains, at least apparently. The northernmost horizon extreme of Venus corresponds with the start of the rainy season in Mesoamerica. Thus it would appear that Chac-Venus brings the rain.

222. Tollan is a Mayan paradisiacal realm, sometimes given a physical location, such as Tula, but whose location is usually left a bit vague and unspecified. Quetzalcoatl the Plumed Serpent is its king and founder. The houses in Tollan are made of green stone or precious metals, turquoise, shells, or bird plumage. Nobody ever goes hungry there, people want for nothing, and everyone can read. Quetzalcoatl lived in a palace comprising four buildings, oriented to the four directions; one was ornamented with gold, another with jade, a third with turquoise, the fourth with shells. The quetzal bird flew around Tollan. At some point Quetzalcoatl voluntarily left Tollan, or was banished, after having been deceived by another god into committing unsuitable sexual actions.

223. Mary Miller and Karl Taube, *An Illustrated Dictionary of the Gods and Symbols of Ancient Mexico and the Maya* (New York: Thames and Hudson, 1993): 141–2.

224. Mike Dixon-Kennedy, *Native American Myth & Legend: An A–Z of People and Places* (London: Blandford, 1996): 195.

225. Susan Milbrath, *Star Gods of the Maya: Astronomy in Art, Folklore, and Calendars* (Austin: University of Texas Press, 1999): 183.

226. Lewis Spence, *The Myths of Mexico & Peru* (London: George G. Harrap, 1913): 79–80.

227. Susan Milbrath, *Star Gods of the Maya: Astronomy in Art, Folklore, and Calendars* (Austin: University of Texas Press, 1999): 177.

228. Wayne van Kirk, "Mayan Ruins and Unexplained Acoustics," 1996, published at: www.mm2000.nu/sphinxw.html

229. David Lubman, "An Archaeological Study of Chirped Echo from the Mayan Pyramid of Kukulkan at Chichen Itza," Acoustical Society of America, October 1998, published at: www.ocasa.org/MayanPyramid.htm

230. Linda Schele and Peter Matthews, *The Code of Kings: The Language of Seven Sacred Maya Temples and Tombs* (New York: Scribner, 1998): 207.

231. Xibalba is a Mayan word that means "place of fright." The term denoted the Mayan Underworld,

also called Mictlan. It consisted of nine levels; the Upper World had 13 levels. The Mayans believed Xibalba lay in the West and could be entered through a cave or standing water. The Underworld contained various hazards that the souls of the dead had to negotiate to arrive in safety, much like the ball-playing twins and their night ordeal in the stations of the Death lords.

232. Susan Milbrath, *Star Gods of the Maya: Astronomy in Art, Folklore, and Calendars* (Austin: University of Texas Press, 1999): 159.

233. J. J. Hurtak, *The Book of Knowledge: The Keys of Enoch* (Los Gatos, Calif.: The Academy for Future Science, 1977): 48, 49, 310–3.

234. Jerusalem means "the foundation of peace," from *Yerushalayim*, meaning *yarah*, "to found," and *shalom*, "peace." However, Jerusalem also means "foundation of Lucifer," from *shalayim*, meaning not peace but Morning Star and Evening Star, an ancient reference to Venus, a planet also once known as Lucifer. Venus was thought of as the last planet to defy the rising of the Sun in the morning. Jerusalem is also known as Zion, God's City, and *Ir Ha-Kodesh*, "the Holy City." Lucifer is described as God's chief archangel, Son of the Dawn *(Helel ben Shahar)*, who "walked in Eden amid blazing jewels, his body a-fire with carnelian, topaz, emerald, diamond, beryl, onyx, jasper, sapphire, and carbuncle, all set in purest gold." Robert Graves and Raphael Patai, *Hebrew Myths: The Book of Genesis* (New York: Greenwich House/Arlington House/Crown, 1983): 57–9.

235. The Pleroma is a Gnostic term to denote "the Fullness of Being, the hierarchy of the divine realm, the 'fully explicated manifold of divine characteristics.' The Pleroma (or prime Aion) is the perfection of God, the fullness of God's being, the circle of divine attributes, the whole completeness of divinity, the fullness of real existence, and the archetypal ideal." There are thirty Aeons, or Aions, arranged in fifteen pairs. Sophia, the goddess of divine wisdom, was the thirtieth Aion, the one who left the Pleroma to see God from the outside. See Richard Leviton, *The Imagination of Pentecost: Rudolf Steiner and Contemporary Spirituality* (Hudson, N.Y.: Anthroposophic Press, 1994): 150.

The twenty-four Elders are a Christian mystical image in which twenty-four spiritual beings, like elder humans, stand about the Throne of God; they wear white robes and a golden crown, and continually praise the Supreme Being.

236. Planets such as Mercury and Venus which exhibit retrograde motion with respect to the

Earth—they seem to go backwards for a while—create "very particular patterns in the sky by their retrograde motions." Venus, as seen from Earth, goes around our planet, "looping in close" five times over the course of eight years, creating a pentagonal pattern around the Earth. Each loop is equally spaced and, after eight years, the pattern is repeated and another five-petaled flower is created. See Keith Critchlow, *Time Stands Still: New Light on Megalithic Science* (New York: Saint Martin's Press, 1982): 160.

237. Susan Milbrath, *Star Gods of the Maya: Astronomy in Art, Folklore, and Calendars* (Austin: University of Texas Press, 1999): 210.

238. Paul Younger, *The Home of Dancing Sivan: The Traditions of the Hindu Temple in Citamparam* (New York: Oxford University Press, 1995): 84.

239. Umapati Sivacarya, *Koyil Purana,* quoted in Paul Younger, *The Home of Dancing Sivan: The Traditions of the Hindu Temple in Citamparam* (New York: Oxford University Press, 1995): 176.

240. Ananda K. Coomaraswamy, *The Dance of Siva: Essays on Indian Art and Culture* (New York: Dover Publications, [1924] 1985): 50.

241. This corresponds approximately to the Western astrological framework of Cancer. Pushya is one of the twenty-seven *nashaktras,* the name for the Hindu way of dividing up the zodiacal wheel in thirteen degree wedges.

242. Paul Younger, *The Home of Dancing Sivan: The Traditions of the Hindu Temple in Citamparam* (New York: Oxford University Press, 1995): 165.

243. E. A. Sivaraman, *Chidambara Mahamyam* (Bombay, India: Bharatiya Vidya Bhavan, 1993): 5–6.

244. Clingman was a prospector, Civil War general, and later a U.S. Senator. He extolled the region's wealth of timber and minerals and suggested the area would also make an excellent health resort.

245. The range of the Eastern Cherokee included North and South Carolina, Virginia, Kentucky, Georgia, Alabama, and principally Tennessee, especially the Great Smoky Mountains. The name "Cherokee" is a foreign graft. They called themselves *Yun-wiya,* or *Ani-Yun'wiya,* which meant "real people" or "principal people"; on ceremonial occasions, they called themselves *Ani-Kitu'hwagi,* or "people of *Kitu'hwa,*" an ancient settlement on the Tuckasegee River and the presumed origin point of the tribe. Their Muskogean neighbors called them *Tciloki,* meaning "people of a different speech"; the Cherokees adopted this name as *Tsalagi,* which later became corrupted to Cherokee.

246. Vicki Rozema, *Footsteps of the Cherokees: A Guide to the Eastern Homelands of the Cherokee Nation* (Winston-Salem, N.C.: John F. Blair, 1995): 189–90.

247. James Mooney, *James Mooney's History, Myths, and Sacred Formulas of the Cherokees* (Asheville, N.C.: Historical Images, [1891,1900] 1992): 264, 325–6.

248. "Clingman's Dome," *Peakware World Mountain Encyclopedia,* 2001, at: www.peakware.com/encyclopedia/peaks/clingmans.htm

249. [no author cited] "Clingmans Dome," Great Smoky Mountains National Park webpage, at: www.imagesbuilder.com/gsmnp/clingmans-dome.html

250. Craig Whitlock and Todd Richissin, "Mountains of Problems," *News & Observer Sunday* (September 1, 1996); Raleigh, N.C.

251. Roger Rowlett, "My Visit to Clingman's Dome," October 27, 1997, published at: www.americasroof.com

252. The approximate extent of this figure stretches west to the Missouri River, north to southern Quebec, south to at least North Carolina, and east a fair distance into the Atlantic. The figure occupies a geometric space in the form of a pentagon, of which there are 12 of equal size on the Earth's surface, covering it like a quilt. Other key points in this figure (eight major chakras, seventy-two minor ones, and an extra feature) are in New York, Arkansas, Kentucky, and Virginia.

253. According to this source, ape-like humanoids came from the destroyed planet Maldek (now the asteroid belt between Mars and Jupiter) some 500,000 years ago to work out "their understanding complexes through a series of what you would call karmic restitutions." These beings are known as Bigfoot and dwell "in your deeper underground passageways." Don Elkins, Carla Rueckert, and James Allen McCarty, *The Ra Material—An Ancient Astronaut Speaks* (Norfolk, Va.: Donning, 1984): 108–11.

254. Michael Dames, *Mythic Ireland* (London: Thames and Hudson, 1992): 167–8.

255. Norbert C. Brockman, *Encyclopedia of Sacred Places* (New York: Oxford University Press, 1997): 56.

256. Edwin Bernbaum, *Sacred Mountains of the World* (Berkeley: University of California Press, 1997): 121.

257. These eight turning points are known as solar festivals and are: *Geerah,* December 22–25; *Imbolc Oimele,* or Candlemas, February 2; *Antharoc,*

March 21; *Beltain,* May 1; *Saura,* Midsummer's Day, June 21–24; *Lughnasadh,* August 1; *Law Aila Miheel,* September 22–24; and *Samhain,* November 1. Obviously two of these festival days correspond to the vernal and autumnal equinoxes; two others to the summer and winter solstices; the other four mark midway points between the equinoxes and solstices. See Peter Dawkins, *Zoence—The Science of Life: Discovering the Sacred Spaces of Your Life* (York Beach, Maine: Samuel Weiser, 1998): 14.

258. Further complicating the solar myth is the fact that *Crochen* is an old Irish name for the setting Sun personified; and *croch* means "saffron or cream," a reference to the color of the Sun as it sets but before it turns red at the horizon. Mebd's primary sacred site was *Sidh Sinche,* believed to be the same as the Cave of the Cats in County Roscommon. In northwest European myth, cats pulled the solar chariot across the sky, and cats came for a drink from the "solar bowl of cream." It is also said that the Midsummer's Sun Maid, Crochen Croderg, descends into the Cave of the Cats at dusk.

259. Peter Harbison, *Pilgrimage in Ireland: The Monuments and the People* (Syracuse, N.Y.: Syracuse University Press, 1991): 68.

260. Joseph Rose, "Virtual Journey—A Passage from My Irish Journal," 1994, published at: www.cbn.ie/reek/virtual2.html

261. Martin Gray, "Mt. Croach Patrick," 2000, published at: www.sacredsites.com

262. Courtney Bayne, in "Croagh Patrick: Pilgrims Worldwide. Stories, Pictures, and Greetings from Croagh Patrick Patrick Pilgrims and the World," maintained by Joseph Rose, Ellensburg, Penn., 2000, published at: www.anu.net/reek/pilgrimsworld.html

263. Lest it seem confusing that dragons and serpents are used interchangeably, it is helpful to conceive of Sesa the cosmic serpent and chief denizen of the Celestial City of Raksovati as a wingless coiled serpent; its progeny, the thirteen "daughters" and their offspring, the 1,053 dragons, gain wings by virtue of existing outside the fullness of potential being and in the world of manifest reality. In this sense, a winged dragon is a second generation wingless cosmic serpent.

264. Miranda J. Green, *Dictionary of Celtic Myth and Legend* (New York: Thames and Hudson, 1992): 135–7.

265. Geomythically, an equivalent image to the spear is that of master geomancer Joseph of Arimathea arriving at Wearyall Hill (another Celestial City of Raksovati) in Glastonbury around 30 A.D., and inserting his staff into the hill, whereupon the staff burst into a flowering thorn tree. See Glastonbury, England.

266. Virgil, *The Aeneid,* trans. Robert Fitzgerald (New York: Random House, 1981): 159,160,161.

267. John Opsopaus, "Pauca Anecdota Neapolitana" and "Ovum Incantatum Neapolis," published at Biblioteca Arcana [no date]: www.cs.utk.edu/~mclennan/BA/JO-AN.html

268. The name Parthenope suggests virgin birth or a virgin female, such as the Greek goddess Athena, who sprang not from a mother but from her father Zeus' forehead. The Parthenon on the Acropolis in Athens was named in honor of the Virgin, Athena. Biologically, parthenogenesis means birth from an unfertilized egg.

269. Hans Biedermann, *Dictionary of Symbolism: Cultural Icons and the Meanings Behind Them,* trans. James Hulbert (New York: Meridian/Penguin, 1994): 331.

270. Brian S. Bauer, *The Sacred Landscape of the Inca: The Cusco Ceque System* (Austin: University of Texas Press, 1998): 6.

271. Anthony F. Aveni, *Between the Lines: The Mystery of the Giant Ground Drawings of Ancient Nasca, Peru* (Austin: University of Texas Press, 2000): 67.

272. The Spanish also installed an insult in the name of the city itself. The original name was Qosqo, meaning navel or center, but after 1533, the Spanish invaders changed that to Cuzco, which is a contemptuous word meaning hypocrite, humpback, and small dog. Later the name slid a little to Cusco, but in 1990, the city government voted to reinstate the original name of Qosqo.

273. Sir Clements Markham, *The Incas of Peru* (London: Smith, Elder, 1911): 21–3.

274. Sanco, quoted in John Hyslop, *Inka Settlement Planning* (Austin: University of Texas Press, 1990): 54.

275. William Montgomery McGovern, quoted in David Hatcher Childress, *Lost Cities & Ancient Mysteries of South America* (Stelle, Ill.: Adventures Unlimited Press, 1986): 63.

276. Adriana von Hagen and Craig Morris, *The Cities of the Ancient Andes* (New York: Thames and Hudson, 1998): 177.

277. William Sullivan, *The Secret of the Incas: Myth, Astronomy, and the War Against Time* (New York: Crown, 1996): 125, 126, 253, 286.

278. Juan de Betanzos [1551], *Narrative of the Incas,* trans. and ed. Roland Hamilton and Dana Buchanan (Austin: University of Texas Press, 1996): 74.

279. As we have seen elsewhere in this book, the very large stone emplacements, the ones in which stones weigh in the dozens or hundreds of tons, have been executed not by humans but the Elohim, an angelic family temporarily incarnate for the purposes of establishing and grounding the Earth's geomantic matrix. Their incarnational form was large—they were the giants of myth—and their engineering talents formidable, such that moving and fitting very large stones was not, to them, a big challenge. Therefore, it is almost a rule of thumb that when you encounter the very large stones, such as at Sacsaywaman, you can assume the Elohim were involved in the construction and that this construction happened a very long time ago, before there were any cultural groups present.

280. Julius D. W. Staal, *The New Patterns in the Sky: Myths and Legends of the Stars* (Blacksburg, Va.: McDonald and Woodward, 1988): 143.

281. Richard Leviton, *Looking for Arthur: A Once and Future Travelogue* (Barrytown, N.Y: Station Hill Openings/Barrytown, 1997): 298.

282. Carol Cumes and Romulo Lizarraga Valencia, *Journey to Machu Picchu: Spiritual Wisdom from the Andes,* 2d. edition (Saint Paul: Llewellyn, 1999): 4.

283. *The Huarochiri Manuscript,* trans. F. Salomon and G. Urioste (Austin: University of Texas Press, 1991): 15.

284. William Sullivan, *The Secret of the Incas: Myth, Astronomy, and the War Against Time* (New York: Crown, 1996): 182.

285. It's further intriguing, though perhaps too far afield for our purposes here, that in the Gnostic myth of creation, the chief archon, cosmic architect, and cosmocrator was called Ialdabaoth. He was depicted as an androgynous lion-faced Demiurge, a sub-creator god, commissioned from on high to create the world, including the seven heavens of the angelic hierarchy. According to the Gnostics, Ialdabaoth was the somewhat unconscious offspring of the goddess of wisdom, Sophia. See Richard Leviton, *The Imagination of Pentecost: Rudolf Steiner and Contemporary Spirituality* (Hudson, N.Y.: Anthroposophic Press, 1994): 152.

286. Ovid, *The Metamorphoses,* trans. A. D. Melville (New York: Oxford University Press, 1986): 10.

287. Specifically, the Nine Muses were: Calliope ("Fair Voice," muse of epic poetry); Clio ("Renown," history); Polyhymnia ("Many Songs," mime); Euterpe ("Gladness," fluteplaying); Terpsichore ("Joy in the dance," dance and light verse); Erato ("Lovely," lyric choral poetry); Melpomene ("Singing," tragedy); Thalia ("Abundance, Good Cheer," comedy); and Urania ("Heavenly," astronomy). An older tradition said there were originally only Three Muses: Melete ("Practice"), Mneme ("Memory"), and Aoede ("Song").

288. Ovid, *The Metamorphoses,* trans. A. D. Melville (New York: Oxford University Press, 1986): 14.

289. "To Apollon," *Homeric Hymns,* trans. Apostolos N. Athanassakis (Baltimore: Johns Hopkins University Press, 1976): 24.

290. Pausanias, *Guide to Greece,* Vol. 1, *Central Greece,* trans. Peter Levi (New York: Penguin Books, 1971): 420.

291. C. Kerenyi, *The Gods of the Greeks* (New York: Thames & Hudson, 1980): 136.

292. Strabo, *Geography,* trans. H. L. Jones, Loeb Classical Library, Vol. 9:3.5 (Cambridge: Harvard University Press, 1954).

293. "To Apollon," *Homeric Hymns,* trans. Apostolos N. Athanassakis (Baltimore: Johns Hopkins University Press, 1976): 20, 23.

294. Diodorus Siculus, *Greek Virginity,* trans. Arthur Goldhamn (Cambridge: Harvard University Press, 1990): 16.26:34–35.

295. Pausanias, *Guide to Greece,* Vol. 1, *Central Greece,* trans. Peter Levi (Baltimore: Penguin Books, 1971): 415–416.

296. Michael Grant and John Hazel, *Who's Who in Classical Mythology* (New York: Oxford University Press, 1973): 38.

297. *The Odes of Pindar,* trans. C. M. Bowra (New York: Penguin Books, 1969): 26.

298. Edwin Bernbaum, *Sacred Mountains of the World* (Berkeley: University of California Press, 1997): 110–1.

299. Alexander Eliot, *Earth, Air, Fire, and Water* (New York: Simon & Schuster, 1962): 14, 87, 89.

300. Roger Lipsey, *Have You Been to Delphi? Tales of the Ancient Oracle for Modern Minds* (Albany: State University of New York Press, 2001): xvii, xviii.

301. In case the idea of visualizing serpents or dragons is either repugnant or scary, be assured Python is not really either. Both are convenient zoömorphic images—metaphors—for a complex, multidimensional reality. If you prefer, visualize a sphere

full of a matrix of interconnecting lines of light. Around its outside is a Celtic torc, a kind of jeweled necklace that doesn't quite clasp in the front. This would correspond to the "mouth" of the dragon, and the jewel to the omphalos stone.

302. This subject is too complex for this book and is handled thoroughly in *The Emerald Modem.* However, the essential point here is that the Earth's grid structure is describable in terms of polyhedra known as the Platonic Solids, of which there are five. The five Solids nest together to form the Earth's grid structure. Two of them—the twenty-sided icosahedron and twelve-sided dodecahedron—comprise the fifteen Oroboros Lines which in fact are the edges of this complex shape.

303. *Star Myths of the Greeks and Romans: A Sourcebook,* trans. Theony Condos (Grand Rapids, Mich.: Phanes Press, 1997): 183–4.

304. Norman Kotker, *The Earthly Jerusalem* (New York: Charles Scribner's Sons, 1969): 6.

305. Benjamin Mazar, *The Mountain of the Lord* (New York: Doubleday & Company, 1975): 262.

306. Roger Garaudy, "Palestine: Land of Divine Revelation," *The American Muslim,* American Muslim Council, Spring 1994, reprinted 1997 as "The Dome of the Rock," ed. A. Zahoor, at: http://users.erols.com/ameen/domerock.htm

307. Raphael Patai, *Man and Temple in Ancient Jewish Myth and Ritual* (London: Thomas Nelson and Sons, 1947): 56.

308. Robert Graves and Raphael Patai, *Hebrew Myths: The Book of Genesis* (New York: Greenwich House/Arlington House, 1983): 31.

309. Louis Ginzberg *The Legends of the Jews,* Vol. I, trans. Henrietta Szold (Phildelphia: Jewish Publication Society of America, 1909): 12.

310. Martin Lev, *The Traveler's Key to Jerusalem: A Guide to the Sacred Places of Jerusalem* (New York: Alfred A. Knopf, 1989): 50, 51.

311. Ibid., 10.

312. Robert Graves and Raphael Patai, *Hebrew Myths: The Book of Genesis* (New York: Greenwich House/Arlington House, 1983): 57.

313. John Michell, *The Temple at Jerusalem: A Revelation* (York Beach, Maine: Samuel Weiser, 2000): 9, 10, 11.

314. Graham Hancock, *The Sign and the Seal: The Quest for the Lost Ark of the Covenant* (New York: Touchstone/Simon & Schuster, 1992): 362, 363.

315. The King Solomon and Grail Knight stories coincide in Sir Thomas Malory's *Le Morte d'Arthur,* Vol. II, ed. Janet Cowen (New York: Penguin Books, 1969): Book XVII, Chaps. 2–7, 331–342.

316. Wolfram von Eschenbach, *Parzival,* trans. A. T. Hatto (New York: Penguin Books, 1980): 240.

317. This is largely the subject of my next book, *The Emerald Modem: A User's Guide to the Geomythic Earth* (Charlottesville, Va.: Hampton Roads, 2003).

318. Ellen Frankel and Betsy Platkin Teutsch, *The Encyclopedia of Jewish Symbols* (Northvale, N.J.: Jason Aronson, 1992): 13.

319. Steiner's new spiritual scientific philosophy, called Anthroposophy, proposed that profound knowledge of the cosmos could be found by studying the esoteric aspects of the human being. This premise was based on the perennial wisdom teaching that the macrocosm (the universe) is replicated in the microcosm (the human), and that all the energies and levels of consciousness in the "outer" world can be found and studied in the "inner" world, that is, the human being. Steiner's Anthroposophy generated numerous practical applications in medicine, agriculture (biodynamic agriculture), education (Waldorf), art, architecture, economics, and special education. Many of these are now practiced worldwide: the Waldorf approach to education is now the second largest private school system in the U.S.; Anthroposophic medicine today is a respected, well-known, and fully accredited form of medicine in the German-speaking countries of Europe.

320. Rudolf Steiner, quoted in Hans Ruedi and Priska Clerc, *The Goetheanum and Its Surroundings* (Dornach, Switzerland: Goetheanum Press, Philosophisch-Anthroposophischer Verlag am Goetheanum, 1987): 18.

321. Johann Wolfgang von Goethe, *Letters from Switzerland,* October 3, 1779, quoted in Rex Raab, Arne Klingborg, and Ake Fant, *Eloquent Concrete: How Rudolf Steiner Employed Reinforced Concrete* (London: Rudolf Steiner Press, 1979): 109.

322. Ibid., 109.

323. Deike and Ean Begg, *In Search of the Holy Grail and the Precious Blood: A Travellers' Guide* (San Francisco: Thorsons/HarperCollins, 1995): 205.

324. Hans Ruedi and Priska Clerc, *The Goetheanum and Its Surroundings* (Dornach, Switzerland: Goetheanum Press, Philosophisch-Anthroposophischer Verlag am Goetheanum, 1987): 84.

325. Trevor Ravenscroft, *The Cup of Destiny: The Quest for the Grail* (York Beach, Maine: Samuel Weiser, 1982): 54.

326. Rudolf Steiner, *The Mission of Folk Souls* (London: Anthroposophical Publishing, 1929): 16.

327. Rudolf Steiner, *The Gospel of Saint John* (Hudson, N.Y.: Anthroposophic Press, 1982): 111.

328. Rudolf Grosse, *The Christmas Foundation: Beginning of a New Cosmic Age* (North Vancouver, BC, Canada: Steiner Book Centre, 1984): 66.

329. Ibid., 70.

330. A dodecahedron is one of the five Platonic Solids, which are five regular polyhedra that have unique geometric properties. The dodecahedron has twelve facets or surfaces, each a pentagon (five-sided shape), all of equal size.

331. Stewart C. Easton, *Rudolf Steiner: Herald of a New Epoch* (Spring Valley, N.Y.: Anthroposophic Press, 1980): 195–7.

332. Rudolf Steiner, *World History in the Light of Anthroposophy* (London: Rudolf Steiner Press, 1977): 146, 147, 149.

333. Rudolf Grosse, *The Christmas Foundation: Beginning of a New Cosmic Age* (North Vancouver, BC, Canada: Steiner Book Centre, 1984): 93.

334. F. W. Zeylmans van Emmichovenm, *The Foundation Stone* (London: Rudolf Steiner Press, 1963): 15, 36, 37.

335. The geometric modeling can be a bit confusing at first. If you look at a six-sided double-terminated crystal from the base, it is a figure of six equal triangles. It is also a cross-section of a cube, which has six sides. Within the theory of Platonic Solids and the five elements, each element, such as earth, air, fire, water, and ether, has one specific geometric shape. The earth element is the cube; ether is represented by the dodecahedron (twelve sides). It can be demonstrated that when you spin or ratchet the cube five times, that is, see the five turns as if frozen in space, you get the dodecahedron. You could say five cubes equals the dodecahedron. For our purposes, this means the cube implies the dodecahedron.

336. Rudolf Steiner, *Karmic Relationships: Esoteric Studies*, Vol. V (London: Rudolf Steiner Press, 1977): 27

Rudolf Steiner, *Life Between Death and Rebirth* (Hudson, NY: Anthroposophic Press, 1968): 97.

Rudolf Steiner, *True and False Paths in Spiritual Investigation* (London: Rudolf Steiner Press, 1985): 8, 202, 217.

337. For more on Steiner's views on the Christ, spiritual development, and the future of Anthroposophy, see my book *The Imagination of Pentecost: Rudolf Steiner and Contemporary Spirituality* (Hudson, N.Y.: Anthroposophic Press, 1994).

338. Rudolf Steiner, *The Four Sacrifices of Christ* (Spring Valley, N.Y.: Anthroposophic Press, 1944): 18.

339. Rudolf Steiner, *An Outline of Occult Science* (Spring Valley, N.Y.: Anthroposophic Press, 1972): 356, 357, 362.

340. Jean Chevalier and Alain Gheerbrant, *A Dictionary of Symbols,* trans. John Buchanan-Brown (New York: Penguin Books, 1996): 472–3.

341. Father Sebastian Englert, *Island at the Center of the World: New Light on Easter Island* (New York: Charles Scribner's Sons, 1970): 31.

342. Katherine Routledge, quoted in Paul Bahn and John Flenley, *Easter Island, Earth Island* (New York: Thames and Hudson, 1992): 51.

343. Liesl Clark, "Lessons Learned," *Secrets of Easter Island, Nova,* May 11, 1998, published at: www.pbs.org/wgbh/nova/easter/dispatches

344. Liesl Clark, "Statue Mold En Route," *Secrets of Easter Island, Nova,* April 22, 1998, published at: www.pbs.org/wgbh/nova/easter/dispatches

345. Father Sebastian Englert, *Island at the Center of the World: New Light on Easter Island* (New York: Charles Scribner's Sons, 1970): 88.

346. Thor Heyerdahl, *Aku-Aku: The Secret of Easter Island* (Chicago: Rand McNally, 1958): 86, 87.

347. Kathrine Routledge, *The Mystery of Easter Island* (Kempton, Ill.: Adventures Unlimited Press, [1919] 1998): 184.

348. Paul Bahn and John Flenley, *Easter Island, Earth Island* (New York: Thames and Hudson, 1992): 120.

349. Thor Heyerdahl, *Easter Island: The Mystery Solved* (New York: Random House, 1989): 111.

350. Jean-Michel Schwartz, *The Mysteries of Easter Island,* trans. Lowell Blair (New York: Avon, 1973): 122, 123, 129.

351. H. P. Blavatsky, *The Secret Doctrine: The Synthesis of Science, Religion, and Philosophy,* Vol. II, *Anthropogenesis* (Pasadena: Theosophical University Press, 1977): 331, 336, 339, 340.

352. Marie Parsons, "Edfu," [no date], published at: www.touregypt.net

353. Dr. Barbara Watterson, "The Temple of Horus at Edfu," *Ancient Egypt Magazine,* Issue 3, September/October 2000, published at: www.ancientegyptmagazine.com

354. R. T. Rundle Clark, *Myth and Symbol in Ancient Egypt* (New York: Thames and Hudson, 1959): 225.

355. George Hart, *A Dictionary of Egyptian Gods and Goddesses* (London: Routledge & Kegan Paul, 1986): 167.

356. Barbara S. Lesko, *The Great Goddesses of Egypt,* (Norman: University of Oklahoma Press, 1999): 84, 87, 113.

357. Dr. Barbara Watterson, "Myth and Ritual in the Temple of Horus at Edfu," *Ancient Egypt Magazine,* Issue 4, November/December 2000. Also see Barry Kemp, "Edfu," in *Atlas of Ancient Archeology,* ed. Jacquetta Hawkes (New York: McGraw Hill, 1974): 160.

358. R. T. Rundle Clark, *Myth and Symbol in Ancient Egypt* (New York: Thames and Hudson, 1959): 122.

359. Remarkably and almost casually, Plutarch in his accounting of the Osiris myth, *De Iside et Osiride,* says Typhon is the Sun, and therefore called Seth, a word meaning "violence and force." E. A. Wallis Budge, *Legends of the Egyptian Gods: Hieroglyphic Texts and Translations* (New York: Dover Publications, 1994): 245.

360. E. A. Wallis Budge, *The Gods of the Egyptians, Or, Studies in Egyptian Mythology,* Vol. I (New York: Dover Publications, [1904] 1969): 476, 477, 478, 479, 485.

361. It is too complex to enter into here, but this statement is based on the contention that Master Jesus and the Christ are two different spiritual beings. Master Jesus, as the sixth Ray Master, works to transmit the Christ essence and, one time, voluntarily embodied it in human form for the benefit of the Earth as part of the Christ Mystery at Golgotha. We might think of Master Jesus (and his other mythic guises) as the active hand of the Solar Logos. For more on this line of thinking, see the works of Rudolf Steiner, and/or my *The Imagination of Pentecost: Rudolf Steiner and Contemporary Spirituality* (Hudson, N.Y.: Anthroposophic Press, 1994).

362. Ekrem Akurgal, *Ancient Civilizations and Ruins of Turkey: From Prehistoric Times Until the End of the Roman Empire,* trans. John Whybrow and Mollie Emre (Istanbul: Haset Kitabevi, 1973): 142–3.

363. Herodotus, *The Histories,* trans. Robin Waterfield (New York: Oxford University Press, 1998): 12, 43, 155.

364. "The Acts of the Apostles" in *The Jerusalem Bible,* ed. Alexander Jones. (Garden City, N.Y.: Doubleday, 1966): 19: 35.

365. "The Acts of the Apostles" in *The Jerusalem Bible,* ed. Alexander Jones. (Garden City, N.Y.: Doubleday, 1966): 19: 23–28.

366. James Harpur, *The Marshall Travel Atlas of Sacred Places: A Guide to the World's Spiritual Oases* (London: Marshall Publishing, 1998): 22.

367. Norbert C. Brockman, *Encyclopedia of Sacred Places* (Santa Barbara: ABC-CLIO, 1997): 76.

368. *The Oxford Dictionary of the Christian Church,* ed. F. L. Cross (New York: Oxford University Press, 1974): 461–2.

369. Colin Wilson, *The Atlas of Holy Places and Sacred Sites* (New York: DK Publishing, 1996): 32.

370. Jessica Amanda Salmonson, *The Encyclopedia of Amazons: Women Warriors from Antiquity to the Modern Era* (New York: Paragon House, 1991): 9.

One of Heracles' twelve labors was to capture the girdle of the Amazon Queen Hippolyta. Irish myth also recounts fierce, warlike women who do battle as peers with heroes such as Cuchulainn. For that matter, in our own times, Carlos Castaneda writes of fierce sorceresses (initiates of Don Juan Matus) with whom he has to "battle," although here the battle was more of a magical than physically combative type. Insofar as Ephesus was said to be a center of the magical arts, however, perhaps the Amazon reference also contains some of the Castaneda nuances. Similarly, several Greek heroines, such as Medea and Circe (both granddaughters of the Sun god, Helios), would qualify for the Amazon title in the Castaneda sense.

371. Pierre Grimal, *A Concise Dictionary of Classical Mythology* (Oxford, UK: Basil Blackwell, 1986): 61.

372. "To Artemis" in *Homeric Hymns,* trans. Apostolos N. Athanassakis (Baltimore: Johns Hopkins University Press, 1976): 65–6.

373. Walter Burkert, *Greek Religion,* trans. John Raffan (Cambridge: Harvard University Press, 1985): 150.

374. Lesley Adkins and Roy A. Adkins, *Dictionary of Roman Religion* (New York: Facts on File, 1996): 60–1.

375. *The Chiron Dictionary of Greek and Roman Mythology,* trans. Elizabeth Burr. Wilmette, Ill.: Chiron Publications, 1994): 77.

376. Buffie Johnson, *Lady of the Beasts: Ancient Images of the Goddess and Her Sacred Animals* (San Francisco: Harper & Row, 1988): 236–8.

Johnson notes that Artemis was the goddess consecrated in the East to the Taurobolium ritual. A high priestess of the Great Mother ritually slaughters a bull inside a cave or darkened space, then pours the blood over the priest, who presents himself to the public. The event (similar in essence, though perhaps more gory because it was literal, to the rites of Mithraism) was believed to purify an entire realm. Johnson, 293.

377. Vincent Scully. *The Earth, The Temple, and The Gods: Greek Sacred Architecture* (New Haven: Yale University Press, 1962): 90–1.

378. W. J. Wilkins, *Hindu Mythology, Vedic and Puranic* (New Delhi: Rupa & Company, [1882] 1975): 296–307.

379. W. J. Wilkins, *Hindu Mythology, Vedic and Puranic* (New Delhi: Rupa & Company, [1882] 1975): 306–310.

380. Margaret and James Stutley, *Harper's Dictionary of Hinduism: Its Mythology, Folklore, Philosophy, Literature, and History* (San Francisco: Harper & Row, 1977): 82.

381. David Kinsley, *Hindu Goddesses: Visions of the Divine Feminine in the Hindu Religious Tradition* (Berkeley: University of California Press, 1988): 95.

382. Nigel Pennick, "The Externsteine: A Germany Sanctuary," in *The Atlas of Mysterious Places,* ed. Jennifer Westwood (New York: Weidenfeld & Nicolson, 1987): 56.

383. Liam Rogers, "Time, Space, and Identity in the Third Reich: The Dangers of Resacralising the Land," in *Place: The On-Line Magazine for Planning in Harmony with the Land* 7: 8, Winter 2001, published at: www.the-cutting-edge.freeserve.co.uk

384. Jeremy Harte, "Taking Leave of Dod— Survey as Metaphor," *The Ley Hunter* 126, 1997.

385. Stephen Cook and Stuart Russell, *Heinrich Himmler's Camelot. The Wewelsburg Ideological Center of the SS, 1934-1945* (Andrews, N.C.: Kressman-Backmeyer Publishing, 1999).

386. Some scholars, such as H. M. Chadwick (1924) identify Eresberg with Marsberg on the Diemel River, but others, such as De Pierrefeu (1955) said that the pillar was at the Externsteine.

387. H. R. Ellis Davidson, *Myths and Symbols in Pagan Europe: Early Scandinavian and Celtic Religions* (Syracuse: Syracuse University Press, 1988): 22.

388. Rudolf Simek, *Dictionary of Northern Mythology,* trans. Angela Hall (Woodbridge, UK: D.S. Brewer/Boydell & Brewer, 1993): 175–6.

389. Peter Dawkins, *Zoence®—the Science of Life: Discovering the Sacred Spaces of Your Life* (York Beach, Maine: Samuel Weiser, 1998): 102–5.

390. Arnbald OR (F), "The Irminsul and the Externsteine: From Yggdrasil to the Irminsul," a speech reprinted from *ORB M,* Issue 2, 2000, published at: www.odinic-rite.org

391. Ehrenfried Pfeiffer, *The Heart Lectures* (Spring Valley, N.Y.: Mercury Press, 1989): 14.

392. Deike and Ean Begg, *In Search of the Holy Grail and the Precious Blood* (San Francisco: Thorsons/HarperCollins,1995): 163–4.

393. Savitri Devi, "Rocks of the Sun," excerpted from *Pilgrimage*, n.p., Calcutta, India, 1958, reprinted at: http://netjunk.com/users/library/rocks_02.htm

394. Robert Burnham Jr., *Burnham's Celestial Handbook: An Observer's Guide to the Universe Beyond the Solar System,* Vol. 1, *Andromeda-Cetus* (New York: Dover Publications, 1978): 585.

395. The term comes from yoga models of the human energy system and from Vedic and Hindu myths about the spiritual center of the world, known as Mount Meru, the cosmic mountain. By Merudanda, yogis mean the subtle vertical sheath parallel with the spinal column along which the seven major energy centers, or chakras, are arrayed. *Danda* means "stick," and this column is regarded as a living stick, the lightning conductor of consciousness from the base of the system, the root chakra, to the top and highest level, the crown chakra, understood to be the bodily equivalent of Mount Meru. A Western equivalent image is the caduceus of Mercury in which two serpents are shown entwining a central column. That central column in the caduceus is the Merudanda; in the Merudanda model, the two entwining serpents are known as the *ida* and *pingala* energy channels which interweave on their way up the pole, passing through all the chakras along the way.

396. In the late 1940s, Ernest Hartmann, M.D., described a tightly woven checkerboard energy grid comprised of naturally occurring charged and magnetically oriented lines running North–South and East–West across the entire surface of the planet. The lines are spaced about 6'6" (north to south) by 8'2" (east to west). Dr. Manfred Curry described a global gridwork of electrically charged lines, also naturally occurring, that run diagonally to the north and south poles—NE–SW and SE–NW. The lines are believed to be about nine feet apart, although the width can vary. Today, dowsers and people studying geopathogenic stress—the ill-health effects of emanations from the Earth—refer to the system jointly as the Curry–Hartmann grid or net.

397. Tomas Venclova, "In Vilnius's Valleys," trans. Ina Navazelskis [no date], published at: www.mediaguide.hu/book/bookID47.html

398. Somewhat confusingly, the Shrine of Divine Mercy in Cracow, Poland, also claims to have the original of this same painting, or perhaps a copy of the original. Both sites claim equal numinosity for this image, and to add to the confusion, its visionary creator, Sister Faustina, lived at neither location nor did she receive her vision at either site. The supposed original at Vilnius was removed from the site in 1948 and was taken to various locations around Europe until it was returned to Vilnius in 1987. For more information about this image, see: Wawel Hill, Cracow, Poland.

399. "Gediminas," *Romuva/USA* 5, Fall 1991, reprinted at: www.geocities.com/Athens/Oracle/2810/castle.html

400. Variations on his name are found in neighboring regions. He is Perkons (Latvia), Pargnus (Prussia), Perun and Perunas (Russia), Pjarun (Byelorus), Piorun (Poland), Perusan (Bulgaria), and Peron (Slovakia).

401. Jonas Trinkunas, "The Baltic Rite: The Basis of the Old Lithuanian Religion," June 20, 1995, Vilnius, Lithuania, published at: www.vinland.org/heathen/pagancee/lithrel.html

402. Mike Dixon-Kennedy, *Encyclopedia of Russian and Slavic Myth and Legend* (Santa Barbara: ABC-CLIO, 1998): 61, 217.

403. Patrick Benham, *The Avalonians* (Glastonbury, England: Gothic Image Publications, 1993): xvii.

404. For more on life and initiation in geomythic Glastonbury, see my *Looking for Arthur: A Once and Future Travelogue* (Barrytown, N.Y.: Station Hill Openings/Barrytown, 1997); and *What's Beyond That Star: A Chronicle of Geomythic Adventure* (London: Clairview Books, 2002).

405. John Michell, quoted in Paul Screeton, *Seekers of the Linear Vision* (Santa Barbara: Stonehenge Viewpoint,1993): 31.

406. *My Dear Alexias: Letters from Wellesley Tudor Pole to Rosamond Lehmann,* ed. Elizabeth Gaythorpe (Jersey, Channel Islands, UK: Neville Spearman, 1979): 51, 160, 124.

407. Phillip Johnson Brown, "Sacred Places," 2000, 3, published at: www.belinus.co.uk/doorsofpeace/Naturesacredplaces.htm

408. Oliver L. Reiser, *This Holyest Erthe: The Glastonbury Zodiac and King Arthur's Camelot* (London: Perennial Books, 1974): 100, 94.

409. John Michell, *New Light on the Ancient Mystery of Glastonbury* (Glastonbury, UK: Gothic Image Publications, 1990): i.

410. Geoffrey of Monmouth, *Vita Merlini,* ed. John Parry, University of Illinois *Studies in Language and Literature,* Vol. X, No. 3 (August 1925): 26.

411. *Trioedd Ynys Prydein: The Welsh Triads,* trans. and ed. Rachel Bromwich (Cardiff, Wales, UK: University of Wales Press, 1978): 217.

412. Nicholas R. Mann, *The Isle of Avalon: Sacred Mysteries of Arthur and Glastonbury Tor* (London: Green Magic, 2001): 18.

413. Gino Gennaro, *The Phenomena of Avalon: The Story of This Planet as Recounted by the Fairies* ([no city given], UK: Cronos Publications, 1979): 30, 31.

414. Wellesley Tudor Pole, *Writing on the Ground* (Tasburgh, England: Pilgrims Book Services, 1968): 97–100.

415. Wellesley Tudor Pole, quoted in *The Awakening Letters,* ed. Cynthia Sandys and Rosamond Lehmann (Jersey, Channel Islands, UK: Neville Spearman, 1978): 72, 73.

416. Adrian J. Ivakhiv, *Claiming Sacred Ground: Pilgrims and Politics at Glastonbury and Sedona* (Bloomington: Indiana University Press, 2001): 116–8.

417. Robert Burnham Jr., *Burnham's Celestial Handbook: An Observer's Guide to the Universe Beyond the Solar System,* Vol. 3 (New York: Dover Publications, [1875, 1876] 1978).

418. In Celtic myths the identity of Gwynn ap Nudd drifts confusingly between grim Lord of the Dead and whimsical King of the Fairies. The fairy attribution is probably a later amendment on Gwynn ap Nudd's essential character, a stage in the process of cultural trivialization whereby the great old myths get knocked down to cartoon status and eventually become entirely disbelieved as "fairy tales." Gwynn ap Nudd as host at the fairy palace feast is more likely a mislabeling of the Gandharvas, whose celestial lifestyle could be described in this way.

419. *My Dear Alexias: Letters from Wellesley Tudor Pole to Rosamond Lehmann,* ed. Elizabeth Gaythorpe (Jersey, Channel Islands, UK: Neville Spearman, 1979): 86.

420. Stephen Jenkins, *The Undiscovered Country: Adventures into Other Dimensions* (Sudbury, UK: Neville Spearman, 1977): 158.

421. William Blake, "Jerusalem. The Emanation of the Giant Albion," *Complete Writings,* ed. Geoffrey Keynes (London: Oxford University Press, 1966): 649.

422. I don't mean to be coy here by not divulging the exact location. The workings of the three aspects of the Earth's chakra are discussed in *The Emerald Modem;* between now and that time geomantic work is being done on the *Ananda-kanda* site before releasing its location to the public. It's a bit like preparing a stage for a grand opera performance; there's no point in letting the audience into the theater if the stage isn't finished—especially in this case as the site has not been worked on since Hyperborean times, which, in rough terms, is more than twenty million years ago.

423. This complex subject receives ample discussion in *The Emerald Modem.*

424. The Kumbh Mela at Allahabad is called the Purna Kumbh, or complete festival, held every twelve years when the planet Jupiter is in the zodiacal sign of Taurus and as the Sun enters Capricorn. The confluence at Allahabad of three rivers, the Ganges, Yamuna, and the mythical Saraswati, affords the festival there extra auspiciousness.

The Ardh Kumbh is held every six years in between two Kumbh Melas which are held every three years. The Magh Mela is an annual Kumbh Mela, attracting two to three million people. The Maha Kumbh Mela happens only once every 144 years (which is a cycle of twelve Jupiter twelve-year cycles). It is held in Allahabad. The Kumbh Mela at Allahabad for 2001 was a Maha Kumbh Mela. January 14, which in Hindu astrology marks the day the Sun enters Capricorn (a sign betokening inner initiation and passing through cosmic gateways), is a major bathing day when millions enter the Ganges.

425. "Millions Plunge into Holy Ganges," *BBC News,* January 24, 2001, published at: www.news.bbc.co.uk

426. One of the major astrological factors in the Kumbh Mela is the planet Jupiter. Its orbital cycle around the Sun takes 11.86 years, which is almost twelve years, the full cycle of the four Kumbh Mela festivals. Jupiter spends almost a year in each of the twelve Houses or Signs of the zodiac, a unit of time called *Parivatsara.* According to classical Hindu time reckonings, Jupiter takes about 4,320 days to complete one orbital revolution around the Sun. The "root" number 432 is of vital significance in Hindu cosmography, as 4,320,000 years comprise the length of the Four Ages, or Yugas, and the fourth, darkest, and present age, the Kali Yuga, is said to last 432,000 years. One thousand of these cycles of 4,320,000 years equals one Day of Brahma, which means,

working backwards, one Kumbh Mela cycle of Jupiter (4,320 days) is symbolically equal to a fraction of a Day of Brahma.

427. Anita Pratap, "Millions of Hindus Bathe in India's Ganges for Purification," CNN Interactive/World News, April 13, 1998, published at: www.cnn.com

428. Margaret and James Stutley, *Harper's Dictionary of Hinduism: Its Mythology, Folklore, Philosophy, Literature, and History* (San Francisco: Harper & Row, 1977): 316.

429. *Hindu Myths: A Sourcebook Translated from the Sanskrit,* trans. Wendy Doniger O'Flaherty (New York: Penguin Books, 1975): 276.

430. Alfred Hillebrandt, *Vedic Mythology,* Vol. 1, trans. Sreeramula Rajeswara Sarma (Delhi, India: Motilal Banarsidass Publishers, 1980): 185, 188, 197.

431. Karapatri, "Sri Siva Tattva," *Siddhanta,* quoted in Alain Danielou, *The Myths and Gods of India* (Rochester, Vt.: Inner Traditions, 1991): 215.

432. David Kinsley, *Hindu Goddesses: Visions of the Divine Feminine in the Hindu Religious Tradition* (Berkeley: University of California Press, 1986): 189, 192.

433. Diana L. Eck, "Ganga, The Goddess Ganges in Hindu Sacred Geography," in *Devi: Goddesses of India,* ed. John S. Hawley and Donna M.Wulff (Berkeley: University of California Press, 1996): 138.

434. Richard L. Thompson, *Vedic Cosmography and Astronomy* (Los Angeles: Bhaktivedanta Book Trust, 1989): 92–5.

435. In due diligence to the Precession of the Equinoxes model, about forty-six hundred years ago Thuban (Alpha Draconis) was the Pole Star, and about twelve thousand years ago it was Vega in Lyra. In the case of the Pole Star and Polaris, we have to think in terms of the original stellar blueprint for the Earth with respect to the galaxy, a reckoning that would take us back into vast reaches of planetary and galactic time, most likely beyond the conceptual reach of current astronomy.

436. Bhagavata Purana, quoted in Giorgio de Santillana and Hertha von Dechend, *Hamlet's Mill: An Essay on Myth and the Frame of Time* (Boston: David R. Godine, 1977): 138.

437. For more on the phase-shifted and elusive tangibility of Mount Meru, see Rene Daumal, *Mount Analogue: A Novel of Symbolically Authentic Non-Euclidean Adventures in Mountain Climbing* (New York: Penguin Books, 1974). Daumal uses the term "Mount Analogue" for Mount Meru, which he places somewhere in the Pacific Ocean.

438. John L. Brooke, *The Refiner's Fire: The Making of Mormon Cosmology, 1644–1844* (New York: Cambridge University Press, 1994): 3.

439. Joseph Smith, *The Journal of Joseph: The Personal History of a Modern Prophet.* Compiled by Leland R. Nelson (Mapleton, Utah: Council Press, 1979): 7.

440. William H. Kelley, "The Hill Cumorah and the Book of Mormon," *The Saints' Herald* (Plano, Ill.) (June 1, 1881): 161–8.

441. Salvatore M. Trento, *Field Guide to Mysterious Places of Eastern North America* (New York: Henry Holt, 1997): 245.

442. Joseph Smith, *The Prophet Joseph Smith's Testimony* (Salt Lake City: Church of Jesus Christ of Latter-day Saints, 1984): 2–5.

443. In Judaic tradition, the *Urim* and *Thummim* was a mystical priestly device used as an oracle as sanctioned by the Torah. The device was kept hidden in a special pouch sewn into the *ephod* (apronlike garment) of the High Priest and consulted when oracular guidance was required. One theory as to the device's mode of operation was that it lit up or pressed out individual letters in the names of the Twelve Tribes of Israel as engraved on the twelve stones of the priest's breastplate. Another theory holds that the *Urim* and *Thummim* were astrological devices associated with the seven planets.

444. H. Donl Peterson, "Moroni, Son of Mormon." *Encyclopedia of Mormonism* Vol 2, Moroni 2 (New York, MacMillan, 1992), reprinted at: www.mormons.org

445. Cory H. Maxwell, "Restoration of all Things," *Encyclopedia of Mormonism* (New York, MacMillan, 1992), reprinted at: www.mormons.org

446. Joseph Smith, *The Journal of Joseph: The Personal History of a Modern Prophet.* Compiled by Leland R. Nelson (Mapleton, Utah: Council Press, 1979): 5.

447. One Mormon scholar mapped the Nephite saga onto a map of ancient Mexico (central Mesoamerica) and claimed that Cumorah (and the older-named Hill Ramah) must have been part of the northern or western extremity of the Tuxtla Mountains, ninety miles from Tres Zapotes, and called Cerro El Vigia (elevation: 3,000 feet). See John L. Sorenson, *An Ancient American Setting for the Book of Mormon* (Salt Lake City: Deseret Book Company, 1985): 347–50.

448. Fawn Brodie, *No Man Knows My History: The Life of Joseph Smith* (New York: Alfred A. Knopf, 1945): 43–4.

449. Ibid., 34.

450. *The Papers of Joseph Smith,* Vol. 1., *Autobiographical and Historical Writings,* ed. Dean C. Jessee (Salt Lake City: Deseret Book Company, 1989): 78–9.

451. Both reviews quoted at www.hillcumorah.com. No publication date or authors given. The Oberammergau is a Passion Play performed every ten years to dramatize the passion of Jesus Christ, and staged by the villagers of Oberammergau in Bavaria, Germany, to fulfill a vow made there in 1663 when the village was saved from the plague.

452. Ingrid Fischer-Schreiber, Franz-Karl Ehrhard, and Michael S. Diener, *The Shambhala Dictionary of Buddhism and Zen,* trans. Michael H. Kohn (Boston: Shambhala, 1991): 222–3.

453. In moxabustion, the acupuncturist burns a small amount of herb, usually mugwort, over a particular acupuncture treatment point on the skin for the purpose of transmitting heated aromatics through the meridian network to benefit the organ system and meridian (or energy channel) associated with that point.

454. Elizabeth Hickey, *The Legend of Tara* (Dundalk, Ireland: Dundalgan Press, 1982): 36.

455. Sean P. O'Riordain, *Tara: The Monuments on the Hill* (Dundalk, Ireland: Dundalgan Press, 1982): 6.

456. The Discovery Programme, directed by Conor Newman, summary published at: www.discovery.programme.ie. The Discovery Programme, a research and archeological initiative, was founded in 1991 and is based in Dublin, Ireland.

457. Miranda J. Green, *Dictionary of Celtic Myth and Legend* (New York,: Thames and Hudson, 1992): 148.

458. In Ireland's original geocosmography, Tara is situated in County Meath; to the north is Ulster; in the east, Leinster; in the south, Munster; and to the west, Connacht. I say "geocosmography" because in Irish lore, each direction and county have a spiritual and political function in the total scheme of Irish identity and destiny.

459. Bob Trubshaw, "The Fifth Direction, Sacred Centres in Ireland." *At the Edge,* no. 2, 1996; republished at: www.indigogroup.co.uk/edge

460. Joseph Jacobs, *Celtic Fairy Tales,* (Belinus Press [1892] 2000) at: www.belinus.co.uk

461. Lady Gregory, *Gods and Fighting Men,* (Belinus Press [1892] 2000) at: www.belinus.co.uk

462. *The Tain,* trans. Thomas Kinsella (London: Oxford University Press and Dublin, Ireland: Dolmen Press, 1970): 150, 153, 156.

463. The terms goblin and gnome of course are not native to Irish speech or description. A more likely term is the English *cluricaune,* from the Irish *cluracan,* which refers to a household or dwarfish sprite or solitary fairy. The cluricaune is usually depicted as a withered little man, like a leprechaun, dressed in red; he is disinclined to work, knows the whereabouts of gold, and may carry a purse of shillings, flowing with silver. Despite the differing terminologies and characterizations, it is likely the cluricaune is a gnome, which is a group of Nature spirits central to human work with the Earth's energy body.

464. Alwyn Rees and Brinley Rees, *Celtic Heritage: Ancient Tradition in Ireland and Wales* (New York: Thames and Hudson, 1961): 163.

465. Tibetan Buddhist legend says that the *cintamani* stone, whose inner radiation is mightier than radium, was brought to Earth on the back of a *Lung-ta,* or winged horse; a Lung-ta was said to be able to travel anywhere in the universe as a messenger of the gods. See Victoria LePage, *Shambhala: The Fascinating Truth Behind the Myth of Shangri-La* (Wheaton, Ill.: Quest Books, 1996): 228.

466. Arthur Avalon, *The Serpent Power* (New York: Dover, 1974): 454.

467. Traditionally the tutelary goddess for Ireland is named Eriu, spelled as Eire in modern Irish and anglicized as Erin. Sometimes she is presented as one of three sister goddesses, and sometimes as a sole personification of the island of Ireland. When the Milesians arrived on the shores, she petitioned them to name the island after her. She is not otherwise particularly distinguished in terms of her qualities as a mythic figure; it is probable that Medb is a later differentiation of the same landscape goddess, or egregor.

468. Patricia Lee Lewis, "Land of Mystical Faith," *Los Angeles Times* (August 8, 1999), published at: www.latimes.com/travel/destinations/19990808/t000070417.html

469. Norman Shanks, *Iona—God's Energy* (London: Hodder & Stoughton, 1999).

470. Anthony Bradshaw, "An Iona Experience," *The Australian Celtic Journal,* Vol. 4, 1993, reprinted 1998 at: www.ogdoad.force9.co.uk/iona.htm

471. Eleanor C. Merry, *The Flaming Door: The Mission of the Celtic Folk-Soul* (Edinburgh, UK: Floris Books, 1983): 221.

472. Fiona Macleod, *Iona* (Edinburgh, UK: Floris Classics/Floris Books, 1982): 41.

473. Eleanor C. Merry, *The Flaming Door: The Mission of the Celtic Folk-Soul* (Edinburgh, UK: Floris Books, 1983): 221.

474. Peter Dawkins, "The Great Vision," *Francis Bacon Research Trust Journal* (Stratford-upon-Avon, UK), series I, vol. 4 (1985): 32–5.

475. Adamnan, *Life of Saint Columba, Founder of Hy,* ed. William Reeves (Lampeter, Wales, UK: Llanerch Enterprises, 1988): 34, 37, 113, 119, 122, 123, 132.

476. Fiona Macleod, *Iona* (Edinburgh, UK: Floris Classics/Floris Books, 1982): 13, 14, 15, 20, 21, 31, 36, 37, 92.

477. *The Awakening Letters,* ed. Cynthia Sandys and Rosamond Lehmann (Jersey, Channel Islands, UK: Neville Spearman, 1978): 90, 91, 94.

478. Ibid., 111.

479. Cynthia Sandys, *The Awakening Letters, Volume Two,* ed. Rosamond Lehmann (Saffron Walden, UK: C. W. Daniel, 1986): 76.

480. Ean Begg, *The Cult of the Black Virgin* (New York: Arkana/Penguin Books, 1996): 131, 133, 134, 144.

481. China Galland, *Longing for Darkness: Tara and the Black Madonna, A Ten-Year Journey* (New York: Penguin Books, 1990): 193, 199, 225, 335.

482. Alan Neame, *The Happening at Lourdes: The Sociology of the Grotto* (New York: Simon & Schuster, 1967): 204.

483. Bernadette Soubirous, quoted in Roy Abraham Varghese, *God-Sent: A History of the Accredited Apparitions of Mary* (New York: Crossroad Publishing, 2000): 101, 102, 104.

484. Ruth Harris, *Lourdes: Body and Spirit in the Secular Age* (New York: Viking/Penguin Putnam, 1999): 53–4.

485. Franz Werfel, *The Song of Bernadette,* trans. Ludwig Lewisohn (New York: The Viking Press, 1942): 24–5.

486. Alan Neame, *The Happening at Lourdes: The Sociology of the Grotto* (New York: Simon & Schuster, 1967): 25.

487. "In the News–February 1999—Paranormal Phenomena/The Unexplained," originally published in *The Mirror,* London, reprinted at: http://french-culture.about.com

488. Ruth Harris, *Lourdes: Body and Spirit in the Secular Age* (New York: Viking/Penguin Putnam, 1999): xiii, xv.

489. Edmond and Jules de Goncourt, *Memoires de la Vie Litteraire,* 1891-1892, Paris, 1956-9, vol. 18 (26 Juillet 1892): 220, quoted in Ruth Harris,

Lourdes: Body and Spirit in the Secular Age (New York: Viking/Penguin Putnam, 1999): 333.

490. Rev. Msgr. Kevin Wallin, "A Visit to Lourdes," published at www.spirituality.org/issue10/10page04.html

491. Jennifer Lash, *On Pilgrimage: A Time to Seek* (New York: Bloomsbury, 1991): 199, 200, 201.

492. James Harpur, *The Marshall Travel Atlas of Sacred Places: A Guide to the World's Spiritual Oases* (London: Marshall Publishing, 1998): 219.

493. Martin Gray, "The Basilica of Lourdes, France," January 2000, published at www.sacredsites.com

494. Claude Viviers, quoted in Alan Neame, *The Happening at Lourdes: The Sociology of the Grotto* (New York: Simon & Schuster, 1967): 176.

495. Martin Scott, The Savvy Traveler, published at: www.savvytraveler.com/show/Features/1999/04.03/lourdes.html

496. For more concepts and information along this line of thinking, see my book *The Imagination of Pentecost: Rudolf Steiner and Contemporary Spirituality* (Hudson, N.Y.: Anthroposophic Press, 1994.

497. The global and geomantic significance and strategy of the Marian sites is discussed in my forthcoming book *Signs on the Earth*, which also discusses UFO sightings and crop circles in the same context.

498. The image here is similar to the Madonna and golden child geomantic structure associated with a hatched Golden Egg. See the discussion in Tetford, England.

499. Peter Frost, *Exploring Cusco*, 5th ed. (Lima, Peru: Nuevas Imagenes S.A., 1999): 209.

500. Carol Cumes and Romulo Lizarraga Valencia, *Journey to Machu Picchu: Spiritual Wisdom from the Andes*, 2d ed. (Saint Paul: Llewellyn Publications, 1999): 183.

501. Peter Frost, *Exploring Cusco*, 5th ed. (Lima, Peru: Nuevas Imagenes S.A., 1999): 156-7.

502. "Historic Sanctuary of Machu Picchu," UNESCO Brief Description, April 2001, published at: www.unesco.org/whc/sites/274.htm

503. Peter Greste, "Peru 'Ignoring Threat' to Inca Site," *BBC News* (June 23, 2001), published at: http://news.bbc.co.uk

504. Jeff. L. Brown, "Rediscovering The Lost City," *Civil Engineering Magazine* (January 2001), American Society of Civil Engineers, published at: www.pubs.asce.org. See also: Kenneth R. Wright and Alfredo Valencia Zegarra, *Machu Picchu: A Civil Engineering Marvel* (Reston, Va.: American Society of Civil Engineers, 2000).

505. David Hatcher Childress, *Lost Cities & Ancient Mysteries of South America* (Stelle, Ill.: Adventures Unlimited Press, 1986): 103.

506. Martin Gray, "Machu Picchu, Peru," July 2000, published at: www.sacredsites.com

507. Vicente Goyzueta, *Qosqo—Inka's Sacred Capital,* information published at: www.bestweb.net/~goyzueta/qosqo/mapi.htm

508. Robert Schneer, "Machu Picchu," Cedar Cottage Media, 1999, published at: www.newagetravel.com/info/machu.htm

509. Gary Urton, *The Legendary Past: Inca Myths* (London: British Museum Press, 1999): 46.

510. Textual evidence suggests that Viracocha and the Sun were the same being for the Inca. The myths say that in the original darkness, the Sun rose out of Lake Titicaca, or Viracocha rose, or Viracocha caused an anthropomorphic Sun to rise. "Thus from the very beginning of the myth, the creator is inseparable from the sun." See Arthur A. Demarest, *Viracocha: The Nature and Antiquity of the Andean High God*, Peabody Museum Monographs, no. 6 (Cambridge: Harvard University, 1981): 31.

511. Carol Cumes, "Machu Picchu: Consecration or Desecration," April 1999, published at: www.planeta.com

512. Faure Duenas Pena, quoted in Carol Cumes and Romulo Lizarraga Valencia, *Journey to Machu Picchu: Spiritual Wisdom from the Andes*, 2d ed. (Saint Paul: Llewellyn Publications, 1999): 150.

513. Peter Frost, *Exploring Cusco*, 5th ed. (Lima, Peru: Nuevas Imagenes S.A., 1999): 114.

514. Grace Cooke, *Sun-Men of the Americas* (Liss, England: White Eagle Publishing Trust, 1975): 22-5

515. A torus is a mathematically defined shape and function, but in simple terms it looks like a ribbed doughnut or the candy called Lifesavers, with the ribs constantly cycling from the inside to the outside to the underside and up through the middle to the outside again. The figure is perpetually turning itself inside out. It is like a white hole and a black hole, as described in astrophysics, merged into one figure and constantly turning itself inside out, cycling between universes, and opening a doorway from one place to another.

516. Thomas Jefferson (1743-1826) was born in Shadwell, Virginia, and was the third president of the U.S., serving from 1801 to 1809. He was also the founder of the University of Virginia.

517. Jack McLaughlin, *Jefferson and Monticello: The Biography of a Builder* (New York: Henry Holt, 1990): 7.

518. Willard Sterne Randall, *Thomas Jefferson: A Life* (New York: A John Macrae Book/Henry Holt, 1993): 346.

519. Anna Maria Thornton, in Jack McLaughlin, *Jefferson and Monticello: The Biography of a Builder* (New York: Henry Holt, 1990): 32.

520. Jack McLaughlin, *Jefferson and Monticello: The Biography of a Builder* (New York: Henry Holt, 1990): 51.

521. *The Garden and Farm Books of Thomas Jefferson,* ed. Robert C. Baron (Golden, Colo.: Fulcrum, 1987): 190–1.

522. Jefferson picked out the parcel of land now called Ashlawn, near Monticello, for his friend James Monroe (1758–1831), fifth U.S. president (1817–1825).

523. Thomas Jefferson, Letter to George Gilmer, August 12, 1787, quoted at www.monticello.org. Edited by Kristen K. Onuf, Monticello Research Department, 1993.

524. Jean Poirier, "Island of Montreal," *Canoma* 5:2 (1979): 6–8.

525. Leo Sultzman, "Iroquois History," [no date], published at: www.tolatsga.org

526. Francois de Belleforest, *Cosmographie Universelle de tout le Monde,* 1575, quoted in "Island of Montreal," Geographical Names, Natural Resources Canada, 1996, published at: http://geonames.nrcan.gc.ca/english/schoolnet/montreal.html

527. Brother Andre Marie, M.I.C.M., "Blessed Brother Andre of Saint Joseph," *From the Housetops* 34, [no date], reprinted at: www.josephsaint.freeserve.co.uk/BrAndre.htm

528. "Why an Oratory?" published at: www.saint-joseph.org

529. Ian Phillips, "Tourists and Development Threaten Mont-Saint-Michel," Associated Press, 1999, published at: www.usatoday.com/life/travel/leisure/1999/t0602ap3.htm

530. Kevin J. Wright, *Catholic Shrines of Western Europe: A Pilgrim's Travel Guide* (Liguori, Mo.: Liguori, 1997): 60–1.

531. The stories of this giant are recorded in the French comic saga by Francois Rabelais (1483–1553), called *Gargantua and Pantagruel,* published in parts between 1532 and 1567. Gargantua is the father of Pantagruel in Rabelais' version.

532. Paul Broadhurst and Hamish Miller, with Vivienne Shanley and Ba Russell, *The Dance of the Dragon: An Odyssey into Earth Energies and Ancient Religion* (Launceston, England: Pendragon Press, 2000): 127.

533. Roger Vercel, *Tides of Mont-St.-Michel,* trans. Warre Bradley Wells (New York: Random House, 1938): 86, 98, 101,103, 198, 225, 277, 278.

534. William Maxwell, "The Gardens of Mont-Saint-Michel," in David R. Godine, *Over by the River, and Other Stories* (Boston: Nonpareil Books, 1984): 177–8.

535. Henry Adams, *Mont-Saint-Michel and Chartres* (Garden City, N.Y.: Doubleday Anchor Books, [1913] 1959): 2, 8, 46.

536. It may seem picayune to point out, but this archangel's name has three syllables, and can be pronounced *My-KAY-el* so as to distinguish it from the common male's name of two syllables.

537. Emmanuel Le Roy Ladurie, *Montaillou: The Promised Land of Error,* trans. Barbara Bray (New York: George Braziller, 1978): viii.

538. Jack Markwardt, "Was the Shroud in Languedoc During the Missing Years?" Published May 1997 at: www.shroud.com/markeward.htm

539. Walter Birks and R. A. Gilbert, *The Treasure of Montsegur: The Secret of the Cathars* (Wellingborough, England: The Aquarian Press/Thorsons, 1990): 150.

540. Wolfram von Eschenbach, *Parzival,* trans. A. T. Hatto (Baltimore: Penguin Books, 1980): 121.

541. Arthur Guirdham, *The Cathars and Reincarnation* (Wheaton, Ill.: Quest Books/Theosophical Publishing House, 1970): 13, 14, 31, 35, 122.

542. Arthur Guirdham, *We Are One Another: A Record of Group Reincarnation* (Wellingborough, England: Turnstone Press, 1974): 89.

543. Deike and Ean Begg, *In Search of the Holy Grail and the Precious Blood: A Travellers' Guide* (San Francisco: Thorsons/HarperCollins, 1995): 53, 55.

544. Kevin J. Wright, *Catholic Shrines of Western Europe: A Pilgrim's Travel Guide* (Liguori, Mo.: Liguori, 1997): 203.

545. Ibid., 204.

546. Stephen Benko, *The Virgin Goddess: Studies in the Pagan and Christian Roots of Mariology* (Boston: Brill Academic Publishers, 1993).

547. Ean Begg, *The Cult of the Black Virgin* (New York: Arkana/Penguin Books, 1996): 257.

548. Deike and Ean Begg, *In Search of the Holy Grail and the Precious Blood* (San Francisco: Thorsons/HarperCollins, 1995): 102.

549. Ibid., 102–3.

550. Rt. Rev. John K. Cartwright, *The Catholic Shrines of Europe* (New York: McGraw-Hill, 1955): 141.

551. Robert Burnham Jr., *Burnham's Celestial Handbook: An Observer's Guide to the Universe Beyond the Solar System*, Vol. 2 (New York: Dover Publications, 1978): 757.

552. Mircea Eliade, *Images and Symbols: Studies in Religious Symbolism* (Princeton: Princeton University Press, 1991): 42, 105; and *The Myth of the Eternal Return, or, Cosmos and History* (Princeton, NJ: Princeton University Press, 1971): 12.

553. Henry Corbin, *Spiritual Body and Celestial Earth: From Mazdean Iran to Shi'ite Iran,* trans. Nancy Pearson (Princeton: Princeton University Press, 1977): 25.

554. "The Bundahishn," *Sacred Books of the East,* Vol. 5, trans. E. W. West (Oxford, England: Oxford University Press, 1897): Chaps. 8:1, 12:1, 3, 28.

555. Ferdowsi, *The Epic of Kings,* "Zal," trans. Helen Zimmerman, 2000, published at: http://classics.mit.edu/Ferdowsi/kings.3.zal.html

556. Henry Corbin, *The Man of Light in Iranian Sufism,* trans. Nancy Pearson (Boulder: Shambhala, 1978): 55–6.

557. Jan Knappert, *The Encyclopaedia of Middle Eastern Mythology and Religion* (Shaftesbury, UK: Element, 1993): 266.

558. Arthur Cotterell, *A Dictionary of World Mythology* (New York: Oxford University Press, 1986): 50.

559. Ferdowsi, *The Epic of Kings,* "The Shahs of Old," trans. Helen Zimmerman, 2000, published at: http://classics.mit.edu/Ferdowsi/kings.html

560. G. A. Gaskell, *Dictionary of All Scriptures and Myths* (New York: Julian Press, 1960): 674.

561. Jaan Puhvel, *Comparative Mythology* (Baltimore: Johns Hopkins University Press, 1987): 31, 120.

562. Dorothy B. Vitaliano, *Legends of the Earth: Their Geologic Origins* (Bloomington: Indiana University Press, 1973): 138.

563. Jan Knappert, *The Encyclopaedia of Middle Eastern Mythology and Religion* (Shaftesbury, UK: Element, 1993): 98, 137, 300.

564. Giorgio de Santillana and Hertha von Dechend, *Hamlet's Mill: An Essay Investigating the Origins of Human Knowledge and Its Transmission through Myth* (Boston: David R. Godine, 1977): 370.

565. Xvarnah is a Persian term to denote the Light of Glory or celestial aura, the paradisiacal, pure light that formed the world, the all-luminous substance with which all beings were constituted at the beginning of Creation. The Xvarnah is the luminous halo that encircles god-kings and high priests; it is also the archetypal image of the soul and its light. The Xvarnah is something "which, having arisen from astral incandescence, remains as a dominating force in the human world; he who is invested with it becomes a hero, a conqueror, a victor." See Henry Corbin, *Spiritual Body and Celestial Earth: From Mazdean Iran to Shi'ite Iran,* trans. Nancy Pearson (Princeton: Princeton University Press, 1977): 125.

566. In the Zoroastrian religious system, Ahura-Mazda is the chief benign divinity, a solar, Christ-like deity who opposes Ahriman (Angra Mainyu), the Evil One and chief of the powers of evil. They are both said to be the progeny of Zervan Akarana, "Endless, Eternal Time."

567. Egerton Sykes, *Everyman's Dictionary of Non-Classical Mythology* (London: J. M. Dent & Sons, 1953): 240.

568. A *manvantara* is 306,720,000 years and consists of four Ages, each of which is diminished in spiritual glory and consciousness; the golden age is called Krtayuga, and lasts 1,728,000 years. As each *manvantara* is presided over by a Manu, an exalted deity, Yima was the Manu for a 306-million-year *manvantara;* his capture by the demon Dahak would refer to the many years that followed the Krtayuga of his reign. See W. Norman Brown, *Man in the Universe: Some Cultural Continuities in India* (Berkeley: University of California Press, 1970): 79–80.

569. This gets into complicated theological territory. But the idea in brief is that too much Light in an insufficiently prepared or matured psychic container can lead to an abuse of that Light (which is also power). This abuse is predicated on the activation of human free will to take actions either "good" or "bad." In one respect, the Fisher King's wound resulted from a "bad" application of magical knowledge (too much Light). His psychic container could not handle the Light in its fullness, and elements in his shadow (the demons underneath Mount Damavand) came to the forefront and became active in the world through his actions.

570. "Mount Etna," [no author cited] at: http://moondancers10.homepage.com/mount_etna.htm

571. The term Gaia (from Ge) in Greek mythology stands for the Earth, but the Earth referred to is not our planet of the same name, but everything in

the realm of matter, from subtle to gross, that lies outside the highest point in Heaven or the celestial world, known to the Gnostics, for example, as the Pleroma. It is more helpful to think of Earth in this context as meaning the primal cosmos and not our planet.

572. Apollodorus, *The Library,* Vol. 1, trans. Sir James George Frazer (Cambridge: Harvard University Press, 1921): 49.

573. Carl Kerenyi, *The Gods of the Greeks* (New York: Thames & Hudson, 1951): 26–8.

574. H. A. Guerber, *The Myths of Greece & Rome* (New York: Dover Publications, 1907, 1993): 12–3.

575. Michael Grant and John Hazel, *Who's Who in Classical Mythology* (New York: Oxford University Press, 1973): 143–4, 244–5.

576. Virgil, *Aeneid,* trans. Robert Fitzgerald (New York: Random House, 1981): 88–9.

577. Homer, *Odyssey,* trans. Robert Fagles (New York: Viking/Penguin, 1996): 275, 281.

578. On account of its triangular shape, Sicily was once known as Thrinacia or Trinacria, meaning "Three Capes," which were Peloro, Passero, and Lilibeo; the capes formed the island's three corners.

579. Ernle Bradford, *Ulysses Found* (New York: Harcourt, Brace & World, 1963): 170–1.

580. H. A. Guerber, *The Myths of Greece & Rome* (New York: Dover Publications, 1907, 1993): 158–61.

581. "Mount Etna," [no author cited] at: http://moondancers10.homepage.com/mount_etna.htm

582. Ernle Bradford, *Ulysses Found* (New York: Harcourt, Brace & World, 1963): 166–7.

583. "Taormina," at: http://www.unime.it/istituti/dmedicin/taormina.htm

584. "Caravella Italia—Ancient Sicily Tour," at: http://www.seeitaly.com/preplan/sicily.html

585. "Introduction," at: http://www.taormina.it.intro.htm

586. "Mount Etna," at: http://moondancers10.homepage.com/mount_etna.htm

587. Lawrence Durrell, *Sicilian Carousel* (New York: Marlowe & Company, 1976): 26–7.

588. Matthew Chance, "Mount Etna Provides 'Awesome, Dramatic Display,'" Cnn.com/World. On the Scene, July 27, 2001, at: www.cnn.com/2001/W...e/07/26/chance.debrief.otsc/index.html. The irony of Chance's conventionally valid observations is that geomantically volcanoes are toxic emission points for the planet, places where the physical Earth can blow off the physical result of astral toxins, mostly from humans and mostly to do with unprocessed, cumulative emotional negativity. In an energy sense, volcanic eruptions are often human produced. The real terror of Nature on display at Etna and other active volcanoes is the power of unprocessed human negativity.

589. Ariadne is famous for having helped Theseus find his way through the Cretan Labyrinth to slay the Minotaur, the bull-headed "monster" of Crete. Some versions say she gave Theseus a thread, but others say it was her golden, bejeweled wreath or crown given to her by Dionysus that Theseus used to light his way through the Labyrinth. Dionysus in turn had received the wreath from Aphrodite, the Greek goddess of love. This is the mythic basis for the constellation Corona Borealis.

590. Robert Burnham Jr., *Burnham's Celestial Handbook: An Observer's Guide to the Universe Beyond the Solar System,* Vol. 2 (New York: Dover Publications, 1966): 699.

591. This identification of course is massively counterintuitive in terms of cultural assumptions. As a Ray Master, however, Jesus had other assignments prior to the Christ incarnation and his assignation with—might we say appropriation by—the Catholic Church. His mastery of the Sun god, its liquid gold energy, and its Time matrix aspect was a requisite for building the Temple—in effect, the Holy of Holies—around the planet in advance of the Christ incarnation, which he would facilitate. The complexities of this identification and further details of his incarnational resume are discussed in my book *The Emerald Modem.*

592. Again, it's too complex to explain in full here, but Rudolf Steiner describes how six Elohim—mythically, the Cyclopes—worked with Jesus—Hephaistos—in the sphere of the Sun preparing the Sun's energy for the Earth, as advance preparation for the incarnation of the Christ. Steiner wrote: The historical appearance of Christ Jesus means that the "forces of the six Elohim, or of the Logos, were incarnated in Jesus of Nazareth . . . [as] the inner force of the sun, the force of the Logos-Love, assumed a physical human form. . . . He Who was there in the visible world is an actual incarnation of the six sun Elohim, of the Logos!" So through the visionary geographic tableau of Hephaistos and his Cyclopes you can perceive the more exalted Mystery of Jesus and the Elohim in the Sun sphere. Rudolf Steiner, *The Gospel of Saint John* (Hudson, N.Y.: Anthroposophic Press, 1962): 54–5. See also Richard Leviton, *The*

Imagination of Pentecost: Rudolf Steiner and Contemporary Spirituality (Hudson, N.Y.: Anthroposophic Press, 1994): 392.

593. "The Pleiades (Alcyone, especially) are thus considered, even in astronomy, as the central point around which our Universe of fixed stars revolves, the focus from which, and into which the divine breathe, Motion, works incessantly during the Manvantara." It is also interesting to note that in Hebrew, *Aleph,* the first letter of the alphabet, means bull or ox. See H. P. Blavatsky, *The Secret Doctrine,* Vol. 2 (Pasadena: Theosophical University Press, [1888] 1977): 551. Blavatsky further notes: "And 'the sun having Alcyone in the Pleiades for the centre of its orbit, consumes 180,000,000 of years completing its revolution' (Maedler)." H. P. Blavatsky, *The Secret Doctrine,* Vol. 1 (Pasadena: Theosophical University Press, [1888] 1977): 501.

Further support of this unusual contention comes from the Mayan tradition, which said that our Sun is part of the orbital system of the Pleiades. In the Mayan *Tzek'er* model of astronomy, our Sun and the stars of the Pleiades are together part of a larger rotational orbit within the galaxy. See Hunbatz Men, "Reconsecrating the Earth," in *Profiles in Wisdom: Native Elders Speak About the Earth,* ed. Steven McFadden (Santa Fe: Bear & Company, 1991).

594. Edwin Bernbaum, *Sacred Mountains of the World* (Berkeley, CA: University of California Press, 1997): 61.

595. W. Y. Evans-Wentz, *Cuchama and Sacred Mountains* (Athens: Swallow Press/Ohio University Press, 1981): 47–9.

596. Dorothy B. Vitaliano, *Legends of the Earth: Their Geologic Origin* (Bloomington: Indiana University Press, 1973): 131–2.

597. F. Hadland Davis, *Myths and Legends of Japan* (New York: Dover Publications, [1913] 1992): 139.

598. *The Awakening Letters,* ed. Cynthia Sandys and Rosamond Lehmann (Jersey, Channel Islands, UK: Neville Spearman, 1978): 161, 165, 166.

599. An Astronomical Unit, or AU, is a convenient term of measurement for objects in our solar system so that 63,240 AU = one light year, or the distance light will travel in one year. At only 1,800 AU apart, the two main stars in M27 are comparatively very close.

600. Robert Burnham Jr., *Burnham's Celestial Handbook: An Observer's Guide to the Universe Beyond the Solar System,* Vol. 3 (New York: Dover Publications, 1978): 2121.

601. Lloyd Motz and Carol Nathanson, *The Constellations* (New York: Doubleday, 1988): 276.

602. To the Greeks, nymphs (from the word *nymphe,* which means "young woman, bride") were considered female spirits of divine or semi-divine origin, usually daughters of Zeus, King of Olympus. They were immortal and resided as nature-goddesses in streams, woods, hills, mountains, lakes, the sea, and other natural phenomena. They correspond to what Japanese Shintoism calls *kami,* the spirits within all natural phenomena. Nymphs were portrayed as beautiful young women of an amorous disposition, likely to accompany the gods but sometimes to sport with humans.

603. W. D. Westervelt, *Legends of Ma-Ui—A Demigod of Polynesia and of His Mother, Hina. The Hawaiian Gazette,* Honolulu, HI (1910): 40–55.

604. Steven Goldsberry, *Maui the Demigod: An Epic Novel of Mythical Hawai'i* (Honolulu: University of Hawaii Press,1984): 270–274. Also W. D. Westervelt, *Myths and Legends of Hawaii* (Honolulu: Mutual Publishing, 1987): 9–13.

605. W. D. Westervelt, *Hawaiian Legends of Volcanoes* (Rutland, Vt.: Charles E. Tuttle, 1963): 13.

606. Martha Beckwith, *Hawaiian Mythology* (Honolulu: University of Hawaii Press, 1970): 167–8.

607. Haumea is a mysterious goddess said to reside originally in the fabled Polynesian paradisiacal land of the gods, called Nu'umealani. She can change form at will, alter her appearance from that of a young woman to a crone using a magical branch called the Makalei.

608. Scott Cunningham, *Hawaiian Religion and Magic* (Saint Paul: Llewellyn Publications, 1994): 42.

609. Tamra Andrews, *Dictionary of Nature Myths: Legends of the Earth, Sea, and Sky* (New York: Oxford University Press, 1998): 148.

610. Mark Twain, *Mark Twain in Hawai'i,* quoted in "Maui Skies—People Come to Haleakala," 2000, at: www.mauiskies.com/people.html

611. Paul Wood, "Dropping Out of Reality into Haleakala Crater," published (2000) at: www.aloha-hawaii.com

612. Linda Alders, "Haleakala: House of the Sun," published (2000) at: http://honolulu.about.com/citiesto

613. Martha Beckwith, *Hawaiian Mythology* (Honolulu: University of Hawaii Press, 1970): 127.

614. H. A. Guerber, *Myths of the Norsemen, From the Eddas and Sagas* (New York: Dover Publications, [1909] 1992): 90.

615. Fred Contrada, "Mount Tom Summit House Spectacle of Valley," *Sunday Republican,* Springfield, Mass. (July 7, 1991).

616. John Riley, "Skinner State Park to Get By with Less Staff," *Daily Hampshire Gazette,* Northampton, Mass. (May 18, 1991).

617. David Graci, *Mt. Holyoke: An Enduring Prospect, History of New England's Most Historic Mountain* (Holyoke, Mass.: Calem Publishing, 1985): vii, viii.

618. Tracy Kidder, *Home Town* (New York: Random House, 1999): 12, 123, 223.

619. At one time, the Pocumtuck Confederacy was a grouping of six different tribes situated between Massachusetts' east coast and the Hudson River near Albany, New York. The Naunawtuks (hence the place name, Mount Nonotuck) occupied both sides of the Connecticut River at Hadley and Northampton. According to research published in 1890, the Pocumtucks were the leading tribe and its "chieftains the acknowledged head of its warlike expeditions." The Pocumtucks were primarily situated on the Deerfield and Connecticut Rivers in Franklin County, Massachusetts. *The Connecticut Valley Indian: An Introduction to Their Archaeology and History,* ed. William R. Young (Springfield, Mass.: Springfield Museum of Science, 1969): 112.

620. The name Pocumtuck comes from *Pocomtakuke,* which means "narrow, swift river" or "clear, open stream." *Nanotuck* means "in the middle of the narrow river," which was the *Quinnitukqut,* or *Quinnecticutt,* now known as Connecticut and meaning "long river."

621. For a descriptive narrative account of this work, see Richard Leviton, "Walking in Albion: Chronicles of Plan-Net Geomancy, Part II: Child of the Maturing Eagle," *The Quest* (Summer 1992).

622. Vincent Scully, *The Earth, The Temple, and The Gods: Greek Sacred Architecture,* rev. ed. (New Haven: Yale University Press, 1962): 15.

623. Hesiod, *Theogony,* trans. Apostolos N. Athanassakis (Baltimore: Johns Hopkins University Press, 1983): Lines 478–480, 483–485, 25.

624. The Titans were conceived as being gigantic celestial beings who ruled the cosmos and Earth in primordial times. They were the offspring of Ouranus (Sky) and Gaia (Earth), and included seven couples, and a few others: Cronos, Rhea, Oceanus, Tethys, Iapetus, Hyperion, Coeus, Crius, Phoebe, Themis, Mnemosyne, Theia, Helios, Prometheus, Epimetheus, and Atlas. They were said to occupy Mount Orthrys in Greece as their stronghold.

625. Pausanias, *Guide to Greece,* Vol. 2, *Southern Greece,* trans. Peter Levi (Baltimore: Penguin Books, 1979): 215.

626. Apollonius of Rhodes, *The Voyage of Argo: The Argonautica,* trans. E. V. Rieu (Baltimore: Penguin Books, 1959): 191.

627. This bull, say the myths, was later subdued by Heracles as one of his Labors; he brought it back to Greece, specifically to Eurystheus of Mycenae, who had commissioned the Twelve Labors; the Cretan bull was later freed by Hera, Zeus' wife, then still later killed on the Plain of Marathon by Theseus (see Acropolis, Athens, Greece).

628. Ovid, *Metamorphoses,* trans. A. D. Melville (New York: Oxford University Press, 1986): 175–6.

629. Apollodorus, *The Library,* Vol. 1, trans. Sir James George Frazer (Cambridge: Harvard University Press, 1921): 305, 307.

630. Homer, *Odyssey,* trans. Robert Fagles (New York: Viking Penguin, 1996): book 19: 201–4, 396.

631. Plato, "Laws" in *The Collected Dialogues of Plato,* ed. Edith Hamilton and Huntington Cairns, Bollingen Series LXXI (New York: Pantheon Books/Random House, 1961): 624a–b, 625a–b, 1226.

632. Lloyd Motz and Carol Nathanson, *The Constellations* (New York: Doubleday, 1988): 294.

633. Richard Hinckley Allen, *Star Names: Their Lore and Meaning* (New York: Dover Publications, 1963): 137.

634. Alice A. Bailey, *Esoteric Astrology,* Vol. 3, *A Treatise on the Seven Rays* (New York: Lucis Publishing, 1951): 165, 168, 265–6.

635. For ease of visual understanding, visualize the Earth's surface divided into twelve equal geometric faces called dodecahedrons, meaning twelve faces. A dodecahedron is a pentagon, a polyhedron with five sides; each of these pentagons occupies one-twelfth of the Earth's surface and is the host for a geomythic figure on the order of (but not identical to) the Bull of Europe. This subject is explained in detail in *The Emerald Modem.*

636. Jean Chevalier and Alain Gheerbrant, *A Dictionary of Symbols,* trans. John Buchanan-Brown (New York: Penguin Books, 1994): 131, 133.

637. J. C. Cooper, *An Illustrated Encyclopaedia of Traditional Symbols* (New York: Thames and Hudson, 1978): 26–7.

638. This insight comes from the psychic observations of Mike Booth, a British colleague of mine in this work since 1984. On a recent visit to Crete, Booth became aware of this pattern around Mount Ida.

639. Of Capricorn's twenty-four described stars, twelve are concerned with Zeus/Cretan labyrinths. In other words, each of the other eleven domes around the Earth that perform the same function as Mount Ida for a Cretan labyrinth is associated with individual stars from Capricorn. Each, like Mount Ida, is a gate of initiation.

640. The perception of Talos as an actual geomantically commissioned celestial being several miles tall was reported to me by Mike Booth, cited above, during a recent trip he made to Crete.

641. John Snelling, *The Sacred Mountain: Travellers and Pilgrims at Mount Kailas in Western Tibet, and the Great Universal Symbol of the Sacred Mountain* (London: East West Publications, 1983): 173, 174.

642. Russell Johnson and Kerry Moran, *The Sacred Mountain of Tibet: On Pilgrimage to Kailas* (Rochester, Vt.: Park Street Press, 1989): 41.

643. Lama Anagarika Govinda, *The Way of the White Clouds: A Buddhist Pilgrim in Tibet* (Berkeley: Shambhala, 1966): 209.

The swastika reference is based on an actual swastika shape on Kailash's southern flank. It looks at first like a huge cross, dividing the mountain into four sections; closer up, you can see the typical hooks or arms of the swastika. Long before the German Nazis adulterated the swastika by reversing it, the glyph was regarded as a profound symbol of occult truths.

644. Lama Anagarika Govinda, *The Way of the White Clouds: A Buddhist Pilgrim in Tibet* (Berkeley: Shambhala, 1966): 201.

645. The five Dhyani Buddhas are five transcendent Buddhas who represent the different aspects of enlightenment. They are five for the purposes of illustration, but Buddhists understand them to be ultimately one Buddha.

646. Robert Thurman and Tad Wise, *Circling the Sacred Mountain: A Spiritual Adventure through the Himalayas* (New York: Bantam Books, 1999): 273.

647. Meru is actually 100,000 yojanas tall, as 16,000 yojanas of it are in the Earth. A *yojana* is eight miles; thus Meru stands 800,000 miles high, or at 84,000 yojanas, at 672,000 miles.

648. *Ramayana*, retold by Krishna Dharma (Badger, Calif.: Torchlight Publishing, 2000): 5, 368.

649. Heinrich Zimmer, *Philosophies of India*, Bollingen Series XXVI, ed. Joseph Campbell (Princeton: Princeton University Press, 1969): 182.

650. John Snelling, *The Sacred Mountain: Travellers and Pilgrims at Mount Kailas in Western Tibet, and the Great Universal Symbol of the Sacred Mountain* (London: East West Publications, 1983): 19.

651. *The Treasury of Good Sayings: A Tibetan History of Bon*, London Oriental Series, Vol. 26, trans. and ed. Samten G. Karmay (New York,: Oxford University Press, 1972): xix, xxviii, xxx, 15.

652. Lama Anagarika Govinda, *The Way of the White Clouds: A Buddhist Pilgrim in Tibet* (Berkeley: Shambhala, 1966): 207, 208.

653. Robert Thurman and Tad Wise, *Circling the Sacred Mountain: A Spiritual Adventure through the Himalayas* (New York: Bantam Books, 1999): 3, 4, 5, 11, 125, 126.

654. Joan Halifax, *The Fruitful Darkness: Reconnecting with the Body of the Earth* (San Francisco: Harper San Francisco, 1993): 70, 73.

655. Stella Kramrisch, *The Presence of Shiva* (Princeton: Princeton University Press, 1981): 43, 44, 45, 48, 50.

656. *The Treasury of Good Sayings: A Tibetan History of Bon*, London Oriental Series, Vol. 26, trans. and ed. Samten G. Karmay (New York,: Oxford University Press, 1972): 5,6.

657. A Chinese text from the ninth century A.D., "The Report Concerning the Cave Heavens and Lands of Happiness in Famous Mountains," lists ten "cave heavens" and thirty-six "small cave heavens" accessed in the mountains of China. Humans who ventured through the passageway to these cave heavens would find when they returned to the human world that centuries had elapsed, seemingly in the space of minutes. The Hindu tradition refers to a place called Bilasvarga, a subterranean heaven similar to the cave heavens. There is no sense of time there, no Sun or Moon, and the scenery is gorgeous, captivating, and seductive. Richard L. Thompson. *Mysteries of the Sacred Universe: The Cosmology of the Bhagavata Purana* (Alachua, Fl.: Govardhan Hill Publishing, 2000): 295–6.

658. Ni Hua-Ching, *The Taoist Inner View of the Universe and the Immortal Realm* (Malibu: Shrine of the Eternal Breath of Tao, 1979): 46, 47, 64.

659. The name Society Islands comes from Captain James Cook, the British explorer who named them this in 1769; in 1767, another English explorer, Samuel Wallis, had claimed them for England. But in 1768, Louis Antoine de Bougainville, asserted France's right to the island chains. They became a French protectorate in 1843, a colony in 1880, and an overseas French territory in 1946. Topographically,

the Society Islands comprise fourteen islands, the Windward Islands and Leeward Islands, or about 650 square miles in all in a 450-mile chain. Only eight of the many islands are inhabited, and nearly all are mountainous. Raiatea is one of the Leeward Islands; the island called Tahiti is part of the Windward Group. The Leewards and Windwards are part of French Polynesia, which comprises 130 islands and whose capital is Papeete in Tahiti.

660. A *marae* is a public square in front of the temple or a chief's demesne; it is typically enclosed by stone or coral rock, and has a shrine for a deity within. Traditionally, Polynesian kings were crowned within the marae. "Thus *marae* came to mean the center of royal power, the most sacred meeting place of the nation." See Jan Knappert, *Pacific Mythology: An Encyclopedia of Myth and Legend* (London: Aquarian/Thorsons, 1992): 182.

661. Robert F. Kay, *Hidden Tahiti* (Berkeley: Ulysses Press, 1997): 268–73.

662. Alexander Russell, *Aristocrats of the South Seas* (London: Robert Hale, 1961): 65.

663. Heather Halstead, "A Trip to Taputapuatea, F.P.," June 1998, published by Reach the World, at: www.reachtheworld.org

664. *The Kumulipo: A Hawaiian Creation Chant*, trans. and ed. Martha Warren Beckwith (Honolulu: University of Hawaii Press, 1951): 161.

665. Initially it may sound confusing, but the island cluster of Hawaii as we know it today was named in honor of the Polynesian Hawaiki, or, according to myth, Raiatea.

666. Johannes C. Andersen, *Myths and Legends of the Polynesians* (New York: Dover Publications, [1928] 1995): 321, 357.

667. Martha Beckwith, *Hawaiian Mythology* (Honolulu: University of Hawaii Press, 1970): 76.

668. Ibid., 307, 468.

669. Donald A. Mackenzie, *South Seas: Myths and Legends* (London: Senate/Random House UK, [1930] 1996): 287.

670. *The Kumulipo: A Hawaiian Creation Chant*, trans. and ed. Martha Warren Beckwith (Honolulu: University of Hawaii Press, 1951): 169,170.

671. Tane was the Polynesian god of light, god of the forest, and lord of the fairies. He was the son of Rangi (heaven, sky) and Papa-Tu-a-Nuku, the mother of all the gods. Tane is probably the Polynesian equivalent to the Greek Zeus, who was the son of Cronos and Rhea.

672. Oro's brothers, Oro-Tetefa and Uru-Tetefa, descend from Heaven to Earth to found this human religious order of celibate warriors drawn from the *ariki* class of Polynesians. Red feathers were traditionally offered to Oro and his mortal wife; these red feathers, called *uru-maru-no-te-Areoi*, became one of the emblems of the Arioi Society.

673. Alice A. Bailey, *Esoteric Astrology*, Vol. 3, *A Treatise on the Seven Rays* (New York: Lucis Publishing Company, 1951): 312.

674. Vedic astrology described twenty-seven *nakshatras*, or lunar mansions; these are equal divisions of the zodiac round of 360°. Each occupies 13'20" of the full circle, and is associated with a Vedic god and various spiritual qualities.

675. Bepin Behari, *Myths and Symbols of Vedic Astrology* (Salt Lake City: Passage Press, 1990): 194.

676. The ancient text called *The Book of Enoch* says that there were two hundred Nefilim, or angels, "Sons of Heaven," who descended upon Mount Harmon in the Mideast for the purpose of mating with human women. Their leader was Samyaza, and seventeen other Nefilim were named. According to this traditional view, once on Earth, they taught humans various things such as sorcery, incantations, foodcraft, warfare, star lore, astronomy, and knowledge of precious gems. (This might be a clue to the nature of the Arioi Society.) Their progeny were unrighteous giants who ate up all the food.

677. *Atlas of Ancient Archeology*, ed. Jacquetta Hawkes (New York: McGraw Hill, 1974): 118.

678. Tholos is an archeological term to describe a tomb, usually round, cut directly into rock and achieving the perfect, intended form—in other words, without accommodating or compromising itself to the resistance of the rock itself.

679. Richard G. Geldard, *The Traveler's Key to Ancient Greece: A Guide to Sacred Places* (Wheaton, Ill.: Quest Books, 2000): 165.

680. Pausanias, *Guide to Greece*, Vol. 1, *Central Greece*, trans. Peter Levi (New York: Penguin Books, 1979): 167–168, 297.

681. David A. Traill, *Schliemann of Troy: Treasure and Deceit* (New York: Saint Martin's Griffin, 1995): 48, 74.

682. Aerope, too, has celestial parentage. Her father was Catreus, the son of Minos, King of Crete. Minos was a son of Zeus and later one of the three Judges of the Dead in Hades. So Aerope is the great-granddaughter of Zeus. For the Homer reference:

Homer, *Odyssey*, trans. Robert Fagles (New York: Viking, Penguin, 1996): Book 2: 133, 97.

683. Carl Kerenyi, *The Heroes of the Greeks* (New York: Thames and Hudson, 1974): 303.

684. Pausanias, *Guide to Greece,* Vol. 1, *Central Greece,* trans. Peter Levi (New York: Penguin Books, 1979): 167–168.

685. Lest this become geographically confusing, the Peloponnese is a large peninsula in Greece; Argos is a political-geographic division somewhat like a shire in England or a state in the U.S.

686. Mythological genealogies are complex, if not vexing, to sort out. Argus is said to be the father of Tiryns, who founded a city of that name built by the Cyclopes two centuries before the Trojan War, "in the infancy of the world." Tiryns is about twelve miles from Mycenae and also has massive, "cyclopean" stone walls. See Will Durant, *The Life of Greece* (New York: Simon & Schuster, 1939): 27–8.

687. Pausanias, *Guide to Greece,* Vol. 1, *Central Greece,* trans. Peter Levi (New York: Penguin Books, 1979): 167.

688. It is believed that King Eurystheus was the last of the line begun with Perseus; after Eurystheus, the House of Atreus took over the rulership of Mycenae.

689. Richard G. Geldard, *The Traveler's Key to Ancient Greece: A Guide to Sacred Places* (Wheaton, Ill.: Quest Books, 2000): 148.

690. Göran Schildt, *In the Wake of Odysseus,* trans. Alan Blair (London: Staples Press, 1953); 149.

691. Henry Miller, *The Colossus of Maroussi* (New York: New Directions, 1941): 86.

692. "Aerial View of Mycenae," at: http://www.furman.edu/~mcknight/g13.htm

693. Homer says that the Cattle of Helios on the slopes of Mount Etna in Sicily numbered 350. One scholar suggests this may be a reference to the days in one year when twelve lunar months are taken together to constitute one incomplete solar year. See Carl Kerenyi, *The Gods of the Greeks* (New York: Thames and Hudson, 1980): 193.

694. For more details, see the entry for Mount Etna. In brief, the Magic Square of the Sun is a number and letter matrix comprising thirty-six numbers arranged in six rows, each of which totals 111; the total for the square is 666, the so-called Number of the Beast, which is a code for the untamed Sun god. It is also a manifestation index for the Archangel Raphael, Archangel of the Sun, who has 666 prime manifestations.

695. The full explanation of this connection requires too much space for this book. But in brief, the Pleiadians, in myth, were called the Sailing ones, the wanderers. The Hyperboreans—you find the term mostly in Greek texts—were mysterious but exalted people living in the far North in a paradisiacal state. Esoterically speaking, the Hyperboreans were the Pleiadians primarily (but other star groups as well) who originally set up the Earth's visionary geography in concert with Merlin and the angelic realm. They wandered from planet to planet over long reaches of time setting up visionary geographic matrices as requested. The griffin, though dismissed by most as a fancy of ancient childlike zoomorphic myths, is an astral reality, and is a prime logo signature and functionary of the Pleiades.

696. *Classical Hindu Mythology: A Reader in the Sanskrit Puranas,* trans. and ed. Cornelia Dimmitt and J. A. B. van Buitenen (Philadelphia: Temple University Press, 1978): 75–6

697. David Elkington, with Paul Howard Ellson, *In the Name of the Gods: The Mystery of Resonance and the Prehistoric Messiah* (Sherborne, England: Green Man Press, 2001): 133–6.

698. Martin Brennan, *The Stones of Time: Calendars, Sundials, and Stone Chambers of Ancient Ireland* (Rochester, Vt.: Inner Traditions International, 1994): 71–73, 118.

699. The same story is attributed to the origin of River Shannon, also in Ireland and its longest river; this river arises in northernmost Connacht, and flows 240 miles to Limerick Bay. The myth is believed to derive from the same mythic account as the Well of Segais. Another version of the same story involves Connla's Well, which does not have a specific worldly site (although one is proposed for Tipperary, Ireland), but is perhaps the archetype of the supernatural well that produces rivers. A maiden named Sinann (a member of the Tuatha de Danann) goes in search of the undersea spring of sacred knowledge; like Boand, after finding Connla's Well, she becomes the river of knowledge itself.

700. Michael Dames, *Mythic Ireland* (London: Thames and Hudson, 1992): 168.

701. Peter Berresford Ellis, *Dictionary of Celtic Mythology* (New York: Oxford University Press, 1992): 41, 171. James Mackillop, *A Dictionary of Celtic Mythology* (New York: Oxford University Press, 1998): 17–18, 45, 61, 103, 382, 415. Miranda Green, *Dictionary of Celtic Myth and Legend* (New York: Thames and Hudson, 1997): 44, 164, 190. Claire

O'Kelly, *Concise Guide to Newgrange* (Blackrock, Ireland: C. O'Kelly, 1984): 25.

702. Chuck Pettis, *Secrets of Sacred Space: Discover and Create Places of Power* (Saint Paul: Llewellyn Publications, 1999): 94–5.

703. "Power and Landscape in Ireland," [no author cited], *Cainteanna na Luise*, 1984, republished at: www.imbas.org/pli.htm, by IMBAS (©2001), 1412 SW 102 Street, PMB 139, Seattle, Wash. 98146.

704. Elizabeth van Buren, *The Sign of the Dove* (Sudbury, England: Neville Spearman, 1983): 10.

705. Michael Baigent, Richard Leigh, and Henry Lincoln, *Holy Blood, Holy Grail* (New York: Delacorte Press, 1982): 8.

706. David Wood, *Genesis: The First Book of Revelations* (Tunbridge Wells, England: Baton Press, 1985): 4, 9, 65, 101, 274–5, 284, 297.

707. Henry Lincoln, *The Holy Place: Discovering the Eighth Wonder of the Ancient World* (New York: Arcade Publishing/Little, Brown, 1991): 15, 17, 67, 70, 125, 135, 160.

708. Henry Lincoln, *Key to the Sacred Pattern: The Untold Story of Rennes-le-Chateau* (New York: Saint Martin's Press, 1998): 145, 174, 199, 215, 218.

709. H. Elie, *Rennes-le-Chateau: Finis Gloriae Mundi, The Message of an Alchemist*, trans. Elizabeth van Buren (Nice, France: Belisane, 1986): 3, 4, 14, 17, 19.

710. These comments are based on an interview by the author with Elizabeth van Buren in November 1989 at her estate near Rennes-le-Chateau.

711. Elizabeth van Buren, *Refuge of the Apocalypse: Doorway into Other Dimensions* (Saffron Walden, England: C. W. Daniel Company, 1986): 164, 171, 179, 188, 301, 332.

712. Richard Andrews and Paul Schellenberger, *The Tomb of God: The Body of Jesus and the Solution to a 2000-Year-Old Mystery* (Boston: Little, Brown, 1996): 423–4.

713. Guy Patton and Robin Mackness, *Web of Gold: The Secret Power of a Sacred Treasure* (London: Sidgwick and Jackson, 2000).

714. David R. Wood and Ian Campbell, *Geneset: Target Earth* (Sunbury-on-Thames, England: Bellevue Books, 1994): 14.

715. Simon Miles, "Conscious Evolution Presents Sacred Landscape Geometry 2000: part one: The Grid of ToMera," 1999, published at: www.consciousevolution.com/Rennes/Part01.htm

716. Lionel and Patricia Fanthorpe, *Secrets of Rennes le Chateau* (York Beach, Maine: Samuel Weiser, 1992): 1, 5, 7, 8, 15, 16.

717. Willy Schrödter, *Commentaries on the Occult Philosophy of Agrippa* (York Beach, Maine: Samuel Weiser, 2000): 127–9.

718. Willy Schrödter, *A Rosicrucian Notebook: The Secret Sciences Used by Members of the Order* (York Beach, Maine: Samuel Weiser, 1992): 193–6.

719. In partial defense of the proposition of structured landscapes is the fact that the network formed by the dome caps (spirals defined by the unfolding of the golden mean, or phi) and straight-running ley lines connecting the domes would reveal some geometric aspects when plotted. Since these energy configurations were the antecedents of the physical landscape, the inherent phi-based geometry would be reflected in the resulting physical terrain, and still later, in the various chapels, chateau, and other monuments put there.

In other words, the placement of these would correspond to the inherent geometry of the energy model, or grid template. Ironically, Lincoln dismisses the idea of a Landscape Zodiac (based on the Glastonbury model), and never mentions (nor do all the Rennes' websites and books) the research of Elizabeth van Buren, who may well be closer to the truth of the Rennes-le-Chateau mystery than all the other researchers.

720. The scallop shell is the principal insignia and logo for the pilgrimage. It gained its significance in relation to the first known miracle performed by Saint James' remains in Spain. As the stone ship bearing Saint James' remains from Palestine arrived at the northwestern tip of Spain at Padron, a horseman was carried by his wild horse into the waves and both were about to drown. Instead, both horse and man emerged from the waters covered with scallop shells; subsequently, the scallop shell was interpreted as a sign of the Apostle's grace.

721. Lee Hoinacki, *El Camino: Walking to Santiago de Compostela* (University Park: Pennsylvania State University Press, 1996): 268. Also Jack Hitt, *Off the Road: A Modern-Day Walk Down the Pilgrim's Route into Spain* (London: Aurum Press, 1994): 22.

722. Antti Lahelma, "A Short Guide for Pilgrims to Santiago de Compostela," April 24, 2000, published at: www.helsinki.fi/~alahelma/santiago.html

723. Blanche Merz, *Points of Cosmic Energy*, trans. Michele Carter Burdet (Saffron Walden, UK: C. W. Daniel, 1983): 26–30, 123, 124. In Merz's system, units between zero and ten thousand are mostly physical and have an effect on the physical body;

those from 11,000 to 13,500 units affect the etheric body; from 13,500 to 18,000 units induct one into a spiritual domain; units beyond this, such as registered at Santiago de Compostela, are exceptional. Her equipment included a Geiger counter, lobe wand, and Bovis biometer (created by a physicist).

724. Nancy Louise Frey, *Pilgrim Stories: On and Off the Road to Santiago* (Berkeley: University of California Press, 1998): 4–5.

725. Ibid., 30, 31, 33.

726. Shirley MacLaine, *The Camino: A Journey of the Spirit* (New York: Pocket Books/Simon & Schuster, 2000): 4, 5, 85, 92, 93.

727. Antti Lahelma, "A Short Guide for Pilgrims to Santiago de Compostela," April 24, 2000, published at: www.helsinki.fi/~alahelma/santiago.html

728. Nancy Louise Frey, *Pilgrim Stories: On and Off the Road to Santiago* (Berkeley: University of California Press, 1998): 29.

729. Jack Hitt, *Off the Road: A Modern-Day Walk Down the Pilgrim's Route into Spain* (London: Aurum Press, 1994): 13, 14, 240, 248.

730. Nicholas Shrady, *Sacred Roads: Adventures from the Pilgrimage Trail* (San Francisco: HarperSanFrancisco, 1999): 168, 202, 204.

731. Adrian J. Ivakhiv, *Claiming Sacred Ground: Pilgrims and Politics at Glastonbury and Sedona* (Bloomington: Indiana University Press, 2001): 167, 173.

732. Robert Scheer, "Experiencing the Sedona Vortexes," January 2000, published at: www.cedarcottage.com/power

733. Adrian J. Ivakhiv, *Claiming Sacred Ground: Pilgrims and Politics at Glastonbury and Sedona* (Bloomington: Indiana University Press, 2001): 176.

734. Dick Sutphen, *Dick Sutphen Presents Sedona: Psychic Energy Vortexes*, ed. Dawn Abbey (Malibu: Valley of the Sun, 1986): 70.

735. Page Bryant, "Sacred Sedona," in *Sedona Vortex Guide Book* (Sedona: Light Technology Publishing, 1991): 3–15.

736. Tom Dongo, *The Mysteries of Sedona* (Sedona: Light Technology Services, 1988): 4, 5, 62.

737. Adrian J. Ivakhiv, *Claiming Sacred Ground: Pilgrims and Politics at Glastonbury and Sedona* (Bloomington: Indiana University Press, 2001): 194–6.

738. Glenn Campbell, "A Visit to Sedona," Rachel, Nev., 1997, published at: www.ufomind.com/misc/1997/jand25-002.shtml

739. Nicholas R. Mann, *Sedona—Sacred Earth* (Prescott, Ariz.: Zivah Publishers, 1991): 42–3.

740. Raymond Mardyks, *Sedona Starseed: A Galactic Initiation* (Sedona: Starheart Publications, 1994): 81–6, 99, 112.

741. Barbara Scott and Carrie Younce, *Sedona Storm* (Nashville: Thomas Nelson Publications, 1994): 49, 66.

742. The identification of guru-beings and their conceptual description is credited to Leon LeGant of San Rafael, California. LeGant is an accomplished clairvoyant reader, healer, and educator; he explains that guru-beings are often found in the astral field of humans where they can control and/or distort many aspects of cognition and spiritual development. They are invited in by a person usually in response to becoming a pupil of a spiritual teacher. Even if a person later officially repudiates the teacher or simply lapses in interest or involvement, unless guru-beings are deliberately "removed" from a person's auric field, they remain, often for lifetimes, LeGant explains.

A well-known cultural example of a guru-being is the figure of Mephistopheles, the so-called Devil in Goethe's *Faust*. I say so-called because in fact this figure has been erroneously demonized; if we think only the Devil or demons can seduce us or offer us power, strength, wisdom, or whatever else we desire, then we can easily miss the seduction by a being who is more developed than a demon. For more information: The Psychic School; website: www.psychicclasses.com; e-mail: staff@psychicclasses.com.

743. Carlos Castaneda, *The Eagle's Gift* (New York: Simon & Schuster, 1981): 179, 180.

744. Harish Johari, *Chakras* (Rochester, Vt.: Destiny Books, 1987): 59, 61.

745. Alice A. Bailey, *Esoteric Astrology*, Vol. 3, *A Treatise on the Seven Rays* (New York: Lucis Publishing Trust, 1951): 154–5, 307, 447, 488.

746. These two terms derive from the clairvoyant development training syllabus of Leon LeGant. Unconscious energy means an energy influence that tries to make you unaware or even put you to sleep so you will not discern its influence or something behind it that is actually the proper goal of your cognitive search. By transmedium energies, LeGant means low-level astral beings, spirit guides, and family beings who temporarily jump into one's cognitive structures and contribute to psychic perception or reporting. Channeling is mostly a case of allowing transmedium beings to jump into one's psychic centers and to displace one's own awareness, which rightfully belongs there, says LeGant. Neither type of energy is desirable or necessary in mature clairvoyance.

747. Bernardino de Sahagun, quoted in Hans Helfritz, *Mexican Cities of the Gods: An Archeological Guide* (New York: Praeger, 1968): 17.

748. Hans Helfritz, *Mexican Cities of the Gods: An Archeological Guide* (New York: Praeger, 1968): 18.

749. David Carrasco, *Religions of Mesoamerica: Cosmovision and Ceremonial Centers* (San Francisco: Harper & Row, 1990): 42–3.

750. Atzlan is the legendary first home of the Aztecs, an island thought to be near a sea-girt mountain called Culhuacan. The Aztecs, also known as the Mexicas, left Atzlan to journey through Mexico, settling and creating structures at many sites, including Teotihuacan. The name Atzlan means "place of whiteness" or "place of herons," while the name Aztec means "people of Atzlan."

751. Andrew Coe, *Archaeological Mexico: A Traveler's Guide to Ancient Cities and Sacred Sites* (Chico, Calif.: Moon Travel Handbooks, 1998): 43.

752. Richard Bluer, "Teotihuacan: Mysterious City of the Gods," in *The Atlas of Mysterious Places,* ed. Jennifer Westwood (New York: Weidenfeld & Nicolson, 1987): 156.

753. Angela M. H. Schuster, "New Tomb Found at Teotihuacan," *Archaeology* (March 2, 1999), published at: www.archaelogy.org

754. Karl E. Meyer, *Teotihuacan* (New York: Newsweek Book Division, 1980): 60.

755. Hugh Harleston Jr., "Did Teotihuacan's Designers, or Their Predecessors, Have a Knowledge of Spherical Trigonometry?" A Research Summary: 1972-1981 (Mexico City: Uac-Kan Research Group, 1981): 1, 18.

756. Peter Tompkins, *Mysteries of the Mexican Pyramids* (New York: Harper & Row, 1976): 321, 322.

757. Vincent H. Malmstrom, *Cycles of the Sun, Mysteries of the Moon: The Calendar in Mesoamerican Civilization* (Austin: University of Texas Press, 1997).

758. Anthony F. Aveni, *Skywatchers* (Austin: University of Texas Press, 2001): 228, 233.

759. Karl E. Meyer, *Teotihuacan* (New York: Newsweek Book Division, 1980): 134.

760. George E. Stuart, "The Timeless Vision of Teotihuacan," *National Geographic* (December 1995), republished online at: www2.mc.maricopa.edu/ anthro/lost_tribes/visionteot.html

761. Hugh Harleston Jr., mentioned earlier, once likened Teotihuacan to a stringed instrument, dubbing it the "Teotihuacan guitar." The strings of this guitar, said Harleston, were 763 meters long, based on the distance between the Pyramids of the Sun and Moon and vibrating at one hundred cycles per second. See: Wesley H. Bateman, "The Musical Message of Teotihuacan," 1998, published at: www.geocities.com/ CapeCanaveral/Hall/3324/nefershouse.htm

762. For more information about the color products, workshops, and agricultural efforts, see: www.aura-soma.net. For information about the Earth mysteries workshops, see: www.primeonthequest.com

763. It is intriguing to note that the Greenwich Meridian (0° 00') passes through most of the Golden Egg; it bisects Little London, the landscape egg itself, and the Shambhala doorway, passing to the west of Somersby and Bag Enderby, and a bit to the east of Maidenwell village at the top end of this figure. Greenwich Meridian is an imaginary line running from the North to South Poles through the "primary transit" instrument (a telescope) at the Royal Observatory in Greenwich, outside London.

The Greenwich Meridian is known as zero longitude, and it is the line from which all the Earth's other longitudinal lines are drawn, including the International Date Line. The Greenwich Meridian was established in 1884 as the "center of time and space" for the Earth and "Prime Meridian of the World" at the request of the U.S. president at a meeting of twenty-five nations in Washington, D.C. For more information, see: www.greenwichmeridian.com

764. The Tetford dome was one of the planet's first domes to receive a renewed wiring to the Great Bear and the fourteen Ray Masters, an event that took place in 1990. Since then, many of the Earth's 1,746 domes have been reconnected with the fourteen-stranded energy filament from Ursa Major; these reconnections, however, can only be done with the participation of humans who simultaneously have their own subtle being bodies similarly "rewired."

765. Carl Kerenyi, *The Heroes of the Greeks* (New York: Thames and Hudson, 1974): 25.

766. Sophocles, *Antigone,* trans. Elizabeth Wyckoff, in *Sophocles I: The Complete Greek Tragedies,* ed. David Grene and Richmond Lattimore (Chicago: University of Chicago Press, 1954): 197.

767. Ovid, *Metamorphoses,* trans. A. D. Melville (New York: Oxford University Press, 1986): 51–4.

768. Apollodorus, *The Library,* trans. Sir James George Frazer (Cambridge: Harvard University Press, 1921): 317.

769. Roberto Calasso, *The Marriage of Cadmus and Harmony,* trans. Tim Parks (New York: Alfred A. Knopf, 1993): 386.

770. Euripides, *The Bacchae,* trans. William Arrowsmith, in *Euripides V: The Complete Greek Tragedies* (Chicago: University of Chicago Press, 1959): 156.

771. Carl Kerenyi, *Dionysus: Archetypal Image of Indestructible Life,* Bollingen Series LXV.2, trans. Ralph Manheim (Princeton: Princeton University Press, 1976): 193.

772. Pausanias, *Guide to Greece,* Vol. 1, *Central Greece,* trans. Peter Levi (Baltimore: Penguin Books, 1979): 325–6.

773. Homer, *Odyssey,* trans. Robert Fagles (New York: Viking Penguin, 1996): book 2, lines 298–300: 258.

774. Cark Kerenyi, *The Heroes of the Greeks* (New York,: Thames and Hudson, 1974): 34, 38.

775. Roberto Calasso, *The Marriage of Cadmus and Harmony,* trans. Tim Parks. (New York: Alfred A. Knopf, 1993): 385.

776. The sphinx is not to be confused with the Egyptian monument at Giza of the same name, although they may derive from the same mythic source. The Greek sphinx (also called Phix, meaning "the Throttler") was the offspring of Typhon (a solar monster buried under Mount Etna in Sicily—see Mount Etna, Sicily, in part 3), and Echidna (half-woman, half-serpent, granddaughter of the Gorgon Medusa—see Troy, Turkey, part 3). The sphinx was sent by Zeus' wife, Hera, to plague Thebes in retribution for an offense committed there against the rites of marriage. The sphinx vowed that if ever anyone answered its question it would either kill itself or leave the citadel.

777. Sophocles, *Oedipus Rex,* trans. Dudley Fitts and Robert Fitzgerald, in *The Oedipus Cycle: An English Version* (New York: Harcourt, Brace & World, 1939): 4.

778. In a variation on the Dionysus story, from the Orphic Mystery tradition, Zeus impregnated the Olympian goddess Persephone; their offspring was called Zagreus. Zeus' wife, Hera, became jealous, and got the Titans to tear Dionysus-Zagreus from limb to limb, and to devour him. They ate all of him except his heart, which Pallas Athena rescued; Zeus gave the heart to Semele to eat and thus Dionysus was able to be conceived afresh—resurrected, as it were.

779. *Greek and Egyptian Mythologies,* comp. Yves Bonnefoy, trans. Wendy Doniger and Gerald Honigsblum (Chicago: University of Chicago Press, 1991): 160.

780. Carl Kerenyi, *Dionysus: Archetypal Image of Indestructible Life,* Bollingen Series LXV.2, trans. Ralph Manheim (Princeton: Princeton University Press, 1976): 194.

781. Vincent Scully, *The Earth, The Temple, and the Gods: Greek Sacred Architecture,* rev. ed. (New Haven: Yale University Press, 1979): 22.

782. L. Sprague de Camp and Cathrine C. de Camp, *Ancient Ruins and Archeology* (Garden City, N.Y.: Doubleday, 1964): 77.

783. David A. Traill, *Schliemann of Troy: Treasure and Deceit* (New York: Saint Martin's Griffin, 1995): 78.

784. Michael Wood, *In Search of the Trojan War* (New York: Plume/New American Library, 1985): 11.

785. Ekrem Akurgal, *Ancient Civilizations and Ruins of Turkey: From Prehistoric Times Until the End of the Roman Empire* (Istanbul, Turkey: Haset Kitabevi, 1973): 48.

786. *Atlas of Ancient Archaeology,* ed. Jacquetta Hawkes (New York: McGraw Hill, 1974): 134.

787. Apollodorus, *The Library,* Vol. 2, trans. George James Frazer (Cambridge: Harvard University Press, 1921): III, xii, 3, 39.

788. The Palladium was believed to have been a magical statue capable of preserving the inviolability of any citadel in which it resided. One version of its origin is that the goddess Athena (born from Zeus' forehead) was raised by Poseidon, the Lord of the Seas, who also had a daughter named Pallas. During a mock combat between the two girls, and as Pallas was about to strike Athena, Zeus intervened and stood between the two (exhibiting his aegis). Pallas, distracted, got hit by a blow from Athena. To honor her stepsister, Athena carved a statue in her likeness and made a miniature of Zeus' aegis for it. The statue remained on Olympus until Zeus attempted to rape Electra and she sought refuge in the statue, after which Zeus threw it down to Troy. Zeus' aegis included the face of the Gorgon Medusa, a monstrous female with snakes for hair and eyes that could turn humans to stone.

Another version of the Palladium's origin is that it was made from the shoulder blade of Pelops, son of Tantalus (a son of Zeus). Pelops had been carved, cooked, and served up to the gods by Tantalos; the gods eventually reconstituted him, finding all the body parts except his shoulder blade. This tradition says that the Palladium was stolen from Sparta along with Helen, thus precipitating the Trojan War.

789. E. R. Dodds, *The Greeks and the Irrational* (Berkeley: University of California Press, 1951): 2–14.

790. Homer, *Iliad*, trans. Robert Fitzgerald (Garden City, N.Y.: Anchor Press/Doubleday, 1974): book 21, 507.

791. Roberto Calasso, *The Marriage of Cadmus and Harmony* (New York: Alfred A. Knopf, 1993): 228.

792. Ibid., 129.

793. *The Atlas of Mysterious Places: The World's Unexplained Sacred Sites, Symbolic Landscapes, Ancient Cities and Lost Lands,* ed. Jennifer Westwood (New York: Weidenfeld & Nicholson, 1987): 184.

794. Ulrich Eberl, "Excavating Troy (Truva)," Daimler-Benz High Tech Report, January 1995, at: http://www.iit.edu/~agunsal/truva/exc.html

795. Vincent Scully, *The Earth, The Temple, and the Gods: Greek Sacred Architecture,* rev. ed. (New Haven: Yale University Press, 1979): 22.

796. Brahma in Hindu thought refers to the All-Creator, but also to the primal creative word, or sound, which is the source of the world. It is coincident with a human's inner consciousness, and means in effect Sound is God and God is Sound. "*Nada Brahma* is one singularity: the primal sound of being. Being itself." *The World Is Sound: Nada Brahma: Music and the Landscape of Consciousness* (Rochester, Vt.: Destiny Books, 1987): 17–8.

797. You find essentially the same story in the Vedic classic *The Ramayana.* Rama's wife, Sita, is abducted by the ten-headed demon Ravana and taken to his half-brother's resplendent palace, Lanka, atop Mount Trikuta somewhere on the island of what we now know as Sri Lanka. Rama, Hanuman, and his monkey troops besiege Lanka and eventually regain Sita. The visual effects are more spectacular than in the *Iliad,* probably because this version of the geomythic story took place far earlier in human planetary experience, but the story line is consistent. Obviously, Rama would be the King Arthur figure, Sita the Guinevere.

798. Uluru rises 340 meters, or 1,115 feet, above the central plains, but it is actually 862 meters, or about 2,586 feet, above sea level.

799. Sarah Titchen, "Cultural Landscapes: Uluru-KatAtjuta," *World Heritage Newsletter,* no. 10 (March 1996): 7–8, published at: www.unesco.org/whc/news/10newsen.htm#story4

800. Josephine Flood, *Archaeology of the Dreamtime: The Story of Prehistoric Australia and Its People* (New Haven: Yale University Press, 1990): 251.

801. A. W. Reed, *Aboriginal Myths, Legends, and Fables* (Chatswood, Australia: Reed/William Heinemann Australia 1982): 152–4.

802. The Dreamtime is an English word for an Aboriginal concept that evokes the Beginning time when the Ancestors, or primal celestial beings, created everything in the world. From a Western viewpoint, it would be the time when mythology or mythopoeisis was the operative description of reality. It was a time when the archetypes of creation—what I would call the geomythics of the galaxy on Earth—were imprinted on the Earth. One of the names for the Dreamtime is *Tjukurrpa* (a Pitjantjatjara word) and it means the beginning creation period when the ancestral beings, known by some tribes as *Tjukaritja,* created the world and traveled all over its surface. These ancestral beings are believed to still reside in the landscape, but in the Dreamtime version of it. The *Tjukurrpa* guides all aspects of Aboriginal life, from ceremonies to food foraging; it embodies history, knowledge, and ritual.

803. Mudrooroo, *Aboriginal Mythology* (London: Thorsons/HarperCollins, 1994): 169, 170.

804. The term "song lines," which of course was popularized by Bruce Chatwin's *The Songlines* (1987), is often interpreted to be what the British call ley lines, lines of connection between sacred sites. But the Aborigines describe song lines as the sonic equivalent of the tracks their ancestors made across the landscape; song lines require regular maintenance, which Aborigines perform as part of their Walkabout. The ancestors sang their way all over the landscape, and "wrapped the whole world in a web of song," says Chatwin. "Each Ancestor, while singing his way across country, was believed to have left a trail of 'life-cells' or 'spirit-children' along the line of his footprints. . . . The song was supposed to lie over the ground in an unbroken chain of couplets." See Bruce Chatwin, *The Songlines* (London: Picador/Pan Books, 1987): 67, 81, 82.

Dreaming tracks are the roads across the landscape along which the primal ancestors journeyed in the Dreamtime; while moving along these tracks, the ancestors created natural features such as lakes and rivers.

805. *Dreamtime Heritage: Australian Aboriginal Myths,* paintings by Ainslie Roberts, text by Melva Jean Roberts (Brisbane, Australia: Rigby, 1975): 27.

806. Mudrooroo, *Aboriginal Mythology* (London: Thorsons/HarperCollins, 1994): 20.

807. Cyril Havecker, *Understanding Aboriginal Culture* (Sydney, Australia: Cosmos, 1987): 7.

808. Charles P. Mountford, "The Rainbow Serpent Myths of Australia," in *The Rainbow Serpent—A Chromatic Piece,* ed. Ira R. Buchler and Kenneth

Maddock (The Hague, Netherlands: Mounton Publishers, 1978): 40-1.

809. Charles P. Mountford, *Brown Men and Red Sand: Journeyings in Wild Australia* (Sydney, Australia: Angus and Robertson, 1962): 92, 95.

810. Bill Bryson, *In a Sunburned Country* (New York: Broadway Books, 2000): 255-7.

811. The Olgas, or Katatjuta, are part of the Uluru park, but not physically related to the Rock. Their name means "many heads," a reference to the thirty-six rounded knobs or rock outcroppings distributed over an area of ten square miles. They are believed to represent a Dreamtime map.

812. Robert Coon, "Uluru—Heart of Australia, Solar Plexus of the World," 2000, published at: http://members.nbci.com/_XMCM/chalice156/uluru.html. Coon also made this association with Uluru in: Robert Coon, *Voyage to Avalon: An Immortalist's Introduction to the Magick of Glastonbury* (Glastonbury, UK: Griffin Gold Publications, 1986): 52.

813. David Mowaljarlai and Jutta Malnic, *Yorro Yorro: Aboriginal Creation and the Renewal of Nature* (Rochester, Vt.: Inner Traditions, 1993): 191.

814. Alan Oken, *Alan Oken's Complete Astrology,* rev. ed. (New York: Bantam Books, 1988): 199.

815. Apollodorus, *The Library,* Vol. I., trans. Sir James George Frazer (Cambridge: Harvard University Press, 1921): 218, 315, 335.

816. This may strike the reader as improbable if not fanciful, but I experienced it during a meditation at Mount Warning in Queensland. Several Aborigines appeared in spirit form and whisked me away on a boomerang into Uluru, telling me that Mount Warning, and other holy sites, were like boomerangs sent out long ago from Uluru.

817. Arthur Avalon, *The Serpent Power* (New York: Dover Publications, 1974): 366.

818. Ibid., 369.

819. Kevin J. Wright, *Catholic Shrines of Central and Eastern Europe* (Liguori, Mo.: Ligouri, 1999): 241.

820. Ibid., 235.

821. Katarzyna Raburska, "Polish Myths and Legends: The Legend of Smok Wawelski," British Studies Web Pages, The British Council, Poland, 1999, published at: www.britcoun.org

822. Corpus Christi day is a Catholic Feast day commemorating the institution of the Eucharist based on visions by Sister Juliana of Liege in the thirteenth century. It is celebrated the Thursday after Trinity Sunday, which is the first Sunday after Pentecost, itself fifty days after Easter.

823. China Galland, *Longing for Darkness: Tara and the Black Madonna, A Ten-Year Journey* (New York: Penguin Books, 1990): 132.

824. Honoré de Balzac, quoted in Janusz Roszko, *Krakow* (Warsaw, Poland: Wydawnictwo/ Sport I Turystyka, [no date]): 16-7.

825. Lenny Karpman, "The Wailing Wall," *Jewish Magazine* 44 (June 2001), published at: www.jewishmag.com

826. Stuart C. Nichols, "Kazimierz and Cracow," *On Every Day Since—A Christian at Auschwitz,* part 6, 1993, published at: www.remember.org/educare

827. Mark Haeffner, *The Dictionary of Alchemy: From Maria Prophetissa to Isaac Newton* (London: Aquarian Press/HarperCollins, 1991): 192-3, 39, 111, 117.

828. Ibid., 260.

829. Edwin Birnbaum, *Sacred Mountains of the World* (Berkeley: University of California Press, 1997): 37.

830. John Blofeld, *The Wheel of Life: The Autobiography of a Western Buddhist,* 2d ed. (Berkeley: Shambhala, 1972): 121-2.

831. Robert M. Gimello, "Chang Shang-ying on Wu-t'ai Shan," in *Pilgrims and Sacred Sites in China,* ed. Susan Naquin and Chün-fang Yü (Berkeley: University of California Press, 1992): 100, 101.

832. Mary Augusta Mullikin and Anna M. Hotchkis, *The Nine Sacred Mountains of China: An Illustrated Record of Pilgrimages Made in the Years 1935–1936* (Hong Kong: Vetch and Lee, 1973): 82.

833. Anthony Tribe, "Manjusri: Origins, Role and Significance (parts 1 and 2)," *Western Buddhist Review,* Vol. 2 (August 1997), Windhorse Publications, Birmingham, UK, at: www.westernbuddhistreview.com

834. The Tibetan Book of the Dead, comp. and ed. W. Y. Evans-Wentz (New York: Oxford University Press, 1960): 113.

835. Lin Sen-shou, "Manjusri," *Mirror of India* (June 9, 2001), published at: http://members.xoom.it/ _XOOM/kundalini/kundalini_eng/manjusri3.html

836. *The Encyclopedia of Eastern Philosophy and Religion,* ed. Stephan Schuhmacher and Gert Woerner (Boston: Shambhala, 1989): 219, 220.

837. Chang Shang-ying, "A Further Record of Ch'ing-liang," in Robert M. Gimello, "Chang Shang-ying on Wu-t'ai Shan," in *Pilgrims and Sacred Sites in China,* ed. Susan Naquin and Chün-fang Yü (Berkeley: University of California Press, 1992): 103-12.

838. Gustav Davidson, *A Dictionary of Angels* (New York: Free Press, 1967): 193-4.

Index

About the Author

Health writer and editor Richard Leviton is the author of nine other books, including *Brain Builders!*, *Physician*, and *The Healthy Living Space*. He served as chief editor of *Alternative Medicine* magazine and senior writer for *Yoga Journal*. Leviton's personal fascination with sacred sites led him to write *Looking for Arthur* (Barrytown, 1997), a mystical adventure delving into the ancient legends surrounding Glastonbury and King Arthur. He is also the author of *What's Beyond that Star: A Chronicle of Geomythic Adventure* (Clairview Books, 2002), recounting some of his exploration into Earth mysteries over 20 years. He lives near Charlottesville, Virginia.

Hampton Roads Publishing Company

. . . for the evolving human spirit

Hampton Roads Publishing Company
publishes books on a variety of subjects,
including metaphysics, health, integrative medicine,
visionary fiction, and other related topics.

For a copy of our latest catalog, call toll-free
800-766-8009, or send your name and address to:

Hampton Roads Publishing Company, Inc.
1125 Stoney Ridge Road
Charlottesville, VA 22902

e-mail: hrpc@hrpub.com
www.hrpub.com